Sourcebook of
Family
Theory
&
Research

Sourcebook of Family Theory & Research

Editors

Vern L. Bengtson
University of Southern California

Alan C. Acock
Oregon State University

Katherine R. Allen
Virginia Polytechnic Institute and State University

Peggye Dilworth-Anderson
University of North Carolina at Chapel Hill

David M. Klein
University of Notre Dame

SAGE Publications
Thousand Oaks ▪ London ▪ New Delhi

For information:

Sage Publications, Inc.
2455 Teller Road
Thousand Oaks, California 91320
E-mail: order@sagepub.com

Sage Publications Ltd.
1 Oliver's Yard
55 City Road
London EC1Y 1SP
United Kingdom

Sage Publications India Pvt. Ltd.
B-42, Panchsheel Enclave
Post Box 4109
New Delhi 110 017 India

Printed in the United States of America on acid-free paper.

Library of Congress Cataloging-in-Publication Data

Sourcebook of family theory and research / edited by Vern L. Bengtson [et al.].
      p. cm.
Includes bibliographical references and index.
ISBN 978-0-7619-3065-5 (cloth) — ISBN 978-1-4129-4085-6 (pbk.)
   1. Family—Research—Methodology. I. Bengtson, Vern L.
HQ728.S639 2005
306.85′072—dc222

2004013736

07   08   09   10   9   8   7   6   5   4   3

Acquiring Editor:	Jim Brace-Thompson
Editorial Assistant:	Karen Ehrmann
Project Editor:	Claudia A. Hoffman
Copy Editor:	Judy Selhorst
Typesetter:	C&M Digitals (P) Ltd.
Indexer:	Molly Hall

Contents

• Foreword

Theories are social constructions based on research, practice, and creative thinking. They are expected to change. The process of theorizing is ongoing. This *Sourcebook* prepares a new generation of scholars for this essential process. With unsurpassed diversity across disciplines and views, this book helps scholars reformulate existing theories and create new ones about how and why contemporary families remain resilient or break down. How do family systems support their children, adults, and elders? I congratulate the editors and contributing scholars of this comprehensive and inclusive volume. It ensures that the process of theorizing about such questions—and others—will continue.

Why is it necessary to continue theorizing about families? Today, more than ever, family scholars need to be curious. To be relevant, we need to ask new questions and generate new hypotheses. We need new frameworks and methods through which to understand differences *and* commonalities in couples and families across the United States and around the world. To analyze the enormity of data, we need linkages to frameworks, but they must be culturally inclusive. Whether we use models or metaphors, we can make sense of old and new knowledge about a diversity of families in diverse contexts—sickness and health, poverty and prosperity, conflict and harmony, and in times of peace and war. Theoretical thinking helps us see the big picture.

It is at the edges between disciplines that new theories tend to emerge, so cross-disciplinary teams are a good idea. The editors and the contributors to this *Sourcebook* illustrate such collaboration. Refreshingly,

they do not hide their diverse viewpoints. Rather, their paradigmatic, methodological, and experiential differences lead us to a confluence of ideas that stimulates new thinking about the delicate balance between family continuity and change. The possibilities for discovery are enhanced.

The process of theorizing also includes self-reflection. What are our own experiences and biases about family life? How do they fit with the particular families we are studying? There exists a range of family forms and functions, but we continue the debate about the definitions of marriage and family. Family processes that do not fit the norm are devalued. Does this mean that Ozzie and Harriet were wrong? Reading this volume and critically discussing its contents will help you know for yourself.

To formulate your own ideas about family research and theorizing, it is essential that you conduct free and independent inquiry. This includes self-reflection, critical thinking, and the opportunity to study the different methods of discovery. The differences in methods only enrich the process of theorizing (Boss, 2004). Elsewhere, I have written:

> There are different ways to search for knowledge. The creative process of theory development requires methods of proof and methods of discovery. The poet shapes a verse; the therapist tries an intervention; the researcher tests or generates hypotheses. But the theorist must be aware of all three possibilities. (Boss, 1999, p. 112)

In this *Sourcebook*, uniquely, all three possibilities are addressed. I encourage you to open your mind to different possibilities as you read. And to help you maintain perspective as you do this work, I add a cautionary note. Johann Wolfgang von Goethe, an 18th-century German poet and philosopher, wrote in his poem *Studier Zimmer,*

> Grau, teurer Freund, ist alle Theorie
> Und grün des Lebens goldner Baum.

May we not limit ourselves to theorizing about families, but also find, in this frenzied world, a real group to call family, and an actual place to call home.

— Pauline Boss
Professor of Family Social Science
University of Minnesota–St. Paul

REFERENCES

Boss, P. (1999). *Ambiguous loss: Learning to live with unresolved grief.* Cambridge, MA: Harvard University Press.

Boss, P. (2004). Ambiguous loss and ambivalence when a parent has dementia. In K. Pillemer & K. Lüscher (Eds.), *Intergenerational ambivalences: New perspectives on parent-child relations in later life* (pp. 207–224). Oxford: Elsevier Science.

• Preface

This is a book about the process of research about families. Its focus is on epistemology in family studies—the origin, nature, and limits of knowledge about families—and on how we can develop more effective theories and methods to advance that knowledge. We call it a *sourcebook*—a source for many ideas and perspectives—because we hope readers will use this volume as a companion while they develop their own studies of families and familylike relationships. This will, we hope, lead to more useful theories and methods in the future.

BACKGROUND

This *Sourcebook of Family Theory and Research* is part of an important and impressive tradition. It is the third publication since the 1970s sponsored by the Theory Construction and Research Methods (TCRM) Workshop and the Research and Theory Section of the National Council on Family Relations (NCFR) to encourage development of research methods and theory in family studies. It builds on the success of the 1993 *Sourcebook of Family Theories and Methods: A Contextual Approach* (edited by Pauline Boss, William J. Doherty, Ralph LaRossa, Walter R. Schumm, and Suzanne K. Steinmetz) and the 1979 two-volume *Contemporary Theories About the Family* (edited by Wesley R. Burr, Reuben Hill, F. Ivan Nye, and Ira L. Reiss). These volumes stimulated many new developments in family research and theory. The traditions they developed are described more fully in Chapters 2 and 3 of this *Sourcebook*.

The current *Sourcebook* extends the earlier projects by emphasizing today's more diverse, eclectic, and process-oriented approaches to theorizing. The contributors demonstrate how crucial the development and use of theory and theorizing are to the future of family research. How family scholars conceptualize and theorize about the issues of the day are keys to addressing the pressing needs that families face in the changing contexts in which they live.

GOALS

Our mission in developing this *Sourcebook* was to generate a text for theorizing about families that, first and foremost, would be useful to both scholars and students throughout the coming decade. We wanted a *Sourcebook* that would not simply sit on shelves but would be engaged and consulted repeatedly by family researchers over the next few years. We wanted to create an environment for the community of scholars generating the materials for this *Sourcebook* that would lead them to become interactive in ongoing theory construction by a community of future family scholars.

A second goal was to create an open process whereby the gates to theorizing could be as wide open as possible, including not simply main chapters in the style of traditional handbooks, but also permutations, elaborations, and challenges to these ideas within each chapter. Authors from many specialties and parts of the world have contributed to this *Sourcebook*. With the addition of a companion Web site for this *Sourcebook* (http://www.ncfr.org/sourcebook), we hope to engage additional interaction in the process of doing theory and constructing cumulative knowledge.

Third, we felt that a text for the 21st century should not have chapters organized around a few selected theoretical frameworks, as did the 1979 and 1993 volumes noted above. Such a format did not seem to be practical or relevant for contemporary theorizing about families. Graduate students, publishers, journal articles, and our own experiences reminded us that theorizing is increasingly eclectic. We wanted this *Sourcebook* not only to ride the wave of what is different about theorizing today but also to chart a new course of action and make the process of theorizing more relevant. Our challenge was to create a road map for a future in which we are unclear about where we want to go, and in which we often seem to go in divergent directions.

PROCESS

We were selected to serve as editors of this *Sourcebook* in spring 2002 as part of a process initiated in 2000 by the TCRM Workshop and the Research and Theory Section of NCFR. A call for nominations, disseminated through NCFR and TCRM Listservs, resulted in the submission of the names of 31 scholars to serve on the editorial board. We were ultimately chosen as volume editors by an editorial selection committee appointed at the TCRM business meeting. The goal was to create an editorial board that optimized both diversity and balance in terms of theoretical and methodological expertise, past experience with other *Sourcebook* projects, disciplinary background, geographic region, and scholarly seniority. All five editors would share equally in editorial responsibilities. We developed a proposal concerning the mission, structure, and budget of the project that was approved by the TCRM Workshop and the Research and Theory Section of NCFR at their annual meetings in November 2002.

As the *Sourcebook* editors, we sent out a broad invitation for individuals to send in proposals for chapters and contributions. We included in this invitation the entire membership of NCFR, the Family Sociology Section of the American Sociological Association, and the Division on Family Psychology of the American Psychological Association. In return, we received 73 chapter proposals—far too many to include in a 700-page volume. How could we accommodate the wealth of material proposed? After lengthy evaluation and dialogue, we decided to use several formats in the *Sourcebook*. It would consist of 25 main chapters, each centered on a specific theoretical and methodological topic; case studies that would elaborate or shed further light on the chapter topics; discussions that would extend the ideas presented in the chapters; and brief pieces on theory and on methods ("spotlights") that would highlight innovation. Thankfully, most of the scholars who submitted proposals agreed to work within these formats. Many struggled with the highly constrained length limitations we placed on them and with a very tight timeline. However, they accepted the challenge of doing things differently, and in record time. Also, as we noted above, we created a companion Web site for the Sourcebook on which the contributors could post additional materials. We look forward to our readers' assessments of these innovations: Have they worked for you? Has this diverse format helped you to learn more?

From the history of the previous *Sourcebook* projects, we knew that producing this volume would be a long-term commitment (3 or 4 years of our time) for which we would receive no financial compensation. All royalties from this volume go to the National Council on Family Relations, the TCRM Workshop, and NCFR's Research and Theory Section. No honoraria or royalties are paid to the 198 authors of chapters or features, the 17 members of the Editorial Advisory Board, or the five editors. Working on the *Sourcebook* has been both a privilege and a labor of love for all of us over the past several years. This project is dedicated to the future of family theory and research methods: The authors and editors—and, most important, those who purchase the *Sourcebook*—are "financing the future" in that proceeds from sales of this volume will go toward financing the next *Sourcebook,* which we hope will be published 10 years from now.

We were able to bring this book to press in record time for two reasons: First, the contributors all made extraordinary efforts to meet the deadlines we imposed; and second, we received support from the TCRM Workshop and NCFR that allowed the editorial team to meet 10 times over several years. We traveled, over weekends and holidays, to many places for meetings: to the University of North Carolina at Chapel Hill (twice); to the University of Southern California (twice); to the University of Notre Dame; to the cities in which the TCRM Workshop, NCFR, and the American Sociological Association were holding their annual meetings; and, in a final spurt inspired by panic over the fast-approaching publication deadline, to a nondescript hotel near Chicago's O'Hare Airport. These meetings were essential for our negotiations of ideas. We needed to meet face-to-face, as a group or in pairs or threesomes, to generate ideas, iron out differences, edit, brainstorm about reviewers or authors, come up with titles, and deal with the endless minutiae that accompany such a large-scale project. Even settling on the design of a cover for the book was a group effort requiring much debate. During our final year of work, we all took part in weekly conference calls that typically took several hours of preparation.

OBJECTIVES

We decided early on that one of our primary objectives for this *Sourcebook* would be *inclusiveness.* Having solicited input from a wide array of students and scholars in the field, we were sure that the volume should allow the voices of many different authors to be heard, authors who vary in ideas and in backgrounds, by race, gender, sexual orientation, age, seniority, religion, and professional affiliation, as well as in other ways that matter.

Therefore, our first objective was to be as inclusive as possible in terms of authors, ideas, and editorial advice. We hope we have achieved that goal. The 198 separate contributors to this *Sourcebook* represent a very diverse group. We wanted to be inclusive in the race/ethnicity of contributors as well as in their age and seniority. We wanted to involve individuals new to the family field as well as seasoned researchers, teachers, and theorists. Consequently, the authors include graduate students working on degrees, part-time instructors at 2- and 4-year institutions, independent scholars without university affiliations, emeritus professors, and widely known professors at research institutions. We also attempted to include the most salient theorizing being done today on as wide a variety of family issues as possible. Further, we attempted to go beyond North American contributors, involving European and Asian family scholars as well. To enhance this inclusiveness, we created an International Editorial Advisory Board, some of the members of which are scholars who reflect areas or issues we had not been able to cover with the group of authors who emerged.

Our second objective was to engage our readers in *interaction*—both with the text and with the volume's companion Web site. In this era of ever-increasing technical sophistication, when our students and our children know more about computers than we do, we knew that a traditional off-the-shelf volume would not suffice. This *Sourcebook* could not be only textually based; *interactive* to us meant that offering examples and "how-to" features was more important than tracing the histories of particular concepts.

We wanted our authors to be as interactive as possible with the students and scholars who read this volume. We attempted to foster such interaction in several ways. We encouraged all authors to post lists of additional readings, exercises, and information on the *Sourcebook's* companion Web site. Most of the chapters feature a "Spotlight on Theory" and a "Spotlight on Methods" in which scholars present important insights from their ongoing research that expand on the ideas discussed in the chapters. Most chapters also include at least one case study that illustrates the experiences of one researcher or team of researchers in regard to research associated with the chapter's topic.

Third, we wanted to *focus on the process rather than the outcome* of theory. We challenged our authors to consider *theory* as a verb (*theorizing*) rather than as a noun. We wanted them to focus on the process of theory building and methods development rather than on summarizing existing findings to date on family issues. We hoped that this would result in a product that is different from other handbook-type publications in family research, in which reviews of the existing literature—presenting findings from as many studies as possible—are the end goal, rather than the discussion of ideas that lead to explanations and the development of research methods to study them.

Fourth, we wanted to *mix methods and theory* in as many chapters as possible. We encouraged the authors to integrate their theorizing with discussions of research methods. We emphasized the value of multimethod approaches in family research. We asked the contributors to join us in our attempt to break down some of the artificial barriers between qualitative and quantitative methods. These have become something like implicit ideologies in family research, creating for many students an "either/or" dichotomy, to the disservice of both approaches.

Finally, we found in implementing our goal of inclusiveness that *collaboration is the key*. Collaboration is both absolutely necessary and much more difficult than is usually acknowledged. Collaboration is a multidimensional and multimethod process. We understand now that it is nearly impossible to cover only *one* theory in a chapter, because family scholars must blend, borrow, mix, and pair theories together.

The Editors
Vern L. Bengtson
Alan C. Acock
Katherine R. Allen
Peggye Dilworth-Anderson
David M. Klein

• Acknowledgments

We want to acknowledge the many organizations and individuals who have contributed to the success of this *Sourcebook* project. Bringing this volume to press has truly been a collaborative process involving hundreds of contributors, and we recognize that we could not have completed it without their assistance.

The TCRM Workshop is the intellectual home base of this *Sourcebook*. Since its inception in 1982 through the work of Reuben Hill and other pioneers in family research, the TCRM has organized a preconference workshop held prior to the NCFR annual meeting as a forum for presenting in-process ideas about theory building and research methods. The workshop is open to anyone who wants to submit an idea or simply attend. This *Sourcebook* was conceived, sustained, nurtured, and launched through the TCRM, which provided not only the necessary funding but also the ideas and insights to keep it going year after year. The intellectual and emotional capital for this volume comes from the TCRM, and for that, we are all grateful and proud. We thank the three most recent chairpersons of the TCRM for their support of this project: Libby Blume, Stan Knapp, and Richard Bulcroft.

We acknowledge also the sustaining support of NCFR, which is the parent organization of the TCRM, and particularly Michael Benjamin, executive director of NCFR, for his willingness to support the *Sourcebook* project and to guarantee its expenses. We also thank John Pepper, financial administrator of NCFR, for his encouragement and guidance concerning many aspects of the *Sourcebook* development. We thank the Research and Theory Section of NCFR, whose officers and members voted to provide financial support for this *Sourcebook* project. Our thanks to Jane Gilgun and Ann Crouter, recent chairpersons for the Research and Theory Section, who responded to our requests for support. As we have noted above, royalties from this *Sourcebook* will go to expand theory and research and to provide support for the next *Sourcebook* project.

Special thanks are due to the members of the Sourcebook *Editorial Advisory Board: Bert Adams, Ana Mari Cauce, David Cheal, Margaret Crosbie-Burnett, Kerry Daly, Thomas Holman, Stan Knapp, Ralph LaRossa, Harriett Pipes McAdoo, Velma McBride Murry, Bernhard Nauck, Jay Teachman, William Turner, Manfred van Dulmen, Alexis Walker, Clare Wenger, and Chin-Chun Yi. All of the member of this international group of highly respected scholars participated in the selection and review of chapters. We are particularly grateful for their suggestions about international data and perspectives.*

We also want to acknowledge the wonderfully smooth and substantively helpful working relationship we have experienced with Sage Publications and Jim Brace-Thompson, Sage's senior editor. Jim, thank you for the amazingly useful suggestions you have offered us throughout this *Sourcebook* project. You are the rare editor who demands academic quality as well as reader accessibility, and who balances these along with guidance about the readership, marketability, and sales for a volume. In addition, we thank Karen Ehrmann, Jim's assistant and Sage's editorial assistant for our volume. Karen, you have nagged us and you have encouraged us and you have helped us meet the unreasonably ambitious production schedule for this volume—which is being published a full year ahead of the original projection. Our thanks also to Claudia Hoffman, Sage's project editor for this *Sourcebook,* and to Margaret O'Connor, Sage's marketing editor. Finally, special thanks are due to Judy Selhorst, the superb copy editor Sage selected for this volume. Judy, your editing has been wonderful. Thank you for your ability to recast sentences to convey more clearly what authors wanted to say, as well as your meticulous attention to details of graphics and references that the editors—as well as the authors—had missed.

From start to finish, we thank Linda Hall at the University of Southern California for coordinating all activities related to the organization, processing, and production of this *Sourcebook.* This is the 13th volume she has shepherded to press from manuscript to finished book in conjunction with Vern Bengtson, the senior editor. Linda's persuasive skills are legendary, particularly with authors (or editors) who fall behind schedule with their contributions. Special thanks also are due to Tanaya Burnham. While a USC undergraduate majoring in sociology and part-time student worker, she handled the responsibility of monitoring the progress of the 97 separate contributions and the 198 individual authors involved in this volume. She devoted countless hours and enormous effort to updating the *Sourcebook*'s table of contents as authors sent in their revised contributions.

A huge thank-you is due to Alan Acock, the editor who took on the responsibility of developing the *Sourcebook*'s companion Web site. The addition of a Web site is one of the most important innovations of this *Sourcebook,* allowing readers to access additional materials posted by the authors to supplement and expand their printed contributions. Thanks to the work of Dr. Acock, these materials will be continually updated over the next 5 years.

Oregon State University provided valuable support for the *Sourcebook* project by allowing us to use the university's conference call facilities. Almost every week over the past 2 years or so, we were all able to talk with one another about the goals and progress of the *Sourcebook* thanks to OSU's teleconference arrangements. The charges for these teleconferences each week were minimal, and we thank the administration of OSU for enabling these transcontinental exchanges among scholars working on a complex project.

Additional acknowledgment is due to the National Institute on Aging, which provided support for this project through training grant 5-T32AG00037 and research grant 2R01-AG007977. These grants enabled predoctoral and postdoctoral students to participate in this project.

We also want to recognize the contributions of students and colleagues who were instrumental in various aspects of this *Sourcebook* project. Special thanks are due to Dr. Norella Putney of the University of Southern California, who assisted with the preparation of chapters 1 and 25. Our thanks also to Allyson Banas and Mayra Alvarez of the University of North Carolina at Chapel Hill; Jana Meinhold and Patricia Meierdiercks of Oregon State University; and Brian Conway, Carl Neblett, Rui Gao, Jonathan Hill, Georgian Schiopu, Maureen Wynne, and Min Zhang of the University of Notre Dame.

Finally, all of us thank our respective universities, as well as our students and colleagues, for supporting the production of this *Sourcebook.* This has truly been a collaborative process, and we recognize that we could not have completed it without your assistance.

The Editors
Vern L. Bengtson
Alan C. Acock
Katherine R. Allen
Peggye Dilworth-Anderson
David M. Klein

Part I

SETTING THE CONTEXT FOR FUTURE FAMILY RESEARCH

• One

THEORY AND THEORIZING IN FAMILY RESEARCH

Puzzle Building and Puzzle Solving

Vern L. Bengtson

Alan C. Acock

Katherine R. Allen

Peggye Dilworth-Anderson

David M. Klein

Often siblings who have had little contact over time come together and reassert family ties when their parents become frail or die. Why? What is the balance between obligatory and voluntary family ties? (Chapter 7)

Some children are similar to their mothers, while others in the same family are more similar to their fathers. Why? With shared genes and a common environment, what accounts for sibling differences in parent-child resemblance? (Chapter 15)

Some men and women say their marriage is very unsatisfying or unloving and has been for a long time. Yet they choose to stay in their marriage. Why? Why are people so reluctant to end difficult relationships? (Chapters 11, 13, and 21)

An increasing number of American families are multiracial. How do their members—especially children—create and negotiate their identities in the context of racial tensions both across society and within families? (Chapter 8)

These are but four examples of the many puzzles that family researchers are trying to understand by building theory.

That theory is important most family researchers today would agree. Yet *what*

Authors' Note: We are grateful to several scholars who have helped us revise draft upon draft of this chapter: Norella Putney, Jonathan Turner, Merril Silverstein, Pauline Boss, Kerry Daly, and David Cheal.

constitutes useful theory, *how* theory can best be developed, and *why* we haven't developed more useful theory by now—these are some fundamental questions confronting family research today. The field of family studies is changing very rapidly. Some scholars feel that we are in the middle of a paradigm shift in family studies (see Chapter 6 and Spotlight 1.3). Others feel that we are not in a paradigmatic shift—we just need to use the best of current knowledge to develop more useful theories (see Case Study 1.1 and Chapter 2). Certainly the debates concerning what is useful knowledge about families and how it should best be pursued have become more heated in recent years (see Chapters 16 and 25).

Over the past half-century our field has accumulated a wealth of data about families and family relationships. We have come to know a great deal about family structures and their increasingly diverse configurations, about the complex relationships of individuals within families, and about their variation within and across societies. At the same time, we still do not know as much as we would like about *why*, or *how,* these relationships and their consequences occur, or why and how there is so much variation in family relationships.

This we believe is the purpose of theorizing—trying to understand and explain the *why* and *how* beyond the *what* of our data about families. We feel it is unfortunate that the increasing wealth of data *about* families and relationships has not resulted in a corresponding increase in helpful *explanations* about the complexities of family relationships and their problems. Nor have we seen this wealth of data result in increasingly effective interventions, in family practice or public policy, in order to ameliorate family problems. The reason, we believe, is inadequate attention to *theorizing*.

The five authors of this chapter have been debating such issues over almost three years, in the process of developing this *Sourcebook.* We have spent hundreds of hours discussing what family theory is, or has been, and how it can be developed so as to be more useful tomorrow for students, researchers, and practitioners in our field. The five of us entered these discussions from quite different perspectives in family research and theory, from qualitative to quantitative research methods, from theories of revolutionary emancipation to traditional science—at least these were the labels we had to deal with at the beginning and negotiate beyond in order to work together. These debates about the nature of theory in family research were quite passionate: sometimes there was shouting, sometimes tears, sometimes angry silences. (We describe some of these debates in Chapter 25.) But from these discussions we arrived at some basic principles, ideas that we have hotly debated and then decided to agree upon.

In this chapter we provide an overview of the multiple perspectives evident today concerning the nature and place of theorizing in the context of our inherently multidisciplinary field. We address four questions, four issues we hope that tomorrow's researchers will consider as they plan their studies:

1. What is theory? What is theorizing in family research?

2. What is knowledge? How do we effectively build knowledge in family research?

3. How does theorizing work? What are the steps in creating explanations from observations?

4. How is theorizing related to research methods in understanding and explaining family issues?

We conclude by suggesting some principles that we believe will be crucial in the development of knowledge about families in the future.

WHAT IS THEORY?
THEORIZING IN FAMILY RESEARCH

Theorizing is a *process of developing ideas that allow us to understand and explain our data.* At least this is the definition we have come to in the course of our three years of work on this project. The term "theory" is used in many ways to describe interpretations of ideas or observations—from theory as a conjecture or guess, to what physicists define as a "coherent group of general propositions used as principles of explanation for a class of phenomena" (Webster, 2001). Even within the same field of knowledge, perspectives on theory change over time. Theory was defined this way 30 years ago in the first Sourcebook on Family Theory project sponsored by NCFR: "Theory [is] a set of logically interrelated *propositional* statements that identify how variables are covariationally related to each other" (Burr, Hill, Nye, & Reiss, 1979, p. 17). We feel this is too restrictive a definition for family research today.

My view: Theory as puzzle-building

- *Theorizing is like putting together a puzzle.* This is one analogy to the process of research in family studies. I think of the data I collect as pieces of a jigsaw puzzle. Each piece by itself is incomplete, mystifying, confusing. But in trying to understand how the pieces fit together I can arrive at a larger and more coherent picture. Everyone who collects data about family issues—from undergraduates to graduate students to assistant professors to emeritus professors publishing tomes—can be, and is, involved in this puzzle building. That is what theorizing means for me: attempting to put together the puzzles resulting from our data in order to explain the *why* beyond what we observe.

- I believe that *theory is absolutely crucial for useful research about families.* Lack of theory leads to one-shot, limited application of our research findings that cannot lead to building cumulative knowledge about an issue. Researchers—whether students or professors, whether using qualitative or quantitative methods—cannot design or plan their studies without ideas about *what* it is they want to find out and *why* that is important, though they may be implicit. Making these explicit is crucial to a successful study design. And at the end of the process, when researchers select the most important results or findings to write about, they are theorizing—developing ideas that are important to share with others. I feel that every family study published should conclude with attempts to explain findings and interpret them within explicit theoretical frameworks.

- *Theorizing is fun.* Puzzle-building is fun. Theorizing is an intellectual game that can be played by everyone involved in family studies, from the neophyte to the experienced scholar. I think every family researcher should enter into this endeavor and enjoy the unexpected insights that can result. Theorizing is like being presented with a puzzle where only some of the pieces are visible or seem to fit together, and making the effort to solve the rest. Fitting the pieces together is fun, though often frustrating, particularly when the overall picture is vague or elusive. And often you have to create your own puzzle, instead of simply solving one that someone handed you. This is where the real creativity lies.

- *Theories are lenses.* Look at an object through one kind of lens and you'll see one thing; look at it through another lens and you'll see something different. I believe that family research is a multiple-paradigm field, with several different paradigms operating and changing all at the same time; several lenses are required to see the complexity and diversity of family processes.

—Vern Bengtson

Theorizing Involves Explanation

"An attempt to explain" is probably the simplest and most direct way to define theory. Theorizing is an attempt to solve some puzzle we have encountered in our experience as scholars (see "My view," p. 5).

Whether in the laboratory or in field studies or in surveys—or indeed in everyday life—humans seek explanations and meanings for *what* they observe or experience. And that leads to questioning the *why* and the *how* beyond their immediate observations. This is theorizing—the search for explanation. For example, Acock and Demo (1994) indicate that many daughters do well academically after their parents' divorce, but have a setback when their custodial mother remarries. Why? Acock and Demo begin their attempt to explain this observation by examining several factors: the age of the mother at the time of the divorce, the emergent relationships the daughter has with her siblings, and how these emergent relationships and expectations are threatened if the mother remarries. The most likely explanation is the one most strongly associated with academic performance in subsequent analyses. Their explanation: family processes that strengthen the role of an adolescent after a divorce are reversed when the mother remarries.

"An attempt to explain" may not be the goal of all family researchers today. But we suggest this should be the goal of research in our field. We acknowledge that "explanation" is not universally accepted in family studies as the outcome of theorizing, since the term is often associated with "scientific theorizing" today (see "My view," this page). As we will discuss later, there are other perspectives about what theory is, what knowledge is, and the process of knowing—important issues within the multi-disciplinary field of family studies. But whatever the definition, we feel that explanation is central to the goals of theory.

My view: Theory is Essential to Science

- A scientific theory is a set of relatively abstract and interrelated statements that attempt to explain a general and repeatable structure or process in nature. This definition, and others quite similar to it, have been offered by philosophers and social scientists for more than 50 years (White & Klein, 2002, p. 2). Theories about the family are useful for assisting people, including researchers as well as family members themselves, to understand the intricacies and mysteries of family life.

- Scientific theories are general. They must be useful across a wide range of specific circumstances. Scientific theories also involve multiple statements rather than just a single assertion or hunch. Understanding nature, including humans and their social ties, requires a fairly complex set of ideas that fit together in some way. The progression of understanding is usually to first describe, next explain, then predict, and finally to attempt to influence outcomes in ways thought to be desirable. But the key is to be able to explain, or answer why. If we can describe something well in an abstract and general way, we have some of the theoretical tools necessary for explanation, and for understanding, but we don't yet have a scientific theory.

- There are two primary ways to explain something: a) to show how it follows logically from a set of premises, and b) to identify what causes it. Some theories employ both deductive and causal reasoning. Burr (1973) was among the first to provide useful examples of how deduction and causation can be systematically employed across a variety of family topics. More resources with definitions of theory and guidance about how to construct theories appear in this *Sourcebook's* web pages.

—David Klein

Theorizing is a Process

We deliberately refer to "theorizing" rather than more passive phrases such as "using theory," "applying theory," or "developing theory" in family research. We want the focus to be on theory as a verb, rather than a noun or a modifier. From our perspective, theory should be considered more as a *process* than as a product (see "My view," this page). Too often "theory" is associated with some abstract set of ideas, disemboweled of the process that led up to these ideas. Or theory is associated with memorizing ideas and names of men long dead. As one of our graduate students said in the course evaluation: "Theory is some arcane body of reasoning associated with a name that you have to memorize in order to appear knowledgeable in this class."

That's not the point of theory. We all theorize, whether we are aware of it or not, in attempting to understand our observations and experiences. This is particularly true of those of us engaged in family research. It is almost irresistible to go beyond describing the *what* of the data we have observed (whether from Census reports or in-depth qualitative interviews or observations of interaction) to explain the *why* and *how* of social and psychological processes underlying them. This is theorizing, whatever else it might be called.

The process of theorizing (see "My view," this page) begins first with intuition and an awareness of ideas, and second with the development of hunches about how they are linked. It is essential to question where and how these ideas emerge, as well as the ideas themselves; their soundness is important to the emerging theory. The third step is empirical research. Research and evidence facilitate the emergence of empirically based associations about hunches that capture the complexity of family life, and developing new theories may require that interactions are examined and dynamic multimethods are used. Fourth, as evidence-based associations are made, new ideas materialize but the confines of the discipline within which they emerge may prevent linking these ideas in nontraditional ways. Fifth, concepts are created that provide structure to the associations that have been made. The key is to create concepts that are inclusive and incorporate the realities of diverse groups. Sixth, understanding the complexity of the associations made allows confidence to emerge when explaining the world. Finally, theory emerges as a tool to help us understand, explain, and give meaning to the data we have collected.

My view: The process of theorizing

Developing Ideas for Getting Out of the Boxes and Into the Circles of Theoretical Thought

How do we arrive at theory?

1. We start with intuition as ideas start to percolate

2. We add hunches about how these are linked

3. We make empirically-based associations about hunches as research evidence emerges

4. New ideas emerge as evidenced-based associations are made

5. We create concepts that provide structure to these associations

(continued)

My view: The process of theorizing *continued*

6. Confidence emerges in explaining the world by understanding the complexity of associations

7. Theory emerges as the tool to help understand, explain and give meaning to phenomena

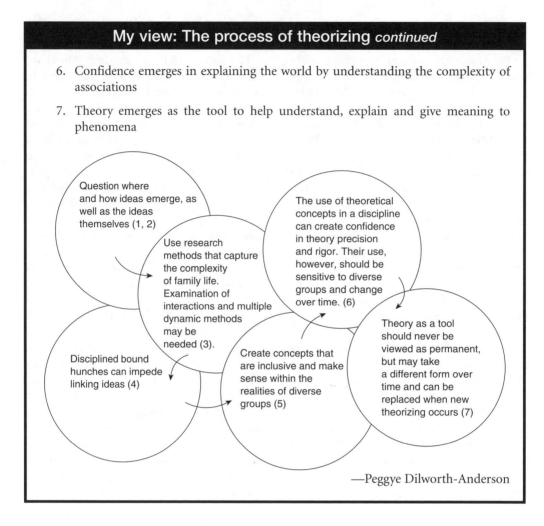

Question where and how ideas emerge, as well as the ideas themselves (1, 2)

Use research methods that capture the complexity of family life. Examination of interactions and multiple dynamic methods may be needed (3).

The use of theoretical concepts in a discipline can create confidence in theory precision and rigor. Their use, however, should be sensitive to diverse groups and change over time. (6)

Disciplined bound hunches can impede linking ideas (4)

Create concepts that are inclusive and make sense within the realities of diverse groups (5)

Theory as a tool should never be viewed as permanent, but may take a different form over time and can be replaced when new theorizing occurs (7)

—Peggye Dilworth-Anderson

This process of developing theory creates confidence in theory precision and rigor. However, it is important that the theory not lose relevance across diverse groups or over time. Therefore, the process of theorizing requires that theories should never be viewed as permanent, regardless of how they help us to understand, explain, and give meaning to phenomena. When theorizing is a process, theories can take different forms over time and can be replaced as new theorizing occurs.

Theorizing Should Be Explicit

We submit that family researchers should be *explicit* in theorizing. We should be aware that the data on families we collect or statistically analyze are not just "social facts," whether they come from our own in-depth interviews or from Census reports about families. They also constitute the essential raw materials of our reasoning and theorizing about our findings.

However, much is published in family research today that makes no reference to theory. Alan Taylor notes in Case Study 1.1 at the end of this chapter that only slightly over one-third of papers published in *Journal of Marriage and the Family* over the decade from 1990 to 2000 contained *any* reference to theory. Too frequently theorizing is covert, or implicit; this can lead to problems in research. Being more explicit will improve our ability to critically analyze the knowledge we produce.

In developing a research project, investigators' "implicit theory" and underlying assumptions about the nature of the phenomena to be studied inevitably guide the selection of research questions as well as the concepts and variables to be measured (Lavee & Dollahite, 1991). If investigators do not recognize or acknowledge these implicit assumptions, this can bias or distort their interpretation of findings.

This can be a problem, for example, with some highly respected, large-scale panel surveys today. The National Longitudinal Study and the National Survey of Households and Families have collected data on thousands of variables over time. However very few of these concern family *processes,* nor do they reflect sibling relationships, gay and lesbian families, or immigrant families' culture clash. What implicit theory led the investigators of these enormously funded federally supported studies to include multiple items used to measure household income, and only a few items to measure gender role beliefs? We do not know. The original designers of the survey were demographers who eschewed social theory; consequently the utility of these highly expensive panel surveys is now limited for family researchers. Similar questions can be asked of many epidemiological or census analyses concerning families, where only a form of implicit theory—often an application of rational choice theory—is used to select the variables to include in prediction models. This is unfortunate, since most family processes are not driven by "rational" choices (Silverstein, Conroy, Wang, Giarrusso, & Bengtson, 2002). Furthermore, the demographic analysis of family change lends itself nicely to theorizing (see Chapter 5), though this has yet to be recognized by some demographers.

We believe family researchers should be explicit about theorizing from start to finish in developing their research. This will occur only if those doing research about families

stop to consider that theorizing is crucial to research and knowledge-building. Whether we start from a hunch or a concern that leads us to collect data, or a question that leads to secondary analysis of a large-scale dataset, we should be explicit about what we are investigating and why—to ourselves and to others. This is true also when we conduct our data analyses, whether this involves assessing patterns from the texts of our interviews or testing best-fit statistical models from survey data. Further, when we report our findings in papers or presentations, we should be explicit in discussing how they contribute to, or modify, existing knowledge about that issue or topic.

THEORIZING IN FAMILY STUDIES TODAY REFLECTS SEVERAL THEORETICAL ORIENTATIONS

We find that studies in the family literature today reflect three basic orientations toward theory.

Theory as explanation of naturally occurring events. This is the "scientific method" perspective of theory. It has proven very useful in the history of physical and natural science and has led to many useful applications of "basic research," from the theory of germs to the inoculation of children for smallpox. From this perspective, theory can lead to prediction, alteration, and eventual control of naturally occurring events and processes (Brown, 1989; Kinkaid, 1996). For family researchers this can suggest directions for intervention, designing programs that promote family well-being.

Note that this is *not* "positivism," which we feel is an outmoded label that inaccurately stereotypes quantitative research and theorizing on families. Nor is explanation of this sort "deterministic." These are outmoded labels, descriptors of scientific theory of 50 or 70 years ago, and we feel these have no useful place in family discourse today.

My view: Contemporary Myths about Theory and Research Methods

The developmental stake of advocates of new approaches can lead to polarized misattributions about other strategies. As approaches mature, advocates should free themselves of these myths. Here are misattributions about quantitative methods we should avoid.

- *Myth 1. Quantitative researchers are deterministic and linear.* Determinism disappeared from most scientific inquiry shortly after the start of the 20th century. Statistics flourished only after determinism vanished. Exclusively linear progress was rejected by historians over a century ago and by science since the work of Kuhn.
- *Myth 2. Quantitative researchers use theory deductively.* In fact, the greater risk is being atheoretical. A graduate student discovering a national dataset needs to be cajoled into thinking theoretically. Quantitative research typically has serendipitous findings leading to inductive theory; some techniques are explicitly inductive.
- *Myth 3. Quantitative researchers are positivists.* Positivism, as an approach to science, all but disappeared with the rise of indeterminism/statistics. Labeling quantitative scholars positivist makes no sense. Positivists did not employ multi-dimensional probabilistic theories.
- *Myth 4. Quantitative researchers study objective variables in static models.* "Objective" variables are often subjective. Age means different things in different cultures. Subjective variables (attitudes, values, and beliefs) are the focus of many quantitative methods. "Processes" are the focus of quantitative methods developed in the last decade.
- *Myth 5. Quantitative researchers are value free.* Values influence the topics we study, the variables we consider, the people we interview or observe, and the theoretical frameworks we use. We should be conscious of our values, try not to be blinded by them, and be open to information that challenges our values.

—Alan Acock

That theorizing and the search for explanation should be explicit—from the design of the study to reporting in publications its findings—is a conviction that we five authors have come to share. This is in contrast to the idea that theorizing—the construction of explanations and understandings—should be left to the reader when we publish our research. From this perspective the responsibility of researchers ends with data anaysis, the results of our statistical modeling or observations. Authors should not go "beyond the data" into explanations or theory, since theories are speculations. This view is reflected in publications of some epidemiologists and demographers as well as ethnomethodologists and

anthropologists. We feel that reports like these are incomplete and should not be accepted by journal editors. We feel that "puzzle solving" should be a norm for journal reviewers to assess—that an evaluation of theorizing is as important as research methodology in considering the merit of a journal submission.

But can there be a "scientific" theory of the family? Are there useful theories *of* the family? Jonathan Turner (Case Study 1.2) answers "no." For Turner theories in the family field should be about general social forces and relationships—as they are manifested in family relationships and configurations. It is a mistake, he argues, to think that there is anything completely unique about family relationships;

rather families reflect general social process in unique contexts.

Theory as narrative ("natural terms"). This is associated with the interpretive perspective in knowledge development (see "My view," this page). Theory can be a story, an account of what we have heard or observed, leading to understanding of some general process. From this perspective we use these narratives to understand or account for the processes or behaviors of individuals or groups we have observed. For example, Stack (1974) presented in her classic ethnography a rich and detailed understanding of urban black families. It reflects what Geertz (1975) called "thick description"—the hermeneutic understanding of a whole culture as an ensemble of socially produced and shared meanings. This procedure uses details from the participants' own voices to elaborate ideas. The description is the evidence; but it is then used to generalize, to generate hypotheses about what is going on in the data. Another example is Rubin's (1976) analysis of marriage for working class men and women. Both of these studies point to the importance of *process* in understanding. These studies emphasize the importance of integrating both interpretation (understanding; *Verstehen*) and explanation in research (Schweizer, 1998). Knapp (2002) has proposed the use of a set of practices grounded in the constructionist approach that advance knowledge claims in an open, self-reflexive process.

My view: Theorizing as contextual, relevant, and imaginative

- I believe that theorizing is a contextual, relevant, and imaginative process. Theory helps me understand the problems that people encounter by living in the mundane and often oppressive circumstances of daily life. Theorizing provides options for solving those problems.

- As a practicing theorist, I have found that scientific ideas work in both progressive (linear) and revolutionary (transformative) ways. By transgressing the boundaries between progressive and revolutionary "camps," I can juggle empiricist *and* social constructionist ways of knowing to help me understand my substantive concern: family diversity over the life course.

- Certainly, there are multiple intellectual traditions, and some scholars are opposed to the category mixing in which I engage (e.g., juggling empiricism and social constructionism). But I cross the borders from positivist to postpositivist to postmodernist and back again because I do not believe science proceeds exclusively in a linear and cumulative fashion.

- My scholarly emphasis is on telling a compelling story. I use theory to construct an argument with evidence that illuminates the poignancy of human life and reveals social processes. I have a political aim—to move readers, participants, and self into action. I want the work I do to make a difference. But to do the work that integrates theory and contextual relevance, I must borrow from multiple traditions and raid other disciplines.

- Theorizing, then, requires me to think *differently* about the issues that capture my imagination. Theorizing is an ongoing and engaging process in which I take chances and make myself intellectually visible and emotionally vulnerable in my work. All of my selves (scholar, scientist, human being) are evident so that my ideas are open to scrutiny, evaluation, and revision.

—Katherine Allen

Sometimes these narratives are used to advocate change on behalf of the individuals or groups providing the data. Dilworth-Anderson and Gibson (2002) gather information from African American and White family caregivers to older persons with dementia, in order to understand caregivers' perceptions of, and the meanings they assign to, demented behaviors. They are using a social constructivist perspective, a grounded theory approach, and family focus groups to help design interventions for the caregivers as well as the older persons themselves.

Theory as empowerment. Another perspective in family research today is that the goal of theory is to provide explanations that assess social problems and offer an activist agenda for social change. Self-reflection on motivations for research and explicit statements of the ideas underlying research are key tools in creating a family social science that matters to the people whose lives are investigated, the students who are training for the profession, and the citizens for whom the knowledge will be influential (Allen, 2000). "Conscientization" (Freire, 1970/1997) is the process of using our own experiences with marginalization to develop a critical consciousness about the possibility of social change. Rather than assuming the social world is "as it should be," and thus accepting oppression in its various forms (sexism, racism, heterosexism, classism, and the like), through action and interaction we come to recognize the malleability of cultural products and to create our own opportunities for liberation. As we all know, the most exciting learning occurs when students feel connected to knowledge that is meaningful to their own lives. As bell hooks [as she spells her name] (1994), suggests in her activist treatise on pedagogy, students want "an education that is healing to the uninformed, unknowing spirit" (p. 19). Similarly, theory as empowerment is linked to participative inquiry, of "living processes of coming to know" (Reason, 1994, p. 325). This has led to changes to redress discrimination against diverse social groups. Theorizing, then, is not simply an academic, ivory tower exercise. Theorizing leads to effective interventions, policies, and solutions to real world problems are critical as well.

These examples of theorizing in family studies today indicate that defining "theory" is complex, and that there is no single definition of theory in family research today. This leads us to some basic questions in examining what constitutes "knowledge"—the concern of epistemology—in studying families today.

WHAT IS KNOWING? BUILDING KNOWLEDGE IN STUDYING FAMILIES

Epistemology is Basic

Epistemology is a term that may seem esoteric and abstract to students. But epistemology is the basic and underlying core of any scholarly inquiry today. Epistemology involves analyzing the nature, origins, methods, and limits of knowledge. Epistemological concerns are basic to any field of scholarship. They are reflected in three very basic questions: (a) What is "knowing?" (b) How do we "know" what we think we know? (c) How useful is what we think we know—how valid, or truthful, or consequential is this knowledge?

Several Ways of Knowing as Applied to Family Studies

Klein and White (1996) have assessed several epistemological approaches as applied to family studies today. They contrast three epistemologies, three paradigms of knowing, that are today preeminent in contemporary family studies.

These are the *scientific* view of knowledge, the *interpretive* perspective, and the *critical* perspective. While there is much overlap among these perspectives, there are important differences. In Table 1.1, these distinctions among and between three major "ways of knowing" about families are discussed in terms of four aspects of "knowing": (a) the values underlying each approach; (b) the criteria for evaluation in terms of family theory; (c) goals of the approach; (d) scholarly style.

Table 1.1   Three Ways of Knowing Applied to Family Studies

1. **Scientific approach to knowing**

   View of knowledge: There are objective truths, processes, or realities to be discovered about families.

   Values: Family science can and should be value-neutral if not value-free.

   Criteria for evaluating family theories: Good theories should be relationally constructed (internally consistent, simple, coherent, clear, explicit, general, abstract). Good theories also should be empirically relevant (testable, fit well with data).

   Goals: Explanation and prediction.

   Scholarly style: Analytic, causal, deductive or inductive, deterministic or probabilistic, factual, logical, materialistic, mathematical, mechanistic, observant, planful, precise, quantitative, structural.

2. **Interpretive approach to knowing**

   View of knowledge: Truth is subjective, and all knowledge about families is created by interpreting actors engaged in conversations with one another.

   Values: Families science is values relevant, and family scientists should become aware of and open about their own values.

   Criteria for evaluating family theories: Good theories should have literary qualities (e.g., elegance, imagination, narrative power). Good theories also should be based on data grounded in the experiences of family members.

   Goal: Understanding.

   Scholarly style: Artistic, evocative, existential, hermeneutic, humanistic, intuitive, metaphorical, phenomenological, postmodern, processual, self-reflective, sensitive, speculative, spontaneous, symbolic.

3. **Critical approach to knowing**

   View of knowledge: Truth is defined by those who are in power, who impose their definition on others.

   Values: Family theories are value laden. Opportunities for change are created only when the values underlying theories are exposed and *challenged.*

   Criteria for evaluating family theories: Good theories contextualize phenomena and allow for pluralism. Good theories also are emancipatory, prescribe changes, display the theorists' ethical stances, and fit well with the theorists' personal experiences.

   Goal: Emancipation or empowerment of oppressed peoples and social groups

   Scholarly style: Constructivist, dialectical, feminist, liberal or radical, macroscopic, pluralistic, postmodern, processual, relativistic.

SOURCE: Adapted from Klein and White (1996).

A substantive example might help clarify this. A scientific theory of spousal abuse is oriented toward how, why, and under what conditions it occurs. An interpretive theory of spousal abuse is oriented toward how victims and perpetrators feel about and make sense of the behavior and the circumstances surrounding it. A critical theory of spousal abuse seeks ways of preventing or minimizing its occurrence. We feel there is no reason in principle why these three points of view could not be blended together. Knowing how social actors make sense of situations can help explain why violence occurs, and knowing why it occurs can help prevent or reduce future occurrences.

Each of these ways of knowing is valuable; each can be useful; neither is "best" or "worst" in our view. They allow us to see different things. They are different lenses through which to view and understand the world of families and intimate relationships. It may be useful to think of them as paradigms, a "fundamental image" of the subject matter within a scholarly field. Paradigms serve to define "what should be studied, what questions should be asked, how they should be asked, and what rules should be followed in interpreting the answers obtained" (Ritzer 1980, p. 7).

There Are Theories and There Are Paradigms, and These Rise and Fall

The progression of scientific knowledge is not as regular or smooth as methods textbooks often make it appear. There are bumps and occasional upheavals. Science is social; it involves the conceptualization of reality in accord with established definitions used by a group of peers in inquiry. The definition of what is "known" or "proven" or "demonstrated" is a social process involving a community of scientists.

No one has argued this more persuasively than Thomas Kuhn (1996). He viewed the history of science, from the Copernican revolution in the 16th Century to the development of the hydrogen bomb, as a series of knowledge revolutions. He termed these the construction and destruction of "paradigms," ways of viewing the observed world. This process, according to Kuhn, is rarely linear, but instead is complex, overlapping, and occurring over time. They are typically negotiated within a discipline by those who benefit most from maintaining the existing paradigm or those who are most negatively affected by its continued use in the discipline. See the spotlight on theory, p. 15 for applying Kuhn's arguments about the structure of scientific revolutions to family science.

The construction of knowledge is an inevitably a social endeavor. As such it is reflective of the concerns and careers of a collective group of practitioners. Theoretical development—and the explanations that ensue from it—are embedded in institutional and historical contexts. There are connections between scientific inquiry and the social milieu at particular points in time that influence how a subject matter is conceived. In recent years, interpretive and critical theorists have called attention to these connections, cautioning researchers to be more reflective on their own values or biases as they interpret findings, develop explanations, and make policy recommendations.

Are there paradigms in family studies? It would seem so. Have there been paradigmatic revolutions in family studies? Perhaps. Family researchers are very well mannered and seldom has there been occasion for spirited debate. But discussions can become heated when it appears that one "world view" is being challenged by another. One recent example of controversy is the family solidarity *versus* ambivalence debate (see chapter 16). Luscher and Pillemer (1998) presented the concept of ambivalence as the basic and underlying dimension of family relationships, since neither the solidarity nor the conflict model were adequate in characterizing adult intergenerational relationships—"anomalies" is the term Kuhn might have used. The debate was taken to another level by Connidis and McMullen (2002a, b), who argued that the concept of ambivalence should have been taken further, to reflect structural aspects of contemporary society that create inequalities and challenged the intergenerational solidarity model, which they suggested was both normative and hegemonic. This led to a response by Bengtson, Giarrusso, Mabry, and Silverstein (2002) arguing that the Connidis and McMullen (2002b) critique had misinterpreted the solidarity model, and challenging the assertion that ambivalence is more basic than solidarity and conflict in family relationships. Does this debate represent a potential paradigm shift in analyzing and explaining intergenerational relationships? Or is it a disagreement about the ways of knowing? Or about the primacy of certain constructs within a common paradigm? In any event it was a wonderful and welcome debate, an explicitly drawn controversy of the sort that is useful and has been too infrequent in family studies.

APPLYING KUHN'S SCIENTIFIC STRUCTURE OF REVOLUTIONS TO FAMILY SCIENCE

Peggye Dilworth-Anderson, *University of North Carolina-Chapel Hill*

In any discipline many factors encourage and sometimes demand that scientists practice their craft in a new or different manner. In American society, and some would argue globally, scientists are faced with the changing demographic landscape of families: different peoples (e.g., new immigrants) and different types of families (e.g., blended families, gay and lesbian families, and multiracial families). Thomas Kuhn's ideas, advanced in his seminal work, *The Structure of Scientific Revolutions* (1970), provide a framework that family scientists can use to conceptualize about these changes and how such changes demand an examination, if not a revolution, in how they practice their science, from theory and methodology to interpretation of findings.

Kuhn's ideas also challenge scientists to understand that science does not progress in the logical manner that we usually talk about. Instead, in reality scientists do not always incorporate new data as data are accumulated; rather, as Kuhn noted, scientists selectively attend to data on the basis of whether or not the data fits into their existing paradigms. This selectivity among scientists is just one way they resist incorporating changes in, for example, social and behavioral changes in their study participants that do not fit how they practice their science. When such changes are embraced, on the other hand, according to Kuhn, scientists are willing to question their paradigms, and if this challenge is fostered by key scientists in the discipline, it is possible that the discipline can approach a paradigm shift. Over time new concepts are introduced into the discipline and maybe even new elements of reality that are open to future investigation will be acceptable in the discipline. Describing this process in such few words here does not give justice to the complexity of how it takes place, the time it takes to evolve, and the identity crisis that ensues in a discipline for both individual scientists and the elements (e.g., theory and methodology) of the discipline.

I believe that family science is uniquely positioned at this time, similar to the field of astronomy in the 1700s, to making a paradigm shift, and possibly move through a "scientific revolution." We are no longer unified around asking similar questions. We do not agree on what types of questions are worth asking and what constitutes an acceptable answer to a question. We are showing signs that we do not share a common paradigm. Critical theory and feminist perspectives would argue that family science is in a crisis where we are dealing with anomalies, which makes it ripe for a revolution.

(continued)

• *SPOTLIGHT ON THEORY continued*

Family scientists are not without blueprints to understand how a shift, and ultimately a "scientific revolution," can greatly advance the practice of science. Using Galileo's observations and discoveries, we can see the power of a scientific revolution, which opens us up to new discoveries, and hopefully more relevant applications. For example, Galileo's use of the spyglass to observe the heavenly bodies opened the field of astronomy to investigate more broadly the stars and the planets; therefore, after Galileo's observations and discoveries other internal properties of the planets became subjects for investigation. Building on the discoveries of Galileo, astronomy became a transformed discipline that allowed different questions to be asked that further developed and expanded the field of astronomy. Because of Galileo's discoveries and his stature in the field, his observations were revolutionary and represented the rise of a new paradigm in astronomy (Hall, 1981). •

HOW DOES THEORIZING WORK? STEPS IN CREATING EXPLANATIONS FROM OBSERVATIONS

Methods of theorizing are as important as methods of conducting research. However, for several reasons, less attention is paid to *how* theories are developed. One reason is that some researchers are trained to feel that they should *apply and/or test existing theories,* rather than to *build or create new theories.* This results in a consumer rather than a producer mentality about theories, a focus on verifying rather than discovering knowledge. We feel this is unfortunate. Second, while the policies of most academic research journals require that papers have a research methods section, they do not require a section on theory or the contributions of the analysis to cumulative explanation. Thus, there are too few models in current family journals about how to theorize one's research results, and how theorizing is important to knowledge development. This too is unfortunate.

Our task as family scholars, operating within the community of family studies, is to contribute to better theoretical knowledge and demonstrate the usefulness of theories through their application to family problems and interventions.

The primary resources about how to build theories in the social sciences come from texts written in the 1960s and 1970s (e.g., Burr, 1973; Chafetz, 1984; Glaser & Strauss, 1967; Hage, 1972; Merton, 1957; Zetterberg, 1964). These texts often drew upon examples from the author's own work. They did not claim that their recommendations were based on widespread practices in the field, but rather advocated strategies that the authors felt should be used to develop knowledge and advance the social sciences. (See the web pages that will accompany this chapter for a synopsis of key texts in the "theory construction movement" of the 1960s and 1970s.)

Science is a continuous, cyclical process of discovery and confirmation (see Spotlight on Methods). It is a process of logical deduction, combinations, and borrowing.

THE CYCLICAL PROCESS OF SCIENCE

David M. Klein, *University of Notre Dame*

Science is a continuous process of transforming information elements into other information elements, and by means of specific methods. This process involves feedback, so it is circular.

Figure 1.4.1, sometimes called "the theory/data wheel," represents the process of science. It is reprinted from Wallace (1971, p. 18), and many similar versions have appeared in countless other books on theory and on research methodology.

Figure 1.4.1 The Principal Informational Components, Methodological Controls, and Information Transformations of the Scientific Process

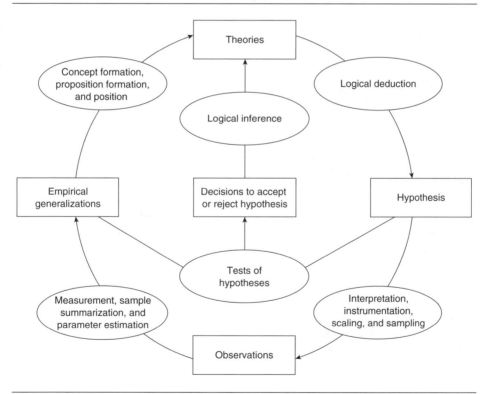

Note: Informational components are shown in rectangles; methodological controls are shown in ovals; information transformations are shown by arrows.

From Wallace, W., The Logic of Science in Sociology; 1971/Aldine, Atherton.

(continued)

The primary elements are theorizing in the top half and doing research in the bottom half. Working inductively is on the left side, and working deductively is on the right side. Several key points are worth keeping in mind about this view of science:

1. The wheel describes a general process in the scientific community, with many participants being engaged over time. The process includes actions as well as products or outcomes (theories and theorizing, data and doing research).

2. Theory and research are intertwined. Eventually, each leads to the other. While theories and methods are often taught in separate courses, they are intimately connected. Indeed, we have "methods of theorizing" (e.g., how to create an explanation) as well as "theories of methodology" (e.g., measurement theory).

3. In a particular project, the process may start with any informational component and end with any informational component. A full cycle is not always required. Also, informational components may be singular or plural. For example, we might start with one theory or several. We might start with one observation of one family, or with much data about many families.

4. Paths not shown may appear (e.g., from observations back to hypotheses via "analytical induction"). Therefore, the process may be reversible. Generally, it goes clockwise, but not always.

5. The lines connecting "tests of hypotheses" with "hypotheses" and with "empirical generalizations" are not paths to be followed. Instead, they are meant to indicate that hypotheses and empirical generalizations are compared when testing hypotheses.

6. The process is normative in the sense that a science is operating well when work progresses through the paths. In practice, some obstacles may arise and dead ends may occur. Additional efforts eventually overcome these problems.

7. Individual scientists may specialize in one aspect of the process, but they are always building upon previous work by others. For some projects, a team of scholars with complementary talents pushes the process along.

Wallace (1971, pp. 25–29) showed how Emile Durkheim used the wheel model in his study of suicide. But, how do we know that the model is adequate for describing how scientists usually work? You could evaluate the adequacy of the model by examining a body of literature developed over time on a particular family topic (marriage, parenting, etc.). You could start with the "hypothesis" that knowledge about the topic has been developed in accordance with the model. Your "observations" would be statements in published works about the topic. If the wheel model does not adequately describe how family science deals with the topic, develop your own model about how family science works. However, what model will you use to develop your own model? If scientists are people and family members are people, perhaps theories and methods about family science should be similar to theories and methods about families. Being "reflexive" means that we as family scientists develop an understanding of ourselves in the same way that we develop an understanding of people in families. And, our theories about science must have some correspondence with our theories about whatever we are studying within our science. ●

1. *Deductive theorizing:* Theories of smaller scope and less generality are deduced from existing theories of larger scope and more generality. Research hypotheses are also deduced from theories. The basic skill here is deductive logic.

Most scientific theory-building is essentially deductive, starting with definitions of general concepts and putting forward a number of propositions about the relationships among concepts. Concepts are linked to empirical phenomena through operational definitions. Derived hypotheses are then tested against empirical observations. A general theory allows investigators to deduce logically a number of quite specific statements, or explanations, about the nature and behavior of a large class of phenomena (Turner, 2003b; Wallace & Wolf, 1991). Because such theories are useful in predicting and hence manipulating our environments, they are considered essential for the design of programs aimed at ameliorating problems of families (especially by government funding agencies).

2. *Inductive theorizing:* Theories of larger scope and more generality are induced from existing theories of smaller scope and less generality. Theories are also induced from confirmed empirical generalizations. The basic skill here is inductive logic.

Many researchers using qualitative methods employ *grounded theory* as an inductive approach to generating theory (Glaser & Strauss, 1967). This method of theorizing starts with the data, and leads in the final stages of analysis to the emergence of key concepts and how they relate to one another. Rather than beginning with a theory and an explicit set of derived hypotheses, a grounded theory approach attempts to create theoretical categories from data generated during the course of the research using an iterative process in which emerging theories shape data collection and analyses throughout an investigation. Research using quantitative methods can also proceed from the bottom up, starting with data and developing theory.

While patterns observed in data can inspire theoretical statements, they do not prove the truth of statements of greater scope or more generality that are created as a result of one's research. What research can do is disconfirm theories, suggest marginal improvements to existing theories, or suggest better theories for future research. One study alone, or several in combination, is seldom adequate to prove the truth of all aspects of a given theory.

These ideas of deduction and induction in the social sciences are explored further by Turner (2003a), a useful source for additional discussion.

3. *Combinations:* Given the existence of two or more theories that are judged to be relevant to a particular problem, aspects of the different theories can be combined. Two basic skills are involved here. One is to read widely enough to know the range of relevant theories. The other is to know a discipline's vocabulary well enough to judge the similarities and differences between the concepts and the relationships between concepts in different theories.

Sometimes, the combination of theories may be eclectic. That is, the theorist will select bits and pieces from different theories in order to arrive at a more comprehensive explanation. At other times, the integration of theoretical insights may be more systematic. Perhaps Theory A is judged to apply well in some explicitly stated situations, while Theory B is judged to apply better in other explicitly stated situations.

4. *Borrowing:* Promising theories and concepts can be borrowed from other topics of study, or even from other disciplines. This can be particularly fruitful in multidisciplinary fields such as family studies. The basic skill here is openness to metaphors and analogies, but also an awareness of their limitations.

In thinking this way, we can envision families as being like other kinds of human social groups in crucial respects (see Jonathan Turner's Case Study 1.2). Alternatively, we might start by imagining that families are like individual persons in some respects. We might even start by thinking about families as nonhuman entities (e.g., forests, molecules, solar systems, rivers, or ant colonies). All that is required is familiarity with other areas of research where theories are used, a willingness to see the heuristic potential of borrowing ideas, and a dose of skepticism so that the boundaries of relevance or of uncertainty are acknowledged.

It is useful to explore other ways of proceeding, other methods of theorizing that might be fruitful beyond those we have been able to discuss here.

HOW IS THEORIZING RELATED TO METHODS IN STUDYING FAMILIES?

Advances in quantitative techniques since the last *Sourcebook* (Boss et al., 1993) have been directed to greater isomorphism between methods and theoretical perspectives. Many of these developments are reviewed in Chapter 3. Other developments such as growth curve modeling focus on developmental processes as more and more theory points to the importance of studying processes over time. Another major development is multilevel analysis, which allows us to focus on contextual and family level variables as well as individual level variables (see Chapter 12). Ecological theory and family process theory call for simultaneously considering family level variables and contextual variables, and early quantitative methods did not perform this task very well. Another advance in quantitative techniques since the last *Sourcebook* is the development of procedures for limited dependent variable analyses that deal with outcomes that are best conceptualized as categorical or ordered categories rather than as measured by a single, underlying continuum. An example is the concept of ambivalence (Luescher & Pillemer, 1998), which denotes the complex and often-contradictory feelings children have toward their parents that do not fall nicely on a single underlying dimension. Quantitative methods have been responsive to these kinds of theoretically driven challenges.

The legitimization of qualitative methods since the last *Sourcebook* (Boss et al., 1993) has been remarkable. Scholars who were prejudiced

against qualitative methods at the time of the last *Sourcebook* are included among their advocates today. These groups have questioned, examined, and documented "stories" that are rarely captured with quantitative methods or surveys. Feminist theorizing as well as the theoretical work of scholars who represent marginalized groups have played a central role in this transformation of methodology (Ferree, 1990). Often this has involved legitimizing strategies that have been used for over a century and stand out among the classic social science studies, such as Thomas and Znaniecki's (1918–1920) analysis of Polish immigrants. Increasingly, graduate programs require training in both quantitative and qualitative methodology. Chapter 3 discusses how the use of mixed methods will allow scholars today and those who are being trained for tomorrow to tell more complete, comprehensive, and inclusive stories about families.

As the construction of knowledge in family studies becomes more inclusive, family studies will include both concordant and discordant views. Moreover, as suggested by Kuhn (1996), discordant views can serve as a catalyst to question, modify, and replace existing theories and scientific practices. Just as jazz represents discordant tones that can be pleasing to the ear, discordant and sometimes opposing views about what we come to "know" about families can also provide a new way to accept what is knowledge and how to advance it in the field of family studies. Thus, speaking metaphorically, different views about the family can produce new knowledge that through time can become accepted ways of knowing or thinking, just as jazz is now considered the only "truly American" music.

Occasionally, theories are used to limit methodological approaches. Some students may have been taught that a feminist needs to do qualitative research or a person from a social exchange perspective needs to take a quantitative approach. Although these are legitimate options, they should not be seen as theoretically imposed methodological blinders. Homans's (1961) original work on social exchange theory was largely qualitative, being based on observation in natural settings and letting questions emerge after extended observation. Quantitative national surveys on the effect of divorce on various measures of efficacy among women are certainly appropriate research methodologies from a feminist perspective. The point is that divergent theoretical perspectives need to be considered and theoretical perspectives should be used to expand our methodological capabilities rather than limit them.

There is certainly no one unified paradigm in family studies today. This means that we are faced with multiple theoretical perspectives and an even larger number of methodological strategies and techniques. This also means that we need to be particularly sensitive to linkages between research and theorizing, methods and theory. Most articles in leading family journals include only very brief tributes to theory, often just one or two paragraphs. It is unusual for the methods section of the articles to discuss linkages between the theory and methods, though they may often be implicit. There is also very limited linkage between the often superficial discussion of theory at the start of the article and the discussion section at the end. Which theory is supported? Is there a need to revise a theory in order for it to be consistent with the results? In short, greater attention needs to be given to theory and the bridge between data and explanations in our journal articles.

CONCLUSION

In this chapter we have reviewed a wide range of issues related to theory and theory development in family research, from basic epistemological concerns to the often-uneasy relationships between theorizing and the research methods we use in family studies. In concluding this chapter we want to be explicit about our own observations, which are based on our many discussions over the three years as we have worked.

1. We believe that *theorizing is crucial* if we want to expand the knowledge base about families and the processes of family relationships. Lack of theorizing leads to one-shot, limited application of research findings, which cannot advance the development of knowledge in our field.

2. We feel that *theorizing should be explicit*—and that too frequently it has not been so in family studies to date. Too often both quantitative and qualitative studies of families and family interactions have been based on implicit explanations of what is important to study and why the results are important. We argue that implicit theorizing should be made explicit—in both the design and reporting of results—so that the knowledge from these studies can be examined in a full and open scholarly debate. This is a debate that will go beyond research methods (qualitative vs. quantitative) and beyond disciplinary boundaries (epidemiological or sociological), toward building knowledge about families at the macro-, meso-, and micro-social levels of scholarly analysis.

3. We suggest that *theorizing is necessary to all research reports about families*. We feel that family scholars cannot design or plan a study without some expectations about *what* it is that we want to find out and *why* that is important. Similarly, when we select the most important results or findings to write about, we are theorizing—developing ideas that we feel are important to share with others.

4. We believe that *theorizing means explanation and understanding*. We suggest that all studies of family issues should conclude with attempts to explain findings and interpret them within explicit frameworks that make transparent the ideas underlying the research process, including the values of the researcher and the ends to which research will be used. We advocate an inclusive stance toward theorizing, in that interpretation and explanation are not positioned in opposition to one another but are integrative. Particularly in a field like family studies, where there are multiple points of view and where lived experiences in families is an obvious source of

insight, meaning, and motivation, we recognize the importance of using all the resources at our disposal to develop theoretical understandings and advance the field.

5. We feel that *theorizing about families is fun*. It's not dull, boring, or mysterious. Theorizing about family processes is a very human process, perhaps more so today than ever before. Now more than ever we need to carefully summarize our ideas so that others can evaluate and scrutinize them—and thus

continue to refine them toward the practical ends that theory should be used. We have the tools in both scientific and humanistic methods to generate good theories that offer plausible explanations of the complex family phenomena we study. We also need good will, humor, forgiveness, and the willingness to create as well as revise our theories. Theorizing is an inclusive, communal process, one in which all of us— participants, students, and scholars—are needed to produce multiple visions of how and why families are the way they are.

CASE STUDY

THE LACK OF EXPLICIT THEORY IN FAMILY RESEARCH

A Case Analysis of the *Journal of Marriage and the Family* 1990–1999

Alan C. Taylor, *Syracuse University*

Aparna Bagdi, *University of Delaware*

Scholars in family studies have been criticized for the lack of interplay between theory, measurement, and analysis in the design, implementation, and reports of family research (Galigun, 1982; Nye, 1988; Schumm, 1982). Lavee and Dollahite (1991) noted that the majority of family researchers do not delineate the theoretical underpinnings guiding their methodology, resulting in a lack of linkage between theory and research in family studies. A 60-year review of family research concluded that a major weakness in the field has been its inadequate development of theory (Bahr, 1990).

A systems approach can help family researchers better understand the necessary interaction between theory and empirical research. Lavee and Dollahite (1991) introduced a

systemic model of scientific activities, describing the necessary relationship between theory and scientific research. In this model the scientific system's input (family phenomena) and the system's output (systematic explanation of family phenomena or consensual knowledge) is described, as well as the interchange between theory and research as it affects the input and outputs. The lack of feedback between theory and research can have lasting effects on the purposes and outcomes of scientific research.

In the field of family studies, little systematic research regarding the connection between research and theory has been attempted, in addition to the limited discussion of the relationship between specific theoretical frameworks and methods (Klein & White, 1996). In

CASE STUDY *continued*

order to more fully evaluate these issues, I examined how explicit theoretical frameworks were employed within empirical studies published in the *Journal of Marriage and the Family* from 1990–1999.

EXAMINING UTILIZATION OF EXPLICIT THEORY

We reviewed empirical articles published in the *Journal of Marriage and the Family* between 1990–1999. An article was judged to be empirical if it manipulated some type of data in its analysis. Of the 886 articles published in the 10-year period of *JMF*, 673 met these criteria. Book reviews, theoretical essays or methodological studies were not included.

The first step was to categorize the theoretical frameworks utilized. Theories were identified when an underlying theoretical perspective was explicitly stated within the content of the empirical research article. We created a list of family interaction and human development theories based on existing literature (Boss et al., 1993; Burr et al., 1979; Klein & White, 1996). All explicit theories not categorized as family or human development theories were initially labeled as "other," and later examined using a constant comparative method to discover any common themes or frequencies. The research team also analyzed whether a study was by design qualitative, quantitative, or a combination of the two. Then we examined the use of explicit theoretical frameworks within each type of method. The table on page 24 summarizes our results.

USING THEORY TO ACCOUNT FOR EMPIRICAL RESULTS

Of the 673 empirical articles examined, 265 (39%) made *no explicit reference to theory* anywhere in the article. Of the articles using explicit theoretical frameworks, exchange theory was most commonly referred to (8%). Life course perspective and gender theory

were also among the most commonly reported theoretical frameworks (5% and 4.6%, respectively).

Of the 673 articles, 635 (94%) used quantitative methodologies exclusively. Eighteen (2.6%) articles employed qualitative methodologies, while 20 (3%) articles involved a combination of both quantitative and qualitative methodologies.

Qualitative articles more frequently used explicit theoretical frameworks.

Seventeen of the 18 qualitative articles (94%) using qualitative methodologies reported explicit theoretical approaches. Symbolic interaction theory and social construction theory were the most frequent explicit frameworks within this category.

Only 381 of the 635 quantitative empirical articles (60%) used explicit theoretical frameworks to account for results. Exchange theory, the life course perspective, and gender theory were the most frequently cited. Exchange theory was used explicitly in 50 articles, while life course and gender were employed in 36 and 30 quantitative articles, respectively. Ten of the 20 articles (50%) employing both qualitative and quantitative methodologies used explicit theoretical frameworks.

A PLETHORA OF "THEORIES"?

This study indicates that explicit theory is being employed in *JMF* empirical research articles only slightly more frequently than over a decade ago (Lavee & Dollahite, 1991). It is worth noting that many *JMF* authors reviewed (35%) chose not to utilize the more common family and human development theories traditionally and currently found in family theory textbooks and sourcebooks (Boss et al., 1993; Burr et al., 1979; Klein & White, 1996). Instead many opted for less commonly used theories, minitheories (such as the "Addictive Theory of Size Constraint"), which are intended to explain specific

Case Study

CASE STUDY *continued*

The Use of Explicit Theories in Empirical Studies Reported in the *Journal of Marriage and the Family,* 1990–1999: Frequencies and Percentages

Theory	Frequency	Percentage
No explicit theory mentioned	265	39.3
Exchange theory	52	8.2
Life-course perspective	38	5.0
Gender theory	31	4.6
Role theory	26	3.8
Systems theory	24	3.5
Ecology/human ecology theory	22	3.2
Social learning theory	22	3.2
Stress/coping theory	22	3.2
Structural/functional theory	22	3.2
Theory named after an individual	21	3.1
Socialization theory	16	2.3
Symbolic interaction theory	13	1.9
Resource theory	12	1.7
Family development theory	11	1.6
Feminist theory	11	1.6
Cultural theory	11	1.6
Social capital theory	10	1.4
Intergenerational theory	10	1.4
Human developmental theory	9	1.3
Power/control theory	9	1.3
Social causation theory	8	1.1
Cognitive development theory	6	.8
Interpersonal theory	6	.8
Identity theory	5	.6
Parenting theory	5	.6
Behaviorist theory	4	.5
Conflict theory	4	.5
Attachment theory	4	.5
Equity theory	4	.5
Identity theory	4	.5

phenomena or interaction and are often less abstract than conceptual frameworks and meta-theories (Doherty et al., 1993). Based on this information, it appears that as the family field grows and expands, so does the number of theories that scholars may employ to explain and interpret family phenomena.

Moreover, some of the empirical articles reviewed simply presented another scholar's name to describe an approach—such as "LeVinge's concepts" or "Blau's perspective." Unfortunately, many of these authors did not go into detail regarding the concepts or assumptions of the approaches they labeled. Without details about concepts or assumptions, a reader may find the approach meaningless without further investigation into the focus or scope of these theories.

CASE STUDY *continued*

A LACK OF THEORIZING?

Given the wide range of theories being used in the family field, it is still puzzling to find that more than one third of the empirical studies published in *JMF* during the 1990s did not include explicit theory in accounting for empirical results. Why?

Publishing an empirical article is a process in which many factors and people influence the end product. Like a general system, an empirical study has multiple components that are important to the whole manuscript. A quality empirical article should include a sound rationale, an explicit theory-research link, a strong methodology, findings, and a discussion section that covers application, implementation, and future research. A weak or missing element in the study influences the whole system, or in this case, the entire manuscript. Outside forces or suprasystems can greatly influence the system as a whole, as well as each interconnected element within the system. Examples of these suprasystems include the authors themselves, the publishers who set guidelines and limitations, as well as the reviewers and editors who judge and critique the system as a whole.

First, some researchers may not value theory usage and do not want to incorporate theory into their findings. Some researchers may not feel there is a connection between theory and the topic on which their article focuses. Others may assume that readers will be able to decipher which implicit theoretical frameworks are being used, just by examining the specific concepts or by a thorough examination of the background or review of literature sections. But with multiple assumptions embedded within the large number of unique theoretical frameworks, it should be the authors' responsibility to be explicit in describing which theoretical approach or approaches they were using in conjunction with their empirical research.

Second, and also from a systemic perspective, professional journals such as the *Journal of Marriage and the Family* have not facilitated the theory/research link. Authors face stringent space constraints about what must be included in a journal article submission (literature review, methods, findings, a discussion and implications of such findings). With such space limitations, theory may be deemed less valuable than other components of empirical research. Within the last decade in the *Journal of Marriage and the Family*, few (less than 25) theoretical, nonempirical articles have been published. The lack of theoretical dialogue within the pages of a well-respected research journal may send a subtle message that theory is less important or of little value in the family field.

Third, it is the editors and peer-reviewers who must assume the role of enforcing theoretical relevance in empirical research. They are the "watch-dogs" of the practice of theory-research integration (Lavee & Dollahite, 1991). The use of explicit theory would be greater if reviewers and editors strongly encouraged more direct theoretical connections to research methodologies, findings, and discussions.

CONCLUSION

Over a decade ago Lavee and Dollahite (1991) issued a call to all family researchers to focus their efforts on forging a stronger link between theory and empirical research. As is evident from this analysis of research published in the *JMF*, this challenge has yet to be fully realized. Family researchers and scholars, as well as journal editorial boards and reviewers, must take responsibility to better incorporate a more explicit theory-research connection. They owe it to their readers, as well as to the future of the family field.

Case Study

CASE STUDY

IS A SCIENTIFIC THEORY OF THE FAMILY DESIRABLE?

Jonathan H. Turner, *Department of Sociology, University of California, Riverside*

Scientific theory seeks to explain the operative dynamics of the universe. Scientific theories first isolate what are considered to be the generic dimensions of the universe, then develop abstract models and principles to explain their operation. In sociology, scientific theory would thus seek to develop principles and models that explain the operation of those fundamental processes directing human behavior, interaction, and social organization.

This "hard science" view of sociological theory is, of course, not accepted by all, but let me pursue the implications of this view of sociological theory in the context of theorizing about family processes. I recognize that many reading these words are not sociologists; and moreover, much scholarly work on the family is not oriented to scientific explanations. There are many other reasons to study family processes, above and beyond efforts to generate scientific explanations. Thus, what I have to say is directed primarily at those who see scientific explanations as *one way* to understand family dynamics. What I say of sociology is also true of other disciplines. And, whether the effort at scientific explanations comes from a sociologist, psychologist, demographer, economist, anthropologist, or from any other related discipline, I believe that my commentary will be relevant.

NO THEORY "OF" THE FAMILY

The most obvious implication of this view of scientific explanation is that it is not possible, or desirable, to have a theory *of* the family. The family is the place where more generic social forces intersect, and theorizing should be about these more generic forces rather than the family as a unit. True, families have existed since humans emerged as a species, and so in this sense the family is universal and generic; but it is not the most generic of forces that drive the formation of the family (and many other social structures). The family is where one studies social processes, but theory is about these processes, not the family per se.

A second implication is that different theoretical models and principles should exist for each of the *generic* processes that drive behavior, interaction, and organization. In trying to explain a particular empirical regularity in families, it is necessary first to isolate the underlying processes involved, and then use the relevant theoretical models and principles on *each* of these processes. Thus, the particular explanation for a set of empirical observations will be somewhat ad hoc because it is necessary to assemble the principles and models that bear on the problem at hand. I have always seen theory as a "bag of principles and models" on fundamental forces driving the formation and operation of the social universe; depending upon the particular problem, one reaches into this bag and pulls out the relevant theoretical principles that are relevant, ignoring those that do not apply to the empirical events that one is trying to explain. Thus, if comparison processes, emotions, justice, and power dynamics are the underlying forces driving empirical observations about some aspect of a family, then the models an principles about these processes are the ones that are pulled from the bag and assembled in an ad hoc way to develop an explanation.

THEORY VS. PERSPECTIVES OR SCHOOLS OF THOUGHT

The big problem with this vision of how scientific theory works is that sociologists do not formulate their theories in this way. Instead, we tend to view theories as part of "schools of thought," "paradigms," or "perspectives"—e.g., functionalism, conflict theory, interactionism, phenomenology, postmodernism, exchange theory, critical theory, and so on, for the dozen or so "perspectives" that can be found in theory textbooks. Explanation tends to revolve around debates among or conflicts between symbolic, conflict, functional, exchange, critical, etc., theoretical interpretations of some process in the family. While interpretations using the eyeglasses provided by one or more of these theoretical perspectives can be quite enlightening, they do not constitute a very mature form of scientific explanation. Moreover, interpretations from multiple theoretical perspectives will yield different explanations that will become the basis for a theoretical argument among theorists and researchers. Unfortunately these kinds of arguments cannot be resolved because each theory operates with different assumptions, sees different things, and forces varying conclusions.

Theoretical explanations about family processes will, therefore, simply replicate the theoretical debates that occur within broader theoretical sociology. Rather than perpetuate replication of old theoretical debates, I believe that sociology needs a fundamental reorientation in how it generates explanation, and empirical work in substantive areas such as family can help in this reorientation. There are many reasons for studying a particular aspect of families that, on the surface, have little to do with theory testing. A client desires data on some dimension of the family; and

researchers develop measuring instruments to gather information desired by a client. Some of these data will, however, provide information on more generic social processes that occur in all interpersonal relations and groups; and it is here that research can feed into theory, if researchers are willing to ask a simple question: "*What are the more generic processes in the social universe operating in the family processes that I am studying?*" This question is not easily answered. But if it is asked, then research can feed into assessments of more generic theories; and theories can provide more useful explanations for empirical events observed in families.

HEAVY LIFTING FOR RESEARCHERS

Unfortunately, even if a researcher is willing to ask and answer this question, the theories themselves are not generally organized around models and principles of discrete social processes. Thus, researchers are forced to scan through various theories and cull out the relevant theoretical models and principles, even assuming that the theories are stated as models and principles (which typically they are not). Thus, the researcher must do additional work by first finding the relevant theoretical ideas and then formalizing these ideas so that they become an explanation of the data. This is heavy lifting for researchers.

It is not surprising that researchers find so much theory irrelevant to their research goals because, in essence, the present state of theory asks researchers to become theorists who do all of the heavy lifting. The researcher must, first of all, decide upon the underlying processes that are being measured in a research design; then, the researcher must find the relevant theories, pull out the key ideas, and formalize them into an abstract principle and model that can then be used to explain the empirical regularities in the data. If the researcher must do all of this work, why do they need theorists?

Case Study

CASE STUDY *continued*

The fault resides in how sociologists visualize the process of developing theories. Relatively few theorists ask the most basic question: *What are the generic and fundamental forces and processes* driving the formation and operation of the social universe? Some theories nibble at the edges of this question because conflict, exchange, structural interdependence, symbolic interaction, and the like are indeed fundamental social processes. And, if we move into areas such as social psychology, theories often appear to be about generic social processes, such as expectation states, attributions, emotions, comparison, justice, status, and the like. Thus, one can find the beginnings of what theory should look like: abstract statements that explain the operation of fundamental social processes.

What, you may ask, is a "fundamental," "generic," or "basic" social force or process? My answer is simple: *Fundamental processes are those that are always evident when humans behave, interact, and organize.* The answer is complex because different processes may operate for behavior, interaction, and organization; and social organization may reveal varying processes depending upon whether it is a micro-, meso-, or macro-level pattern of social organization.

But at a minimum, sociological theorists should ask: What always occurs when humans behave? What always occurs when people interact? And what always occurs when people form micro-, meso-, and macro-level patterns of social organization? If sociological theory had a bag full of models and principles that answered these questions, researchers would have theories that they could use. Theorists rather than researchers would do most of the heavy lifting.

BREAKING DOWN PARTITIONS

In fact, sociology does have many of these principles and models, if only implicitly. The various theoretical perspectives reveal some of them; the traditions within social psychology offer insights into more of them as they affect behavior and interaction; and the relatively few theories in sociology that seek to develop formal models and principles on generic social processes can offer some more of these principles. The problem in current theory is the lack of consolidating and synthesis of what is known about basic social processes. Sociologists know a great deal more about how the social world operates than is often recognized. The problem is that this knowledge is partitioned into theoretical perspectives, or ignored by the many critics of any form of scientific explanation. The end result is that the full explanatory potential of theoretical sociology is not realized, or even recognized.

How, then, can we break this impasse? One answer can come from those who work within delimited specialties, such as the sociology of the family. Most work in the family is focused on some topic; and the overwhelming majority of work on the family is empirical in nature, revolving around collecting data on some aspect of the family that is of interest to researchers or their clients. Only a modest shift in emphasis is required to make data collection more relevant to theory.

If researchers ask what generic processes are in play in the phenomenon under study, they have taken the critical step in making the data useful in developing or testing more general theories. For example, if "family violence" is being studied, the important question is what more fundamental processes are involved in generating violence, or a lack of violence. Power would be one process, arousal of negative or positive emotions would be another, resource distribution and exchange dynamics would be yet another, or so on. Of course, further refinement is necessary: what aspects of power, emotional arousal, and exchange dynamics are relevant? But, in just asking these kinds of questions, a descriptive study can become more theoretically relevant; and theories can offer explanations as to *why* particular patterns of family violence occur.

On the other side, theorists themselves need to ask this same question: "What are the generic social forces of the social universe and how can I conceptualize their operative dynamics?"

Even to phrase the matter in this way invites derision from some quarters about the dangers of "scientism" and "positivism." Yet, what is the alternative?

We can continue offering interpretations of events from some theoretical perspectives that brings in its bag all manner of epistemological, ontological, ideological, and similar baggage without ever offering explicit models and principles. Or, we can continue to collect data that describes some set of events at a given time and place. In the end, we will have more information without knowing very much. For, ultimately, knowledge comes from the ability to explain the specific with the general; that is, we can know why the social universe operates by collecting data on generic social processes and explaining these data in terms of theoretical principles and models on these generic processes.

Well-established research traditions, especially cross-disciplinary ones like the family field, offer great potential for theoretical development. But this will occur only if family researchers take a courageous step: attempting to explain their findings using fundamental social processes.

DISCUSSION AND EXTENSION

THEORIZING FAMILY: FROM THE PARTICULAR TO THE GENERAL

David Cheal, *University of Winnipeg*

The authors of Chapter 1 have opened up for discussion the question of "What is theory?" Theory is a kind of discourse. It is a set of topics and a way of talking about those topics. Not all discourse is theoretical discourse, however. Theory is the kind of discourse that seeks generalization. It moves from the particular to the general, and makes statements that apply to a large number of cases under a variety of conditions. The purpose of theory may be to explain, or to construct a narrative, or to summarize knowledge, but the form of argument is always one of generalization. Theory is that discourse which takes particular cases and places them in a context where they can be compared with other cases having similar or different properties.

The principal means by which generalizations are made in theoretical discourse is through the use of concepts that identify types of objects. Concepts are the heart of any theory, and definitions of concepts therefore rightly receive a great deal of attention in the process of theorizing. A renewal of family theory must include renewed attention to problems of definition in family studies, including the problem of defining family itself.

If the goal of theory is generalization, we need to pay attention to the different levels of theory. This involves including in our

DISCUSSION AND EXTENSION *continued*

repertoire of theories those theories which are general in the sense of applying to aspects of society beyond family relations. Concepts such as industrial society and post-industrial society are relevant here, and seem likely to become more important as we try to develop our theories to take account of changes in family life.

It also includes considering what are the most general concepts in time and space. As Bengtson et al. (2002) note, we need explanations and understandings of family relationships and their diverse processes across time and place. There are many levels of temporal and spatial relevance in our repertoire of theories. However, objects which have the greatest distribution in space and/or the greatest distribution in time deserve special attention in family theory. In relation to space, this means that we must look outside national borders to construct global conceptualizations of family and family issues. Cross-cultural and comparative studies of family life need to be engaged in with renewed vigor, not just from the perspective of data collection but also from the perspective of conceptualization. Similarly, studies that encompass broad regions of time are needed, and these should be more than a collection of discrete historical case studies. Among the most general concepts in time is that of modernity, and its attendant concept of post-modernity. Attempts to theorize the relation between family and modernity should be recognized and encouraged, and family theorists should attempt to broaden the scope of their work by relating it to questions of modernity whenever possible.

Papers on family theory should include examples of theorizing in family studies in order to open up theory for discussion. If theorizing is to receive the attention it deserves, then we need more discussion of substantive theories. This paper therefore includes an illustration of successful theorizing along the above lines taken from the theory of family change as a result of the process of

individualization advanced by Ulrich Beck and Elisabeth Beck-Gernsheim (1995, 2002). Individualization theory maintains that many of the changes occurring in families, such as the increased number of single parent families, can be accounted for by a long-term trend in modern societies to accord more autonomy to individuals. It is a simple, yet powerful, explanation for changes in family structure as well as in gender relations and the contents of family life (see the web pages).

From this point of view, modernization involves not just structural change, but a changing relationship between structures and agents. When modernization reaches a certain level, agents tend to become more individualized, that is to say less constrained by social structures (Beck, 1992). Individualization means that men and women are released from the gender roles prescribed by industrial society for life in the nuclear family (Beck and Beck-Gernsheim, 1995). Responding to the pressures of the labor market, they become free to design their own occupational careers and to adapt the rest of their lives to their careers. When two individuals in the same family adopt this way of thinking, then the potential for conflict emerges as each person struggles to put his or her needs first.

Individualization involves liberation from traditional commitments and personal emancipation, but it also involves loss of stability and increased risk of disappointment. Opportunities and threats must increasingly be perceived, interpreted, and handled by individuals themselves without the intervention of social groups. The individual himself or herself becomes the agent of his or her own biography, in relation to educational institutions and market-based subsistence and the consequent life planning and organization. Individuals must construct their own biographies, and they therefore make decisions about whether and whom they shall marry, whether or not to have children, and what sort of sexual preference they will have, etc.

DISCUSSION AND EXTENSION *continued*

In family life, the result has been to break apart the old togetherness, Beck believes. Viewed from the perspective of the individual life course, a normal biography now appears as a sequence of alternating phases of living in families and other ways of living together or alone. Rules about the indissolubility of marriage are replaced by a new ethic of personal choices, and women are urged to maintain their economic independence inside and outside marriage through a commitment to careers which equals that of men. According to Beck (1992), the family, and family roles, have been dissolved by a surge of individualization. At the extreme, divorce cuts women loose from support as spouses and housewives, and produces new patterns of poverty. Inside the family, responsibilities are constantly being negotiated and renegotiated under the pressures of occupational commitments, educational constraints and individual mobility. According to Beck (1992), the type of family which emerges from this process is the negotiated provisional family.

The point of this extended discussion is to remark that there are examples of successful theorizing that can help us to make sense of a multitude of research findings in the ongoing discourse of family studies. The authors of "Theory and Theorizing in Family Research" complain about the lack of theorizing in the research literature, but we need to pay more attention to the theories which actually exist. Theories such as individualization theory have much to tell us about family issues over the long term, and they are therefore important guides to research on the past and in the present. Individualization theory represents a serious attempt at generalization about family issues, which is the hallmark of family theory.

REFERENCES

Acock, A. C., & Demo, D. H. (1994). *Family diversity and well being.* Thousand Oaks, CA: Sage.

Allen, K. R. (2000). A conscious and inclusive family studies. *Journal of Marriage and the Family, 62,* 4–17.

Beck, U. (1992). *Risk society: Towards a new modernity.* London: Sage.

Beck, U., & Beck-Gernsheim, E. (1995). *The normal chaos of love.* Cambridge: Polity.

Beck, U., & Beck-Gernsheim, E. (2002). *Individualization: Institutionalized.*

Bengtson, V. L., Giarrusso, R., Mabry, J. B., & Silverstein, M. (2002). Solidarity, conflict, and ambivalence: Complementary or Competing Perspectives on Intergenerational Relationships? *Journal of Marriage and the Family, 64,* 568–576.

Boss, P., Doherty, W., LaRossa, R., Schumm, W., & Steinmetz, S. (Eds.). (1993). *Sourcebook of family theories and methods: A contextual approach.* New York: Plenum.

Brown, R. H. (1989). *Social Science as civic discourse: Essays on the invention, legitimation, and uses of social theory.* Chicago: The University of Chicago Press.

Burr, W. R. (1973). *Theory construction and the sociology of the family.* New York: John Wiley.

Burr, W. R., Hill, R., Nye, F. I., & Reiss, I. L. (Eds.). (1979). *Contemporary theories about the family* (2 vols.). New York: Free Press.

Chafetz, J. S. (1984). *Sex and Advantage: A comparative macrostructural theory of sex stratification.* Totowa, NJ: Rowman & Allanheld.

Connidis, I. A., & McMullin, J. A. (2002a). Sociological ambivalence and family ties: A critical perspective. *Journal of Marriage and the Family, 64,* 558–547.

Connidis, I.A., & McMullin, J. A. (2002b). Ambivalence, family ties, and doing sociology. *Journal of Marriage and the Family, 64,* 594–601.

Dilworth-Anderson, P., & Gibson, B. (2002). The cultural influence of values, norms, meanings, and perceptions in understanding dementia in ethnic minorities. *Alzheimer's Disease and Associated Disorders, 16,* S56–S63.

Ferree, M. (1990). Beyond separate spheres: Feminism and family research. *Journal of Marriage and the Family, 52,* 866–884.

Freire, P. (1970/1997). *Pedagogy of the oppressed* (M. B. Ramos, Trans., new rev. ed.). New York: Continuum.

Geertz, C. (1975). *The interpretation of cultures.* London: Hutchinson.

Glaser, B. G., & Strauss, A. L. (1967). *The discovery of grounded theory: Strategies for qualitative research.* Chicago: Aldine de Gruyter.

Hage, J. G. (1972). *Techniques and problems of theory construction in sociology.* New York: Wiley Interscience.

Hall, R. (1981). *From Galileo to Newton.* New York: Dover Publishers.

Homans, G. C. (1961). *Social behavior: Its elementary forms.* New York: Harcourt, Brace & World.

hooks. b. (1994). *Teaching to transgress: Education as the practice of freedom.* New York: Routledge.

Kinkaid, H. (1996). *Philosophies of social science: Individualism and its social and political consequences.* London: Sage.

Klein, D. M., & White, J. M. (1996). *Family theories.* Thousand Oaks, CA: Sage.

Knapp, S. J. (2002). Authorizing family science: An analysis of the objectifying practices of family science discourse. *Journal of Marriage and Family, 64,* 1038–1048.

Kuhn, T. (1962). *The structure of scientific revolution.* Chicago: University of Chicago Press.

Luescher, K., & Pillemer, K. (1998). Intergenerational ambivalence: A new approach to the study of parent-child relations in later life. *Journal of Marriage and the Family, 60,* 413–425.

Merton, R. K. (1957). *Social theory and social structure.* Glencoe, IL: Free Press.

Reason, P. (1994). Three approaches to participative inquiry. In N. K. Denzin & Y.S. Lincoln (Eds.), Handbook of qualitative research (pp. 324–339). Thousand Oaks, CA: Sage.

Ritzer, G. (1980). *Sociology: A multiple paradigm science.* Boston: Allyn and Bacon.

Rubin, L.B. (1976). *Worlds of pain: Life in the working-class family.* New York: Basic Books.

Schweizer, T. (1998). Epistemology: The nature and validation of anthropological knowledge. In H. R. Bernard (Ed.), *Handbook of methods in cultural anthropology* (pp. 39–987). Walnut Creek, CA: Alta Mira.

Silverstein, M., Conroy, S., Wang, H., Giarrusso, R., & Bengtson, V. L. (2002). Reciprocity in Parent-Child Relations Over the Life Course. *Journals of Gerontology: Social Sciences, 57B,* S3–S13.

Stack, C. B. (1974). *All our kin: Strategies for survival in a black community.* New York: Harper Colophon.

Thomas, W. I., & Znaniecki, F. (1918–1920). *The Polish peasant in Europe and America.* Chicago: University of Chicago Press.

Turner, J. H. (2003a). *The structure of sociological theory.* Belmont, CA: Wadsworth/Thomson Learning.

Turner, J. H. (2003b). *Human institutions: A theory of societal evolution.* New York: Rowman & Littlefield.

Wallace, W. (1971). *The logic of science in sociology.* Chicago: Aldine/Atherton.

Wallace, W. L. (1969). *Sociological theory: An introduction.* Chicago: Aldine.

Webster. (2001). *Unabridged dictionary of the English language.* New York: Random House.

White, J. M., & Klein, D. M. (2002). *Family theories* (2nd Ed.). Thousand Oaks, CA: Sage.

Zetterberg, H. L. (1964). *On theory and verification in sociology.* Totowa, NJ: Bedminster Press.

Two

CONTEMPORARY AND EMERGING THEORIES IN STUDYING FAMILIES

Peggye Dilworth-Anderson, *University of North Carolina at Chapel Hill*

Linda M. Burton, *Pennsylvania State University*

David M. Klein, *University of Notre Dame*

I n this chapter, we discuss issues that are important to theorizing about contemporary families. Scholars engaging in such theorizing need to be aware that both past and current approaches are useful and that, regardless of the period, family theorists must address certain basic issues that are fundamental to the process of theorizing. Future theorizing about contemporary families will also require scholars to use great imagination and to seek great inspiration. We suggest that the terrain for this imagination and inspiration is as open as the ocean, in that it includes theorists' personal experiences, cultural information, new technologies, and knowledge of the theoretical traditions in family studies. Even literary works—specifically those that provide metaphors for understanding contemporary families—can inform theorizing.

THE RECENT HISTORY OF THEORIZING IN FAMILY STUDIES

Social scientists, as well as family members and casual observers of family life, have always been interested in understanding how families work and in explaining why families are the way they are. Early commentators (e.g., Engels, 1884/1946) saw families as suffering under or adapting naturally to broader forces of modernization in society (see Lamanna, 2002, on Durkheim) and sometimes as the seedbed of normal and abnormal psychological development in children (Bayer, 1966/1981). However, until about 1950, systematic attempts to develop theories about the family were sporadic, and most were direct applications of ideas borrowed from other disciplines.

During the first half of the 20th century, scholars emphasized the accumulation of research evidence that would be useful for both practical and scientific purposes (Hill, 1980). By 1950, it became widely recognized that the generation of data about families had outpaced the development of theories that could organize the data. Hill's sketch of existing "conceptual frameworks" in 1951 signaled a turning point that influenced the next two decades. This turning point coincided with the inauguration of training programs for scholars interested in family research (e.g., Hill, 1969).

A conceptual framework is a set of loosely connected assumptions and abstract concepts that helps us to understand a particular phenomenon. Several key works in the 1960s showed the promise of such frameworks for the study of families as they charted the ebb and flow of the popularity of various theoretical orientations (Christensen, 1964; Hill & Hansen, 1960; Nye & Berardo, 1981). While attention turned to the identification and usage of general frameworks, the pace of empirical research continued to quicken. Those scholars who produced and published data often did not link their findings explicitly to specific frameworks. By the end of the 1960s, a more concerted effort to theorize carefully about families took hold. The National Council on Family Relations recast its Research Committee as the Research and Theory Section, and the council began holding its annual Pre-conference Workshop on Family Theory Construction, later renamed the Workshop on Theory Construction and Research Methodology.

The initial spark to create formal theories about the family was short-lived. The key works illustrating this emphasis were Burr's *Theory Construction and the Sociology of the Family* (1973) and the two *Contemporary Theories* volumes edited by Burr, Hill, Nye, and Reiss (1979a, 1979b). Few other notable publications appeared during this period.

Since about 1980, several turns in the intellectual climate of the field of family studies have expanded the theoretical landscape. The emergence of family science as a discipline and family psychology as a specialty has brought new perspectives into vogue. New frameworks (e.g., feminism and postmodernism), eclectic combinations of perspectives, growing interest in families among scholars in other disciplines (e.g., history and biology), and the inclusion of viewpoints from previously marginalized minority groups have all added to the richness of the scientific landscape. We now have more ways than ever before to explain family phenomena. However, it is also more difficult than ever to classify the alternatives and to identify their similarities and differences, as well as their virtues and limitations. Klein and White (1996; see also White & Klein, 2002) have suggested that we need to pay attention to the origins of and historical changes in each theoretical tradition. We also need to inspect the variations within each tradition in order to understand better both the existing landscape and the possibilities for future theorizing.

• *SPOTLIGHT ON THEORY*

APPLICATION OF PEPPER'S WORLD HYPOTHESES TO FAMILY THEORIES

Hilary A. Rose, *Concordia University*

"It is just as necessary to ground fundamental concepts at the level of . . . epistemological discourse as it is to ground them at the theoretical and observational levels" (Overton, 1998, p. 128). As educators, we teach our students to be good consumers of research; it is also important that they become good consumers of theory. Being a good consumer of theory means understanding the assumptions, explicit or not, on which

(continued)

● **SPOTLIGHT ON THEORY** continued

theories are based. As one heuristic device, Stephen Pepper's (1942/1970) model of world hypotheses illuminates the underlying assumptions of family theories (for other devices, see Klein & White, 1996; Overton, 1998).

Reese and Overton (1970; Reese, 1991) have applied Pepper's model to child development theories, but no application of the model to family theories has been published, to my knowledge. The value of Pepper's model for family theories lies in its ability to help scholars, educators, and practitioners (a) understand the assumptions of family theories, (b) recognize similarities among family theories, and (c) determine which family theories can logically be combined (i.e., eclecticism). The model is also useful for criticizing family theories, as many criticisms stem not so much from the theories as they do from assumptions on which the theories are based.

Pepper (1942/1970) describes four world hypotheses—*formism, mechanism, organicism,* and *contextualism*—each with its root metaphor. Each of these hypotheses can be categorized as *dispersive* versus *integrative* and as *analytic* versus *synthetic*. Categorizing a theory as analytic implies that it is reductionistic, whereas categorizing it as synthetic implies that it is holistic. Categorizing a theory as dispersive implies that it is descriptive, and categorizing it as integrative implies that it is predictive. Integrative theories are faulted for a lack of scope; dispersive theories, for a lack of precision. Analytic theories are faulted for being too reductionistic; holistic theories, for being too comprehensive.

Pepper's (1942/1970) World Hypotheses

		Type of Theory	
		Analytic *(i.e., reductionistic)*	*Synthetic* *(i.e., holistic)*
	Dispersive *(i.e., descriptive)*	Formism (root metaphor: similarity)	Contextualism (root metaphor: historic event)
Type of Theory			
	Integrative *(i.e., predictive)*	Mechanism (root metaphor: machine)	Organicism (root metaphor: organism)

Formism answers the question "What is it (like)?" and its root metaphor is *similarity* or a *similar type* (Pepper, 1942/1970). Typologies, used in the social sciences to classify (e.g., parenting styles), have their roots in formism, as does structural functionalism. Mechanism answers the question "How does it work?" and its root metaphor is a *machine*. Learning theory is an example of a mechanistic theory (Reese & Overton, 1970); exchange theory is also based in mechanism.

Organicism answers the question "How does it develop?" and its root metaphor is an *organism* (Pepper, 1942/1970). An example is Erikson's theory of psychosocial development (Reese & Overton, 1970). Family development and family systems theories are also based in organicism. Contextualism answers the question "How is it happening?" and its

(continued)

● *SPOTLIGHT ON THEORY continued*

root metaphor is a *historic event* (Pepper, 1942/1970). An example is Bronfenbrenner's ecological theory (Reese, 1991); symbolic interaction and feminist theories are also based in contextualism.

Pepper (1942/1970) asked, given that contextualism and organicism "may almost be called the same theory" (p. 147), why not combine them? He concluded that as world hypotheses have different root metaphors, attempts to combine them are logically confusing; the differing worldviews are simply irreconcilable. For practical purposes, however, he was less concerned about combining theories, opening the door for eclecticism. Practitioners who choose to combine various aspects of different theories should understand the logical implications of theoretical eclecticism; at a minimum, they should be aware of the implications of eclecticism.

When I recently used Pepper's model in a graduate family theories class, the students were receptive to using the rubric to identify their own assumptions and those of the theories we discussed. Although we did not always agree on how particular theories should be classified, Pepper's model provided an excellent starting point for discussion. Reviews of family theories should include Pepper's rubric as a basis for criticizing family theories, as very often scholars (e.g., White & Klein, 2002) actually criticize the philosophical assumptions on which family theories are based. ●

CRITICAL ISSUES FACING THEORISTS

One constant in family theorizing over the past several decades has been a basic set of crucial issues that every theorist must face. We briefly discuss five of these crucial issues below.

Finding an Entry Point

Because theorizing is a process, there is no best place to begin. As theorists, we normally start with curiosity, often about some puzzle that begs to be solved. If no readily available solution appears through our familiarity with the topic, creative theorizing may be essential. However, we rarely create new ideas from scratch. Rather, we borrow ideas and combine them in new ways. If a plausible solution to the puzzle already exists, perhaps in the professional literature about families, we may start with that as an analogy or metaphor. We may also treat it as a more general solution, with our specific puzzle just offering an example of where the solution can be applied.

Along the way, we will likely want to compare alternative solutions. Perhaps there is a widely accepted one, but we decide to challenge it because it does not seem to fit well with our own experiences. Alternatively, we may decide to rely on aspects of two or more existing solutions, viewing them in a new way as being complementary. When we start with an existing theory, we may leave the theory intact and simply apply it to the explanation needed. However, we often discover that we have to enhance, clarify, or otherwise refine the theoretical ideas of others, even when we judge those ideas to offer a useful framework.

Note that the ideas we borrow from previous theorists may be fragments of their theories, not necessarily entire theories. Perhaps we like a particular concept found in a given theory but not much else. Similarly, we can extract from an existing theory a particular assumption or a linkage between two variables in the form of a proposition, such as "X positively influences Y."

Finally, if we start with an existing theory in all of its complexity, we must decide if we want to employ the theory heuristically or as the foundation for a critical test of the theory's accuracy in an empirical research setting. Sometimes, the relevance of a theory to research is that the theory helps us to interpret findings, whatever the findings might be. In this case, the theory is an orienting or sensitizing tool. At other times, the point of our using a theory to guide research is to help us decide, based on the empirical findings, whether or not the theory offers an adequate explanation of the phenomenon being studied. If the theory seems adequate, it is provisionally supported. If not, we will often propose a modification of the theory in a way designed to help the next researcher who comes along with a similar puzzle.

Positioning "Family" in the Argument

Another crucial issue is the positioning of "family" when we are developing or using a family theory. In order to develop or use a family theory, we not only need a working definition of what a family is but we also need to decide where familial concepts or variables belong in the argument. Perhaps we want to explain something about families. In this case, the explanation could be provided by any combination of ideas, some or even all of which are not familial. For example, we might want to argue that an individual's personality influences his or her mate selection. One challenge in this particular case is to decide whether a married couple constitutes a family. For the most part, family scholars see intimate unions between adults as inherently familial. Others, however, believe that a relationship must include two generations (parent and child) to count as a family. It is no surprise, therefore, that the flagship journal in our field is titled the *Journal of Marriage and Family* (emphasis on *and*). However, we also have an important journal called *Family Relations,* which includes articles on unions between adults who are childless.

Another example of the positioning of "family" in family theory involves the question of whether family concepts or variables provide all or part of an explanation. Perhaps we want to argue that the quality of parent-child relationships influences the academic performance of children. In this case, what is being explained is something about persons, not something about families. The fact that a student is a child has nothing to do with families. The basic point that makes this issue relevant to family studies is that the explanation entails family relationships. The important question to ask is, Are you explaining something about families, or are you using something about families to explain something else? The answer might be that you are doing both, but if the answer is that you are doing neither, then you are not operating in the field of family studies.

As long as familial ideas have some relevance to a theory, many other kinds of acting units can also be important. It is always crucial for researchers to specify who the social actors are for each concept or variable. Examples of relevant social actors are individuals, dyads, groups (such as families), organizations, institutions, and societies. A common error that researchers make is to attribute impossible characteristics to actors. For example, families have incomes, but we can measure "family income" only by adding up the incomes of all members and assuming that all members have equal access to all sources of income. Families do not have emotions or attitudes. Some characteristics of persons can be aggregated at the family level and some cannot. Others are better conceptualized as differences between family members. A family can have an attitude or enact a behavior only when the members collectively act in a coordinated way.

Whenever we refer to acting units outside of the family, it is useful to think about how they affect families and about how families affect them. So, for example, if we assert that "societal values influence family interactions," we are forced to think about which people outside of the family have the important values. We must also ponder the thought that those people are also likely to have families. We also may feel compelled to ask why other people's values affect what individuals do. This helps to create a broader picture of the nature of the interaction between family and society.

Taking a Stance on Causality

Because it is usually unethical to perform experiments on human relationships, it is difficult to make a convincing argument that family variables cause or are caused by anything. Some family scholars avoid causal reasoning whenever they theorize. Others say that however elusive the proof might be, it is often useful to think about causality when trying to understand families. We encourage you to develop your own position on this issue.

If you are a determinist, you believe that the presence of one or more conditions guarantees an outcome—few family scholars are determinists, however. Most who allow for causation assume that variables have differing degrees of influence on other variables. The puzzle is how much influence exists under each of the many different conditions. We usually end up thinking in terms of the probability that X will lead to Y. One reason we allow for probabilities rather than think in terms of certainties is that our measurements are always imperfect.

If you agree with the idea that causal factors vary in importance, there are several other interesting issues to consider. Which causal factors are proximal, and which are distal? In other words, is the effect to appear soon, will it be delayed, or will it perhaps be mediated by another factor? Is the cause in the near environment or in the far environment? Do several causes combine? If so, how? Perhaps multiple causes combine in an additive way. This leads to an image resembling a fan, with lines from each of several ideas leading into one effect. Perhaps there is a chain of effects, such that X influences Y, which in turn affects Z, and so on. Finally, some influences may be moderated or contingent: X influences Y only when Z meets certain requirements. If we decide that a particular argument requires some combination of fans, chains, and contingencies to provide an adequate solution to the theoretical puzzle, then we end up with an image of a complex web.

Note that the story of an explanation can be told in different ways. If we render the story as a narrative, we might sacrifice precision in order to plant a vivid image in the reader's mind. Such lack of precision may lead to misunderstandings by others. Ideally, a set of formal assertions and a narrative about the same things tell essentially the same story.

Dealing With Time and Space

Families live through time and in different places. Good theories are clear about these crucial issues. Theorists must decide about the relevance of historical, biographical, and episodical time. Perhaps the puzzle is to understand how families have been changing (or not) across decades or centuries. Alternatively, the focus may be on how family relations change throughout all or part of the existence of families as specific groups, from their formation to their dissolution. The period examined may even be quite narrow, with a focus on events that occur daily, monthly, or annually. The key point is that family theorists have to develop some vision of the flow and boundaries of time. Whenever we witness changes across time, we need to ask whether these changes have been influenced by the ages of the people involved, the period in history being observed, or the fact that the people involved are members of a particular cohort in which individuals experience the same events at the same times in their lives regardless of their ages.

Spatial variation refers to variation in both geographic and cultural location. Does a given family theory apply in the same way everywhere, or does it apply differently (or at all) to families in varying parts of the world? Even when we develop theories to apply within fairly narrow spatial parameters, other theorists can push the limits outward to see if the theories apply more broadly or if they have to be revised before they will apply equally well across key spatial dimensions.

Theories that are stated in broad terms with respect to time and space are *macrotheories*. Theories that focus more on specific times and places are *microtheories*. Both kinds of theories are important. A challenge for future family scholars is to link macro- and microtheories together in a more comprehensive framework.

Handling Structure

The crucial issue of "structure" involves the ways in which relationships are organized at particular points in time. Although few would deny the importance of structure, scholars have dealt with this concept in a wide variety of ways in theories about families. Some theorists apply the concept to the structural elements of the family itself—that is, the family's size, its age and gender composition, and the marital status of members. Other theorists use the term *structure* to refer to the broader society or to the local community in which the family is found—in either case, they are concerned with the organizational features of social units that are outside of families. For still other theorists, the concept of structure involves the placement of families within their environments, such as their social classes. For example, being poor has different implications for families depending on how common it is to be poor. The main point here is that when theorists include structure in their theories, they need to be clear about how they define structure.

Sometimes family theorists choose to emphasize process—that is, how family members interact with each other over time—over structure. A process theory might argue that structure influences process, which in turn influences what is being explained. With an emphasis on proximal causes, the focus is on processual effects, and structural effects fade into the background. Alternatively, theorists may view structures as factors that condition the relationship between processes and outcomes. So, for example, social class may influence the impact that a certain child-rearing style has on child outcomes rather than have any direct effect on the outcomes themselves. In addition, structure can be viewed as the outcome of process. Instead of assuming that structures shape or condition outcomes, a theory may focus on how family members interact to change preexisting structures.

Some theorists conceptualize structure as something distinct from culture. If *structure* refers to organized patterns of relationships, then *culture* refers to shared sets of beliefs, values, preferences, and attitudes. When theorists argue that structure influences culture, or vice versa, they are taking a stand on how structure and culture operate in a more complex explanation.

Regardless of the specific way in which a theorist brings structural concepts to bear, the bigger issue of "choice versus constraint" inevitably arises. Is the overriding image one of people being governed by circumstances outside of their direct control or one of people actively interacting with others to shape their destinies?

OVERVIEW OF FAMILY THEORETICAL TRADITIONS

We have already suggested that the sources of inspiration for family theories are boundless. Scholars may find puzzles in their personal experiences or in those revealed by others. Intensive reading—whether of works in any academic discipline or of nonacademic works—may provoke puzzles. Even television programs and materials found on the Internet may stimulate scholars to ask questions. Whatever sources provide assistance for theorizing about families, there is no substitute for knowledge about the theoretical traditions in family studies. In this section we briefly suggest how the major traditions deal with some of the issues discussed above. More thorough treatments of these and other theoretical traditions can be found in White and Klein (2002) and Boss, Doherty, LaRossa, Schumm, and Steinmetz (1993); other useful reviews are available as well (see, e.g., Ingoldsby, Smith, & Miller, 2004; Nye & Berardo, 1981; Winton, 1995).

One way to look at families is to ask why they take the forms that they take. *Functional theories* seek to find the purposes of existing social structures and to discover how these purposes are achieved. Different ways of achieving a given purpose are often created, and if the purpose changes or if existing structures lose their effectiveness, the structures may change. Structural functionalist theories rely heavily on historical and cross-cultural evidence. Compared with most other kinds of family theories, functional theories tend to focus on macroscopic views of time and space, and on how families are connected with other institutions in a society. These theories often emphasize structure more than process.

A guiding perspective of *symbolic interaction theories* is that humans seek meaning and identities by interacting with other humans. Current and potential family members therefore engage in conversations to cocreate meanings and guidelines for social relationships. Language, and how it is communicated, is central to the construction of social reality. Therefore, symbolic interaction theories rely heavily on conversational evidence. Compared with most other family theories, interactional theories tend to focus on microscopic contexts of time and space. They also are likely to view family life as an origin or cause of change rather than as being pushed by outside forces. These theories emphasize individual actors and the ways they connect with each other, in short but repeatable processes.

Life-course theories and *theories of family development* draw on concepts from other theories, but they have a unique perspective on time. They focus on the changes that occur in families across the duration of the families' existence. Therefore, the scope of time with which these theories are concerned is intermediate, ranging from months to a few decades. Family life appears as a series of fairly structured stages punctuated by periods of potentially disruptive transitions. Life-course theories focus on individuals and the impacts that family experiences have on them; in contrast, developmental theories about families focus on the forces that shape and alter the family unit itself.

Some theories about the family start with the perspective that families are groups whose members struggle to control and protect resources. This perspective arose as an alternative to the more common view that families are bastions of mutual love and harmony. According to these *social conflict theories*, negative emotions and behaviors sometimes arise in families in the course of members' dealing with inevitable differences or disagreements. Such conflicts can be functional, but they also can be destructive. Some conflicts are resolved, whereas others persist as family members avoid or withdraw from them. Family conflicts may yield winners and losers, or they may at least be managed, if not resolved, through compromise or the emergence of new agreements or understandings.

Another way to look at families is to see family members' activities as a series of transactions. Each member has something valued by other members, so the parties engage in bargaining or negotiating, which often results in the exchange of valued resources. It costs each member something to reward another; therefore, one puzzle that scholars examine concerns which exchanges members view as fair or unfair. According to *social exchange theories,* family relationships tend to form and to endure so long as exchanges are sufficiently rewarding to all participants, taking into account the costs of attempting to change or end the relationship. Therefore, participants use some kind of calculus based on information and hunches to assess, rationally, the likelihood that additional commitment and investment will lead to a satisfactory outcome. Like symbolic interaction theories, exchange theories most often deal with microscopic contexts of time and space, even though there may be enduring cultural rituals about proper exchanges.

Some family theories have a structural emphasis without necessarily invoking a functional perspective. One common variety is *family systems theory.* It may be useful to see a family as a set of separate relationships that are all connected in some important way, as the organs of the body or the components of a computer are connected. Each part, as well as the system as a whole, has boundaries that are partially permeable but are also maintained to preserve the integrity of the system. According to systems theories, a family processes information by moving and transforming it through the family's component parts. Compared with most other family theories, systems theories tend to be descriptive rather than explanatory. The goal is to understand how families work, or sometimes fail to work, and the cause of success or failure may not be important. Still, too much or too little information, or perhaps a part's inability to process information, may be a cause of family system failure. Losing a previously important part of the system (e.g., a key member dies or is no longer participating) can be very disruptive.

Another type of family theory emphasizes the connection between families and their environments. Such *ecological theories* may deal with how available natural and human resources affect family life in environments such as communities or neighborhoods. A more macro-level version of these theories has an evolutionary perspective. The puzzle is to discover how family forms and practices are adaptations to biological and social traditions that have survived through many generations of reproductive success. Evolutionary theories are often functionalist in the sense that they assert that humans do what they do because it has worked in the past to help them achieve desired outcomes. However, even human purposes and biological endowments are adaptive to changes in environmental conditions.

Families are unavoidably shaped by the existence of gender and sex, and by ideas about them. A number of *feminist family theories* have emerged to deal with the gendered and sexual context of family life. These theories share the observation that gender inequality exists in every human society to varying degrees. They often draw on ideas from other theories, particularly symbolic interaction and social conflict theories, and they explain how gender inequality either originates in or is maintained by family relationships. Although it is possible to use any family theory to make suggestions about how to improve human relationships, feminist family theories have so far been among the most explicit about using explanations to advocate changes in families.

Given the constraints of space, we have not exhausted the full array of family theories in the above discussion, nor have we provided much detail on the theories mentioned. Our point here, however, is to remind you that a rich tradition already exists, and we expect that future work will build on this tradition. Perhaps you will take one theory as your starting point and show how it works, or fails, to solve a puzzle in your own substantive area of interest. Perhaps you will draw insights from multiple theories, either to show how they combine to work better than one theory alone or to show that one seems to be much better than others for your purposes. If you want to create a new theory, knowing the heritage of theories in your field will help you to guard against making excessive claims about how new your ideas actually are.

● *SPOTLIGHT ON THEORY*

IN SEARCH OF A PHILOSOPHICAL FOUNDATION FOR FAMILY THEORY AND THERAPY

Norbert A. Wetzel, *Center for Family, Community, and Social Justice, Princeton, New Jersey*

Family systems therapy as a clinical orientation is rooted in a series of experiences that therapists from diverse professional backgrounds made in the process of practicing as clinicians:

(continued)

● *SPOTLIGHT ON THEORY continued*

1. Therapists noticed the intense involvement of their patients in networks of personal relationships. Gradually, clinicians became sensitive to the degree to which a family relationship system can determine an individual's experiences and, vice versa, how profoundly an individual can influence a family's relational processes.

2. As soon as therapists learned to consider the unique context of each individual patient, other phenomena became visible. Therapists were able to understand their patients' behavior patterns, emotions, experiences, attitudes, and actions as soon as they explored these areas afresh in the contexts of the individuals' relevant relationships. What therapists had previously often judged as irrational, crazy, neurotic, or psychotic they could now understand as rational within given contexts of meaning.

3. Clinical observers realized, to their surprise, how powerfully individual clients' inner experiences were determined not only by their family contexts, but by broader contextual factors. Adopting a perspective that allowed them to consider in detail their patients' lives in particular social or economic contexts, to explore the diverse worlds and life experiences of men and women, and to be curious about their patients' cultural and ethnic heritages, therapists opened up avenues of understanding that had remained hidden when they focused solely on their patients' inner experiences.

4. Clinicians learned that they themselves are involved in relational processes with their clients, and so they need to understand others, as well as themselves, on many different levels. To understand a description of a picture, you need to know something about the viewer; to comprehend the interpretation of a text, you need to know about the context and the reader; to gauge the depth with which a concerto touches a listener, you need to hear from the listener; to understand the diagnosis of a psychiatric patient, you need to assess the psychiatrist. The diverse horizons of understanding are integrated into a whole view, an image rich in gradations and facets, in a process similar to turning a kaleidoscope. Whatever levels of understanding therapists highlight, whether they adopt individually or relationally oriented perspectives, their choices are always responsible for making some aspects of their clients visible while others remain invisible.

The search for a philosophical foundation for family theory and therapy has to be located on the same level as the epochal movements of the natural and human sciences, of philosophy and socioeconomic development during the past century (Wetzel & Winawer, 2002). To put it differently, family therapy and theory need to be rooted in a new "epistemology" or "first philosophy"—that is, in a fundamental and comprehensive paradigm of thinking that is suited to the conceptualization of the self-reflexive experience of human beings and is capable of serving as orientation toward the universality of the human experience. In this way Newton's paradigm of classic realism, focused on individuals or atoms or inanimate objects, can remain useful, but only as a heuristic perspective among others, not as the philosophical or epistemological foundation of thinking.

(continued)

● *SPOTLIGHT ON THEORY continued*

Philosophical reflection starts with the experience of the reflecting subject in order to avoid standing on uncertain ground from the very beginning. The foundation of philosophy in the experience of the thinking subject was developed by Immanuel Kant and further methodically refined by Edmund Husserl, the founder of the phenomenological method, and his pupils Martin Heidegger and Emmanuel Levinas. Since then, detailed analyses of human experiences have been part of the foundational reflective process of philosophy. In particular, the work of Levinas and his revolutionary philosophy of conceiving of the Self as constituted by the relationship with the Other can be seen as the "epistemology" (in a universal sense) or "first philosophy" that could serve as the foundation of family theory and therapy. Family therapists are invited to follow these traces of a philosophy of relationships and to make their own discoveries on that journey. ●

THEORIZING ON CONTEMPORARY FAMILIES

There are many different ways of developing theory. One of the most common is to frame and explain ideas using traditional theoretical perspectives (such as those discussed above). Another way is to use abstract ideas, such as metaphors. We believe that family theorists can use both of these methods at any given time; however, when little is known regarding families in a particular cultural group, metaphors are especially useful for the conceptual guidance they can provide. Sociohistorically, this is a very good time for family researchers to consider the utility of metaphors, because American families today are best described as representing multiple forms, structures, and configurations that are diverse in race, ethnicity, culture, and sexual orientation. These families are also very dynamic, more political and vocal than ever, and they respond to and are helping to shape definitions of marriage, parenthood, and socioemotional bonds. Family researchers are challenged by these family characteristics when searching for entry points in the theoretical enterprise. For contemporary families, new ideas may emerge from existing theoretical traditions as well as from emerging perspectives.

Issues of time and space are also very significant in theorizing about contemporary families. Changes in families today reflect a transitional period for families. Some may even suggest that we are living in "new times"; however, others have made such claims about families in the past. The question for family researchers today is, How can we understand the relevance of time and space as we search for new ways to theorize about contemporary families? For example, questions may emerge about whether American society at the beginning of the 21st century both recognizes and includes diversity in its definition of family and whether this period will see the establishment of new norms for acceptable family structures and configurations. These questions address time, space, and structure, and they may encourage us to examine processes within families according to the time in which the families are developing and interacting.

Later chapters in this volume help to set the stage for an understanding of the contemporary challenge to family theorists and researchers. In Chapter 4, Bianchi and Casper clearly outline some of the demographic changes that are taking place in contemporary families—changes that will inform theorizing. For example, they describe the trend toward delaying marriage, the dramatic decline in the numbers of marriages, the rise in unmarried heterosexual (and same-sex) cohabitation, the decrease in fertility rates, the rise of "beanpole families" (i.e., families with more grandparents than parents and more parents than children), and the effects on marriage and childbearing of the dramatic increase in the number of women in the workforce.

In Chapter 8, McAdoo, Martínez, and Hughes describe and discuss the diverse families of color that are emerging in American society. The authors suggest that these families reflect varying combinations of both old and new ways of "being" families. Old, familiar value systems are evident in the constantly evolving new family formations. Therefore, in positioning the family in their theorizing, scholars need to take into account the sociohistorical and demographic changes that are evident in contemporary families. As a result, they may need new concepts to capture the changes that are occurring in families. Although old and familiar, concepts such as family, family organization, and family morals and values beg for new definitions and meanings.

In Chapter 6, Oswald, Blume, and Marks discuss such terms as *norms* and *family sexual identity* as well as the concept of gay identity negotiation in families. In Chapter 1, Bengtson, Acock, Allen, Dilworth-Anderson, and Klein also address concerns about family scholars' use of relevant concepts to understand, describe, and define contemporary families. These authors discuss how family scholars are currently challenged by the need to move through a paradigm shift and possibly "revolutionize" how they study families, in part by taking the important step of getting involved in the lives of the families they study. Therefore, in theorizing about families today, scholars must employ methodological rigor to improve the conceptual models, measurement strategies, and analytic approaches applied to the study of the new family landscape, both today and in the future.

THE USE OF METAPHORS
AND THE NEW FAMILY LANDSCAPE

Given the lack of clear consensus among family scholars about various concepts, definitions,

and meanings related to families, we suggest that metaphor is a very useful conceptual tool for beginning to theorize about contemporary families. Through metaphors, we may gain insights into why and how family members behave and interact as they do; we may also be able to see how different factors contribute to typical outcomes of family life. However, the use of metaphors does not always result in information about causal processes in contemporary families (Dilworth-Anderson, Burton, & Johnson, 1993).

As DeJong (2004) notes, in the context of family theory, a metaphor is "not simply a literary device, but a complex array of comparisons based on experiences within families, social settings, and cultural landscapes" (p. 5). A review of several bodies of literature on families across racial, cultural, and geographic boundaries indicates that four basic metaphors can provide conceptual guidance to family researchers: the metaphors of the family circle, the veil, fences, and tapestry. These metaphors, which we discuss briefly in turn below, are not value-neutral; rather, they are value-specific in that they provide meanings, definitions, directions to live by, and structures within which to develop cultural identity. Through qualitative research using a narrative approach, family researchers can begin to understand family life by knowing, first, that metaphors are theoretical tools and, second, that a methodology employing metaphors can help them to gain information about family. Data gathered using metaphors can also lead to the development of quantitative variables that researchers can use in analyzing families. As Acock, van Dulmen, Allen, and Piercy point out in Chapter 3 of this volume, innovations in both qualitative and quantitative methods hold great promise for helping family scholars to recognize that "qualitative versus quantitative" is a false dichotomy.

The Family Circle

The circle is often used as a symbol of connection. As Frederick Douglass points out in his 1846 autobiography, the *Narrative of the Life of Frederick Douglass,* the symbol of the circle has a double meaning: It represents both the confinement of bondage and the community. In most immigrant families today, the family circle is protective and nurturing and may help to create closeness and intimacy, thus binding family relationships (Greenfield, 1984). Within the family circle, members find a reprieve from a hostile society and a source for identity formation. However, the family's communal identity may prevent member individuation. The mutual obligation and cooperation in the family circle ensures that no member "falls through the cracks," but it also makes it difficult for any member to get ahead, because any gains that an individual makes must be divided among members of the family circle.

The Veil

In *The Souls of Black Folk* (1903), W. E. B. Du Bois describes being born Black in America as being born with a veil. The veil is the color line that separates Black America from White America. Applying Du Bois's metaphor to contemporary families today, especially immigrant and marginalized families (e.g., African American, Hispanic, and Native American), the veil may be seen to represent second sight or double consciousness. For African American families, the veil still serves to explicate the duality of self as experienced by most African Americans. To survive, African Americans must function in a society that marginalizes them while they are embracing the values of the larger American culture. Further, African Americans maintain linkages to the past through, among other things, a strong oral tradition. African Americans use their veil to function as Americans while maintaining ties to their African heritage. Similarly, some immigrant families (e.g., those from Middle Eastern countries) also operate through a veil that stratifies their existence. Unlike African Americans, such families may be separated from mainstream Americans by the veil of their religious beliefs.

Fences

Along the same lines of thought as the family circle metaphor, immigrant and other marginalized families are often characterized as being "fenced into their homes." On the surface, the fence that separates family members from the outside world appears negative and impenetrable, but it is necessary to protect members of the household from harm (e.g., racism and discrimination). The fence is also a boundary that limits how far family members may distance themselves from the family; it keeps the dominant society out, but it also keeps family members in. For example, some researchers have suggested that particular groups in the United States, such as Hispanics and African Americans, live on what amount to urban reservations (Waste, 1995). We suggest that these groups also develop imaginary fences around the spaces they inhabit that serve to protect the most vulnerable among them, including the young. Children in these settings are rarely allowed outside to play; they have very little recreational space in which to develop community relationships and their identities within the larger community. Instead, the fence of protection, which is often erected no farther away than outside the family's immediate front door, is used for protection and survival (Leventhal & Brooks-Gunn, 2000).

Tapestry

A tapestry is a woven fabric of intricate design. The metaphor of the tapestry, in which individual threads combine with other threads to form a unified pattern or picture, has been used to represent many culturally diverse families. Like the individual threads in a tapestry, family members' individual traits and characteristics provide them with identities outside of their group, and when family members join together, they form a whole cultural group. Cultural groups exhibit characteristics, rituals, and values that have continuity over time—in other words, a consistent pattern in the tapestry.

THE ROLE OF CULTURAL VALUES IN THE NEW FAMILY LANDSCAPE

In theorizing, the utility of metaphors for helping us to find pieces of the puzzle is enhanced when we connect these pieces to other pieces. Cultural values may be viewed as bridging pieces that allow us to move from the use of metaphors to the larger puzzle of theorizing about the family landscape of today. Values are much more concrete, observable, and measurable than metaphors. They do more than allow us to gain insights; they provide some explanations that can help us to understand family life. We refer to cultural values as "guideposts" of family functioning because they provide direction for individual and group socialization and identification. They also provide direction for behavior and parameters for acceptable and unacceptable behavior within groups. Cultural values tell us what to expect of ourselves and what to expect of others within our families.

In this discussion, therefore, we define values as internal criteria for evaluation (Hechter, 1993). They are standards that guide individual actions, even though they may change over time because of individual, group, historical, and societal factors. As Hechter (1993) notes, values can be defined specifically as "principles, or criteria, for selecting what is good (or better, or best) among objects, actions, ways of life, and social and political institutions and structures. Values operate at the level of individuals, institutions, and entire societies" (p. 15). In this discussion, we are most concerned about addressing values at the individual and family levels.

Similar to metaphors, values help us to understand how individuals within families experience themselves and others. DeJong (2004) suggests that metaphors are imported with values, with a sense of good or bad and right or wrong. Further, values are not independent; instead, they must form a coherent system with the metaphorical concepts we live by (Lakoff & Johnson, 1980, p. 22). The metaphors we live by are created by the values we hold, based in part on the experiences that shape our lives. This clear connection between metaphors and values provides strong, distinct pieces of the theorizing puzzle: Metaphors provide images and meanings, and values provide the vehicle through which these images and meanings become real in everyday life.

THE CASE OF THEORIZING: HOMEPLACE FOR CONTEMPORARY FAMILIES

In this section, we discuss the metaphor *homeplace* as an example of how family researchers can begin finding the pieces of the puzzle as they theorize about the marginalized families, immigrant families, and culturally displaced families that are now a part of the American demographic landscape. Gieryn (2000) outlines three essential features of the homeplace: geographic location, material form, and investment with meaning and value. He contends that home, nested in a definable space, is the crucible from which a person's social identity emerges, transforms, and is internalized and sustained over time.

In her collection of essays titled *Yearning: Race, Gender, and Cultural Politics* (1990), bell hooks discusses the importance of the homeplace relative to the survival and coping strategies of African Americans. Using her memories of childhood visits to her grandparents' home, hooks characterizes the homeplace as a communal experience anchored in a domestic household where "all that truly mattered in life took place—the warmth and comfort of shelter, the feeding of our bodies, the nurturing of our souls" (pp. 41–42). Metaphorically speaking, the homeplace provides both a circle and a fence within which family members can live safely while they learn dignity and integrity of being. According to hooks, African Americans experience a deep sense of yearning when they do not have a homeplace or cannot create one, when they must fight to keep a homeplace, or when they must work to reclaim one. Yearning is an individual's or family's psychological and emotional longing for connectedness to place, for a sense of rootedness and purpose, and for a crucible of affirmation of a sense of social and cultural identity. Other researchers have suggested that for many African American families, the homeplace is a physical, political, social, and personal necessity in their lives (see, e.g., Burton & Lawson Clark, in press; Clark, 1993; Gilbert, 1998).

In her Pulitzer Prize–winning book *Interpreter of Maladies* (1999), Jhumpa Lahiri tells insightful stories about the impacts of immigration on individual and family relationships in an Indian family. She describes the range of experiences and emotions among Indian immigrants who feel dislocated without a homeplace. She writes:

> We are American citizens now, so we can collect social security when it is time. Though we visit Calcutta every few years, and bring back drawstring pajamas and Darjeeling tea, we have decided to grow old here. . . . We have a son that attends Harvard University. Mala no longer drapes the end of her sari over her head, or weeps at night for her parents, but occasionally she weeps for our son. So we drive to Cambridge to visit him, or bring him home for the weekend, so that he can eat rice with us with his hands, and speak Bengali, things we sometimes worry he will no longer do after we die. (p. 197)

Both hooks and Lahiri highlight the importance of the concept of cultural dislocation among immigrant and marginalized families and its connection to historical, political, cultural, racial, and social consciousness. Both describe how cultural dislocation creates a yearning for identity, self-definition, and meaning. Similarly, in her ethnographic work *Call to Home* (1996), Carol Stack discusses feelings of dislocation among African Americans and their yearning for home. She recounts the return migration of adult African Americans to the poor rural South, and in doing so reveals the homeplace as a critical and dynamic developmental process in their lives. The African American families involved in Stack's study experience the homeplace as somewhere that can send you away in early adulthood and call you back in midlife. Like the characters in Lahiri's book, Stack's study participants reveal their attachment to the origins of identity development and self-definition.

The poetry of Marilyn Nelson (1990) and Evelyn Dilworth-Williams (2002) further reveals how family scholars can use the concept of homeplace as a theoretical tool. Both poets artfully depict the cultural ethos of the homeplace. In *Panola: My Kinfolks' Land* (2002), Dilworth-Williams's poems describe how a viable homeplace may serve specific functions for dislocated and marginalized families. They tell stories of how men, women, and children are involved in creating a homeplace, the routines and rituals that embody it, the physical space that gives the homeplace form, and what happens in the lives of African Americans who do not have a homeplace. Thus, just as empirical studies provide conceptual guidance, poetry tells us how the homeplace, in the best of situations, is a sanctuary—a place where African Americans can go for renewal and for physical, mental, and emotional healing from frequent subtle and overt discriminatory assaults.

It is important to note, however, that some family scholars suggest that the significance of the homeplace varies for individuals across time, with some embracing the homeplace all their lives and others rejecting it during critical developmental periods (e.g., adolescence). Individual family members' differing feelings about the homeplace at various times can create relationship tensions that can temporarily compromise the "refuge" quality of the homeplace (Stevenson, Winn, Coard, & Walker-Barnes, 2003; Winn, Nicholson, & Hyman, 2002). Healthy families and the individuals within them are able to weather these tensions, but those without the skills to do so continually flounder as they consciously, and sometimes unconsciously, yearn for a homeplace.

Understanding a concept such as homeplace can allow family researchers to find a context in which they can better use metaphors such as the family circle and the fence to find the pieces in the puzzle of theorizing about contemporary families. Family scholars can use the metaphor of homeplace to inform their theorizing about contemporary families, especially immigrant and marginalized families, regarding identity development, individual and family development processes, conflict in families, and family stress and coping.

CONCLUSION

The ideas that we have explored in the second half of this chapter illustrate how family scholars can usefully pursue symbolic interaction theory and cultural rather than structural traditions of family theorizing to understand contemporary families. Other traditions mentioned in the first half of the chapter might also turn out to be valuable points of entry for future family theorizing and research. We propose that, in addition to using traditional theoretical views, family scholars can also use abstract ideas such as metaphors in the theorizing process. We also suggest that theorizing should be accompanied by an understanding of many changes currently taking place: changes in societal norms and values, changes in population demographics, changes resulting from challenges to long-accepted definitions of family life, and changes resulting from challenges to the ways in which families are studied.

In this chapter, we have challenged you to accept some existing theories about contemporary families and at the same time create new theoretical ideas. We encourage family theorists and researchers to understand that theories develop and change over time, energized by the active participation of many scholars within and across successive generations. We invite you to become a contributor and to learn more about theoretical traditions in family studies by bringing to bear your own creative and questioning spirit. Many resources beyond academic books and journals are available to foster this creative and questioning spirit. The humanities, in particular, offer resources that can inspire creative thinking and provide starting points from which to understand families. You can gain insights about family life from literary works just as you can from empirical findings.

We advise you to be sensitive to the ways in which changes in families enable, if not require, changes in the ways we understand and explain family life. Share your ideas with others; they are eager to receive them. Finally, allow yourself to be challenged by the stimulating ideas you find in the remainder of this volume.

CASE STUDY

AGONY OR ECSTASY? EVOLVING THEORY AND METHODS OF THE CIRCUMPLEX MODEL

Judy Watson Tiesel, *Family Therapy Resources, Minneapolis*

Dean Gorall, *Human Services Inc. of Washington County, Minnesota*

One of the models that family studies students first learn about—the circumplex model (CM) of marital and family systems (Olson, Russell, & Sprenkle, 1989)—is a conceptual diagram that highlights the importance of two dimensions of family functioning: cohesion and flexibility. The model has appeal for many reasons, including the fact that it captures family complexities and condenses them into types based on their levels of cohesion and flexibility. We were so taken by the circumplex model that we became research assistants in the Circumplex Model Center, collecting data from various studies using the CM worldwide. Imagine our surprise, then, when we discovered that several of these studies found that higher scores on the two dimensions were correlated with indicators of *healthier* family functioning, contradicting the model's premise of curvilinear relationships. That is, healthy families were supposed to score in the *moderate* range of cohesion and flexibility, not at the high ends; unhealthy/problem families were supposed to score at either end of the dimensions, not just the low ends.

Our surprise at these findings created some agony that launched us into a recursive cycle: The data challenged our methods, which led to new measures with new findings, which challenged our theory, which led to new hypotheses, which once again challenged our methods, and so on. We experienced varying degrees of agony and ecstasy as researchers during that recursive cycle, the former catalyzing us to generate the latter. Here is an account of how the recursive cycle unfolded.

Believing that the problem must lie in the self-report method, not the theory, we set out to develop a new and improved questionnaire, the Family Adaptability and Cohesion Evaluation Scales IV, or FACES IV (for details, see this volume's companion Web site at http://www.ncfr.org/sourcebook), that would accurately assess those families at the high extremes who were clinically evaluated as chaotic or enmeshed but were escaping detection by FACES II (Olson, Portner, & Bell, 1982) and FACES III (Olson, Portner, & Lavee, 1985). First, we asked clinical members of the American Association of Marriage and Family Therapists (AAMFT) to describe extreme (i.e., enmeshed, disengaged, rigid, or chaotic) families. Second, we had a diverse team generate potential items for FACES IV using the descriptors provided by the AAMFT members. Third, we sent these items to the original developers of the CM and to researchers who were experienced with using

FACES for (ahem) face validity. Fourth, we modified or discarded items based on their feedback. This resulted in a questionnaire that we gave to a sample of 2,400 subjects across the United States. The subsequent findings left us ecstatic (briefly) and then agonized over what the data meant for the theory.

We were ecstatic because it seemed that FACES IV had captured those elusive families at the high extremes of the dimensions. All the construct and discriminant validity tests supported the theory that some unique dynamics characterized those family systems labeled enmeshed or chaotic. The agony was that those high extremes (enmeshed and chaotic) were not independent factors, as the CM theory suggested. Enmeshment *should* have loaded onto the same factor as disengagement. Instead, the data suggested that if families were enmeshed, they were rigidly enmeshed; if they were chaotic, they were chaotically disengaged. That did not at all fit the CM theory, because only two of the four types of extreme families were represented. Rather than enmeshment being an anchor on the cohesion dimension, it seemed to be something else entirely. Aaack!

But wait, wasn't this important information? The revised FACES was obviously capturing crucial family dynamics, given that the scales were able to discriminate between problem and nonproblem families. Was it possible that we needed to adjust our theory rather than attempt yet one more stab at FACES? Perhaps a family system could have aspects of *both* disengagement *and* enmeshment, *both* chaos *and* rigidity. We knew from our clinical experience that families could contain members who were enmeshed with each other yet not feel very close at all. And the phenomenon of "chaotic flippers" (Killorin & Olson, 1984) is frequently witnessed in parents who flip between rigid discipline and chaotic permissiveness.

If we allowed the data to inform the theory, what might we better understand about families? If we examined each of the four "extremes" independently instead of trying to

Case Study

graft them onto two dimensions, would we learn anything new? Each extreme had its own scale, so we analyzed the data by scores on each of those four scales. The picture that emerged revealed that healthy families (measured through the use of other standardized scales) showed low scores on each of the four scales, whereas unhealthy families had high scores on at least one of the scales. The greater the number of scales with high scores, the more unhealthy the families, according to a discriminant function test. (Ecstasy here!) The data were indicating that when families could be characterized as enmeshed, they were more often *rigidly* enmeshed. When they were characterized as chaotic, they were more often chaotically *disengaged*. Perhaps the data were suggesting that enmeshed families need a certain amount of constraint to maintain their enmeshment; perhaps disengagement is the by-product of chronic chaos.

However (mild agony), the new FACES IV methodology did not supply the entire range of functioning. We hit a bull's-eye on the extreme functioning targets, but we neglected to aim at a direct measure of healthy family functioning—presumably the moderate ranges of cohesion and flexibility. If families scored low on the extreme items, we assumed by default that they were healthy—a risky assumption, and one that is incompatible with the strengths-focused zeitgeist in the field. So we returned to the drawing boards (agony) of our theoretical and methodological forerunners and developed another version of FACES IV, combining those already "proven" extreme items with moderate items tapping healthy family functioning (a last methodological attempt at ecstasy?).

If this new attempt at instrument construction was going to reflect methodologically what the model portrays theoretically, then the scales designed to tap each of the two dimensions should load in a manner consistent with the model in factor analysis. That is, three scales representing low, moderate, and high cohesion should group together, as should the scales

representing flexibility. Unfortunately, our shot flew far afield of its intended target. Once again, three of the four extremes (enmeshed, chaotic, and rigid) demanded their own individual factor, as did moderate flexibility. The fourth extreme, disengagement, loaded onto the opposite end of the factor with moderate cohesion, suggesting a dimension ranging from very low to high (but not enmeshed) cohesion. How, then, do these data inform our theory? Our methodological arrow may have missed its objective, but it hit another target we didn't even know existed (an unintended sort of ecstasy). Although the instrument developed to tap the curvilinear nature of the cohesion and flexibility dimensions through self-report "once and for all" fell short of the target (agony), what emerged is an instrument that is useful in assessing both healthy and problematic aspects of family functioning. In our attempts to tap the two key dimensions more fully, we uncovered much more than we ever intended (ecstasy, we think).

The newest incarnation of the CM reflects the impact of research on theory, research that now is creating new theory, which is awaiting validation by further research. Here are some of the agonizingly ecstatic new theoretical components: (a) Curvilinearity has not been empirically supported; (b) enmeshment is quantitatively (and presumably qualitatively) different from cohesion; (c) instead of a standardized flexibility dimension, three separate subconcepts emerged (conflict resolution, organization, and inflexibility); and (d) these scales together proved quite powerful at discriminating healthy from problem-saturated families.

We present this case study to illustrate the recursive nature of theory and research methods, and want to emphasize the overall intention of subjecting ourselves to the agony and the ecstasy of such a process. Simply stated, the global objective in the family science field is to understand families better so that we can provide better service—in its multitude of forms—to families. For us as researchers and therapists, better service is applied primarily in clinical settings, so we explored how these new understandings had relevance for therapeutic practice.

For example, if enmeshment is no longer synonymous with extremely high cohesion, what impact will this have on our work with an incestuous family that presents as very enmeshed? Will we work to decrease enmeshment while concurrently working to increase cohesion? Such a treatment plan would have been theoretically impossible according to the original CM. If disengaged families are more likely than engaged families to lack organization and leadership skills, will we need to address this skills deficit in order to create opportunities for family members to connect emotionally? If we're having trouble understanding a particular family's dynamics, how would the family members' scores on the five crucial scales assist us in our assessment and subsequent intervention? It is not enough to understand—we must also let our understanding inform our service.

Capturing the complexity of family dynamics in this project involved challenging the old methods, creating new methods, challenging the old model, offering new theoretical interpretations, and reexamining both the old and the new. Family work (theorizing, research, and practice) is inherently messy, resistant to tidy compartmentalization. Nevertheless, we believe that the pursuit of a better understanding of families is a cause worthy of the agony and ecstasy.

Case Study

CASE STUDY

ON THE USE OF PROBABILITY IN FAMILY THEORY

Jetse Sprey, *Case Western Reserve University*

The word *emerging* in the title of Chapter 2 implies a transition from an existing discourse to a more complex one. Whether emerging structures are more descriptive or more abstract than previous ones, they reflect a process that is more than just a sum of its parts. In line with this thinking, I will focus here on the idea of probability as a potentially "emerging" component of theoretical practice in family studies.

In *The Taming of Chance,* Ian Hacking (1998) notes that "the most decisive conceptual event of twentieth century physics has been the discovery that the world is not deterministic." He goes on to say: "Quantum physics takes for granted that nature is at bottom irreducibly stochastic. . . . A moment's reflection shows that a similar statement may be attempted in connection with people" (p. 2). As such, "social and personal arrangements" also are matters of probabilities and thus "statistical" in nature. Adding a historian's view to the foregoing, Porter (1995) observes:

On the whole, statistical inference has not made its way down the hierarchy of science, from mathematics and physics to the biological and at last the social sciences. Rather, it was seized most

Case Study

readily by weaker disciplines, such as psychology and medical research, and indeed by their relatively applied subfields. (p. 200)

Probabilistic reasoning must compensate for the virtual absence of experimental research in family studies. This may account for the fact that the use of such reasoning among family scholars so far primarily seems limited to the prevention of judgment errors. This raises the question: Should that be all?

ON PROBABILITY

The chance of any individual ticket holder winning a state lottery is one in millions. Each ticket, however, may either win or lose whatever is at stake. Tossing a coin, buying a lottery ticket, and getting married are *all* binary events: They all have possible outcomes that do or do not happen. This contradiction between *one-in-millions* and *either/ or* reflects the fact that the notions of "probability" and "randomness" are absent from Nature's vocabulary. Instead, they are human inventions designed to help us make sense of a complex, uncertain, and frequently unknown world. "Facts," then, reflect the transition from possibility to "reality." This may account for their dubious reputation of "speaking for themselves." Some facts, however, "speak" more loudly than others. Tossing a coin involves a 50/50 probability space, one much larger than the chance of *any* lottery ticket's becoming a winner. Clearly, *winning* tickets are not bought but "made," and their chances of "becoming" are quite low indeed.

Public lotteries—like other systemic processes—have their own probability spaces. Calculations concerning lotteries, including predictions, do not *directly* involve specific winners or losers. Rather, significant information consists of averages and a range of additional systemic computations.

PROBABILITY SPACES

As I have noted, the probability space of a state lottery is systemic; that is, it involves a "population" rather than a set of unique individuals. The space of buyers, on the other hand, is personal and involves choices made within a specific set. To illustrate: A normal die has a probability space of six equally likely outcomes, whereas a series of throws creates a unique sequence that, given the properties of the die, requires additional information for its ultimate specification (Wicken, 1987, p. 185). What *is* known are the six equally possible outcomes for each throw and the likelihood that during an extended series each separate outcome will appear at least once. In contrast, if a thousand dice are cast all at once, a *system* or *population* emerges. Its unique structure contains a variety of microstates clustered around a mean. Its probability space *lacks* precise information about the qualities and forms within its boundary (see Hayles, 1990, p. 53). Observing *its* path over time involves observing changing rates, means, standard deviations, and the like.

To bring this to bear on family studies, it seems that the growing diversity of marriage and family forms increases the ontological uncertainty of the *institutional* realms of contemporary marriage and the family. Their cognitive realities become more complex. However, their respective probability spaces do not provide the information we need to know the quantity and the quality of newly emerging *relational* forms. Remember state lottery systems, in which individual winners and losers remain irrelevant and, as such, unknown. The lottery will continue to operate regardless of who wins or loses. It might continue, at least for a while, in the absence of a winner. It would be interesting, then, to compare and contrast the role of probability within the *institutional* realms of marriage and the family with that in their respective *relational* forms.

USING PROBABILITY

As I have mentioned, family scholars tend to use "probability" almost exclusively to avoid errors of judgment. Left unexplored is whether the logic of probability may prove useful to scholars seeking a better understanding of populations as systems per se and, as such, to the ontology of systemic uncertainty, vulnerability, and even necessity. Consider, for example, the following statement by a contemporary quantum theorist:

> The failure of quantum theorists to distinguish in calculations between several quite different meanings of "probability," between expectation values and actual values, makes us do things that are unnecessary. . . . We routinely commit the Mind Project Fallacy of projecting our own thoughts out into Nature, supposing that creations of our own imagination are real properties of Nature, or our own ignorance signifies some indecision on the part of Nature. (Jaynes, 1990, pp. 385–386)

This comment touches on the basic distinction between uncertainty and ignorance and, as such, raises the issue of to what extent any given "population" may be a fact of our imagination, of nature, or of both. In the context of this discussion, one might ask, Is a winning lottery ticket a "fact" likely to repeat itself or a quite rare instance of "becoming"? Any rational *expectation* of winning a jackpot and the actual winning of one reflect different meanings of probability. Few sensible persons really expect to win a state lottery, even if they buy several tickets. The choice to purchase a ticket, then, may be based in hope or faith in "Lady Luck." Without such hope or faith, few reasonable people would buy lottery tickets.

Does all this mean, then, that the choice to marry a special person and the chance that the ensuing marriage will last involve different probabilities? Yes indeed. On the face of it, the decision to take a spouse resembles the decision to buy a lottery ticket; the probability spaces of both choices are analogous to the casting of a die. The assumption that the course of a marital relationship is not totally random suggests a process analogous to the repeated rolling of a *loaded* die: The exact outcome of each throw is up to chance, but an awareness of previous events—revealing the nature of the "load" in question—may well allow a growing reflection on what is happening. On the other hand, to explain—let alone predict—the pathway of a given marriage *institution,* one must have information about divorce rates, death rates, marriage rates, and so forth.

IN CONCLUSION

Hacking (1998) refers to the "seemingly unproblematic" notion of populations and argues that "the very notion of an exact population is one which has little sense until there are institutions for establishing what 'population' means" (p. 6). By doing so, he moves probabilistic reasoning from the "random variable" level to the "original logical inference" approach of Bernoulli and Laplace (Jaynes, 1990, p. 387). But what exactly is the probability of a population or any social system? How "risky," for example, is Ulrich Beck's (1992) "risk society" or contemporary American society? Do social institutions, such as marriage and the family, share the risks of their host societies? If so, how and to what extent? The following quote puts such questions in a historical context:

> It is not clear why professionals with graduate degrees including training in Statistics should have so much difficulty solving elementary Bayesian problems. But it is no mystery why such problems

Case Study

do not succumb to the abilities of the "intuitive statistician" once thought to be within us all. Apart from a few games of chance . . . no human ever confronted a stable, quantified probability value, or even the data to construct one, before the seventeenth century. (Porter, 1995, p. 213)

In other words, the growing uncertainty and contingency that seem to characterize the nature of contemporary "modernity" appear to be as much "causes" as consequences of the human inventions of the notions of probability and randomness. What seems lacking, so far at least, is the emergence of the application of these two crucial analytic tools in the realm of theoretical practice. The use of probability in that case would cover, apart from purely research-methodological concerns, the ontological and epistemological realms of explanatory practice. Bayesian probability as a way of "learning from experience" (Hacking, 2001, chap. 15) may be of great use in efforts to understand the "risk" of social systems and/or institutional patterns. The decision of *what* to learn about *what,* however, remains "subjective" and, as such, theoretical.

Probability theory is at the core of statistical inference and therefore reverberates throughout most family research. Its theoretical statements are often echoed by researchers who say "may lead to" rather than "leads to," or who use verbs such as *influence* instead of *cause.* Regrettably, however, linguistic rules for probabilistic reasoning remain poorly articulated. One thing we must do better is to infuse the logic rather than the mere techniques of probability into the substance of our explanatory discourse. I look forward to constructive responses to this challenge throughout the coming years.

REFERENCES

Bayer, A. E. (1981). The psychoanalytic frame of reference in family study. In F. I. Nye & F. M. Berardo (Eds.), *Emerging conceptual frameworks in family analysis*. New York: Praeger. (Original work published 1966)

Beck, U. (1992). *Risk society: Towards a new modernity* (M. Ritter, Trans.). London: Sage.

Boss, P., Doherty, W. J., LaRossa, R., Schumm, W. R., & Steinmetz, S. K. (Eds.). (1993). *Sourcebook of family theories and methods: A contextual approach*. New York: Plenum.

Burr, W. R. (1973). *Theory construction and the sociology of the family*. New York: John Wiley.

Burr, W. R., Hill, R., Nye, F. I., & Reiss, I. L. (Eds.). (1979a). *Contemporary theories about the family: Vol. 1. Research-based theories*. New York: Free Press.

Burr, W. R., Hill, R., Nye, F. I., & Reiss, I. L. (Eds.). (1979b). *Contemporary theories about the family: Vol. 2. General theories/theoretical orientations*. New York: Free Press.

Burton, L. M., Winn, D.-M., Stevenson, H., & Lawson Clark, S. (2004). Working with African-American clients: Considering the "homeplace" in marriage and family therapy practices. *Journal of Marital and Family Therapy, 30*(4), 113-129.

Christensen, H. T. (Ed.). (1964). *Handbook of marriage and the family*. Chicago: Rand McNally.

Clark, H. (1993). Sites of resistance: Place, "race," and gender as sources on empowerment. In P. E. Jackson & J. Penrose (Eds.), *Constructions of race, place, and nation* (pp. 121–142). London: UCL.

DeJong, M. (2004). Metaphor and the mentoring process. *Child and Youth Care Forum, 33*(1), 3–17.

Dilworth-Anderson, P., Burton, L. M., & Johnson, L. B. (1993). Reframing theories for understanding race, ethnicity, and families. In P. Boss, W. J. Doherty, R. LaRossa, W. R. Schumm, & S. K. Steinmetz (Eds.), *Sourcebook of family theories and methods: A contextual approach* (pp. 627–649). New York: Plenum.

Dilworth-Williams, E. (2002). *Panola: My kinfolks' land*. Bloomington, IN: 1st Books.

Douglass, F. (1846). *Narrative of the life of Frederick Douglass, an American slave*. Wortley, near Leeds: J. Barker.

Du Bois, W. E. B. (1903). *The souls of Black folk: Essays and sketches* (2nd ed.). Chicago: A. C. McClurg.

Engels, F. (1946). *The origin of the family, private property, and the state*. New York: International. (Original work published 1884)

Gieryn, T. (2000). A space for place in sociology. *Annual Review of Sociology, 26*, 463–496.

Gilbert, M. R. (1998). Race, space, and power: The survival strategies of working poor women. *Annals of the Association of American Geographers, 88*, 595–621.

Greenfield, T. B. (1984). Leaders and schools: Willfulness and nonnatural order in organizations. In T. J. Sergiovanni & J. E. Cobally (Eds.), *Leadership and organizational culture*. (pp. 142–169). Chicago: University of Illinois Press.

Hacking, I. (1998). *The taming of chance*. New York: Cambridge University Press.

Hacking, I. (2001). *An introduction to probability and inductive logic*. New York: Cambridge University Press.

Hayles, N. K. (1990). *Chaos bound: Orderly disorder in contemporary literature and science*. Ithaca, NY: Cornell University Press.

Hechter, M. (1993). Values research in the social and behavioral sciences. In M. Hechter, L. Nadel, & R. E. Michod (Eds.), *Sociology and economics: Controversy and integration* (pp. 1–28). Hawthorne, NY: Aldine de Gruyter.

Hill, R. (1951). Review of current research on marriage and the family. *American Sociological Review, 16*, 694–701.

Hill, R. (1969). *The Minnesota Family Study Center: Twelve years of development, 1957-69*. Minneapolis: University of Minnesota Press.

Hill, R. (1980). *The status of children, youth, and families 1979* (OHDS Publication No. 80-30274). Washington, DC: U.S. Department of Health and Human Services.

Hill, R., & Hansen, D. (1960). The identification of conceptual frameworks utilized in family study. *Marriage and Family Living, 22*, 299–311.

hooks, b. (1990). *Yearning: Race, gender, and cultural politics*. Boston: South End.

Ingoldsby, B. B., Smith, S. R., & Miller, J. E. (2004). *Exploring family theories*. Los Angeles: Roxbury.

Jaynes, E. T. (1990). Probability in quantum theory. In W. H. Zurek (Ed.), *Complexity, entropy, and the physics of information* (pp. 381–404). Reading, MA: Addison-Wesley.

Killorin, E., & Olson, D. H. (1984). The chaotic flippers in treatment. In E. Kaufman (Ed.), *Power to change: Family case studies in the treatment of alcoholism* (pp. 99–129). New York: Gardner.

Klein, D. M., & White, J. M. (1996). *Family theories: An introduction.* Thousand Oaks, CA: Sage.

Lahiri, J. (1999). *Interpreter of maladies.* New York: Houghton Mifflin.

Lakoff, G., & Johnson, M. (1980). *Metaphors we live by.* Chicago: University of Chicago Press.

Lamanna, M. A. (2002). *Emile Durkheim on the family.* Thousand Oaks, CA: Sage.

Leventhal, T., & Brooks-Gunn, J. (2000). The neighborhoods they live in: The effects of neighborhood residence upon child and adolescent outcomes. *Psychological Bulletin, 126,* 309–337.

Nelson, M. (1990). *The homeplace.* Baton Rouge: Louisiana State University Press.

Nye, F. I., & Berardo, F. M. (Eds.). (1981). *Emerging conceptual frameworks in family analysis.* New York: Praeger.

Olson, D. H., Portner, J., & Bell, R. (1982). *Family Adaptability and Cohesion Evaluation Scales (FACES II).* St. Paul: University of Minnesota, Family Social Science Department.

Olson, D. H., Portner, J., & Lavee, Y. (1985). *Family Adaptability and Cohesion Evaluation Scales (FACES II).* St. Paul: University of Minnesota, Family Social Science Department.

Olson, D. H., Russell, C. S., & Sprenkle, D. H. (Eds.). (1989). *Circumplex model: Systemic assessment and treatment of families.* New York: Haworth.

Overton, W. F. (1998). Developmental psychology: Philosophy, concepts, and methodology. In W. Damon (Series Ed.) & R. M. Lerner (Vol. Ed.), *Handbook of child psychology: Vol. 1. Theoretical models of human development* (5th ed., pp. 107–187). New York: John Wiley.

Pepper, S. C. (1970). *World hypotheses: A study in evidence.* Berkeley: University of California Press. (Original work published 1942)

Porter, T. M. (1995). *Trust in numbers: The pursuit of objectivity in science and public life.* Princeton, NJ: Princeton University Press.

Reese, H. W. (1991). Contextualism and developmental psychology. *Advances in Child Development and Behavior, 23,* 187–230.

Reese, H. W., & Overton, W. F. (1970). Models of development and theories of development. In L. R. Goulet & P. B. Baltes (Eds.), *Life-span development psychology.* New York: Academic Press.

Stack, C. B. (1996). *Call to home: African Americans reclaim the rural South.* New York: Basic Books.

Stevenson, H., Winn, D.-M., Coard, S., & Walker-Barnes, C. (2003). *Towards a culturally relevant framework for interventions with African-American families.* Paper presented at the conference Emerging Issues in African-American Family Life: Context, Adaptation, and Policy, Duke University, Durham, NC.

Waste, R. J. (1995). Concentrated poverty and the city as reservation. *Journal of Urban Affairs, 17,* 315–324.

Wetzel, N. A., & Winawer, H. (2002). School-based community family therapy for adolescents at risk. In F. W. Kaslow (Ed.), *Comprehensive handbook of psychotherapy: Vol. 3. Interpersonal, humanistic, existential approaches to psychotherapy* (pp. 205–230). New York: John Wiley.

White, J. M., & Klein, D. M. (2002). *Family theories* (2nd ed.). Thousand Oaks, CA: Sage.

Wicken, J. (1987). Entropy and information: Suggestions for a common language. *Philosophy of Science, 54,* 176–193.

Winn, D.-M., Nicholson, M., & Hyman, C. (2002). *Strategies to recruit and retain adolescent subjects in university-based research.* Paper presented at the Eighth Biennial Conference of the European Association for Research on Adolescence, New College, Oxford.

Winton, C. A. (1995). *Frameworks for studying families.* Guilford, CT: Dushkin.

• Three

CONTEMPORARY AND EMERGING RESEARCH METHODS IN STUDYING FAMILIES

Alan C. Acock, *Oregon State University*

Manfred M. H. van Dulmen, *Kent State University*

Katherine R. Allen, *Virginia Polytechnic Institute and State University*

Fred P. Piercy, *Virginia Polytechnic Institute and State University*

I n this chapter, we describe research methods that reflect a range of perspectives, values, and preferences that underlie theoretical and methodological choices in family studies. We address methodological issues in practical ways. We do not pretend to have all the answers. We are lifelong students who want to remain teachable, open to change, and willing to embrace new ideas that offer better approaches to study families.

One of the most exciting things about having the opportunity to work with a team of scholars from diverse backgrounds (child development, family studies, gerontology, marriage and family therapy, psychology, sociology, and women's studies) who employ different methods (quantitative and qualitative) is that we have discovered ways in which our partisan concerns have broader application. A major criticism of qualitative methods,

for example, has been that there are no shared evaluative standards by which to judge manuscripts, theses, and grant proposals (Elliott, Fischer, & Rennie, 1999). But as we examined this issue, we found that qualitative and quantitative strategies have many criteria in common. For example, multilevel analysis was developed as a corrective for the tendency for some quantitative researchers to exclude contextual variables. Nor should we expect only qualitative researchers to be concerned with reflexive analysis. A scientific approach regardless of method requires scholars to be aware of how their own values, experiences, and social locations shape their research (Allen, 2000). Our concern, then, is with generating better research that can elaborate family structure, process, context, and diversity over time. We clearly need innovative strategies to address the complex problems facing families in the 21st century.

New forms of data analysis and representation are emerging, and there is plenty of room for multimethod studies of families. More demanding standards for all types of research are evident as well. This chapter is organized topically by recent and emerging developments in the main aspects of research methodological content: research paradigms, design and measurement advances, and analytic issues. Our coverage is not exhaustive, and we suggest that interested readers visit this volume's companion Web site (http://www.ncfr.org/sourcebook) and seek out the excellent sources cited for further reading on these topics.

METHODOLOGICAL CHALLENGES OF COMPETING PARADIGMS IN FAMILY RESEARCH

Research traditions in family scholarship have generated feuds not unlike that between the Hatfields and the McCoys. New neighborhoods are forming, however, where theoretical and methodological clans are beginning to open their doors and get to know one another. In these new neighborhoods, various families are cooperating with one another. Many are finding out that they are not as different from their neighbors as they once thought. Of course, there are differences between and even within methodological clans. To maintain their distinctiveness, some clans choose to live only with members of their immediate families and celebrate their uniqueness, which is just fine.

In this chapter we include discussion of our growing awareness of the interfaces among methodological neighborhoods. Although we try to focus on the parts of the new neighborhood that are beginning to work together and evolve practices that reflect the strength of their neighbors, we also feature particular innovations in each tradition that improve the linkage between theory and research.

Multiple Paradigms and Mixed Methods

Our decision to cover both qualitative and quantitative methods of family research in a single chapter reflects our inclusive stance on social inquiry in the family field. All research methods are referential. Underlying epistemologies and guiding theories may differ, but there are just a few basic methods of social inquiry: interviewing people, observing behavior, and examining documents (Harding, 1987). Whether one uses numbers, autobiography, poetry, drama, art, or photos as data, all of these serve as ways to gain a better understanding of some phenomenon.

Particular elements of some methods (e.g., strict control of variables) may be at odds with the general practices of others (e.g., naturalistic observation, social action), and researchers must keep these distinctions in mind when they plan their studies. Still, we share the view that analytic strategies from quantitative and qualitative traditions can complement one another when they are applied with a little thoughtful reflection (see Lareau, 2003; Lewis, 1950; Seccombe, 1999).

Not all researchers hold a "both/and" stance when it comes to combining methods. Some qualitative researchers, for example, point to the different philosophical traditions of various qualitative methods (Rosenblatt & Fischer, 1993). Some passionately distance themselves from particular paradigms, as in an ethnomethodologist's insistence that the scientific and the phenomenological cannot be combined (Gubrium & Holstein, 1993). Qualitative researchers are aware of the difficulty that some quantitative researchers have in evaluating the veracity of their work, and they are prepared to deal with questions about validity and replicability, even when these criteria are not always relevant (Ambert, Adler, Adler, & Detzner, 1995). Our view is that family researchers need a combination of methods in order to capture the complexity of family life. This is not to say that for a study to meet standards of excellence it necessarily needs to be based on multiple methods. However, for the field to advance—if we are to understand more clearly and ultimately improve the lives of family members in the 21st century—we need to have respect for, knowledge of, and expertise in a variety of methods.

The choice of research methods does not necessarily reflect one or another philosophical assumption. For example, a researcher may use focus groups to generate quantitative questionnaire items, or to come to a better understanding of a group's opinions on certain subjects. The data gathered may be analyzed quantitatively, such as through word counts or interactional patterns (Roberts, 1997), or interpreted through the lens of a feminist social constructionist (Gergen, 1997). Philosophical assumptions are made by people, not by methods, and the combining of analytic methods will improve a study when the researcher is committed to research that combines the best of multiple worldviews (Lincoln & Guba, 2000).

Depending on the questions asked, then, insightful family researchers may choose quantitative methods, qualitative methods, or both. A researcher may use a quantitative questionnaire to learn about condom use patterns in certain communities hand in hand with qualitative interviews to learn about the meaning that condom use has for certain target groups. Likewise, a critical theorist might critique either data set with an eye toward cultural or social influences. We see qualitative and quantitative methods, then, as providing a view of the vagaries of family life through multiple lenses.

Evaluative Standards for Research: Challenges of Methodological Pluralism

We find ourselves in a dilemma regarding the plethora of research options today. Although qualitative research has a rich and important tradition in family studies (Gilgun, 1999), qualitative methods have been marginalized in mainstream journals (LaRossa & Wolf, 1985). Over the past decade, there has been an explosion of interest in qualitative methods, evident in the success of Denzin and Lincoln's *Handbook of Qualitative Research* (2000b). An abbreviated list of the rich qualitative methodological practices available today includes discourse analysis, participatory action research, focus group research, ethnomethodology, autoethnography, narrative analysis, and grounded theory methodology.

The widespread interest in qualitative methods across disciplines has raised many issues regarding research design, epistemology,

researcher standpoint, and intersection with multiple data sources. How can qualitative researchers, with this backdrop, demonstrate rigor and accountability yet also maintain the advantages of qualitative methods? For example, whereas quantitative scholars typically emphasize the importance of probability samples and select participants as representatives of populations, qualitative scholars often sample participants based on their information value. It is, therefore, inappropriate for quantitative reviewers to critique qualitative studies for not employing probability samples.

Consider the focus of just a few of the classic qualitative studies that have provided powerful insights about family life in the 20th century: Thomas and Znaniecki's (1918–1920) study of Polish family immigration in the United States; Cuber and Harroff's (1965) examination of five types of marriage among affluent Americans; Bott's (1971) ethnographic study of London families; Humphreys's (1970) study of impersonal sex between men in public restrooms; and Rubin's (1976) examination of working-class marriage relationships at the end of the modern era. To understand the inner workings of families and the social forces impinging on family lives, we often turn to the richness of meaning provided in such work.

Despite the fact that evaluation criteria have been developed for qualitative and quantitative methods separately, we wish to level the playing field by identifying both common and unique standards for excellence in qualitative and quantitative research. Scholars are wise to translate their intentions, methods, and analyses into language and symbols that a general scientific readership will understand and appreciate (Davis, 1981). Qualitative researchers are competing more aggressively for research dollars today than in the past, yet many reviewers still lack formal training in qualitative methods. They may see these methods as guesswork or as the romanticization or bias of the researcher (Belgrave, Zablotsky, & Guadagno, 2002). The dilemma is how to make qualitative work accessible to scientific evaluators without sanitizing it so much that it loses its power to affect readers and transform social reality (Dill, 1994; Jaffe & Miller, 1994; Krieger, 1991; Stanley, 1990).

Table 3.1   Guidelines for Evaluating Qualitative and Quantitative Research

Guidelines Shared by Most Qualitative and Quantitative Methods	Guidelines Especially Pertinent to Qualitative Methods	Guidelines Especially Pertinent to Quantitative Methods
Contribution to knowledge	Researcher's owning of own perspective	Generalizability
Use of appropriate methods	Situation of the sample through comprehensive description	Reliability
Respect for participants (informed consent, ethical research)	Accomplishment of general versus specific research tasks	Replicability
Specification of methods	Provision of credibility checks	
Appropriate discussion	Coherence	
Clarity of presentation	Grounding of research in examples	
Explicit scientific context and purpose	Resonance with readers	

SOURCE: Adapted from Elliott et al. (1999).

Citing the dramatic rise in the popularity of qualitative methods and the lack of criteria against which to evaluate the merit of studies in psychology and related fields, Elliott et al. (1999) developed a set of evolving guidelines. They assembled 40 quality standards from experts, such as Lincoln and Guba (1985), based originally on Cook and Campbell's (1979) ideas about credibility, transferability, dependability, and confirmability. Other experts had turned to the philosophical literature on truth criteria for evaluating interpretive accounts and developed a triangulation procedure or member check (see Packer & Addison, 1989). Elliott et al. organized this initial list into clusters of similarity and then reduced it to 11 principles. Next, they solicited feedback from qualitative experts and then further refined the guidelines to two lists.

These guidelines propose that there are divergent epistemological and ontological positions among methodologists. Some assumptions and expectations are common to both quantitative and qualitative research, and some are of special importance to either qualitative or quantitative research. Table 3.1 shows Elliott et al.'s guidelines, to which we have added a few criteria that have special importance in quantitative research.

Historically, there has been a quantitative bias in how qualitative research products have been judged. This has meant that qualitative researchers have struggled in the area of publications, but even more so in grant applications. Substantial progress has been made, however. For example, the National Institutes of Health's Office of Behavioral and Social Sciences Research (1999) has published a guide for writing qualitative proposals relating to health, and a number of authors have outlined ways to make the qualitative research process more explicit and credible to external reviewers (e.g., Anfara, Brown, & Mangione, 2002; Belgrave et al., 2002). Also, the use of software designed especially for qualitative research supports both the efficiency and the sophistication of qualitative data analysis, and this has contributed to its greater acceptance in the scientific community (see Matheson's review of qualitative software on this volume's companion Web site).

To facilitate researchers' efforts to capture rich data without relinquishing the flexibility and depth that draws many scholars to qualitative work, Belgrave et al. (2002) have devised some strategies that qualitative researchers can use to communicate successfully with quantitatively oriented scholars who may not share their paradigms or methods. Their suggestions include the following:

1. Provide sufficient detail and explicitly tie methodological strategies to research goals.

2. State the specific aim of the research in a single interrogative sentence.

3. Draw from the quantitative and qualitative literature in preparing a literature review.

4. Give concrete details.

5. Avoid the "terminological jungle" (Lofland & Lofland, 1995) of jargon; explain any technical language.

6. Provide a solid, well-reasoned plan for data collection: Give details for sample and site selection; include numbers; compare across sites.

7. Describe how you will record data and what will count as notes.

8. List the questions you will ask and what the questions are designed to do.

9. Do not romanticize the data analysis process: Describe in detail exactly how you will code data and how categories will emerge.

10. Address issues of credibility and validity.

We believe that quantitative researchers should incorporate many, if not all, of the criteria for judging qualitative studies into their own standards of excellence. For example, quantitative researchers need to situate their samples by providing readers with comprehensive descriptions of their study participants. Quantitative scholarship is enriched when it provides grounding in examples—giving voice to the participants. Walker, Acock, Bowman, and Li (1996), for example, used latent growth curve analysis in a study of caregiving and then interviewed study participants; in their report on their research, they used quotes from these interviews to provide insights into those participants whose growth trajectories departed from the norm. All research should have credibility checks, and coherence is equally important for quantitative and qualitative research. Although reports on quantitative research can be very difficult to read, the best quantitative research should resonate with informed readers. The point is not that the criteria coming from qualitative scholarship are unique, but that all research can benefit from them. Similarly, some large-scale qualitative research studies are now being evaluated on the merits of their "translation research," that is, their ability to generalize and replicate their results in real-world settings (Tubbs & Burton, in press).

● *SPOTLIGHT ON METHODS*

ASKING NEW QUESTIONS OF EXISTING QUALITATIVE DATA

M. Elise Radina, *University of Northern Iowa*

Kimberly J. M. Downs, *University of Missouri–Columbia*

Qualitative research is usually labor-intensive and time-consuming and yields rich information beyond the original research questions. Therefore, many researchers

(continued)

seek to capitalize on the data they collect by reanalyzing them, or conducting secondary analyses (Thorne, 1994). Existing data can answer new research questions that are different from the questions that guided the original study (McCall & Appelbaum, 1991). Although secondary analyses are typically associated with deductive or quantitative approaches (Jacobson, Hamilton, & Galloway, 1993), social scientists have been conducting secondary analyses of qualitative data for some time, whether or not they explicitly identify their work as such (Hinds, Vogel, & Clarke-Steffen, 1997).

Hinds and her colleagues (1997) note that there are four ways of classifying secondary analyses of qualitative data. In *retrospective interpretation,* the researcher revisits the data with questions arising from the original study that were not thoroughly investigated at the time. For example, a researcher who has completed original analysis of a data set might become aware of another aspect of the experience that is unrelated to the study's original purpose. The researcher might then reexamine the existing data in light of this new information. In *analytic expansion,* the researcher uses existing qualitative data as a pilot study in order to refine research questions and methods in future work. For example, a researcher may notice a pattern of responses among similar participants and use the existing data from these participants to develop new research questions to address with new participants. A researcher also asks new questions of existing data through a *unit of analysis modification,* which may involve breaking down a data set from family-level data (e.g., interviews with multiple adult siblings who are providing care for an aging parent) to individual-level data (e.g., interviews with just the primary caregivers). Finally, in *subset analysis,* the researcher selects a subset of data from the original study based on some similarity between the cases and analyzes only these cases as a data set. For example, a researcher may collect data from several adult daughters of breast cancer survivors. Following completion of the original data analysis, the researcher may focus on those respondents who described their experiences as distressing in order to gain a better understanding of this reaction to a mother's breast cancer experiences.

A researcher needs to consider several issues prior to conducting a secondary analysis (Hinds et al., 1997; Thorne, 1994, 1998). First, the integrity of the original data set is of concern, particularly when the analysts were not involved in the original data collection and lack understanding of the original study's nuances (Easton, McComish, & Greenberg, 2000). A secondary analyst's knowledge is limited to the original study records, and if these are flawed or incomplete the subsequent study's rigor will be seriously compromised. A second issue concerns the fit between the secondary research question and the data set. In most cases, the researcher can determine whether the question and the data set are a good fit by comparing the new research question to that used in the original research. A third and related issue is whether the new research question fits the methodological approach to data collection in the original research. That is, data sets generated by grounded theorists may be very different from those generated by ethnographers, and neither may be suitable for analysis by a descriptive phenomenologist. Finally, the researcher must examine the ethics of using participants' data for purposes other than those that were originally intended and to which the participants have not consented (see Hinds et al., 1997). It is imperative that the researcher present participants' data in context, and that he or she ensure that the new questions being asked are congruent with the intent of the original study. •

INNOVATIONS IN RESEARCH DESIGN AND MEASUREMENT

Participatory Research Methods

Family researchers are discovering the value of participatory methods. Strongly advocated by feminist scholars, such methods have become an emerging standard for many qualitative projects. This is a natural outgrowth of the participatory values many of us share—we recognize the importance of collaboration, shared knowledge, multiple perspectives, and empowerment. Participatory research methods are associated with work with oppressed groups (Freire, 1970, discusses these methods in the context of developing countries), but researchers are increasingly applying them to a wide range of questions and settings (e.g., Lindsey & McGuinness, 1998; Minkler, 2000; Park, Brydon-Miller, Hall, & Jackson, 1993; Piercy & Thomas, 1998; Rains & Ray, 1995). Participatory researchers attempt to flatten the researcher-subject hierarchy by involving research participants as active coresearchers.

Whitmore (1994) recruited former participants of a prenatal program for single mothers as interviewers and as coevaluators of that program. The former-participants-turned-researchers were able to connect with the interviewees in a manner that Whitmore, as a university-trained authority figure, could not. They also were involved, with Whitmore, in the analysis of the data and the presentation of the findings. Whitmore reports that although there were challenges in bridging the differences in race and social class between her and her coresearchers, the coresearchers' perspectives were valuable in helping her make sense of the research data.

Such collaboration between researchers and participants empowers, motivates, and increases self-esteem in participants and builds solidarity among all parties. Because participants generate, own, and often help to implement the research findings, they typically feel more committed to the research endeavor and what comes out of it. When applied to intervention, participatory action research models combine the insights of local community members with the technical expertise of professionals (Small, 1995). The resulting interventions better fit the people for whom they are planned (Piercy & Thomas, 1998).

A participatory approach can also enrich quantitative research (Axinn, Fricke, & Thornton, 1991). For example, coresearchers from a target group (e.g., single fathers, women with breast cancer, incarcerated mothers) could help a family researcher both collect and make sense of either qualitative or quantitative data, plan meaningful interventions, and provide insights regarding why certain interventions worked and others did not. (See the case study following this chapter by Woolley, Bowen, and Bowen.)

Research projects also benefit from advisory committees that include representation of study participants. Such a committee informs all aspects of a study, including design, implementation, and interpretation. Participants are a critical resource for researchers, in gaining access to populations and in making sense of outcomes the researchers' theories did not predict.

Aesthetic Forms of Data Representation

Research is art as well as science (Fischer, 1994). Researchers in many fields are increasingly experimenting with forms that storytellers, artists, actors, and poets have used for centuries (Eisner, 1997). Family researchers have begun to include aesthetic methods of data representation, such as creative writing, art, music, performance, and poetry, to connect with both academic and nonacademic audiences (Piercy & Benson, in press). The artistic side of qualitative research in particular relates to family researchers' efforts to capture the multilayered richness of family life.

Unfortunately, aesthetic forms of data representation often are evaluated by standards that do not fit the researchers' goals. Interpretive, artistic, and evocative methods call for standards that acknowledge affective as well as intellectual knowing. That is, the credibility of findings takes on a feeling dimension. For example, Ensler (2001) based her one-woman play *The Vagina Monologues* on more than 200 interviews with women about their vaginas. She could have organized, analyzed, and presented her data in more traditional ways, but she chose drama. The result is a moving production that audiences relate to on many levels. The play's "truth" relates as much to how the participants' stories resonate with audience members as to the intellectual understanding of those stories.

An aesthetic work may be judged on the degree to which it answers these questions: Does the work resonate with the intended audience? That is, is it compelling, powerful, and convincing (Osborne, 1990)? Does it have verisimilitude, the appearance of being true or real? Other standards may be applied as well. Does the work answer the "so what" question? Is it worth doing? Does it support positive change? Is it catalytic, liberating, transformative? Does it empower? Kvale (1996), for example, contends that beneficence should be the primary guideline of interpretive research. Consistent with Denzin and Lincoln's (2000a) description of the "seventh moment" in the development of qualitative research, a text should be judged on its ability to point to a better world. Qualitative family researchers wishing to use aesthetic forms of data representation must be clear about their purpose, so that others do not judge their work using inappropriate criteria (Piercy & Benson, in press).

Accountability should also be part of the planning for alternative forms of presentation. As a family researcher develops a play, or poem, or dramatic reading, for example, he or she might use standard forms of establishing trustworthiness (e.g., audit trails, member checking, triangulation) in going back to the original data. The researcher might also use, for example, qualitative evaluation methods such as focus groups or interviews to gauge audience reaction to a dramatic pilot performance, and to determine whether the issues emanating from the original interviews are captured adequately in the dramatic representation (a process not unlike the backward translations done in cross-cultural research).

Additionally, researchers can apply quantitative standards to the evaluation of the outcomes of aesthetic forms of scholarship. For example, a researcher could identify goals for *The Vagina Monologues* and then conduct pre- and posttests to examine the play's effectiveness. It is reasonable to believe that viewing this play might result in changed attitudes and beliefs about gender among audience members. A researcher could evaluate the play's effectiveness in changing attitudes and beliefs by using standard scales to measure audience members' attitudes and beliefs both before and after they watch the play. Changing attitudes and beliefs is not all the play is designed to do, of course; this is simply one example of a way to evaluate the play's value quantitatively.

Web-Based Surveys

With the development of the Internet, scholars have recognized the opportunities this technology provides for both data collection and analysis (Anderson & Kanuka, 2003). One method of data collection that seems especially attractive to family researchers is the Web-based survey. An obvious advantage of this method is its relative cost-effectiveness. In addition, conducting surveys online virtually eliminates the need for data entry, as the data gathered are directly integrated with database systems through one of the numerous software packages available (e.g., the hotscripts.com Web site allows visitors to search various survey packages).

Collecting data through Web-based surveys has its own unique limitations and caveats. The response formats used, for example, can affect the amount of missing data and the number of people who choose "I don't know" responses (Heerwegh & Loosveldt, 2002). Complex questionnaire formatting has been associated with increased attrition in online surveys, as has asking for personal information about the respondent on a survey's first page (O'Neil, Penrod, & Bornstein, 2003). Maintaining motivation is a special issue when a participant is one mouse click away from refusal.

Mixed findings have resulted from research investigating whether Web-based surveys suffer more from sample nonrepresentativeness than other modes of inquiry. Some studies suggest that response rates are lower for Web-based surveys than for mail surveys (Crawford, Couper, & Lamias, 2001), whereas others indicate that representativeness issues affect mail and Web-based methodologies similarly (Ballard & Prine, 2002). Because of fears regarding spam and viruses, many people avoid opening e-mail or downloading e-mail attachments from unfamiliar senders as well as visiting unfamiliar Web sites to take online surveys. Sample characteristics may also have an impact on attrition in Web-based surveys, as research has shown that non-students are more likely than students to drop out in the middle of such surveys (O'Neil et al., 2003). Questions remain, however, concerning whether access to and familiarity with computers and the Internet affect attrition in online surveys and, if so, how.

The best opportunity for collecting data using a Web-based survey may be one in which the members of a clearly identified population have agreed to take the survey, are familiar with using the Internet, and can be monitored for compliance. A researcher, for example, might arrange for 25 students from each of 100 high schools to go to their schools' computer labs and complete a survey while school personnel monitor their compliance. Or a researcher might acquire a complete list of e-mail addresses for the members of a particular professional group and monitor compliance by sending e-mail reminders to members who do not complete the survey initially. Schaefer and Dillman (1998) have found that personalization and follow-up notes sent quickly are helpful in increasing response rates in Web-based surveys. It is also helpful if the participants are interested in and committed to the subject of the study (Dillman, 1999). For example, Nelson, Piercy, and Sprenkle (in press) obtained a 70% response rate on a Web-based survey concerning the treatment of Internet infidelity by involving experts on infidelity treatment and sex addiction as participants. (For more on Web-based surveys, see Meinhold's contribution to this volume's companion Web site.)

Design Effects in Complex Samples

The samples of families used for research purposes are generally not selected through simple random sampling. Large national surveys (e.g., the National Survey of Families and Households and the National Longitudinal Study of Adolescent Health) use stratified or cluster sampling; for example, they may first sample schools or communities and then sample individuals within those schools or communities. If researchers sample 25 people from each of 50 high schools, the people from each school will be more homogeneous than randomly selected people from the entire population would be. If researchers ask a mother whether each of her children under age 13 receives paid child care, her answers will be highly correlated. If she reports no paid care for her 1-year-old, then she almost certainly will report no paid care for her 10-year-old. The responses are not statistically independent. This kind of sampling creates design effects. Researchers must adjust for such effects, or they will underestimate standard errors and exaggerate the statistical significance of their findings.

As several comparison studies have shown, design effects generally have greater impacts on measures of central tendency than on measures of covariation (Johnson & Elliott, 1998). Researchers, however, should not base their decisions concerning whether or not to incorporate design effects on the magnitude of the impact of correcting for the effects. Correcting for design effects is important in any probability sample that is not strictly random (Kish, 1965). Researchers can correct for design effects by using special statistical software packages such as SUDAAN (Shah, Barnwell, & Bieler, 1996) or Stata (StataCorp, 1997). SAS also has this capability, and SPSS from version 12.0 on has an optional module with some capability for incorporating design effects. Software packages vary in the procedures they use to handle complex samples.

Design effect is the sample variance estimate of the clustered sample divided by the sample variance estimate of the sample if it had been based on simple random sampling. Design effects mean that standard errors are routinely underestimated by a factor of 1.4 to 2 or more. Using 1.4 as the potential bias, a *z* score of 2.74 (rather than the usual 1.96) is needed for the $\alpha = .05$ level of significance. Many published articles have reported statistically significant results that would not have been significant if the researchers had implemented appropriate adjustments for design effects. As procedures for incorporating design effects into statistical packages are becoming increasingly available, reports on research in the future will need to reflect such adjustments.

Nonindependence of Relationship Data

Quantitative data from multiple family members is affected by potential nonindependence of data because the behaviors of family members are intertwined. Similar to nonindependence in clustered samples, nonindependence in family/relationship data can lead to incorrect assumptions about statistical significance (Kenny, 1988). Therefore, it is important that researchers establish whether and to what extent nonindependence affects family data before they conduct explanatory analyses.

There are two different scenarios in determining nonindependence: Either individuals are drawn from the same group (exchangeable case, i.e., siblings) or they are not (distinguishable case, i.e., parents and children) (Gonzalez & Griffin, 1999). In the exchangeable case, nonindependence can be determined through the calculation of a pairwise intraclass correlation (Griffin & Gonzalez, 1995). In the distinguishable case, nonindependence can be assessed through the calculation of a regular Pearson correlation coefficient (Kashy & Snyder, 1995) or through a partial intraclass correlation coefficient that corrects for the differential impact of covariates (Gonzalez & Griffin, 1997). Correlation coefficients larger than $r = .25$ are considered evidence of nonindependence (Kenny & Kashy, 1991). Nonindependence of covariance structures can be tested through structural equation modeling

(Gonzalez & Griffin, 1999). (In Chapter 12 of this volume, Sayer and Klute approach this issue in terms of multilevel analysis.)

Missing Values

Many studies that use large data sets include only a fraction of the total number of cases in their final analyses. Consider a 5-year panel study that started with 150 children but has only 35 children in the analysis. In dealing with missing values, researchers face two important issues: First, what are the attributes of those individuals with missing data? Second, how can the researchers statistically correct for the missing data?

Too often, published reports on studies fail to explain the attrition in the samples. Some attrition is appropriate—for example, single people need to be dropped from a study of marital relations. When reporting on their research, scholars need to explicate the decision trees they used to eliminate such participants. What researchers see as obvious choices, readers may see as ambiguous or even questionable choices. Researchers need to describe their criteria explicitly.

Once a subsample is defined to include everybody who should be eligible, all remaining attrition is problematic. In a longitudinal study involving 10 waves of data collection, many people may be absent during at least one of those waves. In survey research, some participants may not respond to questions about their income or may not answer other sensitive questions. When answering survey questions using multi-item scales, some participants may skip single questions but answer all of the rest. In the past, researchers used listwise deletion in such cases (i.e., any participant who skipped a single item was eliminated). This has been the default with standard statistical packages. In multivariate analysis, listwise deletion typically results in the loss of 30% or more of the participants.

Clearly, eliminating 30% of participants is problematic. If 10 people in a sample answer only 15 items on a 16-item scale, the researchers lose a lot of information by deleting those individuals from the analysis. Their answers to the 15 items they did complete provide information on 120 parameters, including the means, variances, and covariance among the 15 items. Ignoring this information is extremely inefficient.

We know a lot about who skips specific kinds of items. For example, rich people or poor people often skip questions on income. People who are ambivalent about some aspects of a relationship may skip items that touch on those aspects. Men are more likely than women to skip items. Participants in specific age groups may skip questions that they believe are not relevant to them. When we eliminate such people from our analyses, we create serious bias in our estimates. It is remarkable that we relied on listwise deletion for so long, given that inefficiency and bias are two fundamental concerns of statistical inference.

Pairwise deletion (including all cases that answer each pair of items) can produce impossible combinations, because each mean, variance, and covariance (correlation) is based on a different subsample. Mean substitution is usually the worst solution, because it reduces the variance (giving 30% of a sample the identical income value greatly attenuates its variance and covariance with other variables) and because the mean is often a terrible estimate for nonrespondents. For example, because the rich and the poor are most likely to fail to report their income, the mean income may be the worst value to use as an estimate.

Over the past decade there have been enormous advances in the treatment of missing values. SAS now has a multiple imputation procedure that works with many analytic procedures, SPSS has an optional module for missing values analysis that includes single imputation using expectation maximization, and Schafer (1997, 1999) has developed programs for multiple imputation (NORM, CAT, MIX), as have King, Honaker, Joseph, and Scheve (2001) in a program called Amelia. The various SEM programs now have greatly enhanced options for handling missing data, varying from expectation maximization (EM) and casewise maximum likelihood (AMOS) to multiple imputation (LISREL). Each approach has its own special strengths and weaknesses. (A full discussion of these

approaches is beyond the scope of this chapter; for more detailed information, see this volume's companion Web site.)

ANALYTIC ISSUES AND ADVANCES

Limited Dependent Variables

Many parametric statistical analyses make fewer assumptions concerning predictor variables (independent variables) than they do about outcome (dependent) variables. Our predictors do not need to be normally distributed, and they may be categorical or continuous. Our most common parametric methods are not so forgiving when our outcome variables are categorical, skewed, or in some other way problematic. The term *limited dependent variables* (Green, 1997) refers to outcome variables that are not normally distributed, that do not have an underlying continuum such as dichotomous outcomes, that have special distributions such as count variables, or that are measured in a way that censures or truncates the true variance of the outcome.

Over the past decade, researchers have increasingly used logistic regression for the special case of a limited dependent variable that has a binary outcome (e.g., get divorced versus do not get divorced, have a child versus do not have a child). Logistic regression is by far the most widely used of the limited dependent variable procedures, but there are many other situations in which researchers should use specialized analyses for particular types of limited dependent variables.

Many researchers use outcomes that are simple counts. Often, these variables involve behaviors that happen rarely (e.g., How often in the past month did your stepfather strike or hit you?) or that rarely happen more than a few times (e.g., How many times have you been divorced?). In addition to variables concerning interpersonal violence, examples include how often a person gets drunk, how often a person loses a job, or how many nights a year a person is away from home.

Poisson regression assumes that there is an underlying rate—say, 5%—and the count is the product of this rate and the time period. If the rate of being away from home at night is 5%, then we would expect a person to be away from home $.05 \times 365.25 = 18$ nights per year. A Poisson estimation is often appropriate and gives highly interpretable results. The incidence rate ratio (IRR) tells us how much a unit change in a predictor changes the rate of occurrence of the count variable. If the IRR for husbands is 1.80, then the travel rate is 1.80 times higher for husbands than for wives.

Sometimes a count does not conform to a Poisson distribution (under a Poisson distribution, $\mu = \sigma^2$). Overdispersion, $\mu > \sigma^2$, would happen if there were some threshold to behaving in some way so that not too many people behave that way even once. However, those who do the behavior will tend to do it more often once they have overcome the threshold. This happens with some forms of deviant behavior where an outcome is rare, but there are people who still do it very often. For instance, being drunk while pregnant is a rare event for the preponderance of women, but a practicing alcoholic who is pregnant may be drunk 20 days in a month. The negative binomial model is appropriate for such cases. The point of these examples is that we are moving toward much more serious expectations for appropriate estimation procedures. Procedures for limited dependent variables have been around for a long time, but only recently have they entered family scholarship.

Family economists often use a procedure called Tobit regression, which is intended for variables that are censored above, below, or at both ends of the distribution. We may have many outcome variables whose measured values appear skewed because our measuring instruments censor extremely high or low scores. This results in a clump of people at the high or low end of the distribution as we have measured it. For example, a woman's satisfaction with her role as a mother may be measured on a scale of 1 to 5, where 5 represents _very satisfied_. We might have 30–40% of our sample pick 5 on this scale, indicating that they are very satisfied with their roles as mothers. Almost certainly, however, there is considerable variance in role satisfaction among the women

who have picked _very satisfied_. Some of them may have serious questions about their role performance but are reluctant to share that with us. Some may be only slightly more than satisfied and still select 5 on the scale. Still others may be ecstatic about being mothers and see it as the fulfillment of their lives. If we had more response choices to allow for greater discrimination, we might have ended up with a scale that ranged from 0 to 10, on which the scores of those women who selected 5 on the first scale would be spread out over the range of 5 to 10. Because we don't have a measure that is that sensitive, if we use ordinary least squares regression we will seriously underestimate the explanatory power of the model.

Researchers often use measures of attitudes and beliefs that rely on response options that make censoring likely. Response options of _never, sometimes,_ and _often_ have clear lower limits, but the upper limits are vague. Some people who pick _often_ on a scale will mean often, but others will mean always. _Strongly agree_ to _strongly disagree,_ Likert-type response options may censor at both the top and the bottom when the items deal with issues on which opinions are highly polarized.

Tobit regression was developed precisely for this situation. It estimates what ordinary least squares regression would have produced if the measure had not been censored. When working with single items that have a few ordered categories as their response options—such as _never, sometimes,_ and _often_ or _agree, don't know,_ and _disagree_—researchers may feel uncomfortable treating the responses as if they were interval, even though there is an underlying continuum. It is possible to treat these as ordinal categories and do ordered logistic regression.

Second-generation structural equation modeling programs such as Mplus are designed to handle nominal-, ordinal-, and interval-level variables simultaneously in a single model and to go beyond the restrictive assumption of multivariate normality. These developments allow researchers to do confirmatory factor analysis, compare models across different groups, and evaluate complex models without unrealistic assumptions about measurement and without unrealistic assumptions about distributions.

Multilevel Analysis

Family researchers are beginning to use multilevel analysis to analyze both contextual impacts on family relations and dyadic relationships within families (Maguire, 1999; Snijders & Kenny, 1999). Multilevel analysis provides researchers with the opportunity to model random variation for estimated parameters and is more flexible in handling missing data than more traditional techniques such as regression and analysis of variance. Additionally, multilevel analysis enables researchers to distinguish the relative importance of effects at different contextual levels, such as the individual, family, and neighborhood, or to investigate the effect of a particular variable at both the individual and contextual levels.

An example of the application of multilevel analysis to the study of contextual effects is a recent study by Hoffmann (2002), who investigated whether the relation between family structure and adolescent drug use is dependent on community context. In other words, is the relation between family structure and adolescent drug use stronger in some types of communities than in others? The basic multilevel design for this study was necessary because individuals are nested in communities. The advantage of such an approach is that it allows the researcher to analyze individual and community effects simultaneously as well as estimate the moderating effect of community context. The combination of these factors, in addition to the researcher's ability to model error structures of outcomes that vary across levels and to model variation around individual-level predictors, makes multilevel analysis a relatively conservative approach to statistical significance testing (Teachman & Crowder, 2002).

An example of the application of multilevel analyses to the impact of a particular variable at both the individual and group levels is a recent study by Espelage, Holt, and Henkel (2003). These researchers were particularly interested in the impact of peer group membership on individual fighting and individual bullying across two waves of data collection. In other words, they asked whether individual bullying/fighting at wave 2 could be explained by wave 1 individual bullying/fighting or by the average level of aggression within particular peer groups. They found that, despite the fact that there were strong relations between wave 1 and wave 2 individual bullying/fighting, peer group aggression was more important in predicting wave 2 individual bullying than in predicting wave 2 individual fighting. The advantage of using multilevel analysis for this kind of question specifically is that it allows researchers to separate out the relative importance of the same type of behavior (e.g., aggression) at the individual and group levels.

Researchers have also found multilevel analysis useful in handling the methodological issues associated with multiple-informant data. For example, Kuo, Mohler, Raudenbush, and Earls (2000) applied multilevel analysis to multiple-informant data and compared the results with regression analysis results. They found that agreement between parents and children on exposure to violence increased from .43 to .48 (Pearson correlation coefficient) after they took the measurement error and missing data calculations from multilevel analysis into consideration. In addition, standard errors from the multilevel analysis were generally smaller than the standard errors from the regression models, suggesting that the results obtained through multilevel analysis were more reliable than the results obtained through regression.

Studying families inherently involves the investigation of multilevel content. In the past, the vast majority of family researchers either ignored this fact or at least did not make use of it in their studies. Individuals are nested in families, and families are nested in communities. Many theoretical perspectives, including systems theory and ecological theory, point to the relationships among these multiple levels of experience. Multilevel analysis will become a standard for future research on families, and this will greatly enhance the isomorphism between our theoretical perspectives and our methodologies.

Growth Curve Analysis

Most family science theorists and practitioners share a focus on change. The goal of most research is to discover how we can increase or decrease particular outcomes. We are often interested in studying processes that change. For example, a therapist may want to know whether she can convince her client to increase the amount of praise he gives to his wife and whether the increased praise will lead to increased marital satisfaction for the wife. The therapist's goal has a process of change in marital satisfaction by a spouse as an outcome and a process of change in the partner's praise as the cause.

Most family researchers use cross-sectional analyses and can explain only how the current level of an outcome is or is not based on the current level of other variables. Researchers sometimes examine only two waves of data from longitudinal studies, even those with many waves of data collection, using a cross-lagged panel design. As Rogosa (1995) has argued, two waves do not make a longitudinal study, and a reliable investigation of change requires at least three waves of data. Growth curve analyses use three or more waves of data to focus on the rate at which a variable is changing. Rather than explaining the level of marital satisfaction at some arbitrary point, for instance, growth curves focus on the rate at which marital satisfaction changes over time and what other processes explain why some people have increasing satisfaction and others have decreasing satisfaction.

We can use growth curves to describe processes of change (e.g., change in marital satisfaction during the first 5 years of marriage), to use variables to predict processes (e.g., whether premarital cohabitation leads to increasing or decreasing marital satisfaction over time), or to use other processes of change to predict (e.g., whether change in marital satisfaction depends on change in division of household chores). The focus is on change and explaining change. Quantitative research in the past has had limited ability to study processes and has been legitimately criticized by qualitative researchers for this limitation. By focusing on change, quantitative research can address family processes.

In doing a growth curve analysis it is important to distinguish between two types of curves. For the entire sample, there is an overall growth curve. For example, marital satisfaction may decrease in a nonlinear way over time. In addition to this, each individual has his or her own growth curve. Some individuals may duplicate the overall trend, but other individuals may exhibit very different growth patterns. The overall growth curve is described by an intercept (value when the process starts) and a slope (rate of change). Additional slopes may be added if the growth is nonlinear. Marital satisfaction probably has a high intercept starting right after the wedding vows and then a negative slope indicating that satisfaction goes down over the first 5 years. In addition to this overall growth curve, each individual has a curve. Chantell may be extremely satisfied initially but then have a sharp drop in satisfaction. Shige may be only moderately satisfied initially but actually become more satisfied over time. Notice that each individual has his or her own intercept and slope. This variance in intercepts and slopes is what we want to explain. These parameters representing the process of growth may be positive or negative.

The initial level (intercept) may be explained by variables different from those that explain the rate and direction of change (slope). We may use other processes that are changing to explain the rate of change. We could do parallel growth curves to see if changes in how much of the housework a person's partner does or changes in how often the partner praises the person influence changes in the person's marital satisfaction. We are then examining how change in one variable leads to change in another variable, which is, after all, closer to our theoretical interests and to practice.

Integration of Variable-Centered and Person-Centered Research Approaches

Variable-centered analyses have as the unit of analysis one or more variables. The aim of variable-centered analyses is to understand the relations among a limited number of variables. Examples of variable-centered analyses include regression-related procedures, path analysis, analysis of variance, and factor analysis.

Person-centered analyses have as the unit of analysis one or more cases. The case can be an individual, but it can also be a family or an interpersonal relationship. Examples of person-centered analyses include many qualitative methodologies that focus on the in-depth understanding of individual(s) and the use of case studies. Person-centered analysis also plays a prominent role in quantitative methods that have been underutilized by quantitative family scholars. Examples of person-centered quantitative techniques include approaches that focus on the classification of individuals, such as cluster analysis and latent class analyses. Person-centered approaches are also referred to as *profile-oriented methods,* as they focus on the classification of individuals (Bergman, Eklund, & Magnusson, 1991).

Initial efforts to integrate variable-centered and person-centered approaches focused on the integration of quantitative techniques themselves, such as multiple regression and cluster analysis. For example, Masten et al. (1999) investigated adolescent competence and resilience using both linear regression and comparisons between a priori identified groups of resilient, competent, and maladaptive children. They found that competence was predicted by factors such as parenting and child IQ, even after they had controlled for earlier adversity. Group comparisons further showed that the resilient and competent children generally scored higher than the maladaptive children on variables such as parenting and child IQ, thus corroborating the results of the variable-centered analyses.

Current advancements in integrating variable- and person-centered research have taken two directions. First, some scholars are still involved in efforts to combine quantitative methods, for example, through growth mixture models. Second, researchers are becoming increasingly interested in integrating quantitative and qualitative analytic techniques. We examine these two strategies briefly in turn below.

Growth mixture modeling. Growth mixture modeling (GMM) combines the strengths of growth curve modeling with those of latent class analysis (Muthén & Muthén, 2000). Growth curve modeling, as we have explained above, is a variable-centered approach. A potential application of growth curve modeling would be to identify a growth curve for what happens to the husband's marital satisfaction in the first 12 months after the first child is born in a marriage. Latent class analysis is a person-centered approach that aims to classify individuals optimally into a minimal number of subpopulations based on a limited number of categorical variables.

GMM is particularly well suited for the analysis of developmental/longitudinal data in which hypotheses focus on heterogeneity in developmental trajectories and differential impact of covariates. A good source of questions that are relevant for GMM is the literature on childhood and adolescent externalizing behavior problems, as prior research has established that there are different trajectories from childhood to adulthood and that background factors have differential impacts (Moffitt & Caspi, 2001).

The development of the growth mixture modeling technique, and consequent software packages such as Mplus, has benefited greatly from the work of Bengt Muthén and Linda Muthén (2000), who have used GMM to investigate various trajectories of alcohol use. Based on analyses of data from the National Longitudinal Survey of Youth (NLSY), these researchers identified four groups: two groups in which early heavy drinking decreases over time, one group in which heavy drinking increases over time, and one group in which heavy drinking is high during early young adulthood and then declines (see Figure 3.1). In the same study, Muthén and Muthén also used latent class growth analysis (LCGA)

Figure 3.1   NLSY: Heavy Drinking, Cohort 64

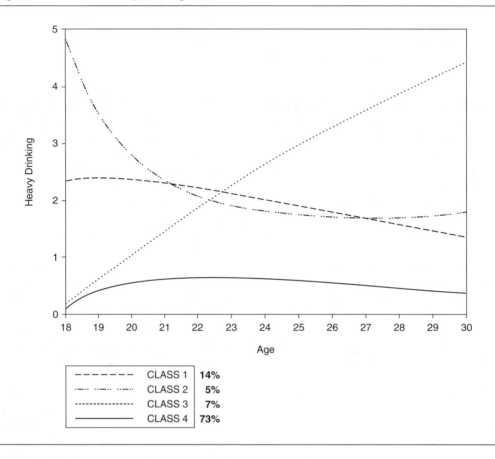

to find different groupings of individuals on alcohol use. They found a nine-class solution using LCGA and a four-class solution using GMM. The discrepancy between the two solutions is primarily a result of the fact that GMM allows for within-group variation, whereas LCGA assumes that there are no within-group differences. As it is unlikely that group members would have the exact same scores on alcohol use at different times, it appears that GMM provides a more accurate reflection of the data than does LCGA. Model fit in growth mixture models is evaluated using the Bayesian information criterion (BIC), although other fit indices may be used with moderate levels of nonnormality

(Muthén, 2003). The model with the largest BIC value "best" represents the data in that it provides an optimal description of the individuals in various subpopulations.

Combining qualitative, case-centered strategies and quantitative, variable-centered strategies. In earlier days, numerous debates focused on the pros and cons of quantitative versus qualitative approaches, leading to potential dichotomies (Smith, 1984). Today, researchers increasingly recognize the unique strengths of both approaches (Grotevant et al., 1998; Sullivan, 1998). An example of such an integrative approach is evident in Grotevant, Ross, Marchel, and McRoy's (1999) study of the adjustment of adopted children (see also Pearce, 2002). These researchers investigated the relation between early adversity and childhood adaptation. They did not find a direct relation between these two variables initially, and they then employed in-depth qualitative analyses with a subsample of children who had high early risk scores. A new variable, collaboration in relationships, emerged from the qualitative analyses. In later quantitative analyses, they found this variable to be related to childhood adjustment.

Quantitative, variable-centered research can be the prelude to qualitative, person-centered research. Many studies rely on regression-related procedures to predict outcome variables (well-being, depression, conflict, divorce, and so on). Often, these studies explain only a small portion of the total variance in the outcome measures. It is not unusual for reports of research published in the *Journal of Marriage and Family* to explain less than 20% of the variance in an outcome. This leaves most, 80% or more, of the variation unexplained. How can researchers improve prediction? One approach we suggest is to identify outliers—that is, individuals for which the prediction is especially bad. We might select 5% or 10% of the cases in a quantitative study for which we have the worst prediction. These are the cases that offer the most information value for in-depth qualitative analysis. In this way, quantitative research is preliminary to qualitative research. Quantitative research based on variable-centered analysis points us to the people who can be most useful for qualitative, person-centered analysis. The qualitative research on these outliers then leads us to reformulated models, which we can test, for example, by regression-related procedures for one level of understanding and ethnographic methods for another.

Abusing the combination of qualitative and quantitative research is always a risk. Quantitative research seeks samples that are based on probability so that they can be representative of a population. Qualitative research seeks persons who have the most potential information value about a process being studied. As more and more large-scale qualitative research projects collect quantitative data, there is a danger that researchers will overgeneralize the quantitative information. A qualitative study of gay couples, for example, may find that the mean education of those in the sample is beyond the level of college graduate. Unless the sample has a probability basis, however, it would be a mistake to conclude from these data that high education is a characteristic of gay couples. Participants in qualitative studies often have a heavy responsibility for contributing a large amount of time and effort to the research, and this results in a significant self-selection bias that also makes quantitative generalizations problematic. As more large-scale qualitative studies gather quantitative data, researchers run the risk of making more generalizations based on quantitative findings that are "shocking but wrong." One solution is to use large-scale national surveys or demographic information to provide contextual background and locational information about participants in qualitative studies (Seccombe, 1999). Indeed, Black, Gates, Sanders, and Taylor (2000) have developed a statistical portrait of gay men and lesbians in the United States based on three large data sets: the National Health and Social Life Survey, the U.S. Census, and the General Social Surveys. Their work provides some of the first analyses of large-scale probability samples on a population that has received attention previously only from researchers using in-depth interview, ethnographic, or nonprobability survey methods.

CONCLUSIONS

Given the trends and innovations we have described in this chapter, current research methods in family studies show great promise for encouraging scholars to reject the false dichotomy of qualitative versus quantitative that is part of our academic heritage. We are starting to use methodologies in such a fashion that they can capture intra- and interindividual variations rather than only simple average differences.

The diversity of the methods discussed here reflects the lack of a unitary theoretical paradigm guiding family scholarship. We believe this theoretical complexity is essential, but it has implications for students and researchers who seek to be fully informed about research methodology. The lack of a single paradigm means that scholars need to understand an enormous variety of methodological strategies. Students today require training in multiple methods, mainly because our awareness of the complexity of the problems we are trying to solve has increased. This poses many challenges for those who are teaching the next generation of family scientists, as there is little opportunity for students to gain expertise in the great variety of specific methods. The next generation of family scientists is receiving snapshot information on various methods, often without having the opportunity to gain any personal experience with many of the different techniques. At the same time, there is an increasing need for current scholars to become knowledgeable about a broad array of methods that were not widely available 20 years ago. In short, this broadening of required methodological skills enforces the need for family studies departments as well as the entire field of family studies to expand the current methodological training opportunities. Perhaps it will be necessary for graduate programs to devote fewer seminars to subject matter and more to the process of generating knowledge.

Some of the classic problems still exist. Family complexity is difficult to model and measure, but we are limited only by our ability to think and work creatively. And our creativity is enhanced by the innovations of scholars working in both qualitative and quantitative methodologies. The theoretical creativity and advancements that have long characterized family studies are increasingly accompanied by qualitative and quantitative methods that can capture the contexts and processes of family life.

As family researchers, we are challenged by the divergent ways of thinking that underlie our choices of methods and analysis, we are interested in methods that reflect traditional science orientations as well as those that derive from the humanities and arts and technological terrains, and we are continually working on ways to resolve the thorniest analytic problems. On top of all this, we generally try to create bridges across disciplinary boundaries and to integrate sometimes different disciplinary standards as to what the salient issues are in sampling, measurement, and data analysis. The evaluation of what is considered "good" methodological work and what the current methodological advancements are for studying families is not dependent on discipline. Useful evaluation standards reflect clarity, precision, and scientific rigor. Useful methodological advancements reflect a body of scholars who, although generally not methodologists by training, become increasingly comfortable with using their creative minds to advance the methodologies for understanding family life. Although each research tradition needs further innovation, our best hope is to work toward engaging our methodological neighbors.

MIXED METHODS: MEANING AND VALIDITY IN THE DEVELOPMENT OF SELF-REPORT ITEMS FOR CHILDREN

Michael E. Woolley, *University of Michigan*

Natasha K. Bowen, *University of North Carolina at Chapel Hill*

Gary L. Bowen, *University of North Carolina at Chapel Hill*

Meaning is a critical issue in social science research. Qualitative researchers often uncover meaning by analyzing interview transcripts. Quantitative researchers interpret meaning from quantitative measurements, including self-report instruments. Mixing qualitative and quantitative methods allows researchers to triangulate meaning from multiple perspectives and at multiple points during their research (Tashakkori & Teddlie, 2003).

Children's developing cognitive abilities differ significantly from the cognitive abilities of researchers, and because of this, children may interpret self-report items differently than researchers intend. The validity of self-report data rests on an assumption of "shared meaning" between respondents and researchers. In this case study, we describe the use of mixed methods to assess the validity of children's interpretations of and responses to self-report items.

The Elementary School Success Profile Child Form (ESSP-CF; Bowen, Bowen, & Woolley, 2004) is a self-report assessment instrument for third- to fifth-grade children. In this report, we describe the application of a qualitative interview methodology, cognitive pretesting (CP), during the development of the ESSP-CF. We also describe a systematic approach to quantifying

item performance with CP interview data that allowed us to conduct an empirical assessment of the reliability of the CP methodology in identifying validity problems in self-report items for children. In this assessment we used a codebook to detail item performance criteria, employed a rater training program, and analyzed interrater reliability.

ASKING CHILDREN WHAT ITEMS MEAN

Cognitive pretesting, an emerging methodology for assessing self-report item performance, can be applied to the development of self-report instruments for children (Bowen et al., 2004; Woolley, Bowen, & Bowen, in press). The CP methodology involves asking children questions that prompt verbal descriptions of the cognitive processes behind reading, interpreting, and responding to self-report items. Researchers can audiotape, transcribe, and analyze CP interviews to assess item performance. However, this qualitative methodology is still evolving; currently, both replicable analysis procedures and convincing demonstrations of its utility are lacking (Foddy, 1998; Willis, DeMaio, & Harris-Kojetin, 1999).

Authors' Note: A 2003 Junior Faculty Development Award to Natasha K. Bowen from the University of North Carolina at Chapel Hill funded the present research. The development of the Elementary School Success Profile has been accomplished in collaboration with Flying Bridge Technologies with funding from the National Institutes of Health, National Institutes on Drug Abuse, grants 1 R42 DA13865-01, 3 R41 DA13865-01S1, and 2 R42 DA013865-02.

Case Study

CASE STUDY *continued*

Because CP is a qualitative methodology applied within a quantitative process, we decided that empirical demonstration of its utility would be the most convincing. We identified three tasks to accomplish that demonstration: (a) operationally define the intent of each item and establish criteria to rate item performance, (b) train independent raters to apply those criteria to a CP data set, and (c) use statistical analysis to evaluate ratings reliability.

Defining What We Mean

We approached the first task by writing a CP codebook in which we specified the intent of each item and established criteria for quantifying item performance using CP text data. Utilizing an information-processing model, we divided the self-report response process into three cognitive components (Woolley et al., in press) that became the rating criteria for item performance: concept, coherence, and congruence (see the codebook sample page).

The first rating criterion was *concept*—the aspect or component of a latent construct a specific item intends to measure. Instrument developers typically define the construct that an entire set of items purportedly measures; however, developers rarely define the intents of individual items. Reaching consensus among ourselves in defining the concept behind each item often required considerable discussion. In rating CP data, children met the concept criterion if their interview responses reflected the concept definition.

The second rating criterion was *coherence*—how the child related the concept to events and experiences in his or her life. In rating CP data, a child demonstrated coherence if he or she reported anecdotes, experiences, or patterns in his or her life that were relevant to the item concept.

The final rating criterion, *congruence*, refers to whether the child chose a valid response option. In rating CP data, we evaluated congruence by comparing the answer option a child chose with the coherent material the child reported.

Sample Codebook Page

ESSP-CF Item 2a	*Item Response Options*		
Adults who live near me are nice to me.	No Adult	One Adult	More Than One Adult
Item Performance Criteria Definitions	*Cognitive Pretesting Data Examples*		

Concept:	Example 1:
Positive social interaction	"Do we have friendly people living nearby?" [concept]
Coherence:	
Descriptions of specific examples or a general pattern of positive interactions with adults who live near the child. These interactions may be described as friendly, polite, generous, kind, and/or helpful.	"More than one adult. 'Cause there are three adults like that. [congruence] Because they are nice to me and I go there and play with my friends." [coherence]
Congruence:	Example 2:
Children who respond "More Than One Adult" should describe specific interactions and/or a consistent pattern of positive interactions with more than one neighborhood adult. Children who choose "One Adult" should report such interactions with one adult. Children who choose "No Adult" will describe no such occurrences or negative interactions with neighborhood adults.	"If adults near us are nice." [concept] "One adult. Because a man [congruence] across the street talks to me when I walk by and he smiles a lot." [coherence]

Case Study

We used the three criteria of concept, coherence, and congruence to create a hierarchical four-point rating scale (0–3). If a child misinterpreted the concept, the rating was 0. If the child met only the concept criterion, the rating was 1. A rating of 2 was given if a child's response met the concept criterion and included a coherent description of relevant memory. To receive a rating of 3, indicating valid item performance, the child had to both meet the criteria for a rating of 2 and choose a response option that was congruent with the coherent memory described.

Training Raters to Assess Meaning

We then recruited and trained CP data raters. Research has shown that training improves rater consistency and accuracy (Weigle, 1998), and in this case, rater training was a critical process because the raters would be quantifying qualitative CP data. We recruited a convenience sample of five raters, all female, ranging in age from 20 to 27; two were African American, two were European American, and one was Latina/Hispanic. Two were bachelor's degree students, two were master's degree students, and one was a doctoral student.

The training program consisted of two 3-hour sessions held a week apart. The first session was devoted to familiarizing the raters with CP procedures and the codebook. The raters completed mock CP interviews and applied the codebook by rating the mock interview data. Group discussion then allowed the raters to process each other's ratings and revealed ways in which the rating procedures and materials could be strengthened.

In the second training session, the raters practiced rating CP data. They also engaged in a group process to build shared interpretations of the rating criteria. Discussions focused on data that evidenced poor interrater reliability. Increased levels of rater agreement were seen after these discussions, reinforcing their benefit. At the end of the second session, each rater was given a packet of ESSP-CF CP interview text data to rate independently.

Reliable and Meaningful Ratings

Our final step was to estimate the interrater reliability of the ratings. After reviewing approaches to assessing reliability, we chose an intraclass correlation coefficient (ICC; Shrout & Fleiss, 1979). The ICC formula assessed rater *agreement* rather than rater *consistency,* meaning raters were treated as a random effect. The interrater reliability coefficient increased only when raters gave the exact same ratings. Estimating agreement always yields a lower coefficient than assessing consistency. Informed by Shrout (1998), we set the benchmarks for interpreting ICC coefficients as follows: above .6 would indicate moderate reliability, and above .8 would indicate substantial reliability.

The raters applied the rating scale's entire range, although a significant proportion of 3-rated child-by-item data skewed the ratings. Because two rounds of cognitive pretesting preceded the current study, we had anticipated this high level of item performance.

Estimating the reliability of all raters' ratings resulted in a reliability ICC coefficient of .85, with a 95% confidence interval from .82 to .89. This coefficient—and the entire confidence interval—exceeded the .8 benchmark, indicating a finding of substantial interrater reliability and revealing a strong pattern of exact agreement in item performance rating when CP interview data were utilized.

DRAWING CONCLUSIONS

The methods and findings in this case study indicate four conclusions. First, the substantial interrater agreement strengthens the argument that a CP methodology can systematically identify validity problems in self-report items for children. Second, generating a codebook detailing self-report item validity criteria has utility for scale developers. Writing a codebook forces researchers to define what each item means and focuses attention on how individual items are interpreted and answered by respondents. Third, the research demonstrates what

CASE STUDY *continued*

researchers can accomplish by mixing methods. The successful application of a system to quantify item performance from CP interview data creates a convincing empirical argument for including qualitative interviews in otherwise quantitative research endeavors. The mixed methods described here augment the tools available to construct valid self-report measures for children. Finally, although the research we have described focused on children, CP can be applied with any population. The methodology seems most beneficial when respondents may interpret items differently than researchers intend—for example, when the respondents are culturally or cognitively different from the researchers.

CASE STUDY

ANALYZING FAMILY INTERACTION PATTERNS FROM VIDEOTAPES OVER TIME

Kurt Kreppner, *Max Planck Institute for Human Development, Berlin*

ENCOUNTERING BARRIERS

When my colleagues and I began our first observations of entire families about 25 years ago, our goal was the microanalytic description of communication patterns and adaptation maneuvers in the family during a critical transition period: when a second child is born (Kreppner, Paulsen, & Schütze, 1982). We went into the families' natural habitats, their homes, with our cameras and recording machines (they were much more visible at that time than they are today) to explore differences in families' socialization practices. We intended not to rely on simple behavior categories but to *create* new categories covering relevant *interactive* aspects of family dynamics (for details, see Kreppner, 1991). Thus we began to focus on those phenomena in everyday situations that we believed were representative of "typical" behaviors in the family.

However, before we were able to create some sort of "new" categories, we ran into a problem that did not appear to be extensively discussed in the literature. Without using any fixed and predetermined categories, we unexpectedly experienced "barriers" that left us with our recorded material in a state of increased helplessness (Kreppner, 1982). We were confronted with two major barriers that kept us from being able to perceive those interaction patterns and recurrent communication exchanges among family members that, at a later stage of our analyses, proved to be the core units defining essential differences in family functioning. The two barriers were *triviality* and *specificity*.

First, during our earliest discussions of what we had observed in the families, we found ourselves trapped by our focus on exceptional events and our neglect of those behaviors that we believed were self-evident and not interesting enough (that is, too trivial) to be registered. At that time, we were still bound to the belief that events worth being registered were those that clearly stand out and are distinct from everyday events.

Later, when we had discovered nontrivial patterns of interaction and communication in a family, we tried to transfer the identified patterns to other families. Again, we found ourselves in a trap: We were unable to transfer family-specific exchange patterns from one family to another, as each family seemed to represent a specific unit with unique patterns of communication.

ADVANTAGES OF USING VIDEOTAPES AND CINEMATIC TECHNIQUES IN ANALYZING COMPLEX FAMILY INTERACTION PATTERNS

After we stopped looking for exceptional, "nontrivial" events, we began to watch the situations we had recorded on tape again and again. During this process, we began to "perceive" recurring formats of exchange among the family members. In addition, the production of exact transcriptions of family communication in the recorded situations was obviously very helpful for bringing us deeper into the internal dynamics of the recurring exchange patterns. These recurring patterns revealed not only some basic structural aspects of family constellations, but also—perhaps more interesting—provided us with information about the *generic process* responsible for the occurrence of these constellations in the family. Thus by using these techniques of repeated viewing and transcribing communication, we began to realize that isolated single behaviors of family members that had seemed "trivial" to us just appeared on the "surface" of everyday behavior. By the same token, families became comparable; we no longer found them totally idiosyncratic in their behavior when we recognized these more basic recurring patterns. Once we established this fundamental differentiation as a basic guideline for analyzing family interaction, we were able to surmount both the triviality and the specificity barriers.

Reflecting these barriers in a more fundamental way, we referred to Kurt Lewin's (1927) differentiation between *phenomenal* and *conditional genetic* observational categories. Lewin

distinguishes between the surface level of categories, depicting the multitude of phenomena as they appear (phenomena), and an in-depth level of classifications, characterizing the underlying structures or conditions that lead to or even cause the observed behaviors on the surface. Once we had recognized the existence of recurring patterns of family interaction and communication in different situations and—as in our longitudinal study—at different developmental stages of the children, we went one step further to gain access to in-depth structures: We began to use cinematic procedures, such as montage technique. For example, we edited together short pieces of tape showing observed situations involving the same family at different times, when the children were at different developmental levels. Watching the edited tape gave us the opportunity to compare directly the surface behaviors of identical family members in quite different contexts over time in a density that is never possible in direct observation. Watching this new tape intensified the impression we had of recurring patterns.

SOME GENERAL CONCLUSIONS

By using cinematic techniques such as repeated viewing and montage, researchers can dramatically refine the choices of abstractions they use to describe typical family interactions and communication patterns. With observed situations conserved on tape in all their detail, researchers can carefully prepare the process of abstraction and develop new categories for description. They can review the recorded situations time and again, without any limitation. This is totally different from situations in which observers with sets of predetermined categories have to decide on the spot which of those categories are appropriate for describing what they are observing at the moment. The idea of using a camera to obtain objectively fixed observations goes back to Arnold Gesell (1928), who was one of the first researchers in the area of human development to emphasize observation as a

Case Study

useful method in infant studies. He argued that the camera is an objective observer:

> The camera is, in a sense, mightier than the psychological eye. The living eye can see but it cannot record. Not even in the visual arcana of the most eidetic cortex can permanent immutable images be stored for retrospective reference. This is just what the camera can do for us. (p. 157)

Moreover, having a multitude of situations frozen on tape gives researchers still another advantage: They can compare situations preserved on tape with other situations by contrasting interaction or behavior sequences directly. This comparison process across varying situations can be likened to the "hypothesis testing procedure" known from experimental research. Thus, with the availability of new video techniques, researchers' problem of making forced and instant abstractions of complex situations is largely eliminated. As Thiel (1991) has put it:

> The invention of cameras and microphones has made it possible for observers to fix objects without directly involving their cognitive systems. Observers can delegate the fixation to the technical process that can perform its task iconically and nonselectively with a completeness that surpasses the observers' own capabilities. (p. 185)

Thus researchers are in the comfortable situation of being able to choose among different approaches for generating appropriate categories for abstraction. Whereas predetermined categories are mandatory in the case of direct observation, the choices of categories can be delayed when the situations of interest have been preserved on tape. Researchers must justify their choices of categories by demonstrating the degree of proper representation of the phenomena under research. An abstraction is a representation of a phenomenon and has to

be both unique and unambiguous (Suppes & Zinnes, 1963). When this condition is not properly met, distortions may occur that may devalue all observational efforts. Statistical methods, as sophisticated and complex as they may be, can never correct misconceptions in the process of representation and abstraction. Thus the use of cinematic techniques may foster the process of abstraction and the generation of appropriate categories.

Thiel (1991) distinguishes two different approaches in the application of cinematic techniques in observational research: the reproductive approach and the productive approach. The *reproductive* approach makes extensive use of the fact that the total situation is fixed on videotape and the researcher can reconstruct what occurred through careful repeated viewing of the tape, slow-motion analysis, and transcription of verbal utterances. The *productive* approach applies advanced cinematic techniques, such as montage, to reveal new aspects of the situation that are possibly blurred or even hidden and may emerge only when individual events are linked together through editing of the videotape.

To date, researchers have widely ignored the advantage of using the technique of montage to create categories, even though it is obvious that this approach could be very helpful for the comparison of longitudinal recordings. Unfortunately, many contemporary researchers seem to categorize what they have observed and preserved instantly from tape as if they had to do the classification during the observation, once and forever. Today, with specialized software offering researchers new possibilities of working with video materials much as with texts, observational methodology may advance to a point where something like in-depth structures producing surface phenomena could be revealed through the use of montage techniques as proposed by Gesell. Thus the story of this "case study" of the attempt to analyze complex interaction patterns may help open new and brighter perspectives for successful microanalytic approaches in family research.

DISCUSSION AND EXTENSION

DEDUCTIVE QUALITATIVE ANALYSIS AND FAMILY THEORY BUILDING

Jane F. Gilgun, *University of Minnesota*

Family scholars have a long-term commitment to theory building. Deductive qualitative analysis is a method, or series of procedures, that is useful for the testing and reformulation of theoretical models (Gilgun, 2001, 2002). In deductive qualitative analysis, researchers begin their research with a conceptual model, then study cases in depth, and then reformulate the model to fit the cases. A key procedure in deductive qualitative analysis is the active search for evidence that undermines the current conceptual model. The disconfirming evidence that leads researchers to reformulate their model can be called *negative instances* or even *negative cases* within a particular case.

This search for disconfirming evidence guards against the possibility that researchers will impose their model on the phenomena they observe while missing other phenomena that could contribute to a useful, viable theory. Popper's (1969) idea of conjectures and refutations and the approaches of the developers of analytic induction (Becker, Geer, Hughes, & Strauss, 1961; Cressey, 1953; Gilgun, 1999, 2002; Lindesmith, 1947; Znaniecki, 1934) provide the foundation for the seeking of evidence that can disconfirm and lead to a reformulation of conceptual models and theories. The goal for reformulated conceptual models is to be more closely aligned with the diverse experiences of the persons who provided the evidence on which researchers build their models.

By analyzing negative cases—that is, cases that are different enough from the cases already analyzed to show promise for the refutation and reformulation of the current model—researchers create concepts and other theoretical constructions that encompass a wide range of variations. In other words, the procedures of deductive qualitative analysis lead researchers to account for diverse patterns in family and social phenomena.

Many people think of qualitative approaches as based on induction—that is, researchers enter the field with open minds in order to identify social processes and to make theoretical sense of them. Yet many researchers have done considerable work in identifying and theorizing about social processes, whereas others have developed conceptual models based on what is already known. Researchers who have developed theoretical models cannot start anew, or act as if they don't already know something about their areas of interest. Thus, in family scholarship as in other social science disciplines, scholars need to develop procedures that allow for the use of conceptual models in the doing of qualitative research when their purpose is theory building.

THEORETICAL SENSITIVITY

As researchers engage in deductive qualitative analysis, they naturally think about theories that fit with and elucidate the processes they are observing. Doing this well requires theoretical sensitivity (Glaser, 1978); that is, the researchers must have knowledge of existing theories that allows them to identify the qualities and processes they observe in the conduct of their research. Researchers develop theory through dialectics—their thinking involves a continual interplay between their observations and the theoretical implications of their observations. (Other dialectics are at play as well, such as researchers' personal biographies and the interactions between

DISCUSSION AND EXTENSION *continued*

researchers and informants, but a discussion of these is beyond the scope of the present commentary.) Different researchers typically do not bring the same theories—and other assumptions—to bear in their research. As Ernest Mowrer (1932) observed more than 70 years ago:

> But facts are not born full bloom to be plucked by anyone. In every perceptive experience there is an infinite number of observations which might be made but which are not. What the individual sees is determined in part, at least, by what he is trained to observe. (p. 281)

As we in the field of family research integrate various theories with our observations, it is important that we keep in mind that the theoretical models that we craft are incomplete. We and other researchers will engage in refutations and reformulations of the models that we develop. We also have to go forward with our incomplete knowledge to create policies and programs, but always with an experimental attitude; that is, when new evidence presents itself, we must be ready to reformulate our models, policies, and programs. Our goal is ongoing responsiveness to the social conditions we wish to ameliorate.

ANALYTIC AND PROBABILISTIC GENERALIZABILITY

Issues related to generalizability discourage some family scholars from using qualitative methods to build theories. Researchers trained in probabilistic thinking, survey research, and group experimental designs find it difficult to shift their thinking to appreciate qualitative approaches. As Cook and Campbell (1979) note, however, qualitative thinking underlies all science. In research that is intended to be applied for the purpose of ameliorating social and family processes, it matters little where the guiding principles come from—whether qualitative or quantitative research, clinical observation, or personal experience. What matters is whether the applications of those principles lead to the outcomes that researchers, policy makers, program developers, and practitioners intend. Many years ago, Cronbach (1975) pointed out that the test of the usefulness of findings is whether they illuminate the social and individual processes of new settings. The application of theories to new settings is a form of analytic generalizability, in which researchers observe how the theories being applied highlight aspects of social processes, test the fit of the theories to new situations, and develop more responsive models of social processes (Gilgun, 1994).

FINAL THOUGHTS

Family researchers and theorists can advance theory building and contribute to the common well-being by engaging in conjecture, refutation, and reformulation. Imagine how much richer our knowledge would be if more researchers and theorists could hold their own ideas lightly and seek evidence that refutes their ideas and leads to formulations that are more responsive to social conditions. The resulting reformulations might be more encompassing, account for more diversity, and contribute more to social and individual well-being.

REFERENCES

Allen, K. R. (2000). A conscious and inclusive family studies. *Journal of Marriage and the Family, 62,* 4–17.

Ambert, A., Adler, P. A., Adler, P., & Detzner, D. F. (1995). Understanding and evaluating qualitative research. *Journal of Marriage and the Family, 57,* 879–893.

Anderson, T., & Kanuka, H. (2003). *e-Research: Methods, strategies, and issues.* Needham Heights, MA: Allyn & Bacon.

Anfara, V. A., Jr., Brown, K. M., & Mangione, T. L. (2002). Qualitative analysis on stage: Making the research process more public. *Educational Researcher, 31*(7), 28–38.

Axinn, W. G., Fricke, T. E., & Thornton, A. (1991). The microdemographic community-study approach. *Sociological Methods & Research, 20,* 187–217.

Ballard, C., & Prine, R. (2002). Citizen perceptions of community policing: Comparing Internet and mail survey responses. *Social Science Computer Review, 20,* 485–493.

Becker, H. S., Geer, B., Hughes, E. C., & Strauss, A. L. (1961). *Boys in white: Student culture in medical school.* Chicago: University of Chicago Press.

Belgrave, L. L., Zablotsky, D., & Guadagno, M. A. (2002). How do we talk to each other? Writing qualitative research for quantitative readers. *Qualitative Health Research, 12,* 1427–1439.

Bergman, L. R., Eklund, G., & Magnusson, D. (1991). Studying individual development: Problems and methods. In D. Magnusson, L. R. Bergman, G. Rudinger, & B. Törestad (Eds.), *Problems and methods in longitudinal research: Stability and change* (pp. 1–27). Cambridge: Cambridge University Press.

Black, D., Gates, G., Sanders, S., & Taylor, L. (2000). Demographics of the gay and lesbian population in the United States: Evidence from available systematic data sources. *Demography, 37,* 139–154.

Bott, E. (1971). *Family and social network* (2nd ed.). New York: Free Press.

Bowen, N. K., Bowen, G. L., & Woolley, M. E. (2004). Constructing and validating assessment tools for school-based practitioners: The Elementary School Success Profile. In A. R. Roberts & K. Y. Yeager (Eds.), *Evidence-based practice manual: Research and outcome measures in health and human services* (pp. 509–517). New York: Oxford University Press.

Cook, T. D., & Campbell, D. T. (1979). *Quasi-experimentation: Design and analysis for field settings.* Chicago: Rand McNally.

Crawford, S. D., Couper, M. P., & Lamias, M. J. (2001). Web surveys: Perceptions of burden. *Social Science Computer Review, 19,* 146–162.

Cressey, D. R. (1953). *Other people's money: A study in the social psychology of embezzlement.* Glencoe, IL: Free Press.

Cronbach, L. (1975). Beyond the two disciplines of scientific psychology. *American Psychologist, 30,* 116–127.

Cuber, J. F., & Harroff, P. B. (1965). *The significant Americans: A study of sexual behavior among the affluent.* New York: Appleton-Century.

Davis, B. H. (1981). Teaching the feminist minority. *Women's Studies Quarterly, 9,* 7–9.

Denzin, N. K., & Lincoln, Y. S. (2000a). Introduction: The discipline and practice of qualitative research. In N. K. Denzin & Y. S. Lincoln (Eds.), *Handbook of qualitative research* (2nd ed., pp. 1–28). Thousand Oaks, CA: Sage.

Denzin, N. K., & Lincoln, Y. S. (Eds.). (2000b). *Handbook of qualitative research* (2nd ed.). Thousand Oaks, CA: Sage.

Dill, A. (1994). Writing for the right audience. In J. F. Gubrium & A. Sankar (Eds.), *Qualitative methods in aging research* (pp. 243–262). Thousand Oaks, CA: Sage.

Dillman, D. A. (1999). *Mail and Internet surveys: The tailored design method.* http://www.amazon.com/exec/obidos/ASIN/0471323543/amurj0b

Easton, K. L., McComish, J. F., & Greenberg, R. (2000). Avoiding common pitfalls in qualitative data collection and transcription. *Qualitative Health Research, 10,* 703–707.

Eisner, E. (1997). The promise and perils of alternative forms of data representation. *Educational Researcher, 26*(6), 4–10.

Elliott, R., Fischer, C. T., & Rennie, D. L. (1999). Evolving guidelines for publication of qualitative research studies in psychology and related fields. *British Journal of Clinical Psychology, 38,* 215–229.

Ensler, E. (2001). *The vagina monologues: The V-day edition*. New York: Villard.

Espelage, D. L., Holt, M. K., & Henkel, R. R. (2003). Examination of peer-group contextual effects on aggression during early adolescence. *Child Development, 74,* 205–220.

Fischer, L. R. (1994). Qualitative research as art and science. In J. F. Gubrium & A. Sankar (Eds.), *Qualitative methods in aging research* (pp. 3–14). Thousand Oaks, CA: Sage.

Foddy, W. (1998). An empirical evaluation of in-depth probes used to pretest survey questions. *Sociological Methods & Research, 27,* 103–133.

Freire, P. (1970). *Pedagogy of the oppressed.* New York: Herder & Herder.

Gergen, M. M. (1997). Skipping stones: Circles in the pond. In M. M. Gergen & S. N. Davis (Eds.), *Toward a new psychology of gender: A reader* (pp. 605–611). New York: Routledge.

Gesell, A. (1928). *Infancy and human growth.* New York: Macmillan.

Gilgun, J. F. (1994). A case for case studies in social work research. *Social Work, 39,* 371–380.

Gilgun, J. F. (1999). Methodological pluralism and qualitative family research. In M. B. Sussman, S. K. Steinmetz, & G. W. Peterson (Eds.), *Handbook of marriage and the family* (2nd ed., pp. 219–261). New York: Plenum.

Gilgun, J. F. (2001). Grounded theory, other inductive methods, and social work methods. In B. Thyer (Ed.), *Handbook of social work research* (pp. 345–364). Thousand Oaks, CA: Sage.

Gilgun, J. F. (2002). Conjectures and refutations: Governmental funding and qualitative research. *Qualitative Social Work, 1,* 359–375.

Glaser, B. G. (1978). *Theoretical sensitivity.* Mill Valley, CA: Sociology Press.

Gonzalez, R., & Griffin, D. (1997). On the statistics of interdependence: Treating dyadic data with respect. In. S. Duck (Ed.), *Handbook of personal relationships: Theory, research and interventions* (2nd ed., pp. 271–302). New York: John Wiley.

Gonzalez, R., & Griffin, D. (1999). The correlational analysis of dyad-level data in the distinguishable case. *Personal Relationships, 6,* 449–470.

Green, W. H. (1997). *LIMDEP Version 7.0 users manual.* New York: New York University.

Griffin, D., & Gonzalez, R. (1995). Correlational analysis of dyad-level data in the exchangeable case. *Psychological Bulletin, 118,* 430–439.

Grotevant, H. D., McRoy, R. G., Dunbar, N., Fravel, D. L., Kohler, J. K., Mendenhall, T. J., et al. (1998). *Bridging epistemological and methodological dichotomies in family research: Implications for research with adoptive families.* Paper presented at the Theory Construction and Research Methodology Workshop, annual meeting of the National Council on Family Relations, Milwaukee, WI.

Grotevant, H. D., Ross, N. M., Marchel, M. A., & McRoy, R. G. (1999). Adaptive behavior in adopted children: Predictors from early risk, collaboration in relationships within the adoptive kinship network, and openness arrangements. *Journal of Adolescent Research, 14,* 231–247.

Gubrium, J. F., & Holstein, J. A. (1993). Phenomenology, ethnomethodology, and family discourse. In P. Boss, W. J. Doherty, R. LaRossa, W. R. Schumm, & S. K. Steinmetz (Eds.), *Sourcebook of family theories and methods: A contextual approach* (pp. 651–672). New York: Plenum.

Harding, S. (1987). Introduction: Is there a feminist method? In S. Harding (Ed.), *Feminism and methodology: Social science issues* (pp. 1–14). Bloomington: Indiana University Press.

Heerwegh, D., & Loosveldt, G. (2002). An evaluation of response formats on data quality in Web surveys. *Social Science Computer Review, 20,* 471–484.

Hinds, P. S., Vogel, R. J., & Clarke-Steffen, L. (1997). The possibilities and pitfalls of doing a secondary analysis of a qualitative data set. *Qualitative Health Research, 7,* 408–424.

Hoffmann, J. P. (2002). The community context of family structure and adolescent drug use. *Journal of Marriage and Family, 64,* 314–330.

Humphreys, L. (1970). *Tearoom trade: Impersonal sex in public places.* Chicago: Aldine.

Jacobson, A., Hamilton, P., & Galloway, J. (1993). Obtaining and evaluating data sets for secondary analysis in nursing research. *Western Journal of Nursing Research, 15,* 483–494.

Jaffe, D. I., & Miller, E. M. (1994). Problematizing meaning. In J. F. Gubrium & A. Sankar (Eds.), *Qualitative methods in aging research* (pp. 51–64). Thousand Oaks, CA: Sage.

Johnson, D. R., & Elliott, L. A. (1998). Sampling design effects: Do they affect the analyses of data from the National Survey of Families and Households? *Journal of Marriage and the Family, 60,* 993–1001.

Kashy, D. A., & Snyder, D. K. (1995). Measurement and data analytic issues in couples research. *Psychological Assessment, 7,* 338–348.

Kenny, D. A. (1988). The analysis of data from two-person relationships. In S. Duck (Ed.), *Handbook of personal relationships* (pp. 185–205). New York: John Wiley.

Kenny, D. A., & Kashy, D. A. (1991). Analyzing interdependence in dyads. In B. M. Montgomery & S. Duck (Eds.), *Studying interpersonal interaction* (pp. 275–285). New York: Guilford.

King, G., Honaker, J., Joseph, A., & Scheve, K. (2001). Analyzing incomplete political science data: An alternative algorithm for multiple imputation. *American Political Science Review, 95,* 49–69.

Kish, L. (1965). *Survey sampling.* New York: John Wiley.

Kreppner, K. (1982). *Zur Interpretation von Alltagshandeln in der Familie: Drei Barrieren vor dem Erkennen?* [On the interpretation of everyday behavior in the family: Three barriers before knowledge?]. Contribution to the discussion group "Experiences with non-standardized research methods" at the 33rd Conference of the German Society for Psychology, Mainz, Germany.

Kreppner, K. (1991). Observation and the longitudinal approach in infancy research. In M. E. Lamb & H. Keller (Eds.), *Infant development: Perspectives from German-speaking countries* (pp. 151–178). Hillsdale, NJ: Lawrence Erlbaum.

Kreppner, K., Paulsen, S., & Schütze, Y. (1982). Infant and family development: From triads to tetrads. *Human Development, 25,* 373–391.

Krieger, S. (1991). *Social science and the self: Personal essays on an art form.* New Brunswick, NJ: Rutgers University Press.

Kuo, M., Mohler, B., Raudenbush, S. W., & Earls, F. J. (2000). Assessing exposure to violence using multiple informants: Application of hierarchical linear model. *Journal of Child Psychology and Psychiatry, 41,* 1049–1056.

Kvale, S. (1996). *Interviews: An introduction to qualitative research interviewing.* Thousand Oaks, CA: Sage.

Lareau, A. (2003). *Unequal childhoods: Class, race, and family life.* Berkeley: University of California Press.

LaRossa, R., & Wolf, J. (1985). On qualitative family research. *Journal of Marriage and the Family, 47,* 531–541.

Lewin, K. (1927). Gesetz und Experiment in der Psychologie [Law and experiment in psychology]. *Symposion, 1,* 375–421.

Lewis, O. (1950). An anthropological approach to family studies. *American Journal of Sociology, 55,* 468–475.

Lincoln, Y. S., & Guba, E. G. (1985). *Naturalistic inquiry.* Beverly Hills, CA: Sage.

Lincoln, Y. S., & Guba, E. G. (2000). Paradigmatic controversies, contradictions, and emerging confluences. In N. K. Denzin & Y. S. Lincoln (Eds.), *Handbook of qualitative research* (2nd ed., pp. 163–188). Thousand Oaks, CA: Sage.

Lindesmith, A. R. (1947). *Opiate addiction.* Bloomington, IN: Principia.

Lindsey, E., & McGuinness, L. (1998). Significant elements of community involvement in participatory action research: Evidence from a community project. *Journal of Advanced Nursing, 28,* 1106–1114.

Lofland, J., & Lofland, L. H. (1995). *Analyzing social settings: A guide to qualitative observation and analysis* (3rd ed.). Belmont, CA: Wadsworth.

Maguire, M. (1999). Treating the dyad as the unit of analysis. *Journal of Marriage and the Family, 61,* 213–224.

Masten, A. S., Hubbard, J. J., Gest, S. D., Tellegen, A. D., Garmezy, N., & Ramirez, M. (1999). Competence in the context of adversity: Pathways to resilience and maladaptation from childhood to late adolescence. *Development and Psychopathology, 11,* 143–169.

McCall, R. B., & Appelbaum, M. I. (1991). Some issues of conducting secondary analysis. *Developmental Psychology, 27,* 911–917.

Minkler, M. (2000). Using participatory action research to build healthy communities. *Public Health Reports, 115,* 191–197.

Moffitt, T. E., & Caspi, A. (2001). Childhood predictors differentiate life-course persistent and adolescence-limited antisocial pathways among males and females. *Development and Psychopathology, 12,* 355–375.

Mowrer, E. R. (1932). *Family, its organization and disorganization.* Chicago: University of Chicago Press.

Muthén, B. (2003). Statistical and substantive checking in growth mixture modeling: Comment on Bauer and Curran (2003). *Psychological Methods, 8,* 369–377.

Muthén, B. O., & Muthén, L. K. (2000). Integrating person-centered and variable-centered analyses: Growth mixture modeling with latent trajectory classes. *Alcoholism: Clinical and Experimental Research, 24,* 882–891.

National Institutes of Health, Office of Behavioral and Social Sciences Research. (1999). *Qualitative methods in health research: Opportunities and considerations in application and review.* Retrieved June 8, 2004, from http://obssr.od.nih.gov/publications/qualitative.pdf

Nelson, T., Piercy, F., & Sprenkle, D. H. (in press). Internet infidelity: A multi-phase Delphi study. In F. Piercy (Ed.), *Handbook on treating infidelity.* Binghamton, NY: Haworth.

O'Neil, K. M., Penrod, S. D., & Bornstein, B. H. (2003). Web-based research: Methodological variables' effects on dropout and sample characteristics. *Behavior Research Methods, Instruments, & Computers, 35,* 217–226.

Osborne, J. W. (1990). Some basic existential-phenomenological research methodology for counselors. *Canadian Journal of Counseling, 24,* 79–91.

Packer, M. J., & Addison, R. B. (1989). Evaluating an interpretive account. In M. J. Packer & R. B. Addison (Eds.), *Entering the circle: Hermeneutic investigation in psychology* (pp. 275–292). Albany: State University of New York Press.

Park, P., Brydon-Miller, M., Hall, B., & Jackson, T. (Eds.). (1993). *Voices of change: Participatory research in the United States and Canada.* Toronto: OISE Press.

Pearce, L. (2002). Integrating survey and ethnographic methods for systematic anomalous case analysis. *Sociological Methodology, 32,* 103–132.

Piercy, F., & Benson, K. (in press). Aesthetic forms of data representation in qualitative family therapy research. *Journal of Marital and Family Therapy.*

Piercy, F., & Thomas, V. (1998). Participatory evaluation research: An introduction for family therapists. *Journal of Marital and Family Therapy, 24,* 165–176.

Popper, K. R. (1969). *Conjectures and refutations: The growth of scientific knowledge.* London: Routledge & Kegan Paul.

Rains, J., & Ray, D. W. (1995). Participatory action research for community health promotion. *Public Health Nursing, 12,* 256–261.

Roberts, C. (1997). A generic semantic grammar for quantitative text analysis: Applications to East and West Berlin radio news content from 1979. *Sociological Methodology, 27,* 89–129.

Rogosa, D. (1995). Myths and methods: "Myths about longitudinal research" plus supplemental questions. In J. M. Gottman (Ed.), *The analysis of change* (pp. 3–65). Mahwah, NJ: Lawrence Erlbaum.

Rosenblatt, P. C., & Fischer, L. R. (1993). Qualitative family research. In P. Boss, W. J. Doherty, R. LaRossa, W. R. Schumm, & S. K. Steinmetz (Eds.), *Sourcebook of family theories and methods: A contextual approach* (pp. 167–177). New York: Plenum.

Rubin, L. B. (1976). *Worlds of pain: Life in the working-class family.* New York: Basic Books.

Schaefer, D. R., & Dillman, D. A. (1998). Development of a standard e-mail methodology: Results of an experiment. *Public Opinion Quarterly, 62,* 378–397.

Schafer, J. L. (1997). *Analysis of incomplete multivariate data.* New York: Chapman & Hall.

Schafer, J. L. (1999). *Software for multiple imputation.* Retrieved June 8, 2004, from http://www.stat.psu.edu/~jls/misoftwa.html#win

Seccombe, K. (1999). *"So you think I drive a Cadillac?": Welfare recipients' perspectives on the system and its reform.* Needham Heights, MA: Allyn & Bacon.

Shah, B. V., Barnwell, B. G., & Bieler, G. S. (1996). *SUDAAN: Software for the statistical analysis of correlated data: User's manual.* Research Triangle Park, NC: Research Triangle Institute.

Shrout, P. E. (1998). Measurement reliability and agreement in psychiatry. *Statistical Methods in Medical Research, 7,* 301–317.

Shrout, P. E., & Fleiss, J. L. (1979). Intraclass correlations: Uses in assessing rater reliability. *Psychological Bulletin, 86,* 420–428.

Small, S. A. (1995). Action-oriented research: Models and methods. *Journal of Marriage and the Family, 57,* 941–955.

Smith, J. K. (1984). Quantitative versus qualitative research: An attempt to resolve the issue. *Educational Researcher, 12*(3), 6–13.

Snijders, T. A. B., & Kenny, D. A. (1999). The social relations model for family data: A multilevel approach. *Personal Relationships, 6,* 471–486.

Stanley, L. (1990). Feminist praxis and the academic mode of production: An editorial introduction. In L. Stanley (Eds.), *Feminist praxis: Research, theory and epistemology in feminist sociology* (pp. 3–19). London: Routledge.

StataCorp. (1997). *Stata statistical software: Release 5.0.* College Station, TX: Author.

Sullivan, M. L. (1998). Integrating qualitative and quantitative methods in the study of developmental psychopathology in context. *Development and Psychopathology, 10,* 377–393.

Suppes, P., & Zinnes, J. L. (1963). Basic measurement theory. In R. D. Luce, R. R. Bush, & E. Galanter (Eds.), *Handbook of mathematical psychology* (Vol. 1, pp. 1–16). New York: John Wiley.

Tashakkori, A., & Teddlie, C. (Eds.). (2003). *Handbook of mixed methods in social and behavioral research.* Thousand Oaks, CA: Sage.

Teachman, J. D., & Crowder, K. (2002). Multilevel models in family research: Some conceptual and methodological issues. *Journal of Marriage and Family, 64,* 280–294.

Thiel, T. (1991). Videotechnique and science: Methodological considerations. In M. E. Lamb & H. Keller (Eds.), *Infant development: Perspectives from German-speaking countries* (pp. 179–195). Hillsdale, NJ: Lawrence Erlbaum.

Thomas, W. I., & Znaniecki, F. (1918–1920). *The Polish peasant in Europe and America* (5 vols.). Chicago: University of Chicago Press.

Thorne, S. (1994). Secondary analysis in qualitative research: Issues and implication. In J. M. Morse (Ed.), *Critical issues in qualitative research methods* (pp. 263–279). Thousand Oaks, CA: Sage.

Thorne, S. (1998). Ethical and representational issues in qualitative secondary analysis. *Qualitative Health Research, 8,* 547–555.

Tubbs, C., & Burton, L. M. (in press). Bridging research: Using ethnography to inform clinical practice. In D. H. Sprenkle & F. Piercy (Eds.), *Research methods in family therapy* (2nd ed.). New York: Guilford.

Walker, A. J., Acock, A. C., Bowman, S. R., & Li, F. (1996). Amount of care given and caregiving satisfaction: A latent growth curve analysis. *Journal of Gerontology: Psychological Sciences, 51,* 130–142.

Weigle, S. C. (1998). Using FACETS to model rater training effects. *Language and Testing, 15,* 263–287.

Whitmore, E. (1994). To tell the truth: Working with oppressed groups in participatory approaches to inquiry. In P. Reason (Ed.). *Participation in human inquiry* (pp. 82–98). Thousand Oaks, CA: Sage.

Willis, G. B., DeMaio, T. J., & Harris-Kojetin, B. (1999). Is the bandwagon headed for the Promised Land? Evaluating the validity of cognitive interviewing techniques. In M. G. Sirken, D. J. Herrmann, S. Schecter, N. Schwarz, J. M. Tanur, & R. Tourangeau (Eds.), *Cognition and survey research* (pp. 133–154). New York: Wiley-Interscience.

Woolley, M. E., Bowen, G. L., & Bowen, N. K. (in press). Cognitive pretesting and the developmental validity of child self-report instruments: Theory and applications. *Research on Social Work Practice.*

Znaniecki, F. (1934). *The method of sociology.* New York: Farrar & Rinehart.

• Part II

CHANGING
FAMILY PATTERNS

• Four

EXPLANATIONS
OF FAMILY CHANGE

A Family Demographic Perspective

Suzanne M. Bianchi, *Maryland Population Research Center*

Lynne M. Casper, *National Institute of Child Health*

Demography is the study of population characteristics and change, and family demographers focus on the intergenerational and gender ties that bind individuals into households and family units. As Goldscheider (1995) has noted, demographers study family change to understand both individual and societal behavior: why individuals behave as they do toward each other and why, once those individual behaviors are aggregated into nations (or other units), societies are similar or dissimilar in their family configurations as well as in their economic, political, and cultural institutions. Sweet and Bumpass (1987) also emphasize how family demography is ultimately a study of individual and societal well-being, for it is through family ties and household groupings that resources are exchanged and less able members are cared for by those who are more able.

The core of family demography describes the composition of families and households using basic demographic information on the numbers of household members, their relationships to each other, and each person's sex, age, and marital status. Family demographers describe the *composition* or *structure* of families and households (the set of statuses and associated roles that are important for the functioning of society) and the demographic *processes* (family-related events such as marriage, divorce, and childbearing) that produce those family structures. Changes in the timing, number, and sequences of demographic events such as marriage transform family and household composition. Family

Authors' Note: We thank Betsy Thorn and Vanessa Wight for research assistance with the preparation of this chapter. The findings and opinions expressed are attributable to the authors and do not necessarily reflect those of the National Institute of Child Health and Human Development.

demographers examine changes in structure and process over time to assess family change (Casper & O'Connell, 2000; Teachman, 1993).

Early family demographic studies documented changes in fertility (childbearing), marriage, and household and family composition, with each of these areas typically studied in isolation. Growing diversity in the number, timing, and sequencing of family events led scholars in the field to study the interrelationships among these events and to incorporate other events (e.g., cohabitation) to develop a more accurate accounting of family change. Instead of studying fertility or nuptiality regimes, family demographers today are more likely to study parenting and partnering. They also focus more on the causes and consequences of family change, including the social and economic contexts in which it occurs. Despite these shifts in focus, the tenets of formal family demography—structure and process—continue to guide "social" demographers in the study of family change.

FAMILY CHANGE

Several key changes in the family that began to occur in developed countries in the latter half of the 20th century have captured the attention of family demographers. The first of these is changing union formation (and dissolution) in the United States, Europe, and Japan. The changes include a dramatic delay in entry into marriage, a decline in marriage in many countries and among some population subgroups in the United States, and a concomitant rise in unmarried heterosexual (and same-sex) cohabitation. Cohabitation increasingly precedes marriage, is an alternative to remarriage after separation and divorce, and, in several European countries, is often a long-term substitute for marriage. An increasing proportion of cohabiting households include children—in 1998, 37% of heterosexual unmarried couple households included children, up from 28% in 1978 (Casper & Bianchi, 2002). Tracking and explaining the increase in cohabiting couples, both heterosexual and same-sex couples,

requires not only a better understanding of cohabitation but also a better understanding of marriage; the meaning, value, and nature of both of these relationships are poorly understood in contemporary developed economies.

A second area of family change has been a decrease in fertility in industrialized economies. Fertility is a subject of long-standing interest to demographers, but until relatively recently most scholarly attention was focused on high fertility in developing regions of the world. The rapid decline in fertility in all parts of the developing world has shifted attention away from high fertility and toward the very low fertility levels of Southern and Eastern Europe and Japan. Most of these countries have fertility levels far below the 2.1 children per woman needed to replace the population. Explanations for these low levels of fertility fall squarely within domains of interest to family demographers and include changing normative, social, and economic contexts, particularly women's changing work and family roles.

Recent increases in child rearing within cohabiting and other nonmarital unions have also heightened researchers' awareness that they cannot study trends in childbearing and child rearing independent of the examination of union (marriage and cohabitation) formation and dissolution. Although it is possible to distinguish empirically the timing of entry into marriage, parenthood, and, to a lesser extent, cohabitation, conceptually and analytically these events are intertwined. In the United States, where fertility levels remain close to replacement (around two births per woman, on average), the questions of greatest interest concern two distinct fertility behaviors that characterize U.S. fertility trends. On the one hand, both marriage and children are being postponed to older ages among the better-educated segments of the population. Will this postponement result in increased childlessness, as "tastes" for children change the longer people delay having children and as the likelihood of infertility looms larger at older maternal age? On the other hand, there seems to be increased willingness to disassociate childbearing from marriage altogether, particularly among less educated, minority groups: to have children relatively early, outside of marriage, and to raise them in environments that do not include two coresidential biological parents. For these groups, why are unions so fragile and often never legalized? Policy makers and researchers are seeking a better understanding of the consequences for children and adults of the separation of marriage and childbearing, on the one hand, and the postponement of both, on the other, and how the consequences vary for different groups within the population.

A third area of family change is found in the intergenerational family, which is changing in form: from a "pyramid" structure, with few living grandparents and many children and grandchildren, to the "beanpole family" (Bengtson, Rosenthal, & Burton, 1990), with more grandparents than parents and, increasingly, more parents than children. Demographically, these changes are occurring when mortality is low, life expectancy is high, and fertility is relatively low in the United States and far below that needed to replace the population in Southern and Eastern Europe and Japan. Who provides financial and caregiving support and who feels obligations to whom when delayed and reduced childbearing and declining mortality among adults result in fewer children per adult; when high life expectancies mean long cosurvival of siblings and more years with parents and grandparents; when adults have more "postchildren" years; and when a healthier elderly population has more independence but increased survival into the "oldest old" years, during which frailty and other health concerns as well as financial concerns require family involvement across generations? Changes in marriage, divorce, and childbearing complicate the intergenerational picture, as financial and care obligations are no longer necessarily dependent on biological or marital ties. In groups where marriage is increasingly fragile, intergenerational ties may supersede nuclear ties in the rearing of children (Bengtson, 2001).

Finally, the steady increase in women's labor force participation, especially among married women, and the accompanying decline in the one-wage-earner, two-parent family, provides a greatly altered context for understanding and interpreting family demographic trends (Bianchi, 2000; Casper & Bianchi, 2002). The interrelationship between increased female employment and changes in union formation, fertility, cross-generation caregiving, and the gender division of labor in nonmarket spheres is receiving increased attention in the family demographic literature addressing both developed and developing economies.

THEORETICAL FRAMEWORKS IN FAMILY DEMOGRAPHY

As Bengtson et al. note in Chapter 1 of this volume, theory is a process by which observation is understood. They state: "Theory is the attempt to move beyond the *what* of our observations . . . to the questions of the *why* and *how* of what we have observed." More so than most other social scientists, demographers believe it is essential to describe the *what* before moving on to the *why* and *how* of social change. After determining the *what* of family change, demographers' interest is in understanding why family organizational units exist in society, how they function, what they do for individuals and for populations, and why they change over time. Family demography is inherently interdisciplinary, with sociology and economics contributing the core of the theoretical perspectives, but with increased attention to perspectives from evolutionary biology, developmental psychology, and anthropology, both anthropological techniques of data collection and anthropologists' focus on culture (Morgan et al., 2003).

Demographers, like ethnographers, are trained to start with the data. Ethnographers use qualitative observational and in-depth interviewing techniques and invest heavily in spending time "on the ground" developing an understanding of the lay of the land. At first blush, demographers would appear the diametrical opposite, yet they too spend inordinate amounts of time in observations of data, in their case using quantitative techniques to refine demographic rates and correct "misleading" data problems. Both approaches result in thick description of family behaviors. Those who employ these descriptive techniques of "knowing" are often criticized for having no theory to guide their empirical work. This criticism focuses on the approach but pays insufficient attention to the goal of the approach. Both ethnographers and demographers use their descriptions to inform and generate theories that can then be tested.

Several theoretical strands are influential in the interpretation of family change in family demographic research. In this chapter, we discuss five areas of theoretical development: (second) demographic transition theory, the life-course perspective, household and family decision-making theories, biodemographic interactions, and the focus on culture and context.

Demographic Transition Theory

The main "theory" in demography used to explain the *how* and *why* of family change is demographic transition theory—the notion that a society moves from a high-mortality, high-fertility regime through a transitional phase in which mortality declines, first creating large population growth. Fertility ultimately follows suit, and the society arrives at a situation in which mortality and fertility reach low levels and are again more or less in balance as they were before the transition. The theory of the "second demographic transition" seeks to explain family change in the West (e.g., very low fertility, delayed marriage) as a function of ideational change, in particular the increased emphasis placed on individual autonomy and self-fulfillment (Lesthaeghe, 1995; van da Kaa, 1987).

This second demographic transition was motivated by the same factors that influenced the first transition from high to low fertility regime (e.g., desires for improved standards of living, investment in the "quality" of fewer children after child survival improved). New to the second demographic transition is

the increased value placed on individual autonomy of adults and on the goal of female emancipation and gender equality. Individuals have also become less willing to accept the institutional control of the state or the church that characterized earlier periods. Finally, as Lesthaeghe (1995) observes, advanced consumerism and an increased market orientation characterize the second demographic transition.

Lesthaeghe (1995) organizes descriptive information on family demographic behaviors into three phases of the second demographic transition. The first, characterizing the 1960s and 1970s, witnessed an accelerated upswing in divorce, fertility decline, and delayed marriage. This was followed by the spread of premarital cohabitation and an increase in nonmarital births. Finally, in the last phase, reached only by some European countries (and the United States), there has been a plateau in divorce rates, more postmarital cohabitation replacing remarriage, some recuperation in fertility (especially at later ages), and an end to the decline in teen fertility.

The second demographic transition places higher "quality" demands on adult relationships. These demands are hard to satisfy, and the end results are less union formation, more wariness about entering unions in the first place, greater dissatisfaction with the unions that are formed, and ultimately more union instability. These changes lead to an increase in single-parent families and thus increased risk of poverty for children, more one-person households, and life-course transitions that are less strictly (or normatively) patterned and more complex than transitions in the past.

Some researchers have developed the second demographic transition theory's focus on gender processes of emancipation to explain the low levels of fertility witnessed in Europe and Japan. For example, McDonald (2000) argues that in many developed countries, workplaces offer women increased autonomy and opportunity for fulfillment of individual goals, whereas family systems remain "traditional," with expectations that women will meet all the caregiving needs of their families with little assistance from men. Under these circumstances (in countries such as Italy and Japan), women who want the recognition, income, and self-fulfillment that market work can bring may feel they have little choice but to eschew marriage and children altogether.

The Life-Course Perspective and Family Demography

Bengtson and Allen (1993) chart the history of the interdisciplinary development of the life-course paradigm, which emanated from the life-span developmental tradition within psychology along with age stratification studies in sociology and family history, and family development (e.g., life-cycle theories) studies. Within demography, the life-course perspective grew out of the "life-cycle approach" first used in 1906 by Roundtree to study poverty and adopted by Paul Glick (1975) to track the average ages at which women in different birth cohorts experience various family "events" such as first marriages and births. As family demographers came to view this life-cycle concept as too static, they increasingly replaced it with a life-course perspective (Teachman, 1993).

The life-course perspective emphasizes transitions and trajectories. People make transitions from being unmarried to being married, from being childless to being parents, from being married to being divorced or widowed, and so forth. Lives are linked across generations and through bonds such as marriage, although the meanings of those linkages change over time and are historically specific. From the life-course perspective, an individual is viewed as following, over the course of his or her life, a life trajectory (Elder, 1985). Each person's life trajectory is marked by a sequence of life events or transitions and is made up of an intertwined bundle of decisions about family and work. Any individual's life trajectory is also interlocked with the trajectories of others, especially significant others such as parents, spouses, and children. Interlocking trajectories connect persons across generations

(consanguineal connections) and by gender (conjugal connections). Because age and sex and the notion of cohorts figure prominently in demographic rates, demographers can begin to interpret and organize rates under the life-course perspective.

This perspective's focus on transitions—including timing of transitions in terms of age and duration between transitions—converges with the "life table thinking" so central to demographers' assessment of mortality, fertility, and nuptiality regimes. The life table focuses on how long a population "lasts" in a certain state (life in the case of mortality, childlessness in the case of fertility, and singlehood in the case of nuptiality) and the rate at which the population surviving in a state makes transitions between states. In life tables, duration in (and sequencing of) states as well as transition probabilities are important, just as they are conceptually to life-course analysis (Moen, Dempster-McClain, & Williams, 1992). Increasingly, these concepts are subject to modeling with a set of tools known variously as event history models, survival analysis, or hazards models.

The life-course perspective also focuses attention on time and space, on the fact that family change or family life trajectories that are typical in one time period or historical setting may not be typical in another time or place. The family life cycle conceptualized by Glick (1975), for example, was well suited to analyzing mid-20th-century U.S. family behavior, with low rates of divorce, relatively high rates of marriage and childbearing, and increasing life expectancy. It was less applicable to family trends after 1965, as divorce rates rose, or earlier in the century, when premature death often broke conjugal partnerships before children were launched.

The life-course approach, with its emphasis on cohorts and intergenerational linkages (Bengtson & Allen, 1993), provides an overarching framework for thinking about family demographic change in the lives of individuals and, when individual data are aggregated, helps to describe and explain family change at the macro level. This perspective's focus on the contexts in which work and family trajectories unfold allows life-course analysts to contemplate the different consequences that may attach to family transitions in different historical settings. For example, the timing of childbearing that is optimal, or at least considered optimal, may vary between settings depending on whether child and maternal mortality is high rather than low. This focus on context fits well with the demographer's traditional focus on cohort—the notion that individuals born in a certain time (and place) may share particular experiences that carry through their lives and shape their later behaviors.

Family and Household Decision Making Theories

Much of the analysis of family processes within family demography has assumed that decisions—about when and whom to marry, whether to have children and how many, whether to remain in a marriage, and so forth—are made by rational actors who weigh the costs and benefits of alternative courses of action and choose optimal strategies. Family demographic analysis of decision making has been heavily influenced by neoclassical economic theory of the family based on the assumption of rational choice. Gary Becker's (1960) economic analysis of fertility, theory of marriage formation (Becker, 1974, 1981), and theories of marital dissolution (Becker, Landes, & Michael, 1977), as well as the analysis of marriage as a market (Becker, 1974, 1981; Oppenheimer, 1988) and the discussion of women's increased labor force participation and family change in terms of "comparative advantages," exchange, and "opportunity costs" (Blau, Ferber, & Winkler, 1998) have flooded the family demographic lexicon and conceptualization of family processes.

As Robert Willis (1987) discusses in an essay titled "What Have We Learned From the Economics of the Family?" the development of family economics in the 1960s was linked to several theoretical streams within economics: life-cycle theories of consumption, theories of

human capital development and labor supply, and work on household production and time allocation. A whole new literature sprang up in which scholars examined marriage and fertility behaviors and decisions about the use of time and goods within the home.

Becker's (1974) theory of marriage formalized the notion of a marriage market and introduced concepts such as the "gains to marriage" and the specialized division of labor in the household. Mincer and Polachek (1974) developed a theory that connects women's family behaviors to their earnings positions in the labor market. Easterlin (1973) explained fertility swings as resulting from changes in preferences for children caused by changing income aspirations and labor market conditions of birth cohorts. Becker et al. (1977) discussed divorce in terms of costs and benefits, expected gains to partnerships, and the role of uncertainty and imperfect information.

Economic theory was particularly influential in the analysis and interpretation of the rise in female employment and its possible connection to marriage and fertility behavior. Economic theorists saw women's increased education and rising employment as increasing the likelihood of divorce and reducing fertility. Labor market involvement raised the value of women's time spent in the labor market and increased the "opportunity cost" (forgone wages) of spending time raising children. According to Becker et al. (1977), women's economic independence contributes to divorce because it erodes the complementarity of what men and women bring to marriage. Marriages, economic theorists argued, are most likely to be formed and least likely to be dissolved when each partner sees an advantage to being married over remaining single. When a woman's comparative advantage in the home relative to the market is greater than her husband's, the couple will allocate more of the wife's time to the home and more of the husband's to the market, and both will have much to gain from marriage and much to lose from divorce.

Researchers have also used the economic theory of labor market search to understand delayed marriage (Oppenheimer, 1988). With increased investment in schooling and poor prospects for entering the labor market, recent cohorts of young men have taken longer than previous generations to get established in the labor market. According to economic theory, this increases the uncertainty concerning their future prospects as good economic providers and thus extends the period between reaching adulthood and entering a first marriage.

The common preference model—that is, the idea that a household maximizes a single, shared utility function—served as the basis for theorizing about the family in economics until the model began to be challenged in the 1980s (Lundberg & Pollak, 1996). Although proponents of the model acknowledged that family members might have divergent preferences, they minimized the problems this afforded by postulating that a family has an altruistic head who allocates resources to members in such a way as to achieve their cooperation (Becker, 1991). This includes pooling the incomes of all family members and allocating the funds to maximize family well-being. From the perspective of the common preference model, what happened within families was more or less a black box: Income flowed in and then family members efficiently allocated resources to the purchase of goods and services, the consumption of leisure, and the production of children, all in accord with a common, shared preference for optimal family output.

Economic theories of the family based on the rational choice assumption were influential because they seemed to provide a conceptually elegant way of thinking about family behaviors and change, especially expenditure patterns and labor supply. However, like the family life-cycle concept, many aspects of the theory ultimately proved too limited and too tautological for the theory to be useful for the analysis of family behavior (Lundberg & Pollak, 1996). Hence this abstraction of family functioning has come under increased scrutiny for failing to theorize adequately those

situations in which adults within families have conflicting preferences or do not follow the rational choice assumption. Empirical evidence showing that families spend money differently depending on who controls the funds, with more allocated to children's needs when women control a greater share, cast doubt on the income-pooling and single-utility-function framework. Empirical work has cast doubt not only on the assumption of income pooling and a common, agreed-upon utility function within families but also on the strength of the causal role of women's economic independence in the movement away from marriage (Oppenheimer, 1997; Sayer & Bianchi, 2000).

Bargaining models, which have arisen out of game theoretic approaches to economic behavior, are increasingly favored by some economists who analyze family behaviors (Lundberg & Pollak, 1996). Researchers who employ such models focus on bargaining processes, recognizing that individuals within families might not always have the same preferences and that power differentials among those engaged in bargaining (over whether to marry or to stay married, for example) need to be studied and modeled explicitly.

Despite increased interest in bargaining processes in family decision making, many of the concepts and other aspects of Becker's (1981) framework remain firmly—perhaps stubbornly—ingrained in the study of family economic behavior. For example, selecting a mate no doubt includes the weighing of costs and benefits of a particular marriage, just as a cost-benefit calculus must also figure into a decision about exiting marriage. The notion of opportunity costs connected to the expenditure of time remains useful. Women (and men) who allocate time to the labor market have less time to allocate to the home. Although perhaps too narrowly economic, the notion that actors behave in certain ways to realize their preferences, within budget constraints, helps to conceptualize family decisions as purposive, rational behavior operating within conditions of uncertainty and constraint. The economic perspective thus has introduced a rigor of thinking into the family demographic literature as well as attention to measurement issues, such as sampling selectivity and unmeasured variables, that have enhanced empirical analysis and theory about family demographic change.

Biology and Family Demographic Processes

Demographers who study family change, particularly union formation and fertility, are increasingly attuned to possible biological underpinnings of human behavior. Evolutionary bases for possible gender differences in investment in offspring and processes of kin selection, as well as possible evolutionary bases of important emotions that form the "glue" of family life (altruism, love, commitment, guilt, honesty) are finding their way into the study of family and fertility processes (Daly & Wilson, 2000; Morgan et al., 2003, pp. 27–28). The thinking is that genetic predispositions interact with the environmental circumstances of individuals to influence behavior, including family formation and maintenance.

The role of endocrines and stress hormones is an active area of research, with sample surveys both within and outside the United States gathering data on biomarkers. In the study of child outcomes, researchers are paying increased attention to brain functioning and hormonal and stress indicators in adolescence. Population researchers are studying the correlation of hormones such as testosterone and the stress hormone cortisol with behaviors such as marital happiness and disruption and the ability to self-regulate and avoid risky behavior in youth.

An increased interest in the ways in which anthropological and biological mechanisms can be combined with economics to enhance understanding of the family is also an influential stream within family economics (Bergstrom, 1997). Particularly as a life-course approach is used in the study of family processes and life trajectories, possible biological influences on decisions and events early in life and their potential effects on later-life outcomes have become the focus of research for a small but growing number of family demographers.

Context and Cultural Theories

As family change comes to be viewed increasingly as specific to time and place—influenced by historical processes and other context—researchers in the family and fertility field are paying greater attention to contextual influences on the family. As family behaviors change rapidly, there is also new emphasis on culture and shared meanings and a heightened sense that nonfamilial influences are increasingly important to the study of changes in fertility (e.g., explaining very low levels of fertility in some parts of Europe).

Social institutions, the *cultural expectations* surrounding institutions such as marriage, and the *shared meanings* that influence family decision making at the individual, micro level have undergone change. Thus family demographers in general are increasingly engaging theoretical perspectives from disciplines not traditionally part of population studies: anthropology, to understand culture; social and developmental psychology, to understand developmental processes that unfold over the life course; and family therapy, to understand couple dynamics that might influence union formation and dissolution.

THE NEW DEMOGRAPHICS OF FAMILIES

Farrell J. Webb, *Kansas State University*

I t is clear from U.S. Census projections that American families are changing. It is also clear that, despite the fact that we have been aware that these changes have been coming for the past 20 years, family scientists have done little in the area of theory development to help us understand how to address these emerging families. Some of the most important issues that researchers need to address center on understanding what the new families will look like. However, one problem with the area of family studies is that we are still using theory and theoretical constructs from the 1950s in the 21st century to explain behaviors that are unique to this era. For example, recent trends in American families suggest the following about families of the near future:

- At least one-half of all children will spend at least one-quarter of their lives in female-headed households.
- The new families will experience severely limited economic growth and growth opportunities.
- The new families will be characterized by a semi–extended family form made up of fictive kin with some ties to the family members' original homelands.
- The new families will more than likely live in households that have two primary languages for at least two generations.
- The new families will involve at least a definite recognition of sexually variant relatives and/or parents.
- The new families will consist primarily of people of color.
- The new families will have social customs, beliefs, attitudes, and communication forms that researchers have not previously examined using the current theoretical constructs.
- The new families will have unique adaptations to currently mainstream religious beliefs—they may not all be "Christians."
- The new families will probably have some form of major involvement with governmental institutions (e.g., immigration, homeland security, criminal justice, public welfare, and social services), not by choice in most cases.
- The new families will be stigmatized in part because we in the scientific community will fail to adapt our research and theories as necessary to understand these families.

Given the above, the challenge I am issuing to all family scientists is that we develop new approaches that are inclusive, responsive, reasonable, fair, and respectful of the new families that are on the horizon. We must make a genuine effort to recognize and acknowledge differences, and we cannot do this through a simple revision of some major theoretical approaches. Rather, we must first focus on the utility of each approach and then see if the approach has merit in terms of understanding the new families.

It is also important that we become more eclectic in our theoretical constructs, research methodologies, and willingness to cross over into other disciplines (economics,

(continued)

• SPOTLIGHT ON THEORY *continued*

sociology, psychology, biology, medicine, public health, political science, law, and philosophy) for input and development. We must also be willing to acknowledge what works and does not work. The new families will not be able to fit the "one size fits all" model that seems to be used in most research. I am not suggesting that we abandon our theoretical and methodological approaches; rather, I am strongly urging that we develop more inclusive ones. I also believe that we must do more careful research and develop theories that value the historical context of these families. A failure to do so will result in the perpetuation of a devalued status for those who do not match the current stereotype of the American family—a family that we know does not really exist. •

Other relevant contextual domains of study include *technology*—for example, as births to older mothers are increasingly assisted through technology, demographers are viewing this development as relevant to understanding fertility processes. Because *geospatial dimensions* of physical environments and communities shape child outcomes, researchers are paying increased attention to neighborhood and community effects on child rearing and adolescent risk taking. The changing *legal and social policy* context also influences family behaviors, such as the decision to marry or cohabit. Whether same-sex marriages will be legally recognized, whether employee benefits will accrue to heterosexual cohabiting partners, whether marriage can be strengthened, particularly among low-income populations,—these are all questions being debated in the policy arena. Rates of union formation, types of unions formed, and stability of those unions may all be affected by policy and legal institutions. All these developments enlarge the domains that family demographic theory must engage if we are to understand change in "core" family demographic phenomena such as union formation and childbearing (Morgan et al., 2003, pp. 32–34).

METHODS OF FAMILY DEMOGRAPHY

Descriptive Analyses

The bedrock of demographic data analysis on family change has been descriptive cross-sectional and trend analysis of family structures and processes, most often using census or survey data. The field of demography has its own tool kit full of measures and methods that are suited to the study of family change. Measures of age and age-related processes figure prominently; change is understood as reflecting age, period, or cohort processes or effects—that is, explanations of change emphasize aging of the population (or life-course change of individuals); broad, sweeping societal or time period effects; and/or the replacement of older cohorts by successively younger birth cohorts with different life experiences. An indispensable measure in family demography, as in other types of demography, is the rate—the number of people experiencing an event out of the population "at risk" of experiencing that event. Another important tool for examining family change is decomposition, in which family change is empirically separated into components: the proportion of change attributable to shifts in population composition versus the proportion caused by change in the likelihood that some family event, such as marriage, occurs.

The measurement of family and fertility transitions in surveys such as the National Longitudinal Survey of Youth, the National Survey of Family Growth, the National Survey of Families and Households, and the Survey of Income and Program Participation and the development of event history data analysis techniques have resulted in an explosion of analyses of the timing of family transitions and the duration of various family statuses over the life course. Measures include duration of time (or person years or months) spent in certain states, such as married and living with a spouse or living in a single-parent family. These measures and methods create a sound empirical foundation for theory building and causal interpretation.

Suppose the goal is to theorize why people are not marrying. Family demographers use these measures and methods to ascertain whether the likelihood of marrying is indeed declining before they develop theories aimed at accounting for the reasons marriage is becoming less popular. If a decline in the number of marriages can be explained by other demographic factors, such as a change in the typical age at marriage, then a grand theory explaining why marriage is no longer valued may be pointless. Given the goal of starting from a firm descriptive foundation, the demographic perspective embodies a tendency to think in terms of rates and composition and a desire to separate these two components in explanations of change.

Demographers often standardize for age composition in order to isolate "true" or "real" rates of behavioral change. In the example of marriage, if the number of first marriages decreases in the United States between two time points, does this change represent a decline in the popularity of marriage? In order to answer this question, one must first determine whether the size of the population eligible to enter, or "at risk" of entering, first marriage has decreased or changed in some other important way that has caused marriages to decrease. To accomplish this task, demographers start with a rate that takes into account the population at risk of actually experiencing the event (e.g., the number of first marriages per 1,000 never-married adults, instead of all adults; or the first marriage rate of never-married females ages 20 to 29, instead of all ages). If the *rate* of first marriage declines between two time points, the evidence that the popularity of marriage may be declining is stronger than if only the number of first marriages declines.

● *SPOTLIGHT ON METHODS*

DOES MARRIAGE MAKE PEOPLE HAPPIER? MARRIAGE, COHABITATION, AND TRAJECTORIES IN WELL-BEING

Kelly Musick, *University of Southern California*

Marriage does indeed improve well-being. According to a review of the evidence by Waite and Gallagher (2000): "In contemporary folklore, marriage may represent the end of the period of happy, carefree youth. But science tends to confirm Grandma's wisdom: On the whole, man was not meant to live alone, and neither was woman. Marriage makes people happier" (p. 77). A growing number of U.S. policy makers clearly agree with this assessment and have increased the attention and resources devoted to marriage promotion.

(continued)

Reports based on survey data are consistent: On average, married men and women score higher on measures of psychological well-being, health, and the quality of social relationships. But are these benefits unique to marriage? Are they stable over time? Relatively little attention is paid to the changes that take place when people move into marriage or cohabitation or, especially, to the trajectories people follow through different stages of couple relationships. The tendency to focus on average differences between the married and the unmarried fails to address why marriage matters, for whom, and for how long.

Early work on the benefits of marriage was based on snapshots of both married and unmarried persons; recent studies incorporate longitudinal designs and more detailed information on living arrangements. Evidence is consistent on the benefits of marriage relative to living alone, but whether benefits are unique to legal marriage is an open question. The association between marriage and well-being may have more to do with intimate relationships—specifically, the *quality* of intimate relationships—than with marriage per se (e.g., Gove, Hughes, & Style, 1983; Ross, 1995). Studies comparing long-lived marriages with short-lived cohabitations may confound the benefits of marriage with the quality of longer-term relationships.

In my ongoing work with Larry Bumpass, we aim to unravel further the associations among marriage, psychological well-being, health, and social relationships (Musick & Bumpass, 2003). We have moved away from static descriptions of single, cohabiting, and married men and women and are examining transitions from being single into cohabitation and marriage as well as trajectories within relationships over time. The life-course perspective provides an overarching framework for our analysis, linking our longitudinal design and the timing and sequencing of life events. We are using panel data from the National Survey of Families and Households to examine how changes in well-being are associated with changes in union status from one wave of data collection to the next. This methodological approach, called a *change score model,* borrows from the experimental method. In the language of experiments, we start with single men and women and divide our sample into a "control" group that remains single and two "treatment" groups that either marry or cohabit by wave 2. Comparing well-being across these three groups gives us the estimated effects of marriage and cohabitation.

To date, we have found more similarities than differences in the effects of marriage and cohabitation on various indicators of well-being: Coresidential partnerships appear to confer benefits irrespective of their legal form. Trajectories over time, however, suggest that these benefits may be short-lived. Recent unions provide relatively large boosts in happiness, health, and relationships; those more than 3 years in duration provide relatively small boosts. As Bianchi and Casper note in Chapter 4, paying attention to variation within the categories "married" and "unmarried" thus sheds light on the "meaning, value, and nature" of marriage and cohabitation. Our results support the sociological notion that institutionalized commitment adds value to relationships, but they also suggest that many of the benefits of marriage extend to informal coresidential relationships. Further, they show that not all marriages last. That half of all marriages end in divorce is perhaps the clearest, most convincing evidence that the benefits of marriage are neither universal nor always for life. ●

The inferential leap is still great, however, because most demographic behaviors, marriage included, are closely related to age and so are sensitive to shifts in the timing of events in individuals' lives. In the marriage example, the rate of first marriage for women in their 20s could decline either because more women remain single throughout their lifetimes or because a greater proportion of women are postponing marriage beyond age 30, perhaps because they are consumed by other activities in their 20s, such as finishing their schooling and getting established in the labor market before they marry. The conclusion that marriage is becoming less popular is supported more readily if the former behavior, more lifetime singlehood, is occurring rather than if the latter behavior, marrying at later ages, is driving down the marriage rate for young women (Oppenheimer, 1997). Hence family demographers are quite attentive to changes in the age patterning of behaviors and to the importance of understanding the effects of shifts in age structure.

Low fertility offers another illustration. "Tempo," or timing, effects are often estimated in the family demographic literature on fertility. Suppose there is no change in lifetime fertility—most women have children, and the societal average is two children per woman. If women in their 20s begin postponing childbearing, it will appear as if fertility is dropping, but this change will be only temporary, lasting until those women age through their childbearing years and the shift to later childbearing is complete in the population. Thus the timing of family demographic events has an important influence on how demographers interpret changes.

These examples show that accounting for family change is complex. This is why demographers, like ethnographers, spend so much time in the beginning of their research on rich description. Description is not the end goal, but standards are high for how much one must know before one travels very far down the road of conceptualization and explanation.

Causal Analyses

Family demography has increasingly moved toward examining the *why* and *how* of family change, incorporating the theoretical perspectives discussed above. In the past three decades, a number of panel surveys have been developed to gather data on families, including the National Survey of Families and Households, the Panel Study of Income Dynamics, the Survey of Income and Program Participation, the National Longitudinal Study of Adolescent Health (known as Add Health), the Fragile Families and Child Well-Being Study, Welfare, and Children and Families. In addition to these, various labor force and educational cohort studies have been conducted. Compared with the data available to demographers previously, the data gathered in these studies include many more "explanatory" variables and provide researchers with prospective sequencing information that is better suited to attempts to draw inferences of causality.

However, the field is now at a crossroads, with opinions diverging widely concerning exactly what evidence one needs to support assertions that causal relationships exist. On the one hand, there is increased circumspection concerning the difficulty of establishing causal claims, which has resulted in a diffusion of methods into the field from economics to approximate the effects of randomized treatment-control experimental designs using nonexperimental data. On the other hand, many demographers have noted the limits of statistical approaches for establishing causality and determining mechanisms of family change, and this has led to increased interest in interpretive, qualitative, anthropological approaches for ascertaining meanings and understanding "culture."

In their contribution to a recent symposium on causal analysis in the population sciences, Bachrach and McNicoll (2003) note that even descriptive findings invite causal interpretation. In family demography, in fact in demography writ large, as in all social sciences, causes are believed to exist but cannot be observed directly. Statistics don't prove causation, as these authors point out; "rather, conclusions about causal effects depend . . . on interpretation, theorizing, or assumptions that are brought into play along with empirical data or observations" (p. 444). They go on to observe that "the problem of causal analysis has always been one of combining observation with theory in order to extract understanding" (p. 446).

As family demography has moved to the use of survey data from panel studies, the tools of causal analysis have shifted from standard descriptive tools of calculation of rates, development of appropriate denominators of the "at risk" population for those rates, and the standardization of rates for age and other relevant attributes of the population to sophisticated statistical modeling techniques for studying change with longitudinal data. Event history models and fixed effects estimation techniques are standard in quantitative analyses of family demographic behavior. Researchers have adapted an arsenal of techniques from the statistical and econometric literature, with the underlying approach based on the idea that to assess causality, one must consider the counterfactual. According to economist Robert Moffitt (2003, p. 448), the counterfactual notion is that whenever one observes an actor's outcome and wants to associate it with a precipitating event, to establish that causal link one must consider the unobserved outcome, the path not chosen. Because an individual cannot simultaneously both choose and not choose an outcome (e.g., marry and not marry), the counterfactual is unobservable. Hence one must ultimately rely on a combination of empirical tests that are interpreted through assumptions, "justified or rationalized on the basis of a priori argument, outside evidence, intuition, theory, or some other informal means," to understand (family demographic) behaviors (p. 449).

Suppose a researcher thinks that religiosity increases the likelihood that a couple will marry rather than cohabit. The researcher cannot randomly assign the "treatment," religiosity, to individuals—individuals develop their own levels of religiosity, and a preference for religious involvement may be associated with other differences that might affect the likelihood of a person's choosing marriage over cohabitation. Thus it is difficult to determine whether it is religiosity or some other unmeasured differences between couples that propel a couple to marry rather than cohabit.

Much of family demographic research has taken a direct approach, with researchers trying to measure other factors that might covary and predict the outcome of interest. However, demographers have become increasingly circumspect about causal language in this instance because it is difficult to be sure that one has observed all of the important sources of variation. Increasingly, demographers are adopting methods from economics that attempt to correct for unobserved, endogenous variation that might affect results and limit their ability to assign causality. Moffitt (2003) and Smith (2003) offer discussions and critiques of these approaches—variously known as instrumental variables approaches, "difference in difference" methods, twin and sibling models that use within-family variation, matching methods, and natural experiments—and both of them assert that none satisfies the conditions of causal analysis and many run the risk of focusing so much attention on internal validity that external validity, or the generalizability of findings to a population, is seriously compromised. This leads Moffitt (2003), among others, to suggest that in developing theories of causation about family demographic behaviors, scholars should use a synthesis of methods, drawing on formal theory as well as informal ethnographic accounts and exploration, as well as a synthesis of evidence and literatures from a number of disciplinary fields and approaches.

There is also expanding interest among family demographers in the interpretive approach to assessing meaning that is used in cultural anthropology. Fricke (2003) emphasizes frameworks of meaning and a focus on coherence in the elements of meaning and culture in the development of causal frames. Causal analysis is always a blend of observation and interpretation, especially when human behaviors are the focus of the analysis, as humans are themselves self-reflective, interpretive beings. Hence anthropologists have joined demographic survey teams in many studies conducted in developing countries. Demographers are also increasingly incorporating observational methods borrowed from anthropology into studies of family behaviors in the United States, such as examinations of cohabitation and its meaning (Manning & Smock, 2003; Sassler & Jobe, 2002); how family dynamics alter decisions about work and welfare in low-income populations (Burton & Lein, 2003); how and when fathers are involved in early, nonmarital births (e.g., analyses of the Fragile Families Study at Princeton); and why marriages are not formed in low-income populations (e.g., Katherine Edin's qualitative component of the Fragile Families Study, called TLC).

CONCLUSION

Family demography has traditionally been concerned with the structure and process of family change. Beginning with careful description is the predilection of proponents of the family demographic approach, but description is not their end goal. Rather, their goals are to understand the meanings behind the observed changes and to develop theory about the mechanisms that lead to alteration in union formation and dissolution, childbearing and child rearing, intergenerational linkages, and the intersection of work and family domains.

Demography has always been an interdisciplinary field. Family demography in particular has been influenced by a number of perspectives, from sociology to economics and, increasingly, anthropology, biology, and psychology. An overarching theory of "ideational" shifts, second demographic transition theory, has influenced family demographic thinking, along with an increasing affinity for the life-course perspective. Theoretical developments and empirical methods in family demography have been influenced greatly in the past few decades by economics, with attention to processes of decision making and bargaining within families. However, the field may well be at a crossroads today—as methods have become increasingly econometrically sophisticated, family demographers are also realizing the limits of such methods for helping them to understand causal processes. This heightens demographers' appreciation of the need for theory that will enable them to make causal inferences as well as opens the door to the use of more interpretive methods in the study of family behaviors.

CASE STUDY

STRENGTHS AND RESILIENCE IN CHINESE IMMIGRANT FAMILIES: AN INITIAL EFFORT OF INQUIRY

Yan Ruth Xia, *University of Nebraska–Lincoln*

Zhi George Zhou, *First Data Corporation*

Xiaolin Xie, *Northern Illinois University*

The landscape of American demography has changed dramatically since the middle of the 20th century. Research indicates that the number of immigrants to the United States will continue to increase rapidly over the next three decades (Day, 1996). As the immigrant population grows, so does the necessity for family researchers to build theories to describe and explain the experiences of the new immigrant families. The research that we present here is aimed at expanding the knowledge base in relation to the resilience of newcomers in the Midwest; this study involved the use of both qualitative (holistic) and quantitative (scientific) methods. Our specific objectives in this case study are to identify the strengths of new Chinese immigrant families and to add to the family strengths model.

FAMILY STRENGTHS MODEL

Stinnett and DeFrain (1985) identified six strengths in their study of Caucasian American families: affection and appreciation, commitment, positive communication, ability to cope with crisis, time together, and a sense of spiritual belief. Studies of family strengths with other cultural samples remain patchy. Xie, DeFrain, Meredith, and Combs (1996) found that families in China perceive a sense of harmony as being a family strength. Nilufer, Larson, and Parul (2000) conducted a similar study in India and identified among Indian families five of the six strengths that Stinnett and DeFrain found among Caucasian Americans as well as three additional strengths: harmony, support and overall well-being, and cooperation and dependability.

METHODS

Because of the scarcity of existing research on the family strengths of new Chinese immigrant families, we began our inquiry with semistructured interviews to examine the perceptions of our research questions among new immigrants from this cultural group. Subsequently, we developed a survey questionnaire based on the strengths identified by the initial interviewees. As a part of the theory-building process, we then conducted a pilot survey. Although it would have been desirable to use structural equation modeling

Authors' Note: The present research was partially funded by the University of Nebraska–Lincoln Layman Award and by a contribution of the University of Nebraska Agricultural Research Division. We want to express our sincere thanks to Dr. John DeFrain, University of Nebraska–Lincoln, for his consultation on this study.

CASE STUDY *continued*

for confirmative factor analysis to determine the construct validity of the measures and test the theoretical model (Bandalos, 1996), we employed exploratory factor analysis owing to the small size of the pilot sample.

Studying immigrant families entails greater challenges than studying nonimmigrant populations. One particular challenge with immigrant families is to secure their participation in the research. Most newcomers are dealing with financial instability, lack of friends and other social supports, discrimination, language and communication barriers, and overwhelmingly unfamiliar social institutions and bureaucracies, such as those dealing with immigration law, schools, health care, and banking (Pipher, 2002). Family members also have to redefine and adjust their roles, responsibilities, and relationships with each other. All too often, these challenges leave them little time or energy to attend to issues that are not essential for survival. Thus taking part in research studies is not a priority. Moreover, it is uncommon in many cultures (including Chinese culture) for individuals to reveal personal information to persons who are not family members or friends, so it can be difficult for researchers to establish trusting relationships with potential participants from such cultures. Given these problems, the recruitment strategies that researchers commonly use to engage study participants may not work well with new immigrant and minority populations, so subject recruitment and data collection can be a lengthy process. For this study, we began building relationships with the Chinese immigrant community prior to data collection; as Chinese Americans, we were able to become involved in the Chinese church and Chinese school as well as various community events. We also offered workshops for the newcomers on parenting, marital relationships, communication, and health care issues.

Another challenge that researchers face when studying immigrant and minority populations is the need to develop culturally sensitive measures. For this study, our success in understanding and describing the resilience of new immigrant families relied on the cultural sensitivity of the measures used. We chose to develop measures by gathering information on immigrants' perceptions of their family strengths through semistructured interviews rather than use existing measures developed for studies of nonimmigrant families. Ideally, the validity and reliability of new measures should be tested with a random sample. However, because of the challenges of collecting data among immigrant populations (as discussed above), researchers studying such groups are likely to find that random sampling and the use of mail surveys result in very low response rates and thus low representative samples. An alternative method is to use "snowball" recruiting followed by survey interviews.

We identified as new immigrants 40 Chinese who had arrived in the United States in the past 20 years and recruited in three midsize cities in Illinois and Nebraska for the initial interviews. Later, we surveyed 94 new Chinese immigrants using the pilot questionnaire (see the table for details on the characteristics of the participants). Unlike the early Chinese settlers, who came to the United States as cheap labor, most new Chinese immigrants follow a path of seeking advanced degrees and establishing careers as professionals in America. The Chinese in our sample reflected this change in demographic characteristics.

RESULTS AND DISCUSSION

Based on our interviews, we were able to identify several major themes related to family strengths among the immigrants in our sample: family support, social support, communication, spiritual well-being, and the balancing of host and heritage cultures. We developed the Chinese Immigrant Family Strengths Survey to measure these five

Case Study

CASE STUDY *continued*

Chinese Immigrant Families: Characteristics of Study Participants

	Interviewees (N = 40)	Survey Participants (N = 81)
Age (years)		
Mean	37	28
Standard deviation	8	6
Gender (%)		
Female	62.5	64.7
Male	37.5	35.3
Years in United States		
Mean	8	11
Standard deviation	5	5
Marital status (%)		
Single	0	8.3
Married	100	86.9
Divorced and missing	0	4.8
Education (%)		
High school/GED	7.5	4.7
Bachelor's degree	20.0	21.2
Master's degree	42.5	24.7
Ph.D.	30.0	49.4

identified constructs. The survey utilized a 5-point Likert scale with 17 indicators that demonstrated high reliability ($\alpha = .80$). Except for the Social Support subscale ($\alpha = .50$), all the subscales showed good or acceptable internal consistency for exploratory study (Family Support, $\alpha = .81$, three indicators; Communication, $\alpha = .64$, three indicators; Balancing Cultures, $\alpha = .73$, four indicators; Spirituality, $\alpha = .61$, two indicators).

Exploratory factor analysis resulted in six principal components with eigenvalues above one. The six components accounted for more than 71% of the total variance. Thirteen indicators had factor loadings greater than .70, and four ranged from .50 to .65. Three components were the family strengths constructs of family support, spirituality, and communication. The multiple measures for each of them clustered, and each component was distinguished from the others, which

suggests empirical evidence for convergent and discriminant construct validity. However, the measures for social support and balancing home and host cultures were not well validated by the statistical results and should be revised.

An inspection of the five indicators on the Social Support subscale revealed that two of them were not worded in a culturally sensitive manner. These were items 5 and 6, which read, respectively, "We can disclose our difficulties to our friends" and "We seldom seek outside help when we have family problems." Keeping face by not airing one's dirty laundry in public is a traditional Chinese value. Higher scores on these items, showing reaching out for help, may indicate greater acceptance of American values, but not necessarily stronger social support as we had expected. These indicators may bear the intended meaning only for those respondents who are relatively assimilated into American culture. It may be that our own values and acculturation levels affected how we designed the meanings of the indicators.

Another observation may also shed some light on the low internal consistency we found. The results showed that the subscales in which all indicators were phrased positively yielded higher reliability (i.e., Family Support, $\alpha = .81$; Balancing Cultures, $\alpha = .73$), whereas those with indicators phrased both positively and negatively tended to have lower scores (Social Support, $\alpha = .50$; Spirituality, $\alpha = .61$; Communication, $\alpha = .64$). One explanation for this is that negative statements are not often used in Chinese Mandarin, and so items worded negatively may have been confusing to Chinese native speakers. Some of the survey participants provided written feedback indicating that they found the negative statements confusing; in addition, we noticed that some participants went back and forth in selecting their responses on these items. This example illustrates how important it is for researchers to go beyond techniques such as back translation (Riordan & Vandenberg, 1994) in their efforts to achieve cultural equivalence in measurement and examine culturally influenced processes such as communication patterns, language structure, and logical thinking as well as the values and acculturation levels of both participants and researchers.

Chinese immigrants, like other immigrants, experience stress engendered by migration (Xie, Xia, & Zhou, in press). Consistent with Stinnett and DeFrain's (1985) findings with Caucasian Americans,

the successful Chinese immigrant families in our sample reported communication and spirituality to be among their family strengths. The strength that we call *family support* in our study is similar to Stinnett and DeFrain's commitment and appreciation. Our study also revealed a family strength that is highly salient for immigrant families: the ability to build social support. As we have noted, migration entails disruption in the family's social environment, loss of social status and support, and feelings of loneliness and isolation, especially during the initial stage. To combat these negative effects, many immigrants strive to reestablish their social groups by becoming involved in ethnic associations and churches. The responses of the participants in this study clearly demonstrated the importance of social support.

In summary, the findings of this study, which utilized both qualitative and quantitative methods, delineate the family strengths of new Chinese immigrant families in the United States. Chinese immigrants represent a growing population that has received scant attention in the study of family strengths and in discussions of cultural sensitivity in methodology. The initial effort reported here, which resulted in a five-construct model, is one of very few to date that have focused on building a theoretical framework to describe Chinese immigrant family strengths. We will use the findings from this study to modify the Chinese Immigrant Family Strengths Survey in preparation for a future large-scale study designed to test the newly built model.

Case Study

DISCUSSION AND EXTENSION

FAMILY CHANGE:
DECLINE OR RESILIENCE?

Paul R. Amato, *Pennsylvania State University*

O f all the changes that Bianchi and Casper describe in Chapter 4, perhaps the most central—and the most controversial—is the transformation that has taken place in the status of marriage. Throughout most of American history, marriage was the fundamental social arrangement that provided structure and meaning in people's lives. Matrimony served as a marker for leaving the parental home, forming one's own household, becoming economically independent of parents, initiating regular sexual activity, and having children. The roles of husband and wife also provided scripts that guided and organized everyday activities such as breadwinning, household labor, and child rearing. Until relatively recently, the great majority of people in the United States married, married relatively early in the life course, and stayed continuously married until the death of one spouse.

But times have changed. The growing popularity of nonmarital cohabitation, the rise in age at first marriage, the increase in nonmarital births, and the continuing high divorce rate indicate that marriage has become a more voluntary and less permanent part of adult life now than it was in the recent past. Changes in public attitudes—involving more positive evaluations of single lifestyles and nonmarital cohabitation—also reflect a decline in the traditional centrality of marriage. After centuries of being the bedrock of the American family system, marriage is losing its privileged status and is becoming one lifestyle choice out of many.

THE FAMILY DECLINE PERSPECTIVE

Some scholars view the retreat from marriage and the corresponding spread of single-parent families as causes for alarm (Glenn, 1996; Popenoe, 1993; Waite & Gallagher, 2000; Whitehead, 1993; Wilson, 2002). According to the *family decline perspective*, American culture has become increasingly individualist, and people have become preoccupied with the unrestricted pursuit of personal happiness. In the past, Americans valued marriage primarily because it provided economic security and a stable environment for raising children. Today, however, most view marriage primarily as a vehicle for self-fulfillment. Because people no longer wish to be hampered by obligations to others, the level of commitment to institutions that require these obligations—such as marriage—has eroded. Consequently, many spouses are unwilling to stick together through the difficult times that arise in most marriages. Instead, marital commitment lasts only as long as both members of a couple are happy and feel that their needs are being met.

Advocates of the family decline perspective frequently cite research findings that show that growing up in a single-parent household is associated with a variety of problems for children, including conduct disorders, emotional disturbances, difficulties forming and maintaining friendships, delinquency, dropping out of school, and having nonmarital

DISCUSSION AND EXTENSION *continued*

births (Amato, 2001; McLanahan & Sandefur, 1994). Other scholars argue that the decline of marriage has created problems for society more generally. For example, Whitehead (1993) states: "Family diversity in the form of increasing numbers of single-parent and step-parent families does not strengthen the social fabric. It dramatically weakens and under-mines society, placing new burdens on schools, courts, prisons, and the welfare system" (p. 77). According to this view, the decline in lifelong marriage has contributed to a variety of social problems, including poverty, delinquency, violence, substance abuse, declining academic standards, and the erosion of neighborhoods and communities.

The cure for this problem, according to advocates of this perspective, is to create a cul-ture that is more supportive of marriage—a culture that values commitment (rather than liberty) and encourages people to accept responsibility for others, including their spouses and children. In terms of specific policies, advocates of this view have called for restrictions on unilateral no-fault divorce, public education programs focusing on the value of marriage, the introduction of courses on relationships skills and conflict resolution into school programs, and greater govern-ment funding for marriage counseling and premarital education services.

THE FAMILY RESILIENCE PERSPECTIVE

Other scholars reject the view that American culture has drifted toward greater individual-ism and selfishness in recent decades (Bengtson, Biblarz, & Roberts, 2002; Coontz, 1992; Demo, 1992; Skolnick, 1991; Stacey, 1996). These scholars also are skeptical of the validity of claims that the proportion of unsuccessful marriages in the population has increased. According to the *family resilience perspective,* marriages were as likely to be troubled in the past as they are in the present. Troubled marriages in the past remained "intact," however, because obtaining a divorce was time-consuming and expensive, and because divorced individuals were stigma-tized. Rather than view the rise in marital instability with alarm, advocates of the family resilience perspective point out that divorce provides a second chance at happiness for adults and an escape from dysfunctional and aversive home environments for many children. Moreover, because children can develop successfully in a variety of family structures, the spread of alternatives to mandatory lifelong marriage poses few prob-lems for the next generation. Feminist schol-ars, in particular, have argued that recent social change has strengthened rather than undermined the quality of intimate relation-ships. In this context, Stacey (1996) states that "changes in work, family, and sexual opportunities for women and men . . . open the prospect of introducing greater democ-racy, equality and choice than ever before into our most intimate relationships, espe-cially for women and members of sexual minorities" (p. 9).

According to the family resilience perspec-tive, poverty, unemployment, poorly funded schools, and lack of government services rep-resent more serious threats to the well-being of children than does the decline in two-parent families. Consequently, advocates of this view do not support policies that would restrict unilateral no-fault or promote mar-riage. Instead, these scholars argue that social policies should provide greater support to adults and children in all types of families and not privilege one form (lifelong marriage) over other arrangements.

Discussion and Extension

DISCUSSION AND EXTENSION *continued*

ASSESSING THE
TWO PERSPECTIVES

Although advocates of the family decline and resilience perspectives agree that marriage and family life in the United States changed dramatically during the second half of the 20th century, they disagree on whether these changes should be condemned (and reversed) or embraced (and supported). To a certain extent, their disagreement is based on their values—that is, on how the advocates of the two perspectives evaluate the relative importance of social stability versus individual liberty. Those who value security and tradition tend to believe that the unrestricted pursuit of self-interest has undermined marriage and the larger social order. In contrast, those who value individualism and freedom tend to believe that the erosion of traditional constraints on sexuality and marriage has increased Americans' potential for happiness and personal development. Because these perspectives are based partly on the values of those who hold them, it is not possible to decide between them entirely on the basis of new research. To a certain degree, these perspectives function as ideologies rather than as scientific frameworks.

Nevertheless, because these two perspectives include arguments based on empirical data, it is possible to evaluate evidence in favor of one or the other. For example, the family decline perspective assumes (a) that children's well-being has declined during the past 50 years, (b) that this decline is correlated with an increase in the proportion of children growing up in households without both biological parents, and (c) that this correlation persists after one controls for other relevant factors, such as changes in the economy. Unfortunately, a full test of these hypotheses has never been reported in the literature, partly because appropriate data are difficult to obtain.

Of course, it is likely that both perspectives contain elements of truth. Ultimately, we may learn that some changes in marriage and family life have been beneficial, whereas others have been harmful. Rather than uncritically accepting one perspective and rejecting the other, we must keep an open mind and follow empirical leads to their logical conclusions. Only then will we be in a position to devise policies and interventions that protect children and adults from the harmful changes that may have occurred while consolidating and strengthening the beneficial changes.

REFERENCES

Amato, P. R. (2001). Children of divorce in the 1990s: An update of the Amato and Keith (1991) "Meta-analysis." *Journal of Family Psychology, 15,* 355–370.

Bachrach, C., & McNicoll, G. (2003). Causal analysis in the population sciences: Introduction. *Population and Development Review, 29,* 442–447.

Bandalos, D. (1996). Exploratory and confirmatory factor analysis. In J. Stevens (Ed.), *Applied multivariate statistics for the social sciences* (pp. 389–420). Mahwah, NJ: Lawrence Erlbaum.

Becker, G. S. (1960). An economic analysis of fertility. In A. J. Coale (Ed.), *Demographic and economic change in developed countries* (pp. 209–231). Princeton, NJ: Princeton University Press.

Becker, G. S. (1974). A theory of marriage. In T. W. Schultz (Ed.), *Economics of the family: Marriage, children, and human capital* (pp. 299–344). Chicago: University of Chicago Press.

Becker, G. S. (1981). *A treatise on the family.* Cambridge, MA: Harvard University Press.

Becker, G. S. (1991). *A treatise on the family* (Rev. ed.). Cambridge, MA: Harvard University Press.

Becker, G. S., Landes, E. M., & Michael, R. T. (1977). An economic analysis of marital instability. *Journal of Political Economy, 85,* 1141–1187.

Bengtson, V. L. (2001). Beyond the nuclear family: The increasing importance of multigenerational bonds. *Journal of Marriage and Family, 63,* 1–16.

Bengtson, V. L., & Allen, K. R. (1993). The life course perspective applied to families over time. In P. Boss, W. J. Doherty, R. LaRossa, W. R. Schumm, & S. K. Steinmetz (Eds.), *Sourcebook of family theories and methods: A contextual approach* (pp. 469–499). New York: Plenum.

Bengtson, V. L., Biblarz, T. J., & Roberts, R. E. L. (2002). *How families still matter: A longitudinal study of youths in two generations.* New York: Cambridge University Press.

Bengtson, V. L., Rosenthal, C. J., & Burton, L. M. (1990). Families and aging: Diversity and heterogeneity. In R. H. Binstock & L. K. George (Eds.), *Handbook of aging and the social sciences* (3rd ed., pp. 263–287). New York: Academic Press.

Bergstrom, T. (1997). A survey of theories of the family. In M. R. Rosenzweig & O. Stark (Eds.), *Handbook of population and family economics.* Amsterdam: North-Holland.

Bianchi, S. M. (2000). Maternal employment and time with children: Dramatic change or surprising continuity? *Demography, 37,* 401–414.

Blau, F., Ferber, M. A., & Winkler, A. E. (1998). *The economics of women, men and work* (3rd ed.). Upper Saddle River, NJ: Prentice Hall.

Burton, L. M., & Lein, L. (2003, June). *The walls of Jericho: Poverty, work, and mothering.* Paper presented at the conference Workforce/Workplace Mismatch? Work, Family, Health and Well-Being, Washington, DC.

Casper, L. M., & Bianchi, S. M. (2002). *Change and continuity in the American family.* Thousand Oaks, CA: Sage.

Casper, L. M., & O'Connell, M. (2000). Family and household composition of the population. In M. J. Anderson (Ed.), *Encyclopedia of the U.S. Census.* Washington, DC: CQ.

Coontz, S. (1992). *The way we never were: American families and the nostalgia trap.* New York: Basic Books.

Daly, M., & Wilson, M. I. (2000). The evolutionary psychology of marriage and divorce. In L. J. Waite, C. Bachrach, M. Hindin, E. Thomson, & A. Thornton (Ed.), *The ties that bind: Perspectives on marriage and cohabitation* (pp. 91–110). New York: Aldine de Gruyter.

Day, J. C. (1996). *Population projections of the United States by age, sex, race, and Hispanic origin: 1995 to 2050* (Current Population Reports No. P25-1130). Washington, DC: U.S. Bureau of the Census.

Demo, D. H. (1992). Parent-child relations: Assessing recent changes. *Journal of Marriage and the Family, 54,* 104–118.

Easterlin, R. (1973). Relative economic status and the American fertility swing. In E. Sheldon (Ed.), *Family economic behavior.* Philadelphia: J. B. Lippincott.

Elder, G. H., Jr. (1985). *Life course dynamics: Trajectories and transition: 1968–80.* Ithaca, NY: Cornell University Press.

Fricke, T. E. (2003). Culture and causality: An anthropological comment. *Population and Development Review, 29,* 470–479.

Glenn, N. D. (1996). Values, attitudes, and the state of American marriage. In D. Popenoe, J. B. Elshtain, & D. Blankenhorn (Eds.), *Promises to keep: Decline and renewal of marriage in America* (pp. 15–33). Lanham, MD: Rowman & Littlefield.

Glick, P. C. (1975). A demographer looks at American families. *Journal of Marriage and the Family, 37,* 15–26.

Goldscheider, F. K. (1995). Interpolating demography with families and households. *Demography, 32,* 471–480.

Gove, W. R., Hughes, M., & Style, C. B. (1983). Does marriage have positive effects on the psychological well-being of the individual? *Journal of Health and Social Behavior, 24,* 122–131.

Lesthaeghe, R. (1995). The second demographic transition in Western countries: An interpretation. In K. O. Mason & A.-M. Jensen (Eds.), *Gender and family change in industrialised countries* (pp. 17–62). Oxford: Clarendon.

Lundberg, S., & Pollak, R. A. (1996). Bargaining and distribution in marriage. *Journal of Economic Perspectives, 10*(4), 139–158.

Manning, W., & Smock, P. (2003). *Measuring and modeling cohabitation: New perspectives from qualitative data.* Unpublished manuscript.

McDonald, P. F. (2000). Gender equity in theories of fertility transition. *Population and Development Review, 26,* 427–439.

McLanahan, S. S., & Sandefur, G. (1994). *Growing up with a single parent: What hurts, what helps.* Cambridge, MA: Harvard University Press.

Mincer, J., & Polachek, S. (1974). Family investments in human capital: Earnings of women. In T. W. Schultz (Ed.), *Economics of the family: Marriage, children, and human capital* (pp. 397–429). Chicago: University of Chicago Press.

Moen, P., Dempster-McClain, D., & Williams, R. M., Jr. (1992). Successful aging: A life-course perspective on women's multiple roles and health. *American Journal of Sociology, 97,* 1612–1638.

Moffitt, R. (2003). Causal analysis in population research: An economist's perspective. *Population and Development Review, 29,* 448–457.

Morgan, S. P., Bianchi, S. M., DiPrete, T. A., Hotz, V. J., Sanders, S., Seltzer, J. A., et al. (2003). *Designing new models for explaining family change.* Proposal submitted to the National Institute of Child Health and Human Development.

Musick, K., & Bumpass, L. (2003). *CDE colloquium to honor Larry Wu: Cohabitation, marriage, and trajectories in well-being and relationships* (CDE Working Paper No. 2003–25). Madison: University of Wisconsin.

Nilufer, M., Larson, J., & Parul, B. (2000). East-Indian college students' perceptions of family strengths. *Journal of Comparative Family Studies, 31,* 407–425.

Oppenheimer, V. K. (1988). A theory of marriage timing. *American Journal of Sociology, 94,* 563–591.

Oppenheimer, V. K. (1997). Women's employment and the gain to marriage: The specialization and trading model. *Annual Review of Sociology, 23,* 431–453.

Pipher, M. (2002). *The middle of everywhere: The world's refugees come to our town.* New York: Harcourt.

Popenoe, D. (1993). American family decline 1960–1990: A review and appraisal. *Journal of Marriage and the Family, 55,* 527–556.

Riordan, C. M., & Vandenberg, R. J. (1994). A central question in cross-cultural research: Do employees of different cultures interpret work-related measures in an equivalent manner? *Journal of Management, 20,* 643–671.

Ross, C. E. (1995). Reconceptualizing marital status as a continuum of social attachment. *Journal of Marriage and the Family, 57,* 129–140.

Sassler, S., & Jobe, T. (2002, May). *To live together . . . as man and wife? The process of entering into cohabiting unions.* Paper presented at the annual meeting of the Population Association of America, Atlanta, GA.

Sayer, L., & Bianchi, S. M. (2000). Women's economic independence and the probability of divorce. *Journal of Family Issues, 21,* 906–943.

Skolnick A. S. (1991). *Embattled paradise: The American family in an age of uncertainty.* New York: Basic Books.

Smith, H. L. (2003). Some thoughts on causation as it relates to demography and population studies. *Population and Development Review, 29,* 458–469.

Stacey, J. (1996). *In the name of the family: Rethinking family values in the postmodern age.* Boston: Beacon.

Stinnett, N., & DeFrain, J. (1985). *Secrets of strong families.* Boston: Little, Brown.

Sweet, J. A., & Bumpass, L. L. (1987). *American families and households.* New York: Russell Sage.

Teachman, J. D. (1993). Family and household research: Life course events. In D. J. Bogue, E. E. Arriaga, D. L. Anderton, & G. W. Rumsey (Eds.), *Readings in population research methodology: Vol. 4. Nuptiality, migration, household, and family research* (pp. 15-1–15-14). New York: United Nations Population Fund.

van da Kaa, D. J. (1987). Europe's second demographic transition. *Population Bulletin, 42*(1).

Waite, L. J., & Gallagher, M. (2000). *The case for marriage: Why married people are happier, healthier, and better off financially.* New York: Doubleday.

Whitehead, B. D. (1993, April). Dan Quayle was right. *Atlantic Monthly,* pp. 47–84.

Willis, R. J. (1987). What have we learned from the economics of the family? *American Economic Review, 77,* 68–71

Wilson, J. Q. (2002). *The marriage problem: How our culture has weakened families.* New York: HarperCollins.

Xie, X., DeFrain, J., Meredith, W., & Combs, R. (1996). Family strengths as perceived by university students and government employees in the People's Republic of China. *International Journal of Sociology of the Family, 26*(2), 7–27.

Xie, X., Xia, Y. R., & Zhou, Z. G. (in press). Strengths and stress in Chinese immigrant families: A qualitative study. *Great Plains Research.*

Five

FAMILY COMPOSITION AND FAMILY TRANSITIONS

David H. Demo, *University of North Carolina at Greensboro*

William S. Aquilino, *University of Wisconsin–Madison*

Mark A. Fine, *University of Missouri–Columbia*

Family composition in the United States is marked by increasing diversity and change. Brandon and Bumpass (2001) have estimated that less than 50% of American children live in "traditional nuclear families," defined as families that have two biological parents married to each other, full siblings only, and no other household members. Family forms continue to proliferate, and children's living arrangements increasingly include unmarried parents, stepfamilies, and multigenerational households. Cohabitation, by both opposite-sex and same-sex couples, has become more prevalent, and the proportion of cohabiting households with children has increased (see Bianchi & Casper, Chapter 4, this volume). Many gay and lesbian parents are raising children. The number of grandparents raising their grandchildren has increased dramatically over the past 30 years.

In addition to the widely variable, pluralistic nature of postmodern family forms, individuals are also increasingly likely to experience fluid, shifting family configurations, movement of relatives in and out of the household, and disruptions in family relationships over the life course.

In this chapter, we describe the nature and consequences of family composition and family transitions for both children and adults. Our objectives are (a) to describe prominent theoretical frameworks for conceptualizing family composition and family transitions, (b) to discuss and assess research evidence on the consequences of family composition for family members, (c) to suggest theoretical directions and methodological tools for investigating family transitions over time, and (d) to advocate for greater attention to family diversity in the study of family composition and change.

Authors' Note: We gratefully acknowledge the helpful comments and suggestions of the editors, the anonymous reviewers, and the students in the fall 2003 graduate seminar in contemporary families at the University of North Carolina at Greensboro.

DEFINING FAMILY AND
FAMILY COMPOSITION

Expanding on the definition used by the U.S. Bureau of the Census, Allen, Fine, and Demo (2000) define a family as "characterized by two or more persons related by birth, adoption, marriage, or choice. Families are . . . defined by socioemotional ties and enduring responsibilities, particularly in terms of one or more members' dependence on others for support and nurturance" (p. 1). We concur with this definition and note that it implies that families are defined primarily by long-term committed relationships, responsibilities, and ongoing support, rather than exclusively by marriage, law, or biological ties.

It is important to draw a number of theoretically relevant distinctions involving the definition of family. First, individual family members' definitions ("insiders' definitions") of who is (and who is not) in their family may differ from those of others (e.g., "outsiders"), including researchers, who attempt to define who is in another individual's family. Thus there are both "subjective" and "objective" definitions of family, and we believe that, depending on the goals of the inquiry, each type of definition has its merits.

Second, "household" needs to be distinguished from "family." The term *household* refers to a residential unit and the individuals who live in that specific home. A family may extend across multiple households, and, in some circumstances, not everyone in a household may be considered to be in the same family. Defining a family by who lives in a particular residential unit may not accurately represent who is actually considered to be in the family. When we consider family transitions, we need to be clear about whether we are examining transitions involving a household or with the family as a whole. Whenever possible, in the following discussion we will refer to changes involving the family as a whole.

Third, a distinction needs to be drawn between individual-level and family-level definitions. At the individual level, definitions of family can differ for members within what outsiders may consider to be a family unit. For example, one child in the unit may consider her mother to be a member of her family, whereas another child in the unit may consider that same woman, who is a stepmother to him, to be outside of his family. Thus the family may be constituted quite differently for different members of the unit. At the family level, because of the different meanings of family for different individuals within the unit, it is difficult to categorize families into types or categories that have the same meaning to all individuals within that unit.

Fourth, it should be noted that individuals who are physically absent may still be considered family members. For example, a nonresidential parent who has no contact with his or her children is not physically available, but some individuals within the unit might still consider that parent to be a member of the family. Some might even consider a deceased individual, because of his or her continued importance to family functioning, to be a member of the family. Considerable research has shown that individuals who are physically absent but still psychologically present in the minds of at least some individuals within the unit can have important influence on individual and family functioning.

Finally, membership in a family is not restricted to individuals who have harmonious relationships with others in the unit. Family members may have conflictual and/or distant relationships with each other, but they may consider themselves to be members of the same family nevertheless, because their lives are intertwined in important ways.

For the reasons noted above, scholars need to conceptualize family composition inclusively. A person's family may extend across generations, households, and marital, legal, and blood ties.

CONCEPTUALIZING
FAMILY COMPOSITION
AND TRANSITIONS OVER TIME

Scholars have used several theories to conceptualize family composition, how it changes over time, and how these changes affect family members. Below, we review three prominent theories, each of which contributes unique insights regarding family composition and transitions: the life-course perspective, the risk and resilience perspective, and the family ecology perspective.

The Life-Course Perspective

The life-course perspective is a valuable tool for conceptualizing changes in family composition over time and for identifying the consequences of those changes for individual family members. Elder (1994) summarizes four central themes of the life-course perspective: the timing of lives, the interdependence of lives over the life span, human agency, and the interplay of human lives and historical times.

The timing of lives refers to the social meanings of age and the many ways that social roles, family events, turning points, and life-course pathways are age related. The impact that a particular family experience (e.g., divorce) has on a family member depends on the individual's age, generation, and life stage. Further, social expectations, values, and beliefs guide individual and family decisions, and also influence how family members and others respond. Thus some family events are considered "on time" (e.g., a marriage occurring after young adults have completed formal education), whereas others are regarded as "early" (e.g., teenage childbearing), "delayed" (e.g., postponed parenthood), "late," or "ill timed." Expectations regarding such events also vary by social class, race/ethnicity, gender, and sexual orientation (Bengtson & Allen, 1993; Demo & Allen, 1996).

A second theme emphasized in the life-course framework is the concept of linked or interdependent lives. In studying family composition and family transitions, scholars have noted that parents' and children's lives are linked through the relationship that parents have with each other, the interactions between parents and children, the relationships among siblings and extended family members, and the impacts that each family member's resources, personal characteristics, and actions have on other members of the family. Although most intergenerational

research to date has concentrated on parental influences on children's development, family influences are better conceptualized as multidirectional and reciprocal.

The third theme of the life-course perspective is human agency, or individuals' ability to make their own decisions, to be efficacious, and to make things happen in their lives. Operating within the constraints of the family and larger society, individuals activate their own skills and resources to choose social relationships, roles, and environments that appeal to them and that are consistent with their self-concepts (Clausen, 1993; Demo, 1992). Further, individuals and larger family units have the capacity to act as agents in responding to, minimizing, or even averting personal or family misfortunes (Hareven, 1987).

The fourth and least studied theme in life-course analyses is the interplay between historical circumstances and personal experiences. The objective here is to understand the intersection between social and historical experiences and personal biography (Elder, 1977; Mills, 1959). Economic opportunities, cultural values, and family experiences are influenced strongly by historical conditions; thus we would expect variations in the life courses of individuals born in different historical periods (e.g., parents who grew up in the 1960s and their children growing up in the 21st century). Smaller differences in historical experiences (e.g., between siblings) may also have profound developmental consequences.

The Risk and Resilience Perspective

Risk involves exposure to experiences or conditions that raise the probability of negative outcomes for individuals, dyads, or groups. For example, children's exposure to hostile, stressful, or otherwise negative family experiences may elevate the probability of developmental or adjustment problems. Resilience is the ability of an individual or group to overcome life's challenges, to rebound from adversity, and to grow stronger as a result of dealing with crises (Walsh, 1998). The risk and resilience perspective posits that an individual's reaction to a stressor reflects an interaction between the nature of the stressor and the individual's capacity to respond (Margolin, Oliver, & Medina, 2001). In research on family composition, the risk-resilience framework poses the question of why some children exposed to family composition transitions appear to be affected adversely whereas others show successful adaptation despite the difficult situations they confront. The risk-resilience approach places the theoretical focus on understanding *diversity* in parents' and children's responses to the challenges posed by family disruption, life in a single-parent household, remarriage, and other family transitions (Hetherington, 1999).

In the risk-resilience framework, differential outcomes to apparently similar stressors result from interactions among risk factors, risk mechanisms, and protective factors (Margolin et al., 2001). *Risk factors* raise the likelihood of negative developmental outcomes (e.g., parental divorce or family economic hardship). *Risk mechanisms,* or vulnerabilities, explain how and why a person is susceptible to a stressor, including personal characteristics and attributes of the stressor (Rutter, 1994). *Protective factors* promote resilience; such factors include individual characteristics, family resources, interactional processes, and environmental-contextual factors that buffer the effects of risk. A family resilience approach emphasizes identification and enhancement of the coping resources—the social, economic, psychological, emotional, and physical assets— that enable individuals and families to overcome disruptive challenges (Walsh, 1998). Important issues include how well families can marshal these resources to respond adaptively to crises and the extent to which families' coping mechanisms are functional.

Much of the extant research on family transitions has focused on linking the experience of particular stressors to developmental outcomes. The risk and resilience perspective is conceptually based on the notion that risk and protective factors interact in their effects on adaptive responses to stressors (i.e., the effects that a risk factor has on adaptive responses may vary depending on the level and type of protective factors present in the family), but researchers have too often considered only the individual (additive) effects that risk

and protective factors have on adaptation. The risk-resilience framework encourages researchers to move away from strictly comparative research designs (e.g., studies using the deficit model, comparing the outcomes for children in a variety of family configurations to children in first-married families) in favor of designs that explore the variability in responses among individuals who experience the same type of stressor.

The Family Ecology Perspective

A primary feature of ecological theories is the premise that development, for individuals and for families, is contextual. According to Bronfenbrenner (1986), individual development is affected by five types of environmental systems: microsystems (proximal contexts that influence the individual directly, e.g., the family), mesosystems (relationships between developmental contexts, e.g., between the family and schools), exosystems (external environments that influence the individual indirectly, e.g., parental work settings and social networks that affect a child indirectly), macrosystems (e.g., societal values), and the chronosystem (e.g., changes over time in the effects of these systems on development).

Although the family ecology perspective does not provide insights into the *mechanisms* underlying how these systems affect families, it directs our attention to factors occurring within the family (e.g., intrafamilial dynamics such as relationship conflict) as well as to the layered influences of factors occurring outside of the immediate family (e.g., extrafamilial dynamics such as interactions between parents and the school system). For example, families that experience parental divorce are affected by societal views of divorce (i.e., a macrosystem) as well as by more immediate factors, such as how work settings adapt to the changing responsibilities of newly single parents (i.e., an exosystem). Thus, when scholars examine the consequences of family composition changes on individuals and families, the family ecological perspective provides a valuable theoretical complement to other theories that offer greater insights into *how* contextual factors affect families and their members.

● *SPOTLIGHT ON THEORY*

FAMILY DISRUPTION—CHAOS VERSUS HAVOC: A CHAOS THEORY (DYNAMICAL SYSTEMS) VIEW OF FAMILY STRUCTURE AND CHANGE

Rory Remer, *University of Kentucky*

Family systems are in perpetual chaos. Only the degree and how the patterns of interaction manifest themselves are at issue. The chaotic characteristics of these dynamical systems should *not* be considered problematic; they are absolutely essential to the systems' functioning. The implications of this fact for family psychologists—both clinicians and researchers—concerning the knowledge and skills they need to address these types of systems cannot be understated.

Families—and all other dynamical systems, human or otherwise—are recursive; that is, they adjust via feedback loops. Families establish and adapt their patterns of behaviors, thoughts, feelings, and interactions in complex, chaotic ways.

THE MATHEMATICAL BASIS OF CHAOS THEORY

$$x_{n+1} = kx_n (1 - x_n)$$

The above equation, or model, is called a logistical map (Wildman & Russell, 1995). It feeds values back into itself (i.e., it is recursive). Although it is seemingly simple, its behaviors—the patterns it generates—evidence all the essential characteristics of a chaotic, dynamical system, such as a family (Butz, 1997; Butz, Chamberlain, & McCown, 1997). If k, called the tuning constant, is small, the patterns produced are stable and predictable. Once reached, they do not change under further iteration. For large values of k, patterns are chaotic. Chaos is highly sensitive, disorderly orderliness (Crutchfield, Farmer, Packard, & Shaw, 1995).

APPLICATION TO FAMILIES

Chaos is not only indicative of but also provides necessary energy for adaptation of dissipative, dynamical systems patterns. Without it, they would stagnate and cease to exist.

From some perspectives (*phase spaces*), family systems (*strange attractors*) evidence short-term predictability and long-term *unpredictability* in patterns of feelings, thoughts, behaviors, and interactions—fluctuating within boundaries (*basins of attraction*). Patterns are both similar (*self-affine*) across situations, levels, and/or processes and more or less different and complex (*fractal*). Due to "linking" of subsystems reciprocally

(continued)

● *SPOTLIGHT ON THEORY continued*

(*resonance*) and nonlinearity/nonindependence, systems can increase in complexity and energy (*bifurcation*), sometimes so quickly that the chaos level can be disconcerting (*cascade*). However, these same characteristics lead to new coherence (*self-organization, autopoiesis*). Depending on the chaos level (*system state*), patterns shift, sometimes dramatically and permanently (*sensitivity to initial conditions*), but never reversibly or controllably. One can only *influence*—and that is what we can do and teach others to do.

Families as strange attractors evidence continual disruptions (chaos) to various degrees and at different levels that scholars can examine, discuss, and address using these ideas and structures. Violent, unanticipated, and unanticipatable external impacts can cause severe disruptions in system patterns—*havoc*. These pattern dissolutions should not be termed *chaotic* (although sometimes differentiation is equivocal). However, the chaotic properties of dynamical systems are required to address havoc.

Although scholars who address dynamical systems disagree about how to approach chaos, they do concur that change cannot occur without it. Thus dynamical systems must be in a ready state. The readiness seems to rely on the tuning constant. How one can know what the state and the tuning constant are for a given system and/or how to influence them is very much open to debate. Complexity theorists believe that "skating on the edge of chaos" is possible; chaoticians see that option as paradoxical, given the tenets of chaos theory. Similarly, scholars differ concerning how to view the production and use of chaos. However, perhaps these seeming differences are more a matter of definition and perspective than actual.

CONCLUSION

Chaos—disruption—is a necessary and sufficient condition for change in families. It is not only part of the dynamics in evolution but also a coping mechanism for addressing havoc, or drastic upheavals. Welcoming chaos—engendering, recognizing, and using it—is incumbent on family psychologists if they are to be effective.

For much more detailed explanations of the concepts discussed above (e.g., definitions and examples of construct applications; see Kossmann & Bullrich, 1997; Mahoney & Moes, 1997), see the articles and books listed in the reference section. In particular, family-related examples and case studies are available in Remer (2000, 2004). ●

IMPORTANCE OF FAMILY
COMPOSITION AND CHANGES
IN FAMILY LIVING ARRANGEMENTS

An extensive literature has documented that family composition is related to the well-being of individuals (particularly children). Most studies have involved comparisons of children living in two or more different family structures, and a smaller number have been designed to track and identify explicitly the consequences of *changes in* family living arrangements over time. In this section, we first review briefly the research evidence on the consequences for family members of three types of family structures—single-parent families, stepfamilies, and lesbian and gay families—evidence that illustrates the theoretical importance of the focal concepts of *family structure* and *family transitions*. We then describe some limitations of this work and discuss important theoretical implications and directions.

Consequences of Family Structure for Family Members

Divorce and single-parent families. For both adults and children, the experience of divorce is associated with a range of adverse consequences. Compared with married individuals, divorced persons report more negative life events, greater social isolation, more difficulties in parenting, and lower levels of psychological well-being (Amato, 2000). Similarly, children in divorced, single-parent families score somewhat lower than children in continuously married families on measures of academic achievement, psychological adjustment, conduct, social competence, and physical health (Amato, 2000). For both children and adults, differences between divorced and nondivorced groups tend to be small, and there is tremendous variability in how individual children and adults adjust to divorce (Amato, 2000; Demo & Cox, 2000).

Although divorce and single parenthood are linked for many individuals, it is important to distinguish the *process* of divorce (and the transitions associated with it) from single-parent *family structure*. Most adults and children who experience divorce live in single-parent families, at least for a period of time. Yet many individuals living in single-parent families have never experienced divorce (e.g., continuously single parents and their children, cohabiting couples). Similarly, many people experience divorce but subsequently live in arrangements other than single-parent families (e.g., in stepfamilies, or living alone as single childless adults). Partly because theory

has not yet strongly emphasized the importance of family transitions, most research to date has involved cross-sectional comparisons of children and adults living in different family structures, providing us with limited understanding of how individuals within and across families respond over time to changes in family composition, family relationships, and family resources.

Remarriage and stepfamilies. A growing number of researchers have examined the effects of remarriage and stepfamily experiences on parents, stepparents, and children (see Coleman, Ganong, & Fine, 2000). Most of the research in this area has focused on the consequences for children of living in stepfamilies, and most of the evidence has suggested that children in stepfamilies, while having outcomes comparable to those of children living in single-parent families, function less well in a number of adjustment domains than do children from first-marriage families. In particular, children in stepfamilies have more externalizing behavior problems (i.e., acting-out behaviors), more internalizing behaviors (e.g., depression, low self-esteem), and poorer academic performance (e.g., more likely to drop out of school) than do children in first-marriage families (Coleman et al., 2000). However, the differences between groups tend to be relatively small, which suggests that factors other than family structure alone must play an influential role in determining children's well-being.

With respect to the effects on adults and parents of living in stepfamilies, the findings are even more equivocal. For example, some studies have found that remarried individuals are less satisfied with their marriages than are first-married individuals, but other studies have found no differences (Coleman et al., 2000). Some studies have suggested that remarriage is associated with high levels of depression, whereas others have not found such effects and have indicated that remarried individuals report greater well-being and health than do divorced, nonremarried adults.

Lesbian and gay families. Family composition varies greatly within what may be termed lesbian and gay families. Common forms include single lesbians rearing children, lesbian couples with or without children, single gay men rearing children, and gay male couples with or without children. Partly because gay and lesbian families have not been considered in theoretical formulations of families, defining what constitutes a lesbian or gay family is a challenge. For example, most lesbian, gay, and bisexual children live in households with heterosexual parents, creating mixed gay/straight or "dual-orientation" families (Laird, 1993). Likewise, many nuclear, extended, and chosen families in which at least one member is gay or lesbian and other members are straight defy simple classification. In any case, many lesbian, gay, and bisexual children and adults simultaneously live in two worlds, typically involving a heterosexual family of origin and a network of chosen lesbian or gay family and friends.

Lesbian and gay couples describe their relationships as happy and highly satisfying. Lesbian couples are particularly likely to value equality and to be relationship centered, and lesbian mothers score as high as or higher than heterosexual mothers on various indicators of psychological well-being (Patterson, 2000; Savin-Williams & Esterberg, 2000). Relationships between gay children and heterosexual parents are described as generally positive, although both lesbian and gay youth report better relationships with their mothers than with their fathers (Savin-Williams, 2001). Recent reviews and meta-analyses document that lesbian mothers are at least as well-adjusted psychologically as heterosexual mothers; their parenting styles, behaviors, and effectiveness are comparable to (or slightly preferable to) those of heterosexual mothers; and children raised by lesbian or gay parents exhibit no disadvantages with regard to self-concept, conduct problems, peer relations, or other widely studied outcomes (Allen & Burrell, 1996; Patterson, 2000; Savin-Williams & Esterberg, 2000).

Limitations and Theoretical Implications

Research on divorce, single-parent families, stepfamilies, and lesbian and gay families has generated many important and consistent findings. In general, however, researchers have employed cross-sectional and comparative research designs that highlight comparisons of one family type with another on measures of family relationships and family members' well-being. Although very useful, such research designs provide limited information regarding family transitions, couple and parent-child relationship trajectories, and changes in parents' and children's social and psychological adjustment over time. Thus we often do not know whether family dynamics (e.g., a low level of parent-child communication) or reports of individual adjustment (e.g., a child having difficulties in school) that are measured subsequent to a family transition (e.g., divorce) are associated with that transition or whether the observed conditions are ongoing, perhaps even long-standing, phenomena that existed prior to the transition of interest. It is important to note that relatively few studies have examined the history, timing, sequencing, and consequences of multiple family transitions for adults and children. An overreliance on comparisons of family structures thus hinders our ability to understand the fluid, shifting patterns of individuals' living arrangements, the changes in their relationships, and the consequences for their well-being. We believe that theoretical considerations of family composition and structure need to place far greater emphasis on transition and change.

• *SPOTLIGHT ON METHODS*

CAUSAL ANALYSIS OF FAMILY STRUCTURE EFFECTS

Tami M. Videon, *Montefiore Medical Center and Albert Einstein College of Medicine*

O ne difficulty with employing cross-sectional data to assess family structure and outcomes is that it leads the researcher to examine structure and outcomes simultaneously, making assertions about the *causal* influence of family transitions tenuous. Although the issues addressed below apply to family transitions in general, for ease of discussion I will use the example of divorce and children's well-being.

The literature indicates that children whose parents divorce are at greater risk for a host of negative outcomes (Amato, 2000). However, demographers have documented that divorce is not randomly distributed. Individuals with less education, who have lower incomes, and who marry at younger ages are more likely to divorce. These characteristics in parents are also negatively associated with children's well-being. Therefore, we would expect poorer outcomes in the children of such parents even if divorce were not to occur. In other words, divorce may be an indicator of disadvantage, not the cause of it.

Compared with cross-sectional data, longitudinal data allow researchers to be more confident in making causal inferences. Presumably, including a measure of children's well-being prior to divorce allows researchers to control for differences that precede the transition and to estimate the independent influence of divorce. A substantial body of research shows that when researchers include measures of children's well-being prior to divorce, the negative impact of divorce is attenuated or becomes nonsignificant (e.g., Cherlin et al., 1991; Sun, 2001). These findings suggest that differences in well-being are present before changes in family structure take place. Some scholars assert that this tempers the conclusion that divorce has negative impacts on children's well-being, because (at least part of) the "divorce effect" is present before divorce occurs.

However, an alternative interpretation is that the coefficient for well-being prior to divorce actually captures the *process* of divorce. Family scholars have long conceptualized divorce as a progression of family disruption that unfolds over time. Tensions and dissatisfaction with the marital relationship build before culminating in divorce. Difficulties within the marital relationship alter family dynamics and affect children's well-being.

Interest in the short- and long-term impacts of divorce has extended our collective view of the effects of divorce far into the future (with some scholars examining the offspring of divorced parents decades after they experienced divorce). However, the view of children's trajectory of well-being preceding divorce is quite shortsighted. Consequently, despite general consensus that divorce is a process of family disruption, very few empirical data have been brought to bear in identifying when the process of divorce begins, or in differentiating among stages in the process (but see Hanson, McLanahan, & Thomson, 1998). Yet how one interprets children's well-being prior to family transitions

(continued)

● **SPOTLIGHT ON METHODS** *continued*

is contingent on when well-being was measured and when the process of divorce is thought to have begun. What is needed, therefore, is scholarship mapping the uncharted territory of children's well-being in the time leading up to divorce.

The issue of whether differences in children's well-being by family structure are caused by parental divorce or attributable to selection effects is critical, not only to theories of family life, but to attempts by policy makers, social workers, and counselors to improve children's well-being. Thus far, researchers have focused on the coefficient for divorce and how it changes (or does not change) when certain variables are controlled. Consequently, children's well-being before transitions has, for the most part, been relegated to the status of a "control" variable—considered important for parsing out variance that precedes transitions, but not given much interpretive attention. However, our interpretation of this coefficient is fundamental to our understanding of the impact of divorce. Although statistical methods provide different lenses through which we can examine family life, ultimately, our understanding of family life—and the answers to our research questions—is formed through the delicate interplay among theory, methods, and the art of interpretation. ●

Comparative studies of different family structures have also typically relied on oversimplified classifications of family structure, such as single-parent families versus two-parent families, first marriage versus remarriage, and heterosexual parent(s) versus lesbian or gay parent(s). In doing so, many cross-group investigations have been restricted in their ability to capture important within-group variations, such as differences between continuously single-parent families and single-parent families formed through divorce, or differences between simple stepfamilies (in which only one spouse has children from a previous union) and complex stepfamilies (in which both partners have children from previous marriages). Implicitly or explicitly, many of these studies also impose a deficit perspective, assuming that a particular family form (usually the heterosexual, first-marriage family) is a benchmark or healthier family unit against which other forms are judged (Coleman et al., 2000; Demo & Cox, 2000; Patterson, 2000; Savin-Williams & Esterberg, 2000). Thus we also advocate for more refined and inclusive ways of conceptualizing family structure so that important within-group differences are not masked.

Other limitations characterize the burgeoning literature on family structure. Our conceptual understanding of the experience of family transitions has been limited because few strong qualitative studies have explored the accounts of children and adults who have experienced various family transitions. Further, there have been many clinical studies of divorce, single-parent families, stepfamilies, and lesbian mother families, but most of them have relied on small, nonrepresentative samples. In addition, the scope of theory has been limited because researchers have tended to study primarily White, middle-class samples. This limitation characterizes the research to date on divorce and single-parent families (Demo & Cox, 2000), remarriage and stepfamilies (Coleman et al., 2000), and lesbian and gay families (Patterson, 2000; Savin-Williams & Esterberg, 2000). We need (a) quantitative studies that more adequately capture the full range of family diversity and transition, particularly on critical dimensions such as race/ethnicity, socioeconomic status, gender, and sexual orientation; and (b) more in-depth qualitative studies that portray the lived experience of family composition transitions.

TRANSITIONS IN PARENTING ARRANGEMENTS OVER THE COURSE OF CHILDHOOD AND ADOLESCENCE

The theories and empirical literature reviewed above suggest that family transitions have important influence on the lives of family members. For example, parenting transitions, such as parents exiting the household upon divorce and entering the household upon remarriage, may have strong influences on children's and adolescents' adjustment. We believe that it is particularly important for scholars to consider three rarely studied aspects of family composition transitions: their *frequency,* their *nature,* and their *timing.*

First, the sheer number of family composition changes is likely to have an impact on family members' well-being, with more frequent transitions likely to have greater effects. The more often children have to adjust to the addition of a new adult to the household (e.g., a stepparent), the loss of an adult from the household (e.g., through divorce and/or separation), geographic moves, changes in the schools they attend, and alterations in their social networks, the more stress they experience. Increased stress, in turn, is associated with a wide range of adjustment problems, although stress also provides opportunities for growth that may not emerge otherwise.

Fluidity refers to the frequency of changes in family composition and the speed with which changes occur (Burton & Jayakody, 2001); this ranges from chaotic (frequent, rapid, and simultaneous transitions) to stable (infrequent, predictable, one-at-a-time transitions). A sizable minority of individuals experience very unstable childhood living arrangements characterized by multiple transitions and the possibility of being separated from both biological parents (Teachman, 2002). Wu and Martinson (1993) identified 187 unique sequences of living arrangement transitions among women under age 50 and found considerable variability in the number of transitions experienced and the rapidity with which they occurred.

Second, family transitions are likely to have differential impacts on family members

depending on the nature of the transitions. For example, characteristics such as the type of transition, how abruptly the transition occurs, how severe a change is involved, the extent to which the change was anticipated, whether the change involved the addition of or the loss of a family member, and the amount of support available to buffer the change are likely to contribute to variations in adjustment.

One particularly important type of transition takes place when children physically move from one residence to another. In a recent meta-analysis, Bauserman (2002) documented the positive effects on children's adjustment of joint physical or legal custody of children following divorce as opposed to sole custody, including positive effects on children's family relationships, self-esteem, and emotional and behavioral adjustment. Joint custody appears to facilitate the ongoing involvement of both parents in children's lives, even though the children may have to move back and forth between their parents. For many children, however, the legal determination of child custody after parents separate is but the beginning of a series of residential transitions. Maccoby and Mnookin (1992) found that among the children of divorced parents in their sample, half the children who were originally (at the time of filing) in dual custody or father custody and one in five children in mother custody had made at least one change of primary residence (moving to the other parent's household) within the 3 years following the divorce. Thus we believe that family scholars need to direct more theoretical attention toward understanding and operationally defining these types of residential changes, including a host of more subtle residential changes, such as when a child changes the proportion of time he or she spends in each parent's home.

Finally, the timing of family transitions is likely to be influential. As the life-course perspective suggests, the same transition can have differing effects depending on when it occurs in the individual's life trajectory and depending on the historical era in which it occurs. In terms of the individual's life trajectory, for example, scholars have paid considerable attention to the question of whether divorce has greater or lesser effects depending on the age of the child at the time of the divorce (and the resulting findings have been quite mixed and complex). With respect to historical influences, some have suggested that there are likely to be fewer negative consequences today for children living in single-parent families or stepfamilies than there were for children in such families 30 years ago, because these family arrangements are now both more common and more normative.

Considerably more research is needed into each of these three dimensions of family transitions, but the least studied dimension has been the frequency of transitions, as we describe in more detail below.

Research on Parenting Transitions

One approach that researchers have used to study the effects of family transitions on children is based on an important assumption of the risk and resilience framework discussed earlier—that change and transition are inherently stressful because they tax the individual's ability to cope. Capaldi and Patterson (1991) hypothesized that because parenting transitions are stressful for children, the greater the number of parenting transitions (e.g., the divorce or [re]marriage of one of their parents) that children experience, the poorer their adjustment should be. In a sample of boys, they found that there was, indeed, a negative linear relationship between the number of parenting transitions experienced and the boys' adjustment. More recent studies using Capaldi and Patterson's approach have yielded similar findings. Kurdek, Fine, and Sinclair (1994, 1995) for example, found that children in their sample who had experienced no parental transitions (in first-marriage families) consistently had the best adjustment, and those in a multiple-parenting transition group (who had experienced at least three parental divorces or remarriages) consistently showed the poorest adjustment.

Although the parenting transition approach has several advantages (e.g., it takes into account the number of times a child has experienced a parental divorce or [re]marriage, unlike traditional definitions of family structure), it can provide only a rough approximation of the amount and nature of the stress children have experienced as a result of family transitions. We need much more sensitive measures of the quantity and nature of family transitions that take into consideration more than just legal (i.e., marriage and divorce) transitions. For example, researchers employing this approach have always defined children who have experienced no parenting transitions as children born to continuously married parents; a conceptual extension of this approach would be to consider children born to continuously single parents also to be in this group.

CONCEPTUALIZING FAMILY DIVERSITY AND FAMILY TRANSITIONS

We believe that to understand family composition and family transitions more fully, scholars need to devote greater theoretical and empirical attention to conceptualizing family diversity. For example, theorists and researchers have often underestimated the heterogeneity of family and household structures that exists among single-parent families. Only about half of all African American single-parent families involve the parent and children living alone in a household (Burton & Jayakody, 2001). Substantial numbers of single parents live with other adults who may become involved in caring for their children, such as dating or cohabiting partners, parents, grandparents, other relatives, and fictive kin (Brandon & Bumpass, 2001). Thus children who begin their lives in single-parent family are very likely to experience other living arrangements as well, including stepfamilies, informal adoptions, and extended family households that include a parent and other relatives. Less than one-fourth of these children live exclusively in single-parent families over the full course of their childhoods (Aquilino, 1996). This underscores the need for scholars to expand the conceptualization of family composition to include greater variation in family circumstances.

Variations Within and Across Race and Ethnicity

Because there is considerable variability in family composition both across and within racial and ethnic groups, as well as considerable changes over time, theorists need to be sensitive to the importance of race and ethnicity. With respect to variations across racial/ethnic groups, African American women and Latinas are less likely to be married and more likely to be single parents than are their European American and Asian American counterparts (McLoyd, Cauce, Takeuchi, & Wilson, 2000). African Americans are also more likely than Whites to live in extended families that include grandparents, parents, and their children.

As we noted earlier with respect to family composition, researchers have devoted more attention to differences among racial and ethnic groups than to variation within them, often assuming that each ethnic/racial group is monolithic (Umana-Taylor & Fine, 2001). However, within-group differences can be substantial. For example, Kellam, Ensminger, and Turner (1977) identified 86 unique family structure configurations in an African American community in Chicago. Illustrating intra-Hispanic variation, Cuban Americans and Mexican Americans tend to have lower rates of single-headed households than do Puerto Ricans (McLoyd et al., 2000).

It is also interesting to note that there is some limited evidence that the *effects* of family structure transitions may differ across ethnic and racial groups. Some scholars have found that the negative effects of divorce and separation are less severe among African American and Hispanic children than among White children (McLoyd et al., 2000). In sum, the variation within racial/ethnic groups in family composition and the potentially differing consequences of family transitions by racial/ethnic group suggest that race/ethnicity is a variable that scholars need to take into account in theoretical and empirical work on family composition.

METHODOLOGICAL IMPLICATIONS AND RECOMMENDATIONS

We have argued that theorists need to find more refined ways of conceptualizing family composition and that transition needs to be a hallmark of these efforts. Such theoretical advancements have methodological implications. To understand the complex nature and consequences of family transitions more fully, researchers need to develop and implement more dynamic definitions of family structure. In this section, we present recommendations to facilitate richer accounts of family history and relationship trajectories.

Triangulation of Research Methods

We believe that there is a need for triangulation of research methods, or methodological pluralism. The complexities of family composition changes and consequences require researchers to employ both quantitative and qualitative methods—not necessarily in the same studies, but in the field as a whole. Below, we make recommendations for both quantitative and qualitative designs, recognizing that (a) individual studies need not have all of these features, nor are all features even relevant for answering particular research questions; (b) the distinction between quantitative and qualitative research is a fuzzy one, and we encourage investigators to combine these approaches; and (c) even researchers engaged in quantitative research need to think in a postpositivist manner, acknowledging that "truths" are not absolute, that there are different realities for different family members, and that family life is heavily influenced by the context in which it occurs.

Recommendations for Quantitative Designs

There is a strong need for quantitative research on family transitions that is sensitive to the nuances of family changes over time. Important directions for such work include longitudinal designs, within-group designs that examine characteristics of particular types of families without necessarily comparing across family types, studies that examine process and interaction variables in addition to composition and structural variables, studies that use multiple informants, research that employs standardized measures across studies and across multiple waves within studies, and samples that are diverse on such dimensions as race and ethnicity, sexual orientation, socioeconomic status, and gender. Echoing Amato's (1993) call for researchers to study family structure and family process variables as they interact with each other, we believe there is considerable potential in studies that examine both sets of variables and that consider, for example, whether family processes have differential effects on family members depending on family composition at various times.

Fortunately, recent advances in statistical analysis have provided the tools that researchers need to conduct studies with the methodological features enumerated above. For example, studying longitudinal data with multiple informants has long been an analytic challenge, but a number of new analytic techniques are especially helpful with such designs, such as structural equation modeling, multilevel models, and growth curve models. Researchers can use multilevel models, for instance, to consider such issues as how children in particular types of families are differentially affected by variations in the characteristics of the schools they attend, consistent with the family ecology model discussed earlier. Growth curve models can test whether there are group differences in individual rates of change in particular domains, such as the possibility that children's academic achievement may change over time at different rates depending on whether or not they have spent any time living with a residential father.

Data Needs

Parent calendars, such as those used in the National Survey of Families and Households (Sweet & Bumpass, 1996), are powerful tools that can help researchers to develop more complete histories of childhood living arrangements. Parent respondents use these calendars to record the ages, from birth to home-leaving, during which children lived with each type of parent (biological parent, stepparent, and adoptive parent) and with grandparents, relatives, fictive kin, foster parents, and other individuals. By examining parent calendars, researchers can determine not only the living arrangements children experienced at each age, but the duration of each living arrangement, age at each transition, and the sequence of transitions. Wu and his colleagues have demonstrated that researchers can use parent calendar data to construct theoretically grounded measures that capture both the experience of instability in family composition and the degree of exposure to particular family configurations over the course of childhood (Wu & Martinson, 1993; Wu & Thomson, 2001). These dynamic measures of childhood experience provide a much fuller picture of family composition effects than can snapshot measures of family structure taken at single points in time.

Although parent calendars can generate a wealth of data, there are limitations to this approach. Such a calendar captures household structure (with whom a child was living at any given age), but it provides no information on transitions in family composition that take place outside the child's household, especially the union transitions and additional childbearing of the nonresidential parent. It also provides no information on whether other family members in the nonresident parent's household become important figures in a child's life. In addition, a parent calendar does not always make clear the events that precipitated a change in living arrangements, such as why a child moved from the home of one parent to the home of the other or was raised by grandparents for a period of time. In addition to gathering parent calendar data, researchers should record the family composition at the time of the child's birth or adoption, the formation and termination of parents' cohabiting relationships, the union and fertility histories of the child's parents and stepparents, changes in the family and household composition of the nonresident parent, changes in the child's custody arrangements and primary residence, and periods in which the child lives in multigenerational households, with stepsiblings, and with half siblings.

Recommendations for Qualitative Designs

Some aspects of changes in family composition and how they affect families are likely to be very subtle, to pose measurement challenges, to ebb and flow over time, and to be heavily influenced by the contexts in which they occur. As a result, we recommend that researchers employ a range of qualitative designs. For example, studies with small samples that involve in-depth interviewing of family members over extended periods of time would be instructive. In addition, narrative approaches that allow family members to tell their "stories" in their own voices would provide useful "insider" information on family changes. Our commitment to methodological pluralism also extends to nontraditional data sources, such as newspapers, magazines, television and radio shows, and Web sites. Researchers may gather useful information about changes in social norms by examining the content of stories in the media on families, how they change, and how the changes affect family members. Further, because laws and social policies are related to social norms and values, it would be useful for scholars to track changes in laws affecting family transitions, such as those concerning divorce, marriage (including marriage between same-sex partners), cohabitation, and parental rights and responsibilities.

CONCLUSIONS AND FUTURE DIRECTIONS

The composition of most families in the United States at the beginning of the new millennium is much more diverse, complex, fluid, extended, nuanced, and ambiguous than the picture painted in prevailing scholarship on family structure would suggest. Family scholars need new and expanded ways of conceptualizing family composition and transition. Further, the population of families we seek to understand is not as White, heterosexual, and middle-class as the families in typical research samples. More than half of American children today are living in family arrangements other than the "traditional nuclear family" consisting of two adults in their first marriage rearing their biological children. Cohabitation, divorce, single-parent families, stepfamilies, lesbian and gay families, multigenerational households, chosen kin, and a broad patchwork of other family forms continue to reshape postmodern family living arrangements. Family scholars have noted that the forces driving pluralistic family forms, forces ranging from struggles for gender equity and gay rights to advances in reproductive technology, are here to stay and are likely to accelerate (Stacey, 2000).

Although thousands of studies have examined the correlates and consequences of family structure, relatively few have charted changes or transitions in family composition over time. Yet, as we have argued, the theoretical, methodological, and statistical tools that scholars need to design and conduct this type of research are available. Although it may be premature to abandon research designs that focus on cross-sectional comparisons of different family structures, particularly if researchers devote adequate attention to measures of family process as they interact with family composition, we argue that scholars will gain more from employing research designs that enable the tracking of relationship trajectories, transitions, disruptions, and reconfigurations in family composition over time. Such investigations, guided by life-course, family ecology, and/or risk and resilience frameworks, will enable more careful and precise estimates of the influence of changing family conditions on individual development and well-being.

Simply stated, our challenge is to enrich our theoretical conceptualizations and reframe our research questions so that our observations more accurately reflect the diversity and fluidity of postmodern families. Rather than searching for differences between family types, we must direct our attention to exploring turning points in family relationships and individual development. This involves investigating the influence of family transitions on family economic circumstances as well as probing a vast array of historical and contextual forces that impinge on family relationships. Individual variability also deserves much more attention, including variability in individual vulnerabilities, protective factors, and coping resources that promote resilience. Pursuing these questions with a variety of research methods and designs promises family scholars a richer understanding of postmodern family composition, family transitions, and individual adjustment.

CASE STUDY

PREDICTING MARITAL SUCCESS OR FAILURE: BURGESS AND BEYOND

Ione Y. DeOllos, *Ball State University*

Ernest W. Burgess, a sociology professor at the University of Chicago from 1916 through 1960, became interested in predicting marital success after he had developed a method of predicting parole success. While acknowledging the greater complexity of predicting marital adjustment, Burgess (1938) argued that the quality of marriage could be determined scientifically and that the procedure for predicting marital success should be essentially the same as that for parole. As a result, he turned his attention to the task of predicting marital adjustment and marriage success using the same scientific procedures he had used in his research on parole success.

Earlier studies that examined factors relating to marital happiness helped form Burgess's research design and theoretical perspective. In a 1926 article in *Social Hygiene,* Hornell Hart reported the optimal ages for happy marriage to be 29 for men and 24 for women. G. V. Hamilton, in his book *Research in Marriage,* published in 1929, reported a high probability of success in marriage when the husband reported that his wife bore a physical resemblance to his mother. Terman, in a 1938 study of "psychological factors in marital happiness," reported correlations between "personality, background and sexual factors and happiness in marriage" (Burgess, 1939, p. 1). Burgess (1939) argued that a major weakness of these studies was the researchers' inclusion of married couples in their samples. Because the shared experience of marriage would bring married couples' answers into closer conformance, Burgess contended that the responses of engaged couples would differ significantly from those of married couples.

Burgess's first systematic investigation of marital success, undertaken in 1931 with Leonard Cottrell, was a study in which an eight-page survey was distributed to 7,000 married couples, with 1,300 couples eventually responding (Burgess & Cottrell, 1936). For their marital adjustment study, Burgess and Cottrell utilized a subsample of 526 couples for analysis. Due to the ambiguous nature of happiness, Burgess and Cottrell included ratings of marital happiness by outsiders to the marriages who were well acquainted with the couples. For each couple, they were able to compare the evaluations of happiness made by the husband, the wife, and the outsider, giving them greater confidence in the married couple's reports of happiness or unhappiness.

The degree of marital adjustment exhibited by the couple was indicated by responses to 20 questions identified by their level of correlation with the couple's happiness ratings. Each couple was given an adjustment score based on their answers to the 20 marital adjustment questions.

The most significant indicators of positive marital adjustment include the reported happiness of the parents' marriage, close attachment of the husband and wife to the other's parents, having four or more siblings, not being an only or youngest child (unless married to an oldest or middle child), similar cultural backgrounds of the partners, attendance at Sunday school, having affiliations with three or more organizations, higher educational levels for both partners, husband's occupation, and the wife's having been employed prior to marriage. When compared to marital status, the adjustment scores were able to discriminate between marriages that ended in divorce or separation and marriages that were not broken. Furthermore, for intact marriages, the adjustment scores were able to discriminate between those who had and had not considered divorce (Burgess, 1938).

To test these predictive factors further, Burgess and P. I. Wolinsky (1937) conducted a study of engaged couples to measure engagement adjustment. The schedule included questions designed to evaluate the engagement relationship, including inquiries into how the individuals preferred to spend their leisure time; whether the engaged couple participated in interests and activities together; whether they confided in one another; the frequency of and satisfaction with demonstrations of affection; the extent of the couple's agreement on money, recreation, and religious matters, and on ways of dealing with family and arrangements for their marriage; and whether they had ever contemplated

breaking their engagement (Burgess & Wallin, 1944). The researchers contacted the same individuals again 3 to 4 years later to determine whether they eventually married and to measure their marital adjustment. In the presentation of their early findings, Burgess and Wolinsky (1937) reported that "two important conditions for adjustment in the engagement period seem to be temperamental compatibility and consensus upon the life organization" (p. 20).

In 1944, Burgess and Paul Wallin conducted a study with a sample of 505 engaged couples from the 1937 study. In analyzing the participants' responses to marital adjustment questions, they were able to differentiate between broken engagements and successful engagements, leading Burgess and Wallin to suggest the usefulness of these items as predictors. Additionally, they reported that the engagement and marriage adjustment scores were correlated, indicating the utility of measures of engagement adjustment for predicting levels of marital adjustment.

Burgess and his colleagues focused primarily on measurable individual characteristics that were correlated with positive marital outcomes. However, acknowledging that not all predictive characteristics of marriage are easily measurable, Burgess attempted, through the use of a third party, to get a measure of the level of expressed happiness within marriage. Unfortunately, the predictive power of the variables that Burgess and his colleagues identified were only strong enough to apply to groups of couples who possess certain characteristics. Burgess (1938) willingly admitted that he could not predict the outcome for any individual marriage.

One possible reason for this limitation may lie in the personal nature of the institution of marriage. When an individual is considering potential candidates for engagement and marriage, external conditions such as the woman's physical similarity to the man's mother, age, educational level, and occupation are important factors. Once the individual is married, however, the factors he or she considers important about the partner may change in focus. Rather than external factors, characteristics such as fidelity to the marriage, willingness to share daily household chores equally, views about child-rearing practices, desire for children, and views concerning the roles of each person in the marriage may be strong determining factors in the success of the marital union.

In recent years, studies of marital adjustment and prediction have once again appeared in the literature. Kaslow and Robison (1996) conducted a cross-cultural study in which they investigated the essential ingredients for long-term satisfying marriages. Nemechek and Olson (1999) reported on the relationship between marital adjustment and spousal similarity in the areas of conscientiousness, agreeableness, and neuroticism. Blum and Mehrabian (1999) investigated the potential for individual temperament factors to be predictive of marital satisfaction.

Many of the characteristics mentioned above could be subsumed under the concept of commitment to the marriage. As recent studies have demonstrated, levels of commitment, although attitudinal in nature, can effectively be measured. One could argue that spouses who are equally committed to their marriage would have an increased likelihood of being happily married. Marriages in which one individual has a higher level of commitment than his or her partner would still have a potential of success, even if lessened by the differences in commitment. Because in the past married women were more likely to be financially dependent on their husbands than is the case today, earlier research might have suggested that as long as the husband has the higher commitment to remaining in the union, the potential for the success of the marriage is generally good. However, today fewer women need to remain in unhappy marriages for financial reasons, so the wife's level of commitment to the marriage is also important.

Spouses' perceptions of reciprocity within their marriage are important factors in predicting marital success as well. Couples do not necessarily need to divide marital chores and responsibilities equally; as long as both spouses are satisfied with the reciprocal relationship they have developed, they will experience high levels of marital happiness. Therefore, each spouse's perceptions concerning the contributions of his or her partner are important in the determination of acceptable reciprocity. When one partner feels that he or she is contributing a disproportionate share of maintenance work within the marriage, that individual is more likely to characterize the marriage as unhappy. In this situation, the unhappy individual will often suggest to his or her spouse that the spouse do more. If acceptable levels of reciprocal equivalence are achieved in response to this request, the expressed levels of happiness within the marriage will increase. Dissonance occurs, however, when both partners feel they are being responsible but feel the other is not contributing enough to the relationship. In such cases, requests for greater levels of reciprocal exchange will likely be met with resistance, thereby increasing the couple's feelings of dissatisfaction or unhappiness. As a result, both spouses will be more likely to identify their marital union as unhappy and potentially seek to escape the relationship so that they may be free to find one that will make them happy.

As the above discussion illustrates, to improve our understanding of what constitutes a happy marital relationship, we need to expand our research beyond the physical or external characteristics of individual marital partners and enter into investigations that examine spouses' perceptions of their commitment to their marriage and the reciprocity within the marriage.

DISCUSSION AND EXTENSION

THE ADJUSTMENT OF CHILDREN IN DIVORCED AND REMARRIED FAMILIES

E. Mavis Hetherington, *University of Virginia*

When I began studying divorced families and mother-headed households almost 40 years ago, this was seen as research on "father absent" families, a label that reflected the predominant theoretical views of the time. Scholars gave little concern to changes in life experiences and family functioning associated with marital transitions other than paternal loss. Both psychoanalytic theory and social learning theory predicted that the absence of a father might lead to deficits in identification or role modeling associated with problems in sex role typing, moral development, self-control, and antisocial behavior, especially in sons. Almost all of the "father absence" studies were cross-sectional, involved sex role typing or delinquency in boys, and relied on information obtained from single reporters. The comprehensive review of family composition and family transitions that Demo, Aquilino and Fine provide in Chapter 5 demonstrates how far we have come in the past four decades in our conceptualizations and in the research-based knowledge available about family structure and transitions and the adjustment of family members. Still, some troubling interpretive, logistical, and methodological problems remain in our studies of family structure and transitions. Some of these problems are not confined to this specific topic but are pervasive in the study of human development. Because of space limitations, I will focus my comments here mainly on family transitions and the adjustment of children. (For a longer version of this discussion that includes a more complete methodological discussion and extensive references, see this volume's companion Web site at http://www.ncfr.org/sourcebook.)

In the immediate aftermath of a parental divorce or remarriage, most children experience emotional distress and behavior problems, including anger, resentment, demandingness, noncompliance, anxiety, and depression, as they cope with the confusion and apprehension stemming from changing relationships in the family and shifts in their life situation. In the vast majority of children, these responses begin to diminish in the second year following divorce and in the third to fifth year following remarriage. However, some children may show severe, enduring adjustment difficulties and others show delayed effects, appearing to adapt well in the early stages following divorce, but exhibiting problems at a later time.

There is considerable agreement in the research literature that children in divorced and remarried families are at increased risk for the development of psychological, behavioral, social, and academic problems in comparison with children in two-parent, nondivorced families, and that the risk is greatest for children who have experienced multiple marital transitions. Moreover, this increased risk continues into adulthood, when youths from divorced and remarried families experience lower socioeconomic and educational attainment and have more problems in relationships with family members, in intimate relations, in marriage, and in the workplace. Furthermore, although a stepparent can offer economic, social, emotional, and child-rearing support, these benefits do not seem to be reflected in enhanced development of stepchildren. The adjustment of children in remarried families is similar to that of children in divorced families.

DISCUSSION AND EXTENSION *continued*

There is less consensus in the literature on the size, causes, and significance of the differences between the adjustment of children in divorced and remarried families and that of those in nondivorced families. Many of the discrepancies in reported research findings on these issues are the results of the investigators' theoretical biases and the methods used.

Scholars who have conducted meta-analyses of the effects of divorce on children's adjustment have reported that for externalizing disorders, where the largest differences usually are obtained, the effect size is only about one-third of a deviation unit and that there is considerable overlap in the adjustment of children from divorced and remarried and nondivorced families. However, much larger effect sizes have been reported by some researchers who have used multiple measures, including observations and composite indices.

The fact that mean differences in adjustment among children in different family types are small, and the fact that there is considerable overlap in the distributions in adjustment for children in different types of families, should not be seen as an indication that marital transitions have a negligible effect on children's adjustment. Some scholars have surmised that small differences occur because of the great diversity in children's adjustment in response to parental divorce and remarriage.

Cluster analyses identifying patterns of adjustment support this position. Children, adolescents, and young adults whose parents have gone through marital transitions are overrepresented both in multiproblem clusters and in high-competence clusters. Girls in divorced, mother-headed families, for example, are especially likely to be exceptionally well-adjusted and socially responsible, although for some this competence comes at a cost and is accompanied by low self-esteem and elevated anxiety and depression. Enhancement following divorce is more likely to be found in mothers and daughters than in fathers and sons. The findings of extremes of competence and of problem behaviors following divorce and remarriage suggest that it is the diversity, not the inevitability of adverse outcomes, that is most striking in the adjustment of children following parental marital transitions.

Researchers examining the increased risk of children's developing specific problems associated with parental divorce or remarriage might draw somewhat different conclusions. This strategy parallels epidemiological methods for identifying the contribution of various risk factors to health outcomes.

Offspring from divorced and remarried families, compared with those from nondivorced families, show a two- to threefold greater risk for psychological and behavioral problems, including school dropout, early sexual activity, having children out of wedlock, unemployment, substance abuse and delinquent activities, and involvement with antisocial peers. These problems tend to go together in a maladjustment cluster. About 20–25% of children in divorced and remarried families, versus 10% in nondivorced families, score above the clinical cutoff in total behavior problems on standardized tests. This is not a negligible risk size—it exceeds the association between smoking and lung cancer. However, it still means that 75–80% of children in divorced and remarried families are functioning within the normal range and have been resilient in coping with the stresses associated with their parents' marital transitions. This is not to underestimate the apprehension, painful feelings, and grief that many children experience in response to the end of their parents' marriage or entry into remarriage. However, in the absence of new stresses and adversity, the vast majority of such offspring are able to cope with their new life situation and eventually emerge as reasonably competent and well-adjusted individuals.

DISCUSSION AND EXTENSION *continued*

THE BEFORE AND AFTER

On the basis of research findings showing differences in children's adjustment following divorce and remarriage, can we assume that these differences are caused by their parents' marital transitions? In order to understand the contributions of divorce and remarriage to children's adjustment, we must examine changes in their adjustment and circumstances of living from before to after these transitions. There is considerable evidence that problems in the adjustment of parents and children, disruptions in family functioning, and inept parenting are present and may take their toll long before divorce or remarriage occurs. In analyses that have controlled for these pretransition levels, researchers have found that the contribution of parental marital transitions to child adjustment is greatly reduced or eliminated.

Some scholars have also proposed that a genetic substrate may underlie the associations among psychological and social problems in parents, divorce, unskilled parenting, and behavior problems in children. Depressed, antisocial, or poorly educated parents are less sensitive and more irritable in interpersonal relationships, which increases their risk of divorce as well as inept parenting. These factors, in addition to genetic links between adjustment problems in parents and children, may contribute to problem behavior in children in divorced and remarried families both before and after the transitions occur.

It seems unlikely that these antecedent conditions or genetic factors entirely explain the association between marital transitions and children's adjustment problems. On the average, stresses and behavior problems in children do increase in the immediate aftermath of parental divorce or remarriage. However, a marital transition also may offer both parents and children an escape from conflict and a move to a more satisfying, supportive, harmonious family situation. When this occurs, the well-being and adjustment of both parents and children are enhanced.

REFERENCES

Allen, K. R., Fine, M. A., & Demo, D. H. (2000). An overview of family diversity: Controversies, questions, and values. In D. H. Demo, K. R. Allen, & M. A. Fine (Eds.), *Handbook of family diversity* (pp. 1–14). New York: Oxford University Press.

Allen, M., & Burrell, N. (1996). Comparing the impact of homosexual and heterosexual parents on children: Meta-analysis of existing research. *Journal of Homosexuality, 32*(2), 19–35.

Amato, P. R. (1993). Children's adjustment to divorce: Theories, hypotheses, and empirical support. *Journal of Marriage and the Family, 55*, 22–38.

Amato, P. R. (2000). The consequences of divorce for adults and children. *Journal of Marriage and the Family, 62*, 1269–1287.

Aquilino, W. S. (1996). The life course of children born to unmarried mothers: Childhood living arrangements and young adult outcomes. *Journal of Marriage and the Family, 58*, 293–310.

Bauserman, R. (2002). Child adjustment in joint-custody versus sole-custody arrangements: A meta-analytic review. *Journal of Family Psychology, 16*, 91–102.

Bengtson, V. L., & Allen, K. R. (1993). The life course perspective applied to families over time. In P. Boss, W. J. Doherty, R. LaRossa, W. R. Schumm, & S. K. Steinmetz (Eds.), *Sourcebook of family theory and methods: A contextual approach* (pp. 469–499). New York: Plenum.

Blum, J. S., & Mehrabian, A. (1999). Personality and temperament correlates of marital satisfaction. *Journal of Personality, 67*, 93–125.

Brandon, P. D., & Bumpass, L. L. (2001). Children's living arrangements, coresidence of unmarried fathers, and welfare receipt. *Journal of Family Issues, 22*, 3–26.

Bronfenbrenner, U. (1986). Ecology of the family as a context for human development: Research perspectives. *Developmental Psychology, 22*, 723–742.

Burgess, E. W. (1938, January 25). *Predicting marriage adjustment.* Lecture presented at the University of Chicago. (Retrieved from Burgess Papers, Box 195, Folder 5, University of Chicago, Joseph Regenstein Library, Special Collections Research Center.)

Burgess, E. W. (1939, January). Predictive factors in the success or failure of marriage. *Living.* (Retrieved from Burgess Papers, Box 23, Folder 4, University of Chicago, Joseph Regenstein Library, Special Collections Research Center.)

Burgess, E. W., & Cottrell, L. S. (1936). The prediction of adjustment in marriage. *American Sociological Review, 1*, 737–751.

Burgess, E. W., & Wallin, P. (1944). Predicting adjustment in marriage from adjustment in engagement. *American Journal of Sociology, 49*, 324–330.

Burgess, E. W., & Wolinsky, P. I. (1937, December 29). *Predicting the adjustment in marriage of engaged couples.* Paper presented at the annual meeting of the American Sociological Society, Atlantic City, NJ. (Retrieved from Burgess Papers, Box 194, Folder 2, University of Chicago, Joseph Regenstein Library, Special Collections Research Center.)

Burton, L. M., & Jayakody, R. (2001). Rethinking family structure and single parenthood: Implications for future studies of African American families and children. In A. Thornton (Ed.), *The well-being of children and families: Research and data needs* (pp. 127–153). Ann Arbor: University of Michigan Press.

Butz, M. R. (1997). *Chaos and complexity: Implications for psychological theory and practice.* Washington, DC: Taylor & Francis.

Butz, M. R., Chamberlain, L. L., & McCown, W. G. (1997). *Strange attractors: Chaos, complexity, and the art of family therapy.* New York: John Wiley.

Capaldi, D. M., & Patterson, G. R. (1991). The relation of parental transitions to boys' adjustment problems: I. A linear hypothesis; II. Mothers at risk for transitions and unskilled parenting. *Developmental Psychology, 27*, 489–504.

Cherlin, A. J., Furstenberg, F. F., Jr., Chase-Lansdale, P. L., Kiernan, K. E., Robins, P. K., Morrison, D. R., et al. (1991). Longitudinal studies of effects of divorce on children in Great Britain and the United States. *Science, 252*, 1386–1389.

Clausen, J. A. (1993). *American lives.* Berkeley: University of California Press.

Coleman, M., Ganong, L. H., & Fine, M. A. (2000). Reinvestigating remarriage: Another decade of progress. *Journal of Marriage and the Family, 62,* 1288–1307.

Crutchfield, J. P., Farmer, J. D., Packard, N. H., & Shaw, R. S. (1995). Chaos. In R. J. Russell, N. Murphy, & A. Peacocke (Eds.), *Chaos and complexity: Scientific perspectives on divine action* (pp. 35–49). Vatican City State/Berkeley, CA: Vatican Observatory Publications/Center for Theology and the Natural Sciences.

Demo, D. H. (1992). The self-concept over time: Research issues and directions. *Annual Review of Sociology, 18,* 303–326.

Demo, D. H., & Allen, K. R. (1996). Diversity within lesbian and gay families: Challenges and implications for family theory and research. *Journal of Social and Personal Relationships, 13,* 415–434.

Demo, D. H., & Cox, M. J. (2000). Families with young children: A review of research in the 1990s. *Journal of Marriage and the Family, 62,* 876–895.

Elder, G. H., Jr. (1977). Family history and the life course. *Journal of Family History, 2,* 279–304.

Elder, G. H., Jr. (1994). Time, human agency, and social change: Perspectives on the life course. *Social Psychology Quarterly, 57,* 4–15.

Hanson, T. L., McLanahan, S. S., & Thomson, E. (1998). Windows on divorce: Before and after. *Social Science Research, 27,* 239–349.

Hareven, T. K. (1987). *Family time and industrial time.* New York: Cambridge University Press.

Hetherington, E. M. (1999). Introduction and overview. In E. M. Hetherington (Ed.), *Coping with divorce, single parenting, and remarriage* (pp. vii–x). Mahwah, NJ: Lawrence Erlbaum.

Kaslow, F., & Robison, J. A. (1996). Long-term satisfying marriages: Perceptions of contributing factors. *American Journal of Family Therapy, 24,* 153–168.

Kellam, S. G., Ensminger, M. E., & Turner, R. J. (1977). Family structure and the mental health of children. *Archives of General Psychiatry, 34,* 1012–1022.

Kossmann, M. R., & Bullrich, S. (1997). Systematic chaos. In F. Masterpasqua &

P. A. Perna (Eds.), *The psychological meaning of chaos: Translating theory into practice* (pp. 199–223). Washington, DC: American Psychological Association.

Kurdek, L. A., Fine, M. A., & Sinclair, R. J. (1994). The relation between parenting transitions and adjustment in young adolescents: A multi-sample investigation. *Journal of Early Adolescence, 14,* 412–432.

Kurdek, L. A., Fine, M. A., & Sinclair, R. J. (1995). School adjustment in sixth graders: Parenting transitions, family climate, and peer norm effects. *Child Development, 66,* 430–445.

Laird, J. (1993). Lesbian and gay families. In F. Walsh (Ed.), *Normal family processes* (2nd ed., pp. 282–328). New York: Guilford.

Maccoby, E. E., & Mnookin, R. H. (1992). *Dividing the child: Social and legal dilemmas of custody.* Cambridge, MA: Harvard University Press.

Mahoney, M. J., & Moes, A. J. (1997). Complexity and psychotherapy: Promising dialogues and practical issues. In F. Masterpasqua & P. A. Perna (Eds.), *The psychological meaning of chaos: Translating theory into practice* (pp. 177–198). Washington, DC: American Psychological Association.

Margolin, G., Oliver, P. H., & Medina, A. M. (2001). Conceptual issues in understanding the relation between interparental conflict and child adjustment. In J. H. Grych & F. D. Fincham (Eds.), *Interparental conflict and child development* (pp. 9–38). Cambridge: Cambridge University Press.

McLoyd, V. C., Cauce, A. M., Takeuchi, D., & Wilson, L. (2000). Marital processes and parental socialization in families of color: A decade review of research. *Journal of Marriage and the Family, 62,* 1070–1093.

Mills, C. W. (1959). *The sociological imagination.* New York: Oxford University Press.

Nemechek, S., & Olson, K. R. (1999). Five-factor personality similarity and marital adjustment. *Social Behavior and Personality, 27,* 309–318.

Patterson, C. J. (2000). Family relationships of lesbians and gay men. *Journal of Marriage and the Family, 62,* 1052–1069.

Remer, R. (2000). Sociatric interventions with secondary victims of trauma: Producing secondary survivors. In P. F. Kellerman & M. K. Hudgins (Eds.), *Psychodrama and trauma: Acting out your pain* (pp. 316–341). London: Jessica Kingsley.

Remer, R. (2004). When a partner is traumatized: Learning to cope with chaos. In D. R. Catherall (Ed.), *The handbook of stress, trauma and the family.* London: Taylor & Francis.

Rutter, M. (1994). Family discord and conduct disorder: Cause, consequence, or correlate? *Journal of Family Psychology, 8,* 170–186.

Savin-Williams, R. C. (2001). *Mom, Dad, I'm gay: How families negotiate coming out.* Washington, DC: American Psychological Association.

Savin-Williams, R. C., & Esterberg, K. G. (2000). Lesbian, gay, and bisexual families. In D. H. Demo, K. R. Allen, & M. A. Fine (Eds.), *Handbook of family diversity* (pp. 197–215). New York: Oxford University Press.

Stacey, J. (2000). The handbook's tail: Toward revels or a requiem for family diversity? In D. H. Demo, K. R. Allen, & M. A. Fine (Eds.), *Handbook of family diversity* (pp. 424–439). New York: Oxford University Press.

Sun, Y. (2001). Family environment and adolescents' well-being before and after parents' marital disruption: A longitudinal analysis. *Journal of Marriage and Family, 63,* 697–713.

Sweet, J. A., & Bumpass, L. L. (1996). *The National Survey of Families and Households—Waves 1 and 2: Data description and documentation.* Retrieved June 10, 2004, from University of Wisconsin–Madison, Center for Demography and Ecology Web site: http://www.ssc.wisc.edu/nsfh

Teachman, J. D. (2002). Childhood living arrangements and the intergenerational transmission of divorce. *Journal of Marriage and Family, 64,* 717–729.

Umana-Taylor, A., & Fine, M. A. (2001). Methodological implications of grouping Latino adolescents into one collective ethnic group. *Hispanic Journal of Behavioral Sciences, 23,* 347–362

Walsh, F. (1998). *Strengthening family resilience.* New York: Guilford.

Wildman, W. J., & Russell, R. J. (1995). Chaos: A mathematical introduction with philosophical reflections. In R. J. Russell, N. Murphy, & A. Peacocke (Eds.), *Chaos and complexity: Scientific perspectives on divine action* (pp. 49–93). Vatican City State/Berkeley, CA: Vatican Observatory Publications/Center for Theology and the Natural Sciences.

Wu, L., & Martinson, B. (1993). Family structure and the risk of a premarital birth. *American Sociological Review, 58,* 210–232.

Wu, L., & Thomson, E. (2001). Race difference in family experience and early sexual initiation: Dynamic models of family structure and family change. *Journal of Marriage and Family, 63,* 682–696.

• Six

DECENTERING HETERONORMATIVITY

A Model for Family Studies

Ramona Faith Oswald, *University of Illinois at Urbana-Champaign*

Libby Balter Blume, *University of Detroit Mercy*

Stephen R. Marks, *University of Maine*

Heteronormativity is an ideology that promotes gender conventionality, heterosexuality, and family traditionalism as the correct way for people to be (Ingraham, 1996). Our goal in this chapter is to help family scholars deconstruct this complex ideology. Toward this end, we propose a model to untangle the gender, sexuality, and family polarities by which heteronormativity is socially constructed.

Before we proceed with our working definition of heteronormativity, we want to note several assumptions that guide our thinking about this project. First, deconstructing heteronormativity is *not* primarily a strategy for studying gays and lesbians, or for comparing them to heterosexuals. Rather, we intend our framework to provide a tool for recognizing how three structural components

merge to constitute heteronormativity as a system of privileging, and to show how individuals may uphold or challenge it as they negotiate daily life.

Second, we offer no systematic summary of the research showing how heteronormativity (or survey proxies for it) fluctuates within this or that population. What is compelling to us is that these surveys show that heteronormativity remains pervasive. For example, Loftus's (2001) report on data from the General Social Survey (the most representative U.S. sample there is) shows that in 1998, a majority of Americans (56%) still believed that "sexual relations between two adults of the same sex is always wrong" (the other response choices were "almost always wrong," "wrong only sometimes," and "not wrong at all"). In the most recent GSS data available, the proportion of participants selecting the

Authors' Note: We thank Elisabeth O. Burgess for her dynamic participation during our writing retreat.

same response to this item decreased only slightly, to 54% in 2000 and 53% in 2002 (Davis & Smith, 2000, 2002).

Third, we are social constructionists who view families as constituted by interaction rather than by nature. We draw heavily from ethnomethodological and feminist scholarship that examines ideologies as interpretive resources that competent members of society reference in order to organize and attach meaning to their lives (Garfinkel, 1967; Gubrium & Holstein, 1990; West & Zimmerman, 1987).

Finally, a definitional note about the term *heteronormativity* for those readers not familiar with it: In current usage, the term does not refer to a statistical "norm" in the sense of a central tendency, or to what is "normal" in a clinical sense. Rather, the *normative* part of the term is drawn from sociology, where something is said to be normative when the majority of people hold it as a value or a moral standard. Heteronormativity, then, is the implicit moral system or value framework that surrounds the practice of heterosexuality. Typically, heteronormativity is buttressed by claims (often implicit) that because heterosexuality is "more natural" than other forms of sexuality, it should be standard sexual practice.

A THEORETICAL MODEL FOR QUEERING HETERONORMATIVITY IN FAMILY RESEARCH

Heteronormativity has historically emerged as a vast matrix of cultural beliefs, rules, rewards, privileges, and sanctions that impel people to reproduce heterosexuality and to marginalize those who do not (Adam, 1998). The core belief of heteronormativity is that males and females are "opposite sexes" who become sexually attracted and bonded to one another through the unfolding of natural forces within them (Ingraham, 1996). Heteronormativity entails a convergence of at least three binary opposites: "real" males and "real" females versus gender "deviants," "natural" sexuality versus

"unnatural" sexuality, and "genuine" families versus "pseudo" families. Each of these binaries is commonly believed to have an unambiguous and stable boundary separating the poles, so that any given individual is located at one pole or the other (Jagose, 1996). Further, these binaries are organized hierarchically, such that those occupying the "real," "natural," or "genuine" positions have more power and legitimacy than those occupying the "deviant," "unnatural," or "pseudo" positions (Ingraham, 1996).

Although it is analytically desirable to see each binary as distinct from the others, we believe that at this phase of history, heteronormativity remains an ideological composite. It fuses together a gender ideology, a sexual ideology, and a family ideology into a singular theoretical complex. Doing sexuality and doing family properly are inseparable from doing gender properly. For example, in a male's life cycle, socializing agents will constantly flood him with messages that to know oneself as a "real" man is to feel attractions to women, to have sex with them, and eventually to make families with them. This prescription is neither inevitable nor universal; rather, it is a product of history (see D'Emilio, 1983/1998a; Katz, 1995; Staggenborg, 1998). Although evidence abounds that many individuals' lived experiences are not (and were not) as constricted as the ideological composite would suggest (Coontz, 1992), we see heteronormativity as a continuing interpretive resource that guides social action at multiple levels. To explain, we address each of the three binaries that constitute heteronormativity in turn below.

The Gender Binary

The gender binary contrasts "real" males and females with persons who do not conform to gender stereotypes. Feminists have elaborately deconstructed and reconstituted notions of "real men" and "real women" since at least the 1970s, as any standard gender textbook will document. Despite these ongoing challenges, heteronormative gendering continues to be upheld across multiple contexts.

For example, children, especially boys, who are perceived as gender "nonconformists" are more likely to be bullied by their peers (Savin-Williams & Cohen, 1996). Even if children are raised in "gender-fair" families, they are likely to believe that boys and girls are opposites and that they are not equal (Risman, 1998). In school settings, adolescents' gendered behaviors typically intensify as a result of peer pressure to conform to traditional masculine and feminine roles (Galambos, Almeida, & Petersen, 1990). The household, caring, and child-rearing work of heterosexual marriage largely continues to replicate heteronorms (Coltrane, 1998). On television talk shows, gays and lesbians who appear to be just like polite conventional middle-class men and women are presented by hosts and responded to by audiences as more acceptable than those with "trashy" self-presentation (Gamson, 2001, p. 73). In the legal arena, criminal defendants whom judges and juries perceive to be conventionally gendered receive lighter sentences than do those perceived as being "deviant" (Renzetti & Curran, 2003). Since the development of sex-change technology, the standard of care for gender-ambiguous infants has been sex-reassignment surgery, even without informed parental consent (Kessler, 1998). In the realm of employment, males in gender-atypical employment are likely to be promoted out of their pink-collar positions, whereas females in gender-atypical jobs face multiple pressures to leave for more female-dominated arenas (Renzetti & Curran, 2003). The gender binary intersects with race and class in that definitions of "real men" and "real women" are based largely on White middle-class values (Collins, 1990). Thus upholding the gender binary may be complicated by other identities and statuses. For example, African American women have been derogated on multiple fronts for failing to be submissive (i.e., "good") women (Collins, 1990). Together these examples illustrate the complex and tenacious gender binary that partially constructs heteronormativity by upholding ideals of "real men" and "real women" that reflect dominant societal biases (see Lester, 2002).

The Sexuality Binary

The sexuality binary marks heterosexuality as "normal" and pathologizes other forms of sexual behavior. Engaging in heterosexual intercourse constitutes the gold standard against which other behaviors and accompanying identities are deemed less natural or valid. Despite numerous challenges, such as the American Psychiatric Association's decision in 1973 to drop homosexuality from its list of "psychiatric disorders," this binary continues to be reproduced. The opposition of many parents to the inclusion of curricular content about gay or lesbian families in their local schools is an example of the upholding of "natural" sexuality against presumed "unnatural" sexuality, as is the current national movement against same-sex marriage (both examples intersect with the family binary, which we discuss below).

Whereas the connection between sexuality and gender binaries is only implicit in our examples, Nielsen, Walden, and Kunkel's (2000) findings make it more explicit. These researchers collected more than 650 gender transgression narratives from undergraduate students over a period of 15 years. Each student violated a gender norm in public and then wrote an account of what he or she did and how people responded (each was assisted by a covert peer observer). The students' departures from gendered behaviors were often seen as showing something about their sexuality. Even seemingly nonsexual acts, such as a woman buying a cigar or a man wearing a dress, were interpreted sexually. Further, males were homosexualized and females were heterosexualized. That is, people responded to the men's gender transgressions by derogatorily labeling them as gay, whereas women received comments about how their transgressions increased or diminished their heterosexual desirability. These comments typically located women as either "sluts" or "dykes." In their reports, many of the students also expressed their own fears of being identified as gay or lesbian or, if female, promiscuous. Nielsen et al.'s analysis demonstrates social processes by which heteronormativity is reproduced through self and social pressures to conform to both gender and sexuality binaries.

The Family Binary

The family binary privileges biological and legal ties as "genuine" family and designates other forms of relations as "pseudo." For example, in most U.S. states, judicial decisions still offer few or no protections to nonbiological parents concerning child custody or visitation following a lesbian or gay couple breakup. In addition, other-mothering and other forms of community parenting found in some ethnic minority communities may be disregarded by policies that use the family binary to mete out benefits and privileges (Collins, 1990).

Oswald and Suter's (2004; see also Oswald, 2000) comparative research on weddings provides some links connecting the gender, sexuality, and family binaries. Based on their comparisons of the ways in which both gay, lesbian, bisexual, and transgendered (GLBT) people and heterosexual people are included and excluded during weddings, Oswald and Suter theorize that heteronormativity shapes the family membership of people across the continuum of sexual orientation diversity. They argue that inclusion and exclusion processes are driven by the degree to which an individual conforms to heteronormativity within the ritual. For example, in the weddings they studied, gay or lesbian-identified people were likely to receive conditional invitations, as when Lucy Gibbons received a telephone call from the bride: "[She] specifically asked me to not bring Karen [her partner] to the wedding. She had this fear that I was going to bring Karen and embarrass her" (Oswald, 2000, p. 356). Heterosexually identified people may likewise be relegated to the periphery of the wedding ritual insofar as they are believed to violate heteronormative standards of self-presentation that mark the genders as opposites. The overall theme that Oswald and Suter's research revealed was that those whose identities and relationships were highly consistent with heteronormativity were pulled closer to the core of family membership, whereas those whose

identities and relationships posed challenges to heteronormativity were either excluded from the domain of family or included with conditions that masked their difference. Inclusion and exclusion processes together produced a veneer of conventionally gendered heterosexual family normality (i.e., heteronormativity).

QUEERING

The term *queering processes* (see Figure 6.1) refers to acts and ideas that resist heteronormativity by challenging the gender, sexuality, and/or family binaries described above. Whereas second-wave feminist and gay liberation movements sought to legitimate the "deviant," "unnatural," and "pseudo" poles of these binary categorizations, queer theories emerged in the 1980s when some people chafed against having to find places on either side of any of these binary oppositions (Adam, 2002).

When sociologists began to study sex in postwar America, they saw sexuality as a property of individuals and the expression of sexuality as shaped by social norms and attitudes (Seidman, 1996). During the 1950s, however, social perspectives on sexuality were articulated by homophile groups (e.g., the Mattachine Society, the Daughters of Bilitis) that viewed homosexuality as natural and tried to legitimate it. During the 1960s and 1970s, social movements in the United States and elsewhere gradually led to the conceptualization of homosexuality as a political identity and to the founding of gay and lesbian studies programs in academe. By the late 1980s, gay activists began to use the word *queer,* reclaiming a once-derogatory term for GLBT people (Blasius, 2001). In the early 1990s, however, researchers stepped back from a focus on GLBT studies to ask the underlying question of how people and desires came to be separated into the two camps of homosexuality and heterosexuality in the first place (Adam, 2002). "Queer theory," strongly influenced by postmodern philosophy and poststructural feminism (see Jagose, 1996), was used to

Figure 6.1   Conceptual Model for Understanding How Heteronormativity Is Resisted and Accommodated

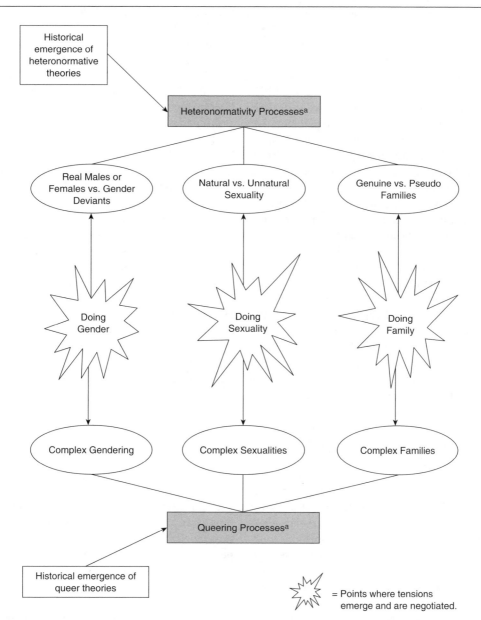

a. The level of analysis may be individual, relational, institutional, historical, or some other level.

examine multiple, socially constructed identities and to question linguistic binaries such as homosexual/heterosexual, male/female, and Black/White (Adam, 2002). Historically, however, queer theory has been a more dominant perspective in philosophy, literary criticism, and history than in the social sciences, probably because of the humanities' primary strategy of deconstruction—reading texts to uncover the "subtexts," or underlying cultural discourses, that constitute the social construction of self and other.

In our conceptual model we identify the process of queering as engaging in complex gendering, complex sexualities, and/or complex families (see Figure 6.1). *Complex gendering* unfolds when humans resist or subvert sex stereotyping. A good example comes from Schwartz's (1994) book *Peer Marriage* (see also Risman & Johnson-Sumerford, 1998). Schwartz's "peer couples" partially queer their families by defying the heteronormative notion of the sexes as opposites. Such couples are steadfastly committed to deep friendship, mutual control over the family economy, and equal responsibility for child care, and for them gender difference no longer figures in how family gets done. Put differently, for peer couples sexual desire is disentangled from the eroticization of gender difference, and the vitality of the partners' sex together must now stand or fall on their inventiveness in creating new forms of sexual tension between them.

Complex sexualities not only include homosexuality and heterosexuality as equally valid ways of being in the world but also encompass bisexuality, asexuality, people who change their sexual identifications, and people who refuse any sexual identification or call themselves queer, as well as other fully consensual ways of complicating sexual identities and practices. Engaging in complex sexualities involves recognizing that sexual identity, sexual attraction/desire, and sexual behavior may not always hang together in one neat package for some individuals. For example, in the 1970s, some women who identified as lesbian feminists and enacted sexual relationships only with other women may have sometimes had sexual *desire* for men, although it is unlikely that they would have acted on it or disclosed the fact of their attraction to their feminist friends (Stein, 1997). In the 1990s, some women who identified as lesbians and who on occasion had sexual desire for men *did* have sex with these men (Stein, 1997), and without any sense of contradiction or apology. One of us knows a female couple who for a long time have been making a life and having sex only with each other, but one of the women refuses any sexual identity: "I don't define myself as a lesbian; I just happen to be in love with a woman."

Complex families include not only families as defined by biological and legal ties but also the many other kinds of relationships that may be considered family by given persons or groups. For example, Gubrium and Holstein (1990, pp. 122–123) tell the story of Maida, an elderly woman who was placed in a nursing home by her son and daughter under circumstances she took to be unfair, capricious, and decidedly contrary to her concept of filial responsibility. Once there, Maida bonded with three other residents so tightly that she (and they) began to make claims about this new group as being her "genuine" family now, much to the consternation of the son and daughter, who were inclined to see these claims more as evidence of her confused state than as a credible alternative perspective on Maida's family composition. Notice how closely this account parallels the idea of networks of friends as "chosen" family (Weston, 1991) within lesbian, gay, and queer studies. Indeed, we would suggest that Maida partially "queered" her family by reconfiguring it in a way that defied conventional claims about what a family is and of whom it is composed.

A QUEER THEORETICAL APPROACH TO FAMILY STUDIES

The starburst elements in Figure 6.1 represent points at which tensions between heteronormativity and queering become salient as people make decisions to resist or accommodate heteronormativity. We are challenging family scholars to bracket all assumptions about what configuration of members qualifies as "family" and to keep their attention focused squarely on family construction processes. The starbursts in the figure represent creative spaces; they are border places where new constructions get crafted and old ones are remade. We envision families in a manner similar to West and Zimmerman's (1987) vision of gender: Family is best understood as something we *do*, because to see it as something we *have* is to beg the question of what family is in advance of knowing what the family-making process has created. This approach may take a variety of forms, two of which we discuss below.

Carrington's Approach

One form is Carrington's (2002) elaboration of doing family as producing and reproducing domesticity—feeding work, consumption work, housework, and kin work. In his study of 52 "lesbigay" (his preferred designator) families in San Francisco, Carrington scrutinized the details of how domesticity is elaborated and maintained, right down to the contents of the refrigerator and which partner gets them there. Borrowing from Dizard and Gadlin's (1990) concept of the "minimal family," Carrington reached the startling conclusion that those families who lack the time or the monetary resources to elaborate domesticity are constrained in their capacity to produce family. The overall heteronormative privileging system results in lesbians' having less disposable income than gay men, who in turn have less than straight men. Lesbigays with children must worry additionally that the shops and other establishments to which they bring their children will not subject them to homophobic hostility. Those lesbigay couples who are not protected by strong domestic partnership regulations have the additional worry that their domesticity may be shattered by illness or other catastrophic personal events that will leave them vulnerable in ways that heterosexually married people typically are not.

Aside from showing the consequences of an overall heteronormative privileging system, Carrington documents the tensions between heteronormativity and queering that are seen within his lesbigay sample. To be sure, the fact that these are same-sex couples shows them to be resisting the "natural" orientation prescribed by the sexuality binary. Side by side with this resistance, however, are myriad accommodations to the prescriptions of heteronormativity. Many lesbigays uphold the "genuine" pole of the family binary by producing and reproducing utterly conventional domestic lives. They buy food and cook meals, trying to honor each other's food preferences.

They shop. They make homes and maintain them (with a queer eye toward aesthetic appeal if they have ample money). They have people over (again depending on how much money they have). Here, readers will look in vain for signs of any difference between lesbigay domesticity and heterosexual domesticity.

Similarly, some lesbigays reproduce "genuine family" by confining their kin work to "biolegal" kin (Carrington, 2002), especially if they are relatively poor, live outside of the central city, have children, and/or have rigid job hours that conspire against the expansion of their family circle. Others, however, queer their families by maintaining forms of kin work that regularly bring them together with chosen family who are drawn from their network of friends. Carrington (2002) cautions us against seeing these chosen families as merely "a rough approximation of the real thing" (p. 141), adding that often these bonds "are far more extensive" than what most heterosexual people understand as friendship. Referring specifically to caring for loved ones with AIDS, he notes:

> Middle-class Americans infrequently take in their friends and provide them housing, food, and medical care while they are dying. Moreover, any number of the lesbigay families in this study would not dream of sacrificing the lesbigay kin ties they have created in favor of some biolegally defined entity. (p. 141)

Along with complex family-making processes, Carrington documents complex gendering within lesbigay families. Many of the couples in his sample showed clear preferences for maintaining the sexes as opposites, and they developed both rhetorical and behavioral strategies for restoring themselves as real men and real women. These couples upheld heteronormative notions of domesticity as "women's work," and so they made reasonable excuses to account for men who did "too much" of it and women who did "too little." Other couples, however, appeared to be indifferent to heteronormative gender prescriptions, if not downright resistant to them, and we see these people as more prone to an unapologetic queering of gender.

Carrington's rich data drive us to an inescapable conclusion: There is no simple continuum with heteronormativity on one end and queering on the other, in large part because the three components of heteronormativity—gender, sexuality, and family constructions—may vary independent of one another. People who enact a queer sexuality may or may not adopt heteronormative standards of gender performance or family composition. People with a queer approach to gender may or may not construct queer families or a queer sexuality. A professional woman who lives alone and never marries or has children is queering heteronormative gendering, but there is no way of knowing from these facts alone if she falls into either the "lesbian" or the "heterosexual" camp, or if her approach to sexuality is "natural" or "unnatural." Similarly, there is no way of knowing if her family-making processes are "genuine" or "pseudo" family constructions. Some people do adopt the "wrong" pole of all three binaries, whereas others violate the heteronormative prescriptions of just one or two of them, but it is senseless to theorize a world consisting of triple queers, double queers, single queers, and nonqueers. People who violate only one of the three prescriptions may be more extreme in their departure from conventionality than people who violate all three of them, and we would be hard-pressed to say who is more thoroughly queer. The fact is that some people thoroughly complicate these binary oppositions, weaving together elements of both sides of each binary in ways that defy any "either/or" logic.

Gubrium and Holstein's Approach

Whereas Carrington's focus is on private households and their production through acts of domesticity, Gubrium and Holstein (1990) see family as waxing and waning purely on the basis of the production of talk (or "discourse") about it. Family is produced as much by judges, social workers, real estate brokers, teachers, nursing home workers, and the residents of institutions as it is by the members of any given household. The list of "producers" of family easily expands to include presidents, presidential candidates, legislators, lawyers, ministers, talk-show hosts, family scholars, queer theorists, and more. In the discursive approach, "family" is reproduced every time it is invoked. Families, like gender and sexuality, are constructed through repetitive performance of the cultural discourse—what Judith Butler (1993) describes as "performativity."

We see much of value in both of these approaches—family as domesticity and family as discursive production. Carrington gets down to the behavioral nitty-gritty of domestic family construction processes, but in so doing, he sometimes comes close to reinstating a "genuine" versus "pseudo" family binary. The starting point of "genuine" family becomes the doing of homemaking activities for and with other people. Much is illuminated by an exploration of these processes, but much is potentially left out. For example, Michael L. (1996), a recovering alcoholic for some 18 years, writes of his "gay AA family": "More than anything, I was given a sense of family as a positive and nurturing place—not the dark and dangerous island I had experienced as a child" (p. 12). In stunning detail, Michael stands the "genuine" family/"pseudo" family binary on its head, elaborating the genuine family values and family membership he discovered among his sober gay friends in Alcoholics Anonymous in contrast to his experiences in his family of origin. Totally absent from his account is any mention of domestic reproduction processes. Family is here constructed and reproduced discursively, and Gubrium and Holstein's approach is better suited to uncovering this kind of discursive reiteration.

Both analytic strategies lend themselves readily to a queering approach to family scholarship. To foster this approach, family scholars must recognize that individuals' very "competence as members of society" is held "hostage" to the way they do family (West & Zimmerman, 1987, p. 126). To do family too queerly, to reveal oneself to be on the "wrong" side of the three binaries we have elaborated, is to expose oneself to risk: risk of rejection by members of one's family of origin, hostility from neighbors and friends, interference from the state, threats to one's livelihood from employers, and physical violence from strangers and acquaintances.

Exposure to risk, however, does not rule out a broad range of responses to that risk, and herein lies the transformative (or what we would call queering) potential of family-making processes. As Moloney and Fenstermaker (2002) assert, following Butler on gender, "What exactly it is that is being iterated and reiterated" can always be changed (p. 199). All families have to be reinvented continuously in the minutiae of everyday life, and the impulse to reinvent family-business-as-usual differently, or queerly, may come from many sources. Here we offer a very provisional list of some fault lines of potential family transformation that may lead people to queer their own patterns of doing family:

- Feeling blocked in the expression of powerful yearnings or desires
- Getting challenged or prodded by someone else, especially a would-be suitor
- Being curious, creative, or inventive
- Feeling that neither side of the sexual binary—straight or gay—speaks adequately to one's desires
- Having models around oneself of diverse approaches to sexuality, gender, and/or family
- Wanting a greater level of couple intimacy and mutuality than is possible when each partner is rendered into an "opposite" of the other

To illustrate, we will focus our attention on just one of these fault lines—the ready availability of diverse models of sexuality, gender, and family configuring. Consider 15-year-old Morgan Green's (2000) account of her family-business-as-usual. Morgan recalls being told at age 3 that her mother's lover, Jamie, was going to have a sex-change operation to become a physical man. By the time she entered the fifth grade, no longer wanting to carry the weighty secret of a lesbian mom and a transsexual dad, Morgan shared her family story with her best friends, Lauren and Briana ("Friends were supposed to tell each other everything, no matter what"; p. 89). The friendships "survived" the news, and although the couple relationship between Morgan's mother and Jamie apparently could not survive Jamie's sex and gender change, Morgan's relationships with both of her parents did. Jamie (now "James") became "Dad," and his transsexual activism became just another "boring" adult thing: "At times, I really can't understand why my dad is so obsessed with his own transsexuality" (p. 91). By the time Morgan was 15, normal family life for her had meant a lesbian mom, a transsexual dad, their fighting and eventual breakup, and a new lesbian relationship for her mom, plus all the publicity associated with her father's having become a well-known activist.

Family scholars can spin this account in at least two different ways: They can focus on how needlessly difficult the challenges were for Morgan (they indeed came in ample supply), or they can begin with Morgan's own claim that "my parents had always taught me to be myself" (p. 90)—Morgan's explanation of why she revealed her family secrets to her teacher via her class journal. In the face of her teacher's stigmatizing response, this 15-year-old remained steadfastly unapologetic: "In reality, of course, the only painful times have been caused by other people's prejudices" (p. 91). Morgan will likely emerge from her adolescence with a much better chance than most of us to select whatever form of sex and gender expression and sexual object choice are most compatible with her inner sensibilities. For its part, family studies should include the Morgans of the world in its canon of knowledge. Family scholarship might redouble its efforts to detail a complete (albeit unfinished) spectrum of gender and "sexual lifeways" (Hostetler & Herdt, 1998), and it should seek to understand the myriad family configurations that arise at various points on this spectrum.

APPLYING A QUEER LENS
TO FAMILY STUDIES RESEARCH

Queer methodology has been widely recognized as an approach to reading existing literature, especially classic texts, from a new perspective (i.e., through a queer lens). Such an approach acknowledges that all texts embody the prevailing social discourse and may shape how readers socially construct understandings of heteronormativity. Although humanities-based queer theory has been widely criticized for not moving "beyond the text" and thus ignoring lived experiences, Stein and Plummer (1994) have argued that a reexamination of social science texts could fruitfully challenge our assumptions of heteronormativity.

We believe that our theoretical model describes phenomena that are happening in the world but that family scholars have not yet addressed. We further believe that our model provides a framework that can help unify family scholarship on gender, sexuality, and family membership. We could use it to examine how individuals negotiate heteronormativity. We could study how organizational practices uphold or resist it. The multilevel repetition of heteronormativity that we have theorized suggests that there is ample opportunity to study it at many levels of analysis. We offer the following three examples of methods successfully employed by family researchers to decenter heteronormativity.

Research on Complex Gendering

Researchers have studied the ways that families challenge heteronormativity through their shared discourse about gender. Matching adolescents' independent narrative accounts with those of their parents, Blume and Blume (2003) documented tensions between the gender binary and complex gendering by comparing parent and child narratives. Both parties recounted ways that the gender binary had been accommodated and resisted over time by children who were performing different gender identities. For example, one

mother, who was open to the idea of gender as fluid, described her daughter's gender appearance as both conforming to and resisting gender norms, sometimes appearing very feminine and sometimes not:

> When she was a child, she loved to wear pink. And she liked to wear dresses. And, she didn't mind wearing dresses, let's put it that way. And then she became pretty conservative, where she would wear pants most of the time, which was fine. But, um, yeah. It changed, 'cause like I said, she loved pink there for quite a while. So, yeah, it did change. (quoted in Blume & Blume, 2003, p. 790)

The daughter's parallel narrative revealed an equally fluid and transitory identification with social discourse on gender in which she sometimes dressed like a "tomboy" and sometimes wore makeup and dresses:

> I was a tomboy. I always played with my brother like we'd play tackle football sometimes with him and his other friends and let's see, I played baseball and tee ball and I was one of the only girls on the baseball team and I always had real short hair. Like I still have my more like tomboyish sides, but I still like love makeup, and I like wearing skirts sometimes but I also like getting in the dirt and like playing rough or something. (p. 791)

Revealing the tension between dualistic positions such as viewing gender distinctions as either natural or cultural, Blume and Blume found that the adolescents in their sample deconstructed heteronormativity by practicing different gender "performances." In the midst of multiple, incompatible messages, the adolescents appeared to be influenced more by a peer culture of experimentation with gender (e.g., hair dyeing, cross-dressing) than by heteronormativity. The parents, at the same time, resisted heteronormative notions that adolescent gender explorations

Chapter tells reader how future study should be directed.

are negative while attempting to negotiate their own new family-level reconstructions of gender. Complementing Blume and Blume's findings is this anecdote: One of us was recently informed by a first grader, over dinner, that the first grader's friends included "girls, boys, girly boys, and boyey girls." Family scholars should study how, and to what consequence, gender is and is not queered within everyday family life.

Research on Complex Sexuality

Researchers have also investigated the construction of (or resistance to) heteronormativity using Gubrium and Holstein's (1990) discourse approach of examining how people attach heteronormative meanings to their experiences through everyday talk. Braun (2000), for example, analyzed 16 different focus group interviews about sexuality for implicit and overt expressions of heterosexual privilege. Braun defined "heterosexism by commission" as participants' equating generic woman and generic man with heterosexual woman and heterosexual man, and as their equating sex with heterosexual intercourse. "Heterosexism by omission" occurred when there was a lack of disagreement with or challenge to heterosexist talk—for example, when participants failed to discuss lesbian topics that were introduced or failed to challenge the equation of sex with heterosexual intercourse. Braun's study effectively questioned *how* the sexuality binary was either maintained or contested by the study participants (see also Namaste, 1996).

We can also apply this discursive approach to families by examining heteronormative discourse as homosexual adolescents come out to their parents. Although teens typically disclose to friends before family and to mothers before fathers (D'Augelli, Hershberger, & Pilkington, 1998), recording family interaction has the potential to reveal teens' awareness of heteronormative talk. For example, Herdt and Koff (2000) describe the "heterosexual family myth" as a belief that only heterosexuals who marry and have children are "normal." In one narrative, a mother told her gay son to try dating (she meant *girls*). Such family discourse may result in adolescents' being reluctant to disclose to their parents despite having come out in other contexts (see Savin-Williams, 2001). Again, family scholars should study how the sexuality binary is upheld and resisted in the minutiae of family life.

Research on Complex Families

As a final example of research that decenters heteronormativity, we have selected a study by Davis and Friel (2001) that used wave 1 data from the National Longitudinal Study of Adolescent Health (known as Add Health). The researchers questioned assertions that growing up in single-parent, stepparent, cohabiting, or lesbian families has negative effects on adolescent sexual behavior. They resisted heteronormative definitions of family structure in their methodology by examining three family structure measures independently: (a) whether the adolescent currently lived in an intact (i.e., two-parent) family, a single-parent family, or a stepfamily; (b) whether the parent had cohabited prior to the focal adolescent's sexual debut; and (c) whether the adolescent currently lived in a lesbian family. They explained:

> For example, if the adolescent lived with her or his lesbian parents (who were in a marriage-like relationship) from the time he or she was born, the respondent would be considered to be in an intact family, to have lived in a cohabiting family, and to be in a lesbian family. (p. 674)

Davis and Friel found that teens' sexual initiation was associated with the mother-child relationship, the mother-child level of interaction, and the mother's attitudes toward and discussion of sex, and *not* with family structure. Through creative operationalization, these researchers were able to measure and assess the lived complexity of their respondents' lives with greater accuracy.

CONCLUSIONS

To end our chapter, we offer the following personal reflections.

Ramona

As someone who has spent the past decade studying gay and lesbian people's families and is chronically annoyed by the continued social marginality and academic invisibility of such families, I am cautious about any theory that challenges identity-based scholarship. When the idea for this chapter first surfaced, I felt excited but incredibly defensive. I was afraid that my contributions and concerns would be eclipsed by queer theory's deconstruction of binaries. Having spent the past year working on this chapter, I can now say that my feelings have totally changed. Our model is powerful because it enables us to talk about complex configurations of both privilege and marginality within and across families, and to intersect those dynamics with race and class. It moves us beyond "gay versus straight" scholarship to a place where we can analyze the ways in which heteronormativity and queering are relevant to anyone. Whether researchers use the model to interpret ethnographic data, to derive measures for quantitative models, or to do something else entirely, my hope is that we have provided a tool that resonates with family scholars who wish to theorize in new directions.

Libby

From my perspective as a human developmentalist, "normal" adolescents who are exploring their identities through gender nonconformity are all too often seen as "deviants" if they transgress heteronormative standards. In 1998, I wrote a working paper for the National Council on Family Relations Theory Construction and Research Methodology Workshop in which I began a feminist project of theorizing gender construction processes in families. As I read sociological theories of the body, psychological perspectives on gender, and feminist philosophical writings on sexuality, however, I "discovered" queer theory. Since that time, applying this interdisciplinary perspective—which we have called queering—to human development and family studies has been both challenging and transformative for me. As a professor of developmental psychology and women's studies, I have found writing this chapter with colleagues from family studies and sociology to be profoundly energizing. The chapter is a reflection of this exciting process of theorizing that may be equally useful to both human development and family scholars who recognize the generational, historical, and disciplinary relevance of decentering heteronormative assumptions in our personal and political lives as well as in our scholarly work.

Stephen

As a sociologist, my passion has always centered on the power of culture and social structure to expand people's options or to constrict them. I seem to be driven to discover the multiplicity of things. More than 25 years ago, I was drawn to considering how people manage their multiple roles, and my bias was rooted in the inner conviction that people can do many different things without necessarily taxing themselves or depriving other people of what is their due. This conviction easily flowed into thinking about what people can be as well as what they can do, and again my bias was that people are as many different things as they want to carve out for themselves. From there it became all too obvious how systems of privilege open doors to some people and close them to others, merely on the basis of assigning them to particular categories. I am drawn to queer theory because it so clearly reveals these categories at the same time it deliberately mucks them up. I enjoy the muck. Writing this chapter with Ramona and Libby has been an exciting reminder to keep on exploring the multiplicity of self and family, and hearing the voices of queer-identified people has been a constant challenge to keep rethinking who I am.

CASE STUDY

BACKWARD SOCIALIZATION AND GAY IDENTITY NEGOTIATION IN FAMILIES

Bertram J. Cohler, *University of Chicago*

The family is the primary source of care and support for young and old alike. A family member's disclosure of an alternative sexual identity represents a highly charged situation that can affect continued family cohesion. In particular, a young adult's "coming out" as lesbian or gay may threaten family cohesion. At the same time, this disclosure has implications for the continued socialization of each generation within the family. Consistent with the model that Oswald, Blume, and Marks present in Chapter 6, such disclosure leads to decentering of the heteronormative family or, in other words, to the "queering" of the family. In this discussion I will provide an illustration of one way in which a family might try to negotiate the meaning for each generation of an offspring's disclosure of gay or lesbian identity.

Nowhere is the challenge of social change for relations within the family more important than in the area of sexuality and "sexual lifeways" (Hostetler & Herdt, 1998), or culturally shaped ideas and emotions, roles, and rituals concerning sexuality that are understood as the foundation for being a person across the life course. Sexual lifeways other than those normatively presumed by the larger society have emerged over the past three decades from a largely secretive and subversive place in society to become socially acknowledged and increasingly accepted alternatives to heterosexuality. Much of this change in understanding of sexual lifeways arose in the wake of the civil rights movement in postwar American society. Although there had been significant protests by men and women enjoying same-gender sexual orientation across the decade of the

1960s (D'Emilio, 1998b), this social movement became more widely visible in the early 1970s following patron resistance in June 1969 to a police shakedown raid of the Stonewall Inn, a homosexual bar in New York's Greenwich Village.

Traditional understanding of socialization across generations within the family and the larger society has presumed "forward" socialization, in which older generations induct younger generations into prevailing norms and values. Hagestad (1981) has portrayed the young adult generation within the family as a cohort bridge linking the family to social changes taking place in the larger society. As a result of the tumultuous social changes that took place in American society between the mid-1960s and the mid-1970s, a time of particularly rapid social change sparked by controversies regarding civil rights and the Vietnam conflict, with young adults seeking to change their parents' views regarding these issues, scholars undertook renewed efforts to understand socialization as a reciprocal process in which each generation within the family attempts to influence other generations. The traditional view of forward socialization was replaced by a perspective that also emphasized backward socialization (Hagestad, 1981).

As Hagestad (1981) has observed, members of generations within the family seek to reconcile their own views with those of other family members in order to maintain the harmony and support so essential for family life. Older generations attempt to influence younger generations regarding their views, while younger generations, connected to social change through school and peer

Case Study

groups, seek reciprocally to influence their elders regarding issues ranging from politics to lifestyles. Offspring attempt to influence their parents regarding new understandings of traditional roles and norms just as parents seek with equal determination to have their offspring conform to their understanding of prevailing norms and values. Greene and Boxer (1986) suggest that this reciprocal socialization takes place in two arenas: within the family itself and in the larger world outside the family, where the offspring have different social roles. The sexual orientation of offspring is an issue that has implications for both of these arenas. Within the family, offspring who adopt alternative sexual lifeways appear to challenge cherished aspects of family life, such as their parents' desire for grandparenthood. In the larger world, the family's having queer-identified offspring poses potential issues of embarrassment and stigma. It may also threaten the family's standing in the community if issues of stigma prevent offspring from gaining employment viewed as commensurate with the family's position in the larger society (Dew, 1994). The offspring's identity with alternative sexual lifeways may disrupt continuing relations across the generations within the family and the family's relations with the larger society. Having queer offspring has the effect of queering the family as a whole.

An individual's disclosure to family members of same-gender sexual orientation and acceptance of a gay or lesbian (or queer) sexual identity is an "ideal type" of backward socialization. Such disclosures, which are often the focus of intense conflict, are at the center of an extensive literature regarding the means that offspring use to renegotiate prevailing familywide understanding of their sexuality (Herdt & Koff, 2000; Savin-Williams, 2001). Beeler and DiProva (1999), for example, studied narratives of offspring disclosure and family response and found that offspring efforts to induct parents into new

understanding of their roles as parents, now of gay or lesbian young adults, were initially a source of conflict and confrontation but led over time to renegotiation of roles for both generations.

In the wake of the sociopolitical movement that led to at least partial normalization of gay and lesbian sexual identity, many gay and lesbian young adults today believe that telling their parents and other family members about their alternative sexual identity is an important means of realizing an enhanced sense of integrity and personal coherence. This announcement almost inevitably leads to enhanced ambivalence within the family as parents struggle to understand the implications of this disclosure for family solidarity. Parents of gay and lesbian young adults often express feelings of consternation and disapproval of their offspring's alternative sexual identities, often accompanied by feelings of guilt for having "produced" gay or lesbian offspring and concern about the implications of the disclosure for the family's status within the community (Dew, 1994; Savin-Williams, 2001). These concerns most often lead to conflict between the gay or lesbian offspring and other family members that threatens to disrupt close ties.

Two accounts of reciprocal socialization have been published, each featuring backward socialization on the part of offspring to induct parents into new understandings of sexuality and sexual orientation, a queering of the family. The first, a mother's account of her college-age son's coming out as gay and the impact of this disclosure on family and community, provides a vivid portrait of the process leading to the queering of the family and the impact of this disclosure on society (Dew, 1994). The second account is reported by a young gay man and his partner together with the young man's parents regarding the young gay couple's effort to arrange a traditional Jewish "wedding" or commitment service in a conservative urban Canadian community (Wythe, Merling, Merling, & Merling, 2000). Both of these accounts provide particularly good illustrations of the process of reverse or backward socialization as well as continuing forward socialization on the part of parents leading to the renegotiation of roles within the intergenerational family (Beeler & DiProva, 1999; Boxer, Cook, & Herdt, 1991).

Even in the liberal, close-knit families involved in these accounts, there are continuing problems as the parents fight against lifetimes of prejudice. Offspring (as well as parent) sexual orientation provides a particularly vivid opportunity to study the process of reciprocal socialization. These two examples show the manner in which, through backward influence, young adults socialize their parents into new conceptions of both same-gender sexual orientation and their role as parents of gay and lesbian offspring. Through backward socialization, these young people have succeeded in queering the family. Parents learn how to relate to a son's life partner and to the partner's parents, now their in-laws (Serovich, Skeen, Walters, & Robinson, 1993). Even as they struggle with their own feelings of shame at having a gay son or daughter, they begin to be activists in the larger community, reaching out to other parents of queer offspring and, ultimately, helping to queer society more generally.

CASE STUDY

GAY MARRIAGE AND SOCIAL SCIENCE

Timothy J. Biblarz, *University of Southern California*

Judith Stacey, *New York University*

In 2001, the Netherlands legalized gay marriage. In 2002, same-sex marriage gained de jure recognition in Ontario and British Columbia and became, de facto, legal in Canada. In 2003, the Supreme Judicial Court of Massachusetts ruled that a state ban on same-sex marriage violated the Massachusetts Constitution. Gains for same-sex marriage have been so dramatic that opponents are currently seeking an amendment to the U.S. Constitution to prohibit it. As same-sex marriage is achieving legal status internationally, this seems to be a propitious time to envision the new research opportunities created by this development. Here we suggest four promising domains for researchers in the sociology of family, gender, inequality, and social policy to pursue.

CHILDREN'S DEVELOPMENT

A preoccupation in political debates but relatively understudied in family research is the relationship between parents' gender and sexual identities and those of their children. Our own work to date suggests that parental genders and sexual identities interact in complex ways to influence children's values,

CASE STUDY *continued*

aspirations, gender repertoires, and sexual interests (Stacey & Biblarz, 2001), but we have been unable to match samples on marital status. When we compared children in families with two heterosexual parents with children in families with two lesbian comothers, for example, most of the heterosexual parents were married whereas the lesbian comothers were not. Alternatively, in studies matching parent groups who are unmarried and cohabiting, only one group has been legally prevented from marrying.

Thus prior research has been unable to examine the effects on parents and children of marriage itself—with its formidable public and material privileges and sanctions. Legal marriage for same-sex couples will enhance our ability to discern whatever unique effects the sexual orientation and gender mix of parents have on family processes and child outcomes. If the gay men and lesbians who choose to marry end up being similar to the groups that have inhabited our samples to date—disproportionately Whites who are comparatively well educated and mature, and who reside in relatively progressive urban centers—differences currently observed between married gay and straight parents and their children may not change much. However, if married gay men and lesbians prove more diverse, currently observed differences—many of which actually favor gay parents and their children (Stacey & Biblarz, 2001)—may diminish as marriage opportunities expand. In either case, the legalization of same-sex marriage will enhance our ability to distinguish the impacts on a host of child outcomes of parental genders, sexual orientations, numbers, and legal statuses.

THE BENEFITS OF MARRIAGE

Will the expansion of marriage increase the well-being of gay couples and their children? At first glance the answer is obviously yes. Researchers who have examined the benefits of marriage argue that, in addition to the extensive legal benefits married couples enjoy, marriage is an institution that helps to stabilize relationships, affords social recognition, and improves health, socioeconomic achievement, civic participation, and involvement with extended family members (Waite & Gallagher, 2000; see also the Spotlight on Methods by Musick in Chapter 4 of this volume). Being denied the freedom to marry conveys the social judgment that same-sex relationships are less worthy than those of opposite-sex couples. Opening marriage to same-sex couples should reduce the prejudice and discrimination they and their children experience.

In addition, legalizing gay marriage should reduce the incentive for closeted lesbians and gay men to instrumentally enter into heterosexual marriages. This should, in turn, diminish the number of marriages that later dissolve because of sexual incompatibility and spare the adults and children involved the hardships associated with those breakups. Legal marriage would also expand lesbian and gay access to adoption and foster care rights, thus reducing the numbers of difficult-to-place children in need of homes. This would create a side benefit for family researchers by enabling us to study more systematically the effects of genders, numbers, legal statuses, and sexual orientations of parents on adoptive children and family relationships.

However, some researchers who have documented the benefits of marriage have been hesitant to infer that similar benefits would apply to married same-sex parents and their children. One suggestion is that it may not be marriage per se but heterosexual marriage that is beneficial, or that spouses' heterosexual sexual orientation may be a precondition for marriage to confer benefits (Nock, 2001). Another is that the benefits to children of married parents depend on the specific gender mix of a man and a woman. Children with married comothers, for example, may not benefit as much from marriage because their households won't receive the breadwinner's bonus in income awarded primarily to

CASE STUDY *continued*

married men (Waite & Gallagher, 2000). Some scholars speculate that married cofathers may be more sexually promiscuous than married heterosexual fathers because they lack the constraints imposed by female spouses. Access to legal marriage for same-sex couples will allow researchers to test these hypotheses and help to untangle the relative impacts of sexual orientations, gender mixes, and legal statuses on associations between marriage and the well-being of adults and their children.

GENDER, MARRIAGE, AND THE DESIRE TO PARENT

The legalization of gay marriage can advance our understanding of the connections among gender, marriage, and the desire to parent. Where same-sex marriage is legal, we will be able to compare the extent to which the desire to marry and the desire to parent coalesce for gay and straight women and men. Some evidence suggests that in advanced industrialized societies, where children represent more an expense than a contribution to family labor and income, men do not desire children as strongly as do comparable women. Marriage provides a route to situational parenthood for many heterosexual men, because they marry women who are more apt to have a strong desire for children.

We suspect that the desires to marry and to parent may be more directly linked for gay men than for heterosexual men. We also hypothesize that a higher percentage of gay men than heterosexual men desire parenthood whether or not they are in committed couple relationships. With legal marriage available, researchers can investigate whether a higher percentage of gay men who choose to marry also choose to become fathers, compared with those who do not marry. The legal marriage option will allow researchers to compare the rate of chosen single parenthood between gay and heterosexual men and between lesbians and heterosexual women.

Inevitably, legal same-sex marriage will also yield a pioneer cohort of same-sex divorce and custody decisions. As unwelcome as these may prove for participants, they will expand researchers' opportunities to study the relationships among gender, marriage, divorce, and parenthood. Comparing postdivorce custody arrangements negotiated by lesbians, gay men, and heterosexual couples should prove particularly illuminating.

THE STRUCTURE OF SOCIAL INEQUALITIES

What is the relationship between the expansion of marriage and other kinds of social inequalities? On the one hand, gay marriage, by reducing institutional discrimination, should help to reduce homophobia and to promote social acceptance of all gay and lesbian people. Such acceptance could have a spillover effect, reducing stigma and increasing tolerance for all kinds of families. Removing gender criteria from the composition of marital dyads represents a bonanza for researchers investigating inequalities in the division of labor, power, emotion work, sexual norms, financial practices, and much more.

Will gender-neutral criteria for marriage help to erode traditional heterosexual marriage patterns and foster greater egalitarianism? Or will the institutional force of marriage trump the more egalitarian patterns that have been documented among same-sex couples? How will the gender composition of conjugal unions affect these patterns? Census data, for example, suggest that gay male parenting couples are more likely than lesbian or heterosexual parents to adopt a full-time at-home parent model during early childhood (Bellafante, 2004). Will marriage reinforce this tendency, and, if so, what impact might this have on other parents and on national family policy agendas?

Another provocative question concerns the potential effect of same-sex marriage on interracial marriage patterns. Census data show that,

Case Study

CASE STUDY *continued*

relative to married heterosexual couples, higher proportions of gay male and lesbian couples are interracial (W. Rubenstein, project director, Williams Project on Sexual Orientation Law, UCLA School of Law, personal communication, February 1, 2003). Will the entry of same-sex couples into matrimony increase interracial coupling and marital heterogamy?

Although the legalization of same-sex marriage might foster a climate of greater tolerance for diversity in some respects, it may do little to change (and may even exacerbate) structural inequalities in the distribution of public and private resources. The gay marriage movement and the conservative promarriage movement both promote a privileged regime for married-couple families that discriminates against the unmarried and their families (Stacey, 2003). Removing the sexual orientation requirement from marriage may do little more than admit to the conjugal club more of the same relatively privileged people—White, middle-class, employed, and so on—who already enjoy higher rates of marriage and marital stability. Thus legal same-sex marriage could shift the axis of

inequality from sexual orientation to marital status as the more significant social divide (Stacey, 2003). In this scenario, single, unmarried, and/or cohabiting citizens of all genders and sexual orientations and their dependents may find that gay marriage does little to channel public resources their way and intensifies the social disadvantages they already suffer. Those who make the conservative case for gay marriage explicitly advocate this agenda: "We should insist on gay marriage. We should regard it as scandalous that two people could claim to love each other and not want to sanctify their love with marriage and fidelity" (Brooks, 2003, p. A15). Some family scholars advocate a similar policy conclusion; for example, Waite and Gallagher (2000) note: "Domestic partners who want partnership benefits have only to marry to get them. Giving the benefits of marriage to people who have refused its responsibilities is neither fair nor wise" (p. 201). If these attitudes prevail, legal same-sex marriage could do more to contract than to expand the ranks of 21st-century families accorded social dignity and public support.

DISCUSSION AND EXTENSION

REFLECTIONS ON QUEER THEORY AND FAMILY SCIENCE

Lawrence A. Kurdek, *Wright State University*

In this discussion I want to raise some general issues regarding the study of gay and lesbian persons in the family in terms of five polarities that Oswald, Blume, and Marks do not explicitly acknowledge in Chapter 6.

HETERONORMATIVE VERSUS HETERONORMAL

Although Oswald et al. clearly define *heteronormativity*, I initially had some trouble understanding the word because *normative* has two layers of meaning for me. First, *normative* can be used in a descriptive sense (in which a norm is an average or typical value) to indicate that the majority of individuals claim a heterosexual identity. Second, it can be used in an evaluative sense to indicate that anything other than heterosexuality is deviant and harmful. To distinguish between these descriptive and evaluative dimensions, I would reserve the term *heteronormativity* to indicate that identifying as heterosexual *is* what most people do (and, therefore, is normative), and I would reserve *heteronormality* to indicate that being heterosexual is by that very fact a facet of the natural (and, therefore, is normal).

I would also suggest that heteronormality be identified as an overarching factor that shapes the developmental context for many individuals who assume the identity of someone who is attracted to a member of his or her own sex. Indeed, a significant developmental milestone in the lives of most gay and lesbian individuals (as well as members of their families) is adapting to the fact that the social paths mapped out for most people will not be available to them (Savin-Williams, 2001) and that they will have to forge their own identities without the benefit of well-worn traditions and support.

Acknowledging, rather than resisting, difference as a context of development is consistent with evidence that many adults who identify as gay or lesbian did not fit in with their peers in childhood (Bell, Weinberg, & Hammersmith, 1981) and justifies the selection of peer group processes as one component of the development of sexual orientation (Bem, 1996). In view of evidence that the construct of minority stress can be used to understand the mental health outcomes of lesbians, gay men, and bisexuals (Meyer, 2003), the very feeling of being different from others will likely have stressful consequences, even if that feeling is not associated with

stigma and prejudice. In short, confronting being different from others, especially during adolescence, when "fitting in" is so important, is a separate process from negotiating the social and cultural consequences of the particular ways in which one is different.

CONTINUA VERSUS CATEGORIES

Oswald et al. regard human sexuality and family interactions as fluid continua that are created in individual acts. However, this dynamic conceptualization of sexuality and the family is at odds with the convention of referring to both individuals (e.g., gay, lesbian, bisexual, or transgendered) and families (e.g., single parent, two parent, or lesbian parent) as members of mutually exclusive groups. Resisting the use of fixed personal and family categories is consistent with a growing body of evidence that sexual behavior and sexual identity are plastic, fluid, and responsive to social-cultural contexts (Peplau, 2001) and that outcomes for children and parents are more strongly linked to what happens in families than to the specific configurations of who resides in families (Patterson, 2000).

NORMS VERSUS HETERONORMS

Oswald et al. argue that the processes of including and excluding that occur in wedding rituals are driven by the degree to which individuals conform to heteronormativity within the rituals. However, I wondered about the extent to which the processes of including and excluding also occur within the contexts regarded as normative for gay men and for lesbians. Why, for example, do few bars cater to both gay and lesbian clientele? Why is there tension between gay men and lesbians? Why do bisexuals and transsexuals report feelings of alienation from gay men and lesbians—the very individuals from whom they might expect acceptance and tolerance to be unconditional? Depending on the context, does it

DISCUSSION AND EXTENSION *continued*

not make sense to refer to "gaynormativity" or "lesbiannormativity," such that each term refers to a set of normative rules or rituals complete with its own processes of inclusion and exclusion for persons from the relevant in-groups and out-groups? From a psychological standpoint, the processes of inclusion and exclusion that occur within groups of gay, lesbian, bisexual, and transgendered individuals are perhaps one way that such individuals cope with being members of a stigmatized and ostracized group (Meyer, 2003).

FRAGILITY VERSUS CHANGE

Oswald et al. appear to regard family reality as a set of fragile practices and usages. Further, they emphasize that the fragility of these practices and usages underscores the importance of behavioral repetitions and discursive iterations. Because families are dynamic systems, I would argue that *change* is the core construct of family science. My emphasis on change is consistent with Oswald et al.'s emphasis on repetition and iteration, but my emphasis also argues for a *prospective* longitudinal perspective on family realities in which the trajectories of change are studied as they occur rather than as they are remembered. From a single snapshot perspective, family reality may indeed appear to be fragile. However, when viewed from the wider lens of change over time, this fragility may actually be part of a stable process in which underlying needs are constant but are expressed in different ways.

QUEER THEORY VERSUS A QUEER PERSPECTIVE

Queer theory is not a theory with a well-articulated set of premises that enables one to make testable predictions that compete with those of other theories. I speculate about two reasons for this (perhaps) controversial

claim. First, queer theory emerged from disciplines other than family studies, such as disciplines within the humanities. As such, different disciplines have developed different strategies for advancing knowledge. Second, queer theory is compatible with a qualitative approach to theory building. As such, studies may not easily be conducted—as they often are from studies using a quantitative approach—with the idea of pitting claims from different theories against each other and then determining which theory provides a better fit to the data.

Perhaps my dubious views regarding the status of queer theory as theory come from my particular stance of "doing family science." As a psychologist, I was trained to be quantitatively oriented. As a psychologist reading the literature in family studies, I am particularly intrigued by empirical studies that address explanations for a phenomenon from perspectives that lead to different predictions and then use replicable methods to assess the extent to which the different predictions are supported. If queer theory is to hold promise for advancing family science, it needs to make *testable* predictions about outcomes of interest to family scientists that *differ* from those of other theories. If queer theory is to make these testable predictions, its proponents need to develop a set of techniques and strategies—queer methodology?—that enable such tests to be conducted. In particular, proponents of queer theory might address whether quantitative methods are necessarily unqueer. From my perspective, the repeated demonstration using quantitative methods that family process is more important than family structure and that gay/lesbian couples are more similar to than different from married heterosexual couples is compelling evidence, consistent with a "queer" perspective, that plurality in form can coexist with common underlying processes that cut across such plurality.

REFERENCES

Adam, B. D. (1998). Theorizing homophobia. *Sexualities, 1*, 387–404.

Adam, B. D. (2002). From liberation to transgression and beyond: Gay, lesbian, and queer studies at the turn of the twenty-first century. In D. Richardson & S. Seidman (Eds.), *Handbook of lesbian and gay studies* (pp. 15–26). Thousand Oaks, CA: Sage.

Beeler, J., & DiProva, V. (1999). Family adjustment following disclosure of homosexuality by a member. *Journal of Marriage and Family Counseling, 23*, 443–459.

Bell, A. P., Weinberg, M. S., & Hammersmith, S. K. (1981). *Sexual preference: Its development in men and women.* Bloomington: Indiana University Press.

Bellafante, G. (2004, January 12). Two fathers, with one happy to stay at home. *New York Times,* pp. A1, A12.

Bem, D. J. (1996). Exotic becomes erotic: A developmental theory of sexual orientation. *Psychological Review, 103*, 320–335.

Blasius, M. (2001). *Sexual identities: Queer politics.* Princeton, NJ: Princeton University Press.

Blume, L. B., & Blume, T. W. (2003). Toward a dialectical model of family gender discourse: Body, identity, and sexuality. *Journal of Marriage and Family, 65*, 785–794.

Boxer, A. M., Cook, J. A., & Herdt, G. (1991). Double jeopardy: Identity transitions and parent-child relations among gay and lesbian youth. In K. Pillemer & K. McCartney (Eds.), *Parent-child relations throughout life* (pp. 59–92). Hillsdale, NJ: Lawrence Erlbaum.

Braun, V. (2000). Heterosexism in focus group research: Collusion and challenge. *Feminism and Psychology, 10*, 133–140.

Brooks, D. (2003, November 22). The power of marriage. *New York Times,* p. A15.

Butler, J. (1993). *Bodies that matter: On the discursive limits of "sex."* New York: Routledge.

Carrington, C. (2002). *No place like home: Relationships and family life among lesbians and gay men.* Chicago: University of Chicago Press.

Collins, P. H. (1990). *Black feminist thought: Knowledge, consciousness, and the politics of empowerment.* New York: Routledge, Chapman & Hall.

Coltrane, S. (1998). *Gender and families.* Thousand Oaks, CA: Pine Forge.

Coontz, S. (1992). *The way we never were: American families and the nostalgia trap.* New York: Basic Books.

D'Augelli, A. R., Hershberger, S. L., & Pilkington, N. W. (1998). Lesbian, gay, and bisexual youth and their families: Disclosure of sexual orientation and its consequences. *American Journal of Orthopsychiatry, 68,* 361–371.

Davis, E. C., & Friel, L. V. (2001). Adolescent sexuality: Disentangling the effects of family structure and family context. *Journal of Marriage and Family, 63,* 669–681.

Davis, J. A., & Smith, T. W. (2000). *General Social Surveys, 1972–2000* [Machine-readable data file] (J. A. Davis, principal investigator; T. W. Smith, director and co–principal investigator; P. V. Marsden, co–principal investigator). Chicago: National Opinion Research Center.

Davis, J. A., & Smith, T. W. (2002). *General Social Surveys, 1972–2002* [Machine-readable data file] (J. A. Davis, principal investigator; T. W. Smith, director and co–principal investigator; P. V. Marsden, co–principal investigator). Chicago: National Opinion Research Center.

D'Emilio, J. (1998a). Capitalism and gay identity. In K. V. Hansen & A. I. Garey (Eds.), *Families in the U.S.: Kinship and domestic politics* (pp. 131–141). Philadelphia: Temple University Press. (Reprinted from *Powers of desire: The politics of sexuality,* pp. 100–113, by A. Snitnow, C. Stansell, & S. Thompson, Eds., 1983, New York: Monthly Review Press)

D'Emilio, J. (1998b). *Sexual politics, sexual communities: The making of a homosexual minority in the United States, 1940–1970* (2nd ed.). Chicago: University of Chicago Press.

Dew, R. F. (1994). *The family heart: A memoir of when our son came out.* New York: Ballantine.

Dizard, J. E., & Gadlin, H. (1990). *The minimal family.* Amherst: University of Massachusetts Press.

Galambos, N. L., Almeida, D. M., & Petersen, A. C. (1990). Masculinity, femininity, and sex role attitudes in early adolescence: Exploring gender identification. *Child Development, 61,* 1905–1914.

Gamson, J. (2001).Talking freaks: Lesbian, gay, bisexual, and transgender families on daytime talk TV. In M. Bernstein & R. Reimann (Eds.), *Queer families, queer politics: Challenging culture and the state* (pp. 68–86). New York: Columbia University Press.

Garfinkel, H. (1967). *Studies in ethnomethodology.* Englewood Cliffs, NJ: Prentice Hall.

Green, M. (with Samuels, E.). (2000). Freak. In N. Howey & E. Samuels (Eds.), *Out of the ordinary: Essays on growing up with gay, lesbian, and transgender parents.* New York: St. Martin's.

Greene, A. L., & Boxer, A. M. (1986). Daughters and sons as young adults: Restructuring the ties that bind. In. N. Datan, A. L. Greene, & H. M. Reese (Eds.), *Life-span developmental psychology: Intergenerational relations* (pp. 125–150). Hillsdale, NJ: Lawrence Erlbaum.

Gubrium, J. F., & Holstein, J. A. (1990). *What is family?* Mountain View, CA: Mayfield.

Hagestad, G. (1981). Problems and promises in the social psychology of intergenerational relations. In. R.W. Fogel, E. Hatfield, S. B. Kiesler, & E. Shanas (Eds.) *Aging: Stability and change in the family* (pp. 11–46). New York: Academic Press.

Herdt, G., & Koff, B. (2000). *Something to tell you: The road families travel when a child is gay.* New York: Columbia University Press.

Hostetler, A., & Herdt, G. (1998). Culture, sexual lifeways, and developmental subjectivities: Rethinking sexual taxonomies. *Social Research, 65,* 249–290.

Ingraham, C. (1996). The heterosexual imaginary: Feminist sociology and theories of gender. In S. Seidman (Ed.), *Queer theory/ sociology* (pp. 168–193). Cambridge, MA: Blackwell.

Jagose, A. (1996). *Queer theory: An introduction.* New York: New York University Press.

Katz, J. N. (1995). *The invention of heterosexuality.* New York: Dutton.

Kessler, S. (1998). *Lessons from the intersexed.* New Brunswick, NJ: Rutgers University Press.

Lester, T. (2002). (Ed.). *Gender nonconformity, race, and sexuality: Charting the connections.* Madison: University of Wisconsin Press.

Loftus, J. (2001). America's liberalization in attitudes toward homosexuality, 1973–1998. *American Sociological Review, 66,* 762–782.

Meyer, I. H. (2003). Prejudice, social stress, and mental health in lesbian, gay, and bisexual populations: Conceptual issues and research evidence. *Psychological Bulletin, 129,* 674–697.

Michael, L. (1996). Gay AA: A family of my own. In J. Preston (Ed., with M. Lowenthal), *Friends and lovers: Gay men write about the families they create* (pp. 11–30). New York: Plume.

Moloney, M., & Fenstermaker, S. (2002). Performance and accomplishment: Reconciling feminist conceptions of gender. In S. Fenstermaker & C. West (Eds.), *Doing gender, doing difference: Inequality, power, and institutional change* (pp. 189–204). New York: Routledge.

Namaste, K. (1996). The politics of inside/out: Queer theory, poststructuralism, and a sociological approach to sexuality. In S. Seidman (Ed.), *Queer theory/sociology* (pp. 194–212). Cambridge, MA: Blackwell.

Nielsen, J. M., Walden, G., & Kunkel, C. A. (2000). Gendered heteronormativity: Empirical illustrations in everyday life. *Sociological Quarterly, 41,* 283–296.

Nock, S. L. (2001). [Affidavit]. Court File Nos. 684/00 and 39/2001, Ontario Superior Court of Justice, *Halpern et al. v. Attorney General of Canada, et al.*

Oswald, R. F. (2000). A member of the wedding? Heterosexism and family ritual. *Journal of Social and Personal Relationships, 17,* 349–368.

Oswald, R. F., & Suter, E. (2004). Heterosexist inclusion and exclusion during ritual: A "straight versus gay" comparison. *Journal of Family Issues, 25*(7), 881–899.

Patterson, C. J. (2000). Family relationships of lesbians and gay men. *Journal of Marriage and the Family, 62,* 1052–1070.

Peplau, L. A. (2001). Rethinking women's sexual orientation: An interdisciplinary, relationship-oriented approach. *Personal Relationships, 8,* 1–19.

Renzetti, C. M., & Curran, D. J. (2003). *Women, men, and society* (5th ed.). Needham Heights, MA: Allyn & Bacon.

Risman, B. J. (1998). *Gender vertigo: American families in transition.* New Haven, CT: Yale University Press.

Risman, B. J., & Johnson-Sumerford, D. (1998). Doing it fairly: A study of postgender marriages. *Journal of Marriage and the Family, 60,* 23–40.

Savin-Williams, R. C. (2001). *Mom, Dad, I'm gay: How families negotiate coming out.* Washington, DC: American Psychological Association.

Savin-Williams, R. C., & Cohen, K. M. (1996). Psychosocial outcomes of verbal and physical abuse among lesbian, gay, and bisexual youths. In R. C. Savin-Williams & K. M. Cohen (Eds.), *The lives of lesbians, gays, and bisexuals: Children to adults* (pp. 181–200). Orlando, FL: Harcourt Brace.

Schwartz, P. (1994). *Peer marriage: How love between equals really works.* New York: Free Press.

Seidman, S. (Ed.). (1996). *Queer theory/sociology.* Cambridge, MA: Blackwell.

Serovich, J. M., Skeen, P., Walters, L. H., & Robinson, B. E. (1993). In-law relationships when a child is homosexual. *Journal of Homosexuality, 26*(1), 57–76.

Stacey, J. (2003, December). *Married to the market? The new haves and have-nots of contemporary conjugal politics.* Paper presented at the annual meeting of the Australian Sociological Association, Armidale, New South Wales, Australia.

Stacey, J., & Biblarz, T. J. (2001). (How) Does the sexual orientation of parents matter? *American Sociological Review, 66,* 159–183.

Staggenborg, S. (1998). *Gender, family, and social movements.* Thousand Oaks, CA: Pine Forge.

Stein, A. (1997). *Sex and sensibility: Stories of a lesbian generation.* Berkeley: University of California Press.

Stein, A., & Plummer, K. (1994). "I can't even think straight": "Queer" theory and the missing sexual revolution in sociology. *Sociological Theory, 12,* 178–187.

Waite, L. J., & Gallagher, M. (2000). *The case for marriage: Why married people are happier, healthier, and better off financially.* New York: Doubleday.

West, C., & Zimmerman, D. H. (1987). Doing gender. *Gender & Society, 1,* 125–151.

Weston, K. (1991). *Families we choose: Lesbians, gays, kinship.* New York: Columbia University Press.

Wythe, D., Merling, A., Merling, R., & Merling, S. (2000). *The wedding: A family's coming out story.* New York: Avon.

• Seven

THEORIZING AND STUDYING SIBLING TIES IN ADULTHOOD

Alexis J. Walker, *Oregon State University*

Katherine R. Allen, *Virginia Polytechnic Institute and State University*

Ingrid Arnet Connidis, *University of Western Ontario*

In this chapter, we theorize adult sibling ties as central relationships across the life course for individuals and families. Drawing from a variety of theories and research to explain why the relationships among adult siblings are key for understanding people's everyday lives, we emphasize the socially constructed nature of family ties. In doing so, we depart from the traditional focus on reproduction and heterosexual relations as the primary axes of family organization (Gittins, 1993). Family research concentrates on two sets of relationships: (a) vertical parent-child ties, typically those of young parents and their dependent children; and (b) the horizontal adult ties of married heterosexual partners. Feminists such as Thorne (1982) have critiqued this narrow conceptualization of intra- and intergenerational ties, which Dorothy Smith (1993) describes as "the standard North American family." They challenge scholars to provide perspectives that capture the full diversity of family life.

By shifting the focus away from parents and children, and wives and husbands, to the actual social networks in which individuals and their kin relate to one another over the life course, the study of sibling ties broadens our ability to explore *family* relationships. Our purpose in this chapter is twofold: Our primary aim is to develop a theoretical framework for studying sibling ties in adulthood, and our secondary aim is to show how scholars can use sibling ties to conceptualize the expanding and contracting boundaries of families beyond narrowly conceived vertical (e.g., parent-child) and horizontal (e.g., husband-wife) ties. Ultimately, we seek new ways of thinking about family relations among kin—including those related by blood, marriage, adoption, and choice—over the life course.

The sibling tie is the family relationship of longest duration. Nevertheless, it has received somewhat limited empirical and theoretical attention, particularly in comparison to marriage and parenthood. Although many studies have been conducted over several decades, sibling research is rarely cited in the family literature. Despite the useful descriptive data and provocative ideas it provides, adult sibling research has tended to be atheoretical, to use specialized populations, to be problem focused, and to lack attention to the other family connections in which sibling relationships are embedded. In effect, adult sibling ties are not central to family studies, and research on sibling relationships has yet to coalesce into a definitive body of work. That researchers have employed a variety of methods in examining these relationships suggests that the use of multiple methods alone is not sufficient to move our understanding of sibling relationships forward. Instead, an overarching theoretical framework is needed for understanding sibling relationships in the context of family ties. This framework must provide a basis for cohesion across a range of research questions and the studies designed to explore them.

Social change and the consequent demographic trends in Western families have brought a new complexity to family relationships over the life course. These changes include structural transformations such as increases in cohabitation, nonmarital childbearing, divorce, and remarriage as well as an elongated life span. Issues once thought to be private have become politicized: In addition to other contested issues, public debates are taking place concerning family rights for gay, lesbian, bisexual, and transgendered people; affirmative action for ethnic/racial minorities; and the right to self-definition for people who are bi- and multiracial. These demographic and social developments have resulted in complex and diverse family structures and processes that require researchers to develop new conceptual and methodological tools. Because these changes are implicated in the very definition of sibling ties, they draw attention to this understudied subject and simultaneously offer a conceptually rich tool for bridging the classic kinship ideas of "family of orientation" and "family of procreation" (Christensen, 1964).

As we have noted, much contemporary family research focuses implicitly on nuclear families, an approach that conflates families and households and draws attention to young married couples with children (Bould, 1993). Family researchers view parents and children, wives and husbands, through a microscope, simultaneously losing focus on the broader family connections that impinge on and are affected by these close kin or primary ties (Rossi & Rossi, 1990). This narrow focus has caused family scholars to view families and households as one and the same. Because most siblings do not coreside in adulthood, then, sibling ties are often invisible to researchers or are relegated to the periphery of families over the life course (for an exception, see Connidis, 2001).

The study of sibling ties encourages a flexible conception of family connections that goes beyond those between parents and children and between wives and husbands. By definition, adult sibling ties are outside of the normatively conceptualized bonds of partnering and parenting; they require researchers to focus on a broader social network (Wellman & Wortley, 1989). This broader view has the potential to lead scholars to include other, even less visible, family ties in their research. By studying siblings, we can see what families actually look like in adulthood, which may enable us to theorize families as something other than nuclear versus extended kin. The notion of an *invisible* family life course helps us to conceptualize and understand families as they really are, including, for example, those who are childless, persons who never marry, individuals without biological siblings, and those who are gay, lesbian, bisexual, or transgendered.

Adult sibling relationships are simultaneously like those of closer kin (e.g., parents, children) and like those of nonkin (i.e., friends). Unlike closer kin relations, sibling relations include a strong element of choice (Allan, 1977). In contrast with friendship ties, however, these ties are not voluntary: "One can have an ex-friend, but not an ex-sibling" (Allan, 1979, quoted in Matthews, 1994, p. 183). Like closer kin relationships, sibling ties represent at least a minimal level of obligation (on structural bases for commitment, see Johnson, 1999), evidenced by the fact that most siblings maintain contact throughout their lives (Cicirelli, 1982). Sibling ties are variable, however. Some are intensely close, whereas others exist in name only (Ross & Milgram, 1982). This intragenerational connection, then, offers family researchers an avenue for examining the expanding and contracting boundaries of families (Johnson, 1995). Further, because of their partly voluntary nature, sibling ties are conceptually linked to kinship extension and conversion (e.g., reliance on collateral fictive kin), which typically occur in African American families (Stack, 1974) as well as in gay and lesbian families (Weston, 1991).

We do not view the study of sibling ties as peripheral to the understanding of family issues, an interesting sidebar arising from more central concerns. Rather, we argue that facets of sibling relations that are unique to them (e.g., their relatively egalitarian, relatively voluntary nature) will help to illuminate the dynamics and processes of relationships common to all family ties. Following the logic of induction and deduction, we view theorizing about sibling ties as an interactive process. We seek to identify core theoretical ideas central to understanding sibling relationships and to combine them into a conceptual framework. At the same time, we keep empirical evidence in view when thinking theoretically. We learn through an iterative process that combines elements from our theoretical tools with what we see. Stepping away from an implicit acceptance of the nuclear model, we are confident that including adult sibling ties in our observational field will enhance theoretical development.

When we place sibling ties in the center of our line of vision, we view them not *indirectly*, from the vertical, normative perspective of the parent-child relationship, but *directly*, from a horizontal perspective. Analyzing sibling ties makes it possible to study family life in ways that question the taken-for-granted elements of more obligatory relationships (Connidis, in press). That sibling ties are simultaneously voluntary and obligatory provides flexibility for relationship partners in interpreting and

responding to social norms. In the sections that follow, we discuss key theoretical ideas and their application to sibling ties, outline a methodological orientation and its connection to theory, discuss how we are applying our methodological orientation to sibling ties, identify key methodological issues in the study of sibling connections, and propose new directions for research by asking questions that should arise for scholars examining sibling relationships.

THEORETICAL ORIENTATION

In considering various theoretical perspectives and concepts, we make systematic choices consistent with our biases and assumptions. We aim to explain processes and dynamics, to treat social structure as embedded in all social relations, to examine siblings in the contexts of their broader social networks, and to explore the variations in sibling relationships that are consequences of the relationships' location in the social structure and also in historical time. We look at siblings in their own right, not only in relation to parents as in much adult sibling research. From life-course, feminist, social constructionist, and ambivalence perspectives, we draw ideas and constructs to theorize about adult sibling relationships. First we examine core assumptions of these theoretical ideas relevant to our subject matter, and then we present our theoretical integration.

Life-Course Perspective

Elder (1974) has identified four key principles of a life-course framework: (a) An individual's life course is intertwined with and influenced by the specific historical time and place in which it is located; (b) the timing of transitions, experiences, and patterns of relating influence their developmental causes and effects; (c) because individuals live their lives in the contexts of other social relations, sociohistorical influences impinge on their interdependence with others; and (d) individuals exercise agency as they relate to specific sociohistorical opportunities and constraints, thus building their own unique life courses. The life-course perspective, then, focuses attention on the individual, familial, and sociohistorical events and transitions that shape lives over time, allowing us to study how transitions and trajectories are linked across family members (Bengtson & Allen, 1993).

A key concept in the life-course perspective is that of the *birth cohort* (Ryder, 1965), which draws attention to the unique experiences of particular cohorts as well as commonalities across cohorts. The postwar baby boom cohort, for example, born roughly between 1946 and 1964, generated the largest sibling pool in the 20th century. Being members of a very large cohort coincided with relative affluence in the early years of baby boomers' lives and job shortages when they entered the labor force. These are among the sociohistorical factors that created a unique cohort experience, with some variations between the older and younger segments of the baby boom. Now in middle age, siblings in the baby boom cohort provide an opportunity for researchers to examine family of origin connections at midlife, a time frame dominated in the literature by issues of children leaving home and, to a lesser extent, the effects of retirement on marriage.

Although the life-course perspective draws attention to dimensions that are important for our understanding of family ties across time, the links among these dimensions, such as the connection between agency and social structure, are not fully realized. Further, this perspective does not articulate how social structure is reproduced in relationships. For these purposes, we rely on feminist constructs.

Feminist Perspective

A feminist perspective draws attention to how individuals in diverse social locations negotiate sociostructural arrangements (Baber & Allen, 1992; Collins, 1990). Feminist principles include (a) the belief that women are capable and valuable, (b) recognition that most knowledge has an androcentric bias, (c) acknowledgment that social change occurs on both personal and collective levels, and (d) an understanding that social locations (e.g., race, class, sexual orientation) intersect to produce differential life experiences such that there is no universal standpoint for women (Freedman, 2002). A feminist perspective calls attention to what is taken for granted in families, such as the unpaid labor of kin keeping and the invisible work of caring for family members and of monitoring family life. Feminism alerts us to inequality in social structures and its reproduction and transformation in families. This attention to inequality parallels discussions in critical theory of how structured sets of social relations are produced and reproduced (Connidis & McMullin, 2002; Tilly, 1998).

Social Constructionist Framework

Compatible with a feminist perspective on the partiality of knowledge, a social constructionist framework moves attention away from a singular view of reality that exists outside the observer's perception and calls into question the notion of a unitary, rational, enlightened view of truth, of morality, and of the self (Gergen, 1999). The experiences of those on the margins of society—who are not White, male, heterosexual, youthful, middle- or upper-middle-class, attractive, married, parents, and so on—have helped to create a crisis of confidence in what once was taken for granted as "the center." Now, "there is no center that can hold" (Gergen, 1999, p. 30).

The constructionist perspective requires us to employ a wide-angle lens, to consider margins, groups, topics, and issues that have been ignored. This means asking how family relationships are negotiated and renegotiated (i.e., constructed and reconstructed) over time and in relation to specific ideologies, practices, and structures. Further, it extends our focus to include sibling relationships within a broader kin network. For researchers and theorists, the social constructionist framework draws attention to the constantly shifting social and historical contexts through which individuals negotiate their lives (Henderson, 1994). Life decisions such as whether to partner, when to partner, whether to have children, and when to have children are situated in relation to and against the beliefs and behaviors of social partners, dominant family ideologies, and structural constraints (Gittins, 1993). Individuals negotiate and renegotiate their social relations always in connection to this multilayered sociostructural context. These negotiations occur at the personal level, as people negotiate their senses of themselves as siblings. They occur also within specific sibling ties, because sisters and brothers, siblings who are older and younger, siblings who are married and unmarried, and so on, face unique structural and ideological constraints. Further, specific sibling ties are negotiated within the broader complex of sibling connections such that a sister with four brothers, for example, is situated differently from a brother with only one brother or from a sister who has both sisters and brothers.

The Concept of Ambivalence

Ambivalence enables us to link key ideas from the theoretical frameworks we have identified for the study of sibling ties in adulthood. These ideas are individual action, family relationships, and social structure (i.e., sets of social relations such as those of gender, class, race, ethnicity, and age). The contradiction of expectations based on differences in sociohistorical time is an additional dimension of ambivalence. Because ambivalence has been developed as both a psychological concept and a sociological concept (Boss & Kaplan, 2004; Connidis & McMullin, 2002; Lüscher & Pillemer, 1998), it is compatible with a multidisciplinary approach that can address emotions, social psychological factors such as stress, and individuals' connections to social institutions (e.g., family) and social structures through their relations with one another (interaction). Together, the two perspectives on ambivalence emphasize the coexistence of harmony and conflict, in the form of mixed emotions, as well as the socially structured contradictions that individuals experience in interactions with others (Connidis & McMullin, 2002). Ambivalence names the process that links individual action with the contradictions created by social structures.

In psychology, the focus of the concept of ambivalence is on contradictory feelings and thoughts. Fingerman (2001), for example, has demonstrated that aging mothers and their adult daughters experience mixed emotions in their relationships with each other. In sociology, the focus is on how embeddedness in socially structured sets of relations creates contradictions among family relationships (Connidis & McMullin, 2002). Willson, Shuey, and Elder (2003) bring these two views together by interpreting the ambivalent feelings of women for parents and in-laws to whom they give care as a function of gendered social relations in which women are more obligated than men to provide care.

Applying Our Theoretical Framework to Sibling Ties

Having identified key theoretical ideas, we now consider how their application leads us to address sibling ties in new ways. To ground our discussion in current research, we use as an example the negotiation of sibling ties when parents need support. On one hand, we are reluctant to rely on the literature on this subject because it repeats the traditional focus on siblings *in relation to parents* rather than in relation to each other and in their own right. On the other hand, this literature provides an empirical basis for our illustrations. Further, several insightful studies have examined sibling ties in the context of siblings' supporting older parents. Here, we show how our research question and consequent understandings are transformed with the integration of each new theoretical idea.

The life-course perspective encourages attention to the implications of critical transition points in individual lives for sibling relationships. The emphasis on linked lives and the assumed willingness to act in response to situational imperatives suggests that a parent's need for care will prompt interaction among siblings as they work out how that care will be provided. Following from our discussion of socially structured relations, however, we know that siblings are not merely interdependent as family members. Their level of interdependence is based on their unique sociodemographic characteristics and their position in the social structure. Research suggests, for example, that because working-class adults depend more on their siblings than do middle-class adults, they are affected more by their siblings' life-course transitions (e.g., divorce, childlessness, retirement; Merrill, 1996). Further, expectations to help parents may be somewhat relaxed for siblings with very young children relative to those whose children are grown.

Matthews (2002) outlines how siblings vary in responding to their parents' need for care. What accounts for this variability? A feminist perspective reminds us that lives are stratified by gender, race, and class. Gender features prominently in the adult sibling literature. Brothers, for example, are more likely than sisters to receive assistance in helping parents, in part because they are more likely to demand it (Merrill, 1996).

Feminist theory emphasizes the significance of gender as structuring the social world. A gendered social world implicates women in caring work of all kinds (e.g., emotional labor, housework). Sibling ties also reproduce gendered social order in that siblings vary in their ability to exercise agency in response to ambivalent structural demands. Because of the simultaneously voluntary and obligatory nature of sibling ties, however, siblings have a heightened possibility of *transforming* the social order, drawing our attention to individual agency. Social change in the form of women's labor force participation, for example, intensifies the ambivalence of gendered expectations that sisters will provide family support in conjunction with paid work and has led to some shifts in caregiving for both adult children and their aging parents. For instance, although women continue to bear greater responsibility than men for caregiving, their style of delivery has changed. The greater diversity of women's experiences, based in part on variability in labor force participation, means that sisters are not alike in responding to parents' needs for care and that demands on brothers may have increased (e.g., Finch & Mason, 1993; Matthews, 2002).

Qualitative research over decades has found consistently that British and U.S. siblings from working-class backgrounds are closer to and more cooperative with one another than middle-class siblings. It is not surprising, then, that working-class adults are more likely than middle-class adults to name a sibling as a best friend (Allan, 1977). Building on Bott's (1971) analysis of social networks, Merrill (1996) argues that the cultural value of family interdependence means that the working classes are more connected to extended families than are the middle classes. In contrast, an individualist orientation of autonomy means that middle-class siblings feel less obligated to help each other and express less conflict when other siblings refuse to join in helping parents.

Social constructionism draws attention to the contested nature of reality and shifting views of truth. The center that does not hold is children's obligation to support their parents *personally*. There is no uniform expectation of filial responsibility. Weakly defined norms may lead to variability among siblings about what each should do, disagreement about their shared commitment, or perhaps a uniform view that caring for parents is not their responsibility. In fact, older adults with geographically proximal children often use fictive kin, social siblings, or other chosen family members to meet their immediate needs (Barker, 2002).

An ambivalence perspective points to structural dimensions, such as gender, socioeconomic status, and culture, that impinge on intragenerational linkages (Connidis & McMullin, 2002; Lüscher & Pillemer, 1998). Unique features of the sibling tie, particularly its relatively voluntary nature, create unique bases for ambivalence (Connidis, in press). In fact, ambivalence may be an expected outcome of the lack of clarity between what is voluntary and what is obligatory. Siblings have overlapping but distinct social networks, and individual siblings face unique sets of social expectations. Consider two married sisters whose parents cannot meet their own daily needs. Whereas one married sister may assist her parents with the help and support of her financially secure husband, the other may limit her assistance because of the time she must spend doing paid work, which is essential to her family's financial well-being. The more helpful sister has more opportunity for agency than does the less helpful sister, who faces greater constraints. The inevitably unequal pattern of aid by these sisters may heighten the ambivalence between them. If the sisters are not cognizant of their differential constraints, hidden and even overt conflict may be one outcome of this heightened ambivalence (Jerrome, 1996).

As we have already noted, constraints do not exist only at the interpersonal level. Recall that working-class siblings receive more assistance than middle-class siblings in providing parent care (Merrill, 1996). Wanting but being unable to share caregiving with siblings also provokes intense feelings, such as anger and disappointment. These intense feelings also are more common among working-class siblings who provide care and have fewer options to hire help than do middle-class siblings. Ambivalence, then, is related to social class, both across families and within sibling sets.

A related factor is the shifting pattern of migration into Western societies. Families from different cultures vary in the extent to which they emphasize vertical and horizontal ties and in the relative importance of older versus younger siblings (Johnson, 1995). This variation has implications for the relative importance and meaning of sibling relationships within and across racial and ethnic groups. Further, both relative importance and meaning are likely to change with immigrants' length of time in the new culture and across generations. Change within any ethnic or cultural group, however, is not likely to be uniform, creating the potential for even more ambivalence for sibling ties.

• *SPOTLIGHT ON THEORY*

THEORIZING ABOUT SIBLING RELATIONSHIPS WHEN PARENTS BECOME FRAIL

Victoria Hilkevitch Bedford, *University of Indianapolis*

One property that distinguishes adult sibling ties from parent-child ties is that the former are less obligatory than voluntary. It may be useful to view the obligatory-voluntary ratio not as a static property, but as a dynamic one that varies over the life course. During the period of caring for aging parents, for instance, the voluntary aspect may diminish, which may explain why filial caregivers often complain that their siblings are not helping them enough. At the same time, however, siblings' sense of obligation may increase, which may account for why sisters whose circumstances prevent them from helping their siblings with parent care often feel guilty (Brody, 1990).

(continued)

● **SPOTLIGHT ON THEORY** *continued*

An essential aspect of sibling relationships is that they share at least one parent (excluding some social siblings). Thus any theorizing about sibling relationships must take the parent-child bond into account, yet most references to siblings neither embrace the full sibling network nor consider its intersection with the parent-child bond. One approach to considering this complexity of inter- and intragenerational family bonds draws heavily on Hochschild's (1973) theorizing, which derives from the work of Durkheim. According to this perspective, siblings engage in equal exchanges; theirs is a side-by-side relationship of similar individuals (generational mates) who are equals. In contrast, the parent-child relationship is complementary, dependent, and based on differences. As Hochschild notes, by being equals, "siblings offer the same things to each other, but they also have the same needs to fill" (p. 147). Thus, despite the advantages of similarity (e.g., its potential for community building), the relationship lacks the quality that provides for need fulfillment. This lack may help explain why the filial care literature is replete with negative feelings about siblings— disappointment, resentment, and conflict. As siblings' resources become depleted during the course of caring for a parent with dementia, even the most caring and interidentified siblings may eventually become protagonists (Lerner, Somers, Reid, & Chiriboga, 1991).

This deterioration of sibling relationships during filial care implies that there are times when sibling solidarity and parent-child solidarity are in direct conflict with one another—that is, the parent's needs wear down the sibling bond. Conversely, in order to preserve the sibling bond, siblings may need to sacrifice optimal levels of parent care. This conflict of needs may be why the stem family form (cohabitation of a parent and one child, usually the eldest) appears to be the optimal family structure for the welfare of older parents (Cowgill, 1986). Perhaps families could reduce generational conflicts by drawing on the resources of the full complement of siblings (including step-, half, social, and rejected siblings). In order for families to engage these siblings, however, there must be greater acknowledgment of siblings from alternative family forms and siblings on the family margins (e.g., rejected due to sexual orientation).

When viewed from a life-course perspective, intra- and intergenerational (sibling and parent-child) conflicts seem to wax and wane. When a parent serves as kin keeper, kinship ties are encouraged. After the death of a parent, a decrease in helping behaviors toward siblings may occur (Eriksen & Gerstel, 2002). This finding seems to suggest that parent bonds strengthen sibling bonds. On the other hand, sibling offspring of deceased parents are likely to be older, and age is also related to fewer sibling helping behaviors (but not a decrease in sibling salience; Gold, 1989). Further, when frail parents die, caregiving that has brought siblings together for a common purpose ceases, thereby eliminating a compelling reason for sibling help.

Clearly, the sibling relationship is not a static one. The conditions, content, and consequences of sibling relationships vary with life-course contexts (e.g., Bedford, 1989). Filial caregiving is a particularly compelling context, and one with increasing prevalence in family life. ●

METHODOLOGICAL ORIENTATION

As is true of any research endeavor, our approach to studying sibling ties is shaped by our theoretical framework; it both informs and limits our choice of research methodology. We are explicit in stating the relations among our theoretical ideas, our research questions, and our method. Our position is that research methodologies have their own theoretical underpinnings, even if unstated. In turn, a theoretical claim to any subject comes to fruition only when the methodology employed can reveal it. For example, much family research described as atheoretical assumes uniformity in family structure and processes. We treat players in and processes of family relations as open questions. Employing both quantitative and qualitative methods, either independently or in combination, we take a stance that problematizes the status quo and approaches data with research questions rather than detailed hypotheses. We acknowledge that family scholars need both large-scale quantitative and intensive qualitative studies to appreciate the landscape and the dynamics of sibling ties.

RESEARCH ON SIBLING TIES

We have noted the existence of an empirical literature on adult sibling relationships, scattered throughout a number of disciplines and appearing in a variety of outlets. With few exceptions, and reviewed superficially, this literature can be characterized as sociological, psychological, or psychoanalytic in orientation. From a sociological perspective, for example, survey researchers have highlighted older adult sibling ties and have shown sociodemographic differentiation by marital status, parental status, age, gender, race, and socioeconomic status, and by sibling configuration, such as gender composition, geographic proximity, and sibling network size. This research suggests that sibling relationships tend to be closer in later life than in earlier adulthood and among sisters, the unmarried, those without children, and the geographically proximal. African Americans are less likely than Whites to exchange aid with siblings, as are those with low income and low education. Yet sibling support and closeness are more prominent in the life histories of African Americans than in those of other racial/ethnic groups (Johnson, 2000). These studies have begun to map the topography of sibling relationships in adulthood.

Some of the sibling research that has taken a psychological perspective, primarily conducted with samples of young adults, often college students, has focused on characterizing sibling relationships. Researchers have created typologies of sibling relationships and identified relationship properties that characterize sibling ties. Retrospectively, researchers also have studied how experiences in childhood affect sibling relationships later in life. These studies have identified key emotional and attitudinal dimensions of adult sibling relationships.

Although few studies have identified any theoretical disposition, a psychoanalytic perspective is implicit in much of this literature. Superficially, this perspective highlights the relation of adult children to parents. It suggests that children interpret their experiences in relation to their connection to their parents and their parents' connection to their siblings. This perspective inevitably leads to questions about constructs such as sibling rivalry and competition. In our view, it has led family scholars to miss more central processes of adult sibling ties. Several small-scale, in-depth, qualitative studies of sibling relationships in adulthood have revealed more complex insights: that siblings negotiate their interactions in the context of the larger sibling network (Matthews, 2002) and that sibling ties are often inactive but activated in times of need (Allan, 1977).

Researchers have examined adult sibling relationships using large-scale survey methods, vignettes, typological approaches, checklists, observation, physiological assessments, and a variety of qualitative approaches, including focused interviews, retrospective accounts, psychodynamic interviews, and ethnography. We propose an overarching framework for interpreting family ties as a basis for cohesion across a range of research questions and their exploration. The combination of both quantitative and qualitative analysis best reveals the variety, dynamics, and processes of sibling relationships. Because we seek diverse information, we require multiple methodologies. We need data from large-scale quantitative studies with representative samples to understand who counts as a sibling, the nature of sibling contacts and exchanges over time, and how these dimensions vary by stage of the life course, social structural factors, and family structure. To study the dynamics of sibling ties within the broader context of family networks as well as the process of relating, which is made evident in the context of particular issues or transitions, we need to use qualitative methods with samples of specialized populations.

METHODOLOGICAL CHALLENGES

Regardless of subject matter, family researchers struggle with many methodological challenges. Any longitudinal study, for example, must disentangle age, period, and cohort effects; confront attrition and instrument decay; and so on. Although sibling research has these same difficulties, the unique characteristics of sibling relationships lead to the special challenges we discuss below.

Who Counts as a Sibling?

Who counts as a sibling is a complex matter (Connidis, in press). Siblings can be biological, through one parent (half siblings) or both parents (full siblings), adoptive, or step. These permutations presume a maximum of two unions for any one biological parent. Some biological parents enter third or subsequent cohabitations or biological unions or have children with multiple partners. Cohabiting and gay and lesbian couples in second or subsequent unions also may have children who are effectively stepsiblings although not recognized as such in law.

These variations do not exhaust the variety of sibling ties. We have thus far identified only those defined through family membership. Fictive kin or social siblings exist as well. African Americans are known to "go for sisters (brothers)," converting friends into kin (Stack, 1974). Furthermore, gay men and lesbians may create siblinglike ties with friends (Weston, 1991). Conversely, some persons legally qualify as siblings but do not view one another as such. We expect time (age when full-, half-, or stepsibling ties are established or revealed) and place (coresidence patterns and length) to influence siblings' self-definition (Connidis, in press).

Researchers cannot simply ask, "How many siblings do you have?" We need quantitative research with representative samples to identify how many people exist in various sibling categories. We need qualitative research to determine the process through which individuals come to recognize others as siblings. Across all forms of sibship there may be commonalities, and within any category of sibship there may be substantial variation. The value of clarifying sibling ties and keeping forms conceptually distinct lies in the opportunity this affords the researcher to determine the conditions under which variation and commonalities exist.

The Illusive Nature of Sibling Ties

Although sibling relationships are likely the social tie of longest duration, they wax and wane throughout adulthood. The study of any sibling tie, then, represents a snapshot of the relationship at a point in time; it cannot capture growth, stability, or decline.

Although most biological siblings coreside throughout childhood, they rarely do so in adulthood. Further, geographic proximity in adulthood may be common among only some siblings. Siblings know one another intimately, as they are linked by childhood experiences unlikely to be known by others. Simultaneously, there may be huge gaps in siblings' intimate knowledge of one another, as in adulthood siblings share some information about themselves only with partners, children, and closest friends. Even when geographically proximal, few siblings have the kind of frequent, routine connection that keeps them in the forefront of each other's daily lives. Such coresidence, proximity, and intimate connection are more common in later life and among particular socioeconomic and racial/ethnic groups.

Family researchers are mistaken when they assume that lack of routine, frequent contact means that sibling relationships are neither close nor important, however. For most adults, siblings are, at the same time, close and distant—in the forefront of their daily experience and simultaneously in the background. Allan (1977) describes sibling relationships as *dormant*, to be activated during times of need or family connection. Perhaps this is why researchers have focused disproportionately on siblings in relation to aging parents' need for care, a situation that may bring siblings into relatively frequent contact. Further, this dormant quality suggests that family rituals (e.g., weddings, reunions, marker birthdays and anniversaries, retirements) are opportunities to study sibling relationships.

The term *dormant* means that sibling ties are suspended or inactive. In effect, sibling relationships are like air mattresses: mostly flattened and hidden away but pumped up for service when needed. Applying the concept of ambivalence, however, we see sibling relationships as neither *on* nor *off*. Instead, we acknowledge that small but significant portion of sibling ties in which siblings are best friends and highlight other sibling ties as significant regardless of activity level. Siblings influence each other's thoughts, feelings, and actions even without being present.

Shared family and interpersonal history means that sibling ties have the potential to be active even without contact. Daily experiences trigger memories of siblings or remind us of things only our siblings would understand. These events are influential; they keep siblings in close proximity even without contact. Further, although not actually present, siblings are likely to be in the forefront in their fellow siblings' interactions with parents and other relatives. For example, a conversation with one's aging parents frequently leads to follow-up conversations with a sibling or two. How to capture this relationship that is at once both close and distant, active and dormant, and its meanings to siblings, is a methodological challenge.

Decisions Regarding the Unit of Analysis

Sibling ties are a special case of relationships, and relationship research is complicated by the perspective of the reporter. Further, the number of relationships varies with the number of siblings. Each of the various perspectives of relationship partners presents unique methodological challenges (Thompson & Walker, 1982):

- One sibling provides a single, subjective perspective on the relationship and the sister (brother) within it.
- When both siblings report, the researcher has the advantage of both perspectives but has analytic problems as well. Quantitative data from sibling pairs are not independent. Qualitative researchers must reconcile distinct perspectives on the same social tie. Depending on the researcher's theoretical orientation and the research question, distinct points of view are important in their own right.
- An outsider (e.g., parent, in-law, researcher) may report on a sibling relationship, but outsiders vary in their access to the insider's view. Yet information both about and from third parties sheds light on the sibling relationship and helps account for variations in perspectives between and among siblings.

All relationship researchers face such unit of analysis issues, and the solutions to these problems reside in the researcher's theoretical perspective. As our perspective situates individuals in relationships within a particular sociohistorical time and a particular set of social structures, we examine sibling relationships from individual, dyadic, and multilevel perspectives.

Problems in combining multiple levels of analysis have led researchers to create new quantitative analytic techniques that are useful in sibling research. Multilevel modeling, for example, enables researchers to analyze data from individuals nested in relationships that are nested in families, eliminating concerns about nonindependent data (e.g., Willson et al., 2003). For qualitative researchers, affordable and powerful software packages now make it possible for them to manage even thousands of pages while minimizing the risk of being swayed by "extraordinary stories" (Fischer, 1994).

Selectivity

Family researchers must address selectivity issues. Geographically proximal siblings, for example, may interact more frequently than siblings who live some distance from each other. Further, geographic proximity may be intentional: Emotionally close siblings or those with particular need for support following life transitions may choose to live in close proximity. Additionally, individuals who volunteer for sibling research may have more positive ties than those who do not volunteer. Researchers should be cognizant of these selectivity factors so that they can control for them in quantitative analyses. Further, selectivity should be a subject for study in sibling research. Controlling for selectivity factors takes them into consideration but tells us little about how they operate in individuals' lives (Johnson, 1995). In sibling research, selectivity factors are linked to key dimensions such as gender, social class, race, and ethnicity, dimensions that might be viewed as lenses through which people see and experience their social worlds (Johnson, 1982).

Differentiating Siblings From Other Kin

Contact and instrumental and socioemotional exchange are key dimensions of all family relations. Survey researchers must ask about specific kin rather than include siblings within an "other kin" category that contains grandparents, grandchildren, aunts and uncles, and so on (Wellman, 1992). Further, surveys must ask about individual sibling connections rather than "*any* brother (sister)" or "your brothers *and* sisters." Survey data must make it possible for researchers to isolate siblings for analysis.

Gender as an Axis for Studying Sibling Ties

Our theoretical perspective highlights gender as a key dimension for interpreting, experiencing, and negotiating sibling relationships. As we have noted, in adulthood, sisters are closer to each other than sisters are to brothers; brother-brother ties are the least close. Mostly, research concerning kin ties has been the study of women, although some researchers, notably Sarah Matthews, have brought men to the center of our understanding. We face a challenge, however, in assessing men's interpersonal closeness, feelings of affection, and activities that express care (e.g., Bank & Kahn, 1997). Similarly, our conceptualization of what women and men do for siblings (and aging parents) is tilted toward women's activities (Matthews, 2002). For these reasons, the study of brother-brother ties provides family researchers with an opportunity to understand men better as socioemotional partners.

Because our theoretical perspective draws attention to gender, we highlight the need to study siblings within a complex network of sibling relationships. When are sisters expected to be responsible for keeping sibling ties active, and under what circumstances do they do so? What is the work of a sibling tie (e.g., emotional labor, relationship management), and how is it carried out? How are sibling ties influenced by this work? Because family work is stratified by gender (Ferree, 1990), sibling work is a key dimension of interest to feminist sibling researchers.

● SPOTLIGHT ON METHODS

TWIN STUDIES AND DEMENTIA

Keith E. Whitfield, *Pennsylvania State University*

Advances in health research suggest that there are substantial individual differences in the causes of poor health and that this variability arises from both genetic and environmental sources. An understanding of these etiologies will have an impact on our knowledge about aging in general and even facilitate our understanding across ethnic and racial groups. Studies with genetically informative data have only begun to increase our understanding of the inter- and intraindividual variability in older adults (Whitfield, 1994).

Quantitative genetic research employs three primary sibling-based designs: the classic twin study, the parent-offspring family study, and an adoption design. The information provided by such research is quite useful for helping us to understand the forces that are involved in shaping the lives of older adults. These methods, which are based on population statistics and genetic theory, are used to assess the impacts of genetic and environmental influences on the traits of individuals.

In the study of health in late life, there is perhaps no greater emphasis than on dementia and individual variability in Alzheimer's disease (AD). Given that researchers have focused a great deal of attention on the familial version of AD, there is implicit interest in both the relationship of family history to AD and the heritable transmission of the disease. Sibling studies have provided some of the most interesting portrayals of the relative importance of genes and environmental influences.

Researchers have used twin studies in two ways to examine dementia among older adults: They have employed traditional quantitative genetic analyses comparing identical to fraternal twins to estimate the heritability of dementia, and they have conducted case control studies to examine concordance for dementia within twin pairs. Heritability of susceptibility to AD has been estimated to be .74, and to any dementia, .43 (Gatz et al., 1997). Researchers have even conducted imaging studies to examine similarities and differences in brain structures associated with dementia.

Although twin studies provide researchers with opportunities to gain important insights about dementia as a process, twin research may have important limitations that need to be acknowledged. Perhaps the most important of these is the assumption that in twin research, typically both members of a pair must participate. Survivorship of members of intact pairs compared with surviving members of nonintact twin pairs may reflect differences in psychosocial and health factors and represent a potential selection bias relative to the general population. Samples may be biased toward healthier individuals because of higher refusal rates when one or both twins are ailing and the removal of the most frail due to mortality of one twin. Among minority populations that experience health disparities, this may be even more common. For example, Whitfield, Brandon, Wiggins, Vogler, and McClearn (2003) compared health, cognition, and well-being

(continued)

● SPOTLIGHT ON METHODS *continued*

among members of African American intact twin pairs with the same characteristics among individuals from nonintact twin pairs. After they controlled for demographic variables, only blood pressures differed between the groups, favoring the members of intact twin pairs. These results are interesting in light of recent findings of potential relationships between cardiovascular disease and AD. Whitfield et al. suggest that, to avoid possible selection biases, future research on the etiology of genetic and environmental influences in adulthood should attempt to extend designs to include siblings or perhaps use missing data procedures.

Twin and sibling studies that include genetically informative information will significantly contribute to our understanding of Alzheimer's disease and other dementing illnesses. In this way, we can begin to understand these diseases as arising from insults to a complex system represented by the interaction between genes and environments that creates gradients in the excess burden of chronic illness and disease. ●

Sibling Ties Within Broader Kin Networks

Earlier, we cited work by Allan (1977) and Johnson (1982) in which they describe sibling ties as embedded within broader kin networks, which is especially important for particular class, racial, and ethnic groups. With the exception of Johnson's work on Japanese American, Italian American, and African American families, sibling researchers have yet to bring in-laws and siblings' broader kin networks (e.g., parents' siblings, cousins) into the equation. Sibling ties are linked to other social connections by definition and in practice. A woman becomes a sister-in-law, for example, through the marriage of her brother. How do in-law connections impinge on, enlarge, stress, and enhance sibling ties? How are sibling relationships transformed when a brother does not like his sister's husband? In what ways are sibling relations enhanced when siblings have children of similar ages and genders?

FUTURE DIRECTIONS

All researchers are interested in change, which makes the study of sibling ties among the most exciting areas in family research.

Variations in sibling relations are pushed by structural change. Baby boomers have many siblings relative to the people in the cohort that follows them. Additionally, they have experienced a relatively high divorce and remarriage rate, complicating their kin ties. The implications of these characteristics for sibling relationships have yet to be determined. In later life, baby boomers will have few adult children on whom to rely. Some, especially fathers who remarried after divorce and then had children with subsequent partners, may be estranged from their older adult children. How will adults in the network of siblings, half siblings, stepsiblings, and siblings-in-law negotiate expectations to help aging family members and the constraints that make it difficult to do so?

Divorce, remarriage, and cohabitation have complicated family lives, and families are becoming diverse in other ways as well. Increasing migration, higher rates of reproduction among immigrant groups, and ethnic and racial diversity also complicate this area of study. For example, Western nations have increasing rates of interracial and interethnic pairings. Siblings now are more likely to be multiethnic and bi- or multiracial, and they are increasingly likely to form diverse partnerships. As sexual orientation becomes more open, individuals must negotiate with gay and lesbian siblings as well as with their siblings' partners and children within kin networks that have varying levels of knowledge, acceptance, and understanding of nonheterosexual ties. Additionally, adult siblings who did not spend much time coresiding as children may be forced to forge connections in adulthood. Examining the complex constellation of sibling ties will help us to identify factors that are essential to understanding these and all family relationships.

The unique properties of sibling ties—intragenerational, shared history, potential egalitarianism, waxing and waning connections—make them interesting in their own right. At the same time, in studying these relationships we may uncover processes and features of relating that are relevant to all family ties. The constancy of sibling ties in terms of duration and generation provides a lens through which we may see more clearly how societal change affects all relationships as well as observe the timelessness of family connections beyond wives and husbands, parents and children. Our overarching theoretical framework provides the cohesion we need to understand sibling relationships in the context of broader social relations, both kin and nonkin. Highlighting gender and other aspects of the social structure facilitates the study of ambivalence among siblings as they negotiate critical transitions in a complex web of linked lives.

CASE STUDY

REACHING BEYOND THE DYAD: RESEARCH ON ADULT SIBLINGS

Sarah H. Matthews, *Cleveland State University*

Imagine what families and societies might be like if no one had siblings. In her intriguing novel *The Children of Men* (1993), P. D. James presents a world in which people have stopped being able to reproduce. She raises to the level of awareness how ingrained in our actions and beliefs is the assumption that others will come after us. Similarly, to understand the effects of having and being a sibling as well as the significance of siblings for the organization of societies, it is instructive to envision a world in which no one has a sibling, where everyone is an "only child." The modifier *only,* of course, would be unnecessary, because no one would have a brother or a sister. Moreover, other kinship ties would exist only in the imagination. Aunts, uncles, and cousins would be nonexistent. All relatives, including in-law relationships, would be intergenerational. There would be no brothers- and sisters-in-law. For a middle-aged, married parent, for example, a complete four-generation kinship network would consist of a spouse, two parents and two parents-in-law, a child, a child-in-law, and a grandchild. This kinship network would comprise the same people regardless of whether the middle-aged person is a father or mother. The only difference would be which parents in the preceding generation are biological and which are in-laws.

The likelihood of a society composed exclusively of one-child families is small. For most of human history, the volume of death across the life span has been so high that limiting reproduction would have threatened the survival of a population. However rational it might be in the short term, such a cultural

Case Study

reproductive strategy is too risky to sustain a human group over the long haul. Siblings and all the other kinship ties that stem from them are very much part of human societies and are likely to continue to be. Nevertheless, imagining a world without siblings not only raises to the level of awareness the integral role of siblings in the structure of kinship relationships in societies but also suggests new research questions.

CURRENT RESEARCH

Most of the research that has been conducted on adult siblings has taken a social psychological perspective. Researchers are interested primarily in knowing the strength of sibling relationships as measured by such things as how close respondents feel to a sibling and the degree to which respondents believe a sibling can be counted on for emotional and instrumental support. Scholars have also explored whether such things as gender and stage in the life course affect individuals' assessment of their siblings.

Sibling respondents typically are asked to choose one sibling on which to focus. This means that the responses of those who have only one brother or sister and have no choice are equated with those who select one sibling from two brothers, or a sister and a brother, or two sisters, and those who select one sibling from three brothers, or two sisters and a brother, or one sister and two brothers, or three sisters, and so on. Size and gender composition are only two of the ways in which sibling groups differ. Age between siblings is another. Asking respondents to focus on the sibling closest in age equates ties with siblings who differ in age by 10 years with those who are only 1 year apart. The assumption that sibling dyads identified in these ways are similar enough to place in one category is questionable.

Moving beyond the dyad, however, creates methodological problems. The fact that respondents have different numbers of siblings challenges the application of statistical techniques that require all respondents to have equivalent data. Furthermore, when someone reports about each of her or his siblings, the researcher cannot treat the resulting data as independent. As noted above, researchers typically solve these problems by focusing on selected dyads, usually from the perspective of only one of its members. The requirements imposed by statistical techniques limit the kinds of research questions that can be addressed and suppress important factors that contribute to an understanding of sibling relationships. The absence of independence challenges siblings as well, but in ways that cannot be as easily suppressed: They are aware that they act within a network of interdependent ties. Although qualitative research is not subject to the same constraints, researchers tend to limit research designs in the same way. Rarely do they ask respondents about all of their siblings or ask siblings about one another. As a result of these limitations, research findings on adult siblings are difficult to interpret and tend not to be particularly revelatory because they require so many caveats.

FOCUSING ON NETWORKS

Although specific ties between adult siblings are worthy of attention, raising questions exclusively about them leaves unaddressed questions about kinship networks across generations that siblings make possible. It is easy to lose sight of the benefits and drawbacks that accrue from the very existence of sibling ties irrespective of feelings, face-to-face interaction, and direct social support. The very existence of siblings increases the size and complexity of kinship groups and the ways in which they are embedded in larger networks of relationships. Aunts, uncles, cousins, nephews, nieces, and the variety of in-law relationships all stem from the existence of siblings. Moreover, siblings serve as indirect links not only to in-laws and nieces and nephews but to all of *their* strong and weak ties as well. Siblings rarely are the same age, but even when they are they are unlikely to have the same friends or employers or to marry into the same families. In short, siblings are important because they connect one another to different networks, which in turn increases opportunities.

Studying sibling ties provides us with the opportunity to ask research questions that link social psychological questions with structural ones. The quality of sibling ties affects whether and in what ways siblings have access to one another's networks of relationships, whether kith or kin. Allan (1979), for example, found that the frequency and enjoyment of brothers' ongoing interaction through the life course was greatly facilitated when the brothers' wives were friends. As another example, O'Bryant (1988) found that for some recent widows, their sisters' husbands were important sources of support. Recent work by Lareau (2003) suggests that the probability of siblings' having a close relationship as adults varies with social class. The "concerted cultivation" to which middle-class children are subjected fosters competition between siblings, whereas the "accomplishment of natural growth" favored by working-class parents encourages children to identify with one another. Ironically, then, middle-class adult siblings, who are likely to have a plethora of potentially useful weak ties, may be less willing to share them than are working-class siblings, who have a preponderance of strong ties that they are more likely already to share. Siblings link one another to both strong and weak ties, but the ways in which they do so vary by social class (Granovetter, 1973).

Social class is important for another reason. For the working class, there is evidence that kinship ties, including parents, grandparents, aunts, uncles, siblings, nieces, and nephews, continue throughout life to have a taken-for-granted quality that the middle class leaves behind with other "childish things." This is one way to interpret Merrill's (1996) finding that "the working classes are

more connected to extended families than are the middle classes," as Walker, Allen, and Connidis put it in Chapter 7. Likewise, the meaning of "voluntary" may be related to social class. This difference suggests that members of the middle class, when compared with members of the working class, may be handicapped in their appreciation of the meaning of sibling ties. Social scientists and their students at the universities where research on families is framed and conducted are usually at least middle-class and are unlikely even to have working-class backgrounds. As a result, their interpretation of research findings may be problematic, and they may even have difficulty posing appropriate research questions.

Another potential bias stems from the fact that the labels for kinship ties remain the same through time, effectively concealing changes in meanings (Gillis, 1996). Throughout history, people have had and been sisters and brothers, but the meanings and consequences associated with those ties have changed and continue to change.

DESIGNING RESEARCH

The appropriateness of particular research designs for studying sibling relationships depends, as in any research, on the research question. I have already noted that researchers using both quantitative and qualitative methods rarely move effectively beyond the dyad. Current research rarely takes into account relationships among all siblings in a group or investigates the larger networks in which sibling groups are embedded. To do so would be to challenge the methods that researchers typically employ.

The kind of intensive research that allows interpretation of the worlds of family, including sibling ties, in specific social locations is increasingly rare (e.g., Young & Willmott, 1960). One of the basic tenets of qualitative research is that the researcher's goal is to discover not only the participants' interpretations of the subject at hand but also to gain a clear understanding *of what the participants are interpreting.* This suggests that when one is doing research on adult siblings, it is important to have a very clear idea of the networks in which the sibling ties are embedded if one hopes to interpret the siblings' responses reliably. A researcher would gain much in studying adult siblings by identifying and keeping in mind the whole network while gathering information about how and why siblings in it behave and believe as they do. Survey instruments alone are not well suited to accomplishing this, although allowing both fixed-choice and open-ended responses to questions (Connidis, 1983) might prevent misinterpretation. By including information in their descriptions and explanations about the contexts within which adult siblings make their decisions, researchers can improve understanding of adult family ties and the relationships between the family and other institutions.

CONCLUSION

My intent in inviting the reader to contemplate a social world in which siblings do not exist has been to show just how significant siblings are for individuals, families, and societies. Without them, kinship networks would be much less complex and the myriad connections among people that rely on kinship would be severely curtailed. My second intent here has been to argue that research on siblings provides us with an opportunity to move beyond the social psychological level of questioning to improve our ability to understand and describe those bonds among social actors that bind people into social networks. An important challenge for family scholars is to frame new questions that reach beyond the level of individuals in roles. Toward this end, the study of adult sibling relationships may prove fruitful indeed.

DISCUSSION AND EXTENSION

SIBLING RELATIONSHIPS IN CHILDHOOD: IMPLICATIONS FOR LIFE-COURSE STUDY

Susan M. McHale, *Pennsylvania State University*

Ann C. Crouter, *Pennsylvania State University*

Siblings are significant in the everyday lives and development of individuals and families. The study of sibling relationships illuminates family dynamics that are often ignored by family scholars and fosters new ways of thinking about both dyadic relationships and family systems. Research on siblings also directs attention to the methodological challenges of studying dynamic social phenomena and complex social groups. Given these facts, all of which Walker, Allen, and Connidis mention in Chapter 7, sibling relationship researchers have long wondered why family scholars so often overlook this area of study. Walker et al. provide some intriguing answers, and in so doing they may turn the attention of the next generation of scholars to these important relationships.

Research on sibling relationships in adulthood is especially limited, but over the

DISCUSSION AND EXTENSION *continued*

past several decades, beginning with Lamb and Sutton-Smith's (1982) edited volume and a seminal review by Dunn (1983/1998), research on sibling relationships in childhood and adolescence has increased steadily in both quantity and sophistication. There is now a substantial body of knowledge about the unique qualities of sibling relationships, how these relationships develop, and how they influence child development. In the following we provide a brief overview of research on sibling relationships during the first two decades of life. Our goals are to ground Walker et al.'s significant conceptual contribution within the larger body of research on childhood sibling relationships, to draw some important distinctions between sibling relationships early in life and those later in life, and to suggest directions for life-course investigation of sibling experiences. Like Walker et al., we hope that our commentary promotes family scholars' interest in investigating sibling relationships both in their own right and in the conceptualization and study of families more generally.

Although sibling relationships become more voluntary in adulthood, siblings are a fixture of family life in childhood. Even in the face of declines in family size among all segments of U.S. society, for example, the overwhelming majority of children grow up in households with at least one sibling (Eggebeen, 1992; Hernandez, 1997); indeed, children today are more likely to grow up in households with siblings than with fathers. Our own work documents that, in middle childhood, children spend more of their out-of-school time with siblings than with anyone else (McHale & Crouter, 1996). Cross-cultural analyses likewise highlight the ubiquity of siblings in children's everyday lives, leading one observer to suggest that what varies across cultures is who *aside from* siblings makes up children's social ecology (Weisner, 1989).

Another unique element of childhood sibling relationships is their role structure: Sibling experiences reflect both the egalitarian structure of friendships, as when sisters and brothers play together, and the hierarchical structure of parent-child relationships, as when older siblings serve as models, advisers, and caregivers for their younger sisters and brothers. Some cross-sectional analyses suggest that sibling relationships become increasingly egalitarian as children mature (Buhrmester & Furman, 1990), but we know little about how changes in these relationship dynamics are negotiated or about how childhood roles color sibling relationships in adulthood.

In addition to dynamics marked by birth order and age, the role structure of childhood sibling relationships is defined by processes linked to the dyad's sex constellation. Although some studies have documented differences in siblings' experiences as a function of sex constellation, small sample sizes, a paucity of longitudinal data, and researchers' failure to "unpackage" sex (e.g., are observed differences due to personality? shared interests? interactional styles?) limit our understanding of what it means to be a sister versus a brother (McHale, Updegraff, Helms-Erikson, & Crouter, 2001). Piecing together available data, we might conclude that sex constellation differences are less pronounced in early childhood; our own data suggest that, by adolescence, same-sex sibling relationships are more intimate than sister-brother ones and that same-sex dyads spend more time together (Updegraff, McHale, & Crouter, in press). It is important to note that the companionship of sisters and brothers in childhood—and exposure to the sometimes different worlds of girls and boys by virtue of having a sibling of the other sex—stands in stark contrast to the sex segregation of the peer group that characterizes this developmental period (Maccoby, 1998). Shrinking family size, however, means that increasing proportions of children may grow up without this important childhood connection to the other sex.

In childhood, sibling relationships are emotionally intense. In one vivid account, Dunn (1983/1998) describes an older sister who was tormented to tears by a toddler-age sibling's claim of having stolen the older girl's *imaginary* companion. Based on evidence like this—of a barely verbal child mustering language and social cognitive skills to recognize and target her sister's special vulnerability—Dunn argues that the emotional intensity of sibling relationships is a motivating force in children's social development. As this example also reveals, emotion in the sibling relationship is not always positive; rather, some have described the tie between siblings as a love-hate relationship (Bryant, 1982), reflecting the emotional ambivalence between siblings that emerges from their roles as constant companions, sources of social comparison, and competitors for family resources.

Furthermore, the emotional intensity of sibling experiences may spill over to affect the broader dynamics of families. Problems with how their children get along, for example, are at the top of the list of mothers' and fathers' parenting concerns (Perlman & Ross, 1997); along these lines, our data show that the most frequent source of conflict between children and parents is how children are getting along with their siblings. In short, the emotion engendered by everyday sibling experiences in childhood contrasts sharply with the waxing and waning of siblings' emotional connections in adulthood. A life-course perspective directs attention to the processes underlying continuity and change in the intensity of siblings' emotional connections from childhood through old age.

Sibling relationships emerge during childhood within the context of larger family dynamics. Although most studies of childhood examine siblings' direct influences on one another in their everyday interactions, siblings also can influence one another indirectly by virtue of their family roles, relationships, and activities. For instance, a body of work examines differences between siblings' family experiences and their implications, through social comparison processes, for child and adolescent well-being and development (e.g., Brody, Stoneman, & McCoy, 1992; Daniels & Plomin, 1985). In addition to highlighting children's nonshared family experiences as central in family life and child development, this work exemplifies a systemic approach to studying families. It also directs attention to family dynamics that the more typical focus on a single parent-child *dyad* cannot—for instance, the sometimes competing interests of siblings and the trade-offs parents must make to balance the needs of two or more children (McHale & Crouter, 1996; McHale, Crouter, & Whiteman, 2003). Even in the face of a "norm" of equal treatment in U.S. society (Parsons, 1942/1974), however, parents' differential treatment (PDT) of siblings is common. Some of siblings' differential experiences may be explained by children's social location in families (e.g., their birth order, sex, and biological relatedness), but children also play an active role in patterns of PDT by virtue of their personalities, interests, and behaviors (e.g., Mekos, Hetherington, & Reiss, 1996; Tucker, McHale, & Crouter, in press). Research on PDT also directs attention to the social construction of family dynamics with findings that children's perceptions of the reasons for and fairness of PDT moderate its negative implications for child well-being and sibling relationships (Kowal & Kramer, 1997; McHale, Updegraff, Jackson-Newsom, Tucker, & Crouter, 2000). How siblings' differential family roles and relationships evolve in adulthood from childhood patterns is an intriguing question for life-span research on siblings.

As this glimpse into the research on childhood sibling relationships suggests, in the everyday lives of families with children, siblings are anything but marginal. Nonetheless, these relationships remain at the margins of theory and research among both family and developmental scholars. Theoretical biases that mark parent-child relationships as primary (e.g., the functionalist tradition in family research, the ethological/analytic tradition within child development) as well as methodological challenges are likely reasons for past neglect. The very ubiquity of siblings, however, may also be responsible for their taken-for-granted status. More than two decades ago, Urie Bronfenbrenner (1979) explained the field's failure to attend to the ecology of human development with a quote from Goethe that would seem to apply here: "What is the most difficult of all? That which seems to you the easiest, to see with one's eyes what is lying before them" (p. 37).

REFERENCES

Allan, G. (1977). Sibling solidarity. *Journal of Marriage and the Family, 39,* 177–184.

Allan, G. A. (1979). *A sociology of friendship and kinship.* Sydney: Allen & Unwin.

Baber, K. M., & Allen, K. R. (1992). *Women and families: Feminist reconstructions.* New York: Guilford.

Bank, S. A., & Kahn, M. E. (1997). *The sibling bond.* New York: Basic Books.

Barker, J. C. (2002). Neighbors, friends, and other nonkin caregivers of community-living dependent elders. *Journal of Gerontology: Social Sciences, 57,* 158–167.

Bedford, V. H. (1989). A comparison of thematic apperceptions of sibling affiliation, conflict, and separation at two periods of adulthood. *International Journal of Aging and Human Development, 28,* 53–65.

Bengtson, V. L., & Allen, K. R. (1993). The life course perspective applied to families over time. In P. Boss, W. J. Doherty, R. LaRossa, W. R. Schumm, & S. K. Steinmetz (Eds.), *Sourcebook of family theories and methods: A contextual approach* (pp. 469–499). New York: Plenum.

Boss, P., & Kaplan, L. (2004). The link between ambiguity and ambivalence in intergenerational relations. In K. Pillemer & K. Lüscher (Eds.), *Intergenerational ambivalences: New perspectives in parent and child relations in later life.* Oxford: Elsevier Science.

Bott, E. (1971). *Family and social network* (2nd ed.). New York: Free Press.

Bould, S. (1993). Familial caretaking: A middle-range definition of family in the context of social policy. *Journal of Family Issues, 14,* 133–151.

Brody, E. M. (1990). *Women in the middle: Their parent-care years.* New York: Springer.

Brody, G. H., Stoneman, Z., & McCoy, J. K. (1992). Associations of maternal and paternal direct and differential behavior with sibling relationships: Contemporaneous and longitudinal analyses. *Child Development, 63,* 82–92.

Bronfenbrenner, U. (1979). *The ecology of human development: Experiments by nature and design.* Cambridge, MA: Harvard University Press.

Bryant, B. K. (1982). Sibling relationships in middle childhood. In M. E. Lamb & B. Sutton-Smith (Eds.), *Sibling relationships: Their nature and significance across the lifespan* (pp. 87–121). Hillsdale, NJ: Lawrence Erlbaum.

Buhrmester, D., & Furman, W. (1990). Perceptions of sibling relationships during middle childhood and adolescence. *Child Development, 61,* 1387–1398.

Christensen, H. T. (1964). Development of the family field of study. In H. T. Christensen (Ed.), *Handbook of marriage and the family* (pp. 3–32). Chicago: Rand McNally.

Cicirelli, V. G. (1982). Sibling influence throughout the lifespan. In M. E. Lamb & B. Sutton-Smith (Eds.), *Sibling relationships: Their nature and significance across the lifespan* (pp. 267–284). Hillsdale, NJ: Lawrence Erlbaum.

Collins, P. H. (1990). *Black feminist thought: Knowledge, consciousness, and the politics of empowerment.* New York: Routledge, Chapman & Hall.

Connidis, I. A. (1983). Integrating qualitative and quantitative methods in survey research on aging: An assessment. *Qualitative Sociology, 6,* 334–352.

Connidis, I. A. (2001). *Family ties and aging.* Thousand Oaks, CA: Sage.

Connidis, I. A. (in press). Sibling ties across time: The middle and later years. In M. Johnson (Ed.), *The Cambridge handbook of age and ageing.* Cambridge: Cambridge University Press.

Connidis, I. A., & McMullin, J. A. (2002). Sociological ambivalence and family ties: A critical perspective. *Journal of Marriage and Family, 64,* 558–567.

Cowgill, D. O. (1986). Kinship systems and family roles. In D. O. Cowgill, *Aging around the world* (pp. 54–69). Belmont, CA: Wadsworth.

Daniels, D., & Plomin, R. (1985). Differential experience of siblings in the same family. *Developmental Psychology, 21,* 747–760.

Dunn, J. (1998). Siblings, emotion, and development of understanding. In S. Braten (Ed.), *Intersubjective communication and emotion in early ontogeny: Studies in emotion and social interaction* (pp. 158–168).

New York: Cambridge University Press. (Original work published 1983)

Eggebeen, D. J. (1992). Changes in sibling configurations in American preschool children. *Social Biology, 39,* 27–44.

Elder, G. H., Jr. (1974). *Children of the Great Depression.* Chicago: University of Chicago Press.

Eriksen, S., & Gerstel, N. (2002). A labor of love or labor itself: Care work among adult brothers and sisters. *Journal of Family Issues, 23,* 836–856.

Ferree, M. M. (1990). Beyond separate spheres: Feminism and family research. *Journal of Marriage and the Family, 52,* 866–884.

Finch, J., & Mason, J. (1993). *Negotiating family responsibilities.* New York: Tavistock/ Routledge.

Fingerman, K. L. (2001). *Aging mothers and their adult daughters: A study in mixed emotions.* New York: Springer.

Fischer, L. R. (1994). Qualitative research as art and science. In J. F. Gubrium & A. Sankar (Eds.), *Qualitative methods in aging research* (pp. 3–14). Thousand Oaks, CA: Sage.

Freedman, E. B. (2002). *No turning back: The history of feminism and the future of women.* New York: Ballantine.

Gatz, M., Pedersen, N. L., Berg, S., Johansson, B., Johansson, K., Mortimer, J. A., et al. (1997). Heritability for Alzheimer's disease: The study of dementia in Swedish twins. *Journal of Gerontology: Medical Sciences, 52,* 117–125.

Gergen, K. J. (1999). *An invitation to social construction.* London: Sage.

Gillis, J. R. (1996). *A world of their own making: Myth, ritual, and the quest for family values.* Cambridge, MA: Harvard University Press.

Gittins, D. (1993). *The family in question: Changing households and familiar ideologies* (2nd ed.). New York: Macmillan.

Gold, D. T. (1989). Generational solidarity: Conceptual antecedents and consequences. *American Behavioral Scientist, 33,* 19–32.

Granovetter, M. (1973). The strength of weak ties. *American Journal of Sociology, 78,* 1360–1380.

Henderson, J. N. (1994). Ethnic and racial issues. In J. F. Gubrium & A. Sankar (Eds.), *Qualitative methods in aging research* (pp. 33–50). Thousand Oaks, CA: Sage.

Hernandez, D. J. (1997). Child development and the social demography of childhood. *Child Development, 68,* 149–169.

Hochschild, A. R. (1973). *The unexpected community.* Englewood Cliffs, NJ: Prentice Hall.

James, P. D. (1993). *The children of men.* New York: Knopf.

Jerrome, D. (1996). Continuity and change in the study of family relationships. *Ageing and Society, 16,* 91–104.

Johnson, C. L. (1982). Sibling solidarity: Its origin and functioning in Italian-American families. *Journal of Marriage and the Family, 44,* 155–167.

Johnson, C. L. (1995). Cultural diversity in the late-life family. In R. Blieszner & V. H. Bedford (Eds.), *Handbook of aging and the family* (pp. 307–331). Westport, CT: Greenwood.

Johnson, C. L. (2000). Perspectives on American kinship in the later 1990s. *Journal of Marriage and the Family, 62,* 623–639.

Johnson, M. P. (1999). Personal, moral and structural commitment to relationships: Experiences of choice and constraint. In J. M. Adams & W. H. Jones (Eds.), *Handbook of interpersonal commitment and relationship stability* (pp. 73–88). New York: Plenum.

Kowal, A., & Kramer, L. (1997). Children's understanding of parental differential treatment. *Child Development, 68,* 113–126.

Lamb, M. E., & Sutton-Smith, B. (Eds.). (1982). *Sibling relationships: Their nature and significance across the lifespan.* Hillsdale, NJ: Lawrence Erlbaum.

Lareau, A. (2003). *Unequal childhoods: Class, race, and family life.* Berkeley: University of California Press.

Lerner, J., Somers, M. J., Reid, D. W., & Chiriboga, D. G. (1991). Adult children as caregivers: Egocentric biases in judgments of sibling contributions. *Gerontologist, 31,* 746–755.

Lüscher, K., & Pillemer, K. (1998). Intergenerational ambivalence: A new approach to the study of parent-child relations in later life. *Journal of Marriage and the Family, 60,* 413–425.

Maccoby, E. E. (1998). *The two sexes: Growing up apart, coming together.* Cambridge, MA: Harvard University Press.

Matthews, S. H. (1994). Men's ties to siblings in old age: Contributing factors to availability and quality. In E. H. Thompson, Jr. (Ed.), *Older men's lives* (pp. 178–196). Thousand Oaks, CA: Sage.

Matthews, S. H. (2002). *Sisters and brothers/ daughters and sons: Meeting the needs of old parents.* Bloomington, IN: Unlimited.

McHale, S. M., & Crouter, A. C. (1996). The family contexts of children's sibling relationships. In G. H. Brody (Ed.), *Sibling relationships: Their causes and consequences* (pp. 173–196). Norwood, NJ: Ablex.

McHale, S. M., Crouter, A. C., & Whiteman, S. D. (2003). The family contexts of gender development in childhood and adolescence. *Social Development, 12,* 125–148.

McHale, S. M., Updegraff, K. A., Helms-Erikson, H., & Crouter, A. C. (2001). Sibling influences on gender development in middle childhood and early adolescence: A longitudinal study. *Developmental Psychology, 37,* 115–125.

McHale, S. M., Updegraff, K. A., Jackson-Newsom, J., Tucker, C. J., & Crouter, A. C. (2000). When does parents' differential treatment have negative implications for siblings? *Social Development, 9,* 149–172.

Mekos, D., Hetherington, E. M., & Reiss, D. (1996). Sibling differences in problem behavior and parental treatment in divorced and remarried families. *Child Development, 67,* 2148–2165.

Merrill, D. M. (1996). Conflict and cooperation among adult siblings during the transition to the role of filial caregiver. *Journal of Social and Personal Relationships, 13,* 399–413.

O'Bryant, S. (1988). Sibling support and older widows' well-being. *Journal of Marriage and the Family, 50,* 173–183.

Parsons, T. (1974). Age and sex in social structure. In R. L. Coser (Ed.), *The family: Its structures and functions.* (pp. 243–255). New York: St. Martin's. (Original work published 1942)

Perlman, M., & Ross, H. S. (1997). The benefits of parent intervention in children's disputes: An examination of concurrent changes in children's fighting styles. *Child Development, 68,* 690–700.

Ross, H. G., & Milgram, J. I. (1982). Important variables in adult sibling relationships: A qualitative study. In M. E. Lamb & B. Sutton-Smith (Eds.), *Sibling relationships: Their nature and significance across the lifespan* (pp. 225–249). Hillsdale, NJ: Lawrence Erlbaum.

Rossi, A. S., & Rossi, P. H. (1990). *Of human bonding: Parent-child relations across the life course.* Hawthorne, NY: Aldine de Gruyter.

Ryder, N. B. (1965). The cohort as a concept in the study of social change. *American Sociological Review, 30,* 843–861.

Smith, D. E. (1993). The standard North American family: SNAF as an ideological code. *Journal of Family Issues, 14,* 50–65.

Stack, C. B. (1974). *All our kin: Strategies for survival in a Black community.* New York: Harper & Row.

Thompson, L., & Walker, A. J. (1982). The dyad as the unit of analysis: Conceptual and methodological issues. *Journal of Marriage and the Family, 44,* 889–900.

Thorne, B. (1982). Feminist rethinking of the family: An overview. In B. Thorne & M. Yalom (Eds.), *Rethinking the family: Some feminist questions* (pp. 1–24). New York: Longman.

Tilly, C. (1998). *Durable inequality.* Berkeley: University of California Press.

Tucker, C. J., McHale, S. M., & Crouter, A. C. (in press). Dimensions of mothers' and fathers' differential treatment of siblings: Links with adolescents' sex-typed personal qualities. *Family Relations.*

Updegraff, K. A., McHale, S. M., & Crouter, A. C. (in press). Adolescents' sibling relationship and friendship experiences: Developmental patterns and relationship linkages. *Social Development.*

Weisner, T. S. (1989). Comparing sibling relationships across cultures. In P. G. Zukow (Ed.), *Sibling interaction across cultures* (pp. 11–25). New York: Springer-Verlag.

Wellman, B. (1992). Which types of ties and networks provide what kinds of social support? *Advances in Group Processes, 9,* 207–235.

Wellman, B., & Wortley, S. (1989). Brothers' keepers: Situating kinship relations in broader networks of social support. *Sociological Perspectives, 32,* 273–306.

Weston, K. (1991). *Families we choose: Lesbians, gays, kinship.* New York: Columbia University Press.

Whitfield, K. E. (1994). The use of quantitative genetic methodology to gain insights into the origins of individual differences in later life. *Experimental Aging Research, 20*(2), 134–143.

Whitfield, K. E., Brandon, D. T., Wiggins, S. A., Vogler, G., & McClearn, G. (2003). Does intact pair status matter in the study of African American twins? The Carolina African American Twin Study of Aging. *Experimental Aging Research, 29*(4), 1–17.

Willson, A. E., Shuey, K. M., & Elder, G. H., Jr. (2003). Ambivalence in the relationship of adult children to aging parents and in-laws. *Journal of Marriage and Family, 65,* 1055–1072.

Young, M., & P. Willmott (1960). *Family and class in a London suburb.* London: Routledge & Kegan Paul.

• Eight

ECOLOGICAL CHANGES IN ETHNIC FAMILIES OF COLOR

Harriette Pipes McAdoo, *Michigan State University*

Estella A. Martínez, *University of New Mexico*

Hester Hughes, *Michigan State University*

New pictures of ethnic families are emerging from the increasing diversity among families that now exists within the United States. The challenges for family researchers are to develop accurate and timely knowledge about ethnic families so as to put them into a national context and to apply this knowledge to the particular theories that frame their research. In this chapter, we provide current information on family demographics as well as basic data on the population of ethnic families of color in the United States to aid family theoreticians and researchers as they examine the dynamics of family interactions. We first provide a contemporary profile of ethnic families of color that scholars can incorporate into their theoretical thinking and writing. We then explain how theorizing about families of color is informed by the meaning of racial diversity beyond demography. We end the chapter with a brief discussion of the challenges that American families of color face today.

A CONTEMPORARY PROFILE OF FAMILIES OF COLOR

American families have changed a great deal in the past 25 years. Between the 2000 U.S. Census and July 1, 2002, the U.S. population increased by 2.5%, from 281.4 to 288.4 million. Half a century ago, roughly 87% of the U.S. population was White, 10% was Black, and the small remainder was Asian, Hispanic, and Native American. Since that time, these proportions have changed significantly owing to increased immigration and high birthrates among groups of color. Changes are also evident in how groups are defined by their racial or ethnic identities. For example, the U.S. Bureau of the Census (2001) considers Asians to be members of a distinct race, whereas it considers Hispanics to be members of an ethnic group. Filipinos, it is interesting to note, may identify as both Asian and Spanish in origin. Thus far, the Census Bureau has not devised a way for people to identify themselves as Arab Americans or of Middle

Eastern ethnicity (Clemetson, 2003). Members of this and other groups need to find ways to identify themselves, or scholars need to find ways to identify them.

Intermarriage has created a growing population of persons in the United States who think of themselves as multiracial or "other" because they have roots in more than one ethnic group (Collins, 2003). In the latest U.S. Census, 7 million Americans refused to place themselves in one of the listed ethnic/racial categories. Although this number represents less than 3% of the total population, the presence in society of such individuals means that more diverse descriptions are needed to reflect Americans' ethnic/racial identities. There have also been marked changes in the numbers of people who see themselves as multicultural, especially among the young (Rodriguez, 2003). This implies that the ethnic and racial classifications currently used in American society may be becoming obsolete (for more on this topic, see this volume's companion Web site at http://www.ncfr.org/sourcebook).

Latino or Hispanic Families

The Latino/Hispanic population in the United States has grown rapidly over the past few decades. As of July 2002, this population numbered 38.8 million (see this volume's companion Web site). Latinos have surpassed African Americans in number and are now considered the country's largest ethnic minority group (U.S. Bureau of the Census, 2003). Latinos/Hispanics account for half of the national increase in population. The rapid rise in this youthful population (with 70% estimated to be under age 40) is attributed to both high immigration rates and high fertility rates (Therrien & Ramirez, 2001). The arrival in the United States of families from various Latin American countries has created the most heterogeneous Hispanic population in history.

Fundamental to understanding Latino families is an understanding of their ethnic or cultural self-identification, which often differs from the labels applied by the popular culture and the U.S. Census Bureau. For example, many people use the terms *Hispanic* and

Latino interchangeably, but in fact these labels refer to a number of distinct groups, the members of which generally prefer to identify themselves in terms of their national origins. The 1980 and 1990 U.S. Census forms used the category "Spanish/Hispanic origin or descent." This nomenclature became controversial because many people consider it inaccurate; they see it as a label that was created for bureaucratic convenience and assert that it is inappropriate to apply it to the members of an extremely diverse subpopulation of North Americans (Martínez, 1999). Many also dislike the term *Hispanic* because of its reference to Spain, a nation that many Latin Americans associate with historical oppression.

The term *Latino* appeared for the first time in the U.S. Census in 2000, as part of the category "Spanish/Hispanic/Latino origin." Additional space was provided along with this category for respondents to write in their national and other ethnic origins, such as Mexican, Puerto Rican, Cuban, Dominican, Central American, South American, or Spanish (Therrien & Ramirez, 2001). Many of those who chose to note their national origins in that space saw themselves as professing their ethnic loyalty or preference rather than as accommodating to European American conformity (Martínez, 1999). People who identify themselves using such terms as *Mexican American, Cuban American,* and *Spanish American* are making a bicultural statement about being American while simultaneously acknowledging their ethnic origins. Latino/ Hispanic persons vary in skin color and other physical characteristics. Some have African ancestors, whereas others are descendants of indigenous peoples of North, Central, and South America; some have roots in the Caribbean region, and still others are of European ancestry (Sullivan, 2000).

Although non-Latinos often seem to treat these various distinctions as unimportant, the differences among the groups involved create confusion and contribute to misunderstandings about individuals and families to whom the distinctions are meaningful. Various people who fall into the general category of Mexican American may self-identify as Chicano,

Xicano, Mestizo, or Méxicano. *Chicano* is a political identifier first adopted during the 1960s by social activists who took pride in their ancestral fusion of Spanish, Mexican, and Native American heritage, and who demonstrated cognizance of their social and political oppression in U.S. society. Individuals refer to themselves as Chicana (feminine) or Chicano (masculine). *Mestizo* is a similar term that simply refers to mixed Spanish and Native American heritage. People who immigrated from Spain or are descended from those who did and now reside in the U.S. Southwest, an area that was under Spanish and later Mexican rule until 1848, may self-identify as Spaniard, Spanish, Spanish American, or Hispano. *Hispano* and *Latino* are global identifiers in the Spanish language, as are *Latino* and *Hispanic* in English (Martínez, 1999; Sullivan, 2000).

The 2000 U.S. Census also allowed individuals to choose more than category in identifying their race. The Pew Hispanic Center found that when Hispanic respondents were asked to declare their race on the census form, 46% simply chose Hispanic or Latino, and another 20% responded "other." According to Roberto Suro, director of the Pew Center, more than half of the persons who make up the Hispanic population do not see themselves as fitting into any of the standard American racial/ethnic classifications (cited in Clemetson, 2003). This lack of identification with established categories does not mean that the people in this population are color-blind or beyond racism; rather, it reveals the difficulty many of them have with the categories commonly in use.

African American Families

Present-day African Americans include descendants of enslaved persons who were brought to North America from Africa as well as people who have immigrated from or are descended from immigrants from the Caribbean Islands, South America, and the 52 nations of Africa. Given their many different origins, African Americans are as culturally different from one another as are people from different European and Asian countries. Family scientists often overlook

these distinctions and attempt to place all Americans of African descent in a similar category regardless of their economic and education status, the regions in which they live, and their cultural backgrounds.

African Americans numbered 36.7 million as of July 2002 (Clemetson, 2003), a rate of increase in this population of 3.1% in 2 years. Among African Americans, some 1.7 million also self-identify as Hispanic (Nasser, 2003). The 2000 U.S. Census was not the first official recognition in U.S. or world history that human reality is too varied and fluid to be shoehorned into racial categories. In the 19th century, the U.S. Census classified people with both Black and White ancestors as mulattos, quadroons, and octoroons.

Asian American Families

Like Latino and African American families, Asian American families vary in their national origins, social classes, generational statuses, and places of birth (Fong, 1994). The U.S. Bureau of the Census subdivides Asian American families into the following categories: Asian Indian, Chinese, Filipino, Japanese, Korean, Vietnamese, and "other Asian." Asian Indians have developed as the newest group in the United States over the past three decades (Segal, 1998).

In the 2000 U.S. Census, Asians showed the highest rate of growth among all racial groups. The combined subdivisions of Asians totaled 10.2 million (9%) in 2000, and this number grew to roughly 13 million in 2002 (Clemetson, 2003). Chinese, Filipinos, and Asian Indians combined account for 58% of all those who reported being Asian. In 2000, half of the 10 million Asian Americans were concentrated in just three states: California, New York, and Hawaii. Asian Americans are the second-fastest-growing ethnic group in the country, behind Hispanics, according to census data, which show that the Asian population grew an impressive 72% between 1990 and 2000. Asian Americans have very sizable purchasing power, given that their average household income in 2000 was $48,614, compared with $39,657 for the U.S. population as a whole (Whelan, 2001).

Native American Families

In the United States, Native peoples number approximately 2.3 million, accounting for about 1% of the population, but they have been described as comprising "50% of the diversity" in this country (Hodgkinson, 1990). This diversity is seen in hundreds of tribally specific languages, traditions, and customs as well as the variance in cultural identities among members of given tribes (Johnson & Lashley, 1989; LaFromboise, Trimble, & Mohatt, 1990). According to current estimates, at least 63% of Native Americans do not live on reservations. Across the United States there are 517 federally recognized Native entities (196 in Alaska and 321 in the lower 48 states), 304 federal reservations, 365 state-recognized tribes, more than 50 tribes without any official recognition, and more than 250 different spoken languages.

Native peoples in North America have experienced a history of misunderstanding of their cultural values by the dominant culture (Herring, 1997). The United States did not grant citizenship to Native Americans until 1924, and it was not until 1978 that federal legislation guaranteed Native peoples' right to practice their traditional religions (Deloria, 1988).

• **SPOTLIGHT ON THEORY**

EMPIRICAL REALITY AND VISION: STUDYING PEOPLE OF COLOR

Tammy L. Henderson, *Virginia Polytechnic Institute and State University*

Scholars may conduct sound research with people of color using the best of several theoretical frameworks along with innovative research methods that examine the intersecting processes of race, ethnicity, culture, socioeconomic status, and multiple contextual environments. For example, Walker (2000) has directed our attention to innovative and empirically sound approaches to family science. In this brief discussion, I report on how different theoretical frameworks have helped to unveil embedded issues that shape the lives of Black grandmothers who are rearing their grandchildren.

Symbolic interactionism focuses on the subjective meaning of human behavior and social processes (LaRossa & Reitzes, 1993), and so I used this approach to analyze the meanings that Black grandmothers raising their grandchildren attach to welfare and poverty. Despite the negative stigma that the wider society assigns to welfare, the Black grandmothers in my sample were less negative. From the meanings participants attached to welfare, a continuum of beliefs about why people are poor emerged, including the beliefs that people need help, that it is each individual's fault and responsibility to address his or her impoverished existence, that structural constraints prohibit people from being economically self-sufficient, and that people have no choice. At no point

(continued)

● *SPOTLIGHT ON THEORY continued*

were the participants' responses dichotomous, either totally negative or totally positive. I used another perspective, the culturally variant perspective, to grasp familial strengths and challenges (Allen, 1978). The Black grandmothers in my sample spoke of personal and financial sacrifices made for the sake of family, which demonstrated family strengths, adaptation, and resilience. Both theories helped to unveil the complexities of being Black, a second-time parent, and economically poor but in other ways rich.

Similarly, critical race theory (see, e.g., Crenshaw, Gotanda, Peller, & Thomas, 1995) provided a theoretical lens through which I examined the effects of race, power, and social structures on the lives of Black grandmothers who are raising their grandchildren. Critical race theory seeks to understand how, for example, equal protection and other "American values" serve to maintain the subordination of people of color and to keep specific groups in the margins of society. Historically, Black families were excluded from safety-net programs such as welfare and social security (Gordon, 1994). In the 1960s, changes in the law gave low-wealth Black mothers access to welfare, but this change came with a price. The increase in the numbers of Black families on welfare fueled Moynihan's (1965) report asserting deficits within the Black family and attached a racial stigma to welfare (Roberts, 2002).

Against these theoretical backdrops, I wanted Black grandmothers to share their experiences and recommendations so that I could examine institutionalized discrimination within social service programs. Such a participatory method places a marginalized group at the center of the research process and makes them the experts of the research. The Black grandmothers raising grandchildren in my sample were keenly aware of the discriminatory treatment they were receiving from the welfare and foster care programs compared with foster parents raising children who are not their relatives. For example, unlike the grandmothers, foster parents do not have to meet stringent income requirements to qualify for food stamps. The grandmothers were also ineligible to receive other resources available to foster parents because of their biological and legal relationship to their grandchildren. Consequently, they recommended important changes in eligibility qualifications for Temporary Assistance for Needy Families, food stamps, and Medicaid.

Findings from this study on Black grandmothers led to the development of another interview protocol designed to explore family routines, coping and stress, and health. The research team developed new research questions, such as, How do race and family structure explain the differential treatment of welfare-reliant families? Smaller in-depth case studies emerged. In sum, the continuing development of research designs that use multiple contexts and several theoretical frameworks may eliminate some limitations that have undermined past research concerning people of color. As committed social science professionals, we must maintain our focus and passion toward this end. ●

THE MEANING OF RACIAL DIVERSITY BEYOND DEMOGRAPHY

Given the increasing diversity in the American population as described above, we can no longer talk about families in general. Many issues that affect families of color may or may not have an influence on other families. We also cannot ignore racial and ethnic diversity, which is adding new dimensions to everything from family demography and political campaigning to advertising. The family research literature currently attempts, on some level, to celebrate the diversity of family experiences, but in looking at diversity we must be careful not to universalize to all families certain American values held by mainstream groups or the most advantaged ethnic families. The trends noted above indicate the need for more realistic theories about families and their cultural environments. All families are more alike than they are different, but the differences that do exist have been shown to have significant effects on life trajectories, interactions, structural patterns, and economic standing, especially in families of color. Ethnic families that are not also families of color face fewer barriers. Social scientists need to understand the factors that affect the lives of families of color (Doherty, Boss, LaRossa, Schumm, & Steinmetz, 1993).

SOCIAL CHALLENGES FACED BY FAMILIES OF COLOR

Effects of Racism

Racism occurs when an array of theories or group practices ensure race-based hierarchies of preference for one group over another (Jones, 1999). It can give birth to claims of cultural and biological inferiority that may endure even when race is no longer considered in the assignment of positive or negative attributes. In reality, however, there are definite racial dimensions to the life opportunities, occupational choices, and education that characterize socioeconomic classes. If society routinely uses race to exclude or include groups, then race is a factor about which social scientists and family researchers need to be mindful. In areas such as health care, incarceration rates, education, family structural types, and employment, race is still a major factor in the United States.

Family researchers and theorists must be careful to avoid cultural racism, or the assignment of inferiority to people who act in ways that may differ from the cultural norm (Jones, 1999). In the past, skin color was the defining characteristic in racism, but today ethnicity and social class are also used to differentiate people

in our society. There is little acknowledgment of the role that racism plays in the assignment of life opportunities and class status regardless of ethnic group. Inferiority was once attributed to biology and culture; although now it is more often attributed to socioeconomics, in many cases attitudes remain the same.

Race and racism continue to be salient issues, even though some critics have attempted to pass legislation prohibiting state and local governments from collecting data on race (Barlow & Duster, 2003). Some social scientists argue that race is increasingly irrelevant, but the American Sociological Association asserts that it remains central to understanding many social processes in the United States. Troy Duster, president of the ASA, maintains that as long as society uses race to stratify groups independent of their genetic, biological reality, the social outcomes of race are of transparent interest to family social scientists, policy makers, and social justice professionals (cited in Dimock, 2003). As Duster further notes, at the level of DNA, humans of all races are alike 99.99% of the time—a fact that should also inform theorizing about individuals and families in that it emphasizes the many similarities that exist among diverse groups.

Tensions Caused by Acculturation

Acculturation occurs when two or more cultures are in persistent contact and each is modified by the other in varying degrees. Assimilation is a form of acculturation in which one culture changes significantly more than the other (Garcia & Ahler, 1992). This process may occur through force, as part of efforts to maintain control over conquered peoples (as in the cases of Native Americans and African Americans), or it may occur voluntarily (as in the adoption of certain elements of Western culture in Japan). For the individual, acculturation may mean "a process of giving up one's traditional cultural values and behaviors while taking on the values and behaviors of the dominant social structure" (Atkinson, Lowe, & Matthews, 1995, p. 131).

An example of one of the challenging issues facing families of color regarding acculturation can be observed among Native Americans, where the acculturation process has created tension between traditional Native cultures and modern U.S. culture. As we have noted above, Native Americans are not a homogeneous group, and members of this population vary greatly in their levels of acceptance of and commitment to specific tribal values, beliefs, and practices, including those concerning customs, languages, and types of family structures. Most Native adults live in two worlds, attempting to retain traditional values but seeking accommodation with the dominant culture, at least materialistically. According to the National Institute of Handicapped Research (1987), most Native Americans do not wish to be assimilated into the larger U.S. culture. Another way in which Native Americans may differ from the mainstream U.S. population is that they may be likely to view employment as secondary in importance to involvement with extended family and their community (Martin, 1991). Garrett and Garrett (1994) observe that a prevailing sense of "Indianness," based on a common worldview, seems to bind Native Americans together as a "people of many peoples."

Current socioeconomic, educational, and cultural challenges to this group can be attributed in large measure to history. Urban Native Americans are likely to move from one city to another or from reservations to urban settings (Sage, 1997). Some are searching for the American Dream, some are looking for economic opportunities and adequate housing, and others are seeking educational opportunities (Witt, 1980). Many are of mixed blood and have limited or no relationship with the reservations of their ancestors (Sage, 1997). One result of Native Americans' living off the reservation has been an increase in intertribal and interethnic marriages.

Maintaining Cultural Values in Parenting Styles

Families of color in the United States have always faced the challenge of parenting at two levels: inside their own culture and outside, in the larger culture. Professionals in the field

of child development describe this process as *biracial socialization.*

Mexican Americans. Research on Hispanic/Latino parenting styles has produced conflicting findings, with some studies indicating permissive parenting and others pointing to authoritarian parenting (Julian, McKenry, & McKelvey, 1994). Vega (1990) asserts that parenting practices among Hispanics are authoritative, but several researchers have noted that Hispanic fathers have begun to play a more nurturing role in comparison to the strict authority figures of the past (Gonzalez, 1982; Hawkes & Taylor, 1975; Zinn, 1982).

In a study of teenage parenting in different cultures, Field, Widmayer, Alder, and DeCubas (1990) found that the Mexican American parents in their sample were less talkative with their children than were the European American parents. Other researchers have found Mexican American parents to be permissive, authoritarian with traditional values, or nurturing within a patriarchal setting (LeVine & Bartz, 1979; Williams, 1990). Recent research reveals more diversity in parenting styles. Family values depend on such factors as socioeconomic status, rural or urban location, and the number of generations the family has lived in the United States. It is not possible to generalize from the samples studied to all Mexican Americans.

Additionally, Mexican American families often include extended family members, but differences among Mexican American families in this respect tend to be a function of social class rather than ethnicity. Finally, the relatively low level of educational attainment among Mexican Americans (in comparison with the U.S. population as a whole) is often attributed to childhood socialization, a factor that in turn depends on the cultural self-identification of the family.

African Americans. In general, the African American parenting style promotes respect for authority figures, a work ethic, achievement, a sense of duty and obligation to kin, and a strong religious sense (Harrison,

Wilson, Pine, Chan, & Buriel, 1990), although poverty conditions can affect these traditional values. African American parents also teach their children the skills they need to survive in a predominantly hostile environment (McAdoo, 2002; Taylor, Chatters, Tucker, & Lewis, 1990). African American parents tend to be stricter than parents in other ethnic/racial groups and place on their children a higher level of responsibility for self-help and for coping with racism and negative stereotypes (e.g., Bell-Scott & McKenry, 1986; Hamner & Turner, 1990).

A variety of contemporary forces shape the African American family today, including the following:

- Rural to urban migration during the 20th century
- Racism
- Poverty
- Urbanization
- Recent immigration

In a presentation of the characteristics of African American families based on research conducted by Oscar Barbarin, Nicholson (2002) lists the following important points:

- The transition from a rural environment to an urban one entailed, for many African Americans, a shift from a cohesive community to a state of relative anonymity.
- The effects of urbanization (long work hours, entry of women into the labor force) disrupted traditional family structures.
- African American families tend to be more hierarchical and are more likely to be strict, to hold demanding behavioral standards, and to use physical discipline.
- Such strictness is balanced, however, within a context of strong support and affection.
  - Physical punishment among African American families usually doesn't result in the same negative outcomes as it does for white children.

In addition, Nicholson lists the following cultural resources for African American families:

- Spirituality
- Mutual support
- Ethnic identity
- Adaptive extended family structures
- Church as offering both ideological and instrumental support

Asian Americans. American-born Asians tend to struggle with problems that are different from those faced by Asian immigrants and refugees. There are also differences among Asian Americans in values and parenting styles depending on cultures of origin. Common to all, however, are the issue of acculturation into the American mainstream and the desire to maintain traditional values and practices.

Variations in parenting styles among Asian Americans are influenced by several factors, including country of origin, reason for immigrating to the United States, religious affiliation, and number of years in the United States (Staples & Mirande, 1980; Sue & Kitano, 1973; Suzuki, 1980). Traditionally, the Asian American family is patriarchal, with father as the undisputed leader to whom all others in the family are subservient (Kitano, 1969), but currently there is a trend toward more joint parental decision making. The mother is still primarily responsible for child rearing. Permissive parenting techniques are common in Asian American families when the children are infants, with a shift to nonphysical discipline as the children age. A strong sense of family obligation continues to be reinforced as the children mature.

Native Americans. Respect is particularly important to Native Americans, and parenting in Native American families extends respect to children as well as to the spiritual nature of all things. Children are taught the value of generosity early on and are encouraged to share with others. Traditional Native American values focus on a sense of connectedness, thankfulness, and the importance of giving back to nature. Native peoples tend to view all things as having spiritual energy and importance. All things are connected; harmony and balance are considered sacred, and individuals invite illness if they fall out of harmony and balance (Garrett & Herring, 2001).

Mothers are the primary transmitters of Native culture, and it has been said that they keep the Indian nations alive. The view that the Native American mother has of herself as being Indian affects the way her children see themselves as Indians (Cheshire, 2001). Men are valued more than women in Native cultures, and children are emotionally and socially dependent on their parents (Cheshire, 2001; Pandya, 2001).

● *SPOTLIGHT ON METHODS*

METHODOLOGICAL CONSIDERATIONS IN THE STUDY OF FAMILIES OF COLOR

Masako Ishii-Kuntz, *University of California, Riverside*

Research on families of color has frequently been based on categorizations of race and ethnicity. This category construction has influenced scholarship on families of color in two ways: It has led to the use of oversimplified categories of race and ethnic groups, and it has contributed to race/ethnic-laden assumptions about families, parenting, and marriage that have led researchers to emphasize certain areas of family scholarship in each group.

First, many researchers compare family experiences across different groups using such categories as African Americans, Latinos, Asian Americans, Native Americans, and European Americans. Although comparisons between and among these groups have generated insightful findings, it is important to recognize the diversity that exists *within* each group. For example, within the large category of Asian Americans there are more than 28 subgroups with diverse cultural and socioeconomic backgrounds (Ishii-Kuntz, 2004); family experiences are thus certain to vary within the population designated as Asian American.

Second, the racial and ethnic categories that researchers use are often accompanied by misleading stereotypes. Because of such stereotypes, various ethnic/racial groups are differentially represented in research addressing particular topics in family scholarship. For example, McLoyd, Cauce, Takeuchi, and Wilson (2000) found that although a great deal of research on marital relations has focused on African Americans, little is known about marital processes among Asian Americans. Perhaps the relatively low divorce rate among Asian Americans and the stereotypical image of Asian American marriages as conflict free have led family scholars to assume that these marriages do not warrant significant research attention.

Given the diversity of experiences across and within families of color, special methodological considerations are important in research with such families. Researchers need to

(continued)

● *SPOTLIGHT ON METHODS continued*

examine their measurement instruments for cultural sensitivity, use both qualitative and quantitative methods in multiple phases, and investigate topics that are not influenced by racial and ethnic stereotypes.

Researchers need to pay special attention to the measurements they use in studying families of color. For example, family scholars often use the categories of *authoritative* and *authoritarian* in examining parenting styles, but the meanings attached to these parenting styles may vary from one ethnic group to another. In a study of Chinese American and European American mothers, for instance, Chao (1994) found that the immigrant Chinese mothers interpreted authoritarian parenting as loving children in order to foster close and enduring parent-child relationships, whereas the European American mothers defined authoritarian parenting as loving children to foster the children's self-esteem.

Researchers studying families of color may also find it fruitful to combine qualitative and quantitative approaches. Not only are ethnic families of color underrepresented in survey research, but when they are represented, researchers tend to oversimplify the differences between and among them. Qualitative methods may yield information on the "unique" experiences of families of color and thus may challenge researchers to compare those experiences with other groups of ethnic families and to generalize about larger groups of families of color. Researchers might use qualitative approaches, such as focus group interviews, to identify important issues faced by families of color and to construct culturally sensitive measurements. They can then use the results from this qualitative phase of research to generate comprehensive survey instruments and sampling schemes to study families of color.

Finally, family researchers need to go beyond the usual stereotypes that surround ethnic families of color. Although research examining African American families headed by single women should be continued, more studies examining the involvement of African American fathers are needed. Research into changing family gender roles among Latino families requires in-depth investigation of the division of housework and child care that goes beyond stereotypes of machismo and submissiveness. Scholars need to get past the stereotypes of Asian American families as problem free and strongly bonded to examine domestic violence among Asian Americans and the extent of marital and parent-child conflicts in these families.

In summary, family scholars who want to learn more about ethnic families of color need to employ cultural sensitivity in their measurements and plan the phases of their research carefully. ●

THEORIZING
ABOUT FAMILIES OF COLOR

Given the current demographic profiles of families of color in the United States, the meanings of racial diversity among these families, and the social challenges such families face, family scholars need culturally sensitive frameworks through which to understand families of color—something Dilworth-Anderson, Burton, and Johnson

(1993) suggested more than a decade ago. We would argue that scholars' continued failure to develop such frameworks reflects how researchers all too often ignore ethnic families, treat them in an offhand manner, or even present them in stereotypical ways based on outdated information and outmoded interpretations of their dynamics.

In conducting research on ethnic families of color, scholars should select theories with conceptual frameworks that will allow them to "predict, explain, define, and provide generalizations about observable phenomena as they exist" (Dilworth-Anderson et al., 1993, p. 639). Such explanations and generalizations are likely to differ from group to group because of the varying cultural interactions that are found in families of color.

Over the years, family scholars have used many different theories to help explain the functioning of families (see, e.g., Boss, Doherty, LaRossa, Schumm, & Steinmetz, 1993). Some proposed the use of family conflict theory (Sprey, 1969) and social exchange theory, with its emphasis on quantitative analysis and a broad focus on micro and macro levels of family life (Nye, 1979; Scanzoni, 1972). Home economists developed models of the family in its ecological environment (Paolucci, Hall, & Axinn, 1977; Westney, 1993). Family psychologists brought to the field their emphasis on empirical research. Eventually, feminist theorists (Osmond & Thorne, 1993), ethnic researchers of color (Dilworth-Anderson et al., 1993; McAdoo, 1993), and some psychologists (Crosbie-Burnett & Lewis, 1993) began to challenge other family theorists' overemphasis on male viewpoints and use of majority middle-class family models, as well as the absence of rigorous quantitative and statistical analysis in their research approaches. Many of these theories were formed without reference to persons of color, although some of them could have been used as approaches to understanding families of color. We believe that some theoretical perspectives in particular, such as symbolic interactionism, the life-course

perspective, feminist perspectives, and conceptual models that capture the multiple worlds that families of color live in, allow for broad and inclusive explanations of families of color. Further, interpretive research methods such as ethnographic approaches can be useful for increasing our understanding of the diversity across families of color.

CONCLUSION

In this chapter we have aimed to facilitate theorizing about families of color by providing discussion of the meaning of racial diversity beyond demography and of the social challenges that families of color face in the United States. In recent decades, some ethnic families have moved up economically and socially and others have moved down, but few have had no alteration in their life circumstances. Theories and research on families of color should reflect this existing knowledge. Further, to build on this knowledge, family scholars must improve their understanding of the cultural norms, beliefs, and interpretations found among various racial/ethnic groups.

Family scientists also need to understand the particular strengths and vulnerabilities of families of color. Theorizing should be informed by the knowledge that attitudinal and behavioral differences between ethnic families and the White middle-class mainstream do not mean that ethnic families are pathological, deviant, or deficient; rather, these differences reflect legitimate and valuable expressions of historical and cultural identities (Coll et al., 1996; Deater-Deckard, Dodge, Bates, & Pettit, et al., 1996). Thus scholars should base any generalizations they make about families of color on the reality of the lives and cultural experiences of these families. Such understanding will help family theorists to gain further knowledge about the social systems and patterns of interactions that exist in families of color.

Demographic trends indicate that the growth in the numbers of families of color in the United States will accelerate in the future, especially among Hispanics/Latinos. In many cities and regions, persons of color now represent half the population. Interracial and intercultural marriages are contributing to an even greater array of patterns, and these changes will continue to add to the complexity of family life in the United States. Will family researchers and theorists recognize these new realities and adjust their work to take into account the major contributions that persons of color make to our society? Only the future will tell.

CASE STUDY

BLACK-WHITE INTERRACIAL MARRIAGE AND MULTIRACIAL FAMILIES

Erica Chito Childs, *Eastern Connecticut State University*

Black-White couples and the multiracial families they create constitute an important area for research within family studies. The experiences of interracial couples and multiracial families can help us to gain insights into the social institution of family as well as the complex intersections of race and family.

Most families in the United States today are still monoracial, and most individuals choose partners of the same race. (Data from the 2000 U.S. Census tell us that interracial marriages account for only 1.9% of all U.S. marriages, with White-Black couplings accounting for only .06%.) When interracial couples come together, they not only create multiracial families of their own but also change the racial dynamics of the families from which they come. Given that it is in families that meanings and attachments to racial categories are constructed and learned, we might expect that families would also be the sources of greatest hostility toward interracial relationships. This includes who is and is not considered to be an acceptable marriage partner. In the following pages, I explore the significance of Black-White couples for the institution of family in the United States by looking at how White and Black families respond when family members date or marry interracially. This discussion is based on extensive qualitative research that I have conducted with Black-White couples as well as focus group interviews conducted in predominantly White and predominantly Black communities.[1]

WHITE FAMILIES

White families often have difficulty accepting a family member's marrying a Black individual, although they often assert that their "concern" has no basis in racial prejudice; rather, they justify it by explaining it as a "preference" or "natural." White families that oppose interracial marriage do so to varying degrees, with some disowning family members outright and others displaying subtler expressions of

CASE STUDY *continued*

support and opposition woven together. In some cases, families ultimately accept their members' interracial relationships or the individuals involved but still have objections to interracial dating and marriage in general.

Some White families express opposition to interracial marriage in subtle ways, such as by questioning their members' relationships or expressing concern. Even family members who appear to be basically supportive may make derogatory comments or fail to support the couple fully when faced with opposition or exclusion from other family members. One example of this contradictory response is illustrated by the experience of Victoria, a White woman married to a Black man:

> My parents have always said they have no problem with Chris being Black, but I guess they say offensive things, without even knowing it, like not about us but whatever, Blacks on talk shows or just little sarcastic remarks.

Even members of White families who advocate for racial equality on a general level may express opposition to individuals in their own families marrying interracially. For example, Jennifer, a White college student who is dating a Black man, describes her parents' difficulty in accepting her relationship, despite the way they raised her:

> They'd always raised us not to judge people on the color of their skin, and my dad always said he didn't care if someone was purple, yellow, Black whatever as long as they were nice, but he has a hard time dealing with my relationship. . . . my mother . . . will say, "I'm not being racist, I'm not saying there is anything wrong with interracial dating but I want you to take into consideration the stress and impact it's going to have on you. It's not going to be a normal relationship."

Jennifer's parents' response is complex. Although her parents espouse color-blind ideals in general, when it comes to their daughter's choice in men, color does matter. Jennifer's mother, by using societal opposition as the basis for her own personal concerns, does not have to acknowledge that she may hold prejudiced or racist views. Still, Jennifer finds it difficult to reconcile what they told her while she was growing up with how they feel about her relationship.

Among White families, opposition to interracial unions can also be explicit and extreme. Black-White couples sometimes must end their contact or have limited contact with various family members who cannot accept their relationships. For example, Kevin, a White man who is married to a Black woman, describes his family's response:

> My father was blatantly racist, Archie Bunker style . . . but basically my whole family disowned me for in general hanging out with people of color. I was always ostracized growing up . . . so I was constantly battling my family about racist remarks.

Some White families refuse to allow their members' Black partners into the home or, in essence, into the family. Such responses can be understood as these families' attempts to protect themselves from "Blackness" by preventing the union of Black and White, two irreconcilable opposites. Ultimately, many Whites' families choose to marginalize their own members rather than accept Black individuals into their primary group.

BLACK FAMILIES

Black families, like White families, often express opposition to interracial relationships, but Black families tend to raise different issues, such as the importance of "marrying

Case Study

CASE STUDY *continued*

Black" and the negative meanings attached to interracial relationships. Black families often have a hard time accepting a family member's getting involved with a White person because of lingering racism and distrust of Whites in general. Black families may question the motives of the White partner or the sincerity of the relationship. Black family members often express their opposition through statements of their own personal convictions never to date interracially, as illustrated by the experience of Sharon, a Black woman married to a White man:

> My older sister was shocked . . . and my younger sister . . . she just doesn't think White and Black should be together, she always says [imitating her sister], "It is hard for me to relate to someone of a race that has killed, belittled, and continues to come into the Black community to break it up, I couldn't do it."

Black families also sometimes mention the issue of rejection; that is, they base their opposition not only on the racism of Whites but on the decision of the Black individual. Chris, a Black man married to a White woman, discusses how his sisters felt offended by his marriage because they saw it as Chris's rejection of them:

> My family likes Victoria [Chris's wife] as a person and they respect her . . . but I can't say that they don't wish she was Black, or really that I married a Black woman on a number of levels. My younger sisters especially feel hurt by my choice because they feel all too much they can't get a date because all the [Black] guys are dating White. . . . [They think] Whites are just different, "Oh White people cookout, they don't barbecue, they're uptight, they can't get their groove on," and all that . . . so

I think they feel sort of confused at why I married a White woman, like "Don't I like my own people?"

The disappointment, confusion, and hurt that Chris describes do not seem to stem from a belief that Whites are inferior; rather, his sisters see interracial marriage as a sign that the Black individual feels his or her own race is inferior. According to his narrative, another part of this opposition comes from a belief that Blacks and Whites are "culturally different," making the idea of having a White person in the family undesirable and uncomfortable for Black family members.

Based on the familial responses noted above, it appears that Black families that object to having a White person within the family and intimate social circle do so because Whites are viewed as the "enemy," and their inclusion in the family is a sign that one is not committed to the Black community or to the family. Not surprisingly, Black families tend to oppose interracial marriage much more strongly than they oppose interracial dating, primarily because marriage represents a legitimation of the union and formally brings the White partner into the family.

WHAT ABOUT THE CHILDREN?

Both White families and Black families raise the issue of biracial children as a central concern and a reason to question and/or oppose interracial unions. This includes particular concern about how the children will identify racially and how they will be accepted by society. White families often argue that interracial marriage is "not fair to the children" because biracial children have "problems," such as confusion over their identity and lack of acceptance among both Whites and Blacks. Kayla, a White woman who is involved with a Black man, describes how her family reacted when they found out she was pregnant:

CASE STUDY *continued*

They told me they didn't think it was a good idea because all the things I would have to go through raising an interracial baby in Maine . . . that other people would be too cruel and that I had to think of the child and that it is not fair to bring a child into this world, interracial, knowing what was going to happen. They told me if I had the baby I was selfish.

Black families also see biracial children as a problem, particularly because of the difficulties of identity they might face ("Am I black, am I white?"). Aisha, a Black woman married to a White man, describes her mother's views on biracial children:

My mom said, "What do you think kids will be like? . . . it is wrong to bring kids into a situation like this, kids will be confused, I Don't Want Polka Dot Grandkids!"

The underlying concerns and fears of both Kayla's and Aisha's families tie into historical beliefs and practices surrounding biracial children, including the traditional image of the offspring of Black-White unions as the "tragic mulatto," predisposed to emotional and psychological problems. Although both Whites and Blacks bring up the issue of biracial children as a reason to object to interracial relationships, the arguments that underlie the objections of the two groups are different. Whereas opposition among many Whites lies in the view that the creation of "Black" children through interracial unions is a form of "pollution" of the White race, Black opposition seems to stem from concerns about maintaining the Black community.

CONCLUSION

This discussion has clearly highlighted some of the intersections of family and race. The familial responses discussed above demonstrate how people's images of themselves and their families are linked to the concept of race and otherness, especially within the construction of families.

White families often object to the idea of a member's dating a Black person, not because they have met that individual and have been confronted by overwhelming "racial" differences, but merely because of their ideas and beliefs about interracial relationships and Blacks in general. Black families also express opposition to Black-White relationships, but their opposition is often based on negative experiences they have had with Whites or on a belief that such relationships are problematic. The responses of their families have many effects on Black-White couples, often resulting in familial tensions and strained (or estranged) relationships. The above discussion demonstrates the centrality of race to our constructions of families and identities, as well as the "norm" of monoracial families, yet Black-White couples and their biracial children are forced to exist somewhere in between, with or without their families.

NOTE

1. This work is based on a larger book project in which I conducted in-depth interviews with 15 Black-White couples, conducted focus groups at churches and universities in predominantly White and predominantly Black communities, and undertook cultural analyses of images of Black-White couples in American popular culture (see Childs, in press). The quotations presented here come from my interviews for that project.

Case Study

DISCUSION AND EXTENSION

THE DEMOGRAPHICS OF THE 21ST-CENTURY FAMILY: EXAMINING RACE, ETHNICITY, AND CULTURE WITHIN GEOGRAPHIC AND GENERATIONAL CONTEXT

Ana Mari Cauce, *University of Washington, Seattle*

More than a decade ago, Graham (1992) noted that the model American family, as represented in the pages of our professional social science journals, was White and middle-class. This depiction was inaccurate a decade ago, and the results of the 2000 U.S. Census clearly show just how far from the American norm the White, middle-class family now is.

The American family is changing, and among the most obvious of these changes is its increasingly multicultural nature. As McAdoo, Hughes, and Martínez demonstrate in Chapter 8, the United States is no longer a country that can be painted in Black and White. Latinos now constitute the largest ethnic minority group in the United States, and Asian Americans and Pacific Islanders no longer represent a trivial portion of the population. The number of those who formally define themselves on census questionnaires as belonging to more than one race remains small, but population projections suggest that the numbers of bi- and multiracial children are increasing, as are the numbers of individuals likely to identify themselves as such.

What needs further highlighting as we struggle to understand what these changes mean, both for our country and for the science of family research, is the degree to which this demographic revolution is as much a regional and local phenomenon as a national one. At the beginning of the 21st century, the United States was about 70% White (non-Hispanic), 12% Black or African American, 12% Latino, 4% Asian American/Pacific Islander, and 1%

Native American (U.S. Bureau of the Census, 2001). There are no states or cities in the nation, however, that approximate this profile. Some cities, such as Atlanta and Detroit, are majority African American. Currently, one state (New Mexico) is approaching half (42%) Latino. In San Francisco, the population under age 25 is about 40% Asian American/Pacific Islander. Although Native Americans make up less than 1% of the entire U.S. population, they make up 16% of the population of Alaska.

The growing diversity within our country is not evenly distributed. A look at how people of color are dispersed reveals that they are much more geographically concentrated than are White European Americans. For example, about half of all Latinos in the United States live in California and Texas. More than three-fourths reside in only 7 states (Ramirez & de la Cruz, 2003). Similarly, 60% of all African Americans reside in just 10 states (McKinnon, 2003), and a little more than half of all Asian Americans/Pacific Islanders live in 10 Western states (Reeves & Bennett, 2003). Some cities and regions may even be getting more White as they become points of emigration for those who feel uncomfortable in a multicultural environment (for a story about White migration out of Dade County, see Booth, 1998).

As of 2000, North Dakota, Iowa, West Virginia, Maine, Vermont, and New Hampshire remained more than 90% White, non-Hispanic. Another 15 states remained more than 80% White, non-Hispanic. In other words, about half of all U.S. states are still overwhelmingly White, whereas the other half *how valuable is (smart in) this study in mia?*

DISCUSION AND EXTENSION *continued*

are rapidly becoming majority-minority (U.S. Bureau of the Census, 2001). These varying demographic patterns make it very difficult for researchers to examine ethnicity, race, and culture outside of specific geographic contexts. The experience of a Latino family in Texas is very different from that of a Latino family in Maine, for instance. Moreover, the experience of a Mexican American family in Texas is very different from the experience of a Mexican American family in Florida. Although both states have large proportions of Latinos, in Texas most of the Latino population is of Mexican origin, whereas most Latinos in Florida are of Caribbean origin.

Two additional factors that scholars need to consider more closely in their attempts to understand ethnic families of color are immigration history and generational status. Just as it is not altogether appropriate to generalize across ethnic groups, it is not appropriate to do so across generational status. Within Latino communities, where most of the research in this area has taken place, generational status has been found to be as strong a predictor of health, mental health, or behavioral outcomes as race or ethnicity. And, although generational status has not typically been a construct given salience in research on African American, or Black, communities, it may well become significant as we begin to study Haitian, Jamaican, Ethiopian, and other Black immigrant populations that constitute significant portions of the populations of some cities and neighborhoods.

As McAdoo et al. note, the growing size and influence of the Latino population, as well as Latinos' desire to define themselves in terms of ethnicity, culture, and national origin rather than race, pits this group against traditional African American political constituencies. If all dark-skinned Latinos were to define themselves racially as Black, then African Americans might well still be the largest minority group in the United States. Yet, although many multicultural visions of the future of America are based on the notion that the significance of race is decreasing, there is some evidence to the contrary. In the long run, race may retain more meaning and predictive power than ethnicity. An examination of intermarriage rates over the past few decades has led some to believe that the future of the United States is less multiracial than it is "Black and Beige" (Lind, 1998). Light-skinned Latinos, Asian Americans/Pacific Islanders, and Native Americans will fall into the latter category, and dark-skinned Latinos may fall into the former. Thus first-generation dark-skinned Dominicans or Panamanians who define themselves as Hispanic may raise children or grandchildren who will define themselves as Black or African American.

Geographic and neighborhood contexts may determine, in large part, the racial and ethnic identifications that individuals take on. Dark-skinned children whose parents emigrate from the Dominican Republic to a New York City Dominican enclave are more likely to retain their identification as Latino (and their knowledge of the Spanish language) than are children from a similar background who grow up in Alabama. Outside of a Latino context, both White Americans and Black Americans will view these children as Black, and that, in turn, will shape their ethnic and racial identities.

The necessity of defining race and culture more contextually is further highlighted when socioeconomic status is added to the mix. One of the key issues facing families of color in the United States is how to raise their children in neighborhoods characterized by concentrated poverty, danger, and violence, a phenomenon that is almost unique to families of color, especially African Americans.[1] Although the emphasis on issues such as respect and obedience found among African and Latino American families is no doubt a reflection of culture, it is impossible to separate this characteristic from the material conditions in which the children of many such families are

DISCUSION AND EXTENSION *continued*

reared. Culture arises from context and is largely a reflection of the geographic and material conditions that have shaped survival for groups of people over generations.

Often overlooked in discussions of the new multicultural America is the role that recent immigration plays in the demographic revolution. According to figures published by the Urban Institute, as of September 2000, one in five children in the United States was the native- or foreign-born child of an immigrant. The vast majority of these children live in mixed-status families, where at least one parent is a noncitizen and at least one child is a citizen (Fix, Zimmerman, & Passell, 2001). The experiences of immigrant families as they adapt to the exigencies of life in different parts of this country may provide family scholars with the best possible laboratory for studying how ethnic and racial identities are shaped and how cultural values are maintained or transformed.

In 1959, at the age of 3, I arrived in the United States with my brother to reunite with our parents, who had left Cuba as political refugees. Today, more than 45 years later, my extended family includes individuals who define themselves primarily as Cuban, Cuban American, Panamanian, Spanish, Latino, Hispanic, Black, Jewish, and White or Anglo. As the next generation grows up, *biracial* and *bicultural* will be added to the mix of identifications. Matching faces to ethnic identifications in this group would not be easy. Yet how each individual chooses to identify him- or herself makes good sense in terms of that person's specific immigration history and the geographic, socioeconomic, and cultural context in which he or she was raised or is being raised. Important challenges for family researchers over the next few decades are to discover and map out the mechanisms that underlie such identifications and to begin to understand how they play out within the family, both shaping and being shaped by family dynamics, generational ties, and place.

NOTE

1. About a quarter of African American youth grow up in neighborhoods characterized by concentrated poverty, as opposed to less than 3% of White Americans (for a discussion, see Cauce, Stewart, Domenech Rodriguez, Cochran, & Ginzler, 2002).

REFERENCES

Allen, W. (1978). The search for applicable theories of Black family life. *Journal of Marriage and the Family, 40,* 117–129.

Atkinson, D. R., Lowe, S., & Matthews, L. (1995). Asian-American acculturation, gender, and willingness to seek counseling. *Journal of Multicultural Counseling and Development, 23,* 130–138.

Barlow, A., & Duster, T. (2003, July/August). Public forum: Researchers challenge California initiative to ban racial data. *Footnotes, 31,* 7.

Bell-Scott, P., & McKenry, P. C. (1986). Black adolescents and their families. In G. K. Leigh & G. W. Peterson (Eds.), *Adolescents in families* (pp. 410–432). Cincinnati, OH: South-Western.

Booth, W. (1998, November 11). America's racial and ethnic divides: Part 5. A white migration north from Miami. *Washington Post.* Retrieved June 11, 2004, from http://www.washingtonpost.com/wp-srv/national/longterm/meltingpot/melt1109.htm

Boss, P., Doherty, W. J., LaRossa, R., Schumm, W. R., & Steinmetz, S. K. (Eds.). (1993). *Sourcebook of family theories and methods: A contextual approach.* New York: Plenum.

Cauce, A. M., Stewart, A., Domenech Rodriguez, M. D., Cochran, B., & Ginzler, J. A. (2002). Overcoming the odds? Adolescent development in the context of urban poverty. In S. S. Luthar (Ed.), *Resilience and vulnerability: Adaptation in the contexts of childhood adversities* (pp. 343–363). New York: Cambridge University Press.

Chao, R. (1994). Beyond parental control and authoritative parenting style: Understanding Chinese parenting through the cultural notion of training. *Child Development, 65,* 1111–1119.

Cheshire, T. C. (2001). Cultural transmission in urban American Indian families. *American Behavioral Scientist, 44,* 1528–1535.

Childs, E. C. (in press). *Navigating interracial borders.* New Brunswick, NJ: Rutgers University Press.

Clemetson, L. (2003, June 19). Hispanic population is rising swiftly, Census Bureau says. *New York Times,* p. A22.

Coll, C. G., Crnic, K., Lamberty, G., Wasik, B. H., Jenkins, R., Garcia, H. V., et al. (1996). An integrative model for the study of developmental competencies in minority children. *Child Development, 67,* 1981–1914.

Collins, G. (2003, June 20). More than Black and White. *New York Times,* p. A24.

Crenshaw, K., Gotanda, N. M., Peller, G., & Thomas, K. (Eds.). (1995). *Critical race theory: The key writings that formed the movement.* New York: New Press.

Crosbie-Burnett, M., & Lewis, E. A. (1993). Use of African-American family structures and functioning to address the challenges of European-American postdivorce families. *Family Relations, 42,* 243–248.

Deater-Deckard, K., Dodge, K. A., Bates, J. E., & Pettit, G. S. (1996). Physical discipline among African American and European American mothers: Links to children's externalizing behaviors. *Developmental Psychology, 32,* 1065–1072.

Deloria, V., Jr. (1988). *Custer died for your sins: An Indian manifesto.* Norman: University of Oklahoma Press.

Dilworth-Anderson, P., Burton, L. M., & Johnson, L. B. (1993). Reframing theories for understanding race, ethnicity, and families. In P. Boss, W. J. Doherty, R. LaRossa, W. R. Schumm, & S. K. Steinmetz (Eds.), *Sourcebook of family theories and methods: A contextual approach* (pp. 627–649). New York: Plenum.

Dimock, S. H. (2003, July/August). ASA briefs Congress on policy role of racial and ethnic data. *Footnotes, 31,* 1, 6.

Doherty, W. J., Boss, P., LaRossa, R., Schumm, W. R., & Steinmetz, S. K. (1993). Family theories and methods: A contextual approach. In P. Boss, W. J. Doherty, R. LaRossa, W. R. Schumm, & S. K. Steinmetz (Eds.), *Sourcebook of family theories and methods: A contextual approach* (pp. 3–30). New York: Plenum.

Field, T. M., Widmayer, S., Alder, S., & DeCubas, M. (1990). Teenage parenting in different cultures, family constellations, and caregiving environments: Effects of infant development. *Infant Mental Health Journal, 11,* 158–174.

Fix, M., Zimmerman, W., & Passell, J. (2001). *The integration of immigrant families in the*

United States. Washington, DC: Urban Institute.

Fong, R. (1994). Family preservation: Making it work for Asians. *Child Welfare, 73,* 331–341.

Garcia, R. L., & Ahler, J. G. (1992). Indian education: Assumptions, ideologies, strategies. In J. Reyhner (Ed.), *Teaching American Indian students* (pp. 13–32). Norman: University of Oklahoma Press.

Garrett, J. T., & Garrett, M. T. (1994). The path of good medicine: Understanding and counseling Native Americans. *Journal of Multicultural Counseling and Development, 22,* 134–144.

Garrett, M. T., & Herring, R. D. (2001). Honoring the power of relation: Counseling Native adults. *Journal of Humanistic Counseling, Education and Development, 40,* 139–160.

Gonzalez, A. (1982). Sex roles of the traditional Mexican family. *Journal of Cross-Cultural Psychology, 13,* 330–339.

Gordon, L. (1994). *Pitied but not entitled: Single mothers and the history of welfare 1890–1935.* New York: Free Press.

Graham, S. (1992). Most of the subjects were White and middle-class: Trends in published research on African Americans in selected APA journals, 1970–1989. *American Psychologist, 47,* 629–639.

Hamner, T. J., & Turner, P. H. (1990). *Parenting in contemporary society.* Englewood Cliffs, NJ: Prentice Hall.

Harrison, A. O., Wilson, M. N., Pine, C. J., Chan, S. Q., & Buriel, B. (1990). Family ecologies of ethnic minority children. *Child Development, 61,* 347–362.

Hawkes, G. R., & Taylor, M. (1975). Power structure in Mexican and Mexican-American farm labor families. *Journal of Marriage and the Family, 37,* 807–811.

Herring, R. D. (1997). Counseling indigenous American youth. In C. C. Lee (Ed.), *Multicultural issues in counseling: New approaches to diversity* (2nd ed., pp. 53–70). Alexandria, VA: American Counseling Association.

Hodgkinson, H. L. (1990). *The demographics of American Indians: One percent of the people; fifty percent of the diversity.* Washington, DC: Institute for Educational Leadership.

Ishii-Kuntz, M. (2004). Asian American families: Diverse history, contemporary trends, and the future. In M. Coleman & L. H. Ganong (Eds.), *Handbook of contemporary families: Considering the past, contemplating the future* (pp. 369–384). Thousand Oaks, CA: Sage.

Johnson, M. E., & Lashley, K. H. (1989). Influence of Native Americans' cultural commitment on preferences for counselor ethnicity and expectations about counseling. *Journal of Multicultural Counseling and Development, 17,* 115–122.

Jones, J. (1999). Cultural racism: The intersection of race and culture in intergroup conflict. In D. Prentice & D. Miller (Eds.), *Cultural divides: Understanding and overcoming group conflicts* (pp. 465–490). New York: Russell Sage Foundation.

Julian, T. W., McKenry, P. C., & McKelvey, M. W. (1994). Perceptions of European American, African American, Hispanic, and Asian American parents. *Family Relations, 43,* 30–37.

Kitano, H. H. L. (1969). *Japanese Americans: The evolution of a subculture.* Englewood Cliffs, NJ: Prentice Hall.

LaFromboise, T. D., Trimble, J. E., & Mohatt, G. V. (1990). Counseling intervention and American Indian tradition: An integrative approach. *Counseling Psychologist, 18,* 628–654.

LaRossa, R., & Reitzes, D. C. (1993). Symbolic interactionism and family studies. In. P. Boss, W. J. Doherty, R. LaRossa, W. R. Schumm, & S. K. Steinmetz (Eds.), *Sourcebook of family theories and methods: A contextual approach* (pp. 135–163). New York: Plenum.

LeVine, E. S., & Bartz, K. W. (1979). Comparative child-rearing attitudes among Chicano, Anglo, and Black parents. *Hispanic Journal of Behavioral Sciences, 1,* 165–178.

Lind, M. (1998, August 16). The beige and the black. *New York Times Magazine,* pp. 38–39.

Martin, W. E. (1991). Career development and American Indians living on reservations: Cross-cultural factors to consider. *Career Development Quarterly, 39,* 273–283.

Martínez, E. A. (1999). Mexican American/ Chicano families: Parents as diverse as the families themselves. In H. P. McAdoo (Ed.), *Family ethnicity: Strength in diversity* (2nd ed., pp. 121–134). Thousand Oaks, CA: Sage.

McAdoo, H. P. (1993). The social cultural contexts of ecological developmental family models. In P. Boss, W. J. Doherty, R. LaRossa, W. R. Schumm, & S. K. Steinmetz (Eds.), *Sourcebook of family theories and methods: A contextual approach* (pp. 298–301). New York: Plenum.

McAdoo, H. P. (2002). African American parenting. In M. H. Bornstein (Ed.), *Handbook of parenting: Vol. 4. Social conditions and applied parenting* (2nd ed.). Mahwah, NJ: Lawrence Erlbaum.

McKinnon, J. (2003). *The Black population in the United States: March 2002* (Current Population Reports No. P20-541). Washington, DC: U.S. Bureau of the Census. Retrieved June 11, 2004, from http://www.census.gov/prod/2003pubs/p20-541.pdf

McLoyd, V. C., Cauce, A. M., Takeuchi, D., & Wilson, L. (2000). Marital processes and parental socialization in families of color: A decade review of research. *Journal of Marriage and the Family, 62,* 1070–1093.

Moynihan, D. P. (1965). *The Negro family: The case for national action.* Washington, DC: U.S. Department of Labor, Office of Policy Planning and Research.

Nasser, H. (2003, June 19). Census confirms stats on Hispanics. *Lansing State Journal,* p. A8.

National Institute of Handicapped Research. (1987). *Cross-cultural rehabilitation: Working with the Native American population* (Rehab Brief No. 9[5]). Washington, DC: Author.

Nicholson, J. (2002). *Characteristics of African American families.* Presentation based on the work of Oscar Barbarin, Ph.D., Professor, University of North Carolina, School of Social Work. Retrieved July 6, 2004, from http://ssw.unc.edu/rti/presentation/pdfs/aa_families.pdf

Nye, F. I. (1979). Choice, exchange and the family. In W. R. Burr, R. Hill, F. I. Nye, & I. L. Reiss (Eds.), *Contemporary theories about the family: Vol. 1. Research-based theories* (pp. 1–41). New York: Free Press.

Osmond, M. W., & Thorne, B. (1993). Feminist theories: The social construction of gender in families and society. In P. Boss, W. J. Doherty, R. LaRossa, W. R. Schumm, & S. K. Steinmetz (Eds.), *Sourcebook of family theories and methods: A contextual approach* (pp. 591–622). New York: Plenum.

Pandya, M. (2001, May). No going back: Indian immigrant women shape a new identity. *The World & I, 16,* 204.

Paolucci, B., Hall, O. A. & Axinn, N. (1977). *Family decision making: An ecosystem approach.* New York: John Wiley.

Ramirez, R. R., & de la Cruz, G. P. (2003). *The Hispanic population in the United States: March 2002* (Current Population Reports No. P20-545). Washington, DC: U.S. Bureau of the Census. Retrieved June 11, 2004, from http://www.census.gov/prod/2003pubs/p20-545.pdf

Reeves, T., & Bennett, C. (2003). *The Asian and Pacific Islander population in the United States: March 2002* (Current Population Reports No. P20-540). Washington, DC: U.S. Bureau of the Census. Retrieved June 11, 2004, from http://www.census.gov/prod/2003pubs/p20-540.pdf

Roberts, D. E. (2002). *Shattered bonds: The color of child welfare.* New York: Basic Books.

Rodriguez, R. (2003, September 12). "Blaxicans" and other reinvented Americans. *Chronicle of Higher Education,* pp. B9–B11.

Sage, G. P. (1997). Counseling American Indian adults. In C. C. Lee (Ed.), *Multicultural issues in counseling: New approaches to diversity* (2nd ed., pp. 33–52). Alexandria, VA: American Counseling Association.

Scanzoni, J. (1972). *Sexual bargaining: Power politics in the American marriage.* Englewood Cliffs, NJ: Prentice Hall.

Segal, U. A. (1998). The Asian Indian-American family. In C. H. Mindel, R. W. Habenstein, & R. Wright (Eds.), *Ethnic families in America: Patterns and variations* (4th ed., pp. 331–360). Upper Saddle River, NJ: Prentice Hall.

Sprey, J. (1969). The family as a system in conflict. *Journal of Marriage and the Family, 31,* 699–706.

Staples, R., & Mirande, A. (1980). Racial and cultural variations among American families: A decennial review of the literature on minority families. *Journal of Marriage and the Family, 42,* 157–174.

Sue, S., & Kitano, H. H. L. (1973). Stereotypes as a measure of success. *Journal of Social Issues, 29*(2), 83–98.

Sullivan, T. A. (2000). A demographic portrait. In P. S. J. Cafferty & D. W. Engstrom (Eds.), *Hispanics in the United States: An agenda for the twenty-first century* (pp. 1–29). New Brunswick, NJ: Transaction.

Suzuki, B. H. (1980). The Asian-American family. In M. D. Fantini & R. Cardenas (Eds.), *Parenting in a multicultural society* (pp. 75–103). New York: Longman.

Taylor, R. J., Chatters, L. M., Tucker, M. B., & Lewis, E. A. (1990). Developments in research on Black families: A decade review. *Journal of Marriage and the Family, 52,* 993–1014.

Therrien, M., & Ramirez, R. R. (2001). *The Hispanic population in the United States: March 2000* (Current Population Reports No. P20-535). Washington, DC: U.S. Bureau of the Census.

U.S. Bureau of the Census. (2001). *Overview of race and Hispanic origin 2000* (Census Brief No. C2KBR/01-1). Washington, DC: Author. Retrieved June 11, 2004, from http://www .census.gov/prod/2001pubs/c2kbr01-1.pdf

U.S. Bureau of the Census. (2003, June 18). *Hispanic population reaches all-time high of 38.8 million, new Census Bureau estimates show* [Press release]. Washington, DC: Author.

Vega, W. A. (1990). Hispanic families in the 1980's: A decade of research. *Journal of Marriage and the Family, 52,* 1015–1024.

Walker A. J. (2000). Refracted knowledge: Viewing families form the prism of social science. In R. M. Milardo (Ed.), *A decade in review: Understanding families in the new millennium* (pp. 52–65). Lawrence, KS: Allen.

Westney, O. E. (1993). Human ecology theory: Implications for education, research, and practice. In P. Boss, W. J. Doherty, R. LaRossa, W. R. Schumm, & S. K. Steinmetz (Eds.), *Sourcebook of family theories and methods: A contextual approach* (pp. 448–450). New York: Plenum.

Whelan, D. (2001, July). The Asian American blind spot. *American Demographics, 23,* 16–17.

Williams, N. (1990). *The Mexican American family: Tradition and change.* New York: General Hall.

Witt, S. H. (1980). Pressure points in growing up Indian. *Perspectives: The Civil Rights Quarterly, 12*(1), 24–31.

Zinn, M. B. (1982). Chicano men and masculinity. *Journal of Ethnic Studies, 10*(2), 29–44.

ADVANCING THEORY THROUGH RESEARCH

The Case of Extrusion in Stepfamilies

Margaret Crosbie-Burnett, *University of Miami*

Edith A. Lewis, *University of Michigan*

Summer Sullivan, *University of Miami*

Jessica Podolsky, *University of Miami*

Rosane Mantilla de Souza, *Catholic University of St. Paul*

Victoria Mitrani, *University of Miami*

O ur purpose in this chapter is fourfold: We want to demonstrate (a) how to advance theory by empirically testing the validity of a theory in a real-life situation, (b) how to advance theory by generating new theory through qualitative methods, (c) how theory guides practical interventions that address problems, and (d) how to address the intersections of three theories, two research methods, and the demographic characteristics (e.g., educational level, ethnicity, race, social class) of researchers and research participants. We will accomplish these goals by focusing on the problem of physical extrusion of adolescents in some stepfamilies. *Extrusion* is defined as individuals' being "pushed out" of their households earlier than normal for members of their cultural group, either because they are forced to leave or because remaining in their households is so stressful that they "choose" to leave.[1]

Authors' Note: The superscripted numerals throughout this chapter refer the reader to expanded discussion, additional references, and/or figures on this volume's companion Web site, at http://www.ncfr.org/sourcebook.

First, we will conceptualize and explain the phenomenon of extrusion through the lenses of three different theories (i.e., the theorizing that Bengtson et al. discuss in Chapter 1 of this volume). Second, we will show how a qualitative component of the research study can enable the researcher to discover new variables that are important for understanding extrusion. Third, we will explain how the relative ability of the extant theories explaining extrusion, augmented by the additional variables identified in the qualitative component, can be tested empirically in a quantitative research design (see Chapter 3, this volume).[2] As a result of the data analysis, the variables that best predict extrusion (i.e., that explain the most variance in the measure of extrusion) form the basis for the new, advanced theory of extrusion.[3] Fourth, we will demonstrate how the new theory can guide clinical interventions, community prevention and intervention programs, and policy. (Note that the case and the study discussed here are hypothetical; we created them for the pedagogical purposes of this chapter.)

THE CASE OF EXTRUSION

During the past 3 years, the Mendota County Juvenile Court Services office has been operating Making a Change, a diversionary program for adolescents who have been in trouble with the law. The program was designed to meet three needs identified by the County Board of Supervisors: County officials and law enforcement officers wanted to (a) lower the number of legal offenses (e.g., truancy, delinquency, smoking, alcohol and drug use) being committed by members of the county's adolescent population, (b) decrease the rate of teen pregnancy, and (c) collaborate with families to ensure that parents and program personnel give adolescents consistent messages concerning illegal activities and pregnancy.

The program entails weekly support group meetings for the adolescents, with each meeting cofacilitated by a staff member and a "graduate" of the program, and multiple family support group meetings. The Board of Supervisors has asked for information about the types of adolescents served, the outcomes of the service, and the involvement of families in the program. The director of Making a Change, Lakshmi Taylor, presents the board with a report summarizing this information. According to the report, in the 3 years of its operation the program has served 122 families: the families of 25 girls who were considered "at risk" for pregnancy and those of another 97 adolescents who were referred for offenses. Only 1 of the 25 girls has become pregnant, and the young offenders who have participated in the program have only a 20% recidivism rate after 2 years. While following up with the families, however, Taylor discovered something curious: Two-thirds of the families referred were stepfamilies—that is, households in which the parent-adolescent relationships predated the couple relationships. These families included married and cohabiting heterosexual couples, gay and lesbian couples, new immigrant families, and families from a variety of cultures and socioeconomic classes.

What made the stepfamilies' data even more disconcerting was that 50% of the adolescents were not living with their custodial parents and stepparents, a higher percentage than that associated with other family structures. It appeared that these adolescents no longer felt comfortable or safe at home; some had been asked to leave by at least one of the adults in the household. Now they were living in a variety of situations, some in the homes of neighbors, peers, or relatives, both in this country and in their countries of origin, and some existing on the streets. They had been extruded. The recidivism rate for these adolescents was more than 70%; they broke panhandling laws, were truant, misused alcohol and other drugs, and engaged in sex acts for money in order to support themselves. These findings led Taylor to ask us to form a research team to try to provide some answers to the community about how to help these families. Although we know that there are many well-functioning stepfamilies, Taylor's discovery suggested that stepfamilies *might* have a particular vulnerability to the problem of extrusion.

To address this issue, we need to answer these questions: How are stepfamilies that extrude adolescents different from those that do not? What are the causes of extrusion of adolescent stepchildren? How can such extrusion be prevented? How can extruded adolescents be reintegrated into their families? As family scholars, we contemplate how we might best assure that our recommendations for interventions will be based on conceptual frameworks and scientific methods that are useful for *this* phenomenon. First, we review the empirical, clinical, and theoretical literatures on home-leaving, particularly extrusion of adolescents, with a focus on stepfamilies.

LITERATURE REVIEW OF EXTRUSION IN STEPFAMILIES

To conduct a good review of the literature on extrusion, a scholar must be like a detective, searching out what aspects of extrusion have been studied, the biases of the studies (e.g., theoretical, sampling, and measurement biases, as well as biases in the interpretation of results), and the gaps in the literature. The literature review shapes the proposed study, and the researcher should write up the results of the review to inform the reader of the relevance of the proposed study and how the study may contribute theoretical and empirically based knowledge to the issue of extrusion in general as well as guide practical interventions in Mendota County. Our literature review revealed the following information.

— More than 30% of minors in the United States spend some time living in stepfamilies before the age of 18 (Bumpass, Raley, & Sweet, 1995). This statistic is an underestimate, because it excludes adolescents older than 17 years who live at home, those who live in stepfamilies part-time, and those who live in gay and lesbian stepfamilies. Living in a stepfamily has been shown to be an important predictor of adolescent adjustment: Compared

with children who live in families with two biological parents, children in stepfamilies are significantly more likely to evidence behavioral and emotional problems (Coleman, Ganong, & Fine, 2000)[4] and to leave home prematurely, which we assume to be extrusion.[5]

Studies of the relationship between family structure and the timing of adolescents' home-leaving have found that adolescents in stepfamilies are at increased risk for "premature home-leaving" (the term used in the literature) when compared with adolescents who live with both biological parents (Aquilino, 1991; Cooney & Mortimer, 1999) and with adolescents who live in single-parent households (Mitchell, 1994).[6] The risk is even greater for girls, but it is lower for African Americans.[7] Leaving the family prematurely disrupts the normal life-course trajectory of adolescents, leading to less favorable outcomes. Premature home-leaving has been associated with adolescents' lower educational attainment, premarital pregnancy, cohabitation, early marriage, homelessness, alcohol and drug use, and living with friends or extended family.[8] Several studies have focused on one outcome of extrusion, homelessness, and its relationship to adolescent adjustment. Homeless adolescents are more likely than other adolescents to use alcohol and drugs, to engage in risky sexual behaviors, to be suicidal, and to have mental health problems (Cauce et al., 2000).[9]

Although studies have demonstrated the direct relationship between living in a stepfamily household and early home-leaving, and other studies have shown the relationship between early home-leaving and negative outcomes, only Mitchell (1994) and Cooney and Mortimer (1999) have explored intrafamilial factors that contribute to early home-leaving. These researchers found that adolescents and young adults in single-parent and stepparent families reported leaving home due to "conflicts with parents" and the "desire to be independent"; in addition, girls who had their own babies and girls who were responsible for doing more housework were more likely to leave. To date, no research has focused on identifying the dynamics of stepfamilies that may cause their increased risk for extrusion.

Our review of the literature reveals that research in this area has been mainly atheoretical, thus there is a need to examine theories that may explain this phenomenon. Although discussion of theory is noticeably absent, there is an assumption in the literature that *any* premature home-leaving from the home of a custodial, biological parent is likely problematic. This assumption of the primacy of the nuclear family may be a product of the worldview of the researchers, who have mainly conducted their studies from the perspective of American culture, which is considered "dominant" or "normal" in the social sciences and public policy.[10] However, no studies have compared outcomes for adolescents across types of postextrusion living arrangements or across various cultural heritages. Perhaps adolescents who leave home to live with extended family or neighbors fare better than they did at home.[11] Perhaps adolescents from nondominant cultures have different outcomes from those identified in the literature.[12] The sampling bias has almost entirely neglected nondominant-culture and immigrant stepfamilies. No qualitative studies have explored the extrusion phenomenon.

In sum, our review of the literature affirmed Mendota County's finding that adolescents in stepfamilies are at higher risk for extrusion than are other adolescents. However, we also found that the literature does not address (a) what is occurring in the intimate environments of the stepfamilies that extrude their adolescents, (b) how stepfamilies that extrude adolescents may be different from stepfamilies that do not, and (c) possible variations in outcomes of extrusion across cultural groups, across groups differing in immigration and acculturation status, across genders, social classes, or sexual orientations, and so on. There may be commonalities among extruding stepfamilies that can be explained by theory, or perhaps each situation is unique. That is an empirical question that we must try to answer, not only for Mendota County, but also to contribute to the knowledge base about extrusion.

First, we will use the classic scientific method. Now that we have reviewed the literature, our next step is to peruse the various theories of family (Boss, Doherty, LaRossa, Schumm, & Steinmetz, 1993) and choose a few grand or middle-level theories that may best explain extrusion. We will then use a deductive method (see Chapter 1, this volume) to explain extrusion by examining it through the "lens" of each theory.

THEORIZING ABOUT EXTRUSION

Attachment Theory

Overview

Origins. Attachment theory has its origins in developmental psychology (Bretherton, 1993). As such, it focuses on the relationship between the child and the child's primary caregiver. The development of attachment theory is most often credited to the work of John Bowlby (1982), who brought forth the notion that the relationship between mother and infant in the first years of life is the key to determining who the infant grows up to be, the individual's ability to develop high-quality relationships in adulthood, and his or her overall future well-being.[13] Bowlby uses the term *attachment* to describe the interaction between parenting behavior and the adaptation of the infant. Because of this interaction, the child develops "working models," or internal mental representations, that drive how he or she will behave and respond in relationships inside and outside of the family. Ainsworth, Blehar, Waters, and Wall (1978) empirically studied the process of attachment and identified three distinct attachment styles in infants: secure, anxious-ambivalent, and avoidant.

Adult attachment styles. Attachment theory has also been applied developmentally, viewed as a life-span phenomenon that influences adults' peer relationships and parenting styles. Attachment styles in adults are theorized to come directly from the mental models of self and others that individuals develop during infancy and childhood. An extensive body of literature focuses on how the attachment style formed in childhood affects the quality of a person's adult relationships.[14] Main and Goldwyn (1985) developed the Adult Attachment Interview to assess adult attachment styles, which they categorize as (a) secure/ autonomous; (b) insecure, dismissing; and (c) insecure, preoccupied.

Attachment styles and parenting. Some scholars have used these classifications to illustrate the influence of adult attachment styles on parenting, the validity of which has strong support in the literature. An individual's childhood attachment style influences his or her adult attachment style, which influences parenting, which then creates the attachment style of the individual's children. For example, securely attached mothers have securely attached children, and insecure, dismissing mothers usually have anxious or avoidant children.[15] This relationship between the primary caregiver's attachment style and the child's attachment style may be explained through the influence that attachment style has on parenting practices. For instance, insecure attachment styles in parents have been linked with child maltreatment. Compared with secure mothers, those with an insecure, preoccupied style have been found to demonstrate more anxious and intrusive behaviors when parenting their adolescent children.[16] Compared with other mothers, mothers with a dismissing style have reported feeling less cohesive with and less supportive of their children in certain scenarios.[17]

Attachment Theory's Explanation of Extrusion

To date, attachment theory has not been applied to stepparents; therefore, our study has the potential to advance attachment theory by including stepparents. When we view extrusion through the lens of attachment theory, we predict that a biological parent with a secure attachment style would be least likely to extrude the adolescent or allow the stepparent to do so. A biological parent with an insecure, dismissing style would be most likely to extrude an adolescent. A biological parent with an insecure, preoccupied style would fall in between these two, because an insecure, preoccupied parent might forfeit the adolescent (extrude) to keep the conjugal relationship intact. Like all adults, stepparents have attachment styles that influence their relationships. We predict the same relative probabilities of a stepparent extruding a stepchild as we do for a biological parent. However, we predict that the relationship between attachment style and probability of extrusion will be weaker for stepparents than for biological parents. In either case, if attachment style of either parent were found to be related to extrusion, the finding would be an important contribution to the stepfamily literature.

Normative-Resource Theory

Overview

Whereas attachment theory focuses on one aspect of psychoemotional adjustment, traditional normative-resource (N-R) theory, based in sociology and economics, focuses on the relative power between the adults in a relationship (Szinovacz, 1987). *Power* in this context is defined as "the ability of an individual within a social relationship to carry out his or her will, even in the face of resistance by others" (McDonald, 1980, p. 842). One can predict power by comparing the resources that each adult brings to the relationship and the dictates of the gender role norms specific to the couple's cultural context(s).

Pioneers in the study of family power theorized that an individual's relative conjugal power is based directly on his or her ability to contribute economic resources to the relationship.[18] Although data collected in Western societies provided support for this resource theory, Rodman (1972) framed the theory within a cultural context and highlighted the relevance of incorporating gender role norms when applying resource theory to non-Western populations.[19] He concluded that both resources and norms interact to determine the level of an individual's power within a conjugal relationship. This proposition led to the refinement of N-R theory, one of several exchange theories (Sabatelli & Shehan, 1993).

Several scholars have conceptualized the variables that might constitute the general category termed *resources*. These variables for each partner include but are not limited to the following: education, income, occupational prestige, age, areas of knowledge (e.g., languages or parenting), mental and physical health, intelligence and other psychological resources, social support and level of independence or dependence, and citizenship and resident status.[20] Resources increase one's power in a relationship only if one's partner values those resources. For example, a Spanish-speaking immigrant may value his partner's knowledge of English and American citizenship, whereas the American citizen may value her partner's membership in a cohesive extended family. Normative variables include gender role attitudes, patriarchal culture, family structure, female participation in the labor force, and religiosity.[21]

Application of N-R theory to stepfamilies. Some scholars have used N-R theory to explain power outcomes between the adult partners and between the generations in stepfamilies (Crosbie-Burnett & Giles-Sims, 1991; Giles-Sims & Crosbie-Burnett, 1989).[22] Although members of newly formed stepfamilies often lack well-defined or socially sanctioned norms to guide them in the roles they will assume within their families, remarried couples have been found to display more egalitarian gender roles than couples in first marriages (Coleman et al., 2000). Power outcomes between the parent and child generations are complex in stepfamilies, because some children gain power during the single-parent phase and are reluctant to share any of that power with their new stepparents.

N-R Theory's Explanation of Extrusion

When we view extrusion through the lens of N-R theory, we predict that the relative power differential between the adult partners,

based on culturally contextualized norms and resources, will determine who has decision-making power to decide if the adolescent may stay in the home or not. (We assume that the stepparent wants the adolescent extruded.) For example, the theory would predict that a stepfather in a traditional (patriarchal) family would likely be able to extrude an adolescent if he wishes, even if his wife has extensive resources, because the community (i.e., intersection of social class, ethnicity, religion, and so on) would support his behavior. Alternatively, a stepfather in an egalitarian, dual-career family would be less able to extrude the adolescent if he wishes, if his wife has extensive resources.

When we expand N-R theory to include the adolescent in the power balance, he or she might have resources that are highly valued by one or both of the adults—for example, physical strength needed to aid a disabled parent, or more income from a part-time job than an unemployed parent. Immigrant families often rely on adolescent members' knowledge of the language and culture of their new country. Cultures vary with respect to family role norms regarding parent-child power relations. For example, Chinese American adolescents have less power relative to their parents than do European American adolescents. Normative bases of power vary depending on families' particular cultural groups; the intersections among variables such as ethnicity, age, socioeconomic status, sexual orientation, gender, acculturation, and religiosity play an important role in determining the norms within any particular family.

Social-Cognitive-Behavioral Theory

Overview

Social-cognitive-behavioral (SCB) theory of families is based in psychology's behavioral paradigm and is an application of Bandura's model of reciprocal determinism (see any one triangle in Figure 9.1) to families (Crosbie-Burnett, Foster, Murray, & Bowen, 1996; Crosbie-Burnett & Lewis, 1993). In Bandura's (1986) social-cognitive theory, an individual's motivations, thoughts, and behaviors are

Figure 9.1   Comparison of Social-Cognitive-Behavioral Theory, Normative-Resource Theory, and
Attachment Theory as Applied to Extrusion in Stepfamilies

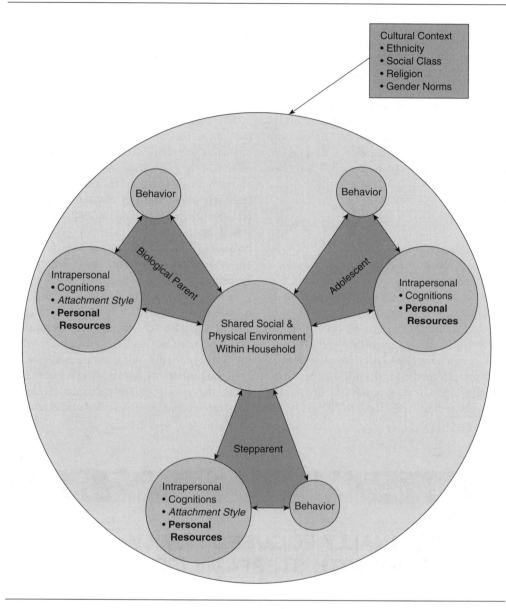

explained by a model of causation in which the individual's behaviors, environmental factors, and *intra*personal factors all operate as interacting determinants of one another. Behaviors include all observable behaviors, environmental factors include physical and social contexts, and intrapersonal factors include genetic makeup, personality and temperament, intelligence, talents, emotions, and cognitions (e.g., perceptions, expectations, beliefs, attributions, values, schemata, learning history).

In Figure 9.1, three individuals are placed together to form a family that shares a social and physical environment. (Given space limitations, the figure shows only a sampling of intrapersonal factors.) SCB theory's focus on individuals' cognitions about and behaviors toward other family members lends itself to explaining the interpersonal relations in families and does so at a more micro level of thought and action than attachment theory or N-R theory. An individual's cognitions mediate between a stimulus and the person's response. Thus SCB theory helps us to understand the nuances of and conditions under which extrusion may be probable in a way that includes cultural context(s), despite the fact that few scholars have applied SCB theory to stepfamilies.[23]

S-C-B Theory's Explanation of Extrusion

Central to SCB theory is the uniqueness of each individual and each family. Therefore, the following possible scenarios are only a few examples of how the causes of extrusion may be viewed through the lens of SCB theory: The probability of extrusion increases if either parent (a) is feeling "punished" (in a behavioral theory sense) by having the adolescent in the home, (b) perceives the adolescent's troublesome behavior as designed to discourage the stepparent from wanting to be part of the family and something that the couple should not have to tolerate, (c) believes that the adolescent's behavior causes arguments or stress between the couple, (d) has low self-efficacy about changing the adolescent's behavior, (e) has a schema of a "good (step)parent" that includes putting "problematic" adolescents out of the home as an appropriate response, and/or (f) anticipates "negative reinforcement" (e.g., relief from stress) if the adolescent is extruded. If any of these types of scenarios are true for both parents, then extrusion is even more likely. If only one parent wants extrusion, then the couple will engage in negotiation in which each will cognitively process and respond to the other's verbal and nonverbal behavior (e.g., pleas, promises, threats, tears, anger), weighing the anticipated rewards and punishments of agreeing or disagreeing with the partner regarding extrusion. In addition, if the social context of the family (e.g., social class, cultural group) includes role models of stepfamilies that have handled "teenage problems" within the home and did not extrude adolescents, then the probability of extrusion is less than it would be in a social context that includes stepfamilies that have extruded adolescents.

• SPOTLIGHT ON THEORY

EMOTIONALLY FOCUSED FAMILY THERAPY WITH STEPFAMILIES

James L. Furrow, *Fuller Theological Seminary*

Brent Bradley, *Indiana Wesleyan University*

Susan M. Johnson, *University of Ottawa*

The strengths of a stepfamily are found in the shared experiences and emotional bonds that tie individuals from different biological families to a new family identity.

(continued)

● *SPOTLIGHT ON THEORY continued*

Relational awareness is required to facilitate these strengths given the preexisting family histories and divided loyalties that can obstruct stepfamily functioning. Because emotional experience and expression both organize and regulate family interaction, therapeutic interventions that engage emotion are likely to be effective in shifting problematic patterns of family interaction (Johnson, 1998). Emotionally focused family therapy (EFFT) is an innovative approach that frames the family's emotional experience in the context of attachment theory (Johnson, 1996). In EFFT practice, family patterns are restructured to enhance the accessibility and responsiveness of family members and thus promote more secure bonds. This approach anticipates many of the challenges that couples and children face when they live in complex family systems.

Stepfamilies often confront the competing needs of members for relational resources, including time, attention, and emotional support. In addition, stressors associated with early stepfamily development interact with unresolved emotional demands from losses encountered through death or divorce. Patterns of availability and responsiveness in the family system affect the relationship functioning of family members as they seek to establish bonds in the new family system. A common stepfamily challenge is the development of a strong couple bond, as couple adjustment in remarriage is influenced by the adjustment of children to the remarriage.

Attachment theory offers a nonpathologizing and practical approach to the conceptualization of problematic relationship patterns. The actions of a disengaged stepchild can be understood as responses aimed at reducing the demands being placed on an attachment figure to improve the safety and security of that relationship, rather than as a personal limitation of that child (Johnson, 2003). Although the child's avoidant behavior may result in conflict in the family, the intent of the behavior is to prompt a restorative response to relational distress.

As the security of a stepfamily increases, members of the family are more likely to share their experiences. A stepdaughter, for example, is more likely to seek support from her stepfather as she begins to see him as safe and worthy of her trust. Families characterized by secure attachments are more adaptive, remaining flexible in their interactions even when under stress. Families must be able to respond to attachment needs in order to maintain a sense of familial security.

EFFT engages family members in a process that addresses these attachment needs. The therapist first reframes the family's presenting problem in light of underlying emotions, interaction patterns, and attachment needs. The therapist then helps family members to strengthen attachment bonds by engaging them in interactions that involve reciprocal attachment-related needs and longings, as illustrated in the following example:

Following their remarriage, Robert and Susan found that Susan's 14-year-old son, Jon, was disengaged from family activities and failing in school. The EFFT therapist noted the frequent conflict escalating between Robert and his stepson. In time, the therapist enabled Jon to experience his previously unspoken grief regarding Susan's divorce from Jon's father. This loss informed Jon's disengaged posture toward his mother and stepfather. The family began to identify the conflict and disengagement as a problematic pattern, rather than blaming Jon. The therapist

(continued)

● SPOTLIGHT ON THEORY *continued*

heightened the expression of Jon's feelings of loss, enabling him to share with Susan his fear that she would abandon him as his father had. Susan softened her stance toward Jon, which had been defensive of Robert and critical toward Jon's irresponsibility at school. In turn, she responded with support and acceptance of Jon's loss and his vulnerability related to the divorce and remarriage. Robert expressed compassion for Jon and shared that he had responded to Jon's defiance, without being aware of his pain and fear. Robert also expressed a hope that he could be a support to Jon, although not a replacement for his father.

This case illustrates how a therapist can use EFFT to engage a stepfamily's emotional experience to assist members in changing patterns that are informed by unexpressed attachment needs and longings. The resulting emotional engagement strengthens the security that members in the stepfamily feel by increasing the emotional responsiveness and availability of family members. ●

COMPARISON OF THEORIES

As the first step in testing the relative power of the three theories described above to explain and predict extrusion, we consider the similarities and differences across theories in concepts and the postulated relationships between concepts. The differences in foci of these three theories are a reflection of N-R theory's roots in sociology and economics, attachment theory's roots in developmental psychology, and SCB theory's roots in behavioral psychology. Figure 9.1 illustrates the comparisons among the theories. SCB theory is the most detailed of the three and encompasses attachment theory, in that attachment style (noted in italics in the figure) is one aspect of personality, an intrapersonal factor in the SCB model. Some of the important concepts of N-R theory (noted in boldface type) are a subset of SCB theory's intrapersonal factors—for example, resources such as intelligence, talents, and physical and mental health, including a secure attachment style. However, other resources, such as an individual's income and valuable possessions, have no direct analogous concepts in SCB or attachment theory. However, in SCB theory, enjoying one's

partner's possessions (and resources, such as physical beauty) can be reinforcing. The *relative* difference in resources between family members that is so central to N-R theory has an analogy in SCB theory, but it is less central. For example, a husband may perceive that he is providing more resources that his wife finds pleasurable (reinforcing) than she is providing for him.

With respect to cultural contexts, SCB theory focuses on (a) role models within an individual's demographic group, (b) rewards and punishments for behavior that come from extrafamilial authority figures or institutions, and (c) an individual's psychological internalization of her or his culture's values and norms, and how this "learning" affects cognitive processing and, therefore, behavior. N-R theory implicitly assumes people's internalization of norms, yet focuses mainly on one dimension of these—gender role norms. Our application of N-R theory adds to these family role norms for power relations between generations in a family. Attachment theory does not address cultural contexts, but it includes a culturally biased implicit assumption that there is one primary caregiver per infant—an inaccurate assumption in some cultures.[24]

THE STUDY OF EXTRUSION

Now that we have explained extrusion as viewed through the lenses of three different conceptual frameworks and have compared the explanations briefly, we want to know which theory or parts of theories can predict extrusion best empirically, allowing us to advance family theory and to create interventions for Mendota County that are theoretically sound and empirically supported. We design a quantitative study that compares the explanatory power of these theories, using concepts from the theories as predictor or independent variables and extrusion as the outcome or dependent variable. Details of the design of this study are beyond the purview of this chapter, but a few points will illustrate some important considerations.

The concepts must have conceptual and operational definitions. Examples of concepts that could serve as predictor variables include adult attachment style (all three theories); gender norms and family role norms for parents and adolescent (SCB and N-R theories); adults' schemata of "good parent" and "bad parent" (SCB theory); anticipated rewards and punishments (from within and outside the family) for extruding the adolescent (SCB theory); presence of stepfamily role models (SCB theory); resources of adults and adolescent (SCB and N-R theories); attributions and expectations about behaviors of family members, related to the adolescent's legal troubles (SCB theory); adults' desires to extrude the adolescent, as a moderating variable (all theories); and demographic variables. *The outcome variable of extrusion will be a composite of two variables:* where the adolescent lives and frequency of contact with parent(s). Various levels of "where" range from living with a close relative or other parent to living with friends to living on the streets. *Psychometrically sound measures of relevant concepts must be identified or created,* and then they must be pilot tested with participants representing the variety of cultures found among the families in our case and modified so that *the measures are culturally*

appropriate.[25] Other issues must also be addressed in the research design, ranging from collecting self-report data from multiple family members without allowing them to influence each other's responses to analyzing data that include multiple measures from multiple family members (see Chapter 3, this volume).

Before we begin the quantitative component of our study, we acknowledge that we really know very little about what is occurring within these stepfamilies that is causing some of them to extrude their adolescents. We know that in order to maximize our ability to advance theory through quantitative methods, *we should include the issues that the families and others in the community deem relevant to extrusion* in addition to those concepts by which our three theories explain extrusion. The best way to identify additional issues or concepts is to conduct the qualitative component of our study next and then add the newly identified concepts to the group of predictor variables in the quantitative component.

The Qualitative Research Component

This particular qualitative approach demonstrates how researchers can study families within a community context while also helping them. It is an example of an inductive method of theory development (see Chapters 1 and 2, this volume), because a theoretical explanation of extrusion will be induced from many pieces of information—the data of qualitative methods. In our qualitative approach, we change our focus from explaining the *problem* of extrusion *within* the family, the perspective of most family theories, to examining the *phenomenon* of extrusion within the whole *community.* The change in unit of analysis from family to community gives us an opportunity to identify extrafamilial factors to add to our theoretical explanation of extrusion. Our goal is to determine the influence of those contexts on extrusion and intervene at the individual, family, and community levels *while we are studying extrusion.* Different research questions guide the qualitative inquiry: Does extrusion, as defined above, actually exist in stepfamilies, or are other social, historical, cultural, or political factors operating in these situations? What are the various causes of the many types of extrusion? If we conceptualize extrusion as a social problem, whose problem is it? Are there any positive outcomes to extrusion? Who knows the most about extrusion in this community? If we find that extrusion exists in this community, will our interventions benefit all affected parties equally, or will factors such as race, gender, sexual orientation, economic class, background, and location influence the type, efficacy, and benefit of the interventions?

Participatory action research (PAR; Minkler, 1999) exchanges the research strategies traditionally used with families for a more organic form of intervention that those most affected by any action taken can participate in and evaluate concurrently.[26] Researchers and representatives of all of the community's stakeholders form a team that is responsible for (a) establishing the research questions; (b) selecting the measures; (c) designing the inquiry processes and structure (i.e., who collects what data, when, and how); (d) carrying out the collection, analysis, and interpretation of data; and (e) planning immediate action and long-term changes. Extruded and nonextruded adolescents and their siblings, parents, and stepparents, as well as other community residents and leaders, describe their reality in their own terms and intervene on their own terms to whatever extent possible. New theory is likely to emerge in the process. It will be shaped by our own standpoints as formally trained researchers, coupled with the standpoints of the various laypersons, professionals, and community institutions involved, because all stakeholders have voices and the traditional hierarchy of power is flattened (see Figure 9.2). When this happens, the interventions developed, the policy implications of the research findings, and the recommendations we make to the County Board of Supervisors will differ from those that would result from the work of researchers operating alone. In PAR, trained researchers join as partners with community human resources and have no

primary hierarchical power over the method. We become *facilitators* of the research instead of its *directors*.

PAR is derived from methods that represent the latest evolutionary development in ethical research practices. These include ethnography, grounded theory, feminist frameworks, multicultural frameworks, and action research (Gutiérrez & Lewis, 1999).[27] Unlike positivist scientific methods that are structured to yield a "truth," these newer methods are structured to reflect the complexities of a phenomenon, with an emphasis on the contextualized experiences of stakeholders; ethical research methods; formally trained researchers as collaborators and facilitators rather than directors; ongoing recognition of the importance of place, power, and voice in the research enterprise; and the linkage of intervention and theory building. This model of research forces us to remain constantly vigilant about the assumptions we researchers are making about families and their communities. For example, a researcher's schema of "family," which is a product of her or his own worldview, may interfere with her or his understanding of the cultural variations of extrusion.[28]

Integrating Knowledge From the Qualitative Component Into the Study

Let's suppose that the PAR study reveals the following findings: First, from the adolescents in Mendota County we learn that one of the differences between the adolescent stepchildren who were extruded and those who were not is that the extruded adolescents "could not tell my mom/dad how hurt and angry I felt about how our relationship changed after my stepfather/stepmother moved in with us, and there was no one else to talk to, so I just gave up and got high or got into trouble." Regardless of family structure, extruded gay, lesbian, and bisexual adolescents reported parental reactions to their coming out ranging from being told to leave the home to being treated "like a misfit" in the family. We identify the lack of communication skills exhibited by the extruded adolescents

Figure 9.2   Model of Participatory Action Research as Applied to the Study of Extrusion in
Stepfamilies

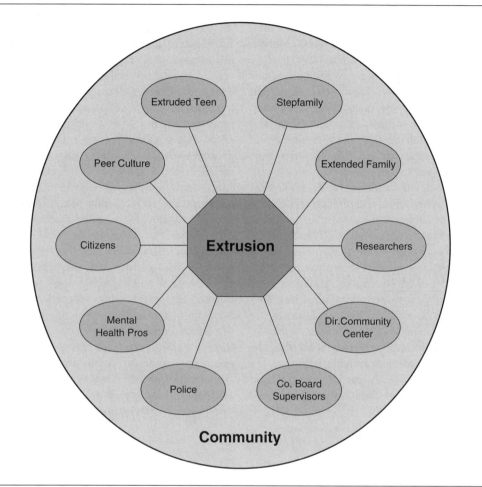

and their parents as an opportunity for intervention. Some of the extruded adolescents reported, "My mom/dad didn't seem to care if I stayed or left." This could be an indication of an avoidant, dismissing type of insecure attachment on the part of those biological parents. Of concern was that some of the adolescents who had left home reported that they were running away from sexual and/or physical abuse; most of these were girls. On a more hopeful note, some of the extruded adolescents had moved in with extended family members, fictive kin, or neighbors; those adolescents were happier than others and were doing well in their new homes. Nearly all of the adolescents in this subgroup are of African, Latin, or Asian descent, including newly immigrated families from Latin American and the Caribbean.[29]

Second, from parents and professionals working with adolescents we learn that it is extremely easy for adolescents to acquire alcohol and drugs in the county. We then decide that we need to target the facilities selling substances to youth as part of this "action" study. And third, from community leaders and police we learn that extrusion has increased the numbers of homeless adolescents; this has become a serious problem not only for the adolescents themselves, but also for community members living in areas where homeless adolescents congregate. Although some of these community members see the homeless adolescent problem as a nuisance that "the police should take care of," others express concern about "this tragedy" and want to help.

Based on the qualitative component of our hypothetical study, we discover that we need to add nine predictor or independent variables to the quantitative component of our study: (a) a measure of adolescent's ability to communicate with parent(s) about family issues, (b) a measure of parent's ability to communicate with adolescent about family issues, (c) adolescent report of sexual abuse and physical abuse, (d) a measure of adolescent use of alcohol and drugs as a mechanism for coping with family problems, (e) adolescent's ease of acquiring alcohol and drugs, (f) gender of adolescent, (g) sexual orientation of adolescent, (h) gender of stepparent, and (i) family ethnicity(ies). The knowledge that some extruded adolescents are successfully living with extended family, friends, or neighbors reconfirms our belief that the outcome or dependent variable, extrusion, is a continuous variable (at least interval level) and not a dichotomous—in or out of the home—variable.

The Quantitative Research Component

To advance theory regarding extrusion, we ask, Which theory, parts of theories, variables identified in the qualitative component, or demographic factors will best predict (i.e., explain the variability in) extrusion in our sample? Let's suppose that we perform a multivariate study (see Chapter 3, this volume) and the results of a multiple regression reveal that a combination of the following predictor variables accounts for most of the variance in our measure of extrusion: both adolescent's and parents' reports of ability to communicate about family issues; biological parent's attachment style; biological parent's beliefs that the adolescent's behavior was threatening the stability of the couple's relationship; gender of the stepparent; relative to the biological parent, amount of resources that the stepparent brings to the family; the presence of abuse; the sexual orientation of the adolescent; the family's ethnicity. All of these variables predicted extrusion in the expected directions, including gender of stepparent. Stepfathers were predicted to be associated with a higher probability of extrusion than were stepmothers.

● *SPOTLIGHT ON METHODS*

EXPLORING THE DIVERSITY OF STEPFAMILY RELATIONSHIPS

Maria Schmeeckle, *Illinois State University*

I n the research reported here, I explored how people define and negotiate family boundaries in stepfamilies. In this brief discussion, I will highlight how my *sample,* my

(continued)

combined use of *qualitative and quantitative methods,* and a *longitudinal* approach enabled me to explore the diversity of family perceptions about stepfamily relationships.

DIVERSE SAMPLE

Much of the research on stepfamilies focuses on coresidential stepparents of minor children (Pasley & Ihinger-Tallman, 1994), but the full spectrum of stepfamilies is broader than this. My research incorporated noncoresidential stepfamily members, minor stepchildren's perspectives, adult stepchildren's perspectives, stepfamily relationships that start when children are already grown, stepfamily relationships based on both marriage and cohabitation, relationships between former steprelatives, and stepfamily relationships across different historical eras. Such a broad sample allows for a more complete understanding of stepfamily relationships. For instance, the breadth of the sample enabled me to detect the strengthening of ties with stepparents that can occur when adult stepchildren have children of their own.

COMPLEMENTARY QUALITATIVE AND QUANTITATIVE METHODS

Initially, I used statistically nonrepresentative stratified interviews (Trost, 1986) to establish a basis for survey questions. I then used survey data to discover the form and range of perceptions of stepparents across a large number of adult respondents. I later returned to interviews to complement and broaden further the insights gained from the survey analysis. Taken together, these methods resulted in findings that confirmed and supplemented each other. For example, through both methods I found evidence of the perceived importance of the stepparent's being in a legally married relationship with the parent.

Research Approach Used to Study the Diversity of Relationships Among Adult Stepfamily Generations

Strategy	Outcome
Exploratory interviews with a convenience sample: 12 qualitative interviews with adults who had living stepmothers; statistically nonrepresentative stratified sample, stratified by gender, age, and timing of stepmother entry	Found a wide range of family perceptions toward stepmothers; established a basis for survey questions; refined interview questions to use in later qualitative interviews
Survey questions: survey about family perceptions of parents and stepparents, in collaboration with the USC Longitudinal Study of Generations (1997 wave); data from 1,603 survey participants (ages 16–70) about relationships with biological parents, stepparents, cohabiting partners of parents, and former stepparents	Found immense diversity of perceptions toward stepparents; explored this diversity with respondents from divorced families with long-term current stepparents; further narrowed pool to 15, stratified by gender (of stepparent and stepchild) and "family" and "parent" perceptions of stepparent

(continued)

● *SPOTLIGHT ON METHODS continued*

(continued)

Strategy	Outcome
Qualitative interviews with selected survey participants, and analysis: open-ended questions about what makes people family members and parents, and what relationship histories contribute to relationship perceptions of stepparents	Recognized themes related to the range of adult children's perceptions of stepparents and related factors contributing to this range
Survey analysis: bivariate and multivariate analysis of factors associated with adult children's family perceptions of various types of stepparents; comparison with perceptions of biological parents	Discovered a wide variety of family perceptions toward various types of stepparents and biological parents; identified significant factors associated with those perceptions
Four-year follow-up with 13 of the 15 previous qualitative interviewees: requested relationship update; tested analysis of previous interviews and significant survey factors against participant experiences	Identified themes of change and continuity across time; deepened understanding of stepfamily relationship dynamics within this subsample; modified previous qualitative and quantitative analyses

LONGITUDINAL APPROACH

I used a longitudinal approach to reveal the *dynamic* nature of the relationships in stepfamilies across time. I examined relationship change from the time of survey completion (1997) to the time of the first interview with a subsample (1999–2000) to the time of follow-up interviews with the same subsample (2002–2003). Across this 7-year period, I assessed changes brought about by deaths, divorces, geographic moves, children being born, children leaving the home, and communication technology.

In conclusion, my research shows that scholars can bring to light the diversity and dynamics of stepfamily relationships by sampling diverse populations, using multiple methods, and taking a longitudinal approach. The findings from such research are an important complement to the normative findings based on limited samples so often described in the literature. ●

THE NEW THEORY OF EXTRUSION

Now we can explain and predict extrusion in stepfamilies with our new, more comprehensive theory better than we could with any one theory or with the qualitative component alone. Our new theory has elements from both psychology and sociology.[30] We would conclude that the probability of extrusion in a stepfamily increases (a) when the adolescent cannot communicate effectively about family issues (behavioral deficit), particularly feelings about a new stepparent entering the family (variable identified by PAR; SCB theory); (b) when the stepparent and biological parent cannot communicate effectively with the adolescent (variables identified by PAR; SCB theory); (c) when the biological parent fears losing the relationship with the stepparent if the adolescent remains in the home (SCB theory); (d) when the biological parent has an insecure, dismissing attachment style, making him or her more likely to "let go of" the adolescent (variable identified by PAR; attachment theory); (e) when the adolescent reports physical or sexual abuse (variable identified by PAR); (f) when the stepparent is male, as men tend to have more power than women in conjugal relationships and are more likely to be abusive (variable identified by PAR; N-R theory); (g) when the stepparent is bringing more resources into the family than the biological parent, giving him or her more power to effect the extrusion (primarily N-R theory, secondarily SCB theory); (h) when the adolescent is not heterosexual (variable identified by PAR); and (i) when the family is from the mainstream individualist American culture as opposed to a culture strong in familism.[31]

The more of the listed predictors a family has, the higher the likelihood of extrusion. For example, the probability of extrusion is high in a mainstream American family in which the mother has an insecure, dismissing attachment style and lacks the skills to communicate with the adolescent, the mother relies on the stepfather for material goods, and the stepfather strikes the gay adolescent during an argument. Alternatively, if a father in a stepfamily newly immigrated from Central America has a secure attachment style, is the sole breadwinner, and can communicate openly with his heterosexual daughter about his concerns regarding his responsibility to protect her from the dangers of adolescent life in America, two outcomes are possible: no extrusion or extrusion in which the daughter is sent back to Central America to live with her aunt in a small town while her father stays in close contact with her.

PRACTICE AND POLICY IMPLICATIONS

Community Interventions

How might our new theory guide interventions in Mendota County? Community centers and schools might add support groups that focus on communication skills for adolescent stepchildren and their parents, and for gay, lesbian, and bisexual adolescents and their parents. The community could seek additional support for adolescents at risk of extrusion through funding at the state level or through community block grant initiatives at the federal level, thus enhancing single parents' access to the resources they need to support their families, helping them to be less dependent on finding new partners as a way of gaining resources. Extruded adolescents could be screened for history of abuse and given appropriate services; tax credits and programmatic support could be given to relatives and concerned citizens willing to house abused adolescents, keeping them out of the foster care system. This would be a shift in policy from a focus on reconnecting extruded adolescents with their families to finding alternative home placements for the adolescents.

Therapeutic Interventions

Knowing how parents' attachment styles can affect extrusion is of limited utility at the community level, but it is relevant for family therapy interventions. Therapists who work with families that are at risk of extruding or have extruded adolescents might focus on the parents' attachment issues as well as on all family members' communication skills related to helping adolescents deal with negative emotions stemming from the integration of stepparents into their families. Parents who are skilled in this type of communication might be employed as peer role models to assist families that are considering extruding adolescents as well as families that are reintegrating previously extruded adolescents.

How Have We Advanced Theory?

We have attempted to show how using extant theories and results of a study with qualitative and quantitative components can advance theory addressing a phenomenon in families. Using the results of the hypothetical study described above, we have advanced family theory by combining into new theory only the parts of the extant theories and the new variables that were related to extrusion statistically. In the narrowest application, we have advanced a family theory of stepfamily extrusion of adolescents who have been in trouble with the law. However, it is possible that this theory may predict conflict in stepfamilies in general; alternatively, it may help explain extrusion in many family structures, including both positive and negative impacts of extrusion. Our next steps in theory development would be to test the new theory with a broader population of stepfamilies and with a broader population of families that have extruded adolescents, so that scholars could use our integrative theoretical model and research method with more confidence when studying families from various ethnic, racial, class, and religious backgrounds. This theory-research-theory cycle advances theory through research and advances research through theory.

CONCLUSIONS

Based on the above discussion, we offer the following advice to family scholars who seek to advance theory through research:

- Use more than one theory when investigating a family issue; try to choose theories from different disciplines within family sciences. The research is likely to be more heuristic in the development of a useful, comprehensive theory.
- Integrate qualitative methods into quantitative studies, for two main reasons: (a) to identify additional salient variables, and thereby improve the appropriateness of the research for the group being studied; and (b) to enrich your understanding of the quantitative results.
- Remember that the practical and policy implications of your research findings should flow logically from the new, advanced theory that your study has produced.

CASE STUDY

IDENTITY ENACTMENT AND VERIFICATION IN GAY AND LESBIAN STEPFAMILIES

Brad van Eeden-Moorefield, *University of North Carolina at Greensboro*

Kari Henley, *University of North Carolina at Greensboro*

Kay Pasley, *University of North Carolina at Greensboro*

In Chapter 9, Crosbie-Burnett et al. note the scholarly interest in outcomes for children who reside in stepfamilies, particularly with regard to factors related to extrusion, such as psychological inclusion of the stepparent into the biological parent-child dyad. They also suggest that resource and normative bases of power might be contingent on the intersectionality of a family member's social positions (e.g., gay, stepparent). Given that little research has been conducted on the effects of intersecting social positions on stepfamily life,

CASE STUDY *continued*

we focus our comments on gay and lesbian (GL) stepfamilies and issues of psychological inclusion. We use identity theory (Stryker, 1968) to frame the discussion, because it provides additional insight into the process of psychological inclusion of stepparents and overall stepfamily formation within the context of social stigma that accompanies being gay or lesbian.

PREVALENCE OF GL STEPFAMILIES

In recent years, the greater visibility of GL families in the United States (see, e.g., Simmons & O'Connell, 2003) has resulted in increased attention from family scholars (Berger, 2000). Here, we use the term *GL step-family* to refer to any GL couple in which at least one of the partners has at least one child from a prior marriage or partnership (heterosexual or homosexual); the child may reside with the couple full- or part-time, and the couple may have formalized their relationship as a civil union (legal stepfamily) or may simply cohabit (i.e., nonlegal stepfamily; Bumpass et al., 1995).

It has been estimated that stepfamilies (legal and nonlegal) account for approximately 30% of households in the United States with children under 18 years (Pasley & Moorefield, 2004) and that 2 to 8 million GL families are raising 3 to 14 million children (Black, Gates, Sanders, & Taylor, 2000). However, these figures do not accurately reflect the number of GL stepfamilies, as they include both families with children born into the union and those with children from prior relationships. Thus our best guess about the prevalence of GL stepfamilies in the United States is that there are millions. Further, these numbers are likely to increase in the future, given the relatively high risk of relationship dissolution among GL couples (Brown, 2003) and the fact that greater numbers of GL couples are having children.

IDENTITY THEORY AND GL STEPFAMILIES

Identity theory asserts that identities are created through individuals' interactions with others; through interaction, shared meanings are created that shape human behavior and sense of self (Stryker, 1968). *Roles* are socially constructed proscriptions that espouse how a person should behave, think, and emote given the social positions or statuses he or she holds (e.g., stepfather, stepmother), and identities are the self-meanings attached to particular roles (e.g., provider, caregiver; Burke, 1991). Given the lack of social norms related to stepfamily roles (e.g., Clawson & Ganong, 2002), particularly for GL stepfamilies (e.g., Berger, 2000), we assume that developing related identities is a more arduous task for GL stepfamilies and includes difficulties both similar to and distinct from those encountered by heterosexual stepfamilies.

To explore these similarities and differences, Lynch (2000) interviewed 45 GL stepfamilies and compared her findings with those in the literature on heterosexual stepfamilies. She found that the two groups were similar in structural factors (e.g., beliefs in stepfamily formation) but not in gender-related issues (e.g., sexual identity development, unique parenting roles). Specific to identity theory, Lynch found that the parenting roles and associated identities of the GL stepparents in her sample developed over time (similar to other stepparent roles; Bray & Kelly, 1998). Similarly, Crosbie-Burnett and Helmbrecht (1993) found that becoming a stepparent was related to unhappiness in the GL couple relationship—a finding also common in heterosexual stepfamilies (Bray & Kelly, 1998). Unique to GL stepfamilies, Lynch's participants felt that they lacked role proscriptions, and this fostered greater flexibility and creativity in their enactment of stepparent roles. Further, they were surprised by

Case Study

CASE STUDY *continued*

the negotiation required to integrate multiple identities (i.e., GL identity, stepparent identity), particularly those related to GL status.

Burke (2003) suggests that the self comprises multiple identities and that each identity is affected by commitment, or the number of relationships associated with the identity and the costs associated with no longer enacting that identity. GL stepfamilies may experience instances in which fewer relationships are available to support stepfamily roles than would be the case in heterosexual stepfamilies because of the stigma associated with being a GL stepfamily (e.g., lack of legal support for GL families [Brown, 2003]; lack of acceptance or acknowledgment of children in GL families by extended family members [Berger, 2000]).

Further, Burke and Stets (1999) contend that commitment to identities emerges from the self-verification process, because people seek to verify their identities (Burke, 1991). Verification is achieved through interaction: An individual exhibits a behavior that he or she perceives as being congruent with the standards he or she holds for a particular identity and then assesses the feedback received from others as a result of that behavior as being congruent or incongruent with the individual's original perceptions. Congruence results in positive verification of an identity and the related behavior, leading to feelings of acceptance and esteem, whereas incongruence creates distress (Burke, 1991). Theoretically, this process creates a feedback loop that reinforces or inhibits identity enactment.

We suggest that self-verification holds additional importance for GL stepfamilies. Consistent with theory, psychological inclusion of the stepparent by the stepchild and the stepparent's partner (a form of verification) is related to relationship satisfaction and feeling accepted (Crosbie-Burnett & Helmbrecht, 1993). Because social support for the stepparent role also is related to acceptance, we agree with Burke (1991) that such feelings result from the verification process. Research also shows that GL stepfamilies report spending time negotiating

the openness of their family status due to negative social reactions (Berger, 2000). Theoretically, a GL stepfamily's not being "out" can reduce the number of possible relationships available to members through which they can verify their identities and so might result in negative outcomes (Lynch, 2000).

AN EXAMPLE

We present a brief example from a study conducted by the first author that examined identity and verification among gay male couples (see Moorefield & Proulx, 2003):

> Jack is a 52-year-old White male who was married for 23 years and had two children from this marriage. He has been in a gay relationship for 7 years, and his partner also brought a child into their partnership from a previous marriage. Jack spoke of the difficult transition from marriage to a gay partnership related to the integration and enactment of new identities: gay partner, gay parent, gay stepparent. For example, he said, "My wife had always known, and, after a very bad breakdown and suicide attempt [referring to his experience with coming to terms with being gay], I decided to come out. She was fully supportive." Jack also discussed the development of new identity standards associated with newly developing roles. He said, "I formed this idea or concept of what the perfect relationship was. And for me that was having someone in my life that essentially filled every aspect of my life, including psychologically, emotionally, and sexually." Jack further spoke about the differences between these ideal standards and those he previously held for his marriage and about the importance of having relationships to support his new identities and roles:
>
> > I have a wonderful relationship with my ex-wife, who is remarried, and Joe and I see them frequently. My children

are very accepting of my partner, spouse, husband . . . and his [child] is of me. We have a grandson, and my daughter is married; her husband is very accepting. His parents are very accepting, so we have a very large extended family. We are all very active together.

Essentially, Jack had relationships that supported his roles and identities (reflective of commitment). As such, he received feedback that his behavior was congruent with his identities, his identities were accepted and verified, and he was able to establish additional relationships (extended family) to continue to support his identities related to being in a GL stepfamily. Thus, from an identity perspective, both commitment and verification are important to GL stepfamily formation, possibly more so than with heterosexual stepfamilies because

of the additional social stigma and reduced relationships available to support GL stepfamily members and their associated identities (Berger, 2000).

CONCLUSION

Research on GL stepfamilies remains scant and often atheoretical, much like the research on extrusion presented in Chapter 9. We have focused here on GL stepfamilies and have situated our discussion within identity theory to provide examples of how theory helps explain research. We have demonstrated the importance of social support as an indicator of identity commitment and have shown how such commitment affects identity verification. Given the stigmatized status of GL stepfamilies, commitment emerges as an essential component for GL stepfamily formation and the psychological inclusion of stepparents.

Discussion and Extension

DISCUSSION AND EXTENSION

LEAVING WHOSE HOME? WHEN STEPCHILDREN LEAVE IS IT ALWAYS EXTRUSION?

Lawrence H. Ganong, *University of Missouri–Columbia*

Marilyn Coleman, *University of Missouri–Columbia*

Early home-leaving by stepchildren is an important issue to study. The small body of research on this subject to date indicates that stepchildren leave home at younger ages, on average, than do their peers who live with both parents. It is not always clear from the reports of these studies where stepchildren

go, but some researchers have found that stepchildren establish independent households at younger ages than do children who live with both parents (e.g., Aquilino, 1991; Kiernan, 1992).

Because the studies conducted thus far have been based on secondary data sets,

Discussion and Extension

researchers have not been able to examine step-family dynamics or intraindividual processes (i.e., thoughts, feelings, attitudes) related to early home-leaving. Instead, they have tried to identify predictors of early home-leaving. Theoretical explanations most often comprise stress or parent involvement models.

STRESS FRAMEWORKS

A major premise of stress models is that the addition of a stepparent into a household increases levels of stress for children and adults. Many changes ensue when a residential parent remarries or cohabits with a new partner—family members encounter new household routines and activities and new expectations for children's behavior. If they move into new residences, stepchildren are faced with more changes—new schools, new friends, perhaps the loss of old friends. There may be alterations in children's relationships with their parents; for instance, children's contact with nonresidential parents often decreases following parental remarriage (Cooksey & Craig, 1998). Relationships with residential parents also may change—some researchers propose that *parental competencies are reduced* when parents enter new relationships because they are so overwhelmed by the need to adapt to their new partners that they neglect their children (e.g., Yeung, Linver, & Brooks-Gunn, 2002).

Stress models generally propose that accumulated changes caused by the addition of a stepparent increase stress, which leads to discordant relationships and eventually to the stepchild's leaving the household. Stepchildren may be forced out by stepparents or parents when household stress and conflict become intolerable, or stepchildren may leave to keep peace in the family and to maintain their own welfare (Hanson, McLanahan, & Thomson, 1996). Some scholars have also hypothesized that stress-induced conflicts between coparents may explain early home-leaving (e.g., Kiernan, 1992).

Some researchers have suggested that stressful effects are heightened for a child when his or her residential parent has had multiple partnerships (e.g., Martinez & Forgatch, 2002). Multiple transitions lead to accumulation of stress, more household conflicts, and deterioration of parenting skills, all of which amplify the likelihood of stepchildren's leaving.

(STEP)PARENT INVOLVEMENT

Another set of explanations for early home-leaving suggests that stepchildren leave households early because their needs are not being met or because they feel neglected. The *social capital hypothesis* is that adults in stepparent households lack time and energy to engage in positive interactions with children because they invest their resources in building relationships with their new partners; stepparents may invest resources in their children from prior relationships instead of in their stepchildren (e.g., Bogenschneider, 1997). Evolutionary scholars postulate that stepparents invest little in stepchildren because they are not genetically related to those children (Daly & Wilson, 1998). The *parental investment/parental discrimination proposition* asserts that stepparents who also are parents discriminate in favor of their genetic children. Although scholars have not yet investigated the effects of (step)parental involvement on early home-leaving, in general researchers have found that stepparents interact less often with their stepchildren than biological parents interact with their children (e.g., Doyle, Wolchik, & Dawson-McClure, 2002) and that remarried parents spend less time with their children than do married parents (Bogenschneider, 1997). Therefore, parental neglect or low parental involvement may result in stepchildren's leaving home earlier than if they were more supported by their (step)parents.

DISCUSSION AND EXTENSION *continued*

The stress and (step)parent involvement models may explain early home-leaving better than the theories that Crosbie-Burnett et al. present in Chapter 9 (i.e., attachment theory, N-R theory, SCB theory). However, all of these theories share problematic assumptions about early home-leaving: (a) Effects are unidirectional (stepparents' or parents' behaviors affect stepchildren's behaviors), (b) a stepchild has only one home, and (c) causes are always negative. These assumptions are embedded in the example of extrusion that Crosbie-Burnett et al. present—they describe an individual, familial, and social problem in which the actions of adult household members create problems for stepchildren, who leave home to escape a hostile, negative environment. However, these assumptions do not fit all stepfamilies.

Rather than conceptualizing only unidirectional effects from adults to children, theories should include *bidirectional or multidirectional effects*. Stepchildren are neither passive recipients of nor merely reactors to adult family members' actions—stepchildren exert enormous influence on parents and stepparents (Ganong & Coleman, 2004). None of the theories that Crosbie-Burnett et al. propose adequately accounts for these influences. Moreover, these theories do not sufficiently consider the effects on stepchildren of non-household kin.

Generally, researchers have assumed that a stepchild resides in only one household. Although this is true for many, countless stepchildren whose parents share physical custody have two residences. Even when an adolescent stepchild resides primarily with one parent, residential shifts occur frequently (Ganong & Coleman, 2004). Residence shifting between parental households is often substantively different from extrusion, but ideology that equates households with families obscures such differences.

Finally, the theories that Crosbie-Burnett et al. propose presume only negative reasons for early home-leaving—stress, conflicts, lack of investment (neglect), poor parenting—but they do not elucidate the processes by which conflicts, stress, or low parental involvement result in early home-leaving. These models ignore nondestructive reasons why stepchildren move. A stepchild may leave a parent's household for many reasons: The parent cannot control the child's behavior, conflicts arise between the residential stepparent and the stepchild, the child wants to spend more time with the nonresidential parent, the family wants to provide the child with opportunities that are unavailable where the family currently resides—the list could go on. Unfortunately, the assumption that all early home-leaving is extrusion functionally precludes researchers from broadly examining the experience and makes it harder for them to investigate holistically why some stepchildren leave home "early" and others do not.

STUDYING EARLY HOME-LEAVING

We agree with Crosbie-Burnett et al.'s suggestion that qualitative studies should precede quantitative investigations. Many research questions centering on interpersonal processes would benefit from more qualitative studies (Coleman et al., 2000). Instead of the qualitative approach that Crosbie-Burnett et al. describe, however, we suggest that three qualitative research traditions are especially useful for the study of early home-leaving: grounded theory methodology (GTM), phenomenology, and ethnography. These approaches are not interchangeable, but any of them may be appropriate depending on the research questions to be addressed.

GTM is compatible with assessing interpersonal processes. GTM researchers would ask, *What family or household dynamics contribute to early home-leaving in stepfamilies?* or *Who initiates home-leaving in stepparent households?*

Phenomenologists want to understand the *lived experience of stepchildren who leave*

DISCUSSION AND EXTENSION *continued*

home early. They would ask questions about the *meanings of the experiences* of stepchildren who leave their parents' households. Phenomenologists might conduct separate studies with stepparents and parents of early home-leaving children to see what the experience means to them. Phenomenology does not necessarily lead to conceptual frameworks, but such an investigation could yield information useful to practitioners and researchers.

Ethnographers would examine the *values, beliefs, and practices associated with stepchildren's early home-leaving.* Ethnography is the study of cultures, and here the culture is the stepfamily system broadly defined or, more narrowly, the stepparent household. Ethnographers would assess the wider cultural context in which home-leaving occurs (i.e., schools, community, peers).

Any of these three methods could yield complex, holistic understandings of stepchildren's early home-leaving. Scholars could pursue answers to the research questions derived from these approaches through quantitative or qualitative studies. We expect that such studies will produce richer and more informative models of stepchildren's home-leaving than extant theories and research designs have generated.

REFERENCES

Ainsworth, M. D. S., Blehar, M. C., Waters, E., & Wall, S. (1978). *Patterns of attachment: A psychological study of the strange situation.* Hillsdale, NJ: Lawrence Erlbaum.

Aquilino, W. S. (1991). Family structure and home-leaving: A further specification of the relationship. *Journal of Marriage and the Family, 53,* 999–1010.

Bandura, A. (1986). *Social foundations of thought and action: A social cognitive theory.* Englewood Cliffs, NJ: Prentice Hall.

Berger, R. (2000). Gay stepfamilies: A triple-stigmatized group. *Families in Society, 5,* 504–516.

Black, D., Gates, G., Sanders, S., & Taylor, L. (2000). Demographics of the gay and lesbian population in the United States: Evidence from available systematic data sources. *Demography, 37,* 139–154.

Bogenschneider, K. (1997). Parental involvement in adolescent schooling: A proximal process with transcontextual validity. *Journal of Marriage and the Family, 59,* 718–733.

Boss, P., Doherty, W. J., LaRossa, R., Schumm, W. R., & Steinmetz, S. K. (Eds.). (1993). *Sourcebook of family theories and methods: A contextual approach.* New York: Plenum.

Bowlby, J. (1982). *Attachment and loss: Vol. 1. Attachment* (2nd ed.). New York: Basic Books.

Bray, J., & Kelly, J. (1998). *Stepfamilies: Love, marriage and parenting in the first decade.* New York: Broadway.

Bretherton, I. (1993). Theoretical contributions from developmental psychology. In P. Boss, W. J. Doherty, R. LaRossa, W. R. Schumm, & S. K. Steinmetz (Eds.), *Sourcebook of family theories and methods: A contextual approach* (pp. 505–524). New York: Plenum.

Brown, L. (2003). Relationships more enduring: Implications of the *Troxel* decision for lesbian and gay families. *Family Court Review, 41,* 60–66.

Bumpass, L. L., Raley, R., & Sweet, J. A. (1995). The changing character of stepfamilies: Implications of cohabitation and nonmarital childbearing. *Demography, 32,* 425–436.

Burke, P. (1991). Identity processes and social stress. *American Sociological Review, 56,* 836–849.

Burke, P. (2003). Relationships among multiple identities. In P. J. Burke, T. J. Owens, R. T. Serpe, & P. A. Thoits (Eds.), *Advances in identity theory and research* (pp. 195–516). New York: Kluwer-Plenum.

Burke, P., & Stets, J. (1999). Trust and commitment through self-verification. *Social Psychology Quarterly, 62,* 347–366.

Cauce, A. M., Paradise, M., Ginzler, J. A., Embry, L., Morgan, C. J., Lohr, Y., et al. (2000). The characteristics and mental health of homeless adolescents: Age and gender differences. *Journal of Emotional and Behavioral Disorders, 8*(4), 230–239.

Clawson, J., & Ganong, L. H. (2002). Adult stepchildren's obligation to older stepparents. *Journal of Family Nursing, 8,* 50–72.

Coleman, M., Ganong, L. H., & Fine, M. A. (2000). Reinvestigating remarriage: Another decade of progress. *Journal of Marriage and the Family, 62,* 1288–1307.

Cooksey, E. C., & Craig, P. H. (1998). Parenting from a distance: The effects of paternal characteristics on contact between nonresidential fathers and their children. *Demography, 35,* 187–200.

Cooney, T. M., & Mortimer, J. T. (1999). Family structure differences in the timing of leaving home: Exploring mediating factors. *Journal of Research on Adolescence, 9,* 367–393.

Crosbie-Burnett, M., Foster, T. L., Murray, C. I., & Bowen, G. L. (1996). Gays' and lesbians' families of origin: A social-cognitive-behavioral model of adjustment. *Family Relations, 45,* 397–403.

Crosbie-Burnett, M., & Giles-Sims, J. (1991). Marital power in stepfather families: A test of normative-resource theory. *Journal of Family Psychology, 4,* 484–496.

Crosbie-Burnett, M., & Helmbrecht, L. (1993). A descriptive empirical study of gay male stepfamilies. *Family Relations, 42,* 256–263.

Crosbie-Burnett, M., & Lewis, E. A. (1993). A social cognitive behavioral model of couples and families: An integration of contributions from psychological theories. In P. Boss, W. J. Doherty, R. LaRossa, W. R. Schumm, & S. K. Steinmetz (Eds.), *Sourcebook of family theories and methods: A contextual approach* (pp. 529–556). NY: Plenum.

Daly, M., & Wilson, M. (1998). *The truth about Cinderella: A Darwinian view of parental love.* New Haven, CT: Yale University Press.

Doyle, K. W., Wolchik, S. A., & Dawson-McClure, S. (2002). Development of the stepfamily events profile. *Journal of Family Psychology, 16,* 128–143.

Ganong, L. H., & Coleman, M. (2004). *Stepfamily relationships: Development, dynamics, and intervention.* New York: Kluwer/Plenum.

Giles-Sims, J. & Crosbie-Burnett, M. (1989). Adolescent power in stepfather families: A test of normative resource theory. *Journal of Marriage and the Family, 51,* 1065–1078.

Gutiérrez, L. M., & Lewis, E. A. (1999). *Empowering women of color.* New York: Columbia University Press.

Hanson, T. L., McLanahan, S. S., & Thomson, E. (1996). Double jeopardy: Parental conflict and stepfamily outcomes for children. *Journal of Marriage and the Family, 58,* 141–154.

Johnson, S. M. (1996). *Creating connection.* New York: Brunner/Mazel.

Johnson, S. M. (1998). Listening to the music: Emotion as a natural part of systems theory. *Journal of Systemic Therapies, 17,* 1–17.

Johnson, S. M. (2003). Introduction to attachment. In S. M. Johnson & V. E. Whiffen (Eds.), *Attachment processes in couple and family therapy* (pp. 3–17). New York: Guilford.

Kiernan, K. E. (1992). The impact of family disruption in childhood on transitions made in young adult life. *Population Studies, 46,* 213–234.

Lynch, J. (2000). Considerations of family structure and gender composition: The lesbian and gay stepfamily. *Journal of Homosexuality, 40*(2), 81–95.

Main, M., & Goldwyn, R. (1985). *Adult attachment classification system.* Unpublished manuscript, University of California, Berkeley.

Martinez, C. R., & Forgatch, M. S. (2002). Adjusting to change: Linking family structure transitions with parenting and boys' adjustment. *Journal of Family Psychology, 16,* 107–117.

McDonald, G. W. (1980). Family power: The assessment of a decade of theory and research, 1970–1979. *Journal of Marriage and the Family, 42,* 841–854.

Minkler, M. (1999). *Community organization and community building for health.* New Brunswick, NJ: Rutgers University Press.

Mitchell, B. A. (1994). Family structure and leaving the nest: A social resource perspective. *Sociological Perspectives, 37,* 651–672.

Moorefield, B. S., & Proulx, C. (2003, November). *Couple identity and couple-verification: Extending identity theory to gay male couples and families.* Paper presented at the Theory Construction and Research Methodology Workshop, annual meeting of the National Council on Family Relations, Vancouver.

Pasley, K, & Ihinger-Tallman, M. (Eds.). (1994). *Stepparenting: Issues in theory, research and practice.* Westport, CT: Greenwood.

Pasley, K., & Moorefield, B. S. (2004). Stepfamilies: Changes and challenges. In M. Coleman & L. H. Ganong (Eds.) *Handbook of contemporary families: Considering the past, contemplating the future* (pp. 317–330). Thousand Oaks, CA: Sage.

Rodman, H. (1972). Marital power and the theory of resources in cultural context. *Journal of Comparative Family Studies, 3,* 50–67.

Sabatelli, R. M., & Shehan, C. L. (1993). Exchange and resource theories. In P. Boss, W. J. Doherty, R. LaRossa, W. R. Schumm, & S. K. Steinmetz (Eds.), *Sourcebook of family theories and methods: A contextual approach* (pp. 385–411). New York: Plenum.

Simmons, T., & O'Connell, M. (2003). *Married-couple and unmarried-partner households: 2000* (Special Report No. CENSR-5). Washington, DC: U.S. Bureau of the Census. Retrieved January 22, 2004, from http://www.census.gov/prod/2003pubs/censr-5.pdf

Stryker, S. (1968). Identity salience and role performance: The relevance of symbolic interaction theory for family research. *Journal of Marriage and the Family, 30,* 558–564.

Szinovacz, M. (1987). Family power. In M. B. Sussman & S. K. Steinmetz (Eds.), *Handbook of marriage and the family* (pp. 651–693). New York: Plenum.

Trost, J. E. (1986). Statistically nonrepresentative stratified sampling: A sampling technique for qualitative studies. *Qualitative Sociology, 9,* 54–57.

Yeung, W. J., Linver, M. R., & Brooks-Gunn, J. (2002). How money matters for young children's development: Investment and family process. *Child Development, 73,* 1861–1879.

• Part III

CHANGING FAMILY
INTERACTIONS WITHIN
AND ACROSS GENERATIONS

Ten

THROUGH THE LENS OF TIME

How Families Live in and Through Time

Kerry J. Daly, *University of Guelph*

John Beaton, *University of Guelph*

Our daily family lives are dominated by an ever-present experience of time: We awake to our clock radios, we carry time on our bodies, our work is orchestrated with time in mind, we are aware of aging (sometimes acutely), and we abide by the organizational rules of time. Although time is pervasive in our lives, we are unsure about whether to call it a natural phenomenon, a measuring device, an oppressive force, a convenient social construction, or a nagging human preoccupation. Symbolically, we have colluded with each other and have arrived at massive consensus about time as a standard measure. As a result, time is real and real in its consequences as expressed every time we feel late, a sense of accomplishment, overloaded, rushed, old, or bored.

This reality of time that we have created is centrally important for our understanding of the way that families live in and through time. In recent years, time has become a more salient concept for understanding the everyday lifeworlds of families because of the accelerated pace of change that affects all of our

cultural institutions. Championed cultural values in the world of work and commerce such as speed, instantaneousness, and efficiency have become key values in family worlds as well. The growing diversity of family life and increases in the numbers of people on nonstandard work schedules have also resulted in more complex daily routines for families. The changing temporal pulse of our globalized world is having real consequences for families: Families need more time to orchestrate and navigate members' often complex work and school schedules, family members must be more vigilant in monitoring the boundaries between their work and family lives, and, for many families, finding time *to be together* as a family has become a challenge.

The growing importance of time in our culture and families' growing preoccupation with managing time provide the context for the development of a theory about time in families. Time is not a newcomer to family theory. Theories of individual and family development are structured by temporal markers and emphasize predictable stages, transitions, and activities. Historians have examined the ways in which roles and activities have changed over time in families in tandem with broader social and economic changes. More recently, theories of work and family have emphasized the challenges and stresses associated with managing the boundaries between the demands of work and the need for family time. In all of these theories time is central to the analysis, but it is often poorly defined, shadowed by other more prominent concepts, and, as a result, incompletely conceptualized.

In this chapter, we focus on time itself as the object of our theorizing about family. We problematize time in an effort to get beyond thinking of time only as a standard measure of counted hours and minutes. For example, in order to deepen our theorizing about time—and, in so doing, deepen our theorizing about families—we need to examine how women and men experience time in different ways, operate under different temporal constraints, come to "possess" time according to different positions of privilege, and come to express different entitlements to use time as they wish. Similarly, theorizing about time directs us to look at the ways in which values and meanings guide individual and collective choices about time in families. Attending to these kinds of issues gives rise to theorizing activity about the politics of time that opens up new pathways for understanding key underlying dynamics and processes in families.

We are deliberate in scrutinizing the way that we understand and conceptualize time according to a number of different standpoints. Specifically, we examine how we *see* time using different theoretical and paradigmatic assumptions, the relationship between the conceptualization and measurement of time, and the way that time can be understood at different levels of analysis, including individual subjectivity, negotiated family interaction, and complex organizational structures. Following this effort to dissect time into its conceptual components, we propose integrating strategies that provide a means for looking at the unified, lived experience of time in families.

THEORIZING ABOUT TIME AND FAMILIES

One of the challenges associated with theorizing about time is that *time* can mean many things and manifest itself in many forms. For example, time has to do with passage, duration, or the punctuation of an event; it can be linear or circular; it has to do with continuity and discontinuity, and with orientation to the past, present, or future; and it is related to issues of possession, power, and control. In the same way that postmodernist ideas direct us to talk about "families" instead of "the family," they direct us to speak of many temporalities instead of a structured monolithic system of time. Given the complexity of time, we propose to look at time from four different vantage points: time as an organizational structure, time as process, time as conflict, and time in practice (pragmatism).

Time as an Organizational Structure

When family members are feeling stressed or overloaded, it is not uncommon for them to complain about time. When we use expressions such as "up against the clock" or "facing a deadline," we treat time as if it had an independent existence outside of ourselves. Through the creation and use of clocks, we have collectively objectified and reified time to have an existence that is external, universal, and apparently unchangeable.

As a central component of social structure, time is part of the regulation of family life. Although individual actors within families make choices about time, it is within the regulated framework of collective life that this agency occurs. There is a sociotemporal order of holidays and workdays, hours of operation, and institutional schedules. The tendency in our culture to use language such as "time squeeze," "harried," and "quality time" reflects the challenges that family members face in trying to manage individual demands within the context of complex and fast-paced temporal structures. This is a problem in families that is rooted in the challenge of coordinating individual choices, preferences, and practices (e.g., the desire to eat meals together) with structured, collective network practices that constrain families in their ability to make these choices (Southerton, 2003). These are emerging problems of "fit" between the needs of dual-earner families for flexibility and the sometimes outdated time structures of the workplace (Moen, 2003).

Embedded in the view of time as an organizational structure is the presence of time norms that provide insight into the standards, rules, and limits of time use. In families, such time norms are present in many forms. For example, as part of the broader socialization process, parents in the United States are expected to teach their children how to manage complex schedules and to be punctual. American families live with a cultural mandate that family members should spend "quality time" together in order to ensure their cohesiveness and solidarity. Family members can be sanctioned or chastised for spending too much or too little time in work-related activities. In all of these examples, time is perceived to reside in an external social structure that has embedded in it a set of normative prescriptions that shape and direct the organization of time in the home.

Although time norms play an important role in shaping how people make decisions about time, little empirical research has examined the ways in which these norms affect family behaviors. Instead, scholars have focused on time-use studies, the findings from which have played a dominant role in efforts to explain and predict patterns of time allocation within families. National time-use studies are premised on the idea that understanding the patterns of time use in different kinds of families is helpful for public policy decision making. For example, policies concerning parental leave, child care, and workplace flexibility can be informed by research that examines how child outcomes are affected by the amount of time parents spend with their children (Hofferth & Sandberg, 2001). Time-use studies document the amounts of time different family members spend in market, nonmarket, and leisure activities; the amounts

of time that women and men spend caring for children or other family members; the amounts of time that families allocate to the maintenance and upkeep of their households; and the different distributions of time in different kinds of families (Robinson & Godbey, 1997). One of the major criticisms of time-use studies is that they often do a poor job of reflecting the fact that individuals frequently engage in more than one activity at a time. Time-use researchers have handled the measurement of time spent in simultaneous activities in a number of ways, including by recording only the primary activity (e.g., folding laundry and watching TV coded as "laundry"), by identifying primary and secondary activities in any given time period, and by coding periods that include more than one activity as periods of "joint" or "compound" activity (National Research Council, 2000). Other limitations of time-use studies include problems with accurate recall of time use among participants, variations in time use depending on individuals' stages in the life cycle, and variations in people's time use across the week.

Time as Process

The experience of time as a process is one that is rooted in our internal awareness of being. To *be*, to live, is to be part of the ever-changing reality that is time. At the most rudimentary level, we experience the passage of time through any and all activity. In this regard, *time* and *process* become interchangeable terms, such that time is process and process is time (Sprey, 2001). As process, time is a social construction that is intersubjectively defined and negotiated on the basis of shared meanings and symbols.

With an emphasis on meaning-making activity, interpretation, emergent action, definition of the situation, identity, and interaction, symbolic interactionism focuses on the ways in which family members individually and collectively assign meaning to time as part of their navigation of their everyday lives. The interpretation of time in any situation serves as a primary mechanism for defining self and guiding action. In families, this interpretive process occurs continuously and on many different levels. Children, for example, quickly become proficient at reading family time cues about promptness, pace of activities, and time limits that are either fixed or open to negotiation. They strategically align their own subjectively constructed behavior with these cues and, as a result, make decisions about whether to linger and be late or respond rigidly in order to align themselves with the family's temporal rhythm. Collectively, family members make decisions about the meaning and importance of family time that involve reading cultural cues about, for example, the importance of mealtimes while responding to their own subjective longing for togetherness. Everyday family routines are executed successfully when family members agree about when and how to get individual members to be at work, school, or lessons and at home for shared meals and activities. Anniversaries, birthdays, and family transitions such as the launching of children serve as temporal markers that are steeped in family meanings. Developmental transitions such as getting a driver's license or retirement symbolically punctuate the passage of time in the lives of individual family members.

Identities within families are situated within a temporal context and shaped by temporal definitions. Presentation of self is contingent on how individuals define the present moment in terms of past and anticipated events, the pressure of concurrent demands, and the way the individuals wish to present themselves in the eyes of others. Hence the mother who comes home from work at 5:00 P.M. and then must respond to the needs of her young children and prepare a meal for the family with an eye on the clock, mindful of family members' planned evening activities, is working to present an identity of mother who is in control, competent, and able to cope with the time pressures of the moment. Through their decisions about time, family members also make decisions about identity salience. Choices about arranging for child care in order to free up a parent's time for paid work and about a parent's shifting to part-time work

so that he or she can spend more time at home reflect the relative salience of identities such as employee, parent, and spouse.

As we operate in the world, time provides us with one of our primary coordinates of meaning. When families plan activities with intention and purpose, they position those activities in an anticipated context conceptualized as the future. When family members are motivated to change how they carry out certain family roles because they wish to be different from previous generations, it is the past that gives shape to their projections and behaviors. To live in family is to live in time in which the past, present, and future exist all at once like juggled balls in the air. However, it is the moment-by-moment unfolding of the present that is the basis on which families interpret (and reinterpret) the past and anticipate the future. From this perspective, time is both process and context, orderly and chaotic, and the unfolding biographies of individual family members are affected by the experiences and transitions of family generations and the broader events and occurrences of historical time (Bengtson & Allen, 1993).

When we assign meaning to time, we also graft value onto time. Judgments about whether particular activities are "a good use of our time" or "a waste of time" reflect our tendencies to evaluate how we use our time. We use the language of time to assess the choices and decisions we make about time allocation. It is not so much time per se that we are evaluating as much as it is the activities that constitute that time. The ways in which individuals assign meaning and value to time is fully contingent on their cultural definitions of time; in modern-day Western societies, those definitions emphasize technological speed, productivity, efficiency, and punctuality. Within a moral economy of time that champions work-related temporal activities, families often lament the difficulties they experience in finding enough family time (Daly, 2001). Hence the collective social values that we hold about time shape our individual constructions and evaluations of activities.

The subjective, emergent nature of time as a process means that the way that we seek to measure or understand time must take these characteristics into account. Qualitative approaches are best suited to the examination of how different family members experience time. Although each family establishes a unique temporal routine and a pace of life that works collectively for its members, all families stand in different relationships to their collective temporal rhythms. Family members' definitions of time and experience of time stress change as families move through stages of individual and family development. Qualitative interviews serve as useful tools for researchers inquiring about the ways in which the experience of time changes as families move through transitions and as individual members age. Methodologically, this means looking at how family members' perceptions of time stress change, for example, from the time when the children are preschoolers with high demands for care to the time when the children are teenagers and looking for independence. The thick description that qualitative interviews produce provides researchers with a means for examining how family members subjectively experience the many temporal dimensions of their lives, including the ways in which they shift pace when moving from one activity to another, how they modify or adjust their rhythms when interacting with other adults or children, and how they experience the duration of events.

The analysis of time as a process cannot be disassociated from individual action, social interaction, and the meaning of the situation. Methodological efforts to understand this experience of time must allow for individual definitions of time that are complex and for multiple and potentially contradictory definitions of what time is.

Time as Conflict

Time becomes a basis of conflict when it is conceptualized as being subject to possession, control, and the relations of power. To possess time is to objectify it as a thing outside of ourselves that can be controlled. We tend to think of time much as we think of money, in that the more time we have, the "richer" we

are—this is especially so within the context of Western culture, which is dominated by discourses of time scarcity, time stress, and time compression. However, like any currency, time fluctuates in value according to supply and demand, such that when time is abundant (e.g., as it is among the unemployed) it is accorded low social value.

We experience conflict over time because we value time, and in the process of negotiating complex schedules, especially in families, the potential for competing interests to attempt to control how time is used is ever present. Within families, this kind of conflict is manifested in many ways: Partners in both gay and heterosexual relationships negotiate responsibilities for housework and child care, separated and divorced couples work out schedules for access to children, children and parents work out complex schedules of programs and meetings, adult siblings work out responsibilities for the care of aging parents, and so on. Underlying all of these negotiations are questions of who controls time, how power is exerted in relation to time and overall within families, and how fairness and equality can be maintained in the balance of responsibilities and entitlements.

Time as conflict is rooted in the assumptions of the critical paradigm. Although time conflicts are manifested at the interpersonal level in families, they are also shaped by broader sociohistorical and cultural conditions that define and legitimate different forms of temporal control. Contemporary Western cultures have developed a mentality about the possession of time that is rooted in the Marxist concept of the commodification of time. Because labor is measured in terms of time, time is commodified and therefore subject to possession, control, and exchange. The identification of sources of power and inequality is a necessary step in finding ways to distribute the balance of power over time fairly in both families and the broader culture. For example, the concept of temporal control is at the root of work-family theories that emphasize the importance of controlling the conditions of work, workplace flexibility to respond to the demands of family life, and individuals' capacity to make choices about when and where they do their work.

Conflict over the possession and control of time has been a central theme in feminist theory. For example, one of the problems of housework, as a traditionally female-dominated activity, is that it has no exchange value in the capitalist market of commodities. Paid labor is therefore a means to bring value to women's time and to change women's position in the decision-making processes within families and society. The distinction between paid and unpaid work time also has implications for entitlements to leisure time (Deem, 1996). Whereas men operate within a tradition of paid work that clearly separates time *on* and time *off* from work, women who spend their time working in the home are less likely to have clear boundaries between *on* and *off* time. Consequently, women who work at home have a more difficult time feeling entitled to leisure time for themselves. There is also a significant body of literature that demonstrates that women continue to carry the primary responsibility for the temporal coordination of housework and family activities, the implication being that women exert a great deal of power and control over the family itself (Daly, 2002).

Scholars have used many methodological approaches to understand the unequal distribution of time between women and men. Researchers have used data from national time-allocation studies to examine gender differences in paid and unpaid work, personal care, and leisure in the United States. They have found that, in general, men continue to give more time to paid work and have more time for leisure than do women, and women give more time to housework and the care of children than do men (Robinson & Godbey, 1997). These studies have provided key evidence regarding the inequalities between women and men in their time use and have spawned a number of critical feminist discourses, such as that concerning the "second shift" (Hochschild, 1989). Feminist scholars have also criticized time-use studies for failing to take into account the gendered experience of time in the domestic sphere. For

example, qualitative researchers have found that although women and men may share household tasks such as cleaning, women are more likely to take a supervisory role in that work; women report more intensity in their experience of carrying out multiple tasks in the home; and women's experience of time is more likely to be fragmented due to interruption (Everingham, 2002).

Time as Pragmatism

Pragmatic philosophy is concerned with the processes by which human beings navigate the environmental conditions of their everyday lives. Human beings are *practical* creatures who must adapt to the conditions of their worlds. As John Dewey and George Herbert Mead describe it, pragmatism is a means to focus on how individuals define situations, think through possible lines of action, and anticipate consequences for those actions. In this regard, pragmatism takes everyday situations and problems as its subject matter and is concerned with finding solutions to problems. Therefore, to think about families and time from a pragmatic perspective is to examine the practical difficulties that families face in their efforts to keep pace with a culture that is increasingly faster, work-intensive, and technologically saturated.

Several theoretical perspectives can be subsumed under the broad umbrella of time as pragmatism. For example, ecosystems theory serves as a basis for looking at how the private experience of time in families is shaped by multiple systems of publicly mediated time, including schools, day-care centers, workplaces, and leisure programs. Life-course approaches that emphasize the interplay between biographical and historical time also serve as a means for examining the navigation of everyday temporal challenges within the context of cohort conditions. Narrative approaches look at the ways in which individuals shape the stories of their practical experience as a way of examining and reinterpreting the flow of temporal experience.

"Time scarcity" has become part of the dominant discourse among families in North

America. Both privately and publicly, families lament the scarcity of time available to them, expressing concerns about lack of leisure time for families to spend together, limited time to connect with people in their communities, and an unshakable malaise that comes from feeling overworked and frenetic. Privately, families experience time scarcity through the everyday challenge of trying to "fit it all in"; publicly, perceptions of time scarcity are reflected in debates about workplace flexibility, government-sponsored employment leave policies, and concerns about shrinking civic participation (Putnam, 2000).

Although there is a general perception of increased time stress among Americans, there is a continued debate in the literature about whether or not individuals are actually involved in more paid work today than in the past (Perry-Jenkins, Repetti, & Crouter, 2000; Robinson & Godbey, 1997; see also MacDermid, Roy, & Zvonkovic, Chapter 20, this volume). However, increases in women's labor force participation have resulted in families' collectively devoting more of their time to paid work. In addition, increases in both the speed of technology and the numbers of people working nonstandard schedules (Presser, 2000) have contributed to the feeling of time crunch.

Contrary to the popular notion that parents are spending less time with their children, however, time-use studies indicate that in many Western countries (Canada, the United States, Great Britain, Australia) the time that parents spend with preadolescent children has actually increased in recent years (e.g., Sandberg & Hofferth, 2001; Sayer, Bianchi, & Robinson, 2002). Although increases in maternal employment may have reduced maternal time with children, in general families are smaller, fathers are more involved with their children, and parents are older and better educated than they were in the past (Sayer et al., 2002). Furthermore, whereas parents tend to feel guilty and express the desire to spend more time with their children, children are relatively satisfied with the amount of time they have with their parents (Galinsky, 1999). These data raise

fundamental questions about the meaning of "time famine in families" (for whom? on what basis?) and the degree to which Western cultures uphold such unsustainable myths as "lost childhood" and the "hurried child" (Lynott & Logue, 1993).

What has changed, however, is the way in which time is structured within the everyday experience of family life. For example, the increased use of computers by both parents and children may make it more difficult for some families to find time for shared activities. Overscheduling of family member participation in community activities has also contributed to the perceived experience of time shortage in families (Doherty & Carlson, 2002). For example, Hofferth and Sandberg (2001), using time diaries from a national longitudinal data set (1981–1997), found that children ages 3–12 had less free time (12 hours per week decline), less play time (3 hours per week decline), and less time at family meals (decline from 9 hours per week to 8 hours) in 1997 than children in that age group had in 1981.

For many years, clinicians have argued that family routines and rituals are important to healthy family functioning. A 50-year review of research on such routines and rituals has shown how they are associated with increased parenting competence, positive child adjustment, and more satisfying marital relationships (Fiese et al., 2002). In the study mentioned above, Hofferth and Sandberg (2001) found that more time at family meals was the strongest predictor of fewer behavior problems in children. The current dilemma for many families is that family routines and rituals are being lost or shortchanged, as family members' increased participation in structured community activities leaves little time for them.

A pragmatic approach to dealing with the issue of time crunch and overscheduling in families is to shift the definition of this experience from a private trouble to a public issue. Recently, there has been growing interest in citizenship models that endeavor to create community initiatives that aim to reclaim control over the way time is spent and organized in personal and family life. Two such initiatives are Take Back Your Time Day (see the Web site at http://www.timeday.org), an international movement to address the problem of overwork and overscheduled families, and Putting Family First (Web site at http://www.familylife1st.org), an organization based in Wayzata, Minnesota. Citizens in some communities have formed partnerships with local organizers of children's sports leagues, church leaders, community leaders, and school officials to develop strategies that can help family members find time for family routines and rituals while at the same time being involved in community activities. To date, little research has examined how individual families go about developing specific strategies to find more time for family rituals and routines.

● **SPOTLIGHT ON THEORY**

FAMILY IN AND BEYOND TIME

Andrew J. Weigert, *University of Notre Dame*

Daly and Beaton present a fruitful framework for understanding family *times* (the plural suggests that it remains a folk term in spite of theorists' best intentions). It seems unlikely that times can be totally integrated into living families or family theories. From a pragmatic social constructionist perspective, symbolically real, yet always contingent, futures remain central empirical issues for families and for theorists.

Persons are individually embodied. Embodiment gives linear grounding to biography: everyone, until now, is born, ages, dies. Technology and genetic sciences are changing embodiment and generating new meanings of time—for example, the lived reality of body perhaps shifting to cyber possibilities (Joy, 2000). Families are collectively embodied. They begin, develop, uncouple, end, or extend into kin ties. Individuals and families are linear temporal trajectories.

A definitive family time is intergenerational. Parenting generates relationships constitutive of family and societal times. Changes in childbearing frequencies such as low fertility in many First World societies suggest that the time frames of persons who do not generate offspring are either shortened by not sequencing through genes and names, or universalized through more inclusive memes or groups, such as nonfamily forms illustrated by celibate religious types.

Prior institutional and cultural times structure family times. They are sometimes at cross-purposes, thus embedding families within temporal pressures and scarcities for realizing members' values. The necessity to gain money through time at work increases time demands on employees, even the privileged and professional. Occupational demands may override family times—a potentially pathological social ordering within which members seek temporal values that institutional and cultural demands make difficult or unattainable.

(continued)

Componential categories, age and gender, stratify within-family times. Enacting these temporal inequalities socializes the young into the naturalness, reproduction, and legitimation of inequalities. Male times likely are valued over female times, middle-aged times over elderly times, parental times over children's times—until children's or dependents' times take on more weight. Increased weight for dependents' times generates additional cross-pressures and scarcities, as for families obligated to both child care and elder care.

Workplace times in contemporary America leave less family time than European, although likely more than Asian, models. Competing institutional and cultural times suggest strong questions: How are contradictions between family and work times culturally valued, institutionally rewarded, and interactionally enacted?

"Family values" include family times that are contradicted by workplace imperatives such as the definition of "overtime." The *over* in *overtime* suggests pointed issues of false consciousness that subordinates family as an interacting group to more powerful institutional constraints. How family times are institutionally pressured, understood, and enacted adds to the reproduction of social inequalities.

How families realize times leads to consideration of more extensive realizations such as religious and alternative cultural times. Strong religious fundamentalisms offer transformed times as powerful family meanings (Almond, Appleby, & Sivan, 2003). At extremes of hopelessness and despair, religious times may motivate violence against other or self as a means to blissful immortality.

Hope in positive imagined futures is a key motivational source in social life (Snyder, 2002, p. 251). A central if underexamined issue arises: What family contexts and dynamics foster projected future times offering hope to, or eliciting despair in, family members? Do relationships among religiously imagined futures and empirical indicators of misery or hope in projected futures beyond individual lifetimes affect childbearing?

Responsibility for a child empirically indicates commitment to a future. Falling birthrates may suggest temporal meanings that are, speculatively, less materially committed to futures than those found in strong religions and groups with high birthrates. Childbearing and child rearing are, whatever the cultural particularities, commitments to futures embodied in children's lives.

In a word, family times as the times of a particular group instantiating the institution of family involve natural, social, and transcendent times. Biographical duration is one socionatural time; extended kin and intergenerational offspring embody others. Encompassing natural and social times, for believers, are symbolically transcendent times of mythic cycles of rebirth or individual and family immortality. A key question today concerns relationships among family times and empirical sources of hope in positive this-worldly futures. ●

TOWARD A THEORETICAL INTEGRATION OF TIME AND FAMILIES

Conceptually, it is meaningful to classify time on the basis of the distinctive elements that allow us to see time as process, structure, conflict, *or* practice. Experientially, however, we are not afforded that same luxury; there is one time that we live in and through, and, as a result, we live with time as a process, a structure, a series of conflicts, *and* a series of ongoing practical challenges. Individual theories of time are therefore helpful for articulating one aspect of our experience, but if our theories are to do a better job of reflecting our "unity of experience" (Bernardes, 1986), they must show how key theoretical dimensions of time are integrated. We live with time in all of its manifestations and forms; our challenge theoretically is to articulate how these forms of experience are related. To this end, we propose three integrating themes that undergird our experience of time: issues of agency and control over time, the relationship between time and values, and the question of perspective.

Agency and Control Over Time

One of the central questions for family members living within the context of fast-paced, complex temporal structures is the degree to which they are able to exert control over time. In each of the four frameworks outlined above, agency is represented in a different form. When viewed as an organizational structure, schedules, calendars, and timetables are perceived as restricting choices and imposing expectations. Personal agency is diminished in the face of time structures that regulate. In contrast, the focus on meaning-making activity within the process approach highlights individual agency by emphasizing the way time is perceived and construed from the various standpoints within families. Viewed from the conflict and pragmatism perspectives, control over time is a function of both the abilities of individual actors to make choices about time and the conditions of the actors' social positions at home, at work, and in the community. From this perspective, agency is the product of the interplay between the individual and social structural positioning.

An integrated theory of time in families seeks to go beyond the distinctions between subjective and objective time or individual and organizational time. If we accept that our subjective experience of processual time is shaped by interactive negotiations and the constraints of broader temporal structures and schedules, then our attention shifts to an iterative conception of time that has both dynamic and fixed forms. Giddens's (1984) theory of structuration focuses attention on time as a dynamic that exists between the individual production of action in time and the reproduction of the temporal structures within which that action occurs. Agency and structure are inseparable in a recursive process.

The lived experience of time in families involves the interplay among individual choices, the negotiated and orchestrated schedules of family members, and the temporal conditions of work, consumption, and community involvement. An integrated theory of time can be seen to have three interdependent dimensions: a subjective experience of time that involves meaning-making activity; interactive time, which involves alignments of time, use of power over time, and negotiations of time in relationships; and organizational time, which constrains, limits, and structures time. Hence family members not only exercise agency in the choices they make about time, but they do so by attending to the other in the situation and, in the process of working within existing schedules, reproduce the temporal structure of their everyday worlds. Although all individuals within families have the opportunity to exercise agency over how they use time and the choices in time that they make, their agency is tempered by the exigencies of their structural positions and relative power. However, these dynamics of time control can manifest themselves in unexpected ways. For example, whereas some of the traditional family research literature emphasizes the role of parents in socializing and controlling the temporal worlds of children, there is an emerging literature that emphasizes the way children's agency in families is playing an increasingly powerful role in controlling the temporal worlds of parents (Thorpe & Daly, 1999). An integrated approach to time involves a complex interplay between individual autonomy and cultural influence.

Time and Values

Underlying all approaches to the conceptualization of time is the question of values. Time is fundamentally a proxy for values. Whether it be a question of balance in pragmatism, entitlements in the conflict perspective, punctuality in the structural perspective, or the definition of time spent as "worthwhile" in the process paradigm, all meanings of time and time usage must ultimately make reference to values. The links between time and values are apparent at the interface between personal agency and temporal structures. As Swidler (1986) has argued, values are the major link between culture and individual action. Agency is expressed through the choices that family members make about time, such as when a father chooses to play with his son rather than wash the dinner dishes. Through this kind of agentic action, a parent expresses values and assigns importance to both time itself and the activities that occur within that time. At another level, individuals' choices about how to use time reflect the internalization of broader cultural values about time. In this example, the voice of cultural values is heard in the form of "a father should be nurturing and should have quality time with his children." Hence the father's decision to play with his son is also part of the process of cultural reproduction. When time choices are made with respect to productivity, efficiency, self-respect, promptness, balance, or frugality, values are manifest at the levels of personal agency and cultural reproduction (Flaherty, 2002). The relationship between time and values is also shaped by the conditions of the historical moment. Technology and globalization have given rise to a discourse that emphasizes speed and efficiency as well as nostalgia for a simpler, slower time.

We cannot understand time without reference to values. Individual actions, relationships, and collective family interactions are all at some level mediated by time and values. Activities that are chosen or forgone, conflicts that arise, and emotions that are generated are all functions of how family members express values that are situated in time. Hence anxiety that arises from uncertainty about the future or anger that lingers because of a past interaction is shaped by conflicts in values and interests, which in turn steer planned courses of action. Values, regardless of whether individuals consciously name or reflect on them in the process of interaction, are inherent in every experience of time; they are the essence of individual motivations, interests, and desired outcomes. Values are the "unmoved mover" in any theory of action (Swidler, 1986).

Whose Time? Questions of Perspective

How we conceptualize any reality, including temporal reality, depends on our perspective. An integrated theory of time in families must therefore take into account the many possibilities for how time is experienced. At the most rudimentary level, scholars must examine how family members' individual standpoints, interests, and perspectives are brought to bear on time within families. For example, children, adolescents, young adults, and older adults experience different meanings of time through the process of aging. This is a function of physiological changes in the body, generational affiliation, and changes in the nature of individuals' roles and responsibilities. Women's experience of time is different from men's, suggesting that scholars need to pay attention to both *his* and *her* time (Daly, 1996).

Time is by necessity relational. Individual family members' perspectives on time are wholly contingent on how others in the family comply with, or react to, their decisions and actions. In relationships of care in families, time is defined less by the task-oriented dictates of the linear clock and more by the processes of attending to the immediate and often unpredictable needs of the other, with the conceptual implication that "time is deeply enmeshed in social relations" (Davies, 1994, p. 280). Another area of emerging interest here is the relationship between time and intimacy in couple relationships (Bennett, 2000). Finding couple time has become increasingly challenging as men and women seek to reconcile their home lives with increasingly complex temporal demands in the workplace (Moen, 2003). Some family therapists have outlined possibilities and creative strategies for couples who wish to map out relational time (Fraenkel, 2001).

At a broader level, families have a collective experience of time that involves clocking, synchronization efforts, scheduling, and routines (Kantor & Lehr, 1975). Through rituals and the marking of key transitions and anniversaries, families map their own histories in the process of creating family narratives that cast them in a favorable light (LaRossa, 1995). "Family time" has also come under critical scrutiny as a collective experience that directs attention not only to the ways in which families create shared time but to the ways in which families seek to reconcile their perceived time famine with outdated expectations regarding an ideal of togetherness (Daly, 2001). An integrated theory of time in families is one that maintains an openness to multiple and potentially incompatible experiences of time within families.

● **SPOTLIGHT ON METHODS**

THE EXPERIENCE SAMPLING METHOD

Jennifer A. Schmidt, *University of Chicago*

One method for measuring the experience of time in families that scholars have used increasingly in recent years is the experience sampling method, or ESM (Csikszentmihalyi & Larson, 1987). The measurement of experience made possible by ESM has been called a *systematic phenomenology* in that it combines a focus on lived experience with an attempt to use the tools of empirical investigation. ESM is a means for measuring multiple facets of time, including the quantity of time family members spend engaged in various activities, subjective evaluations of the quality of this time, and fluctuations in these evaluations as family members move in and through time.

THE PROCEDURE

Each participant is asked to wear or carry a signaling device (watch, pager, or personal digital assistant) for 1 week. The signaling device is programmed to beep or vibrate at randomly selected moments within each 2-hour time block the participant is awake, for

(continued)

● SPOTLIGHT ON METHODS *continued*

a total of eight signals per day. In response to each signal, the participant completes a brief questionnaire in a small diary that he or she also carries during the week (each questionnaire takes 1–2 minutes to complete). The questionnaire, which can be tailored to the research question at hand, typically includes open-ended questions asking the participant to record his or her location, thoughts, and activities at the moment as well as a number of scale items to measure the cognitive, affective, and motivational dimensions of the participant's experience.

The result is an extraordinarily rich and flexible data set that includes multiple observations for each participant, with each "case" representing a particular moment in time for a given individual. The researcher can collapse the data in a variety of ways to answer questions about situations (e.g., How do parents experience their time at work compared with their time at home?) or about persons (e.g., How do employed mothers differ from mothers who are not in the paid workforce in how they experience time with their children?). With its focus on ordinary daily experience rather than on contrived or controlled situations, ESM results in data that have a high level of ecological validity.

APPLICATIONS

Applications of ESM in the study of time in families are numerous (see, e.g., Larson & Richards, 1994). Because the method randomly samples participants' waking hours, the data provide relatively accurate estimates of "time use," as indicated by the number of hours per week individuals spend doing particular activities, such as housework, working for pay, and eating dinner with family members.

Beyond measuring the quantity of time families spend together or in particular activities, ESM provides information about the quality of the time family members spend together. By examining family members' subjective ratings of happiness, enjoyment, anxiety, and affect, researchers have gathered information on conflicting work and family roles and on the quality of family members' time together and have compared and charted patterns in the experiences of different family members as they move through time.

More qualitative analyses of ESM data illustrate temporal and experiential patterns through detailed descriptions of particular persons and families. Such descriptions begin with a focus on a particular moment in time, providing information about a person's physical location, activity, companions, thoughts, and feelings. This rich description then broadens to include fluctuations in the person's experience as a function of time of day, day of the week, activity, companionship, and so on. By using data in this manner, researchers can illustrate general patterns found in their studies or communicate unique features of individuals' or families' experience of time.

The flexibility of the experience sampling method allows researchers to examine the ways that families live in and through time from a variety of perspectives. (For a more comprehensive review of the applications of ESM, see Csikszentmihalyi, Hektner, & Schmidt, 2004.) ●

CONCLUSION

Time is pervasive in the lifeworlds of families. To theorize about time in families is to confront a complex set of processes and perspectives that shape the individual experience of time for each family member, the nature and quality of family members' relationships, and the meanings and expectations that define who the members are as a family. Individually and collectively, the pace of family experience in Western countries is shaped by the cultural values of efficiency, speed, and productivity—with the result being that daily family lives are inundated with complex schedules and routines that are often hard to manage and control.

In this chapter, we have proposed that time can be refracted through many lenses, including paradigms, theories, levels of analysis, and values. Although viewing time and family through each of these lenses can add to our understanding of how families live through different kinds of time, our effort to understand the complex lived experience of time in families means looking at how the many dimensions of time are experienced in concert. This means getting beyond dichotomous ways of thinking in order that we might see time as both process and outcome, natural and social, linear and circular, reversible and progressive, subjective and objective, biological and structural, and involving continuity and discontinuity, quality and quantity. By holding these tensions in play, we may gain a more accurate picture of the challenges, contradictions, and complexities of lived temporal experience in families.

In order to understand fully how families experience time, we must use individual theories that address how primary dimensions of time are integrated. As a result of the escalating pace of family life, individual family members often ask themselves how much *agency* they have over their own lives. An integrated approach to time explores how individual choice, power dynamics, family expectations, and cultural norms influence individual decision making. It is impossible to understand time without exploring how *values* affect individual and family choices. Every day, family members place value on how much time or the quality of time they are going to invest in various activities, such as paid work, family meals, child care, homework, family rituals, and community activities. The multiple and often incompatible realities of how family members experience time are often influenced by gender, age, family structure, income, education, culture, and religion. An integrated approach to time includes space for both collective experience of time in families and multiple realities about time for individual members.

As time becomes an increasingly salient concern in our everyday lives, so too must our theorizing activity about time take a more central place in our efforts to theorize about family life. In a cultural landscape where individual values, workplace practices, and technological conditions are changing rapidly, we need to take a posture of reflexive attentiveness toward time in order to monitor and make sense of the ways in which our changing meaning structures of time affect individual and family life. In contrast with the idea of theory as explanatory product, we need to sustain the dynamic, generative quality of our time theories in order to capture the emerging dynamics and challenges for individuals and families as they live in and through time.

CASE STUDY

VIEWING TIME THROUGH THE EYES OF OVERSCHEDULED CHILDREN AND THEIR UNDERCONNECTED FAMILIES

Yvette V. Perry, *University of Minnesota*

William J. Doherty, *University of Minnesota*

Once upon a time in the Western world, children worked from before dawn until long after dark. There was little time for them to play or engage in other unstructured leisure activities previously associated with childhood, and there was little time for family interaction, as many of these children's parents also worked long hours. Parents were supportive of how their children spent their days: It was not that they did not love their children; rather, the cultural norm of the time dictated that parents who wanted their children to grow up to be contributing members of society should ensure that the children toiled long hours.

We are not describing here the United States of the late 1800s and early 1900s, prior to the establishment of child labor laws that were needed to protect children as young as 7 years old from working in dangerous sweatshops (Zelizer, 1985). We are not describing the plight of children from poor and working-class urban families during this period, often new immigrants who depended for their very survival on the meager earnings of all family members. Instead, we are describing in this "historical" account the situation of many children in middle- and upper-income families in the United States at the start of the 21st century.

In many modern American families, children's lives have become a rat race of tight scheduling, overbusyness, and loss of family time. Especially among middle-class families, some children and adolescents seem to need

daily planners and PDAs to manage their schedules of soccer, hockey, piano, Boy Scouts and Girl Scouts, baseball, football, karate, gymnastics, dance, violin, band, craft clubs, foreign-language classes, academic enrichment courses, and religious youth activities. In such families, parents have become willing and active participants in shaping this phenomenon, often behaving as if they were recreation directors on the family cruise ship (Doherty & Carlson, 2002).

Based on what he has seen in his practice and community work in recent years, one of us has given a name to this phenomenon: "overscheduled kids and underconnected families" (Doherty, 2003; Doherty & Carlson, 2002). The contours and results of this phenomenon are now being documented. For example, a national time-use survey reveals that from 1981 to 1997, the time American children spent participating in structured sports programs doubled, and the time they spent watching siblings and others participate in such programs increased to more than 3 hours per week. During the same period, children lost 12 hours per week in free time, including a 25% drop in playing and a 50% drop in unstructured outdoor activities (Hofferth & Sandberg, 2001).

Another activity that families have forfeited to make room in children's souped-up schedules is the consistent eating of meals at home with family members. This loss is problematic, as there is evidence that eating more meals at home is linked to such positive

Case Study

outcomes as better achievement scores and fewer behavioral problems (Hofferth & Sandberg, 2001), better nutrition (Gillman et al., 2000), and lower rates of alcohol and drug use, early sexual behavior, and suicide (Council of Economic Advisers to the President, 2000).

Beyond these public health concerns, what are the relevant issues of the overscheduled kids/underconnected families phenomenon for theory development and research within the family field, especially regarding the treatment of *time* as an explicit variable? Most broadly, this phenomenon reveals time-related aspects of parenting minor children that are unlike those found in any other family relationships. Parents must employ strategies in the present to assist in the development of future adults, and these parenting actions are intimately influenced by parents' assessments of the past. Thus research that examines cohort changes in the scheduling of children and individual differences between families that overschedule intensely and those that do not may reveal how parents and children living during particular times and in particular places are shaped by and respond to cultural mandates about the proper roles of children and families in society. More important, theory and research concerning this phenomenon will reveal ways in which parents and children help to *shape* the cultural mandate, as such a process is surely bidirectional.

SCHEDULES IN THEORETICAL VIEW

As Daly and Beaton note in Chapter 10, daily activity schedules, in the tradition of the positivist paradigm, are markers of the objectification and reification of time as an external reality. Explorations of children's schedules reveal the boundaries of their structured days: when their "time on" begins and ends. As an example, we know of one mother who was able to mine a rich vein of time when she

arranged for a reading tutor to meet with her son at 6:30 in the morning, leaving his crowded after-school schedule of sports and music lessons intact (Doherty, 2003).

Children's activity schedules reveal more than just how individual families use time as an organizational structure. From a social constructivist viewpoint, the overscheduling of children informs us about recent, collectively developed meanings of adult qualities, with some skills for future adult survival (such as competitiveness and excellence) deemed more valuable than others (say, a sense of balance or the ability to daydream). Further, schedules demonstrate a key pragmatic facet of families and time, as families conduct complex negotiations to coordinate the various temporal needs of different members. The mother mentioned above, for example, was able to "double book" that early-morning tutoring time for one son by setting up her other son in the waiting car to do the homework he previously had no time to complete because of afternoon and evening activities (Doherty, 2003).

Finally, schedules can be examined from critical perspectives. If it is true that time has become a commodity in modern-day Western culture, then the hyperschedules of many children suggests that *childhood* has become commodified, ruled by competition and other marketplace values. Many loving parents find that they are raising their children in a culture that defines good parents as opportunity providers. Part of providing opportunities means keeping children busy, tightly scheduling their time, and closely monitoring them for visible signs of "success." In true market fashion, this becomes parenting as product development (Doherty & Carlson, 2002).

OVERSCHEDULED CHILDREN AND THEORETICAL INTEGRATION

The phenomenon of overscheduled kids and underconnected families is refracted through these paradigmatic lenses of families and time. Future research on this phenomenon, however, might be well served by attention to the theoretical integration that Daly and Beaton pose in Chapter 10, focusing on questions of *agency, perspective,* and *values.* Such integration should aim to place norms for families' scheduling of children in historical context as well as to uncover the experiential unity of time within families of which this scheduling is a major marker.

Many parents who are neck deep in hyperscheduling feel a lack of agency surrounding control of their children's time. Parents often deal with the seemingly stronger agency of their peers and thus can be socially sanctioned for *not* involving their children in many activities. For example, we know of one couple who made the decision to "downsize" their son's schedule by not reenrolling him in league baseball and found that other parents greeted their decision with shock and dismay (Doherty, 2003). It is telling that the most visible efforts to reverse this parental feeling of lack of agency have occurred at the community level (e.g., the Minnesota organization Putting Family First). The organizations making such efforts acknowledge how difficult it is for parents to exercise agency in the midst of strong opposing community sentiment while simultaneously demonstrating how aggregates of individuals can change the course of the community tide.

The overscheduled kids/underconnected families phenomenon is also strongly influenced by perspective. Within families, individual members likely experience high activity levels differently: from the guilt-ridden working mother serving as team chauffeur to the hyperscheduled adolescent contemplating upcoming college admissions to the doting grandparents who find themselves relegated to the sidelines of their grandchildren's lives. An additional perspective on time is revealed when we examine cohorts of individuals and families who are currently experiencing the phenomenon. For example, insights about lived family time may be uniquely informed by the perspectives of families that were formerly characterized by overscheduling and disconnect but that have since cut back, as well as by the perspectives of families that have reared children in the thick of the phenomenon while resisting its pull entirely.

Ultimately, the scheduling of children is a marker of the value that individual families and society at large place on time—and on children, parents, and families. Along with anecdotal evidence of the value placed on the hyperscheduling of children, there is also evidence that new values are being formed and communicated. In one community, a long-time teacher recently went so far as to characterize overscheduled children as "abused." The National Association of Elementary School Principals recommends a level of structured extracurricular activities for elementary school children that is much lower than that found in the schedules that characterize many children's time. And perhaps most persuasive is the fact that in the fall of 2000, the Harvard University admissions office published a report describing arriving hyperscheduled students as decidedly not well-rounded (Doherty & Carlson, 2003).

Family scholarship often lags behind the shifts that families are experiencing in mainstream culture. We hope that this brief excursion into a "now" issue concerning families' use of time helps to illuminate the issues that Daly and Beaton raise in their chapter.

DISCUSSION AND EXTENSION

TIME AND TIME AGAIN: A CRITICAL LOOK AT ORDER IN FAMILY LIFE

Barbara H. Fiese, *Syracuse University*

Time is a mistress, a master, a marauder, and a marker. In Chapter 10, Daly and Beaton masterfully develop several lines of theory using time as a metaphor. Time is considered reflective of changes in family structure, family process, family meaning, and distribution of power. Many of the propositions that Daly and Beaton put forth likely ring true to the reader. The notion that living in the 21st century is marked by a sense of time urgency is widespread, and the dogged feeling of never having enough time is no doubt a common experience. Daly and Beaton propose that this accelerated pace leads to challenges for family members, such as the problem of finding time to be together, and conclude that many families do not effectively meet these challenges.

Without discounting the importance of time pressures and the intuitive appeal of time as imposed from the outside, I suggest that several assumptions need careful consideration here. First, can we reliably access time? Daly and Beaton outline four different ways in which time is construed. Whether through a positivist or constructivist lens, time is accessed through the reports of individuals and their felt experience of time. This is problematic, as individuals are poor judges of time. Indeed, Tourangeau (2000) of the Gallup Organization has found that there is considerable error in reporting on events when they are distant in time, and recollections of individual events are subject to personal beliefs. Personal effects on the recall of

time spent are clearly illustrated by the work of Wagenaar (1986), who recorded more than 2,000 events from his daily life over the course of 6 years. When he then tested his memory for particular events, he found that his recall for who was present at the events was fairly accurate, but his recall of when the events occurred was fairly unreliable. Thus, by its very nature, time is personal, and recollection of its use and influence on others is subject to individual beliefs.

A second assumption is that time use in families has shifted drastically in recent years. If we take a historical perspective and consider shifts in family time over the past century, we see markers that families have increasingly organized more time to be together, rather than less. For example, it was not until the end of the 19th century that special celebrations such as birthday parties, Thanksgiving feasts, and the exchanging of Christmas presents were considered family-oriented activities rather than associated solely with religious institutions (Mintz & Kellogg, 1988). Although one could certainly argue that these kinds of celebrations have become more isolated from extended family members, they are nevertheless one reflection of family time and its enduring nature.

There are incongruities in the data suggesting that families do not spend time together. Daly and Beaton cite Putnam (2000), who reports that over the past two decades there has been a 30% decline in the number of families who report that the whole family

Author's Note: Preparation of this manuscript was supported, in part, by a grant from the National Institute of Mental Health (R01 MH51771) to the author.

usually eats dinner together. However, a recent survey by the *Christian Science Monitor* found that more than 75% of the families participating reported that they frequently eat dinner together. Such discrepancies may result from two assumptions: first, that family time is additive; second, that all families define time in similar fashion.

Is family time additive? Objective time is certainly measured in units that can be added together to make a predictable whole, but family time may not operate in the same way. Noting that the amount of time family members spend together has decreased 10% assumes that there are equivalent decreases in other aspects of family process such that there is a threat to family cohesion, warmth, and support. Yet there is no clear evidence to suggest that there is an absolute amount of time that is essential for good family functioning.

Returning to dinnertime as an example, several studies have examined the frequency of collective family mealtimes and the amount of time families spend eating meals together. The aims of these studies have been relatively diverse, including consideration of the relationships between family dinnertime and children's language development (Gleason, Perlmann, & Greif, 1984), children's socialization (Feiring & Lewis, 1987), family rules (Grieshaber, 1997), interaction in single-parent families (Landesman, Jaccard, & Gunderson, 1991), and conversation patterns across cultures (Martini, 1996). Thus researchers have generally not set out to study family mealtimes per se; rather, they have viewed family mealtimes as context for developmental and social processes. It is interesting to note that the regularity of meals across these studies is strikingly similar. On average, families convene for meals four to five times a week, and, when duration is reported, each gathering lasts, on average, 20 minutes. Added together, this accounts for approximately 80 to 100 minutes per week during which family members are together, or the equivalent of a 90-minute television show. Perhaps 20 years ago the total average weekly amount of time families spent together at mealtimes was closer to 120 minutes, and therefore there may have been a drop of 10% or more over time. Yet these relatively brief interactions appear to be positively related to mental and physical health. If absolute amount of time is not sufficient to explain variability in family functioning, what other aspects might we consider?

One way to integrate these apparent incongruities is to consider two dimensions of family time: practicing and representing. The practicing aspect of family time includes those directly observable and countable aspects of time spent as a family. These practices may vary by stage of life, culture, and current stresses. For example, families with infants spend less time at the dinner table than do families with preschool-age children (Fiese, Hooker, Kotary, & Schwagler, 1993), and members of Hawaiian families spend less time sitting and more time moving around the kitchen than do Filipino American family members (Martini, 1996). Family time practices may constitute one area that reflects the shifting landscape of family life.

Another aspect of family time is its representational or symbolic nature. Time spent together as a family not only reflects patterned interactions but also sets the stage for how individual members create beliefs about and representations of what it means to be a member of a family. Over time, repetitive exchanges among family members become part and parcel of personal memories that encapsulate time spent together. Often these memorable moments are captured during family rituals that are deliberately planned, include expectations for attendance, and have powerful emotional and symbolic elements. There is an ethereal aspect to rituals that places them out of time. Turner (1969) refers to the liminal phase of rituals as "a moment in and out of time" (p. 96). These symbolic

DISCUSSION AND EXTENSION *continued*

gatherings are organized around multiple elements: the preparatory phase, the event, and reminiscence. Different elements may overlap, such that the preparatory phase may include reminiscence of previous occasions, leaving the individual with a sense of bridging two time frames—those of past and future generations. In this regard, family rituals provide opportunities for family members to be transported back in time (Myerhoff, 1978).

The symbolic, or representational, quality of family rituals may be important in explaining how, even under stressful conditions (such as being hard-pressed for time), family members can make emotional connections that reduce the effects of stress. For example, families that practice regular and meaningful family rituals have happier marriages and may experience fewer stresses associated with illness; adolescents in such families report a stronger sense of self than do adolescents in other families (Fiese et al., 2002). This is not to say that family rituals themselves cause healthy functioning. However, the representational aspect of time spent together suggests that the affective residues of family life may not necessarily be measured in temporal units, but rather in complex subjective responses. "Family time" may not always be equivalent to time spent in families.

Daly and Beaton's provocative essay reminds us that family theory is a complex enterprise. The multiple layers of family life call for multiple perspectives on how individuals find meaning in their collective experiences that may or may not stand the test of time.

REFERENCES

Almond, G. A., Appleby, R. S., & Sivan, E. (2003). *Strong religion: The rise of fundamentalisms around the world*. Chicago: University of Chicago Press.

Bengtson, V. L., & Allen, K. R. (1993). The life course perspective applied to families over time. In P. Boss, W. J. Doherty, R. LaRossa, W. R. Schumm, & S. K. Steinmetz (Eds.), *Sourcebook of family theories and methods: A contextual approach* (pp. 469–499). New York: Plenum.

Bennett, J. B. (2000). *Time and intimacy: A new science of personal relationships*. Mahwah, NJ: Lawrence Erlbaum.

Bernardes, J. (1986). Multidimensional developmental pathways: A proposal to facilitate the conceptualization of "family diversity." *Sociological Review, 34*, 590–610.

Council of Economic Advisers to the President. (2000). *Teens and their parents in the 21st century: An examination of trends in teen behavior and the role of parental involvement*. Washington, DC: Author.

Csikszentmihalyi, M., Hektner, J. M., & Schmidt, J. A. (2004). *Measuring the quality of everyday life: The ESM handbook*. Manuscript submitted for publication.

Csikszentmihalyi, M., & Larson, R. (1987). Validity and reliability of the experience-sampling method. *Journal of Nervous and Mental Disease, 175*, 525–536.

Daly, K. J. (1996). *Families and time: Keeping pace in a hurried culture*. Thousand Oaks, CA: Sage.

Daly, K. J. (2001). Deconstructing family time: From ideology to lived experience. *Journal of Marriage and Family, 63*, 283–294.

Daly, K. J. (2002). Time, gender and the negotiation of family schedules. *Symbolic Interaction, 25*, 323–342.

Davies, K. (1994). The tension between process time and clock time in care-work: The example of day nurseries. *Time & Society, 3*, 277–303.

Deem, R. (1996). No time for a rest? An exploration of women's work, engendered leisure and holidays. *Time & Society, 5*, 5–25.

Doherty, W. J. (2003, September/October). See how they run: When did childhood turn into a rat race? *Psychotherapy Networker*.

Doherty, W. J., & Carlson, B. Z. (2002). *Putting family first: Successful strategies for reclaiming family life in a hurry-up world*. New York: Henry Holt.

Everingham, C. (2002). Engendering time: Gender equity and discourses of workplace flexibility. *Time & Society, 11*, 335–351.

Feiring, C., & Lewis, M. (1987). The ecology of some middle-class families at dinner. *International Journal of Behavioral Development, 10*, 377–390.

Fiese, B. H., Hooker, K. A., Kotary, L., & Schwagler, J. (1993). Family rituals in the early stages of parenthood. *Journal of Marriage and the Family, 55*, 633–642.

Fiese, B. H., Tomcho, T., Douglas, M., Josephs, K., Poltrock, S., & Baker, T. (2002). Fifty years of research on naturally occurring rituals: Cause for celebration? *Journal of Family Psychology, 16*, 381–390.

Flaherty, M. G. (2002). Making time: Agency and the construction of temporal experience. *Symbolic Interaction, 25*, 379–388.

Fraenkel, P. (2001). The place of time in couple and family therapy. In K. J. Daly (Ed.) *Minding the time in family experience: Emerging perspectives and issues* (pp. 283–310). Oxford: Elsevier Science.

Galinsky, E. (1999). *Ask the children*. New York: William Morrow.

Giddens, A. (1984). *The constitution of society: Outline of the theory of structuration*. Berkeley: University of California Press.

Gillman, M. W., Rifas-Shiman, S. L., Frazier, A. L., Rockette, H. R. H., Camargo, C. A., Field, A. E., et al. (2000). Family dinners and diet quality among older children and adolescents. *Archives of Family Medicine, 9*, 235–240.

Gleason, J. B., Perlmann, R. Y., & Greif, E. B. (1984). What's the magic word: Learning language through politeness routines. *Discourse Processes, 7*, 493–502.

Grieshaber, S. (1997). Mealtime rituals: Power and resistance in the construction of mealtime rules. *British Journal of Sociology, 48*, 649–666.

Hochschild, A. R. (with MacHung, A.). (1989). *The second shift: Working parents and the revolution at home*. New York: Viking.

Hofferth, S. L., & Sandberg, J. F. (2001). How American children spend their time. *Journal of Marriage and Family, 63,* 295–308.

Joy, B. (2000, April). Why the future doesn't need us. *Wired,* pp. 238–262.

Kantor, D., & Lehr, W. (1975). *Inside the family: Toward a theory of family process.* San Francisco: Jossey-Bass.

Landesman, S., Jaccard, J., & Gunderson, V. (1991). The family environment: The combined influence of family behavior, goals, strategies, resources, and individual experiences. In M. Lewis & S. Feinman (Eds.), *Social influences and socialization in infancy* (pp. 63–96). New York: Plenum.

LaRossa, R. (1995). Stories and relationships. *Journal of Social and Personal Relationships, 12,* 553–558.

Larson, R. W., & Richards, M. H. (1994). *Divergent realities: The emotional lives of mothers, fathers, and adolescents.* New York: Basic Books.

Lynott, P. P., & Logue, B. J. (1993). The "hurried child": The myth of lost childhood in contemporary American society. *Sociological Forum, 8,* 471–491.

Martini, M. (1996). "What's new?" at the dinner table: Family dynamics during mealtimes in two cultural groups in Hawaii. *Early Development and Parenting, 5,* 23–34.

Mintz, S., & Kellogg, S. (1988). *Domestic revolutions: A social history of American family life.* New York: Free Press.

Moen, P. (Ed.). (2003). *It's about time: Couples and careers.* Ithaca, NY: Cornell University Press.

Myerhoff, B. G. (1978). A symbol perfected in death: Continuity and ritual in the life and death of an elderly Jew. In B. G. Myerhoff & A. Simic (Eds.), *Life's career—aging: Cultural variations in growing old.* Beverly Hills, CA: Sage.

National Research Council. (2000). *Time-use measurement and research: Report of a workshop.* Committee on National Statistics. M. Ver Ploeg, J. Altonji, N. Bradburn, J. DaVanzo, W. Nordhaus, & F. Samaniego (Eds.). Commission on Behavioral and Social Sciences and Education. Washington, DC: National Academy Press.

Perry-Jenkins, M., Repetti, R. L., & Crouter, A. C. (2000). Work and family in the 1990s. *Journal of Marriage and the Family, 62,* 981–998.

Presser, H. (2000). Nonstandard work schedules and marital instability. *Journal of Marriage and the Family, 62,* 93–110.

Putnam, R. D. (2000). *Bowling alone: The collapse and revival of American community.* New York: Simon & Schuster.

Robinson, J. P., & Godbey, G. (1997). *Time for life: The surprising ways Americans use their time.* University Park: Pennsylvania University Press.

Sandberg, J. F., & Hofferth, S. L. (2001). Changes in children's time with parents: United States, 1981–1997. *Demography, 38,* 423–436.

Sayer, L., Bianchi, S. M., & Robinson, J. P. (2002). *Are parents investing less in children? Trends in mothers' and fathers' time with children.* Unpublished manuscript (revision of a paper presented at the annual meeting of the American Sociological Association, August 2000, Washington, DC).

Snyder, C. R. (2002). Hope theory: Rainbows in the mind. *Psychological Inquiry, 13,* 249–275.

Southerton, D. (2003). Squeezing time: Allocating practices, coordinating networks and scheduling society. *Time & Society, 12,* 5–25.

Sprey, J. (2001). Time bound. In K. J. Daly (Ed.), *Minding the time in family experience: Emerging perspectives and issues* (pp. 37–58). Oxford: Elsevier Science.

Swidler, A. (1986). Culture in action: Symbols and strategies. *American Sociological Review, 51,* 273–286.

Thorpe, K., & Daly, K. J. (1999). Children, parents, and time: The dialectics of control. In C. L. Shehan (Ed.), *Through the eyes of the child: Revisioning children as active agents of family life* (pp. 199–224). Stamford, CT: JAI.

Tourangeau, R. (2000). Remembering what happened: Memory errors and survey reports. In A. A. Stone, J. S. Turkkan, C. A. Bachrach, J. B. Jobe, H. S. Kurtzman, & V. S. Cain (Eds.), *The science of self-report: Implications for research and practice* (pp. 29–48). Mahwah, NJ: Lawrence Erlbaum.

Turner, V. (1969). *The ritual process: Structure and anti-structure.* Chicago: Aldine.

Wagenaar, W. (1986). My memory: A study of autobiographical memory over six years. *Cognitive Psychology, 18,* 225–252.

Zelizer, V. A. (1985). *Pricing the priceless child: The changing social value of children.* New York: Basic Books.

• Eleven

THEORIZING ABOUT MARRIAGE

Jason S. Carroll, *Brigham Young University*

Stan J. Knapp, *Brigham Young University*

Thomas B. Holman, *Brigham Young University*

Since its inception in the 1920s, research on marriage relationships has attracted widespread attention within a variety of disciplines and has held a central position in the scientific study of families. However, despite marriage scholarship's long tradition and broad interdisciplinary base, a number of scholars believe that this area of research has reached a crossroads at the beginning of the 21st century. This pivotal moment is seen as largely the result of a lack of explicit theory development in the marriage field. In fact, during the past decade several leading marriage scholars have called for the development of broad integrative frameworks to guide research and intervention efforts with married couples (Fincham & Beach, 1999; Holman, 2001; Karney & Bradbury, 1995).

In addition to calling for new theory development, some marriage scholars have also begun to question the dominant theoretical orientations and therapeutic assumptions of the marriage field (Browning, 2003; Cere, 2000; Doherty & Carroll, 2002; Fowers, 2000; Knapp, 2002). In general terms, these scholars have identified the need for more explicit and rigorous dialogue about the implicit assumptions that underlie current conceptual and methodological approaches to the study of marriage.

In this chapter, we present a critical commentary on the current state of theorizing about marriage. Our primary argument is that the process of theorizing is important for high-quality, productive scholarship. The future vitality of marriage scholarship lies in the development of both *theoretical frameworks* that can integrate disparate lines of existing research and *theoretical practices* that can open up new areas of investigation. We argue that both *integration* and *innovation* require a deeper articulation and analysis of the ontological, epistemological, and evaluative assumptions that inform marital scholarship. We also assert that a more explicit focus on theory development in the marriage field will prompt marriage therapists and educators to examine more thoroughly the clinical assumptions that guide their work with premarital and marital couples, thereby leading to better fit among research, theory, and practice.

THEORIZING
(ABOUT MARRIAGE) IS CRUCIAL

We agree with the editors of this volume when they suggest in Chapter 1 that theory is crucial, and we believe this is nowhere more true than in the study of marriage. We also believe that theorizing can take many forms, including formal model building and propositional theory development as well as paradigmatic critique of prevailing assumptions that undergird scholarly investigation. Our focus in this chapter is on the last of these forms of theorizing. We also agree with those who suggest that marital scholarship is at a crossroads and that continued progress in the field depends on improvements in the development and use of theory. The issues, then, are how we can be more theoretically minded and how we can move marital scholarship along through our theorizing.

The systems theory concept of *levels* or *types* of analysis is useful for organizing where we are and where we need to go in theorizing about marriage. Watzlawick, Weakland, and Fisch's (1974) metaphor of changing gears in an automobile with a standard transmission illustrates differing types of analysis. When one is driving a truck, for instance, engaging different gears allows one to produce different kinds of movement. Each gear is limited in the kind of movement it can produce: A low gear may enable more power, and a high gear may enable greater speed. Therefore, if the truck is in the right gear, improving speed or power may be simply a matter of stepping on the gas. However, there is a limit to the power or speed—or both—that the truck can achieve in any one gear. One gear is not necessarily superior to another, but neither is one gear alone sufficient. We increase our power, speed, and range by using multiple gears. Becoming more theoretically minded can be like "stepping on the gas" as we refine and expand existing conceptualizations. But it can also require that we "shift to alternative gears," because we may never get to all the important destinations we need to reach if we use only one of the gears available to us.

THEORIZING ABOUT MARRIAGE
WITHIN THE RECEIVED VIEW

The "gear" currently in use in the study of marriage is grounded in what some have called the "received view" of scientific inquiry (Lincoln & Guba, 2000; Thomas & Wilcox, 1987). This view is similar to what the editors of this volume see as one of the "basic orientations" or overarching approaches to theorizing (see Chapter 1); we use the term *received view* to refer to the mainstream of sociological and psychological theorizing that has been and is being done about marriage. The underlying philosophical position of the received view is positivism (Thomas & Wilcox, 1987), with its attendant ontological, epistemological, and methodological assumptions (Guba & Lincoln, 1994; Lincoln & Guba, 2000). The dominant application of this paradigm in the marriage field is witnessed in the widespread acceptance of a scientific approach that emphasizes "empirical theory," or the idea that descriptive research is objective in nature and, therefore, can and should precede theory in the scientific enterprise. Markman, Notarius, Stephen, and Smith (1981) articulate this paradigm when they state, "A solid data base is a prerequisite to theory development [and] can be best accomplished by descriptive studies which focus on observable behavior" (p. 236). At the core of this "empirical-descriptive" approach is the assumption that observable patterns of behavior can be understood in purely objective ways that will lead to universally accepted interpretations.

Grounded in the received view of scientific inquiry, the past 25 years of research on marriage has focused predominantly on observable patterns of interaction between spouses—particularly interactions around marital conflict (for a review, see Gottman & Notarius, 2000). In general terms, this research has yielded an increased understanding of the "topography of marital conflict" (Fincham & Beach, 1999, p. 49) through a focus on the delineation of sequential patterns of behavior that differentiate distressed marital couples from nondistressed marital couples (Bradbury, Fincham, & Beach, 2000). Specifically, this line of research has shown that, compared with nondistressed couples, distressed couples are characterized by greater amounts of negativity, reciprocity of negative behavior, more sustained negative interaction, and escalation of negative interactions (Gottman & Notarius, 2000). More recent studies in this line of research have focused on less immediately observable aspects of marital interaction, global patterns of interaction, and neglected prosocial dimensions of marital behavior (Bradbury et al., 2000).

Limitations Within the Received View

Although observational research on couple processes has generated rich descriptive accounts of marital interactions and identified a number of behavioral markers of marital distress, some limitations of this empirical-descriptive approach to studying and theorizing about marriage are beginning to emerge. In what follows, we briefly review five such limitations: (a) a lack of theorizing about data, (b) a lack of cross-fertilization of work from researchers with disparate (disciplinary) orientations, (c) a lack of integration and theory development, (d) a commitment to an atheoretical myth that limits rigorous examination of grounding assumptions, and (e) the production of empirical-descriptive work that can sometimes fail to provide full explanations of, and improved theoretical understanding for, the processes described.

Lack of theorizing about data. As in other aspects of family theorizing, theorizing about marriage within the received view suffers from work that is minimally "grounded" in theory, but when grounded, "the association between such theories and research tends to be loose and imprecise and, in some cases, constitutes only a metaphorical connection" (Fincham & Beach, 1999, p. 55). What are sometimes called theories of marriage are often little more than "empirical generalizations" and do not fit the commonly accepted definitions of theory in terms of scope or level of abstraction.

Lack of cross-fertilization. A purely descriptive approach to research tends to discourage "cross-fertilization" of ideas among marriage scholars in different disciplines. One result of this insularity of research to disciplinary frameworks is that the collective knowledge base of marital studies becomes "scattered across a variety of disparate sources," making it difficult for anyone "to access the picture of marriage painted by scientific research" (Fincham, 1998, p. 543).

Lack of integration and theory development. The most central and perhaps most widely voiced criticism of current marital scholarship is the relative lack of development of broad theoretical frameworks to integrate research and clinical intervention (Fincham & Beach, 1999; Karney & Bradbury, 1995). In the past 30 years, marital research has generated a large number of theoretical constructs and midrange models that have proven valuable in helping scholars to understand the success and failure of marriage relationships. However, conceptual work in the marital domain has proceeded in an additive fashion rather than a cumulative one. For example, many current model-building efforts focus on widening the scope of inquiry in an effort to contextualize marital interactions. It appears that although a purely descriptive-empirical approach has proven useful in generating new conceptual ideas, it has been less successful in leading scholars to integrate and synthesize these ideas into integrated theories.

The atheoretical myth. As we have noted, many marital scholars working within the received view of scientific inquiry promote the belief that atheoretical observation is possible and desirable. This assumption limits the kind of theoretical analysis available to scholars and may prevent both theoretical awareness and progress. Theory is always in operation in our work, whether we acknowledge it or not. We concur with Fincham and Beach's (1999) assertion that fundamental to further progress is marital scholars' need to "make explicit and critically analyze the assumptions that informed the choice of what to observe in the first place" (p. 55).

Description without explanation. Perhaps most important is the argument that a purely behavioral account of marriage often leads to "progress" without improved understanding. Thus, although observational approaches may be productive of all kinds of empirical data and models, the data and models often remain undeveloped theoretically and therefore fail to provide fully the kinds of understanding and explanation that scientific scholarship aims to provide. For example, although behavior-oriented approaches have proven useful for generating *descriptions* of types and sequences of interactions that can distinguish distressed from nondistressed couples, such approaches seem to be less effective for generating *explanations* of why these differing interactions occur. We suspect that in order to explain marital processes and outcomes more fully, and not just describe them, scholars will need not only to expand their models but also to deepen them.

The Need to Consider Alternative Views of Theory and Scientific Inquiry

We find the vast majority of contemporary calls for explicit theory development and more careful theorizing of marital relations to be calls simply for "more gas" rather than a "shift in gears." Indeed, much of value can be done within the existing paradigm or received view. For example, Bradbury, Cohan, and Karney (1998) suggest that a social learning/behavioral perspective has served as a foundation for much of psychological research on conceptualizing marital change. They acknowledge the value of this theoretical perspective, but they also assert that it has limitations. They suggest an "alternative view" that incorporates stressful events and individual differences into the behavioral model of marital change. Their alternative is an important contribution to our theoretical understanding of marriage, but it also represents "pressing on the gas" in that it remains within the received view of scientific inquiry.

Such emergent frameworks offer great promise as heuristics for organizing existing findings and identifying new lines of inquiry, but the majority continue to be based in a behavioral account of marriage. Although this allows these models to build on the strengths of existing behavior-oriented research, too much emphasis on observable interaction patterns may continue to constrain theory development.

Much marital scholarship of value has been done and is yet to be done within the paradigmatic boundaries of the received view, but we can do much more. Indeed, the well-documented limitations of positivism and the received view of science (e.g., Slife & Williams, 1995) suggest that a thorough understanding of marriage cannot come only from within the mainstream perspective. Although increasing our speed from 5 miles per hour to 10 miles per hour in first gear is laudable and even important, we need to change gears, to make a "second-order change" (Watzlawick et al., 1974), if we are to come to a fuller theoretical understanding of marriage.

ALTERNATIVE PRACTICES FOR IMPROVING THEORIZING ABOUT MARRIAGE

Despite the fact that marriage scholarship within the received view has hegemony within the academic community (in tenure decisions, for example), within grant-giving institutions, and even within popular culture, there is a long tradition of approaching marriage from different paradigmatic frames (Guba & Lincoln, 1994). In what follows, we suggest that the time is ripe for marital scholars to shift gears and engage in sustained, rigorous theoretical analysis of marital research and scholarship. We attempt to articulate both the process and the value of the kind of theorizing we envision by providing three brief illustrations of the kinds of theoretical practices we view as necessary to advance the field: (a) analysis of basic *ontological assumptions* grounding marital knowledge claims, (b) analysis of basic *epistemological assumptions* informing marital research, and (c) analysis of *evaluative dimensions* of marital scholarship (i.e., what constitutes the "good marriage"). Due to space limitations, we cannot present our argument to the degree or with the depth that we would have preferred. Indeed, our three illustrations must be read as suggestive rather than definitive. Nor should these illustrations be taken as exhaustive of the potential payoff we anticipate from this kind of work. Instead, taken together, they represent our argument for rigorous theoretical examination of grounding assumptions, the kind of theoretical analysis that can offer the field a new "gear" through which to understand marriage.

Examining Ontological Assumptions in Marital Scholarship

All forms of marital scholarship make ontological assumptions that ground their knowledge claims about marriage. Such foundational assumptions about marriage have far-reaching implications for scientific work and intervention on family life. Careful examination of ontological assumptions can form

a "first step toward generating better work" as we "delve deeply into the theories and findings" of contemporary scholarship on marriage (Bradbury et al., 2000, p. 975).

Although current marital scholarship makes a number of important grounding assumptions, here we examine ontological assumptions dealing with how marital scholarship understands the human actor. All forms of marital scholarship make assumptions about what it means to be a human being. In some theoretical frameworks, such as exchange and rational choice theories, these assumptions are clearly formulated and discussed, whereas in others they often remain hidden and unexamined, as in most behavioral models of marital interaction. Nevertheless, how marital scholarship understands the human actor has major consequences for how we understand the marital relationship and what kinds of interventions we might recommend. To illustrate the value of the practice of questioning ontological foundations, we focus our analysis on the grounding assumptions of social exchange and rational choice (SE/RC) theories.

● SPOTLIGHT ON THEORY

THEORY-DRIVEN COUPLE EVALUATION

Luciano L'Abate, *Georgia State University*

A theory of personality socialization is evaluated through models in the laboratory; through the use of self-report, paper-and-pencil tests; and in primary, secondary, and tertiary prevention. It consists of three metatheoretical assumptions: (a) an assumption of horizontality, or *width* of relationships, consisting of emotionality, rationality, activity, awareness, and context, evaluated with the Relational Answers Questionnaire (L'Abate, 2003, in press; L'Abate & De Giacomo, 2003); (b) an assumption of verticality, or *depth* of relationships, described according to the four levels of presentation/public,

(continued)

● **SPOTLIGHT ON THEORY** *continued*

phenotypic/private, genotypic/internal, and historical/developmental, evaluated qualitatively through interviews; and (c) an assumption of settings, such as home, school/work, surplus leisure time, and transit, evaluated objectively through time analyses and subjectively with the semantic differential.

Two requirements are (a) expansion of monadic constructs to intimate relationships and (b) verifiability and accountability for theoretical models. Two major assumptions deal with abilities to love and to negotiate, their combination, and their contents, evaluated with (a) "What Applies to Me That I Agree With?" (WAMTIAW?; L'Abate & De Giacomo, 2003), (b) a negotiation potential enrichment program, (c) a negotiation workbook (L'Abate, 1986), and (d) face-to-face interviews and prescribed tasks in psychotherapy. The contents of what is exchanged between partners are condensed into the Triangle of Living—composed of Being/Presence, Doing/Performance, and Having/Production—and evaluated through a planned parenting workbook.

Personal and couple identity differentiates developmentally through the Likeness Continuum according to a dialectical curvilinear model composed of symbiosis, sameness, similarity, differentness, oppositeness, and alienation, evaluated with the Likeness Scale, the Likeness Grid, and WAMTIAW? In primary prevention, this model is evaluated with an enrichment program; in secondary prevention, it is evaluated with the "Who Am I?" workbook.

From the Likeness Continuum, three styles in relationships are derived: (a) most dysfunctional, Abusive-Apathetic; (b) semifunctional, Reactive-Repetitive; and (c) most functional, Creative-Conductive. These are evaluated with (a) the Problems in Relationships Scale (PIRS), (b) a negotiation potential enrichment program, (c) assignments in a negotiation workbook, and (d) face-to-face interviews in psychotherapy.

The PIRS, with 240 items, measures 20 potentially conflictual couple dimensions matching 20 written homework assignments. Individual partner scores have no meaning except in comparison with scores from the other partner. A discrepancy score between partners correlates significantly and negatively with Spanier's DAS. The PIRS is scored also for the three styles mentioned above.

Importance, as shown by care and concern for self and intimate others, as ascribed and attributed to self and intimates, produces four propensities: (a) Selfulness, positive attribution of importance to self and intimate others; (b) Selfishness, positive attribution of importance to self and negative attribution to others; (c) Selflessness, positive attribution of importance to others and negative attribution to self; and (d) No-Self, negative attribution of importance to both self and others. This model has been evaluated extensively with (a) the Self-Other Profile Chart, showing clear relationships with the attachment model (L'Abate, 2003; L'Abate & De Giacomo, 2003); (b) the Dyadic Relations Test (Cusinato & L'Abate, 2003); and (c) a workbook developed from that test.

Priorities, or what is important to self in relationship to intimates, have been evaluated with (a) the Priorities Grid and the Priorities Inventory, (b) a helpfulness enrichment program, and (c) an assignment in a negotiation workbook (L'Abate, 1986).

(continued)

● *SPOTLIGHT ON THEORY continued*

Intimacy in couples has been evaluated with (a) the Sharing of Hurts Scale, (b) an intimacy enrichment program, (c) an intimacy workbook, and (d) the Sharing of Hurts therapeutic task for couples (L'Abate, 1986; L'Abate & De Giacomo, 2003).

Three additional models derived from the assumptions and models of the theory—the Drama Triangle (victim, persecutor, savior), distance regulation (pursuer, distancer, regulator), and the process of negotiation—are evaluated with matching assignments in (a) a depression workbook for couples (L'Abate, 1986) and (b) a negotiation workbook (L'Abate, 1986). One can evaluate the whole theory using a parenting workbook for couples (L'Abate, in press). ●

Although social exchange theories and rational choice theories have different historical roots (i.e., behaviorism and classical economics, respectively; Rigney, 2001, pp. 101–120), they share a common commitment to understanding social life as reducible to the actions of individuals. This commitment, commonly called *methodological individualism,* assumes that social entities such as marriage can be accounted for primarily or ultimately in terms of individual actions (see Udehn, 2002). For example, George Homans (1970), the main author of social exchange theory, argues that "all social phenomena can be analyzed without residue into the actions of individuals" (p. 325). Other approaches to marriage research also adopt methodological individualism as the mode of explanation, but SE/RC theories incorporate what might be called "ontological atomism," or the view that "basic human needs, capacities, and motivations arise in each individual without regard to any specific feature of social groups or social interactions" (Fay, 1996, p. 31). SE/RC theories start with the assumption that individuals are "the bearers of sets of given, discrete, nonambiguous, and transitive preferences" (Hechter, 1987, p. 30). Individual preferences or needs are independent of social groups, cultures, or social institutions and are located in and derived from the individual.

Beginning with the view that individuals have sets of needs, wants, and preferences, SE/RC theories account for individual action

in terms of how well such action fulfills the needs and preferences of the individual; in other words, human beings are fundamentally self-interested. Individual actions are therefore understood as the results of actors' evaluating possible courses of action in terms of how well they will maximize rewards over costs. Therefore, "every individual voluntarily enters and stays in any relationship only as long as it is adequately satisfactory in terms of his rewards and costs" (Thibaut & Kelley, 1959, p. 37). This approach to understanding marriage assists family scholars in giving accounts of variations in marital stability and marital satisfaction at specific points in time, two common foci of marital research. Yet, if we maintain a commitment to the grounding assumptions of SE/RC theories, the approach struggles to account for change over time in marital satisfactions. Because SE/RC theories reduce social relations to self-interest, they must account for relationship change as either change in the values, wants, or preferences of the individual actor or change in the objective conditions for maximizing some set of stable preferences.

SE/RC approaches have difficulty accounting for how and why marital relationships develop because they lack a fully adequate conception of the human actor. Our argument builds on, but is more than, several common criticisms leveled against SE/RC approaches: (a) that actors don't really engage in rational calculation of costs and rewards in the ways presupposed by the theories (Root, 1993, pp. 100–123), (b) that actors lack sufficient information to make rational choices about alternative courses of action (Procter, 2000), (c) that emotional aspects are more important than SE/RC theorists grant (Peggs & Lampard, 2000), (d) that actors cannot be understood as acontextual or atomistic selves (Regan, 1993), and (e) that actors cannot be reduced to acting out of self-interest without the loss of valuable human motivations, such as morality and altruism (Procter, 2000; Rigney, 2001; Root, 1993, pp. 173–204). We agree with many of these criticisms, but we also assert that SE/RC approaches are of limited utility for increasing our understanding of marital development because they assume features of the self that need to be brought into theoretical and empirical relief. Rather than assuming that the self is composed of a set of values, needs, and preferences and is driven to realize them, marital scholars need to ask why actors have the values and preferences they do at varying points in the course of marriage. In this way, we not only subject our conceptualization of the human actor to theoretical critique, but we also open the door to a fuller empirical analysis of marital change and development. This is the case because the values, needs, and preferences through which spouses determine the attractions and barriers associated with their relationship become areas in need of explanation rather than mere assumption or description. Additionally, rather than assuming that actors act in the name of self-interest, marital scholars can seek to ascertain when, where, and why self-interest might be an overriding concern and when, where, and why other forms of action inform the marital relationship.

Examining Epistemological Assumptions in Marital Scholarship

In this subsection, we examine contemporary behavioral approaches in an attempt to illustrate why rigorous analysis of epistemological assumptions is crucial to theorizing about marriage. To illustrate why a commitment to epistemological assumptions

contributes to the formation of particular knowledge claims about marriage, we contrast the behavioral approach with contemporary feminist, philosophical, and religious approaches to marriage.

Behavioral epistemology. In the past two decades, psychologists have advanced knowledge claims of marital relations by challenging the SE/RC perspective and research findings acquired primarily through survey methods. These challenges have largely centered on the assertion that studying what people say about themselves is not a substitute for studying what they do. The SE/RC approach has been faulted as "a theory in how people *perceive* interaction, not a theory of interaction per se" (Gottman, 1982, p. 950). Instead, psychological researchers propose to study marital interaction as an "exchange of behaviors" (Bradbury et al., 2000, p. 965) and suggest observational and daily diary techniques as the methods of choice (for a review, see Gottman & Notarius, 2000). The aim is not simply to catalog various behaviors prevalent or absent in marital relations but to discover the behavioral sequences productive of (dis)satisfaction in marriages.

The emphasis on behavior has resulted in some important methodological developments in the study of marriage. Although behavioral researchers maintain an allegiance to marital quality as the dependent variable, how they measure marital quality has changed, shifting from a focus on both frequency of certain types of behaviors and evaluations of the marriage to a focus almost exclusively on level of satisfaction. This enables researchers to posit behavioral patterns as predictive of (dis)satisfaction in marital relations rather than confounded with it (Fincham & Bradbury, 1987) and thus to produce evidence for "the guiding premise of the behavioral approach to marital quality," which is "that positive and constructive behaviors enhance marital quality and negative or destructive behaviors are harmful" (Kluwer, 2000, p. 68).

Scholars who take the behavioral approach often pride themselves on being more "scientific" in their work than those who use other approaches to understanding married life and tend to regard other theoretical perspectives on marriage as imaginations "not based on empirical knowledge" (Gottman, 1999, p. 6). Instead, behavioral researchers propose to develop "a real theory of how marriages work and fail to work" through empirical analysis of "what real couples do to accomplish the everyday 'tasks' of being married" (Gottman, 1999, p. 7). However, behavioral theorists adopt an insufficiently critical epistemological framework for the study of married life. Their claims rely on a theory/data split that assumes that a simple recording of observable events produces atheoretical evidence. Such claims are not without their critics and amount to the adoption and championing of one of a number of possible epistemological frameworks for the scientific study of marriage.

By understanding the epistemological commitments of behavioral researchers, we can help to make sense of why they rarely discuss their ontological assumptions explicitly: They seek to present themselves as merely reporting observations and discovering simple behavioral patterns. Nevertheless, the behavioral approach does entail critical ontological assumptions regarding the human actor and what it means to be married.

Alternative epistemologies. When seen from within the received view of scientific inquiry, behavioral epistemology makes sense. However, when it is viewed from alternative epistemological standpoints, certain blind spots start to emerge. In particular, atheoretical observation is revealed to be less benign than it may at first appear. One can see this point most clearly when one adopts the epistemological standpoint offered by *critical theory* (a blanket term often used to describe several alternative paradigms, including neo-Marxism, feminism, materialism, participatory inquiry, poststructuralism, and postmodernism; for reviews, see Guba & Lincoln, 1994; Lincoln & Guba, 2000). Guba and Lincoln (1994) suggest that the "common breakaway assumption" of critical theory from the received view is an epistemological

difference, a difference suggesting that epistemological assumptions are formative claims of knowledge about families. We illustrate this difference through a discussion of feminist and recent religiocultural theorizing on marriage.

Of all the forms of critical theory, feminist theorizing has probably had the largest impact on the field of marriage studies. As Fox and Murry (2000) note, "Across varied disciplinary fields, feminism as an intellectual orientation has taken a critical eye to received traditions of scholarship and epistemology." Thus this perspective provides marriage scholars with new and different concepts, questions, methodologies, and ways of organizing and seeing research and research findings (Thompson, 1993).

A variety of different and even competing views exist within feminist theory, but most scholars suggest that all strands of feminist theory share certain themes or assumptions (Fox & Murry, 2000; White & Klein, 2002), including the following: (a) Women's experiences are central, normal, and as important as men's experiences (Wood, 1995); (b) gender is a basic organizing concept in social life (Thompson, 1993; Wood, 1995); (c) a feminist gender perspective presupposes that gender relations are shaped by historical and cultural contexts and must be studied in those contexts (Lincoln & Guba, 2000); and (d) feminist theory is emancipatory (White & Klein, 2002). These assumptions have allowed feminist-informed scholars to observe and conceptualize aspects of marriage that were previously hidden from view. For example, many feminists see traditional marriage as problematic for women. They assert that traditional gender-structured marriage, with its centrality in patriarchy, devaluation of women's contributions, and hierarchy of gender, is oppressive and costly to women in financial, emotional, and physical terms (Blaisure & Allen, 1995).

As noted above, a behavioral epistemology leads us to explain marriage as primarily a matter of explaining each individual's marital *satisfaction.* A feminist epistemology, on the other hand, enables researchers to ask why women would be "satisfied" with, and not see as unfair, the often imbalanced division of work in the marital relationship (Blaisure & Allen, 1995; Thompson, 1993). Theorizing marriage is no longer reducible to seemingly atheoretical observations of individual spouses' satisfaction. Feminist inquiry calls for critical examination of the ideology and practice of marital relations (Blaisure & Allen, 1995).

A similar critique of behavioral epistemology can be informed by religious and philosophical understandings of marriage. As with feminist and other critical theories, a central aspect of this religiocultural view is that our observations of marriage are informed by our theoretical commitments. In this case, our theoretical commitments can be informed by religious traditions and concepts. This type of mixed discourse is possible because of an often overlooked symmetry between religious thought and secular thought. All types of thinking, whether religious, philosophical, or scientific, involve a complex interweaving of several dimensions of thought. These include foundational metaphors that convey fundamental assumptions about views of reality, human nature, and other aspects of the human condition. A careful analysis of all types of thinking invariably reveals assumptions and judgments at the ontological, epistemological, and teleological levels. As Browning (2003) notes, religiously informed scholars hold that "the deep metaphors of all practical thinking have the status of faith-like assumptions" (p. 3). Therefore, because such metaphors "can be uncovered in all instances of practical thinking, the distinction between explicitly religious practical thinking and so-called secular thinking is not categorical" (p. 3). Both scientific and religious forms of reasoning are based on assumed metaphors about the basic nature and structures of life; therefore, religiously based concepts and perspectives can make valid contributions to family theory development. Of course, for religiously informed theories to influence social scientists, they must be put forward in ways that allow scholars to use scientific methods to establish the credibility of their ideas. This can happen when scholars form mixed discourses in which religiously based concepts are interwoven with theoretical arguments that can be expressed in recognizable forms of scientific theory and philosophy.

An example of this type of theory development in the marriage field is the work of Browning and his colleagues, who have explored the possible relevance of Western religious traditions to contemporary family issues, including marriage (Browning, 2003; Browning, Conture, Franklin, Lyon, & Miller-McLemore, 1997). They use the term *critical familism* to identify a paradigmatic position that abiding themes from religious traditions can be coupled with the best insights of contemporary human sciences to offer a unique understanding of marriage. Critical familism is "critical" in that it "attempts to expose, critique, and reform distortions of social, economic, and political power which function to block or undermine free formation and support of the equal-regard mother-father partnership" (Browning, 2003, p. 4). According to this alternative perspective, the principles supporting such critique can be found within Jewish, Christian, and other faith traditions and gleaned from insights drawn from contemporary moral philosophy. These traditions recognize marriage as a central aspect of both personal and collective religiocultural aspirations and highlight the need for scholars to consider the "mutual regard" (e.g., equality, commitment, self-sacrifice, other-centeredness) and social institution (e.g., community support, social goods) dimensions of the marriage relationship.

Examining the Question of the Good Marriage

What is a good marriage? This deceptively simple question plays a central role in how researchers study marriage and, in turn, how marital therapists and educators focus their intervention efforts.

The received view of the good marriage. Scholars working within the received view have defined the good marriage predominantly in terms of spousal satisfaction and relationship stability. In their review of longitudinal research on marriage, Karney and Bradbury (1995) point out that "marital researchers have rarely explored outcomes other than satisfaction or stability" (p. 16). Indeed, although there has been a recent shift in focus in marriage scholarship (i.e., from status variables to interaction processes), the way current scholars define the "good marriage" has changed little since the early theorizing of the 1940s and 1950s. The conceptualization of marital quality according to the two primary factors of marital stability and marital satisfaction has been one of the most enduring aspects of marital scholarship through the 20th century.

Although marital satisfaction has shown remarkable endurance as the primary criterion used to define the good marriage in the social sciences, it would be inaccurate to say that this construct has not changed or progressed over time. Furthermore, scholars operating within the received view have begun to recognize that we have been overly dependent on the behavioral and social exchange views of "marital satisfaction" as the outcome variable of choice (e.g., Fincham, Beach, & Kemp-Fincham, 1997). During the past decade, scholars have questioned some of the conceptual assumptions that have provided the foundation for how marital satisfaction has traditionally been defined and measured (for a review, see Bradbury et al., 2000). For example, Fincham et al. (1997) have challenged the long-standing assumption that researchers can measure marital satisfaction accurately by using bipolar or single-dimension measures (e.g., dissatisfied versus satisfied). An emerging line of research supports this challenge and suggests that positive and negative evaluations in marriage can be conceptualized and measured as separate, although related, dimensions (see Fincham & Linfield, 1997). Reconceptualizing marital satisfaction in this way has potentially far-reaching implications and will enable more detailed descriptions of change in marital satisfaction over time and the factors that account for these changes.

Theorizing the good marriage. Although recent reconceptualizations of marital satisfaction have invited scholars to view the construct in broader and more nuanced ways, these developments have tended to represent refinements of the existing definition of a good marriage rather than an alternative definition. Recently, however, some scholars have begun to question the assumption that satisfaction and stability should be the primary outcomes in marital research and practice. In particular, they have questioned the assumption that personal satisfaction or happiness is the defining feature of a good marriage (Fowers, 2000). An alternative to this "communication-based satisfaction" definition of marital quality is available in concepts that relate to personal characteristics and focus on what spouses contribute to marriage, such as generosity, loyalty, sacrifice, friendship, devotion, maturity, and goodwill (Fowers, 2000; Gottman, 1999; Stanley, 1998).

Similarly, conceptualizations of the marriage relationship that transcend individual experience and emphasize companionship also provide alternatives to traditional definitions of the good marriage. Fowers (2000) has argued that concepts such as partnership, teamwork, cooperation, collaboration, and coordination represent a view of the good marriage that is couple centered rather than individual centered. Whether or not one agrees with Fowers regarding what constitutes the good marriage is not important; the point we wish to emphasize is that his alternative conceptionalizations are healthy for the field, enabling us to see dimensions of marriage that may have gone unnoticed in the received view. The integration and innovation that Fowers has produced are direct results of the kind of sustained, explicit, and rigorous theoretical analysis we are advocating for the field of marriage scholarship.

We also see the benefits of shifting gears and theorizing the good marriage in another line of critique of marital satisfaction. Loveless (2000) argues that traditional notions of marital satisfaction assume that all happiness is functionally equivalent, when in fact differences in marital satisfaction between spouses and couples may differ not only in *degree*, but also in *kind*. Specifically, he asserts that "all happiness reported by those studied is assumed to be equivalent in kind and varying only in quantity, where in fact it may have distinct types or subtypes with significant qualitative differences" (p. 7). If all reported satisfaction in relationships is treated as equivalent, there is no way to distinguish, for example, between a spouse who is happy because he gets to buy everything he wants and one who is happy because he has a deeply committed friendship with his partner. Drawing from moral philosophy, Loveless identifies three types of happiness that spouses and couples might find in marriage: *hedonism* (the relatively indiscriminate

satisfaction of desires), *individualism* (in which one discriminates between worthwhile desires and harmful ones, and then chooses to satisfy the former), and *altruism* (in which the needs of others, not personal desire, are one's primary concern, and happiness occurs as a by-product of serving others in a perceived human unity). This opening up of the concept of marital satisfaction through rigorous theoretical examination of grounding assumptions enables marital scholars to produce new typologies that may connect well with existing research on attributions in marriage and help explain varying levels of resilience of satisfaction over time in marriage, in that some types of satisfaction may be more stable than others.

● *SPOTLIGHT ON METHODS*

STUDYING MARRIAGES LONGITUDINALLY

Frank D. Fincham, *University at Buffalo*

Thomas N. Bradbury, *University of California, Los Angeles*

With the recent transition among marriage scholars to the study of the development of marital dysfunction, it seems that the prospects for understanding the determinants of marital well-being have never been brighter. Carroll, Knapp, and Holman's analysis of the rudimentary state of theories of marital development, however, provides a welcome counterpoint to this view. Why? Absent identification and clear specification of core constructs and recognition of the limits of longitudinal research for studying causal processes, the value of longitudinal research is moot.

CORE CONSTRUCTS IN LONGITUDINAL RESEARCH

Slaying the Bipolar Bear

Marital scholars typically conceptualize and assess core constructs using bipolar evaluative continua. Such bipolar assessments function like the balance knob on a stereo,

(continued)

which does not allow left (positive evaluations) and right (negative evaluations) speakers to function independently. They therefore necessarily provide a limited picture of change. In studying the development of marital dysfunction, it is theoretically important to know whether happily married spouses who have become distressed spouses first increased in negativity before decreasing in positivity, as opposed to a progression in which negativity increased at the same time positivity decreased. Such a progression may, in turn, differ in important ways from one in which a steady decline in positivity results in marital distress. Documenting the existence of different avenues of change in marital constructs, examining their causes, and exploring their consequences is a program of research that could do much to advance understanding of how marriages succeed/fail. Moving beyond bipolar conceptualizations has the added advantage of drawing researchers' attention to new phenomena, such as ambivalence in marital and family relationships.

Continuity or Discontinuity?

Many researchers assume that marital well-being is a continuous variable, whereas clinicians using a threshold score to define "recovery" following marital therapy imply the existence of a discrete taxon. The continuity/discontinuity of core constructs is critical for longitudinal research because it has implications for the plausibility of linear models versus nonlinear models. Nonlinear models often imply discontinuities, and so a continuous distribution of scores might be taken as a strike against theories based on such models. Likewise, the recent discovery of taxonicity in marital well-being challenges longitudinal findings that have thus far assumed continuity in variables.

LONGITUDINAL RESEARCH AND CAUSALITY

Causal Discovery Versus Causal Inference

Researchers tend to overestimate the value of longitudinal research for illuminating the causes of marital dysfunction. Longitudinal studies of marriage (without randomized experimentation) are not useful for discovering causal relations and, when sample selection bias due to separation/divorce is handled improperly, can even create the appearance of (spurious) effects over time. Such longitudinal data are always subject to more than one interpretation. At best, we find ourselves making causal inferences with greater or lesser confidence. To tip the balance toward greater confidence, we must work as hard at eliminating plausible explanations as we do at working to identify statistically reliable effects.

Testing the Null Model Versus Testing Competing Models

Another way to increase our confidence in our ability to draw causal inferences is to move beyond testing data against the null model. Although it is not trivial to show that a model fits the data, an unknown number of additional models may also fit the data. Comparing the somewhat inconsistent findings of longitudinal research on marital

(continued)

● *SPOTLIGHT ON METHODS continued*

conflict and marital well-being (which tests against the null model) with the fairly consistent findings in comparative treatment outcome research (which tests different theoretical positions) illustrates this point well. Although we can never overcome the third variable problem in longitudinal research, we can and should do more to address this problem by examining competing models. This points to the strong need for a clear theoretical or empirical foundation that outlines expected causal relations among constructs, a characteristic that is all too often absent in longitudinal studies of marriage.

CONCLUSION

Research on marriage has evolved from a reliance on cross-sectional studies to the use of two-wave longitudinal designs, to the recognition that multiwave longitudinal studies may provide the greatest vantage point from which to understand how marriages develop and change. We need refined theoretical frameworks to guide and integrate the data collected in studies using these designs, and Carroll et al. provide welcome grist for this mill. In the same way that a sophisticated theory gains us little when it is combined with a weak research design, a strong design will underperform when its underlying theoretical postulates are vague or poorly conceived. ●

The benefits of applying theoretical analysis to assumptions that are often taken for granted in marital scholarship are also exemplified in recent work on the place of communication skills in the good marriage. In accordance with current definitions of the good marriage that hold that marital satisfaction and stability are largely determined by how well couples handle conflict and exchange positive interactions with each other, many couple-based interventions emphasize increasing relationship satisfaction by improving communication skills. However, Burleson and Denton (1997) note that "a careful review of the relevant literature reveals that *the impact of communication skills on marital satisfaction has been assumed much more frequently than it has been shown*" (p. 886). Their review confirmed their suspicion that the "communication skills-deficit" model of marital competence has been largely assumed. Specifically, they found that spouses' communication skill levels did not differ as a function of marital distress. Distressed husbands and wives were no less skilled in communication than their nondistressed counterparts—a result that contrasts directly with the frequent claim that distressed couples suffer from deficits in communication skills. Although Burleson and Denton found that distressed couples did not have poorer communication *skills* than nondistressed couples, distressed couples did express significantly more negative *intentions* toward each other than did nondistressed couples. These findings support the argument that there are many theoretical reasons for poor communication behavior. Or, put differently, approaches that highlight communication behavior can take us only so far, because they have not adequately theorized marriage. Marital scholars need to shift gears by calling grounding assumptions into question and engaging in theoretical practices that can lead to real progress in our understanding of the dynamics of marital relations.

Improving our understanding of the interpersonal aspects of marriage is not enough, however, and may limit the kinds of theoretical examinations that are brought to bear on marriage. This can be seen in the work of a handful of scholars who have recently called for a more systematic inclusion of the *social domain* in definitions of marital quality (Browning, 2003; Doherty & Carroll, 2002). In essence, these scholars caution marital researchers and practitioners about contributing to the *deinstitutionalization of marriage* and call for a deeper theoretical analysis of the good marriage that recognizes marriage as a social institution that involves important social, intergenerational, and public dimensions. From this perspective, our call for more rigorous theorizing about marriage is not just an academic issue; such theorizing is critical for the well-being of real families, communities, and societies.

When viewed through a moral-social lens, marital health can be expanded beyond traditional approaches that focus almost exclusively on spouses' happiness with the relationship and the permanence of the union. While recognizing the importance of spousal well-being and evaluations of the relationship, socially informed perspectives also stress that marriage is part of a familial and social ecosystem and, therefore, has a number of interdependent stakeholders with interests in the quality of the marriage relationship. The unavoidable connection of marriage to these stakeholders defines much of the social dimension of marriage. Taking this type of perspective, Doherty and Carroll (2002) have developed an ecological model of marital quality that conceptualizes marital health, or well-being, at four ecological levels: the individual, the family, the community, and the society. Within this model, the good marriage is defined as an ongoing process of balancing the mutually interdependent needs of the stakeholders in the marital ecosystem. This type of perspective stands in stark contrast to many of the current conceptualizations in the couples and marital domain that implicitly encourage individuals to operate primarily from self-interest and from concern with maximizing their personal fulfillment and happiness. Instead, socially informed approaches to marital well-being stress the recognition of shared morality that emerges from marital partners' position as relational beings in a social world.

None of the scholars whose work we have reviewed in this section seek to impose value-laden definitions of the good marriage dogmatically on marital scholars, families, or societies. Nor do they fall back on a version of the atheoretical myth and/or a moral relativism, which insists that only individuals can define for themselves what constitutes the good marriage. Instead, they make explicit arguments for their positions and, in so doing, offer us examples of the kinds of theoretical analysis the field of marital scholarship needs to encourage. Whether or not we agree with any or all of these scholars is not the point— the point is that by making arguments that are explicit rather than hidden, sustained rather than fleeting, rigorous rather than indulgent, examined rather than assumed, marital scholars will be able to produce better work and increase our understanding of marriage.

CONCLUSION

Marital scholarship today stands at a crossroads. Like many of our colleagues, we are optimistic for the field given that marriage is currently drawing widespread attention from scholars of diverse disciplinary backgrounds and that the previous generation of marriage scholarship has generated a rich foundation from which to build. However, we also share the doubts expressed by some marital scholars that the descriptive-empirical approaches that have guided marital research for the past 30 years will be sufficient to guide the next generation of research. We believe that the impact of future marriage scholarship—both in research and in application—will depend on an infusion of theoretical-explanatory approaches that can unify and synthesize existing research and guide future studies. We also believe that the field cannot be intellectually honest or professionally responsible unless marital scholars openly grapple with the social and moral meanings of marriage as well as the developmental aspects and contexts that inform such meanings. However, all of that said, our optimism outweighs our pessimism as we look to the future of theorizing about marriage.

CASE STUDY

CULTURAL NARRATIVES AND INDIVIDUAL EXPERIENCES IN RELATIONSHIPS

Richard Bulcroft, *Western Washington University*

Linda Smeins, *Western Washington University*

Kris Bulcroft, *Western Washington University*

The research we discuss here began with a student's question. Soon to be married, she hoped to do a project on marriage rituals, including the honeymoon, but she found that very little research on the topic was available. How could this be? Clearly the honeymoon had been widely overlooked. What few academic references to honeymoons she found were focused on the functional value of honeymoons for society or the significance of the honeymoon as a critical role transition in the development of families (Bulcroft, Smeins, & Bulcroft, 1999). These explanations seemed inadequate, however, as honeymoons appear to be becoming more important in spite of the declining significance of marriage and a reduced need for transitional adjustment due to increased levels of cohabitation.

To help fill the void, we initiated a project that began with a historical analysis of articles in the popular press and evolved to include a cultural analysis of honeymoon locations and a longitudinal survey of newlyweds. What started out as a question about honeymoons grew into a project with greater theoretical significance for understanding marriage and romantic relationships in late-modern society. It also developed into an exemplar of how two quantitative sociologists who are well indoctrinated into the scientific process and survey methods can work together with a qualitative art historian who is well versed in postmodernism and visual cultural analysis.

PHASE I: THE HISTORICAL CONTEXT

Adopting a social constructionist perspective (Bulcroft et al., 1999), we viewed the honeymoon as an event with potentially changing meaning linked to larger social processes and emergent cultural themes. This meant that our first task was to uncover these meanings at the cultural level. We began with a qualitative content analysis of articles about honeymoons published in the popular press since 1880. We then treated the contents of these articles as elements of a story or cultural "narrative" (Bulcroft et al., 1999) involving locations, sets of actors, role relationships, activities, themes, and plots. This approach grew out of the story structure of many of these articles and the adaptation of ideas from cultural studies of architecture and tourism (Bulcroft et al., 1999). We adopted the following assumptions about physical locations: that they provide opportunities for specific types of experiences, that they are imbued with symbolic meanings, and that they are mapped to culturally constructed stories. In particular, we found cultural studies of romanticism and the "myth of the exotic" (Bulcroft et al., 1999) to be useful in guiding our research. The emergence of romantic ideals linked to exotic locations has been attributed in these studies to a growing tension between rationality and emotions—a tension also noted in the postmodernist literature on identity and the sociological literature on modern relationships (Bulcroft et al., 1999).

CASE STUDY *continued*

Although we found similar story elements across the years, we did discern four qualitatively distinct narratives. In the earliest time period examined (pre-1940), the honeymoon story was largely one of domestic role enactment that took place in mostly natural settings and in rudimentary accommodations that facilitated domestic role activities. Beginning around 1940, however, a different story line began to emerge. Still occurring in mostly natural settings, honeymoons began to take on greater interpersonal significance. Increasingly, articles highlighted the intimacy aspects of the experience and alluded to the potential for later marital disaster should the honeymoon not go well. Gone were domestic role activities, as honeymoon locations went from housekeeping cabins to full-service accommodations where the couple was free to explore psychological compatibility. The risks involved in the honeymoon were portrayed as significant, and, for the first time, social scientists and other experts weighed in on the experience. By the 1960s, these concerns had all but disappeared from the cultural narrative, replaced by an emphasis on sexual and emotional gratification in luxurious accommodations filled with symbols of love and romance. Articles published during this time increasingly focused on planning to assure a rewarding experience, with a key element being the selection of a site that provided an unlimited supply of activities and services. This "all-inclusive" honeymoon was also evident in advertising. Today, this evolution has progressed even further, as a more hegemonic picture of the honeymoon has emerged involving exotic locales that provide a context for a narrative involving themes of perfection, authenticity, emotional fulfillment, sensuality, affirmation, and class privilege.

PHASE II: A CULTURAL ANALYSIS OF HONEYMOON SITES AND ADVERTISING

With elements of the contemporary cultural narrative identified, we began to work toward situating couples in this context by asking how they experience the narrative. How is the honeymoon imagined and made personal, and how are these imaginings actualized? These questions led us to research methods applied in visual culture analysis (Bulcroft et al., 1999). They also led us to progress to the micro level of personal experience. We began with analyses of representations in advertisements, then explored symbolic connections with actual experiences posed for couples at specific locations. Using industry studies to determine the most popular honeymoon destinations, we analyzed advertisements to understand how various possibilities for actualizing the imagined honeymoon are presented and how physical tourist settings offer closer scripting of the honeymoon narrative. Tropical locations expand the imaginings of romance, and at each specific location, couples are prompted to assume scripted identities. Using spatial and visual culture analysis, we examined how specific sites script the honeymoon through the organization of architecture, symbolism, and activities. Further, they map the sequence and pace with which the spatial organization will be experienced. Thus the cultural narrative becomes incorporated as part of the couple's personal biography, with the setting providing the necessary meanings of authenticity, heightened emotionality, intimacy, and status.

PHASE III: MOVING FROM MACRO TO MICRO AND FROM QUALITATIVE TO QUANTITATIVE

Returning to the scientific paradigm and concluding our journey from the macro to the micro, the final step in our research involved testing specific hypotheses derived from our cultural observations. Our analyses to this point suggested an alternative to functionalism as well as to many of the emerging modernist perspectives on relationships. Not only was evidence of functionality missing from

Case Study

CASE STUDY *continued*

Case Study

the modern honeymoon, but we found no evidence for the more authentic, less gendered experience that modernist theories would predict. The honeymoon had become more universal, less spontaneous, and more scripted, elaborate, and feminine as society had become more modern. These observations led us to the alternative perspective of "risk society" theory (Bulcroft et al., 1999). Accordingly, we interpreted these narrative changes as a cultural response to the increasing invasiveness of rationality into our most intimate relationships, a growing sense of risk as a result, and, paradoxically, a tendency in late modernity to manage risk through formal, if not substantive, rationality. The honeymoon had become a highly planned and elaborate ritual for managing individual and couple identities, assuring the couple of an authentic emotional experience without the risks of failure, validating each spouse's free choice of a partner, and providing a well-orchestrated reflected appraisal of the couple as successful.

To test this perspective at the level of lived realities, we undertook a study of newlyweds before and after their weddings and honeymoons. As expected, we found that expectations have become highly uniform and that they reflect the cultural narrative of the exotic. Although nearly all respondents expected to take honeymoons, few expressed any specific functional reasons for doing so. Most identified romance and passion as reasons and downplayed the importance of staging, recognition, and symbolism. Paradoxically, a vast majority expressed strong preferences for honeymoon resorts in exotic locales and were more disappointed if these expectations were not fulfilled, although most couples expressed satisfaction with the event regardless of their experiences. Finally, and most important from a risk society theoretical perspective, we found significant effects of perceived risks in

marriage on the importance of honeymoons, thematic accommodations, recognition as newlyweds, symbols of romance, and planning. Those respondents who perceived greater risks in marriage also expected more in the way of interpersonal adjustment and fantasy fulfillment outcomes on their honeymoons.

CONCLUSION: LESSONS ABOUT THEORY AND METHODS

What have we learned and where do we go from here? First, we learned that we have much to gain by exploring seemingly trivial aspects of everyday life. Second, we have come to appreciate the postmodern perspective of reflexivity as was evident in the role played by "experts" and "scientific" theory-building activities (especially functionalism and family development theory) in shaping the honeymoon narrative of the 1940s and 1950s. Third, we found added value in interdisciplinary collaboration. The concept of cultural narratives guided our coding of articles from the popular press, and spatial and visual cultural analyses helped us to understand how cultural narratives frame experiences and build personal biographies. Fourth, we came to understand the difficulties inherent in attempts to move from the macro to the micro. The idea that cultures develop in response to relationship conditions in a society to alleviate concern about those conditions makes it difficult to measure such conditions through individual questionnaires. Finally, we found a body of literature that contains a wealth of ideas for future research into both relationships and the life course (see this volume's companion Web site at http://www.ncfr.org/sourcebook). What began as a simple inquiry into a seemingly mundane everyday event has developed into a program of research into relationship formation patterns and life-course transitions in modern society.

COUPLES UNDER STRESS: STUDYING CHANGE IN DYADIC CLOSENESS AND DISTANCE

Yoav Lavee, *University of Haifa*

Over the past two decades, there has been a growing interest among family researchers concerning the effects of stress on marital relationships. This research has been guided, implicitly or explicitly, by family stress theory (Boss, 2002; Hill, 1949; McCubbin & Patterson, 1983), which posits that adaptation to a crisis in the family social system is dependent on the nature of the event and its hardships, the resources available to the family, and the perception of the situation.

As a focusing lens through which to study marriages under stress, family stress theory has a number of strengths: It is relatively simple, easy to operationalize and test, and is useful for explaining a wide range of situations affecting the family. It also offers a means of predicting when declines in marital satisfaction are likely to occur and is useful for explaining change in marital quality and stability over time (Karney & Bradbury, 1995). Although a number of other theoretical models have been developed that focus on marital relationships under stress (e.g., Bodenmann, 1997; Karney & Bradbury, 1995), family stress theory has continued to guide research on this topic.

Indeed, the majority of research has supported the assertion that stressful events have a deleterious effect on marital relationships. Scholars have found this to be the case with respect to a variety of sources of stress, both normative life transitions and nonnormative and catastrophic events. However, a number of studies have also shown that stressful experiences may actually strengthen marital relationships, resulting in increased cohesiveness and tighter couple bonds. Other studies have found even more complex patterns of change in marital relationships. For example, relationships may change in certain dimensions but not in others, or they may be negatively affected in some aspects and positively in others (Lavee & Mey-Dan, 2003). Indeed, Burr and Klein (1994), who studied family functioning and marital satisfaction along various stages of the coping process, conclude that "considerably more variation is seen in the way family systems respond to stress than is generally recognized in the stress literature" (p. 123).

Given the emphasis of family stress theory on marital *outcomes,* the theory's shortcoming lies in the lack of attention paid to systemic *processes* and interpersonal interactions that may explain different patterns of change. Therefore, a different approach is needed if we are to gain a better understanding of what transpires within couples and how intimate partners interact under stress. Examinations of short-term outcomes and changes in couple relationships under stress may shed light on these patterns and enhance theory building. The two studies reported below utilized different methodologies to investigate interactional processes among couples under stress.

STUDY I. CLOSENESS-DISTANCE IN THE DAILY LIVES OF COUPLES: A REPEATED TIME SAMPLING STUDY

A limitation of many studies that have dealt with the impact of stress on marital

CASE STUDY *continued*

relationships is that they have assessed the effects of a stressful event on the relationship *after* the event has occurred. Thus it is hard to assess *change* in a relationship associated with the event from the findings of such studies. One approach to achieving a better understanding of what transpires within couples in times of stress is to employ a short-term longitudinal design and a repeated time sampling method to examine the repeated sequences of the effects of stress on the couple relationships (Larson & Almeida, 1999). Such a method has been used for estimating the effects of daily stresses and strains on changes in dyadic closeness (Lavee & Gilat, 2000).

Daily reports were collected from a sample of 94 couples over a 7-day period. These reports included checklists of daily hassles, interpersonal conflicts, and positive and negative mood, and a measure of the sense of dyadic closeness. In addition, the couple's marital quality, as a relatively stable characteristic of the marital system, was measured before the couples began reporting on their daily experiences.

The data were analyzed using the hierarchical multivariate linear modeling approach (Raudenbush & Bryk, 2002), which is an application of hierarchical models with repeated observations nested within persons or couples (for a description of the analytic strategy, see Larson & Almeida, 1999).

Excluding the first day of reporting, analyses were based on 564 diary days. A *change model* was estimated, namely, the extent to which a change in dyadic closeness from the previous day, as reported by one spouse, is related to the level of stress reported by the other spouse. In addition, the moderating effect of marital quality was estimated to enable an examination of whether the association of daily stress and change in dyadic closeness is shaped by it.

The analysis showed that for both spouses, sense of closeness was negatively associated with the other spouse's stress: The more stress a person experienced in a certain day, the less closeness (or more distance) his or her spouse reported. This effect, however, was stronger for women than for men.

Marital quality had a significant main effect on the level of closeness: Couples who had high-quality relationships reported more closeness than did those in distressed marriages, regardless of the stress level. However, in both happy and distressed couples, more stressful days were associated with increased dyadic distance.

These findings may suggest that daily stress has a negative influence on relationships. However, greater distance may not necessarily be bad for a marriage. It might be that in some couples, one or both spouses use "relationship-focused coping" (Coyne & Smith, 1991), whereby when one spouse detects stress in the other, he or she avoids behaving in ways that might be burdensome and refrains from making demands on the stressed spouse's time and attention. This may depend on the partners' approach-avoidance strategies and the couple's pattern of distance regulation under stress (Kantor & Lehr, 1975).

STUDY II. MARITAL RELATIONSHIPS AMONG PARENTS OF CHILDREN WITH CANCER: A QUALITATIVE STUDY

A child's life-threatening illness is often characterized not only by its traumatic impact on the parents, but also by ups and downs in the child's condition, which are accompanied by rising and falling stress levels in the family. In a qualitative study of parents whose children had been diagnosed with cancer, in-depth interviews were conducted with 21 couples. A theme that ran through the interviews was that affective communication, supportive behaviors, and emotional closeness changed in times of heightened stress (such as immediately following the diagnosis, during signs

CASE STUDY *continued*

of relapse, and in times of physical deterioration) as well as in times of reduced stress (such as when the child's condition improved, when the child was released from the hospital, when medical treatment was terminated, or when lab tests showed promising results).

Two opposite patterns of relationship changes were observed in stressful times versus less stressful times: *Distancing couples* pulled away from each other when relapse occurred or the child's physical condition deteriorated. Under heightened stress, such couples exhibited escalating tension and a growing emotional and physical distance. However, some of these couples tended to draw closer together again when the child's health improved. In contrast, *bonding couples* felt closer to each other soon after diagnosis and whenever the child's medical condition deteriorated, demonstrating more intimate and supportive communication. Two other couple types did not experience significant changes in their relationships. *Distant couples* had little affective communication and mutual support before the child's illness and remained distant from each other in both "good" and difficult times, and *fluctuating couples* went through periods of closeness and distance that appeared to be unrelated to the child's condition.

The analyses further indicated that these patterns of dyadic closeness and distance were related to the parents' emotional and behavioral reactions in times of heightened stress, their level of comfort with and reactions to their spouse's behaviors, and their approach or avoidance strategies in support seeking and giving.

CONCLUSIONS AND IMPLICATIONS FOR RESEARCH AND THEORY

Although most research indicates that experiencing stress has a deleterious effect on marital quality, studies also show a more complex pattern of relationship change. As the two studies reported above demonstrate, time sampling methodologies may enhance our understanding of the repeated sequences of marital relationship change under stress, and qualitative research may shed light on other processes of dyadic interactions and relationship change.

Some important questions still await further research and theory building: What determines couples' interactions under stress? Under what circumstances do spouses get closer together or become more distant from each other? What accounts for "ups and downs" in a relationship at various points in the stress process? Do different sources of stress and/or stress levels elicit different behaviors and different patterns of couple interaction? Does culture shape the ways in which marital partners regulate distance in time of stress?

Research that focuses on the adaptive process and ways of interaction among couples under stress may enhance theory building and help to increase our understanding of the complex patterns of change in marital relationships.

Case Study

DISCUSSION AND EXTENSION

THEORIZING THE PARTICULARS OF MARRIAGE

Bert N. Adams, *University of Wisconsin–Madison*

In Chapter 11, Carroll, Knapp, and Holman say that marriage is important in the family field and that we need to theorize about it. "Theorizing (about marriage)," they state, "is crucial." Carroll et al. discuss the "received view" of sociological theorizing and "the good marriage." The former is scientific positivism; the latter is the satisfied and stable relationship.

The contributions that make up this *Sourcebook* (and Bengtson et al.'s introductory chapter in particular) attempt to make it clear that positivism in its original form should no longer be considered the "received view." Theorizing includes the standpoints of both qualitative research and feminism, and is much broader than positivism. Even when Carroll et al. discuss the limitations of this supposedly "received view," it is not obvious from their comments that these limitations should be blamed on positivism. The limitations, which include "lack of theorizing about data," "an atheoretical myth," and "empirical-descriptive work," are all related to the fact that findings are often reported without leading to an "improved theoretical understanding." This, however, is not necessarily the result of a positivist philosophy. In fact, case studies, subjective insights, historical studies, and so on may also be left at the descriptive level.

As for the satisfactory and stable marital relationship, there is much to discuss regarding whether this is the current expectation. Carroll et al. suggest that successful lifelong marriage is a highly valued goal for most people. However, recent writings and theorizing on marriage in Western capitalist societies show that economic individualism has made

it possible for individuals and couples to desire/pursue the happy marriage rather than the stable marriage.

Carroll et al. make it clear that they see a particular type of satisfactory, stable relationship as the marital goal. They distinguish distressed couples from nondistressed couples, with the former characterized by negative interactions and negative or poor communication. In fact, their discussion of communication skills shows that their primary focus is the interactional, middle-class marriage, not the parallel lower-class marriage. In the latter, the purposes of marriage are sex and child rearing, not communication and friendship (Kerckhoff, 1974).

Likewise, the discussion of marital communication in general in terms of problem solving and the handling of conflict ignores Cuber and Harroff's (1965) finding that an "adjusted" marriage may, in fact, be conflict habituated. In other words, adjusted marriages may be either weak or conflictual in their communication patterns. Increasing our understanding of such marriages will require a much broader approach to theorizing than Carroll et al. take in Chapter 11.

Over and over, Carroll et al. make it clear that we need to theorize about marriage. Near the end of the chapter they state that "marital scholars need to 'shift gears' by calling grounding assumptions into question and engaging in theoretical practices that can lead to real progress in our understanding of the dynamics of marital relations." I doubt that anyone would disagree with this broad statement. However, aside from communication skills and a mention of systems theory, they

DISCUSSION AND EXTENSION *continued*

do not make it clear what we need to theorize about regarding marriage. Thus, in the remainder of this commentary, I introduce some marital issues that need further theoretical consideration.

What is marriage? The issues of the definition and universality of marriage go back to Kathleen Gough's (1959) discussion of the Nayar. Cross-culturally, the issue of customary versus legal or government-sanctioned marriage has long been of interest. To this has been added the current topic of same-sex marriage. Then we have the irony of the disappearance of common-law marriage at a time when cohabitation is increasing—giving a new logic to the common-law principle. In other words, the theory of marriage itself is unfinished business.

His and hers. The nonadditive nature of marriage is an issue that is broader than the simple descriptive satisfaction level. Carroll et al. note that a feminist epistemology questions why women who do the majority of housework are still satisfied in their marriages. A Marxist might call this "false female consciousness." Thus the theory of marriage, gender, and division of labor is complex (see Sydie, 1987).

Marital power. Discussions of power in the family are confused both in their terminology and in their theory or explanation. Authority, influence, and decision making all contribute to the consideration of power. However, delegation is another issue that makes power more complex. If I delegate a task or decision because I don't want to be bothered with it, does that mean I have little or much power in that area? Obviously, I have power over who does it, but not over the outcome (Adams, 1995). Marital power and gender are, then, closely tied together empirically and theoretically.

Economics and marriage. Despite what W. J. Goode, H. Becker, and others have told us about the relations between the economy and marriage, changes in the economy continue to update the need for theory in this area. Rapid technological changes, which include both biotechnical developments and the increasingly "electronic cottage" (Toffler, 1980), leave us needing to develop more useful theory. And we still lack adequate theories of either consumerism or television and marriage.

Commuter marriages and LATs. The work of Jan Trost on marital relationships in which the couples are "living apart together" (LAT) has increased our cross-cultural understanding of such marriages. Coresidence can no longer be considered an essential characteristic of marriage. This, then, further complicates the first issue raised above—that is, What is marriage?

Marriage/divorce/happiness. Much value-laden ink has been spilled on the issue of whether divorce is a good or bad thing, a problem or a solution to a problem. Although no one has argued that divorce makes people happier, there is a still-open issue of whether divorce is better or worse than staying in a truly unhappy, conflict-filled marriage. And because of the ubiquity of value judgments, the development of theory concerning this issue has lagged.

These are enough points to raise in this commentary. This extension is meant to point out that it is insufficient simply to say, "We need to do more theorizing about marriage." Of course that is true. But there are many specific marital issues that deserve our theoretical attention, and they will require that we employ multiple philosophical perspectives and not presuppose a view of marriage as either stable or communication based.

Discussion and Extension

REFERENCES

Adams, B. N. (1995). *The family: A sociological interpretation*. Fort Worth, TX: Harcourt Brace Jovanovich.

Blaisure, K. R., & Allen, K. R. (1995). Feminists and the ideology and practice of marital equality. *Journal of Marriage and the Family, 57*, 5–19.

Bodenmann, G. (1997). Dyadic coping: A systemic-transactional view of stress and coping among couples: Theory and empirical findings. *European Review of Applied Psychology, 47*, 137–141.

Boss, P. (2002). *Family stress management: A contextual approach*. Thousand Oaks, CA: Sage.

Bradbury, T. N., Cohan, C. L., & Karney, B. R. (1998). Optimizing longitudinal research or understanding and preventing marital dysfunction. In T. N. Bradbury (Ed.), *The developmental course of marital dysfunction* (pp. 279–311). New York: Cambridge University Press.

Bradbury, T. N., Fincham, F. D., & Beach, S. R. H. (2000). Research on the nature and determinants of marital satisfaction: A decade in review. *Journal of Marriage and the Family, 62*, 964–980.

Browning, D. S. (2003). *Marriage and modernization*. Grand Rapids, MI: William B. Eerdmans.

Browning, D. S., Conture, P. D., Franklin, R. M., Lyon, K. B., & Miller-McLemore, B. J. (1997). *From culture wars to common ground: Religion and the family debate*. Louisville, KY: Westminster/John Knox.

Bulcroft, K., Bulcroft, R., Smeins, L., & Cranage, H. (1997). The social construction of the North American honeymoon, 1880–1995. *Journal of Family History, 22*, 462–490.

Bulcroft, K., Smeins, L., & Bulcroft, R. (1999). *Romancing the honeymoon: Consummating marriage in modern society*. Thousand Oaks, CA: Sage.

Bulcroft, R., Bulcroft, K., Bradley, K., & Simpson, C. (2000). The management and production of risk in romantic relationships: A postmodern paradox. *Journal of Family History, 25*, 63–92.

Burleson, B. B., & Denton, D. H. (1997). The relationship between communication skill and marital satisfaction: Some moderating effects. *Journal of Marriage and the Family, 59*, 884–902.

Burr, W. R., & Klein, S. R. (1994). *Reexamining family stress: New theory and research*. Thousand Oaks, CA: Sage.

Cere, D. (2000). *The expert's story of courtship*. New York: Institute for American Values.

Coyne, J. C., & Smith, D. A. (1991). Couples coping with a myocardial infarction: A contextual perspective on wives' distress. *Journal of Personality and Social Psychology, 61*, 404–412.

Cuber, J. F., & Harroff, P. B. (1965). *The significant Americans: A study of sexual behavior among the affluent*. New York: Appleton-Century-Crofts.

Cusinato, M., & L'Abate, L. (2003). The Dyadic Relationships Test: Creation and validation of a model-derived, visual-verbal instrument to evaluate couple relationships. *American Journal of Family Therapy, 31*, 79–89.

Doherty, W. J., & Carroll, J. S. (2002). Health and the ethics of marital therapy and education. In J. Wall, D. S. Browning, W. J. Doherty, & S. Post (Eds.), *Marriage, health, and the professions: If marriage is good for you what does this mean for law, medicine, ministry, therapy, business?* (pp. 208–232). Grand Rapids, MI: William B. Eerdmans.

Fay, B. (1996). *Contemporary philosophy of social science: A multicultural approach*. Oxford: Blackwell.

Fincham, F. D. (1998). Child development and marital relations. *Child Development, 69*, 543–574.

Fincham, F. D., & Beach, S. R. H. (1999). Conflict in marriage: Implications for working with couples. *Annual Review of Psychology, 50*, 47–77.

Fincham, F. D., Beach, S. R. H., & Kemp-Fincham, S. I. (1997). Marital quality: A new theoretical perspective. In R. J. Sternberg & M. Hojjat (Eds.), *Satisfaction in close relationships* (pp. 275–304). New York: Guilford.

Fincham, F. D., & Bradbury, T. N. (1987). The assessment of marital quality: A reevaluation. *Journal of Marriage and the Family, 49*, 797–809.

Fincham, F. D., & Linfield, K. J. (1997). A new look at marital quality: Can spouses feel positive and negative about their marriage? *Journal of Family Psychology, 11*, 489–502.

Fowers, B. J. (2000). *Beyond the myth of marital happiness.* San Francisco: Jossey-Bass.

Fox, G. L., & Murry, V. M. (2000). Gender and families: Feminist perspectives and family research. *Journal of Marriage and the Family, 62,* 1160–1172.

Gottman, J. M. (1982). Temporal form: Toward a new language for describing relationships. *Journal of Marriage and the Family, 44,* 943–961.

Gottman, J. M. (1999). *The marriage clinic: A scientifically based marital therapy.* New York: W. W. Norton.

Gottman, J. M., & Notarius, C. I. (2000). Decade review: Observing marital interaction. *Journal of Marriage and the Family, 62,* 927–947.

Gough, E. K. (1959). The Nayar and the definition of marriage. *Journal of the Royal Anthropological Institute, 89,* pt. 1.

Guba, E. G., & Lincoln, Y. S. (1994). Competing paradigms in qualitative research. In N. K. Denzin & Y. S. Lincoln (Eds.), *Handbook of qualitative research* (pp. 105–117). Thousand Oaks, CA: Sage.

Hechter, M. (1987). *Principles of group solidarity.* Berkeley: University of California Press.

Hill, R. (1949). *Families under stress.* New York: Harper.

Holman, T. B. (2001). *Premarital prediction of marital quality or breakup: Research, theory, and practice.* New York: Kluwer Academic/ Plenum.

Homans, G. (1970). The relevance of psychology to the explanation of social phenomena. In R. Borger & F. Cioffi (Eds.), *Explanation in the behavioural sciences* (pp. 313–329). Cambridge: Cambridge University Press.

Kantor, D., & Lehr, W. (1975). *Inside the family: Toward a theory of family process.* San Francisco: Jossey-Bass.

Karney, B. R., & Bradbury, T. N. (1995). The longitudinal course of marital quality and stability: A review of theory, method, and research. *Psychological Bulletin, 118,* 3–34.

Kerckhoff, A. (1974). The social context of interpersonal attraction. In T. L. Huston (Ed.), *Foundations of interpersonal attraction.* New York: Academic Press.

Kluwer, E. S. (2000). Marital quality. In R. M. Milardo & S. Duck (Eds.), *Families as relationships* (pp. 59–78). New York: John Wiley.

Knapp, S. J. (2002). Authorizing family science: An analysis of the objectifying practices of family science discourse. *Journal of Marriage and Family, 64,* 1038–1048.

L'Abate, L. (1986). *Systematic family therapy.* New York: Brunner/Mazel.

L'Abate, L. (2003). *Family psychology III: Theory-building, theory-testing and psychological interventions.* Lanham, MD: University Press of America.

L'Abate, L. (in press). *Personality in intimate relationships: Socialization and psychopathology.* New York: Kluwer Academic.

L'Abate, L., & De Giacomo, P. (2003). *Intimate relationships and how to improve them: Integration of theoretical models with prevention and psychotherapy interventions.* Westport, CT: Praeger.

Larson, R. W., & Almeida, D. M. (1999). Emotional transmission in the daily lives of families: A new paradigm for studying family process. *Journal of Marriage and the Family, 61,* 5–20.

Lavee, Y., & Gilat, A. (2000, November). *Distance regulation in couples under daily stresses and strains.* Paper presented at the 62nd Annual Meeting of the National Council on Family Relations, Minneapolis.

Lavee, Y., & Mey-Dan, M. (2003). Patterns of change in marital relationships among parents of children with cancer. *Health and Social Work, 28,* 255–263.

Lincoln, Y. S., & Guba, E. G. (2000). Paradigmatic controversies, contradictions, and emerging confluences. In N. K. Denzin & Y. S. Lincoln (Eds.), *Handbook of qualitative research* (2nd ed., pp. 163–188). Thousand Oaks, CA: Sage.

Loveless, A. S. (2000). *Paired conceptions of morality and happiness as factors in marital happiness.* Unpublished doctoral dissertation, Brigham Young University, Provo, UT.

Markman, H. J., Notarius, C. I., Stephen, Y., & Smith, T. (1981). Behavioral observation systems for couples: The current status. In E. E. Filsinger & R. A. Lewis (Eds.), *Assessing marriage: New behavioral approaches* (pp. 234–262). Beverly Hills, CA: Sage.

McCubbin, H. I., & Patterson, J. M. (1983). The family stress process: The double ABCX model of adjustment and adaptation. In H. I. McCubbin, M. B. Sussman, & J. M. Patterson (Eds.), *Social stress and the family: Advances and developments in family stress theory and research* (pp. 7–37). New York: Haworth.

Peggs, K., & Lampard, R. (2000). (Ir)rational choice: A multidimensional approach to choice and constraint in decisions about marriage, divorce and remarriage. In M. S. Archer & J. Q. Tritter (Eds.), *Rational choice theory: A critique* (pp. 93–110). New York: Routledge.

Procter, I. (2000). "I do": A theoretical critique of Becker's rational choice approach to marriage decisions. In M. S. Archer & J. Q. Tritter (Eds.), *Rational choice theory: A critique* (pp. 147–166). New York: Routledge.

Raudenbush, S. W., & Bryk, A. S. (2002). *Hierarchical linear models: Applications and data analysis methods* (2nd ed.). Thousand Oaks, CA: Sage.

Regan, M. C., Jr. (1993). *Family law and the pursuit of intimacy.* New York: New York University Press.

Rigney, D. (2001). *The metaphorical society: An invitation to social theory.* New York: Rowman & Littlefield.

Root, M. (1993). *Philosophy of social science: The methods, ideals, and politics of social inquiry.* Oxford: Blackwell.

Slife, B. D., & Williams, R. N. (1995). *What's behind the research: Discovering hidden assumptions in the behavioral sciences.* Thousand Oaks, CA: Sage.

Stanley, S. (1998). *The heart of commitment.* Nashville, TN: Nelson.

Sydie, R. A. (1987). *Natural women, cultured men: A feminist perspective on sociological theory.* Toronto: Methuen.

Thibaut, J. W., & Kelley, H. H. (1959). *The social psychology of groups.* New York: John Wiley.

Thomas, D. L., & Wilcox, J. E. (1987). The rise of family theory: A historical and critical analysis. In M. B. Sussman & S. K. Steinmetz (Eds.), *Handbook of marriage and the family* (pp. 81–102). New York: Plenum.

Thompson, L. (1993). Conceptualizing gender in marriage: The case of marital care. *Journal of Marriage and the Family, 55,* 557–569.

Toffler, A. (1980). *The third wave.* New York: William Morrow.

Udehn, L. (2002). The changing face of methodological individualism. *Annual Review of Sociology, 28,* 479–507.

Watzlawick, P., Weakland, J. H., & Fisch, R. (1974). *Change: Principles of problem formation and problem resolution.* New York: W. W. Norton.

White, J. M., & Klein, D. M. (2002). *Family theories* (2nd ed.). Thousand Oaks, CA: Sage.

Wood, J. T. (1995). Feminist scholarship and the study of relationships. *Journal of Social and Personal Relationships, 12,* 103–120.

• Twelve

ANALYZING COUPLES AND FAMILIES

Multilevel Methods

Aline G. Sayer, *Harvard University*

Mary Maguire Klute, *University of Colorado*

Family theories are often focused on explicating the complexities of family life, including how individuals interact in dyadic relationships and family groups and how these individuals, relationships, and families are affected by the contexts in which they exist. Until recently, researchers had few statistical tools that would enable them to test such questions directly. With the advent of multilevel models in education, sociology, and psychology, however, interest in applying such models to questions posed by family and relationship theory has grown. Both the *Journal of Marriage and Family* (May 2002) and *Personal Relationships* (December 1999) have devoted special issues to this methodology (for a didactic approach, see Campbell & Kashy, 2002). In this chapter we continue the discussion of multilevel methods, with particular emphasis on models for dyadic data.

Many research questions that are of interest to family scholars are multilevel in nature because family scholars often collect data at more than one unit of analysis. For example, it is not uncommon for family researchers to be interested in *individuals'* own characteristics (e.g., depression, personality) as well as their views of their relationships (e.g., how much they love their partners, how satisfied they are with their marriages). Family researchers also recognize that individuals are part of many *relationships* and are interested in properties of those relationships (e.g., sibling similarity; see Tolson & Urberg, 1993). In addition, family researchers are often interested in the *contexts* in which individuals, dyadic relationships, and families exist (e.g., rates of poverty in neighborhoods,

Authors' Note: We gratefully acknowledge Alan Acock and an anonymous reviewer for their comments on an earlier draft of this chapter. Support to Dr. Klute was provided by an institutional postdoctoral research training grant from the National Institute of Mental Health (5 T32 MH15442).

availability of community resources). All of these examples—individuals, relationships, and contexts—represent different levels of analysis. Family theories often suggest research questions that cut across these levels; for example, Butler (2002) studied the effects of state welfare policies on childbearing decisions. Multilevel models are isomorphic with these theories because they are able to model such cross-level interactions directly.

EXAMPLES OF MULTILEVEL RESEARCH QUESTIONS

The study of relationships has long been a focus of family research. This includes the study of married couples (Klute, Crouter, Sayer, & McHale, 2002), of parent-child dyads (Ceballo, Dahl, Aretakis, & Ramirez, 2001), of caregiver–care recipient dyads (Lyons, Zarit, Sayer, & Whitlatch, 2002), and of siblings (Crouter, Helms-Erikson, Updegraff, & McHale, 1999). The study of relationships is multilevel because individuals (e.g., husbands and wives) are nested in relationships (e.g., marriages), and researchers might be interested in answering questions at both the individual level and the couple level of analysis. That is, researchers might be interested in both properties of the individuals, such as self-disclosure, and properties of the relationships, such as conflict.

Thompson and Walker (1982) explain the importance of being clear about the unit of analysis at all stages of the research process, starting with how the research question is framed. Researchers can study individual-level properties such as love and commitment at the individual level or at the dyad level. An example of an individual-level question is, Are individuals who feel more love for their partners also more committed to their relationships? In contrast, a dyad-level question might be, Are couples who are more in love less likely to divorce? Even when researchers collect data on individual properties, they can use the data to address dyadic research questions.

An interest in studying development in context (Bronfenbrenner, 1979) has fueled another area of research in family studies that is multilevel in nature: the study of community or neighborhood effects on individual or family outcomes. This approach recognizes that families and individuals are nested in communities. Researchers might ask questions about how characteristics of a neighborhood, such as the sex ratio, affect the propensity of individuals to marry early (Teachman & Crowder, 2002) or how communitywide parental monitoring might shape the development of adolescents in that community (Cook, Shagle, & Degirmencioglu, 1997). In these cases, researchers typically collect data at the level of individuals and families through self-reports as well as at the level of the neighborhood, often through census information. (An analysis of multilevel questions of this type is beyond the scope of this chapter, but for good examples see Teachman & Crowder, 2002; see also the Spotlight on Theory in this chapter by Mancini, Bowen, and Martin.)

THE STUDY OF DYADS

In the remainder of this chapter we focus on one multilevel data situation that family researchers commonly face: the study of dyads, when two individuals are nested in a relationship. All of the approaches we discuss are useful for the specific but quite common situation in which researchers have "relational data" (Fisher, Kokes, Ransom, Phillips, & Rudd, 1985). Data are defined as relational when the same information is collected from both members of the dyad, reporting either on their own individual perceptions (e.g., psychological well-being) or on properties of their relationship (e.g., quality of the marital relationship).

All of the methods we describe below are also appropriate for situations in which dyad members are distinguishable. Gonzalez and Griffin (1997) draw the following distinction between distinguishable dyads and exchangeable dyads. *Distinguishable dyads* are those in which dyad members can be differentiated on the basis of some naturally occurring distinction, such as gender, age, or family role status. Some examples of distinguishable dyads are husbands and wives (distinguished by gender), older and younger siblings (distinguished by age), and mothers and children (distinguished by role status). *Exchangeable dyads* are those in which the members cannot be differentiated by some naturally occurring distinction; these include homosexual couples, same-sex friends, and identical twins. The analytic methods we consider in this chapter are not appropriate for use with data on exchangeable dyads. We suggest that readers who are interested in studying correlational methods appropriate for such data see Griffin and Gonzalez (1995).

CHARACTERISTICS OF MULTILEVEL DATA

Multilevel data share common characteristics that can complicate data analysis efforts. First, variables of interest may be measured at different levels of analysis. For example, some variables of interest, such as marital satisfaction and depression, might be measured at the individual level, whereas other variables, such as reciprocity and cohesion, might be measured at the dyad level. The research question may be asked at one level (e.g., a dyad-level research question), but the data may be collected at a different level (e.g., the individual level). This is often the case with relational data. One may be interested in characterizing a dyad based on individual dyad members' responses, such as characterizing a marital dyad based on the husband's and wife's responses to a marital satisfaction questionnaire. All of the methods presented in this chapter are suitable for addressing this challenge.

• SPOTLIGHT ON THEORY

PERSONALITY AND FAMILY PROCESS

James E. Deal, *North Dakota State University*

Charles F. Halverson, Jr., *University of Georgia*

Valerie Havill, *University of Georgia*

As Sayer and Klute note, an alternative way to conceptualize "multilevel" in regard to family scholarship is to view individuals as nested in relationships, which are nested in communities. When scholars conceptualize multilevel research in this manner, it is important that they include personality among the individual-level variables being studied.

In the past 20 years, the multiple models and disagreements on basic issues that characterized personality psychology prior to the 1990s have been reconciled, and researchers have come to a general acceptance of a model that formulates five major facets of adult personality: neuroticism, extraversion, openness, agreeableness, and

(continued)

conscientiousness (McCrae & Costa, 1996). The arrival of researchers from very different backgrounds at the same point has resulted in a great deal of unification in the personality field, allowing for a more concentrated focus, narrowing the "target" of personality considerably and making an examination of the relation between personality and family process much more accessible than in the past.

Such an examination will help to fill in an important empty cell in the literature. Whereas the literature on romantic, dyadic relationships has benefited from the inclusion of both personality and interpersonal variables, the focus in the family process literature has been almost entirely interpersonal, a result, perhaps, of the strong systemic focus in the field. As a result, the literature on marital process, strongly influenced by a variety of social psychological theories, has grown in ways that the family process literature has not. As Bradbury, Campbell, and Fincham (1995) have pointed out, the marital literature has demonstrated that incomplete models—that is, either intrapersonal or interpersonal, but not both—provide incomplete explanations of relationship processes. The incomplete models in the family process literature would be expected to yield incomplete explanations as well.

Hoyle's (2000) work on the relation between personality and problem behaviors can be an important guide to the integration of personality into family process. Hoyle has noted that much of the literature in that area has been foundational, focusing on establishing a relationship between personality and problem behaviors. It is essential, however, that researchers move beyond this foundational research to examine process—that they move from asking whether two variables are related to asking how and under what conditions they are related. Specifically, Hoyle proposes that researchers look for moderators, variables that interact with personality to affect outcome measures, as well as for mediators, third variables to which the relationship between personality and outcome can be at least partially attributed.

If we apply Hoyle's model to the study of personality factors and family process, we can see that the foundational research is still largely lacking. There is still a need for scholars to examine how personality relates to various aspects and measures of family process—global and specific; attitudinal, cognitive, and behavioral; self-report, other report, and observational. The exact nature of the relationship between these two sets of variables remains unclear. Once this relationship is clarified, scholars can focus on understanding its nature and the moderating and mediating relationships that Hoyle discusses. It is important that researchers identify variables that interact with personality to influence family process as well as variables that mediate the relationship between personality and family process. They can use multilevel analyses of the type that Sayer and Klute demonstrate, for example, to explore situations in which the relationship between personality and family process varies according to the level of a third variable. Clearly, no family researchers have yet examined questions of this type, leaving a host of uninvestigated variables at a variety of levels that may work with personality to affect the quality of family relationships. ●

● *SPOTLIGHT ON THEORY*

FAMILIES IN COMMUNITY CONTEXTS

Jay A. Mancini, *Virginia Polytechnic Institute and State University*

Gary L. Bowen, *University of North Carolina at Chapel Hill*

James A. Martin, *Bryn Mawr College*

C ommunity context factors, including families' transactions with other families and with institutions, are significant elements in understanding family life. Families are surrounded by community forces that influence both their everyday life experiences and their individual and collective life trajectories. We believe that community context should have a more prominent place in thinking about families. We also believe that greater elaboration is needed in the conceptualization, measurement, and use of community-level variables when researchers study families and family outcomes. In this brief contribution we extend Sayer and Klute's discussion of multilevel methods to include a broader community focus, which we believe will expand family researchers' abilities to understand important influences on family life.

Many researchers attempt to capture complex community-level processes by using variables that assess various dimensions of the community's social and demographic infrastructure—an approach strong on predictive validity but weak on explanatory potential. These community-level markers (e.g., poverty rate) typically are entered into analyses as a summary index. Although the use of such structural variables may uncover contextual noise, the variables' influence on dependent outcomes often is indirect. In this approach, processes that reflect contexts are left unexamined, and the meanings that researchers attach to contextual effects are addressed largely through conjecture rather than through examination. Investigators are left searching for the process mechanisms that link community structure with outcomes.

Social organization is an instructive concept that identifies and conceptualizes these group effects at the community level. Social organization is how people in a community interrelate, cooperate, and provide mutual support; it includes social support norms, social controls that regulate behavior and interaction patterns, and the networks that operate in a community (Mancini, Martin, & Bowen, 2003). Individual family members and families as collective entities both influence and are influenced by these social organizational processes.

The concept of social organization provides an umbrella for conceptualizing specific group effects that reflect complex community context. *Community capacity* is one group effect that comprises and surrounds families (Bowen, Martin, Mancini, & Nelson, 2000). Two elements of community capacity are a sense of shared responsibility between community members and the collective competence that enables communities to

(continued)

● **SPOTLIGHT ON THEORY** continued

meet important goals and challenges. Community capacity emerges from formal and informal networks that build reciprocity and trust and is linked with the achievement of desired community and family results.

Community capacity as an aspect of social organization reveals the process of community influence on families along these dimensions: how families interact with informal networks of friends, neighbors, and associates; how families interact with formal networks of agencies, organizations, and civic groups; and how the interplay of formal and informal networks shapes family life. Research taking this perspective can also identify actions (reciprocity) and sentiments (trust) resulting from families' network involvement. Reciprocity and trust lead toward the action (collective competence) and sentiment (sense of shared responsibility) dimensions of community capacity. Community capacity positions individuals and families to achieve important results for themselves and for their communities.

The findings from Teachman and Crowder's (2002) recent review of multilevel models in family research support the argument that scholars' central aim should be to exploit rather than simply try to control contextual noise in family functioning models. Sprey (2000) also discusses the examination of macrovariables in family studies, noting that layered approaches to human sociability enable a level of understanding that is otherwise unattainable. Ideally, social organization concepts such as community capacity will enhance the breadth and depth of studies of families in context and will allow family scientists to incorporate dynamic measures of community contexts into their models. ●

Second, when one has multilevel data, observations from individuals within the same group are most likely nonindependent. For example, one would expect that responses from married men and women would not be independent because people tend to marry people who are similar to themselves, because the spouses are likely influenced by similar contextual factors, and because the spouses likely influence one another directly (Kenny, Mannetti, Pierro, Livi, & Kashy, 2002). When data are nonindependent, one has less unique information than the total sample size would suggest. When two scores in the sample are compared, they are more likely to be similar if they have been obtained from two members of the same couple than if they have been obtained from a husband chosen at random from one couple and a wife from another.

Independence of observations is an assumption of most traditional statistical techniques, including correlation, ANOVA, and regression. If one were to ignore the nested structure of the data (e.g., treat a sample of 200 married couples as 400 individuals), the violation of the assumption of independence of observations would not distort the point estimates of the magnitude of the relationships between variables (e.g., as captured by beta coefficients in regression). However, the violation of this assumption would lead to bias in the estimates of the error variance, which would in turn distort the estimates of standard errors, p values, confidence intervals, and effect sizes (Kenny et al., 2002). In situations where dependencies exist, it is critical to use analytic methods such as those described in this chapter that estimate (and control for) the degree of shared variance. It is important for family researchers to be cognizant of the ways in which the data they collect may not be independent and of the dangers of ignoring this nonindependence.

Third, dependence between dyad members is not just a statistical nuisance to be circumvented in family research; rather, it is often considered an important part of the phenomenon under study. The forces behind this dependence (e.g., assortative mating, the effect of a shared context on individuals, the processes whereby spouses influence one another's cognitions, attitudes, and behaviors; Kenny et al., 2002) are the focus of interest in family research and should be modeled explicitly.

TRADITIONAL APPROACHES TO STUDYING DYADS

Before we discuss the application of multilevel modeling to the analysis of dyadic data, we review below "traditional" methods that treat the dyad as the unit of analysis. Each of these methods has its drawbacks, many of which are addressed by the use of multilevel modeling. One class of methods includes measurement approaches that focus on the creation of measures of dyadic properties from individual-level data. The researcher then uses these new measures as outcome or predictor variables in subsequent analyses employing traditional analytic techniques. We also discuss below an analytic approach to treating the dyad as the unit of analysis, a special case of repeated measures ANOVA (RMANOVA).

Measurement Approaches

A researcher uses a measurement approach to construct an observed measure of the dyad from data collected from or about each dyad member. The most common measurement approaches include the creation of the following for each dyad: mean scores, difference scores, ratio scores, grouping variables, and intraclass correlations. These approaches are attractive because these new measures are relatively easy to compute and the researcher can use them as independent or dependent variables in subsequent analyses. The researcher does not need special software because standard statistical techniques (e.g., ANOVA, regression, correlation) are appropriate for

use with such approaches. However, each approach has important limitations.

Mean scores or sum scores are useful when the researcher is interested in the overall dyad level on a variable of interest. However, averages or sums are meaningful only when the scores for both dyad members are similar. If one member of a couple reports a very low level of marital conflict and the other member reports a very high level, for example, the mean would assign this couple a midrange value, which would have limited value as a summary of this couple's scores.

Difference scores correct the problem of discrepancy and are useful when the researcher is interested in the lack of consensus within the dyad but does not care about the location of dyads on the response scale. Difference scores, like mean or sum scores, are a simple linear combination of the two dyad members' raw scores, so it is not possible to use both the difference score and the two dyad members' raw scores in a multivariate linear model (for a more complete discussion of difference scores, see Griffin, Murray, & Gonzalez, 1999).

Ratio scores are most useful when the researcher is dealing with variables that have a true zero point, such as income. As is the case with difference scores, a ratio score provides no information about the location of dyads on the scale. For instance, a wealthy couple in which the wife does not work will receive the same ratio score (i.e., 0%) as a very poor couple in which the wife does not earn any income.

Another measurement approach involves classifying dyads into groups based on the relations between dyad members' scores. The researcher can achieve the groupings in several ways, including by constructing high/low groups through median splits or by employing a cluster analysis routine. The researcher can construct groups by dichotomizing the distribution of scores into high- and low-scoring groups for each dyad member. The researcher then cross-classifies the two dichotomies to create two similarity groups (both members have high values or both members have low values on the variable of interest) and two discrepancy groups (members have opposite scores). This approach is useful when the researcher is interested in both the difference between dyad members and the overall dyad level. However, this approach has all the problems associated with median splits: Variance is lost when continuous variables are dichotomized, and if the distribution of scores is skewed, the groups may not be meaningful.

Another approach to the categorization of dyads is cluster analysis (Everitt, 1993). Using this method, the researcher classifies dyads into groups based on the results of a cluster analysis of the variables of interest. This approach is useful when the researcher is interested in the pattern of dyad members' scores on more than one variable. For example, Aquilino (1999) conducted a cluster analysis using parent and child reports of parent-child closeness, contact, control, and conflict. It is also useful when the researcher is interested in both the difference between dyad members' scores and the overall level of the dyad members on the variables of interest. One important limitation of cluster analysis is that it will provide a solution even when it is applied to random data. It is important that the researcher take steps to assess the quality of the cluster solution and to determine whether the clusters that emerge are conceptually meaningful or interesting (for a discussion of the limitations of cluster analysis, see Haslam, 1999).

Maguire (1999) describes a method for using intraclass correlations (ICCs) as a measure of dyad similarity whereby several individual items from a scale are used to compute an ICC for each dyad. Unlike conventional uses of correlation, where variables are correlated across people, with this method dyad members are correlated across items. The researcher uses the ICC instead of a Pearson product-moment correlation because it is more suited to describing similarity. It can be thought of as a measure of the extent that scores on two variables fail to agree.

ICCs are useful when the researcher is interested in the degree of similarity of dyad members on a construct with multiple items. They provide no information about the direction of difference between dyad members. ICCs also provide no information about the

overall dyad level on the variable of interest. However, unlike difference scores, the ICC is not a simple linear combination of the two dyad members' scores. This feature of the ICC allows the researcher to use dyad members' individual scores in multivariate models along with the ICC.

Traditional Analytic Approach: Repeated Measures Analysis of Variance

Data example. In this section, we use data from the Early Intervention Collaborative Study (EICS) to illustrate a traditional analytic strategy that is sensitive to the multilevel nature of the data. EICS is a longitudinal investigation of the development of young children with disabilities and the adaptive capacities of their families (Hauser-Cram et al., 2001; Shonkoff, Hauser-Cram, Krauss, & Upshur, 1992). Families of children with Down syndrome, motor impairments, and developmental delays were recruited for the study at the time of the children's enrollment in early intervention programs in Massachusetts and New Hampshire. The data we use for this illustration are drawn from home interviews conducted when each target child was 5 years of age. The sample consists of 51 two-earner, married couples, each of which has a child with one type of disability. These data, which have been analyzed extensively (Warfield, in press), are available on this volume's companion Web site (http://www.ncfr.org/sourcebook).

Although many constructs were assessed during the interviews, we focus here on the relationship between parenting role stress for husbands and wives and child demands. Parenting role stress was assessed through the use of the Parent Domain Subscale of the Parenting Stress Index (PSI) (Abidin, 1995), which consists of 54 items with primarily Likert scale responses and includes statements regarding the respondent's reactions to the parenting role (e.g., "I feel trapped by my responsibilities as a parent") and feelings of parental competence (e.g., "I feel capable and on top of things when I am parenting my child"). Mothers and fathers completed the PSI separately. The Cronbach's alpha reliability coefficient was .94 for mothers and .92 for fathers. We refer to this variable as *stress*.

Child demands include characteristics of the child with disabilities that are likely to make the parenting role more challenging. Children with disabilities who have fewer cognitive skills and more behavior problems place more demands on their parents because they need more assistance in performing everyday tasks. Cognitive skills were assessed through the use of the McCarthy Scales of Children's Abilities (McCarthy, 1972), and the Child Behavior Checklist (CBCL) for ages 2–3 (Achenbach & Edelbrock, 1983) was used to assess behavior problems. As cognitive skills and behavior problems were moderately inversely correlated ($r = -.42$), a composite variable was created as follows: The cognitive skills distribution was multiplied by -1, each variable was transformed into a z score, and the two variables were summed. Thus higher scores on the composite variable indicate a more challenging child in terms of demands. We refer to this variable as *demand*.

Table 12.1 presents the descriptive statistics for the key variables in this example. Pooling across dyad members, we note that parenting stress scores range from 68 to 208. The demand composite is a standardized variable with a distribution that ranges from -4 to 3, with a mean of approximately zero. The repeated factor *spouse* is a dichotomous variable that distinguishes the dyad members. It is effects coded $-.5$ for husbands and $+.5$ for wives.

RMANOVA. This analytic approach involves conducting a repeated measures ANOVA in which the dyad member is the repeated factor. The analysis models the mean difference in the outcome between dyad members for the sample as a whole and for subgroups that are defined by the categorical independent variable(s). This approach is useful when the researcher is interested in predicting both the overall dyad level and the similarity between dyad members (e.g., Crouter & Manke, 1997; Gottman & Levinson, 1992).

There are two components to the RMANOVA model: a within-subjects component and a between-subjects component. The within-subjects part of the model is concerned with mean differences for dyad members in the values of the dependent variable for the sample as a whole and for subgroups. The between-subjects portion of the model pools across the repeated measure (e.g., spouse) to estimate mean subgroup differences.

Table 12.2 presents the data record for the first 10 couples. Each line of data represents the record for a single dyad and has four variables: couple identification, husband's report of parenting role stress, wife's report of parenting role stress, and a dichotomous variable that takes on the value of 1 if the couple has a demanding child (created using a median split of the distribution of demand scores). We note that for dyads 202 and 301, the husband did not contribute a stress score.

In this model, the demanding child indicator is the independent variable, and the husbands' and wives' reports of parenting role stress are the dependent variables. Spouse is the repeated factor. The results of the analysis are presented in Table 12.3.

Three specific research questions can be addressed with this model: (a) Is the presence of a demanding child associated with *couples'* parenting role stress? (b) Is there a difference in husbands' and wives' parenting role stress regardless of the presence of a demanding

Table 12.1   Descriptive Statistics for Variables in Example ($n = 51$ dyads)

Variable Name	Mean	SD	Minimum	Maximum
Spouse	0.00	0.50	−0.50	0.50
Stress	119.05	23.64	68.00	208.00
Demand	−0.04	1.65	−4.29	3.07

Table 12.2   Data Records for First 10 Couples in Repeated Measures ANOVA Example

Couple ID	Husband's Parenting Role Stress	Wife's Parenting Role Stress	Demanding Child (1 = have demanding child)
102	111	86	0
109	179	140	1
202	.	135	1
205	110	109.69	0
208	142	146	1
210	115	105	1
211	97	135	0
213	79	77	0
301	.	133	1
306	79	119	0

Table 12.3   Results for Repeated Measures ANOVA Example

Source	df	SS	F	p
Between subjects				
Demanding child	1	7861.16	14.67	.000
Error	43	23036.38		
Within subjects				
Spouse	1	476.81	1.80	.186
Spouse × Demanding Child	1	427.56	1.62	.210
Error	43	11369.43		

child? and (c) Does the difference between husbands' and wives' parenting role stress vary as function of whether or not they have a demanding child? The first question is addressed by the main effect for demanding child. This effect is a test of whether there is a difference in the means between the two groups (those with demanding children versus those without demanding children) pooling across husbands and wives. The F statistic is significantly different from zero (see Table 12.3), indicating that couples who have a demanding child reported higher levels of parenting role stress than did those who do not have a demanding child (see Figure 12.1).

The second question—Is there a difference in husbands' and wives' parenting role stress regardless of the presence of a demanding child?—is addressed by the main effect for spouse. This effect is the test of the average degree of husband-wife difference in the sample as a whole, pooling across the demanding child groups. Inspection of Table 12.3 reveals that the F statistic associated with this effect was not significant at conventional alpha levels, suggesting that husbands and wives reported similar levels of parenting role stress (see Figure 12.2).

The third question—Does the difference between husbands' and wives' parenting role stress vary as function of whether or not they have a demanding child?—is addressed by the Spouse × Demand interaction. This effect was also not significant (see Table 12.3). As Figure 12.3 shows, the magnitude of the difference between husbands' and wives' reports of parenting role stress was similar in both demanding child groups.

Figure 12.1 Repeated Measures ANOVA: Mean Scores for Couples With and Without a Demanding Child, Pooling Across Husbands and Wives (main effect for demanding child)

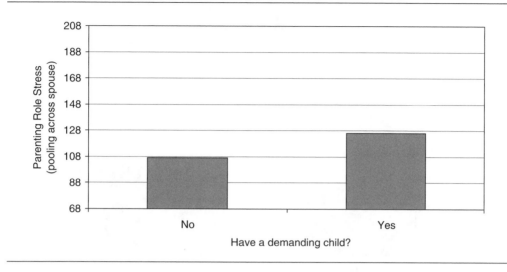

Figure 12.2 Repeated Measures ANOVA: Mean Scores for Husbands and Wives, Pooling Across Demanding Child Groups (main effect for spouse)

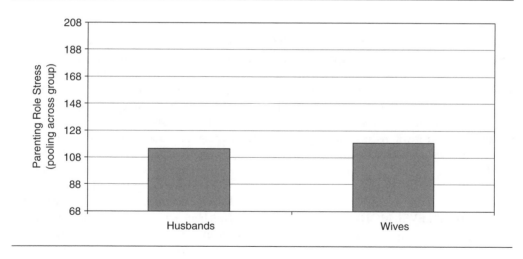

Limitations. The above example illustrates how RMANOVA is useful for addressing several questions of interest to family researchers. However, this approach also has several limitations. First, the researcher is restricted to looking at variation between subgroups as defined by the levels of the categorical predictors in the analysis (e.g., demand subgroups). Within each subgroup, the deviation of any couple from the subgroup mean is treated as error rather than as a source of interesting within-group heterogeneity. Second, RMANOVA requires balanced data. Any dyads with missing data on the outcome variable are omitted

Figure 12.3   Repeated Measures ANOVA: Mean Scores for Husbands and Wives, With and Without a Demanding Child (Spouse × Demand interaction)

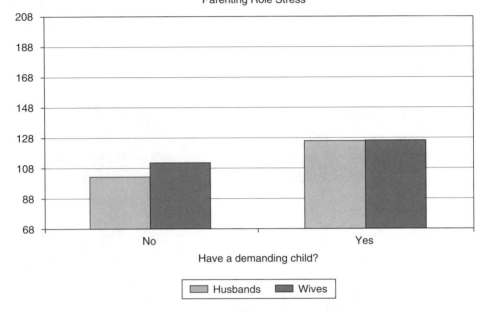

from the analysis. In our example, 2 out of the first 10 cases shown in Table 12.2 had missing data and were therefore omitted from the analysis. Finally, this is an analysis of scores unadjusted for the presence of measurement error: to the extent that the scores are fallible, measurement error will reduce the magnitude of the estimates of the true relations between variables.

USING MULTILEVEL MODELS TO ANALYZE DYADIC DATA

Hierarchical linear modeling (HLM; Raudenbush & Bryk, 2002)—also called mixed linear modeling, multilevel modeling, random coefficient modeling, and variance components modeling—is widely used in educational, social, and health research to study clustered data. Classic examples of clustered data structures include students nested in classrooms (Lee, Loeb, & Lubeck, 1998), patients nested

in therapy groups (Svartberg, Seltzer, Stiles, & Khoo, 1995), and adolescents nested in neighborhoods (Hoffman, 2002). A familiar application of HLM involves formulating a level 1 regression model to account for variation among individuals within each cluster (e.g., a neighborhood). This model is fit to each neighborhood separately, and the coefficients of each neighborhood's regression equation are then allowed to vary randomly over clusters (i.e., take on different values in each neighborhood). Then a level 2 model is formulated to explain variation in these coefficients as a function of neighborhood characteristics. The level 1 and level 2 models are fit to data simultaneously, and the parameters are estimated through maximum-likelihood procedures.

Although the dyad is clearly an example of a clustered (or hierarchical) data structure, the family research community has been slow to utilize multilevel models to address important questions about within- and between dyad variation. The key to understanding the multilevel application to dyads is to view the measurement of latent variables as a special case of clustered data. That is, one must view the responses of each dyad member on some outcome measure as nested within the dyad. Therefore, a level 1 regression equation within each dyad specifies the association between each response contributed by a dyad member and a variable indicating which member contributed the response. The parameters of this level 1 model are regression coefficients that vary randomly (take on different values) across dyads. These coefficients can be viewed as latent variables. It is straightforward then to estimate the variance of each latent variable, the correlation between the variables, and the association of each of the latent variables with selected predictors. Below, we illustrate this approach using two different parameterizations of the basic hierarchical linear model: a univariate formulation that can be compared to the traditional approaches described above and a multivariate formulation that can be contrasted with an analytic approach that splits the sample in half by dyad membership and estimates separate regression equations for each sample.

Advantages of HLM

HLM has several advantages over traditional analytic approaches such as RMANOVA. First, it permits unbalanced data, whereby the number of responses can vary across dyads. All couples can be included in the analysis, even in cases where either the wife or the husband does not supply information on the outcome variable. Recall that two dyads with missing responses for husbands were dropped from the RMANOVA analyses in the example above even though the wife's responses were present. HLM capitalizes on all data available to increase the statistical precision of the estimation of the level 1 regression coefficients. The assumption is that the data are missing at random (Schafer, 1997). This means that it is necessary to have other predictors available that are related to the probability of an individual's missing an observation—that is,

predictors that can explain the missingness. Most researchers will have collected other information about the individuals that they can include in explanatory regression models to meet this assumption. Second, unlike RMANOVA, HLM models variation at two levels: within and between dyads. This permits the explanation of variation by predictors measured at the appropriate unit of analysis: Within-dyad predictors tell us something about why a husband and wife are different from each other, whereas between-dyad predictors tell us how one dyad is different from another dyad. Third, in HLM, outcome scores are adjusted for measurement error. This solves the problem of fallible measures, as latent or true scores become the dependent variables in the level 2 regression model. Fourth, HLM can accommodate any combination of predictors measured on a binary, ordinal, multinomial, or continuous scale. Finally, a hierarchical linear model can readily be expanded to incorporate the nesting of dyads within higher-order settings, such as communities or therapy groups.

Univariate HLM for Dyads

Level 1 model: within-dyad variation. The univariate formulation corresponds to the traditional measurement approaches described previously, where the goal is to create a measure that characterizes the dyad from individual-level scores. The parenting stress scores in the above example are conceived as indicators of two latent variables that characterize the dyad: the dyadic stress level and the extent of dyadic discrepancy in stress. In this way, the level 1 or within-dyad model can be viewed as a measurement model for constructing the latent variables. To build intuition for this model, we display the data record for Couple 109 in Table 12.4 and graph the data in Figure 12.4. Note that there are four responses for parenting stress (two for the husband, two for the wife). These are a result of creating parallel scores (dividing the stress score into two replicate scales).

Figure 12.4 displays the four responses plotted against an indicator that denotes

Table 12.4   Level 1 Data Record for First Couple

Couple ID	Stress	Indicator
109	154	+.5
109	126	+.5
109	208	−.5
109	150	−.5

NOTE: For the variable indicator, +.5 indicates the response was given by the wife and −.5 indicates the response was given by the husband.

Figure 12.4   Fitted Regression Line Superimposed on Observed Data (parallel scores) for Couple 109

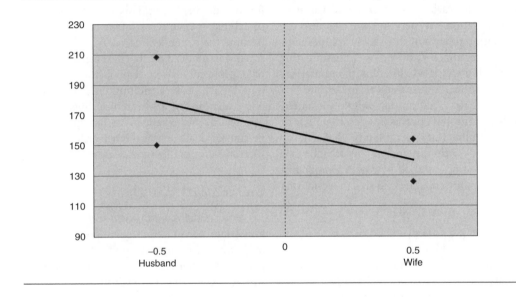

who contributed which response. We can fit a regression line to the four data points that will summarize the information in the four responses. More formally, the following model will be fit to the stress responses for each dyad:

$$\text{Stress}_{ij} = \beta_{0j} + \beta_{1j}\,(\text{Indicator}_{ij}) + r_{ij}. \quad (1)$$

Y_{ij} is the stress response i in couple j (where $i = 1, \ldots, 4$ and $j = 1, \ldots, 51$), and indicator is a dichotomous variable taking on a value of $-.5$ if the response was obtained from the husband and $+.5$ if the response was obtained from the wife. The level 1 or within-dyad regression model expresses the outcome as a function of a single dichotomous variable that indicates whether the score was reported by the husband or the wife, plus a residual term that captures measurement error in the outcome scores. Under this formulation, the model intercept (β_{0j}) represents the expected value of the outcome stress when the predictor indicator is zero. As Figure 12.4 shows, the use of effects coding for the indicator ensures that the predictor is zero when it is at the couple average. β_{0j} is the latent mean stress score for this couple, similar to the traditional mean scores described previously but corrected for both missing data and measurement error.

The model slope (β_{1j}) is the expected difference in the outcome for a one-unit difference in the predictor. In this case, a one-unit change in the predictor (from −.5 to +.5, or from husband to wife) is associated with a β_1 change in stress between the two members of the dyad. β_1 is the latent mean difference score, adjusted for missing data and measurement error. Note that with this model, each dyad can potentially have a different intercept and slope, which in turn can become outcome variables at the next level. The residual term r_{ij} represents the deviation of each observed response from its value predicted by the fitted regression line. These within-dyad residuals, also called the level 1 random effects, are assumed to be normally distributed with a mean of zero and variance σ^2.

Use of parallel scales. This variance parameter σ^2 represents measurement error variance and can be estimated, provided enough information is available within each dyad. We illustrate the use of parallel scales as a means of providing the necessary information. This is a strategy first suggested by Raudenbush, Brennan, and Barnett (1995) in their study of psychological change in married couples. It assumes that the items that constitute a scale can be conceived as replicates and that the scale is unidimensional. It follows that one can construct two parallel scales from the set of items by splitting the item pool in half and assigning half the items to Scale A and half to Scale B. In the EICS data, the 54 items for the mother's PSI were matched based on their sample standard deviations to create 27 pairs of scores. One item from each pair was randomly assigned to one of two parallel scales. This generated two maternal parenting role scales with equal variances and equal reliability. The same procedure was followed to create two parallel scales for fathers. Thus each dyad member had two stress scores available for analysis, for a total of four responses per dyad.

Level 2 model: between-dyad variation. Estimates of couple mean and couple discrepancy

Figure 12.5   Within-Dyad Fitted Regression Lines for Nine Randomly Selected Couples

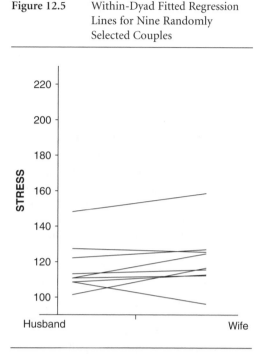

based on fitting the model in Equation 1 are collected for each dyad. Then the first step in the between-dyad analysis is to examine the distribution of these estimates to assess the extent of heterogeneity in the sample. Figure 12.5 displays the fitted regression lines for nine randomly selected dyads. This composite plot displays variability in both couple mean and couple discrepancy. Note the differences in both the intercepts (if we drop a plumb line at zero, we see that the couple means range from about 100 to 160) and the slopes. There is graphic evidence of great discrepancy (steep slopes) as well as lack of discrepancy (flatter slopes). The direction of the tilt of the line is informative: Increasing slopes indicate that the wife is more stressed, whereas decreasing slopes indicate the opposite.

At level 2, the level 1 coefficients become dependent variables, to be explained as a function of level 2 predictors. Formally, we fit the following *unconditional* level 2 model to estimate the population averages of dyad mean and dyad discrepancy and assess heterogeneity around these averages. It consists of two equations that, taken together, model the between-dyad variation in stress:

$$\beta_{0j} = \gamma_{00} + u_{0j}. \qquad (2)$$

$$\beta_{1j} = \gamma_{10} + u_{1j}. \qquad (3)$$

Equation 2 is the model for differences between dyads in mean level of stress, and Equation 3 is the corresponding model for differences in dyad discrepancy in stress. The level 2 intercepts (γ_{00} and γ_{10}) provide estimates of the population averages for each outcome. The level 2 random effects (u_{0j} and u_{1j}) represent the deviation of each dyad from the population average. The u_{0j} and u_{1j} are assumed to have a bivariate normal distribution with zero means, variances τ_{00} and τ_{11}, and covariance τ_{10}. In the unconditional model, these parameters represent the true variance in the outcomes β_{0j} and β_{1j}. The chi-square statistic can be used to test whether the variances are significantly different from zero. If they are, significant heterogeneity exists across dyads.

The *conditional* level 2 model adds the predictor demand to explain the variability across dyads in average stress and discrepancy in stress:

$$\beta_{0j} = \gamma_{00} + \gamma_{01}\,\text{Demand} + u_{0j}. \qquad (4)$$

$$\beta_1 = \gamma_{10} + \gamma_{11}\,\text{Demand} + u_{1j}. \qquad (5)$$

In this model, the effect of demand is captured by the coefficients γ_{01} and γ_{11}. If γ_{01} and γ_{11} are positive and significantly different from zero, then demand is associated with both higher couple means and larger couple discrepancy scores (relative to the average score). If demand is centered on its grand mean, then the intercepts (γ_{00}, γ_{10}) retain the same interpretation as in the unconditional model. (For a discussion of centering options, see this volume's companion Web site.)

Results. Several computer programs are currently available for fitting multilevel models, including HLM, SAS PROC MIXED, Stata, Mplus, LISREL, and MLwiN. A comparison of these programs is outside the scope of this chapter, but we suggest that interested readers see Zhou, Perkins, and Hui (1999) for a review. We used the HLM5 computer program (Raudenbush, Bryk, Cheong, & Congdon, 2000) to estimate the parameters of the level 1 and level 2 models and to obtain standard errors for testing the hypotheses that the parameter was zero in the population. The results from the *unconditional* model indicated that the average couple is moderately stressed ($\gamma_{00} = 118.9$, t ratio $= 46.81$, $p > .001$), and the average difference in the couple's scores was about 4 points, although this was not significantly different from zero in the population ($\gamma_{10} = 4.01$, t ratio $= 1.21$, $p = .231$). The variance components indicated that there was significant variability in both couple means ($\tau_{00} = 264.38$, $\chi^2 = 291.60$, $p < .001$) and couple discrepancies ($\tau_{11} = 294.98$, $\chi^2 = 110.96$, $p < .001$). That is, not all couples resembled the average couple, and the estimation of such heterogeneity opened the possibility that these differences could be explained by the extent of child demands. Results from the *conditional* model indicated that, on average, demand was positively associated with couple means ($\gamma_{01} = 6.25$, t ratio $= 4.79$, $p > .001$) but had no effect on explaining differences in couple discrepancy ($\gamma_{11} = -2.21$, t ratio $= -1.08$, $p = .287$).

Multivariate HLM for Dyads

A two-level hierarchical linear model with multivariate outcomes is an alternative parameterization of the univariate model just presented. Such an approach is useful when the researcher's goal is to model outcomes separately for husbands and wives rather than at the level of the dyad. In the past, the lack of a sound method for handling the dependence of couples' data led researchers to rely on flawed analytic strategies. Some split their samples by gender and conducted separate analyses for husbands and wives, but this strategy results in a loss of power, makes it impossible for the researcher to test explicitly for gender differences, and ignores information

Table 12.5   Level 1 Data Record for Three Couples

Couple ID	Mom	Dad	Stress
102	1	0	86
102	1	0	86
102	0	1	120
102	0	1	102
109	1	0	154
109	1	0	126
109	0	1	208
109	0	1	150
202	1	0	150
202	1	0	120
202	0	1	.
202	0	1	.

that can be gained from estimation of the shared couple variance. Other researchers pooled their samples prior to conducting analyses and included dummy variables to test for gender differences. However, this strategy does not reflect the hierarchical structure of couple data, and so the dependence in scores is not modeled explicitly.

Barnett, Marshall, Raudenbush, and Brennan (1993) have described the superiority of the multilevel approach compared with traditional analysis in which separate regression equations are estimated for husbands and wives. One major advantage of the multilevel approach is that it can incorporate predictors with distinct values for each member of the dyad as well as those with shared values. It also permits the researcher to test explicitly for gender effects and to constrain effects to be equivalent for each member of the couple, thereby increasing power and precision.

Table 12.5 presents the data record for the first three couples for the multivariate formulation. As in the univariate model, there are parallel scores for both mothers and fathers, resulting in four responses for each dyad. Note that, in contrast to the univariate formulation, which relied on a single indicator, two dummy variables are now included to denote which member of the dyad contributed each response.

Level 1 model. The level 1 or within-dyad model postulates that the husband's stress score (Y) is the sum of a latent true score (β_h) plus measurement error. Similarly, the wife's stress score (Y) is the sum of a latent true score (β_w) plus measurement error. It is written as follows:

$$Y_{ij} = (H)_{ij}(B_{hj} + r_{hj}) + (W)_{ij}(B_{wj} + r_{wj}), \quad (6)$$

where

Y_{ij} is the stress response i in couple j (where $i = 1, \ldots, 4$ and $j = 1, \ldots, 51$),

H is an indicator variable taking on a value of 1 if the response was obtained from the husband and 0 if the response was obtained from the wife,

W is an indicator variable taking on the value of 1 if the response was obtained from the wife and 0 if the response was obtained from the husband,

B_{hj} is the husband's true or latent stress score,

r_{hj} is the measurement error associated with the husband's true score,

B_{wj} is the wife's true or latent stress score, and

r_{wj} is the measurement error associated with the wife's true score.

Level 2 model. The level 2 or between-dyad model consists of simultaneous regression equations, with each of the parameters estimated by the level 1 model (i.e., β_h and β_w) serving as outcomes or dependent variables. These equations, taken together, explain husbands' and wives' parenting role stress as a function of individual-level and couple-level predictors.

The following unconditional level 2 model was estimated:

$$\beta_h = \gamma_{10} + u_{hj}. \tag{7}$$

$$\beta_w = \gamma_{20} + u_{wj}. \tag{8}$$

γ_{10} and γ_{20} are the level 2 intercepts or average latent scores for husbands and wives, respectively, and u_h and u_w are the residuals (i.e., individual deviations from the average husband or wife true score). The residuals (u_h, u_w) are assumed to be normally distributed with variances τ_{hh}, τ_{ww} and covariance τ_{hw}. It is the last parameter that estimates the degree of dependence in the outcomes.

The baseline model generates four important pieces of information. First, the intercepts are point estimates of the average true scores for husbands and wives. The researcher can compare them to test whether husbands and wives, on average, have significantly different levels of parenting role stress. Second, the variance components τ_{hh} and τ_{ww} are estimates of the heterogeneity around the mean score for husbands and wives. The chi-square test associated with each variance component assesses the null hypothesis that the variance is zero—that is, there is no variability around the average score. If the null hypothesis cannot be retained (i.e., the chi-square test is significant), then individual husbands' and wives' scores are different from their respective averages. The researcher can then enter predictor variables into the level 2 equations in an attempt to explain the variance in β_h and β_w. Third, the shared variance (within-couple covariance of husband and wife stress scores) is estimated.

Results. The mean stress score for husbands ($\gamma_{10} = 116.95$, $SE = 3.16$) and the mean stress score for wives ($\gamma_{20} = 120.96$, $SE = 2.89$) were not significantly different from each other, as revealed by a multivariate hypothesis test, an option in HLM ($\chi^2 = 1.474$, $p > .10$). This is the same result observed in Figure 12.2 from the RMANOVA analysis. Note that the difference between the two average scores is $120.96 - 116.95 = 4.01$. This value is identical to the point estimate of the average couple gap in the univariate model. It is evident that this model is simply a reparameterization of the univariate model, but useful when interest centers on predicting separate true scores for husbands and wives rather than discrepancy scores for couples. The chi-square test associated with the wives' true score variance ($\tau_{00} = 314.79$, $\chi^2 = 196.20$, $p < .001$) and the husbands' true score variance ($\tau_{11} = 361.45$, $\chi^2 = 205.09$, $p < .001$) indicates that we can reject the null hypothesis that these variances are zero in the population. There is enough variability around each mean score to warrant entering predictor variables into the equation at level 2 in order to explain this variability.

The covariance component τ_{10} was 190.63, which represents a correlation of .565. This indicates that a moderate and positive correlation exists between husbands' and wives' parenting role stress and that ignoring this degree of dependence in a single-level model would have serious consequences for all the hypotheses tests associated with the model.

Conditional level 2 model. The baseline level 2 model was expanded to include the predictor demand, as follows:

$$\beta_h = \gamma_{10} + \gamma_{11} (\text{Demand}) + u_h. \tag{9}$$

$$\beta_w = \gamma_{20} + \gamma_{21} (\text{Demand}) + u_w. \tag{10}$$

γ_{10} and γ_{11} are the level 2 intercepts, representing the expected or average value of the outcomes β_h and β_w when the predictor is equal to zero. In this case, the interpretation of these intercepts can be retained to be equivalent to those in the baseline level 2 model through the centering of the predictor on its grand mean. The regression coefficients γ_{11} and γ_{21} capture the relationship between parenting role stress and having a demanding child for husbands and wives, respectively. Demand is positively associated with the stress scores of husbands ($\gamma_1 = 7.35$, $SE = 1.71$) and wives ($\gamma_{21} = 5.14$, $SE = 1.60$). Although the effect is slightly larger for husbands (i.e., a 1-unit difference in demand is associated with a 7.35-unit difference in stress as opposed to a 5.14-unit difference for wives), a multivariate hypothesis test indicates that the coefficients are not significantly different from one another ($\chi^2 = .99$, $df = 1$, $p > .500$).

EXTENSIONS OF THE MULTIVARIATE MODEL

Several important extensions of the multivariate model can greatly increase the researcher's ability to ask (and answer) interesting questions about dyads and families. First, the model enables the investigator to specify crossover effects by using variables that are characteristics of one member of the dyad as predictors of the outcome for the other member. Barnett, Raudenbush, Brennan,

Pleck, and Marshall (1995) have used this technique with dual-earner couples to investigate whether the quality of the wife's job has an effect on the husband's well-being and vice versa. Second, the model can be expanded to include more than two outcomes. There is no limit on the number of latent true scores that can be estimated as long as there are data to support the model. A third dummy variable can be included to indicate responses given by a child; in this way, the model can be extended to families or other triads, as long as the members of the group are distinguishable. Third, the model is not limited to cross-sectional data but can be expanded to include longitudinal data on group members. Thus individual trajectories of change that differ for members of the dyad can be estimated (Raudenbush et al., 1995). Finally, the model can be expanded to a three-level formulation in which dyads are nested within upper-level units such as neighborhoods or therapy groups, and the researcher can investigate the effects of context on dyad members. This latter model brings us full circle by integrating the relational and ecological perspectives laid out at the beginning of this chapter.

DISCUSSION AND EXTENSION

A COMMENT ON THE USE OF MULTILEVEL METHODS IN FAMILY RESEARCH

James M. White, *University of British Columbia*

Jay D. Teachman, *Western Washington University*

In Chapter 12, Sayer and Klute state that in the study of individuals and families, the forces behind the interdependence of dyad members "are the focus of interest in family research and should be modeled explicitly."

This statement prefaces their clear and concrete introduction to multilevel models for the study of dyadic relationships. Indeed, individuals may be nested not only within relationships, but also within family groups,

DISCUSSION AND EXTENSION *continued*

neighborhoods, schools, and many other geographic and institutional contexts. As Teachman and Crowder (2002, p. 281) point out, micro- and macro-level variables are often not independent. For instance, an individual's social class (individual level) might partially determine the neighborhood (macro level) in which he or she resides, or the social and physical conditions of a neighborhood might influence the degree of trust shown by individuals. Modeling this interdependence has important consequences for family research and theory.

In this comment, we clarify the meaning of *levels of analysis* and the cognate terms *sampling unit* and *reporting unit,* discuss the ramifications of levels of analysis for different forms of explanation, discuss the relationship between models and theoretical formulations, and focus on some problems associated with aggregation and disaggregation. Finally, we argue that one consequence of multilevel modeling may be to prod theorists to more precise specification of theoretical relationships.

LEVELS OF ANALYSIS, SAMPLING UNIT, AND REPORTING UNIT

Bulcroft and White (1997) argue that the term *levels of analysis* refers to the conceptual levels at which explanations are formulated. Levels of analysis are tied to the conceptual positions of "methodological individualism" and "methodological holism." Holism is the perspective that group constructs are necessary to explain group phenomena, whereas methodological individualism assumes that all such "group" phenomena can be explained as aggregations of individual characteristics. Methodological individualism in theories such as rational choice theory explains phenomena such as marriage rates using individual constructs such as profit (see Lichter, LeClere, & McLaughlin, 1991). Holistic positions argue that certain processes in the neighborhood or dyad are necessary to explain phenomena.

A strength of multilevel modeling is that it allows us to move across these traditional distinctions and examine both individualistic and holistic explanations.

The sampling unit (or unit of analysis) is a methodological concept indicating the unit that is sampled. In much of family research the sampling unit is the individual, but it may also be the household or an areal unit such as school district. The sampling unit clearly restricts the researcher's ability to generalize findings and is of special importance for moving to higher-order levels of analysis, as in multilevel modeling when the sampling unit is the individual, as discussed later.

The reporting unit is an important methodological distinction. As Bulcroft and White (1997) note, in many cases the sampling unit is the household and the reporting unit is an individual "person most knowledgeable" reporting on a level of analysis such as family or neighborhood. It is critically important to distinguish among these three in order to avoid fallacious generalizations and to identify the relevant explanatory and conceptual level. Both of these are significant in avoiding problems of theoretical misspecification.

MODELS AND THEORY

To date, theorists calling for multilevel analysis have been less than clear as to the exact nature of these levels. Bronfenbrenner (1979) introduced abstract terms such as *mesosystem* and *exosystem* to capture levels of analysis. These levels include areal units such as neighborhoods and institutions such as schools, but the actual defining dimensions of the levels are vague. White (1991) also refers to levels of analysis, including the levels of the individual, the relationship, the family, social aggregations, and normative institutions. And again, the underlying dimensions are unclear, as they are based either on the number of individual members

DISCUSSION AND EXTENSION *continued*

(individual, dyad, triad) or on norms (family and institutions). So although the calls for multiple-level theory have been clear, the exact meanings of the levels remain theoretically vague. We cannot expect loosely specified levels of analysis to be correctly specified by the models without some further guidance from theory.

AGGREGATION-DISAGGREGATION ISSUES

One potential difficulty is that the level to which we want to aggregate may lack sufficient data (sampling units). Teachman and Crowder (2002) suggest that "some data sets that provide information on both individual cases and broader context in which they are located contain too few individuals sharing a common context" (p. 292). Some scholars have recently extended this same type of thinking to the aggregation of individuals to dyadic groups (Hox, 2002; Newsom & Nishishiba, 2002). They argue that little research has been conducted on the stability and bias of random effects estimators of significance when group size is only two. This is a question that Sayer and Klute do not address, but it is one that other researchers may want to examine before they conduct similar analyses. On the other hand, when individual scores are not independent, this too might result in the underestimation of standard errors and erroneous claims of significance of results (Teachman & Crowder, 2002, p. 292).

A second potential difficulty lies in the determination of the appropriate unit of aggregation and theoretical misspecification. Aggregating to the dyad level is relatively clear, but for other units of aggregation the appropriate unit may not be as readily apparent. For example, how do we define a neighborhood? We might use census data to define a neighborhood, but our definition may not be one to which people actually respond or that has any theoretical meaning. We might also find that

the appropriate unit of aggregation is not constant across all lower-level units. For example, one individual might respond to a very narrow neighborhood whereas another responds to a broader neighborhood. Thus there would be little phenomenal identity even though the concept is "neighborhood."

ECOLOGICAL AND INDIVIDUALISTIC FALLACIES

The two fallacies in regard to levels of analysis are the "individualistic fallacy" and the "ecological fallacy" (Bulcroft & White, 1997; White, 2004). The individualistic fallacy occurs when observations at the individual level are generalized to the dyad, group, or institutional level. For example, measures taken on individual spouses and then generalized to the couple aggregate individual scores, but the "couple" is not measured. The individualistic fallacy is not a relevant methodological criticism of the model Sayer and Klute present because their model incorporates a dyad-level measure. As we shall demonstrate below, the individualistic fallacy is more relevant to the interpretation of findings from these models.

The ecological fallacy occurs when observations at the group level are generalized to the individuals. For example, when we take measures on school districts such as aggregated academic performance scores, we cannot then generalize about students, because we have sampled only districts. Likewise, research dealing with characteristics of the "marriage market" should not generalize macrocharacteristics of the market to individuals in the market. Again, this methodological criticism does not apply to multilevel models, but such fallacies may emerge in interpretations.

Researchers using multilevel models may still commit these errors as they interpret results. For example, Butler (2002) discusses the effects of community tolerance and stigma (macro level) on individuals' premarital

DISCUSSION AND EXTENSION *continued*

childbearing (p. 310). The meanings of such social psychological terms as *stigma* and *tolerance* may be clearer when attributed to individuals than when attributed to communities. Such thinking leads to questions such as, Do communities think and form opinions, or would such concepts as "tolerance" better refer to individuals? Thus we return to the need for well-developed theory in advance of the interpretation of multilevel results.

MULTILEVEL THEORY

We propose that the development of multilevel models may result in theoretical development and refinement. One extension that Sayer and Klute do not mention is that interactions between levels can be modeled (i.e., the effects of an individual-level covariate on an individual-level outcome can be made a function of an aggregate covariate). Another extension is that multilevel modeling can be used to create

models for data on individuals over time (e.g., growth curve models). In essence, with multiple observations on each individual, the person becomes his or her own aggregate unit.

Few social scientific theories offer details regarding how effects occur at different levels or how effects at one level interact with those at another. Coleman (1990) argues that any contemporary social theory must provide specific and detailed analyses of how effects move from one level of analysis to another. Although many theories relevant to the family propose multiple levels, these theories fail to offer precise definition of the levels or to specify how effects move from one level to another. In order for multilevel models to propel social scientific knowledge, we need decent multilevel theory that addresses such details. This need represents new challenge to theorists and researchers. Without the development of detailed multilevel theory, the promise of multilevel models can never be fully realized.

REFERENCES

Abidin, R. R. (1995). *Parenting Stress Index: Manual* (3rd ed.). Odessa, FL: Psychological Assessment Resources.

Achenbach, T. M., & Edelbrock, C. S. (1983). *Manual for the Child Behavior Checklist.* Burlington, VT: University Associates in Psychiatry.

Aquilino, W. S. (1999). Two views of one relationship: Comparing parents' and young adult children's reports of the quality of intergenerational relations. *Journal of Marriage and the Family, 61,* 858–870.

Barnett, R. C., Marshall, N. L., Raudenbush, S. W., & Brennan, R. T. (1993). Gender and the relationship between job experiences and psychological distress: A study of dual-earner couples. *Journal of Personality and Social Psychology, 64,* 794–806.

Barnett, R. C., Raudenbush, S. W., Brennan, R. T., Pleck, J. H., & Marshall, N. L. (1995). Change in job and marital experiences and change in psychological distress: A longitudinal study of dual-earner couples. *Journal of Personality and Social Psychology, 69,* 839–850.

Bowen, G. L., Martin, J. A., Mancini, J. A., & Nelson, J. P. (2000). Community capacity: Antecedents and consequences. *Journal of Community Practice, 8,* 1–21.

Bradbury, T. N., Campbell, S., & Fincham, F. D. (1995). Longitudinal and behavioral analysis of masculinity and femininity in marriage. *Journal of Personality and Social Psychology, 68,* 328–341.

Bronfenbrenner, U. (1979). *The ecology of human development: Experiments by nature and design.* Cambridge, MA: Harvard University Press.

Bulcroft, R., & White, J. M. (1997). Family research methods and levels of analysis. *Family Science Review, 2,* 136–153.

Butler, A. (2002). Welfare, premarital childbearing, and the role of normative climate: 1968–1994. *Journal of Marriage and Family, 64,* 295–313.

Campbell, L., & Kashy, D. A. (2002). Estimating actor, partner, and interaction effects for dyadic data using PROC MIXED and HLM: A user-friendly guide. *Personal Relationships, 9,* 327–342.

Ceballo, R., Dahl, T. A., Aretakis, M. T., & Ramirez, C. (2001). Inner-city children's exposure to community violence: How much do parents know? *Journal of Marriage and Family, 63,* 927–940.

Coleman, J. S. (1990). *Foundations of social theory.* Cambridge, MA: Belknap.

Cook, T. D., Shagle, S. C., & Degirmencioglu, S. M. (1997). Capturing social process for testing mediational models of neighborhood effects. In J. Brooks-Gunn, G. J. Duncan, & J. L. Aber (Eds.), *Neighborhood poverty: Vol. 2. Policy implications in studying neighborhoods* (pp. 94–119). New York: Russell Sage Foundation.

Crouter, A. C., Helms-Erikson, H., Updegraff, K. A., & McHale, S. M. (1999). Conditions underlying parents' knowledge about children's daily lives in middle childhood: Between- and within-family comparisons. *Child Development, 70,* 246–259.

Crouter, A. C., & Manke, B. (1997). Development of a typology of dual-earner families: A window into the differences within and between families in relationships, roles, and activities. *Journal of Family Psychology, 11,* 62–75.

Everitt, B. S. (1993). *Cluster analysis* (3rd ed.). London: Edward Arnold.

Fisher, L., Kokes, R. F., Ransom, D. C., Phillips, S. L., & Rudd, P. (1985). Alternative strategies for creating "relational" family data. *Family Process, 24,* 213–224.

Gonzalez, R., & Griffin, D. (1997). On the statistics of interdependence: Treating dyadic data with respect. In S. Duck (Ed.), *Handbook of personal relationships: Theory, research and interventions* (2nd ed., pp. 271–302). New York: John Wiley.

Gottman, J. M., & Levinson, R. W. (1992). Marital processes predictive of later dissolution: Behavior, physiology, and health. *Journal of Personality and Social Psychology, 63,* 221–233.

Griffin, D., & Gonzalez, R. (1995). Correlational analysis of dyad-level data in the exchangeable case. *Psychological Bulletin, 118,* 430–439.

Griffin, D., Murray, S., & Gonzalez, R. (1999). Difference score correlations in relationships research: A conceptual primer. *Personal Relationships, 6,* 505–518.

Haslam, N. (1999). Taxometric and related methods in relationships research. *Personal Relationships, 6,* 519–534.

Hauser-Cram, P., Warfield, M. E., Shonkoff, J. P., Krauss, M. W., Sayer, A. G., & Upshur, C. C. (2001). Children with disabilities: A longitudinal study of child development and parent well-being. *Monographs of the Society for Research in Child Development, 66*(3, Serial No. 266).

Hoffman, J. (2002). The community context of family structure and adolescent drug use. *Journal of Marriage and Family, 64,* 314–330.

Hox, J. (2002). *Multilevel analysis: Techniques and applications.* Mahwah, NJ: Lawrence Erlbaum.

Hoyle, R. (2000). Personality processes and problem behavior. *Journal of Personality, 68,* 953–966.

Kenny, D. A., Mannetti, L., Pierro, A., Livi, S., & Kashy, D. A. (2002). The statistical analysis of data from small groups. *Journal of Personality and Social Psychology, 83,* 126–137.

Klute, M. M., Crouter, A. C., Sayer, A. G., & McHale, S. M. (2002). Occupational self-direction, values and egalitarian relationships: A study of dual-earner couples. *Journal of Marriage and Family, 64,* 139–151.

Lee, V., Loeb, S., & Lubeck, S. (1998). Contextual effects of prekindergarten classrooms for disadvantaged children on cognitive development: The case of Chapter 1. *Child Development, 69,* 479–494.

Lichter, D. T., LeClere, F. B., & McLaughlin, D. K. (1991). Local marriage markets and the marital behavior of Black and White women. *American Journal of Sociology, 96,* 843–867.

Lyons, K. S., Zarit, S. H., Sayer, A. G., & Whitlatch, C. J. (2002). Caregiving as a dyadic process: Perspectives from the caregiver and receiver. *Journal of Gerontology: Psychological Sciences, 57,* 195–204.

Maguire, M. C. (1999). Treating the dyad as the unit of analysis: A primer on three analytic approaches. *Journal of Marriage and the Family, 61,* 213–223.

Mancini, J. A., Martin, J. A., & Bowen, G. L. (2003). Community capacity. In T. P. Gullotta & M. Bloom (Eds.), *Encyclopedia of primary prevention and health promotion* (pp. 319–330). New York: Kluwer Academic/Plenum.

McCarthy, D. (1972). *McCarthy Scales of Children's Abilities.* New York: Psychological Corporation.

McCrae, R. R., & Costa, P. T., Jr. (1996). Toward a new generation of personality theories: Theoretical contexts for the five-factor model. In J. Wiggins (Ed.), *The five-factor model of personality: Theoretical perspectives* (pp. 51–87). New York: Guilford.

Newsom, J. T., & Nishishiba, M. (2002). *Nonconvergence and sample bias in hierarchical linear modeling of dyadic data.* Unpublished manuscript, Portland State University, Portland, OR. Retrieved June 14, 2004, from http://www.upa.pdx.edu/IOA/newsom/mirdyad4.doc

Raudenbush, S. W., Brennan, R. T., & Barnett, R. C. (1995). A multivariate hierarchical model for studying psychological change within married couples. *Journal of Family Psychology, 9,* 161–174.

Raudenbush, S. W., & Bryk, A. S. (2002). *Hierarchical linear models: Applications and data analysis methods* (2nd ed.). Thousand Oaks, CA: Sage.

Raudenbush, S. W., Bryk, A. S., Cheong, Y. F., & Congdon, R. T. (2000). *HLM5: Hierarchical linear and nonlinear modeling.* Chicago: Scientific Software International.

Schafer, J. L. (1997). *Analysis of incomplete multivariate data.* New York: Chapman & Hall.

Shonkoff, J. P., Hauser-Cram, P., Krauss, M. W., & Upshur, C. C. (1992). Development of infants with disabilities and their families: Implications for theory and service delivery. *Monographs of the Society for Research in Child Development, 57*(6, Serial No. 230).

Sprey, J. (2000). Theorizing in family studies: Discovering process. *Journal of Marriage and the Family, 62,* 18–31.

Svartberg, M., Seltzer, M., Stiles, T., & Khoo, S. T. (1995). Symptom improvement and its temporal course in short-term dynamic psychotherapy: A growth curve analysis. *Journal of Nervous and Mental Disease, 183,* 242–248.

Teachman, J. D., & Crowder, K. (2002). Multilevel models in family research: Some conceptual and methodological issues. *Journal of Marriage and Family, 64,* 280–294.

Thompson, L., & Walker, A. J. (1982). The dyad as the unit of analysis: Conceptual and methodological issues. *Journal of Marriage and the Family, 44,* 889–900.

Tolson, J. M., & Urberg, K. A. (1993). Similarity between adolescent best friends. *Journal of Adolescent Research, 8,* 274–288.

Warfield, M. E. (in press). Family and work predictors of maternal and paternal parenting role stress among two-earner families of children with disabilities. *Infant and Child Development.*

White, J. M. (1991). *Dynamics of family development.* New York: Guilford.

White, J. M. (2004). *Advancing family theories.* Thousand Oaks, CA: Sage.

Zhou, X., Perkins, A., & Hui, S. (1999). Comparisons of software packages for generalized linear models. *American Statistician, 53,* 282–290.

• Thirteen

THEORIZING ABOUT AGGRESSION BETWEEN INTIMATES

A Dialectical Approach

Loreen N. Olson, *University of Missouri–Columbia*

Mark A. Fine, *University of Missouri–Columbia*

Sally A. Lloyd, *Miami University*

For millions of people across the United States and around the world, the image of a family is one of possibility, hope, love, and support. Unfortunately, however, family life for thousands of others has a darker, more malevolent connotation—one filled with an odd, paradoxical mixture of aggression and tenderness. In this chapter we define this darker side, which we refer to as *aggression*, as Gelles and Straus (1979) have defined it: "any malevolent act, i.e., an act carried out with the intention of, or which is perceived as having the intention of, hurting another. The injury can be psychological, material deprivation, or physical pain or damage" (p. 554).[1]

Without diminishing the importance of other types of family violence (e.g., child abuse and neglect, elder abuse, sibling violence,

child-to-parent abuse), we have chosen to focus our attention on aggression between heterosexual adult partners because of its frequency and unique set of characteristics. Although it has existed for centuries, intimate aggression first came to be recognized as a social problem in the latter part of the 20th century, with this recognition leading to increased attention from researchers, practitioners, and community advocates. As a result of this attention, our understanding of the phenomenon has grown substantially in recent years. It appears, however, that after several decades of focused scholarly attention, the field of intimate aggression research is at a crossroads. The literature presents numerous paradoxical, contested, and/or contradictory findings. In a now classic article, Johnson (1995) identified several of these, including contradictory findings related to per couple frequency, reciprocity, gender (a)symmetry, power and control, and escalation. We suggest that such differences persist within the literature in part because of artificially created binary opposites.

We believe that an integrated theoretical approach, one that highlights both contradiction and dynamic change, offers the greatest utility for helping scholars to understand the paradox of intimate aggression. A dialectical perspective focuses on the contradictory aspects of intimate aggression. Therefore, our purpose in this chapter is to advance understanding of aggression between intimates by using a dialectical perspective to integrate multiple theoretical approaches and empirical findings in hopes of developing a comprehensive framework for theorizing. The structural lens provided by dialectics also affords us a preliminary vantage point from which to view the empirical and theoretical landscape of intimate aggression. As such, our ideas are primarily conjecture at this stage. We are not proposing a new theory of intimate aggression; rather, we are using the dialectical approach to build a flexible architecture (or a metatheory) that scholars can use for both theoretical and empirical purposes in the future. Toward that end, we begin by listing the theories we used to inform our dialectical view of intimate aggression and by explaining why we chose these theories. This discussion is followed by a summary of the dialectical perspective, which informs the final section— a presentation of the main features of dialectics and a discussion of how this metatheoretical perspective makes new theorizing possible by providing a new lens through which to view intimate aggression.

RELATIONAL AND CONTEXTUAL THEORIES OF INTIMATE AGGRESSION

Scholars have used multiple theoretical perspectives to explain intimate aggression, ranging from early notions of female masochism to recent evolutionary explanations of the biological roots of aggression. Although all of these have helped inform our understanding of aggression between romantic partners, we have chosen seven to form the underpinnings of our dialectical integration: social learning theory, social exchange and investment models, family systems theory, relational control and communication models, conflict theory, feminist theory, and life-course theory (see Table 13.1 for a summary of the theories' major assumptions and a review of theory-related findings related to intimate aggression). Our purpose here is to provide only brief synopses of the major tenets of these theories, particularly those aspects that have most informed work on intimate aggression. We encourage interested readers to visit this volume's companion Web site (http://www.ncfr.org/sourcebook) for references to additional literature in which these theories are more fully explicated.

Beyond the practical issue of limited space, the question becomes, Why did we choose these theories? More than 25 years ago, Gelles and Straus (1979) drew on 15 theories, ranging from intraindividual to social psychological to sociocultural, to create 45 propositions to explain intimate aggression in the family. Rather than undertaking such a broad approach, we chose to employ a more focused perspective, emphasizing theories that provide *relational* (i.e., "the interpersonal dynamics that both surround the use of aggression and characterize the overall relationship between perpetrator and victim"; Lloyd & Emery, 2000b, p. 19) and/or *contextual* (i.e., the social structures, time periods, and discourses within which intimate aggression is embedded) explanations of interpersonal aggression. This reflects our belief that these levels of explanation are the most helpful for explaining intimate aggression from a dialectical perspective. Specifically, as interpersonal scholars, we view intimate aggression as a socially constructed, relational dynamic enacted by and between partners who are embedded within various familial, social, and institutional systems that both sustain and resist its existence. We chose to focus on theories that emphasize these

Table 13.1   Summaries of Theories That Scholars Have Used to Understand Intimate Aggression

Social learning theory

Interpersonal aggression is learned through experience and/or modeling in the family, with peers, in media, in society.

The family is viewed as a training ground that provides rewards and punishments that may encourage the use of aggression.

Children who witness/receive aggression in the family of origin learn that aggression is appropriate and effective as a way to solve interpersonal conflict, that the use of force is legitimate, and that those who love you hit you.

Interpersonal aggression is also related to other negative aspects of the parent-child relationship, including disturbed attachment, poor supervision, and lack of opportunity to learn appropriate problem-solving skills.

Social exchange and investment models

Individuals enter relationships, find them satisfying, and stay committed when they perceive a high ratio of rewards to costs, an equitable balance, a high investment of resources, and few alternatives that would be more rewarding.

Although aggression constitutes a severe cost to the relationship, when it is embedded within a relationship that is otherwise high in rewards and/or low in alternatives, the relationship is likely to continue despite the aggression.

Women who return to aggressive partners report substantial investments (dependent children, longer duration of the relationship), some satisfaction in and commitment to their relationships, and few alternatives (economic dependence, limited education and labor force experience).

Family systems theory

The family system is understood in terms of processes, patterns, and mutually contingent interaction.

The family system is embedded within, and has transactions with, other social systems (e.g., work, school, neighborhood).

Dysfunctional interaction patterns may provide the source and momentum for aggression; aggression may be part of a larger pattern of coercive interaction.

The system may keep tight controls on information transmission, keeping aggression invisible to those outside the family.

Positive feedback loops may produce an upward trend when aggression leads to the achievement of the goals of the perpetrator; negative feedback loops may stabilize the use of aggression and the relationship itself.

The family system is characterized by periods of both adaptation and stability; change in intimate aggression may be triggered by internal and/or external disruptions to the system.

Relational control and communication models

Aggression is viewed as a form of interpersonal communication.

These models draw on systems theory; they use the metaphor of "dance" to emphasize the patterns of interaction between individuals and emphasize processes whereby interpersonal behavior is mutually contingent.

Interpersonal aggression is associated with control-related conflict and unhealthy/ineffective conflict behaviors; aggression, as a coercive communication strategy, serves to establish and maintain control.

Communication patterns of partners who use aggression are characterized by higher levels of competitive symmetry, nonsupport statements, negative reciprocity, escalating cycles, rigid communication patterns, attempts by both husband and wife to exert control, rejection of influence, dominance and power hierarchies, and withdrawal.

(Continued)

Table 13.1 (Continued)

Conflict theory

Conflict occurs in all social relationships and at all levels of social organization; the family is a system in which family conflict is inevitable.

Individuals act to further their own interests and goals; due to the competing interests of members, the family does not seek system equilibrium but rather the management of conflict.

Emphasizes power differentials among family members, particularly gender, race, class, and age stratifications, that create structural inequalities.

Interpersonal aggression is a conflict strategy that family members enact when other tactics for achieving their interests break down or fail; aggression is a powerful means of achieving one's goals.

The family has a dualistic quality, characterized by both conflict and harmony, competition and cooperation; order is maintained in the family through coercion and force and/or negotiation and bargaining.

Feminist theory

Emphasizes the centrality and value of women's experiences, the analysis of gender and power relationships, gender as socially constructed, and the importance of historical and sociocultural contexts.

Brings to the forefront the intersections of gender and power/control with interpersonal aggression.

Systems of patriarchy have legitimated interpersonal aggression as a tactic of male control over women; this has been reinforced by women's differential access to resources and specialized male and female roles in families.

Men may use interpersonal aggression to denigrate and intimidate, prevent women's autonomous action, and maintain male dominance; men explain their use of aggression in terms of desire for control, fear of abandonment, jealousy, and fear of women's independence.

The family, helping professions, and criminal justice system are all embedded in and affected by discourses that construct aggression against women as legitimate.

Life-course perspective

Emphasizes the ongoing processes of intimate relationships as they are embedded in the broader context of social structure and history.

Focuses on transitions in relationships and on the socially constructed meanings attached to family processes, including aggression and intimacy.

Intimate aggression is a process, rather than an event; aggression is woven into normal family interaction, which may make it difficult to identify the beginning and end of an aggressive episode.

The development, maintenance, and demise of an aggressive relationship are processes that are characterized by adaptation, nonlinear change, and heterogeneity.

Life-course transitions may interact with family processes to produce increasingly severe and frequent acts of interpersonal aggression (e.g., when the abused partner takes steps to leave, or during periods of unemployment).

The occurrence and aftermath of intimate aggression varies depending on the life-course history of the relationship.

SOURCES: On social learning theory: Gelles and Straus (1979), O'Leary (1988), Rosen (1998). On social exchange and investment models: Rusbult and Martz (1995), Sabatelli and Shehan (1993). On family systems theory: Giles-Sims (1983), Montgomery and Fewer (1988), Whitchurch and Constantine (1993). On relational control and communication models: Rogers, Castleton, and Lloyd (1996), Olson (in press-a), Sabourin and Stamp (1995). On conflict theory: Farrington and Chertok (1993), Gelles and Straus (1979), Sprey (1999). On feminist theory: Baber and Allen (1992), Lloyd and Emery (2000b), Stark and Flitcraft (1996), Yllö and Bograd (1988). On the life-course perspective: Bengtson and Allen (1993), Kirkwood (1993), Olson (2001), Williams (2003).

relational and social contexts because we believe they are poised especially well for a dialectical analysis of intimate aggression. Thus the metatheoretical framework of relational dialectics is paradigmatically aligned with the theories we summarize here. Moreover, it is important to note that these seven theories are interrelated. Rather than forming discrete and disparate perspectives, they have numerous crosscutting themes and connections. For example, the concept of power is integral to feminist, conflict, systems, and relational control theories; interpersonal communication is integral to social learning, relational control, and systems theories; and the larger social context is integral to life-course, feminist, and conflict theories.

Although each of these seven theoretical perspectives has contributed significantly to our understanding of intimate aggression, we believe that greater understanding can be achieved through the integration of these perspectives. In this way, the unique aspect of intimate aggression that each perspective brings to light is integrated into the "both/and" perspective, creating a newly woven tapestry that uses the strengths of each individual theory to fill gaps that other theories leave open (Goldner, Penn, Sheinberg, & Walker, 1990). Thus our choice of these seven theories reflects our particular dialectical perspective on what is essential to an understanding of intimate aggression: an emphasis on *both* interpersonal dynamics *and* the larger social context.

Ultimately, we believe that a dialectical perspective allows us to hold multiple theories in our hands simultaneously, acknowledging the dynamic and changing nature of intimate aggression and the contexts that surround it. Note that a dialectical perspective should not be confused with an eclectic perspective that picks and chooses, often based on the theorist's personal experience, the "best" features of particular theories. Rather, a dialectical perspective encourages a theoretically guided approach to highlighting certain aspects of existing theories—in particular, those that are consistent with the principles of contradiction, holism, totality, and praxis.

THE DIALECTICAL PERSPECTIVE IN UNDERSTANDING PERSONAL RELATIONSHIPS

Dialectics has been a part of theorizing for more than a century, dating back to such classical theorists as Karl Marx. The specific dialectical stance that we use in this chapter is grounded in Bakhtin's philosophical foundation of dialogism, which Baxter and Montgomery (1996) imported into the study of personal relationships. "Relational dialectics" is a metatheory that focuses on the dynamic interplay of opposing tendencies as they are enacted in interaction. Montgomery (1993) formally defines dialectical opposition as "the simultaneous presence of two relational forces that are interdependent and mutually negating" (p. 207). Each force is known and defined only in contrast to the other. According to the dialectical perspective, much of social life is grounded in a series of contradictory pulls and tugs, or oppositional forces. Although Baxter and Montgomery (1996) emphasize that these forces are located in a relationship, they also acknowledge that dialectical tensions are intertwined with social, historical, and environmental contexts.

As Baxter and Montgomery (1996) note, four assumptions are central to the dialectical perspective: contradiction, change, totality, and praxis. First, *contradiction*, the dynamic interplay between oppositions, is at the heart of this perspective and captures the "both/and-ness of social life" (Baxter & West, 2003, p. 494). The focus on the interplay between contradictory forces is what differentiates dialectics from dualism. Although both perspectives emphasize the presence of opposites, the dialectical approach explores how the parties manage contradictory forces simultaneously, whereas a dualistic stance investigates the opposites in parallel (Baxter & Montgomery, 1996).

According to Baxter and Montgomery (1996), the two diametrically opposed tensions are in constant motion with respect to each other. The domination of one pole over the other leads to a desire to seek equilibrium

(Baxter & Simon, 1993). This results in a focus on *change*, the second assumption of the dialectical approach. Change is the result of the struggle to resolve the tension of the contradiction and is essential for growth to occur (Baxter, 1993). The dialectical perspective posits that relationships are constantly changing.

Tensions need to be understood in their *totality*, the third assumption of dialectical theory (Baxter & Montgomery, 1996). The concept of totality has three features. First, contradictions do not exist in isolation from one another, but instead are often experienced as a knot of contradictions, interdependently coexisting in a weblike fashion (Baxter, Braithwaite, Golish, & Olson, 2002). The second feature of totality is location. From a dialectical perspective, tensions are located within the relationship, although there is often little commonality between partners' perceptions of the relational contradictions (Baxter & Montgomery, 1996). The third feature, situatedness, also known as

in situ, highlights the need to be attentive to unique tensions indigenous to particular relationships and to recognize their embeddedness within time, space, and social contexts (Baxter & Montgomery, 1996).

The fourth assumption of the dialectical perspective is *praxis*. This concept acknowledges that people are simultaneously proactive actors and reactive objects within their social worlds (Baxter & Montgomery, 1996). It focuses attention on the concrete practices people use to manage their lives and negotiate myriad contradictions. Although dialectical theorists vary in where they situate praxis (e.g., Marxist dialectical theorists focus on materialism; Marx & Engels, 1848/1998), our discussion of praxis is guided by the work of those who consider it to be a symbolic, communicative activity (e.g., Baxter & Montgomery, 1996). Thus communication is the vehicle through which parties respond to dialectical exigencies in their lives.

● SPOTLIGHT ON THEORY

FAMILY RESILIENCE

Charles H. Huber, *New Mexico State University*

For most of the history of mental health practice, and particularly in recent decades concerning the "right way" to intervene in cases of domestic violence, practitioners have placed primary emphasis on pathology and dysfunction. It has been assumed that certain diagnoses are the norm for both victimizer (e.g., intermittent explosive disorder) and victim (e.g., posttraumatic stress disorder). Practitioners have then used these diagnoses to instruct intervention efforts by presupposing corresponding prescribed remedial processes. Within this practice perspective, individuals and families have generally been viewed only as service recipients rather than as also being capable, active partners in the change process. Indeed, those clients who do not accept professionals' expert diagnoses and corresponding therapeutic recommendations are all too often labeled resistant, and their potential contribution to the change process is even further minimized (Christensen, Todahl, & Barrett, 1999). Research and practice addressing issues of

(continued)

● *SPOTLIGHT ON THEORY continued*

domestic violence have become informed by the principles of family resilience within this ecology (Huber, 1998).

The concept of family resilience offers a contextual view from which scholars can consider how families confront and manage disruptive experiences, buffer stress, effectively reorganize, and then move forward with life. This view recognizes that the family interactions inherent in these processes influence immediate and long-term adaptation for both family members as individuals and the family as a unit. From the family resilience perspective, damaged families are seen not only as damaged, but also as challenged and able to address challenges adaptively. This perspective further shifts scholars away from a tendency to perceive family health or normality as residing in mythologized, problem-free families and toward understanding how families can and do survive and regenerate even in the midst of overwhelming stress and crises. Finally, the family resilience perspective affirms families' capacities for self-repair by identifying and amplifying family transactional processes that make it possible for families to emerge from adversity functioning more adaptively than before, not in spite of their experience, but rather strengthened by it (Walsh, 1998).

Research findings supporting resilience as a theoretical framework for prevention and intervention programs and policies have asserted that such a framework is appealing because it "emphasizes the promotion of positive outcomes while not ignoring risk-focused strategies" (Masten, 2001, p. F2). Likewise, it offers a balanced perspective relative to the many dichotomies within mental health fields (e.g., deficit/pathology versus collaboration/competence, victim versus victimizer, individual versus family). Scholars, however, have emphasized the inherent theoretical assertion that primary intervention efforts are best aimed at promoting competence. Of particular relevance to domestic violence, this contemporary family resilience framework encompasses the following (Kragh & Huber, 2002):

1. Interactions that lead families to "cope well" and those that contribute to serious problems are both considered; the former, however, are highlighted relative to intervention efforts.

2. Intervention goals are defined in both promotional terms (e.g., promoting competence) and remedial terms (e.g., reducing or preventing pathology and problems); again, the former are highlighted.

3. Assessments to guide and evaluate interventions include considerations of competence, strengths, and assets as well as symptoms, deficits, and risks; the former are emphasized relative to intervention efforts.

4. Intervention strategies emphasize building strengths, increasing resources, and mobilizing positive processes while simultaneously reducing deficits and treating symptoms.

5. Intervention programs are designed to incorporate both development and risk reduction, in that order of priority. ●

A DIALECTICAL APPROACH
TO THEORIZING ABOUT
AGGRESSION BETWEEN INTIMATES

The dialectical perspective is ideal for capturing the paradoxical nature of theorizing, studying, and experiencing intimate aggression. Using the four assumptions of the dialectical approach (contradiction, change, totality, and praxis), we present below some ways in which this perspective can help make sense out of contradictory findings, resolve artificially created binaries, create new ways of theorizing about aggressive relationships, and inform methodological improvements.

Contradiction and
Intimate Aggression

Contradiction and theory. Central to the notion of contradiction is the presence of *opposing* forces—*each* present, *each* pulling and pushing. Unlike a binary construction, the dialectical construction of contradiction emphasizes the simultaneity of "both/and." It also acknowledges the "knot" of multiple contradictions and tensions. Many of the theories used to explain intimate aggression are limited by their tendency to create mutually exclusive opposites, isolating or privileging one of the potentially dialectical forces (or poles) or not adequately accounting for the presence of the other. For example, the investment model suggests that an individual has a single level of commitment to a particular relationship, as opposed to the dialectical perspective's suggestion that an individual may have both high levels and low levels of commitment toward a particular relationship at different times and in different circumstances, or even at the same time. With its emphasis on the dyad and the family, the family systems perspective suggests that aggression is rooted in the relationship and not in the individual, as opposed to the dialectical perspective, which suggests that intimate aggression is simultaneously embedded within individual, relationship, and social levels. The social learning perspective suggests that observing aggression leads an individual to be more likely to engage in violent behavior. In contrast, the dialectical perspective suggests that an individual's observing aggression may lead to a number of contradictory tensions (e.g., the sense that aggression is acceptable versus the sense that it is horrifying and unacceptable), with potentially differing effects on the likelihood of the individual's behaving aggressively in the future.

A dialectical perspective encourages us to look for areas of overlap between apparently contradictory aspects of theory. For example, the family systems approach is often considered antithetical to feminist analysis of intimate aggression. Feminist theorists examine the roles of gender and patriarchal structures of dominance and, as a result, emphasize the differing contexts and consequences of men's versus women's use of aggression. On the other hand, systems theorists place intimate aggression in a context of coercive interaction; the locus of aggression lies not in a particular individual, but rather within the dysfunctional relationship. Although many scholars have pointed out the inconsistencies between these two theoretical perspectives, it is possible to take a both/and perspective that emphasizes how aggression is simultaneously embedded within relational patterns of communication and control, within a gender/power context that supports male dominance, *and* within social constructions of "appropriate" victims, "good" relationships, and forgiveness for violent behavior (Lloyd & Emery, 2000b). The dialectical aspect of contradiction pushes us to look for ways to resolve the apparent contradictions among multiple theories so that we can use them to shed helpful light on the problem of intimate aggression.

Contradiction and empirical findings. Findings within the domestic violence literature are noted for their polarity on various issues (Johnson, 1995). Much of this research can be characterized by its tendency to create "either/or" distinctions between types of samples drawn, kinds of aggression studied, and gender of perpetrators and victims. For example, there is a sharp dichotomy in findings between studies that have utilized samples of women who sought shelter from their severely battering husbands and studies that have examined physical aggression in representative samples of U.S. households (Johnson, 1995). Although there are some notable exceptions, such bifurcation of samples, theoretical perspectives, and findings continues to engender heated debate about the nature, extent, severity, and mutuality of intimate aggression.

Additionally, whereas researchers acknowledge that intimate aggression takes many forms, studies of verbal, psychological, physical, and sexual aggression have taken place in relative isolation from one another. Many scholars tend to study one type of aggression at a time, and the results of their work appear in disparate publications, causing a low level of cross-fertilization. Further, scholars most commonly use acts of physical aggression as markers for defining aggressive relationships and delineating when aggression occurs. On the other hand, when researchers have examined multiple forms of aggression simultaneously, their studies have at times been plagued with methodological problems, including weak operationalization of some constructs (e.g., the verbal aggression score within the Conflict Tactics Scale; Olson, in press) and assumptions of linearity (e.g., verbal aggression necessarily *leads* to physical aggression).

Most, but not all, researchers have focused primarily on physical aggression, which is limiting when viewed through a dialectical lens. For instance, using physical aggression as the primary way to define aggressive relationships downplays the grooming or seduction process, which is more verbal and psychological in nature, occurs long before the physical aggression begins, and better explains the entrapment process and why it is so difficult for abused women to disengage (Olson, 2004). Additionally, because physical aggression is empirically studied most often, it has been inadvertently positioned as the most serious or important form of aggression. Such a stance potentially minimizes the damage that other types of aggression may cause.

Contradiction and methodology. Certainly, conceptualizing aggression as all or nothing, one type or the other, is both limiting and incomplete. We acknowledge, however, that this practice may be the result of the difficulty in operationalizing the many forms that aggression takes, researchers' desire to maintain a cogent focus within their work, and the differing theoretical perspectives that drive research on intimate aggression. Yet we also suggest that a dialectical perspective is sorely needed in the conceptualization, measurement, and study of intimate aggression. A both/and perspective would begin with a different set of assumptions, most notably that we need to understand the deep interrelationships among the many forms of intimate aggression. A dialectical perspective would also de-emphasize a hierarchy among kinds of aggression. Instead of a rank-ordering approach, the emphasis would be on the deleterious impacts of verbal, physical, psychological, and sexual aggression and the ways in which these forms of aggression intersect and interplay to form a very tight web of control.

A dialectical perspective also raises many questions regarding the thorny theoretical and measurement problems associated with issues of mutuality versus gender asymmetry in intimate aggression. For example, to what extent is the issue of symmetry tangled up in our understanding of the impact of the severity of aggression, the social construction of "appropriate" responses to relational transgressions for men versus women, and the dynamics of control within relationships? When do women initiate aggression in their intimate relationships, and how is their use of aggression both different from and similar to men's aggression in context, impact, and meaning? A dialectical perspective alerts us to the possibility that both poles or positions may have some merit—that is, relational aggression may be characterized by both gender symmetry and asymmetry and the reflexive relationship between initiator and recipient.

The study of aggression in relationships understandably leads to a tendency to study the aggressive encounters themselves, as well as the situations that occur before and after such encounters. However, a dialectical perspective encourages us to contextualize intimate aggression, for example, by understanding how positive interactions and discourses serve to tie the knot that encourages partners to stay together despite aggressive behavior. A dialectical perspective also directs us to examine multiple poles of experience rather than focus solely on the negative pole. For example, researchers need to study not only hate, but also love, pain and joy, violence and peacefulness, in the same relationship.

Change and Intimate Aggression

Change and theory. According to the dialectical perspective, it is essential to recognize the role that change plays in the human experience. Many of the theories reviewed earlier consider changes over time to be an integral part of intimate aggression. However, change has a more central role in the dialectical perspective. For dialectical theorists, change is the norm. Rather than taking a cross-sectional view, dialectical theorists view change as an essential component of the process of intimate aggression. For example, in the investment model, a woman's decision concerning whether to stay in an abusive relationship or leave it is posited to be based on her concurrent calculation of rewards, costs, investments, satisfaction, and commitment to the relationship. Indeed, her calculation of these factors may change in the future, which may affect her ultimate decision, but from the investment perspective, change is not a necessary part of the process. A dialectical theoretical framework, in contrast, would integrate the life-course perspective's emphasis on process, change, and transition with other theoretical perspectives to enable better understanding of how aggression develops, changes over time, is maintained or disrupted, and (hopefully) ends.

Change and empirical findings. Although researchers have acknowledged the dynamic aspect of intimate aggression, relatively few have taken a process perspective on aggression among intimates. Instead, scholars have often conceptualized aggressive relationships from a static perspective, tending to focus on the crisis event (i.e., a physically violent episode). However, notable exceptions do exist. For example, Johnson (1995) and Lloyd (1999) have noted that the progressive nature of aggression varies by relationship or couple type, Olson and Golish (2002) have delineated the different pathways that the course of aggression takes during conflicts, and Kirkwood (1993) and Olson (2001) have focused on the process abused women go through as they disengage from their abusers, capturing the nonlinear processes involved in leaving.

Also related to change is one of the most commonly cited "facts" in the area of intimate aggression: the "intergenerational transmission of violence." This concept focuses on individuals' tendencies to repeat with their partners the aggressive patterns they were exposed to in their families of origin. Such a mechanism is consistent with a social learning explanation, which emphasizes the role of observation and modeling of aggressive behavior. Still, recent research indicates that the predictive ability of the cycle of violence has been greatly overstated, and that a number of factors may mediate and even "break" the cycle of violence (Johnson & Ferraro, 2000).

Results such as these suggest that scholars need to account more fully for how and why aggression changes over time. In addition, there is a particularly acute need for research that explores the period before aggression begins, as we know even less about the processes that take place during this period than we do about those that occur during and after aggression. Long before physical abuse occurs, an abuser "grooms" his victim, communicatively seducing her and slowly gaining control over her (Olson, 2004). During this time, the abused woman's identity is reconstructed, becoming subordinated to and enmeshed with the male partner's view of reality (Kirkwood, 1993; Olson, 2004). Our understanding of aggressive relationships would be greatly enhanced by additional knowledge about these early, preaggressive stages and by a broadening of our perspective to account more fully for how aggression (of all types) evolves over time. For instance, how is it that some couples are able to redirect the trajectory of aggression toward a healthier, more constructive pattern, whereas others are not? How do aggressive, nonaggressive, and potentially aggressive relationships compare and contrast in their developmental paths?

Change and methodology. A dialectical perspective prompts us to situate our understanding of physical aggression within processes of emotional, psychological, verbal, and sexual aggression, with particular emphasis on how this web of control develops and changes over time. We also need to broaden our lens to examine more of the everyday interactions and daily functioning in aggressive relationships compared with nonaggressive relationships, with an emphasis on how relational aggression occurs with the presence of some periods of relational harmony. Finally, a change/process model prompts us to question the logic that given that aggression has occurred, the couple (or individual) will always be aggressive. Olson and Golish (2002), for example, found that some couples who had experienced aggression during conflict (even very severe instances of aggression) were able to change and create nonaggressive ways of interacting.

The study of everyday life processes and events that we recommend can be achieved through the use of some (relatively) new methodological techniques. For example, researchers can have participants use personal digital assistants to keep electronic diaries; with such technology, researchers have the option of cuing participants to provide their thoughts, feelings, and/or behaviors at particular times to obtain concurrent, rather than retrospective, information on individuals' experiences. Similarly, researchers can gather change information through daily telephone interviews (Lloyd, 1999) or by first videotaping couples' behavioral interactions and then asking the partners, separately and/or together, to view the tapes and reflect on how they were feeling and thinking during

particular moments during the interactions (Jacobson & Gottman, 1998).

Finally, researchers need to employ longitudinal designs to capture the dialectics of family processes in aggressive (and potentially aggressive) couples, to understand day-to-day interactions in addition to crisis episodes, and to examine both micro (relational) and macro (social) cultural influences on the conceptualization and experience of interpersonal aggression. Although cross-sectional designs are useful for the examination of focused research questions (e.g., the frequency with which aggression occurs in dating relationships), studying the ebbs and flows of the process requires the use of longitudinal approaches.

Totality and Intimate Aggression

The third assumption of the dialectical perspective guiding our presentation is the concept of totality. Although empirically informative (and methodologically simpler), examining one tension in isolation from others provides a limited view of intimate aggression. For instance, as Goldner et al. (1990) have argued, it is remiss to focus solely on the dark side of domestic aggressiveness without looking at its other side, "the face of atonement and redemption" (p. 359). The honeymoon phase after an aggressive episode is infused with both reconnection and bonding. Further, because of the shameful aspect of the abuse, the act becomes the couple's "little secret" (p. 359). Therefore, the alliance that is formed between the partners following an abusive episode is a powerful bonding ritual in which the partners must deal simultaneously with tensions at intrapersonal, interpersonal, and social levels. The dialectical perspective's notion of totality prompts us to examine how tensions such as these are experienced in relation to others and how certain tensions are indigenous (in situ) to specific relationships (e.g., love and hate for an abusive partner).

Totality and theory. Theories that scholars have used to describe and explain intimate aggression have tended to focus on particular aspects or issues rather than on the totality of the experience. For example, the social learning perspective tends to focus on cognitions that relate to the process of role modeling. Here, the cognitive processes involved in the intergenerational transmission of aggressive behavior are privileged, and other aspects of the experience, such as the factors that maintain aggressive patterns of behavior, are not centrally considered. Relational control theory and the investment model also focus on targeted issues, such as how control in relationships both influences and is influenced by aggression and the cost-benefit calculus victims use in deciding whether to stay or leave, rather than the totality of the experience and process. Family systems theory, in its emphasis on the reverberating effects of changes in any of the family's subsystems, partially considers the totality of the experience. However, family systems theory focuses on the system and its subsystems, downplaying factors that are influential at the individual level or the societal level. A dialectical approach encourages the consideration of factors at all levels—cultural, familial, relational, and individual.

Totality and empirical findings. One of the most useful ways of incorporating the concept of totality into the study of aggressive relationships is to look at how intimate aggression is related to social locations such as class, race, and sexuality. The concept of intersectionality involves the ways in which various social locations intersect with one another and with aggression and power. In describing structural intersectionality, Crenshaw (1996) emphasizes that "the location of women of color at the intersections of race and gender makes our actual experience of domestic violence, rape, and remedial reform qualitatively different from that of white women" (p. 95). Renzetti (1997) has presented similar analyses of the intersections

of sexuality and gender with aggression. The concept of intersectionality meshes perfectly with a dialectical analysis of intimate aggression, for the both/and emphasis of dialectics makes room for and encourages careful intersectional analysis.

The totality assumption also invites exploration of how intimate aggression is embedded in structural and institutional contexts. Intimate aggression occurs in a context of low social control and high familial privacy. Generally, the social costs of perpetrating intimate aggression are low, because the controlling forces that usually restrain people from committing verbal, physical, or sexual assault are weak for such behaviors committed within a family. A lack of social sanctions is exacerbated by the fact that most intimate aggression is enacted in privacy (Gelles & Straus, 1979). Low social control and high familial privacy intersect with patriarchal structures to shape institutional responses to aggression that encourage trivialization and/or non-criminalization of aggressive acts (Stark & Flitcraft, 1996).

Another key concept that could profit from scholars' consideration of totality is that of control. Researchers (particularly those using feminist or relational control theories) acknowledge that power and control are at the heart of intimate aggression and have focused their attention on the negotiation of power within aggressive relationships (for a review, see Lloyd & Emery, 2000a). Unfortunately, much of the literature in this area is vague in its conceptualization of control; most problematic from a dialectical stance is that researchers have tended to consider control a unidimensional construct, ignoring its multidimensionality or totality. By recognizing the multidimensional nature of control, researchers and practitioners become better equipped to describe the variety among aggressive couples and individuals (Johnson, 1995; Johnson & Ferraro, 2000; Lloyd & Emery, 2000a; Olson, in press).

HOLDING MULTIPLE THEORIES IN OUR HANDS: ADVANCED DIALECTICAL RESEARCH METHODS

Deborah A. Davis, *Michigan State University*

Edward Read Barton, *Michigan State University*

The dialectical dynamic of interacting opposites is the integrative pattern of life. This dynamic unites cosmological and biological evolution with cultural, social, psychological, and spiritual evolution through symbols that convey the reality of a dynamic occurring everywhere between pairs of opposites. Dialectical tensions are not only located in intimate relationships but are intertwined with social, historical, cultural, and environmental contexts (see the discussion of Wilber's "Four Quadrants" on this volume's companion Web site, http://www.ncfr.org/sourcebook). Scholars should study families in all aspects of their existence: behavioral, social, cultural, and intentional/ mythopoetic (i.e., personal work with introspection, intuition, inner awareness, and insight).

Although at first very challenging, complex frameworks make the dynamic and changing interactiveness between and among multiple layers of influence on families more visible: the surfaces and depths (quantitative and qualitative) and the individual and collective (micro and macro) levels of families. According to Wilber (2002), the overall movement of cultural transformation is from individual human intelligence to the collective worldview, which at first is marginalized but eventually becomes embedded in social institutions, at which point these basic institutions automatically help reproduce the transformed worldview and socialize people in succeeding generations. Human biospiritual intelligence is the dialectical engine of cultural and social transformation.

Although Baxter and Montgomery (1996) do not seem to emphasize interiors in their relational dialectics, Wilber, the biocultural paradigm, mythopoetic women, and mythopoetic men know them well—and know the intentional/mythopoetic to be not only the dialectical engine of cultural and social transformation but the origin of the healing impulse as well (Wilber, 2002). Rather than just describing exteriors (even fluidly and paradoxically with dialectics), mythopoetic women's work and mythopoetic men's work (Barton, 2000) delve into psyche, spirit, and emotional healing by drawing from art, dance, initiation, support groups, ritual support groups, myth, and quasi-myth. In the New Warrior Training Adventure and subsequent integration groups, for example, men from the ManKind Project devote much time and energy to accessing long-denied and buried emotions (glad, mad, sad, and sacred) and discharging them in ritual space, to recognizing the distinctive presence (subtle physical feeling) of each of these emotions in their own bodies and developing a vocabulary for these feelings, and

(continued)

● *SPOTLIGHT ON METHODS continued*

then to articulating these emotions in their lives. Thus mythopoetic praxis results in new, emotionally more mature, abilities ("feeling through the lived body") for men and women—they can grieve their losses and love more fully.

Mythological images spring from the deepest recesses of the psyche, unmolested by the cultural and social systems of domination that have shaped the intellect, suppressed serotonin levels, and generated neurochemical patterns of fear, anxiety, and violence. Most emotional and spiritual healing therapies are directed toward reintegration and realization of the psyche's endowed power, which in turn generates healthy neurochemical patterns of self-empowerment, trust, respect, and the ability to learn continually (Pearce, 2002).

The central relationship of all healthy whole systems is an integration of dialectical opposites. Our ability to process this kind of information clearly is often compromised by our attitudes, traditions, beliefs, and linguistic habits. This compromising of clarity leads to social, psychological, and scientific errors—evident in our tendency to produce toxic (violent) relationships and environments. When the special "neurochemistry of trust" cascades through interior landscapes, new neural networks are self-generated, dysfunction dissolves, and personal, psychological, and spiritual growth result. We recognize previously hidden relationships between our interior states and our exterior behaviors. This is the advanced dialectical information of clarity that family scholars need for research methods and theory construction, so that families of any configuration can be more healthy and whole.

Advanced Dialectical Research Methods

1. Select a wholistic framework that

2. Makes visible the dynamic interactiveness of dialectical opposites.

3. Recognize that intentional/mythopoetic work is the engine of transformation and healing.

Practical test: Are relationships between interior states and exterior behaviors being revealed? ●

Totality and methodology. One of the most important implications of the totality assumption for the study of intimate aggression is the entreaty to consider both multiplicity and intersectionality. Aggression and control are likely to differ not only along single dimensions of diversity, but also across multiple, interacting dimensions (e.g., race/ethnicity, gender, socioeconomic status, rural versus urban geographic area). Thus, despite the methodological and practical challenges inherent in studying how the multiple dimensions interact and mutually influence one another, it is imperative that scholars attempt to undertake such research.

Before we can design and conduct such studies, however, we need to expand our theoretical lens to accommodate multiple dimensions. For example, hooks (1984) argues that to understand intimate aggression between Black men and women, one must look beyond interpersonal relationships and begin instead with the psychological abuse that Black men, especially, experience in the public world. For the "cycle of violence" to end, hooks asserts, Black men must challenge the notion of masculinity as created by the dominant group, question the role that capitalism plays in their lives, and understand the degree to which they are alienated and exploited in the workplace. In her work, hooks underscores the multivocality of intimate aggression—how the many voices of those abused and those who do the abusing vary according to the individuals' social, economic, and racial standpoints.

Praxis and Intimate Aggression

In the context of intimate aggression, *praxis* refers to the communication activities and agentic behaviors that human beings use at both the interpersonal level and the societal level to negotiate a variety of aggression-related contradictions. For example, an abused woman is likely to be faced with processing the prevailing discourses that frame the abuse she endures as simultaneously justifiable and unjustifiable. In order to manage this contradiction, she may choose several communication strategies, such as talking to friends or family members about the abuse, staying silent out of fear of being beaten, or coming to the conclusion that the aggression was her fault (Lloyd & Emery, 2000b). She may also engage in any of a number of behavioral strategies to manage the contradiction, such as leaving her abuser or attempting to change her own behavior in the hope that he will be less likely to abuse her.

Praxis and theory. Among the theories guiding our discussion, feminist theory has emphasized more than any other the social construction of intimate aggression, the language of aggression, and the symbolic and agentic strategies that victims use to negotiate and make sense of the paradoxes of intimate aggression. Feminist theorists have asked key praxis questions, including how intimate aggression is perpetuated and minimized through the language used to describe it, how victims of aggression resist/reconstruct the

dominant discourses of blaming the victim and excusing the aggressor, and how battered women display multifaceted components of agency (Lloyd & Emery, 2001; Mahoney, 1994).

Feminist theoretical work on praxis has emphasized both social construction and agency. Analyses of the social construction of intimate aggression seek to understand the ways in which individuals actively manage the paradoxical nature of such aggression, focusing on how their meaning-making processes and strategic choices are embedded within the larger social context. Discourse is an important concept here, with its emphasis on the meanings that are constructed from everyday features of life, conversations, statements, and cultural practices. These discourses are not constructed in isolation, nor are they immutable; rather, they are socially constructed along locations of gender, race, class, sexuality, and power (Hare-Mustin, 1994; Yllö & Bograd, 1988).

The concept of agency is also a theoretically important aspect of praxis. Agency, as Mahoney (1994) explains, is acting for oneself as an individual. Feminist theorists have called for a renewed emphasis on agency and a de-emphasis on constructing battered women as helpless and dependent victims. Mahoney effectively argues that the agency of women who are physically and sexually assaulted must be understood in the context of oppression; unfortunately, all too often, women who are battered are assumed to be "unproblematically independent actors today, or if we are not, the main obstacle is our own consciousness" (p. 62). More nuanced views of agency acknowledge the dialectics of victim/survivor (see also Reich, 2002) and agency in the face of oppression and limited choices.

Praxis and empirical findings. Analyses of the "language of intimate aggression" illustrate the concept of praxis. The language used to describe aggression influences the ways in which we perceive and react to it (Reich, 2002). For example, the word *victim* conveys the sense that the recipient of violent behavior passively receives it and has very little opportunity to respond with agency (Mahoney,

1994). Use of the term *untoward behavior* as a synonym for *aggression* conveys a sense that the behavior is not all that devastating. Both the scholarly literature and the popular media are replete with "linguistic avoidance" in the case of intimate aggression—that is, language that renders issues of perpetrator/victim/gender/harm invisible (Lamb & Keon, 1995).

Delineation of the discourse of intimacy and the discourse of intimate aggression provides a context for how both perpetrators and victims make sense of intimate aggression and actively construct responses to it (Lloyd & Emery, 2000b). The discourse of intimacy is imbued with the language of equality, romance, and sexuality. The discourse of intimate aggression emphasizes excusing the aggressor, blaming the victim, and rendering intimate aggression invisible. These narratives reinforce the complementarity of men and women, construct relationships as magical and romantic, and emphasize notions of the male sexual drive as urgent and uncontrollable. They also belie the presence of male domination and power inequities in relationships and encourage couples to construct negative interactions (even severe physical and sexual aggression) as externally produced (Lloyd & Emery, 2000b).

Research on agency and intimate aggression has also examined the binaries of "stay versus leave" and the "good victim versus the bad victim." Mahoney (1994) asserts that, in law, media, and professional discourse, staying in an abusive relationship is set up in opposition to leaving the relationship; a woman has only these two choices, and if she stays, she is presumed to lack agency and to accept the aggression. Furthermore, the "good victim" of abuse is one who can exact our full sympathy and therefore deserves our protection; she is White and middle-class, does not fight back, and lacks culpability for her predicament. In other words, she is constructed as a person without agency. Lloyd and Emery (2001) present a counternarrative by examining the intricate ways in which abused women display agency in the face of oppression.

Praxis and methodology. Many of the methodological implications of attending to praxis include the need for qualitative, mixed-method, and longitudinal designs as well as the importance of examining multiple poles of experience. In addition, attention to praxis calls for a reconceptualization of the very ways in which intimate aggression has been elucidated and named. Scholars must deconstruct and reconstruct the binaries of stay/leave and accept/fight using methodologies that will allow them to examine staying/leaving as processes and victims as resisting and active agents. Questions such as "Why does she stay with the batterer?" and "Why didn't she fight harder to prevent sexual assault?" would be less relevant in such a reconceptualized framework. Similarly, the binary of victim/agent would be rejected in favor of a dialectical analysis of the contradictions and tensions inherent in the experience of aggression.

Further examination of praxis and aggression is sorely needed. Such work would seek to make visible the behavioral and communicative strategies that people use to negotiate the presence of intimate aggression in their lives. It also would simultaneously examine the ways in which these strategies are embedded within a rich discourse about how partners are supposed to act in loving relationships, perform as gendered beings, and react to and understand intimate aggression. Finally, there is much potential in searching out the ways in which victims of intimate aggression do enact agency and creating a discourse around those acts of agency that make them visible and acknowledged.

SOME FINAL THOUGHTS

In this chapter, we have attempted to clarify and advance our understanding of the dynamics of intimate aggression from a dialectical perspective. Our work here builds on key relational and contextual theories as well as on a wealth of empirical studies of intimate aggression. The dialectical assumptions of contradiction, change, totality, and praxis serve to integrate current knowledge about intimate aggression and to advance both theory and methodology in the future. This discussion also highlights the tensions inherent in theory and research on intimate aggression and points to the increasingly complex frameworks/methodologies that scholars will need to develop to advance this field of inquiry. As Gilgun (2003) has noted, "Entering the field means entering chaos" (p. 3). Applying a dialectical lens to the inquiry process means that researchers must be willing to enter a world that is complex and chaotic. We must remain mindful not only of the interplay between theory and practice, but also of the dynamics between researcher and researched. The constantly changing nature of intimate aggression and our understanding of it also implies another dialectic—the continuous motion between the known and the unknown. Taking all of these dynamics into account means increasing the complexity of our explorations exponentially. Yet we must be willing to accept this inevitability, trusting that, by embracing a both/and approach, we are gaining a more elaborate awareness of what it means to experience intimate aggression and the knowledge that our understanding will never be complete.

Finally, we come to an interesting question for self-reflection: What are *our* particular dialectical lenses? As we theorize about intimate aggression and conduct research on this compelling topic, what really speaks to us as scholars? Certainly, our own perspectives are infused throughout this chapter (in the very choices of the theories and research we emphasize). Still, we would like to end with a brief treatise on our current working, dialectical

assumptions about intimate aggression. We assume that control is at the heart of intimate aggression. We assume that intimate aggression is simultaneously situated as a learned behavior; as a pattern of interaction; as a phenomenon that perpetrators and recipients react to, understand, and act on within prevailing discourses of gender, intimacy, sexuality, and violence; and as an occurrence that is deeply rooted in hierarchy, patriarchy, racism, heteronormativity, and inequity. We assume that intimate aggression is filled with contradictions and tensions: It occurs in the context of a loving relationship, it is shocking and hurtful behavior, and it may be preceded and followed by everyday acts of care/hostility/concern/control. We construct perpetrator/victim and/or mutually aggressive partners as active agents who are embedded in a context of romance and joy, control and dominance, patriarchy and equality. In addition, we assume that a both/and perspective can advance our understanding of the paradoxes and processes of intimacy and aggression.

NOTE

1. We have chosen to use the term *aggression* throughout this chapter because it maintains a relatively narrow focus on the acts themselves and, in so doing, also encapsulates a broader range of behaviors. Additional terms, such as *battering, abuse,* and *violence,* add important relational and social dynamics to the construct but do so in ways that exceed our thesis here. We encourage readers to view an extended list of definitions on this volume's companion Web site (http://www.ncfr.org/sourcebook) and to join us in a dialogue about such terms.

Case Study

CASE STUDY

AN ECOLOGICAL PERSPECTIVE ON AN INTERGENERATIONAL FAMILY PROBLEM

Lawrence B. Schiamberg, *Michigan State University*

Daphna Gans, *University of Southern California*

The increasing rate of elder abuse by adult children is an example of intimate family violence with significant repercussions for families as caregivers of older adults. Because the relevant risk factors for such abuse are related to individuals (i.e., adult child as caregiver and older adult as care recipient), the social/cultural contexts of individuals, and the interactions between persons and contexts over time, both human ecological and life-course perspectives provide effective frameworks for explaining elder abuse as an intergenerational family problem (Bronfenbrenner, 1997; Elder, Johnson, & Crosnoe, 2003). In this case study we utilize an ecological, bifocal model of elder abuse by adult children, focusing simultaneously on the adult child and the aging parent as a familial dyad. The model posits the essential role of the intergenerational relationship between an adult child and an aging parent, over the life course, as a primary basis for understanding elder abuse as well as the development of relevant and effective community prevention and intervention programs (e.g., Schiamberg & Gans, 2000). Research on elder abuse increasingly points to the need for theoretical explanations that address the problem in context (Kosberg & Nahmias, 1996).

HUMAN ECOLOGICAL PERSPECTIVE

From a human ecological perspective, both positive and negative outcomes occur in a framework of four locational/spatial contexts and one time-related context (Bronfenbrenner, 1997):

1. *Microsystem:* The immediate context of development involving person-to-person interaction (e.g., family, community, or work setting).

2. *Mesosystem:* The relationships between two or more microsystems. For example, if an aging parent is the focus of the model, the mesosystem might include relationships between family interactions and potential formal support such as social service agencies.

3. *Exosystem:* Environments that are influential by virtue of the participation of other family members but that are external to the focal person. For example, an aging parent does not participate in his or her adult child's workplace, but the policies of that workplace, such as those concerning family leave, may affect the parent's well-being.

4. *Macrosystem:* The broad ideological values, norms, and institutional patterns of a particular culture.

5. *Chronosystem:* The time-related dimensions of person-context interaction over the life course.

CASE STUDY *continued*

LIFE-COURSE PERSPECTIVE

The life-course perspective is embedded in Bronfenbrenner's notion of the chrono-system, but it has also received considerable attention from other theorists and researchers as both a developmental and a historical framework for the study of intergenerational relations (Bengtson & Allen, 1993). The life-course perspective emphasizes aging as shaped by social contexts, cultural meanings, and cohort/historical periods (Bengtson, Burgess, & Parrott, 1997). A major principle of the life-course perspective, essential to this case study, is the concept of linked lives, wherein individual life trajectories are interdependent (Elder et al., 2003). Furthermore, the principle of linked lives includes the norm of reciprocity, which suggests that people will stay in exchanges as long as the benefits are greater than the costs and the level of satisfaction is higher than the comparison level of alternatives (Bengtson et al., 1997).

THE ECOLOGICAL, BIFOCAL MODEL: RISK FACTORS OF ELDER ABUSE

In an ecological, bifocal model, risk factors for elder abuse in the home care setting are related to individuals (i.e., adult child as caregiver and older adult as care recipient), the immediate family and social/cultural contexts of those individuals, and the interactions between persons and contexts.

The Microsystem

Characteristics of Elderly Victims

- *Gender:* Although some research has found evidence that women are more likely than men to be abused because of increased vulnerability to sexual molestation, other studies point to the high risk of abuse for older men because they are likely to be living with family and therefore with potential abusers (Pillemer & Finkelhor, 1988).
- *Chronological age and health:* Because increased age is often associated with the presence of health problems and such problems may complicate the caregiving relationship, older adults are at higher risk for abuse (Kosberg & Nahmias, 1996).
- *Dementia/Alzheimer's disease:* Abuse is estimated to be higher for dementia patients than for elderly persons in other groups, possibly due to the provocative or aggressive behavior of some dementia patients (Paveza et al., 1992).
- *Psychological factors and social isolation:* Psychological problems such as depression may lead elderly parents to accept abuse without seeking help; such problems may also hinder detection of abuse (Kosberg & Nahmias, 1996).

Characteristics of Abusive Adult Children

- *Substance abuse:* Alcoholism is associated with family violence, including elder abuse (Anetzberger, Korbin, & Austin, 1994).
- *Caregiver experience and burden:* Stressed and overburdened caregivers are more likely to abuse the elderly relatives they care for than are caregivers who are able to handle their stress (Kosberg & Nahmias, 1996).
- *Personality traits:* Hypercritical behavior and impatient behavior are associated with caregiver abuse, as are the tendency to blame the older person for caregiving problems and the tendency to hold unrealistic caregiving expectations.
- *Absence of social support:* Caregivers who are not linked to formal or informal support networks (e.g., family, friends, coworkers) may be at increased risk for committing elder abuse.

Case Study

CASE STUDY *continued*

Family Factors: The Linked Lives of the Abusive Adult Child and the Abused Parent

- *Dependency relationships:* Although some abused elders may feel powerless or vulnerable in their relationships with their family caregivers, some family caregivers may actually be more dependent on, and resentful of, their aging relatives than vice versa, especially with regard to finances and housing (Pillemer & Finkelhor, 1988).

- *Living arrangements:* Overcrowded living spaces and lack of privacy are frequently associated with intrafamily conflict, including elder abuse (Kosberg, 1988).

- *Intergenerational transmission of abuse in the family:* Abuse of older adults is more common in families with long-term patterns of violent behavior. There is no evidence, however, of a cycle of abuse wherein a previously abused child strikes out at his or her own abusive parent when the parent is aging. In fact, the concept of intergenerational transmission of family violence is more useful in explaining child abuse by parents than elder abuse by adult offspring (Korbin, Antezberger, & Austin, 1995).

- *Demands of multiple generations:* Typically, the care of older adult parents has fallen on the shoulders of middle-aged women, who are sometimes labeled the "sandwich generation" because of their responsibilities in caring for both their own children and their parents. Although such demands may increase the risk of abuse by increasing caregivers' stress and subjective burden, evidence for this relationship is inconsistent (Loomis & Booth, 1995).

The Mesosystem and the Exosystem

When we view these systems from the bifocal perspective, some of the factors that appear in the mesosystem of one focal person may appear in the exosystem of the other person and vice versa.

- *Employment status and financial resources of the adult child:* Inadequate financial resources for caring for a dependent elder family member may foster caregiver resentment against the older adult, creating a situation conducive to abuse (Kosberg & Nahmias, 1996).

- *Social isolation and lack of formal support for the adult child:* Lack of social support for caregivers from family members, friends, and associates has been linked with abuse of older adults. As a result, a wide range of programs have been developed that aim to provide support for families, including in-home respite and support groups.

- *Social isolation and lack of formal support for the aging parent:* Abused elders tend to be more socially isolated than non-abused elders, and their limited contact with community support systems reduces the likelihood of detection and effective intervention (Gelles, 1997).

The Macrosystem

- *Cultural norms:* Cultural attitudes and values such as ageism, or the view of older adults as "less worthy" than younger persons, may create a climate within families that is favorable to elder abuse (Kosberg & Nahmias, 1996).

- *Public policy:* In the 1987 amendments to the Older Americans Act, a provision for elder abuse prevention activities mandated the development of public education and outreach to identify abuse, neglect, and exploitation of elderly persons as well as procedures for investigating reports of such abuse (Neale, Hwalek, Goodrich, & Quinn, 1996).

In summary, the focus of the human ecological and life-course perspectives on linked lives provides a useful framework for understanding and eventually addressing the multiple contexts that contribute to elder abuse by adult children.

DISCUSSION AND EXTENSION

THE CHALLENGES AND PROMISE OF A DIALECTICAL APPROACH TO THEORIZING ABOUT INTIMATE VIOLENCE

Claire M. Renzetti, *St. Joseph's University*

I remember the first time I learned about dialectical theory. I was a sophomore in college, enrolled in a classical sociological theory course in which the focus of discussion was the work of Karl Marx. Today, when I teach Marx in my sociological theory course and discuss how he developed his dialectical theory from the work of philosophers such as Hegel and Feuerbach, my students look at me much the same way I looked at my instructor in 1976. Their eyes ask, "Why do I need to learn this? I'll never use it." Later, I grew to appreciate the richness and practicality of dialectical theory—and I hope my students will too. Certainly, one of the strengths of Olson, Fine, and Lloyd's chapter is their demonstration of the utility of a dialectical approach for understanding intimate partner violence. Although they discuss dialectical theory in terms of its application to interpersonal relationships, the fundamental components—the emphasis on inherent contradictions, constant change, social and historical contexts, and human agency—are the same as those found in the classical dialectical approaches that Marx and others developed to explain social structures and the material conditions of social life.

Olson et al. accurately name many of the issues that have long frustrated researchers and practitioners in the field of intimate partner violence, such as the bond between the victim and the abuser, and the fact that women, although far more often than men on the receiving end of abuse, may sometimes initiate violence against their intimate partners. They correctly point out that much of the difficulty

scholars have had in understanding such issues lies in the tradition of viewing intimate partner violence in binary or dualistic terms when, in reality, social life is dynamic and fluid, and what makes human beings distinctively human is our ability to make decisions that allow us to be "simultaneously proactive actors and reactive objects within [our] social worlds." Dialectical theory captures, as they put it, this "both/and" character—or the *nonlinearity*—of social interaction.

Olson et al., however, focus primarily on the couple or relationship level, giving far less attention to structural or institutional issues that are as much a part of—and, indeed, impinge on or constrain—interpersonal interaction in everyday life. For instance, in discussing change, they rightly suggest that researchers need to investigate how and why intimate partner violence changes over time, looking not only at crisis periods but also at the previolence stage, when, they state, an abuser "grooms" his victim by "communicatively seducing her" into compliance. This depiction implies that abusers plan their abuse well in advance and deliberately "set up" their victims. Perhaps this is true in some cases, but such a characterization overlooks the fact that men's control of women in intimate relationships is, in many cultures, *normative* and thus positively sanctioned by the larger society as well as by men's smaller social peer groups. A dialectical approach to intimate partner violence requires us to examine the normative embeddedness of gendered interactions in intimate partner

Discussion and Extension

relationships—and this is done at the structural, not the interpersonal, level of social life.

Further, the need to move beyond the interpersonal to the structural is more apparent in the discussions of totality and praxis. Social locations (e.g., gender, class, race/ethnicity, sexuality, age, disability, and geography) do not intersect only with one another; they also intersect with the structural and institutional contexts that Olson et al. mention briefly. The issues generated by these structural and institutional contexts go beyond the question of "low social control and high familial privacy." In our everyday lives, we interact constantly with institutions, but the institutions with which we interact and the character of these interactions are directly influenced by our respective social locations. For example, because women and members of racial minority groups are disproportionately represented among the poor, they are more likely than men, Whites, and the more affluent to interact with the state through welfare offices. The goal of recent welfare "reforms" is to move people off welfare, supposedly by transitioning them to work. But if a woman is experiencing intimate partner violence, she is (in most states) eligible for a waiver from welfare-related work requirements. As research indicates that 20–30% of welfare recipients are involved in violent intimate relationships (Browne & Bassuk, 1997; Raphael & Tolman, 1997) and that such violence typically inhibits their ability to maintain employment (Riger, 2003), the waiver—or the Family Violence Option (FVO), as it is officially called—can be a significant institutional response to intimate partner violence for poor women. Seeking answers to such questions as "Do most welfare recipients or poor women receive information from welfare offices about the FVO?" and "What impact has the FVO had on women's experiences of intimate partner violence?"

puts the researcher at the *intersection of the interpersonal and the structural* and highlights the nexus of social locations, institutional/structural contexts, and intimate relationships (see, e.g., Lein, Jacquet, Lewis, Cole, & Williams, 2001; Postmus, 2003).

Similarly, by focusing their discussion of praxis at the level of interpersonal communication and social discourse, Olson et al. largely overlook *institutional* responses to both battered women and abusers. These institutional responses impinge on women's agency in dealing with the abuse as well as other aspects of their lives. For instance, mandatory arrest, no-drop prosecution, and mandatory sentencing policies take much decision making away from victimized women and result in men's not only being arrested for abuse, but also receiving jail time. Supporters argue that such policies relieve women of fear of retaliation from their abusers were they to prosecute and hold men accountable for their behavior. But others argue that such policies do not represent what some women want to have happen to their abusers, nor do they necessarily benefit women or make them safer (Ford, 2003). If a woman needs her abusive intimate partner's income to support herself and her children, then she may not see jail time for him as an optimal outcome. A woman who has to travel several hours a day by public transportation to a low-paying job may also reject arrest, prosecution, and jail for her abuser if she relies on him or members of his family for child care that she cannot afford to pay for in the public sector. Again, these examples draw researchers to an examination of the interplay between the interpersonal and the institutional/structural levels of everyday life, which is central to a dialectical approach to any social problem.

Of course, we are left with the question of how such examinations should be conducted empirically. What specific measurement tools or methods would allow social scientists to gather the data necessary to

DISCUSSION AND EXTENSION *continued*

answer the complex research questions that a dialectical theory poses? I am intrigued by Olson et al.'s suggestion of having research participants use PDAs to keep electronic diaries, recording their thoughts, feelings, and behaviors at precise moments in time in response to preprogrammed cues. Equally provocative is their suggestion of daily telephone interviews to gather "change information." Nevertheless, I am concerned that such methods are too intrusive, particularly for women who must struggle daily to support themselves and their children. Such methods also raise safety concerns: What are the risks to women involved in controlling or physically abusive relationships

of participating in studies that use such methods of data collection?

I have raised here only a few of the challenges inherent in taking a dialectical approach to understanding intimate partner violence. That the task of addressing these challenges is daunting makes it no less worthwhile. To the contrary, given the potential practical and theoretical gains that may be achieved through the use of a dialectical approach to intimate partner violence, we should embrace these challenges enthusiastically. Olson et al.'s chapter is our springboard and, as such, represents a significant contribution to our collective efforts to end violence in intimate relationships.

Discussion and Extension

REFERENCES

Anetzberger, G. J., Korbin, J. E., & Austin, C. (1994). Alcoholism and elder abuse. *Journal of Interpersonal Violence, 9,* 184–193.

Baber, K. M., & Allen, K. R. (1992). *Women and families: Feminist reconstructions.* New York: Guilford.

Barton, E. R. (2000). Parallels between mythopoetic men's work, men's peer mutual support groups and selected feminist theories. In E. R. Barton (Ed.), *Mythopoetic perspectives of men's healing work: An anthology for therapists and others* (pp. 3–20). Westport, CT: Bergin & Garvey.

Baxter, L. A. (1993). Dialectical contradictions in relationship development. In S. Petronio, J. K. Alberts, M. L. Hecht, & J. Buley (Eds.), *Contemporary perspectives on interpersonal communication* (pp. 88–103). Madison, WI: Brown & Benchmark.

Baxter, L. A., Braithwaite, D., Golish, T. D., & Olson, L. N. (2002). Contradictions of interactions for wives of elderly husbands with adult dementia. *Journal of Applied Communication Research, 30,* 1–26.

Baxter, L. A., & Montgomery, B. M. (1996). *Relating: Dialogues and dialectics.* New York: Guilford.

Baxter, L. A., & Simon, E. P. (1993). Relationship maintenance strategies and dialectical contradictions in personal relationships. *Journal of Social and Personal Relationships, 10,* 225–242.

Baxter, L. A., & West, L. (2003). Couple perceptions of their similarities and differences: A dialectical perspective. *Journal of Social and Personal Relationships, 20,* 491–514.

Bengtson, V. L., & Allen, K. R. (1993). The life course perspective applied to families over time. In P. Boss, W. J. Doherty, R. LaRossa, W. R. Schumm, & S. K. Steinmetz (Eds.), *Sourcebook of families, theories and methods: A contextual approach* (pp. 469–499). New York: Plenum.

Bengtson, V. L., Burgess, E. O., & Parrott, T. M. (1997). Theory, explanation and a third generation of theoretical development in social gerontology. *Journal of Gerontology: Social Sciences, 52,* 572–588.

Bronfenbrenner, U. (1997). Ecology of the family as a context for human development: Research perspectives. In J. L. Paul, M. Churton, H. Rosselli-Kostoryz, W. C. Morse, K. Marfo, C. Lavely, et al. (Eds.), *Foundations of special education* (pp. 49–83). Pacific Grove, CA: Brooks/Cole.

Browne, A., & Bassuk, S. S. (1997). Intimate violence in the lives of homeless and poor abused women: Prevalence and patterns in an ethnically diverse sample. *American Journal of Orthopsychiatry, 67,* 261–278.

Christensen, D. N., Todahl, J., & Barrett, W. C. (1999). *Solution-based casework: An introduction to clinical and case management skills in casework practice.* New York: Aldine de Gruyter.

Crenshaw, K. (1996). Mapping the margins: Intersectionality, identity politics, and violence against women of color. In J. L. Edleson & Z. C. Eisikovits (Eds.), *Future interventions with battered women and their families* (pp. 93–118). Thousand Oaks, CA: Sage.

Elder, G. H., Jr., Johnson, M. K., & Crosnoe, R. (2003). The emergence and development of life course theory. In J. T. Mortimer & M. J. Shanahan (Eds.), *Handbook of the life course.* New York: Kluwer Academic.

Farrington, K., & Chertok, E. (1993). Social conflict theories of the family. In P. Boss, W. J. Doherty, R. LaRossa, W. R. Schumm, & S. K. Steinmetz (Eds.), *Sourcebook of family theories and methods: A contextual approach* (pp. 357–381). New York: Plenum.

Ford, D. A. (2003). Coercing victim participation in domestic violence prosecutions. *Journal of Interpersonal Violence, 18,* 669–692.

Gelles, R. J. (1997). *Intimate violence in families* (3rd ed.). Thousand Oaks, CA: Sage.

Gelles, R. J., & Straus, M. A. (1979). Determinants of violence in the family: Toward a theoretical integration. In W. R. Burr, R. Hill, F. I. Nye, & I. L. Reiss (Eds.), *Contemporary theories about the family: Vol. 1. Research-based theories* (pp. 549–581). New York: Free Press.

Giles-Sims, J. (1983). *Wife battering: A systems theory approach.* New York: Guilford.

Gilgun, J. F. (2003, November). *Deductive qualitative analysis and the testing of conceptual models: Commentary on "A dialectical approach to theorizing about violence between intimates."* Paper presented at the annual meeting of the National Council on Family Relations, Vancouver.

Goldner, V., Penn, P., Sheinberg, M., & Walker, G. (1990). Love and violence: Gender paradoxes in volatile attachments. *Family Process, 29,* 343–364.

Hare-Mustin, R. T. (1994). Discourses in the mirrored room: A postmodern analysis of therapy. *Family Process, 33,* 19–35.

hooks, b. (1984). *Feminist theory: From margin to center.* Boston: South End.

Huber, C. H. (1998, February). *Family resilience and domestic violence: Panacea or pragmatic therapeutic perspective?* Paper presented at the midwinter convention of the American Psychological Association, La Jolla, CA.

Jacobson, N., & Gottman, J. M. (1998). *When men batter women: New insights into ending abusive relationships.* New York: Simon & Schuster.

Johnson, M. P. (1995). Patriarchal terrorism and common couple violence: Two forms of violence against women. *Journal of Marriage and the Family, 57,* 283–294.

Johnson, M. P., & Ferraro, K. J. (2000). Research on domestic violence in the 1990s: Making distinctions. *Journal of Marriage and the Family, 62,* 948–963.

Kirkwood, C. (1993). *Leaving abusive partners.* Newbury Park, CA: Sage.

Korbin, J. E., Anetzberger, G. J., & Austin, C. (1995). The intergenerational cycle of violence in child and elder abuse. *Journal of Elder Abuse & Neglect, 7*(1), 1–15.

Kosberg, J. I. (1988). Preventing elder abuse: Identification of high risk factors prior to placement decisions. *Gerontologist, 28,* 43–50.

Kosberg, J. I., & Nahmias, D. (1996). Characteristics of victims and perpetrators and milieus of abuse and neglect. In L. A. Baumhover & S. C. Beall (Eds.), *Abuse, neglect, and exploitation of older persons: Strategies for assessment and intervention* (pp. 31–49). Baltimore: Health Professions Press.

Kragh, J. R., & Huber, C. H. (2002). Family resilience and domestic violence: Panacea or pragmatic therapeutic perspective? *Journal of Individual Psychology, 58,* 290–304.

Lamb, S., & Keon, S. (1995). Blaming the perpetrator: Language that distorts reality in newspaper articles on men battering women. *Psychology of Women Quarterly, 19,* 209–220.

Lein, L., Jacquet, S. E., Lewis, C. M., Cole, P. R., & Williams, B. B. (2001). With the best of intentions: Family Violence Option and abused women's needs. *Violence Against Women, 7,* 193–210.

Lloyd, S. A. (1999). The interpersonal and communication dynamics of wife battering. In X. Arriaga & S. Oskamp (Eds.), *Violence in intimate relationships.* Thousand Oaks, CA: Sage.

Lloyd, S. A., & Emery, B. C. (2000a). The context and dynamics of intimate aggression against women. *Journal of Social and Personal Relationships, 17,* 503–521.

Lloyd, S. A., & Emery, B. C. (2000b). *The dark side of courtship: Physical and sexual aggression.* Thousand Oaks, CA: Sage.

Lloyd, S. A, & Emery, B. C. (2001). *The missing/misguided discourse of agency in the analysis of intimate violence against women.* Paper presented at the meeting of the International Network on Personal Relationships, Prescott, AZ.

Loomis, L. S., & Booth, A. (1995). Multigenerational caregiving and well-being: The myth of the beleaguered sandwich generation. *Journal of Family Issues, 16,* 131–148.

Mahoney, M. R. (1994). Victimization or oppression? Women's lives, violence and agency. In M. A. Fineman & R. Mykitiuk (Eds.), *The public nature of private violence* (pp. 59–92). New York: Routledge.

Marx, K., & Engels, F. (1998). *The communist manifesto: A modern edition.* London: Verso. (Original work published 1848)

Masten, A. S. (2001). The power of the ordinary: Resilience in development. *National Council on Family Relations Report, 46*(2), F1–F3.

Montgomery, B. M. (1993). Relationship maintenance versus relationship change: A dialectical dilemma. *Journal of Social and Personal Relationships, 10,* 205–223.

Montgomery, J., & Fewer, W. (1988). *Family systems and beyond.* New York: Human Sciences.

Neale, A. V., Hwalek, M., Goodrich, C. S., & Quinn, K. M. (1996). The Illinois elder abuse system: Program description and administrative findings. *Gerontologist, 36,* 502–511.

O'Leary, K. D. (1988). Physical aggression between spouses: A social learning theory perspective. In V. B. Van Hasselt, R. L. Morrison, A. S. Bellack, & M. Hersen (Eds.), *Handbook of family violence* (pp. 31–55). New York: Plenum.

Olson, L. N. (2001). Survival narratives: A feminist analysis of abused women's stories of disengagement. *Speech Communication Annual, 15,* 53–79.

Olson, L. N. (2004). The role of voice in the (re)construction of a battered woman's identity: An autoethnography of one woman's experiences of abuse. *Women's Studies in Communication, 27,* 1–23.

Olson, L. N. (in press). Relational control-motivated aggression: A typology based theory of violence between intimates. *Journal of Family Communication.*

Olson, L. N., & Golish, T. D. (2002). Topics of conflict and patterns of aggression in romantic relationships. *Southern Communication Journal, 67,* 180–200.

Paveza, G. J., Cohen, D., Eisdorfer, C. E., Freels, S., Semla, T., Ashford, J. W., et al. (1992). Severe family violence and Alzheimer's disease: Prevalence and risk factors. *Gerontologist, 32,* 493–497.

Pearce, J. C. (2002). *The biology of transcendence: A blueprint of the human spirit.* Rochester, VT: Park Street.

Pillemer, K., & Finkelhor, D. (1988). The prevalence of elder abuse: A random sample. *Gerontologist, 28,* 51–57.

Postmus, J. (2003). Valuable assistance or missed opportunities? Shelters and the Family Violence Option. *Violence Against Women, 9,* 1278–1288.

Raphael, J., & Tolman, R. (1997). *Trapped by poverty/trapped by abuse: New evidence documenting the relationship between domestic violence and welfare.* Chicago: Taylor Institute and University of Michigan, Research Development Center on Poverty, Risk, and Mental Health.

Reich, N. M. (2002). Towards a rearticulation of women-as-victims: A thematic analysis of the construction of women's identities surrounding gendered violence. *Communication Quarterly, 50,* 292–311.

Renzetti, C. M. (1997). Violence and abuse among same-sex couples. In A. P. Cardarelli (Ed.), *Violence between intimate partners* (pp. 70–89). Needham Heights, MA: Allyn & Bacon.

Riger, S. (2003, October). *Domestic violence, poverty, welfare, and employment.* Paper presented at the Fourth Trapped by Poverty/Trapped by Abuse Conference, Austin, TX.

Rogers, L. E., Castleton, A., & Lloyd, S. A. (1996). Relational control and physical aggression in satisfying marital relationships. In D. D. Cahn & S. A. Lloyd (Eds.), *Family violence from a communication perspective* (pp. 218–239). Thousand Oaks, CA: Sage.

Rosen, K. H. (1998). The family roots of aggression and violence: A life span perspective. In L. L'Abate (Ed.), *Family psychopathology* (pp. 333–357). New York: Guilford.

Rusbult, C. E., & Martz, J. M. (1995). Remaining in an abusive relationship: An investment model analysis of nonvoluntary dependence. *Personality and Social Psychology Bulletin, 21,* 558–571.

Sabatelli, R. M., & Shehan, C. L. (1993). Exchange and resource theories. In P. Boss, W. J. Doherty, R. LaRossa, W. R. Schumm, & S. K. Steinmetz (Eds.), *Sourcebook of family theories and methods: A contextual approach* (pp. 385–411). New York: Plenum.

Sabourin, T. C., & Stamp, G. H. (1995). Communication and the experience of dialectical tensions in family life: An examination of abusive and nonabusive families. *Communication Monographs, 62,* 213–242.

Schiamberg L. B., & Gans, D. (2000). Elder abuse by adult children: An ecological framework for understanding contextual risk factors and the intergenerational character of quality of life. *International Journal of Aging and Human Development, 50,* 329–359.

Sprey, J. (1999). Family dynamics: An essay on conflict and power. In M. B. Sussman, S. K. Steinmetz, & G. W. Peterson (Eds.), *Handbook of marriage and the family* (2nd ed., pp. 667–686). New York: Plenum.

Stark, E., & Flitcraft, A. (1996). *Women at risk: Domestic violence and women's health.* Thousand Oaks, CA: Sage.

Walsh, F. (1998). *Strengthening family resilience.* New York: Guilford.

Whitchurch, G. G., & Constantine, L. L. (1993). Systems theory. In P. Boss, W. J. Doherty, R. LaRossa, W. R. Schumm, & S. K. Steinmetz (Eds.), *Sourcebook of family theories and methods: A contextual approach* (pp. 325–352). New York: Plenum.

Wilber, K. (2002). *Sex, ecology, and spirituality: The spirit of evolution* (2nd ed.). Boston: Shambhala.

Williams, L. M. (2003). Understanding child abuse and violence against women: A life course perspective. *Journal of Interpersonal Violence, 18,* 441–451.

Yllö, K., & Bograd, M. (Eds.). (1988). *Feminist perspectives on wife abuse.* Newbury Park, CA: Sage.

• Fourteen

FATHERHOOD AND FATHER INVOLVEMENT

Emerging Constructs and Theoretical Orientations

Randal D. Day, *Brigham Young University*

Charlie Lewis, *Lancaster University*

Margaret O'Brien, *University of East Anglia*

Michael E. Lamb, *National Institute of Child Health and Development*

Our purpose in this chapter is to highlight several thematic changes that characterize how the focus on men in family life has matured and shifted emphases over the past 30 years. We first explore how fatherhood and father involvement have been conceptualized, and then we provide a short survey of how men influence their families in general and their children in particular. Finally, we show the ways in which the concerns of policy makers and practitioners have come to affect the perspectives of scholars and researchers.

As family historians have shown, any analysis of fatherhood requires awareness of the specific cultural, economic, and social conditions that give rise to the norms and behavior shaping the conduct of fathers (LaRossa, 1997). The contemporary study of fathers is strongly influenced by the concept of a *caring father,* an active, "hands-on" sharer of childcare responsibilities, who embraces nurturant expectations studied in earlier historical periods (e.g., Johansen, 2001). During much of the 20th century, the concept of a *breadwinning father* predominated in most North American and Western European societies, whereas in the two preceding centuries, the primary emphasis was on the religious and moral education provided by fathers, even though the actual practices of men living in colonial America and many European countries were more uneven and varied (Pleck & Pleck, 1997). Accordingly, current research on fathering is no longer defined solely by concerns about discipline, religious education, provisioning, or protection. Today, fathers in the United

States and Europe are expected to be nurturant and accessible as well.

Indeed, research on fathering has increased in visibility partly because men's involvement in family life has become a featured element in policy and intervention strategies designed to promote child well-being (Day & Lamb, 2004; Tamis-LeMonda & Cabrera, 2002). Even though policy makers and researchers have long recognized the need for research on men in families, until recently most studies were characterized by poorly articulated constructs and theories (Day & Lamb, 2004). Furthermore, as Roggman, Fitzgerald, Bradley, and Raikes (2002) remind us, no "Grand Unifying Theory" about men in family life yet exists, and the implicit definitions of fatherhood adopted by researchers and policy makers vary considerably, largely depending on the agendas being pursued.

This definitional variance underscores a key feature of current fathering research: Much of it has been driven by pragmatic issues rather than by theory. For example, more pragmatically driven agendas foster efforts to increase men's awareness of their financial responsibility toward their children in cases of divorce, separation, or other transitory relationships. Additionally, such practical research agendas often promote concerns about welfare assistance and transfer payments to disadvantaged families. Fathering research is also motivated by political/ideological agendas; Blankenhorn (1995) and Popenoe (1993), for example, emphasize the "natural" path to paternity (i.e., fatherhood *not* through adoption, stepparenting, or sperm donor strategies) while proposing that nonbiological fathers have difficulty making the same connections with, contributions to, and investments in children that biological fathers do. Such an ideological position seeks to place biological fatherhood at the fore of the ongoing debate about the centrality of marriage as a core and "essential" institution in our society (see Silverstein & Auerbach, 1999). Conversely, the "social constructionist" definition of fatherhood also has an inherent political/ideological agenda, as its emphasis on the "social father" (rather than the biological father) both legitimates and allows consideration of a wide range of marital and nonmarital arrangements.

CONCEPTUALIZING FATHERHOOD AND FATHER INVOLVEMENT

The constructs relevant to the study of fathers are more complicated than they first appear. Early research about fathers was somewhat simplistic. Often researchers used the terms *fatherhood* and *father involvement* interchangeably, even though they clearly refer to different constructs (Marsiglio, Day, & Lamb, 2000). In this chapter, we emphasize conceptions of *fatherhood* at the individual level, as they pertain to a man's motivations when entering the fathering role, the nature of the man's behavior, and his internalized image or role identity, rather than at the macrocontextual level, where fatherhood is viewed with respect to a set of cultural, legal, and social norms. We consider the definitional and motivational aspects of fathering with respect to the man's status as a biological, social, or adoptive father, which in turn reflects the societal, cultural, and/or community role images that prescribe and proscribe what men can and should do when fathering and convey the contemporary norm that fatherhood implies responsibility and an intention to be part of the child's life.

In contrast, *father involvement* refers to the man's behaviors as he *enacts* the paternal role. When studying father involvement, therefore, researchers record what men do (or say they do) in relation to their children on a daily basis, whether this involves relatively undemanding activities (e.g., simply being present in the lives of their children) or more specific and purposeful activities designed to enhance the father-child relationship or promote child-centered goals. It has become increasingly apparent that men's involvement in the lives of their children occurs within diverse contexts and family structures (Marsiglio, Amato, Day, & Lamb, 2000).

The occurrence of father involvement may also respond to culturally defined role prescriptions and proscriptions that focus on paternal identity (see, e.g., Roopnarine, 2004). For example, Hewlett (1992) points out that most of the research about men and children in Western cultural settings has quite ethnocentrically ignored the key effects of culture and situation. Harkness and Super (1992) have drawn attention to the emphasis on economic provisioning in sub-Saharan Africa, where fathers' paramount obligation is to "take care of" their children. The subtle differences between "taking care of" and "caring for" are telling. Whereas Westerners emphasize strategies that engender close affection and participation in child-centered activities, groups such as the Kokwet of Kenya emphasize safety, survival, and the acquisition of life's basics needs.

WHO ARE "FATHERS"?

As several researchers have suggested, it is difficult to define *who a father is* (see Day & Lamb, 2004; Lewis, 1986; Roggman et al., 2002). At the most basic level, the term *father* sometimes implies a biological connection but always indicates some form of relationship, given that, as Palkovitz (2003) reminds us, there is "no such thing as a father independent of relationships" (p. 3). Social relationships are only part of what one needs to consider in defining what makes a father, however. In addition to social relationships, even the biological aspects of paternity are proving to be much more complex than scholars once believed.

Table 14.1 helps to illustrate the character and complexity of father-child relationships by identifying two central components of fathering: fatherhood and father involvement. The first, fatherhood, focuses on the claim of *paternity* (i.e., biology), which has taken on greater significance as increasing numbers of putative fathers and mothers have come to question or insist on paternity establishment even as researchers rarely consider the complicated assessment of paternity. For example, practitioners, policy makers, and scholars often consider fathers' views about pregnancy options (including abortion and technologically assisted pregnancy) only superficially, even though legal scholars are beginning to discuss differences between "genetic fathers" and "birth fathers" (Bainham, 2003). In addition, researchers and theorists have paid relatively little attention to men's decisions, feelings, responses, and behaviors about such topics as condom use (or nonuse), abortion, assisted reproductive techniques, involvement (or reasons for noninvolvement) during pregnancy or the period immediately following childbirth, and response (or lack of response) to out-of-wedlock pregnancy. We also know very little about men's views, responses, and feelings about contested paternity, although legal paternity is often seen as "the sine qua non of responsible fathering" (Doherty, Kouneski, & Erickson, 1998, p. 278). Only recently have policy makers, interventionists, and academics alike begun to grapple with the moralistic and value-laden overtones of paternity establishment and responsibility.

Table 14.1 suggests that scholars need to consider how father involvement and fatherhood interact. As several researchers have noted, the decision to become involved

Table 14.1 Fatherhood and Father Involvement: Biological and Social Aspects

Level of Involvement	Biological Connection Present	Biological Connection Absent
High	1. Highly involved biological father	3. Highly involved nonbiological father (e.g., involved stepfather)
Low	2. Underinvolved biological father (e.g., disengaged father)	4. Underinvolved nonbiological father (e.g., casual transitory relationship)

as a social father can be independent of procreation (see Cowan & Hetherington, 1991; Doherty et al., 1998; Palkovitz, 2003). Therefore, a key aspect of defining what we mean by *social father* involves *intentionality* (Doherty, 1997). Intentional motivated fatherhood implies aims, goals, and plans about that role that translate into action and relationship creation.

Table 14.1 illustrates several possibilities. Cell 1 represents situations in which men chose fatherhood *and* are highly involved as they perform fathering roles. Cell 2 describes circumstances in which there was a chosen (or accidental) biological beginning that was followed by a choice to be uninvolved or less involved. These fathers are usually absent socially and have little or no intention of providing for, connecting with, or participating in their children's lives. Cell 3 describes stepfathers or adoptive fathers and those whose partners were artificially inseminated *and* who are strongly committed to higher levels of involvement. Cell 4 illustrates living situations in which multiple fatherlike figures move in and out of the family without making long-term commitments to either partners or children. Each of these types of fatherhood/involvement has its own texture, and each poses unique challenges for scholars and researchers. When scholars overlook the diversity and differences among the fathers represented by these different cells, they muddy the theoretical, conceptual, and empirical waters.

Although Table 14.1 describes two key dimensions of fathering, it is only a starting point. These dimensions need to be embedded within a framework of other relationships and social contexts. Parenting is necessarily relational. Both acceptance of a fatherhood role and father involvement are central to scholars' understanding of the well-being of children. For example, one could build a similar 2 × 2 matrix and explore other dimensions of fatherhood (e.g., motivation, role identity clarity) with more specific examples of father involvement (such as how a father enacts a felt need to transmit moral/ethical values).

MEASURING AND ASSESSING FATHERHOOD AND PATERNAL INVOLVEMENT

Over the past 15 years, efforts to refine the conceptualization of fatherhood and father involvement have been paralleled by burgeoning efforts to assess men's contributions to family life more thoroughly, with researchers asking about the amounts of time men and women devote to household duties and child care as well as how men's contributions to family life affect women's personal potential (Pleck & Masciadrelli, 2004). Other researchers have searched for linkages between father involvement and target child outcomes. The scholarly landscape is dotted with examinations of men's lives, their interactions with women and children, the distribution of resources and responsibilities within families, and clarion calls for more and better involvement of fathers with children (Day & Lamb, 2004; Lamb, 2004; Parke, 2001; Tamis-LeMonda & Cabrera, 2002).

The Binary Approach

Although the dominant child welfare concern in the postwar period was maternal rather than paternal deprivation, some child psychologists began to wonder toward the end of the 1940s about the effects of men's long-term absence (to participate in World War II) on the psychological well-being of their children. For example, Stolz (1954) studied families in which fathers had been absent. Driven by a Freudian psychodynamic perspective that led to a focus on gender role identification, breadwinning, and family stability, Stolz's work provides an early example of what might be labeled a *binary* approach to the study of fatherhood. Conceptually, this early research approach was simple: Was/is father present or absent in the household? Stolz and many other researchers adopting this approach made little reference to the quality and diversity of fathering or father involvement. Despite the central emotional role of the father in Freud's concept of the

Oedipus complex, most psychodynamic theorists have not paid much attention to father-child relationships until recently.

The binary approach dominated research through the 1970s but shifted focus from war-related absence to concerns about the escalating divorce rate. This research was also fueled by increasing concerns about teen problem behaviors (including early pregnancy) in the late 1950s and the 1960s. Fatherhood research during this stage was again dominated by psychoanalytically rooted assumptions that fathers' absence affects children's sex role development and inner psychic development (see Biller, 1974). Because such deficit models focused primarily on the negative aspects of father involvement (absence), few researchers at the time systematically examined the benefits associated with variations in paternal presence (involvement) (Hawkins & Dollahite, 1997).

Fathers and Child Well-Being

During the 1980s, the pace quickened as many researchers began exploring how divorce (and comparable transitions to fatherlessness) influences child well-being (Amato & Sobolewski, 2004). Understanding of the role men play in the lives of their children took a conceptual leap forward during this period as researchers began to describe more accurately how paternal absence affects the socialization process in diverse and complex ways. For example, researchers began using rich theoretical perspectives such as symbolic interaction and identity theory (e.g., Pasley, Furtis, & Skinner, 2002; Rane & McBride, 2000), neopsychoanalytic theory from an Eriksonian perspective (Palkovitz, 1997), social capital theory (Hofferth, Boisjoly, & Duncan, 1999), cultural and anthropological change perspectives (Mackey, 1985), feminist theory (Silverstein, 1996), and family processes orientations (Boss, 1986; Day, Gavazzi, & Acock, 2001).

Also, during the 1990s some researchers began employing large national data sets (e.g., in the United States, the National Longitudinal Survey of Youth, the National Survey of Families and Households, the National Survey of Adolescent Health, and the Panel Study of Income Dynamics) to complement the smaller convenience samples that had been used to study the effects of father involvement/absence on children's well-being. These theoretical, conceptual, and methodological contributions have pushed the fatherhood research forward and have provided greater clarity and richness. Additionally, these efforts have helped scholars move the study of fatherhood from a focus on pragmatic issues to more theoretically based endeavors.

The Multifaceted Nature of Father Involvement

It is clear that father involvement can take many different forms. Palkovitz (1997) lists 15 general ways in which fathers become involved in their children's lives (e.g., planning, teaching, physical care), and Hawkins and Palkovitz (1999) further differentiate among activities that are cognitive (e.g., thinking about one's child), affective (e.g., showing affection), and behavioral (e.g., playing ball). Other theorists have suggested that father involvement should include economic provisioning (Lamb, Pleck, Charnov, & Levine, 1987), moral and ethical guidance (Day & Lamb, 2004), and emotional and psychological support for female partners. Hawkins et al. (2002) have taken measures of these diverse domains and attempted to develop both short and long versions of the Inventory of Father Involvement (IFI). It is too early to tell whether use of the IFI will facilitate insightful research, although it is clear that researchers are increasingly attempting to measure the multifaceted aspects of fatherhood and father involvement more inclusively and precisely.

In part, these efforts reflect dissatisfaction with the earlier focus on only the amounts of time that fathers spend with their children. These time-use analyses were initially prompted by attempts to compare and examine gender differences in the ways in which mothers and fathers invest time in paid work, family work, and housework. To facilitate these comparisons, Lamb et al. (1987) distinguished among the amount of time parents spend directly interacting with their children, the amount of time they spend being accessible to their children, and the amount of time they spend making arrangements for the care of their children; these distinctions were very helpful in explaining and clarifying apparently contradictory findings (Pleck & Masciadrelli, 2004). Unfortunately, however, these efforts led researchers to focus narrowly not only on time use but also on child care, rather than the diverse aspects of father involvement (including breadwinning and qualitative indices of commitment). Recent efforts to redress this obvious imbalance should lead to more insightful research in the future.

PATERNAL INFLUENCES ON CHILD DEVELOPMENT

As theoretical paradigms have shifted over the past 50 years, so too have the aims, types, and interpretations of research on paternal influences. In the 1950s and 1960s, psychoanalysis, social learning theory, and structural functionalist approaches dominated research on how fathers influence their children's development. All these theories shared an assumption that mothers are the primary parents, particularly early in development, and that fathers are important only in their supportive function. Partly to challenge such assumptions, a group of American researchers began in the 1970s to explore the early development of father-child relationships. Using longitudinal and innovative methods, the researchers confirmed the primary significance of mothers but also demonstrated that fathers affect child development both directly and indirectly.

Early observational studies found that American fathers tended to engage in more physically stimulating and unpredictable play with infants and toddlers than did American mothers (for a review, see Lamb & Lewis, 2004). Mothers were found to hold their infants in the course of caregiving, whereas fathers were more likely to do so while playing or in response to the infants' requests to be held. Likewise, infants responded more positively (by smiling and laughing) when held by fathers than when held by mothers. These observations appeared to support social learning theorists' hypothesis that parents model gender-typed behaviors that their children imitate. As Lamb and Lewis (2004) note, research in a variety of cultures showed that African American, Hispanic, English, and Indian men also specialized in play with their children, although Swedish, Chinese, German, and Israeli fathers were not found to be significantly more playful than their female partners.

Other observational studies in this era also found that babies formed attachments to both of their parents at the same time, even when they spent much more time with their mothers than with their fathers (Lamb & Lewis, 2004). However, although these infants protested when separated from either of their parents and gained comfort from the presence of either, the infants' preferences for their mothers were clear, especially under stress.

Other research in the attachment tradition has focused on the quality or security of attachments rather than on whether or not attachments have formed. Meta-analyses reveal a consistent link between paternal sensitivity and infant-father attachment, although the association appears to be weaker than the corresponding link between maternal sensitivity and infant-mother attachment (DeWolff & van IJzendoorn, 1997; van IJzendoorn & DeWolff, 1997). In addition, earlier assessments of child-mother attachment security predict the children's later behavior and adjustment better than does the security of child-father attachment in the United States, Belgium, and Germany, although not in Sweden or Israel (Lamb & Lewis, 2004).

Of course, many of these studies were conducted before major secular changes took place in the roles assumed by mothers and fathers, but the results nevertheless underscore that parent-child relationships are much more variable and multifaceted than researchers initially imagined. Contemporary scholars thus emphasize the need to consider cultural variation and reject simplistic, mechanistic models of parental "effects" in favor of models that explore the family system and its social context.

The Demise of "Traditional" Theories

Cross-cultural diversity has given added credibility to the work of those scholars who doubt that the different interactional styles of mothers and fathers foster gender-appropriate behavioral repertoires in children (e.g., Block, 1976). Early meta-analyses such as Lytton and Romney's (1991) examination of 27,000 children in 72 studies revealed almost no links between parental style and child behavior. At the same time, psychoanalytic approaches became less popular because their claims were not testable, although many psychodynamic assumptions have been incorporated into attachment theory (Main, 1996).

Dynamic/Systemic Theories as Alternatives to Traditional Theories

Research conducted in the 1970s also pushed the boundaries of social learning approaches by emphasizing patterns of indirect influence within the family and wider social community. Not only does each parent influence the nature and degree of the other's involvement, but the quality of father-infant interaction is highly correlated with levels of engagement between the parents (Belsky, Gilstrap, & Rovine, 1984) and both partners' attitudes about paternal involvement (Beitel & Parke, 1998). These dynamics are influenced by the family's connections to the outside world, especially with respect to both parents' employment patterns and commitments. For example, work demands strongly influence how involved Swedish (Lamb et al., 1988), Asian (Ishii-Kuntz, 2000), and American (Hyde, Essex, & Horton, 1993) fathers become. More fine-grained analyses of parental occupational characteristics suggest that maternal work hours and maternal income are

associated with higher levels of father involvement in child care (Fuligni & Brooks-Gunn, 2004; Sandberg & Hofferth, 2001), although the psychological implications of such patterns can be counterintuitive. For example, Crouter, Perry-Jenkins, Huston, and McHale (1987) found that, at least in dual-earner families, increased paternal involvement in child care was related to lower marital satisfaction, although other research has indicated that higher levels of paternal participation in child care enhance mothers' marital satisfaction (Brennan, Barnett, & Gareis, 2001).

The Dynamics of Paternal Influence Over Time

Researchers have reported considerable stability in levels of paternal involvement within the first 30 months of their children's lives (Lamb et al., 1988; Pruett & Litzenberger, 1992), although other data suggest that the amount of time fathers spend interacting with their children decreases as their children age and that individual differences are not stable (Lamb, Chuang, & Hwang, 2004; Pleck & Masciadrelli, 2004). Early involvement is correlated with variations in child adjustment, however. For example, Yogman, Kindlon, and Earls (1996) found a general link between paternal involvement in infancy and the children's later IQs, even after controlling for socioeconomic differences, and others have reported associations between father-toddler reading and children's later interest in books (Lyytinen, Laakso, & Poikkeus, 1998). Similarly, father-child scaffolding (i.e., giving indirect help) has been shown to predict independent problem solving by 18-month-olds (Labrell, 1990). Indeed, Grossmann et al. (2002) found that paternal sensitivity during 10 minutes of free play at age 2 predicted German children's attachment at 16 years of age better than did the security of infant-mother attachment.

As paternal involvement declines in childhood and adolescence, family members in cultures as diverse as the United States and Korea report that fathers, like mothers, become less salient (for a review, see Lamb & Lewis, 2004). Paradoxically, longitudinal research suggests that it is at these stages in development that men's early influences on their children are most discernible. For example, earlier paternal involvement has been found to predict the children's self-assessed parenting skills as adults (Franz, McClelland, Weinberger, & Peterson, 1994), the reported hostility of the "child" at age 25 (Allen, Hauser, O'Connor, & Bell, 2002), and relationship satisfaction and psychological integrity at age 33 (Flouri & Buchanan, 2002). The sleeper effect of positive paternal involvement in the early years, and its role in promoting later child well-being, clearly requires further empirical inquiry. Conspicuously absent from these kinds of analyses have been systematic attempts to understand the nonrecursive aspects of parent-child interaction. That is, we know very little about how a child's behavior (whether a young child or a teen) affects the well-being of the parents, the relationship between the two parents, and/or the future relationship between the parents and the child or between the parents and other children within the family.

Where Have Studies of Paternal Influence Taken Us?

Perhaps Roggman et al. (2002) could find no unifying theory of fatherhood because the factors mentioned above interact in dynamic ways, producing changing patterns and diffuse connections that vary over historic time, over the life course, and across cultures, often in unexpected ways. For example, there is some evidence that "traditional" fathers who engage in more robust play (Parke et al., 2004) or who clearly have different parenting styles than their partners (Zaouche-Gaudron, Ricaud, & Beaumatin, 1998) have more positive effects on their children's development, especially the quality of their peer relationships. It may thus be that paternal influence is enhanced by fathers' relative distinctiveness, which means that a secular trend toward symmetrical parenting might change fathers'

impacts on their children's development. Clearly, additional longitudinal research is needed to tease out the particular contribution to child development of fathers' early involvement in child care (in terms of style and time) and of any distinctive features of the ways fathers behave. Intrafamily preferences regarding child-care arrangements and material resources may also affect both the nature and the impact of paternal influence.

POLICY IMPLICATIONS

In recent years, policy makers and practitioners have paid increasing attention to fathers, especially with respect to family support services, child welfare interventions, and family-related employment policies. In their recent review of European parental leave policies, Deven and Moss (2002) remark, "If we consider the developments since 1998, the most striking trend is a growing emphasis on fatherhood" (p. 4). Services have been developed for fathers in diverse contexts and life-course stages, with particular focus on new and nonresident fathers. Most interventions have been concentrated on fathers "at risk," both "troubled fathers" and "fathers who cause trouble," including low-income or workless fathers, abusive fathers, and, in the American context, unwed fathers (Cabrera et al., 2002; Carlson & McLanahan, 2002). However, the emphasis on problem fathers has been complemented by efforts to promote more positive relationships between fathers and their children through parenting and fatherhood programs that enhance emotional sensitivity and cognitive/educational investment (McBride & Lutz, 2004; Mincy & Pouncy, 2002). Networks of practitioners who provide services to fathers have permitted extensive exchanges and discussion about ways of increasing fathers' utilization of services, the development of appropriate fathering interventions, staff training innovations, and new approaches to support minority ethnic fathers. For example, the National Center on Fathers and Families has developed the

Fathering Indicators Framework, "a tool for quantitative and qualitative analysis," to facilitate the design and evaluation of multifaceted interventions with fathers (Gadsden, Fagan, Ray, & Davis, 2004).

Interventions to Enhance Father Involvement

The growing realization that positive paternal involvement promotes child development and adjustment has inevitably underscored the inability of dyadic mother-child models to explain contemporary relationships within families adequately. Clearly, family support approaches that concentrate on mothers or mother-child relationships, to the exclusion of fathers, may ignore significant emotional supports or stresses for children and parents. Indeed, a recent meta-analysis of interventions designed to enhance positive parental behaviors, such as responsiveness, toward children younger than 54 months of age suggests that those involving fathers as well as mothers are more effective than mother-only approaches (Bakermans-Kranenburg, van IJzendoorn, & Juffer, 2003).

Where paternal behavior has negative features, as in cases of child abuse, there is debate about the benefits of including fathers in interventions, although problems can emerge when practitioners focus too narrowly on mothers in their work (Gadsden et al., 2004). Most important, fathers who are ignored by practitioners may later establish relationships with other mothers of young children in which they repeat previous patterns of abusive behavior. A more systemic approach to family and child welfare suggests that fathers, "good" and "bad," should be served wherever possible.

Similarly, family-related employment policies based in the view that the work-family balance is a maternal issue overlook the predominance of dual-earner families in most modern economies (Hertz & Marshall, 2001). With the rapid growth of maternal employment since the 1970s, a caring dimension has become more central to the social construction of fathering because engagement in caring and economic provisioning are increasingly expected of both mothers and fathers. Public anxiety since the 1990s about the impact of parents' long working hours on children and the concurrent interest in "family-friendly" employment policies for mothers and fathers has to be seen in this context (Brannen & Moss, 1998).

Research Based on Nationwide Policy Initiatives

At national levels, a focus on fathers is still quite rare, notwithstanding the pioneering introduction in 1974 of paternity leave in Sweden, where, as in the other Nordic countries, such policies were explicitly designed to foster a societal environment in which women and men have equivalent opportunities for occupational and familial fulfillment. In this context, the Fatherhood Initiative introduced in the United States by the Democratic presidential administration in 1995 represents a significant departure from mainstream policy and practice; however, this initiative was motivated more by uncertainty about the predictability and permanence of fathers in the lives of American children and a desire to promote "responsible" fatherhood than by commitment to equal opportunities (Coltrane, 2001). Under the leadership of the Interagency Forum on Child and Family Statistics, a collaborative alliance of scholars and policy makers, the Fatherhood Initiative promoted a wide-ranging review of national policies and practices and produced an influential report titled *Nurturing Fatherhood* (Federal Interagency Forum on Child and Family Statistics, 1998). The initiative also spawned a series of large-scale studies designed to explore fathering in some depth: the Early Head Start Research and Evaluation Project Fatherhood Study, the Fragile Families and Child Wellbeing Study, and the Early Child Longitudinal Study Birth Cohort. In an analysis of data from the Early Head Start study, Cabrera, Shannon, Tamis-LeMonda, and Lamb (2003) found that, for low-income fathers, positive outcomes for children were associated with fathers' capacities to earn and to care for their children sensitively, thereby demonstrating that the exclusive focus on men's economic provisioning in social policy is insufficient. One implication is that a "welfare to work" strategy that concentrates on fathers' work may not be in children's interests unless it is complemented by a concern with "child care."

In the United States, as in other modern economies, balancing welfare-to-work policies and child-care policies has been a challenge for government and practitioners. Many European governments support working fathers' parental responsibilities through directives on working hours and paid paternity leave (O'Brien, 2004), but fathers continue to work many hours (for example, more than a third of British fathers usually work 48 hours or more per week, and a minority, 12%, usually work 60 hours or more per week—excluding commuting). The dilemma for contemporary couples is that parenthood demands the maximization of resources, and the earning capacity of fathers is typically greater than that of mothers.

Fathers at the Margins of Society

Policy makers have also focused on support for fathers who live apart from their children because the increase in divorce and repartnering that began toward the end of the 20th century has shaped contemporary parenting. Over time, fathers are likely to experience more than one family type, with many fathers ceasing to reside with the children resulting from their first relationships. As a consequence, the preservation of children's relationships with biological and social fathers is emerging as a key preoccupation of legal jurisdictions throughout the world (Bainham, Lindley, Richards, & Trinder, 2003). Since 1989, contact with parents has been enshrined as a basic human right for children under the United Nations Convention on the Rights of the Child, although the principle is difficult to implement when conflicts about contact

exist between a residential parent (usually the mother) and a nonresidential parent (typically the father). Lobbyists for fathers' rights often complain that courts tend to underplay fathers' child-caring competencies, whereas advocates for mothers assert that fathers want to have contact with their children without also fulfilling their responsibilities. As the debate continues, some legal scholars have argued that, as Bainham (2003) puts it, "the answer is not to remove the rights but to promote and if necessary attempt to force the obligations which go with them" (p. 86). Because it is difficult to intervene successfully in private family life, particularly on relationship issues, Bainham argues, the law needs to play an educative function in setting guidelines for normative behavior.

Another looming political debate focuses on men (and women) who are in prison but will return to family life (Petersilia, 2003). The issue of promoting and maintaining contact between prison fathers and their children is slowly attracting the attention of both policy makers and practitioners. As male prison populations in the United Kingdom and the United States reach their highest levels ever, practitioners in these countries are developing programs to support imprisoned fathers' relationships with their children (Brooks-Gordon, 2003), but the courts often respect the rights of such fathers—for instance, in relation to contested contact or adoption procedures—less than they respect those of imprisoned mothers. For example, in England, if the mother of a child whose biological father is in prison wishes to give her child up for adoption, local authorities are not obliged to seek the imprisoned father's permission for the adoption if it can be shown that he has not "established a family life" with the child and mother.

In many developing nations, of course, fathers lose regular contact with their children not only because of divorce or imprisonment but because they are forced to migrate in search of work. Unfortunately, although such "missing fathers" are common in Latin America, the Caribbean, Africa, and Asia, this phenomenon has received little attention from academic researchers.

CONCLUSION

In this brief review of recent conceptual and empirical work on fatherhood and father involvement, we have shown that the study of men in families has finally come of age: Scholars no longer study family life almost exclusively from the perspective of mothers. Significant multidisciplinary and multinational efforts to examine and understand men's roles and influences in their families have particularly elucidated the varying nature and significance of father-child relationships. Over the past few decades, furthermore, researchers have recognized the inadequacy of emphasizing deficits and have instead sought to understand the contributions made by fathers. As a result, increasing numbers of researchers and practitioners are articulating the diverse ways in which fathers can promote family well-being instead of cataloging the negative effects of their absence.

This emergent body of work reveals the increasingly diverse types of relationships that men develop with children. Probably more than at any other time in history, both biological and social fathers today confront a range of decisions about how to conduct their kin and nonkin fathering relationships. To illustrate the interaction among the roles of biology and social agency, we have proposed a two-dimensional model in terms of which fathers can be classified with respect to both their biological connections with children and their involvement in child-paternal relationships. This model underscores that these two aspects of fathering are separate, involve different processes, and require different research strategies. Whatever

defines the relationship between fathers and children, however, fatherhood and paternal involvement in the early years can have demonstrably positive effects as children pass into the teen years and beyond, although researchers still need to explore how fathers' roles and contributions vary depending on the ages of their children. Similarly, the range of family practices that researchers have identified shows that neither breadwinning nor caring activities sufficiently capture the essence of fatherhood. The scholarly stage is set for more sophisticated qualitative and quantitative measures of father involvement in specific context-dependent settings.

We have also emphasized the ways in which fathers' other relationships, particularly those with their children's mothers and with the labor force, facilitate or constrain fathers' involvement with their children. It is interesting to note that the ways in which fathers facilitate or constrain maternal involvement with children have yet to be explored in any depth. A systems approach to father involvement may initially generate more questions than answers, but such an approach promises to advance our understanding of men's behavior in families. Similarly, the social context beyond the household needs to be the focus of much more research.

As we have shown, family policies have become increasingly sensitive to both the provisioning and caring roles assumed by fathers. Future policy makers will be challenged to develop instruments that are responsive to an ever-changing set of paternal behaviors and aspirations, even as public policy agendas continue to pay increasing attention to fathers in important decisions about welfare, child well-being, and efforts to reduce poverty. These trends, building on the legacy of earlier research and scholarship, represent a coming of age in the study of men in family context.

CASE STUDY

INCARCERATION AND REENTRY OF FATHERS INTO THE LIVES OF THEIR FAMILIES

Joyce A. Arditti, *Oregon State University*

Alan C. Acock, *Oregon State University*

Randal D. Day, *Brigham Young University*

BACKGROUND AND SIGNIFICANCE

Currently, as many as 10 million of America's children have at least one parent, usually a father, who is imprisoned or under the supervision of the criminal justice system (Reed & Reed, 1998). We care about this issue because fathers who maintain family ties and reenter family life successfully after incarceration are less likely to be rearrested (Petersilia, 2003). The following is a case study in the making in an area of research that few family scholars have explored. Most research about prisoners and recidivism is conducted by scholars working from either an institutional (or macro-level) perspective or a deviance perspective. We use a family perspective—examining family processes, support mechanisms, and the reconstitution of family structures following periods of ambiguous parental absence and presence.

The outcome of an individual's going through the prison system in the United States has been described as a "stigma that never fades," effectively locking ex-convicts (especially poor Blacks) out of participation in important opportunity structures and viable employment opportunities (Barak, Flavin, & Leighton, 2001). Felony offenders are systematically disenfranchised from social welfare benefits such as public housing and educational loans, and in some states they are barred from full participation in the political process. Most of the 600,000 prisoners released annually are undereducated and have limited employment skills, high rates of illiteracy, and histories of substance abuse and health problems (Austin & Irwin, 2001; Uggen, Thompson, & Manza, 2001). Furthermore, family-hostile prison policies that isolate incarcerated fathers from community and family as a punishment strategy contribute to the difficulty of familial reentry after prison; Nurse (2002) labels these policies the "deep break."

Little is known about the impacts on women and children of formerly incarcerated fathers' reentry into their families' lives. Preliminary findings from our pilot project suggest that the nature of men's family involvement after prison is diverse.

RESPONSIBLE FATHERING AND THE ECOLOGY OF INCARCERATION

Father involvement research is broadly concerned with responsible fathering and the promotion of positive family outcomes (Marsiglio, Amato, et al., 2000). Additionally, fatherhood research has moved beyond simplistic dichotomous conceptualizations of father presence versus father absence and now acknowledges the complex variations of biological and social father-child involvements. Yet, despite recent emphasis on the importance of understanding fathering roles in diverse, "hard to reach" samples, family scholars have failed to give attention to the significant threat that incarceration poses to father involvement. It is unclear how a responsible fathering framework may apply to this growing number of fathers and their families, and how such a framework should be refined to reflect this unique familial situation.

Ecological models, which are sensitive to contextual factors and diverse family structures and residential patterns (see, e.g., Doherty et al., 1998), hold theoretical promise in terms of informing our understanding of the experience of incarceration and how it affects families. An ecological framework also recognizes that incarcerated fathers and their families are embedded in a broader sociocultural network that stigmatizes involvement in the criminal justice system (Arditti, 2003). Relative to incarceration, we theorize that context takes on heightened salience, given the highly stigmatized nature of incarceration. Unlike other contexts of family disruption, such as death or illness, loss of a family member because of incarceration seldom elicits sympathy and support from others. The tendency for stigma and the resultant shame to extend from the stigmatized prisoner to family members may contribute to a lack of social support, ambiguous relationships, and the avoidance of relations with the incarcerated father.

Contextualizing imprisoned fathers' relationships with their family members during confinement and after release thus necessitates a reconsideration of the idea of responsible fathering. Relative to Doherty et al.'s (1998) conceptualization, context overwhelms the model of responsible fathering because of stigma and the "deep break." Harsh institutional practices, lack of family preservation policies, mandatory sentencing laws, and cultural emphasis on "punishment" preclude the possibility of father presence for significant periods of time and undermine the possibility of responsible fathering upon reentry.

PRISONIZED FATHERS

Identity theory focuses on the emerging nature and profile of a person's identity within a specified role (Pasley & Minton, 1997). *Prisonization* refers to identity transformation that results from an individual's becoming acculturated into the prison environment, whereby the person's perspective and view of self become "a reflection of the overregulated, upside-down, violence prone, hyper masculine, and extraordinarily routinized lifestyle common to such institutions" (Terry, 2003, p. 2). This process is also influenced by institutional practices aimed at keeping prisoners isolated, controlled, and contained. Thus the identities of incarcerated fathers are likely to be altered dramatically during their imprisonment, such that they come to mirror the norms and values of the prison. We contend that in order to promote responsible fathering in formerly incarcerated men, society needs to find a way to reconstruct and redefine ex-prisoners' identities in terms of the roles and responsibilities of parent-child and parent-parent interaction. Such a change may be monumental, depending on the extent of the individual's prisonization and his potential for building social capital upon release.

According to social capital models, resources exist inherently within relationships and connections and can be generated by both strong and weak ties (see Coleman, 1988). The "deep break" policies of prisons create separation and isolation, both of which hamper former prisoners' successful reentry into society. Prisonized fathers have few resources, and their unemployability makes it difficult for them to provide for their families financially. It is no surprise, then, that the systematic incapacitation associated with prison life and reentry is incompatible with responsible fathering. The resultant outcomes—rootlessness, social alienation, and mistrust of government and authority—are reminiscent of Howell's (1973) "hard living" families.

Families are potential pathways to reestablishing relationships that can generate social capital. Indeed, Terry (2003) emphasizes that,

Case Study

CASE STUDY *continued*

however challenging the situation, it is plausible to assume that the longer an ex-inmate is able to maintain new and meaningful associations and activities, the more likely it is that he can avoid a "regression." However, ex-prisoners must cope with "hangover identities"—ghosts left over from prison that cloud and affect their current roles, giving rise to contradictory meanings between life within prison walls and life outside. Reintegration is often hindered by such hangover identities, which may be easily triggered by situations in which ex-prisoners perceive that others are disrespecting them (Terry, 2003). Rebuilding or, in some cases, creating a fathering identity in the presence of these ghosts is difficult. Concept development related to prisonization and the ecology of the "deep break" represents a first step in theorizing about incarceration, reentry, and fathering.

METHODOLOGICAL CONSIDERATIONS

The study of marginalized prison populations is fertile ground for research employing a "qualitative consciousness." Such a consciousness is an implicit aspect of a feminist epistemology that seeks to expose disadvantage and "multiple jeopardy" (Few, Stephens, & Rouse-Arnett, 2003) and is appropriately applied to prisonized fathers, their partners and ex-partners, and their children. Bringing a qualitative consciousness to the study of marginalized populations also exposes the unavoidable place of values in scholarship. In acknowledging their own values, scholars must examine the research process in terms of how they obtain access to the worlds of those they study as well as reflect on any emotional difficulties they may experience in the field. Indeed, a feminist epistemology is useful in this work because it forces scholars to raise their own consciousness about the people they study

through emancipatory knowledge. Such research offers the "studied" something of value in telling their story and requires the researchers to reflect politically and possibly view their own lives differently as a result (Fonow & Cook, 1991). Such a consciousness also requires researchers to develop "cultural competence"; in our case, this meant developing an awareness of the politics of location relative to prisonization and the criminal justice system.

Family relations are extraordinarily complex for "hard living" families, as our pilot study clearly confirmed. The inmates in our sample had difficulty responding to global, Likert-type questions that rely on a single underlying dimension of positive to negative. Their worlds are complex, and the isolation they have experienced has left them with a great deal of ambiguity and ambivalence about relationships. Several inmates described relationships that were extremely sad, but also chose responses of "good" or "very good" on Likert-type survey items designed to measure the quality of their relationships. Thus we recommend that researchers conducting quantitative analyses on fragile populations interpret their findings with great care; we also recommend the use of open-ended survey questions to allow participants to qualify their answers.

For a review of specific aspects of our experience in conducting our research, see this volume's companion Web site (http://www .ncfr.org/sourcebook). Researchers undertaking work in this area need to be prepared for the impacts of human subjects policies, institutional barriers related to gaining entry, and characteristics and inconsistencies related to the interview setting itself. It is our hope that our frustrations and our successes will aid other scholars who plan research on stigmatized families and facilitate the study of "hard to reach" fathers.

CASE STUDY

THE UNANTICIPATED CONSEQUENCES OF PROMOTING FATHER INVOLVEMENT: A FEMINIST PERSPECTIVE

Yoshie Sano, *Oregon State University*

In the past two decades, there has been increased political and scholarly interest in fathers. In the United States, federal government policies focus on fathers' earning capacity, with the objective of enforcing fathers' financial contribution to their children and penalizing noncontribution. Much scholarly research on fatherhood has been conducted from the standpoint of encouraging father involvement, sometimes with moral overtones. Underlying these policies and research is the assumption that increased father involvement promotes positive outcomes in children. Although research does indicate that *positive* father involvement is beneficial to child development (Marsiglio, Amato, et al., 2000), some previously unanticipated negative consequences have been identified, particularly by feminist researchers.

Scholars working from a feminist perspective, using the concepts of gender and power, have raised questions about the ideology underlying current policies and research. Feminists value the experiences of socially disadvantaged populations such as women, children, and low-income families, and research based in this perspective has demonstrated that father involvement may not always be desirable, especially when fathers are violent; it is not uncommon for women receiving public assistance to be victims of domestic violence (e.g., Tolman & Raphael, 2000).

One of the biggest concerns raised by feminists is that strict enforcement of child support laws may unintentionally endanger families of abusive fathers. Most mothers and children, especially those of low-income families, are more financially stable when nonresident fathers pay regular child support. In order to collect child support under current welfare regulations, women need to establish the paternity of their children. Paternity establishment, however, may lead to retaliation by currently or previously abusive partners, or to attempts by the partners to gain custody and/or visitation rights. This may put mothers and children in danger through increased contact with the abusers. Although "good-cause" waivers of child support enforcement are available, only a small number of the women who qualify for such waivers actually obtain them (Pearson, Thoennes, & Griswold, 1999). Requirements for such waivers are so stringent that many women who are at risk do not qualify. In these cases, the negative consequences of child support collection may outweigh the economic benefits to these families.

The Personal Responsibility and Work Opportunity Reconciliation Act (PRWORA) of 1996 has been criticized because it represents a shift in the federal government's focus from cash assistance to promoting self-sufficiency through employment and marriage (Lipscomb, 2001). Feminist researchers

Author's Note: I would like to acknowledge suggestions from Ted Futris on an earlier draft of this contribution.

Case Study

have documented that, due to PRWORA's time limit on the receipt of welfare and strict work requirements, some mothers have had to remain in undesirable relationships as a survival strategy, relying on abusive partners for financial and social assistance (e.g., transportation and child care) as they struggled to move from welfare to work (e.g., Scott, London, & Myers, 2002). By promoting marriage to reduce out-of-wedlock births and to create heterosexual-parent families, PRWORA may pressure mothers to marry undesirable partners. In addition, the policy ignores "nontraditional" family forms, including single-parent households and same-sex unions, which may be equally if not more effective in providing necessary social and financial support.

Some have argued that the problem of domestic abuse in welfare families has been exaggerated, but Raphael (2000) found that 20–30% of current welfare recipients are victims of domestic violence. Some scholars have speculated that domestic violence is underreported or may even go unrecognized (Roulet, 1999). Even though the overall number of nonresident fathers with risk factors for abuse is comparatively low, such men constitute a significant minority whose negative impacts on mothers and children cannot be ignored (Sano & Richards, 2003).

The unanticipated consequences of father involvement go beyond abuse and violence. A nonresident father's increased contact with his child(ren) may intensify continuing conflict with the child's mother or create new conflicts, and parental conflict has been found to be one of the most detrimental factors affecting children's adjustment to divorce (Kelly, 2000). Without substantial effort to promote supportive mother-father relationships, nonresident fathers' involvement may not be in the best interest of the children.

Furthermore, both policy makers and researchers may overemphasize biological fathers' involvement with their children, paying little attention to the important roles that other father figures can play in children's lives.

Current policies may also reinforce a gender ideology that supports the traditional patriarchal family/culture, in which men are expected to be providers and women are expected to be caregivers. Despite the fact that fathering includes many aspects such as emotional support and caregiving, current policies emphasize fathers' economic contributions to families almost exclusively. Focusing on certain aspects of fathering may indirectly reinforce men's dominant position in the employment market, creating wider gender inequality in paid work and family life. Overemphasis on economic contributions may in fact undermine a man's identity as a father. Despite the image of the selfish "deadbeat dad" found widely in the popular media, the majority of fathers whose children are on welfare are also struggling financially. The association between nonpayment of child support and having a low income or being unemployed is significant (Garfinkel, McLanahan, Meyer, & Seltzer, 1998). Punishing these fathers may not only be ineffective, it may also generate negative psychological stress for poor fathers.

A feminist perspective cautions us not to overvalue fathers' contributions to their children's lives. Just as mothers' problematic behaviors can be detrimental to families, increased father involvement is not universally beneficial. Social policy makers and fatherhood researchers need to recognize the potential dangers of increased father involvement for some families and take every reasonable precaution not to sacrifice the well-being of any family member—man, woman, or child.

DISCUSSION AND EXTENSION

FATHERS, FATHERHOOD, AND FAMILIES: (RE)CASTING ISSUES OF DIVERSITY INTO FORMING AND RE-FORMING CONCEPTUALIZATIONS

Vivian L. Gadsden, *University of Pennsylvania*

R. Karl Rethemeyer, *State University of New York at Albany*

As Day, Lewis, O'Brien, and Lamb suggest in Chapter 14, the academic, service, and public landscapes in which child and family well-being is studied have expanded within recent years, widening scholars' perspectives on and understanding of the range and complexity of issues facing children and families, both nationally and cross-nationally. These changes demand new paradigms and models to demonstrate the shifts in structural and functional identities of families and parents, their representation in different public and private settings, and the chronicling of their culturally and socially diverse experiences and transitions. The full story of these shifts is still to be scripted. Family practitioners and researchers are challenged to form and re-form conceptualizations, assumptions, and definitions that have historically informed the field. Discussions of the father's role in the family and in the lives of his children have become a central part of this re-formed and emerging story.

Day and his colleagues provide a convincing analysis of the major issues in the field of fatherhood and family research over the past decade. As they note, although research on fathers has a history that predates the 1990s, only recently have scholars undertaken sustained multidisciplinary and multidomain efforts. Day et al. focus on three areas: conceptualizations of fatherhood and father involvement, the influence of men on their families and children, and the impacts of policies and practices on the perspectives of researchers

and scholars. These three areas capture the core of critical areas of inquiry in an emerging field. Appropriately, the authors highlight the significant role that practice has assumed in current discussions. They also focus on the dominance of policy and political agendas that frame national attention to problems, whether in small town halls and community meetings or in the mass media. Threaded throughout their chapter are references to the complex nature of defining images of fathers, fatherhood, and father involvement. Similarly, Day et al. position the importance of research in unpacking these images in the field against the need to examine multiple dimensions of the problems, issues, and possibilities that are associated with them.

In this brief discussion, we focus on a problematic and relatively underaddressed theme in research on fathers and fatherhood: diversity. Here, we construct *diversity* in a broad sense to include discussions of race and culture as well as issues of age, income, education, work, sexual orientation, and social stereotypes. We address the ways characteristics of fathers and diversity create opportunity for fathers, their children, and their families.

ADDRESSING DIVERSITY

Day et al. cover many cross-cultural issues related to fathers, particularly in their references Ishii-Kuntz's (1994) work on Japanese fathers and Harkness and Super's (1992) work

DISCUSSION AND EXTENSION *continued*

Discussion and Extension

on fathers in sub-Saharan Africa, with similar attention to multicultural issues (see also Nsamenang, 2000; Seward, Yeatts, & Zottarelli, 2002; Smit, 2002), such as urban fathers, fathers from minority groups, Caribbean fathers, and immigrant fathers (Hossain, Field, Pickens, Malphurs, & Del Valle, 1997; Hossain & Roopnarine, 1994; Roopnarine, Talukder, Jain, Joshi, & Srivastava, 1992; see also Allen & Doherty, 1998; Coley & Morris, 2002; Mincy & Pouncy, 1997; McLanahan & Garfinkel, 2002). Their focus on marginalized fathers makes prominent the ways in which the diversity of fathers is unaddressed in the current literature, raising questions about whether there is a demise of traditional theories, discussed briefly. Both the separation of cultural definitions and the reference to fathers at the margins, while calling attention to the absence of a rigorous discourse about non-Western fathers, also highlight the exclusionary nature of discussions in the field—discussions that place fathers who differ by ethnicity, race, and culture on the outside and reinforce negative perceptions of their difference.

What has been striking from a developmental and educational perspective is that, from the outset of the fathering impetus in the 1990s, discussions have referred to father absence as a problem without acknowledging in equally provocative ways the child as the source, recipient, and context of changes in father presence and family sufficiency. Even in their chapter, Day and his colleagues refer to "troubled fathers" and "fathers who cause trouble." Such labeling reflects most substantively the stance of policy makers, who until recently were more likely to focus on fathers' material and financial contributions, with less regard for the emotional and nurturing contributions they make, and who were likely to examine the role of fathers based on long-held images of detached breadwinners whose significance was appended to the "real work" of parenting and mothering.

As fathering becomes a new emphasis in family studies, debate on the nature of fathers'

roles—particularly in reference to mothers' roles—will no doubt flourish in the literature. Since 1994, the numbers of published studies and articles on fathering have increased significantly, and they now cut across a range of disciplines and domains (National Center on Fathers and Families, 2004). A number of studies are under way that will expand the limited literature on diverse kinds of fathers: fathers from ethnic minority groups; low-income fathers; noncustodial, nonresidential fathers; never-married fathers; adolescent fathers; and working poor fathers. However, within this growing literature, the status of diversity issues is oddly situated. Most of the focus, even to date, has been on low-income men who are fathers and disproportionately on low-income men of color who are labeled as "troubled fathers" and "fathers who cause trouble." Such characterization is troubling, particularly when the group "low-income fathers" is conflated with "low-income fathers of color," and when superficial efforts to solve entrenched problems such as educational limits, poverty, social vulnerability, intergenerational father absence, and joblessness within short time frames have become par for the course.

At the same time, minority men in the United States are seen as both the same as Western fathers and different from them. The umbrella term *urban fathers* is used to capture the full gamut of characteristics associated with limited opportunity and social problems in urban settings. It reflects the tendency in both academic and popular discourse to link urban-related issues with poverty, hardship, crime, incarceration, and a series of harsh life circumstances and negative characteristics. In discussions about fatherhood, the word *urban* typically serves as code to designate African American and Latino fathers whose profiles include being poor, having grown up in mother-headed households, having received poor schooling, and having fathered children out of wedlock. However, some argue that the broad use of the term *urban fathers* to denote

DISCUSSION AND EXTENSION *continued*

the wide range of young fathers who are members of minority groups, poor, and living in urban settings is informative as well as problematic—narrowly depicting the nuanced experiences of the members of this diverse population whose individual practices as fathers are derived from both individual and shared contexts that have shaped their images of fatherhood (Gadsden & Ray, 2002).

Racial and ethnic differences, although the most visible and most easily identified factors among fathers, account for only a small subset of the possible differences. Fathers differ in their notions of fatherhood and fathering practices by virtue of age, income, social class, and sexual orientation, which is perhaps the last frontier. In other words, fathers experience and respond to issues around fathering differentially by virtue of age, culture, ethnicity, gender/masculine identity, race, and class. The interplay of these characteristics is complex for a number of reasons—biological, psychological, and social (Gadsden, Wortham, & Turner, 2003). Societal stereotypes of different racial, cultural, and ethnic groups further complicate the experiences of fathers who are represented by these other descriptors. Add to these images poor schooling (not just years of schooling but quality of schooling) and employability and employment, and the picture transforms our understanding and assessment of the "average father," making it unlikely that we can identify such a person.

CLOSING CONSIDERATIONS

Day and his colleagues paint a portrait that is outlined but unfinished. They identify several issues, but we have yet to determine the salience of these issues. Among the issues in need of further examination are the following:

- *Multidimensionality of minority status:* Minority status combines culture, social opportunity, and financial and educational opportunity, among others. Studies of fathers tend to focus on subsets of these rather than the entire bundle, within and outside noncustodial, nonresidential relationships.
- *The way in which partial images of minority status inform policy and practice:* Our research suggests that stereotyping of minority fathers and families affects policy and practice, but how and in what ways?
- *The role and place of nontraditional "father figures":* What status do men who assume responsibilities without legal or biological relationships with their children have in research, practice, and policy? How does policy affect men's willingness to assume these nontraditional but critical roles?

What would it take for scholars to consider diversity more broadly in conceptualizations of fatherhood and fathering? First, as Day et al. suggest, researchers need better data from multiple sources, collected longitudinally and linked to child measures, so that they may trace children and fathers together, evaluate child outcomes within the home and at school, measure and evaluate fathering behaviors, and link fathering behaviors and child outcomes in a dynamic framework that is sensitive to changes in children's needs over their developmental life course.

However, before this can happen, scholars need to determine what constitutes positive improvements for children, what constitutes fathering behaviors, and how those behaviors are related to and distinct from mothering behaviors. In part, determining child outcomes in a global fashion may not be possible in a country as culturally diverse as the United States. Instead, it may be necessary to specify the universe of factors that affect child outcomes and measures that faithfully report differences in those factors.

Discussion and Extension

REFERENCES

Allen, J. P., Hauser, S. T., O'Connor, T. G., & Bell, K. L. (2002). Prediction of peer-rated adult hostility from autonomy struggles in adolescent-family interactions. *Development and Psychopathology, 14,* 123–137.

Allen, W. D., & Doherty, W. J. (1998). "Being there": The perception of fatherhood among a group of African American adolescent fathers. In H. I. McCubbin, E. A. Thompson, A. I. Thompson, & J. A. Futrell (Eds.), *Resiliency in African-American families* (pp. 207–244). Thousand Oaks, CA: Sage.

Amato, P. R., & Sobolewski, J. (2004). The effects of divorce on fathers and children: Non-residential fathers and stepfathers. In M. E. Lamb (Ed.), *The role of the father in child development* (4th ed., pp. 341–367). New York: John Wiley.

Arditti, J. A. (2003). Locked doors and glass walls: Family visiting at a local jail. *Journal of Loss & Trauma, 8,* 115–138.

Austin, J., & Irwin, J. (2001*). It's about time: America's imprisonment binge.* Belmont, CA: Wadsworth.

Bainham, A. (2003). Contact as right and obligation. In A. Bainham, B. Lindley, M. Richards, & L. Trinder (Eds.), *Children and their families: Contact, rights and welfare.* Portland, OR: Hart.

Bainham, A., Lindley, B., Richards, M., & Trinder, L. (Eds.). (2003). *Children and their families: Contact, rights and welfare.* Portland, OR: Hart.

Bakermans-Kranenburg, M. J., van IJzendoorn, M. H., & Juffer, F. (2003). Less is more: Meta-analyses of sensitivity and attachment interventions in early childhood. *Psychological Bulletin, 129,* 195–215.

Barak, G., Flavin, J., & Leighton, P. (2001). *Class, race, gender, and crime: Social realities of justice in America.* Los Angeles: Roxbury.

Beitel, A. H., & Parke, R. D. (1998). Parental involvement in infancy: The role of maternal and paternal attitudes. *Journal of Family Psychology, 12,* 268–288.

Belsky, J., Gilstrap, B., & Rovine, M. (1984). The Pennsylvania Infant and Family Development Project, I: Stability and change in mother-infant and father-infant interaction in a family setting at one, three, and nine months. *Child Development, 55,* 692–705.

Biller, H. B. (1974). *Paternal deprivation.* Lexington, MA: Heath Lexington.

Blankenhorn, D. (1995). *Fatherless America: Confronting our most urgent social problem.* New York: Basic Books.

Block, J. (1976). Issues, problems and pitfalls in assessing sex differences: A critical review of *The psychology of sex differences. Merrill Palmer Quarterly, 22,* 283–340.

Boss, P. (1986). Psychological absence in the intact family: A systems approach to a study of fathering. *Marriage and Family Review, 10,* 11–32.

Brannen, J., & Moss, P. (1998). The polarization and intensification of parental employment in Britain: Consequences for children, families, and the community. *Community, Work and Family, 1,* 229–247.

Brennan, R. T., Barnett, R. C., & Gareis, K. C. (2001). When she earns more than he does: A longitudinal study of dual-earner couples. *Journal of Marriage and Family, 63,* 168–182.

Brooks-Gordon, B. (2003). Contact in containment. In A. Bainham, B. Lindley, M. Richards, & L. Trinder (Eds.), *Children and their families: Contact, rights and welfare.* Portland, OR: Hart.

Cabrera, N., Brooks-Gunn, J., Moore, K., West, J., Boller, K., & Tamis-LeMonda, C. S. (2002). Bridging research and policy: Including fathers of young children in national studies. In C. S. Tamis-LeMonda & N. Cabrera (Eds.), *Handbook of father involvement: Multidisciplinary perspectives* (pp. 489–524). Mahwah, NJ: Lawrence Erlbaum.

Cabrera, N., Shannon, J., Tamis-LeMonda, C. S., & Lamb, M. E. (2003, April). *Determinants of father involvement: Presence/absence and quality of engagement.* Early Head Start Research and Evaluation Project presentation, University of Michigan, Ann Arbor.

Carlson, M., & McLanahan, S. S. (2002). Fragile families, father involvement, and public policy. In C. S. Tamis-LeMonda & N. Cabrera (Eds.), *Handbook of father involvement: Multidisciplinary perspectives* (pp. 461–488). Mahwah, NJ: Lawrence Erlbaum.

Coleman, J. S. (1988). Social capital in the creation of human capital. *American Journal of Sociology, 94*(Suppl.), S95–S120.

Coley, R. L., & Morris, J. E. (2002). Comparing father and mother reports of father involvement among low-income minority families. *Journal of Marriage and Family, 64,* 982–997.

Coltrane, S. (2001). Marketing the marriage "solution": Misplaced simplicity in the politics of fatherhood (Presidential address to the Pacific Sociological Association). *Sociological Perspectives, 44,* 387–418.

Cowan, P. A., & Hetherington, E. M. (Eds.). (1991). *Family transitions.* Hillsdale, NJ: Lawrence Erlbaum.

Crouter, A. C., Perry-Jenkins, M., Huston, T. L., & McHale, S. M. (1987). Processes underlying father involvement in dual-earner and single-earner families. *Developmental Psychology, 23,* 431–440.

Day, R. D., Gavazzi, S., & Acock, A. C. (2001). Compelling family processes. In A. Thornton (Ed.), *The well-being of children and families: Research and data needs* (pp. 103–126). Ann Arbor: University of Michigan Press.

Day, R. D., & Lamb, M. E. (Eds.). (2004). *Conceptualizing and measuring father involvement.* Mahwah, NJ: Lawrence Erlbaum.

Deven, F., & Moss, P. (2002). Parental leave in Europe. *Community, Work and Family, 5,* 237–255.

DeWolff, M. S., & van IJzendoorn, M. H. (1997). Sensitivity and attachment: A meta-analysis on parental antecedents of infant attachment. *Child Development, 68,* 571–591.

Doherty, W. J. (1997). *The intentional family: How to build family ties in our modern world.* Reading, MA: Addison-Wesley.

Doherty, W. J., Kouneski, E. F., & Erickson, M. F. (1998). Responsible fathering: An overview and conceptual framework. *Journal of Marriage and the Family, 60,* 277–292.

Federal Interagency Forum on Child and Family Statistics. (1998). *Nurturing fatherhood: Improving data and research on male fertility, family formation, and fatherhood.* Washington, DC: Author.

Few, A. L., Stephens, D. P., & Rouse-Arnett, M. (2003). Sister-to-sister talk: Transcending boundaries and challenges in qualitative research with Black women. *Family Relations, 52,* 205–215.

Flouri, E., & Buchanan, A. (2002). What predicts good relationships with parents in adolescence and partners in adult life: Findings from the 1958 British birth cohort. *Journal of Family Psychology, 16,* 186–198.

Fonow, M., & Cook, J. (1991). *Beyond methodology: Feminist scholarship as lived research.* Bloomington: Indiana University Press.

Franz, C. E., McClelland, D. C., Weinberger, J., & Peterson, C. (1994). Parenting antecedents of adult adjustment: A longitudinal study. In C. Perris, W. A. Arrindell, & M. Eisemann (Eds.), *Parenting and psychopathology* (pp. 127–144). New York: John Wiley.

Fuligni, A. S., & Brooks-Gunn, J. (2004). Measuring mother and father shared caregiving: An analysis using the Panel Study of Income Dynamics–Child Development Supplement. In R. D. Day & M. E. Lamb (Eds.), *Conceptualizing and measuring father involvement* (pp. 341–358). Mahwah, NJ: Lawrence Erlbaum.

Gadsden, V. L., Fagan, J., Ray, A., & Davis, J. E. (2004). Fathering indicators for practice and evaluation: The fathering indicators framework. In R. D. Day & M. E. Lamb (Eds.), *Conceptualizing and measuring father involvement* (pp. 385–452). Mahwah, NJ: Lawrence Erlbaum.

Gadsden, V. L., & Ray, A. (2002). Engaging fathers: Issues and considerations for early childhood educators. *Young Children, 57*(6), 32–42.

Gadsden, V. L., Wortham, S. E. F., & Turner, H., III. (2003). Situated identities of young, African American fathers in low-income urban settings: perspectives on home, street, and the system. *Family Court Review, 41,* 381–399.

Garfinkel, I., McLanahan, S. S., Meyer, D. R., & Seltzer, J. A. (1998). *Fathers under fire: The revolution in child support enforcement.* New York: Russell Sage Foundation.

Grossmann, K., Grossmann, K. E., Fremmer-Bombik, E., Kindler, H., Scheurer-Englisch, H., & Zimmermann, P. (2002). The uniqueness of the child-father attachment relationship: Fathers' sensitive and challenging play as a pivotal variable in a 16-year long study. *Social Development, 11,* 307–331.

Harkness, S., & Super, C. M. (1992). The cultural foundations of fathers' roles: Evidence from Kenya and the United States. In B. S. Hewlett (Ed.), *Father-child relations: Cultural and biosocial contexts* (pp. 191–211). Hawthorne, NY: Aldine de Gruyter.

Hawkins, A. J., Bradford, K. P., Palkovitz, R., Christiansen, S. L., Day, R. D., & Call, V. R. A. (2002). The Inventory of Father Involvement: A pilot study of a new measure of father involvement. *Journal of Men's Studies, 10,* 183–196.

Hawkins, A. J., & Dollahite, D. C. (1997). Beyond the role-inadequacy perspective of fathering. In A. J. Hawkins & D. C. Dollahite (Eds.), *Generative fathering: Beyond deficit perspectives* (pp. 3–16). Thousand Oaks, CA: Sage.

Hawkins, A. J., & Palkovitz, R. (1999). Beyond ticks and clicks: The need for more diverse and broader conceptualizations and measures of father involvement. *Journal of Men's Studies, 8,* 11–32.

Hertz, R., & Marshall, N. L. (Eds.). (2001). *Working families: The transformation of the American home.* Berkeley: University of California Press.

Hewlett, B. S. (1992). Husband-wife reciprocity and the father-infant relationships among Aka Pygmies. In B. S. Hewlett (Ed.), *Father-child relations: Cultural and biosocial contexts* (pp. 153–176). Hawthorne, NY: Aldine de Gruyter.

Hofferth, S. L., Boisjoly, J., & Duncan, G. J. (1999). The development of social capital. *Rationality and Society, 11,* 79–110.

Hossain, Z., Field, T., Pickens, J., Malphurs, J., & Del Valle, C. (1997). Fathers' caregiving in low-income African American and Hispanic American families. *Early Development and Parenting, 6,* 73–82.

Hossain, Z., & Roopnarine, J. L. (1994). African-American fathers' involvement with infants: Relationship to their functional style, support, education, and income. *Infant Behavior and Development, 17,* 175–184.

Howell, J. T. (1973). *Hard living on Clay Street: Portraits of blue collar families.* Prospect Heights, IL: Waveland.

Hyde, J. S., Essex, M. J., & Horton, F. (1993). Fathers and parental leave: Attitudes and expectations. *Journal of Family Issues, 14,* 616–641.

Ishii-Kuntz, M. (1994). Paternal involvement and perception toward fathers' roles: A comparison between Japan and the United States. *Journal of Family Issues, 15,* 30–48.

Ishii-Kuntz, M. (2000). Diversity within Asian American families. In D. H. Demo, K. R. Allen, & M. A. Fine (Eds.), *Handbook of family diversity* (pp. 274–292). New York: Oxford University Press.

Johansen, S. (2001). *Family men: Middle-class fatherhood in early industrialization.* New York: Routledge.

Kelly, J. B. (2000). Children's adjustment in conflicted marriage and divorce: A decade review of research. *Journal of the American Academy of Child and Adolescent Psychiatry, 39,* 963–973.

Labrell, F. (1990). *Educational strategies and their representations in parents of toddlers.* Paper presented at the Fourth European Conference on Developmental Psychology, Stirling, Scotland.

Lamb, M. E. (Ed.). (2004). *The role of the father in child development* (4th ed.). Mahwah, NJ: Lawrence Erlbaum.

Lamb, M. E., Chuang, S. S., & Hwang, C. P. (2004). Internal reliability, temporal stability, and correlates of individual differences in paternal involvement: A 15-year longitudinal study in Sweden. In R. D. Day & M. E. Lamb (Eds.), *Conceptualizing and measuring father involvement* (pp. 129–148). Mahwah, NJ: Lawrence Erlbaum.

Lamb, M. E., Hwang, C. P., Broberg, A., Bookstein, F. L., Hult, G., & Frodi, M. (1988). The determinants of paternal involvement in primiparous Swedish families. *International Journal of Behavioral Development, 11,* 433–449.

Lamb, M. E., & Lewis, C. (2004). The role and significance of father-child relationships in two-parent families. In M. E. Lamb (Ed.), *The role of the father in child development* (4th ed., pp. 272–306). New York: John Wiley.

Lamb, M. E., Pleck, J. H., Charnov, E. L., & Levine, J. A. (1987). A biosocial perspective on paternal behavior and involvement. In J. Lancaster, J. Altmann, A. S. Rossi, & L. R. Sherrod (Eds.), *Parenting across the lifespan: Biosocial dimensions* (pp. 111–142). Hawthorne, NY: Aldine de Gruyter.

LaRossa, R. (1997). *The modernization of fatherhood: A social and political history.* Chicago: University of Chicago Press.

Lewis, C. (1986). *Becoming a father.* Milton Keynes, Eng.: Open University Press.

Lipscomb, A. (2001, May). *The legislative marriage agenda and its potential meaning for programs serving low-income families.* Madison, WI: Center on Fathers, Families, and Public Policy. Retrieved August 26, 2003, from http://www.cffpp.org/publications/marriage_agenda.html

Lytton, H., & Romney, D. M. (1991). Parents' differential socialization of boys and girls: A meta-analysis. *Psychological Bulletin, 109,* 267–296.

Lyytinen, P., Laakso, M. L., & Poikkeus, A. M. (1998). Parental contribution to child's early language and interest in books. *European Journal of Psychology of Education, 13,* 297–308.

Mackey, W.C. (1985). A cross-cultural perspective on perceptions of paternalistic deficiencies in the United States: The myth of the derelict daddy. *Sex Roles, 12,* 509–533.

Main, M. (1996). Introduction to the special section on attachment and psychopathology: Overview of the field of attachment. *Journal of Consulting and Clinical Psychology, 64,* 237–243.

Marsiglio, W., Amato, P. R., Day, R. D., & Lamb, M. E. (2000). Scholarship on fatherhood in the 1990s and beyond. *Journal of Marriage and the Family, 62,* 1173–1191.

Marsiglio, W., Day, R. D., & Lamb, M. E. (2000). Exploring fatherhood diversity: Implications for conceptualizing father involvement. *Marriage and Family Review, 29,* 269–293.

McBride, B. A., & Lutz, M. M. (2004). Intervention: Changing the nature and extent of father involvement. In M. E. Lamb (Ed.), *The role of the father in child development* (4th ed., pp. 446–475). New York: John Wiley.

McLanahan, S. S., & Garfinkel, I. (2002). *Unwed parents: Myths, realities, and policymaking* (Working Paper No. 2002-15-FF). Princeton, NJ: Center for Research on Child Wellbeing.

Mincy, R. B., & Pouncy, H. (1997). There must be fifty ways to start a family: Social policy and the fragile families of low-income, noncustodial fathers. In W. Horn, D. Blankenhorn, M. Pearlstein, & D. Eberly (Eds.), *The fatherhood movement: A call to action* (pp. 83–104). Berkeley: University of California Press.

Mincy, R. B., & Pouncy, H. (2002). The responsible fatherhood field: Evolution and goals. In C. S. Tamis-LeMonda & N. Cabrera (Eds.), *Handbook of father involvement: Multidisciplinary perspectives* (pp. 555–598). Mahwah, NJ: Lawrence Erlbaum.

National Center on Fathers and Families. (2004). *NCOFF FatherLit Database.* Retrieved July 28, 2004, from http://fatherfamilylink.gse.upenn.edu/fatherlit

Nsamenang, A. B. (2000). *Fathers, families, and child well-being in Cameroon: A review of the literature.* Philadelphia: University of Pennsylvania, Graduate School of Education, National Center on Fathers and Families.

Nurse, A. M. (2002). *Fatherhood arrested: Parenting from within the juvenile justice system.* Nashville, TN: Vanderbilt University Press.

O'Brien, M. (2004). Social science and public policy perspectives on fatherhood in the European Union. In M. E. Lamb (Ed.), *The role of the father in child development* (4th ed., pp. 121–145). New York: John Wiley.

Palkovitz, R. (1997). Reconstructing "involvement": Expanding conceptualizations of men's caring in contemporary families. In A. J. Hawkins & D. C. Dollahite (Eds.), *Generative fathering: Beyond deficit perspectives* (pp. 200–216). Thousand Oaks, CA: Sage.

Palkovitz, R. (2003). *Involved fathering and men's adult development: Provisional balances.* Mahwah, NJ: Lawrence Erlbaum.

Parke, C. S. (2001). An approach that examines sources of misfit to improve performance assessment items and rubrics. *Educational Assessment, 7,* 201–225.

Parke, R. D., Coltrane, S., Borthwick-Duffy, S., Powers, J., Adams, M., Fabricius, W., et al. (2004). Assessing father involvement in Mexican-American families. In R. D. Day & M. E. Lamb (Eds.), *Conceptualizing and measuring father involvement* (pp. 17–38). Mahwah, NJ: Lawrence Erlbaum.

Pasley, K. B., Furtis, T., & Skinner, M. L. (2002). Effects of commitment and psychological centrality on fathering. *Journal of Marriage and Family, 64,* 130–138.

Pasley, K. B., & Minton, C. (1997). Generative fathering after divorce and remarriage: Beyond the "disappearing dad." In A. J. Hawkins & D. C. Dollahite (Eds.), *Generative fathering: Beyond deficit perspectives* (pp. 118–133). Thousand Oaks, CA: Sage.

Pearson, J., Thoennes, N., & Griswold, E. A. (1999). Child support and domestic violence: The victims speak out. *Violence Against Women, 5,* 427–448.

Petersilia, J. (2003). *When prisoners come home: Parole and prisoner reentry.* New York: Oxford University Press.

Pleck, E. H., & Pleck, J. H. (1997). Fatherhood ideals in the United States: Historical dimensions. In M. E. Lamb (Ed.), *The role of the father in child development* (3rd ed., pp. 33–48). New York: John Wiley.

Pleck, J. H., & Masciadrelli, B. P. (2004). Paternal involvement by U.S. residential fathers: Levels, sources, and consequences. In M. E. Lamb (Ed.), *The role of the father in child development* (4th ed., pp. 222–271). New York: John Wiley.

Popenoe, D. (1993). American family decline 1960–1990: A review and appraisal. *Journal of Marriage and the Family, 55,* 527–556.

Pruett, K., & Litzenberger, B. (1992). Latency development in children of primary nurturing fathers: Eight-year follow up. *Psychoanalytic Study of the Child, 4,* 85–101.

Rane, T. R., & McBride, B. A. (2000). Identity theory as a guide to understanding fathers' involvement with their children. *Journal of Family Issues, 21,* 347–366.

Raphael, J. (2000). *Saving Bernice: Battered women, welfare, and poverty.* Boston: Northeastern University Press.

Reed, D. F., & Reed, E. L. (1998). Children of incarcerated parents. *Social Justice, 24,* 152–169.

Roggman, L. A., Fitzgerald, H. E., Bradley, R. H., & Raikes, H. (2002). Methodological, measurement, and design issues in studying fathers: An interdisciplinary perspective. In C. S. Tamis-LeMonda & N. Cabrera (Eds.), *Handbook of father involvement: Multidisciplinary perspectives* (pp. 1–30). Mahwah, NJ: Lawrence Erlbaum.

Roopnarine, J. L. (2004). African American and African Caribbean fathers: Level, quality, and meaning of involvement. In M. E. Lamb (Ed.), *The role of the father in child development* (4th ed., pp. 58–97). New York: John Wiley.

Roopnarine, J. L., Talukder, E., Jain, D., Joshi, P., & Srivastav, P. (1992). Personal well-being, kinship tie, and mother-infant and father-infant interactions in single-wage and dual-wage families in New Delhi, India. *Journal of Marriage and the Family, 54,* 293–301.

Roulet, M. (1999, November). *Fatherhood programs and domestic violence.* Madison, WI: Center on Fathers, Families, and Public Policy. Retrieved August 26, 2003, from http://www.cffpp.org/publications/father hood_programs.html

Sandberg, J. F., & Hofferth, S. L. (2001). Changes in children's time with parents: United States, 1981–1997. *Demography, 38,* 423–436.

Sano, Y., & Richards, L. N. (2003, November). *Are mothers really gatekeepers of children? Mothers' perception of nonresident fathers' involvement after separation.* Paper presented at the annual meeting of the National Council on Family Relations, Vancouver.

Scott, E. K., London, A. S., & Myers, N. A. (2002). Dangerous dependencies: The intersection of welfare reform and domestic violence. *Gender & Society, 16,* 878–897.

Seward, R. R., Yeatts, D. E., & Zottarelli, L. K. (2002). Parental leave and father involvement in child care: Sweden and the United States. *Journal of Comparative Family Studies, 33,* 387–399.

Silverstein, L. B. (1996). Fathering is a feminist issue. *Psychology of Women Quarterly, 20,* 3–37.

Silverstein, L. B., & Auerbach, C. F. (1999). Deconstructing the essential father. *American Psychologist, 54,* 397–407.

Smit, R. (2002). The changing role of the husband/father in the dual-earner family in South Africa. *Journal of Comparative Family Studies, 33,* 401–411.

Stolz, L. M. (1954). *Father relations of war-born children.* New York: Greenwood.

Tamis-LeMonda, C. S., & Cabrera, N. (Eds.). (2002). *Handbook of father involvement: Multidisciplinary perspectives.* Mahwah, NJ: Lawrence Erlbaum.

Terry, C. M. (2003). *The fellas: Overcoming prison and addiction.* Belmont CA: Wadsworth.

Tolman, R. M., & Raphael, J. (2000). A review of research on welfare and domestic violence. *Journal of Social Issues 56,* 655–685.

Uggen, C., Thompson, M., & Manza, J. (2001). *Crime, class, and reintegration: The scope and social distribution of America's criminal class.* Unpublished manuscript, University of Minnesota.

van IJzendoorn, M. H., & DeWolff, M. S. (1997). In search of the absent father— meta-analyses of infant-father attachment: A rejoinder to our discussants. *Child Development, 68,* 604–609.

Yogman, M. W., Kindlon, D., & Earls, F. (1996). "The role of fathers": Reply. *Journal of the American Academy of Child and Adolescent Psychiatry, 35,* 700.

Zaouche-Gaudron, C., Ricaud, H., & Beaumatin, A. (1998). Father-child play interaction and subjectivity. *European Journal of Psychology of Education, 13,* 447–460.

• Fifteen

INFLUENCES OF PARENTS AND SIBLINGS ON THE DEVELOPMENT OF CHILDREN AND ADOLESCENTS

Martin Pinquart, *Friedrich Schiller University*

Rainer K. Silbereisen, *Friedrich Schiller University*

In this chapter we relate parent-child interactions and sibling-child interactions to the development of children and adolescents. Given the focus on families and child development, we refer to both family and child development theories. We limit our attention to the most prominent theories and their core assumptions and to interrelations between these theories rather than try to include all specific topics that have been raised with regard to these theories. We distinguish global metatheories that make general assumptions about the roles of parents and siblings for child development from more specific theories that focus on particular aspects of parent-child or sibling relationships. We start with a discussion of four general theories (developmental contextualism, family systems, behavioral genetics, learning), followed by four specific models of the role of parent-child relationships (attachment, coercion,

family stress, parenting) and two theories on the role of siblings (confluence and resource dilution). We then derive methodological consequences for the study of how parent-child interactions and sibling interactions influence child development. We do not cover the effects of single-parent families, stepfamilies, grandparents, or extended families. As our main focus in this chapter is the effect of the family on child development, we do not discuss in depth the factors that influence parenting and the broader family environment.

METATHEORIES

Contextualistic Theory

In developmental science, contextualistic, biopsychosocial theories, such as Lerner and Ford's developmental systems theory and Thelen's dynamic systems approach, have become most prominent during recent decades (for an overview, see Lerner, 2002). According to these theories, development occurs in a multilevel context (genes, neurobiological processes, psychological processes, social context), and changes at one level promote changes at the others. Developmental changes occur as the consequences of reciprocal (bidirectional) relations between the active organism and the active context. By being producers and products of their contexts and by setting and pursuing developmental goals, individuals affect their own development. Because of the complexity of the interactions among developmental contexts, the same change (e.g., birth of a sibling) can have different effects on individuals, depending on the interplay of the change with other developmental contexts. For studying the influence of family on child development, contextualistic theory suggests that the effect of parental or sibling behavior on the development of the child is also influenced by the child (e.g., by child's temperament) and by the broader social context (e.g., parental control may be more critical for child development in high-risk neighborhoods). As contextualistic theory is formulated at a very abstract level, it would be difficult to derive specific hypotheses concerning what effects an individual parental behavior would have on the child under which circumstances.

Family Systems Theory

The interplay between specific developmental contexts and child development is the focus of other theories and paradigms, but these concepts focus on a narrow range of contexts or even on just one context. The general assumption that not only do parents influence their children but children also influence their parents has also been formulated in family systems theory. According to this theory, the family is characterized by wholeness and order, a hierarchical structure, and self-organization. Changes can arise at any level of the family system (including that of the child), and change at any one level can stimulate change in an individual member.

Transactions across the multiple levels of a family system are important in regulating child behavior, and continuity or discontinuity in child characteristics has to be located in the relationship between the child and the family system (Cox & Paley, 2003). As family systems theory emphasizes the dynamics within the family, it has a narrower focus than do contextualistic biopsychosocial theories.

Behavioral Genetics Framework

According to the framework of behavioral genetics, human development results from the interplay between genes and environments, such as the family, although some proponents of behavioral genetics put more emphasis on the effects of genes than on the effects of environment (e.g., Scarr, 1992). Similarities between parents and children or between siblings cannot be explained exclusively by joint family environment; rather, they are, in part, mediated through shared genes and the interaction between genes and environment. Three forms of such interactions are distinguished. *Passive* genome-environment covariance is based on the facts that the child shares 50% of his or her genes with each parent and that parents build a family environment that corresponds to their own genetic dispositions. Thus the child is born into a family environment that generally fits his or her inborn dispositions. For example, gifted children are likely to be born into family environments that stimulate their talent. *Evocative* genome-environment covariance indicates that children's genes lead to behavior that evokes corresponding responses by their family environments. In this way, when parents perceive a child's talent they will promote its development through the provision of stimulation and support. Finally, *active* genome-environment covariance indicates that children can actively change their environments or even select environments that fit to their genes (e.g., by choosing particular schools or universities). Research suggests that active genome-environment covariance increases in importance as the child gets older.

Behavioral genetics provides evidence for the influence of family and other environments, but it also shows that environment works in a surprising way. Common environmental factors (e.g., similarities in child-rearing practices toward siblings, the so-called shared environment) are less important for interindividual differences between siblings than are nonshared environmental factors, such as differential parental behaviors toward individual children (e.g., related to child gender, birth order, temperament) and differential perceptions of the same aspect of the family among siblings (Plomin, Asbury, & Dunn, 2001). As parents often do not act in the same ways toward all of their children, and as siblings may react differently to the same parental behavior, children experience a significant amount of nonshared family influences. Behavioral genetics offers methods for estimating the average explained variance by genes, shared environment, and nonshared environment on child development (e.g., based on twin studies and adoption studies).

From a behavioral genetics point of view, Scarr (1992) has proposed that parenting may have low impact on child development as long as parents provide a good-enough environment that helps children to become themselves, and as long as opportunities for normal development are not particularly limited. Normal genes and normal environments promote species-typical development, and individuals make their own environments based on their heritable characteristics. Nonetheless, it may be difficult to specify the criteria for a good-enough environment, given cultural differences and social-historical change. In addition, Scarr's position would not be applicable when parents want to promote optimal development rather than normal, average-expected development.

Learning Theories

Learning theories provide another general framework for the study of child development within the family. According to such theories, child psychological development is based primarily on learning processes, such as classical and operant conditioning (reinforcements and punishments), or on children's modeling of the behavior of their parents. Parents demand age-appropriate behavior from their children, and they reinforce desired and punish undesired behavior. Parents are also considered to be the most salient role models to guide the behavior of young children because of the intensity and duration of the parent-child relationship. Whereas proponents of behavioral genetics have suggested that nonshared family influences are more important for child development than shared influences, social learning theories (Bandura, 1977) assume that the family environment influences psychological development, with the result that shared experiences lead to similarities among siblings (Plomin et al., 2001). Pure learning theories have difficulty explaining why all children do not react in the same ways to particular parental behaviors or role models. As we have learned from developmental contextualism and behavioral genetics, not all interindividual differences in reactions to role models or parental teaching can be explained by previous learning history or social-environmental variables.

SPECIFIC THEORIES ON THE ASSOCIATION BETWEEN PARENT-CHILD RELATIONSHIP AND CHILD OUTCOMES

The four theories discussed below make more specific assumptions about the role of parent-child relationships in child development. These theories agree that children have age-associated developmental needs and that the satisfaction of those needs promotes positive development. In infancy, the needs for food, shelter, comfort, and warmth dominate. Recognizing and satisfying these needs are important behaviors for parents (e.g., parental responsiveness and attentiveness), and such is the main focus of attachment theory. Older children have to acquire a large number of cognitive and social competencies, so their parents need to provide adequate stimulation/learning opportunities, supervision, and support. These aspects of parenting are the central focus of Baumrind's model of authoritative parenting. As gaining autonomy is an important developmental goal in adolescence, parents' granting of autonomy is a central component of Steinberg's reformulation of Baumrind's model.

Attachment Theory

Attachment theory is the most prominent theory on early parent-child relationships. Attachment is the emotional security that children derive from their perceptions of their relationships with their primary caregivers. Attachment patterns emerge at the end of the first year of life, when, it is suggested, the child develops an inner working model that represents the self in relation to others. The model is based on the primary relationship, usually with the mother as the primary caregiver (Bowlby, 1969). Based on empirical studies (e.g., Ainsworth & Bell, 1970), theorists have distinguished a secure type of attachment and three insecure types (insecure resistant, insecure avoidant, and disorganized). Ideally, the attachment figure provides a secure base from which the child can explore the world.

Patterns of attachment are thought to develop as a function of parental behavior in relation to the characteristics of the child. As the infant's competence to express needs and to regulate interactions with the mother or other caregivers is still very limited, parents need to be responsive to the infant's signals, to be prompt in their response, and to be supportive. In line with these assumptions, a meta-analysis by DeWolff and van IJzendoorn (1997) revealed that maternal sensitivity, synchronicity, and mutuality of positive emotions and reactions showed the highest correlations with infant's attachment security. In line with contextualistic theories of development and family systems theory, however, the development of attachment is also influenced by characteristics of the child, such as temperament. For example, it is more difficult to establish interactional synchronicity with fearful infants or with infants who become upset very easily. Early established attachment patterns influence development of later close social relationships, although longitudinal research has shown that attachment patterns may change over time in response to new relational experiences (Cassidy & Shaver, 1999).

• **SPOTLIGHT ON THEORY**

PARENTAL ACCEPTANCE-REJECTION THEORY

Ronald P. Rohner, *University of Connecticut*

Parental acceptance-rejection theory (PARTheory) is an evidence-based theory of socialization and life-span development that seeks to predict and explain major causes, consequences, and other correlates of parental acceptance and rejection worldwide. The theory is divided into three distinguishable subtheories: *Personality subtheory*

(continued)

● **SPOTLIGHT ON THEORY** *continued*

attempts to predict and explain major personality or psychological consequences of perceived parental acceptance-rejection in childhood and adulthood; *coping subtheory* deals with factors associated with the fact that some children and adults cope emotionally with the experience of rejection more effectively than others; and *sociocultural systems subtheory* attempts to predict and explain why some parents are warm and loving whereas others are cold, aggressive, or neglecting/rejecting. Sociocultural systems subtheory asks, In what way is the total fabric of a society as well as the behavior and beliefs of individuals within that society (e.g., people's religious beliefs and artistic preferences) affected by the fact that most parents in that society tend to either accept or reject their children? (For evidence regarding details about PARTheory's subtheories, see this volume's companion Web site at http://www.ncfr.org/sourcebook.)

Parental acceptance and rejection together form the warmth dimension of parenting. One end of this dimension is marked by parental acceptance, which comprises the warmth, affection, care, comfort, concern, nurturance, support, and simply love that parents can feel and express toward their children. The other end is marked by parental rejection, or the absence or significant withdrawal of these feelings and behaviors, and by the presence of a variety of physically and psychologically hurtful behaviors and affects. Scholars have found that, anywhere in the world, parental rejection can be seen in any combination of four principal expressions: (a) cold and unaffectionate (the opposite of warm and affectionate), (b) hostile and aggressive, (c) indifferent and neglecting, and (d) undifferentiated rejecting. The term *undifferentiated rejection* refers to individuals' beliefs that their parents do not really care about them or love them, even though there might not be clear behavioral indicators that the parents are neglecting, unaffectionate, or aggressive toward them.

Because personality subtheory is the most highly developed aspect of PARTheory, it is highlighted here. This subtheory begins with the assumption that humans have an enduring, biologically based emotional need for positive response from the people most important to them. This need includes an emotional wish, desire, or yearning (whether consciously recognized or not) for comfort, support, care, concern, nurturance, and overall positive regard from people with whom they have affectional bonds of attachment. The emotional need for positive response from significant others, including attachment figures, is a powerful motivator; when individuals do not get this need satisfied adequately they are predisposed to respond emotionally and behaviorally in a specific way. In particular, rejected individuals are likely to feel (a) anxious and (b) insecure. Additionally, they are likely (c) to be hostile, aggressive, or passive-aggressive, or to have problems with the management of hostility and aggression; (d) to be dependent or defensively independent, depending on the form, frequency, and severity of rejection; (e) to have impaired feelings of self-esteem and (f) impaired self-adequacy; (g) to be emotionally unresponsive and (h) emotionally unstable; and (i) to have a negative worldview.

Taken together, these personality dispositions constitute a measure of psychological adjustment that is postulated to vary directly and universally with children's experience of parental acceptance-rejection. More than 50 studies within the United States and

(continued)

• SPOTLIGHT ON THEORY *continued*

across cultures have tested these assumptions (see Khaleque & Rohner, 2002; Rohner, 1986, 2004), and virtually all of them—despite great variations in culture, language, race, gender, and geographic boundaries across the studies—have come to the conclusion that the experience of parental acceptance or rejection is associated universally with the form of psychological (mal)adjustment postulated in PARTheory's personality subtheory. •

Model of Authoritative Parenting

Despite the fact that assumptions from attachment theory about effective parental behavior focus mainly on a narrowly defined criterion (attachment to the parent or other caregivers) and psychological development in infancy, some aspects of parenting from attachment theory relate to models of effective parenting of older children and adolescents. Baumrind (1973) and Maccoby and Martin (1983) offer a very influential typology of parenting styles. As these scholars derive detailed expectations about the effectiveness of different forms of parental behavior and make theoretical suggestions concerning why these behaviors are effective, we can speak of a parenting theory. Baumrind conceptualizes parenting as varying on two dimensions. The first, *demandingness,* corresponds to the degree to which parents try to control how their children behave (behavioral control, parental monitoring) and the extent to which parents expect mature, responsible behavior from their children. The second, *responsiveness,* corresponds to the degree to which parents respond to their children's needs in an accepting, supportive manner and the amount of affection parents display toward their children. The meanings of these dimensions are supported by the fact that both dimensions are usually found in factor analyses of parenting questionnaires. Certainly, parental sensitivity as a key component of attachment theory overlaps with the concept of monitoring (parents' being informed about their children's needs, problems, activities, and whereabouts), although, in Baumrind's theory, monitoring is not limited to parents' adequate perception of

their children's needs. Similarly, parental responsiveness from the Baumrind model and mutuality of positive emotions from the attachment model represent the socio-emotional dimension of the parent-child relationship. However, parents' expecting mature, responsible behavior from their children, which is a core component of the model of authoritative parenting, is not developmentally appropriate for infants and therefore plays no role in attachment theory.

In the model of authoritative parenting, parental responsiveness and demandingness are considered to be more or less independent of each other (Baumrind, 1973). Thus it is possible to conceptualize four combinations (see Table 15.1):

- *Authoritative parents* are warm and supportive but firm. They provide clear standards by explaining their rules or decisions and by reasoning with their children rather than using physical punishment and stressing obedience to authority as a virtue in itself. They are willing to consider the children's points of view, even if they do not always accept them.
- *Authoritarian parents* place high value on obedience and conformity. They tend to use more punitive, absolute, and forceful disciplinary measures than do other parents. They expect their children to accept the rules and standards established by the parents without question. Such parents tend not to encourage independent behavior and place a good deal of importance on restricting their children's autonomy.

Table 15.1   Two-Dimensional Model of Parenting Patterns

		Responsiveness (Support/Involvement/Warmth)	
		Accepting, responsive, child centered	Rejecting, unresponsive, parent centered
Demandingness (Strictness, Supervision)	Demanding, controlling	Authoritative	Authoritarian, power assertive
	Undemanding, low control attempts	Indulgent, permissive	Indifferent, uninvolved, neglecting, ignoring

SOURCE: Adapted from Maccoby and Martin (1983).

- *Permissive or indulgent parents* behave in an accepting and sometimes relatively passive way in matters of discipline. They take low explicit control over their children's behavior and give their children a lot of freedom to determine their own activities. They do not demand the same level of achievement and mature behavior that authoritative and authoritarian parents do.

- *Indifferent or uninvolved parents* minimize the time and energy they spend in interacting with their children. They know little about their children's whereabouts and activities; they are parent centered in that they structure their home life primarily around their own needs and interests. In extreme cases, they may be neglectful.

Theorists have suggested that authoritative parenting is the most effective parenting style because authoritative parents make demands that fit with their children's ability to take responsibility for their own behavior, keep control that appears fair and reasonable (i.e., not arbitrary) to their children, and provide a warm and supporting relationship that promotes children's internalization of parental demands. Further, by modeling parents who are secure in the standards they set, children may gain emotion regulation skills, emotional understanding, and social understanding. Children learn that they are competent individuals who can do things successfully for themselves, which may foster emotional

maturity, high self-esteem, and cognitive development (Baumrind, 1973).

Surprisingly, very few longitudinal studies have examined the effects of authoritative parenting. Those that have been conducted have shown positive associations between authoritative parenting and children's increases in self-reliance, self-esteem, and academic competence as well as a lower age-associated increase in delinquency, although the sizes of the effects are usually small (Steinberg, Lamborn, Darling, Mounts, & Dornbusch, 1994). Even so, many textbooks on child development and parenting advise parents to be authoritative, despite the fact that the effects of parenting may also vary by ethnicity, family structure, child's age, personality, and other factors. First, for example, as parenting practices are linked to cultural values, African American, Asian American, and Hispanic families often combine a very high degree of strictness (similar to White authoritarian parents) with warmth (similar to White authoritative parents). Authoritative parenting seems also to have lower effects among ethnic minority adolescents than among their European American counterparts (Steinberg, Darling, & Fletcher, 1995). Second, research on stepfathers has shown that permissive parenting (high responsiveness/low demandingness) of stepfathers may be as functional for children's development as authoritative parenting, probably because stepparents have no formal obligation to put high demands on their stepchildren (Crosbie-Burnett & Giles-Sims, 1994). Third, effects of parenting also vary by child's temperament, and different parenting strategies may be needed to bring about the same outcome in different same-aged children. For example, Bates, Pettit, Dodge, and Ridge (1998) found that firm restrictive parental behavioral control was more likely to inhibit later externalizing behavior in early difficult, unmanageable children, thus supporting the goodness-of-fit perspective between early adolescents' temperaments and their parents' demands and behavior. Fourth, research on parenting usually conceptualizes authoritative parenting as a uniform family construct, for example, by asking adolescents how parents behave in general or by focusing on the mother-child dyad. From the perspective of family systems theory and developmental contextualism, however, it is also important to study how processes of coparenting (e.g., interparental agreements and disagreements, mutual support versus active undermining of a partner's parenting) influence child development (McHale, Kuersten, & Lauretti, 1996). Finally, behavioral genetics researchers have asked whether parenting styles may, in part, reflect genetic effects. Adoption research shows that parental warmth has such a component, probably indicating that the emotional element of the parent-child relationship is partly influenced through child effects on parental affect. In contrast, parental behavioral control appears to have no genetic component and is influenced primarily by parental attributes, such as education and child-rearing attitudes (e.g., Deater-Deckard, Fulkner, & Plomin, 1999).

As the model of authoritative parenting was first formulated and tested in childhood, it was later reformulated with regard to adolescents through the addition of a third dimension: parental support for autonomy (i.e., parents' granting of psychological autonomy to adolescents, such as encouragement to be individualistic and independent; Steinberg, Elmen, & Mounts, 1989). The psychological autonomy dimension does not emerge as a critical variable until the child reaches early adolescence, around age 10 or 11, and begins to establish an independent psychological identity.

Coercion Theory

According to the model of authoritative parenting, dysfunctional parenting is characterized by low levels of demandingness, responsiveness, and autonomy support (e.g., parents who show very low levels of involvement with their children). However, other theories highlight the fact that there are further forms of dysfunctional parental behavior, such as inconsistent and ineffective control, that may explain the development of problem behavior in children and adolescents. Patterson (1976) first formulated coercion theory to explain the role of dysfunctional parent-child and sibling interactions in the development of antisocial behavior. This theory suggests that a pathway of antisocial behavior development begins when a child's aversive response is rewarded by the termination of parents' and siblings' undesired behavior. For example, when the parent asks the child to help with household tasks, the child may at first ignore the request. The request then becomes more intense but the child still refuses to comply, yells at the parent to stop asking, and finally runs out of the room. If this behavior effectively stops the repetition of the undesired parental request, it is likely that the child will repeat it in the future because the behavior was reinforced by the termination of an undesirable stimulus. The more frequently such interactions occur, the more likely the child is to become difficult to handle. The major regulator of coercive interactions is the parent's lack of skill and effectiveness in setting limits. If there are no countervailing measures, the child may progress from the display of trivial aversive behaviors to behaviors with the potential to harm people. Antisocial behavior learned within the family may be generalized to other social contexts, such as school and peer relations. Coercion theory relates to basic assumptions of developmental contextualism and family systems theory (as parent and child are suggested to influence one another reciprocally) and learning theory (the role of reinforcement in developing and stabilizing problem behavior). Empirical support for coercion theory is available from research on preschoolers, older children, and adolescents (e.g., Dishion, Patterson, & Kavanagh, 1992; Eddy, Leve, & Fagot, 2001). Nonetheless, because of its focus on antisocial behavior, this theory is smaller in scope than most other theories on family and child development.

Family Stress Model

From a methodological point of view, parenting theories view parental behavior as an independent variable that influences child outcomes. As parental behavior is embedded in the family and even broader social contexts, however, parenting may also mediate or moderate the effects of other variables, such as economic stress, marital conflict, or parental psychopathology. Family stress theory focuses on the roles that stress and coping play in family development. Ineffective forms of coping within the family may erode family resources and even produce new stressors, such as problem behavior in children (McCubbin & Patterson, 1983). This theory appears to be too unspecific to be useful for studying the impact of family stressors on child development. Thus scholars have derived more specific models from general theories on stress and coping. Most relevant of these may be the family stress model developed by Conger and Elder (1994). This model suggests that family stressors impair parents' mental health and the quality of their marital relationship. As parents become preoccupied with their own problems, they show less effective parenting (high levels of harsh, inconsistent parenting or low parental involvement). Problems in parenting are then reflected in poor child adjustment. There is much empirical evidence showing that the effect of parental stressors on the development of the child is mediated through impaired parenting quality (Conger & Elder, 1994). Similarly, influences of parental disorders, such as mental illness, on child development have been found to be mediated by the quality of parenting, mainly through high levels of parental negativity and various forms of ineffective discipline practices (Berg-Nielsen, Vikan, & Dahl, 2002). Nonetheless, other mediators, such as genetic factors, must

also be taken into consideration (Plomin et al., 2001). The effects of family stressors on child development vary from child to child depending on individual differences in sensitivity to these stressors, among other differences based on genetic risk factors and prior experiences. For example, in a Finnish adoption study, Tienari et al. (1994) found that being adopted into dysfunctional families was associated with an increased risk for multiple psychiatric disorders (including schizophrenia) only in adoptees who had a biological risk for psychiatric disorders (children who had a schizophrenic biological parent). In addition, parental influences cannot be limited to parenting: As research on associations between parental substance abuse and children's substance use has shown, parental behavior may also serve as a role model for child behavior (Petraitis, Flay, & Miller, 1995).

Finally, in line with the developmental contextualistic perspective, we have to be aware that some parental influences are rather indirect, mediated by other social contexts. Parents are managers of their children's social environments, for example, serving as gatekeepers and facilitators of children's opportunities to interact with others outside the family (Furstenberg, Cook, Eccles, Elder, & Sameroff, 1999). With regard to peer relations, parents influence children's experiences with age-mates in several ways. During elementary school, parents propel their children toward certain peers by organizing and encouraging social activities that increase contact with some peers and decrease contact with others. In general, during childhood, parents actively steer their children toward certain friends and away from others. Parents' influences on their children's peer contacts are also indirect, mediated through children's attitudes, motives, and personalities (Collins, Maccoby, Steinberg, Hetherington, & Bornstein, 2000). In older children and adolescents, parents' indirect regulation of children's experiences outside the home becomes more important through choices of environments, agencies, and individuals who enter the children's lives (Furstenberg et al., 1999). Family variables can moderate the effects of other social contexts on child development (although other social contexts may moderate the impacts of family variables on child development as well). For example, adolescents whose parents are authoritative are less susceptible to peer pressure to misbehave than are adolescents from authoritarian families (Fuligni & Eccles, 1993).

INFLUENCES OF SIBLINGS ON CHILD DEVELOPMENT

Most theories on the influence of families on child development concentrate on relations between parents and their children. Given that in North America as well as in other countries most families include at least two children, the influence of sibling relationships on child development needs to be considered. Most theoretical work has focused on explaining the negative correlation between a structural characteristic of the family (namely, number of siblings) and cognitive outcomes for the child, rather than on how interaction processes between siblings may influence children's cognitive development and educational success.

Confluence Theory

As a first explanation of sibling influence, Zajonc and Markus (1975) suggested the confluence theory, which states that a child's intelligence is a function of the intellectual milieu in which the child develops. The intellectual milieu is defined as the unweighted average of the intellectual levels of all members of the child's family. The arrival of a new sibling drops this average, as the infant does not yet possess the same mental abilities as older family members. Thus the addition of siblings to the family, and closely spaced siblings in particular, negatively affects intellectual development by lowering the average quality of the intellectual milieu in which the child grows up. Within the family, this theory suggests that the firstborn profits intellectually not only because he or she is born into a family with a higher average intellectual level (no older siblings are available to lower the family's intellectual level), but also because later he or she has the opportunity

to teach younger siblings. Confluence theory postulates that teaching a younger sibling stimulates the intellectual development of the older child. For example, the teaching child must understand the topic being taught, know how to explain it to the younger sibling, and show flexibility when his or her first explanation fails. Empirical support for assumed associations between cognitive development and number of siblings or birth order, however, has generally been weak (Retherford & Sewell, 1991).

Resource Dilution Model

The resource dilution model offers an alternative explanation for the effect of number of siblings on intellectual performance. It assumes that parental resources (e.g., amount of personal attention and teaching available for children, the number of cultural objects in the family) are finite. As the number of children in the family increases, the proportion of parental resources accrued by any one child decreases (Blake, 1981). In support of this model, Downey (1995) found that the family resources each child received declined with increasing numbers of siblings. Frequency of talk with parents, parental educational expectations, money saved for college, and the number of educational objects in the home explained the effect of the number of siblings on a child's school grades. Finally, the effect of these resources on school grades declined in larger families.

Not all family resources are finite as the resource dilution model suggests. For example, the birth of a sibling may motivate a mother to stop working outside the family, and this may actually increase the amount of parental time available for each child. Although the change in family resources is probably a core component of the effect of the birth of a younger sibling on the development of older children, it is not sufficient to explain all observed effects. A complete explanation must include *processes* of adaptation over time and moderating variables, such as the child's gender. Almost all longitudinal studies of transition to siblinghood have found increases in some problem areas of preschoolers in the first weeks following the birth of a second child (e.g., sleep disturbance, anxiety, dependency, regression, withdrawal, and aggressiveness) that are typically related to a decrease in the amount of maternal attention given to the older child and perhaps to a decrease in the amount of positive interaction between mother and firstborn (Teti, 2002). However, many of these disturbances tend to dissipate over time, and a great deal of inter-individual variability has been observed in the reactions of older siblings. For example, Stöhr, Laucht, Ihle, Esser, and Schmidt (2000) found that in the first 3 years after the birth of a second child there was an increase in closeness of mother's relationship with firstborn daughters but a decrease in closeness with firstborn sons. In turn, they found negative effects of the birth of a sibling on cognitive development only in sons. Girls even showed a smaller increase in behavior problems than only children. Mothers were more likely to include daughters than sons in the care of the younger child, which caused positive effects for girls.

As already suggested by confluence theory, sibling interactions provide incentives for learning for the older and the younger child. Direct effects of older siblings on the socialization of the younger child are most obvious in agricultural societies, where much of the child care is performed by older siblings. In Western societies, children have less responsibility for their younger siblings, but older siblings act as teachers, helpers, and role models when they play with their younger brothers and sisters. Experiences with older siblings relate to the development of social competence, but also to younger siblings' problem behavior, such as alcohol and drug use. In line with confluence theory, there is empirical evidence that teaching younger siblings promotes the development of the older sibling. For example, Smith (1993) found that seventh- to ninth-grade students who reported spending an amount of time teaching their younger siblings earned higher language and reading achievement scores than did same-aged older siblings who did not engage in such teaching.

According to family systems theory, each family member has to find his or her position in the family. In late childhood, siblings, especially firstborns versus secondborns, actively try to be different from each other ("sibling deidentification"; Teti, 2002). Finding a niche in the family is not only a means of maximizing parental attention and reducing sibling rivalry, it also directs the development of interests and activities and, thus, influences the siblings' development. Conflicts between unsupervised siblings may also provide a training ground for antisocial behavior, as posited by coercion theory. Negative sibling interactions, however, may also facilitate the development of conflict management skills that are useful in peer relations.

FUTURE DIRECTIONS FOR THEORY DEVELOPMENT

The complexity of family influences on child development and of the interplay between family variables and other developmental contexts is probably too great to be explained by a single theory, although most parental influences are based on parenting processes. Figure 15.1 summarizes the theories concerning the roles that parent-child and sibling interactions play in child development. Scholars often suggest models that help to order potentially relevant variables rather than develop more comprehensive theories that can provide explanations and meanings for *what* they observe. Many of the reports of empirical studies on family influences on child development do even not refer to theories. Nonetheless, as the German psychologist Kurt Lewin noted more than six decades ago, there is nothing more practical than a good theory (see Lück, 1996), and we need more theorizing about the role of the family and the interplay between family and other influences on the development of children and adolescents.

Family scholars need to translate general theories, such as developmental contextualism, to testable hypotheses. As biological, social, and psychological changes interact during adolescence, it would be of interest to discover how early or late pubertal timing relates to different parenting practices, and how interactions

Figure 15.1   Theories on the Roles That Parent-Child and Sibling Interactions Play in Child
Development

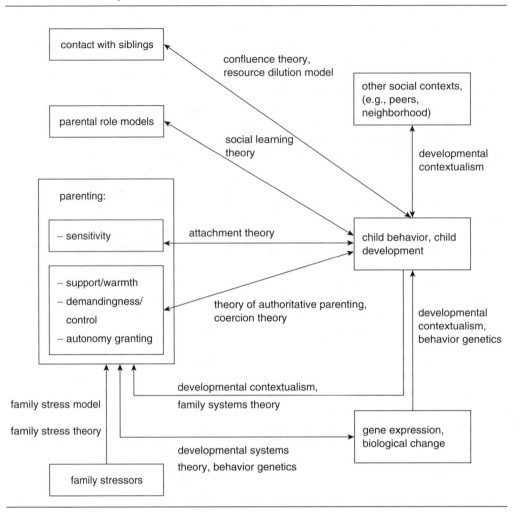

between these biological and social factors influence adolescent development. Recently, Weichold, Silbereisen, Schmitt-Rodermund, Vorwerk, and Miltner (in press) analyzed videotaped daughter-mother conflict discussions and found that both early and late maturers were higher in striving for individuation than were on-time maturers, but only mothers of early maturers reciprocated the behavior of their children in a symmetric way. We need theory-based hypotheses on how symmetry versus asymmetry of biological maturation and parental autonomy granting relate to adolescent psychological outcomes.

In the past few decades, scholars have offered new theoretical concepts about life-span development, such as the model of primary and secondary control processes (Heckhausen, 1997), that could guide further theoretical development on the role of family. Researchers could take these models and ask how parents and siblings contribute to these developmental processes, such as by helping the child to set developmental goals, providing a stimulating environment, offering guidance and support, and providing a model for goal striving.

More specific theories about the role of parents in child development will allow scholars to derive specific hypotheses on the association between parental behavior and child outcomes; such theories will also serve as useful guides for research and for family interventions. To develop these theories, scholars need to conduct more theoretical and empirical work to specify moderators and mediators (e.g., as discussed with regard to ethnic differences or differential effects of parenting in safe versus dangerous neighborhoods). Models on the influences of parenting (Abidin, 1992; Belsky, 1984) can be useful for guiding further theorizing.

With regard to the impacts of siblings on child development, theories that focus exclusively on family structure (number of siblings and birth order) are too unspecific to account for what happens in the individual family over time following the arrival of a new sibling. Although existing theories and models suggest potential mediators of the availability of siblings, such as change in family resources, opportunities to teach younger siblings, and modeling the behavior of older siblings, these factors still have to be integrated into a more comprehensive process-oriented theory.

• SPOTLIGHT ON METHODS

OBSERVATIONAL METHODS FOR STUDYING FAMILIES

Lorraine C. Taylor, *University of North Carolina at Chapel Hill*

Melissa A. Barnett, *University of North Carolina at Chapel Hill*

Observational methods for studying families capture the essence of the systems perspective by allowing researchers to understand the behavior of individual family members (e.g., mother, husband, sibling) in the context of the family as well as to make comparisons of whole families as units. Because they enable researchers to make both within- and between-family comparisons, observational methods are useful for identifying family processes that can be linked to a variety of individual and family outcomes. Examining connections between family-level processes and individual-level outcomes is important for understanding resilience, because features of the family system may operate in ways that promote positive outcomes for children, adults, and families considered to be "at risk" for negative developmental outcomes. Prevention and intervention strategies can be derived from research that uses observational methods.

Depending on the unit of analysis of interest, several observational methods are available. Most common are macroanalytic (global) approaches, in which the level of analysis is the overall level of behaviors for an individual, dyad, or whole family. For example, videotaped observations of parent-child interactions may be coded for the global level of parental warmth, the child's positive or negative mood, or dyadic information on behaviors such as conflict resolution or mutual task engagement. Microanalytic approaches focus on the sequential dynamics of an interaction. Here, the unit of analysis

(continued)

• SPOTLIGHT ON METHODS

is the particular pattern of behaviors and responses observed in the interaction. Microanalytic research is often time-consuming and requires volumes of data, but it is useful for understanding the minute-by-minute sequencing of particular interactions. As in other methods of studying families, reliability and validity are important considerations in observational research. Reliability determinants indicate the extent of agreement among multiple observers or coders. Some common statistical indices of interobserver reliability include percentage of agreement, Cohen's kappa coefficient, and correlation (Lindahl, 2001).

How well do observations of family interactions represent what families are like when they are not being observed? Do coding systems reflect the cultural, ethnic, and socioeconomic diversity that exists in families? Establishing the validity of observational coding systems is another important methodological consideration. Researchers can determine construct validity by comparing an observed code with another indicator of the same construct. For example, converging scores on self-reports of maternal depression and observational scores on coded depression would indicate construct validity.

The ecological validity of observational data, or the extent to which observational data are meaningful across different ethnic, cultural, or socioeconomic niches, has emerged as an important consideration. Some studies have suggested that it is important for coders' ethnicities or backgrounds to be similar to those of the families under study to prevent biased judgments of family interactions (Gonzales, Hiraga, & Cauce, 1998). Other research has focused on the development of culturally sensitive observational coding systems that capture family diversity in an ecologically valid way. Taylor (2004), for example, uses separate codes for observations of maternal sensitivity/responsiveness and warmth/positive affect. Studies have suggested that ethnic/cultural differences in emotional expressiveness may result in differences in levels of expressed positive affect during various types of child interactions. Some coding systems used to study parent-child relationships combine the dimension of sensitivity/responsiveness with warmth/positive affect, which may result in some ethnic families' being rated as "less sensitive" when the difference may actually reflect variations in the affective dimension of the interaction.

Observational methods are especially useful for research aimed at understanding the mechanisms through which the family system affects the development of individual members as well as understanding variations across families. The use of observational methods poses clear challenges for researchers, in that they must develop valid coding systems, train reliable coders, acquire and maintain the equipment needed to record family interactions, and invest a great deal of time in coding, but it also can lead to invaluable insights into family relationships that self-report measures alone cannot provide. •

RECOMMENDATIONS
FOR FUTURE RESEARCH

First, longitudinal studies are needed to allow scholars to assess bidirectional influences in the parent-child relationship. Until now, most studies that have examined the association between family variables and child development have used correlational designs, and researchers have interpreted concurrent correlations between parental behavior and child behavior as environmental effect on the child, assuming that the environment provided by the parents is the cause of the outcome of child development. These correlations, however, may also indicate that parents adjust their behavior in response to the observed competence and maturity of the child (the influence of the child on the parents; see the above discussions of developmental contextualism and family systems theory). We recommend the use of cross-lagged models for testing how parenting behaviors or styles and changes in these behaviors or styles relate to changes in child competence over time and how child competence and its change relate to changes in parenting. Because parenting observed at the first point of measurement may have been a reaction to previous child behavior, however, even longitudinal studies are not sufficient to allow researchers to conclude that family processes play a causal role in children's adaptation. Nonetheless, longitudinal studies can show that associations between family and child variables are not only due to the effect of children on the family in general or to confounding variables that correlate with family and child variables at the first time of measurement.

Second, because parenting and other aspects of the family environment (e.g., number of siblings) may reflect, at least in part, the influence of socioeconomic status, parental intelligence, and other variables, researchers should measure these potentially confounding variables and statistically control for them (e.g., through analysis of covariance or multiple linear regression analysis).

Third, proponents of the behavioral genetics framework have raised questions about the extent of genetic influence on measures of family environments. For example, a positive association between low parental warmth and child's behavior problems may be related to the fact that parents pass on their genes to the child (passive genome-environment covariance) and the fact that behavior problems in the child evoke negative parental behavior (evocative genome-environment covariance; Deater-Deckard et al., 1999). Twin studies and adoption studies can disentangle the effects of nature and nurture, allowing scholars to estimate the average effects of genes and family environment on developmental outcomes. For example, if parents do not differ in their treatment of identical and fraternal twins, stronger similarities between identical twins (who share 100% of their genes) than between fraternal twins (who share approximately 50% of their genes) would be interpreted as indicating genetic influence. Because parenting is more similar for identical twins than for fraternal twins, twin studies may overestimate heritability (Collins et al., 2000). By combining twin studies with other behavioral genetic designs, such as adoption studies, researchers can reduce this source of bias. Another option for testing causal relations between family variables and child development is the use of intervention trials. In such research, families are randomly assigned to either an intervention condition, which is aimed at changing parental behavior or the broader family environment, or a control condition. Because the genetics of parents and children is held constant in these studies, the intervention effect can be interpreted as an effect of changed family environment (Cowan & Cowan, 2002). Adoption studies, twin studies, and intervention trials are all very costly to conduct, so many researchers will be unable to use these techniques. However, researchers using simpler designs should check to see whether it is possible to include proxies for genetic influences. For example, when studying associations between the level of cognitive stimulation of the family and cognitive development in childhood, researchers must test whether they can find meaningful associations between these variables after they have statistically controlled for parental intelligence. Otherwise, they need to exercise caution when interpreting associations between family environment and child development.

Fourth, based on the distinction between shared and nonshared environmental influences in behavior genetics, it is not sufficient to measure only familywide variables, such as a mother's report about her general parenting. Rather, the researcher should collect information on the treatment of the child and on child-specific aspects of the family environment (e.g., different levels of intellectually stimulating toys in the siblings' rooms) and analyze whether the associations of family variables with developmental outcomes vary between children (e.g., between children with "easy" and "difficult" temperaments).

Fifth, many studies on associations between the family and child development have used only one informant per family. When information on both family variables and child outcomes comes from the same respondent (usually the parent), any associations found may reflect perception biases in the mind of the person making the ratings rather than causal effects. Researchers need to employ multiple measures and gather information from multiple informants (e.g., parental reports, child reports, observations of family interactions).

Finally, the parent-child relationship and the relationship between siblings cannot be considered in a vacuum; rather, they must be examined in the context of other relationships inside and outside the family (Abidin, 1992; Belsky, 1984). Given the complex interplay among different social contexts (e.g., family, peer group, neighborhood), researchers have to assess not only direct (bivariate) associations between family variables and psychosocial development but also indirect effects (e.g., when parents influence the child's choice of peer groups, which in turn influences child development) and interaction effects between contexts (e.g., whether the impact of family variables on child development varies depending on other contexts, such as the safety of the neighborhood or the child's affiliation with a particular peer group). The results of such research will help to specify theoretical assumptions concerning the role that parent-child interactions play in the psychological development of the child.

CASE STUDY

PARENT-ADOLESCENT RELATIONSHIPS: INTEGRATING ATTACHMENT AND BOWENIAN FAMILY SYSTEMS THEORIES

Mark J. Benson, *Virginia Polytechnic Institute and State University*

Adolescents and children adapt to their environments through the aid of both direct experience and transmission across generations. The mechanisms of this transmission include genetic inheritance, socioeconomic transfer, and behavioral processes. Theories explaining behavioral transmission emphasize modeling, reinforcement, and generalization. Beyond these mechanistic views, two organismic theories emphasize emotional and instinctual processes as vehicles for transmission. Both Murray Bowen's family systems theory (Kerr & Bowen, 1988) and John Bowlby's (1969, 1973, 1980) attachment theory explain transmission as nested within close, intimate relationships in the family. In this case study, I compare these theories to advance conceptualizations for future research.

FAMILY SYSTEMS THEORY AND ATTACHMENT THEORY

In Bowen's family systems theory, anxiety is a primary mechanism for transmission. Anxiety is a property of families and individuals that regulates the amount of emotional closeness

CASE STUDY *continued*

and distance within the family. When family members experience excessive emotional distance, anxiety increases because of abandonment fears. Family members reduce anxiety by seeking increased togetherness. Conversely, if family members experience excessive togetherness, anxious fears increase over loss of autonomy. Such anxiety prompts family members to distance themselves from one another. Anxiety, then, is the mechanism through which family members monitor and manage emotional distance. Family members in healthy relationships tolerate minor variations in closeness and distance without overly reactive anxiety. In dysfunctional families, however, anxiety surfaces with minor changes in closeness and distance, resulting in reactive behaviors, automatic patterned thinking, and charged emotions. With chronic anxiety, dysfunctional families divert or project the anxiety onto one or more individual members. Family members collude in this process by integrating or incorporating the anxiety as part of them, and they carry this anxiety into subsequent relationships. Through these projection and introjection processes, anxiety is transmitted across generations.

In Bowlby's attachment theory, the internal working model fuels the transmission process. The internal working model develops instinctually to organize the environment. In infancy, behaviors such as crying, smiling, and babbling maintain the infant's proximity to the caregiver. During development these attachment behaviors lead to "affectional bonds," which, according to Bowlby (1969, p. 224), represent the product of a historical transaction process. Secure attachment enables an adolescent to face the challenges of exploration and adaptation in the environment. Attachment processes that result in internal working models of security and trust lay a foundation for confident exploration.

These brief summaries imply several differences between Bowen's and Bowlby's theories. Whereas Bowlby emphasizes the dyadic relationship, Bowen views the triangle as the primary relationship building block. In attachment theory, security is emphasized as the internal working model emerges. Bowen's theory, in contrast, emphasizes fusion and triangulation as central processes. The foundational methods differ markedly between the two theories as well, with observation emphasized in early attachment theory and the clinical interview emphasized in Bowenian theory.

Despite these differences, the theories also parallel each other. In both theories, close, intimate relationships emerge from evolutionary processes that serve adaptation at both the individual level and the human species level. Both theories are systems oriented, acknowledging the multiplicity of intersecting elements. Both theories provide lenses through which one may examine the nexus between individual- and family-level analysis, which holds potential for integration across disciplines (Benson & Deal, 1995). For both Bowen and Bowlby, emotional or instinctual processes are central to an understanding of close relationships. These processes modulate and regulate the level of connection and autonomy. Finally, both theories view individual differences in major areas of functioning as inherently tied to these intimate processes in relationships.

RESEARCH DIRECTIONS

The similarities and differences noted above lead to some suggestions for future research. For instance, differentiation in Bowen's theory and secure attachment in Bowlby's theory suggest a straightforward research question: In what ways are these constructs empirically similar or different during adolescence? In addition to this readily apparent question, other suggestions for research emerge from the theories' common assumptions and contrasting features as well as from the findings of previous research.

Research concerning attachment in adolescence has burgeoned, in part, because of the clarity of attachment theory's core causal construct. Whereas Bowenian theory presents an

CASE STUDY *continued*

array of complexly interconnected constructs, *security* provides a coherent core construct for generating related research. The early emergence of observational methods such as the strange situation and adult attachment interview provided an empirical grounding across research disciplines. Further, in recent years effective questionnaire methods, appropriate for use with adolescents, have emerged based on theory and these founding methods. This contrast suggests that limited Bowenian research could blossom through the development of methods focused on differentiation. Bowen's clinical interview provides a seminal method for generating a foundational core.

Attachment theory and subsequent research also emphasize multiple potential outcomes. Outcomes in attachment theory relate to models of self and other. Parental attachment during adolescence, for example, is related to identity achievement (Benson, Harris, & Rogers, 1992) and peer relations (Schneider, Atkinson, & Tardif, 2001). Extending Bowenian research to include models of self and other constructs during adolescence holds potential for extending the impact of Bowenian concepts.

The dyadic emphasis in attachment theory prompts research on both mother-child and father-child relationships. For example, Benson et al. (1992) found that adolescents experience greater security with their mothers than with their fathers. Bowenian research that employs dyadic analyses with mothers, fathers, daughters, and sons has the potential to increase our understanding of complex triadic relationships in families.

In addition to these advantages of attachment theory and research, Bowenian theory provides a useful tool for advancing attachment research. Attachment research that includes constructs such as fusion and triangulation could extend the understanding and interpretation of attachment relationships. Prior research using Bowen's theory, for example, has confirmed the role of fusion in suppressing open communicating and fostering aversive communication in romantic relationships (Benson, Larson, Wilson, & Demo, 1993). Triangulation has also been found to be related to more aversive romantic communication (Benson et al., 1993) and more dour views of marriage (Larson, Benson, Wilson, & Medora, 1998).

Aside from triadic and family-level analysis, an emphasis in Bowenian theory on mediation processes holds potential for the extension of attachment research. Using Bowen's theory, for example, Benson et al. (1993) found that anxiety mediated the relationship between fusion and communication problems in romantic relations. Similarly, Rosen, Bartle-Haring, and Stith (2001) found that Bowen's construct of differentiation partially mediated the impact of family of origin violence on dating violence. By examining mediational processes between felt attachment security and outcomes, scholars could clarify mechanisms of attachment influence.

Whereas both Bowen's and Bowlby's theories assume the fundamental potency of the emotional, instinctual process, the role of cognition provides an avenue for future research. The way in which conscious awareness affects shifts in internal working models or differentiation remains an important area for research. Research using Bowenian theory, for example, indicates that conscious awareness of triangulation in the family of origin mitigates triangulation's influence on anxiety (Benson et al., 1993). Such conscious processes reflect individual- and family-level perceptions (Benson, Curtner-Smith, Collins, & Keith, 1995) and indicate potentially greater malleability in the attachment and differentiation constructs than was originally assumed in the theories.

The related assumptions of stability for attachment and differentiation concepts raise questions for research. To what extent do family changes make attachment and differentiation malleable? What features of family dynamics and life events result in shifts? Emerging research suggests that changes in attachment classification do occur over time

CASE STUDY *continued*

that link to changes in the family and life events (Waters, Weinfield, & Hamilton, 2000). In addition to this potentially evolving nature, an important question concerns the changes that take place from childhood through adolescence. In a recent meta-analysis, for example, Schneider et al. (2001) found that the association between attachment and peer relationships is stronger during adolescence than in early childhood. The hypothesis that attachment and differentiation become more influential as family and individual processes mature is an important area for investigation.

Hypotheses that extend attachment and Bowenian theories emerge when scholars expand beyond the focus on close, intimate family relationships. Both theories ignore the larger social context in which these intimate relationships in the family occur. As I have noted elsewhere, social norms for parenting and child behavior vary culturally and have important impacts on adolescent development (Benson, 2004). Parents interpret cultural norms and the norms in their own referent groups. These parental interpretations involve meaning making and interpretation of

the social environment for the developing adolescent. Through these interpretations, parents provide a template for the adolescent's understanding and interpretation of his or her social world. Understanding the interior world of the family is critical, as the same behaviors can have vastly different meanings at different levels of family differentiation (Prest, Benson, & Protinsky, 1998).

The common assumptions and contrasting features of the two theories discussed above, as well as previous research findings, provide clues for advancing research concerning parent-adolescent relationships. Just as adolescents adapt to perturbations in their environments, researchers, too, adapt to changes provoked in their conceptual systems. The analysis of related theories and research provides a catalyst for new research. In addressing greater complexity, researchers, like the adolescents and families they study, develop new levels of system organization and conceptualization. Evolving research sharpens adaptation for the next generation of researchers and answers questions that promote transmission to improve the lives of adolescents and families.

DISCUSSION AND EXTENSION

THE ROLE OF FAMILIES IN DEVELOPMENTAL CONTINUITY AND CHANGE DURING ADOLESCENCE

Jennifer L. Matjasko, *University of Texas at Austin*

Katherine A. Paz, *University of Texas at Austin*

How malleable are developmental trajectories during adolescence? Some have argued that the time between conception

and 3 years of age represents a "critical" or "sensitive" period in development when the individual must achieve basic milestones in

Discussion and Extension

DISCUSSION AND EXTENSION *continued*

order to develop optimally. If an individual does not get the proper cognitive stimulation and nutrition and become securely attached to a primary caregiver during this time, he or she cannot make up for these deficiencies later in life (Carnegie Task Force, 1994). According to some scholars, adolescence represents another such sensitive period in development. Because teenagers are undergoing multiple changes—physically, cognitively, and emotionally—some view this time as an opportunity for developmental change (Graber & Brooks-Gunn, 1996). In this brief discussion, we consider how researchers have used the person-centered approach to observe developmental continuity during adolescence and how families facilitate or disrupt developmental trajectories throughout adolescence.

DEVELOPMENTAL CONTINUITY DURING ADOLESCENCE

Various studies have examined developmental continuity during adolescence. Some researchers have found that the transition to adolescence is marked by an increase in emotional distress for girls and an increase in behavioral problems for boys (Angold, Costello, & Worthman, 1998; Hoyt & Scherer, 1998). Once these changes occur, adolescence is characterized by a high degree of developmental continuity on behavioral and emotional measures. In more recent longitudinal studies, scholars have used the person-centered approach—which incorporates multiple aspects of the adolescent, as opposed to one characteristic, as the unit of analysis—in assessing developmental continuity in adolescence. One of the main strengths of person-centered analysis is that it allows researchers to characterize adolescents according to their functioning in multiple domains (e.g., psychological, behavioral, and academic), so that they can capture a more holistic picture of adolescent well-being.

The person-centered approach also provides unique insights into processes related

to continuity in development over time (Asendorpf, 1992; Cairns, Cairns, Rodkin, & Xie, 1998). Researchers can assess continuity with longitudinal data by classifying individuals on functioning variables at each time point and then comparing the classifications over time. Individuals display continuity if they fall into the same theoretical classifications at each point (Bergman, 1992). For example, Roeser, Eccles, and Freedman-Doan (1999) used the person-centered approach to characterize children and adolescents on measures of mental health and academic functioning. They identified four different types of adjustment profiles: one in which individuals were functioning well in all domains, another in which individuals were not functioning well in any domain, and two groups that showed mixed patterns of adjustment. Roeser et al. found that the groups that displayed consistently negative and consistently positive patterns of adjustment during adolescence showed the developmental precursors of such patterns during childhood, whereas the other groups' functioning was not as strongly linked to childhood measures of adjustment. In other words, certain groups of individuals were more likely than others to show developmental continuity. Thus studies using the person-centered approach have found strong evidence for developmental continuity while at the same time they have elucidated subtle nuances about developmental change during adolescence.

FAMILIES AND ADOLESCENT CONTINUITY AND CHANGE

Given that a majority of adolescents show evidence of developmental continuity over time, what would cause some adolescents to change their patterns of functioning over time? Research has uncovered two possible family mechanisms for change: (a) Parents fail to grant more autonomy to their adolescents at a stage in development when they need more freedom, which results in a lack of "stage-environment fit" (Eccles, Lord, &

DISCUSSION AND EXTENSION *continued*

Midgley, 1991); and (b) increasing family risk is responsible for changes in well-being (Sameroff, Seifer, & Bartko, 1997). Adolescence is a time when individuals are trying out different identities, exploring who they are and who they would like to be. The concept of stage-environment fit has to do with whether adolescents' parents grant them the freedom to experiment with different looks and, as they get closer to adulthood, the independence to make some of their own decisions regarding rules for their behavior. When parents do not grant their adolescents more autonomy at appropriate times, a "developmental mismatch," a lack of stage-environment fit, can occur; such adolescents are more likely than others to show increased behavioral, emotional, and social problems. For example, Barber (1996) found that parental psychological control (attempts to control that intrude on the thinking and emotional development of the adolescent) was predictive of depression and externalizing problems in adolescents, whereas parental behavioral control (attempts to control or manage the adolescent's behavior) was related to externalizing problems. As Pinquart and Silbereisen emphasize in Chapter 15, parents need to consider the developmental changes that occur in adolescence and adapt their parenting to meet their children's needs.

The second mechanism, family risk, has been linked to diminished adolescent well-being. In particular, several studies have captured the family environment using a "cumulative risk model" in which family stressors such as poverty, single parenthood, and poor parent-adolescent relationships are used to predict various facets of adolescent adjustment (e.g., Jones, Forehand, Brody, & Armistead, 2002; Sameroff et al., 1997). Typically, studies have found that higher numbers of family stressors predict more adolescent emotional distress and behavioral problems. In some cases, however, the presence of family risk factors is not static over time, and few studies have used a *longitudinal* cumulative risk model and *multiple* measures of adolescent adjustment simultaneously (i.e., the person-centered approach). In one of our studies, we utilized the longitudinal cumulative family risk model and its relationship to adolescent discontinuity using the person-centered approach (Matjasko, 2004). We found that changes in the number of family risk factors that adolescents faced were significantly related to adolescent developmental discontinuity. Furthermore, the relationship between changes in family risk and developmental discontinuity was not a linear one—those adolescents who experienced no change in family risk faced a one in five probability of discontinuity, those whose family risk index changed by one factor faced a one in three probability of discontinuity, and those whose index changed by more than two factors faced slightly more than a one in two chance of discontinuity between data collection points.

CONCLUSION

Developmental continuity is the norm during adolescence, but change can occur for a small number of young people. Are families driving change? In all likelihood, yes. In order to understand how families influence developmental continuity, researchers must model both adolescent functioning and family processes dynamically. For example, do parents adapt their parenting strategies to the specific needs of adolescents? Furthermore, scholars must assess cumulative family risk *and* changes in this risk in order to understand the role of family risk in developmental change. The person-centered approach offers scholars an innovative way to use conceptual models that employ stage-environment fit and dynamic cumulative family risk to predict adolescent developmental discontinuity.

Discussion and Extension

REFERENCES

Abidin, R. R. (1992). The determinants of parenting behavior. *Journal of Clinical Child Psychology, 21,* 407–412.

Ainsworth, M. D. S., & Bell, S. M. V. (1970). Attachment, exploration and separation: Illustrated by the behavior of one-year-olds in a strange situation. *Child Development, 41,* 49–67.

Angold, A., Costello, E. J., & Worthman, C. (1998). Puberty and depression: The roles of age, pubertal status, and pubertal timing. *Psychological Medicine, 28,* 51–61.

Asendorpf, J. B. (1992). Continuity and stability of personality traits and personality patterns. In J. B. Asendorpf & J. Valsiner (Eds.), *Stability and change in development: A study of methodological reasoning* (pp. 116–142). Newbury Park, CA: Sage.

Bandura, A. (1977). *Social learning theory.* Englewood Cliffs, NJ: Prentice Hall.

Barber, B. K. (1996). Parental psychological control: Revisiting a neglected construct. *Child Development, 67,* 3296–3320.

Bates, J. E., Pettit, G. S., Dodge, K. A., & Ridge, B. (1998). Interaction of temperamental resistance to control and restrictive parenting in the development of externalizing behavior. *Developmental Psychology, 34,* 982–995.

Baumrind, D. (1973). The development of instrumental competence through socialization. In A. D. Pick (Ed.), *Minnesota Symposium on Child Psychology* (Vol. 7, pp. 3–46). Minneapolis: University of Minnesota Press.

Belsky, J. (1984). The determinants of parenting: A process model. *Child Development, 55,* 83–96.

Benson, M. J. (2004). After the adolescent pregnancy: Parents, teens, and families. *Child and Adolescent Social Work Journal, 21,* 433–453.

Benson, M. J., Curtner-Smith, M. E., Collins, W. A., & Keith, T. Z. (1995). The structure of family perceptions: Individual satisfaction factors and family system factors. *Family Process, 34,* 323–336.

Benson, M. J., & Deal, J. E. (1995). Bridging the individual and the family. *Journal of Marriage and the Family, 57,* 561–566.

Benson, M. J., Harris, P., & Rogers, C. (1992). Identity consequences of differential attachment to mothers and fathers among late adolescents. *Journal of Research on Adolescence, 2,* 187–196.

Benson, M. J., Larson, J. H., Wilson, S. M., & Demo, D. H. (1993). Family of origin influences on late adolescent romantic relationships. *Journal of Marriage and the Family, 55,* 663–672.

Bergman, L. R. (1992). Studying change in variables and profiles: Some methodological considerations (Commentary on Asendorpf). In J. B. Asendorpf & J. Valsiner (Eds.), *Stability and change in development: A study of methodological reasoning* (pp. 143–149). Newbury Park, CA: Sage.

Berg-Nielsen, T. S., Vikan, A., & Dahl, A. A. (2002). Parenting related to child and parental psychopathology: A descriptive review of the literature. *Clinical Child Psychology and Psychiatry, 7,* 529–552.

Blake, J. (1981). Family size and the quality of children. *Demography, 18,* 421–442.

Bowlby, J. (1969). *Attachment and loss: Vol. 1. Attachment.* Harmondsworth: Pelican.

Bowlby, J. (1973). *Attachment and loss: Vol. 2. Separation.* New York: Basic Books.

Bowlby, J. (1980). *Attachment and loss: Vol. 3. Loss.* New York: Basic Books.

Cairns, R. B., Cairns, B. D., Rodkin, P., & Xie, H. (1998). New directions in developmental research: Models and methods. In R. Jessor (Ed.), *New perspectives on adolescent risk behavior* (pp. 13–40). Cambridge: Cambridge University Press.

Carnegie Task Force on Meeting the Needs of Young Children. (1994). *Starting points: Meeting the needs of our youngest children.* New York: Carnegie Corporation.

Cassidy, J., & Shaver, P. R. (Eds.). (1999). *Handbook of attachment: Theory, research, and clinical applications.* New York: Guilford.

Collins, W. A., Maccoby, E. E., Steinberg, L. D., Hetherington, E. M., & Bornstein, M. H. (2000). Contemporary research on parenting: The case for nature and nurture. *American Psychologist, 55,* 218–232.

Conger, R. D., & Elder, G. H., Jr. (1994). *Families in troubled times: Adapting to change in rural America.* New York: Aldine de Gruyter.

Cowan, P. A., & Cowan, C. P. (2002). What an intervention design reveals about how parents affect their children's academic achievement and social competence.

In J. G. Borkowski, S. L. Ramey, & M. Bristol-Power (Eds.), *Parenting and the child's world: Influences on academic, intellectual, and social-emotional development* (pp. 75–97). Mahwah, NJ: Lawrence Erlbaum.

Cox, M. J., & Paley, B. (2003). Understanding families as systems. *Current Directions in Psychological Science, 12,* 193–196.

Crosbie-Burnett, M., & Giles-Sims, J. (1994). Adolescent adjustment and stepparenting styles. *Family Relations, 43,* 394–399.

Deater-Deckard, K., Fulkner, D. W., & Plomin, R. (1999). A genetic study of the family environment in the transition to early adolescence. *Journal of Child Psychology and Psychiatry, 40,* 769–775.

DeWolff, M. S., & van IJzendoorn, M. H. (1997). Sensitivity and attachment: A meta-analysis on parental antecedents of infant attachment. *Child Development, 68,* 571–591.

Dishion, T. J., Patterson, G. R., & Kavanagh, K. A. (1992). An experimental test of the coercion model: Linking theory, measurement, and intervention. In J. McCord & R. E. Tremblay (Eds.), *Preventing antisocial behavior: Interventions from birth through adolescence* (pp. 253–282). New York: Guilford.

Downey, D. B. (1995). When bigger is not better: Family size, parental resources, and children's educational performance. *American Sociological Review, 60,* 746–761.

Eccles, J. S., Lord, S., & Midgley, C. (1991). What are we doing to early adolescents? The impact of educational contexts of early adolescents. *American Journal of Education, 13,* 521–542.

Eddy, J. M., Leve, L. D., & Fagot, B. I. (2001). Coercive family processes: A replication and extension of Patterson's coercion model. *Aggressive Behavior, 27,* 14–25.

Fuligni, A. S., & Eccles, J. S. (1993). Perceived parent-child relationships and early adolescents' orientation toward peers. *Developmental Psychology, 29,* 622–632.

Furstenberg, F. F., Jr., Cook, T. D., Eccles, J. S., Elder, G. H., Jr., & Sameroff, A. J. (1999). *Managing to make it: Urban families and adolescent success.* Chicago: University of Chicago Press.

Gonzales, N. A., Hiraga, Y., & Cauce, A. M. (1998). Observing mother-daughter interaction in African-American and Asian-American families. In H. I. McCubbin, E. A. Thompson, A. I. Thompson, & J. A. Futrell (Eds.), *Resiliency in African-American families* (pp. 259–286). Thousand Oaks, CA: Sage.

Graber, J. A., & Brooks-Gunn, J. (1996). Transitions and turning points: Navigating the passage from childhood through adolescence. *Developmental Psychology, 32,* 768–776.

Heckhausen, J. (1997). Developmental regulation across adulthood: Primary and secondary control of age-related challenges. *Developmental Psychology, 33,* 176–187.

Hoyt, S., & Scherer, D. (1998). Female juvenile delinquency: Misunderstood by the juvenile justice system, neglected by social science. *Law and Human Behavior, 22,* 81–107.

Jones, D. J., Forehand, R., Brody, G., & Armistead, L. (2002). Psychosocial adjustment of African American children in single-mother families: A test of three risk models. *Journal of Marriage and Family, 64,* 105–115.

Kerr, M. E., & Bowen, M. (1988). *Family evaluation: An approach based on Bowen theory.* New York: W. W. Norton.

Khaleque, A., & Rohner, R. P. (2002). Perceived parental acceptance-rejection and psychological adjustment: A meta-analysis of cross-cultural and intracultural studies. *Journal of Marriage and Family, 64,* 54–64.

Larson, J. H., Benson, M. J., Wilson, S. M., & Medora, N. P. (1998). Family of origin influences on marital attitudes and readiness for marriage in late adolescents. *Journal of Family Issues, 19,* 750–768.

Lerner, R. M. (2002). *Concepts and theories of human development* (3rd ed.). Mahwah, NJ: Lawrence Erlbaum.

Lindahl, K. M. (2001). Methodological issues in family observational research. In P. K. Kerig & K. M. Lindahl (Eds.), *Family observational coding systems* (pp. 23–32). Mahwah, NJ: Lawrence Erlbaum.

Lück, H. F. (1996). *Die Feldtheorie und Kurt Lewin* [Field theory and Kurt Lewin]. Weinheim: Beltz.

Maccoby, E. E., & Martin, J. A. (1983). Socialization in the context of the family: Parent-child interaction. In P. H. Mussen (Series Ed.) & E. M. Hetherington (Vol. Ed.), *Handbook of child psychology:*

Vol. 4. Socialization, personality, and social development (4th ed., pp. 1–101). New York: John Wiley.

Matjasko, J. L. (2004). *Stability, continuity, and change in patterns of adolescent adjustment over time.* Manuscript submitted for publication.

McCubbin, H. I., & Patterson, J. M. (1983). The family stress process: The double ABCX model of adjustment and adaptation. In H. I. McCubbin, M. B. Sussman, & J. M. Patterson (Eds.), *Social stress and the family: Advances and developments in family stress theory and research* (pp. 7–37). New York: Haworth.

McHale, J. P., Kuersten, R., & Lauretti, A. (1996). New directions in the study of family-level dynamics during infancy and early childhood. *New Directions for Child Development, 74,* 5–26.

Patterson, G. R. (1976). The aggressive child: Victim and architect of a coercive system. In E. J. Marsh, E. A. Hammerlynck, & L. C. Handy (Eds.), *Behavior modification and families* (pp. 267–316). New York: Brunner/Mazel.

Petraitis, J., Flay, B. R., & Miller, T. Q. (1995). Reviewing theories of adolescent substance use: Organizing pieces in the puzzle. *Psychological Bulletin, 117,* 67–86.

Plomin, R., Asbury, K., & Dunn, J. (2001). Why are children in the same family so different? Nonshared environment a decade later. *Canadian Journal of Psychiatry, 46,* 25–233.

Prest, L., Benson, M. J., & Protinsky, H. (1998). Codependency in families: Family of origin and current relationship influences. *Family Process, 37,* 513–528.

Retherford, R. D., & Sewell, W. H. (1991). Birth order and intelligence: Further tests of the confluence model. *American Sociological Review, 56,* 141–158.

Roeser, R. W., Eccles, J. S., & Freedman-Doan, C. (1999). Academic functioning and mental health in adolescence: Patterns, progressions, and routes from childhood. *Journal of Adolescent Research, 14,* 135–174.

Rohner, R. P. (1986). *The warmth dimension: Foundations of parental acceptance-rejection theory.* Beverly Hills, CA: Sage.

Rohner, R. P. (2004). [Home page]. Ronald and Nancy Rohner Center for the Study of Parental Acceptance and Rejection Web site: http://vm.uconn.edu/~rohner

Rosen, K. H., Bartle-Haring, S., & Stith, S. M. (2001). Using Bowen theory to enhance understanding of the intergenerational transmission of dating violence. *Journal of Family Issues, 22,* 124–142.

Sameroff, A. J., Seifer, R., & Bartko, W. T. (1997). Environmental perspectives on adaptation during childhood and adolescence. In S. S. Luthar, J. A. Burack, D. Cicchetti, & J. R. Weisz (Eds.), *Developmental psychopathology: Perspectives on adjustment, risk, and disorder* (pp. 507–526). Cambridge: Cambridge University Press.

Scarr, S. (1992). Developmental theories for the 1990s: Development and individual differences. *Child Development, 63,* 1–19.

Schneider, B. H., Atkinson, L., & Tardif, C. (2001). Child-parent attachment and children's peer relations: A quantitative review. *Developmental Psychology, 37,* 86–100.

Smith, T. E. (1993). Growth in academic achievement and teaching younger siblings. *Social Psychology Quarterly, 56,* 77–85.

Steinberg, L. D., Darling, N. E., & Fletcher, A. C. (with Brown, B. B. & Dornbusch, S. M.). (1995). Authoritative parenting and adolescent adjustment: An ecological journey. In P. Moen, G. H. Elder, Jr., & K. Lüscher (Eds.), *Examining lives in context: Perspectives on the ecology of human development* (pp. 423–466). Washington, DC: American Psychological Association.

Steinberg, L. D., Elmen, J., & Mounts, N. S. (1989). Authoritative parenting, psychosocial maturity, and academic success among adolescents. *Child Development, 60,* 1424–1436.

Steinberg, L. D., Lamborn, S. D., Darling, N. E., Mounts, N. S., & Dornbusch, S. M. (1994). Over-time changes in adjustment and competence among adolescents from authoritative, authoritarian, indulgent, and neglectful families. *Child Development, 65,* 754–770.

Stöhr, R. M., Laucht, M., Ihle, W., Esser, G., & Schmidt, M. H. (2000). Die Geburt eines Geschwisters: Chancen und Risiken für das erstgeborene Kind [The birth of a sibling: Chances and risks for the first-born child]. *Kindheit und Entwicklung, 9,* 40–49.

Taylor, L. C. (2004). *Families with young children observational coding system.* Unpublished manuscript, University of North Carolina at Chapel Hill.

Teti, D. M. (2002). Retrospect and prospect in the psychological study of sibling relationship. In J. P. McHale & W. S. Grolnick (Eds.), *Retrospect and prospect in the psychological study of family* (pp. 193–224). Mahwah, NJ: Lawrence Erlbaum.

Tienari, P., Wynne, L. C., Moring, J., Lahti, I., Naarala, M., & Sorri, A. (1994). The Finnish adoptive family study of schizophrenia: Implications for family research. *British Journal of Psychiatry, 23,* S20–S26.

Waters, E., Weinfield, N. S., & Hamilton, C. E. (2000). The stability of attachment security from infancy to adolescence and early adulthood: General discussion. *Child Development, 71,* 703–706.

Weichold, K., Silbereisen, R. K., Schmitt-Rodermund, E., Vorwerk, L., & Miltner W. (in press). Links between timing of puberty and behavioral indicators of individuation. *Journal of Youth and Adolescence.*

Zajonc, R. B., & Markus, G. B. (1975). Birth order and intellectual development. *Psychological Review, 82,* 74–88.

• Sixteen

THEORIZING INTERGENERATIONAL FAMILY RELATIONS

Solidarity, Conflict, and Ambivalence in Cross-National Contexts

Ruth Katz, *University of Haifa*

Ariela Lowenstein, *University of Haifa*

Judith Phillips, *Keele University*

Svein Olav Daatland, *Norwegian Social Research*

One of the most enduring puzzles in family research is how to conceptualize and theorize intergenerational relationships. One of the most intriguing and exciting scholarly exchanges in family sociology in recent years has been the debate about the solidarity-conflict and ambivalence models of intergenerational relationships (Bengtson, Giarrusso, Mabry, & Silverstein, 2002; Connidis & McMullin, 2002a; Lüscher, 2002). In this chapter we do not offer a critique of the relative merits of either conceptual model. Rather, our aim is to theorize each of these models further and offer empirical evidence testing their manifestations.

To understand the complex and diverse intimate family relationships in societies undergoing rapid social changes, scholars require several conceptual and theoretical lenses, especially when discussing micro interpersonal relations and macro structural forces and the interactions between them (see Chapter 1, this volume). No single theoretical approach can facilitate such understanding, and no one can claim that his or her theoretical viewpoint is "truer" than the viewpoints of others. To the contrary, an understanding of the complexity of a social phenomenon such as intergenerational family relations in later life will only be enriched by the theorizing and verification of more than one theoretical model. This is imperative in light of changing family structures encompassing not only different family types, such as one-parent families, but also the childless old or elderly living in multigenerational households. Population aging adds to the diversity and complexity of family lives by virtue of the growing numbers of four- and five-generation families.

We have just completed a cross-national study examining these issues: the OASIS project (Old Age and Autonomy: The Role of Service Systems and Intergenerational Family Solidarity), with data from national samples in England, Germany, Israel, Norway, and Spain. In this study, we examined the relevance of the theoretical concepts of solidarity-conflict and ambivalence in order to conceptualize relations between older parents and their adult children when the parents are becoming frail. In this chapter we discuss the theoretical bases and roots of the solidarity-conflict and ambivalence theoretical models, examine their perspectives and contributions to the enhancement of understanding of intergenerational family ties in later life, and present empirical evidence from our cross-national study to evaluate these concepts critically while further theorizing them and their implications across the diverse societies studied.

In all societies, the family holds a crucial position at the intersection of generational lines and gender. Because individuals today live longer and thus share more years and experiences with members of other generations, intergenerational bonds among adult family members may be even more important today than in earlier decades (Bengtson, 2001). The value attached to sociability makes the family a main reference point in the aging process, and the needs of older people are best understood within the context of the family.

Population aging is caused by three factors: a growth in the proportion of people age 65 and older, an increase in the absolute number of older people, and improvement of life expectancy at birth. All of these factors are evident today in Europe and the United States, creating challenges for individuals, families, and societies (Kinsella, 2000).

A process parallel to that of aging societies can be observed in the changing family structures, social networks, and living arrangements of older people. These are seen in the growing numbers of elderly one-person households, in the increased geographic distances between parents and adult children, in the smaller numbers of children per family, in the increased rates of divorce and remarriage, and in the growing labor force participation of women (Bengtson, Lowenstein, Putney, & Gans, 2003). Combined with these transformations are broader societal and technological changes, such as internal and external migration, shifts in social policies, and changing care preferences. To understand the implications of these changes, we must analyze more traditional patterns of family intergenerational relations and how they are changing. In the discussion that follows, we highlight the theoretical bases of models that conceptualize intergenerational family relations and their development over time.

THEORETICAL PERSPECTIVES

Concerns about family solidarity and conflict have followed humans throughout history. Each era has had its own version of generational conflicts. Religious and other forms of authority have imposed norms about respect for elders, such as the Bible's commandment to "honor thy father and thy mother." Such norms would hardly have been necessary if there had been no concern about this issue. The very idea of insisting on not only respect but also affection for elderly parents points to the ambivalences found in family relationships and the family institution.

In the 1950s and 1960s, concerns about family solidarity were rooted in modernization and the isolated nuclear family thesis. More recently, such concerns have been connected to debates on the expanding individualism of late modernity and the rise of postmodernist societies. The earlier concerns were based in the assumption that loss of functions since modernization made the family retreat from an extended form to the nuclear unit, with the result that both horizontal and vertical lines beyond that nucleus lost importance and consequently weakened

(Parsons, 1955). The more recent concerns about threats to the family from individualism have a different basis: the assumption that individualism corrupts the moral character, leading from a concern for others to a concern for oneself. Wolfe (1989) relates this specifically to welfare state expansion, calling it a moral risk that may have impacts on the very foundation for societal and family solidarity. Empirical studies have failed to support either of these two theories. To be sure, intergenerational relationships are affected by modernization, but the changes are not uniformly in the direction of weaker ties between generations. Moreover, studies from several countries indicate that family solidarity is still strong but may seek other expressions when circumstances change (Daatland & Herlofson, 2003).

THEORIZING INTERGENERATIONAL FAMILY SOLIDARITY

The conceptual framework of the intergenerational family solidarity model represents an enduring attempt to examine and develop a theory of family relations for adult family life (Roberts, Richards, & Bengtson, 1991). It is reflected in the framework developed by Rossi and Rossi (1990) based on the life-course model. The paradigm of solidarity in intergenerational relationships reflects several theoretical traditions, including classic theories of social organization, the social psychology of group dynamics, and the family sociology approach. Table 16.1 summarizes these theoretical traditions. Below, we provide a more detailed history of the theoretical roots of the intergenerational solidarity model.

Classic Theories of Social Organization and Relationships

Understanding the nature of the bonds that create cohesion between individuals is a concern that has long occupied social researchers. More than a century ago, Durkheim (1933) made an important distinction between two solidarity types. *Mechanical solidarity* is the

traditional family cohesion that characterized ties between individuals in the preindustrial era, based on internalization and endorsement of traditional norms and customs. This type, according to Durkheim, was weakened by industrial society and was replaced by *organic solidarity,* typified by mutual dependence of individuals as imposed by their relations to the division of labor. The differences between traditional and industrial societies, in Durkheim's view, form the basic normative solidarity that leads to social cohesion. Parsons (1973) widened this theory by suggesting that several types of solidarity can exist simultaneously in various social interactions.

The central contribution of these theories to later models of solidarity lies in their description of the relevant bases of group solidarity: normative perceptions internalized by group members, functional interdependencies among group members, and consensus between group members over rules of exchange.

Exchange Theory

The basic assumption underlying exchange theory is that interactions between individuals or collectivities reflect attempts to maximize rewards, both material and nonmaterial. Drawing on economic cost-benefit models of social participation, Thibaut and Kelley (1959), Homans (1961), and Blau (1964) expanded this observation into a view of social behavior as exchange. As in economic exchange, the profit one derives from social exchange is equivalent to the difference between rewards and costs.

Family scholars applied the social exchange framework as a starting point for explanations of relationships between parents and their adult children characterized by multidimensional resources, costs, and benefits (Dwyer, Lee, & Jankowski, 1994; Roberts et al., 1991). The intergenerational solidarity model integrates exchange theory in that individuals with resources to exchange are those who can provide various types of help and support, while the recipients are made dependent on the providers, which thereby weakens their power in the relationship (Hirdes & Strain,

Table 16.1   Family Solidarity: Summary of Theoretical Traditions

Classic Sociological Theories	Social Psychology of Group Dynamics	Family Sociology Approach
Mechanical solidarity (normative)	Interactions Activity Affection	Structural integration Affectual integration Consensus
Organic solidarity (functional) Consensus over rules of exchange (Durkheim, 1933)	Norms (Homans, 1950)	Normative integration Goal integration (Nye & Rushing, 1969)
Possible existence of several forms simultaneously (Parsons, 1973)	Similarity (consensus) Sentiment (Heider, 1958)	Associational solidarity Affectual solidarity Consensual solidarity Functional solidarity Normative solidarity Structural solidarity (Bengtson & Schrader, 1982)

1995). Family members who provide more assistance than they receive may perceive the supportive exchange as less desirable over time. In turn, the family member receiving assistance may want to avoid feeling dependent on the support provider and seek to reciprocate with other forms of assistance, such as emotional support or advice, thus "balancing" the support exchange in an effort to reciprocate (Parrott & Bengtson, 1999).

Social Psychology of Group Dynamics

Research in group dynamics includes a cogent theoretical taxonomy of group solidarity elements developed by Homans and later amplified and extended by Heider. Homans (1950) identified four components: (a) interactions between group members, based on functional interdependence as described by Durkheim (1933) in organic solidarity; (b) shared activity involving group members; (c) sentiment (the affective dimension) between group members; and (d) norms for behaviors in interacting. The fundamental proposition from the theory is this: The more cohesive the group, the more its members interact, like each other, and share similar normative expectations and commitments to group activities. Heider (1958), expanding this theory, emphasized the importance of "contact," "liking," and "similarity,"

and noted that these should be in balance in order for the group to be effective.

These social psychologists contributed to the development of the intergenerational solidarity model by extending the classic definition of consensus over rules of exchange to incorporate the notion of similarity among group members. When the classic sociological and the social psychological definitions of family solidarity are combined, five elements may be identified: normative integration, functional interdependence, similarity or consensus, mutual affection, and interaction.

Family Sociology Approaches

In the 1960s, when interest in defining and measuring the components of family internal relationships emerged, Nye and Rushing (1969) proposed a conceptual framework in which findings from previous research could be integrated. It posited six dimensions of family integration: associational, affectual, consensual, functional, normative, and goal integration. Bengtson and Schrader (1982) refined these components and proposed a model of intergenerational family solidarity as a multidimensional construct with six elements of solidarity: associational, affectual, consensual, functional, normative solidarity, and family structure. Subsequently, research empirically demonstrated that each of the multiple dimensions of solidarity is distinct (orthogonal) and each represents a dialectic, as Bengtson et al. (2002) point out: "(1) intimacy and distance (affectual); (2) agreement and dissent (consensual); (3) dependency and autonomy (functional); (4) integration and isolation (associational); (5) opportunities and barriers for interaction (family structure); (6) familism and individualism (normative solidarity)" (p. 571). In further analyses, the model has reflected statistically independent components that divide substantially into two general dimensions: (a) structural-behavioral (associational, functional, and structural) and (b) cognitive-affective (affectual, consensual, and normative) (Bengtson & Roberts, 1991; Silverstein & Bengtson, 1997). Thus the solidarity model has been supported by quantitative evidence as a way "to characterize the behavioral and emotional dimensions of interaction, cohesion, sentiment and support between parents and children, grandparents and grandchildren, over the course of long-term relationships" (Bengtson, 2001, p. 8).

THE INTERGENERATIONAL SOLIDARITY MODEL: ADVANTAGES AND CRITICISM

Subsequent research has demonstrated several advantages of the solidarity model. It focuses on family cohesion as an important component of family relations, particularly for successful adjustment to old age (Silverstein & Bengtson, 1994). The family solidarity model emphasizes that intergenerational relations are multidimensional (Bengtson & Schrader, 1982; Silverstein, Giarrusso, Gans, & Bengtson, in press). Family researchers have used the paradigm widely to study relations between parents and their adult children in various ethnic groups (Kauh, 1997) and in cross-national contexts (Katz et al., 2003).

Some scholars have criticized the conceptual framework of family solidarity because of its normative underpinnings—indicating how intergenerational relations "should be" rather than how they "are" (Marshall, Matthews, & Rosenthal, 1993). Others have objected that it assumes that individuals' personal feelings, such as affection, attraction, and warmth, serve to maintain cohesion in the family system (Sprey, 1991). Some have pointed out that the term *solidarity* itself implies an emphasis on consensus (Marshall et al., 1993). In this framework, negative aspects of family life are interpreted as an absence of solidarity. Thus, critics argue, the solidarity model contains normative implications that lend themselves to idealization (Lüscher, 2000). In addition, some scholars assert that the solidarity model provides little insight concerning conflictual relationships (Connidis & McMullin, 2002b; Lüscher & Pillemer, 1998).

Theorizing Conflict in Parent-Child Relations in Later Life

As a result of criticisms such as those noted above, the family solidarity paradigm has been modified to become the "family solidarity-conflict model," which incorporates conflict and focuses also on the possible negative effects of too much solidarity. Conflict theory views the "superstructure" as containing religious, moral, legal, and familial values that are created, implemented, and modified in accordance with the vested interests of those controlling the economy. Theorists in this tradition maintain that a capitalistic economy makes each family responsible for its own members and that the levels and intensities of family violence are directly associated with social stress. Conflict theory as applied to the family has highlighted issues such as isolation, caregiver stress, family dysfunction, and abuse (Marshall et al., 1993; Webster & Herzog, 1995).

In revising the solidarity model, Bengtson and others have argued that conflict is a normal aspect of family relations and that it influences how family members perceive one another and consequently their willingness to assist one another (e.g., Bengtson et al., 2002; Parrott & Bengtson, 1999; Silverstein et al., in press). Conflict can also mean that some difficult issues eventually get resolved, and the overall quality of relationships improves rather than deteriorates following episodes of conflict. Moreover, solidarity and conflict do not represent a single continuum from high solidarity to high conflict. Rather, intergenerational relationships can exhibit both high solidarity and high conflict, or low solidarity and low conflict, depending on the family dynamics and circumstances. Bengtson et al. (2002) see conflict as a natural and inevitable part of human life, a view that is the basic assumption of conflict theory. Social interaction, such as experienced within family units, always contains elements of both harmony and conflict. Groups cannot exist in total harmony, because that would require them to be completely static (Klein & White, 1996).

By positing the family solidarity-conflict model recently, Bengtson and Silverstein are part of the group of contemporary theorists of aging who emphasize conflictual relations and understanding aging as part of a system of age stratification, where relations between different age groups are not necessarily based on equality of exchange. Because exchange relations between generations may never balance, it has been suggested that "beneficence" (Dowd, 1984) rather than reciprocity characterizes contemporary generational relations (Turner, 1999). This revision of the previous solidarity theoretical model is an example of the scientific approach to theory building, which attempts to be cumulative and use empirical testing as a means of enhancing a model or theory.

Theorizing Ambivalence in Parent-Child Relations in Later Life

The theoretical model of family solidarity and conflict has been challenged by a new concept for studying parent-child relations in later life: the concept of "family ambivalence" (Connidis & McMullin, 2002b; Lettke & Klein, 2004; Lüscher, 2002; Lüscher & Pillemer, 1998), which suggests that intergenerational relations may generate ambivalence between family members. This concept is based on postmodern approaches to the family, which argue that because contemporary society is characterized by rapid social change, individuals are unsure about their roles in family life, especially those associated with intergenerational relations. Lüscher (2000, 2004) has proposed the term *intergenerational ambivalence* to reflect the contradictions in relationships between older parents and their adult children along two dimensions: contradictions at the level of the macrosocial structure in terms of roles and norms, and contradictions at the psychological-subjective level in terms of cognition, emotions, and motivation. Lüscher (2000) defines ambivalence as follows: "Polarized simultaneous emotions, thoughts, volitions, actions, social relations, and/or structures that are considered relevant for the constitution of individual or collective identities and are (or can be) interpreted as temporarily or permanently irreconcilable" (p. 15).

Lüscher's concept and its development by Lüscher and Pillemer (1998) present some advantages in the study of intergenerational relations. The concept of intergenerational ambivalence attempts to avoid the pathological perspective of conflict as well as the assumption that family solidarity is normative. It provides a way to look at everyday life issues around relationships such as caregiving and divorce, and it connects disciplines such as sociology and psychology. In Lüscher's (2000) view, the definition "allows us to operationalize" ambivalence and to "organize empirical observation, integrate research results and connect insights" (p. 15). However, some have criticized the ambivalence model as being too static and too abstract. They assert that Lüscher's definition limits individual agency to adapting to structural conditions rather than changing them. In defining ambivalence as irreconcilable (either permanently or temporarily), they argue, the model limits the scope for action (Bengtson et al., 2002).

Connidis and McMullin (2002b) propose a reconceptualization of ambivalence that draws on critical theory and symbolic interactionism perspectives. Ambivalence, in their view, is a condition of social structure conceived as a set of social relations. They emphasize "socially structured" ambivalence as opposed to Lüscher's "structured ambivalence." Individuals negotiate structurally created ambivalence in their relations with family members. In this way ambivalence can be related to both individual agency and structured social relations.

Critics of this reformulation of the ambivalence model, such as Marshall (2002), suggest that Connidis and McMullin may be "pumping too much into the concept of ambivalence," because ambivalence does not necessarily tie individual agency and social structure together. Ambivalence may be a motivator simply to do nothing. This has resulted in one of the most lively debates in recent years about concepts and conceptual models in family research. In the *Journal of Marriage and Family,* Bengtson et al. (2002) critique the ambivalence concept on a number of fronts. They see little difference between the concept of ambivalence and traditional symbolic interactionist approaches to role conflict, with both featuring negotiation and attempts at change. They see the concept of ambivalence as similarly normative with the concepts of solidarity and conflict. They see the intergenerational ambivalence model as not competing with the solidarity and conflict model, but instead complementing it. They argue that "from the intersection of solidarity and conflict comes ambivalence, both psychological and structural" (p. 575).

Several studies have provided empirical evidence to support the ambivalence concept (Lorenz-Meyer, 2004; Lüscher, 2004). A study by Lüscher and Lettke supports the utility of the distinction between the structural and personal dimensions of relationships in regard to ambivalence (Lüscher, 2004). Lorenz-Meyer's (2004) study of parental care by young German adults has drawn attention to overlapping personal and structural ambivalences. Connidis (2002) has similarly demonstrated ambivalence in relation to divorce and gay and lesbian relationships. However, these researchers have had little to

say about the causes of ambivalence—or indeed whether such sentiments should be treated as independent or dependent variables to explain intergenerational relations.

Two studies of ambivalence have focused on old age, attempting to use the concept in quantitative analysis providing an empirical assessment of the model. Pillemer and Suitor (2002) suggest that the characteristics of parent-child relationships that predict intergenerational ambivalence are to a great extent distinct from those that predict positive and negative relationship quality. They are especially manifested during status transitions experienced by both adult children and older parents. However, Pillemer and Suitor warn us that their "findings are best viewed as suggestive rather than definitive" (p. 611). In the second study, Willson, Shuey, and Elder (2003) conclude that ambivalence may be produced within the context of social relations structured by gender and kinship. These two studies demonstrate the potential usefulness of further examination and theorizing of the ambivalence concept.

We have outlined above the theoretical bases of the solidarity-conflict and ambivalence models. We agree with Bengtson et al. (2002) that "each is a lens through which one can look at family relationships" (p. 575). Our goal in the OASIS study was to respond to the challenge of empirically testing both lenses in a comparative cross-national context.

TESTING THE MODELS: THE OASIS PROJECT

Most family studies may have an unacknowledged ethnocentric bias, given that they are conducted in only a single country. The OASIS project represents a comparative perspective and draws on data from five countries: Norway, England, Germany, Spain, and Israel. These countries reflect a diverse range of welfare regimes (institutional, conservative, residual) (Esping-Andersen, 1990) and familial cultures (family-oriented and individualist), and also reflect elements of a north-south divide (Reher, 1998). These differences are likely to be reflected in intergenerational family relationships.

Methodological Issues in Comparative Cross-National Research

Comparative studies are driven by two contrasting goals: One is the search for generalities, the structuralist approach; and the other is the search for distinctiveness, the culturalist position. Both approaches have their virtues and problems. Structuralists assume that similar macro structures will produce similar micro (individual)-level outcomes. Culturalists assume that country characteristics modify effects of social structure and produce culturally distinct patterns. Demonstrating cross-national similarities is an avenue to more general knowledge. Any cross-national differences and national idiosyncrasies that are found must be understood and interpreted in the appropriate historical and political contexts. The OASIS study adopted both approaches in a comparative focus on the intergenerational solidarity-conflict and ambivalence paradigms.

The OASIS project was a cross-sectional study that incorporated both quantitative and qualitative methods. (For details about the research instruments used, see this volume's companion Web site at http://www.ncfr.org/ sourcebook; see also Lowenstein, Katz, Mehlhausen-Hassoen, & Prilutzky, 2002; Phillips & Ray, 2003.) The quantitative data were collected through face-to-face structured interviews with an urban representative sample of 1,200 respondents (800 ages 25–74 and 400 ages 75+) in each of the five countries, for a total sample of 6,000. The qualitative data were gathered through in-depth interviews with 10 dyads (an older parent of 75+ and one of his or her adult children) in each country, for a total of 50 dyads.

Solidarity

Intercorrelations between the six solidarity dimensions revealed low correlations (.26 to .34), which supports the multidimensionality of family solidarity claimed by the model (Silverstein & Bengtson, 1997). Thus the data in Figure 16.1 present the distribution of the six dimensions, based on Longitudinal Study of Generations measures (Bengtson & Schrader, 1982). To facilitate comparisons among the five countries, we transformed the dimensions into dichotomous indicators, as used by Silverstein and Bengtson (1994). Differences on all dimensions between all samples, assessed by chi-square tests, were significant at .001.

A general conclusion from these data is that family intergenerational solidarity appears to be very strong in all five countries. This indicates that older people are firmly embedded within their families across these societies, although there are variations in the strength of the various dimensions in the different countries. High percentages of respondents in all countries reported high levels of affectual solidarity (emotional relations), although the percentage was relatively low in Germany. There were also high levels of consensus (although this figure was relatively low in Spain). Most respondents lived relatively close to their children, and most reported frequent face-to-face contact with them (although the percentages were somewhat lower in Germany). Normative solidarity was highest in Spain, followed by Germany and Israel; the lowest reported normative solidarity was in England. Functional assistance received by parents from children was higher than functional assistance provided by parents to children. The qualitative data from face-to-face interviews supported the quantitative evidence that older people and their children experience strong feelings of solidarity. These data across nations indicate that older parents feel safe and secure because of these positive reciprocal feelings.

Looking at the associations between background attributes and the six solidarity dimensions, four personal resources stand out as affecting the most dimensions: number of children, financial situation, gender, and physical functioning. This corresponds to findings in other studies.

Figure 16.1   Distribution of the Six Solidarity Dimensions for the OASIS Participants Ages 75+

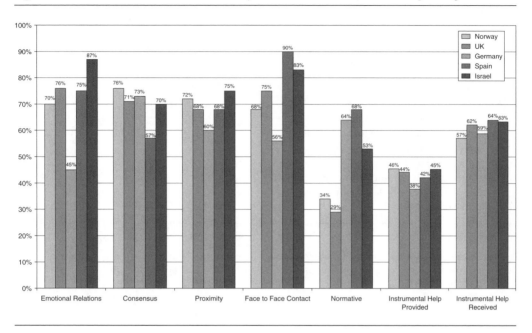

The OASIS study explored family norms and ideals as part of intergenerational family relations—namely, normative solidarity—in terms of three kinds of relationships: between adult children and older parents, between the family and the welfare state, and between oneself and one's family. The first is the main focus here—the level and character of filial obligations. These issues are of theoretical interest because of the controversy about the isolation of the nuclear family and aged members in postindustrial society. Filial responsibility reflects the extent to which adult children feel obligated to meet the needs of their aging parents and can be seen as one component of normative family solidarity.

A number of researchers who have conducted studies in the United States have concluded that filial responsibility norms are still strong and to a large extent are shared across class, gender, age, and ethnicity (Hamon & Blieszner, 1990; Lee, Peek, & Coward 1998). What about filial responsibility in contemporary European countries? In the OASIS study, filial responsibility norms were measured as agreement with the four scale items shown in

Table 16.2. The majority of respondents in all five countries acknowledged some degree of filial obligations, but there were important cross-societal differences: Respondents in Spain and Israel showed more agreement with these items than did those in Germany, England, and Norway. The differences are moderate, however, and if we assume that we can generalize from the findings for familistic Spain, we may conclude that filial obligation norms are quite vital also in northern European countries. This is so in the large urban areas from which the OASIS samples were drawn, and in a universalistic welfare state such as Norway, this indicates that neither urbanization nor expansion of the welfare state has eroded filial obligations.

Country differences are more evident in the *character* of filial norms than in the *strength* of those norms. Attitudes concerning whether or not adult children should live close to their elderly parents (item 1 in Table 16.2) follows the north-south division of countries, attracting far more support in Spain and Israel than in England and Norway. The latter two nations seem to subscribe to a

Table 16.2   Percentages in Agreement With Filial Obligation Items, by Item and Country

Item	Norway	England	Germany	Spain	Israel
1. Adult children should be willing to sacrifice some of the things they want for their own children in order to support their frail elderly parents.	41.0	46.6	35.5	43.6	37.0
2. Adult children should live close to their older parents so they can help them if needed.	28.5	30.7	40.2	57.1	55.4
3. Older people should be able to depend on their adult children to help them do the things they need to do.	58.3	41.0	55.2	59.8	51.1
4. Parents are entitled to some return for the sacrifices they have made for their children.	37.9	47.9	26.1	55.4	63.8
Total (agree with at least one item)	76.0	74.6	65.8	82.3	84.3

SOURCE: The OASIS project; scale adopted from Lee, Peek, and Coward (1998).

NOTE: This table shows the percentages of respondents in agreement ("agree" or "strongly agree") with each item and the total scale (= agree with at least one item). Weighted samples, population ages 25 and older living at home in large urban settings (100,000+); $n \approx 1,200$ for each country.

norm of independence regarding living arrangements. In fact, the majority of respondents in all of the countries except Spain prefer residential care over living with one's child if one can no longer live alone in old age. The north-south division appears also in attitudes toward reciprocity as a guide for parent-child relationships (item 4). Again the majority of respondents in Spain and Israel were in favor, whereas those in Norway and Germany gave little support to the reciprocity norm.

Conflict

Intergenerational conflict was measured through three items related to tension in parent-child relations and prevalence of arguments and criticism. These conflict measures were based on other intergenerational studies (Silverstein & Bengtson, 1997). The levels of conflict in these cross-national samples were low compared with the levels of the solidarity dimensions. But conflict is clearly

an important component of intergenerational family life. Between one-third and one-half of the older parents in the OASIS sample in each country reported the existence of some conflict and tension in their relationships with their children. The qualitative interview data suggested that many of the conflicts that existed had to do with the issue of the older parents' autonomy. However, basically these conflicts were "positive" in that the children wanted to help the parents, but the parents did not want to be a "burden" to the children.

Ambivalence

Ambivalence was measured through three items related to mixed feelings in parent-child relations, evaluation of the relationships regarding pleasant and unpleasant aspects, and degree of trying to preserve family harmony. Levels of ambivalent feelings were quite low when compared with the solidarity-conflict dimensions, given that only 27% of respondents exhibited feelings of ambivalence.

• SPOTLIGHT ON METHODS

QUALITATIVE APPROACHES TO STUDYING INTERGENERATIONAL RELATIONS

Gay Becker, *University of California, San Francisco*

Qualitative research can illuminate our understanding of intergenerational relations because it emphasizes the meanings that people attach to their experiences. Qualitative studies explore new directions, examine phenomena that are little understood, and provide in-depth data on a wide range of topics. Qualitative research that is done in combination with quantitative research can flesh out quantitative findings and facilitate further interpretation of results.

Several methodological considerations arise in the application of qualitative research to intergenerational relations. If different cultural groups are being compared, attention needs to be paid to the development of research questions and interview guides that cover the full extent of the topic under study while leaving room for unanticipated cultural factors to emerge. Each cultural group to be included should be adequately sampled. Marin and Marin (1991) outline a process for making social science research culturally appropriate for specific cultural groups.

A key question is which generations should be included in a study. Intergenerational studies may be conducted solely from the perspective of one generation (Becker, Beyene, Newsom, & Mayen, 2003), they may consist of dyads (as in this chapter), or they may be done with triads or greater numbers. Two or more generations may be included, depending on the research design.

Matching the methods to the research inquiry is of critical importance. Interview studies are most common. Ethnographic interviewing methods include both directive and nondirective strategies; in in-depth interviews, researchers "reframe" respondents' statements as further questions, following the respondents' lines of thinking and following their leads (Rubinstein, 1987). Hammersley and Atkinson (1983) suggest that it is inaccurate to think of ethnographic interviewing as unstructured and survey interviewing as structured; rather, a more appropriate way of viewing these practices is as "reflexive" and "standardized."

Scholars have also used participant observation of family interactions in conducting in-depth analyses of family dynamics across generations (Henry, 1973). Participant observation is a traditional social science technique that includes observation of participants in their environment as well as the researcher's participation in those aspects of the daily lives of participants that are relevant to the study (Keith, 1981). These techniques may be used in combination; for example, a researcher may follow a small number of cases from a large number of interviews with participant observation for a closer look at family dynamics.

Qualitative content analysis is commonly used to analyze data. Several specific approaches have been developed, such as ethnographic analysis and grounded theory (Strauss & Corbin, 1997). Dividing the data first by ethnic group and then by generation (and perhaps gender) is the first step in such an analysis. Within-group comparisons are made after each data segment is analyzed. If more than one cultural group is studied, cross-group comparisons follow.

(continued)

● **SPOTLIGHT ON METHODS** *continued*

A thematic analysis emerges directly out of the data. The process of code development may be conducted by a solo researcher or by a team of researchers working together. Core categories that repeatedly reappear in the data are identified first, followed by an elaboration of code categories that may be expanded subsequently and developed for use with a data-sorting software program. Codes may then be linked to each other, and the researcher may revisit the data with these codes in mind for further analysis on a case-by-case basis (Becker, 1997). Further comparisons by generation and cultural group are useful at this stage of data analysis.

NOTE: Preparation of this article was supported by grants from the National Institute on Aging, National Institutes of Health, R37 AG11144 and RO1 AG16608. ●

Ambivalent relationships were relatively difficult to capture in the quantitative survey data; the qualitative study was more successful in revealing them. Data from the in-depth interviews showed how the older parents, in their attempts to negotiate, manage, and reorganize their lives as a result of the onset of chronic illness and disability, often identified experiences of ambivalence at an individual level. Ambivalence, like conflict, was mostly reflected during periods of transition (moving toward dependency) in the life course, when older parents and adult children were attempting to renegotiate roles.

Relationship Types

In order to understand the complexity of intergenerational family relations relating to solidarity, conflict, and ambivalence, we used a typological approach that reflects a holistic empirical perspective, as advocated by Silverstein and Bengtson (1997). We used correspondence and cluster analyses, identifying the groups of parents whose responses were as closely related as possible within each group and as different as possible between each group, making no a priori assumptions about the number or nature of classes that might emerge (for details about the procedures used, see this volume's companion Web site). This procedure yielded four category types: close,

steady, ambivalent, and distant (Phillips, Ogg, & Ray, 2003), as shown in Table 16.3.

Close relationships were found in 24% of the respondents. These were characterized by parents' feelings of extreme closeness to their children. There is room for mixed feelings in a close relationship, but these mixed feelings do not seem to "harm" the relationship in any substantial way. For example, one parent respondent stated about his daughter, "When she comes here she might be here for 3 hours and we talk and talk and we laugh and she's got the same sort of humor that I've got" (Stan, England).

Steady relationships form the largest category, representing 32% of the parents. These parent-child relationships are more emotionally distant than the relationships categorized as close, although they might still be described as close. The parents in this category generally get on well with their children, but perhaps they like to keep some emotional distance from them.

The *ambivalent* group is the second largest, representing 27% of the parents. Those in this group show signs of a generational gap emerging between parents and their children. These parents tend to feel neither emotionally close to nor distant from their adult children. They get along with and communicate pretty well with their children. There is conflict in these relationships that seems to result more

Table 16.3   Cluster parent-child relationships by country

Relationship Type	Norway	Germany	England	Spain	Israel
Type 1: Close (24%)	21	12	27	11	51
Type 2: Steady (32%)	32	29	40	41	16
Type 3: Ambivalent (27%)	32	41	11	35	16
Type 4: Distant (17%)	15	18	23	13	17
Base	*645*	*708*	*697*	*694*	*7407*

NOTE: Numbers in parentheses show the percentages of the specific type among all respondents.

$p < 0.01$

from distancing than from closeness. The mixed feelings that characterize this group begin to show significantly when the group is compared with the close and steady groups, although the majority say they seldom or never have mixed feelings. The comments of one daughter illustrate:

> I argue with my mother and I shout at her a bit, because if I don't shout at her she blows my top, and from time to time if you shout a bit at her, she calms down. . . .
> No, it doesn't affect our relationship. I argue with her and the next day I continue talking to her and caring for her; those arguments, but then they're forgotten. (Fabiana, Spain)

The *distant* group is the smallest, representing 17% of the parents. This is clearly the group where relationships show signs of emotional distancing and where conflicts, mixed feelings, and differences of views are likely. More than one-third of these parents report holding opinions and values that are not similar to those of their children.

Regarding intercountry differences, the survey data reflect important differences in relationship styles across the five study countries (see Table 16.3). Ambivalent relationships were most evident in Germany, Spain, and Norway; distant relationships were most evident in England; and close relations were most evident in Israel. The German parents differed from those in all the other countries in that the majority portrayed their parent-child relations as either ambivalent or distant.

It is of interest to note that similar types—and distributions—have been demonstrated by American studies employing the solidarity-conflict model. Silverstein et al. (in press; see Web site for this volume) used latent class analysis that yielded four types of intergenerational relationships: amicable (37% of the sample), ambivalent (28%), disharmonious (21%), and civil (14%). That Silverstein et al.'s analysis and the OASIS analysis resulted in such similar types provides justification for the typological modeling approach to theorizing.

CONCLUSIONS: LINKING SOLIDARITY, CONFLICT, AND AMBIVALENCE

In this chapter we have focused on analyzing and further theorizing the conceptual models of family solidarity-conflict and family ambivalence. We have presented empirical evidence testing the utility of each model, and we have summarized how these concepts were exemplified empirically within our cross-national study (the OASIS project). We hypothesized that styles of parent-child relationships differ from country to country, reflecting both the influence of individual agency and social structure. We used a combined methodological approach of triangulating quantitative and qualitative data to apply the models across multinational contexts. The OASIS design allowed us to test the more problem-oriented model of solidarity-conflict, which has been measured by quantitative methods. Some of the key components of ambivalence, stemming from critical and interactionist theories, such as contradictions in relationships that cannot be reconciled or the simultaneous presence of positive and negative perceptions by an individual, became more apparent in the OASIS qualitative data.

Analyses of the empirical OASIS data confirmed once more, in broad cross-cultural contexts, what family sociologists have previously argued: The extended family has maintained cross-generational cohesion despite massive social changes over the past century (Bengtson, 2001). But our data also supported a newer perspective, the solidarity-conflict model (Bengtson et al., 2002; Silverstein et al., in press). Thus, as Clarke, Preston, Raskin, and Bengtson (1999) suggest, further study of the balance between solidarity and conflict is warranted.

Two tentative conclusions can be drawn from our analyses and the typologies. On the one hand, it is clear that there are both intra- and intercountry differences in styles of parent-child relationships. On the other, in all the study countries we found persuasive evidence that parents and children differ qualitatively in the ways in which they relate to one another. These differences are important enough to have an impact on flows of intergenerational support. However, it should be remembered that the majority of families show strong signs of intergenerational family solidarity. In this respect, our analysis confirms previous findings (Silverstein & Bengtson, 1997; Wenger, 1989).

Scholars should consider the possible paradigmatic changes in the social fabric of families and societal networks. However, the main story that emerges from the OASIS study is one of stability more than change as far as global family norms are concerned. There are considerable variations in how these family norms are translated into preferences and practices. The norms are sufficiently open to allow accommodation to new social realities, such as gender equality and increased female participation in the workforce. Families seem to be less duty driven and more open to individual adaptation. Personal affection and attachments will then grow more important for family cohesion and intergenerational family ties. Normative obligations will live on, but may increasingly be transcribed

into affection and choice, giving family relationships a more personal and less structural flavor. The high scores on affectual solidarity in all of the OASIS project countries point in this direction, and the potential for adaptation may in fact be one of the major reasons the family is so persistent and resilient as a social institution.

In trying to link the testing of solidarity-conflict and ambivalence models on the micro level of the individual and the family within the macro perspective of the cross-national study, one must pay attention to the unique historical and familial developments in each of the five countries. Thus, for example, the higher rates of close parent-child relationships found in Israel may have much to do with that country's recent history and the current geopolitical situation. Similarly, the apparent generation gap between current cohorts of older parents and their adult children in Germany may have something to do with the polarization (along generational lines) of traditional/radical attitudes that occurred in the 1960s. To take another example, the low rates of close parent-child relationships alongside the highest rates of steady relations found in Spain may be due to enduring norms of traditional respect for elders common to Mediterranean cultures. However, Spain is undergoing rapid modernization (reflected, for example, in low fertility rates). Younger generations are more exposed to this process, in addition to being better educated and more well-off than their parents. This could result in the emergence of a large generation gap, as reflected in Spanish respondents' scoring the lowest on consensus.

The qualitative interviews in the OASIS study highlighted the dynamics of conflict and ambivalence. These dyadic interviews provided important insights into the ways different actors perceive and experience change and transition along the life course. It would be beneficial for scholars to consider how intergenerational dyadic relations operate within the whole context of family networks and roles (Connidis & McMullin, 2002b). Our data highlight the importance of individuals in an intergenerational context actively negotiating and renegotiating solutions or management strategies in response to change and transitions over the life course. This is similar to what Boss (2004) has termed "ambiguous loss" in referring to the psychological loss of a loved one, as in cases of Alzheimer's disease. Little support has been found for the notion that dyadic strategies may exist to deal with ambivalence (Lüscher, 2000). Although members of a dyad might discuss the same experience of transition and change, each does so from his or her own individual context and in relation to his or her perception and experience of the other. Individual strategies rather than dyadic strategies were evident in the OASIS respondents' processes of dealing with or resolving transitional situations. This leads to a further observation that resolution of ambivalences is possible, albeit temporarily. Rather than focusing attention on whether or not ambivalences are unsolvable, it would appear to be more fruitful for scholars to attend to the ways in which ambivalences emerge in family relationships and the processes and strategies family members use to address these issues. This approach has potential in terms of implications for further theorizing the concept of ambivalence and for practice and policy in respect to intergenerational ties and family relationships.

We found the solidarity-conflict model and the instruments to measure it useful in evaluating the strength of family relationships, as suggested by Bengtson and Roberts (1991). At the same time, the solidarity-conflict model does not capture the whole complex and diverse picture of family late-life relations, as noted by Bengtson et al. (2002). This is especially so in times of transitions along the life course, such as failing health of older parents or changing needs of working caregivers. Thus ambivalence may be a complement to solidarity and conflict. Dyads who had experienced their relationships as effective and essentially harmonious tended to identify ambivalence or conflict as part of the process of their relationships.

As we found that ambivalence was best captured through qualitative data and researchers to date have measured solidarity-conflict for the most part through quantitative data, we recommend that scholars use both methods and triangulate databases in order to capture these different concepts. Clearly, further work needs to be done on validating the concept of ambivalence, operationalizing it, and capturing its individual and structural dimensions in central transition periods of the life course. The accumulation of additional empirical evidence would facilitate further theorizing of the ambivalence model along with the solidarity-conflict model to determine if the two could be incorporated into a broader conceptual paradigm.

Case Study

CASE STUDY

TESTING THEORIES ABOUT INTERGENERATIONAL EXCHANGES

Merril Silverstein, *University of Southern California*

Gerontology and family studies are often described as multidisciplinary sciences. Scholars can fully understand the phenomena each seeks to explain—human aging and family behavior—only by bringing to bear the concepts and theories of at least several of these fields' constituent disciplines. In the study of aging and families, theory forms a

Case Study

natural bridge, linking disciplinary perspectives and presenting exciting opportunities for theoretical development and synthesis. The potential of these fields to draw on multiple theoretical orientations also presents challenges to scholars by placing a burden on them to choose wisely among the theories at their disposal and to combine those theories creatively. Perhaps because these two areas of inquiry originated as applied sciences, they have come late to developing the abstract concepts and principles that form the foundation of traditional disciplines in the human sciences. Thus it is not surprising that much of the early and, to some extent, current empirical research in social gerontology and family science has eschewed formal theory testing.

In this case study I present, as an example, the results of an ongoing effort to blend theoretical perspectives from several quarters in the social and behavioral sciences to inform a program of research on intergenerational exchange in the aging family (Silverstein, Conroy, Wang, Giarrusso, & Bengtson, 2002). This research, which lies at the intersection of family and aging studies, draws on ideas from the disciplines of economics, sociology, social demography, and social psychology to model intergenerational exchange dynamics as comprehensively as possible. Through a unique collaboration of scholars trained in these disciplines, a general unified model of life-course reciprocity was developed and tested using data collected on multigenerational families over three decades.

THEORIES OF INTERGENERATIONAL EXCHANGE

How are we to understand the extraordinary efforts made by adult children to serve the needs of their older parents? In the absence of a strong bioevolutionary imperative, we are drawn to social explanations rooted in normative structures, principles of reciprocity, and models of families as systems of exchange. Here I briefly review perspectives from the disciplines noted above. To be sure,

these perspectives share a common set of assumptions in proposing reciprocity as the central mechanism guiding intergenerational transfers. Yet each discipline contributes uniquely from its theoretical base to emphasize certain aspects of reciprocity over others. Therefore, the disciplines to be discussed may be viewed more as complementary than competing, and together they produce a deeper understanding of intergenerational exchange than would any one discipline alone.

Exchange perspectives in economics are based on the premise that individuals tend to engage in actions that maximize their personal rewards and minimize their personal costs—the basic assumption of rational choice theory. In general, the economic perspective emphasizes the family as an institution that smooths risk by reallocating goods and services to where they are needed most. In this context, the family is considered an efficient resource distribution system that insures against adverse outcomes among its members. Investments in children are viewed as an alternative to investments in private markets to reduce the risk of having unmet health and economic needs in later life (Pauly, 1990).

The sociological approach to intergenerational transfers as an exchange process is rooted in the fundamental precept that reciprocity is enforced by a normative principle that obligates the repayment of an incurred social or economic debt (Gouldner, 1960). This insight gained new power through the concept of social capital, a repository of goodwill and trust instilled in others through social interaction, common group membership, and provision of favors (Coleman, 1988). The obligation to return a favor is a fundamental normative principle of society and the basis of small group solidarity. Yet, as a durable asset, social capital is a latent resource that is typically consumed only when it is needed. For instance, adherence to norms of filial responsibility by adult children is a form of social capital that can be converted into supportive behavior when triggered by the frailty of an aging parent.

CASE STUDY *continued*

A related approach in social psychology uses the concept of a "support bank" to model how social capital is produced and consumed between generations over the life course of the family (Antonucci, 1990). A support bank is a latent reserve of social capital that parents build early in the family life cycle by investing time, labor, and money in their children. The parents later draw on this social capital in the form of social support from children when the parents develop age-associated dependencies. Thus partners in the intergenerational relationship variously play the roles of provider and of receiver, depending on the type and timing of their developmental needs. Exchange theory within a social psychology framework also proposes that valued resources other than financial assets may be used as currencies of exchange, including affirmation, empathy, and group solidarity (Emerson, 1981); transfers need not be of the same type to attract reciprocation. This perspective goes far toward explaining why families are able to tolerate long periods of latency before reciprocation is activated.

Social demography provides a related perspective from which to view intergenerational exchange. This perspective emphasizes the provision of mutual aid across generations as the basis for family survival, especially in developing nations where formal mechanisms of support for families are weak or nonexistent. Contemporaneous time-for-money transfers have been observed between generations in developing nations, where younger family members provide monetary support to older persons in exchange for household and child-care labor (Frankenberg, Lillard, & Willis, 2002). In addition, these studies infer a long-term strategy for ensuring old age care from the observed association between parents' investment in the higher education of their children and the likelihood of later receiving support from them—a parental strategy also discussed by scholars in the field of microeconomics. Long-term serial patterns of intergenerational exchange have also been found in the United States. For instance, one study found that parents who provided financial assistance to their children in early adulthood tend to receive support from them in old age, suggesting a quid pro quo in transfers over the life course (Henretta, Hill, Li, Soldo, & Wolf, 1997). That demographic analysis tends to focus on the temporal dynamics of intergenerational exchange is consistent with the field's general emphasis on the *timing* of family transitions and events.

APPLYING THEORIES OF INTERGENERATIONAL EXCHANGE

So where does this leave the application of theory to empirical research on intergenerational exchanges in the family? My colleagues and I assessed how parents' transfers of sentiment, time, and financial assets to their adolescent/young adult children affected the children's propensity in middle age to provide social support to their parents in later life (Silverstein et al., 2002). We implicitly appropriated five general propositions from the aforementioned disciplines to develop a set of hypotheses that could be tested against empirical data:

1. Parents accumulate social capital by transferring valued resources in their children.

2. Children feel that they should repay parents for transfers made to them earlier in life.

3. Reciprocity characterizes intergenerational family transfers such that the balance of transfers strives toward equilibrium over the long term.

4. Children will tend to reciprocate for the receipt of earlier parental transfers when the needs of their parents are elevated.

5. Valued resources transferred across generations include both economic and noneconomic reserves.

Case Study

CASE STUDY *continued*

Using family data collected over almost three decades, we operationally defined "lagged reciprocity": when the provision of emotional and instrumental support to an older parent was proportional to that parent's earlier transfers to the child. We defined transfers to children in terms of emotional support, time commitments, and financial contributions. An investment model was said to hold when earlier transfers to the child were unconditionally reciprocated regardless of parental need. An insurance model was said to hold when earlier transfers to the child were returned primarily in the event of parental need. Both hypotheses were confirmed. Thus the availability of long-term longitudinal data made it possible to test dynamics of intergenerational family exchange based on theories integrated across several disciplines in the social and behavioral sciences.

Theoretical Depiction of Two Intergenerational Exchange Mechanisms

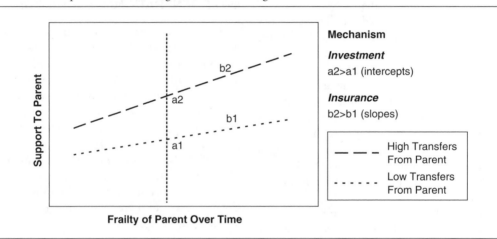

CONCLUSION

Theory is an invaluable tool that social and behavioral scientists use to assemble data into meaningful patterns that make sense of the infinite complexity of human behavior. However, the theories we most often apply are those we learn in our disciplinary training rather than those that best fit the requirements of the research problem. This case study illustrates how synthesizing perspectives across several disciplines increases the utility of data by widening the explanatory power of the resulting empirical model. Indeed, cross-disciplinary collaborations may bring to fruition novel paradigms for better understanding social processes in the family.

None other than the founding father of free market economics, Adam Smith, recognized the limits of rational self-interest for explaining the motivations behind interpersonal transactions in families. In his book *The Theory of Moral Sentiments* (1790), Smith writes, "How selfish soever man may be supposed, there are evidently some principles in his nature which interest him in the fortune of others and render their happiness necessary to him though he derives nothing from it except the pleasure of seeing it." This venerable text provides fuel, as well as comfort, to scholars who wish to bridge disciplinary divides and widen their theoretical lenses in studying family relations.

Case Study

RECENT SHIFTS IN FAMILY SUPPORT FOR OLDER PEOPLE IN GHANA

Isabella Aboderin, *University of Oxford*

THE PROBLEM, KEY QUESTIONS, AND AIMS

A central issue in current debates about aging in Ghana, as in other African nations, is concern about the apparent decline in customary material family support for older people. In the absence of comprehensive formal welfare systems, such family support has been responsible for ensuring economic security for the old. The duty of the young, especially of adult children toward their elders, is enshrined in this Ghanaian proverb: When your elders take care of you while you cut your teeth, you must in turn take care of them while they are losing theirs. Today, however, although most older Ghanaians continue to live with and rely on material help from younger kin, indications are that the adequacy of such help has declined, exposing increasing numbers to deprivation and poverty, especially in the cities. In light of this, and the predicted sharp growth in the older population, increasing stress is being placed on the urgent need for appropriate policy responses to ensure the economic welfare of older people now and in the future. A vital prerequisite of such policy development is a solid understanding of how and why old-age family support has declined and of how family support systems have evolved and operate today. Such an understanding, however, does not yet exist.

ANALYTIC CHALLENGE: GAPS IN CURRENT EXPLANATIONS

The point of departure for the empirical investigation that I undertook in 1997–1998 (Aboderin, in press) was a critical examination of the content and limitations in the two main explanations for family support declines currently advanced in the literature. The first, pointing to modernization and aging perspectives in line with idealist views, emphasizes the key role played by a weakening of traditional norms of family and filial obligation as a result of Western individualist influences and an emphasis on the conjugal family. Support, no longer compelled by the force of custom, is seen to have become increasingly dependent on younger people's discretion— that is, their *wish* to support older kin. Ultimately, support declines are thus seen as the result of an increasing *unwillingness* of the young to provide for the old.

In contrast, interpretations drawing on political economy and materialist perspectives emphasize the crucial role played by growing material constraints among the young. In the context of worsening economic strain and poverty in Ghana, as in Africa more generally, they imply an increasing *incapacity* (rather than unwillingness) of the young to provide adequate support for their aged kin.

Although both interpretations undoubtedly capture some of the important factors involved, two crucial limitations curb the understanding they offer. Conceptually, both explanations fail to illuminate the *interrelationships* between normative and material factors in causing declines in support from younger kin. Underlying this conceptual gap is a more fundamental epistemological limitation: Neither of the two perspectives takes into account evidence on individuals' perspectives and motives.

The analytic challenge for my research was thus to illuminate how changes in individuals'

Case Study

and families' perspectives have been related to changes in their wider structural context and, in doing so, to shed light on the relative roles played by cultural and material changes in driving the support shifts.

METHODS AND APPROACH

In order to meet this challenge, I used an interpretive approach informed by a life-course perspective and a generational sequential design (Aboderin, 2004). This generated an understanding of the recent shifts in family support by allowing me to explore and compare the life experiences and perspectives of three successive generations: the older (G1), the middle (G2), and the youngest (G3). I conducted in-depth interviews with a three-generation sample of respondents (*N* = 51) purposely selected to include older parent–adult child dyads and, where possible, triads with grandchildren and stratified to capture a broad spectrum of income, gender, and ethnic groups. From the themes raised by respondents and through systematic comparison between generations, I inductively generated three "building blocks" of evidence:

1. A picture of *why* and *how* younger people provided material support to older parents or relatives in the "past," based on the older generation's accounts of (a) their past motives, interests, and experiences in providing such support; (b) the types and sources of support given to or received by aged kin; and (c) the social and material context surrounding them at the time. (The "past" roughly spans the late 1930s to the 1960s, with G1 respondents' birth dates ranging from 1914 to 1932.)

2. A similar appreciation of the basis, patterns, and context of support in the "present" (the late 1990s), based on the older generation's current experiences of receiving such support

and on (a) the middle generation's experiences, motives, and attitudes in providing it; and (b) both younger generations' expectations of such support in the future

3. A systematic comparison of "past" and "present," taking into account the older generation's own interpretations of the changes that have occurred

PROPOSING ANSWERS

Using these building blocks, I developed three main accounts in answer to the key research questions: (a) why and how old-age support was provided (more adequately) in the "past"; (b) the extent, nature, and causes of the decline in support; and (c) the emerging expectations for the future. The findings indicate that there has indeed been a decline in support from adult children and extended kin in general. This has been caused by a complex interplay between economic constraints and changing normative ideas that has given rise to two main shifts and is not captured by either modernization or political economy accounts.

The most important shift, as political economy perspectives imply, has undoubtedly been a reduction in the resource capacity of the middle generation. Many younger people simply do not have enough resources to care for themselves, their children, and their aged parents, let alone for more extended kin. The main reasons for this change have been the growing economic strain and spiraling cost of living in Ghana. However, two other factors, not hitherto discussed, have also played important roles. The first is an apparent shift in status criteria toward an emphasis on modern material goods and lifestyles, which has raised younger people's "need" for such goods, thus further narrowing their capacity to give to the old. The second crucial factor is a seemingly fundamental hierarchy of priorities that underpins the middle generation's resource allocation decisions. This hierarchy, crystallized in the current situation of economic scarcity, gives clear priority to the needs of the young over those of the old. The underlying principle, it seems, is that the old have no "right" to absorb the resources that the young need for their lives—a principle echoing the notion of a "transitive order" or "processional nature" of intergenerational justice discussed in the West.

The second shift underpinning the decline specifically in filial support is a change in its normative basis. In contrast to the past, when adult children largely supported their aged parents regardless of their judgment of them, children today increasingly make their support dependent on their assessment of their parents' past conduct and thus their personal relationships with them. This shift is not, as modernization views would hold, the result of weakening filial obligation norms per se. The customary, proverbial *reciprocal* obligation (mentioned above) to repay parents *if* they cared in the past, and the conditionality it expresses, persists and, in fact, is increasingly emphasized. What has weakened is the absolute duty—backed up by potent sanctions and enshrined in biblical commandment—that in the past compelled children to honor their parents *no matter what* and thus overrode the conditionality in the customary obligation. That this duty has weakened is not a result of secularization: Christian worship has become more marked with the continued economic strain in Ghana. The primary reason, rather, is Ghana's worsening employment and economic situation. This has raised the importance of parents' providing good education or training, as well as the resentment of adult children whose parents fail to provide it. Blaming their parents for their hopeless situation, such children now reject a duty to honor and support parents who, they feel, do not deserve it. Moreover, economic hardship has weakened the threat of divine and family sanctions that formerly enforced this duty. In a context where individuals can no longer

hope for economic backing from extended family anyway and now see God as their loving protector, these sanctions have lost their bite. Nonetheless, growing economic problems are not solely responsible for the shift in filial support. The increasing emphasis on the judgment of parents' conduct has also been supported by the growing prominence of the notion of children's rights, as established in the United Nations Convention on the Rights of the Child, which Ghana ratified in 1989.

Together, the identified processes of change clearly suggest that the alteration in families' material circumstances has been the dominant driver of shifts in the support of older parents. Yet a wholly materialistic explanation is not enough: Changes in broader societal values and ideas have also played a role. They have interacted with deteriorating material conditions and served to exacerbate their effects. The dominance of material processes in driving change is further reflected in the emergent expectations of material old-age support in the future. The increasing value that all generations now place on self-reliance, away from filial and kin support, is, above all, a response to the worsening economic situation. The principle, it seems, is that if material conditions change to such an extent that fulfillment of a particular family norm becomes harmful to the younger generation, it is no longer tenable and must change.

CONCLUDING REMARKS

Despite their limited application to the respondents studied and the specific context and time frame experienced by them, the research findings discussed above may point to processes that have occurred more widely in urban or rural Ghana or in other African nations. If so, they may carry crucial implications for old-age economic security policy. They may, moreover, contribute to wider theoretical debates on the nature and drivers of change in family norms and behaviors.

Case Study

DISCUSSION AND EXTENSION

THEORIZING INTERGENERATIONAL RELATIONS ACROSS SOCIETIES

G. Clare Wenger, *University of Wales, Bangor*

In Chapter 16, Katz, Lowenstein, Phillips, and Daatland illustrate theoretical perspectives on intergenerational relationships in family life with findings from the OASIS project involving England, Germany, Israel, Norway, and Spain. In analyzing existing theories of intergenerational relationships, their focus is on the theoretical model of family solidarity, with acknowledgment of later research on parent-child conflict and ambivalence in later life. The intergenerational relationships of concern to Katz et al. are those between adult children and their older parents in need of help. Both the chapter and some of the literature these authors review tend to have a negative tone: asking if elders are abandoned by their families rather than addressing the nature of intergenerational relationships and, in terms of conflict, researching isolation, caregiver stress, family problems, and abuse, although Katz et al. do note that most conflict concerns elders' being constrained by their children. The findings of the OASIS project emphasize diversity in the distribution of outcomes within and between countries, and the chapter presents a typology of relationships as close, steady, ambivalent, and distant.

Katz et al.'s general conclusion is that family solidarity is alive and well. In discussing and expanding on their chapter, I consider here (a) what aspects of intergenerational relationships are missing from the discussion, (b) whether the findings can be generalized, and (c) what questions arise for the further development of intergenerational research.

One of the stated concerns of the editors of this *Sourcebook of Family Theory and Methods* is to ensure that it does not represent only a U.S.-based view of families and family research

today (see the preface). This is not an easy task, given that much of the theorizing of family sociology recently has come from the United States and from those other developed nations from which academic research in this area is published in the English language. Although none of the authors of Chapter 16 is American, the theoretical perspectives addressed in the chapter come primarily from the United States, with some from Europe, and as such have been developed on the basis of data on U.S. or (less frequently) European populations.

Although the OASIS project was cross-national (conducted in the countries listed above), it included six developed countries, five of which are in Western Europe, all of which have cultures within the Judeo-Christian tradition. The United States inherited family structures and cultural traits from all of these countries. Thus the approach to intergenerational relationships presented in theory and in Chapter 16 is inevitably biased toward a minority of the world's population, despite the authors' claims to the contrary.

Some U.S. publications in English have paid attention to the differences between cultures (Holmes & Holmes, 1995; Keith et al., 1994). It is possibly difficult to find theoretical approaches to intergenerational relationships emanating from less developed countries, and literature in languages other than English may be less accessible. However, it is possible to find descriptive analyses of data relating to such relationships and to references to solidarity, conflict, and ambivalence in populations in Africa (e.g., Keith et al., 1994), South America, Australia (e.g., Kendig, 1986), the Far East (e.g., Chang, 1992; Keasberry, 2002; Wenger & Liu, 1999, 2000), the Middle East, and South

DISCUSSION AND EXTENSION *continued*

Asia (e.g., Bhat & Dhruvarajan, 2001; Kabir, 2001). Such data can give indications about the fit or lack of fit of existing theories in these other areas of the world and suggest hypotheses for testing in a broader context.

It is important for researchers and practitioners in the developed world to understand the patterns, expectations, and obligations that accrue to people from different cultures, because it is from these cultures that immigrants come to the developed world. They become our neighbors, our colleagues, our patients and clients, our customers, and occasionally our in-laws. The recognition of differences between, say, White Baptists in Virginia and White Roman Catholics in Austria is important, but even more difficult to come to grips with are differences between, say, African American Evangelicals in California and Hindus or Muslims or tribal peoples in India. Further, understanding the range of human responses to relationships between generations can help us to understand and theorize better about our own society.

From the U.S. Pacific Coast to the Bosporus, women are generally the kin keepers and those who tend to be expected to take responsibility for the care of other generations. East of the Bosporus, more vulnerable generations are the responsibility of male family members, although often it is female members of the family who provide care. In the East, most marriages are still arranged or influenced by the parents. Women tend to be married into the families, communities, and households of their husbands. Some never or only rarely see their parents again. For such married women, intergenerational relationships are with their children and the older generations of their husbands' families. Women who do not marry are the responsibility of their fathers, then their brothers, then their nephews. Widows become the responsibility of their fathers-in-law, then their brothers-in-law, then their nephews. In the absence of a welfare state, these relationships are critical. The nature of these relationships is likely to be quite different from the same relationships in the West. Some acknowledgment of these differences is important in theorizing intergenerational relationships and should be included in the development of theory.

Family sociology may be able to learn interesting things from anthropology. Anthropologists who study kinship and family relationships have identified different types of kinship structures and terminologies. In classificatory kinship systems, uncles and aunts may be classified as fathers and mothers in some cultures, and cousins as siblings. (Note that the classifications are generational.) Expectations for these relationships are different from those with which we are familiar. These systems of terminology are clearly significant in terms of the rights, duties, and responsibilities as well as the expectations associated with particular types of relationships. For instance, responsibilities to all family elders may fall on all those in a particular kinship position in relation to them, such as children and classificatory children (i.e., nieces and nephews). The situation of all generations under the one-child family policy in China raises another set of questions about intergenerational relationships. Any theory of intergenerational relationships should take into account the wide range of family types, and scholars should recognize that a theory has only limited cultural application until it is tested more widely.

Another area for study is consideration of the intergenerational relationships of elders without children. Those who do not marry or marry but do not have children also have intergenerational relationships. They have relationships with their parents, and many develop close relationships with nieces and nephews, who may be the children of the siblings to whom they are closest. These close relationships can cause ambivalence and conflict—for instance, among mother, aunt, and daughter/niece (Wenger, Scott, & Patterson, 2000). In some more traditional cultures, parents with many children may "give" or

DISCUSSION AND EXTENSION *continued*

assign a child to a childless sibling (as, for example, among Indian Hindus) or assign a child to a grandparent (as is traditional among the Navajo). There are often special kin terms to denote such relationships. Research in Wales has shown that intergenerational relationships between aging parents and adult children become more distant with the passage of time and the need for support (Burholt & Wenger, 1998), which indicates the importance of longitudinal studies and a broader age range of dyads in theory construction.

The study of intergenerational relationships is not new. Social scientists have been concerned about parent-child relationships for a long time. What is a more recent development, as a result of demographic shifts, is the emphasis on older people. Chapter 16 focuses on intergenerational relationships primarily between older people and their adult children—more specifically, not middle-aged parents but old parents and an underlying assumption of the need for care. The whole area of intergenerational relationships includes a much wider range than this, for example: (a) parents and dependent children, parents and (young) adult but not married children, parents and young married children in the family-building phase of the life cycle, parents and the partners and ex-partners of children, and parents and aging children; (b) grandparents and infant grandchildren, grandparents and grandchildren at each of the stages listed

above; and (c) aunts and uncles with their nieces and nephews as above. This age range of relationships between generations also emphasizes the need for a longitudinal theory of intergenerational relationships.

The OASIS project has drawn attention to variation and diversity among countries primarily in Europe, presents a typology of intergenerational relationships, and raises questions concerning the factors that influence differences. It also raises new questions for further exploration and research:

- How do existing theories of intergenerational relationships fit or need to be adjusted or changed to include different cultures and religious contexts and to cover both developed and developing countries?
- Do different types of cultures demand subtheories of intergenerational relationships?
- Do different types of kinship structures and terminologies affect the nature of intergenerational relationships?
- Are intergenerational relationships different for fathers and mothers, sons and daughters?
- What is the nature of intergenerational relationships for families separated by emigration?
- How do intergenerational relationships change over time?

REFERENCES

Aboderin, I. (2004). Modernisation and ageing theory revisited: Current explanations of recent developing world and historical Western shifts in material family support for older people. *Ageing and Society, 24,* 29–50.

Aboderin, I. (in press). Decline in material family support for older people in urban Ghana, Africa: Understanding processes and causes of change. *Journal of Gerontology: Social Sciences.*

Antonucci, T. (1990). Social supports and social relationships. In R. H. Binstock & L. K. George (Eds.), *Handbook of aging and the social sciences* (3rd ed., pp. 205–226). New York: Academic Press.

Becker, G. (1997). *Disrupted lives: How people create meaning in a chaotic world.* Berkeley: University of California Press.

Becker, G., Beyene, Y., Newsom, E., & Mayen, N. (2003). Creating continuity through mutual assistance: Intergenerational reciprocity in four ethnic groups. *Journal of Gerontology: Social Sciences, 58,* 151–159.

Bengtson, V. L. (2001). Beyond the nuclear family: The increasing importance of multi-generational bonds. *Journal of Marriage and Family, 63,* 1–16.

Bengtson, V. L., Giarrusso, R., Mabry, J. B., & Silverstein, M. (2002). Solidarity, conflict, and ambivalence: Complementary or competing perspectives on intergenerational relationships? *Journal of Marriage and Family, 64,* 568–576.

Bengtson, V. L., Lowenstein, A., Putney, N., & Gans, D. (2003). Global aging and the challenge to families. In V. L. Bengtson & A. Lowenstein (Eds.), *Global aging and challenges to families* (pp. 1–24). New York: Aldine de Gruyter.

Bengtson, V. L., & Roberts, R. E. L. (1991). Intergenerational solidarity in aging families: An example of formal theory construction. *Journal of Marriage and the Family, 53,* 856–870.

Bengtson, V. L., & Schrader, S. (1982). Parent-child relations. In D. Mangen & W. A. Peterson (Eds.), *Research instruments in social gerontology* (Vol. 2, pp. 115–186). Minneapolis: University of Minnesota Press.

Bhat, A. K., & Dhruvarajan, R. (2001). Ageing in India: Drifting intergenerational relations, challenges and options. *Ageing and Society, 21,* 621–640.

Blau, P. (1964). *Exchange and power in social life.* New York: John Wiley.

Boss, P. (2004). Ambiguous loss and ambivalence when a parent has dementia. In K. Pillemer & K. Lüscher (Eds.), *Intergenerational ambivalences: New perspectives on parent-child relations in later life* (pp. 207–224). Oxford: Elsevier Science.

Burholt, V., & Wenger, G. C. (1998). Differences over time in older people's relationships with children and siblings. *Ageing and Society, 18,* 537–562.

Chang, P. J. (1992). Implications of changing family structure on old age support in the ESCAP Region. *Asia-Pacific Population Journal, 17*(2), 49–66.

Clarke, E. J., Preston, M., Raskin, J., & Bengtson, V. L. (1999). Types of conflicts and tensions between older parents and adult children. *Gerontologist, 39,* 261–270.

Coleman, J. S. (1988). Social capital in the creation of human capital. *American Journal of Sociology, 94*(Suppl.), S95–S120.

Connidis, I. A. (2002, June 21). *Bring outsiders in: Conceptual and research challenges in the study of gay and lesbian family ties.* Plenary address presented at the International Symposium Reconceptualising Gender and Ageing, University of Surrey, Guildford.

Connidis, I. A., & McMullin, J. A. (2002a). Ambivalence, family ties, and doing sociology. *Journal of Marriage and Family, 64,* 594–601.

Connidis, I. A., & McMullin, J. A. (2002b). Sociological ambivalence and family ties: A critical perspective. *Journal of Marriage and Family, 64,* 558–567.

Daatland, S. O., & Herlofson, K. (2003). "Lost solidarity" or "changed solidarity"? A comparative European view on normative family solidarity. *Ageing and Society, 23,* 537–560.

Dowd, J. J. (1984). Beneficence and the aged. *Journal of Gerontology, 39*(1), 102–108.

Durkheim, É. (1933). *The division of labor in society* (G. Simpson, Trans.). New York: Free Press.

Dwyer, J. W., Lee, G. R., & Jankowski, T. B. (1994). Reciprocity, elder satisfaction, and caregiver stress and burden: The exchange of aid in the family caregiving relationship. *Journal of Marriage and the Family, 56,* 35–43.

Emerson, R. M. (1981). Social exchange theory. In M. Rosenberg & R. H. Turner (Eds.), *Social psychology: Sociological perspectives* (pp. 30–65). New York: Basic Books.

Esping-Anderson, G. (1990). *The three worlds of welfare capitalism.* Cambridge: Polity.

Frankenberg, E., Lillard, L., & Willis, R. J. (2002). Patterns of intergenerational transfers in Southeast Asia. *Journal of Marriage and Family, 64,* 627–641.

Gouldner, A. W. (1960). The norm of reciprocity: A preliminary statement. *American Sociological Review, 25,* 161–178.

Hammersley, M., & Atkinson, P. (1983). *Ethnography: Principles in practice.* London: Tavistock.

Hamon, R. R., & Blieszner, R. (1990). Filial responsibility expectations among adult child older parent pairs. *Journal of Gerontology: Psychological Sciences, 45,* 110–112.

Heider, F. (1958). *The psychology of interpersonal relations.* New York: John Wiley.

Henretta, J. C., Hill, M. S., Li, W., Soldo, B. J., & Wolf, D. A. (1997). Selection of children to provide care: The effect of earlier parental transfers. *Journal of Gerontology: Social Sciences, 52,* 110–119.

Henry, J. (1973). *Pathways to madness.* New York: Random House.

Hirdes, J. P., & Strain, L. A. (1995). The balance of exchange in instrumental support with network members outside the household. *Journal of Gerontology: Social Sciences, 50,* 134–142.

Holmes, E. R., & Holmes, L. D. (1995). *Other cultures, elder years* (2nd ed.). Thousand Oaks, CA: Sage.

Homans, G. C. (1950). *The human group.* New York: Harcourt, Brace & World.

Homans, G. C. (1961). *Social behavior: Its elementary forms.* New York: Harcourt, Brace & World.

Kabir, Z. N. (2001). *The emerging elderly population in Bangladesh: Aspects of their health and social situation.* Stockholm: Karolinska Institute.

Katz, R., Daatland, S. O., Lowenstein, A., Bazo, M. T., Ancizu, I., Herlofson, K., Mehlhausen-Hassoen, D., & Prilutzky, D. (2003). Family norms and preferences in intergenerational relations: A comparative perspective. In V. L. Bengtson & A. Lowenstein (Eds.), *Global aging and challenges to families* (pp. 305–326). New York: Aldine de Gruyter.

Kauh, T. O. (1997). Intergenerational relations: Older Korean-Americans' experiences. *Journal of Cross-Cultural Gerontology, 12,* 245–271.

Keasberry, I. N. (2002). *Elder care, old-age security and social change in rural Yogykarta, Indonesia.* Wageningen, Netherlands: Wageningen University.

Keith, J. (1981). Participant-observation. In C. L. Fry & J. Keith (Eds.), *New methods in old age research.* Chicago: Loyola University Press.

Keith, J., Fry, C. L., Glascock, A. P., Ikels, C., Dickerson-Putman, J., Harpending, H. C., et al. (1994). *The aging experience: Diversity and commonality across cultures.* Thousand Oaks, CA: Sage.

Kendig, H. (1986). *Ageing and families: A support networks perspective.* Sydney: Allen & Unwin.

Kinsella, K. (2000). Demographic dimensions of global aging. *Journal of Family Issues, 21,* 541–558.

Klein, D. M., & White, J. M. (1996). *Family theories: An introduction.* Thousand Oaks, CA: Sage.

Lee, G. R., Peek, C. W., & Coward, R. T. (1998). Race differences in filial responsibility expectations among older parents. *Journal of Marriage and the Family, 60,* 404–412.

Lettke, F., & Klein, D. M. (2004). Methodological issues in assessing ambivalence in intergenerational relations. In K. Pillemer & K. Lüscher (Eds.), *Intergenerational ambivalences: New perspectives on parent-child relations in later life* (pp. 85–114). Oxford: Elsevier Science.

Lorenz-Meyer, D. (2004). The ambivalence of parental care among young German adults. In K. Pillemer & K. Lüscher (Eds.), *Intergenerational ambivalences: New perspectives on parent-child relations in later life* (pp. 225–254). Oxford: Elsevier Science.

Lowenstein, A., Katz, R., Mehlhausen-Hassoen, D., & Prilutzky, D. (2002). *The research instruments in the OASIS project: Old age and autonomy, the role of service systems and intergenerational family solidarity.* Haifa: University of Haifa, Center for Research and Study of Aging.

Lüscher, K. (2000). *Family issues between gender and generations* (Seminar report, European

Observatory on Family Matters). Vienna: Austrian Institute for Family Studies.

Lüscher, K. (2002). Intergenerational ambivalence: Further steps in theory and research. *Journal of Marriage and Family, 64,* 585–593.

Lüscher, K. (2004). Conceptualising and uncovering intergenerational ambivalence. In K. Pillemer & K. Lüscher (Eds.), *Intergenerational ambivalences: New perspectives on parent-child relations in later life* (pp. 23–62). Oxford: Elsevier Science.

Lüscher, K., & Pillemer, K. (1998). Intergenerational ambivalence: A new approach to the study of parent-child relations in later life. *Journal of Marriage and the Family, 60,* 413–425.

Marin, G., & Marin, B. V. (1991). *Research with Hispanic populations.* Newbury Park, CA: Sage.

Marshall, V. W. (2002, November 21). *Solidarity and/or ambivalence?* Paper presented at a symposium during the annual meeting of the Gerontological Society of America, Chicago.

Marshall, V. W., Matthews, S. H., & Rosenthal, C. J. (1993). Elusiveness of family life: A challenge for the sociology of aging. In G. L. Maddox & M. P. Lawton (Eds.), *Annual review of gerontology and geriatrics: Focus on kinship, aging and social change* (pp. 39–72). New York: Springer.

Nye, F. I., & Rushing, W. (1969). Towards family measurement research. In J. Hadden & E. F. Borgatta (Eds.), *Marriage and family.* Itasca, IL: Peacock.

Parrott, T. M., & Bengtson, V. L. (1999). The effects of earlier intergenerational affection, normative expectations, and family conflict on contemporary exchange of help and support. *Research on Aging, 21,* 73–105.

Parsons, T. (1955). The American family: Its relations to personality and the social structure. In T. Parsons & R. F. Bales (Eds.), *Family, socialization and interaction process.* Glencoe, IL: Free Press.

Parsons, T. (1973). Some afterthoughts on *Gemeinschaft* and *Gesellschaft*. In W. J. Cahnman (Ed.), *Ferdinand Tönnies: A new evaluation* (pp. 140–150). Leiden, Netherlands: Brill.

Pauly, M. V. (1990). The rational nonpurchase of long-term care insurance. *Journal of Political Economy, 98,* 153–168.

Pillemer, K., & Suitor, J. J. (2002). Explaining mothers' ambivalence toward their adult children. *Journal of Marriage and Family, 64,* 602–613.

Phillips, J., & Ray, M. (2003). The qualitative phase. In A. Lowenstein & J. Ogg (Eds.), *OASIS: Final report* (pp. 103–126). Haifa: University of Haifa, Center for Research and Study of Aging.

Phillips, J., Ogg, J., & Ray, M., (2003). Ambivalence in intergenerational relations. In A. Lowenstein & J. Ogg (Eds.), *OASIS: Final report* (pp. 193–226). Haifa: University of Haifa, Center for Research and Study of Aging.

Reher, D.S. (1998). Family ties in Western Europe: Persistent contrasts. *Population and Development Review, 24,* 203–234.

Roberts, R. E. L., Richards, L. N., & Bengtson, V. L. (1991). Intergenerational solidarity in families: Untangling the ties that bind. *Marriage and Family Review, 16,* 11–46.

Rossi, A. S., & Rossi, P. H. (1990). *Of human bonding: Parent-child relations across the life course.* Hawthorne, NY: Aldine de Gruyter.

Rubinstein, R. (1987). In-depth interviewing and the structure of its insights. In S. Reinharz & G. Rowles (Eds.), *Qualitative gerontology.* New York: Springer.

Silverstein, M., & Bengtson, V. L. (1994). Does intergenerational social support influence the psychological well-being of older parents? The contingencies of declining health and widowhood. *Social Science & Medicine, 38,* 943–957.

Silverstein, M., & Bengtson, V. L. (1997). Intergenerational solidarity and the structure of adult-child parent relationships in American families. *American Journal of Sociology, 103,* 429–460.

Silverstein, M., Conroy, S., Wang, H., Giarrusso, R., & Bengtson, V. L. (2002). Reciprocity in parent-child relations over the adult life course. *Journal of Gerontology: Social Sciences, 57,* 3–13.

Silverstein, M., Giarrusso, R., Gans, D., & Bengtson, V. L. (in press). Aging parents and adult children: New perspectives on intergenerational relationships. In M. Johnson, V. L. Bengtson, P. Coleman, & T. Kirwood (Eds.), *Cambridge handbook of age and ageing.* Cambridge: Cambridge University Press.

Smith, A. (1790). *The theory of moral sentiments* (6th ed.). Retrieved January 17, 2004, from the Library of Economics and Liberty Web site:http://www.econlib.org/library/Smith/smMS1.html

Sprey, J. (1991). Studying adult children and their parents. In S. K. Pfeifer & M. B. Sussman (Eds.), *Families: Intergenerational and generational connections* (pp. 221–235). Binghamton, NY: Haworth.

Strauss, A. L., & Corbin, J. M. (Eds.). (1997). *Grounded theory in practice.* Thousand Oaks, CA: Sage.

Thibaut, J. W., & Kelley, H. H. (1959). *The social psychology of groups.* New York: John Wiley.

Turner, B. S. (1999). Aging and generational conflicts: A reply to Sarah Irwin. *British Journal of Sociology, 49,* 299–304.

Webster, P. S., & Herzog, A. R. (1995). Effects of parental divorce and memories of family problems on relationships between adult children and their parents. *Journal of Gerontology: Social Sciences, 50,* 24–34.

Wenger, G. C. (1989). Support networks in old age: Constructing a typology. In M. Jeffreys (Ed.), *Growing old in the twentieth century* (pp. 166–185). London: Routledge.

Wenger, G. C., & Liu, J. M. (1999). Support networks in Beijing (China) and Liverpool (UK): Differences and similarities. *Hallym International Journal of Aging, 1*(2), 47–57.

Wenger, G. C., & Liu, J. M. (2000). Family support in Beijing (China) and Liverpool (UK): Differences and similarities. *Hallym International Journal of Aging, 2*(1), 85–91.

Wenger, G. C., Scott, A., & Patterson, N. (2000). How important is parenthood? Childlessness and support in old age in England. *Ageing and Society, 20,* 161–182.

Willson, A. E., Shuey, K. M., & Elder, G. H., Jr. (2003). Ambivalence in the relationship of adult children to aging parents and in-laws. *Journal of Marriage and Family, 65,* 1055–1072.

Wolfe, A. (1989). *Whose keeper? Social science and moral obligations.* Berkeley: University of California Press.

• Part IV

FAMILIES AND LARGER SOCIAL FORCES

• Seventeen

CULTURE, COGNITION, AND PARENTHOOD

Ralph LaRossa, *Georgia State University*

Wendy Simonds, *Georgia State University*

Donald C. Reitzes, *Georgia State University*

THINKING ABOUT THINKING

The central premise of this chapter is that a cognitive pluralistic approach to mental processes can contribute significantly to the development of family social science. A cognitive pluralistic approach ties cognition to culture—with *culture* defined as a "historically transmitted pattern of meanings embodied in symbols" (Geertz, 1973, p. 89)—and assumes that "what goes on inside our heads is affected by the particular *thought communities* to which we happen to belong" (Zerubavel, 1997, p. 9). A cognitive pluralistic approach underscores the fact that across different thought communities, people may perceive things that others may not perceive, focus on issues that others consider immaterial, attach significance to historical moments that elsewhere are deemed ordinary, and collectively remember events that happened before they were born, or maybe never happened at all.

Cognitive pluralism is related to, but notably different from, both cognitive individualism and cognitive universalism. Cognitive individualism examines the cognitive inclinations and skills of a specific person, and cognitive universalism looks at the cognitive abilities of humankind. By contrast, cognitive pluralism essentially is about the social manufacture and distribution of ideas. Taken together, cognitive pluralism, cognitive individualism, and cognitive universalism encompass the field of cognitive science.

The theoretical roots of cognitive pluralism may be traced to symbolic interactionism, as well as to cultural studies, social phenomenology, and the sociology of knowledge. Among the first symbolic interactionists, the two who were the most influential, Charles Horton Cooley and George Herbert Mead, were clearly cognitive in their orientation. Cooley (1902/1956) went so far as to argue that "the imaginations which people have of one

Authors' Note: We appreciate the written comments on this chapter provided by Katherine R. Allen, Vern L. Bengtson, Bernard Nauck, Constance L. Shehan, and Gloria D. Warren.

another are the *solid facts* of society, and that to observe and interpret these must be a chief aim of sociology" (p. 121). George Herbert Mead (1934, p. 156) repeatedly strove to connect the study of society to the study of mind and the self, and maintained that only by taking the attitude of the whole community can a person think at all. Max Weber and Émile Durkheim, in their historical and comparative works, also examined the relationship between communal thought and collective action. Weber (1904–1905) moved culture from the periphery to the center in the theorizing process, advancing the proposition that the intersubjective world is not simply an epiphenomenon but a powerful explanatory variable. Durkheim (1915) showed how consciousness could be studied at the aggregate level and how classificatory schemata (e.g., divisions between the sacred and profane) contribute to both solidarity and conflict. The early phenomenologists Alfred Schutz (1962) and Harold Garfinkel (1967) called for the investigation of the epistemologies of everyday life and motivated scholars to explore how social realities are constructed, objectified, and internalized (see also Berger & Luckmann, 1966). Critics of social phenomenology—Erving Goffman (1974) among them—contributed as well to the development of cultural pluralism by elucidating how complex and multilayered intersubjectivities can be. Finally, the subfield generally referred to as the sociology of knowledge is predicated on cognitive pluralistic principles. In his introductory volume, published some time ago, Karl Mannheim (1929/1936) outlined the three branches of cognitive science when he made the point that it is imperative to study not only how isolated individuals think or how humans in general think, but also how people "in certain groups" think. "The principal thesis of the sociology of knowledge," stated Mannheim, "is that there are modes of thought which cannot be adequately understood as long as their social origins are obscured" (p. 2).

A variety of family research projects rely, at least in part, on cognitive pluralism. Examples may be found in family-centered

theoretical reviews of symbolic interactionism, phenomenology, feminism, and the life-course perspective (see Boss, Doherty, LaRossa, Schumm, & Steinmetz, 1993). For the most part, however, cognitive pluralistic principles are not applied in family social science as much as they could be. We would like to see this change.

Although cognitive pluralism can be useful in any area of family studies, in this chapter we show how the orientation can be applied to the study of parenthood. We further restrict our discussion to several key phases of parenthood, namely, parenting decision making, pregnancy and birth, and infant care. Our goal is not to offer an exhaustive review, but to demonstrate the theoretical value of an approach that we hope to advance.

MINDS AND SOCIETIES

Mental processes may be divided into six interrelated cognitive acts: perceiving, focusing, classifying, symbolizing, timing, and remembering (Zerubavel, 1997; for a similar, although not identical, set of acts, see Cerulo, 2002). From a cognitive pluralistic perspective, the basic question is, How are the cognitive acts connected to thought communities; that is, how are minds and societies linked?

Perceiving

Although people live in a physical environment that they are able to sense (i.e., touch, hear, smell, taste, and see), they also are immersed in an interpretive world (Blumer, 1969, p. 11). The English letter *A* on a chalkboard is not on the chalkboard at all but in the minds of the English-reading community. People can see the scribbled lines, but they must interpret what they see in order to "know" that the lines are an *A*. Thus *perceiving* (not to be equated with seeing) is a mediated act.

Some of what people perceive can be understood in cognitive universalistic terms. Newborns, for example, "know" how to suckle. Most of what people perceive, however, is contingent on *optical socialization,* a process that entails being taught both "what to look at" and "what to ignore." A 4-year-old child at a restaurant who turns and gawks at a diner in the next booth often is instructed to stop. An adult doing the same would be considered an *optical deviant* (Zerubavel, 1997).

Focusing

Cognition also involves the ability to define some things as foreground and other things as background. A teacher's directive "Please look at the board" generally refers to the information available in the writing on the board rather than to the board itself. Whether the board is black or white is irrelevant and not supposed to be "in focus." With a very different thought community, however, the shade of what is in view can be paramount. If someone at a pro-segregation rally were to say, "Look at *that* guy," color would be highly relevant—perhaps *the* object of focus. In a significant sense, racial profiling is politically motivated focusing.

Another way to conceptualize focusing is to employ a *framing* metaphor (Goffman, 1974; see also Zerubavel, 1991, pp. 10–13). Swiveling a picture frame (absent a picture) a few degrees shifts some objects from "in frame" to "out of frame." When one person accuses another of making an irrelevant point in an argument, the comment in question is pushed "out of frame." The power to decide what should be in frame clearly is an important factor in society. Patriarchy rests, in part, on men's inordinate control over how women's issues are framed in political circles.

Classifying

Creating boundaries, or *classifying,* is built on the complementary processes of lumping and splitting. As Zerubavel (1991) describes it: "On the one hand, it involves grouping 'similar' items together in a single mental cluster. At the same time, it also involves separating in our mind 'different' mental clusters from one another" (p. 21). Thus in some thought communities, lambs are considered groceries and dogs are not, despite the fact that both may be lumped together as sources of protein. From a cognitive pluralistic perspective, the boundaries between and around objects are social constructions residing in an intersubjective world. To apprehend these boundaries, or any other social phenomena, "*as if* they were something else than human products" is to *reify* them (Berger & Luckmann, 1966, p. 89).

Creating boundaries also involves the application of what may be called "the law of the excluded middle." Carving boundaries out of the flux of human experience means separating physically proximate objects from one another. In order to lend legitimacy to arbitrary distinctions, thought communities mentally work to emphasize the distances between lumps or groupings (Zerubavel, 1991, pp. 21, 46). Gender stratification hinges not only on the separation of babies into girls and boys—two nonoverlapping categories—but also on the bipolarization of presumed male and female "traits" (Kessler & McKenna, 1978).

Boundary work, in addition, entails boundary transcendence: norms and regulations for moving from one grouping to the next, and perhaps back again (Nippert-Eng, 1996). "Rites of passage" (Van Gennep, 1960) allow travel across a mental divide while reinforcing the social facticity of that divide.

Symbolizing

A woman enters a room with an infant dressed in pink, and others in the room conclude that the child is a girl. In their judgment, pink means—or *symbolizes*—girl. This association, however, is not universal, for the meanings of colors vary across cultures and time. The process of "gendering" an infant on the basis of what the child wears assigns meanings to the child, but the meanings arise from the work that people *do* (West & Zimmerman, 1987).

Central to symbolizing is the social construction of identities, or *identifying.*

Identifying entails two cognitive subprocesses, *identification of* and *identification with,* both of which require the affirmation of others in order to be successful (Stone, 1962, p. 90). "Identification of" announces or establishes *who* the person is. It signifies the appropriate meanings that characterize a person and cognitively connects that person to other similarly identified persons. "Identification of" also is related to the "presentation of self" (Goffman, 1959). A mother may "present" her "self" verbally or nonverbally, either by saying, "Did you know that I'm a mother?" or by wearing a button emblazoned with a child's picture or a necklace made of colored macaroni. "Identification with" announces or establishes the *extent* of a person's involvement or investment in an identity. A man who covers the walls of his office with pictures of his children announces the salience of his identity as a father. "Identification of" and "identification with" enable mothers and fathers to perceive connections with other parents and to discern what is distinctive about their own parenting.

Timing

People often mistakenly assume that time is *only* a physical reality, a flowing river of sorts that individuals hop into when they are born and hop out of when they die. Astronomers also seem to talk about time exclusively in a material sense when they refer to how many years the universe has existed, or include the speed of light—700 million miles per hour or 186,000 miles per second—in mathematical equations ($E = mc^2$). When it comes to time, however, the physical and the social are fused. Years, hours, and seconds are mental constructs, as are weeks, months, decades, centuries, and millennia.

Time reckoning—or *timing,* for short—is "one of the most central dimensions of the social world" (Zerubavel, 1981, p. ix; see also Daly, 1996). The yearly calendar or schedule—with its division of days, weeks, and months—allows for mental "lumps" to be designated as work time and family time, or

public time and private time. Likewise, synchrony in groups—indispensable to many religious and secular celebrations and a source of solidarity—would be harder to achieve were it not for clocks and calendars.

Remembering

The process of remembering is crucial to thinking, and to survival. Without the capacity to store experiences, humans would find the simplest tasks to be perpetual challenges. More than an isolated act, however, *remembering* is a social endeavor, because people do not always naturally remember; rather, they are often taught what to recall. Different *rules of remembrance* and variable forms of *mnemonic socialization* help to explain why one nation's report of an episode can diverge from another nation's description of presumably the same event. Collective memories are instrumental to a country's identity and pride (Zerubavel, 1997, 2003).

Identity and pride in families also rely on narrative elements. Holiday dinners are *autobiographical occasions* (Vinitzky-Seroussi, 2000) during which relatives "relive" what they have been doing since they were last together. Children are fed anecdotes—"memory bites"—about their grandparents to connect them to their ancestors. When intimate partners separate, they often give conflicting *vocabularies of motives* (Mills, 1940) for why their relationship failed (Hopper, 1993).

Plotlines in historical narratives can vary as well. A *progressive story* says that things were better at time 2 than they were at time 1, whereas a *regressive story* says that things were better at time 1 than they were at time 2 (Zerubavel, 2003; see also Gergen & Gergen, 1997). Chronicles of how parenthood has changed generally employ one of these plotlines or a combination of the two. Also, it may be asked, at what temporal point does the "true" story about something begin? Family members often periodize chronicles to suit their own purpose, with each side *mnemonically decapitating* self-incriminating elements from the past (Zerubavel, 1997).

THE SOCIAL REALITIES
OF PARENTHOOD

The full benefits of cognitive pluralism become evident only when the six cognitive acts, considered as a whole, are applied to a substantive topic. How do these acts, operating together and in relationship with culture, expose the social realities of parenthood?

Parenting Decision Making

For as long as humans have recognized the connections between particular sexual activities, pregnancy, and having a baby, they have sought to mediate or control the terms of these connections. Scholars have explored, for example, how perceptions of abortion can vary and change. Research indicates, for example, that it was not until the beginning of the mid-19th century that abortion was classified as a moral issue in the United States (Luker, 1984) and that, up until the 1950s, contraception was lumped with abortion and framed as a morally deviant act rather than as a responsible antidote to abortion (Luker, 1997).

Scholars also have elucidated how thinking about bodies, personhood, gender, and rights contributes to cultural notions about abortion. Sonography and high-tech methods of photographing the interiors of people's bodies have altered how pregnancy is conceptualized. Representing a fetus as a baby, as opposed to part of a woman's body, means focusing on the inside of the woman's body, visually denying and thus disconfirming the woman's existence (Hartouni, 1997, pp. 66–67). Using sonograms, antiabortion activists have succeeded in cognitively "lumping" fetuses with babies and in "splitting" fetuses and babies from women (Isaacson, 1996). They have also "split" fetuses and babies from women to classify and symbolize babies (but not women) as entities worthy of sympathy—to be portrayed as helpless, innocent, endangered. Abortion workers and abortion rights activists strive to void such language and narratives by refocusing viewpoints to make women central (Simonds, 1996).

In her work on differential procreative rights for White women and women of color, Dorothy Roberts (1997) has unpacked conventional framing techniques and made historical connections to reveal a racist ideology underlying a wide range of state policies impeding procreative freedom in the United States. She notes that, since the country's origin, Black women and other women of color have been denied procreative rights and publicly symbolized as inadequate mothers. For instance, White women are as likely as Black women to use drugs that can harm fetuses during pregnancy, yet they are far less likely than Black women to be arrested and publicly vilified for doing so (Roberts, 1997, pp. 175–178). Medical evidence also challenges media claims that crack use during pregnancy is as dire for babies as was reported in the late 1980s and 1990s. Nonetheless, Roberts notes, "the image of the crack baby—trembling in a tiny hospital bed, permanently brain-damaged, and on his way to becoming a parasitic criminal—is indelibly etched in the American psyche" (p. 159). The "crack baby" also became a racist symbol of Black women as deficient, even lethal, mothers.

Similarly, Julien S. Murphy's (2001) discussion of physicians' freedom to discriminate against lesbians seeking donor insemination services (by refusing to treat them) and Susan E. Dalton's (2001) critique of second-parent adoption laws have helped to reveal institutional perceiving, classifying, and focusing practices. Law and medicine have framed heterosexual marriage as *the* morally valid structure for mediating adult sexuality and child rearing. Taking this family form for granted, medical and legal agents ironically view the denial of equal services as ethical rather than discriminatory.

Another approach to understanding the cognitive significance of parenthood is to consider the ramifications of its undesired absence. In her analysis of new reproductive technologies, Gay Becker (2000) shows how women and men experience infertility differently. The quest for a child becomes a symbolic representation of people's commitment to a broad spectrum of societal ideas regarding gender, genetic procreation, "normal" adulthood, and happiness. Monica Casper's (1996) investigation of fetal surgery similarly reminds us of how perceiving, focusing, symbolizing, and timing can be used to coerce women into having surgeries that are not in their best interests because of the health risks involved—surgeries that are motivated by a profound devotion to achieving one particular outcome: a biological child.

Ways of defining and framing the value of relationships influence whether infertility is classified as culturally acceptable or unacceptable. For instance, the popularity of donor insemination has declined with the advent of techniques of sperm and egg manipulation that, although less successful, offer the slight chance of preserving men's biological parenthood. Becker (2000) describes how the timing of various procedures socializes couples experiencing infertility into the process of medicalization. Repeated failures may cause couples to shift their focus from achieving genetic parenthood to achieving parenthood through adoption. Roberts (1997) proposes that African Americans are more critical than Whites of genetic thinking and of medicalization. Black women are about twice as likely as White women to experience unwanted infertility, yet they are less likely to have financial access to medical treatments and less likely to trust such treatments. They also are less likely to view the achievement of genetic parenthood as a solution to infertility. Black women thus are a resistant thought community striving to offer a critique of contemporary classifications of parenthood, fertility, and infertility.

Pregnancy and Birth

Cognitive pluralism also can be applied to pregnancy and birth. Scholars have closely examined the belief systems inherent in obstetrics and midwifery; contrasted the ways in which doctors and midwives focus, perceive, classify, and symbolize women, women's bodies, pregnancy, and birth (and the ways these conceptualizations vary with time and culture); and articulated how social timing and scheduling impact all aspects of procreative and parenting experiences (e.g., see Martin, 1987/1992; Rothman, 1982/1991; Simonds, 2002).

Barbara Katz Rothman (1986) has demonstrated how prenatal testing—an unquestioned aspect of obstetric thinking—affects women's perceptions of pregnancy. She found that women who had amniocentesis were prone to delay feeling fetal movement and wearing maternity clothes or publicly acknowledging their pregnancies until they received negative test results (i.e., results that showed no signs of genetic anomalies). Coining the term "tentative pregnancy" to refer to this phenomenon, Rothman shows how cognitive shifts in perceiving and focusing can be imposed by a powerful thought community and how these social cognitions can shape people's bodily experiences. Medicine generally views the baby as the most important outcome or product (testable in utero); in other words, in a medical frame, pregnancy and birth precede what "truly matters." Midwifery, on the other hand, focuses on process (while not ignoring outcome). Pregnancy and birth are something women *do;* that is, they are activities that shape not only fetuses but also women themselves. Dutch midwives, for example, lament how prenatal testing "spoils the pregnancy" (Rothman, 1998/2001, p. 183). Such a characterization would be unlikely among obstetricians, who generally focus intensively on birth outcomes.

THE EVOLUTION OF PARENTING

David C. Bell, *Affiliated Systems Corporation*

Evolution occurs because of genetic changes that affect physical structures. The brain is one of these structures, so that psychological and social processes also undergo evolutionary change (Tooby & Cosmides, 1992). Evolution is the cumulative effect of small mutations that increase the probability that an organism will survive to pass on the underlying genes. These mutations in most cases make an existing system more complex, but at the same time they preserve the original functions of the system. Like other evolving social processes, parenting shows both change and continuity.

Animals in all species can produce offspring, but only mammals routinely act like parents—that is, feeding and caring for their children. *All* mammals can be parents in this sense, but the quality, extent, and distribution of parenting differ among mammals (Bell, 2001). In some species, such as rabbits, parenting is limited to mothers and to feeding. Among rats, mothers retrieve wandering pups as well as feed them. In some herd animals, parenting extends further, to protection of own and other offspring. In canines, parenting is performed by mothers, fathers, and other relatives and includes feeding, retrieval, protection, and emotional support. In humans, parenting is provided by mothers, fathers, and unrelated persons and encompasses the meeting of a wide range of physical, emotional, and social needs in the child. The fundamental psychological principles of the caregiving system as evolved in humans are the parent's empathy and felt responsibility for the child.

In the 1950s, John Bowlby began to present a view of the parent-child relationship in evolutionary terms (see Bowlby, 1982). He identified an "attachment behavioral control system" in the child and a "caregiving behavioral control system" in the parent. This early speculation about parental and child psychology was subsequently substantiated by brain researchers, who have identified separate attachment and caregiving circuits in all mammalian brains (Panksepp, 1998). The brains of human females on the average have a greater number of neurons in their caregiving systems than do the brains of men, and they increase this advantage during pregnancy. However, both men and women develop additional caregiving neurons as a result of physical contact and interaction (Hrdy, 1999). Thus fathers who hold their infants and interact with their children develop additional caregiving neurons, as do lovers who hold each other.

Parental caregiving is not just biological. All humans have the gene to produce a caregiving structure for parenting in the brain, but not all humans become good parents. As humans live in a social environment, their genes are also expressed in a social environment. The caregiving structure in the brain will emerge fully functional if the prenatal environment is congenial, so that genes are "turned on" in the developing fetus at the appropriate time and underlying brain structures are laid down; if appropriate social or other environmental stimulation occurs that leads the brain structures to consolidate and develop; and if there is no trauma (such as the death of a parent or rejection by a parent). Once all biological prerequisites are in place, responsive caregiving will be expressed if an emotional caring bond develops to the child and if the person has the resources to carry out the intention to give care.

(continued)

● *SPOTLIGHT ON THEORY continued*

Furthermore, caregiving is not just an individual phenomenon. As good parents are motivated by their caregiving neurosystems to nurture their children, social norms arise mandating that all parents *should* nurture their children. For those parents whose caregiving neurosystems have not developed or are misdirected because other motivations are dominant, social norms provide further impetus toward nurturance of the child.

NOTE: An extended discussion of this topic with additional references can be found on this volume's companion Web site (http://www.ncfr.org/sourcebook). ●

Taking a historical approach, Jo Murphy-Lawless (1998) has outlined how the obstetrical world developed a perception of itself as a "science with a provable logical basis" in relation to women and fetuses. Obstetricians classified birth as profoundly painful and dangerous, and presented themselves as "the sole experts" who could offer an antidote to suffering and pathology (p. 6). Obstetricians purported that they could rescue women from death when they claimed birth as solely their arena around the end of the 19th century. (Ironically, at that time physicians had not yet accepted germ theory, and obstetricians were far more likely than midwives to cause puerperal fever.) They also denounced midwives as unfit providers, symbolizing midwifery as a dirty, backward, premodern artifact in contrast to obstetrics as a rational, progressive, status-conveying practice (Murphy-Lawless, 1998; Rothman, 1982/1991). Joseph B. DeLee's (1920) article in the inaugural issue of the *Journal of Obstetrics and Gynecology* epitomizes obstetric thinking in the early 20th century (Rothman, 1982/1991, pp. 57–58). According to DeLee, for women, being in labor is like being impaled with a pitchfork, and for the infant, it is like having the head slammed in a door (pp. 39–40). This perception of labor and birth cast doctors' interventions as crucial acts of rescue in a race against danger and pathology—a line of thought that persists to this day.

Gertrude Fraser (1998) conducted interviews with older Black Virginians in one town to document the ways that they remembered the shift from home to hospital birth and from midwifery to obstetrics. Her informants located temporal changes in women's and newborns' physiologies, casting herbal remedies and midwifery as uniquely appropriate to bodies of the past and obstetrics as appropriate to bodies of the present. In this way, they accepted the present and remembered the past without fully invalidating it. Although they expressed nostalgia for some long-ago elements, they focused on the shift to hospital births as an achievement of equal access to health care that was once denied Blacks—and so perceived it as remediation of racial injustice rather than as a hegemonic system of control (as some feminists have done).

Women's health care activism led to shifts in self-presentation—if not ideology—within the obstetric community. Hospital rooms now look like hotel rooms; "labor" is not split from "delivery"; doctors and nurses no longer automatically drug laboring women with amnesiacs and strap them to hospital beds. But current medical methods of time reckoning during pregnancy demonstrate that the power dynamics between procreating women and obstetrics—and the perceptions, classifications, and symbols that shape them—have not changed all that much. In the 1950s, obstetricians took Friedman's curve, a statistical measure of average lengths of parts of labor and birth, and made it into a standard with which birthing women still must contend (Rothman, 1982/1991). Today, superimposed time constraints still serve as the rationale for medical intervention during pregnancy and birth, despite medical evidence that such interventions create rather than remove risks (Simonds, 2002). Medical thinking often involves the reification of rigid time measurement, because controlling time means being able to manage patients' bodies in ways that doctors believe are in women's best interests. Research has shown, however, that these practices lead to more invasive deliveries and cesarean sections, and to higher rates of morbidity for women and babies, than do in-home or birth-center births or hospital births attended by midwives (Gaskin, 2003; Goer, 1995).

Infant Care

It generally is recognized that human infants are relatively helpless, requiring a tremendous amount of attention in order to survive. The concentration directed to infants, and the prioritization of their apparent needs, demonstrates how social focusing lies at the heart of any infant care system. Also interesting is how much the level of focusing can vary, depending on the circumstances and the values and beliefs of the people involved. In a neonatal intensive care unit (NICU), for example, the quantity and quality of focusing can be extremely high, with the babies occupying much of the staff's attention. But it can be extremely low, too. Removing a terminally ill child from life support may be defined as a shift in the hospital's focus vis-à-vis that child.

The social world of the NICU can also be mentally different for parents than it is for the hospital staff. Whereas the doctors and nurses perceive a complex range of objects and rely on subtle divisions of labor, the optical spectrum of the parents is much more restrictive. Staff members, for example, make fine distinctions among residents, fellows, attendings, and consultants. Mothers and fathers, on the other hand, are likely to lump these collectivities into a single category, with the result that the parents may perceive the comings and goings in the NICU "as 'noise' rather than as different, but orderly and predictable, patterns" (Heimer & Staffen, 1998, p. 69).

Social constructions of time and memory are also important in the NICU. Having a baby generally is viewed as the beginning of a long-term commitment. In the NICU environment, however, a different sociotemporal reality may be enforced, in that parents often are "urged by hospital staff members not to think about the future and the uncertainties it holds but instead to take things one day at a time" (Heimer & Staffen, 1998, pp. 335–336). What is remembered or narrated is central to how the NICU operates as well. When briefing parents, staff members are likely to keep technical jargon to a minimum and to discard or modify "bad news" if it appears the parents are not ready to be told "the awful truth." When a family ultimately confronts the fact that a baby will die, the positive stories told about the child ("She put up a great fight") and self-sustaining vocabularies of motive offered for the decision to "let her go" are instrumental to the family's identity and pride.

The moment a newborn leaves the hospital, household members quickly discover, or are soon reminded, how much an infant can change people's lives. It is not just the level of attention directed to infants but also the seemingly unrelenting nature of that attention, in that infant care systems typically are set up as *continuous coverage social systems*. Thus, similar to other organizations that provide round-the-clock care (e.g., fire departments in major cities), someone *always* must be either "on duty" or "on call" (LaRossa & LaRossa, 1981; Zerubavel, 1979). Because one person alone cannot *be there* 24 hours a day, 7 days a week, continuous coverage social systems rely on a division of labor to give people "downtime" while still getting the job done.

Who does *what, when, how,* and *why* in infant care is of utmost importance to infants, parents, and the community at large. From a cognitive pluralistic perspective, thinking about the division of infant care does more than reflect a division of infant care; it creates the division of infant care. First, what does infant care look like? Does picking up a crying baby constitute care? Might there be occasions when *not* holding a baby would be perceived as care? (For a critical look at the concept of care, see Dressel & Clark, 1990.) Second, how do people know when they or others are engaged in care? Research indicates that mothers and fathers overestimate their own involvement and minimize how much their partners interact with (or do for) their children (Deutsch, Lozy, & Saxon, 1993). One study found that, in earlier times, research on father involvement relied almost exclusively on women's self-reports, thus undervaluing men's connections with their daughters and sons (LaRossa & Reitzes, 1995). Another study, concentrating on the present day, found that "fathers were not useful sources of information for the routines of family life." Men seemed to know little about daily home activities, and "most of what they knew came from their wives" (Lareau, 2000, p. 407).

Cognitive pluralists would argue that reports of parental behavior are historical narratives—*stories* of what fathers and mothers have done while enacting their parental roles (LaRossa, 1995). During the transition to parenthood, narratives can play a significant part in how infant care is divided. The accounts that parents offer for reneging on promises to take care of middle-of-the-night feedings serve not only to defuse tensions but also to facilitate change. At first, the accounts help to mend the break between culture and conduct. Over time, however, as the accounts for "not doing enough" are repeatedly offered and subsequently honored, expectations fall in line with behavioral patterns, negating the need to explain the misconduct. Thus the traditionalization that occurs in some families during the first few months postpartum, whereby mothers take on an increasingly greater share of the infant care load, can be fueled by the *child-care tales* that fathers and mothers relate to each other (LaRossa & LaRossa, 1981).

ISSUES IN NEED OF FURTHER RESEARCH

Childhood Memories

A central proposition in the parenthood field is that fathers and mothers will remember how they were brought up and use their own parents as positive or negative role models when they interact with their own children (e.g., see Daly, 1993). It is difficult, however, to gauge the accuracy of people's reports about how they were raised. Historical narratives are invariably tied to the politics of identity; consequently, we generally do not know how much the stories parents tell about their upbringing are based on who they think they are or on who they would like to be. We thus would ask, as Milkie, Simon, and Powell (1997) have, "Do children's perceptions and evaluations of maternal and paternal roles reflect their parents' actual behavior or their selective perceptions of those behaviors—both of which are shaped by cultural beliefs about motherhood and fatherhood?" (p. 235).

Studies have found that men's interactions with children sometimes are not remembered. Fathers and kids in public settings, for example, may not make an impression on people's minds. One explanation is that "men-interacting-with-kids" is outside the mental lens that people generally use to perceive parenthood: "[Because] most people have schemas that associate young children with women, . . . everyday observations of men with young children may go unnoticed or may be interpreted as exceptional events" (Amato, 1989, p. 987).

Rather than accepting at face value what people say about their own fathers or mothers, researchers would do well to examine the contents of the narratives themselves. What kinds of stories are being told? What differences appear by race and class, or by historical period? How are the stories connected to past and future identities?

The Parental Division of Labor

The division of labor in families is directly related to power dynamics and levels of satisfaction and well-being (Walker, 1999). At the center of the issue is the question of fairness. What is considered "fair" comes down to the measurement of the parity of activities on the one hand and the parity of opportunities and constraints on the other. A parity-of-activities measure would count tasks and determine whether they are equally distributed. A parity-of-opportunities-and-constraints measure would not only count tasks but also assess the relative difficulty of the tasks (e.g., messy diapers would register higher than nonmessy diapers). When opportunities and constraints are entered into the equation, as they often are, what is fair and what is not fair is open to debate (LaRossa & LaRossa, 1981; Rapoport & Rapoport, 1975).

● *SPOTLIGHT ON METHODS*

STUDYING FOSTER AND ADOPTIVE PARENT-CHILD RELATIONSHIPS

Katharine P. Leslie, *Brand New Day Consulting, Pittsboro, North Carolina*

Foster and adopted children who have been exposed to early traumatization in their birth homes often find it effortful, awkward, and frightening to use parent-child relationships as a positive context for development, and as a result they suffer from a variety of developmental and relationship problems. These problems often persist even when the children are placed in healthy, safe environments with surrogate parents.

Many books and journal articles have described the developmental problems of traumatized children and why they occur. However, little information is available concerning the relationship problems of these children, particularly in their relationships with surrogate parents, and the transactional effects that traumatized children have on the parents. For example, we know little about why many foster and adoptive parents find relationships with traumatized children stressful and unsatisfying. After all, many birth children also engage in undesirable behaviors, and parents still find their relationships with these children satisfying.

It is a fact that traumatized children's negative behaviors differ from those of non-traumatized children in terms of quantity, intensity, duration, frequency, and maturity level, and that some of traumatized children's behaviors are actually abusive. But, in addition to experiencing these negative behaviors, foster and adoptive parents feel taken advantage of by these children; they give but the children do not give back. And they sense that their foster/adopted children do not love them. There is no reciprocity, which makes sense—if traumatized children are not exposed to positive family functioning in their birth homes, then their negative social engagement capacities become solidified and their positive social engagement capacities are not developed or become damaged. This results in the lack of a repertoire of positive relationship behaviors, which appears to be more disturbing to foster and adoptive parents than a plethora of negative behaviors.

Furthermore, it appears that reducing the quality and quantity of these children's negative behaviors through appropriate parenting strategies and/or medication does not automatically increase or activate the children's positive social engagement capacities.

(continued)

• SPOTLIGHT ON METHODS *continued*

This is most likely because negative and positive behaviors are not on a single continuum. A single continuum implies that the more positive behaviors one employs, the fewer negative behaviors one employs, and vice versa. Instead, positive and negative behaviors are on two separate continua (they are exclusive factors), each of which ranges from high to low. Furthermore, we can infer from this conceptualization that behavior checklists are insufficient instruments for capturing the whole nature of the child (any child), because they indicate only presence or absence of negative behaviors; they do not indicate presence or absence of positive behaviors.

It is also hypothesized that the child's positive behaviors, as opposed to negative behaviors, predict relationship quality. In other words, if a child exhibits high or low levels of negative behaviors and high levels of positive behaviors, the relationship quality will be good. Conversely, if a child exhibits low or high levels of negative behaviors and low levels of positive behaviors, the relationship quality will be poor. This may explain the lack of satisfaction in parent-child relationships between surrogate parents and traumatized children, and the high incidence of foster and adoptive placement disruptions, even with children who exhibit low levels of negative behaviors.

To study the parent-child relationships of traumatized children, then, scholars need to identify the negative behaviors and the positive behaviors that the children are and are not demonstrating. However, no tool exists that describes these positive behaviors (what children are supposed to give/provide/reciprocate in parent-child relationships that creates in others the knowledge and feeling of being loved and that presumably leads to relationship satisfaction). In research aimed at creating such a tool, 70 parents of non-traumatized children completed a survey in which they were asked to list five behaviors that their children bring into the parent-child relationship that make them happy, satisfied, or proud to be the parent (70 equaled saturation). Their answers were analyzed for redundancy and relationship orientation (personal attributes were removed) and then sorted into categories. The result is a new survey tool that researchers and practitioners can use (a) as a companion to behavior checklists when studying and/or assessing child functioning and relationship quality of traumatized children and their significant others, (b) to educate and support parents, and (c) to encourage and inform a therapeutic practice of coaching child clients in executing positive behaviors (as opposed to extinguishing negative behaviors). •

The manner in which parents classify care activities determines how much work they *imagine* themselves and others to be doing. All other things being equal, the more elements in an act, the more effort the parent will feel he or she has expended to complete the act. How much effort the parent perceives he or she has expended will determine how much the parent believes he or she is owed, and the relative balance or imbalance in the "exchange" will affect child well-being and parental satisfaction. Lesbian couples, for example, report a more equal division of child care than do heterosexual couples, and the greater the sharing, the better adjusted are the children and the more satisfied are the parents (Patterson, 1995). How parents and children in different thought communities "lump" and "split" family care is an important issue.

Child Development

In the early 20th century, child psychologists advanced the notion that the stages of childhood should be divided into smaller and smaller increments. In sociotemporal terms, the life course of children was *chronometricalized*. Whereas before, parents were told to monitor their children's maturation on a yearly basis, experts increasingly encouraged fathers and mothers to plot their children's growth and development on a monthly basis, especially when the children were very young. Because specialists in metropolitan areas were the first to adopt growth charts, children living in large cities were more likely to be perceived in chronometrical terms. Conversely, the Great Depression mitigated the extent to which parents chronometricalized their children's lives. When financial survival was at stake, developmental nuances were less salient (LaRossa & Reitzes, 2001).

How parents perceive and classify their children can have impacts on both children and parents. Children whose growth and development are meticulously observed may get a sense that they are special, but they may also feel burdened by the scrutiny. Parents who analyze their children's every move may believe that they are doing whatever they can for their daughters and sons, but they may also become exhausted by the intensity of attention they are providing.

Chronometricalization is especially intense during hospital labor and delivery, when the fetus's and then the newborn's development is assiduously charted. An expanding chronometricalized hospital culture is one of the factors that have contributed in recent years to the significant increase in the numbers of cesarean births. With the status of a fetus measured literally by the second, hospital staff have more opportunities to perceive danger (where often there is none). Might the same thing happen once a baby is born? If an infant's development is plotted on a daily or weekly basis, are new parents more likely to live in a state of apprehension?

FUTURE THEORY BUILDING

Culture has been a central variable in the social sciences for years. Typically, however, it has been studied as a dependent rather than an independent variable. Thus scholars have often examined how the economy influences culture but have not as often investigated how culture influences the economy. These two orientations capture the difference between the *sociology of culture* and *cultural sociology* (Alexander, 2003; see also Griswold, 1994).

Family theorists who take a cognitive pluralistic perspective should recognize the value of both orientations. Clearly, it is important to understand how demographic factors, or economic or technological change, may alter how people classify families. Different racial and ethnic groups conceptualize parenthood in a variety of ways. New medical machinery and the creation of psychometrics have reconfigured pregnancy and infant care. It is equally important, however, to study how cultural shifts can reshape racial and ethnic dividing lines and set in motion social change. The 2000 U.S. Census allowed Americans, for the first time, to classify themselves as multiracial or multiethnic. Feminist reconstructions of the birth process transformed how hospitals organize labor and delivery.

Although we believe that it is critical to acknowledge the reciprocal relationship between culture and other structures, we also believe that, in the immediate future, the most challenging theoretical work within a cognitive pluralistic perspective lies in explaining how culture and cognition construct social life. Two key elements are vital to such an effort (see Alexander, 2003). The first is a commitment to mapping the complexities of culture and cognition. Thus we would encourage scholarship that shows not just how perceiving *or* focusing influences the social life of families but how perceiving, focusing, classifying, symbolizing, timing, and remembering, *operating together*, structure family relationships. The closest we have come to illustrating this process in this chapter is in our discussion of what happens in neonatal intensive care units. The same kind of manifold analysis, however, could be applied to other domains. Disciplining a child, for example, involves creating misbehavior by perceiving, focusing on, and classifying a particular slice of a child's life. The value of what the child has done is simultaneously assessed, through symbolizing, and judgments are made about the timing of the misbehavior in question ("Your actions would have been okay at 2:00 P.M., but not at 2:00 A.M."). Finally, the reasons for—or stories about—the child's conduct are offered and then either accepted or rejected, thus determining (or, more accurately, producing) the child's level of guilt.

The second key element in explaining how culture and cognition construct social life is a research agenda that places a premium on the close study of people's words. From a cognitive pluralistic perspective, "an understanding of language is essential for any understanding of the reality of everyday life" (Berger & Luckmann, 1966, p. 37). Hence examining, in intricate detail, how family members speak

about distinctions and narrate the past will go a long way toward illuminating how culture and cognition penetrate family relationships. Interpretive strategies that advocate "thick description" (Geertz, 1973) and qualitative methods that encourage line-by-line coding—grounded theoretical methods, for example (Glaser, 1978; Glaser & Strauss, 1967; Strauss, 1987)—are especially well suited to this kind of research. In-depth interview transcripts, ethnographic field notes, personal diaries, family correspondence, and commercial media accounts (e.g., newspaper and magazine articles) are rich sources from which researchers can glean information about how social realities are made and remade.

In conclusion, much has been said about the recent cultural turn in the social sciences (e.g., see Friedland & Mohr, 2004). Family scholars would do well to pay heed. As we have tried to show, cognitive pluralism can clarify and expand perennial issues in family social science, as well as generate basic and policy-oriented hypotheses. It is a perspective admirably suited to family research.

CASE STUDY

RIVER OF GRIEF: HEARING PARENTS AND SIBLINGS FOLLOWING CHILD DEATH

Colleen I. Murray, *University of Nevada at Reno*

Kathleen R. Gilbert, *Indiana University*

What happens when society says that you are no longer a parent or, in the case of prenatal loss, that you never were a parent? How does child death influence spousal or remaining parent-child relationships? When families' experiences run counter to cultural expectations, the language of the culture does not accurately describe their experiences, and

theories do not match their reality. How can families reconstruct meaning in a way that enables them to function within that culture? If a parent's grief is a river, how should we plan a crossing in order to understand that river? Do we swim, row a boat, build a bridge, or hang glide above? What strategy enables us to hear the river?

We each pondered these questions when we began to study the experiences of bereaved parents and siblings during the 1980s. The dominant theories of grief at that time assumed the existence of phases that bereaved individuals followed when moving from attachment to detachment (for more on this topic, see this volume's companion Web site at http://www.ncfr.org/sourcebook). Healthy grief was seen as having an ending point: acceptance of loss and relegation of the deceased child to the past. Most research had been conducted with samples of individuals in clinical situations or widows, with the assumption being that death had occurred after a long productive life with relatively uncomplicated resultant grief.

Bereaved families often heard "If you just had enough faith, you could cope," or "Time heals all." As scholarly theories or public recipes for recovery, these views did not match what we observed in bereaved families. Healthy bereaved families seemed to have continuing emotional or cognitive bonds with deceased children, even years after the deaths. This ran contrary to the common recommendation that parents "let go, move on, and don't cling to your dead child's memory," yet it seemed to make sense in the context of the ongoing nature of intimate family relationships. We each approached our study of loss by viewing bereaved parents and siblings not as a clinical population but as normal families facing an abnormal situation—death of a child prior to parents' deaths. It was in this climate that we separately undertook systematic ways of learning more about bereaved families.

By 1980, most research concerning bereaved parents involved parents whose children had previously been hospitalized for illnesses, a "captive audience" for researchers. However, the majority of child deaths have sudden or accidental causes. As graduate students, we both wondered how we could reach bereaved parents whose only contact with a hospital took place when they had to identify their child's body in the middle of the night, or those parents whose

losses came in maternity units. An opening came when Colleen was asked to talk about coping with sudden or accidental death at local and national meetings of support groups for bereaved parents and siblings. Although the research sample this led to was neither random nor representative, it was a start.

As was common in the early 1980s, Colleen used quantitative methods to conduct her study (for details, see this volume's companion Web site). Although symbolic interaction theory was an appealing framework for studying loss, it did not lend itself to the dominant quantitative methodologies. Role theory variations did not seem to address the complex dynamics and contexts associated with loss. Eventually, Colleen used various scales based on concepts from family stress and crisis theory.

Kathleen also struggled with the dominant research paradigm of the time, repeatedly returning to the underresearched idea of grief as a dyadic phenomenon (Gilbert, 1997; for additional related references, see this volume's companion Web site). What was it that couples who stayed together after child death did to maintain intact and, often, satisfying marriages? Research that purported to examine couples' experiences consisted of data collected from mothers, who were asked to describe both their own experiences and those of their husbands. It was not surprising that mothers' experiences were richly detailed, whereas fathers' were sketchy and stereotypical. If scholars were ever to understand the experiences of bereaved couples, they would need to include in their research data from fathers *in those couples*.

Existing models clearly focused on individual bereavement, and the study of grief as a family phenomenon was in its infancy. What theoretical orientation and method would be appropriate to address this little-studied phenomenon? Family systems theory at that time downplayed the unknowable past in order to focus on current communication and processes, and so seemed ill suited for examining grief as a systemic process. How could

CASE STUDY *continued*

scholars effectively use a theory that was so focused on the present to address losses that required acknowledgment of the importance of past relationships?

A MOVE FROM
THE QUANTITATIVE VIEW

Structured questionnaires and scales did not touch on aspects of the bereavement process that parents and siblings appeared to need to tell us. In Colleen's early studies, parents often attached narratives of their losses, describing their resulting situations; some parents added maps showing the circumstances of their children's deaths rather than rely on words (for more on these studies, see this volume's Web site). In multiple-informant studies, what parents were saying about their surviving adolescents was not in accord with what the adolescents said. One clue we had to the importance of looking at context and avoiding viewing elements in isolation came from Colleen's attempts to use linear models with interaction effects to examine factors related to adaptation (Murray, 1991). The ultimate result of this was a sense that closed-ended questionnaire items and traditional theoretical models were not doing justice to the experiences of bereaved parents, siblings, or couples. It was at this point that we both came to the recognition that only through open dialogue with participants could we represent the complexity and depth of the loss experiences of bereaved parents and siblings.

The field began a shift toward viewing loss in the family as complex and broader than the loss itself, addressing the importance of intergenerational transmission of values and beliefs about loss, and viewing grief as an element of current family dynamics (for references related to these changes, see this volume's Web site). At that point, we grappled with the potential of family systems theory and the question of whether grief could be a family-level variable. However, rather than looking for some aspect of the family system that was shared by all members, we identified the dynamic of "differential grieving," in which family members who have experienced the same objective loss individually experience a unique subjective loss (Gilbert, 1996).

By the 1990s we were searching for ways to understand more fully the intersection of contexts of grief, meanings that societies give to child death, and families' reconstruction of meanings of loss (for related references, see this volume's Web site). We explored professional paradigms and scholars' understandings of grieving families (Murray, 2000) as well as the stress experienced by research assistants who worked with information on losses, surrounded by the grief of others but unable to respond to those families (Gilbert, 2001).

Another context that concerned us was derived from the extensive media coverage of mass tragedies. We became increasingly aware that the types of images shown could further complicate grief for family members as well as for other viewers. Our mutual interest in the social construction of meaning was facilitated by the opportunity to develop a content analysis in order to compare media reporting in each country of two mass tragedies, the Oklahoma City bombing and the Dunblane, Scotland, school massacre (Murray & Gilbert, 1997; see also this volume's Web site).

As we increasingly recognized the importance of context, we also began to challenge whether there could be a single operational definition of grief. To incorporate elements of diversity, the definition needs to include recognition of differences in *what* constitutes loss, *when* a loss is perceived to take place, and whether grief is seen as predominantly cognitive-emotional or somatization (Murray, 2003). Information on continuing bonds between parents and deceased children may raise questions about long-held assumptions regarding boundary ambiguity (see this volume's Web site). Perhaps some individuals may experience comfort from maintaining such bonds, and for them the psychological

CASE STUDY *continued*

presence of the child may serve a positive function rather than a negative one.

With our interest in the contexts, meanings, and experiences of bereaved families, we have moved toward a social constructionist approach and so have incorporated qualitative methods, which allow the voices of the bereaved to be heard. Narrative analysis, which emphasizes hearing and telling of participants' stories, suggests a socially constructed hierarchy of family members who are most entitled to grieve (Gilbert, 2002). Rather than relying on clinical psychology as our basis for understanding grief, we now ground our work in the context and processes associated with a social psychology of loss and the constructivist view of loss and grief (for related references, see this volume's Web site).

At this point our work also involves deconstructing the study of parent and sibling grief. We still know more about problems of coping than we do about the process of coping, and more about what inhibits grief than about what facilitates it (Murray, 2000). Even though thanatology is moving away from reliance on grief theories based on attachment, and researchers acknowledge the somatizations of grief, theory and conceptualizations continue to be biased toward a view of grief as largely a cognitive phenomenon. With a focus on intellect, will Western theorists keep developing cognitive approaches that replace one another in the study of grief and loss? We are working toward building models of grief that are broad enough to take a truly systemic view, in which somatic, cognitive, emotional, social, and even spiritual elements are included. As family scholars, our goal is also to ensure that these models reflect the complexity of the elements coming together in the family context—to understand the river of grief.

DISCUSSION AND EXTENSION

PARENTHOOD, PARENTING, AND MARITAL INTERACTIONS

Debra Umberson, *University of Texas at Austin*

Belinda L. Needham, *University of Texas at Austin*

The structure of a family shapes the interactions within that family. Thus changes in structure lead to changes in interactions. Parental status and parenting transitions (birth of a child, launching adult children from the home) constitute some of the most common structural influences and changes that occur in families over time. In this brief contribution, we describe some of our recent research on the effects of parenting on marital quality to illustrate the importance of family structure and social context for family interactions. We follow this with a discussion of promising research strategies for investigating changes in family interactions as they unfold over time.

DISCUSSION AND EXTENSION *continued*

PARENTHOOD
AND MARITAL QUALITY

The transition to parenthood has long been associated with a decline in marital quality, presumably because the strains of parenthood undermine interactions between the new parents (Orbuch, House, Mero, & Webster, 1996). Several recent longitudinal studies that have followed newlywed couples over time have found that marital quality does diminish following the birth of a child (e.g., Helms-Erickson, 2001). However, Kurdek (1993) found that marital quality dipped to a similar degree for couples over a 4-year period *whether or not* they had a child. In our recent research on change in marital quality over the life course, we used data from a national longitudinal survey to conduct growth curve analyses of marital quality change. We found that, on average, marital quality tends to diminish over time; however, parental status and parenting transitions can serve to slow or to accelerate the rate of change in marital quality.

The birth of a child is one of the factors that accelerates the decline in marital quality. Adults who make the transition to parenthood experience a greater increase in negative marital interactions over an 8-year period than do other individuals. We also considered how other parenting transitions that tend to occur later in the life course might affect marital quality. Previous studies that relied on cross-sectional data have suggested that launching adult children from the home might be beneficial to parents' marital quality (White & Edwards, 1990) and that living with adult children might undermine parents' marital quality (Umberson & Gove, 1989). In our growth curve analyses, we found that launching adult children served to slow the usual rate of increase in negative marital interactions over time. Moreover, having an adult child move back into the parents' home accelerated marital quality decline. These findings suggest that certain parenting transitions not only undermine

marital interactions, but also have lasting effects in the years following the transitions.

Parenthood may have different effects depending on adults' positions in the life course. The context of parenting shapes the socioemotional experience of parenting, as LaRossa, Simonds, and Reitzes point out in Chapter 17. Presumably, the context of parenting differs for individuals at different ages. Adults who become parents at a very young age may be disadvantaged in terms of financial stability, emotional maturity, and social support. In our research, we did not find that the transition to parenthood affects younger parents more than older parents, but we did find that living with a minor child is associated with higher initial levels of negative marital interaction for younger parents compared with older parents. Older parents have more resources that ease the strains of parenting young children. We also found that adults who have adult children who live apart from the parents experience less marital quality decline over time than do their childless counterparts, and this benefit to marital quality is greater for older than for younger parents.

In sum, our analysis strongly suggests that parenthood and parenting transitions initiate change in marital interactions. Why is this the case?

THEORETICAL WORK
ON FAMILY INTERACTIONS

Many sociological theories provide explanations for the impact of social structure or social contexts on marital interactions. We work from a social structure and personality framework that emphasizes that the social context is shaped by social position (e.g., as defined by gender or age or social class). One's social position shapes the sorts of social opportunities and rewards one is likely to encounter as well the demands and constraints one is likely to face. Clearly, parenthood and parenting transitions shape the daily

DISCUSSION AND EXTENSION *continued*

and long-term opportunities and constraints that might influence marital interactions. Of course, social contexts also influence the way any particular individual comes to perceive the meanings of marriage and family. For example, in Chapter 17 LaRossa et al. emphasize that the meaning of parenthood differs for men and women. If parenthood were to inspire more of a sense of meaning and purpose in life for women than for men, this might alter the meaning of marriage for men and women as well as their subsequent marital interactions.

To understand more fully how parenthood affects marital interactions, we must take into account multiple theoretical perspectives. This is because different perspectives tend to focus on different layers of the parenthood or marital experience even while they tend to have much in common. Almost all sociological perspectives somehow take into account that social structures influence individuals— even while different perspectives emphasize one layer of analysis over another. Social structure and personality views tend to emphasize the power of social structures to shape opportunities and demands of parenthood for individuals (Umberson, 1989), stress and coping perspectives tend to emphasize how social structures impose more stress of parenting for some individuals than others (Aneshensel, 1992), and the cognitive pluralism view tends to emphasize how social structures shape individuals' cognitions and perceptions in ways that shape the experience of parenthood (LaRossa et al., Chapter 17).

METHODOLOGICAL APPROACHES TO FAMILY INTERACTIONS

Just as we can enrich understanding by considering how multiple theoretical perspectives overlap to influence family interactions, we can also enrich understanding by blending and layering different methodological approaches to the study of family interactions. An example from our work on how marital quality changes over time illustrates this. We began our study on how marital quality changes over time by analyzing longitudinal data from a national survey. Using this approach and standard regression procedures, we considered how parenting transitions affected change in marital quality between two time points. This told us *how much change in marital quality* occurred following the birth of a child. Although the amount of change following this parenting transition is interesting, it does not give us any information about where people start on marital quality. This is important because each spouse starts from a different baseline of marital quality. If a woman begins with an extremely high score on marital quality that then drops by 20 points over time, she still actually ends up with a pretty good marriage (even though her marital quality has declined). It is a very different experience to begin with a below-average marriage and drop 20 points in marital quality, because the end point may land one in the divorce-prone category. Next, we used growth curve analysis to study change in marital quality over an 8-year period. This approach allowed us to take into account *initial levels of marital quality* as well as the *rate of change in marital quality* over time. The rate of change is important because it can tell us how slowly or quickly marital quality declines over time. For example, we found that those individuals who introduced a new child into the family experienced a more rapid decline in marital quality over time than did their peers who did not experience this transition.

Our quantitative analyses of longitudinal data tell us a lot about patterns of marital quality change in the general population and structural features of parenthood that might facilitate change, but they leave a lot of questions unanswered. For example, they cannot tell us about individuals' perceptions of the meaning of parenthood and how those perceptions might influence marital interactions. Qualitative data are often better suited to

DISCUSSION AND EXTENSION *continued*

addressing patterns of process, meaning, and change. To that end, we are now conducting in-depth interviews with couples to explore their life-course experiences of marriage and parenting as well as the meaning of marriage and parenting for individuals. In addition, we would like to know more about how the *daily dynamics* of marital interactions might differ for men and women over the life course. To that end, we are conducting a daily diary study of family experiences and marital interactions for 60 individuals. This allows us to consider daily fluctuations in marital quality and couple dynamics, stress levels, and individual well-being, both within individuals and across age groups.

CONCLUSION

Qualitative data help us to assess the subjective meanings and dynamic processes associated with the statistical patterns we see from our quantitative analyses of longitudinal data. Merging qualitative and quantitative research offers scholars a unique opportunity to extend knowledge about how family structures and dynamics change over the life course. Qualitative studies can address empirical questions raised by quantitative studies of family change (over years in surveys or days in diary studies) and can serve as theory-building tools to help us understand how family structures and contexts come to affect family interactions.

REFERENCES

Alexander, J. C. (2003). *The meanings of social life: A cultural sociology.* New York: Oxford University Press.

Amato, P. R. (1989). Who cares for children in public places? Naturalistic observation of male and female caretakers. *Journal of Marriage and the Family, 51,* 981–990.

Aneshensel, C. S. (1992). Social stress: Theory and research. *Annual Review of Sociology, 18,* 15–38.

Becker, G. (2000). *The elusive embryo: How women and men approach new reproductive technologies.* Berkeley: University of California Press.

Bell, D. C. (2001). Evolution of parental caregiving. *Personality and Social Psychology Review, 5,* 216–229.

Berger, P. L., & Luckmann, T. (1966). *The social construction of reality: A treatise in the sociology of knowledge.* New York: Anchor/Doubleday.

Blumer, H. (1969). *Symbolic interactionism: Perspective and method.* Englewood Cliffs, NJ: Prentice Hall.

Boss, P., Doherty, W. J., LaRossa, R., Schumm, W. R., & Steinmetz, S. K. (Eds.). (1993). *Sourcebook of family theories and methods: A contextual approach.* New York: Plenum.

Bowlby, J. (1982). *Attachment and loss: Vol. 1. Attachment* (2nd ed.). New York: Basic Books.

Casper, M. (1996). *The making of the unborn patient: A social anatomy of fetal surgery.* New Brunswick, NJ: Rutgers University Press.

Cerulo, K. A. (Ed.). (2002). *Culture in mind: Toward a sociology of culture and cognition.* New York: Routledge.

Cooley, C. H. (1956). *Human nature and social order.* Glencoe, IL: Free Press. (Original work published 1902)

Dalton, S. E. (2001). Protecting our parent-child relationships: Understanding the strengths and weaknesses of second parent adoption. In M. Bernstein & R. Reimann (Eds.), *Queer families, queer politics: Challenging culture and the state* (pp. 201–220). New York: Columbia University Press.

Daly, K. J. (1993). Reshaping fatherhood: Finding the models. *Journal of Family Issues, 14,* 510–530.

Daly, K. J. (1996). *Families and time: Keeping pace in a hurried culture.* Thousand Oaks, CA: Sage.

DeLee, J. B. (1920). The prophylactic forceps operation. *Journal of Obstetrics and Gynecology, 1,* 34–44.

Deutsch, F., Lozy, J. L., & Saxon, S. (1993). Taking credit: Couples' reports of contributions to child care. *Journal of Family Issues, 14,* 421–437.

Dressel, P. L., & Clark, A. (1990). A critical look at family care. *Journal of Marriage and the Family, 52,* 769–782.

Durkheim, É. (1915). *The elementary forms of the religious life.* New York: Free Press.

Fraser, G. (1998). *African American midwifery in the South: Dialogues of birth, race, and memory.* Cambridge, MA: Harvard University Press.

Friedland, R., & Mohr, J. W. (Eds.). (2004). *Matters of culture: Cultural sociology in practice.* New York: Cambridge University Press.

Garfinkel, H. (1967). *Studies in ethnomethodology.* Englewood Cliffs, NJ: Prentice Hall.

Gaskin, I. M. (2003). *Ina May's guide to childbirth.* New York: Bantam.

Geertz, C. (1973). *The interpretation of cultures: Selected essays.* New York: Basic Books.

Gergen, K. J., & Gergen, M. M. (1997). Narratives of the self. In L. P. Hinchman & S. K. Hinchman (Eds.), *Memory, identity, and community: The idea of narrative in the human sciences* (pp. 161–184). Albany: State University of New York Press.

Gilbert, K. R. (1996). We've had the same loss, why don't we have the same grief? Loss and differential grief in families. *Death Studies, 20,* 269–283.

Gilbert, K. R. (1997). Couple coping with the death of a child. In C. R. Figley, N. Mazza, & B. Bride (Eds.), *Death and trauma: The traumatology of surviving* (pp. 101–122). Bristol, PA: Taylor & Francis.

Gilbert, K. R. (2001). Collateral damage? Indirect exposure to emotions among students and staff. In K. R. Gilbert (Ed.), *The emotional nature of qualitative research* (pp. 147–161). Boca Raton, FL: CRC.

Gilbert, K. R. (2002). Taking a narrative approach to grief research: Finding meaning in stories. *Death Studies, 26,* 223–240.

Glaser, B. G. (1978). *Theoretical sensitivity.* Mill Valley, CA: Sociology Press.

Glaser, B. G., & Strauss, A. L. (1967). *The discovery of grounded theory: Strategies for qualitative research.* Chicago: Aldine.

Goer, H. (1995). *Obstetric myths versus research realities: A guide to the medical literature.* Westport, CT: Bergin & Garvey.

Goffman, E. (1959). *The presentation of self in everyday life.* New York: Doubleday/ Anchor.

Goffman, E. (1974). *Frame analysis: An essay on the organization of experience.* New York: Harper & Row.

Griswold, W. (1994). *Cultures and societies in a changing world.* Thousand Oaks, CA: Pine Forge.

Hartouni, V. (1997). *Cultural conceptions: On reproductive technologies and the remaking of life.* Minneapolis: University of Minnesota Press.

Heimer, C. A., & Staffen, L. R. (1998). *For the sake of the children: The social organization of responsibility in the hospital and home.* Chicago: University of Chicago Press.

Helms-Erickson, H. (2001). Marital quality ten years after the transition to parenthood: Implications of the timing of parenthood and the division of housework. *Journal of Marriage and Family, 63,* 1099–1110.

Hopper, J. (1993). The rhetoric of motives in divorce. *Journal of Marriage and the Family, 55,* 801–813.

Hrdy, S. B. (1999). *Mother nature: A history of mothers, infants, and natural selection.* New York: Pantheon.

Isaacson, N. (1996). The "fetus-infant": Changing classifications of in utero development in medical texts. *Sociological Forum, 11,* 457–480.

Kessler, S. J., & McKenna, W. (1978). *Gender: An ethnomethodological approach.* New York: John Wiley.

Kurdek, L. A. (1993). Nature and prediction of changes in marital quality for first-time parent and nonparent husbands and wives. *Journal of Family Psychology, 6,* 255–265.

Lareau, A. (2000). My wife can tell me who I know: Methodological and conceptual problems in studying fathers. *Qualitative Sociology, 23,* 407–433.

LaRossa, R. (1995). Stories and relationships. *Journal of Social and Personal Relationships, 12,* 553–558.

LaRossa, R., & LaRossa, M. M. (1981). *Transition to parenthood: How infants change families.* Beverly Hills, CA: Sage.

LaRossa, R., & Reitzes, D. C. (1995). Gendered perceptions of fatherhood in early 20th century America. *Journal of Marriage and the Family, 57,* 223–229.

LaRossa, R., & Reitzes, D. C. (2001). Two? Two and one-half? Thirty months? Chronometrical childhood in early 20th century America. *Sociological Forum, 16,* 385–407.

Luker, K. (1984). *Abortion and the politics of motherhood.* Berkeley: University of California Press.

Luker, K. (1997). *Dubious conceptions: The politics of teenage pregnancy.* Cambridge, MA: Harvard University Press.

Mannheim, K. (1936). *Ideology and utopia: An introduction to the sociology of knowledge.* New York: Harcourt, Brace & World. (Original work published 1929)

Martin, E. (1992). *The woman in the body: A cultural analysis of reproduction.* Boston: Beacon. (Original work published 1987)

Mead, G. H. (1934). *Mind, self, and society.* Chicago: University of Chicago Press.

Milkie, M. A., Simon, R. W., & Powell, B. (1997). Through the eyes of children: Youths' perceptions and evaluations of maternal and paternal roles. *Social Psychology Quarterly, 60,* 218–237.

Mills, C. W. (1940). Situated actions and vocabularies of motives. *American Sociological Review, 5,* 904–913.

Murphy, J. S. (2001). Should lesbians count as infertile couples? Understanding the strengths and weaknesses of second-parent adoption. In M. Bernstein & R. Reimann (Eds.), *Queer families, queer politics: Challenging culture and the state* (pp. 182–200). New York: Columbia University Press.

Murphy-Lawless, J. (1998). *Reading birth and death: A history of obstetric thinking.* Bloomington: Indiana University Press.

Murray, C. I. (1991). Misuse of linear models in the study of families. *Family Science Review, 4,* 145–163.

Murray, C. I. (2000). Death, dying, and grief. In P. C. McKenry & S. Price (Eds.), *Families and change: Coping with stressful events* (2nd ed., pp. 120–153). Thousand Oaks, CA: Sage.

Murray, C. I. (2003). Grief, loss, and bereavement. In J. J. Ponzetti, Jr. (Ed.), *International encyclopedia of marriage and family* (2nd ed., pp. 782–788). New York: Macmillan.

Murray, C. I., & Gilbert, K. R. (1997, June). *British and U.S. newspaper reporting of the Dunblane School Massacre.* Paper presented at the 5th International Conference on Grief and Bereavement in Contemporary Society, in conjunction with the 19th Annual Conference of the Association for Death Education and Counseling, Washington, DC.

Nippert-Eng, C. (1996). *Home and work: Negotiating boundaries through everyday life.* Chicago: University of Chicago Press.

Orbuch, T. L., House, J. S., Mero, R. P., & Webster, P. S. (1996). Marital quality over the life course. *Social Psychology Quarterly, 59,* 162–171.

Panksepp, J. (1998). *Affective neuroscience: The foundations of human and animal emotions.* New York: Oxford University Press.

Patterson, C. J. (1995). Lesbian and gay parenthood. In M. H. Bornstein (Ed.), *Handbook of parenting: Vol. 3. Status and social conditions of parenting* (pp. 255–274). Mahwah, NJ: Lawrence Erlbaum.

Rapoport, R., & Rapoport, R. N. (1975). Men, women, and equity. *Family Coordinator, 24,* 421–432.

Roberts, D. (1997). *Killing the Black body: Race, reproduction, and the meaning of liberty.* New York: Vintage.

Rothman, B. K. (1986). *The tentative pregnancy: Prenatal diagnosis and the future of motherhood.* New York: W. W. Norton.

Rothman, B. K. (1991). *In labor: Women and power in the birthplace.* New York: W. W. Norton. (Original work published 1982)

Rothman, B. K. (2001). *The book of life: A personal and ethical guide to race, normality, and the implications of the Human Genome Project.* Boston: Beacon. (Original work published 1998)

Schutz, A. (1962). *Collected papers I: The problem of social reality.* The Hague: Nijhoff.

Simonds, W. (1996). *Abortion at work: Ideology and practice in a feminist clinic.* New Brunswick, NJ: Rutgers University Press.

Simonds, W. (2002). Watching the clock: Keeping time during pregnancy, birth, and postpartum experiences. *Social Science & Medicine, 55,* 559–570.

Stone, G. (1962). Appearance and the self. In A. Rose (Ed.), *Human behavior and social processes* (pp. 86–118). Boston: Houghton Mifflin.

Strauss, A. L. (1987). *Qualitative analysis for social scientists.* New York: Cambridge University Press.

Tooby, J., & Cosmides, L. (1992). The psychological foundation of culture. In J. H. Barkow, L. Cosmides, & J. Tooby (Eds.), *The adapted mind: Evolutionary psychology and the generation of culture* (pp. 19–136). New York: Oxford University Press.

Umberson, D. (1989). Parenting and well-being: The importance of context. *Journal of Family Issues, 10,* 427–439.

Umberson, D., & Gove, W. R. (1989). Parenting and well-being: Theory, measurement, and stage in the family life course. *Journal of Family Issues, 10,* 440–462.

Van Gennep, A. (1960). *The rites of passage.* Chicago: University of Chicago Press.

Vinitzky-Seroussi, V. (2000). "My God, what am I gonna say?": Class reunions as social control. *Qualitative Sociology, 23,* 57–75.

Walker, A. (1999). Gender and family relationships. In M. B. Sussman, S. K. Steinmetz, & G. W. Peterson (Eds.), *Handbook of marriage and the family* (2nd ed., pp. 439–474). New York: Plenum.

Weber, M. (1904–1905). *The protestant ethic and the spirit of capitalism.* New York: Scribner's.

West, C., & Zimmerman, D. H. (1987). Doing gender. *Gender & Society, 1,* 125–151.

White, L., & Edwards, J. N. (1990). Emptying the nest and parental well-being: An analysis of national panel data. *American Sociological Review, 55,* 235–242.

Zerubavel, E. (1979). *Patterns of time in hospital life.* Chicago: University of Chicago Press.

Zerubavel, E. (1981). *Hidden rhythms: Schedules and calendars in social life.* Chicago: University of Chicago Press.

Zerubavel, E. (1991). *The fine line: Making distinctions in everyday life.* New York: Free Press.

Zerubavel, E. (1997). *Social mindscapes: An invitation to cognitive sociology.* Cambridge, MA: Harvard University Press.

Zerubavel, E. (2003). *Time maps: Collective memory and the social shape of the past.* Chicago: University of Chicago Press.

• Eighteen

MULTICULTURAL AND CRITICAL RACE FEMINISMS

Theorizing Families in the Third Wave

Lee Ann De Reus, *Penn State Altoona*

April L. Few, *Virginia Polytechnic Institute and State University*

Libby Balter Blume, *University of Detroit Mercy*

T he dramatic evolution of feminist theories over the past decade necessitates an epistemological transformation in the study of women and families. Multicultural and critical race feminist theories have created a political space for theorizing diversity that challenges conceptual boundaries, centers marginalized ideas and people, decolonizes knowledges, and compels the creation of innovative research questions, methods, and praxis. Instead of "*Where* are the women?" as posed by Osmond and Thorne (1993, p. 591), the question now becomes, *How* do women "do" gender, experience difference, create identity, and negotiate intersectionality in the multiple contexts of changing families, diverse cultures, and rapid social change? (see Moloney & Fenstermaker, 2002; West & Zimmerman, 1987). These divergent questions represent particular feminist ideologies that can be located in separate "waves" of the U.S. women's movement. Dividing this movement into particular time periods, some feminists and historians refer to the 19th-century women's rights movement as the *first wave*, the women's liberation movement of the 1960s as the *second wave*, and the movement guided by today's younger, post–baby boom feminists as the *third wave* (see Heywood & Drake, 1997).

Our purpose in writing this chapter is to integrate U.S. multicultural and critical race feminist theories into a third-wave feminist framework for examining the multiplicity, fluidity, and intersectionality of social phenomena in individuals' and families' lives. A critical premise of this project is our recognition that aspects of self-identity such as race, ethnicity, class, gender, sexuality, nationality, ability, age, and religion are not fixed but dynamic. This conceptualization has enabled us to transcend limiting categories, thereby creating a unique space from which to understand the lived experiences of diverse people.

Given our emphasis on the diversity of experiences, we would be remiss as feminist authors if we did not position ourselves relative to this text and acknowledge our own biases. We are three well-educated, middle-class, feminist women employed as faculty in comparable positions at different universities. One of us is Black, two of us are White, one of us is Jewish, and each of us represents a different birth cohort. While we recognize that our writing is limited by our own personal and intellectual biases, we celebrate the similarities and differences in our perspectives and value the exchange of ideas that has culminated in this chapter. Collectively, our work is informed by postmodernism and framed by a poststructuralist perspective resulting in a feminist epistemology that is guided by the following five assumptions:

1. The diverse experiences of women and families are constructed by dynamic cultural discourses concerning gender, race, ethnicity, nationality, class, sexual orientation, age, ability, and religion.

2. Identity is not a biologically inherent feature of individuals, families, or social groups; rather, it is contingent on relationship to self and others.

3. Human experiences are not universal and cannot be essentialized across or within groups; rather, individuals are situated and negotiate the intersections of multiple locations.

4. Personal, lived experiences are valid sources of data and can be theorized by critical feminism.

5. Research can be liberatory for both researchers and participants.

It is important to note that the vocabulary used by postmodern and poststructural feminists may pose some confusion for family studies scholars who are not familiar with the use of particular terms. The words *difference, identity,* and *intersectionality,* for example, possess particular meanings for postmodern feminists that may be new to readers. *Difference* in this context refers to the distinctions made between and within groups based on socially constructed categories such as class and family. This term is similar to *diversity* as often used by family studies scholars. A person's or family's identity is embedded in difference; in this context *identity* refers to socially constructed self-definitions or labels applied by others. These are typically static characteristics or traits, such as "Black" or "woman." *Intersectionality* refers to the process by which social phenomena such as race, class, and gender at the individual (identity) and family (difference) levels co-construct one another (Crenshaw, 1993).

THEORIZING DIFFERENCE

Theorizing difference is not a simple endeavor in a postmodern world. For women and families of various locations, the related questions of who defines difference, how various categories of people are represented within the discourses of difference, and how much power is granted to (or stripped from) individuals and groups based on these classifications are powerful determinants of people's lived experiences (Brah, 2001). The ability to name one's own identity empowers women and families to define themselves and to center relevant issues that may have been marginalized previously. A postmodern feminist approach to the study of diverse families stresses the importance of cultural variation, historical change, and power relations (Baber & Murray, 2001). For example, a postmodern researcher would describe and critique the wide-ranging cultural changes for women and families resulting from the colonialism, racism, patriarchy, homophobia, and ageism prevalent in popular culture (St. Pierre & Pillow, 2000). These issues are central to what some indigenous peoples and scholars refer to as the *decolonization* (i.e., de-Westernization) of knowledge and research about diverse individuals. Long before the existence of postmodern critiques, indigenous peoples were questioning "the institutions, vocabulary, scholarship, imagery, doctrines, even colonial bureaucracies and colonial styles" (Smith, 1999, p. 2) used to determine and describe their lives.

Whereas a postmodern feminist approach questions the definition of social categories, such as women or families, thereby problematizing the notion of *difference* (Weedon, 1999), poststructuralism represents a shift toward theorizing the relations between specific social or cultural discourses and the multiple identities of subjects. Poststructural feminism is largely academic in nature and is concerned primarily with language and discourse. From a poststructural perspective, individuals and families are viewed as constructed by the social discourses of gender, ethnicity, race, and so on. When employed, poststructural practices deconstruct conventional categories of difference—such as race and gender—by carefully examining the social meanings that are often hidden within the dominant cultural discourse. A basic assumption is that language itself may lead to oppression, depending on the power relations within which discourse is produced (Weedon, 1999). Poststructural methodologies, therefore, criticize the use of linguistic categories (e.g., gender, race, class) that are fixed, unitary, and essentializing. Consequently, poststructural feminists question the very existence of restrictive social categories by recognizing the fluidity and contextual embeddedness of identities.

THEORIZING IDENTITY

Poststructural feminists have challenged the unified category of "woman" as the basis for a general theory of oppression of *all* women because it obfuscates within-group variation. To theorize identity from a poststructural feminist perspective is to capture the fluidity of identities by examining socially constructed individual and group differences. In this approach to identity, two processes of self/other representation are typically addressed: agency and subjectivity. Women's *agency*, for example, is used to account for the individual's existence as a thinking, feeling social agent who is able to reflect on the prevailing cultural discourse and on the options available to her (Weedon, 1999). Women's *subjectivity*, on the other hand, is seen not only as

the result of a person's *lived* experiences but also as a result of *discursive* experiences—the meanings assigned by her family or society as they interpret and discuss her conformity or resistance to social norms (see Blume & Blume, 2003). Poststructural feminists, therefore, claim that the relationship of experience to discourse is what is at issue (Mohanty, 1999). By recognizing that all knowledge is situated and therefore partial, poststructural feminists also theorize the intersectionality of *multiple* identities.

THEORIZING INTERSECTIONALITY

Collins (1998) posits that as a heuristic device, intersectionality references the ability of social phenomena such as race, ethnicity, class, gender, sexuality, nationality, ability, and religion to mutually construct one another. The concept of intersectionality requires us to examine how social institutions, organizational structures, patterns of social interactions, and other social practices on all levels of social organization influence the choices, opportunities, and identities that individuals and groups make and claim as their own (Collins, 1998). Intersectionality, then, is the negotiation of a *politics of location*.

Mohanty (1999) describes the politics of location as "specific historical, geographical, cultural, psychic and imaginative boundaries that shape our definitions of self and the other" (p. 74). This focus on location insists on a standpoint perspective, yet it does not essentialize. Instead, the research process provides only a "partial story." Sudbury (1998) argues that in theorizing the politics of location faced by our participants and ourselves as co-conveyers and cocreators of their stories, we "create the space for critical analysis of subordinated voices without re-centering those voices which have been deposed" (pp. 32–33). In their efforts to reclaim epistemological voice and to name experience in their own words, some racial/ethnic minority women who identify themselves as woman centered or feminist have organized in grassroots movements and in academe, and this has resulted in various multicultural feminisms.

Some multicultural feminists, however, have argued that deconstructing linguistic and social categories may lead to a conceptual descent to "nothingness" by fragmenting women's experiences. This criticism is at the heart of the tension between poststructural and standpoint theories. The source of this tension is the perception that standpoint theories, including multicultural feminisms, are essentialist and lead to false generalizations, whereas poststructural theories are antiessentialist and deconstructive to a fault. We assert that multicultural feminisms, when viewed through a poststructural lens, are *not* necessarily essentialist but rather represent collective standpoints of diverse experiences and voices. This perspective enables us to recognize that Latina/Hispanic families, for example, include a wide variety of ethnic groups with different historical and social experiences while still presenting a Latina perspective. In the spirit of postmodernism, we have intentionally resisted perpetuation of a poststructural versus standpoint dichotomy that serves only to create a theoretical impasse. Rather, we embrace this discord and construe it as an additional space for theorizing diverse women's and families' lived experiences. We concur with Derrida (1995), who explains that deconstruction does not imply the "liquidation of the subject" but rather permits a subject that "can be reinterpreted, re-stored, reinscribed" (p. 256). When used to frame the integration of U.S. multicultural and critical race feminisms, then, poststructuralism requires the adoption of an epistemology of difference and diversity as well as a methodology for the deconstruction of singular, unified categories (see Sandoval, 2000).

MULTICULTURAL AND CRITICAL RACE FEMINIST THEORIES

Multicultural Feminisms

Contemporary U.S. multicultural feminisms represent a (r)evolution in U.S. feminist thought and action. This movement, which was given voice in 1981 with the publication of the groundbreaking anthology *This Bridge Called My Back: Writings by Radical Women of Color* (Moraga & Anzaldúa, 1981), represents racial/ethnic women's attempt to embrace the contradictions and complexities of postmodern life, envision nondichotomous possibilities, challenge cultural constructions of sex and gender, decolonize knowledges, and ultimately reclaim and redefine gender in a way that is empowering for their affiliated groups. Multicultural feminists do not necessarily set out to transcend static labels such as "Black" or "woman," but they do purposely negotiate difference because it is a reality to be contended. Given its emphasis, this work specifically challenges the White, middle-class, typically heterosexual, Western feminism that characterized the women's movement of the 1960s. In addition, the artificial segmentation of the U.S. women's movement into waves has received criticism for its erasure of racial/ethnic women's activism and scholarship, which existed long before the organized White feminist movement of the 19th century. For example, White women such as Elizabeth Cady Stanton first learned about women's empowerment from indigenous women such as the Iroquois of New York, who had respect, authority, and power in their nations (Wagner, 1996).

In fact, work that depicts "languages and images that account for multiplicity and difference, that negotiate contradiction in affirmative ways, and that give voice to a politics of hybridity and coalition" (Heywood & Drake, 1997, p. 9) is evidenced throughout U.S. history. Sojourner Truth's 1852 speech "Ain't I a Woman?" is an example of racial/ethnic women's theorizing of difference, identity, and intersectionality. Truth's words, which she delivered in response to the Seneca Falls conference of 1848 that initiated the White women's rights movement, constituted her attempt to raise the consciousness of these early White suffragists about their privilege. Truth wanted them to understand that by ignoring the intersection of race and gender and by excluding Black women from the suffrage movement, they were complicit in her bondage and oppression (Lewis, 2003).

Like Truth, the Mexican nun Sister Juana Inés de la Cruz wrote the "Response to Sister

Filotea" in 1691 in an attempt to develop the critical consciousness of women and men regarding the appropriateness of women's education, scholarship, and intellectual pursuits. Through her poetry, plays, and letters, she exposed the constraints and prevalence of patriarchy and contributed to the discourse on intersectionality by integrating her indigenous Mexican and Basque backgrounds in her use of gendered language, rules of communication, and religion (Lewis, 2003).

The work of contemporary multicultural and third-wave feminists is evidenced in anthologies such as Rebecca Walker's *To Be Real: Telling the Truth and Changing the Face of Feminism* (1995) and Barbara Findlen's *Listen Up: Voices From the Next Feminist Generation* (1995). These books are primarily anecdotal and represent attempts by the contemporary generation of feminists to articulate the complexities and contradictions inherent in their lives, thereby moving beyond the notion of a single "female experience." Although the White feminist motto of the second wave, "The personal is political," is still applicable, multicultural and third-wave feminists are asking, "Which personal?" and "Whose politics?" (Siegel, 1997).

Also illuminated by current multicultural feminist and third-wave writings is the evolution of issues confronting different cohorts of women. Earlier, primarily White feminists critiqued beauty culture, sexual and wife abuse, power structures, and the wage gap, for example. Black feminists, while also invested in many of these issues, were working alongside African American men on such issues as racial oppression and differential treatment and expectations (McAdoo, 2003). Contemporary feminists—from both the second and third waves—are tackling issues such as equal access to technology, HIV/AIDS, child sexual abuse, colonization, self-mutilation, globalization, sex trafficking, eating disorders, immigration, and gay rights (Baumgardner & Richards, 2000). Various multicultural feminisms are models of how contemporary racial/ethnic women have theorized difference and intersectionality from differing standpoints. Standpoint theories suggest that social and epistemic location influences how individuals and groups have assigned meaning to identity and foment strategies to negotiate the politics of difference (see also McAdoo, Martínez, and Hughes, Chapter 8, this volume).[1]

● **SPOTLIGHT ON THEORY**

VEILED HEADS: A MIDDLE EASTERN FEMINIST PERSPECTIVE

Manijeh Daneshpour, *St. Cloud State University*

"**H**ard-core feminist" I called my mother in front of my skeptical and surprised classmates, as I was presenting my family's three-generation genogram years ago. There are no other words to describe my stereotype-shattering maternal half. My

(continued)

classmates were astounded that I would use these two simple words to describe my mother, the veiled Iranian Muslim woman standing before them. The question that still rings in my memory from that distant day is, "Don't you think being Muslim and being feminist are mutually exclusive?"

At the time, my defenses were triggered, and I adamantly insisted that if my mother believes in the equality of men and women, if she advocates for women's rights, and if she challenges the oppressive ways of men worldwide, then regardless of her culture or religion she can be a feminist to the very core. Even today, as I stand before American society in my power-inducing and symbolic veil, I insist that this outer shield, which I feel is the very essence of my feminist strength, is truly not oppressive and that there is no man with a stick waiting for me to come home and make sure that my hair is still neatly pleated beneath the simple fabric. The irony is in the fact that this symbolic piece of material has been interpreted as incompatible with a woman's being emancipated, modern, and open-minded.

Many first- and second-wave Western feminists and secular feminists from the Middle East also claim that Islam and feminism are mutually exclusive. They argue that under Islamic fundamentalism (a term with roots in Western colonial tradition), veiled women experience a life of oppression and that the true symbolism of the veil is that of vile inequality. This discourse that equates being veiled with being oppressed and insists on the urgency of emancipating the claustrophobic heads of Muslim women from their burdening fabric continues to be part of a major debate among Western colonizers, Western feminists, and many secular Middle Eastern feminists (Ahmed, 1992).

To counter this problem, third-wave feminists use postmodernism framed by a post-structuralist perspective to interpret our veiled lives quite differently given the fact that both colonial powers' and fundamentalists' interpretations of Islam and women's lives are very much the same. Actually, it is ironic that Islamic fundamentalists, by embracing the female body as the symbolic representation of communal dignity, and by drawing only on the Qur'an and orthodox texts to explain, as divine, the historically developed subjugation of women in Islamic societies, recycle the totalizing colonial conception of Islam and women's right as a static, unchanging, and unchangeable order. As with other forms of extremism, the two opposing poles end up on the same side on certain important issues. By manipulating the female body and using it as a playing card in oppositional politics, fundamentalists embrace the views of the Western colonizer, however unsought and uncomfortable. Third-wave feminists are challenging both the fundamentalists and Western colonial interpretations of women's lives by using an epistemology that redefines, reinterprets, reclaims, and restores lived experiences and by inventing new visions and revisions of Islam. Simultaneously constituting themselves as the "greening hands" of secular feminism, veiled Islamic feminists have audaciously messed up our comforting categories of *Islamic* and *secular* (Najmabadi, 1998).

Now knowing that the success of forward-thinking feminist praxis is the ability to embrace contradictions, veiled Islamic feminists are challenging the fundamentalists' interpretation of Islam on many grounds. For example, Iranian feminists are proposing several changes, including making women's contributions more visible; forming women's

(continued)

organizations; encouraging women's skepticism concerning the existing condition of women; changing women's and men's perceptions of women; ending inequalities, not only at the level of laws but in actual social practice, through provision of equal opportunities for women; and, most important, transforming cultural concepts about men and women. Taking into consideration such a recipe for the perfect blend of feminism at its best, I still cannot imagine labeling my mother anything other than a "hard-core feminist." ●

Critical Race Feminism

U.S. legal scholars developed critical race theory during the 1980s as a response to two related problems: (a) the lack of critical analysis in existing civil rights scholarship and (b) the lack of race consciousness in the prominent critical legal studies movement. Critical race theorists also emphasize the ways that majority groups racialize different minority groups at different times in response to shifting needs (e.g., global labor market, economic flux, social and legal movements) to maintain power within a hierarchical social matrix (Delgado & Stefancic, 2001). The writings of critical race scholars reveal the ways in which racial/ethnic individuals and groups negotiate intersectionality by reexamining American legal history and offering an alternative interpretation of history from the perspective of minorities' experiences.

Because of the historical exclusion of racial/ethnic legal women scholars by their male peers and by White feminist legal scholars, critical race *feminist* theory emerged from the broader perspective of critical race theory. Informed by the writings of various multicultural feminists and activists, critical race feminists are antiessentialists whose legal writings reflect the multiplicity of women's identities (Crenshaw, 1993). Critical race feminists conduct research that investigates how the law and social policies have created a "multiplicative legal praxis" to help or oppress racial/ethnic women and their families. Further, they assert that minority status presumes a competence for minority writers and theorists to

speak about race and the experiences of multiple oppressions without essentializing those experiences. The research foci of critical race feminists include welfare reform, domestic violence, grandparenting and parental rights, adoption, education, immigration, poverty, environmental issues, women's rights, human rights, mental and physical health issues, and sexual practices as these pertain to the law (see Wing, 1997). Studies of family policy in particular could benefit from critical race feminist theory as a guiding theoretical framework for explaining the choices that racial/ethnic families make in regard to social and legal policies.

CRITICISMS OF MULTICULTURAL AND CRITICAL RACE FEMINIST THEORIES

Critiques of multicultural feminisms and critical race feminist theories consist of charges—often by postmodernists and poststructuralists—that standpoint theories and the identity politics that they invoke are essentialist, constrictive in nature, and difficult to apply methodologically. We argue, however, that multicultural feminisms and critical race feminist theories actually *transcend* identity politics by engaging scholars in an analysis of the politics of location and intersectionality. As Alcoff (1988) asserts:

Identity politics provides a decisive rejoinder to the generic human thesis and the mainstream methodology of

Western political theory. . . . If we combine the concept of identity politics with a conception of the subject as positionality, we can conceive of the subject as nonessentialized and emergent from a historical experience. (pp. 432–433)

Thus a politics of location is the process of individuals and groups operating from the various—sometimes competing—standpoints of multiple identities (e.g., woman/Jewish/ lesbian) that may privilege or reject some or all of these identities to varying degrees. We believe, however, that these intersecting identities do not necessarily perpetuate marginalization, subordination, or privilege. For example, Collins (1998) has suggested that individuals and the groups of which they are a part are imbued with subjugated, partial knowledges to be shared with others in an open dialogue where no one voice has more resonance or power than others.

THEORIZING FAMILIES

The contemporary application of feminist theories in the field of family studies has been characterized primarily by a second-wave epistemology (i.e., White, middle-class, heterosexual). Consequently, the work of White feminist scholars in the 1970s and 1980s has been credited with recognizing women as separable from their families and shifting them to the center of empirical analyses about marriage, roles, power, and work. In this work, the ideological split between "public" and "private" spheres was questioned, gender was regarded as a social structure and ideology inherent in every institution, and the unitary notion of "the family" was challenged (see Osmond & Thorne, 1993).

Yet the positioning of this research at the center of family discourse ignores the work of early racial/ethnic family activists and scholars. Missing, for example, is the work of Ida B. Wells Barnett, who founded a national network of African American women's clubs in the 1880s. Although the initial concern

of such work was the lynching of African American men, these women soon expanded their focus to include other family problems. They initiated the first federal infant nutrition programs and the first residential programs for the aging in the United States (Macht & Quam, 1986). Such efforts are an excellent example of feminist *praxis*, which refers to developing critical consciousness about an issue and working to articulate and institutionalize a strategy for change.

Also absent from most feminist accounts of second-wave family scholarship is the landmark work of Robert Staples (1971, 1985), who reinterpreted the findings of the 1965 Moynihan congressional report. This rereading challenged the establishment of a "deficit model" as the standard for study of African American families. By contextualizing the report's findings, Staples revealed how institutional racism, unequal educational and economic opportunities, public assistance policies that lock families into a cycle of poverty, and the mischaracterization of adaptive African American family strategies perpetuated pathological stereotypes of African American family life in academia, on Capitol Hill, and in the mass media. Staples's method of revisionist history, like the work of indigenous scholars, represents an often-ignored yet major contribution to the field of family studies and serves as a model for contemporary family scholars of the application of critical race theory. Only through our recognition and inclusion of marginalized works such as those by Barnett and Staples can we shift to a center that more accurately theorizes diversity.

Black feminist Patricia Hill Collins (1990) provides an example of such a shift in her writings on "motherwork" and its relation to physical survival, power, and identity. Collins notes that for racial/ethnic women, the mother-child relationship is shaped by the necessity for mothers to work in order to provide for family well-being. Consequently, her emphasis is on collective identity (e.g., extended kinship networks) for means of survival. Motherhood is theorized not only as a biological event but also as a social event in which any woman (e.g., community mothers, "othermothers") can participate without giving birth. Motherhood is viewed as a communal event as opposed to solely an individual or family event. Finally, motherwork involves racial/ethnic women's ability to foster meaningful racial/ethnic identities in their children, imparting wisdom to challenge multiple oppressions. Thus family scholars can use (re)visioned concepts such as motherwork to redefine and contextualize the reality of motherhood by incorporating the experiences of racial/ethnic women and their families.

A recent example of family scholarship that theorizes intersectionality is a project by Hill and Thomas (2000) on interracial partnerships. In this qualitative study, the researchers used racial identity development, social constructionist, and feminist theories to describe an empowering process by which participants transformed racist narratives. By recognizing that a woman in an interracial relationship may be managing multiple racial identities because of her cross-racial affiliation, Hill and Thomas examined the intersectionality of race as it occurs in the context of a larger social discourse. They successfully theorized race by asking questions such as the following: "Has being in this relationship changed what it means to you to be a White/Black woman and how you think about race? How? What did you do to get to this understanding of yourself?" Citing the power and privilege of race, Hill and Thomas concluded that participants negotiated their multiple identities through "restorying" their identities "in the space between personal agency or self-construction and social discourse within a larger contextual setting" (p. 194).

FEMINIST RESEARCH METHODS

Feminist research is about revealing intersectionality in the lives of participants and transcending dichotomous positions, as Baber and Allen (1992) note, "in a way that acknowledges the interdependence and legitimacy of each conflicting position" (p. 4). Baber and Allen

recommend, for example, that the study of women's intimate adult relationships be expanded from women's experiences as wives and mothers to include their connections to other women as friends and lovers. Feminist researchers also consciously examine how the researcher and the researched interact based on the consistent negotiation of the politics of location throughout the research process. For example, researchers carefully monitor their own position (i.e., subjectivity) throughout the research process (e.g., sampling, interviewing, analyzing data, and presenting data) as well as their relationships with participants. As Lorraine Code (1995), a prominent feminist scholar, has observed, the "politics of speaking for, about, and on behalf of other women is one of the most contested areas in present-day feminist activism and research" (p. 30).

We propose that multicultural feminisms and critical race feminist theories can provide a framework with which family scholars can conceptualize, design, and conduct research as well as interpret and contextualize their findings. To illustrate how scholars can use both critical race and feminist perspectives to study and theorize about families, we have selected the topic of intimate partner violence. Researchers examining this topic could use critical race theory to analyze how limited resources (i.e., social, educational, political, economic) in certain racial/ethnic communities or biased legal and police responses to intimate violence may influence the choices women make in violent relationships. With this approach, intersectionality could be observed at multiple levels—intrapersonal, interpersonal, and community. Whereas critical race theory specifically contextualizes the experiences of different racial/ethnic families by examining within-group variation, researchers could use feminist theories such as Johnson's (1995) patriarchal terrorism and common couple violence theories to explain mutual couple violence across racial/ethnic groups. From this perspective, researchers would involve multiple constituencies to construct a holistic picture of intimate violence among different racial/ethnic groups. For instance, they might recruit both female and male participants to determine the frequency, severity, and type of violence as well as the coping strategies of family members. If social service agencies, battered women's shelters, counseling centers, or probation and parole departments are sources for participant recruitment, researchers could also interview staff members about departmental policies and legal responses to intimate violence in their communities. In addition, research that addresses the educational and training needs of professionals who may interact with violent couples could contribute to a more holistic picture of intimate violence in the community.

Methodologically, both multicultural feminist and critical race feminist theories are conducive to qualitative, quantitative, and mixed-method designs. Interviews, narratives, and nontraditional data, for example, have informed researchers about how intersectionality affects the lives of women and their families (Bell-Scott, 1994). Multicultural feminist, critical race feminist, and family scholars have also recognized the validity of integrating narrative documents and nontraditional data to understand human experience. In analyzing intersectionality, no one methodological approach—qualitative or quantitative—is better than the other. For example, in the hypothetical study of mutual couple violence described above, researchers could use a mixed-method approach to investigate the interaction of cultural factors and to develop intervention models for specific groups of abuse victims or violent couples. In addition to collecting data through surveys consisting of multiple empirical measures, researchers could also utilize the following methods:

- Semistructured individual interviews with both women and men that may allow researchers to co-construct the meaning of a phenomenon or theoretical concepts in a social context
- Q-sort methodologies that offer an opportunity for participants to explain their viewpoints by sorting items on

cards, after which the researcher groups and labels differing perspectives
- Genograms that track intergenerational patterns of family violence
- Nontraditional and nonliteral data (e.g., poetry, storytelling, diaries, photographs, creative art) that document the personal experiences of the participants
- Critical ethnographies (e.g., case studies, oral histories) that document or characterize family and community values toward intimate violence
- Focus groups that encourage brainstorming and inform changes in current cookie-cutter policies that may not meet the unique needs of racial/ethnic families
- Decolonizing methods that include research participants and community elders/leaders in the design of projects, interpretation and dissemination of results, and development of strategies for self-determination and community/ societal change

Feminist methods, then, entail mining these fields of intersectionality for individual and collective "partial stories" as well as examining the dynamic relationship between the researcher and study participants. Interdisciplinary, mixed-method designs utilizing nontraditional data offer inventive and fresh approaches to this task. As Allen (2000) reminds us, at both the analysis and representation stages of research we need to be conscious not only of how others negotiate intersectionality but also of how we "do" intersectionality. As researchers, we are also interpreters of participant experiences for consumption by our own communities (i.e., academia, social services, shelters). Our interpretations of the data we gather must be informed by the theories we use to contextualize the experiences of different racial/ethnic families. Otherwise, we risk inaccurately interpreting the voices of our participants and thus contribute to the distortion and/or marginalization of those stories.

KENTUCKY HOMELESS MOTHERS

Joanna M. Badagliacco, *University of Kentucky*

How can researchers give voice to impoverished families whose public identities are often politicized, misunderstood, and sometimes demonized? Which methodological tools must we use to present families accurately, respecting their lives and histories, without contributing to the war against the poor?

With regard to homeless families, there is little agreement on the actual number of such families or even what constitutes a homeless family. Scholars usually describe a "homeless family" as an undomiciled parent(s) with a child or children present, but it is most often a mother with her children. We know little about the characteristics of these families, the roots of their homelessness, their social support networks, or the prevalence of abuse and psychosocial problems among them. If we expect to help homeless mothers and children to become and remain housed, we need to know more about the causes and consequences of family homelessness, especially within a larger framework of poverty.

At the same time, deciding what constitutes "homelessness" presents substantial definitional and methodological problems. For example, are families that "double up" with relatives and/or friends homeless? If researchers or public agencies construct definitions of groups as "families," or as "homeless," how does this social construction fit with the way impoverished individuals feel about themselves and their situations? Understanding the concept of family and how it is socially constructed for different groups is central to understanding how an individual defines her or his own social statuses, such as parent or spouse, and actively or passively makes decisions concerning such issues as childbearing, child rearing, and marriage. Snow, Anderson, and Koegel (1994) argue that researchers must present a more balanced portrait of the conditions of homeless persons to redress the "distorting tendencies" that medicalize and decontextualize them.

In my work with impoverished mothers in Kentucky, I use ethnographic techniques, having them tell their own life histories. Thus far, I have interviewed 125 such mothers using an open-ended semistructured 1- to 3-hour protocol; three-quarters of these mothers are rural or Appalachian. They are not a monolithic group. They cross racial and regional boundaries in conceptualizing their personal and public identities as they navigate their relationships with men, their means of resolving their homelessness, and their reliance on the social welfare system. Through these women's discussions of their definitions of their situations and their proposed solutions, a needed counterpoint emerges to many of the commentaries on poor mothers currently offered.

My work redresses portrayals of poor women with children as pitiful, problematic, or immoral by validating their strength in dealing with their current situations and by identifying their survival strategies. The importance of gender in any analysis of poverty is central here. I argue that the reason for differences among the women in my study rests

(continued)

● **SPOTLIGHT ON METHODS** *continued*

in the degree to which they think about their lives as revolving around men or symbolic men (e.g., the state or the Christ figure) as opposed to seeing *themselves* at the core of their families. The women act in accordance with their internalized beliefs within the context of societal conceptualizations of families in poverty (Badagliacco, 1999).

In articulating the voices of homeless families, I am aware that the sequencing of topics, the particular questions asked, and the specific language used, as well as the overall tone of the interview, are extremely important. I use both open and closed questions in the interviews, and I encourage the mothers to talk about the issues that are important to them so that they can help others to understand how they view their situations.

The women have said that being interviewed was enjoyable, difficult, and even painful at times. Some have said that no one ever asked them about their lives before, and several have acknowledged the opportunity to speak for other women and children who preceded and will follow them. Most have been reflective before answering questions, and some have said that they were glad to have the chance to think about particular issues.

The methodological lesson of this work is that scholars and practitioners must *hear* the varied stories of homeless women with children in order to support such women effectively rather than punish them—to work *for* rather than merely *on* homeless mothers. ●

FEMINIST RESEARCH AS ACTIVISM

As activists, feminist family scholars frequently have advocated for research that is designed to improve women's lives and for reflexivity in the research process (e.g., Allen, 2000). *Reflexivity* refers to researchers' critical self-reflection on their own experiences and responses to others during the theory construction, research, or teaching/learning process. Just becoming aware of gendered, racial, or class inequities through reflexivity (i.e., *critical consciousness*) is not sufficient for accomplishing a feminist political agenda, however. The goals of feminist scholarship also include consciously improving the lives of women and families by advocating personal, institutional, or social change (e.g., Allen, Floyd-Thomas, & Gillman, 2001). In feminism, the practice of activism is called *praxis*. In praxis, action is to critical self-reflection as practice is to theory (see Galura, Meiland, Ross, Callan, & Smith, 1993).

A commitment to praxis requires family scholars to consider the interactive role of theory and research in feminist struggle. Praxis is difficult to define, and its meaning is usually left vague and intentionally undertheorized in most feminist writings, possibly because the concept of praxis bridges interests in both theory and methods. For example, "How do we find what women *qua* women have in common for a struggle against the oppression of women while not losing sight of the role of class and/or race privilege in the lives of some women and class and/or race oppression in the lives of other women, especially when they are systematically related?" (Johnson-Odim, 2001, p. 111). Thus the praxis goals of multicultural/critical race feminists demand that we reject a static, untheorized category "woman" and work toward improving the lives of women who are oppressed by the inequities of power relations in a variety of social locations—constituted by such intersecting identities as gender, race, ethnicity, and class.

Most feminist activists and scholars work toward eliminating women's subordination and disadvantage in families and conduct research that is based on feminist values and liberatory ideologies (Thompson & Walker, 1995). Feminist researchers, therefore, frequently adopt the strategy of action-oriented research. Related to the feminist goal of praxis, action research is designed to inform policy and practice and lead to social change (Small, 1995). Action researchers work collaboratively with study participants to shape the focus of the inquiry, to design the methodology, to interpret the results, and to craft a solution to a practical problem. Although likely to use diverse methods, action-oriented feminist researchers attend to their mutual interdependence with the people being studied, to their own reflexivity during a participatory research process, and to the ethical tensions that often emerge in the study of families (e.g., Few, Stephens, & Rouse-Arnett, 2003).

Feminist researchers have long been attracted by the ideals and methodologies developed in the "participatory research" and "participatory action research" traditions (e.g., Gutiérrez, Alvarez, Nemon, & Lewis, 1996). Based in the liberation politics of the 1960s, participatory research is committed to the emancipation of marginalized and oppressed groups through the upholding of principles of respecting, valuing, and centering the lived experiences and indigenous knowledge of those being studied (Olesen, 1994; Rose, 2001). Participatory researchers have developed methods and models that minimize hierarchical relationships in the participant-researcher relationship and that involve a collaborative approach throughout all stages of the research process (Reason, 1994). Participatory action researchers challenge traditional research models by inviting community-based stakeholders or activists to define the questions and topics that they believe are important based on their own experiences and histories. Hence their research questions are not derived from prior research or from theoretical considerations, but from "everyday experiences" of people who themselves are seeking creative solutions to the challenges they face (Lather, 1988).

CONCLUSION

In this chapter, we have advocated using multicultural feminist theories to encourage the careful analysis of within-group diversity and to promote debate of the politics of location within family studies. We have also advocated using critical race feminist theories as a link to applications that can take theorizing out of academe and contextualize it within political or legal settings. Although critical race perspectives have not often been used explicitly as theoretical frameworks in family studies, we propose that they may serve as a model for contemporary family scholars. For example, family policy researchers might use critical race feminist theory to explain the choices that racial/ethnic families make with respect to social and legal concerns, such as welfare reform or affirmative action policies.

Weedon (1999) has observed that "one of the strengths of recent feminist thought is the possibilities that it offers for thinking difference differently" (p. 196). In this chapter, we have located those possibilities in the integration of multicultural and critical race feminist theories as a viable, meaningful approach to thinking differently about the diversity among women and families. The central and key component of this third-wave framework is *transcendence* of identity politics to a metalevel of analysis that examines both the politics of location and the intersectionality of multiple identities. In this unique space, family studies scholars can attend to the complexities and contradictions of women's and families' lives through an epistemology that redefines, reinterprets, reclaims, and restores lived experience.

We also believe that poststructuralist theories, although often criticized for fragmenting identity, can help family theorists recognize the fluidity of identities by shifting the debate from micro-level essentialized notions of identity to more macro-level issues of sexism, racism, and classism in diverse cultures. Some feminist critics have argued that the tension between poststructuralist and standpoint or multicultural feminisms may lead to a divided feminist movement, pitting Eurocentric and multicultural feminisms against each other. On the other hand, we think that an integrated multicultural/critical race perspective provides an expanded third-wave feminist framework that allows for the reconciliation of feminist politics with identity politics *by recognizing that difference is relational rather than categorical.* In this poststructural view, deconstructing the category *other* means that we are all "other" to one another. The potential of family studies research, theory, and praxis to recognize the concrete, material conditions of diverse women and families lies in the successful integration and application of multicultural and critical race feminist theories. We hope that the feminist framework theorized in this chapter may serve as a promising approach to a reconfigured, empowering, and accountable understanding of identities and intersectionalities in family life.

NOTE

1. See this volume's companion Web site (http://www.ncfr.org/sourcebook) for descriptions of Arab American and Islamic feminisms, Asian American feminisms, Black feminisms, Latina/Hispanic feminisms, Native American feminisms, and White ethnic feminisms.

CASE STUDY

CHALLENGES FACED BY NONELITE WOMEN IN HIGHER EDUCATION

Norma Burgess, *Syracuse University*

The challenges that women in higher education face raise significant questions regarding the intersection of race, class, and gender. Vaguely defined standards, requirements, and guidelines are often used to the detriment of those outside of educational institutions' inner circles. Although much has been said about the value of inclusion, the numbers of persons in administration and faculty positions who are members of societally underrepresented groups continue to be slight in majority institutions of higher education, where the greatest resources and prestige reside.

It is clear that the advancement of an educational culture that is representative of the larger culture is stagnated by the lack of commitment evidenced by institutions of higher learning. We continue to hear about the lack of a pool of "qualified" candidates from which to select. *Qualified* is a term that the powers that be conveniently define to fit the situation. It serves to help them maintain a status quo that is present only in the minds of those to whom it belongs. A metaphor similar to status quo is "the good old days," which were good only for those who were privileged. In the good old days, tenure and promotion votes reflected whether the candidate was well liked, or they were payback from some of those who had gone on to make it in the big leagues in the "Mavory Tower," a place where the radicals have breached the gate and are making their own rules for themselves. Although it seems that academics should want to "do the right thing" and make their ranks in higher education more representative of society at large, just the opposite appears to be the case

CASE STUDY *continued*

in contemporary universities and colleges. The maintenance of elite status, devoid of the flavor that women scholars and African, Asian, and Latino scholars bring, has taken hold in the system.

Considerable hope was present several decades ago, as the old boys' network started to show signs of age. Many expected that as the old boys retired, they would be replaced by women and men who would be different from them. To some degree this happened: Many of the new professors who had been taught by the old boys brought a richness in background and culture to their universities. But look closer at the playing field today—it has not been leveled, except for a select few. The seemingly elite "minority" scholars that institutions chase each year somehow get presented as "all there is." They cost too much, and if they are hired at all, the level of resentment rises against them and the victory is bittersweet. When they arrive on campus, they are unlikely to establish camaraderie with other scholars. The elites at the top of the scholarly pyramid pay little attention to what their colleagues think in this day and age.

What does all this mean for the new junior faculty member who arrives with the requirement for collegiality looming even larger than the nationally funded external grant and the recommended numbers of publications in the very best journals and then some? The quality of life for such a scholar is diminished until he or she masters the game and adjusts to the new environment, which includes learning who did and did not vote for him or her to join the faculty. What would happen if this junior faculty member were to start out like the majority of young old boys in training? He or she would be welcomed, taken to the club, and shown the ropes; colleagues would publish and write grants with him or her. What is the price the nonelite faculty member pays to maintain contact with an extensive network of editorial boards, to learn who extends the best

invitations to publish, to find colleagues with whom he or she can collaborate?

FOLLOWING SHERLOTTA ON THE FELLOW BRICK ROAD TO THE LAND OF NOZ

The ultimate prize in the field of higher education is a tenured position at a research university. There are certainly other equally important jobs in many places, but in the Ph.D.-granting institution, tenured professors are allowed the privilege of certifying candidates as worthy of the responsibility of certifying others with similar training. One might expect that the process of attaining a tenured position would be open to all, and that all persons would have equal opportunity to achieve that goal. However, individuals from different backgrounds experience the journey to the "Land of Noz" on the "Fellow Brick Road" quite differently.

In Sherlotta's senior year at Prestige University, her mentors encourage her to continue her education and pursue a master's degree. She searches for the most prestigious university that offers the programs in which she is interested.

> *Step 1:* Examine individual graduate students' process of entry—who is asked for recommendations, who is there to write them, who encourages them to attend, and who encourages them to remain optimistic in the application and waiting process, makes phone calls for them, and so on.

Sherlotta keeps her dream alive and begins to believe that she can become a professor like her favorite mentor, who discusses the process with her. Her mentor tells her how her own graduate education and career in academia came about, but she leaves out many of the

Case Study

Case Study

pitfalls she faced because of her concern that such brutal honesty may discourage the potential student (or perhaps she assumes that Sherlotta's experience will be different).

Sherlotta's application is successful—she is accepted at graduate school. Once she arrives, excitement takes hold, and Sherlotta decides to pursue a doctoral degree, because her mentors recognize potential in her. The course work and exams are a breeze; Sherlotta completes all of her assignments on time. She then begins the dissertation process, the final step on the way to the Mavory Tower, the ultimate dream for all those who are seeking wisdom's crown. A doctoral degree is the key to success, a license to speak with authority and candor, and it is reserved only for those who dream big and know the rules of the game.

Step 2: Learn the rules. Who are the players? What are the rules of the game? How does one know that there is a game? Who defines the rules of the game? Do the rules ever change and, if so, how? To benefit whom? What triggers rule changes? How are opportunities granted? Who gets recognition and acknowledgment as the best graduate student? Who gets invited to work on research projects? Who gets to teach classes? Who gets to attend conferences? (Who even *knows* about the conferences?)

Sherlotta completes her dissertation and enters the job market, seeking the ultimate position of member of the Mavory Tower in the Land of Noz. The fellows define the Mavory Tower in many different ways. Those who are involved in significant ways see their roles differently than do those who simply follow the Fellow Brick Road. The road to the Land of Noz is filled with unthinkable land mines, real and imagined (e.g., self-doubt, negative and prejudicial people), that travelers

may anticipate or not, depending on how well they have answered the questions above.

Along the Fellow Brick Road and in the Land of Noz, education is the best equalizer. Sherlotta meets colleagues on the way to the Land of Noz, as they travel the Fellow Brick Road. They begin to share stories. Despite the divergent paths and different experiences that have brought them to the same place, they find that they have many things in common. As they share, they realize that they have both learned three things in their journeys:

1. They have come to understand the importance of networking in their field.

2. They have learned how to get along with other fellows in the Mavory Tower in the Land of Noz.

3. They have learned that, although each of them brings a different culture and language to the Mavory Tower, it is important for them, as fellows, to be like the group of fellows; that is, it is important that they "fit in."

CASE STUDY ANALYSIS

What important insights might be gained from a discussion of Sherlotta's journey to professorship in higher education? What might be the consequences of such a conversation between junior fellows who entered the Mavory Tower at the same time but in different departments? What lessons might such a conversation reveal? What can a junior fellow gain by taking the time to figure out the games being played in his or her institution, who the players are, and the strategies they are using? What factors and opportunities account for success in higher education?

DISCUSSION AND EXTENSION

INTEGRATING YOUTH INTO OUR FEMINIST THEORY, RESEARCH, AND PRACTICE

Kristine M. Baber, *University of New Hampshire*

The recent proliferation of theory and research focused on women and their experiences has resulted in an extensive body of work that is striking in its complexity, richness, and diversity, as well as in its need for synthesis and integration. In Chapter 18, De Reus, Few, and Blume take on the challenge of integrating multicultural and critical race feminist theories with the goal of influencing family studies research, theory, and practice to better serve the needs of all women and their families. Accomplishing this integration is a daunting task, but one that holds great promise for linking various groups' efforts to end oppressive power relations and to ensure equal access to political, economic, and social benefits. De Reus et al.'s poststructuralist approach also allows us to have optimism for the future. If power arrangements in our society are socially constructed and maintained, they can be deconstructed and reconstructed in ways that are more supportive of social equality. Such an assumption encourages us to extend our theory, research, and practice to include children and adolescents.

Adolescence is a critical time during which the individual constructs a sense of self and integrates multiple identities in relationship to a broad range of people and institutions. Most feminist theories and research, however, neglect to include youth explicitly, and thereby miss opportunities to work for change by developing strategies to reduce power struggles and promote equality among future generations. In this brief discussion, I consider how multicultural/critical race feminist theorists, researchers, and practitioners can work together to identify ways to socialize young people to support and expect equality. If power constructs difference (Kimmel, 2000), how do we equalize power in future cohorts of young people to reduce the social construction of differences that oppress certain groups to the benefit of others? How do we address the social construction of difference with youth in a manner that helps them understand the intersectionality of identity categories?

Interdependent systems of power and dominance and the resulting intersectionality of identities such as race/ethnicity, class, gender, and sexual orientation have captured the attention of scholars working to end oppression among adults (Collins, 1998; Johnson-Odim, 2001). Recent research that has included children and adolescents demonstrates how some scholars are exploring the relational constructions of race, class, and gender prior to adulthood. This work emphasizes the importance of bringing youth into theorizing and interventions for equality.

Pyke and Johnson (2003) investigated the simultaneous construction of gender and race in interviews with daughters of Korean and Vietnamese immigrants. Their participants' narratives constructed Asian women as submissive, quiet, and diffident in relation to American women, who were assumed to be independent, self-assured, outspoken, and powerful. Based on this construction, assimilation into the White mainstream was presumed to be the only path to gender equality, and assertive Asian American young women were "caught in a marginalized space that is

DISCUSSION AND EXTENSION

neither truly white nor Asian" (p. 50). In their multicultural research on girls' self-regard, Erkut, Fields, Sing, and Marx (1996) confirmed that although gender may be the primary site for struggle and negotiation for many White girls, this is not necessarily true for White girls living in poverty or for girls of other races and cultures.

Several studies suggest possibilities for bridging theory into practice. Moore (2001) found that "kids" (Moore's term, employed to denote active agency in children) used a racialized and genderized sense of age to organize their peer interactions in both traditional and "cultural awareness" summer camps. Moore's observations about the greater gender flexibility of the campers of color in the sample, the dynamics of inclusion and exclusion, and the ways in which adults' efforts assisted youth in relating across boundaries of difference can inform feminist theory, research, and practice. Other research has identified the importance of working on Whiteness and understanding how it intersects other categories of privilege. Fine, Weiss, Addleston, and Marusza (1997) documented how poor and working-class White boys and men constructed their identities in opposition to White women and African American men as they attempted to preserve vestiges of their presumed privilege. These authors urge us to identify or create spaces where White boys and men can construct identities that do not rest on opposition to and privilege over others.

A multicultural/critical race feminist approach requires us to actively and explicitly problematize and theorize Whiteness and the meanings, dynamics, and consequences of White racism (Frankenburg, 1993; Johnson, 1997; Maynard, 2001). We then should be better able to help White youth recognize their own privilege and not only develop a positive White racial identity but also take a stance against racism (Tatum, 1997). Young White males present a particular challenge because their White privilege is exacerbated by the

"unspoken solidarity around gender privilege" (Johnson, 1997, p. 224) that bonds all males regardless of other determinants of status and power.

Studies such as those noted above can help us understand how we might interrupt the intergenerational transmission of ideas that maintain hierarchical categorizations. An important part of breaking the cycle of oppression is sharing what we know with the next generation and helping youth explore and construct positive identities (Tatum, 1997). We also want to understand and resist discourse and other social practices that use difference to keep those of various ethnicities and those in positions of lesser power separated to reduce the likelihood of their working together as allies. If we agree that oppression operates through interdependent systems of power that are intertwined, mutually constructing, and intersecting, we can see that experiences of oppression are not discrete and separate (Collins, 1998). As a result, to paraphrase Johnson-Odim (2001, p. 123) and extend her reasoning to youth, White girls can be helped to see how antiracist work is critical to the struggle against sexism, and heterosexual youth can be assisted in understanding why addressing homophobia is their responsibility also.

The experiences of girls and women of color suggest potentially effective approaches for addressing multiple forms of exploitation. For example, the truth telling and other resistance strategies that Black mothers use for liberatory purposes in socializing their children (Basow & Rubin, 1999; Ward, 1996) can be employed more widely to acknowledge problems and demand change. Allied groups can confront the disparaging messages of the broader culture by using "intentional, overt, consistent activity that challenges prevailing patterns of oppression, makes privileges that are so often invisible visible, and facilitates the empowerment of persons targeted by oppression" (Ayvazian, 2001, p. 609). Schools,

DISCUSSION AND EXTENSION *continued*

communities, religious institutions, and families can develop preventive strategies to promote the value of diversity, transform discourse, and build strengths and skills in culturally sensitive ways (Vasquez & de las Fuentes, 1999).

If our ultimate goal is to improve the lives of all women and their families, our work needs to go beyond documenting difference based on race/ethnicity, class, sexual orientation, and other identity categories. We need to challenge the categories and constructions of difference that are generated in everyday interactions in our society and focus on racism, sexism, heterosexism, classism, and other social relations that interact to convert difference to oppression (Maynard, 2001). Including youth in our theory, research, and activism both increases the usefulness of this work and provides additional promise for transforming the future of our society.

Discussion and Extension

REFERENCES

Ahmed, L. (1992). *Women and gender in Islam.* New Haven, CT: Yale University Press.

Alcoff, L. (1988). Cultural feminism versus post-structuralism: The identity crisis in feminist theory. *Signs, 13,* 404–436.

Allen, K. R. (2000). A conscious and inclusive family studies. *Journal of Marriage and the Family, 62,* 4–17.

Allen, K. R., Floyd-Thomas, S. M., & Gillman, L. (2001). Teaching to transform: From volatility to solidarity in an interdisciplinary family studies classroom. *Family Relations, 50,* 317–325.

Ayvazian, A. (2001). Interrupting the cycle of oppression: The role of allies as agents of change. In P. S. Rothenberg (Ed.), *Race, class, and gender in the United States* (5th ed., pp. 609–615). New York: Worth.

Baber, K. M., & Allen, K. R. (1992). *Women and families: Feminist reconstructions.* New York: Guilford.

Baber, K. M., & Murray, C. I. (2001). A postmodern feminist approach to teaching human sexuality. *Family Relations, 50,* 23–33.

Badagliacco, J. M. (1999). "He's not Mr. Right, he's more like Mr. Now": Matrifocal and patrifocal discourses among homeless mothers in Kentucky. *Journal of Sociology and Social Welfare, 26,* 71–104.

Basow, S. A., & Rubin, L. R. (1999). Gender influences on adolescent development. In N. G. Johnson, M. C. Roberts, & J. Worell (Eds.), *Beyond appearance: A new look at adolescent girls* (pp. 25–52). Washington, DC: American Psychological Association.

Baumgardner, J., & Richards, A. (2000). *Manifesta: Young women, feminism, and the future.* New York: Farrar, Straus & Giroux.

Bell-Scott, P. (1994). Black women writing lives: An introduction. In P. Bell-Scott (Ed.), *Life notes: Personal writings by contemporary Black women* (pp. 17–26). New York: W. W. Norton.

Blume, L. B., & Blume, T. W. (2003). Toward a dialectical model of family gender discourse: Body, identity, and sexuality. *Journal of Marriage and Family, 65,* 785–794.

Brah, A. (2001). Difference, diversity, differentiation. In K.-K. Bhavnani (Ed.), *Feminism and "race"* (pp. 456–478). Oxford: Oxford University Press.

Code, L. (1995). How do we know? Questions of method in feminist practice. In S. D. Burt & L. Code (Eds.), *Changing methods: Feminists transforming practice* (pp. 13–44). Peterborough, ON: Broadview.

Collins, P. H. (1990). *Black feminist thought: Knowledge, consciousness, and the politics of empowerment.* New York: Routledge, Chapman & Hall.

Collins, P. H. (1998). *Fighting words: Black women and the search for justice.* Minneapolis: University of Minnesota Press.

Crenshaw, K. (1993). Demarginalizing the interaction of race and sex: A Black feminist critique of antidiscrimination doctrine, feminist theory, and antiracist politics. In D. Weisberg (Ed.), *Feminist legal theory: Foundations* (pp. 383–411). Philadelphia: Temple University Press.

Delgado, R., & Stefancic, J. (2001). *Critical race theory: An introduction.* New York: New York University Press.

Derrida, J. (1995). "Eating well," or the calculation of the subject. In E. Weber (Ed.), *Points . . . Interviews, 1974–1994* (P. Kamuf, Trans.) (pp. 255–287). Stanford, CA: Stanford University Press.

Erkut, S., Fields, J. P., Sing, R., & Marx, F. (1996). Diversity in girls' experiences: Feeling good about who you are. In B. J. R. Leadbeater & N. Way (Eds.), *Urban girls: Resisting stereotypes, creating identities* (pp. 53–63). New York: New York University Press.

Few, A. L., Stephens, D. P., & Rouse-Arnett, M. (2003). Sister-to-sister talk: Transcending boundaries and challenges in qualitative research with Black women. *Family Relations, 52,* 205–216.

Findlen, B. (Ed.). (1995). *Listen up: Voices from the next feminist generation.* Seattle: Seal.

Fine, M., Weiss, L., Addleston, J., & Marusza, J. (1997). (In)secure times: Constructing White working-class masculinities in the late 20th century. *Gender & Society, 11,* 52–68.

Frankenberg, R. (1993). *White women, race matters: The social construction of whiteness.* Minneapolis: University of Minnesota Press.

Galura, J., Meiland, R., Ross, R., Callan, M. J., & Smith, R. (1993). The meaning of praxis. In J. Galura, R. Meiland, R. Ross, M. J. Callan, & R. Smith (Eds.), *Praxis II: Service-learning resources for university students, staff and faculty* (pp. 1–26). Ann Arbor: University of Michigan Press.

Gutiérrez, L. M., Alvarez, A. R., Nemon, H., & Lewis, E. A. (1996). Multicultural community organizing: A strategy for change. *Social Work, 41,* 501–509.

Heywood, L., & Drake, J. (Eds.). (1997). *Third wave agenda: Being feminist, doing feminism.* Minneapolis: University of Minnesota Press.

Hill, M. R., & Thomas, V. (2000). Strategies for racial identity development: Narratives of Black and White women in interracial partner relationships. *Family Relations, 49,* 193–200.

Johnson, A. (1997). *The gender knot: Unraveling our patriarchal legacy.* Philadelphia: Temple University Press.

Johnson, M. (1995). Patriarchal terrorism and common couple violence: Two forms of violence against women in U.S. families. *Journal of Marriage and the Family, 57,* 283–294.

Johnson-Odim, C. (2001). Who's to navigate and who's to steer? A consideration of the role of theory in feminist struggle. In M. deKoven (Ed.), *Feminist locations: Global and local, theory and practice* (pp. 110–126). New Brunswick, NJ: Rutgers University Press.

Kimmel, M. S. (2000). *The gendered society.* New York: Oxford University Press.

Lather, P. (1988). Feminist perspective on empowering research methodologies. *Women's Studies International Forum, 11,* 569–581.

Lewis, E. A. (2003, November). *Another case of "where you stand determines what you see."* Paper presented at the Theory Construction and Research Methodology Workshop, annual meeting of the National Council on Family Relations, Vancouver.

Macht, M., & Quam, J. (1986). *Social work: An introduction.* Columbus, OH: Merrill.

Maynard, M. (2001). "Race," gender and the concept of "difference" in feminist thought. In K.-K. Bhavnani (Ed.), *Feminism and "race"* (pp. 121–133). Oxford: Oxford University Press.

McAdoo, H. P. (2003, November). *A second-wave feminist looks at the intersectionalities of third-wave feminism.* Paper presented at the Theory Construction and Research Methodology Workshop, annual meeting of the National Council on Family Relations, Vancouver.

Mohanty, C. T. (1999). Feminist encounters: Locating the politics of experience. In L. Nicholson & S. Seidman (Eds.), *Social postmodernism: Beyond identity politics* (pp. 68–86). Cambridge: Cambridge University Press.

Moloney, M., & Fenstermaker, S. (2002). Performance and accomplishment: Reconciling feminist conceptions of gender. In S. Fenstermaker & C. West (Eds.), *Doing gender, doing difference: Inequality, power, and institutional change* (pp. 189–204). New York: Routledge.

Moore, V. A. (2001). "Doing" racialized and gendered age to organize peer relations: Observing kids in summer camp. *Gender & Society, 15,* 835–858.

Moraga, C., & Anzaldúa, G. (Eds.). (1981). *This bridge called my back: Writings by radical women of color.* New York: Kitchen Table/ Women of Color.

Moynihan, D. P. (1965). *The Negro family: The case for national action.* Washington, DC: U.S. Department of Labor, Office of Policy Planning and Research.

Najmabadi, A. (1998). Feminism in an Islamic republic: "Years of hardship, years of growth." In Y. Y. Haddad & J. L. Esposito (Eds.), *Islam, gender, and social change* (pp. 59–84). New York: Oxford University Press.

Olesen, V. (1994). Feminisms and models of qualitative research. In N. K. Denzin & Y. S. Lincoln (Eds.), *Handbook of qualitative research* (pp. 158–174). Thousand Oaks, CA: Sage.

Osmond, M. W., & Thorne, B. (1993). Feminist theories: The social construction of gender in families and society. In P. Boss, W. J. Doherty, R. LaRossa, W. R. Schumm, & S. K. Steinmetz (Eds.), *Sourcebook of family theories and methods: A contextual approach* (pp. 591–622). New York: Plenum.

Pyke, K. D., & Johnson, D. L. (2003). Asian American women and racialized femininities: "Doing" gender across cultural worlds. *Gender & Society, 17,* 33–53.

Reason, P. (1994). Three approaches to participative inquiry. In N. K. Denzin & Y. S. Lincoln (Eds.), *Handbook of qualitative research* (pp. 324–339). Thousand Oaks, CA: Sage.

Rose, S. (2001). Reflections on empowerment-based practice. *Social Work, 45,* 403–420.

St. Pierre, E., & Pillow, W. (Eds.). (2000). *Working the ruins: Feminist poststructural theory and methods in education.* New York: Routledge.

Sandoval, C. (2000). *Methodology of the oppressed.* Minneapolis: University of Minnesota Press.

Siegel, D. L. (1997). Reading between the waves: Feminist historiography in a "postfeminist" movement. In L. Heywood & J. Drake (Eds.), *Third wave agenda: Being feminist, doing feminism* (pp. 55–82). Minneapolis: University of Minnesota Press.

Small, S. A. (1995). Action-oriented research: Models and methods. *Journal of Marriage and the Family, 57,* 941–955.

Smith, L. T. (1999). *Decolonizing methodologies: Research and indigenous peoples.* New York: Zed.

Snow, D. A., Anderson, L., & Koegel, P. (1994). Distorting tendencies in research on the homeless. *American Behavioral Scientist, 37,* 461–475.

Staples, R. (1971). Towards a sociology of the Black family: A theoretical and methodological assessment. *Journal of Marriage and the Family, 33,* 119–138.

Staples, R. (1985). Changes in Black family structure: The conflict between family ideology and structural conditions. *Journal of Marriage and the Family, 47,* 1005–1013.

Sudbury, J. (1998). *"Other kinds of dreams": Black women's organizations and the politics of transformation.* London: Routledge.

Tatum, B. D. (1997). *"Why are all the Black kids sitting together in the cafeteria?" and other conversations about race.* New York: Basic Books.

Thompson, L., & Walker, A. J. (1995). The place of feminism in family studies. *Journal of Marriage and the Family, 57,* 847–865.

Vasquez, M. J. T., & de las Fuentes, C. (1999). American-born Asian, African, Latina, and American Indian adolescent girls: Challenges and strengths. In N. G. Johnson, M. C. Roberts, & J. Worell (Eds.), *Beyond appearance: A new look at adolescent girls* (pp. 151–173). Washington, DC: American Psychological Association.

Wagner, S. R. (1996). *The untold story of the Iroquois influence on early feminists.* Fayetteville, NY: Sky Carrier.

Walker, R. (Ed.). (1995). *To be real: Telling the truth and changing the face of feminism.* New York: Doubleday.

Ward, J. V. (1996). Raising resisters: The role of truth telling in the psychological development of African American girls. In B. J. R. Leadbeater & N. Way (Eds.), *Urban girls: Resisting stereotypes, creating identities* (pp. 85–99). New York: New York University Press.

Weedon, C. (1999). *Feminism, theory, and the politics of difference.* Oxford: Blackwell.

West, C., & Zimmerman, D. H. (1987). Doing gender. *Gender & Society, 1,* 125–151.

Wing, A. K. (Ed.). (1997). *Critical race feminism: A reader.* New York: New York University Press.

• Nineteen

SOCIOECONOMIC STATUS AND CHILDHOOD EXTERNALIZING BEHAVIORS

A Structural Equation Framework

Robert Flynn Corwyn, *University of Arkansas at Little Rock*

Robert H. Bradley, *University of Arkansas at Little Rock*

Technological innovations are propelling rapid changes in the world of work, with economic structures scrambling to keep pace and families struggling to position themselves so as to become beneficiaries of whatever new alignments emerge. As we stand at this crossroads of history, social scientists once again are challenged to clarify relations among socioeconomic status (SES), family functioning, and child development. In this chapter we take up the challenge, and we do so with considerable enthusiasm. Four factors contribute to our enthusiasm for future studies: historic significance, theoretical developments, the availability of relevant data, and vastly improved statistical tools. In a sense, the historic significance forcefully outlines the importance of the research question, theoretical developments represent what is known about the topic, and available data

and statistical techniques determine the boundaries of what questions can be addressed. We interweave these four factors to provide a broad outline of our current research agenda on the topic of family process mediators of relations between SES and child development. We highlight three aspects of the literature that may prove to be among the most exciting developments in the field: including assets as a measure of SES, theoretical integration, and supplementing traditional research with a person-centered approach. Throughout the chapter, we refer readers to supplemental material provided on this volume's companion Web site (http://www.ncfr.org/sourcebook).

HISTORIC SIGNIFICANCE

Just as historic forces were the catalyst for theoretical and empirical breakthroughs after the Great Depression and the farm crisis of the mid-1980s (Conger et al. 2002), today's scholars are wrestling with the same basic questions as they pertain to new social realities. Census statistics show that since the late 1970s, the only group gaining in aggregate share of household income has been the top one-fifth of the household income distribution (see the U.S. Bureau of the Census Web site, http://www.census.gov). The distribution of wealth now shows vastly greater disparities. Moreover, evidence suggests that education and health care systems have become increasingly bifurcated, with affluent families receiving superior educations and health care. Accordingly, it is time to revisit conceptualizations of SES that were in vogue when the construct was first introduced. In particular, assets (or wealth) have been neglected in family and child development scholarship for several decades despite evidence that assets have a significant independent effect on child well-being (Conley, 1999; Oliver & Shapiro, 2001). Refocusing on assets and how they matter in children's lives has huge potential to energize the research agenda for the upcoming decades. Consider, for example, if assets where shown to matter more than income, parental occupation, and parental education. This alone could force policy makers to reform welfare so that it shifts from an income maintenance program to an asset-building one, as several have suggested (Shapiro & Wolff, 2001). In other words, it could be that a better long-term solution to poverty is to facilitate the passing on of economic assets from one generation to the next.

SYSTEMS THEORIES

Central to developmental systems theory is the idea that human activity and human development reflect ongoing exchanges between individuals and their multifaceted, multilayered contexts, with each aspect of context constraining and potentiating the others (Lerner & Walls, 1999). Closely related is general system theory, or GST (von Bertalanffy, 1968), which posits that human behavior is shaped in a context of multiple systems of influence

(e.g., family, school, peers, neighborhood, biological). For example, childhood externalizing problems are viewed as being influenced by child characteristics (e.g., temperament, attachment security, competence, peer acceptance, negative attribution bias), family characteristics (e.g., poverty status, maternal depression, harsh discipline, marital discord), and community circumstances (e.g., neighborhood crime, quality of child care). In GST, *interdependence,* the interconnectedness of component systems (e.g., child, parent) within a system (e.g., family), is considered a fundamental concept. So is the concept of *mutual influence:* the idea that behaviors of one component reverberate across the whole system. For example, maternal depression has a negative effect on parenting practices, parent-child relationships, and the marital relationship. The concept of *hierarchy* stipulates that all systems (e.g., family system) are made up of smaller subsystems (e.g., sibling system). Likewise, all systems are subsystems of larger suprasystems (e.g., community system). The concept of *holism* states that a system is more than the sum of its parts. One cannot understand a family system, for example, by looking at parent(s) and child(ren) in isolation. Relationships and patterns of interaction among parents and children are also critical.

Of particular interest to research on parenting processes involved in relations between SES/poverty and child outcomes is the concept of *equifinality.* It means that a system may achieve a particular goal in more than one way. For example, parents may foster behavioral control of a child by being responsive to the child's needs, by using strict discipline, or by keeping the child engaged in productive activities. An important companion concept is *multifinality:* the idea that the same process can influence multiple outcomes. This suggests that, although a particular set of parenting behaviors (e.g., affording opportunities for learning) may tend to act most directly on one developmental outcome (e.g., cognitive), the probability of spillover into other forms of development is likely to be high (e.g. behavioral).

The bidirectional child → parent relationship underscores a key proposition of systems thinking: Specifically, children are a source of their own development. That is, they induce particular behaviors from others and, as they age, they increasingly select the environments in which they spend time (Harris, 1995). Likewise, parents are conscious active agents who react to and affect their children's environments. The ongoing interplay among family members means that the family system is a dynamic entity characterized by constant change at all levels (Lerner & Walls, 1999). These tenets of developmental systems thinking focus the attention of researchers on the relations between different levels of the developmental system, and changes in these relations are depicted as the primary cause of developmental change.

FAMILY PROCESS MODELS

For decades, evidence has accumulated that social and economic resources connected with family life have a significant effect on child development. Much of the effect appears to be mediated by what children are exposed to at home (Bradley & Corwyn, 2002). In general, children living in poverty receive less stimulation and support at home than do nonpoor children; they are also exposed to more negative conditions and events. An excellent exemplar of a theoretical model depicting the home environment as a mediator is the family process model. Under the umbrella, family process models are both "resource" models and "deficit" models. The former consider resources as exogenous variables and are derived using such theoretical frameworks as Coleman's (1988) notions about capital. Specifically, Coleman argues that children need three types of capital in order to thrive: financial (money for food, clothing, shelter, and so on), human (instrumental assistance), and social (supportive networks). Deficit models, on the other hand, include such perspectives as the "stress and coping perspective" the "economic deprivation perspective," and the "welfare culture perspective." Each of these perspectives is concerned with the negative effects of chronic diversity on child development. However, models developed in the two traditions were designed to answer somewhat different questions. SES researchers typically focus on the positive effects of economic and social resources, whereas poverty researchers focus on the negative effects of material hardship. Even so, the interests of both converge on many of the same outcomes and mediators.

The family stress model is perhaps the most widely used deficit model. It emerged from studies of families during the Great Depression and the great farm crisis in the rural Midwest (Conger et al., 2002). It depicts a series of mediating processes: perceived economic pressure → emotional distress of caregivers → damaged parent-child and spousal relationships and dysfunctional parenting practices → and maladaptive child outcomes. Economic hardship (poverty) is the exogenous variable in such models. Particularly revealing are studies linking chronic low income to harsh and neglectful parenting via stress-induction (Conger et al., 2002).

Family process models are mediating models. For example, one hypothesized *mediating effect* is that high SES has a positive influence on the provision of productive activities, which, in turn, influences child cognitive and behavioral development. Thus productive activities mediate the relation between SES and child development.

RESILIENCE

Research on child poverty generally approaches relations between low income and child well-being from a "deficit perspective." However, a recent paradigm shift has resulted in research aimed at understanding how children thrive despite exposure to adverse circumstances. This new focus draws from evolutionary views pertaining to human adaptation and recognizes self-righting tendencies and the capacity of humans to act consciously in ways that offset the pernicious effects of adversity. Resilience scholars posit

[handwritten: how stressed you are about your financial situation?]

that certain characteristics of individuals and families are associated with a resilience process. For example, a parent with a high level of agreeableness might be able to treat a child in a warm and nurturant way despite the family's living in poverty, thereby offsetting the generally negative impact of poverty on child well-being. Consistent with evolutionary theory, resilience processes are considered to be normally occurring functions of human adaptational systems (Masten, 2001).

Research has identified both mediation and moderation models of the resilience process. With regard to the effects of poverty status on externalizing behaviors in children, adaptive parenting (e.g., assistance, support, agreeableness) would be a mediator (adaptational system) of the effect of parental characteristics (e.g., SES) on children. Characteristics of the child, the family, or the broader environment are potential *moderators* of the effects of adversity. To illustrate, positive assets of the child may condition the effect of adversity on child outcomes whereby those children possessing high levels of the asset may not be negatively influenced by adversity, whereas those children who do not possess the asset are negatively affected.

ISSUES TO CONSIDER

Prior to developing empirical examples, we derived a list of important issues to consider (see this volume's companion Web site). First, it is important to keep the theoretical and modeling issues related to resource models (e.g., SES) and deficit models (e.g., poverty) separate, as they are designed to address different research questions. Second, it is a serious mistake to use a single component of SES as a proxy for the total array of resources implied by SES. This practice tends to overestimate the effects of the single component used. More specifically, it is more accurate to call maternal education "maternal education" than to treat it as equivalent to SES. Relatedly, composite measures may better represent the amalgam of social and economic resources implied by SES than any

one of its components, but their use can obscure how access to particular financial and social capital influences child well-being. Consistent with the systems concepts of equifinality and multifinality, recent studies confirm that each component operates through somewhat different mechanisms to affect the same outcome, and the same mechanism can influence multiple outcomes (Bradley & Corwyn, 2002). Fourth, the use of yearly household income as an index of family economic well-being is not wholly satisfactory in many research situations. Because household income can be quite unstable, it is often beneficial to use averaged income over multiple years or persistent poverty. However, wealth (or accumulated assets) represents a separate dimension of financial resources, one that family members can draw on when income falls short of needs (Oliver & Shapiro, 2001).

A particularly difficult problem is keeping SES effects separate from ethnicity effects. Ethnicity is confounded with economic status, so it isn't always clear whether specific patterns of human behavior (e.g., parenting practices) reflect ethnicity or social class or some combination. Research establishes two things: (a) Relations between socioeconomic factors and parenting practices vary by ethnicity and (b) the mediating pathways linking SES to child outcomes vary across ethnic groups. A systems theory view reveals just how difficult it is to tease apart SES effects and ethnicity effects (see this volume's Web site). Stated succinctly, if child development is a relational process among the child, parents, school, and peers across different contexts (e.g., home, school, peer group) that is characterized by constant change, then they become fused so that they are more than the sum of the two parts (i.e., the concept of holism).

STRUCTURAL EQUATION MODELING: A VARIABLE-CENTERED APPROACH

Most quantitative research has been conducted using a variable-centered approach to data analysis. That is, the interest has been in the relations between variables (e.g., maternal education and child IQ). In structural equation modeling (SEM), relations between variables are prespecified, and the variances and covariances of variables are written as functions of the hypothesized model. The purpose of SEM is to determine how well the actual covariations among variables in the model fit the hypothesized model. Following three examples in which we use SEM to examine key theoretical propositions concerning relations among SES/poverty, parenting, and child outcomes.

Empirical Example 1: Path Analysis From the SES (Resources) Perspective

Data for the first example were taken from the 1998 combined mother and child National Longitudinal Survey of Youth (NLSY; see the U.S. Bureau of Labor Statistics Web site at http://www.bls.gov/nls/nlsy79.htm). The children ranged from 6 to 9 years old and the mothers from 34 to 41 years old. NLSY is a cohort study of a nationally representative group of women who entered their childbearing years in 1979. Beginning in 1986, biennial assessments of the children of the NLSY cohort were conducted. Because multiple siblings were surveyed in many households, within-family dependencies (i.e., children in the same household were not independent) had to be addressed. One commonly used approach is to correct parameter estimates using robust standard errors. Another common choice, the approach we took, is to randomly select only one child from each family. That decision, although it reduces technical problems connected with data dependency, reduces the representativeness of findings in that children living in large families are disproportionately eliminated.

Among the child outcome measures available in NLSY, we focused on two: the Behavior Problems Index (BPI) and the PIAT-Math score (Dunn & Markwardt, 1970). Previous research shows that each is associated with SES (Bradley & Corwyn, 2002). In accordance with theory, we selected two quite different aspects of children's home environments that

appear implicated in children's behavior and achievement: parental responsivity and learning stimulation. These two constructs were measured using items from the short form of the Home Observational Measure of the Environment (HOME-SF; Caldwell & Bradley, 1984). Exogenous variables for the analyses were three components of SES: averaged net family income (1994, 1996, 1998), assets, and maternal education (see Figure 19.1).

Missing data can present severe problems for multivariate procedures. The question arises: How does one treat missing data so as to limit its damage? Ad hoc procedures such as listwise, casewise deletion and mean substitution are rarely the best choice. Advanced statistical software often includes better options. For example, the AMOS program (Arbuckle & Wothke, 1999) used in this example offers a full-information (casewise) maximum-likelihood technique that maximizes a likelihood function from observed data. However, we elected to use the NORM program by Schafer (1997). NORM uses the EM algorithm for covariance matrices as a starting point to impute multiple data sets using a data augmentation procedure. Despite the fact that it is based on the normal distribution model, it is robust to violations of normality.

Note that both equifinality and multifinality are modeled in Figure 19.1. Each component of SES can operate through different paths to influence children (equifinality), and each series of paths can influence more than one outcome (multifinality). One assumption of family process models is that SES exerts influence primarily through parenting and the home environment. However, it is always the case that responsivity and learning stimulation only partially mediate the relation between SES and child outcome. Specifically, direct paths from SES components to child outcomes may be as strong as indirect paths through these two mediators. However, extant theory does not stipulate precisely which SES component will directly influence which outcome. For this reason, we tested only indirect paths. In order to see whether direct paths may provide a better fit to the data, we asked the AMOS program to provide suggestions to

Figure 19.1   Family Process Model

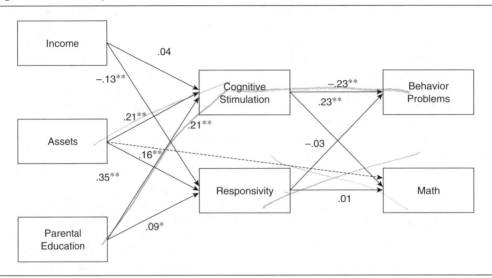

NOTE: Dotted line added per modification index.

*p < .05; **p < .01.

improve the model via modification indices. (*Note:* Rather than specifying a direct path from an SES resource to a child outcome, theories stipulate the processes connecting the two. Finding evidence for a "direct path" generally indicates that there is at least one unspecified mediator.)

Caution is advised when using modification indices. It is an exploratory process that does not derive from a conceptual framework. A risk of respecifying a model based on modification indices is that the new model may reflect chance (or idiosyncrasies of the data) rather than real and replicable associations among model elements. Hayduk (1987, p. 177) suggests that refinements to tested models should be based 90% on theory and 10% on data. Following suggestions by Hayduk, we split the data in two equal halves, tested the model in the first half, and used the second half to cross-validate the model using multiple-group analysis. Multiple-group analysis is used to determine whether a hypothesized model fits the same for two or more groups. When models are analyzed simultaneously across different groups, the equality of one or more parameters across groups can be statistically tested with a χ^2 difference test (see this volume's Web site).

Based on previous work with these data, we were not surprised that modification indices suggested adding a path from assets to math (see example1.doc on the volume's Web site; note that all citations of such documents in this chapter refer to materials linked to the Web site). To cross-validate these findings, we "stacked" models for both groups into a single AMOS file (see Basic1.doc) and analyzed them simultaneously. The combined χ^2 was 62.576 (*df* = 14). If there were no capitalization on chance, the model would fit similarly across both random halves of data. When all regression paths were constrained to be equal across groups, χ^2 increased to 68.451 (*df* = 25) (example1d.doc). The change in χ^2 ($\Delta\chi^2$) was 5.875 (i.e., 68.451 − 62.576) with a change of 11 degrees of freedom. Because 5.875 is less than the critical value for 11 degrees of freedom (i.e., 19.68 at .05 level of significance), we concluded that the model-building process did not capitalize on chance.

We performed checks for collinearity and outliers and found no serious problems. (In example1d.doc, under the section labeled "standardized regression weights" for group 2, you will find the standardized regression coefficients that are shown in Figure 19.1.)

Of the three components of SES, assets had the second-highest effect on cognitive stimulation ($\beta = .21$, $t = 4.848$) and the highest effect on responsivity ($\beta = .16$, $t = 3.276$). Given that responsivity was not significantly related to either behavior problems or math, the effects of SES components are not mediated through responsivity. Notice, too, that cognitive stimulation had a significant negative effect on behavior problems. This finding has emerged in several studies (e.g., Yeung, Linver, & Brooks-Gunn, 2002); we discuss it in the next example.

Reciprocal Effects

Systems theory posits bidirectional influence between child and environment. However, adding reciprocal effects increases the demands of theoretical justification and the technical complexity of modeling (see the volume's Web site). Some researchers argue that models should specify a specific amount of time between cause and effect (i.e., causal lag). They argue that a model that specifies bidirectional effects in cross-sectional data will not incorporate the time ordering of effects (i.e., the causal lag). For example, cross-lag panel designs are particularly useful for studying reciprocal effects. However, from a systems perspective, it could be argued that a cross-sectional measure is the result of a *history* of interactions between arrays of influences. Thus, for example, a single measure of behavior problems can be both the cause *of* and caused *by* a concurrent measure of parental responsiveness. For illustrative purposes, we added a reciprocal path to Figure 19.1 from BPI to responsivity (see reciprocal .doc). These results are quite interesting. Before the reciprocal effect was added, the responsivity to BPI path was only −.03. This changed to −.44 with a corresponding .446 path from BPI to responsivity. If modeled correctly, the results suggest that two significant processes may be taking place simultaneously in the population that canceled out when only the path from responsivity to BPI was considered. Although the negative effect of responsivity on behavior problems

was expected, the positive effect of behavior problems on responsivity was not. Perhaps this positive effect represents highly active children who elicit more reaction from the parent (i.e., talking to the child). In the preceding example, we assumed that the causal process is highly stable. If replicated in a longitudinal design, these effects may prove quite revealing.

Mediating Effects

One of the most useful aspects of path analysis is the ability to decompose total effects into direct and indirect effects (see the volume's Web site). One obtains indirect effects (or mediating effects) simply by multiplying the two path coefficients represented in the indirect effect. For example, the indirect effect of education on behavior through stimulation is $.350 \times -.226 = -.0791$ (Figure 19.1). Using this multiplicative rule, the important mediating effects can be gleaned from Figure 19.1. First, responsivity is not a mediator because it has no effect on either outcome, and income is not mediated because it has no effect on stimulation. Therefore, the salient mediating effects are those of assets and education through stimulation. Finally, because the direct effect of stimulation on behavior is nearly the same as its direct effect on math, the indirect effects of SES components on both outcomes are approximately the same— illustrating the concept of multifinality. Moreover, the influence of assets on math suggests that some other (unspecified) mediator explains the process by which assets influence math ability.

Empirical Example 2:
Hybrid SEM Model Integrating
the Stress Model and Resilience Theory

The National Institute of Child Health and Human Development Study of Early Child Care (NICHD-SECC) contains a rich array of contextual variables for investigating possible additions to the family stress model (see the NICHD Web site at http://public.rti.org/secc).

Figure 19.2   Expanded Family Stress Model of Child Externalizing Behavior

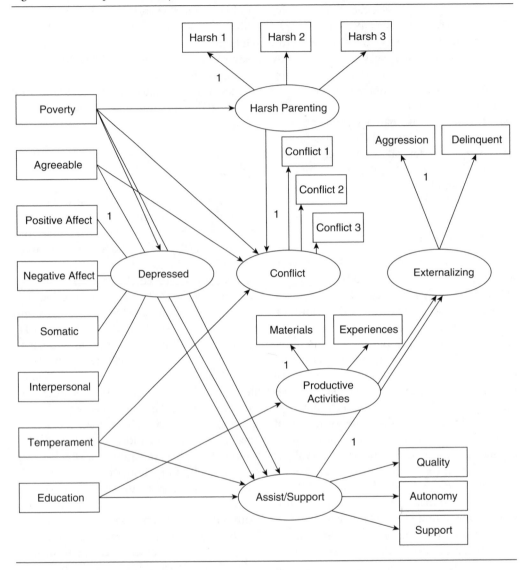

Another valuable feature of this study is that it follows families longitudinally over regular intervals, allowing researchers to investigate questions of stability, change, intraindividual variability, and individual differences in intra-individual variability. The second phase of NICHD-SECC followed 1,226 children from age 3 through first grade between 1995 and 2000.

Figure 19.2 shows a family stress model with additional elements representing potentially interesting paths derived from positive psychology and findings from the resilience literature. In the basic stress model, living in poverty affects child outcomes through maternal depression, harsh parenting, marital discord, mother-child conflict, and low parental involvement (Conger & Elder, 1994). This basic model lends itself to theoretical elaboration. Resilience literature proposes that characteristics of the child and the environment mediate (and/or moderate) the detrimental effects of living in adverse circumstances. Based on this literature, maternal agreeableness and maternal education were added to the family stress model as potential compensatory factors. Child temperament was also added in that temperament is construed by ecological/developmental theorists as having the potential to increase the damaging effects of adversity (i.e., difficult children are more likely than easy children to succumb to challenging circumstances) or to decrease the negative impacts (i.e., easy children tend to secure help in dealing with adversity and are not as prone as difficult children to overreact emotionally to adverse circumstances). Potential moderators discussed in the literature include child competence, attachment to caregiver, gender, and hostile attribution bias (see Masten, 2001). The Child Behavior Checklist (CBCL) was used to measure externalizing behavior (Achenbach & Edelbrock, 1981) because it has been shown to be valid and reliable and because it was administered to multiple informants (mothers, fathers, and teachers). With multiple informants on the same measure, it is possible to investigate reporter bias—a crucial issue in the current study. Moreover, the factor structure of the CBCL has also been investigated in several previous studies (see the volume's Website), providing evidence that it has the same meaning across informants and across some cultural groups.

One beneficial feature of SEM is that it addresses the issue of measurement error directly by including information from multiple measures of unobserved (latent) constructs and extracting the variance that is common to the factor on which all load. Other statistical techniques, such as regression analysis, assume that all constructs are measured without error. Unfortunately, this powerful feature of SEM has a potential downside. If researchers use measures of the same putative construct that do not all measure that construct, then SEM (in looking for common variance among the measures) may create a construct that has no real meaning (i.e., a faux construct). Because of this risk, researchers

must take great care to include only valid measures of theoretically relevant constructs.

Because data sets often do not contain multiple bona fide indicators of key constructs in a model, researchers may wish to consider a hybrid SEM model. Hybrid models include both single-indicator (manifest) and multiple-indicator constructs (latent).

The majority of well-regarded scales consist of multiple items using a binary format or a format allowing three to five response choices. Thus using single items can be problematic because it violates the normality assumption of maximum-likelihood estimation (the estimation procedure most often employed in SEM). Theoretically, asymptotic distribution-free estimators can be used with categorical data, but they require very large sample sizes (Yung & Bentler, 1994). One option is to use the summary scores from scales as single manifest variables in a model. Another option is to create parcels by combining two or more items. Summing scores usually improves the distributional properties over single-item measures and decreases the number of parameters that must be estimated. These item parcels can be used as multiple indicators of a construct and allow researchers to incorporate error in the analysis. Researchers should be cautious when considering item parcels and should be aware of the arguments for and against parceling (see the volume's Web site). Parceling is particularly troublesome in scale development studies and should be used only in studies of relations between latent constructs when the constructed item parcel scales are shown to be unidimensional. For the research discussed in this chapter, we formed parcels by randomly selecting items from two scales, one that measured mother-child conflict and a second that measured harsh parenting.

A crucial issue to consider is reporter bias. For example, the way a reporter rates a child's behavior depends on the relationship between reporter and child and the context in which the behavior is most often observed. Not surprisingly, there is often only a modest correlation between ratings given by different reporters. This issue is central to

Table 19.1   Results of Family Stress Model for Paths Directly Related to CBCL for Three Reporters

| | Path From | | |
	Mother	Father	Teacher
Harsh parenting	.20	.08	.48
	(.05)	(.08)	(.09)
	4.38	.94	5.25
Mother-child conflict	.42	.19	.15
	(.03)	(.03)	(.03)
	15.97	6.50	5.17
Productive activity	−.14	−.22	−.33
	(.03)	(.05)	(.05)
	−5.45	−4.92	−6.55
Support	.00	.00	.07
	(.02)	(.04)	(.05)
	.20	.08	1.44

NOTE: Standardized coefficients; standard errors appear in parentheses, and *t* values appear below standard errors.

a developmental systems perspective on child development. The mother-child, father-child, and teacher-child relationships consist of uniquely shared influences and histories. Thus there should be differences in the factors that influence the perceived conduct of the child according to the reporting source. It is important to note that behavior in a particular context will generally be more strongly related to characteristics and relationships of persons from that context than to characteristics of persons and relationships outside that context. However, systems theory also postulates connections between systems that people inhabit. Thus characteristics of persons and relationships in one system (e.g., the family) can influence behavior in a second system (e.g., the school). In our model where teacher-reported CBCL was used as the outcome measure, we proposed that the family stress model would have an influence on child externalizing behavior in school.

Because NICHD-SECC included CBCL data on the same child from mothers, fathers, and teachers, we were able to analyze the family stress model for three separate relationships by simply changing the dependent variable to mother-, father-, or teacher-reported CBCL. The hope was to provide a more complete picture of emerging behavioral difficulties in young children. We performed the analysis with LISREL 8.54 (Jöreskog & Sörbom, 1996), using maximum-likelihood estimation. (Although the LISREL output files are available for examples in this chapter, and explanations of the technical aspects of the analyses are provided on this volume's Web site, interested readers are encouraged to consult other excellent sources to learn more about SEM and LISREL.)

The results for mother-, father-, and teacher-reported CBCL are available in example2_mom.doc, example2_dad.doc, and example2_teacher.doc, respectively. Table 19.1 summarizes the standardized coefficients, standard errors (in parentheses), and *t* values (above 1.96 is significant) for all paths leading directly to child externalizing behavior. There is evidence of reporter bias; that is, mother-child conflict was much more strongly related to mother-reported behavior problems than to father-reported or teacher-reported problems. Although this finding is consistent with systems theory, the nature of the two constructs suggests something more: Specifically,

Table 19.2   Total Effects of Exogenous Variables on Mother- and Teacher-Reported CBCL

	Poverty	*Agreeableness*	*Temperament*	*Education*
Teacher CBCL	0.23	−0.02	0.01	−0.08
	(0.08)	(0.00)	(0.03)	(0.01)
	9.57	−1.55	1.47	−4.08
Mother CBCL	0.19	−0.11	0.04	−0.06
	(0.06)	(0.00)	(0.06)	(0.01)
	8.76	−4.41	1.65	−4.28

NOTE: Standardized coefficients; standard errors appear in parentheses, and *t* values appear below standard errors.

if a mother perceives conflict with a child, she may also view the child as having behavior problems (a bias in perception). Interestingly, the provision of productive activities in the home had a significant relation with teacher's report of externalizing behaviors. Extensive opportunity for productive activity may enable children to find a fit with a broader array of environments, thus reducing the likelihood they will manifest behavior problems. This finding is consistent with precepts from positive psychology and, specifically, self-determination theory (Ryan & Deci, 2000). Having opportunities for productive activity increases the likelihood of engaging intrinsic motives, which, in turn, induces positive affect. The more frequently intrinsic motives and positive affect are induced, the less likely it is that children will engage in aggressive, noncompliant, and mischievous behavior.

A review of paths from exogenous variables to endogenous variables for teacher-reported CBCL reveals that poverty had a positive influence on harsh parenting ($\beta = .37$, $t = 8.56$), a negative influence on opportunities for productive activities ($\beta = −.43$, $t = −11.15$), a negative influence on parental support ($\beta = −.29$, $t = −7.89$), and a positive influence on maternal depression ($\beta = .31$, $t = 9.52$). Maternal agreeableness had a negative effect on conflict with child ($\beta = −.14$, $t = −4.04$) and a positive effect on maternal support ($\beta = .14$, $t = 2.47$). Child temperament had a positive influence on maternal conflict ($\beta = .08$, $t = 2.35$) and a nonsignificant negative influence on maternal support

($\beta = −.05$, $t = −1.62$). Maternal education had a positive influence on productive activities ($\beta = .35$, $t = 9.19$) and maternal support ($\beta = .25$, $t = 12.52$).

Table 19.2 summarizes effects of exogenous variables on teacher-reported and mother-reported externalizing behaviors. With the exception of agreeableness, model variables had quite similar influences on both mother- and teacher-reported externalizing behaviors. Results pertaining to agreeableness, however, suggest the possibility of reporter bias (mothers reported on their own feelings as well as their children's behavior). The effect for mothers was −.11 ($t = −4.41$), and the effect for teachers was −.02 ($t = −1.55$). Among the exogenous variables, chronic poverty had the most pronounced influence ($\beta = .23$, $t = 9.57$ for teachers; $\beta = .19$, $t = 8.76$ for mothers). Overall, results indicate that family demography has similar effects on child behavior at home and at school.

Mediating Effects

Although these paths were in accord with theory and previous research, the indirect and total effects provide a more complete accounting of how exogenous variables influence child behavior through the home environment. For example, chronic poverty has its strongest influence on teacher-reported problem behaviors through productive activities (i.e., $−.44 \rightarrow −.17 = .0748$), but it has almost as strong an effect through harsh parenting (i.e., $.37 \rightarrow .14 = .0518$) and depression via mother-child conflict (i.e., .31 → .26 → .73 = .0588). Thus this example shows that the same factor can influence an outcome through different mechanisms (i.e., equifinality). Note that when the small effect through depression and harsh parenting (i.e., .31 → .07 → .14 = .0003) is added to all the indirect effects, the sum equals the total standardized effect of poverty shown in Table 19.2 (.0748 + .0518 + .0588 + .0003 = .1884).

Child Characteristics That May Interact With Adverse Environmental Conditions

Resilience theory and precepts from positive psychology stipulate that characteristics of children may moderate negative effects of adverse environmental conditions on child externalizing behavior. Using multiple-group analysis, we tested the hypothesis that intellectual competence may moderate the relation between mother-child conflict and externalizing behavior. Scores on the Woodcock Johnson Picture Vocabulary test (Woodcock & Johnson, 1990) were dichotomized: 1 = top one-third ($n = 342$) and 0 = all remaining children ($n = 661$). When both groups were analyzed simultaneously, the χ^2 and df were 842.55 and 342, respectively (see mom_intell_inter.doc). After the path from conflict to externalizing behavior was constrained to be equal for both groups, the $\chi2$ and df were 852.93 and 343, respectively. The change in χ^2 ($\Delta\chi^2 = 10.38/1df$) was significant, indicating that the relationship between mother-child conflict and externalizing behaviors is less strong for more intelligent children (see mom_intell_inter2.doc). To understand more fully the complex relation between mother-child conflict and externalizing behavior, we identified several other child characteristics that seemed likely (based on theory) to affect that relation: attachment (more securely attached children are generally less likely to externalize) and hostile attribution bias (children with a tendency to suspect the motives of others are more likely to aggress). We found evidence that both attachment

security and attribution bias moderated the relation between mother-child conflict and child externalizing behavior. These results further delineate the complex connections between environment and behavior where stress is implicated. Despite the fact that the stress model has been the subject of many investigations, much about this model remains undetermined.

STRUCTURAL EQUATION MODELING: A PERSON-CENTERED APPROACH

To complement what scholars can learn from variable-centered approaches to analysis, researchers steeped in systems and life-course traditions have recommended the use of person-centered approaches to data analysis (Bergman, Cairns, Nilsson, & Nystedt, 2000). Three propositions of the person-centered approach are as follows: (a) Models likely do not apply to everyone, (b) relations are frequently not linear, and (c) patterns of values often have more meaning than variables considered individually. The holistic, interactive view of the individual as a self-correcting organized whole has been strengthened by findings from studies utilizing longitudinal designs and general system theory. These factors, along with impressive methodological developments in pattern analyses (e.g., Muthén & Muthén, 1998) allow researchers to address new person-oriented questions.

Person-oriented approaches to analysis generally begin by identifying "classes" of individuals who share common characteristics or common longitudinal patterns on a particular characteristic. General growth mixture modeling (GGMM) is useful for determining such classes. In order to ascertain the number of qualitatively distinct classes, one usually begins with a series of preliminary latent class growth analyses (LCGA; similar to GGMM, but with no within-class variation) with an increasing number of classes. The analysis with the lowest Bayesian information criteria value provides a

Figure 19.3   General Growth Mixture Analysis of Externalizing Behavior

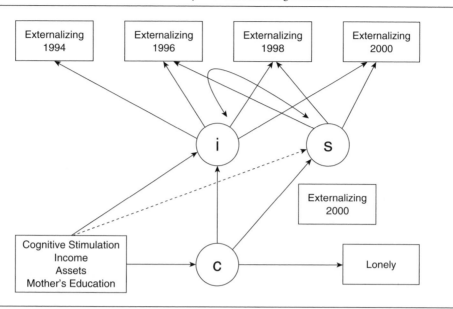

NOTE: Dotted line not estimated based on unconditional analysis.

useful indication of the number of distinct classes. Not surprisingly, one also considers the meaningfulness of the classes and the quality of classification when choosing the number of classes. Mplus software was used in this example (Muthén & Muthén, 1998).

Empirical Example 3: Growth of Externalizing Problems With Covariates and Distal Outcome

Figure 19.3 shows a model of growth in externalizing behavior measured in 1994, 1996, 1998, and 2000. Measures were obtained from the National Longitudinal Survey of Youth. Trajectory class (labeled c) is predicted by averaged income, maternal education, and cognitive stimulation. Externalizing behavior is a mother-report scale, based on the CBCL. Cognitive stimulation is the sum of 14 dichotomous items taken from HOME-SF. Averaged family income is the mean of 1991 through 1994 total net family income (logarithmically transformed).

The series of LGCA point to five qualitatively distinct classes (nlsy_lcga5.txt).

In addition to determining the number of qualitatively distinct classes, LGCA shows how much variation there is in the intercepts and slopes of each class. There was no significant variation in slope within any of the five trajectory classes, and only the first and third classes showed significant variation in the slope (in nlsy_lcga5.txt, see the "Model Results" section under the "Variances" subsection of the output, where the last column is a z value). Because there was little within-class variation in the slope, we did not try to account for this variation using predictor variables in the final analysis. Likewise, we only estimated paths from predictor variables to the intercepts of the first and third classes and set the variance to zero for the other three classes.

The final analysis adds the four covariates of class membership and uses class membership to predict loneliness (nlsy_growth_lgca5e.txt). Figure 19.4 shows the plotted estimated mean curves for the five classes. Class 1 is consistently very low (7% of total sample), Class 2 is medium to higher (32%), Class 3 is low to lower (30%), and Class 4 is high to lower (19%). Class 5 is the comparison

Figure 19.4   Estimated Externalizing Mean Curves

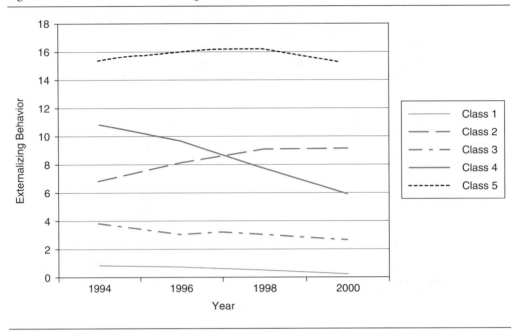

group (consistently very high, 12%). None of the predictors was related to initial status (intercept) for Class 1, but assets was positively related to initial status for Class 5 ($z = 3.347$). There was a significant relation between initial status and slope for Class 2 ($z = 2.69$), Class 4 ($z = 2.48$), and Class 3 ($z = -1.98$). This means, for example, that children with higher initial status in Class 2 also have steeper rates of change in externalizing behaviors.

In regard to covariates, the "latent class regression model part" of the output shows that the odds of belonging to Class 1, Class 2, Class 3, and Class 4 are greater for children receiving more cognitive stimulation at home. Averaged income is related to being in Class 1 and Class 4 and close to significance in Classes 2 and 3. Assets and maternal education did not differentiate among the classes. As expected, the probability of being lonely (and wishing one had more friends) was highest for Class 5 (.44). Class 3 had the lowest probability (.13), with Classes 1 (.22), 2 (.34), and 4 (.30) in between.

DISCUSSION

Just as theory drives and structures the use of statistical and measurement methodologies, advances in statistical and measurement techniques allow researchers to address more penetrating questions and, in the process, facilitate theory building itself. With a basic family process model as a starting point, we have demonstrated here the interplay between theory and analytic strategies using data from two publicly available data sets. We have provided empirical examples that investigate theoretically driven hypotheses about complex and dynamic relations involving children's access to resources. Results showed that family processes such as cognitive stimulation and harshness might function as mediators. Consistent with systems theories, this chapter provides evidence for complex causal pathways involving child characteristics, maternal characteristics, and mother-child relations as implicated in basic SES → parenting → child outcome relations. Also consistent with theory, it provides evidence of reciprocal causation, moderation, and the unique significance of each component of SES in regard to child well-being.

In this chapter we have also showed the advantage of using the person-centered approach. Knowledge of complex relations that change through time has been stifled by an overreliance on research methods and analytic techniques that assume stability rather than intraindividual variability. Nesselroade and Ghisletta (2000) point out that the reason researchers have focused so heavily on individual differences is found in the assumption that individuals are highly stable. However, systems theories hold that people change throughout the life course. Specifically, it is neither the person nor the context that is the cause of functioning or development. Rather, it is the structure of the system (i.e., pattern of relations) that predicts functioning at any given time, and changes in this structure are the primary cause of developmental change (Lerner & Walls, 1999).

Future studies of children and families will benefit from taking into consideration the *history* of influences in the lives of children and families. The superior performance of averaged income and averaged poverty in comparison with single-year assessments supports the value of this approach. New methods for examining trajectories also represent a great advance. The five distinct classes of behavior trajectories identified in this chapter provide strong support for the value of examining class profiles through time. The fact that the five classes were linked to different predictors and were differentially predictive of a distal outcome (loneliness) attests to the value of person-centered approaches.

In effect, while these results partially confirm the "old truths" that having greater resources leads to better outcomes for children, they confront the idea that relations between resources and patterns of development are simple or universally applicable. And just as important, they give researchers a reason to entertain many new possibilities regarding the nature of those relations.

The results presented in this chapter make clear the need to expand current family process models. For example, the "direct effects" of assets on math achievement suggest that other important mediators and moderators are operative (e.g., neighborhood effects). Moreover, the considerable amount of unexplained variance in even the most variable-rich models suggests that the models tested are still lacking key constructs. What are the candidates for expansion? On the deficit/poverty side, perhaps expansion can come in further consideration of physiological responses to stress (i.e., allostatic load) and resilience. On the assets/SES side, perhaps expansion can come from positive psychology (Seligman & Csikszentmihalyi, 2000) and developmental assets (see the Search Institute's Web site at http://www.search-institute.org). On both sides, there may be advantages to the simultaneous consideration of multiple outcomes and their interplay rather than a focus on a single outcome. Such expansion may ultimately lead to the kind of knowledge that enables policy makers and practitioners to design the kinds of programs that reduce the negative consequences of poverty and harness the promotive value of positive socioeconomic assets.

Dr. Greder

CASE STUDY

MULTISITE, MIXED-METHODS STUDY OF RURAL LOW-INCOME FAMILIES

Bonnie Braun, *University of Maryland*

Elaine A. Anderson, *University of Maryland*

The purpose of this case study is to illustrate how researchers organized to investigate the lived experiences of a sample of rural low-income families. We address here both process and observations about the factors contributing to success.

BACKGROUND

Following engagement by family scientists in welfare reform legislation in 1996, a multi-state group collaborated to conceptualize, organize, fund, and conduct research to test the legislation's assumptions. The researchers sought to understand whether rural families, a segment of the assistance population largely ignored, could reasonably achieve economic self-sufficiency—a goal of P.L. 104-193, the Personal Responsibility and Work Opportunity Reconciliation Act of 1996. They wanted to test the feasibility of the assumption that through marriage and employment, rural families could earn income adequate for economic self-sufficiency, and they wanted to understand an array of conditions affecting the families' daily struggles and well-being.

The family scientists committed to produce and disseminate findings in a timely and useful ways for citizens, public policy makers, human service personnel, Cooperative Extension faculty, and scholars. In 1998, they launched the 5-year study Rural Low-Income Families: Tracking Their Well-Being in the Context of Welfare Reform, also known as Rural Families Speak.

The researchers used a continuum model of family economic functioning with the categories "in crisis," "at risk," "safe," and "thriving" to assess family economic well-being, based on income in relation to number of family members (Bauer, Braun, & Olson, 2000). The team members reasoned that they should study a range of rural families to be able to describe and understand conditions along the continuum and to determine the odds that families living below the poverty line, in crisis, could earn sufficient income to rise above poverty, and whether those living at risk of slipping below the poverty line could maintain or improve their economic well-being and live without assistance. Rural families currently receiving or eligible for food stamps and/or the Supplemental Nutrition Program for Women, Infants and Children were selected for the study. Mothers were interviewed.

The team carefully identified critical areas of well-being to be measured through mixed methods that incorporated standardized quantitative measures and qualitative in-depth interviews. Many of the quantitative measures were selected from the Urban Institute's study of urban families, as well as standardized measures of the perception of quality of life. To help them understand the lived experiences of these rural families, the researchers also gathered oral life descriptions. The collection of qualitative data was critical to capture the dynamics and complexity of the family system in the changing welfare policy environment. Qualitative data are viewed as a powerful tool for expanding the knowledge of policy makers, community leaders, and others about the challenges of obtaining and maintaining economic self-sufficiency.

The research design team, composed of members from diverse disciplines, discussed appropriate theories for the study. Through the process of theory examination, the team chose multiple theoretical perspectives as a means of understanding the complexity of the families' situation: ecological, family and community development, human and social capital, and theories of poverty. The work of several theorists from a variety of disciplines guided the investigation. Based on these perspectives, the research team selected appropriate measures for a mixed-method longitudinal investigation of changes over 3 years (Bourdieu, 1986; Bronfenbrenner, 1979; Bubolz & Sontag, 1993; Deavers & Hoppe, 1992; Putnam, 1993, 1995; Weber & Duncan, 2000).

FACTORS AFFECTING
RESEARCH SUCCESS

The researchers who responded to the call to engage in this unprecedented study faced numerous challenges. Their success in overcoming these challenges is attributable to three key components: communication, competence, and commitment.

Communication

Communication was vital at all stages. Open, honest, and regular communication along multiple lines was critical to maintaining the project over time and distance. Discussing problems and celebrating successes kept the team members engaged and encouraged. Discussion and deliberation reduced the problems often inherent in group dynamics. In clarifying semantics and meanings, the team members became unified.

The team members represented five major disciplines and had research, Cooperative Extension, and resident instruction assignments at 15 land-grant universities in all regions of the United States. Each member was expected to recruit faculty and students at

his or her institution to form a state team. The 2000 annual report on this research noted that 54 faculty and student researchers and more than 100 Cooperative Extension educators, community leaders, and/or volunteers were engaged in the study.

The multistate team faced internal challenges caused by diverse disciplinary theories, research methods, professional practices, and semantics—challenges that would be difficult to handle even if members were residentially colocated. Although some members had served on regional research teams, the multiregional approach was new for all.

The team members tackled the logistical challenges by using a mix of communications methods:

- An annual meeting of principal investigators and some state team members
- An elected executive committee whose members were charged with thinking through and proposing processes
- A Listserv used for sharing minutes, updates on public policy, and information involving the study's execution and findings
- Periodic conference calls among members of the executive committee and/or principal investigators to handle team business
- An FTP (file transfer protocol) site for internal posting of instruments, data, communiqués, and findings
- A Web site that made the project accessible to interested and targeted members of the public, researchers, and public policy makers

The team handled methodological, language, and professional practice challenges primarily through work groups organized around bodies of knowledge and areas of interest, such as public policy, economic well-being, and health. These work groups determined priorities for analysis and prepared proposals for presentation of papers, wrote

Case Study

lower has 10% of high dual-income families compare to ITBS s (over D's)

CASE STUDY *continued*

research briefs, and authored manuscripts to publish findings. Plans were shared so that each group's work could be integrated with work from others to fulfill the goal of holistic examination of findings.

Given the potential for conflict over use of the data, the team developed protocols for informing members of different groups' intent to examine the shared data set (e.g., students doing theses and dissertations, colleagues external to the team) and for determining authorship. With an estimated 900 quantitative variables and more than 50,000 pages of qualitative data from 414 families living in 24 rural counties, the research team acknowledged there was enough work to share and almost more than could be completed in a timely way!

Competence

The competence of the team members was foundational to the quality of the study as conceived, executed, and reported. Although all members acknowledge that they were continually learning from each other and from involvement in the project, each researcher, including the students, brought expertise that made the study more than the sum of its parts.

An interdisciplinary protocol development team worked over several months to develop the wave 1 interview protocol. Modifications were made after a pilot test. Standardized interview training was provided for each state team on field use of the protocol. Training was done through conference calls and enhanced by e-mail instructions and personal consultation. Principal investigators agreed to comply with standards adopted by vote—that is, all questions accepted by the research team were to be included; states could include additional questions; interviews were audiotaped; pseudonyms, provided by a central team, were used to protect the identities of all family members.

Changes in protocols for waves 2 and 3 were based on both wave 1 experiences and initial findings. The second, third, and proposed

fourth waves of data collection reflected the responses of those interviewed, analysis of data, and opinions of interviewers about effective questions. Ineffective questions were eliminated or modified. Researchers identified mention of religion or a higher being by many mothers in wave 1, and a dissertation revealed religion as a resilience factor. As a result, the team added a standardized set of measures of religiosity and spirituality in wave 2. After two waves of data collection and analysis, the team decided that social support items were not specific enough, and so a new standardized instrument was added in wave 3. To gather stronger evidence of health status, additional standardized measures were incorporated in wave 3.

To strengthen the study's rigor further and to reduce error and bias, one state team received funds to code both quantitative and qualitative data and to provide tests of reliability. States then checked the coding for accuracy. The multistate team members discussed any problems with data collection or submission. A continual improvement process was followed—that is, when coders found delays occurring because data were not transferred from the interview protocol to the interview transcript, team members were informed. Omissions were greatly reduced in succeeding waves. Improvement in data submission reduced coding time and costs and additionally improved standardization and accuracy.

Quantitative data were entered into SPSS by the central team, which provided codebooks for each wave. Qualitative data were entered into WinMax, a software analysis program selected and purchased by the entire team. Ongoing WinMax training and guidance were provided by the coding team.

The multistate team selected 18 major codes for the qualitative data set. These codes represented a range of concepts contributing to family well-being. Subcoding became the responsibility of the individuals or teams doing specific analyses—for example, one researcher working on a dissertation coded data for stress-protective and crisis-recovery resilience factors; another working on a thesis coded data for health-related factors in the mothers' well-being.

Data analysis challenges were tackled through work groups devoted to such areas as economic well-being, food security, health, and public policy. The researchers could self-identify with one or more work groups convening during the annual meeting, periodically at conferences, or by phone to identify research questions, create subteams of analysts, or prepare presentations or articles for publication or policy briefs. Progress was reported at the annual meeting through written state and work group reports. In 2003, members submitted an inventory of products produced: 8 published articles, 7 student theses and dissertations, and 43 presentations.

Beyond the work groups' analyses, state teams, including additional faculty and under-graduate and graduate students, were encouraged to select research questions for analysis and were required to post their intended analyses and outlets on the multistate team's Listserv and FTP site. Other than analyses for student reports, theses, or dissertations (which required participation of only one member of the multistate team), any analysis that used multistate data required participation of team members from at least two states and notification of the entire multistate team. Cross-discipline analyses were encouraged. Abstracts were posted when analysis was completed for either oral or published presentation.

Commitment

Commitment was an essential part of this ambitious project. The team members were committed to providing sound research findings in a timely manner. They wanted the research to inform public policy making and to expand the knowledge base of family science. They were committed to equipping student researchers to conduct multimethod, multistate, multidisciplinary research that will

contribute to the well-being of children, adults, their families, and the nation. One indicator of the team's commitment was that all but two of the first 5-year team members signed on for a second 5-year study. Three new states joined the 2003–2008 team. Another indicator of commitment was the team members' willingness to work together to obtain funding.

A major challenge was the daunting need for financing to support team communications, data collection, coding, and processing. Each state's team members sought funding from their own universities, Cooperative Extension and Agricultural Experiment Stations, and/or private foundations for data collection, cleaning, coding, and analysis. Collectively, the team submitted proposals for national sources of funds to support the Web site, the FTP site, and some analysis. Some team members led the proposal development and processing while others contributed to conceptualizing, editing, and developing sub-contracts. The team submitted five proposals for which it was awarded a total of a quarter of a million dollars. As of early 2004, proposals were pending to increase the adequacy and availability of funds for the next 5 years.

CONCLUSION

Taken together, the communication, competence, and commitment of the multistate team described above is a tribute to the concept that determined and committed people can change the world. However, without the rural mothers who participated in this study, giving generously of their time to tell about their lives, challenges, and successes, the study would not have been possible.

Findings from this study can inform policy, contribute to program change, and add to the body of knowledge for current and future scholars. The valuable lessons learned, both about the families examined and the process of conducting a multistate, longitudinal, multimethod study, can enrich future research.

Case Study

DISCUSSION AND EXTENSION

PROMOTING POSITIVE YOUTH DEVELOPMENT ACROSS VARIATIONS IN SOCIOECONOMIC STATUS: FRAMING THE STRUCTURAL EQUATION MODELING APPROACH WITHIN A DEVELOPMENTAL SYSTEMS PERSPECTIVE

Christina Theokas, *Tufts University*

Richard M. Lerner, *Tufts University*

Discussion and Extension

Contemporary developmental science embraces an integrative, developmental systems approach to conceptualizing the *relations* between people and contexts as the basic unit of analysis in human development and in the function of institutions (e.g., Lerner, 2002). In Chapter 19, Corwyn and Bradley present an erudite analysis of the research traditions associated with the study of the socioeconomic status and of poverty on family functioning and child and adolescent development. Their presentation is consistent with many aspects of developmental systems theory. In addition, the chapter constitutes a superb tutorial for developmental scientists about how structural equation modeling procedures may integrate and extend theory and research about SES and poverty effects, especially when considered from the perspective of developmental systems theory.

Corwyn and Bradley note that SES research and poverty research have typically been directed to addressing different questions, but, nonetheless, they have often indexed the same mediator and outcome variables. We agree. However, we suggest a recasting of their phrasing of the two questions they present in regard to the SES and the poverty traditions, respectively.

In regard to SES, we believe that this research has been directed to addressing the issue of how variation in SES is associated with differences in family and individual processes and outcomes. Not all research has documented positive effects of material resources. For example, Luthar and Latendresse (2002) describe the problems of psychosocial adjustment that may occur among youth developing in upper-class suburban contexts.

In turn, although most poverty research has been directed to specifying the range of negative influences of low-material-resource contexts on child development, an emerging interest of scientists has been to identify the often formidable strengths that may exist within poor families and, especially, poor families of color (e.g., McAdoo & Martin, 2003; Spencer, 1990). Moreover, the fact that some poor youth "overcome the odds" against them and develop in positive ways is impressive evidence that the equifinality and the multifinality that Corwyn and Bradley correctly depict as part of the developmental systems perspective in fact exist.

Thus both literatures converge in indicating that across SES levels, and even within the most material-resource-restricted settings, there is optimism for the positive development of individuals and families. Both positive and negative outcomes may derive from what Corwyn and Bradley correctly note

DISCUSSION AND EXTENSION *continued*

are seen, within developmental systems theories, as bidirectional, mutually influential relations between individuals and contexts (represented as individual → context relations). Moreover, interlevel relations within the developmental system both facilitate and constrain opportunities for change (e.g., change is constrained both by past developments and by contemporary contextual conditions). As a consequence, contemporary developmental systems theories stress that *relative plasticity*—the potential for systematic change in structure and/or function—exists across life (Lerner, 2002). Given the ethical commitments of developmental scientists, the presence of such plasticity means that the key questions of scholars interested in either SES or poverty effects on youth development are five interrelated "what" questions: (a) What attributes → of (b) what individuals → in relation to (c) what set of contextual/ecological attributes and conditions? at (d) what points in ontogenetic, family, or generational, and cohort or historical, time? may be integrated to promote (e) what instances of positive human development?

In other words, developmental scientists concerned with the links between poverty and/or SES variables and family and child functioning should aim their scholarship at discerning the individual → context relations associated with positive youth development. Indeed, such a focus on the production of positive development within the developmental system is not just a matter of ethical necessity. The focus on positive human development enables developmental science to be applied in ways that inform public policies and shape social programs about how to enhance human life. Such a focus involves identification of the best means known (through research and program evaluation) to capitalize on the strength present in all individuals and families to change in positive ways, a strength constituted by the plasticity of the individual → context relations within the developmental systems (Lerner, 2004).

Contemporary research associated with what has been termed the positive youth development (PYD) perspective (e.g., Lerner, 2004) provides a model of how such applied developmental science may be conducted and how, as well, the ideas about the use of SEM forwarded by Corwyn and Bradley may be used to extend PYD scholarship. Across all levels of the ecology of human development, resources may exist for the promotion of positive development. These resources are what Benson (2003) describes as "developmental assets," that is, the social "nutrients" that young people need for healthy growth. When these developmental assets (e.g., positive and sustained adult-youth relationships. opportunities for civic participation and leadership, opportunities for skill building) are integrated over time, then individual youth → community context relations are created in manners that capitalize on the strengths of young people and promote their positive development (Lerner, 2004).

The focus on developmental assets within the ecology of the developmental system can be a means to synthesize the SES and the poverty research traditions around the concept of PYD, in that developmental assets may exist across all SES and poverty levels (e.g., Benson, 2003). Indeed, data from Search Institute indicate that developmental assets are present across the diversity of families and communities in the United States and that higher levels of assets are associated with indicators of positive development among young people (Benson, 2003). These data suggest that if developmental assets in the ecology of youth are aligned with their individual strengths, then PYD will occur among individuals across all portions of the SES distribution.

The SEM procedures that Corwyn and Bradley suggest may be especially useful for modeling and testing this idea, particularly when they include hierarchical techniques that enable modeling of multiple levels of organization within the developmental

Discussion and Extension

DISCUSSION AND EXTENSION *continued*

system (i.e., the characteristics of—and, theoretically most important, the strengths or assets of—individuals, families, and communities). The general growth mixture modeling that Corwyn and Bradley suggest and the multilevel modeling procedures that may be computed through LISREL may potentially be especially helpful here.

To maximize the use of such procedures, scholars need rich and objective measures of ecological assets. Search Institute measures young people's perceived ecological (and individual) assets (Benson, 2003) and, while such measures are theoretically important and, as noted, have empirical associations with indicators of PYD, they should be coupled (triangulated) with assessments of developmental assets that derive from other than youth self-reports. For example, researchers can utilize census data or information about communities that has been published or is available online to operationalize and objectively index resources that have been shown to support the positive development of youth (e.g., the presence and characteristics of youth-serving community-based organizations in communities).

In sum, a key next step for researchers is to synthesize from across available models of neighborhood and community effects objective measures of these ecological developmental resources. Using SEM procedures as a means to model the positive youth developments that are outcomes of individual → context relations in asset-rich settings, the developmental systems theoretical approach may be a productive frame in which to integrate the SES and poverty research traditions that Corwyn and Bradley discuss.

Discussion and Extension

REFERENCES

Achenbach, T. M., & Edelbrock, C. S. (1981). Behavioral problems and competencies reported by parents of normal and disturbed children aged four through sixteen. *Monographs of the Society for Research in Child Development, 46*(1, Serial No. 188).

Arbuckle, J. L., & Wothke, W. (1999). *AMOS 4.0 user's guide.* Chicago: SmallWaters Corporation.

Bauer, J. W., Braun, B., & Olson, P. D. (2000). Welfare to well-being framework for research, education and outreach: From welfare for the few to well-being for the many. *Journal of Consumer Affairs, 34,* 62–81.

Benson, P. L. (2003). Developmental assets and asset-building communities: Conceptual and empirical foundations. In R. M. Lerner & P. L. Benson (Eds.), *Developmental assets and asset-building communities: Implications for research, policy, and practice* (pp. 19–43). New York: Kluwer Academic.

Bergman, L. R., Cairns, R. B., Nilsson, L. G., & Nystedt, L. (Eds.). (2000). *Developmental science and the holistic approach.* Mahwah, NJ: Lawrence Erlbaum.

Bourdieu, P. (1986). The forms of capital. In J. G. Richardson (Ed.), *Handbook of theory and research for the sociology of education* (pp. 241–258). New York: Greenwood.

Bradley, R. H., & Corwyn, R. F. (2002). Socioeconomic status and child development. *Annual Review of Psychology, 53,* 371–399.

Bronfenbrenner, U. (1979). *The ecology of human development: Experiments by nature and design.* Cambridge, MA: Harvard University Press.

Bubolz, M. M., & Sontag, M. S. (1993). Human ecology theory. In P. Boss, W. J. Doherty, R. LaRossa, W. R. Schumm, & S. K. Steinmetz (Eds.), *Sourcebook of family theories and methods: A contextual approach* (pp. 419–448). New York: Plenum.

Caldwell, B. M., & Bradley, R. H. (1984). *Home observation for measurement of the environment.* Little Rock: University of Arkansas.

Coleman, J. S. (1988). Social capital in the creation of human capital. *American Journal of Sociology, 94*(Suppl.), S95–S120.

Conger, R. D., & Elder, G. H., Jr. (1994). *Families in troubled times: Adapting to change in rural America.* New York: de Gruyter.

Conger, R. D., Wallace, L. E., Sun, Y., Simons, R. L., McLoyd, V. C., & Brody, G. H. (2002). Economic pressure in African American families: A replication and extension of the family process model. *Developmental Psychology, 38,* 179–193.

Conley, D. (1999). *Being Black, living in the red: Race, wealth, and social policy in America.* Los Angeles: University of California Press.

Deavers, K. L., & Hoppe, R. A. (1992). Overview of the rural poor in the 1980s. In C. M. Duncan (Ed.), *Rural poverty in America* (pp. 3–20). New York: Auburn House.

Dunn, L. M., & Markwardt, F. C. (1970). *Peabody Individual Achievement Test manual.* Circle Pines, MN: American Guidance Services.

Harris, J. R. (1995). Where is the child's environment? A group socialization theory of development. *Psychological Review, 102,* 458–489.

Hayduk, L. A. (1987). *Structural equation modeling with LISREL: Essentials and advances.* Baltimore: Johns Hopkins University Press.

Jöreskog, K. G., & Sörbom, D. (1996). *LISREL 8 user's reference guide.* Chicago: SPSS.

Lerner, R. M. (2002). *Concepts and theories of human development* (3rd ed.). Mahwah, NJ: Lawrence Erlbaum.

Lerner, R. M. (2004). *Liberty: Thriving and civic engagement among America's youth.* Thousand Oaks, CA: Sage.

Lerner, R. M., & Walls, T. (1999). Revisiting individuals as producers of their development: From dynamic interactionism to developmental systems. In J. Brandtstädter & R. M. Lerner (Eds.), *Action and development: Theory and research through the life span* (pp. 3–36). Thousand Oaks, CA: Sage.

Luthar, S. S., & Latendresse, S. J. (2002). Adolescent risk: The costs of affluence. In R. M. Lerner, C. S. Taylor, & A. von Eye (Eds.), *Pathways to positive development among diverse youth* (pp. 101–122). San Francisco: Jossey-Bass.

Masten, A. S. (2001). Ordinary magic: Resilience process in development. *American Psychologist, 56,* 227–238.

McAdoo, H. P., & Martin, A. (2003). Families and ethnicity. In R. M. Lerner, F. Jacobs, &

D. Wertlieb (Eds.), *Handbook of applied developmental science: Vol. 1. Applying developmental science for youth and families: Historical and theoretical foundations* (pp. 305–318). Thousand Oaks, CA: Sage.

Muthén, L. K., & Muthén, B. (1998). *Mplus user's guide*. Los Angeles: Authors.

Nesselroade, J. R., & Ghisletta, P. (2000). Beyond static concepts in modeling behavior. In L. R. Bergman, R. B. Cairns, L. G. Nilsson, & L. Nystedt. (Eds.), *Developmental science and the holistic approach* (pp. 121–135). Mahwah, NJ: Lawrence Erlbaum.

Oliver, M. L., & Shapiro, T. M. (2001). Wealth and racial stratification. In N. J. Smelser, W. J. Wilson, & F. Mitchell (Eds.), *America becoming: Racial trends and their consequences* (Vol. 2, pp. 222–251). Washington, DC: National Academy Press.

Putnam, R. D. (1993). *Making democracy work: Civic traditions in modern Italy*. Princeton, NJ: Princeton University Press.

Putnam, R. D. (1995). Bowling alone: America's declining social capital. *Journal of Democracy, 6,* 65–78.

Rank, M. R. (1994). *Living on the edge: The realities of welfare in America*. New York: Columbia University Press.

Ryan, R. M., & Deci, E. L. (2000). Self-determination theory and the facilitation of intrinsic motivation, social development, and well-being. *American Psychologist, 55,* 68–78.

Schafer, J. L. (1997). *Analysis of incomplete multivariate data*. New York: Chapman & Hall.

Seligman, M., & Csikszentmihalyi, M. (Eds.). (2000). Positive psychology: An introduction [Special issue]. *American Psychologist, 55*(1).

Shapiro, T., & Wolff, E. (Eds.). (2001). *Assets for the poor: The benefits of spreading asset ownership*. New York: Russell Sage Foundation.

Spencer, M. B. (1990). Development of minority children: An introduction. *Child Development, 61,* 267–269.

von Bertalanffy, L. (1968). *General system theory: Foundations, development, applications*. New York: George Braziller.

Weber, B. A., & Duncan, G. (2000). *Welfare reform and food assistance in rural America*. Congressional research briefing on welfare reform and rural poverty, Washington, DC.

Woodcock, R. W., & Johnson, M. B. (1990). *Test of achievement, WJ-R: Examiner's manual*. Allen, TX: DLM Teaching Resources.

Yeung, W. J., Linver, M. R., & Brooks-Gunn, J. (2002). How money matters for young children's development: Investment and family process. *Child Development, 73,* 1861–1879.

Yung, Y. F., & Bentler, P. M. (1994). Bootstrap-corrected ADF test statistics in covariance structure analysis. *British Journal of Math and Statistical Psychology, 47,* 63–84.

Twenty

DON'T STOP AT THE BORDERS

Theorizing Beyond Dichotomies of Work and Family

Shelley M. MacDermid, *Purdue University*

Kevin Roy, *Purdue University*

Anisa M. Zvonkovic, *Oregon State University*

Frustration is the mother of this chapter. The isolation and fragmentation of the research literatures that guide us, the authors of this chapter—even though we all study families and work—are frustrating. Despite repeated calls for greater inclusiveness (e.g., Perry-Jenkins, Repetti, & Crouter, 2000), research on macro and micro influences on work and family, paid and unpaid work, and poor and minority families is still conducted by scholars who publish in different places and who may be unaware of one another's research and theoretical frameworks. In addition to lacking common language and

theoretical tradition, we sense that the field of families and work is "haunted by the lives it excludes" (Wacquant, 1999, as cited in Thorne, 2001). More than 35 million individuals, over a third of them children, currently live in poverty and off the radar screen of the literature (U.S. Bureau of the Census, 2003). The number of long-term unemployed individuals in the United States has grown persistently, nearly tripling in recent years. Because the experiences of many families are left untouched, research and theory on families and work are less likely to be externally (and perhaps internally) valid, less likely to be influential, and more likely to be dismissed.

Authors' Note: An early version of this chapter was presented at the 2003 Pre-conference Workshop on Theory Construction and Research Methodology at the annual meeting of the National Council on Family Relations. We are grateful to David Klein, anonymous reviewers, Rob Palkovitz, and Rudy Seward for their suggestions and guidance during the preparation of this chapter, and to Andrew Behnke, Sherri Brown, Ashley Harvey, Young In Kwon, and Chun Hong Zhang for their helpful comments.

Why does this happen? An informal focus group that we conducted with a small number of graduate students offered some insights. We learned that formal training in theory construction is rare. The students in our group found theories useful when they helped to narrow focus and make a research project feasible, or when they helped to interpret findings. Often, the students "retrofit" theories to account for results after analyses were completed. They also "false started," intending to conduct theory-driven research but finding available theories too confining. Finally, when we asked the students to tell us about themselves as theorists, we heard "theory worship." The students felt that it was almost presumptuous for them to build their own frameworks in the face of respect for institutionalized theories.

Based on our observations, we speculate that three factors may be slowing the development of theory about families and work. First, theorizing based on past demographic realities has left the field of families and work with ways of thinking about work, family, and the connection between them that are constrained and incomplete. Second, some scholars may need to be empowered to "do" theory and to develop theory actively from research findings. Finally, theory development may sometimes be constrained by scholars' adherence to traditional metaphors that are too narrow, too static, or too out of touch with lived reality to be useful. We direct our discussion in this chapter specifically to those who consider themselves novice theory builders; our goal is to make theory—and theory building—more relevant to the act of conducting research.

We define research on families and work as the study of the relationships among aspects of family life and paid and unpaid work. We are attentive to dynamic relationships in families and in the domain of work, which is implicitly attuned to relations between those who work and those for whom work is done. For example, a parent may iron a shirt for her child (unpaid work), her partner (unpaid work), or her customer (paid work). Although the work activity is basically unaltered, the different relationships in which it takes place frame how we envision the domain of work to include paid and unpaid labor. Links between work and family life exist at multiple levels, from the macro level of domestic and global economies to the micro-level processes of daily life. The study of paid work necessarily includes the study of access to it and thus families both in the mainstream and at the margins of the economy. Finally, we recognize that family life includes relationships defined by "biological ties, marriage, social custom, or adoption" (Edwards & Rothbard, 2000, p. 179).

PROBLEMS WITH ESTABLISHED THEORY

According to the recent decade review in the *Journal of Marriage and Family* (Perry-Jenkins et al., 2000), three of the major foci in the literature on families and work are multiple roles, maternal employment, and work-related stress. We agree with other scholars that—although it is seldom acknowledged—each of these streams of research continues to be influenced by structural functionalist propositions (Barnett & Hyde, 2001). Like all theories, structural functionalism operates as a lens to focus researchers' attention and reveal important aspects of phenomena. But like all lenses, it can also be used in ways that obscure or distort users' vision.

• SPOTLIGHT ON THEORY

CROSS-CULTURAL PERSPECTIVES ON WORK-FAMILY CONFLICT

Josip Obradovic, *Ivo Pilar Institute of Social Research, Zagreb, Croatia*

Mira Cudina, *Teachers' College, University of Zagreb, Croatia*

During the past 20 years, family scholars have paid a great deal of attention to conflicts between work and family life, a subject of theoretical and practical importance in most countries. The main reason for this attention has been the increase in the numbers of women taking jobs outside of the home, which has created significant changes in family roles and a new set of problems for family functioning. The main questions that researchers have posed concern whether or not the job engagement of both marital partners has an effect on the family and how these new family relationships influence work outside of the home. Scholars have also examined whether any such influence is negative or positive; that is, are work and family roles in conflict, or are they mutually enhancing? Because research data show that, for most employed persons, family satisfaction takes priority over work satisfaction (Kiecolt, 2003), we limit our attention here to out-of-home work influences on family life.

Many studies have been aimed at finding out the antecedents and consequences of work-family conflict, or WFC (see, e.g., Allen, Herst, Bruck, & Sutton, 2000). The majority of studies have found the consequences to be negative for individual and family processes. Studies of the antecedents of WFC have covered individual-level variables while almost always ignoring higher-level variables. In addition, most of the studies to date have been conducted in the social and cultural context of the United States. Some scholars have made valuable attempts at systematization, theoretical integration, and model elaboration (Voydanoff, 2002), but all of their research findings are valid mostly for European and North American social and cultural contexts.

Obviously, enormous variation exists among countries in relevant aspects of sociocultural context (work ethics, work involvement, family values), so there is a questionable fit between the models offered and the realities of various cultures or societies. If scholars desire an unambiguous picture of WFC, they must incorporate into that picture the full gamut of sociocultural variables. An ecological cross-cultural approach could be a possible answer (Bronfenbrenner, 1986). Such an approach should include three levels of variables: macro, meso, and micro. The macro-level variables comprise social context. The specific societal value systems, differing especially along an individualist/collectivist dimension (Hofstede, 2001), could seriously affect WFC in a particular society. Social policies aimed at securing family integrity (maternity leave, financial aid for children, accessible preschool and after-school care) could be a strong buffer against severe WFC. The legal infrastructure of work includes all of the relevant laws and regulations at the societal level and defines the power and position of labor unions. Unions can regulate working hours and work overload, two major causes of WFC.

(continued)

Further, we assume that all three groups of variables influence micro-level variables (i.e., both work and family involvement of individual employees), with collectivist societies producing more family involvement than work involvement. It is also plausible that individual work involvement may be strongly influenced by the legal infrastructure of work and family policy. And it is well documented that both work involvement and family involvement influence the intensity of WFC (Kiecolt, 2003).

We further argue that the influence of macro-level variables is mediated by two meso-level variables: family support and work context (type of job, peer and supervisor support, and so on). Also, the system of values influences family support, thus indirectly affecting WFC. Finally, family policy and the legal infrastructure of work in a society affects work context variables and, indirectly, WFC as well.

If we start from the research results obtained in the cultural context of the United States and elaborate them using the ecological cross-cultural approach, we can gain important new insights into the mechanisms of work-family conflict. ●

Multiple roles. Structural functionalism conceptualizes roles as the fundamental building blocks of social systems, and researchers who focus on roles have displayed three limiting tendencies. The first is the tendency to take an atomistic approach rather than a holistic one (Marks & MacDermid, 1996). That is, scholars have posed many more questions about individual roles than about systems of roles, even though well-being and stress are logically products of the entire role system. Second is the tendency to assume (and not test) that individuals' role identities are organized into a stable priority order. Although research participants have often reported such hierarchies, closer examination reveals that they usually have done so only to comply with researchers' requests. The final and perhaps most persistent tendency is to assume that resources expended in one role are no longer available for use in others. This hydraulic model—the well-known "scarcity" hypothesis (Marks, 1977)—persists despite considerable evidence that it does not uniformly apply (Daly, 1996).

Maternal employment. The best-known legacy of functionalism is the notion of "separate spheres," in which well-functioning families and societies feature husbands who specialize in instrumental activities such as market work and wives who specialize in expressive activities such as domestic work (Kingsbury & Scanzoni, 1993). Early research on mothers' employment was spawned by concerns about the children of mothers who stepped beyond their expressive roles to participate in paid work (primarily White mothers, given that only the participation of White women in the workforce was increasing at the time; Sundstrom, 2001). Few if any reliable differences between the children of employed mothers and those of nonemployed mothers have emerged, however. Striking today is researchers' persistent interest in the connections between marital stability and *wives'* employment (e.g., Schoen, Astone, Rothert, Standish, & Kim, 2002). Such studies may be out of step with demographic realities, given that the labor force participation rates of wives and husbands are closer today than ever before (60% and 74%, respectively; U.S. Bureau of the Census, 2003). It is time for more even-handed consideration of the implications for marriage of wives' and husbands' employment conditions (Perry-Jenkins et al., 2000).

Work stress. According to Kingsbury and Scanzoni (1993), stress theories reveal structural functionalist roots whenever they focus on equilibrium. Early family scholars saw a metaphor for social systems in the physical functioning of the body, where the body activates to restore a condition of normal functioning in response to stress produced by disorganization or deviance. This metaphor ignores the ability of individuals and families to *initiate* changes in social systems, even through such simple acts as choosing where to work or live.

In the literature on families and work, the key indicator of stress is work-family conflict. One legacy of functionalism here is an overwhelmingly negative focus, perhaps an extension of the "disruption is bad" notion. Work-family conflict is typically conceptualized as the result of demands in roles that individuals already occupy as opposed to the demands of trying to gain access to or increase involvement. Work-family conflict is usually about having too much work or family, not too little.

HISTORICAL REALITIES

Some elements of functionalism may be a poor fit for the new demographic realities of families and work. Scholars have observed that the decade prior to the publication of Parsons's 1951 classic volume was a period of "return to normalcy" (Doherty, Boss, LaRossa, Schumm, & Steinmetz, 1993). World War II caused the size of the U.S. active-duty military force to explode from 1.8 million to 12.1 million troops between 1941 and 1945, when almost 1 in every 10 Americans was on active duty (U.S. Bureau of the Census, 1999). The U.S. birthrate plunged to a historic low of 76 births per 1,000 women of childbearing age in 1936, then rocketed from 86 to 102 in a single year, 1945–1946. The divorce rate more than doubled, from 2 per 1,000 population in 1940 to 4.3 in 1946, subsiding to 2.6 in 1950 (U.S. Bureau of the Census, 1975). During World War II, women flowed into the workforce, raising their labor force participation rate from 28% in 1940 to 36% in 1944 (U.S. Bureau of the Census, 1975). After the war,

many women left the labor force, the divorce rate dropped, the birthrate rose, the economy did well, and family incomes rose. Given these events, perhaps anyone would have concluded that societies benefit from gender specialization.

Today's demographic realities are different: Lives are longer, families are smaller, and, although the population is more racially diverse, gender roles have become more similar. The American labor force has bifurcated into a privileged class of highly educated workers whose wages have been rising and a disadvantaged working class whose members' wages have been stagnant or declining (Perrucci, 1999). Within this present reality we must theorize for a new future and be judicious and explicit about the elements of the current and ancestral theories we take with us.

ACTIVE MODES OF THEORIZING ABOUT FAMILIES AND WORK

In 1979, Urie Bronfenbrenner asserted that "there is nothing so useful as a good theory." In preparing to write this chapter, we asked ourselves about the sorts of activities that constitute theory construction: What exactly do theorists *do* to construct theory? Our discussion generated a list of active words, "-ing" words that characterize the functions of theory in our work and in the work we admire. In our view, these gerunds reflect active, engaging processes that have the potential to lead to theory that "explains, predicts, and delights" (Weick, 1995, as quoted in Sutton & Staw, 1995, p. 378). They also indicate that the field is moving toward "strong theory," reflected in what Sutton and Staw (1995) see as "burrow[ing] deeply into microprocesses, laterally into neighboring concepts, or in an upward direction, tying itself to broader social phenomena" (p. 378).

The words on our list of gerunds describe three distinct approaches to building theory. Each approach, or mode, includes two "gerund strategies" that have characterized theorizing about families and work in recent decades: axiomatic theory construction (building and explaining), interactive theory construction (integrating and transferring), and critical theory construction (surfacing and problematizing). We discuss each of these modes in detail below.

Axiomatic Construction: Building and Explaining

One way to construct theories about families and work actively is to follow traditional axiomatic processes. This mode of theory construction is based on positivist goals of objective measurement and separation of data and theory. Most theories in this mode are inductive, moving "up" toward explanation from empirical results that are limited at first. Commitment to explanation and to building theory in the field of families and work often obligates researchers to draw on "what came before." In this way, axiomatic construction usually allows theories to emerge slowly and incrementally.

By identifying, analyzing, integrating, and, ultimately, improving propositions, theorists in the field of families and work have built frameworks that go beyond general propositions. Some researchers have invested in a long-term process of incremental accumulation of empirical generalizations and causal models across studies and over time. As scholars have systematically linked propositions, middle-range theories have emerged, usually focused on specific phenomena within the field. Barnett's work offers a good example of theory building through this slow, systematic process. In her early research, Barnett described the rewards and concerns that women in different role configurations perceived. Her studies suggested that it was not the number of roles but the quality of experience within them that was significant in how individuals make decisions about families and employment (Barnett & Baruch, 1987). Building on these basic descriptions of roles, Barnett, Marshall, and Pleck (1992) then attempted to explain how experiences in one type of role compensate for experiences in another role. Finally, Barnett and Hyde (2001) moved on to efforts at prediction by

developing an expansionist theory in which individuals do not suffer from role strain or conflict with multiple work and family roles but experience a "net gain" because of the benefits associated with multiple roles.

Barnett's efforts to explain her findings about work and family role compensation reflect one of the most traditional goals of theory construction. Taking their theoretical frameworks back for application in the "real world," theorists strive to explain how and why certain phenomena occur. Researchers who strive to explain dynamics in the families and work field return repeatedly to data to fine-tune and revise their theoretical models. Barnett (1999) recently has expanded her efforts to offer explanatory frameworks by reviewing and critiquing three outdated models of work-family interaction: the separate spheres model, the overlapping spheres model, and the work-life integration model. Drawing on her studies on work and family roles, she suggests a work-life systems explanatory framework in which individuals are part of an interactive social system that does not distinguish sharply between work and family roles. As White and Klein (2002) assert, this type of theory construction is conducted in the "context of justification" of a long line of accumulated findings.

Explaining theory about families and work can also happen without reference to multiple related generalizations rooted in prior studies. This "whole cloth" explanation contrasts conventional frameworks with an alternative vision of thinking about families and work. Campbell Clark's (2000) work/family border theory in the discipline of organizational behavior is an example of this approach. Using the interdisciplinary sensitizing concept of "border crossing," Campbell Clark has drawn on prior qualitative studies that included stories of work and family dynamics, supplemented by 15 of her own interviews with individuals who were employed full-time and shouldered "significant family responsibilities." Although her theory retains one conventional concept—borders—she contends that it is "designed to remedy the criticisms and gaps of previous theories of work and family" (p. 750). Detailing dynamics of border keepers and border crossers, Campbell Clark suggests that work/family border theory has important implications for organizations and individuals who seek to balance these two demanding domains.

Normative assumptions about families and work often have permeated axiomatic theorizing. Research on spillover effects between work and family has kept the focus on individuals and families who are active participants in employment and in family life (see Edwards & Rothbard, 2000). Although the potential of extending theory to new populations is promising, the field in general has developed models that address daily choices between work and family activities, not structural constraints on family and work options that may shift and change over time. To the extent that axiomatic theorizing is tied to "what came before," it can limit efforts to extend findings about families and work into new contexts or new populations.

Interactive Construction: Transferring and Integrating

Every discipline has blind spots—phenomena that are poorly understood and explanations that do not go far enough. Interactive methods of theory construction, which fall under the larger umbrella of "borrowing," help scholars to find solutions outside their areas of study. We define transferring as using an element of one theoretical perspective to enrich another. Integrating, perhaps one of the most difficult theoretical strategies to execute, involves bringing together elements of multiple theoretical perspectives to create a new insight or perspective. Integration is transformative because it generates something new as opposed to enhancing an existing perspective.

Transferring and integrating can be driven by the same motives as other methods of theory construction and can be combined with them. For example, a scholar engaged in axiomatic theorizing might look to other areas of study for concepts, propositions, or methods to fill the gaps. A scholar

taking a critical stance toward an established perspective might integrate ideas from several fields to propose a new way of thinking.

With borders as amorphous as those of the study of families and work, it can be hard to say with certainty which ideas originate within and outside those borders. We think that the objective definition of these strategies is probably less important than the subjective one. In other words, transferring and integrating are sometimes in the eye of the beholder. They are the result of a point of view or a stance—a position of openness and eagerness toward ideas from other disciplines that might address gaps in one's own area of study.

Transferring involves looking at a phenomenon through the lens of a different field or subfield. A scholar already versed in the study of families and work might transfer ideas by developing expertise in an additional discipline, but most often transfer occurs when scholars already trained in one area turn their gaze toward families and work. This is the case with Williams's (2000) significant elaboration of a legal perspective about conflict between families and work.

Integration also can take several forms. For example, theoretical statements can integrate across individuals, such as Pleck's (1977) famous article placing husbands' and wives' jobs within a work-family role system, or across contexts, such as Kossek, Colquitt, and Noe's (2001) hypotheses linking caregiving decisions at home to personal well-being and performance at work. Integration also can be used to link levels of analysis, such as organizations and the individuals and families with whom they interact. For example, scholars have studied "family-friendly" benefits at both the individual and organizational levels. Studies of individuals have focused on role conflict as a function of the availability and use of such benefits, whereas studies of organizations have focused on connections between such policies and organizational performance. Lee, MacDermid, and Buck (2000) integrated these approaches in their study of voluntary reduced-load work by managers and professionals. Prior research had focused very much on the characteristics of individual managers or professionals, "highlighting attributes such as competence, flexibility, clear priorities, responsiveness, and initiative" (p. 1211), but Lee et al.'s study uncovered organizational themes in the ways employers responded to requests for reduced-load work, the factors facilitating and hindering success, and the outcomes of the arrangements. Integrating organizational learning and systems perspectives has generated new insights both about the conditions *within* firms under which family-friendly arrangements are likely to spread beyond isolated cases and about patterns *across* firms in their responses to forces of change.

Sociologist Phyllis Moen has made notable progress in integrating factors related to organizations and marriages while also taking the passage of time into account. Under the umbrella of the life-course perspective, she and her colleagues have recognized the dual trajectories of life at work and at home both within individuals over time and across marital partners whose lives are linked (Moen, 2003). Their study of families' strategies for managing multiple demands acknowledges the active role that families play in shaping their experiences, but their simultaneous recognition of the gendered nature of work, family, and family strategies embeds the agency of families within the opportunities and constraints posed by social systems.

Critical Construction: Surfacing and Problematizing

An important element of critical theorizing is bringing unexamined issues to the surface. Critical theorizing can include surfacing assumptions that guided previous work in an area, surfacing previously unexamined phenomena, and problematizing common ways of thinking about phenomena.

Surfacing assumptions is the act of bringing to awareness assumptions that can then be evaluated for their accuracy and utility in the contemporary context. Perlow (1995) coined the phrase when she "surfaced" assumptions that physical presence at work ("face time") is critical for productivity. Critical theorizing makes it possible to surface assumptions about what types of families and what types of work "count" for analysis, and about the nature of families and the nature of work. The process illuminates the lives of women and men whose jobs are not full-time, year-round jobs, or of families with diverse racial/ethnic/class backgrounds and with different structures, such as those without children or with aging parents. Surfacing also prompts researchers to question seriously how the dynamics of work and family may operate in different ways for different populations. For example, Roy, Tubbs, and Burton (in press) delineate daily rhythms that African American, Latina, and European American mothers in Chicago construct in the face of demands for work and child care under welfare reform requirements. Such studies challenge common assumptions about balance and trade-offs between employment and parenthood. In particular, low-income parents who are unemployed or underemployed in time- and wage-limited jobs have limited "work/family" options. Typically, they must craft survival strategies based on shifting resources for child care and daily sustenance.

● **SPOTLIGHT ON METHODS**

METHODOLOGICAL CHALLENGES IN THEORIZING THE WORK-FAMILY COMPLEX

Suraj Commuri, *University of Missouri–Columbia*

O f all the methodological challenges that await a theorist with an interest in the work-family dyad, three rise to the top. First, given the undefined boundaries of the dyad, the theorist must become accustomed to handling a wide variety of theories. Second, given the many subtle and yet unexplored interactions between work and family, the theorist must be willing to explore unconventional research designs and methods. Finally, given that sometimes the roles individuals play at work may be incongruent with those they play in families, the theorist must examine any phenomenon from multiple perspectives.

THEORIES AS BUILDING BLOCKS

As MacDermid, Roy, and Zvonkovic remind us, the work-family dyad is characterized by undefined boundaries. This affects how much reliance the theorist may place in any one theoretical argument, for that argument can be easily challenged by a new interpretation of what constitutes the work-family dyad. On the bright side, this very characteristic makes the dyad a fertile ground on which to build theory. In dealing with a domain that has undefined boundaries, the theorist must make a habit of collecting theories from overlapping domains and confronting and contrasting them against each other. Although scholars often teach theories as if they are serious and infallible, resulting in "theory obfuscation" (Klein & White, 1996, p. xv) and "theory worship" (MacDermid et al.'s term), theories are inherently playful. They are building blocks and, therefore, are cast with creative and playful uses in mind. A theory builder must first learn to take a current theory apart, turn it upside down, use it out of context, confront it, and contrast it against other theories. This promotes in the theorist levels of confidence and comfort that are critical for theory building, and it reveals to the theorist various gaps that are in need of new theoretical explanations.

RESEARCH DESIGNS OUTSIDE THE BOX

In the work-family dyad, the iterative effects of the dynamism of one sphere on the other are often not readily apparent. Therefore, unlike in the case of what is common in theory testing, the theory builder should pause to analyze, interpret, and plan the next step after each and every case/data point. In other words, building theories in multifaceted domains such as the work-family dyad involves a persistent dialogue between the theorist and the data, even as those data are being gathered. Accordingly, a theorist working in this domain must cast away rigid research designs and be prepared to defend bold

(continued)

● **SPOTLIGHT ON METHODS** *continued*

decisions to use unconventional research designs and methods or decisions to turn conventional research designs on their heads to enable articulation of evasive theoretical explanations.

MULTIPLE PERSPECTIVES

In navigating role systems (Marks & MacDermid, 1996), wives and husbands sometimes feel a need to disguise the baggage of work from family and vice versa, especially when the activities in one sphere bear the potential to disturb equilibrium in the other. A theorist must examine such cases from multiple perspectives to aid any meaningful theory construction. For example, today, about one-third of all wives in the United States earn more than their husbands. Although some of these wives perceive the status as normal, their husbands view the situation as transient (Commuri, 2003). Further, although one pattern of power sharing in marriage is declared overtly, investigations of behind-the-scenes money management reveal a very different picture (Commuri, 2003). In order to build a theory, a theorist needs all this information. The told and the untold are both important, as are the wife's narratives and the husband's narratives. Similarly, interpretations of family from the vantage point of work and vice versa are equally important—not just because multiple perspectives must be represented, but because the differences between perspectives often turn out to be the crux of a new theory. ●

Another way to surface assumptions about how work relates to family is to study families that are statistically rare, but that have work-family connections that are perhaps extreme in some way or otherwise worthy of study. Intentional studies on exemplar occupations can "identify the processes of interest in a specific, theoretically relevant sample" (Perry-Jenkins et al., 2000, p. 993). For example, although they receive no income from their work, wives of commercial fishermen are heavily involved as bookkeepers, contacts, and advocates for their husbands (Mederer, 1997). Gender ideology, gender strategies, and power are each socially constructed and responsive to the individual ideological, marital, occupational, and policy contexts of these relationships (Mederer, 1997). In addition, Zvonkovic, Manoogian, and McGraw (2001) provide a detailed analysis of the cycle of departure, separation, homecoming, and reunion among commercial fishing families and long-haul truckers that illuminates such comings and goings in other families (Zvonkovic, Richards, Humble, & Manoogian, 1998).

Not just the populations but also the phenomena selected for study can be expanded through critical theorizing. Surfacing illustrates that not only does work affect family, but family can affect work, in positive *and* negative ways (Barnett, 1998, 1999). For instance, the fact that informal interpersonal support at work is not systematically considered reflects an assumption that work is a cold, cruel place and family is the source of warmth and support for people (Marks, 1994). Hochschild's book *The Time Bind* (1997) is an example of critical research that did not take such assumptions as its starting point. Daly (1996) has critiqued assumptions that all people experience time in the same ways, demonstrating the element of subjective perception and negotiated contexts of time. By exploring individual meanings of time,

Daly was able to move out of the economic metaphor in which time is a commodity to be spent into an analysis of how individuals, couples, and families construct time.

Problematizing a phenomenon extends the work of surfacing. Problematizing not only surfaces a concept, but also takes a value stance on unfairness in the concept. There are many examples of problematizing in feminist literature and in the literature on families in poverty (Thompson, 1993). Feminists have problematized the division of labor in homes through analyses of unpaid labor within households as a form of work (see Walker, 1999). Researchers who have adopted a critical stance have seen that unpaid work includes emotion work (Delphy & Leonard, 1992), defined as managing one's own and other family members' emotions, including encouraging, nurturing, or facilitating interaction among family members, both within the family and in family members' interfacing with outside institutions. Seery and Crowley (2000) identified work that mothers do in families to manage relationships between fathers and children as another distinctive way in which women perform emotion work in families. Theorists who view emotion work as an activity that requires energy and skill problematize it by raising it to the surface and criticizing the assumption that such work is more "natural" for women than for men.

Hallmarks of problematizing a concept would be the illumination that the concept is not determined by biology, by society, or by law, but is instead socially constructed and thus, able to be negotiated and changed. Coltrane's (1998) analysis of the division of household labor, by including consideration of broader contexts that help to determine the division and by including a consideration of the consequences of division, problematizes the way most couples divide such labor. Similarly, Garey's (1999) analyses of how women strategize to accomplish parenting and paid work demonstrate the problems in the larger society that limit women's choices. In general, problematizing a concept broadens our vision, placing it in a larger context and demonstrating the way it has been shaped by particular circumstances.

NEW VISIONS FOR CONTEMPORARY THEORIZING ABOUT WORK AND FAMILY LIFE

The strength and viability of the field of families and work rests on rigorous and varied "acts" of theorizing. In order to encourage new visions for contemporary researchers, we turn to the metaphors that undergird researchers' and other people's thinking about how work and family relate to each other. We disagree with Edwards and Rothbard (2000), who state that metaphors are poorly suited for advancing research.

Because metaphors are so prevalent in the theoretical and empirical literature on families and work, we seek to analyze the visions they hold. Thorne (2001) evokes several metaphors in her argument for stronger theoretical integration in the field:

> Note the telling vocabulary and syntax that organize this area of research: two nouns linked by a hyphen and by an array of other words signaling connection ("work-family nexus," "relations between work and family," "balancing work and family," "juggling work and family")... . Most of the literature on work and family takes these categories to be self evident, using them in ways that gloss complex, contradictory, and shifting realities even as the categories continue to order perceptions of the world. (p. 373)

We believe that through the systematic examination of metaphors, assumptions that researchers carry forth can be made explicit, and new metaphors and visions for analyzing families and work can be intentionally developed.

The first set of metaphors includes juggling and balancing. These visions of families and work were prevalent in the 1970s and persist today. In this way of conceiving of the connection between families and work, individual actors are seen as being presented with too many obligations, as if their role demands are balls they need to juggle. Of course, the juggling metaphor implies that individuals will be unable to keep all the balls in the air simultaneously, thus role strain (if not total disaster) is the consequence of juggling. The image of balancing seems to hold a similar idea, in that actors are seen on a fulcrum atop which they can only change their bodies in space to respond to demands from the family or the work side of their lives.

A more recent metaphor that we include in this category is that of navigating, which positions the actor with more intent and a direction toward which he or she is navigating. The evolution of these metaphors reflects well the way the field has moved away from assumptions of role scarcity and toward models that emphasize individuals' choices in arranging their work and family lives (Barnett, 1998, 1999; Marks, 1977). The navigation metaphor has sparked research about families' goals, about how individuals and families can change course to adapt to changing circumstances, and how they can monitor their progress (Zvonkovic & Moon, 1997). The metaphor of navigation can overemphasize individuals' choices, to the detriment of recognition of the constraints in the lives we study. It may reflect the nature of our daily experiences with families and work: decisions about day care, transportation, and flextime are made by individuals in families sitting around the kitchen table, and not through formal national policies across workplaces.

Yet the experience of navigating and of attempting to find balance in our lives is at best a partial explanation, and, under some circumstances, it is illusory and misleading. The images of balancing and navigation may not resonate with the life experiences of a large number of U.S. families. Recognizing historical and sociocultural contexts included in ecological and even conflict theories can provide theorists with a host of topics suggesting that intentionality is embedded in structure. A focus, then, would be less on choice and alternatively on strategies, resources, and survival (see Collins, 1999). Some promising directions may emerge from research in the public policy field on how poor families' work experiences are managed or regulated (as in recent work

on globalization and movement of service workers—particularly women—across national boundaries to pursue employment; e.g., Ehrenreich & Hochschild, 2003).

The broad theme that is reflected from consideration of these metaphors is the theme of choice and constraint in families and work. Table 20.1 traces the connection from metaphors, important dimensions of inquiry stemming from issues raised from the metaphors, and overarching themes. New visions for considering families and work can be sparked by the limitations of these metaphors and the overarching theme of intentionality, choices, and constraints. In particular, researchers may explore questions of power as it is related to resources available or not available to individuals in families and at work. The line of research into strategies for balancing work and family could be transformed into examination of strategies for managing family life in the face of shifting resources due to periods of underemployment or unemployment. Many of these dimensions suggest that explicit recognition of social structural constraints due to race/ethnicity, class, and gender in particular are important (Dilworth-Anderson, Burton, & Johnson, 1993).

The second set of metaphors we have identified is made up of those that envision connected, and not separated, spheres. These metaphors include weaving, physical or spatial transitions, and the margins between family and work life. The metaphor of weaving shows how the threads of personal and work life can be arranged together, positioning actors as artisans, creating their own unique patterns in response to circumstances and preferences (Garey, 1999). Margins and transitions depict individuals as moving through the physical spaces of work and family worlds. More recently, the metaphor of gatekeeping has been used as a way to understand how family members might protect their turf and prevent others from walking along their lawns.

We suggest that researchers and theorists carefully consider the definitional borders of each phenomenon to be studied, explicitly acknowledging the quadrants of the landscape that will—and will not—be considered.

Table 20.1   Metaphors and Thematic Dimensions of Diverse Work/Family Life Experiences

Metaphors	Dimensions	Themes
Balancing	Power and resources	Choices and constraints
Juggling	Social structure	
Navigating	Intentionality and strategies	
	Agency/structure	
Weaving	Unique nature of work activity	Definitions of borders
Transitions	Shifting family configurations	
Margins		
Gatekeeping		
Rhythms	Continuity and change	Temporal orientations
Pathways	Daily experiences	
Trajectories	Work and family careers	
	Timing	
	Trajectories	
Bricoleur	Mixed method	Methodological diversity
	Longitudinal methods	
	Intentional sampling	
	Generalizability versus particularization	

This is especially important because of the difficulty of defining the borders of the field of families and work. Considering the borders may lead researchers to pay close attention to the nature of particular work activities along a full range of engagement: paid work (from wage contract labor to part-time, cash-in-hand jobs) and unpaid work (from caregiving to personal maintenance). Diverse dimensions of family life are addressed through consideration of border definitions as well, including extended kin networks, multiple households, parenting across residences, and shifting family configurations. New visions of work and family can be sparked by the understanding that researchers and the public commonly make assumptions about the borders between the work and the family world.

The third set of metaphors is made up of those that consider work and family life in a temporal dimension. A driving thrust behind these metaphors is researchers' interest in how families use time (Zvonkovic, Notter, & Peters, in press). These metaphors include images such as clocks, pathways, and trajectories, stemming from life-course perspectives, as well as the more recent image of rhythms. Researchers who make use of these metaphors tend to be grounded in a life-course perspective, in which they visualize work and family life as occurring in daily routines, across life careers, and in historical contexts. Life-course researchers have detailed the pathways of individual careers in work and family and, in particular, the conceptualization of "dual careers" as braided work and family careers of married couples (Moen & Han, 2001). Recently, Fraenkel (2001) has described the dyadic coordinated and discontinuous beats mapped out in couples' work and family lives, and Roy et al. (in press) have examined the improvisation of daily rhythms for families whose lives extend beyond the normative 9-to-5 workday schedule.

If we continue to prioritize time as a theoretical tool, we would pursue life-course perspectives and question how work and family roles change over the life course and how individuals imbue these roles with meaning. Transitions in these domains, and the timing of these events, such as entry into the labor force, transition to parenthood, transition to elder care, empty nest, and retirement, are integral to our conceptualization of the dynamics of work and family life. Emerging interest in the notion of ambivalence also suggests that expectations of work and family roles may diverge sharply between parents and children, and intergenerational relationships may be strongly shaped by such shifting expectations over time. Attention to temporal orientations highlights the importance of work and family dynamics in families in "the long view," in which individuals move from poverty to self-sufficiency, choose to invest and later benefit from training and education, or encounter historical downturns and economic shifts, such as economic restructuring, recessions, and boom periods.

Dimensions that can be addressed through a focus on temporal orientations are also in line with many of the major threads of research in life-course and ecological frameworks. In particular, researchers would be encouraged to weigh what is considered to be change and what is considered to be continuity. These dynamics can be traced out over daily experiences, as well as across important work and family transitions, and through careers. Researchers and theorists must carefully consider the temporal character and context of each phenomenon to be studied. Recent studies of everyday work and family activities, using a variety of new methodological approaches, have provided researchers with new windows onto the inner workings of work and family processes (e.g., Almeida, Wethington, & Chandler, 1999).

So far, our treatment of metaphors has shown that when they are examined systematically, they can be expanded or opened up to provide clues for studying more diverse populations and more diverse phenomena. The final metaphor related to a theme has been coined by Denzin and Lincoln (1994): a "bricoleur." This word describes an individual who creates a close-knit collection of practices that provide solutions to real-world problems. In French, it means "handyman." This image suggests that we must be equipped to pursue research directions on individuals with work and family issues that are broad, and we must devise strategies to study them creatively. What are the dimensions that merit consideration for a bricoleur looking at work and family? Diversity of methodological approaches touches on a number of dimensions for future research on families and work. Mixed methods, in particular nesting qualitative components within larger quantitative surveys, may provide theorists in the field with rich new insights into contextual and dynamic processes (Tashakkori & Teddlie, 2003). Enacting the bricoleur metaphor, the final theme calls for us to seek methodological diversity, especially important to the field of work and family.

ENVISIONING EXCELLENT THEORY AND THEORY-DRIVEN RESEARCH

Research on families and work holds the potential to address everyday experiences in two of life's most significant domains. Like other scholars, we recognize the limits of training, research, and dialogue about families and work, limits reflected in the common metaphors that researchers have come to rely on to represent definitions for work and family.

As alternatives, we have offered here four themes that scholars can use to frame theories and studies about families and work. These themes offer alternative and complementary views of the contextualized dynamics of work and family life. They also push us further in our understanding and conceptualizing of work and family life. Current metaphors are limited in their recognition of the paradox of choice and constraint, and in their limited understanding of the borders around work and family. We call for increasingly sophisticated attention to contexts, and we believe this will contribute to opening researchers' eyes to the diversity of families and work situations that face adults in the contemporary world.

Evidence about demographic changes in family and work over time foretells an increasingly dynamic landscape. We call for continued application of temporal orientations, consonant with life-course perspectives, applied to individuals at different stages of life, and sensitive to different dimensions of time. We believe that the complexity of work and family phenomena for diverse individuals requires us to be bricoleurs, relying on different vantage points to be relevant to contemporary work and family situations in context.

How do the four themes we have described help us to move beyond "work/family" as it has traditionally been framed? In part, the themes recognize the everyday nature of lived experiences with families and work (Daly, 2003). We believe that useful theorizing about work and family challenges the ancestral ways of looking at individuals' and families' experiences. Theories that recognize all families and individuals and the dynamic variation in how they relate to paid and unpaid labor activities may

begin to shape a common language for "a sprawling domain" of research in multiple disciplines. We urge future researchers to contribute to theorizing by pushing themselves to look beyond static, deterministic vantage points on work and family toward greater inclusion, as suggested by the themes displayed in Table 20.1.

Creative, innovative perspectives on the relationships between families and work can invigorate and bridge disconnected bodies of research. However, emerging frameworks and decades of research can be used to ground new theories. Although no one study or research program can tell the whole story of connections for the diverse personal and work lives of individuals today, scholars can contribute to building the field of families and work through purposeful, active engagement in the modes of theory construction discussed in this chapter. We hope that this chapter, which was birthed from our collective frustration, will prove useful to a new generation of scholars pursuing dynamic and contextual approaches to families and work, yielding new visions and metaphors of the ways people experience work and personal lives.

CASE STUDY

THE INTERFACE OF ELDER CAREGIVING AND PAID EMPLOYMENT

Judy L. Singleton, *College of Mount St. Joseph*

When analyzing the interface of paid employment and elder caregiving, scholars must look at the role employers play in the relationship. Employers may make demands, such as overtime, that limit family members' ability to provide care; at the same time, they may offer support and benefits, such as flextime or referral services, that

enhance employees' ability to take care of relatives. Understanding the complexities of the role that the workplace plays in helping or hindering elder care is increasingly important, as many family caregivers are in the labor force. Likewise, there has been tremendous growth in the aging population as life expectancy has increased. The oldest-old, those age 85 and older, constitute the fastest-growing segment of the U.S. population, and it is these individuals who are most likely to require assistance.

What are the effects of elder caregiving on paid employment and vice versa? How can an employer help an employee to remain in the workforce while simultaneously providing care for an aged family member? This case study examines some of the methodological and theoretical challenges researchers may face when attempting to address these questions.

METHODOLOGICAL CHALLENGES IN RESEARCH ON WORK AND FAMILY

In Chapter 20, MacDermid, Roy, and Zvonkovic discuss their frustration with the research methods used in the field of families and work, and I concur with their assessment. I optimistically (unrealistically?) thought that I could overcome some of the problems with previous research and contribute something new and unique to the study of paid employment and elder caregiving. I attempted to do so, and, based on my experience, I offer this word of warning to others: You will encounter far more obstacles than even the most creative mind could imagine.

I wanted a large amount of data for my study on the interface between elder caregiving and caregivers' paid employment so that I would be able to analyze the breadth of elder caregiving among paid employees considering various factors, including full- and part-time status, different industries, numerous size categories (i.e., number of employees) of companies, diverse occupations, and a variety of demographic items. I decided that the cross-sectional survey method, although limited for examining changes over time, would serve the purpose of collecting at one time the large volume of data I needed.

To combat the limitations of the single-workplace setting found so often in studies, I planned to survey a stratified, cluster sample

of companies, using the local Chamber of Commerce listing as a sampling frame. I treated the Standard Industrial Classification (SIC) categories as clusters and the size groupings (number of employees per firm) as the strata. I chose three SIC groupings to investigate, and I categorized each SIC by the number of employees at each company. I collapsed the size categories into three groupings—50–99 employees, 100–249 employees, and 250 or more employees—to differentiate among small, medium, and large companies. I planned to randomly select one company per industrial classification in each size category, giving a total of nine companies for the study.

This process did not seem difficult—or so I thought. The first snag I encountered was in finding companies willing to participate in the study. I predicted neither the time it would take to finalize the sample nor the difficulty involved in asking employees about their use of company-sponsored benefits to assist them with caregiving. One of the most time-consuming processes I encountered was that of contacting the appropriate person in each company and getting the study approved or disapproved. Because this was a random sample, I had not established relationships with the companies. In fact, the whole sampling method was somewhat like making cold sales calls. Typically, I first contacted the human resources director and from there proceeded to speak with individuals in higher-level positions to obtain an answer. Companies expected to be able to review the questionnaire, and rightly so, and wanted to meet with me personally to discuss the research procedure before I could begin. This process in some cases took 8 to 10 weeks, and often resulted in upper management's ultimate refusal to participate in the study. This, in turn, led to my randomly selecting another company and starting the whole process over again. In hindsight, I realize that I may have had more success if I had mailed a detailed letter of explanation to each company before the initial phone contact.

After 6 months of working on acquiring the sample, I proceeded with seven companies, not nine. I still had three different industrial classifications, but not three separate size categories for each. Then, before the study began, two companies withdrew from participation for reasons that had nothing to do with my research methodology (one because of a unionizing attempt and the other because of changes in personnel). I was left with five companies, but at least I still had three industrial classifications.

Companies that declined to participate in the study cited two common reasons. One was that, according to the human resources director, the company had no job-related problems involving employees who are providing care for elderly relatives. In other words, if an HR director had not heard from any employees about their elder caregiving concerns, then surely such problems did not exist. Another common reason that HR directors gave was their concern that a survey dealing with employees' non-work-related responsibilities as well as company-sponsored benefits would "stir things up" in the workforce. One HR director said, "I don't want to deal with the issues that this topic may bring up." Two other HR directors were concerned that workers might become involved in attempts to unionize if they really analyzed their current benefits. In fact, one company that refused to participate asked me if I was working for a union. I never dreamed that someone would envision me as Sally Field's character in *Norma Rae*.

Another challenge I encountered in this research was the limited access I was given to employees. I was not allowed any means of identifying employees (companies would participate only if the study was completely anonymous), so I took a census at each company and distributed a questionnaire to each employee with his or her paycheck. At each of the five companies, I was permitted to send only one follow-up postcard with paychecks to all employees, 3 weeks after the initial distribution of the questionnaire. This anonymous approach eliminated any hope I had of extending the study later by interviewing caregiving employees and their care recipients to look at their reciprocal relationships. It is impossible to compare the reciprocity between caregiver and care recipient and between employer and caregiving employee if the parties are not identified. A blend of qualitative and quantitative methods could have provided a wealth of information about such relationships, but circumstances did not permit me to use such methods in this study.

My research was further affected in that I had to change my original questionnaire dramatically to meet the restrictions imposed by the HR directors and their superiors at the two largest companies. These companies refused to participate if I questioned all employees about job performance. I was permitted to ask job performance questions of caregiving employees only, because the companies assumed that the number of these employees would be minimal. Both companies were concerned, however, that employees would be threatened by a survey that asked about their attendance, distractions, missed appointments, overtime declined, and so on, in addition to questions focused on work satisfaction and loyalty to the company. By this time, my sampling frame was nearly exhausted. Hence, in order to maintain large companies for the survey process, I eliminated most questions on company loyalty and work satisfaction. In addition, although I retained all job performance questions directed specifically at caregiving employees, I eliminated all but two of those measures for questions directed at all employees. This essentially crushed my attempt to compare employees who were not providing care to elders with those who were on specific job issues.

Would I approach employers again to try to conduct a study? Most definitely, but I would structure my approach differently. I would consider a combined quantitative and qualitative approach in order to obtain large

CASE STUDY *continued*

masses of data while at the same time acquiring in-depth answers to some of the specific survey questions. I could have collected data that I wanted along with specific information the employers needed, regardless of whether that information was applicable to my study. In essence, by structuring the data collection process to be a "win-win situation" for both the employer and me, I might have eliminated some of the difficulties I encountered in obtaining my sample.

THEORETICAL CHALLENGES IN RESEARCH ON WORK AND FAMILY

There is little in the quintessential work and family theory that is related to the interface of elder caregiving and paid employment. I rooted this particular study primarily in social exchange theory, a theory seldom used in work and family research. The theory's concept of reciprocity provided the grounding for this study, particular in the domain of employer and caregiving employee. The reciprocity of the exchange between employees providing production and employers providing wages might seem to be a sufficient enough exchange. However, in a competitive labor market, the transfer of money from employer to employee may not be enough to continue the exchange process—that is, the transfer of labor from employee to employer. Benefits and support enhance the exchange process for employees, encouraging their continued production with

one company versus another. However, it becomes difficult for researchers to assess some of this reciprocity, such as the outcome of loyalty to the company, when they are not permitted to ask the necessary questions.

An alternative approach to social exchange theory for this research design could have been systems theory. In looking at the issue of elder caregiving among paid employees, a researcher could focus on the multiple systems that have impacts on the social environment of all parties in these situations. For example, an individual may be a caregiver to both an older person and a child, multiple family members may serve as caregivers to a single older person, or a caregiver may hold more than one paid job. Many systems come into play, and there are interrelationships among the systems and their components. For example, an older parent's condition may worry the caregiving adult child so much that he or she becomes distracted at work, potentially contributing to tensions with fellow workers or superiors and poor job performance. That adult child, in turn, may feel so distraught over work conditions that he or she places unrealistic demands on his or her spouse, creating problems in the marital system. The possible cycle of events is endless among the different systems.

Conducting research on work and family issues has its challenges. However, there are many approaches yet to be tried, and the knowledge gained from scholars' attempts will no doubt be helpful to future researchers.

DISCUSSION AND EXTENSION

SUGGESTIONS FOR A MULTILEVEL REFRAMING OF WORK-FAMILY THEORY

Joseph G. Grzywacz, *Wake Forest University School of Medicine*

Angela J. Hattery, *Wake Forest University*

Patricia Voydanoff, *University of Dayton*

Our goal in this brief contribution is to help readers respond to MacDermid, Roy, and Zvonkovic's call for scholars to advance dynamic and contextual theories of families and work. We argue that persistent gaps in the work-family literature result from conceptual "ruts," and that these ruts preclude clear theorizing. We offer here four suggestions for breaking out of these conceptual ruts with the hope of helping scholars reframe families and work theory.

In *Conceptual Blockbusting* (1986), Adams outlines several common conceptual ruts that are exemplified in the work-family literature. The first of these, seeing what is expected, is driven by entrenched beliefs that work and family are inherently at odds. This rut is exemplified by an almost exclusive empirical focus on conflict and strain and by enduring quests to locate the harmful effects of maternal employment on marriage and children. The next rut, delimiting an issue too closely, is illustrated by MacDermid et al.'s argument in Chapter 20 that scholars tend to define "work" and "family" too narrowly. Studying paid activity through an employer as the only indicator of "work" systematically omits a corps of volunteers as well as the 15% of U.S. adults who are self-employed or work in "nonstandard" jobs. Likewise, the dominant focus on dual-earner couples with children suggests that "family" is exclusively about maintaining the marital dyad and parenting. The last perceptual rut, looking at an issue from one point of view, is reflected in the tendency of work-family scholars to study highly valued professional and middle-class workers and to overlook populations on society's margins. Advancing comprehensive theories of families and work requires breaking out of these three conceptual ruts.

Identifying the ruts that undermine understanding of families and work is easy, but identifying and executing solutions is difficult. There are literatures devoted to critical and creative thinking, as well as published works offering an array of strategies for "getting out of conceptual ruts" (e.g., Adams, 1986). Below, we offer four broad suggestions for breaking out of conceptual ruts that we see as essential for the genesis of comprehensive work-family theories.

Question the assumption that work and family are inherently conflicted. A small but growing body of literature is examining the possibility that work and family, while occasionally conflicted, are also allies. Barnett and her colleagues, for example, have been advancing role enhancement theory in their research for nearly 20 years, and their evidence indicates that people (frequently trained professionals) report that the benefits of combining work and family outweigh the strains (see, e.g., Barnett & Hyde, 2001). Likewise, concepts such as positive spillover (Grzywacz & Marks, 2000) and work-family facilitation (Grzywacz, 2002; Voydanoff, 2004) are gaining increased attention. Although some theoretical ideas are further evolved than others, this issue is fertile

DISCUSSION AND EXTENSION *continued*

ground for theorizing because it remains overshadowed and underdeveloped.

Remember that social structural and cultural contexts matter. Work-family scholarship frequently follows macro-level changes, such as the growth of women's labor force participation and, more recently, the shift toward a 24/7 economy and changes in the structure of families. These changes cannot be viewed acontextually because macro-level changes are more pronounced for members of some social structural groups than for others. For example, although some segments of the world may benefit from the 24/7 economy, it has costs that are borne disproportionately by women, the poorly educated, and members of racial and ethnic minority groups. Additionally, macro-level changes cannot be viewed as culturally universal. Belief systems and patterns of behavior surrounding "work" and "family" vary across cultures and are shaped by physical attributes of the broader environment (suburban Boston is very different from rural Appalachia or sub-Saharan Africa) as well as by regulated local customs regarding such things as appropriate care of children and adults' responsibilities to the larger community. The clearest theorizing about families and work will emerge when scholars examine both social structural and cultural variations.

A methodological strategy for emphasizing context is to *deliberately expand sampling* of observations or units of analysis to reflect the widening diversity of work and family situations emerging in the United States and around the world. Work-family theory to date has been driven primarily by small samples of people in specific occupational (i.e., professionals) and familial (i.e., nuclear families) arrangements. Although clearly important, these observations reflect only a portion of the universe of possible observations. To the extent that theories arise from the analysis of observations, if observations systematically omit segments of a given universe, the

resulting theory will have limited internal and external validity.

Consider ethnographic techniques such as cultural immersion, community observation, and in-depth personal interviews. When aptly applied, ethnography circumvents conceptual ruts by elucidating the meanings that real people ascribe to "work" and "family" as well as their beliefs about the relative separateness between work and family. Data from the Sloan Centers on "ethnographies of daily life" suggest that the conventions frequently imposed by the quantitative study of work and family do not map onto people's everyday lives. For example, Darrah (2003) found that, although people can clearly discern work activities from family activities (filing is, after all, very different from changing diapers), they view the worlds of work and family as simply elements of a larger whole with myriad interconnections. That is, just as people can discern the difference between minutes and seconds, they are also keenly aware that both are elements of a broader concept (i.e., time) and that they differ more in degree than in substantive meaning. These types of insights are essential for building usable theories of families and work.

Finally, *identify and focus on processes that link different levels of analysis.* Symbolic interactionists argue that interaction, negotiation, and ideological work are the mechanisms that link macro-level expectations such as those imposed by economic conditions or cultural norms with micro-level phenomena (LaRossa & Reitzes, 1993). This enactment is made visible in the strategies that families and workplaces develop to address the dilemmas associated with combining responsibilities, commitments, and activities from two domains that until recently have been considered as separate from each other. For example, Hattery's (2001) recent work demonstrates how mothers negotiate the dominant socially sanctioned motherhood ideology, which suggests that "good mothers"

DISCUSSION AND EXTENSION *continued*

are primary caretakers for their children. Hattery found that all the women in her study endorsed motherhood ideology; however, the strategies they employed to enact the ideology (e.g., working nonoverlapping shifts with spouses, working from home) were shaped by situational circumstances. By identifying and focusing on strategies that individuals, families, and organization use to "do work and family," theorists can gain a better understanding of the linkages between macro- and micro-level phenomena.

In their chapter, MacDermid et al. call scholars to engage in dynamic and contextual theory building. To aid this call, we have echoed here MacDermid et al.'s criticisms by arguing that theorists and scholars need to break out of their conceptual ruts, and we have offered the following suggestions for accomplishing this: Scholars should (a) directly question entrenched views that work and family are inherently conflicted, (b) place context at the center of theory building and deliberately expand the view of work and family by widening the sampling of "work" and "family" observations, (c) use ethnographic techniques for forming and refining theoretical ideas, and (d) identify and focus on activities that reflect the connections between macro and micro levels of analysis. These suggestions, of course, are not new, but we are hopeful that our repackaging and reframing of these ideas will stimulate dynamic and contextual theories of families and work that, in MacDermid et al.'s language, "don't stop at the borders."

Discussion and Extension

REFERENCES

Adams, J. L. (1986). *Conceptual blockbusting: A guide to better ideas.* Reading, MA: Perseus.

Allen, T. D., Herst, D. E. L., Bruck, C. S., & Sutton, M. (2000). Consequences associated with work-family conflict: A review and agenda for future research. *Journal of Occupational Health Psychology, 5,* 278–308.

Almeida, D. M., Wethington, E., & Chandler, A. L. (1999). Daily transmission of tensions between marital dyads and parent-child dyads. *Journal of Marriage and the Family, 61,* 49–61.

Barnett, R. C. (1998). Toward a review and reconceptualization of the work/family literature. *Genetic, Social, and General Psychology Monographs, 124,* 125–182.

Barnett, R. C. (1999). A new work-life model for the twenty-first century. *Annals of the American Academy of Political and Social Sciences, 562,* 143–158.

Barnett, R. C., & Baruch, G. K. (1987). Social roles, gender, and psychological distress. In R. C. Barnett, L. Biener, & G. K. Baruch (Eds.), *Gender and stress* (pp. 122–143). New York: Free Press.

Barnett, R.C., & Hyde, J. S. (2001). Women, men, work, and family: An expansionist theory. *American Psychologist, 56,* 781–796.

Barnett, R. C., Marshall, N. L., & Pleck, J. H. (1992). Men's multiple roles and their relationship to men's psychological distress. *Journal of Marriage and the Family, 54,* 358–367.

Bronfenbrenner, U. (1979). *The ecology of human development: Experiments by nature and design.* Cambridge, MA: Harvard University Press.

Bronfenbrenner, U. (1986), Ecology of the family as a context for human development: Research perspectives. *Developmental Psychology, 22,* 723–742

Campbell Clark, S. (2000). Work/family border theory: A new theory of work/family balance. *Human Relations 53,* 747–770.

Collins, P. H. (1999). Shifting the center: Race, class, and feminist theorizing about motherhood. In S. Coontz (Ed.), *American families: A multicultural reader* (pp. 197–217). New York: Routledge.

Coltrane, S. (1998). *Gender and families.* Thousand Oaks, CA: Pine Forge.

Commuri, S. (2003). *Intrahousehold resource allocation.* Manuscript in preparation.

Daly, K. J. (1996). *Families and time: Keeping pace in a hurried culture.* Thousand Oaks, CA: Sage.

Daly, K. J. (2003). Family theory versus the theories families live by. *Journal of Marriage and Family 65,* 771–784.

Darrah, C. N. (2003, June). *Anthropology and the workplace/workforce mismatch.* Paper presented at the conference Workplace/Workforce Mismatch? Work, Family, Health and Wellbeing, Washington, DC.

Delphy, C., & Leonard, D. (1992). *Familiar exploitation: A new analysis of marriage in contemporary Western societies.* Cambridge, MA: Polity.

Denzin, N. K., & Lincoln, Y. S. (1994). Introduction: Entering the field of qualitative research. In N. K. Denzin & Y. S. Lincoln (Eds.), *Handbook of qualitative research* (pp. 1–17). Thousand Oaks, CA: Sage.

Dilworth-Anderson, P., Burton, L. M., & Johnson, L. B. (1993). Reframing theories for understanding race, ethnicity, and families. In P. Boss, W. J. Doherty, R. LaRossa, W. R. Schumm, & S. K. Steinmetz (Eds.), *Sourcebook of family theories and methods: A contextual approach* (pp. 627–649). New York: Plenum.

Doherty, W. J., Boss, P., LaRossa, R., Schumm, W. R., & Steinmetz, S. K. (1993). Family theories and methods: A contextual approach. In P. Boss, W. J. Doherty, R. LaRossa, W. R. Schumm, & S. K. Steinmetz (Eds.), *Sourcebook of family theories and methods: A contextual approach* (pp. 3–30). New York: Plenum.

Edwards, J. R., & Rothbard, N. P. (2000). Mechanisms linking work and family: Clarifying the relationship between work and family constructs. *Academy of Management Review, 25,* 178–199.

Ehrenreich, B., & Hochschild, A. R. (Eds.). (2003). *Global woman: Nannies, maids, and sex workers in the new economy.* New York: Metropolitan.

Fraenkel, P. (2001). The place of time in couple and family therapy. In K. J. Daly (Ed.), *Minding the time in family experience: Emerging perspectives and issues* (pp. 283–310). Oxford: Elsevier Science.

Garey, A. I. (1999). *Weaving work and motherhood*. Philadelphia: Temple University Press.

Grzywacz, J. G. (2002, November). Toward a theory of work-family facilitation. Paper presented at the Theory Construction and Research Methodology Workshop, annual meeting of the National Council on Family Relations, Houston.

Grzywacz, J. G., & Marks, N. F. (2000). Reconceptualizing the work-family interface: An ecological perspective on the correlates of positive and negative spillover between work and family. *Journal of Occupational Health Psychology, 5,* 111–126.

Hattery, A. J. (2001). *Women, work, and family: Balancing and weaving*. Thousand Oaks, CA: Sage.

Hochschild, A. R. (1997). *The time bind: When work becomes home and home becomes work*. New York: Holt.

Hofstede, G. (2001). *Culture's consequences: Comparing values, behaviors, institutions, and organizations across nations* (2nd ed.). Thousand Oaks, CA: Sage.

Kiecolt, K. J. (2003). Satisfaction with work and family life: No evidence of cultural reversal. *Journal of Marriage and Family, 65,* 23–35.

Kingsbury, N., & Scanzoni, J. (1993). Structural-functionalism. In P. Boss, W. J. Doherty, R. LaRossa, W. R. Schumm, & S. K. Steinmetz (Eds.), *Sourcebook of family theories and methods: A contextual approach* (pp. 195–217). New York: Plenum.

Klein, D. M., & White, J. M. (1996). *Family theories: An introduction*. Thousand Oaks, CA: Sage.

Kossek, E. E., Colquitt, J. A., & Noe, R. A. (2001). Caregiving decisions, well-being, and performance: The effects of place and provider as a function of dependent type and work-family climates. *Academy of Management Journal, 44,* 29–44.

LaRossa, R., & Reitzes, D. C. (1993). Symbolic interactionism and family studies. In P. Boss, W. J. Doherty, R. LaRossa, W. R. Schumm, & S. K. Steinmetz (Eds.), *Sourcebook of family theories and methods: A contextual approach* (pp. 135–163). New York: Plenum.

Lee, M. D., MacDermid, S. M., & Buck, M. L. (2000). Organizational paradigms of reduced-load work: Accommodation, elaboration and transformation. *Academy of Management Journal, 43,* 1211–1226.

Marks, S. R. (1977). Multiple roles and role strain: Some notes on human energy, time and commitment. *American Sociological Review, 42,* 921–936.

Marks, S. R. (1994). Studying workplace intimacy: Havens at work. In D. L. Sollie & L. A. Leslie (Eds.), *Gender, families, and close relationships: Feminist research journeys* (pp. 145–168). Thousand Oaks, CA: Sage.

Marks, S. R., & MacDermid, S. M. (1996). Multiple roles and the self: A theory of role balance. *Journal of Marriage and the Family, 58,* 417–432.

Mederer, H. J. (1997). Gender and fishing families. *Fisheries.*

Moen, P. (Ed.). (2003). *It's about time: Couples and careers*. Ithaca, NY: Cornell University Press.

Moen, P., & Han, S. K. (2001). Gendered careers: A life course perspective. In R. Hertz & N. L. Marshall (Eds.), *Working families: The transformation of the American home* (pp. 42–57). Berkeley: University of California Press.

Parsons, T. (1951). *The social system*. New York: Free Press.

Perlow, L. A. (1995). Putting the work back into work/family. *Group and Organization Management, 20,* 227–239.

Perrucci, R. (1999). *The new class society*. Lanham, MD: Rowman & Littlefield.

Perry-Jenkins, M., Repetti, R. L., & Crouter, A. C. (2000). Work and family in the 1990s. *Journal of Marriage and the Family, 62,* 981–998.

Pleck, J. H. (1977). The work-family role system. *Social Problems, 24,* 417–425.

Roy, K., Tubbs, C., & Burton, L. M. (in press). Don't have no time: Daily rhythms and organization of time for low-income families. *Family Relations.*

Schoen, R., Astone, N. M., Rothert, K., Standish, N. J., & Kim, Y. J. (2002). Women's employment, marital happiness, and divorce. *Social Forces, 81,* 643–662.

Seery, B., & Crowley, M. S. (2000). Women's emotion work in the family. *Journal of Family Issues, 21,* 100–127.

Sundstrom, W. A. (2001). Discouraging times: The labor force participation of married Black women, 1930–1940. *Explorations in Economic History, 38,* 123–146.

Sutton, R. I., & Staw, B. M. (1995). What theory is not. *Administrative Science Quarterly, 40,* 371–384.

Tashakkori, A., & Teddlie, C. (Eds.). (2003). *Handbook of mixed methods in social and behavioral research.* Thousand Oaks, CA: Sage.

Thompson, L. (1993). Conceptualizing gender in marriage: The case of marital care. *Journal of Marriage and the Family, 55,* 557–569.

Thorne, B. (2001). Pickup time at Oakdale Elementary School: Work and family from the vantage points of children. In R. Hertz & N. L. Marshall (Eds.), *Working families: The transformation of the American home* (pp. 354–376). Berkeley: University of California Press.

U.S. Bureau of the Census. (1975). *Historical statistics of the United States: Colonial times to 1970* (Bicentennial ed., pt. 2). Washington, DC: Government Printing Office.

U.S. Bureau of the Census. (1999). *Statistical abstract of the United States: 1999.* Washington, DC: Government Printing Office.

U.S. Bureau of the Census. (2003). *Statistical abstract of the United States: 2003.* Washington, DC: Government Printing Office.

Voydanoff, P. (2002). Linkages between the work-family interface and work-family and individual outcomes: An integrative model. *Journal of Family Issues, 23,* 138–164.

Voydanoff, P. (2004). The effects of work demands and resources on work-to-family conflict and facilitation. *Journal of Marriage and Family, 66,* 398–412.

Wacquant, L. (1999, April). *What work, whose family? The ideology of "working families" in an age of liberal paternalism.* Workshop presentation delivered at the University of California, Berkeley, Center for Working Families.

Walker, A. (1999). Gender and family relationships. In M. B. Sussman, S. K. Steinmetz, & G. W. Peterson (Eds.), *Handbook of marriage and the family* (2nd ed., pp. 439–474). New York: Plenum.

Weick, K. E. (1995). Theory. In N. Nicholson (Ed.), *Blackwell dictionary of organizational behavior.* Oxford: Blackwell.

White, J. M., & Klein, D. M. (2002). *Family theories* (2nd ed.). Thousand Oaks, CA: Sage.

Williams, J. (2000). *Unbending gender: Why family and work conflict and what to do about it.* New York: Oxford University Press.

Zvonkovic, A. M., Manoogian, M. M., & McGraw, L. A. (2001). The ebb and flow of family life: How families experience being together and apart. In K. J. Daly (Ed.), *Minding the time in family experience: Emerging perspectives and issues* (pp. 135–160). Oxford: Elsevier Science.

Zvonkovic, A. M., & Moon, S. F. (1997). *Constructing a fishing family: Wives' perspectives on their marital lives.* New York: Family Firm Institute.

Zvonkovic, A. M., Notter, M. L., & Peters, C. L. (in press). Family studies research: Approaching the study of work and family time and family relationships. In E. E. Kossek, S. Sweet, & M. Pitts-Castophes (Eds.), *The work-family handbook.* Mahwah, NJ: Lawrence Erlbaum.

Zvonkovic, A. M., Richards, C., Humble, A., & Manoogian, M. M. (1998, February). *The ripple effect: Lessons about time and work for working families from commercial fishing families.* Paper presented at the Business/Professional Women and Sloan Foundation Conference on Work and Family, San Francisco.

• Twenty-one

RELIGION AND FAMILIES

Linda M. Chatters, *Institute for Social Research*

Robert Joseph Taylor, *Institute for Social Research*

The topic of religion and families has generated scholarly interest within several academic (e.g., sociology, psychology, religious studies) and professional (e.g., family studies, social work, nursing, public health, medicine, child development) disciplines. Research on the relationship between religion and family examines such diverse phenomena as fertility patterns, dating behavior and mate selection, religious intermarriage, and child-rearing practices. In this chapter we present a selective review and integration of research findings on religion and family using three frameworks: role theory, stress and coping, and social networks and social support. We also discuss existing conceptual, methodological, and analytic challenges to this area of research, with a focus on the connections among different research methods (e.g., qualitative studies, personal histories) and their contributions to our understanding of religion and family. We argue here for theory development and research that mirror the diversity of religious traditions and family forms, and we conclude by identifying some resources that are essential to such theory development and research.

OVERVIEW OF RESEARCH ON RELIGION AND FAMILY

Although empirical investigations of the connection between religion and family date back at least to the 1930s, there has been a recent upsurge of interest in this topic (Dollahite, Marks, & Goodman, 2004; Jenkins, 1991; Thomas & Cornwall, 1990; Thornton, 1985). Critical reviews of the literature on religion and family have identified limitations in the research with regard to conceptual, measurement, and analytic issues (Dollahite et al., 2004; Thomas & Cornwall, 1990). Theoretical expectations as to the nature and direction of the relationship(s) between religion and family are often unclear, indicating that scholars need to develop coherent theoretical and conceptual frameworks and appropriate

Authors' Note: Work on this chapter was supported by a grant from the National Institute on Aging, "Church-Based Assistance and Older Blacks" (R01 AG18782), Linda M. Chatters, principal investigator, and Robert Joseph Taylor, co–principal investigator.

analytic models that describe the specific linkages and mechanisms through which religion and family are connected (Thomas & Cornwall, 1990; Thornton, 1985). In their recent critique and review, Dollahite et al. (2004) note three challenges to the development of a coherent assessment of religion-family connections. First, research has not adequately addressed the diversity in religious traditions (e.g., non-Christian) and family types. Second, it is difficult to reconcile the different disciplinary and scholarly traditions (e.g., macro versus micro foci) represented in religion-family research. Third, the role of the broader context (e.g., cultural, societal) in influencing religion and families is largely unacknowledged in the research.

Conceptualization and Measurement of Religion

The methodological rigor of research on religion and family has substantially improved through scholars' development and use of conceptual models, measurement strategies, and analytic approaches that are informed by theory. Although conceptualizations of religious involvement (Chatters, Levin, & Taylor, 1992; Fetzer Institute/National Institute on Aging [NIA], 1999; Levin, 1989; Levin, Chatters, & Taylor, 1995) emphasize the multiple, functionally distinct dimensions of such involvement (e.g., private versus public behaviors, subjective religiosity), researchers often routinely employ single measures of religious attendance or affiliation, such as service attendance (see reviews by Ellison & Levin, 1998; Williams, 1994). Further, studies that are solely concerned with religion's direct effects on outcomes leave open questions concerning possible mediating constructs (e.g., social support) and whether religion itself moderates relationships of interest (Levin & Chatters, 1998).

Several theoretical and conceptual frameworks have been proposed that explicitly link religion (through biobehavioral and psychosocial explanations and mechanisms) to family life and behaviors (Ellison, 1994) as well as other health and social phenomena

(Ellison & Levin, 1998; Fetzer/NIA, 1999; Idler & George, 1998; Levin, 1996). These frameworks suggest multiple connections between religion and family behaviors and phenomena, including the following: (a) Religion proscribes unacceptable individual and interpersonal behaviors (social control) while at the same time promoting specific beliefs, customs, and practices (e.g., communication, conflict resolution) that are conducive to marital and family satisfaction, family solidarity, affection, and assistance; (b) religion provides a framework of beliefs, social norms, and practices that reinforce basic family role identities (e.g., parent, spouse) and invest special meaning in the fulfillment of these roles (Ellison, 1994); (c) religion is important for individuals' handling of life difficulties and stressors, including those associated with the execution of family and other roles (e.g., conflict between family and work roles and responsibilities); (d) religious settings provide particular benefits for families, such as accessible systems of support and identification of needs for assistance; and (e) religion fosters positive emotions (e.g., hope, optimism, empowerment) and orientations that promote family characteristics or schemata (e.g., family resilience or hardiness) that have positive impacts on family process and functioning.

Perspectives on Religion and Family

The frameworks we have selected for discussion in this chapter—role theory, stress and coping perspectives, and social networks and social support—represent fundamental paradigms whose core constructs and processes (e.g., social roles, coping resources, social support) share important commonalities across diverse family theories. Despite theoretical reformulations and apparent differences in the specific applications of these constructs across individual family models and theories, the constructs provide a common language and discourse for understanding the linkages between religion and family. It is our hope that this discussion will encourage the broader application of information about religion-family relationships to other traditions of family scholarship.

Several cautions are worth noting regarding this review. First, the relationships between religion and family are complex and subject to variability with respect to how different denominations and religious subcultures structure and pattern personal and public religious activities (e.g., theological foundations and tenets, centralized and hierarchical versus decentralized and lay-based authority and worship practices). Second, differences in the broader social context, such as concentrations of coreligionists in other social networks and regional variations in religious climate, may moderate the associations between religion and family (Woodbury & Smith, 1998). Finally, despite scholars' efforts to develop theoretically and conceptually grounded links between religion and family phenomena, empirical tests of specific linkages and mechanisms are slow to emerge (Ellison, 1994; Ellison & Levin, 1998; Fetzer Institute/NIA, 1999).

Role Theory Framework

Role theory concerns the ways in which roles define and regulate social life and relationships and give meaning to individual self-conceptions and actions. The concept of role can be traced to symbolic interactionism and its focus on the individual operating within the family context and the prominent place of social interactions in providing meaning and defining the self (LaRossa & Reitzes, 1993). Roles are expected patterns or collections of behaviors that are associated with particular positions or statuses and that provide information about the knowledge, ability, motivation, and emotions and feelings (i.e., extent, duration, direction) associated with roles (LaRossa & Reitzes, 1993). Role theory encompasses several important concepts, including formal versus informal roles, degree of flexibility in roles, and changes in the nature of roles over time. Aspects of roles that individuals experience include role identity, role careers, role conflict, role burden, and role negotiation. Role theory perspective incorporates the idea that both the focal person (the role incumbent) and important others contribute their expectations and beliefs in defining the nature of the role.

Religious content, meaning, and behaviors are important in defining family role identities, relationships, and behaviors. Religious tenets and scriptural teachings provide guidance regarding the appropriate attitudes and behaviors associated with family roles. Religious values affirm and validate positive norms of filial obligations and assistance to family members, particularly younger generations' responsibilities for the provision of care to their elders. As Ellison (1997) notes, scriptural teachings provide important social and moral norms and behavioral role models for family role identities (e.g., father, adult child). Individuals who have been exemplars of family piety or have successfully overcome family crises and difficulties are admired. The successful enactment of family roles and relationships is associated with the attainment of highly valued spiritual qualities and moral characteristics. Conversely, scriptural materials provide warnings about the negative consequences of family conflict and of neglecting family duties and responsibilities.

Religious teachings provide specific guidelines for the performance of marital (e.g., wife, husband) and family roles that act to define role identities and shape role behaviors and attitudes. Religious settings constitute environments in which participants can informally sanction and reinforce valued attitudinal and behavioral norms (Ellison, 1994; Ellison, Bartkowski, & Anderson, 1999). This is accomplished through negative sanctions by fellow church members, the internalization of religious norms regarding lifestyle and family conduct, and the position of religious settings as reference groups that define self-identities (Ellison, 1994). Specifically, participation in religious communities exposes individuals to particular beliefs and attitudes about family relationships as well as provides models of appropriate marital and family behavior that are consistent with group norms. Formal educational programs and ministries (e.g., family life education, marital counseling) often focus on family concerns and issues, making family role expectations explicit. However, it is also the case that individuals may find it difficult to fulfill family roles when those roles are defined and regulated by religious content and institutions (Ellison, 1994). Role incumbents may find it difficult to meet role expectations (e.g., those associated with marital and parental roles) and experience conflict between family and other roles (e.g., worker). Further, problems in enacting marital and parental roles (e.g., differences in marital role definitions) may have direct negative influences on family outcomes (e.g., marital satisfaction).

Major milestones of family life (e.g., marriage, birth, death) are recognized and commemorated in religious rituals and ceremonies that enhance the sense of family cohesion and identity and connection to the religious collective (Howe, 2002). Family events that occur within the context of religious ritual emphasize the notion of family continuity and the family life cycle as well as family members' awareness of their position as part of a larger body. Religious events and milestones (e.g., baptisms and christenings, bar and bat mitzvahs) not only are defined within the context of the family but also emphasize the functions of both the biological and the religious family in directing the spiritual and religious growth of the individual (e.g., coming-of-age observances). These religious and family rituals that mark major life transitions are often accompanied by changes in expectations with respect to individuals' family roles, responsibilities, and capacity to engage in family life as adults (Howe, 2002, p. 439). Special religious holidays and observances (e.g., Rosh Hashanah, Pesach, Christmas) represent occasions for reflection and commemoration that reinforce the primacy of the family as well as individual family members' particular roles within the family. Religious observances and holidays reunite families in time and space, reestablish and reinforce family bonds, and help to construct autobiographical family memory (Howe, 2002). Finally, common family rituals such as the blessing of meals, Sabbath observance, and evening prayers reinforce a basic family identity and foster notions of predictability, stability, regularity, and continuity in family life.

Several studies have focused on the intersection of religion and family roles within the context of relevant social environments, self-perceptions, and gender, marriage, and family ideologies. In their study of linkages (i.e., behavioral, affiliation, beliefs) between religion and domestic violence, Ellison et al. (1999) found that reports of violence were lower among those who attended religious services more frequently. Further, neither simple religious affiliation designations (e.g., conservative Protestant) nor denominational homogamy of a couple was associated with domestic violence. However, couple differences in terms of beliefs (e.g., biblical inerrancy), specifically when husbands held more conservative views, were associated with greater domestic violence on the part of men. Ellison et al. suggest that couple differences in religious beliefs and levels of conservatism reflect fundamental differences in ideas regarding marital power, masculine and feminine roles, and domestic arrangements (i.e., role identities), which are the real sources of conflict. Similarly, Mahoney et al. (1999) found that proximal measures assessing beliefs about the sacredness of marriage (e.g., manifestation of God in marriage) were more important than distal religious indicators (i.e., couple religious homogamy) in predicting marital adjustment and perceived benefits from marriage. In an earlier study, Ellison, Bartkowski, and Segal (1996) found that corporal punishment of children was associated with conservative theological views, whereas effects for denominational affiliation were negligible. Similarly, conservative Protestants were less likely to use verbal reproof (parental yelling) as a means of child discipline, and this effect was mediated by theologically conservative views (Bartkowski & Wilcox, 2000). These findings challenge family researchers and practitioners to consider the underlying beliefs, behaviors, and circumstances associated with child discipline strategies and whether the effects of punitive discipline practices on child outcomes vary across particular social ecologies and contexts.

Stress and Coping Perspective

Theory on stress and coping processes is represented in several disciplines in the biological, behavioral, and social sciences (Wenzel, Glanz, & Lerman, 2002). Within family theory, formulations such as family stress theory, family adjustment and adaptation theory, and family resilience frameworks trace their heritage to questions of how families respond and adapt to stress. Stress and coping models seek to understand how and why families differ in their abilities to negotiate and cope with normative transitions (e.g., parenthood, retirement), major life difficulties and nonnormative events (e.g., illness, job loss), and catastrophic incidents (e.g., disasters, wars). Family theorists have identified family strengths and resources that assist families in enduring difficulties (i.e., family coping resources and coping behaviors). In addition, scholars have used family characteristics (e.g., family coherence, family hardiness) to elaborate family typologies (e.g., balanced, resilient) that may be more or less vulnerable to the impact of stressors (McCubbin & McCubbin, 1989).

Constructs and processes common to the stress and coping paradigm include stressors, appraisals, resources, and coping behaviors and outcomes. Wenzel et al.'s (2002) formulation of the stress and coping paradigm includes *primary appraisals* of the stressor that involve the individual's assessment of the features of the situation in terms of his or her personal susceptibility to and the potential severity of adverse effects resulting from the stressor. In contrast, *secondary appraisals* involve the individual's beliefs about what can be done to change the situation, efforts to manage emotional reactions to the event, and perceptions about the effectiveness of coping efforts. Primary and secondary appraisals are mediated by actual *coping efforts* (i.e., coping behaviors) that are enacted to handle the stressor. Direct problem management (e.g., active coping, information seeking) and attempts to regulate one's emotional reactions (e.g., changing one's feelings about the stressor) are two primary coping strategies.

Individuals also differ with respect to whether they directly engage the stressor or, alternatively, disengage from the stressor (e.g., avoidance, distraction). Coping efforts can also involve attempts to derive meaning from threatening events and to enlist personal and social resources to manage difficult situations. *Meaning-based* coping efforts involve reinterpretations of threatening situations in terms of their ultimate significance for the person. They often involve attributions of religious explanations and causes that can be either positive (e.g., spiritual growth) or negative (e.g., divine punishment) (Pargament, 1997). Similarly, social and personal resources and processes such as social support (e.g., aid, affirmation, and affect), negative social interactions (e.g., social undermining), and enduring dispositional coping styles (e.g., optimism, hope, purpose, pessimism) may influence the stress and coping process for better or for worse.

Ellison's (1994) description of the basic components of the stress and coping paradigm as it relates to the topic of religion was later elaborated to allow for the examination of the relationships between religious involvement (e.g., religious participation, private devotion) and outcomes such as family role performance, closeness, and satisfaction (Ellison, 1997). Religion influences the individual constructs (e.g., primary and secondary appraisals) that constitute this perspective as well as the overall process of coping with stressors. Whether and how individuals evaluate particular occurrences as threatening and likely to occur (i.e., primary appraisals) may be determined by the individuals' religious beliefs. Families in which the members regard themselves as being protected by a loving and benign God may be less likely to view stressful occurrences as specific threats to family functioning and well-being. Religious content is similarly important with respect to secondary appraisals of stressors (i.e., beliefs about changing the situation, managing emotional reactions, and perceptions about coping effectiveness). Religious orientations can cultivate attitudes and beliefs that all problems can be solved (e.g., "With God, all things are possible"); provide intrapsychic defenses against concerns about objective events, chronic stressors, and daily hassles (e.g., "Too blessed to be stressed"); and provide strategies and orientations for addressing problematic situations (e.g., "Prayer changes things"; "Let go and let God").

Religion also plays a part in the coping process with respect to specific coping behaviors and strategies (e.g., spiritual support from others, prayer) as well as the enhancement and use of coping resources (Ellison, 1993; Ellison & Taylor, 1996; Koenig, McCullough, & Larson, 2001; Pargament, 1997; Taylor, Chatters, & Levin, 2004). Although religious coping is often depicted as passive, fatalistic, and acquiescent (i.e., to God's will), in recent research Pargament (1997) has identified several types of religious coping strategies (e.g., deferring, collaborative) and attributions (e.g., negative versus positive coping attributions) that are associated with different emotional sequelae. Religious coping functions in a variety of ways, such as through anxiety reduction, search for meaning, and social cohesiveness (Koenig et al., 2001). Further, religious scripture and belief provide behavioral guidelines for coping with problematic family relationships. Religious settings themselves provide models for religious coping behaviors as well as informal and formal sources of assistance, such as clergy (Taylor, Ellison, Chatters, Levin, & Lincoln, 2000). Church-sponsored activities, such as family life education workshops and classes (e.g., marriage and parenting classes), provide novel information that individuals may use to evaluate problem events and resources for developing new coping skills

and strategies to deal with problematic family interactions.

Prayer is by far the most widely recognized religious coping behavior (Ellison & Taylor, 1996; Krause, Chatters, Meltzer, & Morgan, 2000b; Poloma & Gallup, 1991; Taylor et al., 2004). Prayer is a complex process that involves a range of orientations, motivations, and expectations and functional linkages to outcomes (e.g., reductions in anxiety and worry, personal and spiritual growth, threat reappraisals). Recent research examining the nature of prayer and its role in individuals' coping with adversity indicates that prayer is a transformative personal experience that changes individuals in fundamental ways (e.g., forgiveness, stress reduction) and helps them to manage problems, whether the problems are life crises or daily hassles (Krause et al., 2000b; Taylor et al., 2004). As a religious coping behavior, requesting prayer from others unambiguously signals the need for assistance from coreligionists and facilitates the provision of social support. Further, prayer from others reinforces social bonds and enhances group cohesion (Taylor et al., 2004). Finally, family prayer provides a model of coping behaviors and orientations, reinforces family cohesion and connectedness, and provides opportunities for the exchange of social support (e.g., emotional and spiritual support). Family prayer during stressful circumstances is an important ritual that provides information about the nature of the event (i.e., primary and secondary appraisals) and reinforces existing and emergent family role expectations (Howe, 2002).

• SPOTLIGHT ON THEORY

"GOOD ENOUGH" THEORIZING ABOUT FAMILIES, SPIRITUALITY, AND RELIGION: FACING OUR OWN FUNDAMENTALISM

Carla M. Dahl, *Center for Spiritual and Personal Formation, Bethel Seminary*

More than 15 years ago, Jetse Sprey (1988) challenged our theorizing about families and spirituality, saying that it "must be extended, when appropriate, beyond the realm of the proximate into that of ultimate causality. If family scholars continue to delegate such issues to philosophy, religion, or even the realm of politics, our field will lose much of the credibility that was earned over the past fifty years" (p. 888). Thomas and Cornwall (1990) have also affirmed that our research must address "issues regarding the purposes of life, humankind's relationship to the divine, or the whys of births, deaths, and other intimate family experiences" (p. 990). As we respond to these challenges, the adequacy of our theory development will depend in part on our capacity for conceptual precision and our willingness to monitor and move beyond our own strong personal and professional reactions.

CAPACITY FOR CONCEPTUAL PRECISION

Chatters and Taylor allude to the problematic theoretical and methodological issues related to the conflation of spirituality and religion. We must be careful to define our terms in ways that do not assume that these words represent exactly the same domains. A family's religiosity may either support or undermine the family members' spiritual experience (and vice versa). Both religiosity and spirituality may be significant in a family's management of stress: Religious behaviors and communities may provide support, as Chatters and Taylor note, and spirituality, as part of the family's internal philosophical context (Boss, 2001), will influence the family's perceptions of both the stressor events and the resources available to manage those events. The nature of the particular contributions of religion and spirituality will be better understood through careful, precise definition and exploration of each dimension.

WILLINGNESS TO ENCOUNTER OUR OWN FUNDAMENTALISM

The construction of meaning is an ongoing process underlying much of a family's experience. This process provides rich opportunities for conversation and ritual, intimacy and empowerment, that can be responded to more with fluidity and intellectual flexibility or more with rigidity and fundamentalism (Dahl, 1994). *Fundamentalism* here refers not to a particular set of conservative, sectarian religious beliefs but to a *systemic process* characterized by what Moore (1992) describes as a tendency to "freeze life into a solid cube of meaning" (p. 236). Families whose meaning-making processes

(continued)

● *SPOTLIGHT ON THEORY continued*

are characterized more by fundamentalism desire certainty where there can be little or none. They tend toward rigidity, intolerance of difference, suspiciousness, and extreme deference to ideology. Their inability to carry on meaning-making conversations with others who differ results in mutual misunderstanding, polarization, and entrenched conflict.

A parallel process of meaning construction happens in family research and practice. As researchers, theorists, and practitioners, we are invited to identify and respond to fundamentalism as it emerges in our field and perhaps in ourselves. Like families, fundamentalist professionals may also tend toward rigidity, intolerance, and ideological defensiveness—on *either* "side" of significant family issues. Identifying and moving beyond our own fundamentalist reactions enables us to understand and engage persons from different perspectives and thus avoid either of two extremes: (a) ignoring and denying differences, thereby abdicating our responsibility to engage in dialogue; or (b) resorting to caricature and polemic in ways that overstate and reify differences, thereby reinforcing polarization.

As we take care to develop and maintain conceptual precision and to identify and manage our personal and professional fundamentalism, we will be more able to provide "good enough" theorizing about families, spirituality, and religion. Perhaps we will come to share the perspective offered by a participant in Dahl's study: "Families, whether they know it or not, come together to work out their spirituality." ●

Social Networks and Social Support

Although they do not constitute a formal theory, the constructs of social networks and social support have been explored extensively in the social, behavioral, and health sciences (Heaney & Israel, 2002). Social networks, or the collections of relationships that surround individuals, are described in terms of characteristics such as size, homogeneity (member similarity), proximity, and reciprocity. Social support is defined in relation to the functional aspects of an individual's social relationships (Heaney & Israel, 2002, pp. 185–186). Typically, definitions and typologies of support refer to social interactions that involve aid, affirmation, and affect that are meant to be positive and beneficial to the recipient. Other social support typologies focus on manifest helping behaviors, or so-called enacted support (e.g., actual exchanges of emotional, tangible, or informational support),

in contrast to perceived support, or subjective perceptions of helping relationships (e.g., anticipated support, satisfaction, adequacy) (Krause, Liang, & Keith, 1990). Perceived support also encompasses negative social support, problematic support, and negative social interactions (Lincoln, 2000; Rook, 1998) as exchanges or relationships that involve criticism, social undermining, intrusion, shame, and other negative emotions. Negative or problematic social interactions are distinct aspects of social relationships that occur within families (Lincoln, Chatters, & Taylor, 2003; Lincoln, Taylor, & Chatters, 2003) and religious settings (Krause, Chatters, Meltzer, & Morgan, 2000a; Krause, Ellison & Wulff, 1998; Taylor et al., 2004).

In programmatic research, Taylor and others have investigated church-based informal social support within African American churches (e.g., Krause, 2002a; Taylor & Chatters, 1986a, 1986b, 1988; Taylor et al.,

2004). Similar to the findings of other research with majority samples (Krause et al., 1998), these studies have shown that greater involvement in church networks is associated with more received support (Taylor & Chatters, 1988). With respect to linkages between family and church, adult children appear to facilitate support exchanges from church members to their elderly parents (Taylor & Chatters, 1986a). However, marital and family events such as divorce and separation may be stigmatized occurrences that may curtail support from church networks (Taylor & Chatters, 1988). Finally, anecdotal evidence suggests that churches often fail to address the needs of stigmatized persons and families (e.g., victims of domestic violence, HIV/AIDS patients, substance abuse). Further research is needed to explore how family events and circumstances are associated with support from clergy and members.

In one of the few studies of patterns of support exchanges from family, friends, and church members, Taylor and Chatters (1986b) found that total support or instrumental assistance was most likely to be provided by family; church members provided help during illnesses, prayer support, and advice and encouragement; and friends provided companionship. In a more recent study, Chatters, Taylor, Lincoln, and Schroepfer (2002) found that close to half of their respondents received assistance from both family and church, one-fourth received help from family only, and approximately 1 in 10 received assistance from church members only or did not receive help from either group. Family and religious correlates of receiving assistance from both family and church included greater levels of family closeness, family interaction, and church participation; those not involved with family or church tended not to receive assistance from either. Finally, religious settings provide both informational and instrumental support in the form of formal, church-sponsored programs on family life, marital counseling, parenting skills, and an array of basic assistance services, such as help obtaining food and clothing (Billingsley & Caldwell, 1991; Thomas, Quinn, Billingsley, & Caldwell, 1994).

Negative forms of social interaction and group dynamics also occur within churches (e.g., unwelcoming climate, church factions, gossiping), and these detract from individual and family well-being (Krause et al., 1998, 2000a; Taylor et al., 2004). Negative social interactions within church settings may be especially injurious to well-being outcomes because they are rare and unexpected events given the purported mission and orientation of religious institutions (Lincoln, 2000). Research on the extent and impact of negative social interactions within religious institutions is limited. However, anecdotal evidence indicates that problem areas include internal church schisms and poor interpersonal relationships involving church members and clergy. Further, social support from church members may be problematic if recipients and providers differ in their attributions as to the origin of a problem (e.g., moral failing versus psychological issues) and its solution (e.g., religious versus concrete assistance), or if there is a lack of reciprocity in the support relationship. Finally, helper beliefs about the ability of adversity to bring about positive spiritual and personal growth (e.g., "God never gives us more than we can bear") may be problematic for support recipients who have a different perception of the event and its aftermath (e.g., victim of serious trauma) and who may come to view these sentiments as empty religious platitudes.

CONCEPTUAL, METHODOLOGICAL, AND ANALYTIC ISSUES

Several literature reviews and critical essays have addressed problems of definition and measurement of religious involvement, underscoring its multifaceted nature and functional implications for family and other social and behavioral outcomes (e.g., Chatters, 2000; Dollahite et al., 2004; Ellison & Levin, 1998; Fetzer Institute/NIA, 1999; Idler & George, 1998; Williams, 1994). A number of current research programs are involved in examining verifiable religion-family linkages. These efforts are informed by relevant conceptual models and theories and seek to identify the discrete mechanisms by which religious involvement affects family outcomes and processes. For example, religious involvement could affect family outcomes (e.g., satisfaction, conflict) through enhancement of social support (e.g., instrumental aid), by providing beliefs that serve to define and regulate family relationships and interactions (e.g., spousal, parental), or by elaborating specific family norms and expectations that are conducive to family life (e.g., cooperation, harmony, forgiveness). By focusing attention on the mechanisms for religious effects on family life, such research can help us to understand the underlying processes involved.

The majority of religious research in the health and social sciences has focused on Christian denominations (Protestant) and primarily White Americans (Koenig et al., 2001). The systematic exploration of different family forms and religions will not only enhance our understanding of the linkages between religion and family life and underlying theoretical frameworks but also position this information within a much broader social and cultural context. We currently lack appropriate theoretical and conceptual frameworks for appreciating the influences of racial, ethnic, and cultural diversity with respect to these and other issues. This has been a long-standing issue in the social and behavioral sciences, the result of scholars' failure to take into account the role of context (e.g., social, cultural, historical) in the investment of meaning in primary constructs and in shaping behavior (Chatters, in press; Chatters & Taylor, 2003; Dilworth-Anderson, Burton, & Johnson, 1993; Dilworth-Anderson, Williams, & Gibson, 2002; Doherty, Boss, LaRossa, Schumm, & Steinmetz, 1993; Taylor et al., 2004). Instead, researchers have relied on what has been termed an acontextual approach, which is characterized by a focus on simple group differences and a failure to explore within-group variation in defined population groups (Chatters, in press). Further, this approach assumes that social and psychological factors and processes operate similarly ("racial/ethnic similarity") across specific racial and ethnic groups (Lincoln, Chatters, & Taylor, 2003). We argue that by employing the notion of context (e.g., social, cultural, historical) scholars can gain a better understanding of the nature and meaning of religion and family across diverse groups and illuminate the antecedents and consequences of important group distinctions.

Explorations of religion's effects on family phenomena must be sensitive to issues of sample comparability to detect both similarity and differences in the processes and mechanisms that link religion and family (Chatters, 2000; Dollahite et al., 2004; Ellison & Levin, 1998). Research has often focused on specialized samples of the population (e.g., Mormons, Seventh-Day Adventists) that pose problems with respect to generalizing the effects of religion to other segments of the population. Typically, analytic models of religion's influences on family phenomena have used a religious factor as one of several predictor variables to examine its direct and independent effects (i.e., direct effects model) on an outcome of interest. However, theoretical paradigms such as stress and coping suggest that alternative models of these relationships should be explicitly tested (Ellison & Levin, 1998; Levin & Chatters, 1998). For example, in the presence of a stressor, individuals and families may increase or mobilize religious activities and resources (i.e., suppressor or stressor response model), which then reduces the harmful effects of stress on family outcomes. Alternatively, the prevention model suggests that religion protects families from exposure to stressful circumstances and promotes positive lifestyle and interpersonal behaviors that reduce the risk of problematic family outcomes. These theoretical developments indicate the need for structural equation modeling techniques to assess direct and indirect influences of religion, as well as hierarchical regression models. Prospective study designs are also required to explore change and development in religious orientations over time and to explore topics such as religious or spiritual life histories and how they may be related to important family events.

MEASUREMENT ISSUES IN THE STUDY OF RELIGION AND SPIRITUALITY

Jacqueline S. Mattis, *New York University*

Contemporary studies of religion and spirituality have spawned new questions about the strategies that are best suited for the study of religious and spiritual life. Emerging research points to several important areas for methodological elaboration.

First, much of the mainstream social science literature on religious and spiritual life continues to focus on samples that are White, Christian, college attendees, or members of very distinct religious communities (e.g., Mormons). As Chatters and Taylor note, we need to broaden the sampling frames of our studies.

Second, although qualitative studies have distinguished between religiosity and spirituality (Mattis, 2000; Zinnbauer et al., 1997), those conceptual distinctions are often ignored in empirical research on religiosity and spirituality. The disjunction between conceptualizations of religiosity and spirituality and empirical studies of these topics impedes our efforts to examine nuanced differences in the ways that these constructs operate in family life.

Third, although researchers have created increasingly expansive schemes for categorizing religious identity/affiliation, we need schemes that effectively capture the complex interplay among identity labels, formal theologies, and individuals' private devotional beliefs.

Fourth, researchers must continue to use sophisticated multivariate analytic techniques to both invite and address new questions about religiosity and spirituality.

Fifth, we often fail to acknowledge that although some aspects of religious and spiritual experience and knowledge are explicit and may be expressed in language, many aspects of these domains of life are tacit and inexpressible. We need methodologies that will allow us to bridge the divides that separate people's experiences of, cognitions about, and expressions of religion and spirituality. We also need methodologies that draw on and integrate knowledge from the various forms of texts through which religious meaning is communicated (e.g., music, prayers, private testimonials).

Sixth, we must attend to social and sociopolitical contexts in which discourses about religion and spirituality operate. For example, we must attend to the ways that social location (e.g., race, gender, class) and practices of power shape participants' beliefs about the aspects of their religious and spiritual lives that are safe to share and their thoughts about who can be trusted with, or will be persuaded by, the "truths" of their religious and spiritual lives. Attention to these concerns will shed light on the ways that participants respond to open-ended as well as closed-ended questions about their religious and spiritual lives.

(continued)

• *SPOTLIGHT ON METHODS* continued

Seventh, if we accept Geertz's (1973) assertion that religion is a cultural system, then we must identify strategies for studying religiosity and spirituality as cultural-level phenomena. That is, we must identify methodologies for studying the ideological (e.g., beliefs, values, norms), representational (e.g., languages, symbols, icons), expressive (e.g., literature, music, textual, rituals), and social organizational aspects of religious and spiritual life. For example, we need methodologies that will allow us to examine what culture-bound discursive traditions and practices (e.g., storytelling styles, use of metaphor) reveal about religious and spiritual life.

Eighth, we must move beyond thinking of religion and spirituality as individual-level phenomena in our quest to understand the ways in which religion and spirituality emerge within individuals' social ecologies (e.g., in families, friendships).

Finally, we have a plethora of cross-sectional studies from which to draw in our work on religion and spirituality, but there is a dire need for studies that allow us to explore religious and spiritual development across the life span. •

INTERACTIVE THEME

A number of rich sources of information are available that scholars can use to study religion and families, including sociohistorical accounts of particular groups, contemporary ethnographic data, survey investigations, detailed analyses of religious artifacts (e.g., popular Christian texts), and personal spiritual autobiographies. Qualitative information, which has been used to explore basic conceptions of religion and family, provides new perspectives on these constructs and additional interpretive power for understanding observed empirical relations (Bartowski & Ellison, 1995; Dollahite et al., 2004; Ellison & Levin, 1998; Krause, 2002b; Krause et al., 2000a, 2000b; Mattis, 2002; Taylor et al., 2004). Krause (1993, 2002b) has outlined a systematic set of procedures for using combined methods (e.g., focus groups, in-depth interviews, community surveys) to develop and refine measures of religious involvement. Taylor et al. (2004) used a multiple-method strategy involving sociohistorical accounts, national survey research data, and focus group information to examine religion in relation to the physical, social, and psychological status and well-being of African Americans.

The study of family rituals—their initiation and cessation, changes in frequency and duration, manifest and deep meaning, and timing and patterning in connection with family events—offers scholars important opportunities to explore how ritualized aspects of religious behavior coincide with family life and events. Narrative theory, narrative psychology, and self-narratives (Crossley, 2000) may be important tools for studying religion's role in helping families understand and cope with normative and nonnormative events. Narrative approaches are concerned with the knowledge bases and stories that people and groups use to give meaning to their experiences and the ways that families can "reauthor" their own lives in line with alternative and preferred stories of identity and ways of life. Researchers can examine family narratives to understand how families use religious meaning and symbols to construct meaning out of events in their lives and to develop the sense of self as a family. These and related approaches (e.g., religious/spiritual history or religious biography) provide important information about continuities and discontinuities in religious beliefs, patterns, and practices across time and their relation to family events and processes.

FUTURE DIRECTIONS

Future research on religion and family should continue current work on the conceptualization and measurement of religious involvement, as well as the development and refinement of theoretical models used to understand connections between religion and family. Researchers should explore how religion influences families' relationships to other institutions and groups—that is, how religion and family characteristics (singly and in combination) pattern relationships with external institutions (e.g., health care, social welfare, education). Investigations along these lines would help us to understand how and under what circumstances family and religious institutions respond to expressed need.

Family theorists, researchers, and practitioners are confronted with religious orientations that diverge significantly from the primarily White Protestant orientation currently represented in the research literature. Researchers must begin to address issues of religion and family life within groups that are currently not well represented in the literature (e.g., Judaism), that do not derive from a Judeo-Christian tradition (e.g., Islam), that are polytheistic (e.g., Hinduism) or animistic (e.g., Hmong), and that adhere to diverse religious beliefs, practices, rituals, and meanings and emanate from diverse cultural settings. Future studies should explore the presence of subgroup and subcultural differences in manifestations of religion and its association with family outcomes and phenomena (e.g., work on Evangelical Christian groups) to determine whether the relationships between religion and family life vary across different groups. Along these lines, focused research is needed on the interplay among family behaviors, religious attitudes, and family and gender role conceptions within the context of a broader set of normative religious beliefs and practices found in coherent religious subgroups and communities (e.g., Bartkowski & Wilcox, 2000; Ellison et al., 1999; Mahoney et al., 1999; Wilcox, 1998). Finally, approaches that explore the phenomenological or "lived meaning" of religion and family would be useful for improving our understanding of these basic constructs and how they interrelate within diverse population groups. These and similar approaches can help to clarify the connections between religion and families within diverse and dynamic racial, cultural, and historical contexts.

CORE RESOURCES

Dollahite et al.'s (2004) recent chapter in the *Handbook of Contemporary Families* critiques the literature on religion and family life and discusses current resources for this area of research. The joint report of the Fetzer Institute and the National Institute on Aging titled *Multidimensional Measurement of Religiousness/ Spirituality for Use in Health Research* (1999) is the result of a collaborative effort involving leading scholars and researchers in the area of religion and health. This report focuses on religious involvement and its theoretical and empirical links to social and health-related outcomes and includes discussion of many core constructs, such as social support and coping behaviors. The authoritative *Handbook of Religion and Health,* by Koenig et al. (2001), explores the connections between religion and health and health-related factors. Of particular note for family researchers are the chapters in that volume devoted to religion and marital instability (chap. 13) and religious coping (chap. 5), as well as the chapters focused on positive and negative effects of religion (chaps. 3 and 4). Pargament's book *The Psychology of Religion and Coping* (1997) remains one of the most important and comprehensive volumes on the nature of religion and the search for meaning in the sacred. Pargament's discussion of client-practitioner fit with respect to religious attitudes and beliefs and collaborative relations between clergy and specialty mental health professionals is both thoughtful and timely. Finally, the contextually derived approach to examining religion and family connections that we have advocated in this chapter is supported by a number of divergent resources that provide insights into different aspects of religious expression and family life.

Taking an example from the study of religion among African Americans, in their book *Religion in the Lives of African Americans,* Taylor et al. (2004) present empirical research on the topics of religious beliefs and practices, patterns of religious involvement, functional aspects of religion for health and mental health outcomes, and the use of resources found in religious settings (e.g., informal church support, use of clergy).

CASE STUDY

LINKS BETWEEN FAMILIES AND RELIGION

Don Swenson, *Mount Royal College*

Jerry G. Pankhurst, *Wittenberg University*

Sharon K. Houseknecht, *Ohio State University*

C hatters and Taylor note in Chapter 21 that the research to date on the links between religion and the family suffers from both theoretical and methodological limitations. They urge scholars to make efforts to correct this situation. In this brief discussion, we address some theoretical and conceptual issues that may help to clarify the connections between family and religion. To begin, we present a definition of religion that is multidimensional in nature. The various dimensions then serve as a conceptual framework to link religion with different elements of the family.

WHAT IS AT THE HEART OF RELIGION?

An important question to ask of any social phenomenon, including religion, is, What is its essence? That is, what makes it distinct from all else? In regard to the phenomenon of religion, the answer needs to encompass the many types of religion in various societies—folk, archaic, oriental, and occidental. Common to all these types of religions is the concept of the *sacred*. The sacred is that unique element that distinguishes religion from nonreligion. It is that which is set apart, unique, different from every other phenomenon. The sacred inspires two

responses: one of awe and the other of desire. The awe response takes place when the believer moves away from the holy because it is too inspiring and too far removed from normal human experience. The desire response beckons the believer to come, to see, to touch, and to experience the sacred (Swenson, 1999).

THE MANY DIMENSIONS OF RELIGION

It is important to see religion in all of its various dimensions, and a definition of religion that seems to cover these dimensions is this: "the individual and social experience of the sacred that is manifested in mythologies, rituals, and ethos, and integrated into a collective such as a community or an organization" (Swenson, 1999, p. 69). The *individual experience* of the sacred is the basic dimension of religion that may be termed religious experience or spirituality. The *social experience* or *ritual* reminds us that we are a forgetful people. Ritual is a vehicle through which we remember the sacred stories, the historical religious events. A third dimension emphasizes that the sacred is manifested in *mythologies*. It should be made clear from the outset that mythologies are to be seen not as anything

CASE STUDY *continued*

false but, rather, as belief systems. A fourth element of religion is *ethos*. This concept refers to codes of behavior and how these codes are to be lived out in everyday life. Ethos includes such components as values, norms, ethics, codes of conduct, and laws. There is no known religion that does not offer directions for living out sacred experiences or belief systems. Examples include almsgiving in Islam and the Sermon on the Mount in Christianity. The dimension of *religious groups, communities, and organizations* is the last element essential to a full understanding of religion. Being social beings, we want to belong to, be connected to, be bonded with others. In addition, sociologists recognize that collectivities are driven by logics that go beyond their members' individual needs. Societies and other collectivities need individuals to belong to them, and they develop religious means to keep members attached and fulfilling social functions.

CONNECTING DIMENSIONS OF RELIGION WITH FAMILY LIFE

Individual religious experiences. Three measures of religious experience are personal prayer, spirituality, and meditation. Swenson (1995) found that all were predictive of both marital quality and sexual satisfaction among Canadian Evangelical ministers and their spouses.

Ritual. Ritual is another dimension of religion that has received substantial attention from researchers. Some measures include participation in religious services, attending rites of passage, and public prayer. Using data from the 1995 General Social Survey, Clark (1998) found that 20% of Canadians attended religious services once a week. In comparison with nonattenders and occasional attenders, weekly attenders placed more importance on home life, emphasized lasting relationships, were more likely to be married and to have at least one child, were more likely to be happy in their marriages, and were at lower risk of divorce.

Using data from the 1998 General Social Survey, Clark (2000) revisited the possible relationships between a range of familial phenomena and religious service attendance. He found that young married couples were more than twice as likely as single individuals to attend services once a month. Further, married couples with young children were more likely to attend on a regular basis than were those without children. Divorced and separated men and women were also less likely to attend religious services than were married persons.

Mythologies or belief systems. One indicator of a belief system is the image of God. Swenson (1989), in an American national study of Roman Catholic believers, found that those who viewed God as a judge were more likely to have traditional familial attitudes than were those who did not. Further, Swenson (1995) found links between divine images and marital quality. Ministers who viewed God in intimate terms had higher levels of marital quality than those who did not.

Christiano, Swatos, and Kivisto (2002) recently reviewed arguments about the influence of God imagery on gender dynamics in the Abrahamic traditions. One argument was that biblical literalism is strongly associated with traditional family values and suggests how important religious beliefs are in shaping role patterns and behavior in the family.

Ethos. Another path into the domain of religion is the study of ethos. A religious ethos is expressed in several ways in families, and it appears that familial aspects of the Judeo-Christian ethos are related to the intensity of religious ritual life. Islam provides a striking example of a religious ethos that guides behavior in the family realm. Houseknecht (2000) examined five Islamic prescriptions regarding the family to determine whether family life in Egypt in recent times has reflected religious doctrine. These principles were those of marriage as both a religious duty and a social necessity, the prohibition of sex

CASE STUDY *continued*

outside of marriage, the husband's obligation to provide for his wife, the wife's obligation to obey her husband, and the obligation to be kind to one's relatives of whatever degree and to have concern for their well-being. Houseknecht concluded that, although some changes are occurring, there is no question that Islamic doctrine is widely reflected in Egyptian family life.

Sacred communities or organizations. One may consider communities and organizations of a religious nature as *sacred spaces* for families. Communities and organizations are spaces in which rituals are celebrated, where people go through their sacred/familial rites of passage, where participants learn about their faith, and where bonds of friendship and support are constructed. Using sacred spaces as a dimension of religion that one can measure and then test for relationships to family phenomena is difficult but possible. One way to do this is to consider whether and how these communities and organizations support experiences of the sacred. In Canada, Bibby (2002) found that some religious denominations have recently grown significantly because they have emphasized family, child, and youth ministries and thus encouraged family-religious ties.

In the dynamic global community in which we now live, the waxing and waning of sacred communities can sometimes be seen in clear relief. Danzger (2000) studied the reconstitution of the Orthodox Jewish community of Kiev, Ukraine, after the fall of Communism. He found that the key to reestablishing the local faith community was in connecting the largely faithless Jews with their forgotten heritage of religio-familial life. An emphasis on the family role in religion through the observance of kosher dietary rules, household Sabbath rituals, and the like served to cement the developing community. It is also clear that the Christian religion of Russia could not have been preserved through the 73 years of Soviet Communism, reemerging over the past 15 years as a reinvigorated

sacred community, were it not for the surreptitious work of generations of grandmothers. These women had their grandchildren baptized and taught them the basics of Eastern Orthodoxy, even in the face of political and social opposition (see Pankhurst, 1996).

In diverse, multiethnic communities, maintaining religious identity also can present a major challenge, especially for children. Larson (2000) found that Punjabi children in Britain, whether Hindu, Sikh, or Muslim, explored, compared, and contrasted their various religio-ethnic identities in play with each other but preserved their distinct religious identities because of their attachments to communities of orientation in which fundamental religious and ethnic traditions were cultivated.

CASE STUDY

In a culture and a society embedded in a vigorous secular ethic, the Dosani family stands out. As a middle-class, two-parent family, the Dosanis struggle with many of the same challenges that other families face. However, they meet these struggles with a courage that comes from their various links to a sacred image that is personal, and they all know that they are loved.

Their links to the God who loves them are multidimensional. Jake and Jill, the parents, meditate every day using the Christian sacred text, the Bible. They also pray together and with their children, Catherine, Rodrigo, and Joanne. All of the family members realize that the ethical call of their religion is high (faithfulness, commitment, chastity, respect, and honor), yet they are committed to approximate these high standards in spite of the barrage of the mass media and secular ethical values at work and school.

An additional source of the Dosanis' strength comes from their regular participation in religious services. This link enables each of the family members to connect to a peer group that supports the family's faith walk. On the other hand, the family members comment that the support they feel they need

CASE STUDY *continued*

is not as forthcoming from their church as they would like it to be. They continue to face dilemmas. Difficulties at work encourage Jake and Jill to talk together a lot. The children also face issues that are in contrast to what they want to do. They share quality time with their parents to seek support and wisdom. With many successes and failures, the Dosanis continue to grow together as a family unit and enjoy the bonds of love and care that are exhibited in their relationships.

CONCLUSION

In sum, there are clear and important linkages between the five dimensions of religion considered here and various family-related phenomena as shown in the case study.

According to Pankhurst and Houseknecht (2000), the institutions of religion and family interact in reciprocal ways. A vigorous religious system cannot exist without families, who provide members and socialize them into the ways of the faith. Likewise, religion provides families with the symbolic legitimation that validates cultural patterns. In contrast to other institutions, religion and family are both unique in pursuing interests for their own sake, not for instrumental reasons (MacIver, 1970). It is little wonder, then, that they have such a fundamental interconnection in sociocultural life. We hope that this discussion will serve to stimulate further research and critical thinking about the vital, but often neglected, linkages between family and religion.

Discussion and Extension

DISCUSSION AND EXTENSION

HOW HIGHLY RELIGIOUS FAMILIES STRIVE TO FULFILL SACRED PURPOSES

David C. Dollahite, *Brigham Young University*

Loren D. Marks, *University of Maine*

In this essay, we present a research-based conceptual model that focuses on the processes at work in highly religious families as they strive together to fulfill the sacred purposes suggested by their faith. Here we contribute to the goal of this volume to "do theory" as well as discuss theory.

Authors' Note: Generous support for the research discussed in this essay was provided to the first author by the Family Studies Center and the Religious Studies Center at Brigham Young University, and by a sabbatical research leave provided by the BYU College of Family, Home, and Social Sciences, and to the second author by the LSU Council on Research. We are grateful to Tom Draper for helpful feedback on a previous draft.

PROCESS: THE MISSING BRIDGE BETWEEN RELIGIOUS CONTEXTS AND FAMILY OUTCOMES

Little is known about the *processes* that operate between developmental and relational contexts and outcomes. Our research efforts center on qualitatively exploring process-oriented, "how and why" questions. Consistent with the work of both Emmons (1999) and Day (2003) on the importance of goal-oriented striving, our research indicates that religious families have central "sacred purposes" that family members strive together to fulfill. We use qualitative methods to interview families from a variety of religions, races, and geographic locations with a focus on, as Chatters and Taylor put it in Chapter 21, the "lived meaning of religion and family."

CONTEXTS, PROCESSES, AND OUTCOMES OF FAMILIES STRIVING TO FULFILL SACRED PURPOSES

The figure presented here illustrates a conceptual model of the contexts, processes, and outcomes associated with religious families whose members are striving together to fulfill spiritual goals or "sacred purposes." The model is based in part on a review of the religion and family literature (Dollahite et al., 2004) and draws primarily on our ongoing research with more than 60 highly religious Jewish, Christian, and Muslim families. Although not exhaustive, the model presents central contexts, processes, and outcomes. Given space limitations, we focus here on processes and make only cursory comments about contexts and outcomes.

Contexts: Spiritual and Religious Purposes and Involvement

Three dimensions of spiritual and religious purposes and involvement serve as contexts for religious families and provide the context for, or the content of, the spiritual goals or "sacred purposes" that families strive to fulfill:

- *Spiritual beliefs* include religious ideas, ideals, identity, and intentions; a sense of relationship with God; doctrine; sacred meanings; and goals.
- *Religious practices* include sacred rituals and traditions, prayer, study, holy days, rites, vows and covenants, and religion-based abstinence and sacrifice.
- *Faith community* includes public worship, financial and temporal contributions, organizational involvement, offers of service and support, the meeting of faith community obligations, and acceptance of opportunities to be part of something "bigger" than the self and family.

Processes: Families Striving Together to Fulfill Sacred Purposes

Below we define and describe each process and briefly illustrate it with examples from our interviews with highly religious families.

Process 1: Turning to God for support, guidance, and strength involves looking to and relying on God in ways that are intended to provide aid, strength, and healing to family relationships. Turning to God often includes prayer, reading sacred texts together to understand God's will, and attending worship services together. Examples from our study include the members of a Catholic family saying the rosary or novenas together, the members of a Muslim family turning toward Mecca to pray in their home, and the members of an Evangelical Christian family reading the Bible together around the kitchen table.

Process 2: Sanctifying the family by living religion at home involves integrating religious ideas and ideals into home and family life so that religion is not confined to a place of worship or a day of the week. Sanctifying the family

The Contexts, Processes, and Outcomes of Families Striving to Fulfill Sacred Purposes

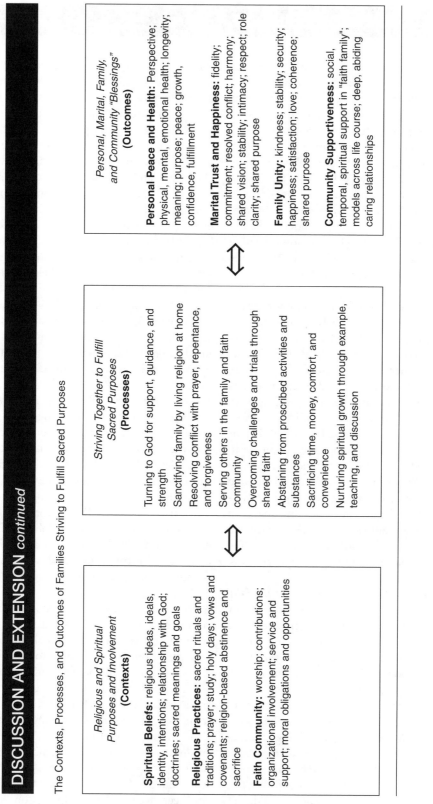

Religious and Spiritual Purposes and Involvement
(Contexts)

Spiritual Beliefs: religious ideas, ideals, identity, intentions; relationship with God; doctrines; sacred meanings and goals

Religious Practices: sacred rituals and traditions; prayer; study; holy days; vows and covenants; religion-based abstinence and sacrifice

Faith Community: worship; contributions; organizational involvement; service and support; moral obligations and opportunities

Striving Together to Fulfill Sacred Purposes
(Processes)

Turning to God for support, guidance, and strength

Sanctifying family by living religion at home

Resolving conflict with prayer, repentance, and forgiveness

Serving others in the family and faith community

Overcoming challenges and trials through shared faith

Abstaining from proscribed activities and substances

Sacrificing time, money, comfort, and convenience

Nurturing spiritual growth through example, teaching, and discussion

Personal, Marital, Family, and Community "Blessings"
(Outcomes)

Personal Peace and Health: Perspective; physical, mental, emotional health; longevity; meaning; purpose; peace; growth, confidence, fulfillment

Marital Trust and Happiness: fidelity; commitment; resolved conflict; harmony; shared vision; stability; intimacy; respect; role clarity; shared purpose

Family Unity: kindness; stability; security; happiness; satisfaction; love; coherence; shared purpose

Community Supportiveness: social, temporal, spiritual support in "faith family"; models across life course; deep, abiding caring relationships

DISCUSSION AND EXTENSION *continued*

also includes creating sacred times, places, and meanings at home by setting aside times in the schedule and places in the home for religious activities, such as Sabbath observances, prayer, and reading sacred texts together, and finding sacred meaning in daily domestic activities. Examples include an Orthodox Jewish family keeping a kosher home to fulfill the Torah, a Jewish mother and daughter lighting the Sabbath candles on Friday evening, a Muslim family observing Ramadan to honor Allah, a Mormon family holding Family Home Evening each Monday night, and an Episcopalian family singing grace each evening at dinner.

Process 3: Resolving conflict with prayer, repentance, and forgiveness involves utilizing religious thought, word, and action to address relational conflicts through praying individually or together, expressing sorrow for actions against God and others, and forgiving others (including family members) for wrongs they have committed. Religious conflict resolution differs from secular approaches in that there is a sense that God expects family members to repent and to forgive. Examples include an African Methodist Episcopal couple holding hands and praying for God to bless their marriage and to forgive them for hurting each other and a Catholic family experiencing a transcendent healing moment while standing together at Mass singing a hymn of forgiveness.

Process 4: Serving others in the family and faith community involves acts of service done by family members (as individuals, in pairs, or as a group) on behalf of others in the family, faith community, or larger community (e.g., feeding the poor, building or repairing homes, working for peace, and working with disabled persons). Examples include the members of a Methodist family working together in a soup kitchen, a Muslim family helping another Muslim family find housing, a Mormon couple working together at a church facility to can food for the poor, and a Jewish family making and delivering treats to neighbors for Purim.

Process 5: Overcoming challenges and trials through shared faith involves family members' attempts to cope with life's adversities through their beliefs, practices, and communities. Consistent with previous research, our work demonstrates that many families rely heavily on religious resources in coping with challenges, and that these resources are subsequently important to their marital and family well-being. Examples include families gathered with others in a prayer vigil after the September 11, 2001, terrorist attacks on the United States, a Pentecostal couple getting serious about their religion to help them avoid a divorce, a Jewish family mourning the loss of a grandfather and saying Kaddish each Sabbath in his memory to "keep his faith alive in them," and a Muslim mother and her daughters wearing the *hijab* (head covering) in public in spite of anti-Islamic taunts and threats.

Process 6: Abstaining from proscribed activities and substances involves obeying one's faith's proscriptions against participation in certain activities and ingesting certain substances. Examples include a Muslim family abstaining from alcohol, a Jehovah's Witness family not participating in Christmas or birthday celebrations, a Seventh-Day Adventist family abstaining from meat, a Catholic family not eating chocolate during Lent, and a newly converted Mormon husband struggling to overcome substance abuse and addiction.

Process 7: Sacrificing time, money, comfort, and convenience involves personal or family giving of time and substance for religious reasons, including donation of money, food, clothing, and service. Both the parents and the children we interviewed spoke of various ways they made sacrifices for their faiths and their families and described how this influenced their connections to God and to each other. Examples include an Evangelical Christian family giving time and money for mission work, the children in a Catholic family giving up sleeping or playing soccer on Sunday

DISCUSSION AND EXTENSION *continued*

morning to attend services, a Baptist family giving up many of "the nicer things" to contribute more money to their church, a large Mormon family tithing 10% of the family income despite significant economic needs, a Muslim family contributing a significant amount of money as *zakah* to relieve the suffering of the poor, and an Orthodox Jewish family walking several miles to pray at a synagogue on the Sabbath.

Process 8: Nurturing spiritual growth through example, teaching, and discussion involves efforts by family members to encourage spiritual development by teaching religious values, "practicing what they preach," and engaging in discussions about the nature, meanings, purposes, importance, complexities, joys, and challenges of religious and spiritual issues. Research, including our own, shows that parental teaching, example, and dialogue about religious matters are important predictors of whether children come to endorse the faith of their parents, a major sacred objective for most highly religious parents. Examples include a Jewish family newly committed to Orthodox observance teaching and discussing the challenges and joys of greater religious observance, the members of a Latino Catholic family talking together around the dinner table about the meaning of the rosary and novenas, and an African American Methodist couple responding to their adolescent daughter's questions about racial discrimination in a congregation. Many of our adult respondents spoke about the importance of "being a good example" for their children.

Outcomes: Personal, Marital, Family, and Community "Blessings"

Here we identify, but do not discuss, four beneficial outcomes repeatedly found in the literature on religion and family (Dollahite et al., 2004) as well as in our studies:

- *Personal peace and health* includes perspective; physical, mental, and emotional health; longevity; meaning; purpose; peace; and growth, confidence, and fulfillment.
- *Marital trust and happiness* includes increased fidelity, commitment, common values, conflict resolution, harmony, shared vision, marital stability, intimacy, respect, role clarity, and shared purpose.
- *Family unity* includes kindness, family stability, security, happiness, satisfaction, love, coherence, and shared purpose.
- *Community supportiveness* includes social, temporal, and spiritual support in the "faith family"; positive role models for family members across the life course; and deep and abiding caring relationships.

CONCLUSION

Our research indicates that much of religion's power lies in sacred familial processes that take place primarily out of public view, on "the other six days of the week." Our work supports and extends the ideas that Chatters and Taylor propose in Chapter 21 concerning the importance of context and process in the study of religion and family as well as ideas from Emmons (1999) and Day (2003) on the importance of attending to the processes that individuals and families use to achieve valued objectives. The processes discussed here represent the largely unconstructed empirical and theoretical bridge between religious contexts and family outcomes. Cogent theory and research aimed at identifying and illuminating processes are needed to complete the bridge.

Discussion and Extension

REFERENCES

Bartkowski, J. P., & Ellison, C. G. (1995). Divergent perspectives on childrearing in popular manuals: Conservative Protestants vs. the mainstream experts. *Sociology of Religion, 56,* 21–34.

Bartkowski, J. P., & Wilcox, W. B. (2000). Conservative Protestant child discipline: The case of parental yelling. *Social Forces, 79,* 365–290.

Bibby, R. (2002). *Restless gods: The renaissance of religion in Canada.* Toronto: Stoddart.

Billingsley, A., & Caldwell, C. H. (1991). The church, the family, and the school in the African American community. *Journal of Negro Education, 60,* 427–440.

Boss, P. (2001). *Family stress management: A contextual approach* (2nd ed.). Thousand Oaks, CA: Sage.

Chatters, L. M. (2000). Religion and health: Public health research and practice. *Annual Review of Public Health, 21,* 335–367.

Chatters, L. M. (in press). Race and ethnicity in religion and health. In K. W. Schaie & N. Krause (Eds.), *Religious influences on health and well-being in the elderly.* New York: Springer.

Chatters, L. M., Levin, J. S., & Taylor, R. J. (1992). Antecedents and dimensions of religious involvement among older Black adults. *Journal of Gerontology: Social Sciences, 47,* 269–278.

Chatters, L. M., & Taylor, R. J. (2003). The role of social context in religion. *Journal of Religious Gerontology, 14*(2/3), 139–152.

Chatters, L. M., Taylor, R. J., Lincoln, K. D., & Schroepfer, T. (2002). Patterns of informal support from family and church members among African Americans. *Journal of Black Studies, 33,* 66–85.

Christiano, K. J., Swatos, W. H., Jr., & Kivisto, P. (2002). *Sociology of religion: Contemporary developments.* Walnut Creek, CA: AltaMira.

Clark, W. (1998, Autumn). *Religious observance: Marriage and family* (Canadian Social Trends).Ottawa: Statistics Canada.

Clark, W. (2000, Winter). *Patterns of religious attendance* (Canadian Social Trends). Ottawa: Statistics Canada.

Crossley, M. L. (2000). *Introducing narrative psychology: Self, trauma, and the construction of meaning.* Buckingham, Eng.: Open University Press.

Dahl, C. M. (1994). *A phenomenological exploration of the definition and understanding of spirituality within families.* Unpublished doctoral dissertation, University of Minnesota.

Danzger, M. H. (2000). The rebirth of Judaism in Kiev after Babi Yar and communism: The interplay of family and religion. In S. K. Houseknecht & J. G. Pankhurst (Eds.), *Family, religion, and social change in diverse societies* (pp. 267–282). New York: Oxford University Press.

Day, R. D. (2003). *Introduction to family processes* (4th ed.). Mahwah, NJ: Lawrence Erlbaum.

Dilworth-Anderson, P., Burton, L. M., & Johnson, L. B. (1993). Reframing theories for understanding race, ethnicity, and families. In P. Boss, W. J. Doherty, R. LaRossa, W. R. Schumm, & S. K. Steinmetz (Eds.), *Sourcebook of family theories and methods: A contextual approach* (pp. 627–649). New York: Plenum.

Dilworth-Anderson, P., Williams, I. C., & Gibson, B. E. (2002). Issues of race, ethnicity, and culture in caregiving research: A 20-year review (1980–2000). *Gerontologist, 42,* 237–272.

Doherty, W. J., Boss, P., LaRossa, R., Schumm, W. R., & Steinmetz, S. K. (1993). Family theories and methods: A contextual approach. In P. Boss, W. J. Doherty, R. LaRossa, W. R. Schumm, & S. K. Steinmetz (Eds.), *Sourcebook of family theories and methods: A contextual approach* (pp. 3–30). New York: Plenum.

Dollahite, D. C., Marks, L. D., & Goodman, M. A. (2004). Families and religious beliefs, practices, and communities: Linkages in a diverse and dynamic cultural context. In M. Coleman & L. H. Ganong (Eds.), *Handbook of contemporary families: Considering the past, contemplating the future* (pp. 411–431). Thousand Oaks, CA: Sage.

Ellison, C. G. (1993). Religious involvement and self-perceptions among Black Americans. *Social Forces, 71,* 1027–1055.

Ellison, C. G. (1994). Religion, the life-stress paradigm, and the study of depression. In J. S. Levin (Ed.), *Religion in aging and health: Theoretical foundations and methodological frontiers* (pp. 78–121). Thousand Oaks, CA: Sage.

Ellison, C. G. (1997). Religious involvement and the subjective quality of family life among African Americans. In R. J. Taylor, J. S. Jackson, & L. M. Chatters (Eds.), *Family life in Black America* (pp. 117–131). Thousand Oaks, CA: Sage.

Ellison, C. G., Bartkowski, J. P., & Anderson, K. L. (1999). Are there religious variations in domestic violence? *Journal of Family Issues, 20,* 87–113.

Ellison, C. G., Bartkowski, J. P. & Segal, M. L. (1996). Do conservative Protestant parents spank more often? Further evidence from the National Survey of Families and Households. *Social Science Quarterly, 77,* 663–673.

Ellison, C. G., & Levin, J. S. (1998). The religion-health connection: Evidence, theory and future directions. *Health Education and Behavior, 25,* 700–720.

Ellison, C. G., & Taylor, R. J. (1996). Turning to prayer: Religious coping among Black Americans. *Review of Religious Research, 38,* 111–131.

Emmons, R. A. (1999). *The psychology of ultimate concerns: Motivation and spirituality in personality.* New York: Guilford.

Fetzer Institute/National Institute on Aging. (1999). *Multidimensional measurement of religiousness/spirituality for use in health research.* Kalamazoo, MI: John E. Fetzer.

Geertz, C. (1973). *The interpretation of cultures: Selected essays.* New York: Basic Books.

Heaney, C. A., & Israel, B. A. (2002). Social networks and social support. In K. Glanz, B. K. Rimer, & F. M. Lewis (Eds.), *Health behavior and health education: Theory, research, and practice* (3rd ed., pp. 185–209). San Francisco: Jossey-Bass.

Houseknecht, S. K. (2000). Social change in Egypt: The roles of religion and family. In S. K. Houseknecht & J. G. Pankhurst (Eds.), *Family, religion, and social change in diverse societies* (pp. 79–106). New York: Oxford University Press.

Howe, G. W. (2002). Integrating family routines and rituals with other family research paradigms: Comment on the special section. *Journal of Family Psychology, 16,* 437–440.

Idler, E. L., & George, L. M. (1998). What sociology can help us understand about religion and mental health. In H. G. Koenig (Ed.), *Handbook of religion and mental health* (pp. 51–62). San Diego, CA: Academic Press.

Jenkins, K. W. (1991). Religion and families. In S. J. Bahr (Ed.), *Family research: A sixty-year review 1930–1990* (Vol. 1, pp. 235–288). Lexington, MA: Lexington.

Koenig, H. G., McCullough, M. E., & Larson, D. B. (2001). *Handbook of religion and health.* New York: Oxford University Press.

Krause, N. (1993). Measuring religiosity in later life. *Research on Aging, 15,* 170–197.

Krause, N. (2002a). Church-based social support and health in old age: Variations by race. *Journal of Gerontology: Social Sciences, 57,* 332–347.

Krause, N. (2002b). A comprehensive strategy for developing closed-ended survey items for use in studies of older adults. *Journal of Gerontology: Social Sciences, 57,* 263–274.

Krause, N., Chatters, L. M., Meltzer, T., & Morgan, D. L. (2000a). Negative interaction in the church: Insights from focus groups with older adults. *Review of Religious Research, 41,* 510–533.

Krause, N., Chatters, L. M., Meltzer, T., & Morgan, D. L. (2000b). Using focus groups to explore the nature of prayer in late life. *Journal of Aging Studies, 14,* 191–212.

Krause, N., Ellison, C. G., & Wulff, K. (1998). Emotional support, negative interaction, and psychological well-being in the church. *Journal for the Scientific Study of Religion, 37,* 726–742.

Krause, N., Liang, J., & Keith, V. (1990). Personality, social support, and psychological distress in later life. *Psychology and Aging, 5,* 315–326.

Larson, H. (2000). We don't celebrate Christmas, we just give gifts: Adaptations to migration and social change among Hindu, Muslim and Sikh children in England. In S. K. Houseknecht & J. G. Pankhurst (Eds.), *Family, religion, and social change in diverse societies* (pp. 283–302). New York: Oxford University Press.

LaRossa, R., & Reitzes, D. C. (1993). Symbolic interactionism and family studies. In P. Boss, W. J. Doherty, R. LaRossa, W. R. Schumm, & S. K. Steinmetz (Eds.), *Sourcebook of family theories and methods: A contextual approach* (pp. 135–163). New York: Plenum.

Levin, J. S. (1989). Religious factors in aging, adjustment, and health: A theoretical overview. In W. M. Clements (Ed.), *Religion, aging and health: A global perspective* (pp. 133–146). New York: Haworth.

Levin, J. S. (1996). How religion influences morbidity and health: Reflections on natural history, salutogenesis and host resistance. *Social Science & Medicine, 43,* 849–864.

Levin, J. S., & Chatters, L. M. (1998). Research on religion and mental health: An overview of empirical findings and theoretical issues. In H. G. Koenig (Ed.), *Handbook of religion and mental health* (pp. 33–50). San Diego, CA: Academic Press.

Levin, J. S., Chatters, L. M., & Taylor, R. J. (1995). Religious effects on health and life satisfaction among Black Americans. *Journal of Gerontology: Social Sciences, 50,* 154–163.

Lincoln, K. D. (2000). Social support, negative social interactions, and psychological well-being. *Social Service Review, 74,* 231–252.

Lincoln, K. D., Chatters, L. M., & Taylor, R. J. (2003). Psychological distress among Black and White Americans: Differential effects of social support, negative interaction and personal control. *Journal of Health and Social Behavior, 44,* 390–407.

Lincoln, K. D., Taylor, R. J., & Chatters, L. M. (2003). Correlates of emotional support and negative interaction among older Black Americans. *Journal of Gerontology: Social Sciences, 58,* 225–233.

MacIver, R. M. (1970). *On community, society, and power.* Chicago: University of Chicago Press.

Mahoney, A. M., Pargament, K. I., Jewel, T., Swank, A. B., Scott, E., Emery, E., et al. (1999). Marriage and the spiritual realm: The role of proximal and distal religious constructs in marital functioning. *Journal of Family Psychology, 13,* 321–338.

Mattis, J. S. (2000). African American women's definitions of spirituality: A qualitative analysis. *Journal of Black Psychology, 26,* 101–122.

Mattis, J. S. (2002). The role of religion and spirituality in the coping experience of African American women: A qualitative analysis. *Psychology of Women Quarterly, 26,* 308–320.

McCubbin, M. A., & McCubbin, H. I. (1989). Theoretical orientations to family stress and coping. In C. R. Figley (Ed.), *Treating stress in families* (pp. 3–43). New York: Brunner/Mazel.

Moore, T. (1992). *Care of the soul: A guide for cultivating depth and sacredness in everyday life.* New York: HarperCollins.

Pankhurst, J. G. (1996). Religious culture. In D. N. Shalin (Ed.), *Russian culture at the crossroads: Paradoxes of postcommunist consciousness* (pp. 127–156). Boulder, CO: Westview.

Pankhurst, J. G., & Houseknecht, S. K. (2000). Introduction: The religion-family linkage and social change—a neglected area of study. In S. K. Houseknecht & J. G. Pankhurst (Eds.), *Family, religion, and social change in diverse societies* (pp. 1–40). New York: Oxford University Press.

Pargament, K. I. (1997). *The psychology of religion and coping: Theory, research, practice.* New York: Guilford.

Poloma, M. M., & Gallup, G. (1991). *Varieties of prayer.* Philadelphia: Trinity Press International.

Rook, K. S. (1998). Investigating the positive and negative sides of personal relationships: Through a lens darkly? In B. H. Spitzberg & W. R. Cupach (Eds.), *The dark side of close relationships* (pp. 369–393). Mahwah, NJ: Lawrence Erlbaum.

Sprey, J. (1988). Current theorizing on the family: An appraisal. *Journal of Marriage and the Family, 50,* 875–890.

Swenson, D. (1989). *Cultural and structural factors of family attitudes in Roman Catholic parochial environments.* Unpublished doctoral dissertation, University of Notre Dame.

Swenson, D. (1995, November). *The religious bases of marital quality: A study of ministers and their spouses.* Paper presented to the Religion and Family Section at the annual meeting of the National Council of Family Relations, Portland, OR.

Swenson, D. (1999). *Society, spirituality and the sacred: A social scientific introduction.* Peterborough, ON: Broadview.

Taylor, R. J., & Chatters, L. M. (1986a). Church-based informal support among elderly Blacks. *Gerontologist, 26,* 637–642.

Taylor, R. J., & Chatters, L. M. (1986b). Patterns of informal support to elderly Black adults: Family, friends, and church members. *Social Work, 31,* 432–438.

Taylor, R. J., & Chatters, L. M. (1988). Church members as a source of informal social support. *Review of Religious Research, 30,* 193–203.

Taylor, R. J., Chatters, L. M., & Levin, J. S. (2004). *Religion in the lives of African Americans: Social, psychological, and health perspectives.* Thousand Oaks, CA: Sage.

Taylor, R. J., Ellison, C. G., Chatters, L. M., Levin, J. S., & Lincoln, K. D. (2000). Mental health services in faith communities: The role of clergy in Black churches. *Social Work, 45,* 73–87.

Thomas, D. L., & Cornwall, M. (1990). Religion and family in the 1980s: Discovery and development. *Journal of Marriage and the Family, 52,* 983–992.

Thomas, S. B., Quinn, S. C., Billingsley, A., & Caldwell, C. H. (1994). The characteristics of northern Black churches with community health outreach programs. *American Journal of Public Health, 84,* 575–579.

Thornton, A. (1985). Reciprocal influences of family and religion in a changing world. *Journal of Marriage and the Family, 47,* 381–394.

Wenzel, L., Glanz, K., & Lerman, C. (2002). Stress, coping and health behavior. In K. Glanz, B. K. Rimer, & F. M. Lewis (Eds.), *Health behavior and health education: Theory, research, and practice* (3rd ed., pp. 210–239). San Francisco: Jossey-Bass.

Wilcox, W. B. (1998). Conservative Protestant childrearing: Authoritarian or authoritative? *American Sociological Review, 63,* 796–809.

Williams, D. R. (1994). The measurement of religion in epidemiologic studies: Problems and prospects. In J. S. Levin (Ed.), *Religion in aging and health: Theoretical foundations and methodological frontiers* (pp. 125–148). Thousand Oaks, CA: Sage.

Woodbury, R. D., & Smith, C. S. (1998). Fundamentalism et al.: Conservative Protestants in America. *Annual Review of Sociology, 24,* 25–56.

Zinnbauer, B., Pargament, K. I., Cole, B., Rye, M., Butter, E., Belavich, T., et al. (1997). Religiousness and spirituality: Unfuzzying the fuzzy. *Journal for the Scientific Study of Religion, 36,* 549–564.

Twenty-two

FAMILIES, THEORIES, AND SOCIAL POLICY

Phyllis Moen, *Cornell University*

Scott Coltrane, *University of California, Riverside*

Social policies are (a) purposive courses of action, taken by (b) actors or sets of actors, about (c) particular issues or problems of concern. Family theories shape both actors' definitions of "problems of concern" and their proposed "purposive courses of action." Good theories (that is, theories that capture key ·components of family relations, resources, and dynamics) are prerequisite to the design of effective family policies. But even bad (inaccurate) or poorly articulated family theories intrude on the policy process (see Aldous & Dumon, 1990; Moen & Forest, 1999). A social problems approach (Schneider, 1985; Spector & Kitsuse, 1987) points out that implicit family theories define both problems and proposed solutions, even though these theories may be weak, inappropriate, or at odds with empirical evidence. The taken-for-granted family theories guiding how policy makers, the public, and social researchers define "problems of concern" typically remain just that: taken for granted. And yet these "theories" have enormous influence on policy making—shaping what gets on the policy agenda, the range of solutions considered, and how programs and policies are evaluated. Such theories can therefore have profound impacts on families and individuals. In this chapter we examine how family issues become defined as social problems in the first place, how implicit theories about families shape subsequent policy development, and how actors or sets of actors shape the policy process. Throughout, we discuss how family scholars use theory to inform policy debates, drawing on the "work-family" arena as a case example.

"Theory" means *explanations*. Sometimes formal theories are explicitly stated (such as conflict theory, exchange theory, and labeling theory), but this occurs mostly in scholarly articles and books (see Chapters 1 and 2, this volume). Far more common are the "theories" people have about all kinds of circumstances. These are the cultural beliefs that people use as a kind of shorthand way of making decisions or understanding the world. For example, most Americans believe that parents' spending time with their children promotes the children's optimal development, that stress at work "spills over" into stress in family life, and that a family's eating meals together is "good" for the emotional health of family members. But note how such shared understandings of what *is* can spill over into shared understandings of what *should be*. Many Americans would argue that parents *should* spend considerable (or "quality") time with their children, that parents (mothers especially) *should* "balance" their lives to reduce stressful spillover from work, and that families *should* eat dinner together. It is in this way—in movement from what is to what should be—that theories become *scripts for living*. They may or may not be "true"; what matters is that most people come to believe they are true and act, try to act, or feel guilty about not acting, accordingly.

Where do these shared theories and scripts come from? Most are what we call "culture," passed on, directly or indirectly, from one generation to the next. This occurs in the form of direct instructions (from parents, teachers, bosses, doctors, ministers, and so on), media messages (including claims of social science experts), observations of what others do, institutional controls (rules, laws, and moral codes), and interpersonal negotiations or ritualized interactions. George Lakoff (2002) explains that implicit theories influence people's family lives as well as shaping their political views. Policy debates are often shaped by deep-seated and often unacknowledged metaphorical ways of understanding the world. For example, conservatives tend to embrace a "strict father" morality, whereas liberals tend to embrace a "nurturant parent" morality. Although such implicit theories are rarely consistent or rational, they provide symbolic resonance and emotional energy to contentious debates about families and politics (Bennett, 1992). Family researchers and practitioners often claim that scientific objectivity and professional training can protect them from errors of inference associated with folk beliefs and moral symbolism, but, as we discuss below, academic and professional "experts" (a group in which we include ourselves) are not immune from the cognitive and emotional biases that influence the larger public (including faith in the power of science to solve society's problems). Although experts have come to play an increasingly important

role in the cultural production of knowledge and the development of family policy, implicit and often unexamined theories continue to undergird such processes. Shared theories are also promulgated through the development and implementation of social policies affecting families. The passage of legislation (in the early part of the 20th century in the United States) prohibiting child labor, for example, reinforced the theory that paid work is harmful to children's development, effectively limiting this as a work-family strategy in hard economic times.

DEFINING ISSUES OR PROBLEMS OF CONCERN

Why do some personal troubles become the focus of social policy initiatives, whereas others remain neglected? How do "new" issues of concern get on the policy agenda? Understanding this process is a fundamental challenge to family scholars. Here we can only introduce a few concepts used in policy research that shape the framing of family issues.

What matters is not what "family" may mean to family theorists or how it may be operationalized in empirical studies, but how policy makers and other influential actors (or sets of actors) define the term. Most often, policy makers have an image of "family" as consisting of two or more related individuals, usually a breadwinner husband married to a homemaker wife with biological children. Definitions matter, because they frame the problems that policies address.

According to the *social constructionist* approach (see Chapter 2, this volume), similar social conditions do not necessarily produce social problems; rather, it is the collective *definition* of a condition as troubling that constructs it as a social problem (Blumer, 1971). Thus, for example, Americans now talk about a work-family "problem" because two-earner couples and single-parent families do not fit the idealized image of a family in which the mother stays home to take care of the children. Any family issue could be used to illustrate this process, but here we focus on the work-family issue as an example of how family social problems come to be socially defined and redefined.

At the beginning of the Industrial Revolution, wives and children, along with men, were expected to earn their keep through wage labor, but there were seldom enough jobs to go around. The rise of capitalism and the growth of unions promoted a "family wage" that could support a whole family, enabling mothers and children to remain out of the workforce. Concerns about unsafe workplace conditions prompted this framing of the issue, but an implicit theory about the vulnerability and fragility of children and women also undergirded this approach. Eventually, this resulted in protective legislation that contributed to the gendering of work in the 20th century in several ways. First, men gained social approval as (paid) workers, whereas women's work became invisible because it was done at home. Second, social values that encouraged employers to ban women from many jobs made sex discrimination commonplace. Third, employers could justify paying women low wages because men presumably supported them. Indeed, people came to define pay as what one earned for going to work; women's relegation to the home put them outside the system of pay for labor. Finally, the sexual division of labor that assigned men to the labor force and women to the home encouraged employers to structure jobs on the assumptions that all permanent workers were men and that all men had stay-at-home wives (Coltrane, 1998; Moen, 2003; Reskin & Padavic, 1994). Not all families could afford to adopt this breadwinner-homemaker family pattern (immigrant women, working-class women, and women of color routinely engaged in paid labor), but the model of "separate spheres" for men and women became the dominant cultural template (for more on this topic, see this volume's companion Web site at http://www.ncfr.org/sourcebook). By the 1930s, the theoretical notion of a single-family breadwinner with a full-time homemaking wife was firmly ensconced as the dominant cultural model in American society.

With the advent of the Great Depression of the 1930s, the "work-family" issue became how to maintain men's employment. Married women in some states lost their jobs because their employment was "taking jobs away" from male breadwinners. Poor families were not seen as "problem families" so much as "families with problems." Almost everyone was suffering some deprivation, and the poor could not be blamed for their circumstances. Even single-parent families were seen as "deserving" (see this volume's Web site).

The groups that are most successful at defining social problems are those with strong interest in the issues, the resources to promote their problem definitions, and the credibility to do so. As groups make claims about social conditions, others respond; this "dance" of claims making and counterclaims making is the process that turns a particular phenomenon (which may or may not have attracted prior attention) into a social problem (Best, 1990; Holstein & Miller, 2003; Schneider, 1985). Advocacy groups have always attempted to promote their interpretations of social problems through public discourse, but the context in which those claims have been advanced has changed dramatically over the past century (Coltrane & Adams, 2003).

With America's entry into World War II, issues linking families and work were again redefined, mostly in light of the high demand for, and scarcity of, labor. Married women's employment came to be defined as patriotic. Government-subsidized day-care centers made it possible for even mothers of young children to help with the domestic war effort by building military equipment or by participating in civilian industries to "free" able-bodied men to serve overseas.

The booming postwar economy of the 1950s, along with pent-up demands for family building and home buying, brought a renewed emphasis on the breadwinner-homemaker ideal. New social science concepts such as "maternal deprivation" suggested that mothers' employment might jeopardize children's development. In the 1960s and 1970s, the second wave of the women's movement promoted equal rights for women, focusing on parity in education, salaries, and career advancement. In other words, the "problem" was defined as the right of women to have access to, and reap equal rewards from, jobs in the *primary* sector—that is, "men's" jobs (Moen & Roehling, 2004).

Although most American families now live on two incomes, and workplaces are populated by workers from dual-earner couples, employers and government policy makers have been reluctant to embrace the two-earner family as the new norm. Work-family issues garnered mild public attention during the 1970s and 1980s, but policy initiatives aimed at dealing with these issues achieved only limited success, in part because of the implicit assumptions remaining about breadwinning, homemaking, and gender.

FAMILY SCHOLARSHIP

The work-family "problem" has been constructed and reconstructed, often in light of prevailing labor market needs and in keeping with conventional gender schemata. For the most part, family scholars have uncritically adopted commonly accepted popular definitions of the problems of working families. Thus scholars in the 1940s wrote about families confronting unemployment and stress (Hill, 1949; Komarovsky, 1940). Scholars in the 1960s and 1970s studied the impacts of working mothers and work-family conflict on children, husbands, wives, and families. Stress and feminist theorists (Hoffman & Youngblade, 1999) have shown that having women in the workforce is good/bad/inconsequential for women/men/children, depending on their theoretical (and political) stances. More recently, the theory behind the problem of working families has been defined as one of overload and "balance" (Aldous, 1996). The career mystique embodied in the lockstep model of continuous full-time-plus employment (male breadwinner model) remains intact—for men and for the few women (often single or child free) who can pursue it (Moen, 2003; Moen & Roehling, 2004). It is women who typically do the balancing, by scaling back on their occupational aspirations or hours of paid work.

Contemporary liberal feminism's first front (including feminist scholars) was the workplace, where the battle was the push for equal opportunity—the cessation of gender discrimination in education, hiring, promotion, and pay. But this, as Arlie Hochschild (1989) has phrased it, is a "stalled revolution," fundamentally changing women's equal access to primary sector careers, but not fundamentally challenging the social organization of those careers (Moen, 2003; Moen & Roehling, 2004; Williams, 2000). When the "issue" is defined exclusively as equal opportunity in the labor market, all adults in families, and especially women, are expected to pursue long-hour, lockstep occupational careers *and* do the hidden domestic and care work at home. Many scholars, like Hochschild, have come to redefine the issue in terms of the unequal allocation of domestic work (Coltrane, 1996).

Still another redefinition has occurred that emphasizes the time squeeze that working families experience. Stress and liberal feminist theories spawned policies based in recognition of the time constraints that families face, most notably the Family and Medical Leave Act, and various private sector "family-friendly" initiatives, such as flextime and flexplace (telecommuting), with child-care policies "freeing up" employees from family work. But such a framing ignores the way that jobs offering benefits and future prospects come prepackaged: in 40-hour or more weekly time expectations, and with continuous uninterrupted attachment to the workforce. Unless employees can afford, and choose, to hire others (often less privileged women with families of their own) to meet their obligations, or else have partners who are willing to scale back their own career investments, conventional occupational career paths are difficult for those with family responsibilities.

Today, life-course scholars and feminists are once again reframing the work-family issue by focusing on particular ages and stages as they intersect with gender and play out in long-term consequences (Moen, 2003; Moen & Roehling, 2004; Williams, 2000). For instance, they show how motherhood exacts a tremendous cost on career progression (England, 1992) and within-couple equality (Moen, 2003). Apart from feminist theorists, few scholars have sought to reconstruct how work-family issues are defined. For example, until recently social scientists generally accepted the concept of "work" as paid work; only now are issues about unpaid care work coming to the fore (Harrington Meyer, 2000).

PURPOSIVE COURSES OF ACTION: PRIVATE TROUBLES VERSUS PUBLIC ISSUES

Sometimes, as was the case with unemployment during the Great Depression, policy actors (such as Franklin D. Roosevelt) define family circumstances as *public issues* requiring public solutions. At other times, much the same circumstances (such as the unemployment of *part-time* workers) are either not acknowledged or are defined as *private troubles,* and thus not requiring policy action. When are family difficulties seen as requiring societal, rather than simply private, courses of action? And how do those with the power to effect change decide what society (or the state, or corporations) should do about them?

Both the definitions of social problems and the adoption of policies designed to address them are strongly influenced by the "claims making" process (Spector & Kitsuse, 1987). "Claims makers" are those who seek to define, publicize, and ameliorate social problems; they typically include advocates for specific causes, their detractors, and a cast of various experts and politicians, along with representatives of relevant government, corporate, and nonprofit sectors. Social problems researchers often focus on the purposive framing of issues, categorizing the rhetoric of various claims makers into grounds, warrants, and conclusions (Best, 1990; Coltrane & Hickman, 1992). *Grounds* provide the basic facts about an issue and serve as the foundation for discussion of the problem (Best, 1987). Grounds statements typically include definitions, supposedly "representative" examples (most often horror stories or vivid extreme cases), and numerical estimates (usually very large numbers intended to dramatize the extent of the problem). *Warrants* are statements that justify drawing conclusions from the grounds and usually include value judgments (Best, 1987). Warrants bridge the gap between grounds and conclusions, providing justification for claims makers' demands for particular actions or social policy changes that they assert will alleviate the social problem (Best, 1987; Coltrane & Adams, 2003).

● *SPOTLIGHT ON THOERY*

FAMILIES AND POLICY: HEALTH ISSUES OF OLDER WOMEN

Karen A. Roberto, *Virginia Polytechnic Institute and State University*

The majority of older women have at least one chronic health problem, and coping with multiple conditions is common with advancing old age. My research focuses on one condition prevalent among older women, osteoporosis (Roberto, 1988; Roberto & Reynolds, 2001). This chronic, progressive disease is a public health threat for an estimated 44 million Americans, accounting for more than 1.5 million fractures annually and costing the United States more than $17 billion annually in direct medical care. The

(continued)

● **SPOTLIGHT ON THEORY** *continued*

consequences of osteoporosis would be severe enough if they were limited to the skeleton, but women with osteoporosis must also contend with associated problems, such as the inability to complete activities of daily living. These functional limitations have complex psychosocial and economic consequences. As Moen and Coltrane assert, the multidimensionality of the human experience requires family scientists to move beyond simple and implicit assumptions about the causes and consequences of social problems, such as those attributed to declining health. To illustrate, in this brief discussion I integrate constructs from three frameworks—the life-course perspective, the trajectory model of chronic illness, and an ethic of care model—to consider the functional, psychological, and social aspects of chronic illness in late life.

The life-course perspective provides a broad-based analytic foundation for studying the individual and social context of health and illness (George, 2003). It recognizes that aging reflects a lifetime accumulation of interacting social, behavioral, and biomedical processes that shape beliefs about health, responses to illness, and reliance on family and the health care system. These processes are influenced by individual factors such as race and ethnicity, education, and socioeconomic status; family processes, including collective attitudes, activities, and actions; and societal norms and support. The onset of a chronic condition represents a life transition for the older woman. Incorporating constructs from Corbin and Strauss's (1988) trajectory model furthers the theoretical unfolding of chronic illness by focusing on the active role the older woman plays in shaping the course of her illness within the context of everyday life.

To understand a change in health status effectively, one must understand the key problems imposed by the health condition and the basic strategies used to manage these problems. *Key problems* such as controlling symptoms and carrying out prescribed regimes vary from person to person, but to some degree they are persistent and relatively permanent. To manage the key problems, *basic strategies* must be developed and implemented. These strategies often depend on assistance from *agents,* or members of the older woman's social network. The *consequences* or effectiveness of the strategies and arrangements depend on how well the older woman and her social network have organized their efforts to handle the key problems. This network of care is influenced by societal norms and government support. Thus, to lend further sophistication to the theoretical framework, I suggest incorporating elements from an ethic of care model to analyze the interactions of older women with the health care system. An ethic of care involves attending to older persons needing help through various caring acts and involves inclusion, empowerment, and deconstruction of myths of bureaucratic operation (Tronto, 2001). This model creates a moral imperative for active government engagement that involves application of a *care collective* to address health care needs.

Theorizing using multiple frameworks requires family scientists to move beyond traditional theoretical boundaries and integrate constructs from diverse perspectives and disciplines to address the complexity of multilayered, intertwining health issues in late life. To ensure that policy makers consider the power and influence of their initiatives on the evolving health-related demands of an aging society, scholars must make explicit the theoretical assumptions that guide the discovery and affirmation of new knowledge. ●

Historical research shows that when a situation comes to be seen as a social problem, a particular discourse is applied to it, and policies are channeled in particular directions (Gusfield, 1996). The language applied leads to different meanings and evaluations; for example, government aid to farmers is called "parity," government aid to businesses through tax cuts is called "economic incentives," but government aid to poor people is called "welfare" (Edelman, 1977). In defining a social problem, claims makers also seek figurative "ownership" of it. Once a particular problem definition becomes generally accepted, former claims makers become authorities on the issue, taking control over policies and programs designed to correct it (Best, 1990). If the members of an interested group have been involved in the political process of defining a social problem, it is easier for them to mobilize support for their framing of potential solutions (Best, 1990). Those in authority (the "experts") are generally able to create an implicit and taken-for-granted "legitimating frame" that governs the problem, and "would-be challengers face the problem of overcoming a definition of the situation that they themselves may take as part of the natural order" (Gamson, 1985, p. 616).

IMPLICIT THEORIES ABOUT SOLUTIONS

How actors define problems affects how they theorize about solutions. For example, how we, as a nation, respond to "family poverty" or "working families" depends on what we see as the problem. The theory behind the Great Society's "War on Poverty" in the 1960s was the economic viability of the family breadwinner. If there was no (male) family breadwinner, then the solution was for government to act as a breadwinner of sorts, providing support (welfare) to dependent mothers and their children (see this volume's Web site). Unemployment insurance, minimum-wage policies, and pension reforms were enacted as solutions to the viability of working families (defined as those with a single [male]

breadwinner). In the 1960s, issues related to dual-earner households had not yet made it to the policy agenda.

By the 1990s, however, after decades of debate about the "deserving" and "undeserving" poor, a new theory emerged. Poverty came to be defined as a consequence of the absence of paid work by family members. The solution implied by this theory was to make sure that working families were just that: All adults in a household, except those of retirement age, were expected to be in the workforce, regardless of the ages of their children. Welfare reform signaled a retheorizing of family life as much as a retheorizing of poverty. If poor single mothers were expected to support their families, and if seeing one's mother go out the door to a job was a good thing for children, then shouldn't all mothers be in the workforce? In this way, feminist theories about gender equality and conservative welfare-to-work theories came to the same conclusion: It is good for women (and men) to be employed, regardless of family circumstances (see this volume's Web site).

Other framings have challenged this "solution." Stress theorists have focused on potential problems of role conflict and overload, but policy makers have most often responded with platitudes rather than concrete policies related to work-family conflict or overload. Feminist theorists have pointed out the disadvantaged position of women (especially mothers) in the labor market (Moen, 2003; Reskin & Padavic 1994), but most government policies continue to be based on the assumption that any job, no matter how low the pay, will permit poor parents to work their way out of poverty (Hays, 2003).

Another example of a policy enacted to address work-family issues is the Family and Medical Leave Act (FMLA). This law (enacted in 1993) offers parents the possibility of unpaid leave from their jobs to care for newborns or sick children (or other family members) for 12 weeks; it applies to employees in organizations with 50 or more employees. The "problem" underlying this policy is defined as a lack of time for family care, but, according to the legislation, this lack of time is seen as a limited, short-term problem. That the "solution" is defined in terms of *unpaid* leave suggests that policy makers hold an implicit theory about family care. Even though the actual act is phrased in gender-neutral terms, family care is presumed to be the province of women, whose earnings are secondary and, hence, not essential to the family. At the same time, the act is targeted to cover employees within the primary sector of the labor market, who are more likely than those in other sectors to have access to financial and family resources and to be White, middle-class, and married (Elison, 1997; Marks, 1997). Note who is left out of this legislation: poor employees (especially single parents) as well as family breadwinners who cannot afford to take unpaid time off, people who are not eligible by virtue of having contingent work or no paid jobs, and employees who work for small companies (see Bornstein, 2000; Gerstel & McGonagle, 1999). This example shows that the framing of the "problem" can lead to policy "solutions" that fail to address the needs of many families who might otherwise be considered most in need. Many additional factors entered into the problem definition and specific policy formation processes that resulted in the FMLA; our point is the significance of the unexamined assumptions ("theories") about men as bread-winners and women as family caregivers that underlie the act's formulation.

WE TOO LIVE IN THIS TAKEN-FOR-GRANTED WORLD

Implicit theories about problems and solutions are frequently in the heads of academics as well as in the heads of policy actors. Because even the most partisan advocacy organizations now invoke their own objective-sounding "experts," it is increasingly important for academics to examine their own implicit theories and taken-for-granted legitimating frames.

Like most Americans, family scholars tend to accept the American Dream, the idea that hard work in a "good" paid job will produce

family as well as individual success (Moen & Roehling, 2004). Taking the social organization of paid work as given, they study ways that women can "manage" to squeeze into the existing lockstep full-time career template by getting equal pay for comparable work (Reskin & Padavic, 1994) and having affordable, accessible, high-quality child care. Both are worthy goals, but neither questions the fundamental theory behind the career mystique: that working long hours continuously throughout the prime adult years pays off in economic and job security. Scholars even differentiate between the "primary" labor market (populated by those following such paths) and the "secondary" labor market (populated by women, minorities, unskilled workers, and immigrants). Clearly, the yardstick that American society uses to gauge success is the taken-for-granted one that may have been characteristic of White, married, middle-class men climbing organizational ladders in the 1950s. Unfortunately, scholars too often unwittingly employ the same cultural yard-stick, income or prestige, to workers today as they did in the 1950s, when seniority was in fact a signal of job security, benefits, and rising wages, if not advancement. But the social contract behind the American Dream has disappeared in a global economy where offshore outsourcing and layoffs are commonplace. Moreover, theoretical models of individual attainment are predicated on employees' having others (wives) serving as full-time home-makers whose unpaid care work enables the employees' unwavering concentration on their (paid) jobs. But even few contemporary employees, male or female, have anyone to do their family and personal care work. Although care work remains hidden, excluded in most discussions about models of career paths and attainments, family scholars are increasingly including the concept of care work in their theories, especially those concerning gender inequality. Still, the lockstep career mystique route to the American Dream remains deeply embedded not only in the ways jobs, benefits, and rewards are organized, but also in the ways most Americans, including policy makers and academics, theorize about them.

RECONSTRUCTING SOCIAL CONSTRUCTIONS

Feminist scholars are reshaping the work-family discourse by theorizing about paid *and* unpaid work, the gendered nature of both, and the costs to anyone (effectively women) of taking time out from the lockstep life course and its typically long-hour work-week (Moen, 2003; Moen & Han, 2001). What kinds of no-cost career path options would be possible if employers were to presume that all employees simultaneously engage in unpaid care work as well as their paid work? What would be possible if policy actors were to recognize the ebb and flow of family care work, factoring that into the ways paths are organized and rewarded? How could occasional detours, "time-outs," retooling, and "second acts" be incorporated as legitimate components of career paths in theories of job commitment and success made tangible in actual benefit, promotion, and reward systems? Detours and postponements are, in fact, a reality for most of the members of today's workforce, but they remain on the fringes of discourse that assigns legitimacy to "primary" uninterrupted career trajectories. How could those on uncertain, unskilled, or obsolete career paths gain the skills to launch new careers at various life stages? Our social problems perspective suggests that the taken-for-granted career mystique is at the root of the paucity of research and policy development that aims to broaden the range of legitimate career options. What most Americans engage in, and what most scholars investigate and theorize about, are essentially private family solutions to the work-family interlock (such as having one person [the wife] scale back on occupational investments; delaying having a first, second, or third child; or having husbands share in housework; see Becker & Moen, 1999; Coltrane, 1996; Moen, 2003). Scholars are only beginning to challenge the apparent invisibility of the clockwork of careers in their definitions of the work-family "problem" and potential "solutions."

POLICY ACTORS DEFINING THEORIES, PROBLEMS, AND SOLUTIONS

Thus far we have discussed how underlying theories shape the formulation of policies intended to address them and how issues come to be defined as social problems. Next we focus on the actors involved in these processes. Looking closely at the actors (or sets of actors) driving policy reveals just how ad hoc the process is. Often issues come to the fore because of the experiences of elected officials: a son who has cancer, a father with Alzheimer's disease. When there is little empirical evidence and few established theoretical axioms (as is usually the case with policies about families), policy actors' own beliefs and experiences tend to drive decision making. Similarly, social network and social influence theories suggest that people's attitudes and beliefs are strongly influenced by their social milieu, so that individuals readily view the experiences of their friends and neighbors, who typically occupy similar positions in the social hierarchy, as normative and "natural."

To date, most policy makers have been (White, upper-middle-class) men with full-time homemaking wives. Their perspectives on both how families are and how they *should be* are inevitably colored by their own personal biographies (Smith, 1993). Men in powerful positions who themselves are in dual-earner arrangements (such as Bill Clinton or Bob Dole) or women in the policy arena (such as Hillary Clinton or Elizabeth Dole) may well define both family issues and family solutions differently from those in traditional (breadwinner-homemaker) households. (But even policy makers in dual-earner or even single-parent families are somewhat removed from the "real world" of work and family in that they often pay others to manage their domestic activities.) Research shows that women who hold positions of authority (in media, civil service, politics) are the most likely to enact policies that address work-family issues. Similarly, countries in which women hold powerful government positions are likely to enact family-friendly policies (Chafetz, 1990). Such findings alert us to the fact that who makes policy affects the policy formation process as much as the research evidence supporting particular problem definitions or solutions.

We use the phrase *actors or sets of actors* deliberately, to remind the reader that policies are made and sustained at a number of levels, and most frequently by groups rather than by individuals. People tend to equate social policies with public policies established by federal, state, and local governments. But there are other policy actors as well, including the large nonprofit sector (consisting of religious and other interest groups as well as foundations), the even larger business sector, the mass media, government employees ("bureaucrats"), and academic researchers. All of these "actors" are constructors of theories about problems and policy remedies as well as stakeholders in which theories prevail. Consider, for instance, the ways that professional organizations and lobbyists operate, sometimes to stave off policy changes and sometimes to promote them, depending on which is most advantageous to the people (or corporations, or industries) they represent. Social movements of particular groups also tend to follow gendered scripts as well as focusing on the concerns of particular regions, ethnic groups, social classes, religious groups, or political parties. Social problems are thus *constructed,* constituted by groups asserting grievances and making claims about harmful social conditions (Spector & Kitsuse, 1987). In other words, social problems arise when advocacy groups advance claims that generate public concern. Issues become social problems when they are defined publicly as disagreeable social conditions (Goode & Ben-Yehuda, 1994). The fact is that people who are engaged in policy debates typically have fuzzy ideas about what the problems are, what the solutions should be, and how to get there. These vague ideas are translated into policy directives according to political expediency and are then refined by regulators and other groups (e.g., states or courts). Even if the product (a law, a regulation, an executive order) mirrors the goals of policy actors, it often has unanticipated consequences that, with good theories, might have been avoided, or at least considered, in the policy-making process. The most important stakeholders in family policy debates, the nation's families, are rarely present at the proverbial policy table, except indirectly through their elected representatives, who have overriding agendas of their own.

• *SPOTLIGHT ON METHODS*

INVESTIGATING CHILD ABUSE INVESTIGATIONS

Jennifer A. Reich, *University of California, San Francisco*

We arrive at Cindi's home, a two-level apartment in a subsidized complex. I stand behind Julie, the social worker from child protective services (CPS) I have been following as part of my research on how parents and the state negotiate power and meaning in the child welfare system. This is one stop among many during which Julie must investigate allegations of child maltreatment and decide whether children are in imminent danger and should be placed in the state's care or remain with their parents. In the car, before we approached Cindi's front door, Julie had commented that the

(continued)

mother, who had threatened her the week before, has "mental health issues." It is 9:45 A.M. when two police officers meet us and, after brief introductions, Julie knocks on Cindi's door. Cindi answers wearing a stained pink nightshirt; her 3-year-old son, Jerome, plays on the floor behind her.

Julie is what sociologists call a "street-level bureaucrat" (Lipsky, 1980), a public service worker who interprets and executes public policy on an interactive level. Federal law, which specifies how child maltreatment allegations should be handled, informs state law, which is interpreted on a local level, dictating how Julie—standing in this mother's living room— should evaluate child well-being. Will Julie believe that Cindi's children are adequately cared for and safe? Indeed, Julie's job is to distinguish "family problems" from "problem families."

At one point Julie walks outside with Jerome—with me following—to ask him the usual questions about his home life, but he is nonresponsive, seeming unable to speak, and Julie returns Jerome to his mother. We then walk to the apartment complex's on-site recreation center to find Cindi's 7-year-old daughter, Amber. Julie tells the teacher to whom Amber is clinging that she would like to speak with the girl alone, and although I expect Amber to seem nervous, she is instead chatty and appears to thrive on the attention that accompanies Julie's questions. In her many answers, Amber explains that she is not allowed to go home until 3:00 that afternoon, that she heard her mom up during the night, and that she saw her mom pick something off of Jerome's leg that made him cry.

In Julie's efforts to assess whether Cindi is an adequate parent, she finds that Cindi has many liabilities. Reports to CPS over the past 6 years, although they have not resulted in her children being removed, have included the following observations: "volatility," "belligerent attitude," "self-admission of crank [methamphetamine] use," "son has lice," and "house is dirty." I wonder how many of these things are about Cindi's material poverty rather than bad parenting. After all, since Jerome's biological father—a man Amber considers to be her father as well—was incarcerated earlier this year, Cindi has alone been responsible for her children. Today's visit added "not a lot of food" and "burn on leg of boy that appears to be a cigarette burn" to the list of maternal failings. Julie also interprets Amber's story of her mom's picking something off of Jerome's leg to mean that Cindi picked at a scab, making the healing burn bleed again. Such behavior would be consistent with methamphetamine use, which creates nervous energy that results in users' fidgeting and "picking." By now, Cindi's presumed "mental health issues" have given way to a vision of her as a drug addict. We head back to Cindi's apartment with Amber.

When we arrive, Julie tells Cindi that she is placing the children in protective custody. Cindi begins to cry, which inspires Amber to do the same. Throughout, Jerome seems oblivious. As a researcher, my only job is to watch this emotionally charged interaction and make theoretical sense of it. One of the police officers, who presumes I am a social work trainee, leans in to tell me that kids should be taken away in such cases so they will have "half a chance." I stand silent. Tony, Julie's colleague, has arrived to transport the kids to foster care. As he puts them in the car, Cindi—with tears streaming down her face—leans inside the car to check that Jerome's car seat is installed correctly, a gesture that is both ironic and an important reminder that people act in complex and contradictory ways. Amber and Cindi hug tearfully until Julie stops them and closes the car door. Cindi and Julie stand watching as Tony, the children, and I drive away. We are going to the receiving home, a stone building with toys, tattered books, and peanut butter sandwiches where the children will have beds for the night. ●

Why have policy actors been so slow in responding to the needs of working families? Some speculate that neither the U.S. government nor corporations are willing or eager to adopt the notion of mothers, as well as fathers, being in the labor force as the new "normal" for American families (Aldous, 1990; Moen, 1989). Laws against gender discrimination are readily enacted, but they do not challenge the primacy or legitimacy of the career mystique (Moen & Roehling, 2004); they simply enable women to pursue (men's) lockstep life course if they "choose" to do so. When the topic moves from working men and women to working fathers and mothers, old value-laden theories about men's and women's distinctive roles of breadwinning and caregiving are often implicitly invoked. The mommy track of neotraditional arrangements that permit employed married women to prioritize family at a cost to their careers is often the implicit solution (Clarkberg & Moen, 2001; Moen & Sweet, 2003; Moen & Yu, 2000; Schwartz, 1989), precisely because this arrangement permits their husbands to remain primary breadwinners.

Most corporations adopt the rhetoric of "family-friendliness," but their policy enactments tend to be symbolic (Still & Strang, 2003). Those businesses offering options for time off, for example, find few takers, given that employees see exercising such options as a path away from security or advancement. Studies have shown that the threat of federal action is a powerful motivator for corporate actors to change their policies on the books (see, e.g., Dobbin & Kelly, 1999). Note, however, that most work-family scholars focus on individuals, not families, and even less on corporate or government policy actors. Thus we know something about how individuals and couples manage the multiple strands of their lives, but very little about the impediments to policies facilitating this integration. Moreover, most research by family scholars does not make its way to the desks of policy makers, meaning that policy actors' own implicit theories and beliefs continue to drive their decision making.

WHY THEORY NEEDS POLICY AND VICE VERSA

Urie Bronfenbrenner frequently recalled the statement of his own mentor, Kurt Lewin, that nothing is so "useful" as a good theory. We have thus far made the point that there are always theories behind proposed policies, theories about both the nature of the problem and what will "fix" it. Social scientists can make valuable contributions to the policy process by *helping to frame the issues or matters of concern.* This entails summarizing what we know and what we have good theoretical reasons to believe in particular substantive domains. For example, research has documented that employment has positive implications for men and women, as well as for children, but only under certain conditions. Clarifying those conditions can do much to qualify the "all or nothing" dichotomies so common in policy making (such as pigeonholing the "employed" versus the "unemployed," or "welfare recipients" versus those who are "self-supporting"). Life-course scholars have shown that people and families move in and out of such categories, pointing to the importance of considering the *pathways, risks,* and *contingencies* that shape what are defined as "problem families" or "families with problems." Research evidence is rarely definitive; the state of our knowledge is such that we will always talk in terms of probabilities and possibilities, not "truths." But we have much to contribute.

Bronfenbrenner and Lewin also pointed out that nothing is more useful to theory advancement than social policy. Like Bronfenbrenner and Lewin, leading family scholars (such as Hill, 1964) have seen no need to divorce theory development from policy development and vice versa. That is because policy issues force us to scrutinize our own theories, both explicit and implicit, against the backdrop of real-world concerns.

Academic researchers have special skills, methodologies, and perspectives that can illuminate the logic of various problem definitions and policy solutions, and such scholars can make real contributions by participating in ongoing policy debates (see Featherman & Vinovkis, 2001). But to do so requires a willingness to move beyond "pure" theory and "interesting" questions to bring the weight of theory and evidence to bear on compelling social and societal concerns. This means using concepts that can be operationalized in ways that are meaningful to those outside academia and developing multidisciplinary theories framed in ways that have clear policy relevance. It also requires a commitment to outreach and dissemination; simply publishing in peer-reviewed outlets is insufficient for joining policy issues. As family scholars we can also strive to understand our own theoretical blinders, the ways all of us unwittingly accept and perpetuate the legitimacy of taken-for-granted assumptions about the ways things are and the ways things should be.

INTEGRATING THEORY, RESEARCH, AND POLICY

Theory, research, and policy are integrally linked to one another and to the dominant cultural models of the good life. Returning to our work-family example, the dynamic nature of family life, producing shifts in both family needs and resources, has been a central theme of family sociology since its beginnings, as the dynamic concept of career has been in occupational and organizational sociology. Both the "family cycle" and "careers" concepts focus attention on the temporal dimensions of social relations and social behavior as well as corresponding shifts in subjective evaluations of them. But family sociologists have concentrated almost exclusively on changes in family composition (e.g., Aldous, 1996; Hill, 1970) while occupational and organizational sociologists have emphasized occupational ladders (e.g., Barley, 1989). Scholars from both camps, however, have tended to equate "success" with income and occupational attainment, with biographical time a key consideration as the breadwinner (in family sociology) or the worker (in occupational sociology) advances up or remains stalled on the earnings/prestige hierarchy.

Until the 1970s, scholars typically viewed work and family as separate topics (Kanter, 1977). Since then, work-family conflict, spillover, and overload have mostly been theorized as individual or family problems, with little attention to their life-course dynamics or their embeddedness in the clockwork careers of unencumbered breadwinners. Only recently have scholars given theoretical attention to the simultaneous unfolding of occupational career stages in tandem with stages of parenting and family development. And yet the implicit relationship between family "careers" (Aldous, 1996) and occupational "careers" has a long history of exploration in the social sciences. Changing family composition and needs occur in the context of changing socioeconomic status and earnings (see Modell, 1978), frequently producing a disjunction between demands on the one hand and resources on the other. Family strategies of consumption and labor market behavior can, therefore, be seen as efforts to deal with a family's shifting economic fortunes over time (Goode, 1960). The emergence of the multidisciplinary life-course paradigm has produced an emphasis on the interlocking nature of work and family careers, placing them in the context of history, relationships, and strategic action (Elder, 1974). The family cycle theoretical framework, criticized for its focus on an invariant progression along a culturally prescribed path, has given way to a more realistic depiction of a range of interlocking work/family/leisure career paths, dynamically juxtaposed with one another and located in particular historical contexts (Moen, 2003). Life-course concepts of agency, planning, and synchronization serve to underscore families' strategies in seeking to fit between occupational and family careers (Moen & Wethington, 1992), suggesting that as family and occupational environments change across the life course, so do families' risks and vulnerabilities.

Drawing on this framework, a potentially useful theoretical model requires locating the work-family interlock on a moving platform of social and personal change. Such a life-course theoretical model proposes that we cannot understand the shifts in family and occupational circumstances without first understanding the deeply embedded gender schemata made visible by feminist theory (e.g., Becker & Moen, 1999; Bem, 1998; Coltrane, 1998; Moen, 2003; Moen & Roehling, 2004). Shifts in work, family, and gender inequality that occur over the life course produce gaps between resources and demands as well as corresponding shifts in individual family members' sense of control, possibility, and well-being. These shape men's and women's evaluations of their own performance and achievements. Thus institutionalized biographical patterns and adaptive strategies (shaping occupational and family conditions and experiences at different ages and stages) elicit gender-, class-, and race-linked self-perceptions and reflections about how well one is doing or has done in terms of occupations, family, or life generally as well as establish the frame for what one perceives to be possible in the future.

A life-course theoretical argument, augmented with feminist and social constructionist insights, locates work and family roles, relationships, effectiveness, and options within a multilayered potpourri of taken-for-granted rules and expectations as well as the dynamisms of biological, biographical, and institutional change. Consider the historical, political, economic, relational, and biographical embeddedness of the intersections between paid work and unpaid family work. *Historical* refers to particular times and places in which families and family members are located. *Political* relates to the body of existing law and norms that are either "on the books" or "in the heads" of people in the form of shared meanings and expectations. *Economic* points to the way the work-family interlock is vastly different in the global, risk economy of the 21st century than it was in the booming post–World War II economy of the 1950s. *Relational* captures the fact that seems to elude most contemporary thinking about this topic: that occupational and family "careers" are invariably negotiated between family members (such as couples) or arranged with an eye to existing or future family exigencies (such as becoming a parent or becoming a caregiver to one's own parents). *Biographical* emphasizes that prior decisions (to drop out of school, to return to school, to have or not have a child, to marry or divorce, to change jobs or remain with the same employer, to move in and out of the workforce, or to remain either in or out) shape current and future options, goals, and assessments.

Academic researchers are well positioned to explain the work-family "problem" as emanating from complex relations among labor markets, career trajectories, divisions of domestic labor, and parenting. Although these arrangements are often assumed to be determined by biological sex or cultural tradition, scholars now commonly see them as negotiated and renegotiated, constantly shifting in response to the exigencies of everyday family and work life. The pushes and pulls of family and work, in turn, are shaped by complex interactions among economic, political, social, and individual forces.

Social theories and methods of inquiry have advanced dramatically over the past 50 years, but scholars have just begun to figure out how to model social processes related to change over the life course and have barely begun to isolate probable causes and possible interventions. Only by moving beyond simple assumptions about individual causes of family problems will we be able to achieve policies that promote the life chances and life quality of all families. (For further discussion, see this volume's Web site.)

THEORETICAL THREADS WEAVE THE FOUNDATION FOR FAMILY POLICY RESEARCH

Lydia Blalock, *Rutgers, the State University of New Jersey*

Pamela A. Monroe, *Louisiana State University*

M. E. Betsy Garrison, *Louisiana State University*

Case Study

The most challenging point in most doctoral students' academic preparation is The Dissertation. I (Lydia Blalock) humbly approached this experience eager to demonstrate my superior intellect and advanced research skills. I knew I was fully prepared to engage in cutting-edge policy research, as I had completed (and excelled in) my graduate course work. The only challenge visible on the horizon was determining how to deflect the well-meaning guidance I expected to receive from my mentors (my coauthors). Let's face it, how long had it been since Monroe or Garrison had completed *their* graduate research methods courses? Ah, the haughtiness of inexperience!

My major professor (second author here and senior researcher) wisely offered me the incredible opportunity to design and implement Phase II of a multiyear study on the effects of the Personal Responsibility and Work Opportunity Reconciliation Act of 1996 (PRWORA; P.L. 104-193) on rural Louisiana families. I likened "my" project to a tapestry. The collected data would provide the threads, and I would serve as the master weaver to create a composite that would beautifully depict the women's shared post-PRWORA experiences so clearly that *any* policy maker would understand these women's lives. In other words, I would (in great humility) create a work of research art!

This project focused on the rural women's journey from welfare reliance to wage work. The primary research questions were as follows: Did the decline in Louisiana welfare caseloads translate into women in nonmetro parishes (counties) finding and keeping jobs? Were there any identifiable predictors for women who got jobs? Would these women be able to sustain employment and reach self-sufficiency?

The first step in producing any work of art is to start with a well-crafted design supported by a strong framework. I selected human ecology theory as the foundation for this research because it would allow me to emphasize the importance of adaptation and environmental context relative to the study of families and social policy. The family resource management model seemed the ideal version of the theory to use, as it focuses on the relationships among three systems: the family's microenvironment, the societal macroenvironment, and the natural/structural macroenvironment. Major shifts in any of the systems may cause a disruption in the family unit that requires an adaptive response.

I will digress a moment to inform you of my biases (not necessarily shared by my coauthors). I expected to find women and families who were in desperate straits because their environments had failed to provide them with the resources they needed to make a successful transition from welfare dependence to work reliance. In my humble opinion this view was totally supported by the chosen theoretical framework.

I used human ecology theory to guide my data collection choices. The theory supports the use of qualitative *and* quantitative approaches to triangulate information, which would allow me to capture the dynamics at work in the lives of families and to understand the complicated processes and interactions resulting from social policy. The research team collected macro-level, quantitative data to describe the larger environmental contexts of the women's lives. The data included information about the geographic area: population, community resources, economic opportunities, adult education facilities, transportation infrastructure, and poverty rates. The research team members also recorded their subjective impressions of the geography and culture to enrich the contextual picture of where the women carried out the tasks of their daily lives.

Individual micro-level data were provided by the research participants, collected through the qualitative research method of semistructured interviews on a variety of topics related to the women's experiences since the implementation of PRWORA. I developed a questionnaire to guide the interviews, and the research team was armed and ready to locate the original 84 participants from Phase I of the study. I discovered at this point that I knew little about the research *process*. I had assumed it would be relatively easy to find the original participants, as they had been interviewed only 12–18 months prior. I was forced to return often (much to my chagrin) to the senior researcher for suggestions on how to track down these rather elusive women. (Research methods courses do *not* cover everything!) Eventually, the team located and interviewed 52 women.

The interviews were tape-recorded, and once the tapes were transcribed I had all the materials I needed to weave my masterpiece. Well, not quite. After several false starts, my coauthors pointed out that the amount of data I had to deal with was too overwhelming—I had too many threads to keep together. Ouch, another blow to my image as crack researcher. We settled on a subset of cases that was much more manageable, and I was finally ready to unravel the secrets hidden within the data. I mined the transcripts carefully for matching and/or discordant threads and themes, and then drafted a case summary for each woman. I used these summaries as the starting point for further analyses.

The next step was to identify the threads that, when woven together, would most clearly predict women's work status, defined as either engaged in work-related activities or not engaged in such activities (i.e., employment, volunteer work, or vocational education). The socioeconomic threads for each woman included her age, the number of children living in the home, her previous employment, her educational attainment, and whether she had received vocational training and/or job readiness training. The contextual threads suggested by human ecology theory included region of residence, job availability, transportation infrastructure, and child-care availability.

I used a predictor-outcome matrix to display the data, as this is a useful tool for explaining differences between program or policy outcomes. I began the cross-case analysis eager to glimpse the design I knew would be revealed. My anticipation soon turned to dismay—there were no clear threads to follow! I was unable to identify any relationships between predictors and specific work-related activities. I had most certainly *not* envisioned this scenario. The difficulty lay in cases that did not fit the expected patterns—the disconfirming cases. I had failed to include some unidentified factors that could help predict the women's work status as well as provide clues as to whether these women would be able to sustain their efforts. The tapestry would not take shape if I could not identify the appropriate threads.

I returned to the original transcripts and individual case summaries, prepared to humble myself enough to completely trust the women's voices to guide my efforts. It was

CASE STUDY *continued*

during this pass through the data that an additional dimension, women's motivation to work, was revealed. Four specific threads were identified: receipt of government benefits, rent obligations, child support, and support from family members. These new threads, labeled "motivators," were added to the predictor-outcome matrix. A more focused picture began to emerge as I sorted the cases alternately by each predictor, motivator, or outcome variable. The "motivation" threads proved to be important!

But motivation did *not* fit my theoretical framework. I was forced to put aside my "I can do it myself, thank you" attitude and consult yet again with my coauthors. They suggested that I explore rational choice and behavioral change theories. Rational choice theory postulates that an individual will choose, from all known alternatives, the option that provides the most benefit for the least investment. That is, people act based on their assessment of risk, level of investment, and choice of consequences. Change theories emphasize that anyone engaged in the change process must be *motivated* to change. A concurrent shift in the individual's values is also required in order to achieve a permanent, second-order behavioral change.

I realized that for these women, engaging in work-related activities was the first-order change required by PRWORA, but the ability to find and sustain employment would require a second-order change. I assumed, in my haste to demonstrate the overall utility of my favorite theoretical perspective, that these formerly welfare-reliant women *could only react* to policy changes based on their environmental contexts. I had conveniently overlooked the "change" side of the "social policy produces behavioral change" equation.

A richer and more distinct portrait of the effects of PRWORA on these women and their families was produced through a careful interweaving of human ecology, behavioral change, and rational choice theories. Rational choice and behavioral change theories provide important guidelines for understanding

behavior *within any given environmental context*. The societal macroenvironment is critical for encouraging, facilitating, and sustaining second-order behavioral change, as the need for change is culturally and socially determined. For second-order change to be sustained, however, *the systems in which the family acts must also be changed*. Therefore, adapting to social policies requires (a) a motivation or stimulus, (b) a shift in values/beliefs, (c) the individual or family to make a rational choice between competing alternatives, and (d) an alteration of the individual's or family's environmental conditions. If these conditions are not successfully achieved, adaptation fails and individual or family well-being is threatened. The participants in this research project who were motivated to work would require an environment that would be supportive of their efforts in order to achieve the second-order change of sustained employment. These women at the very least needed access to jobs, transportation, and affordable child care, and that only barely begins to address the supports that formerly welfare-reliant women require to achieve the ultimate goal of family self-sufficiency.

The disparate threads finally blended into a tapestry that was rather different from, but no less compelling than, the one I had originally envisioned. The analyses were completed and the findings were more robust and relevant as a result of my listening to the data, reevaluating the theoretical perspective, and understanding (admitting?) the personal biases I had introduced into the research.

Another image was reconstructed during the course of this project. I learned that it takes much more than a few research methods courses and a well-defined ego to make an outstanding social scientist engaged in policy research. When I finally used the threads provided by my experienced mentors, interweaving them with my own foundation threads, *and* added several hefty threads of humility, it became clear that my personal tapestry will be a work in progress for some time to come.

Case Study

THOUGHTS ON FAMILIES AND PUBLIC POLICY AS VIEWED BY PHYLLIS MOEN AND SCOTT COLTRANE

Joan Aldous, *University of Notre Dame*

Phyllis Moen and Scott Coltrane deserve our commendation and perhaps our sympathy for attempting to place perceived social problems and perceived solutions within some theoretical framework. They define theory as "explanations" of relationships between various dimensions of the human experience. They describe social policies as "purposive courses of action, taken by . . . actors or sets of actors, about . . . particular issues or problems of concern." Although their definition of theory is adequate, I would specify social policy to make it "family policy," the focal concern of their policy discussion. To me, *family policy* refers to "objectives concerning family well-being and the specific measures usually taken by some public body to deal with them" (Aldous & Dumon, 1990, p. 1137). Thus my emphasis would be on the broad-based situation definition as problematic and the pressures on an institutional unit, often a state legislature or Congress, to do something about it. But my definition also includes workplace actions and those in other institutions relevant to families.

In her review of family policy developments in the 1990s, Karen Bogenschneider (2000, p. 1137) rightly criticizes various definitions of family policy as being too tied to action taken by government bodies, too restrictive as to the family areas covered, or too limited as to the types of families focused on. Thus, along with Moen and Coltrane, I assume the inclusion in family policy-making bodies of religious institutions, economic institutions, education institutions, and other agencies along with political bodies whose actions and reactions constitute portions of the family landscape.

The explanation of what goes on that makes an issue become an object of concern for some members of the public, and their public agitation the reason for some lawmakers to consider doing something about the matter, involves historical accounts and political service theorizing. As Moen and Coltrane note, what helps to explain the change from a situation of concern to only a few individuals to that situation's becoming a social problem would ideally be a theory. Alas, such ready-made and applicable theories do not currently exist in sociology. Thus we sociologists who are interested in family policy must make do with ideas and concepts developed and applied in other areas or turn to political science.

With respect to sociology, the concept of *human capital* that enables individuals to make a broader public aware of their judgment concerning troubling situations can be useful. If individuals have the education to be able to present their concerns in ways that can convince influential others or to be acquainted with who those others are, this is an advantage. Other human capital variables, such as higher income and professional/managerial occupations with the associated possibility of membership in social networks that include elected officials or persons in touch with such officials or persons in agencies in the areas of concern, also play a part in public policy making. The *social capital* concept of interpersonal skills that enable persons to present their concerns about a family issue to a broader audience or to interact effectively

DISCUSSION AND EXTENSION *continued*

with influential persons or persons close to the latter also is useful (Coleman, 1990). In the process, policy could be an outcome.

The focus on human and social capital variables widens the perspective on family policy. In their discussion of work and family issues, Moen and Coltrane wisely place these in a historical and social class perspective. They note such variables' effects on gender, with the lower education and greater economic dependence of women making them less likely to be hired and more likely to be fired during the period of the Great Depression in the 1930s. Even in today's world of higher unemployment and jobs lost to low-wage developing countries, White women (although not women in other racial/ethnic groups) are less apt to be recipients of dismissal slips in the United States. More highly educated than in the 1930s although still underpaid relative to men but benefiting from the equality push of the 1960s women's movement, they are not as likely to be dismissed as a group as they were in the past.

The opponents of defining a situation as problematic and in need of policy action should also be considered in family policy discussions. Thus it was not until the hard times of the Great Depression that much of the major social legislation in the United States became public policy. This includes social security, the minimum wage, the 40-hour workweek, and child labor laws.

My own work on family policy has included the child labor issue. Until the Fair Labor Standards Act of 1938, state laws regulated at what age children and youths could be gainfully employed. In 1920, for example, only 13 U.S. states required children under age 16 to have an eighth-grade education before holding a job, and 7 of those states granted exemptions to these laws. Thus 8.5% of children and youth 10 to 16 years of age were gainfully employed then (Abbott, 1924, pp. 18–19). An attempt to regulate child labor through an amendment to the U.S. Constitution was made in June 1924,

when both houses of Congress passed such an amendment supported also by President Calvin Coolidge. However, the required number of states never ratified it. Anti–women's suffrage groups, as well as factory and farming groups organized by the National Association of Manufacturers, encouraged those holding sentiments against the amendment to get out and vote. In addition, religious bodies with church schools, such as the Catholic Church, urged their members to vote against the amendment, fearing it would threaten their schools. The Catholic Church was especially influential in Massachusetts, where citizens against the amendment voted it down in a statewide referendum (Aldous, 1997, p. 80).

As Ridgeway (1997) has observed, a theory that might prove useful in policy research and/or analysis is that *expectation states theory*. It would seem useful for an examination of the issues and policies concerning paid employment, single mothers, and absent fathers that Moen and Coltrane commendably raise. It would also help to make sense of my own research on the failure of the Child Labor Amendment mentioned above. In a simplified form of the argument, Ridgeway's point is that our "taken-for-granted" ways of interacting with persons according to their ethnicity, power, and especially gender affect institutional processes. Ridgeway focuses primarily on the area of paid employment. She points out that the combination of outside employment and the household division of labor places women at a disadvantage. The gender hierarchy results in daily interaction patterns that devalue women's activities and are accepted without question. Interacting persons draw on widely accepted cultural scripts in their behaviors. These cultural scripts are especially well formulated and influential with respect to the dichotomous categories of gender. Such scripts lead both women and men to expect men to be more competent and powerful (Ridgeway, 1997, pp. 219–221).

DISCUSSION AND EXTENSION *continued*

What do these status expectations have to do with family policy? Much of the activity in this area, including volunteerism, is initiated and led by women (Wilson & Musick, 1997). Women continue to be the gender most responsible for interacting with family members, whether in the area of child care or that of household tasks (Aldous, Mulligan & Bjarnason, 1998; Coltrane & Adams, 2003). Thus they are more likely to be aware of, or to experience directly, family problems.

Before the Industrial Revolution and continuing after it well into the 20th century, family farms were how most American families made their livings. In 1900, farmers constituted 40% of the U.S. labor force, compared with 2% in 2000 (Goodloe, 2000). In farm families, women were involved in outside as well as inside activities, activities having to do with the paying products from the enterprise and that kept it going (Barnett & Rivers, 1998, p. 143). Thus the dual-earner family is not a recent development. And, as

Moen and Coltrane wisely note, low-income women have long been in the paid labor force, often working cleaning the houses of the more affluent or doing factory work, as did their children (Coontz, 1992, pp. 12–13).

However, as in the case of single mothers, there is no ready-made theory to make sense of dual-earner families. Again, human capital and social capital factors such as women's increased education and the lesser economic interdependence of women and men assist in accounting for the increasing numbers of single mothers and dual-earner couples in the body politic. Certainly feminism, as a consequence of the expectation states that persons have in dealing with one another, is a movement that has affected family policy. But feminism is more an orienting perspective than a full-blown theory and is more associated with political policy than with family policy. And so we are sadly left with the conclusion that the theoretical spotlight on families and social policy is noteworthy more for its darkness than for its light.

REFERENCES

Abbott, G. (1924). [Testimony]. In *Hearings before the Committee on the Judiciary, House of Representatives, Proposed Child Labor Law Amendment to the Constitution of the United States* (pp. 17–28, 30–58). Washington, DC: Government Printing Office.

Aldous, J. (1990). Specification and speculation concerning the politics of workplace family policies. *Journal of Family Issues, 11,* 355–367.

Aldous, J. (1996). *Family careers: Rethinking the developmental perspective.* Thousand Oaks, CA: Sage.

Aldous, J. (1997). The political process and the failure of the Child Labor Amendment. *Journal of Family Issues, 18,* 71–91.

Aldous, J., & Dumon, W. (1990). Family policy in the 1980s. *Journal of Marriage and the Family 52,* 1136–1152.

Aldous, J., Mulligan, G., & Bjarnason, T. (1998). Fathering over time: What makes the difference? *Journal of Marriage and the Family, 60,* 809–820.

Barley, S. R. (1989). Careers, identities, and institutions: The legacy of the Chicago school of sociology. In M. B. Arthur, D. T. Hall, & B. S. Lawrence (Eds.), *The handbook of career theory* (pp. 41–65). Cambridge: Cambridge University Press.

Barnett, R. C., & Rivers, C. (1998). *She works/he works: How two-income families are happy, healthy and thriving.* Cambridge, MA: Harvard University Press.

Becker, P. E., & Moen, P. (1999). Scaling back: Dual-career couples' work-family strategies. *Journal of Marriage and the Family, 61,* 995–1007.

Bem, S. L. (1998). *An unconventional family.* New Haven, CT: Yale University Press.

Bennett, W. J. (1992). *The de-valuing of America: The fight for our culture and our children.* New York: Summit.

Best, J. (1987). Rhetoric in claims making. *Social Problems, 34,* 101–121.

Best, J. (1990). *Threatened children: Rhetoric and concern about child-victims.* Chicago: University of Chicago Press.

Blumer, H. (1971). Social problems as collective behavior. *Social Problems, 18,* 298–306.

Bogenschneider, K. (2000). Has family policy come of age? A decade review of the state of U.S. family policy in the 1990s. *Journal of Marriage and the Family, 62,* 1136–1159.

Bornstein, L. (2000). Inclusions and exclusions in work-family policy. *Columbia Journal of Gender & Law, 10*(1), 77–124.

Chafetz, J. S. (1990). *Gender equity: An integrated theory of stability and change.* Newbury Park, CA: Sage.

Clarkberg, M., & Moen, P. (2001). Understanding the time-squeeze. *American Behavioral Scientist, 44,* 1115–1136.

Coleman, J. S. (1990). *Foundations of social theory.* Cambridge, MA: Belknap.

Coltrane, S. (1996). *Family man: Fatherhood, housework, and gender equity.* New York: Oxford University Press.

Coltrane, S. (1998). *Gender and families.* Thousand Oaks, CA: Pine Forge.

Coltrane, S., & Adams, M. (2003). The social construction of the divorce "problem": Morality, child victims, and the politics of gender. *Family Relations, 52,* 363–372.

Coltrane, S., & Hickman, N. (1992). The rhetoric of rights and needs: Moral discourse in the reform of child custody and child support laws. *Social Problems, 39,* 400–420.

Coontz, S. (1992). *The way we were: American families and the nostalgia trap.* New York: Basic Books.

Corbin, J., & Strauss, A. L. (1988). *Unending work and care: Managing chronic illness at home.* San Francisco: Jossey-Bass.

Dobbin, F., & Kelly, E. (1999). Civil rights law at work: Sex discrimination and the rise of maternity leave policies. *American Journal of Sociology, 105,* 455–492.

Edelman, M. J. (1977). *Political language.* New York: Academic Press.

Elder, G. H., Jr. (1974). *Children of the Great Depression.* Chicago: University of Chicago Press.

Elison, S. K. (1997). Policy innovation in a cold climate. *Journal of Family Issues 18,* 30–54.

England, P. S. (1992). *Comparable worth: Theories and evidence.* New York: Aldine de Gruyter.

Featherman, D. L., & Vinovkis, M. A. (Eds.). (2001). *Social science and policy-making: A search for relevance in the twentieth century.* Ann Arbor: University of Michigan Press.

Gamson, W. A. (1985). Goffman's legacy to political sociology. *Theory and Society, 14,* 605–622.

George, L. K. (2003). What life-course perspectives offer the study of aging and health. In R. A. Settersten, Jr. (Ed.), *Invitation to the life course: Toward new understandings of later life* (pp. 161–188). Amityville, NY: Baywood.

Gerstel, N., & McGonagle, K. (1999). Job leaves and the limits of the family and medical leave act. *Work and Occupations, 26,* 510–534.

Goode, E., & Ben-Yehuda, N. (1994). *Moral panics: The social construction of deviance.* Oxford: Blackwell.

Goode, W. (1960). A theory of role strain. *American Sociological Review, 25,* 483–496.

Goodloe, C. (2000). *Where have all the oats and horses gone? Changes in U.S. agriculture over the 20th century.* Washington, DC: U.S. Department of Agriculture.

Gusfield, J. R. (1996). *Contested meanings: The construction of alcohol problems.* Madison: University of Wisconsin Press.

Harrington Meyer, M. (Ed.). (2000). *Care work: Gender, labor, and the welfare state.* New York: Routledge.

Hays, S. (2003). *Flat broke with children: Women in the age of welfare reform.* New York: Oxford University Press.

Hill, R. (1949). *Families under stress.* New York: Harper.

Hill, R. (1964). Methodological problems with the development approach to family study. *Family Process, 3,* 5–22.

Hill, R. (1970). *Family development in three generations.* Cambridge, MA: Schenkman.

Hochschild, A. R. (with MacHung, A.). (1989). *The second shift: Working parents and the revolution at home.* New York: Viking.

Hoffman, L. W., & Youngblade, L. M. (1999). *Mothers at work: Effects on children's well-being.* Cambridge: Cambridge University Press.

Holstein, J. A., & Miller, G. (2003). *Challenges and choices: Constructionist perspectives on social problems.* New York: Aldine de Gruyter.

Kanter, R. M. (1977). *Men and women of the corporation.* New York: Basic Books.

Komarovsky, M. (1940). *The unemployed man and his family.* New York: Dryden.

Lakoff, G. (2002). *Moral politics: How liberals and conservatives think.* Chicago: University of Chicago Press.

Lipsky, M. (1980). *Street-level bureaucracy: Dilemmas of the individual in public services.* New York: Russell Sage Foundation.

Marks, M. R. (1997). Party politics and family policy: The case of the Family and Medical Leave Act. *Journal of Family Issues, 18,* 55–70.

Modell, J. (1978). *Patterns of consumption, acculturation, and family income strategies in late nineteenth-century America.* Princeton, NJ: Princeton University Press.

Moen, P. (1989). *Working parents: Transformations in gender roles and public policies in Sweden.* Madison: University of Wisconsin Press.

Moen, P. (Ed.). (2003). *It's about time: Couples and careers.* Ithaca, NY: Cornell University Press.

Moen, P., & Forest, K. B. (1999). Strengthening families: Policy issues for the twenty-first century. In M. B. Sussman, S. K. Steinmetz, & G. W. Peterson (Eds.), *Handbook of marriage and the family* (2nd ed., pp. 633–663). New York: Plenum.

Moen, P., & Han, S. K. (2001). Gendered careers: A life course perspective. In R. Hertz & N. L. Marshall (Eds.), *Working families: The transformation of the American home* (pp. 42–57). Berkeley: University of California Press.

Moen, P., & Roehling, P. V. (2004). *The career mystique: Cracks in the American Dream.* Lanham, MD: Rowman & Littlefield.

Moen, P., & Sweet, S. (2003). Time clocks: Couples' work hour strategies. In P. Moen (Ed.), *It's about time: Couples and careers* (pp. 17–34). Ithaca, NY: Cornell University Press.

Moen, P., & Wethington, E. (1992). The concept of family adaptive strategies. *Annual Review of Sociology, 18,* 233–251.

Moen, P., & Yu, Y. (2000). Effective work/life strategies: Working couples, work conditions, gender, and life quality. *Social Problems, 47,* 291–326.

Reskin, B., & Padavic, I. (1994). *Women and men at work.* Thousand Oaks, CA: Pine Forge.

Ridgeway, C. L. (1997). Interaction and the conservation of gender inequality: Considering employment. *American Sociological Review, 62,* 218–235.

Roberto, K. A. (1988). Women with osteoporosis: The role of the family and service community. *Gerontologist, 28,* 224–228.

Roberto, K. A., & Reynolds, S. (2001). The meaning of osteoporosis in the lives of rural older women. *Journal of Health Care for Women International, 22,* 599–611.

Schneider, J. W. (1985). Social problems theory: The constructionist view. *Annual Review of Sociology, 11*, 209–229.

Schwartz, F. N. (1989). Management women and the new facts of life. *Harvard Business Review, 67*(3), 65–76.

Smith, D. E. (1993). The standard North American family: SNAF as an ideological code. *Journal of Family Issues, 14*, 50–65.

Spector, M., & Kitsuse, J. I. (1987). *Constructing social problems.* Hawthorne, NY: Aldine de Gruyter.

Still, M., & Strang, D. (2003). Institutionalizing family-friendly policies. In P. Moen (Ed.), *It's about time: Couples and careers* (pp. 288–309). Ithaca, NY: Cornell University Press.

Tronto, J. C. (2001). An ethic of care. In M. B. Holstein & P. B. Mitzen (Eds.), *Ethics in community-based elder care* (pp. 60–68). New York: Springer.

Williams, J. (2000). *Unbending gender: Why family and work conflict and what to do about it.* New York: Oxford University Press.

Wilson, J., & Musick, M. (1997). Who cares? Toward an integrated theory of volunteer work. *American Sociological Review, 62*, 694–713.

• Part V

PREPARING THE
NEXT GENERATION
OF FAMILY SCHOLARS

• Twenty-three

COLLEGE PROFESSORS' CONVERSATIONS ABOUT TEACHING FAMILY THEORIES

Velma McBride Murry, *University of Georgia*

Paul C. Rosenblatt, *University of Minnesota*

Elizabeth Wieling, *University of Minnesota*

This chapter is a summary of conversations among the three of us regarding our personal experiences as college professors teaching family theory courses to graduate students. In these conversations, we discussed our philosophical views about teaching such courses and the issues with which we have grappled in our family theory teaching. We gave particular attention to our goals for students enrolled in these courses. We shared some thoughts about establishing a classroom environment in which we are able to express our own views about the courses, including defining *theory* and *family*, without holding back our own voices and opinions (Marks, 1995) while empowering students to claim their rightful authority over their own thinking and learning. We spent much time discussing the importance of recognizing the significance of social and historical context in theory construction, as well as the need to consider a variety of perspectives in applying theoretical concepts to families' everyday lives. We also examined the practical issues we face in developing our courses. We questioned whether greater consideration should be given to teaching about family theory or to giving students tools to develop their own theories in terms of usefulness, flexibility, and clarity. We discussed other teaching issues as well, particularly ways to incorporate theory into courses that emphasize research on particular topics in family science. We ended our dialogue by summarizing the main ideas we had addressed.

We began our discussion by sharing our philosophical views about teaching family theory courses. We agreed considerably about the purpose and usefulness of family theories, and about the appropriate terms to describe these concepts. *Theories* are tools that organize information, make managing large bodies of research easier, and guide study design. As Wieling noted, "Good research requires a theoretical underpinning of what's worth focusing on and knowing." Murry extended this, remarking, "Theories also provide guidance on what, how, and where to intervene." Theories direct communication and the exchange of information by establishing a common language. They are used to build frameworks for understanding and extending knowledge in ways that enable individuals not only to explain but also to cope with changes in themselves, their families, and the larger society.

Our conversation ended with a discussion of our views about communicating our personal philosophies to students. What "take-home" messages do we want to give the students enrolled in our courses? Rosenblatt's comment summarizes our responses: "My goal is to challenge the basic assumptions that students bring to the course that society imposes on them, in addition to having students learn how to think, see, question, organize, and make sense." To this observation, Wieling added, "Not only to understand how I, as their instructor, and other scholars understand theory but also to make the theories their own and think about how the theory can help them deal with their own issues." The conversation about philosophical views ended with Murry emphasizing the importance of students' becoming critical consumers of theory in ways that encourage questions about what is considered "normal" or "appropriate" and the extent to which theories are inclusive versus exclusive in explaining families' experiences. In the following sections, we blend our philosophical views with issues related to teaching family theory.

ISSUES IN DEFINING FAMILY THEORY

One of the first tasks in teaching a family theory course is to sell theory to students, because in the family field many scholars focus on research findings to the exclusion of theory (Knapp, 2002). Furthermore, much of today's work rejects the sweeping, generalized view that family theory typically provides (Daly, 1997; Rosenau, 1992). A teacher can

honor a great deal of family research and accept the insights it provides while making a case for the value of family theory. Family theories are, among many things, starting places for understanding families, generating research, critiquing family publications, and providing overviews of specific writings.

After students learn to appreciate the value of family theory, the teacher must decide which theories they should learn. Theory education in any field is partly about teaching students the theories, and the texts that define them, that are considered most important. In the family field, however, there is no consensus concerning which theories are most important (Daly, 1990). Although the family theoretical canon has been defined in textbooks and articles since the early 1970s (e.g., in White & Klein, 2002), its content is fluid and changing. Theories that some family scholars consider central are ignored by others. Some theories are tied to narrow areas of empirical research, such as marital satisfaction. Even when scholars agree on the canon's contents, they still may disagree on the exact versions and forms of the theories that should be included. For example, many different versions of family systems theories exist.

Teachers, therefore, have many options from which to choose when deciding which theories to include in their courses. In choosing the family theories they teach, instructors may review widely cited works, such as those by Thomas and Wilcox (1987) and White and Klein (2002) or the collections edited by Burr, Hill, Nye, and Reiss (1979) and Boss, Doherty, LaRossa, Schumm, and Steinmetz (1993). We have used these and other sources to decide what to teach as well as what to include in this chapter.

A teacher's choice of theories to include in a course is governed by many factors. For example, there may be an established course curriculum for which an outline already exists. The teacher's academic unit may have a particular emphasis, such as combining human development with family studies, which would make developmental and socialization theories that have implications for family relationships valuable to include in the course.

THEORY AND CONTEXT
ARE INSEPARABLE

Just as families do not function in a vacuum but are influenced by the social systems in which they reside, theories are constructed within social and historical contexts (Hill, Murry, & Anderson, in press). Theory construction is inseparable from contextual processes. Theoretical assumptions, propositions, concepts, and ways of thinking about family phenomena, purposes, functions, and relations to society are all influenced by events occurring in the world and in the particular society in which the theory was formed.

During our development of this chapter, we talked about the strategies that we have used in our courses to help students understand the connection between theory and context. "What I have found that works," Murry noted, "is to introduce each theory by inviting students to take a trip back in time, relying on their history courses, and share with the class anything that comes to mind about the period of time in question." The students' ideas often are related to specific social movements, political ideologies, and economic circumstances. To further the inquiry, Murry asks her students to link the theory's intellectual context with opinions about family life and human behavior and with definitions of ideal family functioning. Finally, she asks the students to think critically about the generalizability of the theory and its applications across family composition, ethnic/racial groups, economic groups, family types, gender, sexual orientation, and so forth. Through this process, the students often become aware that certain subgroups are not well represented in family theories. For example, students often discover that theory development gave little attention to the historical significance of the civil rights movement in the United States and other major social and political events of the 1960s and 1970s. This recognition often serves as a bridge to the final orientation exercise, in which Murry poses questions that encourage students to think critically about the theory's

usefulness for today's families and society. To illustrate this point, Murry has included an assignment in which students examine a specific proposition from a theory developed decades ago, and the class discusses ways in which the proposition does or does not apply to a contemporary family issue. In a follow-up discussion, students critically evaluate the proposition and provide suggestions regarding how it could be revised to be more applicable to today's families.

This exercise emphasizes the importance of critiquing theoretical scope to determine whether the theory reaches beyond historical time. The following comment from a student during this activity illustrates the interdependence of theory and context quite clearly:

> Actually, connecting what was happening in society at the time the theory was constructed not only helps me remember the theory and how to use it but it also helps me see how theories, families, and society have changed over time.

Another student noted:

> Like the movies we see, the music we listen to, the clothes we wear, the food we eat, and the way we view the world during our lifetime, theories are a reflection of the times in which they are embedded. . . . theories and the field of family studies reflect the evolution of intellectual thoughts about family and how this "family thought" is influenced by other aspects of our social life.

Murry noted that over her years of teaching family theory, this activity has helped students to develop critical thinking skills by emphasizing that the explanations offered in various theories are not unconditional. Families influence and are influenced by the contexts in which they live. For this reason, scholars need to be aware of the significance of time and place when using theory. Time and place are central to the explanations that theories offer concerning family characteristics and events. Cultural, political, religious, organizational, and historical influences all contribute to theories. Essentially, "the specification of a theory's boundaries, conditions or domains of applicability revolves around the historical or cultural conditions under which the theory applies" (Knapp, 1984, p. 35).

For these reasons, it is important for instructors in family theory courses to give their students opportunities to "think outside the box." For example, students can test a theory's flexibility by applying it to current family processes, behaviors, and ideas about the behaviors' causes. Given that events and new technologies have inspired a variety of research studies, teachers can encourage students to think critically about a theory's usefulness in a culture of widespread social unrest, terrorism, and economic downturns. Such a culture provides a natural setting in which students can examine whether particular theories remain useful over time as well as explore the challenges that confront families in the 21st century.

Many of the social, political, and economic events that make up the contexts in which family theories are formed, however, are not new. Families developed relationships, reared children, and organized their daily lives before the specific situations that exist in today's world arose. Although the recent occurrence of particular events in the United States has led social scientists to pay increased attention to such events, decades ago family theoreticians did not have the opportunity to base their work on such experiences. Recent historic occurrences in the United States have inspired much scientific inquiry, but they have had less impact on the development of family theory.

When family scholars do not consider the ways in which context shapes theory development and application, inaccuracies result. In fact, leaving out context when applying family theory leads to overgeneralization about families and their experiences (Pratto, 2002). Teachers must tell their students clearly that

most family theories were developed by men of European descent who held strong views about the best ways for families to work and grow. Their value systems were built on deep-seated ideas about economic and political equality, assimilation, and racial/ethnic minorities (Dilworth-Anderson, Burton, & Johnson, 1999). Those who teach the next generation of family scientists are responsible for encouraging them to restructure theoretical assumptions, expand key concepts, and define "family" and "marriage" in ways that reflect social diversity. New scholars also must reframe theoretical ideas that explain and predict families' characteristics and experiences, exploring the give-and-take between family and society in designing new theories that include "uniqueness," "sameness," and "relevance." This process will create new ways of using family theory by getting away from overgeneralizations. For example, rather than assuming that families' problems arise solely from their members' personal problems, family scientists should explore the conditions and contexts associated with particular family outcomes.

Finally, those who teach family theory courses must recognize the influence of their own experiences, histories, and individual worldviews on their teaching. In our dialogue about this chapter, we discovered that although we share similar philosophies about the importance of theory to family studies, in our teaching we draw on experiences from our own personal journeys. Our experiences have influenced our choices about which theories to include and which to exclude, course designs, supplemental readings, structured learning activities, and so forth. Our discovery of the sameness and the distinctiveness in our teaching of family theory courses reminds us that, as Pratto (2002) observes, just as historical, social, and political contexts influence human behavior, they also shape the "actor's" (in this case, the instructor's) viewpoint.

● **SPOTLIGHT ON THEORY**

WALKING THE WALK: TEACHING SYSTEMS THEORY BY DOING THEORY

Gail G. Whitchurch, *Indiana University–Purdue University Indianapolis*

For the first 17 years I taught family courses, I unintentionally covered *systems* in a *linear* fashion. Grouping systems concepts in logical order, I defined terms and gave relevant family examples. I used a mobile (Satir, 1972) to demonstrate systems concepts visually, and I gave students an assignment in which they had to use systems concepts for an analysis of a family interview. I thought I was teaching effectively, but I was often disappointed that students' *thinking* about families as systems was perfunctory.

About a year ago, I literally smacked myself in the forehead when I came to the realization that I had been assuming that students could use a list of concepts and examples to develop "systems thinking" (Whitchurch & Constantine, 1993), which I had long emphasized over systems as a formal theory. I had taken it for granted that once students knew systems concepts, they could use the concepts to think about families as systems. To describe that approach in current vernacular, I was talking the talk, but I was not walking the walk. Since my forehead-smacking incident, I now help students develop systems *thinking* by having them *do* theory: They now observe families initially and learn systems terms afterward.

Emphasizing research ethics, human subjects protections, and the utilization of all five senses in conducting observations, I assign students to observe, in public places, groups of strangers that they perceive to be families. I have them conduct their observations in pairs, and they can take field notes in any format they choose.

At the next class meeting, I hang a mobile in the front of the classroom without comment and ask the students about the locations where they did their observations. Shopping malls are invariably mentioned, so I relate families to socioeconomic circumstances and introduce the term *suprasystem*. I then ask the students to share some of the specific observations in their notes. I write these observations across the full width of the blackboard, covertly grouping observations that are conceptually similar. For example, I record the observation "The mother said 'no' when the children wanted to have a friend stay overnight" near "The parents smiled when their son showed them the necklace he had bought for his girlfriend."

When clusters of observations appear, I introduce relevant systems concepts. Continuing with the example above: Using leading questions if necessary, I ask the students what these observations might indicate about these two families. Eventually, someone ventures that these parents are communicating their feelings about family members interacting with non–family members. I then introduce the term *boundaries* and define it, using the mobile to demonstrate. I dovetail related systems concepts such as *homeostasis* and *cybernetic* feedback, introducing concepts in logical order, just as

(continued)

● *SPOTLIGHT ON THEORY continued*

I once did when I taught from an unintentionally linear perspective. After all major systems concepts have been covered, I introduce general system theory, its sociohistorical context, and midrange family systems theories that are descended from family research and practice in various disciplines and specialty areas.

Teaching family systems this way takes three or four class meetings, but the time is well invested. Students taught with this approach are comfortable with family systems concepts and use systems terms in asking questions and giving opinions. Most significant is the fact that I see them developing systems thinking: They develop a complex understanding of family relationships as systemic rather than cause and effect, and they also think systemically about families at macro levels. Compared with their predecessors, students in my family courses since I gained my forehead-smacking insights are walking the walk. As one student told me recently while she was working on her family interview project, "This paper is taking a long time—there sure was a lot less to write about before systems thinking." ●

THE CORE CURRICULUM
FOR FAMILY THEORY

One challenge that family theory instructors confront is deciding which theories to emphasize. Many decide by following their own personal values and scholarly priorities. We emphasize theories that are widely taught in the family field, that are broadly usable, and that embrace diversity across and within families. We include both theories that have long histories in the field and theories that have emerged relatively recently. Thus our courses might include systems/ecology, symbolic interaction/social construction, feminist, conflict, and exchange theories as well as family life-course and developmental theories.

Systems/ecology theory is valuable because it provides insights into interactions among family members and highlights the effects of family ecology. Exploration of family ecology can address diversity, including the effects of discrimination toward families of color and families formed by gay adults. Ecology theory also deals with the challenges facing immigrant families and other families that carry out their daily activities as part of more than one culture, as well as the circumstances that make the lives of blue-collar families quite different from those of white-collar families. Ecology theory also addresses the problems that low income creates for families, including poor housing, dangerous surroundings, inferior schools, inadequate health care, and underemployment.

HUMAN ECOLOGY THEORY FOR THE 21ST CENTURY

Lillian A. Phenice, *Michigan State University*

Robert J. Griffore, *Michigan State University*

The human ecological approach is a viable method for scholars who seek to understand humans but realize that all individuals are nested within families and other contexts, such as the social-cultural environment, the human-built environment, and the natural physical-biological environment (Bubolz & Sontag, 1993). This intricate complexity of relationships has been called the web of life as well as a nonlinear dynamics of processes and patterns. A basic assumption of the human ecological approach is that we can improve our understanding of the family by describing and studying the principles that underlie all social organizations and systems.

The human ecological approach can be a unifying force in that it can help to build a bridge between the human sciences and ecological sciences. Family studies can encompass the fields of family ecology, social ecology, and psychological ecology, as well as other ecological areas. To accomplish the goal of bridging the gap between the current state of the human sciences and the science of family systems, we need a common language. That language is found in general system theory, the underlying concepts of which are based on universal system processes. These processes are found in all systems, such as human ecological systems and family ecosystems.

The foundation of the human ecological approach is an understanding of the universal general systems of processes and patterns that are common to all human ecosystems, including family ecosystems (Griffore & Phenice, 2001). The relationships among these processes and patterns can be described as a synthesis of structural, dynamic, governing, information-processing, interrelationship, disruptive, and life process component parts. Although each of these components is separately identified, in actuality all of the components form a web of relationships that is more than the sum of its parts: an ecosystem.

In family ecology, the term *structural* refers to the structure of the family. *Dynamic* refers to flows of energy through the family system, leading to change. *Governing* variables, such as goals, values, rituals, needs, and strategies, regulate the family system. *Information-processing* refers to information sources and how information is used. *Interrelationship* refers to the quality of social interactions and decision-making processes. *Disruptive* variables affect dynamic processes and may impinge on the future of the family. *Life process* refers to the development and growth of an adaptive system and quality of life.

Although not acknowledged as elements of general systems, discrete theoretical orientations for each of these component parts make up a family. These orientations are

(continued)

● *SPOTLIGHT ON THEORY continued*

represented in various chapters of the 1993 *Sourcebook of Family Theories and Methods* (Boss et al., 1993); they include structural functionalism, symbolic interactionism, social conflict, family development theory, and communication theory. Researchers working from these separate orientations have established the groundwork for understanding family systems; however, they have studied only particular aspects of the whole. The human ecological approach takes a step toward uniting all of these component parts in the interest of developing a better understanding of the complex family system as it adapts to a rapidly changing environment. It promotes a synthesis of these separate approaches, a major paradigm shift in the human sciences, that will lead to investigation of the family as an ecosystem.

As Stephanie Coontz (1998) has noted, America's families are changing. Family scientists need a new perspective from which to study individuals who are tightly subordinated within their families and have little identity outside their families as well as individuals whose identities rest heavily on influences outside their families. We need a framework that allows for variations in processes and patterns in any family ecosystem. This way of thinking requires a major paradigm shift, one that will result in theory that can accommodate the intricate complexity of human ecosystems. ●

Symbolic interaction/social construction theories are essential partly because they deal with family members' disagreements about what is real, true, or important in life and the ways in which they reach common understandings. These theories emphasize the importance of social processes in creating, maintaining, and changing viewpoints so that families can work out agreements about the situations they face. Teaching these theories provides instructors with considerable freedom to deal with student diversity and scholarly understanding. When students become comfortable working with these theories, the atmosphere in the classroom often changes from "My way is right and yours is wrong" to "We can learn a lot from one another's differences."

Feminist theory is an essential topic because gender is of major importance in society and in students' lives. Some instructors may think that feminist theories are too ideological; however, many other theories are just as ideological, perhaps covertly rather than openly, about gender and the ways in which it intersects with race, class, and other variations. By teaching feminist theory, we expose students to systems of thinking that are critical of other theories and of the society in which they live (Daly, 1990). Learning about feminist theory stimulates students to consider viewpoints that may be new to them without demanding that they do more than understand those viewpoints. Feminist instruction (Blaisure & Koivunen, 2003) also can create an atmosphere that gets students involved and brings vitality to the whole course.

Conflict theory has received less attention from scholars than the other theories we have discussed. Nevertheless, its inclusion in a family theory course is useful because it goes against widely held ideas that conflict is abnormal and wrong.

Exchange theory is useful partly because it is built around a central value in Western societies: the maximization of personal profit, even in our most intimate relationships. Teaching this theory also provides opportunities for students to explore power in relationships.

Family life-course and family development theories have long-standing links to the study of families. In teaching these theories, instructors can help students explore several domains of family life and describe the dynamic systems of social interchanges and interdependencies that exist across and within families. These theories emphasize that family members have interlocking lives and developmental trajectories that are influenced by one another's differentially changing worlds (Bengtson & Allen, 1993).

● *SPOTLIGHT ON THEORY*

TEACHING THEORY 101A

Denise Berg, *Santa Monica College*

Learning takes place both inside and outside of the classroom; it takes place in ways we understand and in ways we do not. Here, I provide suggestions concerning the learning that takes place in the petri dish we call the classroom, looking for combinations that lead to almost alchemical reactions. Teachers matter, teaching styles matter, and the mixture of students in a class matters. Recent findings in the study of pedagogy suggest that alternative methods of teaching can be valuable. From a Vygotskian perspective, mentoring in its various forms can assist learners. Learning ought to be an interesting, exciting, and collaborative process.

Just as Picasso was a classically trained artist before he began to experiment, we should learn theory before we attempt to move beyond it. It is easy to say, "I am eclectic," but what that often really means is "I am not well versed in any theory." When we study child development, for example, we need to understand the fundamentals before we can build on them or alter them. The underpinnings of many theories of child development lie in whether they are based on nature, on nurture, or on a bit of both. The significance of genes versus the environment is a key theme in child development theory. In the film *Rock a Bye Baby,* we see in the case of monkeys (with regard to the research of Harry Harlow) the pivotal role of contact comfort as well as how different kinds of monkeys vary temperamentally. Over the course of the British documentary films *Seven Up, 14 Up,* and *21 Up,* we see a group of children grow into adults, and we can observe how they change and how they remain the same over time. We can ask, What impacts do class, gender, culture, mental illness, attachment, temperament, and education have on development?

Classroom and small group discussions afford teachers and students the opportunity to explore such concerns in depth. Additionally, assigned outside readings of the works of feminist authors such as bell hooks, Kathy Weingarten, and Dorothy Allison can breath life into the subjects of class, race, feminism, and narrative theory for students. Such authors help to make "the other" more real through their personal explorations.

At the colleges where I teach, the classrooms are filled with diversity of almost every sort. Students from many different backgrounds interact with one another in many

(continued)

• SPOTLIGHT ON THEORY *continued*

ways, including interviewing, debating, and participating in group projects. One of the activities I use is to have different groups study and then present to the entire class various theories about basic psychological concepts, such as psychoanalysis, behaviorism, and cognitive constructs. I also set up debates in which students compare and contrast theories of language learning. I assign Bowenian genograms to help students better understand family patterns, including unconscious processes that can be changed only through awareness. Students share their findings with one another and increase their understanding of both similarities and differences.

Teachers can also explain theory by exposing students to memoirs and fictional works, whether books or films, that present lived or potentially livable examples. For instance, Maya Angelou's *I Know Why the Caged Bird Sings* offers students living in Southern California the vicarious experience of being Black in the Deep South. They can also see how Angelou was shaped by both nature and nurture, and how her resilience allowed her to triumph personally and professionally. Films such as *Iris* can demonstrate the limits of brilliance when nature overtakes anything that nurture might have helped to create.

Classroom exercises and activities should be both relevant and engaging. In one exercise, I give students candy to help them understand the Gibsons' notion of perceived affordances of infants. I ask the students to pretend that they have just come from Mars; as they suck on lollipops, they can understand how infants perceive graspability and hardness. I have also worked with an English instructor to create a multidisciplinary class in which students wrote essays based on child observations, focusing on writing and behavioral skills, both important to academic learning.

I have found that there are endless ways to motivate and stimulate students. To what I have implied or suggested above, let me add my strongest recommendations for teachers:

1. Attend to issues of culture, class, race, and gender that arise in the classroom and *talk* about them.

2. Think about how *you* best learn. What have been your most effective active and passive methods?

3. Make students agentic. Give them the opportunity to take part actively in their own learning process through in vivo experiences both inside and outside the classroom. •

No one course can cover everything, but instructors can teach many theories in ways that bring in elements of other theories. For example, a teacher can add a radical/critical or feminist perspective to the discussion of almost any theory. Whatever theories an instructor may choose to teach, he or she must remember that the overall purposes of the course are to give students tools for examining their world, to help them to live satisfying lives, and to prepare them for continued learning and future professional careers. In preparing their curricula, instructors also must choose among theories they know relatively well and those with which they are less familiar. Teachers should not be criticized for including primarily those theories with which they are more familiar, but they should be encouraged to adopt strategies to expand their lists of "familiar theories." For instance, those who teach the same courses repeatedly might add new material each time a given course is offered. We all agree that one of the delights of teaching is the opportunity to explore new areas of knowledge with each offering, balancing those areas with theories that are more familiar. In this way, teaching a family theory course can become a personal and professional developmental process.

In teaching family theory courses, particularly at advanced levels, we have found that there are advantages to using primary sources—writings in which the theories being taught were originally defined, explained, and advocated. However, students may find such writings hard to read because of outdated language and the sexism, ethnocentrism, or other culture-bound features of the times in which they were written. Distinguishing between primary sources and the secondary sources that clarify and redefine theories can also be challenging. Some sources that technically are secondary are so groundbreaking that they are more appropriately classified as primary. Furthermore, primary sources are not necessarily superior to secondary sources in quality, wisdom, usefulness, interest, or timeliness; some may have been developed by people who simply knew how to use political power effectively within their fields. On the other hand, some wonderfully insightful and useful older primary sources may be overlooked. Nevertheless, it is important for students to learn how to read historically significant material, and material that contains offensive or difficult concepts—for example, the sexism evident in Berger and Kellner's "Marriage and the Construction of Reality" (1964)—can help students to understand the social context in which a theory was formed. Even if instructors use primary sources that are dated, their teaching does not have to be old-fashioned. The sources that teachers use can change in meaning and interpretation with time and context.

Some teachers may question the idea that students should learn a particular set of theories. Teaching theory, they may argue, is not a process of pouring knowledge into the minds of passive students; rather, it involves helping students to think confidently, insightfully, and creatively from multiple perspectives. We believe that knowledge of theories gives students credibility in the field and helps them to communicate with other family scientists, but in teaching theory courses, instructors must choose topics, readings, and tasks that stimulate rather than stifle the thinking process. From this perspective, the outcome of a theory course for students should not be the ability to recite memorized theoretical statements but the power to think flexibly.

Language is another issue. Each theory has its own language, a particular set of terms and definitions, and learning the language of a theory can tend to drown out other languages. Many family theories were developed between 1960 and 1990 by European American men (except for feminist theories, which were developed mainly by European American women). Teachers must consider the extent to which the languages of family theories make it difficult for students to use their own languages and make them less attuned to the insights that can come from considering various viewpoints (for example, those of hooks [1992, 1993] and other authors of color who are seldom cited in family studies). It is important to recognize that several key family theories tend to explain the concepts within them using a one-size-fits-all kind of language. Learning this language may lead students to pay less attention to the experiences of those who are oppressed, less powerful, and less likely to put their words into writing, to write in English, to have the power to get their ideas published, or to have the influence to become well-known in the family field.

The very definition of *theory* is itself an issue. Some critics assert that family theories are just wordy speculations or statements of common sense. Deciding what constitutes a theory becomes even more important if we are teaching students how to theorize. How do we teach students what theories are like? What belongs in the theory curriculum? Should we teach students a specific formula for making a set of ideas into a theory or building a theory on research findings? Should we give students a variety of models to define theory, or should we give them carte blanche to define theory for themselves?

TEACHING THEORY: APPROACHES AND STRATEGIES

Teaching family theory effectively is a complex task, in part because the individual, family, and community contexts in which theory is taught are unavoidably influenced by the teachers' own experiences of human life and the social world in artistic, biological, physical, social, historical, religious, and many other areas. We believe it is important to emphasize these seemingly unrelated areas because they play a potentially critical role in improving the content and process of the teaching of family theory. Although we see ourselves as systems thinkers, too often we do not incorporate knowledge from other fields of study into our course content and scholarly frameworks.

In our discussions while we were preparing this chapter, Wieling noted that some of her most successful teaching experiences have occurred when she used teaching strategies that drew both intellectual and emotional responses from students. By bringing out different levels of experience and knowledge, instructors can help students identify their own ideas by leading them to provide in-the-moment personal data that they can link to their studies. When students identify and understand the implications of different ways of comprehending, organizing, and synthesizing knowledge, they can form a basis for evaluating existing theories and developing new ones.

Another benefit that can come from teachers' awareness of their own positions regarding theory is that they can often readily translate this awareness into behavioral change and activism. For example, an instructor might integrate various forms of art, music, poetry, dance, and other types of expression into course curricula to provide students with an alternative language for understanding human relationships and family experiences. Each of us contends that our goal in the classroom is to become "multilingual," capturing as many expressions of experience as possible while helping students develop the skills necessary to work with diverse families. Lewis (1995) encourages family studies instructors to implement creative learning strategies that heighten students' awareness of issues of diversity, such as highlighting differences, pointing out instances of societal oppression, and recognizing one's own biases. Adding to this list, we emphasize that establishing respectful, challenging, and supportive relationships in the classroom is essential if family theory courses are to promote growth and mutual understanding. To develop such relationships, and to implement the kinds of teaching approaches that Thompson (1995) refers to as a "pedagogy of care," teachers must have an intimate understanding of themselves, of their students, and of the many interactions between themselves and their students. We believe that instructors can further these relationships by considering the issues raised in the following questions.

Language and Communication

- What types of information and sources are included in the course? Are nontraditional authors, journals, videos, and art considered, for example? (Instructors may want to consider including works by women and persons from a variety of cultures on their reading lists. Instructors might also present case examples in class that portray various family structures and values.)
- How is the course information communicated? That is, what teaching techniques are used to convey information?
- Is information shared back and forth between instructors and students as well as among students?
- How is the classroom structured, and how does that structure affect learning?
- Does patriarchy influence class structure or operations? If so, in what ways?
- Is diversity highlighted or hidden in the classroom? In what ways?

Self-Knowledge

- Do instructors thoroughly understand their own personal orientations, biases, prejudices, strengths, and limitations as they approach and interact with students and the course material?
- How do instructors perceive their influence on students through personal attributes such as ethnicity, gender, age, and political views?

- What fears or anxieties do instructors have about teaching the material?
- On what basis do instructors consider themselves qualified to teach family theory? How can they grow as they continue to teach the course?
- What unique contributions do instructors make to students' learning experiences? How can instructors evaluate their contributions?

• SPOTLIGHT ON METHODS

LINKING THEORY, METHODS, COMMUNITY WISDOM, AND LOCAL NEED

James M. Frabutt, *University of North Carolina at Greensboro*

When university-based family scholars collaborate with community practitioners, residents, and families, a host of opportunities arise to build family science *and* strengthen our local communities (Sherrod, 1999; Small, 1996). Among these are opportunities to teach, apply, and refine family theories. In an example of this phenomenon, community members (school principals, juvenile justice professionals, pastors, social service providers, residents, and law enforcement partners) and university-based faculty combined their resources and expertise to address youth violence (MacKinnon-Lewis & Frabutt, 2001). After a local needs assessment identified youth crime and violence as central community concerns, a diverse, multidisciplinary task group began strategizing ways to examine the issue systematically so that effective interventions could be developed.

The university partners in this collaboration were instrumental in couching the youth violence prevention initiative within a broader theoretical and conceptual framework: the "development and risk together" (DART) model (Williams, Guerra, & Elliott, 1999). This integrated framework draws on life-course development approaches and social-ecological theories of development, emphasizing the importance of developmental stages, multiple social contexts, and person-by-environment interactions.

The DART model provided an effective framework for the task group to pose research questions, select and implement appropriate methods, and interpret findings. Initially, the university team outlined the framework, but it came alive through the community partners' examples, insights, and reflections. One component of the task group's work was to identify locally relevant risk and protective factors for youth violence. Through that effort, a teaching opportunity emerged: to demonstrate how a sound theoretical

(continued)

● *SPOTLIGHT ON METHODS continued*

foundation can help to identify a suitable methodology. Community partners and researchers collaboratively designed a multimethod protocol to gather information from court-involved youth and their primary caregivers.

A "learn by doing" ethos emerged throughout the youth violence initiative. Various community members—including a pastor, a youth group leader, an outreach center coordinator, a guidance counselor, and a grandmother—were trained to conduct qualitative, open-ended interviews with youth and caregivers. Each interview lasted about 1 hour, and all interviews were conducted in the homes of the youth and their caregivers. The use of community-based interviewers increased the quality and overall validity of the one-on-one interviews. The experience exposed community members to a participatory method and to involvement in family research. One result was increased community capacity, so that participants were empowered to frame, construct, and begin to answer their own questions about youth and family development.

The community-based initiative provided instruction on how theory and conceptual frameworks help to interpret key findings. Findings from the youth interviews were framed according to the domains and developmental challenges outlined in the DART model. For example, the qualitative interviews revealed that youths' interpersonal conflicts within their peer group were often the triggers for conflicts that carried over into another context—that of the family. Moreover, the DART model encouraged the task force to ask questions about which contexts (e.g., school, neighborhood, or family) would be the best locations for preventive interventions. As with any good conceptual foundation, the DART model formed the basis for new and better research questions that could build on the information already collected.

The use of theory-based approaches in community projects such as the one described here is not without its share of obstacles and challenges. The university partners in such collaborations must be able to show the usefulness and relevance of their theories and discussions of methods, or they run the risk of sounding detached, esoteric, and overly academic. They must constantly link theory to reality by discussing how theory applies, by sharing insights, and by offering meaningful (often local) examples. When academic and community partners are able to engage in that manner, the thoughtful infusion of family theory into such projects leads to enhanced scholarship, action, and community change. ●

The Classroom "Audience"

- Do instructors understand the diverse range of "languages" spoken in the classroom?
- Can instructors speak these languages and communicate effectively with students?
- How can instructors recognize the diversity of languages in the class while making room for the creation of a common language?
- Have some students been left out of this process completely? If so, what are the instructors' responsibilities to them?
- How do instructors approach languages that they or their students have no interest in learning?
- Is the course designed to help students understand a variety of languages?
- What are the students' developmental stages—age, enrollment status, and life experiences?

Content

- Do instructors understand the political and educational implications of the material they present to students? (Resources for examining this issue include the course syllabus, class structure, highlighted objectives, order of topics, selection of readings, videos, texts, and so forth.)
- Does the course content present diversity in family types, theoretical perspectives, research methods, scholarly journals, videos, guest lecturers, and so forth?
- What ethical principles determine the course content and the ways in which it is presented? To what extent have instructors considered and developed strategies for dealing with highly sensitive and personal content that might be painful to some students? For example, if a student's religious values directly oppose the instructor's beliefs, how can the instructor protect that student from negative bias and prejudiced grading in the course?

Process

- How do instructors encourage dialogue about students' learning, thoughts, feelings, and experiences in the classroom?
- Are instructors committed to a lifetime of critical thinking and learning?
- How are instructors accountable for the quality of their teaching?
- How do instructors improve their knowledge, skills, and academic environment?

PRACTICAL CLASSROOM EXERCISES

We have found the following two exercises to be useful in our own classroom work. Both exercises highlight the importance of process in the creation of a classroom environment that encourages not only learning but critical thought.

Exercise 1. This exercise provides students with the opportunity to examine the processes involved in theorizing. Ask students to write down their own theories as far as they have developed them. Encourage them to record the processes they have gone through in developing and writing their theories. Have the students share drafts of their theories with others and then facilitate students' working together to identify each other's areas of improvement in the theorizing process and the language used to communicate the emerging theories. Ask those students who have borrowed and applied existing theories to present and justify their choices in class, both verbally and in writing. If students have combined theories, ask them to demonstrate how they merged different concepts and constructs across frameworks.

Exercise 2. This exercise is designed to stimulate students' thinking about multicontextual and context-specific theories. Ask one set of students to create a theory on a particular topic to apply to a cultural majority group, and ask another set of students to create a theory on the same topic to apply to one or more minority groups. When they have finished, have the class compare the theories. Are the theories so different that they cannot be combined into a single theory? This exercise can alert students to the ways in which theories may or may not benefit from the inclusion of contextual variables. A variation on this exercise is to ask racial majority students to write a majority family theory and a minority family theory while racial minority students do the same. When they are done, compare the theories. What do the students conclude about attempting to theorize outside of their own cultural groups? What are the implications and potential dangers of their conclusions?

HOT TOPICS: A BALANCING ACT IN THE CLASSROOM

In a classroom where diversity is valued and promoted, almost any subject can become a hot topic. Part of the challenge of teaching is becoming open to the many ways in which individuals' situations differ and contexts intersect. When teachers guide discussions, they often, in the same breath, oppress, liberate, reject, and accept those with whom they speak. Thus it is vital that instructors be aware of the topics their students may consider conflictual as well as the ways in which students face or avoid these topics. It is helpful for instructors to be clear about the frameworks that guide them when hot topics arise in the classroom.

We might envision instructors' approaches to hot topics as falling on a continuum. On one end, we find instructors who believe that their role is to facilitate discussion around difficult topics while maintaining a neutral stance to avoid influencing students' expressions and opinions. At the other end of the continuum are instructors who want to encourage open dialogue in the classroom while being as transparent as possible about their own beliefs. These instructors make their assumptions and biases explicit in the classroom and discuss with their students how power affects the discussion process and the topics that are addressed. Regardless of an instructor's position on this continuum, students' perceptions of the levels of safety and trust in the classroom environment typically determine the nature and scope of discussion when hot topics arise. Instructors must also be aware of any patterns that form in the classroom when particular topics are discussed—the groups who talk and those who are silenced, and the groups who feel powerful or powerless.

We believe that one of the major hindrances to productive engagement in difficult discussions in the classroom is the instructor's discomfort with tension and conflict. We encourage instructors to recognize their personal anxieties and learn to manage them in the classroom. This requires practice, ongoing consultation with colleagues, feedback from students, and a firm commitment to meaningful and challenging conversation in the classroom.

Instructors should also decide whether or not they believe that the classroom is an appropriate place to promote social activism. If they believe it is, do they promote or impose particular political agendas, and do they do so openly or subtly? More and more often, we hear students expressing the desire to "do something" in addition to talking about the problems facing families and society. We encourage activism as part of the classroom experience when it is openly integrated into the curriculum and used to help students learn critical thinking, experience the conversion of thoughts into action, and address the many facets of "real world" situations.

We find it helpful to examine the connection between teaching family theory and promoting social justice and activism at different levels and sublevels. For example, one may look at a course syllabus and notice that it is comprehensive in terms of its inclusion of multicultural sources and representation of diverse perspectives. How could an instructor evaluate the ways in which students might view this material? The process of reading itself takes on many different dimensions and levels. Further, how might the instructor interpret class discussion based on the readings? Will students and teachers be moved toward social justice and activism as a result of their classroom experiences? What would constitute activism in this setting? The broader point we want to emphasize is that although it is critical to develop a strongly diverse curriculum that is attuned to issues of social justice, it is not enough. The process through which the curriculum is implemented often defines its impact on student learning and adoption of social justice principles.

Topics that commonly elicit deep emotional reactions in family science classrooms include anything related to religion, race and ethnicity, social class, gender, political affiliation, sexual orientation, marriage, adoption, abortion, globalization, and war. (Another dimension that is seldom mentioned in discussions of classroom hot topics is appearance; this includes issues of weight, height, attractiveness, and health.) When these topics are considered in conjunction with such issues as domestic violence, substance abuse, family finances, teen pregnancy, unemployment, resilience, stress, and family strengths, they often become politically charged in ways that drive students to take extreme positions. This makes meaningful discussion difficult. We acknowledge the challenge that teachers face in attempting to create safe places for open discussions across such a vast range of topics while learning effective ways to confront and discuss these issues in the classroom.

To place the handling of hot topics in the classroom in some context, we invite instructors to consider how they might handle the following situations.

Case 1. Conflicting values: How to find a voice. In a graduate-level family theory course, a student expresses grave concern about the current status of families and asserts, "Families are deteriorating these days because we are a society without morals. . . . As long as we legalize abortion, condone same-sex relationships, and take religion out of the classroom, we will not be able to revert back to good family values." As the instructor, you are aware through your reading of the students' journals that other students in the classroom have ideas about and have had experiences involving abortion, homosexuality, and religious diversity. How do you respond to this student's comment in a way that respects this view without silencing others? What are the implications of your simply turning things over to the class by asking them to respond to this student? How can you use this situation to promote critical thinking and open communication? Is it possible to create a classroom environment in which each student feels he or she has a voice? How about an equal voice? How can you relate the knowledge you and your students gain through this experience to existing family theories? How can this knowledge inform the development of students' personal theories?

Case 2. The instructor's authority is challenged. Halfway through the semester in a graduate course on family theory, a student challenges you, the instructor, during class by saying, "You know, you talk a lot about multiculturalism and about respecting everyone's opinion . . . but I don't see you doing that in this class. You use examples that reinforce racist stereotypes, and I don't see you putting into practice what you teach." How do you respond? How do you hear and try to understand this student's frustration? How do you deal with your own frustration, anxiety, or anger in this situation? What implications does your response have for class interactions in the future? How do issues of respect and hierarchy influence your response? How can you use this experience to launch a discussion and evaluation of existing family theories that are also criticized for their lack of multicultural sensibility?

CONCLUDING REMARKS

We began developing this chapter by conversing about teaching family theory. From our conversations, we developed and exchanged ideas by outlining various topics and issues that we thought would be useful to our colleagues who want to guide students and add to their own professional toolboxes by providing learning opportunities that foster students' understanding and use of family theories. Thus this chapter reflects themes that emerged as we shared our own experiences, including issues with which we have grappled for years in developing and teaching family theory courses. Our conversations were challenging, supportive, validating, and refreshing. At the completion of this project, it was apparent to each of us that we would have benefited greatly from having this chapter to guide us when we began designing and teaching family theory courses. We also realized, however, that the experiences we gained because we did not have this information brought about the learning that provided the material for this chapter.

This project gave us a forum in which to reflect on those experiences that extend our thinking about the approaches we will use as we continue to grow and develop as family scholars, designing courses that will benefit those who enroll in them. After years of teaching family theory courses, we are still seeking the best and most effective ways of enhancing our own scholarship as we educate the next generation of family scholars. As we completed this chapter, each of us pondered the question of teaching effectiveness. How effectively have we taught the next generation? Our continuing efforts can be assessed in the following areas (Alpine & Harris, 2002; Marks, 1995):

1. *Proficiency in the subject matter,* including the completeness of an instructor's mastery of family theories and the selection of course materials to extend students' understanding of the subject

2. *Course design skill,* including the ability to grasp theories' main tenets, the planning and organization of the syllabus and course materials, and the clear formation and application of relevant course objectives

3. *Delivery skills,* including strategies for carrying out instruction plans, providing students with learning activities that are available both in and out of class, activities that encourage application of course material

4. *Management skills* that reflect the ability to organize and connect instructional

opportunities, including finding a balance between assuming the instructor role and giving students active voices in the classroom

5. *Effectiveness in mentoring students* in ways that encourage understanding, critical thinking, and application

6. *Professional development* that reflects the ability to plan and carry out activities that further students' professional development and personal growth

We agree with Stephen Marks (1995) that "all teachers know there is no magic formula in teaching" (p. 147). Like other instructors, we create our course designs through trial and error. This project convinced us that, although we are adept in many areas of instruction as a result of our years of teaching family theory courses, we and our courses are still developing. We are not only facilitators training the next generation of family scholars; we are also very much a part of that generation ourselves.

CASE STUDY

A FAMILY WITH GENDER INEQUALITY: THEORY IN CLINICAL TEACHING

Thomas W. Blume, *Oakland University*

Charles Lee Cole, *University of Louisiana at Monroe*

For family therapy students, theorizing has a special status in the curriculum; intervention with couples and families revolves around theories. Clients arrive with their own multiple understandings of what they need, and a family therapist, a supervisor, and/or team members may have different perspectives. Successful use of theory (Patterson, 1997) not only helps professionals to sort

through information and select among options for helping, it also provides a common language through which professionals can communicate with clients. This creative, dynamic use of theory is modeled in the live supervision setting, where beginning therapists learn to theorize in order to reduce confusion, find a way of describing a situation that provides a reasonable match with the

CASE STUDY *continued*

clients' language and culture, and work toward reconciling multiple theories into a shared process that will meet the family's goals. The following case demonstrates this kind of theoretical exploration, integration, and application.

Ray and Debbie Brown called the clinic for help with their younger child.[1] They described their firstborn, Ray Junior, 16, as a model child who had never caused them any problems—popular, good-looking, a star in sports and in the classroom, newly driving, and exemplifying responsibility. They identified Julie, 14, as the problem child. The current crisis dated from the day when Debbie walked into the house and found Julie having sex with her 17-year-old boyfriend on the floor in the family room. Since that incident, the parents had been watching Julie like a hawk, invading her privacy by reading her diary and going through her bedroom during surprise inspections. Julie had become more defiant, and most recently she had tried to slip out of the house by crawling out her bedroom window after everyone had gone to bed.

INITIAL THEORIZING ABOUT THE SITUATION

During the initial session, mother, father, and older brother agreed that Julie was "out of control." Previously viewed as sweet and innocent, she was now viewed in a new light as the "wild child." Julie offered a different perspective, describing the incident with her boyfriend as an innocent, one-time moment of passion. She protested that she was neither sexually active nor out of control.

The family therapist was a second-year trainee under the supervision of a senior-level therapist. The university marriage and family therapy clinic provided live supervision using a treatment team of two or three interns and the supervisor. In the *reflecting team* format used in this case (Andersen, 1991), the team members observed from another room through a one-way mirror but met with the

family for a few minutes midsession to share their observations.

The team presented a theory that gender inequality was leading to a family crisis, based on the following observations: The family seemed male dominated, with privileges and statuses accorded to the husband/father and brother/son that were not shared by mother and daughter. Parental expectations were apparently higher for Ray Junior than for Julie; Ray and Debbie encouraged him to succeed academically as well as socially, and they hired a tutor to help him when he had problems in math and physics. On the other hand, Ray and Debbie had apparently valued Julie (until recently) for her childishness. They did not encourage her to be smart or to take honors courses; they expected her to graduate from high school, get married, and have a family, as her mother had done. Julie seemed to get attention only when she did something "bad." Julie was pleased by the team's observations. She said that she was tired of being the family mascot and wanted to be taken seriously and given the same privileges that her brother had when he was 14.

In this reflecting team format, the family therapist was free to distance himself from the team. He acknowledged to the family that there seemed to be gender issues, but he offered them an alternative theory. His theory of family change, based on the classic approach of the Mental Research Institute (MRI; Watzlawick, Weakland, & Fisch, 1974), was that the family needed to disrupt its current interactional patterns but would not respond to directives that were inconsistent with their goal (helping Julie fit into the family). Therefore, he said simply that the family was developmentally *stuck* in treating Julie as younger than she was. He instructed Debbie to spend time with Julie and teach her how to be a woman. This intervention, supported by the less provocative, more inclusive theory, was expected to disrupt the gender imbalance by strengthening the female voices in the family.

CASE STUDY *continued*

INTEGRATING, ENHANCING, AND APPLYING THEORIES

In subsequent sessions, the therapist and the team worked together to coordinate their theories with the family's theories and to bridge the gaps between theories. The therapist and the treatment team paid attention to the language that the family used in describing the problem, and the therapist framed interventions in a context that mirrored the language of the family. Decision making concerning the best-fit approach for the case was achieved in a collaborative manner, through a dialogue among the supervisor, the therapist, and the other treatment team members.

Several theoretical sources were helpful in shaping interventions for this family that addressed patterns that were codetermined by cultural norms and family traditions:

- Feminist family therapy sensitized the team to the *inequalities of power* that shaped the family's organizational patterns (Rampage, 2002; Walters, Carter, Papp, & Silverstein, 1988).
- Transgenerational family therapy helped the team to see the importance of respecting *family legacies* (Boszormenyi-Nagy & Spark, 1973).
- Interactional theories (Watzlawick et al., 1974), as well as postmodern approaches focused on language (Anderson, 1997) and narratives (White & Epston, 1990), illuminated the *politics of family interaction.*
- Minuchin's (1974) structural family therapy contributed the idea of *components* of family interaction that performed *symptom-organizing* and *system-maintaining* functions.
- Keeney's (1983) ecosystemic perspective called for respecting ebbs and flows as the family sought to *balance change with predictability and coherence.*

Interventions focused on disrupting the family's language patterns that located Julie in a less valued and less privileged status in relation to other family members. Even though Julie initially used language that paralleled her parents' descriptions, saying things such as, "I guess I'm not as smart as Ray Junior" and "I couldn't do that because I am a girl," the family members began to recalibrate their organizational pattern. The interventions included theory-driven elements such as the following:

- Support for a more active role for the mother that elevated her positions on issues to being as important as the father's positions
- Strengthening of systemic linkages between mother and daughter to accent the uniqueness of being a woman
- Expression of the rights and privileges of women in the family
- Elevation of the choices available for both mother and daughter beyond the stereotyped scripts the family had previously followed

Debbie and Julie began to perceive the actions of Ray and Ray Junior as less dominating. Ray and Ray Junior initially attempted to maintain their privileged status, but gradually they began to see advantages in the new style. The family began to acknowledge the coparenting authority as more equal. By the end of treatment, the family used different language in describing each member. Although Julie still had a history that fit into "bad girl" or "problem child" narratives, those stories were less powerful.

THE SUPERVISION PROCESS AS A THEORY SEMINAR

In this case the supervision process was intertwined with service delivery. Such a

CASE STUDY *continued*

model provides an ideal setting for teaching marriage and family therapy theory. In each meeting of the treatment team, this supervisor seized on teachable moments to challenge the members to think creatively and conceptualize the case using a variety of clinical and nonclinical theories. The team members examined alternative theoretical perspectives in light of multiple goals; in communication with the family, they used primarily a gender perspective, whereas their own exploration of narrative and interactional theories helped them to design and deliver interventions that had the desired impact. The resulting multitheoretical process was productive both for the clients and for the therapists in training.

NOTE

1. All names and identifiers used in this case study have been changed to protect the confidentiality of the clients. The case study was taken from actual clinical work with permission of the clients and the therapist.

Case Study

REFERENCES

Alpine, L., & Harris, R. (2002). Evaluating teaching effectiveness and teaching improvement: A language of institutional policies and academic development practices. *International Journal for Academic Development, 7,* 7–17.

Andersen, T. (Ed.). (1991). *The reflecting team: Dialogues and dialogues about the dialogues.* New York: W. W. Norton.

Anderson, H. (1997). *Conversation, language, and possibilities: A postmodern approach to therapy.* New York: Basic Books.

Bengtson, V. L., & Allen, K. R. (1993). The life course perspective applied to families over time. In P. Boss, W. J. Doherty, R. LaRossa, W. R. Schumm, & S. K. Steinmetz (Eds.), *Sourcebook of family theories and methods: A contextual approach* (pp. 469–499). New York: Plenum.

Berger, P., & Kellner, H. (1964). Marriage and the construction of reality. *Diogenes, 46,* 1–24.

Blaisure, K. R., & Koivunen, J. M. (2003). Family science faculty members' experiences with teaching from a feminist perspective. *Family Relations, 52,* 22–32.

Boss, P., Doherty, W. J., LaRossa, R., Schumm, W. R., & Steinmetz, S. K. (Eds.). (1993). *Sourcebook of family theories and methods: A contextual approach.* New York: Plenum.

Boszormenyi-Nagy, I., & Spark, G. (1973). *Invisible loyalties: Reciprocity in intergenerational family therapy.* New York: Harper & Row.

Bubolz, M. M., & Sontag, M. S. (1993). Human ecology theory. In P. Boss, W. J. Doherty, R. LaRossa, W. R. Schumm, & S. K Steinmetz (Eds.), *Sourcebook of family theories and methods: A contextual approach* (pp. 419–448). New York: Plenum.

Burr, W. R., Hill, R., Nye, F. I., & Reiss, I. L. (Eds.). (1979). *Contemporary theories about family: Vol. 2. General theories/theoretical orientations.* New York: Free Press.

Coontz, S. (1998). *The way we really are: Coming to terms with America's changing families.* New York: Perseus.

Daly, K. J. (1990). Issues in teaching family theory at the undergraduate level. *Family Science Review, 3*(2–3), 87–96.

Daly, K. J. (1997). Re-placing theory in ethnography: A postmodern view. *Qualitative Inquiry, 3,* 343–365.

Dilworth-Anderson, P., Burton, L. M., & Johnson, L. B. (1993). Reframing theories for understanding race, ethnicity, and families. In P. Boss, W. J. Doherty, R. LaRossa, W. R. Schumm, & S. K. Steinmetz (Eds.), *Sourcebook of family theories and methods: A contextual approach* (pp. 627–649). New York: Plenum.

Griffore, R. J., & Phenice, L. A. (2001). *The language of human ecology: A general systems perspective.* Dubuque, IA: Kendall/Hunt.

Hill, N. E., Murry, V. M., & Anderson, V. D. (in press). Sociocultural contexts of African American families. In K. A. Dodge, V. C. McLoyd, & N. E. Hill (Eds.), *African American family life in 21st-century America: Changes, challenges, and opportunities.* New York: Guilford.

hooks, b. (1992). *Black looks: Race and representation.* Boston: South End.

hooks, b. (1993). *Sisters of the yam: Black women and self-recovery.* Boston: South End.

Keeney, B. P. (1983). *Aesthetics of change.* New York: Guilford.

Knapp, P. (1984). Can social theory escape history? Views of history and social change. *History and Theory, 23,* 34–53.

Knapp, S. J. (2002). Authorizing family science: An analysis of the objectifying practices of family science discourse. *Journal of Marriage and Family, 64,* 1038–1048.

Lewis, E. A. (1995). Toward a tapestry of impassioned voices: Incorporating praxis into teaching about families. *Family Relations, 44,* 149–152.

MacKinnon-Lewis, C., & Frabutt, J. M. (2001). A bridge to healthier families and children: The collaborative process of a university-community partnership. *Journal of Higher Education Outreach and Engagement, 6*(3), 65–76.

Marks, S. R. (1995). The art of professing and holding back in a course on gender. *Family Relations, 44,* 142–148.

Minuchin, S. (1974). *Families and family therapy.* Cambridge, MA: Harvard University Press.

Patterson, T. (1997). Theoretical unity and technical eclecticism: Pathways to coherence in family therapy. *American Journal of Family Therapy, 25,* 97–109.

Pratto, F. (2002). Integrating experimental and social constructivist social psychology: Some of us are already doing it. *Personality and Social Psychology Review, 6,* 194–198.

Rampage, C. (2002). Working with gender in couple therapy. In A. S. Gurman & N. S. Jacobson (Eds.), *Clinical handbook of couple therapy* (3rd ed., pp. 533–545). New York: Guilford.

Rosenau, P. M. (1992). *Post-modernism and the social sciences: Insights, inroads, and intrusions.* Princeton, NJ: Princeton University Press.

Satir, V. (1972). *Peoplemaking.* Palo Alto, CA: Science & Behavior.

Sherrod, L. R. (1999). Giving child development knowledge away: Using university-community partnerships to disseminate research on children, youth, and families. *Applied Developmental Science, 3,* 228–234.

Small, S. A. (1996). Collaborative, community-based research on adolescents: Using research for community change. *Journal of Research on Adolescence, 6,* 9–22.

Thomas, D. L., & Wilcox, J. E. (1987). The rise of family theory: A historical and critical analysis. In M. B. Sussman & S. K. Steinmetz (Eds.), *Handbook of marriage and the family* (pp. 81–102). New York: Plenum.

Thompson, L. (1995). Teaching about ethnic minority families using a pedagogy of care. *Family Relations, 44,* 129–134.

Walters, M., Carter, B., Papp, P., & Silverstein, O. (1988). *The invisible web: Gender patterns in family relationships.* New York: Guilford.

Watzlawick, P., Weakland, J. H., & Fisch, R. (1974). *Change: Principles of problem formation and problem resolution.* New York: W. W. Norton.

Whitchurch, G. G., & Constantine, L. L. (1993). Systems theory. In P. Boss, W. J. Doherty, R. LaRossa, W. R. Schumm, & S. K. Steinmetz (Eds.), *Sourcebook of family theories and methods: A contextual approach* (pp. 325–352). New York: Plenum.

White, J. M., & Klein, D. M. (2002). *Family theories* (2nd ed.). Thousand Oaks, CA: Sage.

White, M., & Epston, D. (1990). *Narrative means to therapeutic ends.* New York: W. W. Norton.

Williams, K. R., Guerra, N. G., & Elliott, D. S. (1999). *Supporting youth by strengthening communities: Helping children grow and preventing problem behaviors. The DART model: Linking development and risk together.* Boulder: University of Colorado, Institute of Behavioral Science, Center for the Study and Prevention of Violence.

• Twenty-four

TEACHING METHODS OF FAMILY RESEARCH

Constance L. Shehan, *University of Florida*

Theodore N. Greenstein, *North Carolina State University*

Research is formalized curiosity. It is poking and prying with a purpose.

—Zora Neale Hurston,
Dust Tracks on a Road, 1942

Social scientists—like journalists, private investigators, and lawyers—are professional pokers and pryers. We go about our poking and prying with a purpose. The tools we use to poke and pry differ in some significant ways from those used by other professional researchers. It is our theories and methods that distinguish us, and as teachers of future scholars we are entrusted with the responsibility of making sure that our students learn to use these tools effectively. In this chapter, we present our ideas about designing a course in methods of family research. Additional material posted on this volume's companion Web site (http://www.ncfr.org/sourcebook) provides suggestions regarding the techniques that instructors teaching such a course might use. We are family sociologists who have taught research methods courses and have worked with hundreds of students, at both graduate and undergraduate levels, over our 20-year careers. We believe that our generalizations are applicable to other social science programs in family studies, however, because research on families, households, and/or intimate relationships is interdisciplinary by nature.

DECISIONS IN COURSE DESIGN

Training in research methods plays a central role in most programs in the social sciences. All of us have taken methods courses, and many of us will teach them at some point during our careers. Methods instruction has changed substantially over the past 20 years, however, as the result of technological advances in computing and shifts in epistemological paradigms. Thus the way in which we—and other professors trained in the 1960s and 1970s—were taught research methods differs substantially from the ways we must now teach our own students. For instance, many of us learned statistical analysis using mainframe computers, which required frequent walks to distant buildings to resubmit "jobs" that had minute errors in syntax. Some of us even remember communicating with the mainframes through keypunched data cards that were fed through mechanical readers. Analyses occurred at a laborious and time-consuming pace. Large secondary data sets and the software packages used for analysis were stored on magnetic tapes, which were expensive and typically purchased by universities. Today, of course, students can download data sets and software from the Internet and, with the click of a mouse, instantaneously process and reprocess complex statistical analyses on their laptop computers in their apartments or even in coffee shops. Qualitative analysis has also been affected by changes in computer technology. When Connie Shehan was coding transcripts from the in-depth interviews she conducted as part of her dissertation research in the early 1980s, she did it "by hand." Today, many qualitative researchers use software programs such as Ethnograph to assist in the systematic coding of responses.

Changes in the ways in which research methods courses are taught, however, go far beyond those demanded by technological advances. Paradigm shifts regarding epistemologies, occurring along with the emergence of feminist perspectives, have also had major impacts on methods courses. Until relatively recently, the dominant paradigm in social research emphasized the scientific method. When we were graduate students in the late 1970s, the conventional wisdom was that scholars used qualitative methods (e.g., interviews or observations) primarily during the exploratory stage of research (in order to determine what concepts and processes

were important to study). They then used quantitative methods (i.e., statistical analyses of large data sets) to describe and test hypotheses about the phenomena of interest.

Today, family researchers recognize that qualitative methods offer more than just a way to gather the preliminary information they need before launching quantitative studies. Researchers can use qualitative methods after—or instead of—quantitative analyses to obtain more detailed information. For example, Yoshinori Kamo (2000) of Louisiana State University has done some fascinating quantitative work on extended family households using data from the 1990 U.S. Census. However, in a personal communication with Ted Greenstein, Kamo said that he suspected that the extended family living arrangements meant very different things to members of different ethnic groups. He felt that the census data could not answer questions about the meanings of extended family households or give information about the motivations people have for living in such households. To answer those questions, he plans to conduct unstructured qualitative interviews with members of extended family households of differing ethnic backgrounds. In general, it appears that qualitative methods have assumed a central place in family research over the past two decades.

The proliferation of methods used to collect and analyze data challenges instructors to provide adequate coverage in semester-long methods courses. We often struggle with decisions about what material to include in—and to exclude from—our courses. Below, we offer some guidelines, based on our own experience, to aid instructors in designing research methods courses for the 21st century. We begin with a brief overview of the issues that you, the instructor, must consider as you design your courses. These are summarized in Table 24.1.

Characteristics of the Student Audience

The first issue you must take into account pertains to the characteristics of your student audience. The students' academic backgrounds (e.g., previous course work and other types of

Table 24.1   Issues to Consider in Course Design

1. Determine and understand characteristics and needs of student audience (e.g., previous training, career goals).
2. Identify course goals and learning objectives.
3. Define and limit course content.
4. Organize course content (i.e., order of topics, pace of coverage).
5. Design activities and assignments that address learning objectives (i.e., balance between student-centered and instructor-centered activities).
6. Determine methods of evaluating students' learning and providing feedback (i.e., formative or summative).

research experience) and career plans are central to this decision. Will your students be undergraduates who have had no previous training in methods? Are they likely to enter jobs after graduation that will not require them to conduct independent research? Or will they be graduate students who have completed several "survey" courses and are seeking advanced training in particular methods of data collection and analysis? Is your goal to train the students to be *producers* of research or informed *consumers* of research? You must consider the nature of your audience in order to determine the depth of coverage you will offer, the types of assignments you will make, and the ways in which you present information.

Course Goals and Objectives

Another issue that is closely related to the nature of the student audience pertains to the goals and objectives of your methods course. What will you expect your students to know or be able to do after completing your course? Will you be concerned primarily with mastery of content, development of hands-on skills, or acquisition of particular attitudes (e.g., an appreciation of the way in which well-designed social research can provide information that contradicts "common sense" or personal experiences or observations)? At what cognitive level will you expect your students to perform—recall, comprehension, application, analysis, synthesis, or evaluation? Your answers to these questions will provide you with an indication of the primary teaching techniques you should use (i.e., lectures for recall and discussions for other cognitive levels).

In addition, are there prerequisite skills that your students will need in order to succeed in the course? Will you have to spend time helping students acquire this information before you can move on to your course objectives? Finally, how can you, as the instructor, best use your own areas of interest and expertise in the course to benefit your students and to maximize the interplay between your scholarship and teaching responsibilities?

Course Content and Organization

A third consideration pertains to the selection of course content. Increasingly, this involves identifying interesting and important information that you will *exclude* from consideration in your course because of time and resource limitations. What material do you have to include because of curriculum requirements? What optional materials can you provide to students who have special skills or interests that go beyond the basics of your course?

Once you have selected the course content, organizing it is your next challenge. What order of topics will most effectively aid students' understanding? Textbooks provide excellent clues concerning which topics are considered essential in the field and also suggest a logical ordering of topics. (See this volume's companion Web site for a detailed example of another strategy we have found useful when selecting topics and reading material for inclusion in methods courses and in determining the order of coverage. We refer to this strategy as a *thematic-based* approach. The example provided on the Web site focuses on a wide range of research that deals with sexuality.)

As an instructor you also have to consider the pace that will be most appropriate to cover all requisite material while accommodating variations in student backgrounds and interests. Your own prior experiences or those of your colleagues in teaching the course at the same institution may be your best guide as you decide on an appropriate pace.

Although the topics covered in your methods course might not differ depending on your audience, the depth of coverage probably will. For example, consider the topic of summated indices. For future *producers* of quantitative research, it will be essential that you include discussion of measures of internal reliability, missing data issues, item standardization, and perhaps measurement models using structural equation modeling. You might devote one class meeting to each of these topics to cover it sufficiently. For a class composed primarily of future *consumers* of research, however, this level of detail may be optional. Such students will need to know enough to recognize summated indices when they see them, and something about the properties of major statistical measures that are typically reported in support of such indices, but they do not necessarily need to know how to calculate them.

Course Activities

Another element you will need to consider in course design pertains to the selection of in-class and out-of-class activities that will best enable students to achieve the learning objectives of the course. A basic distinction can be made here between *teacher-centered* activities (i.e., lectures or demonstrations) and *student-centered* activities (e.g., debates, case studies, role plays, discussions). As we argue in more detail below, we believe that a student-centered approach that highlights active-learning strategies is most effective in helping students to understand methods of research.

Promoting active learning and critical thinking. Research about teaching effectiveness consistently shows that teaching styles in which students are treated as "passive learners" are not nearly as effective as those that incorporate "active learning." The term *active learning* refers to an array of classroom practices that promote student learning through guided and increasingly independent investigation of questions and problems. This approach is particularly beneficial in family research methods training because there is usually no single "correct" answer to questions of research design and analysis.

Traditional methods courses rely on the relatively passive approach of teaching the results of others' investigations. Students in these courses are expected to learn the principles of research primarily by reading textbook accounts of research techniques or published reports in their original form. In contrast, instructors using an active learning model assist students in mastering course material through the process of active investigation itself. This process involves opportunities to practice formulating research questions, identifying and/or collecting appropriate data, presenting results systematically, analyzing and interpreting results, drawing conclusions, and evaluating the validity and substantive importance of those conclusions. In short, students take an active role in the learning process and, in doing so, learn to take responsibility for their own professional and intellectual development.

We want our students to be critical consumers of the research they read, and the only way they can do this is to ask questions about the research process and learn how to answer those questions. We know that we've done something right in the classroom when a student brings us a research article from a professional journal and says, "I don't think this was done correctly." In fact, you might build such a task into an informal, ungraded assessment or a formal evaluation of students' progress. For example, you could ask students to bring in articles about family issues that they find in newsmagazines and evaluate the ways in which the relevant social research is presented. You could assign graduate students the task of finding the original published reports addressed in the newsmagazine articles and comparing the journalists' accounts of the research with those of the scholars.

In making decisions about course activities you must also address more mundane, but important, questions, such as the *number* of assignments that students can reasonably complete and you can evaluate in the given time frame. A related question pertains to *uniformity* in assignments. Will you make a range of activities available to accommodate differences in students' interests and abilities, or will you require all students to complete the same assignments and participate in the same activities?

Small group activities and peer teaching. A variety of teaching strategies are consistent with active learning, but the research team approach is an especially good way to get students actively involved in the learning process. Students gain experience in working together on research teams, and, as part of the process, they review the work of other teams of students and have their own work reviewed by peers. They also take part in the collaborative presentation of their research findings in a variety of forms—written and oral presentations that may involve several kinds of media, including computer-generated slides and the creation of Web sites to present their findings.

Using films to teach qualitative methods. Within the constraints of a typical classroom setting, it can be difficult to teach students how to conduct systematic observations of social situations that occur in the field. LeBlanc (1998) suggests the use of feature films to train students in methods of ethnographic observation and analysis. The advantages of this technique include the following: Students typically respond positively to feature films, the films are appropriate for classroom use because of their length and accessibility, and the films provide a common basis for communication. Using films in this way allows instructors to monitor closely their students' development of observational and analytic skills; it also gives instructors control over the conditions of observation. In addition, it is quite a bit easier

to arrange to use a film in the classroom than it is to arrange for students to conduct individual field projects. Two major disadvantages of this technique are that films rely on narrative conventions rather than on "reality," and students can conduct only passive, nonparticipant observation. We believe that some films might have scenes that instructors could use to train students in microanalysis, similar to scenes that might be observed in a laboratory. In any case, the use of films is a convenient, low-cost way to give students more active training in observational techniques.

Semester-long projects. A tried-and-true component of methods instruction is a semester-long class research project in which students conceptualize, design, and execute a study and analyze the data. This activity often serves as the focal point of the course: All instruction is keyed to the development of the project. At the beginning of the semester, the class develops a research question and then learns how to search the literature on the topic. Class discussions of issues in the selection of appropriate research strategies are framed within the context of lessons concerning the advantages and disadvantages of different strategies. Measurement issues come into play as the students develop the research instrument. Training in specific techniques of data collection (e.g., interviewing, observation, focus groups) comes into play during the data collection phase. Class members then analyze the data gathered in the project, either by hand or with available statistical software. Finally, students might present the research report to the class much as a convention paper would be presented (more on this below), with each student preparing an article-length manuscript reporting the findings. Integrated into the design of such a project should be discussions of issues in research ethics, particularly the protection of human subjects. The instructor might ask a representative of the local institutional review boards to speak to the class concerning the required procedures and forms (these can usually be downloaded from university Web sites). Students can be assigned the task of completing these forms for their proposed projects. The Office for Human Research Protections at the U.S. Department of Health and Human Services maintains an informative Web site (http://www.hhs.gov/ohrp); the instructor may want to incorporate that information into the class reading list.

Evaluation and Feedback

Finally, you must determine the kind(s) of feedback you will be providing to students about their participation in activities and/or performance on assignments. Alternatives include evaluations classified as *formative* (e.g., ongoing assessment designed to assist in further development of skills) and those referred to as *summative* (e.g., a one-time assessment used for determination of grades). Summative evaluation puts a great deal of pressure on students and may not approximate the situations they will face later in their careers. The use of formative evaluations—frequent ungraded evaluations of written assignments submitted to instructors and peers at various points in the students' development—enables students to develop ideas and skills without "penalty" while providing instructors with valuable feedback about the students' level of understanding (Angelo & Cross, 1993). The obvious drawback of this type of assessment, of course, is that it places a considerable burden on the instructor. To reduce this somewhat, you might include peer reviews in informal as well as formal assessment of students. You may want to discuss the exact procedures and the "weight" you will be giving to peer reviews at the beginning of the semester, before you implement this type of evaluation procedure.

Additional issues pertaining to evaluation include the impact of group-based assignments. If students complete assignments in small groups or teams, will you evaluate them individually or collectively? You need to ensure that your methods of evaluation mesh with your methods of instruction and with course goals and objectives. Courses that are taught primarily through discussion, for example, might not prepare students for recall-based objective exams. You also need to consider what types of evaluation will allow you to provide students with adequate feedback, given other demands on your professional time. Finally, will you evaluate student progress relative to some fixed standard that you apply to everyone? Alternatively, will you compare individual students to the norm achieved by their classmates or to their own progress relative to where they started in the course?

To summarize, we believe that a full range of research methods, both quantitative and qualitative, should be covered in survey courses and in the other components of undergraduate and graduate training. Family scholars need to be conversant in all of the major research strategies. They should be able to pick up any major family journal and at least feel comfortable reading published reports of research using many different types of strategies. We also believe that methods training should not be limited to the analysis stage of the research process; students should learn about study design and data collection as well. We encourage instructors—and programs as a whole—to provide training in research methods that is based on principles of active, student-centered learning rather than passive, teacher-centered instruction.

PEDAGOGICAL CHALLENGES ASSOCIATED WITH METHODS INSTRUCTION

The challenges of teaching research methods are unlike those in any other course in the curriculum. Some of these challenges—students' anxiety over the supposed mathematical or technical nature of the material, the limited amount of time in a semester to accomplish many goals, and diversity in student interests and abilities—are common to methods instruction in all social and behavioral sciences. Others are more specific to the teaching of family research methods.

General Challenges

Students—even those enrolled in graduate degree programs—often approach research methods courses with a fair amount of apprehension. Many perceive these subjects, particularly social statistics, as inherently uninteresting and difficult—a necessary but unpleasant component of professional training (Hubbell, 1994; Markham, 1991). Fear of the subject may prompt students to postpone taking methods courses until late in their program, which can impede their performance in advanced substantive courses. Anticipated student anxiety may also make faculty reluctant to teach required methods courses (McBride, 1994; Stacks & Hickson, 1991), in part because students' evaluations of such courses tend to be lower than those for other kinds of courses (Gillmore & Greenwald, 1994). Thus one of the major challenges in teaching methods is assuaging student anxiety.

• SPOTLIGHT ON METHODS

MAKING STATISTICS COME ALIVE

Walter R. Schumm, *Kansas State University*

To bring family theories alive in the classes I teach, I role-play various dead theorists and try to use visual models (Schumm, 2003a), but I use a different approach for research methods courses. Over the years, I have shifted my approach from lecturing to a focus on learning—with specific attention to higher-order cognitive skills that students must demonstrate objectively. The lecture approach made some students feel successful with knowledge alone, even if they could not apply the knowledge. Now, I teach and evaluate with very practical examples.

Of course, students know that they have to pass their required statistics courses and that they need to use statistics to get published, to get tenure, to develop grants, and so on. But many question whether knowledge of statistics is "really" useful. One problem is that the use of statistics in the social sciences is often, of necessity, rather abstract. For example, predicting later marital satisfaction from various aspects of individuals' premarital counseling experiences involves abstract concepts for both the dependent and independent variables. Starting out with abstract concepts and abstract statistics, often from large data sets, is a heavy burden for some students. I have discovered that using more concrete variables, often from historical situations with a smaller number of data points, helps students understand the meaning of statistics as well as their genuine value and usefulness and helps them transfer their learning to more abstract, complex situations.

For example, at the most concrete level, I have used the *Challenger* space shuttle disaster to illustrate the value of standard deviations, *t* tests, correlations, linear regression, and logistic regression. The expected launch temperature for *Challenger* was more than two standard deviations below the lowest previous launch temperature as well as being below the lowest temperature authorized (40 degrees Fahrenheit) for use of the rocket's

(continued)

engines. Whenever you exceed the limits of a variable by so many standard deviations or violate "the equipment's manual," you are in a range where the unexpected is much more likely to occur, regardless of previous research done within a smaller range of variation. Using almost any bivariate measure of association reveals a significant pattern between launch temperature and mechanical (O-ring) failure for the 23 shuttle flights before *Challenger* and thus a very high risk of failure on the *Challenger* flight if launched at the expected temperature (information known and debated the night before the flight that exploded, except that incorrect statistics were applied). An exciting role play can be set up in which the students are given the actual data for the 23 previous flights (available in Schumm et al., 2002; see also Hamilton, 2003, p. 216) and told they have 15 minutes to save the crew with statistics.

Turning to more abstract examples in social science, a recent reanalysis of data from Islamic nations comparing Islamic political culture with support for human rights (Schumm, 2003b) could be used as a teaching exercise on the dangers of testing curvilinear hypotheses with linear statistics. Another reanalysis of widely cited family studies data that compared child outcomes for lesbian versus single-parent mothers (Schumm, 2004) raises questions about the risks of using small samples to "prove null hypotheses" and can be used to set up a practical exercise in the careful use of simple statistics with data on controversial topics.

In conclusion, statistics are helpful for making decisions that are somewhat freed from otherwise purely subjective criteria. For example, a leader might make decisions based on astrology or random chance. Even though other approaches might, through luck, lead to better decisions, statistics can help us, in a more objective manner, improve our decision making in any endeavor, including family social science. •

Some instructors have proposed a curriculum change that would reduce student anxiety by integrating coverage of methods and statistics into substantive courses. These introductory "doses" of methods and statistics would meet the needs of undergraduate students enrolled in "terminal" degree programs and reduce their anxiety. Proponents of this approach argue that the cumulative effect could potentially equal what students attain in traditional semester-long courses in methods. As students move from introductory-level courses to more specialized courses for majors, their sophistication and skill levels would presumably increase (Bridges, Gillmore, Pershing, & Bates, 1998).

All research methods instructors face two kinds of time limitations. The first is the severe limitation imposed by the length of the academic semester. It is difficult—if not impossible—to develop a meaningful research question, design the protocols or instruments for it, and gather and analyze the data in a 15-week semester. For this reason, many departments now routinely schedule their required methods courses as a two-semester integrated sequence, a system that works well as long as the composition of the class remains essentially stable across the two semesters.

Time constraints are exacerbated if statistics and methods instruction are combined into a single course. In 1990, the American Sociological Association recommended that these subjects be taught as separate courses, but resource limitations have precluded this in some programs. When only one course is required of majors, some of the course time must be devoted to statistics, so that graduates can make sense of the flood of statistics they encounter in news reports, on the job, and in journal articles.

A second form of time limitation comes from the length of a class period: Research is not typically done in 50-minute blocks. Those of us who are active researchers know all too well how projects can eat up huge chunks of time, often for unanticipated reasons. Students need to learn that they will have to routinely reserve 3- or 4-hour blocks of time to work on their research projects, and that they must try not to allow other activities to displace the research during those periods.

Diversity in student ability levels also poses a challenge to the methods instructor. Some of our incoming students have had little or no training in research methods and statistics, whereas others have already presented papers at conferences or published papers in professional journals. How can instructors deal with such diversity? One technique that Ted Greenstein uses is to create three- or four-person student research teams. He has found that if he allows students to form their own teams, the teams tend to be homogeneous with respect to student ability level, so instead he assigns students to teams, including in each at least one student with a documented high skill level, one with a moderate level of skill, and one at the lower end of the skill continuum. In general, this seems to work well. Less skilled students benefit from their interaction with more skilled students, and an additional benefit is that the more skilled students develop some valuable teaching skills. There are, of course, the usual complaints from more skilled students about free riders and being "held back" by less skilled students, but Greenstein reminds them that once they complete their degrees and enter the professional world they will often have to work with colleagues not of their own choosing. When implementing this strategy, however, instructors should be aware of the potentially negative "labeling" effect this type of assignment might have on student performance.

Challenges Specific to Family Research Methods Instruction

Although the fundamentals of research on families are similar to those of the more general methodologies found in sociology, political science, psychology, and anthropology, there are important differences. In our opinion, these differences are substantial enough to warrant the use of some distinctive approaches in the teaching of family research methods (for additional discussion of these points, see Gelles, 1978; Larzelere & Klein, 1987). We discuss below the implications of the following for instruction in family research methods: lack of agreement over the definition of "family," the systemic nature of families as small groups, family members' simultaneous fulfillment of multiple roles and statuses, the rights of privacy granted to family behavior, and widespread preconceptions about families and family life. (For a more in-depth discussion of these issues, see Greenstein, 2001, chap. 1.)

Lack of consensus about the definition of "family." A fundamental problem in our field is that no generally agreed-upon definition of "family" exists (for a detailed discussion of this issue, see Gubrium & Holstein, 1990). The U.S. Bureau of the Census defines a family as "a group of two or more people (one of whom is the householder) related by birth, marriage, or adoption and residing together." This definition excludes many groups and ties that function as, and are experienced as, families. The lack of consensus about what constitutes a family causes major problems for researchers. Without a definition of "family," how can family scholars know which groups and individuals they should study and which they should exclude from their research? Methods instructors can use this fundamental issue as an extended lesson in measurement. We encourage instructors to confront it directly, early in the semester, through student assignments. For instance, an instructor could assign students the task of interviewing a small number of persons about those individuals' definitions of "family"; this could include asking interviewees to identify the persons they consider to be part of their families. Alternatively, students could look at secondary data sets or opinion polls that ask respondents to select a definition of "family" that seems most accurate. Class discussion could focus on the implications of measurement for accuracy in both population description and delivery of social services.

The systemic nature of families and the unit of analysis. Perhaps the most important difference between research on families and most other social science research is that the primary focus of the former is on small primary groups rather than on individuals. Researchers are faced with the question of how to use multiple sources of information about each unit of analysis. A classic example pertains to the determination of social class. If we want to measure an individual's social class, we typically look at his or her occupation, education, and income. How, then, do we measure the social class of a family? This became an especially pressing question in the 1970s, when millions of American women entered the labor force. How could researchers integrate these women's occupational status and earnings into determinations of their families' socioeconomic status? A similar question pertains to calculation of household income for children of divorced parents. Should researchers count only the custodial parent's income, or should they include the noncustodial parent's characteristics as well? (For a discussion of some of the methodological approaches to handling dyads as the unit of analysis, see Maguire, 1999.) Family methods courses need to spend a fair amount of time on discussion of the unit of analysis and its implications for study design and data analysis. Detailed examination and discussion of studies in which multiple perspectives are presented is useful. Examples could include research pertaining to the division of household labor. Hochschild's (1989) qualitative examination of wives' and husbands' differential framing of their allocation of labor and quantitative analyses of men's and women's time in housework using large national data

sets (e.g., the Panel Study of Income Dynamics) clearly illustrate the limitations of using only one family/household member's perspective.

Multiple statuses and multiple roles. As Gelles (1978) points out, "Families are made up of individuals occupying multiple statuses and enacting multiple roles" (p. 408). Each member of a family is potentially a parent, a sibling, an employee, a spouse, and a son or daughter simultaneously. When we collect data about a member of a family, we have to be sensitive to the fact that the kinds of responses we get may depend on which roles and statuses the individual is occupying at the time of the interview. Power differences among family members may "privilege" one perspective over another. Interviewing adults in the presence of their children, for example, might produce very different results than interviews with the same adults conducted in the presence of their own parents.

Privacy and backstage behavior. Another problem in studying families is the fact that much of what goes on in families is hidden from public view. Activities such as child abuse, domestic violence, and child rearing are not generally visible to persons outside the family. Students need to be sensitized to issues of selective reporting by family members—overreporting of "desirable" family behaviors and underreporting of "undesirable" behaviors—and the possibility of family members' simple refusal to respond at all to interviewers' questions. We suspect, however, that current trends in the popular media and in the larger culture may greatly affect the "public's" willingness to reveal private information to researchers. The most obvious trend involves people's apparently increasing willingness to expose their most intimate behaviors (e.g., childbirth, marriage proposals, cosmetic surgery) and personal problems (e.g., family feuds) in the electronic media. The barriers between public and private seem to be dissolving. In one sense, this may become a teaching resource, in that instructors may be able to use these performances to train students in observational methods. Another current trend pertains to the erosion of privacy that is occurring due to concerns about national security. The increasing surveillance of everyday life in the United States may make potential research participants less likely to refuse researchers' requests for private information. A third development, however, may work against researchers' access to information about family-related behavior—the rights of consumers to restrict solicitors' phone calls. Discussion of these sociocultural developments in methods courses will allow instructors to integrate considerations of ethics and the impacts of social change on the nature of social science.

Familiarity with the subject matter. Another issue that emerges in the study of families is that our personal experiences and observations shape our ideas about "typical" or "appropriate" family behaviors and structures. At the very least, researchers' own personal experiences can influence the questions they choose to study. A key point of discussion in methods courses should concern the advantages and disadvantages of researchers' allowing their own beliefs and experiences to influence the research experience. The writings of feminist scholars on this issue are particularly insightful, and instructors should include some of these in required readings, especially in graduate courses.

PROFESSIONAL SOCIALIZATION IN FAMILY METHODS COURSES

The required family methods course provides an excellent opportunity for professional socialization for graduate students. As established academics, we often take for granted many aspects of our profession that can be sources of mystery to our students. It is important that instructors introduce students to the various venues through which our research gets disseminated to researchers, teachers, practitioners, and the general public.

At some point in methods courses, instructors should address how a manuscript for submission to a professional journal should be formatted and structured. They can reinforce the importance of students' understanding this structure by requiring that term papers be formatted as "publication ready." An initial step in such an assignment would be to have students identify appropriate journals and collect the "Instructions to Authors" sections from them.

One issue that instructors should discuss is the peer review process for family journals. We often spend one or two class meetings in our methods courses talking about how the review process works. One particularly effective strategy is for the instructor to take one of his or her own published articles, along with accompanying reviews and correspondence with the journal editor, and talk about the "story" of the article—how the idea for the article originated; any problems that arose during the data collection, analysis, or other phases of the project; the nature of the reviews of the manuscript (and the instructor's responses to them); and so on, right up to the appearance of the article in print. Quite apart from the substance of the paper, students are fascinated by the actual nuts-and-bolts of the authoring and publication process.

This is also a great time for the instructor to discuss the importance of the peer review process to the discipline. Having students review journal articles is an excellent way to encourage their professional development. A good classroom exercise is to provide students with a rough draft of a manuscript and show how it might be reviewed. The National Council on Family Relations posts guidelines for reviews (and details of the editorial process in general) on its Web site (http://www.ncfr.org). The *Journal of Marriage and Family* has developed a "reviewer-in-training" program that allows advanced graduate students and new professionals to develop their reviewing skills and potentially join the list of *JMF*'s "occasional reviewers." The *Journal of Family Issues* also invites graduate students to review manuscripts and provides mentoring about the process.

In our own courses, we also like to provide students with opportunities to develop familiarity with various types of presentations common to professional meetings. For example, students' presentations of the findings of the semester-long research project can take several forms. One student group might present the findings in the typical 15- to 20-minute conference paper format. Another group might develop a poster version of the presentation. Still another group could organize a roundtable discussion of the findings. All of these different formats should include the opportunity for feedback, not only from the instructor but from the students' peers as well. Undergraduates, too, benefit from training and experience in professional presenta-

tion skills, even if their intended careers fall outside academia.

Another excellent exercise that provides an opportunity for professional socialization among graduate students is the preparation of grant proposals using actual forms provided by agencies or foundations. The instructor might ask colleagues who have received external funding and/or who have served as reviewers or panel members for funding agencies to speak to the class about their experiences. Students can also serve as "review panels" that make comments and recommendations concerning their classmates' proposals.

• SPOTLIGHT ON METHODS

DEVELOPING PROFESSIONAL SKILLS IN METHODS: WRITING GRANT PROPOSALS

Chalandra M. Bryant, *Pennsylvania State University*

S hehan and Greenstein argue—and correctly so—that methods training should include experience with both research design and data collection. Students should also be exposed to another step that occurs before data collection: preparing a grant proposal. Here is an outline that may help you facilitate such an activity. Before beginning this activity, you should have the students read some "real" grant proposals.

INITIAL INSTRUCTIONS FOR STUDENTS

The purpose of this assignment is for you to gain grant-writing experience. We have talked about the various components of a grant proposal, including (a) specific aims, (b) background and significance, (c) preliminary studies, (d) research design, (e) measures, (f) data analytic plans, (g) participant recruitment, and (h) human subject protections/concerns. As you work on this assignment, please also think about timelines. You have seen examples of timelines in other proposals. This project will be completed in teams, and I have assigned each of you to teams based on your research interests. Working in teams will help you learn how to collaborate with "coinvestigators."

When you receive the students' proposals, organize them by topic. For example, if Teams X and Y have written about the effects of divorce, group those two proposals together. The teams grouped together will have read similar articles, so they will be better able to make appropriate suggestions during the peer review process.

(continued)

● SPOTLIGHT ON METHODS *continued*

Tell the paired teams that they are responsible for providing written and verbal peer reviews for each other. Each student should receive his or her own copy of each proposal. Encourage the students to write their comments *on* the proposals themselves.

SAMPLE QUESTIONS FOR THE PEER REVIEW SHEET

- Is the proposal worthy of funding? Why or why not? Are the authors addressing an important issue? How will the work contribute to the field?
- How can the "Background and Significance" section be improved? What did you like about that section? (Critiques underscore what the authors did well in addition to pointing out mistakes.)
- How appropriate are the proposed measures? What changes would you suggest?
- How will the sample be recruited? How can that process be improved?

After *each* student on *each* team has independently answered the questions on the Peer Review Sheet, all students should meet with their *own* team members to discuss the feedback they are going to provide. Are the members in agreement with regard to the suggestions they will make during the meeting?

The members of Team X should then meet with the members of Team Y. At that time, both teams explain their written feedback to each other. During this open discussion, you will notice that even more ideas are exchanged.

The written feedback takes place outside of class. The meetings are best held in class, so that you can visit each of the paired teams. This will give you an opportunity to (a) ensure that feedback is exchanged in a collegial manner and (b) provide additional feedback. After the feedback (written and verbal) is exchanged, give the teams 1 week to revise their papers before submitting them to you.

HOW TO MAKE THE EXPERIENCE REAL FOR UNDERGRADUATES: SERVICE LEARNING AT ITS BEST

I tried a version of this exercise with undergraduates who want to work in social service agencies. I asked the director of one such agency if my students could help prepare proposals for him. I explained to my students the difference between research proposals and proposals written to obtain equipment or establish a program for an agency. The director provided a list of services and equipment that his agency needed, and we then recruited teams to work on the various needs. One team wrote a proposal to establish a community babysitting program, and another wrote a proposal to help the agency secure defibrillators. The teams included sections in their proposals that could be used to evaluate the effectiveness of the programs. The teams were even instructed to find funding sources. The students found this assignment meaningful because they knew that their work was going to be used by an agency. It required hard work, so they did grumble. However, semesters later, I received e-mail messages from some students thanking me for providing them with this opportunity. One student earned an internship with the agency for which the class had written the proposals. ●

METHODS TRAINING BEYOND THE CLASSROOM

No matter how engaging and encompassing our family research methods courses are, the fact remains that an important arena for methods training is the world outside the classroom. We can provide training in the basics of family research, but the hands-on experience a student receives by working with faculty mentors during the preparation of a thesis or dissertation or as a research assistant is extremely valuable. Out-of-classroom experiences are critical to professional socialization in a number of ways: They are authentic experiences, they illuminate the ways in which knowledge is constructed, they involve active rather than passive learning, and they are often collaborative. Training programs that allow greater student-faculty interaction in and out of class increase students' satisfaction with their institution, persistence, educational aspirations, academic growth, knowledge acquisition, and career interest and selection (McKinney, Saxe, & Cobb, 1998).

One of the true innovations in training graduate students in recent years has been the development of the Preparing Future Faculty (PFF) program. PFF aids graduate students in preparing for the full range of faculty activities, including research, teaching, professional service, and outreach/extension. At North Carolina State University, for instance, doctoral students participate in two very different forms of PFF activities. Each PFF participant "shadows" a faculty member at a partner institution, usually on two different occasions. This gives the student the opportunity to see what a faculty member actually does beyond the more obvious research and teaching roles.

Of more direct relevance to methods training, however, is the PFF research team, in which faculty and advanced graduate students mentor students with less experience. Faculty members initiate the teams, but participation is voluntary, unpaid, and open to all students. The research projects conducted by PFF teams run the gamut from highly quantitative secondary analyses to qualitative interview studies and even purely theoretical projects.

Students gain practical, hands-on experience in designing and executing research projects that have a very high potential for publication. A number of universities have also begun to develop faculty-supervised research opportunities for undergraduate students because they recognize the value of such experiences in the development of critical thinking skills.

CONCLUSION

Training undergraduate and graduate students in methods of family research is a major challenge in our preprofessional programs. National trends in higher education affect methods courses in much the same way they affect other aspects of the curriculum and faculty load. Shrinking budgets and ballooning student populations, for example, tax already strained resources. Some programs may find that they must respond to these dual pressures by eliminating separate courses in research methods for undergraduates and integrating methods training in substantive courses. Others may respond by increasing class sizes in undergraduate courses and eliminating hands-on teaching strategies. In addition, growing demands for public accountability in the area of teaching effectiveness and increasing pressures on faculty to publish may result in a decrease in the numbers of faculty members who are available to teach these courses. Untenured faculty especially may shy away from teaching methods courses, not only because such courses are labor-intensive but also because they typically result in lower student evaluations than do other kinds of courses.

The epistemological shifts that have been occurring across the disciplines also affect views about what should be taught in research methods courses. Some programs may continue to emphasize the scientific canons and offer qualitative methods only as electives. Programs that include training in qualitative methods may feel the impact of taxed resources even more intensely as they struggle to provide the high level of mentoring necessary to teach methods of observation, interpretation, and analysis. Remedial training in writing skills may join remedial training in basic calculation as additional drains on resources and additional sources of anxiety for students.

Although we are well aware of these concerns, we urge instructors and curriculum administrators to provide training for the next generation of family scholars that includes a wide range of methods (both qualitative and quantitative), emphasizes hands-on learning strategies, and covers study design and data collection as well as analysis. The investment of scarce resources in this type of training will produce incalculable benefits in the quality of future research producers and consumers.

CASE STUDY

GETTING TO THE BOTTOM OF THE SPANKING DEBATE: BRINGING IN THE ETHICS OF RESEARCH

Robyn L. Mowery, *University of Georgia*

Lynda H. Walters, *University of Georgia*

Case Study

Ethics does not consist in knowing the answers but instead in knowing how to inquire; in particular, in knowing what counts as a possible answer, what questions are appropriate and constructive ones to ask, what tendencies in one's own thinking need to be kept in check, et cetera. (Card, 2002, p. 20)

All researchers are concerned with ethics. The question is, at what point do ethics enter the research process and how do we think about ethics?

Typically, we think of *research ethics* merely as compliance with regulatory guidelines (e.g., those of institutional review boards) established for research on human subjects during the implementation of a study. Macklin (1999) argues that most ethical guidelines for research are procedural, and so do not assist researchers in recognizing any underlying ethical influences overtly or covertly shaping their practices. According to Richardson, Fowers, and Guignon (1999):

> Few [social scientists] critically evaluate the metaphysical and moral underpinnings of their methods or theories. They are not taught to inquire into these matters, and there is little encouragement or support for doing so. . . . Acknowledging that social inquiry may be indelibly linked to ethical reflection touches on some of our deepest hopes and fears and raises all sorts of difficult questions. (pp. 173–174)

What we are calling the *ethics of research* reaches beyond regulations and addresses underlying ethical assumptions and implications associated with the whole of the research process, from initial choice of topic, theory,

Authors' Note: We would like to thank John Hardwig, Ph.D., bioethicist and chair of the Philosophy Department at the University of Tennessee, Knoxville, for his helpful review of this essay.

design, recruitment, data collection, and analysis to write-up, dissemination, and application of findings. Thus, although compliance with *research ethics* is critical, ethically sensitive researchers are concerned with more than just ethics regulations. Because regulatory guidelines are so widely discussed in the research literature (for an excellent resource, see Sieber, 1992), and given space constraints, we focus here on one aspect of the ethics of research. Specifically, we use the empirical literature on spanking to explore ethical issues related to the role of research in the recommendations that scholars make to families and policy makers.

THE CASE

The belief that spanking, or corporal punishment, will extinguish unwanted behaviors in children has a long history in the United States. Diana Baumrind, a psychologist, has spent almost three decades studying the ways in which parents interact with their children and the outcomes for different interaction patterns. Since the early years of her work, Baumrind has taken the position that the authoritative parenting style (i.e., firm control combined with warmth and respect for the child) is the most constructive (see Baumrind, 1971). Within this style, spanking is not considered detrimental; it is viewed as a minor component of a balanced style of parenting in which the parent is acknowledged as the authority but power is expressed in the context of high regard.

Taking a more radical position, based on decades of studying violence in families and more than a decade of studying adult discipline of children, specifically spanking, family sociologist Murray Straus has concluded that spanking in and of itself is damaging to children. Straus (1994, 2001a, 2001b) takes the position that any amount of spanking/hitting is detrimental to a child. Spanking occurs in contexts in which adults who must resort to spanking are less likely to engage with children in positive, constructive ways

than are parents who do not perceive a need to resort to spanking.

Baumrind (2001) is critical of Straus's argument for several reasons. First, she contends that the strength of his research findings does not support such a prohibition against "normative" spanking (i.e., what a majority of parents use without being abusive), and that her more moderate position (i.e., some spanking in certain contexts is permissible) is empirically verifiable. Second, Baumrind takes exception to Straus's beginning his research with the assumption "that corporal punishment, by itself, has harmful psychological effects for children and hurts society as a whole" (Straus, 1994, p. xii). She worries that research that starts with an already formed conclusion is likely to confirm that initial bias; rather, Baumrind suggests, it is best to start with a hypothesis that is open to revision based on empirical evidence. Nevertheless, Baumrind states, "Although a value judgment that spanking is wrong is properly defended by its adherents on ethical grounds, a blanket injunction against disciplinary spanking is not warranted by causally relevant scientific evidence" (p. 14).

DISCUSSION

What role does social science research play in the recommendations scholars make to parents regarding disciplinary practices? In this scientific age, we frequently look to empirical research to tell us how we *ought* to behave (e.g., to spank or not). Although science focuses on careful description and explanation of what "is," increasingly it is playing an authoritatively prescriptive role (i.e., asserting what "ought" to be). To attempt to move directly from "is" (i.e., scientific description) to "ought" (i.e., normative prescription), however, is to commit a "fallacious step in deductive reasoning" (*Stanford Encyclopedia of Philosophy*, 2003, sec. 3.3.3) known in moral philosophy as the "naturalistic fallacy."[1] The jump from empirical data (e.g., spanking is linked to X, Y, or Z) to a recommended course of action (e.g., spanking should or should not occur), at the practical level, *always* involves the presence of value judgments and other sorts of moral claims. In other words: (A) *empirical facts* + (B) *values statements* = (C) *prescriptive conclusions*. In considering A and C only, one commits the naturalistic fallacy, whereas considering B and C only amounts to mere opinion. If the facts (A) are inconclusive and yet there are recommendations (C), such advice must be coming from somewhere (e.g., B). Even if there is scientific consensus (A), there still cannot be a recommended course of action (C) without the presence of value judgments (B).

Baumrind and Straus, both basing their conclusions on extensive research, make vastly different recommendations as to how parents *ought* to discipline their children. In doing so, does either of them commit the naturalistic fallacy of moving from a descriptive "is," based on empirical data, to a prescriptive "ought," based on implicit or explicit value judgments? We suggest that at the very least there is confusion about the relation between the roles of facts and values, and this, even more than methodological concerns, may come close to getting to the bottom of the spanking debate. Baumrind is concerned that Straus has insufficient evidence to support a blanket injunction against spanking. Yet what the naturalistic fallacy alerts us to is that scientific evidence *alone* will *never* be sufficient to produce an injunction for or against a recommended position. Baumrind, who asserts that she is *not* an advocate of spanking, even though she resists a blanket injunction against it, implies that nonabusive spanking within the context of authoritative parenting is acceptable. Thus she too is importing an assumed value position into her recommendations. In other words, Baumrind's attempts to distinguish empirically the types of parents for whom spanking may be morally permissible based on the lack of negative outcomes suggest that she may be as guilty as Straus in confirming her initial bias (i.e., that at least some spanking is appropriate).

We suggest that Baumrind is not doing anything other than what most of us have been trained to do, for we use our research as the basis for recommendations all the time. We applaud Baumrind's caution against overstating claims based on empirical evidence. We further suggest an ethical as well as a methodological application of such wisdom.

In the context of socially sensitive research (e.g., research on spanking), it is easier than in more basic research to recognize the relevance of ethics. Most research methodology courses include an emphasis on regulatory-institution-based *research ethics*. This essay constitutes a narrow introduction to the broader notion of the *ethics of research*. Using the scientific method, we, as researchers, make our factual and theoretical assumptions clear so that others may respond to them. We suggest that it is no less incumbent on researchers to be transparent about the values-based presuppositions they blend with their empirical data when making recommendations. It may well be that we can all agree on the values claims involved in our research (e.g., violence is bad), but in a pluralistic society or across cultures, we may or may not be able to take such consensus for granted. Only by making our values positions explicit can we be sure to avoid the naturalistic fallacy in our recommendations. Without commenting on Straus's value assumption itself, we suggest that it is illustrative of part of the process we have been advocating. Thus we believe that Straus's willingness to reveal his position to his readers directly is exemplary.

NOTE

1. Even if it is true that some analytic philosophers believe that the naturalistic fallacy is not *always* a fallacy in the technical sense, at the practical level for social scientists it serves as a warning signal, cautioning us to account for our value positions in the recommendations we make.

Case Study

REFERENCES

American Sociological Association. (1990). *Liberal learning and the sociology major: A report to the profession.* Washington, DC: Author.

Angelo, T., & Cross, P. (1993). *Classroom assessment techniques: A handbook for college teachers* (2nd ed.). San Francisco: Jossey-Bass.

Baumrind, D. (1971). Current patterns of parental authority. *Developmental Psychology Monograph, 4*(1, pt. 2), 1–103.

Baumrind, D. (2001, August). *Does causally relevant research support a blanket injunction against disciplinary spanking by parents?* Invited address presented at the 109th Annual Meeting of the American Psychological Association, San Francisco.

Bridges, G. S., Gillmore, G. M., Pershing, J. L., & Bates, K. A. (1998). Teaching quantitative research methods. A quasi-experiment analysis. *Teaching Sociology, 26,* 14–28.

Card, R. F. (2002). Using case studies to develop critical thinking skills in ethics courses. *Teaching Ethics, 2*(1), 19–27.

Gelles, R. J. (1978). Methods for studying sensitive family topics. *American Journal of Orthopsychiatry, 48,* 408–424.

Gillmore, G. M., & Greenwald, A. (1994). *The effects of course demands and grading leniency on student ratings of instruction* (OEA Report 94-4). Seattle: University of Washington, Office of Educational Assessment.

Greenstein, T. N. (2001). *Methods of family research.* Thousand Oaks, CA: Sage.

Gubrium, J. F., & Holstein, J. A. (1990). *What is family?* Mountain View, CA: Mayfield.

Hamilton, L. C. (2003). *Statistics with Stata: Updated for Version 7.* Belmont, CA: Thomson/Brooks/Cole.

Hochschild, A. R. (with MacHung, A.). (1989). *The second shift: Working parents and the revolution at home.* New York: Viking.

Hubbell, L. (1994). Teaching research methods: An experimental and heterodoxical approach. *PS: Political Science and Politics, 27,* 60–64.

Kamo, Y. (2000). Racial and ethnic differences in extended family households. *Sociological Perspectives, 43,* 221–229.

Larzelere, R. E., & Klein, D. M. (1987). Methodology. In M. B. Sussman & S. K.

Steinmetz (Eds.), *Handbook of marriage and the family.* New York: Plenum.

LeBlanc, L. (1998). Observing reel life: Using feature films to teach ethnographic methods. *Teaching Sociology, 26,* 62–68.

Macklin, R. (1999). *Against relativism: Cultural diversity and the search for ethical universals in medicine.* New York: Oxford University Press.

Maguire, M. C. (1999). Treating the dyad as the unit of analysis: A primer on three analytic approaches. *Journal of Marriage and the Family, 61,* 213–223.

Markham, W. T. (1991). Research methods in the introductory course: To be or not to be? *Teaching Sociology, 19,* 464–471.

McBride, A. (1994). Teaching research methods using appropriate technology. *PS: Political Science and Politics, 27,* 553–557.

McKinney, K., Saxe, D., & Cobb, L. (1998). Are we really doing all we can for our undergraduates? Professional socialization via out-of-class experiences. *Teaching Sociology, 26,* 1–13.

Richardson, F. C., Fowers, B. J., & Guignon, C. B. (1999). *Re-envisioning psychology: Moral dimensions of theory and practice.* San Francisco: Jossey-Bass.

Schumm, W. R. (2003a). Comments on marriage in contemporary culture: Five models that might help families. *Journal of Psychology and Theology, 31,* 213–223.

Schumm, W. R. (2003b). A reanalysis of Price's "Islam and human rights: A case of deceptive first appearances." *Psychological Reports, 93,* 1335–1338.

Schumm, W. R. (2004). What was really learned from Tasker and Golombok's (1995) study of lesbian and single-parent mothers? *Psychological Reports, 94,* 422–424.

Schumm, W. R., Webb, F. J., Castelo, C. C., Akagi, C. G., Jensen, E. J., Ditto, R. M., et al. (2002). Enhancing learning in statistics classes through the use of concrete historical examples. *Teaching Sociology, 30,* 361–375.

Sieber, J. E. (1992). *Planning ethically responsible research: A guide for students and internal review boards.* Newbury Park, CA: Sage.

Stacks, D. W., & Hickson, M. (1991). The communication investigator: Teaching research methods to undergraduates. *Communication Quarterly, 39,* 351–357.

Stanford Encyclopedia of Philosophy. (2003). The naturalistic fallacy and the open question argument. Retrieved November 2, 2003, from http://plato.stanford.edu/entries/moral-epistemology

Straus, M. A. (1994). *Beating the devil out of them: Corporal punishment in American families.* Lexington, MA: Lexington.

Straus, M. A. (2001a). *Beating the devil out of them: Corporal punishment in American families and its effects on children* (2nd ed.). New Brunswick, NJ: Transaction.

Straus, M. A. (2001b, September/October). New evidence for the benefits of never spanking. *Society, 38,* 52–60.

• Twenty-five

CONTROVERSIES AND FIRESTORMS

An Epilogue

Vern L. Bengtson, *University of Southern California*

Katherine R. Allen, *Virginia Polytechnic Institute and State University*

David M. Klein, *University of Notre Dame*

Peggye Dilworth-Anderson, *University of North Carolina at Chapel Hill*

Alan C. Acock, *Oregon State University*

This *Sourcebook* is a testament to scholarship as a communal effort. We five editors have worked together to coordinate the contributions of nearly 200 authors, many of whom are new to the scene of theory and research. Ever present in our minds as we have organized and edited this volume have been those we anticipate will be the readers and users of this text.

In this chapter we discuss some of the controversies that have energized and troubled us during the *Sourcebook* project. We have rediscovered something about theorizing in the course of debating these issues (we call them firestorms): that people make commitments to ideas, strong commitments, and in that sense, theorizing is inherently political. Each of us also shares his or her own

reflections on editing the *Sourcebook* (see the "My View" boxes in this chapter). We conclude with some thoughts about the next *Sourcebook,* which a new generation of family researchers will publish in 10 years or so.

Scholars who theorize about marriages, families, and relationships are deeply invested in their work. Negotiating across these subjects takes intellectual, interpersonal, and intuitive finesse. This process was clearly evident among the *Sourcebook* authors, whose contributions often reflect contradictory stories about families and the individuals within them. This process was frustrating and at the same time closer to the way things really happen than family scholars have often admitted. Compared with family scholars in the past, today we have more sophisticated research methods, more theoretical insights, and more interdisciplinary teams that are able to handle the complexity of the way families really are. The controversies we discuss in this chapter suggest that family scholars are better positioned than ever before to solve our field's theoretical puzzles, using the very tools we are helping to create.

The controversies we describe reflect differences in definitions, assumptions, and labels in studying families. Several also reflect conflict concerning the moral ends toward which theory should be directed. Some of these issues have generated firestorms of debate among our colleagues and occasionally among the five editors. Some will kindle debate in the future. Each issue reflects divisions of opinion concerning theory and epistemology—how we define families, the questions we ask, the knowledge we have about families, and the methods we use to gain such knowledge. As we argue in Chapter 1 of this volume, epistemology is a crucial but often neglected aspect of current family scholarship. Epistemological issues frame the ways we approach and define families. Definitions, assumptions, labels, and moral stances have powerful implications. They can be picked up by the mass media and misconstrued as pronouncements on "family values" and the "decline of the family" (as the authors of Chapters 4 and 16 discuss). They can also cause us to bicker angrily among ourselves, absorbing energy that could be directed toward more constructive scholarship.

Below we describe five controversies in current family research that we encountered in this *Sourcebook* project. We frame them as divergent paradigmatic or epistemological assumptions. It will be interesting to see how these controversies turn out—will they be resolved, continue to fire debate, or spiral off in unanticipated directions of family research 10 years from now?

CLASHING PARADIGMS: POSITIVISM AND POSTMODERNISM

The first controversy we encountered involved the terms *positivism* and *postmodernism* as code words for the conduct and interpretation of research. We were confronted by these terms—as labels, as systems of thinking, or as pejoratives aimed at particular scholars' (inappropriate) methods of research—as soon as we started reading the 73 proposals we received for *Sourcebook* contributions. We presented a draft of Chapter 1 for discussion at the 2003 Theory Construction and Research Methods Workshop in which we suggested that these labels might be archaic, stereotyping, and possibly damaging to the open exchange of ideas in family research (see Alan Acock's "My view" in Chapter 1). But we discovered in the discussion that followed that the labels of *positivism* and *postmodernism* are still alive and polarizing in family research and theory. Some of us argued that these are such value-laden terms that they are virtually meaningless and should not be used in scholarly discourse about families. Others argued that they do reflect divergent epistemological perspectives—paradigms, perhaps—about the nature of our subject matter, the goals of our research, and the methods we use to gain cumulative knowledge. We editors struggled among ourselves in trying to resolve the "either/or" assumptions on which those using these terms seem fixated. We consulted with our students, our colleagues, and members of our Editorial Advisory Board. We revisited historic schools of thought and discovered inadequacies in our own ideas. We tried to arrive at new ways of theorizing that are less stereotypical.

My view

The Power of Theory

Working on this project has brought home to me the power of theorizing. Theory is the best tool we have to expand our research findings into a cumulative body of knowledge and to enhance their applications. Theorizing forces us to ask "why," to construct explanations about what we have observed in empirical data. Theory enables us to summarize what is already known and to organize the mass of research findings from multiple studies. Theory also helps to suggest research issues that should be pursued, and to correct common myths or misconceptions—"conventional wisdom" about the social world. Theory helps us to build cumulative knowledge in our field—to stand on the shoulders of the giants who have come before us. Perhaps most important, theory can help us change things for the better through public policy and the helping professions: If we know *why* an undesirable condition exists, we can better define *how* it can be ameliorated.

My message to graduate students, the family researchers and scholars of tomorrow, is to take advantage of the power of theory by doing the following:

- Remember that *the development of cumulative knowledge* is our goal. Powerful theory starts with previous explanations, cumulative knowledge from past studies. We use findings from our research to go beyond those explanations, to break new ground. That's what makes theorizing creative and exciting.
- Focus on *theorizing as a process,* not on theory as a final end product. Theories should be evolving, always in the process of changing, as new data come to the fore and new explanations are developed.
- Think of theory without the capital *T.* Too often scholars consider theory as an esoteric historical exercise—trying to fit research findings to theories associated with past giants in our field such as Durkheim, Marx, Weber, Burgess, and Hill. But everyone can theorize; everyone can construct explanations that help us understand research findings.
- Recognize that research methods—whether qualitative, quantitative, or a combination of the two—are a means to an end, not the end itself. The end is the development of cumulative knowledge. Theorizing is important in qualitative studies and in quantitative studies, although demographers and epidemiologists currently place less emphasis on theory (see Bianchi and Casper, Chapter 4, this volume).
- Approach theorizing as though you are putting together a puzzle or playing a game. We hope that, after reading this book, you will be eager to join in this game.

—Vern L. Bengtson

In the end, we feel we can claim little success in breaking down the positivist/postmodernist dichotomy that has caused many heated exchanges in family research recently. But we did have some fun with defining "positivism." One of the editors developed a minitest to assess the degree to which we, as family researchers, follow the "positivist perspective" based on traditional notions of positivism from the scholarly literature. We reproduce this test as a Spotlight on Methods at the end of this chapter so that readers can examine their own notions of positivism in family theory and research. Taking this test can be an illuminating experience. When the five of us compared our scores, we found that the editor who considered himself most "quantitative" and the editor who was most "qualitative" had scored exactly the same on this survey. This suggests that the use of qualitative research methods may not be antithetical to "positivist" perspectives about scholarly knowledge.

In this *Sourcebook* we have tried to make sure that all of the contributors are clear and explicit about their underlying assumptions. However imprecise or archaic, labels such as *positivism, modernism,* and *postmodernism* can reflect quite different epistemological assumptions about social phenomena, the nature of families, and theorizing. Some of us feel that the family studies field is in the midst of a paradigm shift (see Peggye Dilworth-Anderson's "My View" box in Chapter 1). Others feel that family studies is a multiple-paradigm field, with several different paradigms operating and changing all at the same time (see Vern Bengtson's "My View" box in Chapter 1). This situation can create problems in communication. Ritzer (1980) notes that a defining characteristic of a multiple-paradigm science is that supporters of one paradigm are constantly questioning the basic assumptions of those who accept other paradigms: "Thus scientists have a difficult time conducting 'normal science' because they are constantly defending their flanks against attack from those who support other paradigms" (p. 12). Ritzer does not agree that paradigms are applicable only to entire disciplines, that a paradigm is characterized by hegemony in the entire field. Rather, "multiple paradigms can, in a sense, co-exist within a given science" (p. 45). But they do not coexist peacefully. Advocates are engaged in political efforts to gain power within the discipline:

> The struggle between paradigms for preeminence within a field has a clearly political character, underscoring the importance of irrationality in the development of the sciences. Paradigms do not simply gain hegemony because they are better than their predecessors. Paradigms gain the center stage because they are able to attract adherents and ward off attacks from those who support other positions. (Ritzer, 1980, p. 45)

The message is this: Science is social. Paradigms are promoted and persuaded by scholars who live and work in groups and have vested interests in advancing their own causes. Any claim that one paradigm is "better" than another should be viewed with the same caution as a political commercial on American television should be evaluated.

QUEERING VERSUS HETERONORMATIVITY IN THE FAMILY

Another controversy emerged when all chapter drafts had been completed and some colleagues wanted to publish a rejoinder to one of the chapters. This request came after the other submissions had gone through the prescribed review and decision process. As editors, we had made the spirit of inclusion our watchword, and we did not want to silence any voice without considering all sides. At the same time, we did not want to single out any particular chapter or issue for a special, after-the-deadline critique. This firestorm concerned the issues of gender heteronormativity and discrimination on the basis of sexual orientation. Whenever scholars make arguments for new ways of theorizing, redefining fundamental concepts, or creating radically new research methods, controversial reactions are to be expected. This was the case with Oswald, Blume, and Marks's contribution (Chapter 6) on decentering heteronormativity, or "queering family theory," the title they originally proposed.

A draft of Oswald et al.'s chapter was submitted to and presented at the 2003 Theory Construction and Research Methodology (TCRM) Workshop. The TCRM chair asked Camille Williams to be a discussant of the paper. Later, he asked that the rebuttal Williams had written be published in the

Sourcebook with Chapter 6 as an additional "Discussion and Extension" feature. This created a dilemma for the editors. Our goal for the features accompanying each *Sourcebook* chapter was to extend or illustrate the ideas in the chapter, not to challenge the credibility of the chapter or to question it on moral grounds. From this perspective, we did not feel that the critique of Oswald et al.'s chapter presented at the TCRM should be published within the chapter itself (as a "Discussion and Extension" or otherwise) because it neither extends nor illustrates the chapter, but only challenges it. However, it does represent a heated debate in our field that stems from differing paradigmatic or epistemological assumptions. The relevance of this issue to current political and moral debate is reflected in the fact that, around the same time this *Sourcebook* is published, American citizens in 13 states will vote on amendments to their state constitutions to ban same-sex marriage.

My view

Understanding, Stamina, and Respect

The dilemma in theoretical work is the difficulty of understanding others. This theme has emerged as we have worked through the thorny issues of organizing the structure of this book and negotiating with authors. We have witnessed misalignments in meanings and beliefs along with communicative eruptions among scholars. Achieving clarity is not easy. I now know profoundly that others do not share *my* definitions of positivism, postmodernism, paradigm, qualitative research, quantitative research, reflexivity, spirituality, and epistemology. Even with my fellow editors, people I've come to trust and love, understanding is brief and partial. In their presence, I have spent hours ironing out wrinkles of misunderstanding, pressing into performance new creases of thought, only to see unexpected folds emerge when the next challenge comes.

I find this process of theorizing in a collaborative venture to be both exciting and unnerving. As a child, I recited a rhyme: "The bear went over the mountain, to see what he could see . . . the other side of the mountain, is what the bear could see." Like that bear, I am willing to climb again. I have worked hard for my place on this trek because I believe that this expedition can too easily become an exclusive club that keeps people like me out. With me here, it is more diverse. But to keep an open and inclusive process to our theorizing, we need to be better skilled at communication, reflection, and dialogue. Stamina helps, too.

We have fought battles over language and meaning in this *Sourcebook*. Underneath are values, attitudes, behaviors, and laws governing how and with whom people can live, work, and love. Ever mindful that theorizing is a political process, we have tried to be deliberate, relevant, and fair. Future scholars will continue to struggle with meaning and politics as well. With respect for the genius that moves in all of us and the desire to seek new understandings and explanations, we will be closer to knowledge that can inform families and transform lives if we keep alert to these dilemmas and the opportunities they bring.

—Katherine R. Allen

The argument about heteronormativity can serve as a good starting point for classroom discussions of epistemology, of what constitutes theorizing, of how religion and ideology relate to theory and research, of the relationship between theorizing and current cultural norms and trends, and of the excruciating difficulty inherent in any attempt to delimit the family. How well does a "model" of family that is social constructionist and considerably flexible regarding family composition and roles fit today's experience? How well does a model of the family that is restricted to traditional norms of composition and roles work in today's fast-changing world?

The discussion about printing Knapp and Williams's comments created yet another firestorm (see the Spotlights on Theory at the end of this chapter). The debates we encountered as editors forced us to consider current challenges to the prevailing normative categories in family studies, such as marriage and parental rights for same-sex couples. These controversies demonstrate that theorizing in family studies is *not* just an abstract, distant, armchair activity. Family scholars are theorizing about issues that affect people in their bedrooms, around their kitchen tables, in the courts, and in places of worship; thus family theories are entwined with the political nature of those ideas. In Chapter 6, Oswald et al. critique theory, politics, religion, patriarchy, sexuality, gender, marriage, and family in ways that challenge many assumptions that have been at the core of our discipline.

Given the highly contested nature of this controversy, and the fact that we chose to keep alive the open (although difficult and often painful) dialogue we have described here, queer theory is certainly one of the most hotly debated issues we faced in developing the *Sourcebook*. In their Spotlight on Theory at the end of this chapter, Knapp and Williams present arguments in opposition to "queering the family." In a second Spotlight on Theory, one of the editors, Katherine Allen, shares her dissenting view and her thoughts about confronting this debate. We anticipate that family scholars will continue to face differences of opinion such as this. Ideas, morals, and politics are increasingly intertwined with family theory and research in explicit and contested ways.

FAMILY THEORY OR GENERAL SOCIAL SCIENCE THEORIES APPLIED TO FAMILIES?

The third controversy is not as frequently reflected in today's family research literature as the first two we have discussed, but we predict it will be more prominent in the next decade. This controversy concerns whether we should stop attempting to develop "family theory" per se and instead direct our attention to existing social-behavioral theories about social relationships to families. This is the argument made by Jonathan Turner (2002, 2003; see also his case study in Chapter 1). Turner has recently developed a theory of macrosociology that is particularly applicable to the family as a social institution. He presents six "laws," sociological principles that have been verified again and again over decades of research, that can help us understand social change and macrosocial arrangements. The family is one of the most ubiquitous and basic of social institutions, but understanding and explaining the massive changes that families are undergoing does not require theory unique to the family. Rather, family processes and changes can be explained as applications of more general social laws.

Another example is the recent work of social theorist Randall Collins (2004), who has developed a general theory of "interaction ritual chains" that attempts to explain social behavior as diverse as sex, smoking, and social stratification. Collins calls this "radical microsociology." The theory proposes that successful rituals create symbols of group membership and energize individuals with emotional energy (failed rituals drain energy). Individuals flow from situation to situation, drawn to those interactions in which their cultural capital gives them the best payoff in emotional energy. Thinking—social cognition—can be explained as the internalization of conversations within the flow of situations;

individual selves are thoroughly and continually socially constructed, from the outside in. Collins bases his theory on the classic analyses of Durkheim, Mead, and Goffman. This is a theory of general, universal social processes, yet it can be applied easily to specific social contexts and social institutions, such as families. Although Collins does not address family relationships specifically, others can use his theory to explain family behaviors. Collins does address the emotional and symbolic nature of sexual exchanges—from handholding to relations with prostitutes—by analyzing the interaction rituals they involve. Collins does not need "family theory" to explain the interactions he observes; he can apply his general interaction ritual chains theory to most, if not all, behaviors.

Some may feel that this *Sourcebook* illustrates the fragmentation as well as the elaboration of theoretical frameworks to construct explanations for family phenomena. Where does this controversy leave "family theory" today and in the future? In earlier years, family scholars sometimes focused on the search for a grand theory of the family, but now that search has been abandoned, given the recognition that one grand scheme cannot accommodate all aspects and conditions of family life, particularly in a multifaceted and constantly changing world. This leaves us with the challenge of continuing to identify what it is about families that makes this a unique area of study. How do families differ from other primary groups? Why are different theories needed to understand families than to understand other primary groups? What unique perspectives do *family* scholars offer for conceptualizing and understanding relationships, interactions, and structures in these intimate pairings and groups of people who are related to each other by blood or by choice? This controversy illustrates the continuing dilemma family scholars face in defining our subject matter.

My view

Toward a Multiplicity of Perspectives

I've had the privilege of contributing to the 1979 and 1993 family theory and methods projects as well as to the current one, so I believe I can provide some perspective on how the family field has changed during recent decades in its approaches to theorizing.

The *Contemporary Theories* project (Burr, Hill, Nye, & Reiss, 1979a, 1979b) had a dual emphasis. In addition to highlighting the familiar frameworks (Volume 2), the project devoted much attention to formal methods of theorizing (Volume 1). Based mostly on causal modeling and deductive reasoning, the project integrated several substantive areas of research by explicitly connecting concepts and statements, with the goal of explaining important outcomes. Contributors to the *Contemporary Theories* volumes touted the methods of formal theorizing as the best way of clarifying and evaluating theoretical arguments.

By the time of the 1993 *Sourcebook* project (Boss, Doherty, LaRossa, Schumm, & Steinmetz, 1993), much of the previous enthusiasm for formal methods had waned. More exciting seemed to be a return to narrative methods, inspired by emergent perspectives derived from family members themselves, adding legitimacy to previously unheard voices. Nevertheless, the 1993 project continued to emphasize theoretical frameworks, covering even more than the earlier project had covered. Instead of dealing very much with methods of theorizing, the 1993 project was very thorough in covering a range of research methods. This helped to reinforce the idea that theories and research go hand in hand.

(continued)

My view *continued*

At about the time the 1993 project was finished, a colleague and I conducted a study of the attitudes and activities of family theorists by surveying 104 participants at the 1992 TCRM Workshop. Among our purposes was to find out about similarities and differences in family theorists' own philosophies of science (Klein & Janning, 1997). The findings were somewhat surprising.

We discovered that as many as seven different epistemological or philosophical orientations characterized the theorists who participated. The most popular was a "rational-empirical" perspective, one that was congenial to the earlier formal period of theorizing. The second most popular was a "feminist" perspective. The remaining philosophies were not very popular. They included what we called "emotive-creative," "qualitative," "quantitative," positivistic," and "constructivistic" approaches to theory.

The most surprising aspect of the survey's findings was that the participants seldom viewed their philosophies as either/or choices. Instead, they tended to subscribe to elements of several perspectives and to reject few altogether. One conclusion was that family scholars in the early 1990s saw theorizing about families as requiring a diverse "tool kit" of ways to proceed, and that most drew on a variety of philosophical principles according to the situation at hand.

In reflecting on the current *Sourcebook* project, I think that we are observing a continuation of the ecumenical spirit that prevailed more than a decade ago. Few if any of the authors in this volume attempt to make a case that only one theoretical perspective or philosophical orientation is sufficient to provide an adequate explanation or understanding of any family phenomenon. In the future, we may see more attempts by scholars to advocate strongly for one approach and to criticize others. I believe, however, that multiple viewpoints will continue to coexist for the next decade or two, and that more of us will capitalize on this development instead of aligning ourselves into opposing camps.

—David M. Klein

Related issues include whether family studies is a science and what exactly we mean by "science." These, too, are paradigmatic issues. The term *family science* did not arise until the last quarter of the 20th century, preceded in the third quarter by some who identified themselves as "family sociologists." Among family scholars trained in sociology, some may have been attracted to some versions of "positivism," and some family scientists in other disciplines may have followed suit. Even today, family science is a multidisciplinary and somewhat interdisciplinary field rather than an independent discipline in its own right. Some family scholars have wanted to legitimate family studies as a unique discipline, such as "family science," but their arguments have yet to persuade very many university administrators or faculty members who create and change the labels placed on departmental units.

DEFINING "FAMILY"

The controversy about who can marry legally in the United States today goes to the heart of the matter of what most, if not all, societies consider "the family." Family life has traditionally been viewed as beginning with a "legitimate" couple whose union is sanctioned by rules and laws (both informal and formal) in a society. Today, however, the definition of "family" that family theorists and researchers have traditionally used has been challenged by major changes in the American family and family research within the past 75 years that go beyond the issue of what constitutes a legitimate couple. These include changes in the structure and organization of the family, trends toward interracial and same-sex marriages as well as cohabitation outside of marriage, and changes in researchers' approaches to examining households versus families (see Demo, Allen, & Fine, 2000).

Although nuclear families based on heterosexual marriage have not been the norm for many Americans throughout history, the nuclear family structure has long been the gold standard for defining the family in American public policy. The new millennium has brought a broad array of changes in families that are forcing scholars to redefine the concept, but a new standard by which to define families remains elusive. The incongruence between current family structures and the theories available for interpretation may require a paradigm shift in family scholars' theorizing to take the changing family landscape into account. Scholars will have to rethink definitions and understandings to make this shift possible.

Data on families in the United States today indicate a rise in the numbers of never-married women with children, especially among African Americans; a decrease in the numbers of couples with dependent children; an increase in the numbers of divorced and separated parents as well as stepfamilies, or "blended" families; and an increase in the numbers of family members living in different households, especially among immigrant and poor families. Contemporary families are also more diverse in sexual orientation than families in the past, with traditional mother and father roles not present in many families. These and many other characteristics of today's families will continue to challenge what we mean when we use the term *family*. As we approach this challenge, we will need new and refined conceptualizations of family dynamics, structures, and organizations to arrive at a viable definition of family. If we are going to advance our theorizing in family studies, we need to update and broaden our definition of "family."

My view

Theorizing Is Community Work

We cannot create, reframe, and refine theoretical ideas without keeping context in mind. Working on this *Sourcebook* reaffirmed my belief that contexts (e.g., social, historical, and developmental) are critical to good theorizing. Additionally, coupled with contexts is the issue of inclusion. Good theorists and, ultimately, good theories develop within a community; thus theorizing is "community work."

As the editors of this volume, we have created a sense of community among ourselves, and inclusion is a central feature of this community. This inclusion entails having respect for differences, sharing multiple voices, and knowing the value of personal biographies in intellectual discourse. We parlayed our sense of community into how we conceived the *Sourcebook*. As a result, I believe that we all (editors and contributors) have created a book that includes people from varied and overlapping contextual backgrounds and thereby represents a large community of diverse scholars.

The contributors to this volume represent multiple disciplines, ethnicities, and sexual orientations. They honor varied intellectual traditions that go beyond their academic training. As a result, we—the editors and authors—have achieved inclusiveness, both through the varied kinds of theoretical thinking presented and through the diversity of the scholars whose contributions are contained here. As we enter into this new

(continued)

My view *continued*

millennium, the need for inclusion in family scholarship will increase. We need to approach theorizing with inclusion at the forefront of our thinking—we need diverse ideas from diverse people. Through such inclusion, the community of family scholars will grow, and our research and theories will become even more relevant and useful to families, researchers, students, and policy makers.

—Peggye Dilworth-Anderson

Equally challenging to family scholars is the concept of the identity development of individuals within today's diverse families (James & Tucker, 2003). As McAdoo, Martínez, and Hughes note in Chapter 8 of this volume, changes have occurred in how various groups in the United States define their racial and ethnic identities. The census and other research standard for many years was to offer people three choices within which to categorize themselves: White, Black, and other. Today, organizations that collect data are aware that these three categories are no longer sufficient. In 2001, the U.S. Bureau of the Census began to consider Asians as a race, whereas it considered Hispanics as an ethnic group. But Filipinos can identify as both Asian and Spanish in origin. In addition, the increase in interracial marriage has created a new generation of people who think of themselves as multiracial or "other" because they identify with more than one racial or ethnic group. Population projections suggest that the numbers of bi- and multiracial children in the United States are increasing, as are the numbers of individuals who openly identify themselves as such.

Challenges such as those outlined above will continue to require current and future family scholars to include in their theories concepts and assumptions that reflect contemporary definitions of families as well as the identities of individual members within them (Omi, 2001). Census figures do not reflect culture. Race, ethnicity, and culture matter in conceptualizing the family.

MULTILEVEL ORIENTATIONS FOR BOTH THEORY AND RESEARCH

A fifth controversy concerns the "individualization" of the family in research and theory today. Hagestad and Dannefer (2001) refer to this trend as "microfication." Family theorizing has been criticized for being overly individualistic in its methods and its subject matter. It has not paid sufficient attention to structural factors and has ignored influences across multiple levels—individual, family, school, and community. From the content of this *Sourcebook*, it is clear that our theories should be advancing beyond this criticism. Almost all of the theorizing presented in this volume involves the examination of multiple levels of influence. Yet as we look at our journals and textbooks, we see that many of the theories and methods being used are still at one level, that of individual analysis.

My view

Basics of Methodology in Family Research

This project has taught me two important things about methodology that I would like to pass on to the family researchers of tomorrow:

First, we need multiple methodological lenses through which to view and understand families. Some of us are lousy at one or another methodology and have little chance of getting our work published using that methodology. This does not exempt us from the need to use the methods we are not very good at as part of our research process. The limitations of any one method argue for the necessity of collaboration. The best scholarship integrates multiple methodologies, and methodologically diverse research teams are essential for making this work. Every method has both strengths and limitations, and we would do well to be aware of both. We need a moratorium on scholars' attacking all methods but their own. Methodologies are justified by the understandings they offer, not by their users' ridicule of other methodologies that offer other understandings. Each lens we use to study families gives us new findings and new ideas. Choices that limit the lenses we use are self-inflicted blinders. There is no room in family scholarship for methodological bigotry.

Second, serious scholars need to expand their methodological skills during and after graduate school. Virtually none of the quantitative methods discussed in this volume were even imagined when I was a graduate student. Without a lifelong commitment to keeping methodologically current, scholars will fall into a rut that eventually renders their work unpublishable. We need a structure to keep researchers well informed and proficient in new methods. The search for new methodologies and the investment in mastering them will allow scholars to strengthen their contributions throughout their careers. Their final publications will rank among their very best. This is my message to graduate students and family scholars.

—Alan C. Acock

In the period when family scholarship was dominated by overly individualized theories, most of the data and quantitative methods were similarly focused. We had "family" data from a single informant, usually the mother. We had almost no information on the neighborhood or community level. For example, an African American father in a community with a 20% unemployment rate, where 25% of the fathers have been incarcerated, and where enforcement of child support is ineffective was not distinguished from an African American father living in a middle-class community with low unemployment, where incarceration of fathers is rare, and where child support is not an issue. Data collection has changed dramatically with the development of national surveys, and data collected using global positioning satellite systems make it possible for scholars to link individual, family, school, and community variables. Today, family researchers complete interviews with both parents (even when one is nonresident) and their adolescent children. They integrate children's school records with reports from teachers and the children's scores on standardized tests. Our data have become extraordinarily ripe for multilevel theories.

As our theories and data have advanced over the past few decades, so too have our quantitative methods. Multilevel modeling, hierarchical linear modeling, growth mixture modeling, and related techniques make it possible to establish isomorphism among multilevel theory, multilevel data, and multilevel methods. Data sets are becoming more complex, and to use them, researchers need increasingly sophisticated analytic and statistical skills. In the past, the methods available to analyze such data were either inadequate for the task or too complicated for most family scholars to use. The analytic methods available today are up to the task, and computer software packages make them relatively user-friendly. Still, the demand of keeping up with technical changes is a major challenge for people already in the field. It is also a challenge for family studies educators to incorporate these new methods into existing graduate curricula.

Despite these simultaneous developments in theory, data, and quantitative methods, most empirical research published in our major journals is still overly individualistic theoretically, ignores data available on multiple levels, or uses quantitative methods that are individualistic. Researchers may collect data from parents, their children, and the children's teachers and link these data to census data, but they too often ignore these multiple windows. For example, the first wave of the National Survey of Families and Households includes data from mothers and fathers, but most published analyses rely on reports from just mothers or fathers. The second wave of the NSFH includes data from mothers and fathers, their former spouses or partners, adolescent children, adult children, and grandparents, along with data on communities and neighborhoods. However, the preponderance of researchers who have used these data sets have ignored the multiple windows available into the lives of these families, even when their theories would appear to call for them.

We need a systematic way to incorporate the changes noted above into our graduate education and to help people already in the field to become facile in the latest analytic techniques or to collaborate with people who can use them. Graduate training in family studies often does not cover the newest techniques that students will need to conduct multilevel analysis. Knowledge of analysis of variance and multiple regression are not sufficient. Many scholars who have been active in family research for some time have not kept current with theoretical or methodological developments. This is not a new problem, but it does impede progress. Several chapters in this *Sourcebook* can help to move us beyond these limits. In Chapter 12, Sayer and Klute introduce readers to the literature on multilevel analysis, and in Chapter 19, Corwyn and Bradley review advances in structural equation modeling. In Chapter 3, Acock, van Dulmen, Allen, and Piercy provide an overview of recent methodological advances.

CONCLUSION

The next *Sourcebook* project is likely to repeat some of the themes in the present volume, but new themes surely will arise in the decades ahead. Likewise, some of the current controversies in family scholarship may be resolved in future years, but some may prove to be intractable, and new controversies are certain to arise. Will we reach the point where it is routine for a scholar to use both quantitative and qualitative methods in a given research project? Will we witness a revival of formal methods of theorizing using propositional logic? Will we ever overcome disagreements about what "family" means? We certainly cannot agree on the importance of a particular explanation if we do not agree about one or more elements in that explanation, whether the disagreement is about the meaning of concepts in the explanation itself or about what we are trying to explain.

We cannot anticipate in any detail what the landscape of family scholarship will be like in the future. We are convinced, however, that those of us who actively participate in theorizing about families will find our involvements to be enormously exciting and rewarding.

ARE YOU A "POSITIVIST"? AN EPISTEMOLOGICAL SELF-ASSESSMENT

David M. Klein, *University of Notre Dame*

Answer the following about *your own beliefs* concerning family research.

6 = totally agree
5 = mostly agree
4 = somewhat agree
3 = no opinion
2 = somewhat disagree
1 = mostly disagree
0 = totally disagree

_____ 1. Improvements in knowledge about families are what increase the quality and stability of family life.

_____ 2. All sound knowledge about families is grounded in observation.

_____ 3. All sciences can be integrated into a single natural system.

_____ 4. I belong to a secular religion of humanity devoted to the worship of family life.

_____ 5. The motor of progress that guarantees the emergence of superior family forms is the competition among increasingly differentiated individuals.

_____ 6. Family studies as a science consists of the collection and statistical analysis of quantitative data about families.

_____ 7. To be meaningful, a proposition about families must be verifiable.

_____ 8. A carefully crafted plan to unify all sciences syntactically and semantically is worth pursuing.

_____ 9. Family studies as a science consists of a body of interrelated, true, simple, precise, and wide-ranging universal laws that are central to prediction and explanation.

_____ 10. Family studies as a science tries to discover causal laws about families for the purposes of prediction and explanation.

_____ 11. Family science progresses by inducing lawlike statements from observational and experimental evidence.

_____ 12. Family science progresses by conjecturing hypotheses and attempting to refute them, so that false conjectures are eliminated and corroborated ones are retained.

Total up your points. The higher your score, the more your views reflect historical "positivism" (a score over 36 indicates a strong leaning toward positivism).

(continued)

The statements above are adapted from Peter Halfpenny's *Positivism and Sociology: Explaining Social Life* (1982). Statements 1–4 represent four different ideas advanced by Auguste Comte in the 19th century. Statement 5 reflects the position of Herbert Spencer, and statement 6 is associated with Émile Durkheim, both also 19th-century thinkers. Statements 7–9 are associated with philosophers of science during the first half of the 20th century who were often called "logical positivists." Statement 10 is an application of earlier ideas of David Hume that were first taken up after the mid-20th century by causal modelers such as O. Dudley Duncan and Herbert Blalock. Statement 11 is from Francis Bacon near the end of the 16th century, and Statement 12 is the perspective of philosopher Karl Popper in the mid-20th century.

We don't envision that many family researchers would score over 36 points on this "positivism" test. However, we hypothesize that agreements would most often be found for Statements 2 and 10, and that occasional agreements would be found for Statements 6, 7, 11, and 12. If this conjecture is corroborated, the conclusion is that although family scientists may differ in how positivist they are, most are close to being on the fence or positivist in some ways but not in others. Antipositivism may not be very common in practice.

What is your score, and how might it affect your attitudes toward theory, theorizing, and research methods? If you are completely against positivism, you would probably think that our little test is completely worthless (and not take it). But if that is the case, how *would* you examine how "positivist" family scholars are? ●

WHERE DOES QUEER THEORY TAKE US?

Stan J. Knapp, *Brigham Young University*

Camille S. Williams, *Brigham Young University*

Family scholars seek to produce knowledge that advances our understanding of family in the hope that such knowledge will also facilitate improved living conditions for families and individuals. It is to this end that proponents of queer theory and other postmodern theories call for the deconstruction or decentering of "heteronormativity" (Oswald, Blume, & Marks, Chapter 6, this volume), gender (Blume & Blume, 2003), and gendered heteronormativity (Nielsen, Walden, & Kunkel, 2000).

(continued)

Queer theory seeks to destabilize the categories of sex, gender, and family, displacing mainstream heterosexuality as a baseline for judging family normality and denaturalizing the entangling of sexuality with gender and with prescribed family configuration (see Oswald et al., Chapter 6, this volume). Queering the family means a commitment to no necessary connections among gender, sexuality, and family. The desired result would be family configurations that accommodate whatever desires, sensibilities, and opportunities happen to arise. Connections among gender, sexuality, and family are only to be justified through recourse to individual desires and consent. What are the grounding assumptions of this perspective, and does queering the family improve our understanding of family life?

First, calling for the deconstruction of notions of gender, heterosexuality, and their connections to family amounts to claiming that one can understand each category as socially constructed and therefore ultimately *nothing more than* the result of contingent and provisional social practices. Thus heterosexual unions are nothing more than the configuration of social practices currently operative in various societies. But if we are utterly and completely social constructed, then on what grounds do advocates call for the "deconstruction" of gender and heterosexuality? At the heart of queer theory lies an assumption that individual "desire" and "inner sensibilities" are free from processes of social construction. Subverting the heterosexual norm depends on the premise that all people have the capacity and right to define themselves and their relationships. In this way, a "disentangled" sexuality can set individuals free to unfold in accordance with desire, inner sensibility, and the opportunities provided by an unencumbered set of social arrangements. Just where such desires come from remains unanswered and unanswerable; ultimately, they just happen to arise (see Oswald et al., Chapter 6, this volume).

Second, is decentering family in the name of individual desire the best way to transform family studies? How is it that heterosexual desires are socially constructed and therefore "forced" (Nielsen et al., 2000, p. 283), whereas nonheterosexual desires are not? Queer theory seeks to destabilize all categories of sexuality and yet uses such a position primarily in the defense of and affirmation of categories of sexual minorities: gays, lesbians, bisexuals, transsexuals, transgendered persons, and individuals questioning their sexual identity. Queer theory seeks to countermand centering family studies in any kind of "normativity," replacing it with "creativity." Yet can creativity become the primary baseline for judging family practices, arrangements, structures, relationships, identities, and so forth? Is creativity in sexuality, gender, and family, by definition, only present when it challenges heteronormativity? How can the deconstruction of heteronormativity avoid reinscribing the existing binary of the heterosexual and the queer?

Third, queer theory's affirmation of individual creativity seems to avoid empirical and theoretical questions about the limits of our capacity to construct ourselves. Is it possible that heterosexual coupling has been dominant partly because it is sustainable, it can reproduce itself, whereas same-sex coupling cannot? Could the desire to decenter the heteronormative family itself be an ethnocentric project—indeed, perhaps a "normative" project—for a particular group in contemporary societies?

Duh !

Fourth, queer theory seems less interested in theorizing family than in destabilizing, deconstructing, and decentering it. Instead of focusing on how family life is constructed and reproduced, queer theory appears to aim at providing grounds for change rather

(continued)

● *SPOTLIGHT ON THEORY continued*

than grounds for explanation of family forms and practices. Despite the fact that the heterosexual family has been dominant across all cultures throughout all historical periods about which we have knowledge, queer theory provides little focus on why the heterosexual family has been so common other than to accuse previous family forms of "enforced heterosexuality" (Nielsen et al., 2000, p. 283).

Finally, attempts to decenter heterosexuality may exhibit unwillingness to examine the moral and practical consequences of such a move for individuals, families, and the field of family studies itself. It may be that queer theory is ill suited to family studies and better suited to the humanities. A theory of family that encourages creative experimentation with sexual identities will have significant consequences for individuals, families, and society. Before we deconstruct the heterosexual family, we should give more thought to the means and the costs of reconstruction. ●

● *SPOTLIGHT ON THEORY*

PUSHING THE BOUNDARIES OF THE *SOURCEBOOK*

Katherine R. Allen, *Virginia Polytechnic Institute and State University*

I served as the corresponding editor for the contribution to this volume by Oswald, Blume, and Marks (Chapter 6), which was originally presented at the 2003 Theory Construction Research and Methodology Workshop. Stan Knapp, the chair of TCRM, invited attorney Camille Williams of Brigham Young University to be a discussant of the paper, and he later asked if we would include Williams's piece (the preceding Spotlight on Theory) in the *Sourcebook* because it offers a perspective so different from that offered by Oswald et al. Initially, I felt this "rejoinder" was not suitable for the *Sourcebook*. I attended the TCRM session at which Williams gave her discussant comments, and I believed that she had engaged neither the substantive issues nor the spirit of Oswald, Blume, and Marks's work. Rather, I believed, as did Oswald and her coauthors, that Williams's comments were a religiously and politically motivated attack on the subjects of Oswald et al.'s chapter: gay, lesbian, bisexual, and transgendered people and their families.

In keeping with the inclusive mandate established by the editorial team, however, I was obligated in my role as an editor to consider this request. Oswald et al. expressed feelings of shock and betrayal that their chapter (alone among all the chapters in this volume) would be subject to rebuttal at the last minute. Outrage continued to mount as it became apparent that their marginalized perspective might not be protected.

(continued)

The editorial team's debates throughout this process were agonizing, because the editors disagreed with one another about the appropriateness of publishing the rejoinder to the Oswald et al. chapter. We agreed, however, in our feeling that the authors of Chapter 6 may have been blindsided by this request, given that none of the other *Sourcebook* authors had to deal with such a considerable challenge to their scholarship or integrity. We also agreed that we wanted to be as inclusive as possible by considering all requests for features that were presented to us.

The Knapp/Williams piece appears in the *Sourcebook* as part of the chapter on controversies and firestorms, an example of an apparently irresolvable difference in paradigmatic or epistemological perspectives. We feel that the next generation of family scholars must continue to deal with the deep fissures in our society about who gets to count as family, how politics and religion are used to construct and/or distort family bonds, and how gatekeepers (including *Sourcebook* editors) use power implicitly and explicitly to maintain or change the status quo.

Queering family theory pushed the boundaries for many of us involved in this *Sourcebook,* and I believe that is a very good thing. Oswald et al. had the courage to put forward ideas in their chapter that can help others understand and make sense of the different ways in which families live. Their contribution to this volume, like many other chapters and features in this book, challenges prevailing assumptions and offers new possibilities for how to theorize about and study families in the coming years. This is one of the goals of the *Sourcebook*—to challenge old ideas and inspire new conceptualizations, particularly for those who dare to think and act on their insight, knowledge, passion, and lived experience.

It is both a privilege and a risk to air some of these backstage activities for all to consider, including the editors' disagreements about the intellectual goals of the project, the amount of time we spent negotiating a solution to one controversial issue, the misunderstandings we faced on the editorial team, and the need for responsible communication. In past years, the issues of gender inequality and racial inequality have taken center stage in our scholarly debates. These issues continue to be contested as well, but the issue of sexual orientation inequality among families has had particular salience in this iteration of the *Sourcebook* as well as in our communities at large. What I find so promising about our process of collaboration as editors, theorists, and researchers at this moment in time is that we are willing to leave some of the fragments of our thinking on the table for others to see as well. What hot-button issues will the next *Sourcebook* editors and contributors face?

The fear of difference and the inadequate response of indifference to the issues that divide us affect the communities in which we live and the scientific communities in which we work. Although I disagreed with the editorial decision to publish Knapp and Williams's rejoinder to Oswald et al.'s chapter, in the end, I stand with my fellow editors on the whole of this book. At no time did the editors of this *Sourcebook* choose an easy way out of this dilemma (for example, we could have ignored the request to include the Knapp and Williams piece, or we could have included it without comment). Ultimately, this community of scholars consciously worked for change and inclusion in family studies, the study of all families. Together we tried to put difficult issues up front so that the theorizing we do can be as explicit, inclusive, and collaborative as possible. ●

REFERENCES

Blume, L. B., & Blume, T. W. (2003). Toward a dialectical model of family gender discourse: Body, identity, and sexuality. *Journal of Marriage and Family, 65,* 785–794.

Boss, P., Doherty, W. J., LaRossa, R., Schumm, W. R., & Steinmetz, S. K. (Eds.). (1993). *Sourcebook of family theories and methods: A contextual approach.* New York: Plenum.

Burr, W. R., Hill, R., Nye, F. I., & Reiss, I. L. (Eds.). (1979a). *Contemporary theories about the family: Vol. 1. Research-based theories.* New York: Free Press.

Burr, W. R., Hill, R., Nye, F. I., & Reiss, I. L. (Eds.). (1979b). *Contemporary theories about the family: Vol. 2. General theories/theoretical orientations.* New York: Free Press.

Collins, R. (2004). *Interaction ritual chains.* Princeton, NJ: Princeton University Press.

Demo, D. H., Allen, K. R., & Fine, M. A. (Eds.). (2000). *Handbook of family diversity.* New York: Oxford University Press.

Halfpenny, P. (1982). *Positivism and sociology: Explaining social life.* Sydney: Allen & Unwin.

Hagestad, G., & Dannefer, W. D. (2001). Concepts and theories of aging: Beyond microfication in social science approaches. In R. H. Binstock & L. K. George (Eds.), *Handbook of aging and the social sciences* (5th ed., pp. 217–237). New York: Academic Press.

James, A. D., & Tucker, M. B. (2003). Racial ambiguity and relationship formation in the United States: Theoretical and practical considerations. *Journal of Social and Personal Relationships, 20,* 153–169.

Klein, D. M., & Janning, M. (1997, November 18). *Family theorists' philosophies of science.* Paper presented at the Theory Construction and Research Methodology Workshop, annual meeting of the National Council on Family Relations, Orlando, FL.

Nielsen, J. M., Walden, G., & Kunkel, C. A. (2000). Gendered heteronormativity: Empirical illustrations in everyday life. *Sociological Quarterly, 41,* 283–296.

Omi, M. A. (2001). The changing meaning of race. In N. J. Smelser, W. J. Wilson, & F. Mitchell (Eds.), *America becoming: Racial trends and their consequences* (Vol. 1, pp. 243–263). Washington, DC: National Academies Press.

Ritzer, G. (1980). *Sociology: A multiple paradigm science.* Boston: Allyn & Bacon.

Turner, J. H. (2002). *Face to face: Toward a sociological theory of interpersonal behavior.* Stanford, CA: Stanford University Press.

Turner, J. H. (2003). *Human institutions: A theory of societal evolution.* New York: Rowman & Littlefield.

• Author Index

• Subject Index

Abortion, 427
Accountability:
  data presentation, alternate forms of, 66
  See also Evaluation
Acculturation pressures, 196-197
Activism, 12, 458-459
Add Health Study, 9, 67, 105, 153
Adolescents:
  developmental continuity/
    change, family role in, 385-387
  family risk and, 387
  feminist theory applications and, 463-465
  parent-adolescent relations, attachment/family
    systems theories integration and, 382-385
  positive youth development, 488-490
  stage-environment fit and, 387
  teen pregnancy and, 345
  See also Child/adolescent development
Adoptive parent-child relationships, 433-434
Adult Attachment Interview, 217
Adult sibling ties, 167-168
  aging parents, caretaking responsibilities and,
    172, 173-174
  ambivalence concept and, 171, 172-173
  childhood relationships, life-course
    implications of, 184-186
  cultural/ethnic factors and, 173
  family connections, flexibility and, 168, 169
  feminist perspective and, 170, 172
  gender and, 172, 178
  illusive/dormant nature of, 176-177
  interdependent states and, 172
  kinship networks and, 180
  life-course perspective and, 169-170, 171-172
  obligations of, 168-169, 172
  psychoanalytic perspective and, 175
  research on, 175-181
  selection issues, 178
  sibling dyads/kinship network research, case
    study, 181-184
  siblings, definition of, 176, 178
  social changes and, 168
  social constructionist framework
    and, 170-171, 172
  theoretical perspectives on, 169-173
  twin studies, dementia and, 179-180

  units of analysis, decisional difficulties
    and, 177-178
Advisory committees, 65
Aesthetic representation of data, 65-66
African American families, 193
  church-based social support and, 524-525
  deficit model of, 454
  family composition/transitions and, 130, 131
  fence metaphor and, 47
  homeplace, significance of, 48-49
  motherwork and, 454-455
  parenting styles and, 197-198
  veil metaphor and, 47
  See also Ethnic families of color;
    Interracial marriages
Agency, 121, 250-251, 329
  ambivalence, intergenerational
    relations and, 398-399
  self-other representation and, 449
Age patterning, 103, 105, 121
Aggression between intimates, 315-316
  change, human experience and, 324-325
  contradiction, simultaneity of both/
    and, 322-324
  dialectical perspective and, 319-320,
    322-331, 335-337
  elder abuse/ecological perspective,
    case study, 332-334
  empirical findings on, 322-323, 324-325,
    326, 329-330
  family resilience and, 320-321
  institutional/structural elements and, 336
  interpersonal elements and, 335-336
  praxis and, 329-330
  relational/contextual theories of, 316-319,
    317-318 (table)
  study methodology and, 323-324, 325,
    328-329, 330
  totality approach and, 325-326, 328-329
  welfare families and, 355-356
  See also Adoptive parent-child
    relationships
Ambivalence model, 14, 20
  adult sibling ties and, 171, 172-173
  intergenerational family
    relations and, 398-399, 402, 404

• About the Editors

Vern L. Bengtson (Ph.D., University of Chicago) is the AARP/University Chair in Gerontology and Professor of Sociology at the University of Southern California. He has published 15 books and more than 220 articles in gerontology, the sociology of the life course, family sociology, social psychology, and ethnicity and aging. The honors he has received include the Reuben Hill Award from the National Council on Family Relations (1980 and 1986), the Distinguished Scholar Award from the American Sociological Association's Section on Aging (1995), the Robert W. Kleemeier Award from the Gerontological Society of America (1996), and the Ernest W. Burgess Award from the NCFR (1998). He was elected President of the Gerontological Society of America and has been granted a MERIT Award from the National Institute on Aging for his 35-year Longitudinal Study of Generations. In addition, he has received several awards for teaching, which has provided his greatest satisfaction throughout his career.

Alan C. Acock (Ph.D., Washington State University) is Professor and former Chair of Human Development and Family Sciences at Oregon State University. He has also taught at Louisiana State University, Virginia Polytechnic Institute and State University, and the University of Southern California. He has published 4 books, 20 book chapters, and 120 articles. He is a Fellow of the National Council on Family Relations and has held elected offices in the American Sociological Association and the National Council on Family Relations. He has been the recipient of the NCFR's Reuben Hill Award as well as several awards for teaching. His book *Family Diversity and Well-Being* (coauthored with David H. Demo) received the 1995 Choice Award for Outstanding Academic Book. He has served on the editorial boards of several substantive journals, including the *Journal of Marriage and Family*. Currently, he is a member of the editorial board of the *Journal of Structural Equation Modeling*. His substantive research has examined the effects of family structure on the well-being of family members and on intergenerational relations. He is currently investigating the effects on families of fathers' return after incarceration. His methodological research has focused on structural equation modeling and missing values. He is currently writing a book on Stata, a statistical software package.

Katherine R. Allen (Ph.D., Syracuse University) is Professor of Family Studies in the Department of Human Development at Virginia Polytechnic Institute and State University. She coordinates the Human Development Master's Program and also serves as an affiliate of the Center for Gerontology and as Adjunct Professor in Women's Studies. With an interest in family diversity over the life course, qualitative research methods, feminist pedagogy, and social justice work in the family field, she currently studies adult sibling ties, life histories of older gay men and lesbians, and the retention of women and people of color in educational environments. Her books include *Handbook of Family Diversity,* coedited with David H. Demo and Mark A. Fine (2000); *Women and Families: Feminist Reconstructions,* coauthored with Kristine M. Baber (1992); and *Single*

Women/Family Ties: Life Histories of Older Women (1989). A charter Fellow of the National Council on Family Relations, she serves on the editorial boards of the *Journal of Marriage and Family, Family Relations, Journal of Family Issues,* and *Journal of Aging Studies.*

Peggye Dilworth-Anderson is Director of the Center for Aging and Diversity in the Institute on Aging and Professor of Health Policy and Administration in the School of Public Health at the University of North Carolina at Chapel Hill. After earning her Ph.D. from Northwestern University in 1975, she received training in family therapy from the Family Institute of Chicago, Institute of Psychiatry, Northwestern University. In 1989 she received additional training in family issues and Alzheimer's disease from the Harvard Geriatric Education Center. Her research and publications have included both theoretically and empirically based topics on ethnic minority families, with emphasis on older African Americans. In addition to being cited in professional journals, her work has been cited in the *New York Times,* the *Wall Street Journal, USA Today,* the *Christian Science Monitor,* and numerous local and regional newspapers. She serves on the editorial boards of the *Journal of Gerontology: Social Sciences, Psychology and Aging,* and *Aging and Mental Health.* Her research has been funded by the National Institute on Aging, the Administration on Aging, the March of Dimes Birth Defect Foundation, the Alzheimer's Association, and GlaxoSmithKline.

David M. Klein is Associate Professor and Director of Graduate Studies in the Department of Sociology, University of Notre Dame. He has been Department Chair at Notre Dame and has served the National Council on Family Relations as Treasurer, as Chair of the Theory Construction and Research Methodology Workshop, and as Chair of the Research and Theory Section. His recent scholarship has emphasized family theories, methods of studying intergenerational ambivalences, dating and mate selection measurement, and the philosophies of family scientists.